Luxemburger Juristische Studien –
Luxembourg Legal Studies

edited by

Faculty of Law, Economics and Finance
University of Luxembourg

Volume 13

Jenny Weinand

# Implementing the EU Audiovisual Media Services Directive

## Selected issues in the regulation of AVMS by national media authorities of France, Germany and the UK

Nomos

**The Deutsche Nationalbibliothek** lists this publication in the Deutsche Nationalbibliografie; detailed bibliographic data are available on the Internet at http://dnb.d-nb.de

a.t.: Luxembourg, Univ., PhD, 2017

ISBN 978-3-8487-3911-0 (Print)
978-3-8452-8247-3 (ePDF)

**British Library Cataloguing-in-Publication Data**
A catalogue record for this book is available from the British Library.

ISBN 978-3-8487-3911-0 (Print)
978-3-8452-8247-3 (ePDF)

**Library of Congress Cataloging-in-Publication Data**
Weinand, Jenny
Implementing the EU Audiovisual Media Services Directive
Selected issues in the regulation of AVMS by national media authorities of France, Germany and the UK
Jenny Weinand
843 p.

ISBN 978-3-8487-3911-0 (Print)
978-3-8452-8247-3 (ePDF)

1st Edition 2018

*To Marco*

# Preface

The birth of EU(ropean) Media Law was the "Television without Frontiers"-Directive in 1989, and its further development since still make this Directive the main cornerstone of media law and policy in the European Union. Although a wide range of additional areas of regulation and harmonized approaches followed in the meanwhile, such as in Telecommunication, IT or IP law, the current version of the EU "Audiovisual Media Services Directive" (AVMSD) shows the most advanced level of harmonization with a fundamental impact on the media landscape both in terms of available content for viewers as well as economic opportunities for operators. The introduction of a "country of origin-principle" already in the original Directive of 1989, which allows providers – first of television and now more extended of audiovisual media content beyond traditional television – to operate according to the legal requirements of the Member State under which jurisdiction they fall, whilst being able to transmit and disseminate all across the EU without having (in principle) to meet further conditions, was crucial for this success.

The Directive was last reformed a decade ago in 2007 and the codified version of that Directive (2010/13/EU) is the topic of this publication which is based on the thesis prepared by Jenny Weinand as Ph.D. candidate at the University of Luxembourg. Not only the sheer volume of this work but also the comparative view on how a EU Directive is applied in practice in different Member States show that the analysis was a huge effort to be undertaken by a junior researcher. In achieving this goal, she could profit from having worked previously and in parallel on the AVMSD I and II-research projects funded by the University of Luxembourg. This project provides English translations of all AVMSD-transposing acts of the 28 EU Member States, has made them available on the website *www.medialaw.lu* (which was meanwhile expanded and integrated into a database with more functionalities at the European Audiovisual Observatory, available at *avmsd.obs.coe.int*) and used them to prepare a comparative commentary on the national laws concerning the Directive which will also be published by Nomos in the near future. For now, the Research Unit in Law of the University of Luxembourg is very pleased that the analysis of Jenny Weinand is becoming more widely available through publication as Volume 13 of the „Luxemburger Juristische Studien – Luxembourg Legal Studies“ with Nomos publisher.

The title of this volume *"Implementing the EU Audiovisual Media Services Directive – Selected issues in the regulation of AVMS by national media authorities of France, Germany and the UK"* shows the two key features in approaching the topic. Firstly, this analysis does not only look at the national transposition of the AVMSD in selected Member States, but focuses on the actual implementation of the national law – and thereby indirectly the Directive – by the competent national regulatory authorities for the media. Secondly, two main issues in regulating audiovisual media services providers are analysed in detail and with a comparative view to the practices in three of the major EU Member States which at the same time host a large number of all relevant transnationally active providers in the sector in Europe. This approach allows a very telling illustration of how complex EU law is even after its creation: initially there is a text, but there may be interpretation issues that need to be resolved in final instance by the Court of Justice of the EU (CJEU) – such as has been the case e.g. for the question of what constitutes an audiovisual media service in the meaning of the Directive. Then there may be national transpositions which are not only diverse but possibly in violation of the Directive or EU law in general, again a question potentially to be decided by the CJEU. And in the actual practical application of the law there is the different regulatory approaches, in which the implementation can again violate EU law standards and ultimately be reviewed by the CJEU, if the Commission takes action or a Member State court requests clarification. Jenny Weinand's work shows how relevant this last level of diversity is across Europe even in issues, which have seemingly been harmonized in relative detail by EU law.

This publication starts out in chapter 1 with explaining why at all and how audiovisual media services are regulated, after which chapter 2 identifies different regulatory models that are applied. As media regulation is by its nature sensitive in view of the fundamental right to freedom of expression/media freedom, one finds more complex regulatory approaches such as co-regulation in this area. In order to better understand potential differences between the regulatory practices in the three Member States selected for comparison here, the competent media authorities in the United Kingdom, Germany and France are described in chapter 3. Already from this, one can see that administrative structures are diverse, which in turn can impact the administrative work undertaken.

The following two chapters give an in-depth analysis of the regulatory approach for two key sections of the AVMSD. Chapter 4 deals with the actual *materiae* of the Directive, namely what an on-demand audiovisual media service is about and how this actually expands the scope from what was covered previously by reference to television broadcasting. The Directive uses the categories of linear and non-linear services to differentiate and also gives a number of indications both in the recitals and substantive part to be applied when deciding whether or not a specific service is covered by the Directive. These criteria have proven to leave a lot of questions open and therefore it is very valuable to understand how regulators have dealt with the fundamental question of whether or not they can at all monitor a specific service. Chapter 5 deals with one of the substantive areas of regulation: the protection of minors in audiovisual media services. Again, on-demand services are used for illustration. This analysis is important because the provision in the Directive is relatively vague and leaves the details to national transposition and implementation. Although the general approach can build on the experience of protection of minors in television the expectation towards on-demand service providers in ensuring that minors are not confronted with harmful content is somewhat lower, which makes it even more interesting to understand what in practice regulators impose on providers. Already with this explanation and comparison, Jenny Weinand's thesis would be an important contribution to the academic debate because of its thorough analysis. But the author does not only present the challenges in light of the continuing media convergence and changing viewer habits, but uses the comparison to derive best practices from the regulators' approaches and delivers valuable guidance for practice: the work allows comparison with the regulatory monitoring efforts done elsewhere as well as being able to judge which setting or location may be most advantageous for a provider.

The publication does not end here. In addition, the most recent development is also reflected which makes the thesis' publication arrive in a very timely manner: chapter 6 deals with the future regulation of services by the AVMSD. This chapter picks up the current reform debate, launched by the Commission proposal of May 2016. An amended AVMSD as proposed will – if agreed on by European Parliament and Council – inter alia expand some of the rules to so-called video-sharing platforms and update provisions concerning jurisdiction, protection of minors, commercial communication and others. All of this is not only presented in comprehensive form in the final part of the work, but analysed against the backdrop of her recommendations on regulatory strategies in view of media convergence. The suggestions she offers for the future EU legal framework in the AVMSD deserve attention already in the current debate and I am convinced that these, together with the analysis of the current practices, offer a fruitful read and deserve to be regarded in any discussion on the AVMSD.

And even if (as is likely) some of the aspects discussed here will not be resolved in the current reform debate, the value of the work will uphold for the coming years, because:

> "Nach der Reform ist vor der Reform."
> (literally: "After the reform is before the reform.")

– in variation of a famous saying attributed to the former coach of the German national football team Sepp Herberger. During the World Cup 1954 in Switzerland, which the German side went on to win, he said this after a match to indicate that nothing was achieved as the next game is around the corner ("Nach dem Spiel ist vor dem Spiel."). It was one of the matches played in Geneva which is where Jenny Weinand now works for the European Broadcasting Union (EBU) as legal expert on the AVMSD and related issues and can apply her knowledge in practice. With this publication, her theoretical analysis is made available to the public and I am sure readers will share the view that they mark important contributions to discussions about how to regulate audiovisual media services in the future!

*Dr. Mark D. Cole*
Professor for Media and Telecommunication Law
University of Luxembourg and
Director for Academic Affairs
Institute of European Media Law (EMR)

## Acknowledgements

This book would never have been written if one person had not put his faith in me, in the summer of 2010. Professor Mark D. Cole offered me the opportunity to work with him on a research project at the Faculty of Law, Economics and Finance (FDEF) of the University of Luxembourg. This research project laid the basis for my PhD study and helped shape my research skills. For his bottomless trust and support, I am infinitely thankful. I am also grateful for the numerous discussions we have had and during which he has unfailingly widened my perspective and made me look across and beyond my original standpoint. He has nurtured my independence and encouraged my participation in conferences, projects and other events. He has been a role model, both professionally by sharing his vast knowledge and expertise and personally by treating me on equal footing. I have never met a more empathic or kinder person and I hope that one day I get the chance to give back a tiny bit of what he gave me during my time at the FDEF.

I would also like to express my sincere gratitude to my PhD committee at the University of Luxemburg: Professor Herwig Hofmann and Professor Mahulena Hofmann. During our joint meetings, both not only challenged me with tricky questions but provided immensely helpful comments which guided my research and improved this book. I thank them for the time they dedicated to preparing these meetings. I also thank Professor Herwig Hofmann for his additional work as chair of my PhD defence which took place in November 2016 in Luxemburg.

I wish to extend my deepest thanks to the external members of my jury committee: Professor Peggy Valcke, Professor Nico van Eijk and Professor Eva Lievens. It was extremely gratifying to count these three leading scholars in the field as experts at my PhD defence. Not only did they meticulously read this book in the shortest possible time frame, prioritizing my work over other commitments, they also enriched this book by their questions and their fruitful comments during my PhD defence. To have discussed my research with them and to get their stake on the issues I elaborate on in this book was a great honour and fills me with sincere gratitude. I genuinely thank them for their support of my research, with a particular thank you to Professor Valcke for her kind opening remarks which I will never forget.

A great number of people deserve special thanks for accompanying me throughout my academic career. At the University of Luxembourg, I had the pleasure of meeting some wonderful people who motivated me, cheered me up or offered valuable suggestions if ever I found myself in a corner. I thank them all for being there for me and sharing unforgettable years at the FDEF. These friendships are dear to my heart. I would like to express my special thanks to Professor Cole's team at the FDEF and at the Institute of European Media Law in Saarbrücken. I have enjoyed working with every one of them on different projects and getting to know them all has made a lasting impression. Thank you for this. I also would like to thank the University of Luxembourg and its administrative staff for supporting my research.

A few names need nonetheless to be mentioned explicitly: Millions of thanks go to my kind, generous and patient reviewers who made this book easier to follow and definitely more readable: Dr. Bernd Justin Jütte, Dr. Lawrence Siry, Suzanne Larsen and Amy Van Elderen. I thank Justin and Lawrence for their improvements on the substance and Amy for her kindness (and discipline) in getting through the longest chapter of this book.

I would also like to thank my parents as well as my sister for supporting me throughout my entire life. I am infinitely grateful for my parent's substantial financial as well moral support of my academic career, from the first day of school to my PhD defence. I thank the three of them for being there for me and for believing in me at every moment.

Finally, I would like to thank my dear husband Marco who has been at my side throughout this journey, from the first lines to the last footnote. Without his continuous selfless support, this book would never have seen the light of day. As a token of my love and endless gratitude, this book is dedicated to him.

# Abbreviations

| | |
|---|---|
| Art. | Article |
| Arts. | Articles |
| Article 29 WP | Article 29 Data Protection Working Party |
| ARD | Arbeitsgemeinschaft der öffentlich rechtlichen Rundfunkanstalten der Bundesrepublik Deutschland [Germany] |
| ARCEP | Autorité de Régulation des Communications Electroniques et des Postes (Authority for the Regulation of Electronic Communications & Postal Services) [France] |
| ATVOD | Authority for Television On Demand [United Kingdom] |
| AVMS | Audiovisual media services |
| AVMSD | Audiovisual Media Services Directive |
| AVS | Age verification system |
| BEREC | Body of European Regulators in Electronic Communications |
| BKS | Bundeskommunikationssenat [Austria] |
| BGH | Bundesgerichtshof (Federal court of justice) [Germany] |
| BLM | Bayerische Landeszentrale für neue Medien [Germany] |
| BPjM | Bundesprüfstelle für Jugendgefährdende Medien (Federal Review Board for Media Harmful to Minors) [Germany] |
| BVerfG | Bundesverfassungsgericht (Federal Constitutional Court) [Germany] |
| BverwG | Bundesverwaltungsgericht (Federal Administrative Court) [Germany] |
| CA | Communications Act [United Kingdom] |
| CAC | Content access control |
| Cc | Conseil constitutionnel (Constitutional Council) [France] |
| CFR | EU Charter of Fundamental Rights |
| CJEU | Court of Justice of the European Union |
| CNCL | Commission nationale pour la communication et les libertés (National Commission for the Communication & Freedoms) [France] |
| Commission | Commission of the European Union |
| Community | European Community |
| CoE | Council of Europe |

| | |
|---|---|
| CPC | Consumer Protection Cooperation |
| CSA | Conseil Supérieur de l'Audiovisuel [France] |
| CTT | Convention on Trans-frontier Television [Council of Europe] |
| CULT | Committee on Culture & Education of the European Parliament |
| DLM | Direktorenkonferenz der Landesmedienanstalten (Conference of Directors of the Media Authorities) [Germany] |
| DSM | Digital Single Market Strategy of the European Commission |
| The Court | Court of Justice of the European Union |
| EAO | European Audiovisual Observatory |
| EBU | European Broadcasting Union |
| ECD | E-Commerce Directive |
| ECHR | European Convention for the Protection of Human Rights |
| ECtHR | European Court of Human Rights |
| EP | European Parliament |
| EPRA | European Platform of Regulatory Authorities |
| ERGA | European Regulators Group for Audiovisual Media Services |
| EU | European Union |
| FERG | Fernseh-Exklusivrechtegesetz [Austria] |
| FSM | Freiwillige Selbstkontrolle Multimedia Dienste e.V. (Voluntary Self-Monitoring of Multimedia Service Providers) [Germany] |
| GG | Grundgesetz (German Basic Law) [Germany] |
| GVK | Gremienvorsitzendenkonferenz (Conference of Chairpersons of the Decision-Taking Councils of the Media Authorities) [Germany] |
| HACA | Haute Autorité de la communication audiovisuelle (High Authority for Communication, HACA) [France] |
| HRA | Human Rights Act [United Kingdom] |
| IRIS | Imaginons un réseau Internet solidaire |
| IWF | Internet Watch Foundation [United Kingdom] |
| JMStV | Jugendmedienschutzstaatsvertrag (Interstate Treaty for the Protection of Minors) [Germany] |
| JSP | Jugendschutzprogramm (Technical System for the Protection of Minors) [Germany] |
| JSPs | Jugenschutzprogramme [Germany] |
| JuSchRiL | Jugendschutzrichtlinien (Guidelines for Guaranteeing the Protection of Human Dignity and Young People) [Germany] |

| | |
|---|---|
| KEK | Kommission zur Ermittlung der Konzentration im Medienbereich (Commission on Concentration in the Media) [Germany] |
| KJM | Kommission für Jugendmedienschutz (Commission for the Protection of Minors) [Germany] |
| KommAustria | Kommunikationsbehörde Austria [Austria] |
| LCA | Loi sur la communication audiovisuelle (Law on Audiovisual Communication) [France] |
| LG | Landgericht (District court) [Germany] |
| LLC | Loi relative à la liberté de communication (Freedom of Communication Act) [France] |
| LMA | Landesmedienanstalt (state media authority) [Germany] |
| LMK | Landeszentrale für Medien und Kommunikation Rheinland-Pfalz [Germany] |
| MEP | Member of European Parliament |
| NDR | Norddeutscher Rundfunk |
| NRA | National regulatory authority |
| NRAs | National regulatory authorities |
| OCA | Office of Communications Act [United Kingdom] |
| ODPS | On-demand programme service [United Kingdom] |
| OJ | Official Journal (of the European Union) |
| OLG | Oberlandesgericht (Appeal court) [Germany] |
| Para. | Paragraph |
| PP | Product placement |
| PSB | Public service broadcasting/er |
| PSM | Public service media |
| RStV | Rundfunkstaatsvertrag (Interstate Treaty on Broadcasting & Telemedia) [Germany] |
| SVOD | Subscription-based video-on-demand service |
| TEU | Treaty on the European Union |
| TFEU | Treaty on the Functioning of the European Union |
| TKG | Telekeommunikationsgesetz (Telecommunications Act) [Germany] |
| TMG | Telemediengesetz (Telemedia Services Act) [Germany] |
| TT | Tiroler Tageszeitung |
| TWFD | Television Without Frontiers Directive |
| UCPD | Unfair Commercial Practices Directive |
| UG | User-generated |

| | |
|---|---|
| UGC | User-generated content |
| Union | European Union |
| UWG | Gesetz gegen den unlauteren Wettbewerb (Unfair Competition Act)<br>[Germany] |
| VG | Verwaltungsgericht (Administrative Court at State Level) [Germany] |
| VGH | Verwaltungsgerichtshof (Administrative Court) [Austria, Germany] |
| VOD | Video-on-demand |
| VSP | Video-sharing platform |
| VSPs | Video-sharing platforms |
| ZAK | Kommission für Zulassung und Aufsicht (Commission on Licensing & Supervision) [Germany] |

Table of Contents

# Introduction

## A. The raison d'être of this study

### I. Context

> "The unprecedented variety and virtually infinite quantity of information available, the lack of State borders as significant barriers to the flow of that information, the ease of producing any information on any subject and its reach to a virtually unlimited number of recipients, and, (…) the detachment of the virtual, digital world from the material world – all this calls for new legal instruments, often built on entirely new bases. In addition, that reality is changing at a huge speed, significantly outstripping the legislature's ability to react to it, in particular in democratic countries. Applying rules devised for an analogue reality in the digital age is causing a number of difficulties."[1]

This quote from Advocate General (AG) Szpunar's opinion in the *New Media Online* case gets to the heart of this study: the convergence of media, which allows for instant, seamless and immersive communication, has radically challenged the current sector-specific approach to regulating various kinds of different media such as the printed press, broadcasting/ audiovisual media services and the Internet. Media convergence therefore constitutes the factual backdrop to this study. However, this phenomenon is neither predictable nor homogeneous across sectors, in particular the audiovisual media services market. Certain trends can nonetheless be identified. The value of the audiovisual market, which includes broadcasting and on-demand services, video and cinema was € 107 billion in 2014. The vast majority of revenues was derived from broadcasting (85 percent), while 8 percent of the revenues were attributed to the on-demand segment.[2] The market's potential is further illustrated by the large number of TV channels (about 5,300) on the air in the European Union (EU) in 2015,

1 Opinion of Advocate General Szpunar delivered on 1 June 2015 in case C-347/14 *New Media Online GmbH*, EU:C:2015:434, para. 2.

2 Cabrera Blázquez et al., *Yearbook 2015, Television, Cinema, Video and On-Demand Audiovisual Services – The Pan-European Picture, Key Trends*, ed. European Audiovisual Observatory (Strasbourg, France, 2016), p. 44.

compared to about 3,000 on-demand services.[3] It is certainly true that on-demand services have mushroomed over the past five years and mass consumption of simultaneously received content (TV) is dropping, in particular among younger audiences.[4] Competition is fierce between subscription-based on-demand services (SVOD) provided by the five well-established European brands NowTV (Sky), Maxdome (Pro Sieben/Sat1), CanalPlay (Canal+ Group), Viaplay (MTG), Infinity (Mediaset), and several smaller regional SVOD providers (such as CME's Voyo or Liberty Global's MyPrime). Competition has further been increased by the arrival of three global players on the EU market: Netflix, which is now available throughout Europe and attracted more than 50percent of EU subscribers in 2015; Amazon, which has launched its Amazon video platform in the UK, Germany and Austria; and Time Warner, whose HBO Now is available in the Nordic countries (Finland, Denmark, Norway and Sweden).[5] The interest of these US heavyweights provides an indication of the markets' potential, which continue to grow. The development of new business models is beneficial for consumers who engage with services and applications "in new ways and on new devices anywhere and anytime".[6]

---

3 Agnes Schneeberger and Gilles Fontaine, "Linear and on-Demand Services in Europe 2015, Mavise Extra," ed. European Audiovisual Observatory, June 2016, pp. 14, 30, http://www.obs.coe.int/documents/205595/264629/MAVISE+EXTRA_TV+and+ODAS+in+Europe+2015.pdf/6f081c35-b205-4cb2-8214-366f7d5bc500 (accessed 25.9.2016); Cabrera Blázquez et al., *Yearbook 2015*, p. 28.

4 Schneeberger and Fontaine, "Linear and On-Demand Services in Europe 2015," pp. 15–16; Winfried Kluth and Wolfgang Schulz, "Konvergenz und regulatorische Folgen. Gutachten im Auftrag der Rundfunkkommission der Länder, Arbeitspapier Nr. 30" (Hans Bredow Institut, 2014), pp. 80–81, http://www.hans-bredow-institut.de/webfm_send/1049 (accessed 10.2.2015).

5 Media Intelligence Service, "Market Insights SVOD in Europe," ed. European Broadcasting Union, June 2016, pp. 20–22, 23–26, https://www.ebu.ch/news/2016/06/european-svod-reach-50-mil-2020. The report is only accessible for EBU Members.

6 Ofcom, "Ofcom Response to the European Commission Green Paper 'Preparing for a Fully Converged Audiovisual World: Growth, Creation and Values'" (European Commission, September 27, 2013), para. 2.7-2.9, pp. 8–11, http://ec.europa.eu/digital-agenda/en/news/consultation-green-paper-preparing-fully-converged-audiovisual-world-growth-creation-and-values (accessed 14.10.2013).

However, broadcasting has been resilient and it remains the general public's main viewing device.[7] In 2014, Europeans watched on average 03:57 hours of TV per day, 20 minutes more than in 2008.[8] So, even in the Internet era, TV remains an important medium in everyday life, and above all for its role in democracy.[9] It is the primary communication and information resource for social opinion-forming: "media policy creates the communicative space within which all public and decision-making discourse takes place".[10] TV therefore fulfils a function paramount to democracy. Average TV viewing time is, however, deceptive in that it conceals the major differences between age groups. It is important to note that younger audiences (aged 15-24), in particular, only spent an average about 02:15 hours watching TV,[11] which is roughly half the time spent by their parents. In addition to on-demand services, younger audiences increasingly turn to other forms of video provided by video-sharing platforms (VSPs) or social networks.[12] In September 2016, the average viewing session on YouTube lasted 40 minutes, a 50 percent rise in one year.[13] Inter-

---

7 ERGA, "Report on Material Jurisdiction in a Converged Environment," December 18, 2015, p. 18, http://ec.europa.eu/newsroom/dae/document.cfm?action=display&doc_id=13287 (accessed 13.1.2016); Francisco Cabrera Blázquez Javier et al., *On-Demand Services and the Material Scope of the AVMSD*, IRIS Plus 1/2016 (Strasbourg: European Audiovisual Observatory, 2016), p. 8.

8 Media Intelligence Service, "Consumption Trends," ed. European Broadcasting Union, 2015, p. 9; Cabrera Blázquez et al., *On-Demand Services and the Material Scope of the AVMSD*, p. 8.

9 Christian Katzenbach, "Media Governance and Technology. From 'Code Is Law' to Governance Constellations," in *Routledge Handbook of Media Law*, ed. Monroe E. Price, Stefaan Verhulst, and Libby Morgan (London and New York: Routledge, 2013), p. 399. Media consumption trends of 2016 show that 93 percent of total viewing (4:14 hours) of an average UK adult was done on a TV set in the first quarter of 2016, the same proportion as in 2014. Four percent was viewed on a computer, 2 percent on a tablet and 1 percent on a smartphone. See Media Intelligence Service, "Consumption Trends," ed. European Broadcasting Union, 2016, pp. 12, 18.

10 Sandra Braman, "Where Has Media Policy Gone? Defining the Field in the Twenty-First Century," *Communication Law and Policy* 9, no. 2 (2004): p. 169.

11 Cabrera Blázquez et al., *On-Demand Services and the Material Scope of the AVMSD*, p. 8.

12 Cabrera Blázquez et al., *Yearbook 2015*, p. 26.

13 IBC: YouTube goes up against TV as average view time passes 40 minutes. Available at http://www.digitaltveurope.net/597132/ibc-youtube-goes-up-against-tv-as-average-view-time-passes-40-minutes/ (accessed 18.9.2016).

estingly, YouTube views are driven by mobile consumption amounting to 60 percent of the total.[14] This shows that YouTube and similar VSPs are evolving from "bitesized content" of 30-second or two-minute clips to longer forms of entertainment that has the potential to replace (parts of) the TV experience, at least for certain parts of the population.[15] Social networks, such as Facebook, Twitter and Instagram, also want to climb on the bandwagon and are increasingly placing video at the heart of their strategies.[16] In contrast to links to videos hosted on other websites, more and more content is being uploaded to or created on social networks (so-called native content), especially on Facebook.[17] This indicates a "demographic split in the use of the Internet" and underscores the state of flux of the audiovisual media services market.[18]

---

14 IBC: YouTube goes up against TV as average view time passes 40 minutes, 2016.

15 IBC: YouTube goes up against TV as average view time passes 40 minutes, 2016.

16 Facebook has also launched a livestreaming tool similar to Snapchat, Periscope and Meerkat. While it was at first only available to "public figures", who Facebook frequently paid to publish live content through verified pages, it is now rolled out and "ordinary" users are animated to share live videos that are uploaded to users' timeline for catch-up. See https://live.fb.com/about/ (accessed 30.8.2016). The amount of live videos posted has soared between January and June 2016. At the beginning of 2016, approximately 10 percent of the top 500 media publishers posted live videos on Facebook, the percentage has climbed to about 50 percent of publishers six months later. It is also interesting to note that video consumption becomes one of the key user activities on Facebook. In the second quarter of 2016, almost 50 percent of Facebook users of 13 European countries watched a video while almost 70 percent clicked the "like button" and 45 percent messaged a friend. See Media Intelligence Service, "Consumption Trends," 2016, pp. 31–38; European Audiovisual Observatory, ed., "On-Demand Audiovisual Markets in the European Union, Final Report," 2014, p. 27, https://ec.europa.eu/digital-agenda/en/news/demand-audiovisual-markets-european-union-smart-20120028.

17 Media Intelligence Service, "Consumption Trends," 2016, pp. 34, 35.

18 Ofcom, "Response to Commission Green Paper," para. 2.25, p. 13; Zahra Rahvar, *Die Zukunft des deutschen Presserechts im Lichte konvergierender Medien* (Baden-Baden: Nomos, 2011), p. 22. In its staff working document to the Digital Single Market Strategy, the Commission also highlighted that younger generations of viewers watch less linear TV. See European Commission, "Commission Staff Working Document, A Digital Single Market Strategy for Europe – Analysis and Evidence, Accompanying the Document Communication from the Commission on A Digital Single Market Strategy for Europe, SWD(2015) 100 Final," June 5, 2015, para. 4.2, p. 43.

It also highlights the complexities of the audiovisual value chain.[19] In addition to providers of legacy media (broadcasting), new players have entered the audiovisual media services market. Infrastructure operators that have traditionally provided the networks for distributing audiovisual content (terrestrial, cable, satellite and telecommunications) are increasingly diversifying their business, engaging in activities comparable to those of media service providers, such as aggregating and packaging content.[20] In addition, new operators now distribute content "over-the-top", meaning they provide content over the Internet, by-passing those players that have traditionally provided the (telecommunications) infrastructure.[21] Similarly, hosting providers play a growing role in the media ecosystem, in particular those that store content (e.g. on their own servers) or VSPs to which content may be uploaded free-of-charge. Smart TVs, which combine TV and the Internet, are also on the rise and provide proprietary platforms that integrate TV channels, own content and content purchased from partners.

In the midst of these market developments and as part of its Digital Single Market Strategy (DSM),[22] the European Union (EU)[23] has embarked on a reform process, including its principal legislative instrument regulating the audiovisual media services market. The Audiovisual Media Services Directive (AVMSD) of 2007, which was codified in 2010[24] sets minimum requirements for certain aspects of broadcasting and on-demand ser-

19 ERGA, "Report on Material Jurisdiction," p. 24; Cabrera Blázquez et al., *On-Demand Services and the Material Scope of the AVMSD*, pp. 11–12.

20 ERGA, "Report on Material Jurisdiction," para. 1.4, pp. 23–24; Cabrera Blázquez et al., *On-Demand Services and the Material Scope of the AVMSD*, p. 11.

21 Cabrera Blázquez et al., *On-Demand Services and the Material Scope of the AVMSD*, p. 11.

22 European Commission, "Communication from the Commission to the European Parliament, the Council, the European Economic and Social Committee and the Committee of the Regions, A Digital Single Market Strategy for Europe, COM(2015) 192 Final," June 5, 2015.

23 This study will generally employ the term European Union and only refer to the European Community in historical context.

24 Directive 2007/65/EC of the European Parliament and of the Council of 11 December 2007 amending Council Directive 89/552/EEC on the coordination of certain provisions laid down by law, regulation or administrative action in Member States concerning the pursuit of television broadcasting activities, OJ of 18.12.2007, L 332, p. 27, as codified by Directive 2010/13/EU of the European Parliament and of the Council of 10 March 2010 on the coordination of certain provisions laid down by law, regulation or administrative action in Member States concerning the provision of audiovisual media services (Audiovisual Media Ser-

vices, such as the protection of minors, the prohibition of hate speech, advertising rules, listed events, and short news reports. This study focuses on the Directive in a bid to contribute to discussions about the revision of the AVMSD. It explains the methodology and scope below after highlighting its relevance, both, for society and academia.

## II. Rationale

This study has evolved from a research project on the transposition of the AVMSD at the University of Luxembourg. The project systematically compared the English translations of national laws adopted by all 28 EU Member States to transpose the AVMSD.[25] Differences and similarities in wording were examined and the implications set out. The term "transposition" is used here to mean the transfer of rules outlined in an EU Directive into national legal acts. By virtue of Art. 288 TFEU, Directives are binding on Member States "as to the result to be achieved (...) but shall leave to the national authorities the choice of form and methods". The Directive as an instrument of Secondary Union law typically outlines policy objectives, granting Member States a margin of discretion as to the way in which the pre-determined goal is reached. The research project on the AVMSD demonstrated that many Member States transposed the AVMSD in large parts into national legal orders verbatim. Consequently, the wording of national provisions corresponds (in many instances almost to the letter) to the terms of the Directive. More differences, however, came to light when investigating how the national laws were applied and enforced in practice. To implement the AVMSD as transposed into national law, Member States refer to national regulatory authorities (NRAs), specialised bodies that act as intermediaries between the industry and the State. This study employs the term "implementation" to describe the role of the

vices Directive), codified version, OJ of 15.4.2010, L 95, p. 1. See also Corrigendum to Directive 2010/13/EU of the European Parliament and of the Council of 10 March 2010 on the coordination of certain provisions laid down by law, regulation or administrative action in Member States concerning the provision of audiovisual media services, OJ of 6.10.2010, L 263, p. 15.

25 The English translations and original laws are published under www.medialaw.lu and can be freely accessed. Synopses which juxtapose the text of the national law and the corresponding rule contained in the AVMSD are additionally made available.

NRAs. More specifically, this study analyses the cases brought before NRAs by third-party complainants or investigated by their own motions (i.e. NRA practice) as well as the measures they take in the form of guidelines, codes, recommendations, etc. to specify the provisions set out in national laws in certain fields coordinated by the AVMSD: the notion of an on-demand audiovisual media service and the protection of minors in such services. While the term "transposition" is used to denote the legislative measures by Member States in order to give effect to EU Directives within a national framework, the term "implementation" is used more broadly to describe the range of executive measures (practice and guidance) adopted by NRAs. The term "regulation", as used here, indicates that, rather than leaving it to market forces, the State or the EU intervenes in a sector to manage or run an activity (i.e. providing audiovisual media services). While the State or the EU set out common rules (by adopting legislation), these are enforced by NRAs. Regulation therefore refers to executive measures taken to apply specific laws.

## III. State of the art

To date, research has focused on the scope, effect and implications of the rules set out in the AVMSD.[26] To this end, several studies trace the devel-

---

26 Some of the most important handbooks on European media law which treat different aspects of the AVMSD include Oliver Castendyk, Egbert Dommering, and Alexander Scheuer, eds., *European Media Law* (Alphen aan den Rijn and London: Kluwer Law International, 2008); Emmanuel Derieux and Agnès Granchet, *Droit des médias, Droit francais, européen et international*, sixth edition (Paris: LGDJ, 2010); Udo Fink, Mark Cole, and Tobias Keber, *Europäisches und Internationales Medienrecht* (Heidelberg: Müller, 2008); Goldberg, David, Sutter, Gavin, and Walden, Ian, eds., *Media Law and Practice* (Oxford: Oxford University Press, 2009); Jackie Harrison and Lorna Woods, *European Broadcasting Law and Policy* (Cambridge and New York: Cambridge University Press, 2007); Perry Keller, *European and International Media Law, Liberal Democracy, Trade, and the New Media* (Oxford: Oxford University Press, 2011); Michael R. Kogler, *TV (On Demand)*, Europäische Content-Regelungen für audiovisuelle Mediendienste (Wien: Manz, 2010); Price Monroe, Stefaan Verhulst, and Libby Morgan, eds., *Routledge Handbook of Media Law* (London and New York: Routledge, 2013); Ursula Smartt, *Media and Entertainment Law*, first edition. (Milton Park, Abingdon and Oxon: Routledge, 2011); David Ward, ed., *The European Union and the Culture Industries, Regulation and the Public Interest* (United Kingdom: Ashgate Publish-

opment of the AVMSD and inquire about its suitability for converged media.[27] Since the expiry of the deadline for transposing the AVMSD in December 2009, scholarly attention has shifted from the European to the national level. Some studies therefore examine particular aspects of the AVMSD (e.g. product placement) in national contexts.[28] More frequently, NRAs and their activities have become the subject of the analysis.[29] This is indubitably furthered by the European Platform of Regulatory Authorities (EPRA), which has published comparative studies on many of the issues regulated by the AVMSD (and beyond).[30] Similarly, the Council of

---

ing, 2008); see also the legal commentaries examining the transposition of the AVMSD in national law, for example Reinhard Hartstein et al., *Rundfunkstaatsvertrag, Kommentar*, Looseleaf commenatry (Köln: Rehm, n.d.); Kogler, Michael, Traimer, Matthias, and Truppe, Michael, *Österreichische Rundfunkgesetze, Recht der audiovisuellen Mediendienste und des Hörfunks*, third edition (Wien: Verlag Medien & Recht, 2011).

27 Max Schoenthal, *Von der Fernsehregulierung zur Inhalteregulierung, Die Konzeption der Einstufung von Mediendiensten im Recht der europäischen Gemeinschaft und die "Mediakabel"-Rechtsprechung des Europäischen Gerichtshofes*, Schriftenreihe zum Kommunikations- und Medienrecht 12 (Hamburg: Verlag Dr. Kovac, 2009); Philip Kempermann, *Content-Regulierung in konvergierenden Medien*, vol. 1, Schriftenreihe der Kölner Forschungsstelle für Medienrecht (Frankfurt am Main: Peter Lang, 2010).

28 On the country of origin principle, see Martina Blasi, *Das Herkunftslandprinzip der Fernseh- und der E-Commerce-Richtlinie, Unter Berücksichtigung des Herkunftslandprinzips auf der Ebene des Primärrechts*, Schriftenreihe zum gewerblichen Rechtsschutz 132 (Köln: Carl Heymanns Verlag, 2004); on product placement see Stephan Leitgelb, *Product-Placement, Verfassungs- und gemeinschaftsrechtliche Bestandsaufnahme vor dem Hintergrund der europäischen Liberalisierung integrativer Werbeformen durch die Richtlininie über Audiovisuelle Mediendienste*, Schriften zum Medienrecht 22 (Hamburg: Kovač, 2010); Jannis Müller-Rüster, *Product Placement im Fernsehen, Die Legalisierung programmintegrierter Werbung im Lichte der deutschen und europäischen Kommunikationsgrundrechte*, Jus Internationale et Europaeum 40 (Tübingen: Mohr Siebeck, 2010); on the protection of minors see Eva Lievens, *Protecting Children in the Digital Era, The Use of Alternative Regulatory Instruments*, International Studies in Human Rights 105 (Leiden, Boston: Martinus Nijhoff Publishers, 2010); on the right to short news reports see Claudia Wildmann, *Das Europäische Kurzberichterstattungsrecht im Lichte der Richtlinie über audiovisuelle Mediendienste*, Schriften zum Medienrecht 28 (Hamburg: Kovač, 2011).

29 Peggy Valcke and Jeff Ausloos, "'What If Television Becomes Just an App?' Re-Conceptualising the Legal Notion of Audiovisual Media Service in the Light of Media Convergence" (ICRI Research Paper 17, December 20, 2013), http://papers.ssrn.com/sol3/papers.cfm?abstract_id=2375666 (accessed 27.12.2013).

Europe's European Audiovisual Observatory (EAO) has commissioned several publications on specific areas overned by the AVMSD,[31] linking its analysis to national reports about how the standards of the Directive are applied.[32]

---

30 See for example Emmanuelle Machet, "Comparative Background Document on Content Regulation and New Media: Exploring Regulatory Boundaries between Traditional and New Media, 33rd EPRA Meeting" (EPRA, 2011), http://www.epra.org/attachments/ohrid-plenary-1-exploring-regulatory-boundaries-background-document (accessed 23.9.2011); Emmanuelle Machet, "Comparative Background Document on New Media & Regulation: Towards a Paradigm Shift? New Services and Scope: What's In, What's out Revisited, 35th EPRA Meeting" (EPRA, 2012), http://www.epra.org/attachments/portoroz-plenary-1-new-services-and-scope-what-s-in-what-s-out-revisited-paper--2 (accessed 15.10.2012); Emmanuelle Machet, "Comparative Background Document on The Protection of Minors in a Connected Environment, 37th EPRA Meeting," 2013, http://epra3-production.s3.amazonaws.com/attachments/files/2195/original/protectionofminors_final_publicversion.pdf?1372087443 (accessed 17.9.2013).

31 Susanne Nikoltchev, ed., *Jurisdiction over Broadcasters in Europe*, IRIS Special (Strasbourg: European Audiovisual Observatory, 2002); Susanne Nikoltchev, ed., *Audiovisual Media Services without Frontiers, Implementing the Rules*, IRIS Special (Strasbourg: European Audiovisual Observatory, 2006); Susanne Nikoltchev, ed., *Editorial Responsibility*, IRIS Special (Strasbourg: European Audiovisual Observatory, 2008); Susanne Nikoltchev, ed., *Ready, Set...Go? The Audiovisual Media Services Directive*, IRIS Special (Strasbourg: European Audiovisual Observatory, 2009); Susanne Nikoltchev, ed., *The Regulation of On-Demand Audiovisual Services: Chaos or Coherence?*, IRIS Special (Strasbourg: European Audiovisual Observatory, 2011); Susanne Nikoltchev, ed., *Video On Demand and the Promotion of European Works*, IRIS Special (Strasbourg: European Audiovisual Observatory, 2013); Maja Cappello, ed., *New Forms of Commercial Communications in a Converged Audiovisual Sector*, IRIS Special (Strasbourg: European Audiovisual Observatory, 2014); Susanne Nikoltchev, *Legal Aspects of Video On Demand*, IRIS Special (Strasbourg: European Audiovisual Observatory, 2007).

32 Susanne Nikoltchev, ed., *Product Placement*, IRIS Plus 3/2010 (Strasbourg: European Audiovisual Observatory, 2010); Susanne Nikoltchev, ed., *Exclusive Rights and Short Reporting*, IRIS Plus 4/2012 (Strasbourg: European Audiovisual Observatory, 2012); Susanne Nikoltchev, ed., *Protection of Minors and Audiovisual Content On-Demand*, IRIS Plus 6/2012 (Strasbourg: European Audiovisual Observatory, 2012); Susanne Nikoltchev, ed., *Converged Media: Same Content, Different Laws?*, IRIS Plus 3/2013 (Strasbourg: European Audiovisual Observatory, 2013); Susanne Nikoltchev, ed., *What Is an On-Demand Service?*, IRIS Plus 4/2013 (Strasbourg: European Audiovisual Observatory, 2013); Francisco Cabrera Blázquez Javier and Amélie Lépinard, eds., *Enabling Access to the Media for All*, IRIS Plus 3/2014 (Strasbourg: European Audiovisual Observatory, 2014).

However, no comprehensive and detailed scrutiny of the measures by NRAs has yet been conducted. To make up for this, this study examines certain aspects of the Directive's implementation from the perspective of NRAs in certain Member States. Despite a considerable degree of harmonisation, there "has always existed a rich variety of national 'styles' of regulation, reflecting significant differences of historical experience and regulatory culture. Subtle but important differences [are] found in the heritage of assumptions and practices about broadcasting".[33] This observation of diversity in connection to broadcasting is equally true for audiovisual media services. National particularities such as "ideological factors, party incumbency of government, differences of economic structures, differences of cultural and state traditions"[34] underlie and shape the audiovisual media services sector. What is more, content distributed through audiovisual media services is "essentially national in nature, being directly and closely connected to the cultural, social and democratic needs of a particular society".[35] Linguistic barriers contribute to the fragmentation and territorialisation of the market. Although younger generations of users are increasingly interested in and able to understand content produced in a foreign language (meaning in English) due to ease with which information flows globally, the vast majority of audiovisual works cater to national audiences respecting national languages. It is therefore essential to consider the national contexts in which NRAs function and the specific national structures if we are to understand the measures they take to implement the AVMSD. This includes the precise composition of the regulatory scheme including alternative forms of regulation, namely co- or self-regulation.

## IV. Methodology and scope

The research question of this study is, why does media convergence challenge traditional regulatory strategies and content regulation of audio-

33 Kenneth Dyson and Peter Humphreys, "Deregulating Broadcasting: The West European Experience," *European Journal of Political Research* 17 (1989): p. 138.

34 Dyson and Humphreys, "Deregulating Broadcasting: The West European Experience," p. 139.

35 Communication from the Commission to the Council, the European Parliament, the Economic and Social Committee and the Committee of the Regions, Principles and guidelines for the Community's audiovisual policy in the digital age, COM(1999) 657 final, 14.12.1999, para. 3 (5), p. 14.

visual media services? It addresses two interlinking axes that highlight the effects of media convergence.

First, it examines States' choices regarding the type of regulation, and second, it looks at certain content standards. In order to answer this question, this study analyses the measures taken by the UK, German and French regulatory bodies to implement certain aspects of the AVMSD. These countries have been selected owing to their significance for the internal market[36] and the organisation of the State, which has led to a variety of regulatory models that are embedded in national regulatory cultures. The regulators in the countries selected have, moreover, been very active in issuing guidance to providers on their territories. Where possible, the activities of other NRAs are taken into account.

The regulatory measures investigated relate to two issues covered by the AVMSD. First, this concerns the Directive's scope of application and what exactly is covered by the notion of an on-demand audiovisual media service, and second, the protection of minors in on-demand audiovisual media services. These two case studies have been chosen for in-depth analysis as they highlight the problems caused by media convergence in relation to the scope of the Directive and the application of one of the Directive's normative provisions. The case study on the protection of minors illustrates the fundamental rights dimension of this study. In comparing the approaches, positions and interpretations of NRAs, this study aims to pinpoint the shortcomings of the AVMSD in the light of media convergence. It describes best practices and draws conclusions for the future regulation of audiovisual media services at the EU level. In line with the research question, these conclusions are two-fold and relate to the regulatory architecture (i.e. the type of regulatory models employed) as well as to regulatory objectives (i.e. content standards).

The scope of this study inevitably remains limited. A horizontal analysis of the measures taken by all 28 NRAs to implement all aspects regulated by the AVMSD would be highly relevant to assessing the Directive's impact and enhancing an understanding of the practical difficulties in implementing it in order to inspire better regulation in the future but would go well beyond the scope of this research. In addition, although the

36 The UK, Germany and France host the highest number of broadcasters as well as on-demand providers, accounting for almost fifty percent of all providers established in the EU. See Schneeberger and Fontaine, "Linear and on-Demand Services in Europe 2015," pp. 8, 12, 31.

AVMSD applies indiscriminately to public and private/commercial providers of audiovisual media, the regulation of public service media (PSM) is generally excluded given the specificities as PSM are typically subject to specific laws and/or supervisory authorities at the Member State level in contrast to commercial operators. PSM, furthermore, have a special status in the audiovisual sector, safeguarding public service values such as pluralistic programme offers and impartial and accurate reporting to enable the public to form independent opinions, which constitutes the bedrock of democratic societies. In order to fulfil this public service mission, PSM are typically funded by the State. On account of the public interest at stake, the State's involvement is stronger than in commercial media. In many EU Member States, the rules applicable to PSM are stricter (e.g. advertising ban on TV) than those concerning commercial operators. Accordingly, there are often special regulatory arrangements (agreements with providers of public services) and distinct oversight mechanisms. Owing to these fundamental differences, this study is solely concerned with the implementation of the AVMSD for commercial audiovisual media. Still, the application of the AVMSD to public service media merits a separate, comprehensive study to which future research could be devoted.

## V. Outline

This study comprises six chapters. The first chapter explores the reasons for regulating the audiovisual media services market and traces the EU's involvement in this sector. The genesis of the AVMSD therefore constitutes an integral part of this chapter. The second chapter conceptualises various forms of regulation, including co-regulation and self-regulation, outlining the advantages and disadvantages associated with these 'alternative forms of regulation'. It establishes the theoretical basis for the third chapter which sketches the regulatory models employed in the UK, Germany and France. The third chapter thus refers to "media authorities" in an attempt to capture all types of regulatory bodies including the national regulatory authority, co-regulatory bodies as well as other regulatory bodies involved in the implementation of the AVMSD. Understanding the complex structures of national regulatory regimes is essential to an understanding of regulators' choices when implementing the AVMSD. The specific measures adopted by NRAs are subjected to a detailed analysis in chapters four and five. The fourth chapter maps out NRAs' measures regarding the concept of an on-demand audiovisual media service, while the fifth chapter outlines regulatory measures taken to protect minors using such services. The two case studies are similarly structured and conclude with a comparison of the regulators' approaches. Each case study starts by analysing the measures of the UK authorities as these are the most comprehensive, encompassing regulators' practices, their guidance notes and other policy documents including research reports. This facilitates cross-references between the different sub-sections of each case study.

Finally, best practices are derived from the two case studies in the sixth chapter which also entails reflections on the design of the future EU regulatory framework. This chapter also discusses current developments at the EU level,[37] and in particular it takes a critical view of the Commission's 2016 proposal for a revised Directive. Finally, the conclusion provides a summary of the study's main findings in terms of the research question. Before going into detail, the remaining part of this introduction provides an overview of the phenomenon of media convergence and its specific effects for the audiovisual sector.

## *B. The phenomenon of media convergence*

### I. Conceptualising media convergence

Media convergence constitutes the de facto state of the industry, the backdrop for this study. The Commission's 2013 Green Paper "Preparing for a fully converged audiovisual world" suggests that convergence is a continuous process rather than a single event in time and that full media convergence has not yet been achieved. Media convergence has been a buzzword for the past two decades and debates have resurfaced again and again.[38] Although the bursting of the dot.com bubble at the turn of the new millen-

---

37 This study takes into account the state of play until the end of 2016.

38 Kempermann, *Content-Regulierung in konvergierenden Medien*, p. 8; Wolfgang Schulz, "Eine neue Medienordnung im Zeichen der Konvergenz," in *Neuordnung des Medienrechts, Neuer rechtlicher Rahmen für eine konvergente Technik?*, ed. Alexander Roßnagel, Schriftenreihe des Instituts für Europäischens Medienrecht (EMR) 30 (Baden-Baden: Nomos, 2005), p. 37.

nium in 2000/2001 slowed down developments,[39] it seems like we are currently witnessing a phase of enhanced or accelerated convergence. New kinds of services emerge everywhere, are immediately consumed and distributed in users' networks. By the same token, consumers "receive entertainment and other content from a multitude of sources".[40] Specifying a precise definition of media convergence is unnecessary as convergence is a heterogeneous phenomenon that takes place in different ways at different levels, all of which mutate, transform and intertwine with unprecedented rapidity.[41] Although convergence occurs inconsistently, some clarification of this concept is nonetheless needed to put this study in context.

A certain understanding can be achieved by reference to the various levels or contexts in which convergence occurs. On a technical level, convergence of platforms and distribution modes is furthered by digitisation.[42] Thanks to data compression, the size of data packages transported over networks is reduced allowing much greater amounts of data to be distributed in contrast to analogue transmission techniques.[43] In addition, the transmission capacity of networks and platforms has increased, thereby reducing the strain on finite resources (e.g. frequencies).[44] As a result, certain types of content are no longer tied to specific modes of transmission. Instead, content can be distributed by a variety of technologies.[45] Nowadays, for instance, digital telephone networks transport not only calls but also audio and audiovisual material such as videos. Providers of technological infrastructure have therefore coined the term "triple play", which

---

39 Kempermann, *Content-Regulierung in konvergierenden Medien*, p. 9; Karl-Heinz Neumann, "Technische und wirtschaftliche Konvergenz," in *Neuordnung des Medienrechts, Neuer rechtlicher Rahmen für eine konvergente Technik?*, ed. Alexander Roßnagel, Schriftenreihe des Instituts für Europäischens Medienrecht (EMR) 30 (Baden-Baden: Nomos, 2005), p. 33.

40 Thomas Crane, "OFCOM – a New Order for Communications Regulation or a Bureaucratic Nightmare?," *Computer and Telecommunications Law Review* 9, no. 2 (2003): p. 37.

41 Neumann, "Technische und wirtschaftliche Konvergenz," p. 30.

42 Neumann, "Technische und wirtschaftliche Konvergenz," p. 31; Ofcom, "Response to Commission Green Paper," para. 2.6, p. 8; Rahvar, *Die Zukunft des deutschen Presserechts*, p. 17.

43 Kempermann, *Content-Regulierung in konvergierenden Medien*, p. 12.

44 Rahvar in quoting Bullinger speaks of a situation of abundance ("Überflusssituation") which could be reached in the future. See Rahvar, *Die Zukunft des deutschen Presserechts*.

45 Kempermann, *Content-Regulierung in konvergierenden Medien*, pp. 11–12.

encompasses a single service for Internet access, broadcasting and telephony.[46] Consequently, "an end-user has an increased choice in the equipment he or she can use to carry out a particular task".[47] Importantly, the conventional distinction of services according to technical transmission has been abandoned and distribution networks and systems are now content-neutral.[48]

Furthermore, the notion of media convergence entails content convergence or "the interplay of content from various sources"[49] as stated by the Commission. More generally, content authors mix components of conventional sources in innovative ways or combine them with novel elements engaging consumers in new ways. As a consequence, new kinds of offers are emerging that blur the lines between previously distinct services.[50] Traditional legal categories therefore no longer appear appropriate.[51] Today, electronic magazines or newspapers available online typically offer audiovisual content in addition to their "traditional" business of written content.[52] Technology providers engage in content provision and content providers supply technology, leading to horizontal (between companies operating on the same level of the value chain) as well as vertical (companies operating at different levels of the value chain) market integration and the emergence of new business models.[53] Owing to compatible tech-

---

46 Kempermann, *Content-Regulierung in konvergierenden Medien*, p. 17. Today, the notion of "quadruple play" is also used encompassing the triple play service of Internet, TV and telephone including wireless services (e.g. for mobile phones).

47 Stuart Weinstein, "The Medium is the Message: The Legal and Policy Implications of the Creation of OFCOM in the Age of Convergence," *Computer and Telecommunications Law Review* 9, no. 6 (2003): p. 162.

48 Rahvar, *Die Zukunft des deutschen Presserechts*, p. 18; Weinstein, "The Medium is the Message," p. 162.

49 European Commission, Project factsheets: Convergence and social media, available at http://ec.europa.eu/digital-agenda/en/node/72984 (accessed 11.2.2015).

50 Weinstein, "The Medium is the Message," p. 162.

51 European Commission, "Green Paper Preparing for a Fully Converged Audiovisual World: Growth, Creation and Values, COM(2013) 231 Final," April 24, 2013, para. 1, p. 3; Kempermann, Philip, *Content-Regulierung in konvergierenden Medien*, p. 15.

52 Kempermann, *Content-Regulierung in konvergierenden Medien*, p. 15; Marcus Theurer, "Das Ende der Sofakartoffel," *Frankfurter Allgemeine Zeitung*, August 27, 2007, 198 edition.

53 Kempermann, *Content-Regulierung in konvergierenden Medien*, p. 8.

nologies, economic operators previously active in a particular field of the media environment may wish to expand into different sectors.[54]

Moreover, there is evidence that user behaviour is also converging. This type of convergence implies that users no longer differentiate between different media platforms and readily substitute one type for another.[55] The exclusive association of a particular media with entertainment, information or education is no longer maintained. Despite a gradual shift in consumption patterns, true convergence of user behaviour has not so far occurred.[56] It follows that the line between active "desk viewing" on the Internet and passive/lean-back "couch viewing" on the TV screen is still present,[57] albeit crumbling. Instead of an outright substitution of media, users seem to indulge in supplementary services offered in addition to the original service (e.g. videos complementing online magazines).[58] The supplementary use of services on various devices may also be explained by "consumers automatically defaulting to consuming content on the best screen available at the time of watching".[59] When at home, the TV screen appears most attractive to consumers while a mobile device obviously trumps any fixed screen when consumers are "on the go". What is more, no single converged device has yet been produced, regardless of the number of hybrid or smart devices such as smart phones or Connected TVs that have conquered the market in recent years thanks to their providing multiple services on a single device.[60] Furthermore, an interesting question is whether factual convergence requires or promotes regulatory convergence. As Craufurd Smith notes "in the converging media environment the boundaries between different types of media content and different media regulatory bodies are fading, putting pressure on the current

54 Rahvar, *Die Zukunft des deutschen Presserechts*, p. 20.
55 Kempermann, *Content-Regulierung in konvergierenden Medien*, p. 15.
56 Kempermann, *Content-Regulierung in konvergierenden Medien*, p. 15.
57 Kempermann, *Content-Regulierung in konvergierenden Medien*, p. 17; Ofcom, the UK communications regulator notes the stability and resilience of audience figures of traditional television as well as TV advertising revenues. Confer Ofcom, "Response to Commission Green Paper," paras. 2.11-2.22, 2.40, pp. 9, 11–12, 17.
58 Kempermann, *Content-Regulierung in konvergierenden Medien*, p. 16.
59 Ofcom, "Response to Commission Green Paper," para. 2.24, p. 13.
60 Kempermann, *Content-Regulierung in konvergierenden Medien*, p. 16.

regulatory structure".[61] In response to such developments, countries, such as Australia[62] and Canada,[63] have successfully launched converged or "connected"[64] regulators emulated in Europe, for example in Italy, Spain and the United Kingdom, where converged regulators that are mandated to oversee infrastructure and content have been established.

The consolidation of the various strands and constellations of media convergence is a complex endeavour. In its Green Paper, the Commission refers to "the progressive merger of traditional broadcast services and the [I]nternet".[65] The Commission's definition appears to fall short of the plethora of developments that contribute to media convergence as explained above. Nonetheless, it establishes a framework for the analysis conducted in this study, which is limited to the audiovisual sector. In this vein, Connected TV (or Smart TV as it has been called by European institutions) constitutes the epitome of media convergence. These are television sets that connect to the Internet and therefore merge the broadcast and broadband environments on one platform, on one screen.[66] Smart TVs are equipped with computer-like processors and a reverse channel that enables two-way communication and numerous network opportunities, if activated by viewers. Device manufacturers assume the role of gatekeepers for the kind of services integrated in their platforms and the manner in which they

---

61 Rachael Craufurd Smith et al., "The Independence of Media Regulatory Authorities in Finland and the UK: An Assessment," in *The Independence of the Media and Its Regulatory Agencies, Shedding New Light on Formal and Actual Independence against the National Context*, ed. Wolfgang Schulz, Peggy Valcke and Kristina Irion (Bristol, UK and Chicago, USA: Intellect, 2013), pp. 297, 298.

62 For the Australian Communications and Media Authority, see http://www.acma.gov.au/ (accessed 13.2.2015).

63 For the Canadian Radio-television and Telecommunications Commission, see http://www.crtc.gc.ca/eng/home-accueil.htm (accessed 13.2.2015).

64 The Australian Communications and Media Authority refers to "connected regulation" on its website. See About, The AVMA story, Connected regulation, available at http://www.acma.gov.au/theACMA/About/The-ACMA-story/Connected-regulation (accessed 13.2.2015).

65 European Commission, "Green Paper Preparing for a Converged Audiovisual World," para. 1, p. 3.

66 Patrick Godefroid et al., "Smart TV – ein interdisziplinärer Überblick," *Medien-Wirtschaft* 3 (2013): p. 3; Jürgen Sewczyk and Holger Wenk, "Mehr als Fernsehen: Smart TV, HbbTV & Co," *Media Perspektiven* 4 (2012): p. 178.

are presented to the user.[67] Apart from regular broadcasts, users may access additional services in the form of applications (apps) or connect to the World Wide Web. In fact, various windows may be opened simultaneously on the television screen to show an episode of a TV series in the left corner and Twitter feeds about the marriage of one of the main actors in the right corner. To enhance user experiences, services and applications are extended to a second screen offering supplementary information and other extras.

Currently, device manufacturers are improving the presentation of Internet content on the television screen (which needs to be adapted to the environment in which it is consumed) and introducing user-friendly navigation systems. There are no limits to new business models in a burgeoning but still volatile market. Penetration by Connected TVs is increasing[68] and the Commission expects that by 2016 the majority of EU households will have Connected TVs.[69] However, the actual use of the "smart" functions lags behind the production and purchase of such TVs.[70]

## II. The EU Audiovisual Media Services Directive in light of Connected TV

Against this background, the rules and standards set out in the AVMSD have come under enormous pressure. From the outset, the AVMSD and its predecessor the Television Without Frontiers Directive (TWFD) were brokered compromises that both took years to achieve. Torn between the poli-

---

67 Thomas Hess and Christian Matt, "Gatekeeper in der digitalen Medienwelt," *MedienWirtschaft* 3 (2012): p. 48; Ralf Kaumanns, "Der Smart TV-Markt: Akteure, Strategien, Geschäftsmodelle, in: Die Medienanstalten (Hrsg.), Wie smart ist die Konvergenz? Markt und Nutzung von Connected TV," ed. Hans Hege and Andreas Hamann (Die Medienanstalten, 2014), p. 11.

68 European Commission, "Staff Working Document, A Digital Single Market Strategy," para. 4.2, p. 42. For the penetration of smart TV in the UK, see Ofcom, "Response to Commission Green Paper," paras. 2.13, 2.16, pp. 9, 10.

69 European Commission, "Green Paper Preparing for a Converged Audiovisual World," para. 1, p. 3.

70 Hans Hege and Andreas Hamann, eds., "Wie smart ist die Konvergenz? Markt und Nutzung von Connected TV" (Die Medienanstalten, 2014), p. 4, http://www.die-medienanstalten.de/fileadmin/Download/Publikationen/Studie_ConnectedTV.pdf (accessed 10.2.2015); see also in this report Michael Wörmann, "Verhaltensmuster vernetzter TV-Nutzer: Eine ethnografische Studie", p. 37.

cy objectives of the European institutions and discrepancies about fundamental national understandings about the regulation of audiovisual media services (which continue to exist), the text of the Directive was watered down to give Member States room to manoeuvre at the national level. At the heart of the Directive lies an "inherent tension (…) which seeks to achieve a compromise between the (industrial policy) aim of ensuring broadcasters do not need 28 licences, and the (social/democratic) aim of respecting cultural diversity among Member States and the ability of their respective regulatory authorities to protect their citizens accordingly".[71]

However, the adoption of the AVMSD, despite quite considerable opposition, has been a success. The number of TV channels and VOD services has considerably grown throughout the past 20 years and many providers also supply services cross-border.[72] Of approximately 3,000 VOD services offered within the EU in 2015, more than 20percent operated cross-border.[73] Importantly, the prescription of minimum standards such as the prohibition from inciting hatred, conditions for commercial communications, and the screening of events of major importance exemplify the far-reaching effect of the Directive and its significance for the freedom of expression and the right to receive information. The basic standards, above all the country of origin principle crafted in the late 1980s and outlined in the TWFD, have been preserved in the AVMSD. Nevertheless, the gradual convergence of media would appear to necessitate a more profound recalibration of the Directive to make it future-proof. The current "toolbox" of the AVMSD seems ill-suited for the digital environment as will be shown in the sixth chapter.

In spite of similar reasoning by Member States regarding regulatory objectives, it appears that "regulatory creativity" is employed to make the AVMSD apply to new hybrid services. In its Green Paper of April 2013, the Commission acknowledged the weaknesses of the current legal framework and commissioned a public consultation from April to the end of

71 Ofcom, "Response to Commission Green Paper," para. 4.14, p. 26.

72 Schneeberger and Fontaine, "Linear and On-Demand Services in Europe 2015," pp. 24–27; see also André Lange, "Vers une révision a minima de la Directive SMA" (academia.edu, 2016), p. 10, https://www.academia.edu/27935361/VERS_UNE_REVISION_A_MINIMA_DE_LA_DIRECTIVE_SMA (accessed 28.8.2016).

73 Schneeberger and Fontaine, "Linear and On-Demand Services in Europe 2015," pp. 35, 41.

September 2013. The more than 200 responses that the Commission summarised in a feedback paper published in September 2014 make abundantly clear the sharp divisions over whether and to what extent the AVMSD should be revised.[74] For the current term of the *Juncker* Commission, which came to office at the beginning of November 2014, a REFIT exercise of the AVMSD was carried out "to test the regulatory fitness of the Directive".[75] Similarly, the Commission's Digital Single Market Strategy of May 2015 recognised the need to review the AVMSD to "ensure that it fully keeps up with market and technological developments".[76] After a public consultation from July to September 2015, the Commission published its proposal for a revised AVMSD in May 2016 (2016 AVMSD proposal). This study aims to contribute to the current debate on the revision of the Directive by testing its topicality and suitability. By analysing executive measures taken by NRAs, it identifies deficiencies in the Directive and endeavours to formulate proposals for its adjustment to the needs of a converged media environment.

74 The replies to the consultation are available at http://ec.europa.eu/digital-agenda/en/news/consultation-green-paper-preparing-fully-converged-audiovisual-world-growth-creation-and-values (accessed 12.2.2015). See also the feedback paper summarising stakeholders contributions: European Commission, "Summaries of the Replies to the Public Consultation Launched by the Green Paper 'Preparing for a Fully Converged Audiovisual World: Growth, Creation and Values,'" 2014, https://ec.europa.eu/digital-agenda/en/news/publication-summaries-green-paper-replies (accessed 12.2.2015).

75 European Commission, Media and Content Policies, available at http://ec.europa.eu/dgs/connect/en/content/implementation-audiovisual-media-services-directive (accessed 12.2.2015).

76 European Commission, "Communication on a Digital Single Market Strategy," para. 3.2, p. 11.

# Chapter 1. The regulation of audiovisual media services

Audiovisual media services have been regulated for many reasons. Traditionally, states have intervened and have established common rules for those providing audiovisual media services for economic as well as socio-cultural objectives. This intervention was justified as it has been considered that the market, left unregulated, would not be able to deliver these objectives. In addition to the national level, other layers of regulation have been added stemming from supra-national (EU) and international legal orders (Council of Europe, CoE). While initially the legal instruments adopted by the EU and CoE, were developed in parallel, their "mind-sets" have always been slightly different. Due to the distribution of competences, the EU's early regulatory involvement was predominantly driven by market considerations, even if gradually other general interest objectives, not least, fundamental rights have been taken into account. By contrast, the legal instrument negotiated at the CoE level is anchored firmly on the fundamental right to freedom of expression, while it acknowledges the economic dimension of broadcasting. Since the EU has, however, expanded the scale and scope of its regulation (notably by adopting the Audiovisual Media Services Directive, AVMSD), the CoE, given the blockage of negotiations, has not modernised its legal framework, which has lagged behind ever since.

Regulation of audiovisual media services has thus developed at different policy levels for different, sometimes overlapping reasons. Understanding the motives for regulation, as well as the purpose and objectives pursued thereby, will aid in the analysis, set forth below, of the measures taken by NRAs to implement the EU Directive. The first section of this chapter therefore sketches the general context in which the regulation of audiovisual media services takes place. It highlights the complex coexistence of rights and freedoms that have influenced regulatory choices. It then sheds light on the common rationales that motivate regulation of audiovisual media services, first at the state level and second at the European level. At the European level, the Council of Europe's Convention on Trans-Frontier Television (CTT) is worthy of investigation. First and foremost, however, this section will focus on the European Union and the development of a European media policy by the adoption of a Directive that, albeit in modified form, still constitutes the essential building block for the Union's involvement in the market for audiovisual media services.

### A. *The fundamental right of freedom of expression as a justification for regulating audiovisual media services*

The freedom of expression constitutes a fundamental right and is explicitly enshrined in national and European sources of law. In many states, it is constitutionally protected or, where no constitution exists, it has an essentially equivalent value. At the European level, the freedom of expression is recognised by two legal instruments, the Council of Europe's European Convention on Human Rights (ECHR) and the EU's Charter of Fundamental Rights (CFR).[77] While the relationship between these two instruments is complex, it has to be stressed here that the CFR is interpreted in light of the ECHR to the extent that the former contains rights that correspond to those included in the ECHR.[78] While individuals may directly invoke the rights outlined in the ECHR (after exhausting national remedies), the CFR is addressed to the EU bodies and institutions as well as Member States where they implement Union law.[79] Due to the limited case law on

---

77 See Art. 10 ECHR and Art. 11 CFR.

78 See Art. 52 (3) CFR. Art. 6 (2) TEU stipulates that the Union shall accede to the ECHR. On the EU's accession to the ECHR, see Eleanor Spaventa, "Fundamental Rights in the European Union," in *European Union Law*, ed. Catherine Barnard and Steeve Peers (Oxford: Oxford University Press, 2014), pp. 246–52; see also Paul Gragl, *The Accession of the European Union to the European Convention on Human Rights* (Oxford: Hart Publishing, 2013).

79 See Art. 51 (1) CFR. In its case law, the CJEU has broadly interpreted Art. 51 (1) CFR. It underscored that Member States are bound by the CFR when implementing EU law (case C-279/09 *DEB Deutsch Energiehandels- und Beratungsgesellschaft mbH v Bundesrepublik Deutschland*, Judgment of 22.12.2010, EU:C:2010:811, para. 32). The CFR is thus applicable to the EU's fields of competence (case C-370/12 *Pringle v Government of Ireland, Ireland and the Attorney General*, Judgment of 27.11.2012, EU:C:2012:756, para. 179). Within the fields of competence, the CJEU has clarified that the CFR is applicable "in all situations governed by EU law" (case C-617/10 *Åklagaren v Hans Åkerberg Fransson*, Judgment of 26.2.2013, EU:C:2013:105, para. 21). It follows that "applicability of European Union law entails applicability of the fundamental rights guaranteed by the Charter" (case C-617/10 *Åkerberg*, para. 21). In matters of shared competence, Member States may rely on national standards of protection as long as the protection afforded by the CFR is not compromised (case C-399/11 *Stefano Melloni v*

Art. 11 CFR, the freedom of expression is conceptualised here predominantly by reference to the jurisprudence of the European Court of Human Rights (ECtHR). The following section provides a brief overview of the meaning of the right to freedom of expression and its significance for the audiovisual sector. It makes also clear that the exercise of the freedom of expression may be legitimately restricted by other fundamental rights.

## I. The freedom of expression and information

The freedom of expression "constitutes one of the essential foundations of a democratic society, one of the basic conditions for its progress and for each individual's self-fulfilment". [80] This quote from the jurisprudence of the ECtHR shows that the freedom of expression contributes to the functioning and flourishing of democracies. It also fulfils a social function in relation to the personal development of the individual citizen, who is enabled to seek information and, on this basis, form an opinion in order to actively participate in social life. The freedom of expression therefore entails the right to hold and communicate[81] one's opinions and to seek, receive and impart information. Importantly, the notion of expression is interpreted broadly covering not only information or ideas "that are favourably received or regarded as inoffensive or as a matter of indifference, but also to those that offend, shock or disturb the State or any sector

---

*Ministerio Fiscal*, Judgment of 26.2.2013, EU:C:2013:107, para. 60). See also Jörg Gerkrath, "En tant que clé de voûte du système de protection des droits fondamentaux de l'Union européenne la Charte demande une application large et décentralisée," 2012, pp. 13, 16; Craig, Paul and De Búrca, Gráinne, *EU Law, Text, Cases, and Materials*, fifth edition (Oxford: Oxford University Press, 2011), pp. 415–19.

80 ECtHR, *Lingens v Austria*, Judgment of 8.6.1986, Application no. 9815/82, para. 41. On Art. 10 ECHR, see generally Monica Macovei, *Freedom of Expression, A Guide to the Implementation of Article 10 of the European Convention on Human Rights*, ed. Directorate General of Human Rights, Council of Europe, second edition, Human Rights Handbooks 2 (Strasbourg, 2004), http://rm.coe.int/CoERMPublicCommonSearchServices/DisplayDCTMContent?documentId=090000168007ff48 (accessed 18.1.2016).

81 On the right to communicate, see Daithi Sithigh, "From Freedom of Speech to the Right to Communicate," in *Routledge Handbook of Media Law*, ed. Monroe Price, Stefaan Verhulst, and Libby Morgan (London and New York: Routledge, 2013), pp. 175–92.

of the population".[82] Broadly, a distinction has been made between political, artistic and commercial speech, although the boundaries are not clear-cut and the latter typically enjoys a lower level of protection.[83] Freedom of expression thus implies "pluralism, tolerance and broadmindedness without which there is no 'democratic society'".[84] The right to freedom of expression does not only protect the type of information but also its form. It applies regardless of whether the expression is encapsulated in a written document,[85] a broadcast,[86] a film,[87] advertising[88] or communicated via the Internet[89]. The Internet, in particular, as a means of communication, is a facilitator and enabler of free speech and allows citizens unprecedented degrees of access to information as well as involvement in democratic processes and opinion forming.[90] Yet, the Internet also bears challenges for the free dissemination of speech, especially where it is hateful or defama-

---

82 ECtHR, *Handyside v United Kingdom*, Judgment of 7.12.1976, Application no. 5493/72, para. 49. Krenc is, however, critical of the Strasbourg jurisprudence and underscores its incoherence regarding offensive speech, see Frédéric Krenc, "La liberté d'expression vaut pour les propos qui 'heurtent, choquent ou inquiètent'. Mais encore ?," *Revue trimestrielle des droits de l'homme* 106 (2016): pp. 311–50.

83 Lorna Woods, "Article 11," in *The EU Charter of Fundamental Rights, A Commentary*, ed. Peers et al. (United Kingdom: Hart Publishin, 2014), para. 11.28, p. 322; on commercial speech and advertising, see Andrew Nicol, Gavin Millar, and Andrew Sharland, *Media Law and Human Rights*, second edition (Oxford: Oxford University Press, 2009), paras. 12.01-12.36.

84 ECtHR, *Handyside v United Kingdom*, Judgment of 7.12.1976, Application no. 5493/72, para. 49.

85 ECtHR, *Handyside v United Kingdom*, Judgment of 7.12.1976, Application no. 5493/72, para. 49.

86 ECtHR, *Groppera Radio AG a.o. v Switzerland*, Judgment of 28.3.1990, Application no. 10890/84, para. 59. The ECtHR made clear in this case (paras. 60-61) that the freedom of expression as stipulated by Art. 10 ECHR does not preclude states from requiring broadcast licenses in line with the third sentence of Art. 10 (1) ECHR. See also Nicol, Millar and Sharland, *Media Law and Human Rights*, paras. 11.02-11.09.

87 ECtHR, *Otto-Preminger Institut v Austria*, Judgment of 20.9.1994, Application no. 13470/87, para. 42.

88 ECtHR, *Murphy v Ireland*, Judgment of 3.12.2003, Application no. 44179/98, para. 61; ECtHR, *Verein gegen Tierfabriken v Switzerland*, Judgment of 28.6.2001, Application no. 24699/94, para. 48.

89 ECtHR, *Delfi AS v Estonia*, Judgment of 16.6.2015, Application no. 64569/09, para. 110.

90 ECtHR, *Times Newspapers Ltd v United Kingdom*, Judgment of 10.3.2009, Applications nos. 3002/03 and 23676/03, para. 27. See also Barata, Verhulst and Mor-

tory and thus considered unlawful. Any kind of expression "can be disseminated like never before, worldwide, in a matter of seconds, and [it] sometimes remain[s] persistently available online".[91] While the right to freedom of expression applies to the Internet, the specific characteristics of the medium will be taken into account when balancing the rights of affected parties.[92]

Furthermore, the media, above all, audiovisual media, has been a channel through which opinions and ideas are communicated to the general public. Audiovisual media (radio and broadcasting and on-demand audiovisual media services), like other types of media (the press) performs the role of public watchdog.[93] It reports on developments and event of public interest in order to allow citizens to form opinions and hold the state accountable for its actions. Due to the force of the moving image in conveying information,[94] it is vital to establish safeguards that prevent the emergence of a monopoly of information which would have an overwhelmingly one-sided influence on the public.[95] Such safeguards aim at ensuring media pluralism.[96] The objectives of media pluralism and media freedom are expressly prescribed by Art. 11 (2) CFR. Media freedom implies edito-

---

gan, "The Different Concepts of Free Expression and its Link with Democracy, the Public Sphere and Other Concepts," in *Routledge Handbook of*, ed. Price (London and New York: Routledge, 2013), p. 135.

91 ECtHR, *Delfi AS v Estonia*, Judgment of 16.6.2015, Application no. 64569/09, para. 110.

92 For a concise overview of the EHtCR's jurisprudence in relation to the Internet, see Council of Europe, ed., "Internet: Case-Law of the European Court of Human Rights," up-dated 2015 , http://www.echr.coe.int/Documents/Research_report_internet_ENG.pdf (accessed 10.8.2015).

93 ECtHR, *Jersild v Denmark*, Judgment of 23.9.1994, Application no. 15890/89, para. 31. See also Woods, "Article 11," para. 11.22, p. 320; Ronan Fathaigh and Dirk Voorhoof, "The European Court of Human Rights, Media Freedom and Democracy," in *Routledge Handbook of Media Law*, ed. Price, Verhulst and Morgan (London and New York: Routledge, 2013), p. 109.

94 ECtHR, *Jersild v Denmark*, Judgment of 23.9.1994, Application no. 15890/89, para. 31; ECtHR, *Murphy v Ireland*, Judgment of 3.12.2003, Application no. 44179/98, para. 74.

95 ECtHR, *VgT Verein gegen Tierfabriken v Switzerland*, Judgment of 28.6.2001, Application no. 24699/94, paras. 73,75; ECtHR, *Informationsverein Lentia a.o. v Austria*, Judgment of 24.11.1993, Application nos. 13914/88; 15041/89; 15717/89; 15779/89; 17207/90, para. 39.

96 Fathaigh and Voorhoof, "The European Court of Human Rights, Media Freedom and Democracy," p. 109.

rial independence of service providers, especially their independence from governmental or other influences. Media pluralism means that citizens have access to a range of sources and therefore encounter diverse opinions and ideas which nourish their own viewpoints. It is a simple but fundamental truism "that there can be no democracy without pluralism".[97] Given the importance attributed to media pluralism, interference by the state regulating the circulation and dissemination of audiovisual media services has been considered acceptable.[98] What is more, the ECtHR even carved out a positive duty for the state "to ensure, first, that the public has access through television and radio to impartial and accurate information and a range of opinion and comment, reflecting inter alia the diversity of political outlook within the country and, secondly, that journalists and other professionals working in the audiovisual media are not prevented from imparting this information and comment".[99] Public service media plays a particularly crucial role in providing independent and trustworthy information, reflecting a wide spectrum of viewpoints and ideas.[100]

As the dissemination of hate speech demonstrates, there are limits to the freedom of expression. According to Art. 10 (2) ECHR, the restrictions must be prescribed by law and be necessary in a democratic society. The provision also explicitly and exhaustively lists the grounds on which the right to freedom of expression may be restricted. These are "national security, territorial integrity or public safety", "the prevention of disorder or

97 ECtHR, *Manole a.o. v Moldova*, Judgment of 17.12.2009, Application no. 13936/02, para. 95.

98 At the EU level, the CJEU has recognised media pluralism as a general interest objective capable of restricting the fundamental freedom to provide services. See cases C-353/89 *Commission of the European Communities v Kingdom of the Netherlands*, Judgment of 25.7.1991, EU:C:1991:325, para. 29; C-288/89 *Stichting Collectieve Antennevoorziening Gouda and others v Commissariaat voor de Media*, Judgment of 25.7.1991, EU:C:1991:323, para. 23; C-148/91 *Vereniging Veronica Omroep Organisatie v Commissariaat voor de Media*, Judgment of 3.2.1993, EU:C:1993:45, para. 9.

99 ECtHR, *Manole a.o. v Moldova*, Judgment of 17.12.2009, Application no. 13936/02, para. 100. See also ECtHR, *Centro Europa 7 S.R.L. and Di Stefano v Italy*, Judgment of 7.6.2012, Application no. 38433/09, para. 134.

100 See the Council of Europe's Recommendation Rec(2007)2 of the Committee of Ministers to member states on media pluralism and diversity of media content, adopted on 31 January 2007, para. 3.

crime", "the protection of health or morals",[101] "the protection of the reputation or rights of others", "preventing the disclosure of information received in confidence", or "maintaining the authority and impartiality of the judiciary". On account of the structural differences,[102] Art. 11 CFR does not set out the limits to the right to freedom of expression and information. Instead, Art. 52 (1) CFR applies horizontally and specifies that any limitation to the fundamental rights "must be provided for by law and respect the essence of those rights and freedoms".[103] In addition, restrictions must conform to the principle of proportionality[104] and may only be made "if they are necessary and genuinely meet objectives of general interest recognised by the Union or the need to protect the rights and freedoms of others". It has been considered that the notion of legitimate public interest objectives is interpreted in light of the grounds stipulated in Art. 10 (2) ECHR and cannot be wider than the latter.[105] The following section demonstrates the interplay of fundamental rights and freedoms and the potential for conflict inherent in the provision of audiovisual media services.

---

101 ECtHR, *Mouvement Raelien Suisse v Switzerland*, Judgment of 13.1.2013, Application no. 16354/06. On the conflict between freedom of expression and public morals and religious freedom, see Mercedes Candela Soriano and Alexandre Defossez, "La liberté d'expression face à la morale et à la religion: analyse de la jurisprudence de la Cour Européenne des Droit de l'Homme," *Revue trimestrielle des droits de l'homme* 68 (2006): pp. 817–37.

102 Woods, "Article 11," para. 11.37, p. 327.

103 While the CJEU commonly determines the incompatibility of a restriction on fundamental rights on the basis of its proportionality analysis, it has so far been exceptional that the CJEU finds that the essence of a fundamental right enshrined by the CFR is affected. Interestingly, in the field of data protection and in the context of transatlantic data flows, the CJEU held in a case of October 2015 that the restrictions imposed on the right to respect for private life (Art. 7 CFR) and the right to effective judicial protection (Art. 47 CFR) compromised the core of these rights and were thus unlawful. See case C-362/14 *Maximillian Schrems v Data Protection Commissioner*, EU:C:2015:650, paras. 94-95. On the CFR's scope of application, see Spaventa, "Fundamental Rights in the European Union," pp. 240–42; on the *Schrems* case, see Nico Van Eijk, "Annotatie bij Hof van Justitie 6 oktober 2015 (C-362/14 *Maximillian Schrems v Data Protection Commissioner*)," *Tijdschrift voor Consumentenrecht en handelspraktijken* 4 (2016): pp. 189–99.

104 Woods, "Article 11," para. 11.40, pp. 328–29.

105 Woods, "Article 11," para. 11.37, p. 327.

## II. An area of tension between fundamental rights and fundamental freedoms

The dissemination of information by audiovisual media potentially clashes with other fundamental rights guaranteed at the national or European level (i.e. by the ECHR and the CFR).[106] In the EU, a "fully fledged [unique] legal order",[107] several layers of protection may be distinguished: fundamental rights, general principles[108] and fundamental freedoms. These interact with each other, forming a complex legal construction.[109] It is the task of legislatures as well as judiciaries (in retrospect) to carry out a balancing exercise in order to determine how much weight is attributed to a value and which right or freedom trump in specific circumstances. In the EU, the regulation of audiovisual media services is anchored in the freedom to provide services across national borders as guaranteed by Art. 56 TFEU. While the motifs of the EU for adopting measures to regulate certain aspects of audiovisual media services are detailed below, the following section illustrates the balance struck in individual cases.

---

106 On the complexity of rights protection in Europe and the relationship between the ECHR and the EU legal orders, see Pedro Cruz Villalón, "Rights in Europe: The Crowded House, King's College Papers in European Law, No. 1," 2012, https://www.kcl.ac.uk/law/research/centres/european/research/CELWPEL012012FINAL.pdf (accessed 25.1.2016); Bucura Mihaescu Evans, "The 'gaps' in Protection Stemming from the (Problematic) Coexistence of Fundamental Rights' Sources in the EU Legal Order," *Cahiers de Droit Européen*, no. 1 (2016).

107 Cruz Villalón, "Rights in Europe: The Crowded House," p. 10.

108 General principles are unwritten sources of EU law that stem from the jurisprudence of the CJEU. Fundamental rights have been regarded as general principles, although they have become part of EU Primary Law (Art. 6 (1) TEU in conjunction with the CFR). For a comprehensive overview of the EU's general principles, see Herwig Hofmann, Gerard Rowe and Alexander Türk, *Administrative Law and Policy of the European Union* (Oxford: Oxford University Press, 2011); see also Takis Tridimas, *The General Principles of EU Law*, second edition (Oxford: Oxford University Press, 2006); Spaventa, "Fundamental Rights in the European Union," p. 229.

109 On the interaction between fundamental rights and general principles, see Herwig Hofmann and Bucura Mihaescu, "The Relation between the Charter's Fundamental Rights and the Unwritten General Principles of Law: Good Administration as the Test-Case," *European Constitutional Law Review* 9, no. 1 (2013): pp. 73–101.

### 1. Free movement of services

Within the EU legal order, the free circulation of services constitutes one of the four fundamental freedoms.[110] Its inclusion in the Treaties dates back to the origins of European (economic) integration and the conception of the European Coal and Steal Community in 1950. Ever since, the free movement of services has been a crucial aspect of the single market and constitutes the legal basis for the EU's involvement in the regulation of broadcasting, as shown below. Directive 2006/123/EC on services in the internal market (Services Directive) complements the EU Primary Law provisions and sector-specific legislation.[111] As with other fundamental freedoms, the CJEU has shaped this freedom by its jurisprudence.

The notion of "service" contains an autonomous meaning within EU law and implies an intangible, tactile object.[112] Art. 57 TFEU specifies that an activity is considered as a "service" where it is "normally provided for remuneration". This highlights the economic nature of services which must not necessarily be traded for money as long as they can be valued in money.[113] Importantly, the remuneration must not be paid directly by the recipient of the service.[114] Moreover, for the fundamental freedom to be triggered, a cross-border element is necessary. Thus, the free movement of services applies to situation where the service provider and the service recipient are established in different Member States or where the service it-

---

110 The four freedoms are the free movement of goods, persons, services and capital.

111 On the Services Directive, see Catherine Barnard and Jukka Snell, "Free Movement of Legal Persons and the Provision of Services," in *European Union Law*, ed. Catherine Barnard and Steeve Peers (Oxford: Oxford University Press, 2014), p. 426 et seq.

112 Damian Chalmers, Gareth Davies and Giorgio Monti, *European Union Law*, second edition (Cambridge: Cambridge University Press, 2010), p. 787; Daniel-Erasmus Khan and Dominik Eisenhut, "Dienstleistungen," in *Europäisches Unionsrecht*, ed. Christoph Vedder and Wolff Heintschell von Heinegg (Baden-Baden: Nomos, 2012), para. 9, p. 392.

113 Paul Craig and Gráinne De Búrca, *EU Law, Text, Cases, and Materials*, p. 824; Chalmers, Davies and Monti, *European Union Law*, p. 790; Khan and Eisenhut, "Dienstleistungen," para. 12, p. 393; Barnard and Snell, "Free Movement of Legal Persons and the Provision of Services," p. 409.

114 Case C-422/01 *Försäkringsaktiebolaget Skandia (publ) and Ola Ramstedt v Riksskatteverket*, Judgment of 26.6.2003, EU:C:2003:380, para. 24. See also Barnard and Snell, "Free Movement of Legal Persons and the Provision of Services," p. 409.

self travels across borders (as is the case for audiovisual media services).[115] In contrast to the freedom of establishment, which requires a certain level of economic integration in the host Member State, the freedom to provide services applies where the provider moves to another Member State to "[pursue] his activity on a temporary basis".[116] In general, Art. 56 TFEU is addressed to Member States but the CJEU has confirmed that it may also apply horizontally between private actors in certain circumstances.[117]

Furthermore, the free movement of services may be restricted by virtue of the express justifications stipulated in Art. 62 TFEU in conjunction with Art. 52 TFEU (i.e. public policy, public security or public health).[118] In its *Gebhardt* decision, the CJEU broadly interpreted the notion of "restriction" as encompassing all national measures "liable to hinder or make less attractive the exercise of fundamental freedoms".[119] Such measures may be justified if they are "equally applicable to the national and the for-

115 Craig and De Búrca, *EU Law, Text, Cases, and Materials*, p. 824; Chalmers, Davies and Monti, *European Union Law*, p. 788; Khan and Eisenhut, "Dienstleistungen," para. 21, pp. 395–96; Barnard and Snell, "Free Movement of Legal Persons and the Provision of Services," p. 410.

116 Case C-55/94 *Reinhard Gebhard v Consiglio dell'Ordine degli Avvocati e Procuratori di Milano*, Judgment of 30.11.1995, EU:C:1995:411, para. 26. See also Khan and Eisenhut, "Dienstleistungen," para. 16, p. 394; Barnard and Snell, "Free Movement of Legal Persons and the Provision of Services," p. 409.

117 Case 36/74 *Walrave and Koch v Association Union Cycliste Internationale*, Judgment of 12.12.1974, EU:C:1974:140, paras. 19 and 20; Chalmers, Davies and Monti, *European Union Law*, p. 797.

118 Case 352/85 *Bond van Adverteerders und andere gegen Niederländischer Staat*, Judgment of 26.4.1988, EU:C:1988:196, paras. 32-33; Case C-288/89 *Collectieve Antennevoorziening Gouda and Others v Commissariaatvoor de Media*, Judgment of 25.7.1991, EU:C:1991:323, para. 11. See also Barnard and Snell, "Free Movement of Legal Persons and the Provision of Services," p. 421.

119 Case C-55/94 *Reinhard Gebhard v Consiglio dell'Ordine degli Avvocati e Procuratori di Milano*, para. 37. See also Chalmers, Davies and Monti, *European Union Law*, p. 793; Barnard and Snell call this the "market access approach" which is also followed by the CJEU in case C-384/93 *Alpine Investments BV v Minister van Financiën*, Judgment of 10.5.1995, EU:C:1995:126, see Barnard and Snell, "Free Movement of Legal Persons and the Provision of Services," pp. 403–42; see also Khan and Eisenhut, "Dienstleistungen," para. 34, p. 399; Chalmers, Davies, and Monti, *European Union Law*, p. 793.

eign;[120] [are] justified by some legitimate public interest objective[121] and [are] proportionate to that objective".[122] In the *Gouda* case, the CJEU recognised cultural policies aimed at safeguarding the freedom of expression and maintaining pluralism as an "overriding requirement relating to the general interest" that is, in principle, capable of justifying a restriction on the free movement of services.[123] Yet, the Court considered that the Dutch measure laying down conditions for the cable transmission of broadcasts from other Member States containing advertising directed at the Dutch public, was discriminatory and went beyond what was necessary.[124]

The case of *ARD v Pro Sieben*[125] may serve as another illustration of how the CJEU balanced the freedom to provide services with general interest objectives in the audiovisual sector. The case arose between the German public service broadcaster ARD and its commercial opponent Pro Sieben on the interpretation of an advertising rule regulating the calculation of the number of advertising interruptions. Accordingly, feature-length films, which lasted longer than 45 minutes, could be interrupted once for each period of 45 minutes. An additional advertising break was permissible if the duration was at least 20 minutes longer than 90 minutes. This rule is still applicable today but the time intervals have been relaxed

120 See also Craig and De Búrca, *EU Law, Text, Cases, and Materials*, pp. 828–30.

121 Overriding reasons in the public interest which the CJEU has already recognised include professional rules intended to protect recipients of the service, protection of intellectual property, the protection of workers, consumer protection as well as the conservation of the national historic and artistic heritage. See C-288/89 *Collectieve Antennevoorziening Gouda and Others v Commissariaat voor de Media*, para. 14. See also Khan and Eisenhut, "Dienstleistungen," para. 35, p. 399; Barnard and Snell, "Free Movement of Legal Persons and the Provision of Services," p. 422.

122 Chalmers, Davies and Monti, *European Union Law*, p. 803. See also Case C-55/94 *Reinhard Gebhard v Consiglio dell'Ordine degli Avvocati e Procuratori di Milano*, para. 37.

123 Case C-288/89 *Collectieve Antennevoorziening Gouda and Others v Commissariaatvoor de Media*, paras. 22-23.

124 Case C-288/89 *Collectieve Antennevoorziening Gouda and Others v Commissariaatvoor de Media*, paras. 25, 28-29.

125 Case C-6/98 *ARD v Pro Sieben*, Judgment of 28.10.1999, ECLI:EU:C:1999:532.

by successive revisions of the Directive.[126] The decisive question was whether the time of advertising was included in the period of time used for the calculation (so-called gross principle) or whether the calculation was to be made solely on the basis of the length of the film (so-called net principle). The gross principle would allow for more advertising breaks.

In its judgment of October 1999, the CJEU pointed out that the wording of the Directive was equivocal[127] and that the ambivalence could neither be resolved by reference to the different language versions of the Directive nor by history of the Directive and its preparatory documents.[128] The Court underpinned that the primary objective of the Directive is to "ensure freedom to provide television broadcasting services".[129] Any restriction on that activity should be formulated in clear terms and where this is not the case, it must be interpreted strictly.[130] The restriction outlined in the advertising provision must therefore be given a restrictive interpretation.[131] Consequently, the Directive provides for the gross principle.[132] In addition, the referring German court inquired whether Member States could

126 Article 11(3) of the TWFD of 1989 provided as follows: "The transmission of audiovisual works such as feature films and films made for television (excluding series, serials, light entertainment programmes and documentaries), provided their scheduled duration is more than 45 minutes, maybe interrupted once for each period of 45 minutes. A further interruption shall be allowed if their scheduled duration is at least 20 minutes longer than two or more complete periods of 45 minutes".
Art. 20 (2) AVMSD requires that the "transmission of films made for television (excluding series, serials and documentaries), cinematographic works and news programmes may be interrupted by television advertising and/or teleshopping once for each scheduled period of at least 30 minutes. The transmission of children's programmes may be interrupted by television advertising and/or teleshopping once for each scheduled period of at least 30 minutes, provided that the scheduled duration of the programme is greater than 30 minutes. No television advertising or teleshopping shall be inserted during religious services".

127 On the topic of linguistic varieties of Secondary Union law, see Mark Cole and Florian Haus, "Dienstleistungsfreiheit brutto oder netto? Probleme der europäischen Sprachenvielfalt am Beispiel der EG-Fernsehrichtlinie," *Juristische Schulung*, 2001, pp. 435–40.

128 Case C-6/98 *ARD v Pro Sieben*, paras. 26-27.

129 Case C-6/98 *ARD v Pro Sieben*, para. 28.

130 Case C-6/98 *ARD v Pro Sieben*, paras. 29-30.

131 Case C-6/98 *ARD v Pro Sieben*, para. 31.

132 Case C-6/98 *ARD v Pro Sieben*, para. 33.

prescribe the net principle as a stricter or more detailed rule.[133] The Court clarified that Member States were authorised to lay down stricter rules in relation to the provision at issue as the freedom to provide services was not "affected in any way if Member States impose stricter rules on advertising".[134] Furthermore, the Court was asked whether the adoption of the net principle by one Member State was compatible with Primary EU law, namely the cross-border circulation of services. The CJEU noted that the net principle constitutes a restriction on the freedom to provide services as it sets limits for advertisers established in other Member States.[135] Yet, this restriction could be justified by overriding reasons relating to the general interest such as the protection of consumers from excessive advertising as well as the "maintenance of a certain level of programme quality" as an "aim of cultural policy".[136] The Court also considered that the restriction was proportionate.[137] The case thus demonstrates the importance of the fundamental freedom to provide services for the audiovisual media services market and how it interrelates with other general interest objectives, such as the protection of viewers' interests and the preservation of the specificities of the European audiovisual model, which highly values the integrity of programmes. In a similar vein, the Court referred to consumer protection in subsequent cases concerning the Directive's advertising rules to justify proportionate restrictions to the freedom to provide services.[138] The preamble to the Directive reflects this objective, too.[139]

---

133 Given the minimum harmonisation approach of the Directive, it has expressly granted Member States to adopt more detailed or stricter rules in the coordinated fields. See Art. 3 (1) TWFD of 1989 and Art. 4 (1) AVMSD.

134 Case C-6/98 *ARD v Pro Sieben*, para. 42.

135 Case C-6/98 *ARD v Pro Sieben*, para. 49.

136 Case C-6/98 *ARD v Pro Sieben*, para. 50.

137 Case C-6/98 *ARD v Pro Sieben*, para. 51.

138 Cases C-195/06 *Kommunikationsbehörde Austria v Österreichischer Rundfunk*, Judgment of 18.10.2007, EU:C:2007:613, paras.26-27; C-281/09 *European Commission v Kingdom of Spain*, Judgment of 24.11.2011, EU:C:2011:767, paras. 44-46; C-234/12 *Sky Italia Srl v Autorità per le Garanzie nelle Comunicazioni*, Judgment of 18.7.2013, EU:C:2013:496, para. 17; C-314/14 *Sanoma Media Finland Oy – Nelonen Media v Viestintävirasto*, Judgment of 17.2.2016, EU:C:2016:89, para. 34.

139 Recital 83 AVMSD.

## 2. Other fundamental rights

Apart from fundamental freedoms, other rights that may be implicated and conflict with the right to freedom of expression are the right to respect for private life (confer Art. 8 ECHR and Art. 7 CFR), the right to privacy (confer Art. 8 ECHR and Art. 8 CFR), the rights of the child (confer Art. 24 CFR), the freedom of thought and of religion (confer Art. 9 ECHR and Art. 10 CFR), intellectual property rights (confer Art. 1 Protocol no. 1 to the ECHR and Art. 17 CFR) and due process rights (confer Art. 6 and 13 ECHR and Art. 47 CFR).[140] This exemplary list underpins the context of constant frictions with other fundamental rights and freedoms. In the fifth chapter, the clash between the freedom of expression and the rights of the child will become apparent. Where societies consider that audiovisual content is inappropriate for minors due to their state of development, the freedom of expression may be legitimately restricted provided the restrictions are proportionate. This is for instance the case when pornographic or extremely violent content is disseminated. It follows that the freedom of expression, though being of paramount importance for a functioning democracy, is not absolute and will have to be balanced with other, equally valid fundamental rights or freedoms. In other words, there is no hierarchy of rights and the prevalence a fundamental right will have to be established on a case-by-case basis.

The *Sky Österreich*[141] ruling of the CJEU may serve as an example of the rights which may collide with the freedom of expression. The case concerns the right to short news reports as stipulated by Art. 15 Audiovisual Media Services Directive (AVMSD). This provision ensures that the public is informed, by means of short reports, about events of high interest to the public that are broadcast on exclusive basis.[142] Art. 15

140 On the right to an effective remedy, see Herwig Hofmann, "General Principles of EU Law and EU Administrative Law," in *European Union Law*, ed. Catherine Barnard and Steeve Peers (Oxford: Oxford University Press, 2014), p. 219.

141 Case C-283/11 *Sky Österreich v Österreichischer Rundfunk*, Judgment of 22.1.2013, EU:C:2013:28.

142 On short news reporting, see Peter Matzneller, "Short Reporting Rights in Europe: European Legal Rules and their National Transposition and Application," in *Exclusive Rights and Short Reporting*, ed. Susanne Nikoltchev, IRIS Plus 2012/4 4 (Strasbourg: European Audiovisual Observatory, 2012), pp. 7–24; Claudia Wildmann, *Das Europäische Kurzberichterstattungsrecht im Lichte der Richtlinie über audiovisuelle Mediendienste.*

AVMSD does not, as such, prevent the exclusive dissemination of such events, for example by pay-TV operators.[143] It grants broadcasters access to important events for the purpose of short reporting. In practice, broadcasters are typically given access to the transmitting broadcaster's signal to produce the brief extracts broadcast during their news programmes.[144] Art. 15 AVMSD reconciles the rights and interests of various parties including rights holders, broadcasters, event organisers and viewers. The dispute in *Sky Österreich* opposed the pay-TV provider Sky to the Austrian public service broadcaster ORF. Sky had acquired exclusive rights to broadcast the Europa League matches spending several million euros on licence and production costs. It had concluded an agreement with ORF granted the latter the right to produce short news reports against payment of € 700 per minute. Art. 15 (6) AVMSD specifies that "where compensation is provided for, it shall not exceed the additional costs directly incurred in providing access". ORF therefore requested an investigation in the amount of remuneration by the Austrian regulatory authority, KommAustria that decided that Sky was not entitled to demand remuneration. Sky appealed KommAustria's decision before the Austrian courts which referred a preliminary question to the CJEU on the interpretation of Art. 15 AVMSD.

The CJEU examined whether Art. 15 AVMSD was compatible with the right to conduct a business (Art. 16 CFR)[145] and the right to property (Art. 17 CFR). It held that Sky cannot rely on Art. 17 CFR as Union law, in particular Art. 15 AVMSD as transposed by Member States precluded the broadcaster from exercising its rights autonomously.[146] Furthermore, the Court acknowledges that Art. 15 (6) AVMSD interferes with the right to choose with whom to do business and under what terms as conferred under Art. 16 CFR. The Court then appraises the proportionality of the re-

143 Art. 15 AVMSD complements Art. 14 AVMSD which provides for the live or quasi-live free-to-air transmission of events of major importance for society in line with certain conditions.

144 See Art. 15 (3) and (4) AVMSD.

145 On the scope and meaning of the right to conduct a business, see for example European Union Agency for Fundamental Rights, "Freedom to Conduct a Business: Exploring the Dimensions of a Fundamental Right," 2015, paras. 2.1 et seq., http://fra.europa.eu/sites/default/files/fra_uploads/fra-2015-freedom-conduct-business_en.pdf (accessed 15.8.2016).

146 Case C-283/11 *Sky Österreich*, para. 38.

striction on the right to conduct a business.[147] It makes clear that the interference does not affect the "core content of the freedom to conduct a business".[148] The CJEU also clarifies that the provision on short reporting pursues a legitimate objective in the general interest[149] and allows every broadcaster, regardless of its commercial power, to access important events for the purpose of producing short reports.[150] In addition, the Court confirms the necessity of the rule contained in the Directive as less restrictive measures would not have achieved the objective pursued as effectively as Art. 15 AVMSD.[151] It is interesting to note that the CJEU also comments on the allegedly disproportionate nature of Art. 15 (6) AVMSD. It underscores that the "European Union legislature was required to strike a balance between the freedom to conduct a business, on the one hand, and the fundamental freedom of citizens of the European Union to receive information and the freedom and pluralism of the media, on the other".[152] According to the Court, the conditions laid down in Art. 15 AVMSD for the use of short reports ensure that "the extent of the interference" is "confined within precise limits".[153] Short news reports are, for instance, restricted to general news programmes and their duration is limited.[154]

This case thus underpins the need to reconcile the different rights of the parties concerned. Similar to the CJEU in the *Sky Österreich* case, the fol-

---

147 In its jurisprudence, the CJEU has developed a three-step proportionality test. It assesses first, whether acts adopted by EU institutions "do not exceed the limits of what is appropriate and necessary to attain the objectives". Secondly, "when there is choice between several appropriate measures, recourse must be had to the least onerous" and thirdly, the "disadvantages caused must not be disproportionate to the aims pursued". See case C-343/09 *Afton Chemical Limited v Secretary of State for Transport*, Judgment of 8.7.2010, EU:C:2010:419, para. 45. See also Hofmann, "General Principles of EU Law and EU Administrative Law," pp. 204–5.

148 Case C-283/11 *Sky Österreich*, para. 49.

149 Case C-283/11 *Sky Österreich*, para. 52.

150 Case C-283/11 *Sky Österreich*, para. 53.

151 Case C-283/11 *Sky Österreich*, para. 55. Less restrictive measures in the form of higher compensations (based, for instance on the price paid for the exclusive rights or the scale of the event) could have had an adverse effect, "deter[ing] or even prevent[ing] certain broadcasters from requesting access for the purpose of making short news reports".

152 Case C-283/11 *Sky Österreich*, para. 59.

153 Case C-283/11 *Sky Österreich*, para. 61.

154 See Art. 15 (5) and recital 55 AVMSD. Recital 55 AVMSD which is not binding recommends that short reports should not exceed 90 seconds.

lowing sections illustrate the balance that legislatures at the state and European levels have historically found. This balance is not static and has slightly shifted over time, especially in the EU, where fundamental rights have moved from the periphery of non-existence to becoming a central aspect when drafting legislation.

## *B. Regulation by the Member States*

States have "traditionally played a pivotal role in the development of the communications sector".[155] The origins of television broadcasting go back to the 1920s when the first channels where launched in European countries.[156] By the end of the 1960s, colour television was introduced[157] and broadcasting gradually evolved into a mass medium. Until the 1980s, governmental regulation of such transmissions remained a national-level activity and, due to the limited number of broadcasters, which were generally (and firmly) held in public hands, such regulation was primarily "centrali[s]ed" and from the "top-down".[158] The market was characterised by few media outlets or, rather, monopolies entrusted with public service missions.[159] With the emergence of commercial television and technological progress facilitating broadcast transmission by cable and satellite came a tendency to deregulate[160] or, more precisely, a shift away from the "broad and entrenched philosophy of public service values" to the more-liberal

---

155 Natascha Just and Michael Latzer, "Self- and Co-Regulation in the Mediamatics Sector: European Community (EC) Strategies and Contributions towards a Transformed Statehood," *Knowledge, Technology & Policy* 17, no. 2 (2004): p. 39.

156 Gareth Grainger, "Broadcasting, Co-Regulation and the Public Good, 1999 Spry Memorial Lecture," October 28, 1999, p. 18, http://citeseerx.ist.psu.edu/viewdoc/download ;jsessionid=BE2305C10940D3243FF6AB6AA2627117?doi=10.1.1.198.1521&rep=rep1&type=pdf (accessed 25.10.2013); Kogler, *TV (On-Demand)*, p. 3.

157 Kogler, *TV (On-Demand)*, p. 3.

158 Eva Lievens and Peggy Valcke, "Regulatory Trends in a Social Media Context," in *Routledge Handbook of Media Law*, ed. Monroe E. Price, Stefaan Verhulst and Libby Morgan (London and New York: Routledge, 2013), p. 570.

159 Dyson and Humphreys, "Deregulating Broadcasting: The West European Experience," p. 139.

160 Sophia Kaitatzi-Whitlock, "Changing Media Ontology and the Polity," in *Nouveaux Écrans, Nouvelle Régulation?*, ed. Pierre-Francois Docquir and Muriel Hanot, (Brussels: Larcier, 2013), p. 31.

"'market model' of broadcasting".[161] This trend was further reflected in the transfer of regulatory competence and tasks from the state, narrowly defined, to independent regulatory authorities in the 1980s and 1990s[162] and, subsequently, to other self-regulatory bodies in order to accommodate the demands of an increasingly international and technology-driven, dynamic market.[163] To understand the motives for regulating broadcasting from a nation-state perspective, one must first understand its characteristics. Broadcasting still constitutes a mass medium with both economic and cultural implications; due to its scale and enormous reach, broadcasting remains a highly lucrative business. In 2014, the size of the EU's audiovisual market amounted to almost € 107 billion and 85 percent was derived from broadcasting compared to 4 percent from video-on-demand services (VOD).[164] The leading European private television companies, British Sky Broadcasting Ltd and Luxembourg's RTL Group earned consolidated net revenues of € 13.1 million and 5.8 million respectively in 2014.[165] In addition, spending devoted to advertising is mostly directed to the broadcasting market, reaching € 29.2 million in 2014, a five percent increase compared to 2010.[166]

These figures make both the economic potential of that market, as well as the (economic) power its individual players garner from it, blatantly clear. Moreover, broadcasting has, since its inception, been embedded in

161 Dyson and Humphreys, "Deregulating Broadcasting: The West European Experience," p. 139.

162 Kaitatzi-Whitlock, "Changing Media Ontology and the Polity," p. 31; Michael Latzer et al., *Selbst- und Ko-Regulierung im Mediamatiksektor. Alternative Regulierungsformen zwischen Staat und Martk* (Wiesbaden: Westdeutscher Verlag, 2002), p. 29.

163 Latzer et al., *Selbst- und Ko-Regulierung im Mediamatiksektor*, pp. 29, 46; Monroe E. Price and Stefaan Verhulst, "In Search of the Self, Charting the Course of Self-Regulation on the Internet in a Global Environment," in *Regulating the Global Information Society*, ed. Christopher Marsden (London: Routledge, 2000), p. 57.

164 Cabrera Blázquez et al., *Yearbook 2015*, p. 17.

165 Cabrera Blázquez et al., *Yearbook 2015*, p. 18.

166 The aggregated EU advertising expenditures amounted to € 87.795 million in 2014, a four percent increase compared to 2010. Apart from TV advertising as the major expense, expenditures for newspapers was € 21.361 and for online advertising amounted to € 16.326 in 2014. Cabrera Blázquez et al., *Yearbook 2015*, p. 35.

"discourses of nationhood, democracy and the public sphere".[167] Broadcasting is, therefore, also viewed as a cultural commodity, ensuring the formation of independent opinions and a vivid, flourishing public debate about current affairs. The public at large has shown continued trust in, and acceptance of, television as a means of mass communication.[168] As opposed to the printed press, which are permitted to report subjectively, television news programmes are required to cover public affairs in an impartial manner, thereby leaving room for viewers to form their own opinions and ideas, which is important for a functioning democracy (particularly during election campaigns). Furthermore, the nature of the broadcast medium and its effects differ considerably from those of written materials. The power of the medium arises from the images conveyed (especially in contrast to the printed press), their potential intrusiveness, and the passive way in which those images are consumed.[169] Broadcasting is "capable of addressing a mass audience in the privacy of their own homes"[170] and, hence, constitutes an "all-pervading and powerful medium of communication having a direct effect on people's attitudes and behaviour".[171] Indeed, a television programme may reach millions of households simultaneously and often in real time. The direct coverage of events by television preserves the topicality of an event and allows for immediate reactions and

---

167 Marc Raboy and Aysha Mawani, "Are States Still Important? Reflections on the Nexus between National and Global Media and Communication Policy," in *Routledge Handbook of Media Law*, ed. Monroe E. Price, Stefaan Verhulst, and Libby Morgan (London and New York: Routledge, 2013), p. 343.

168 Valérie Schüller-Keber, "Rundfunkfreiheit," in *Medienrecht, Lexikon für Praxis und Wissenschaft*, ed. Peter Schiwy, Walter Schütz and Dieter Dörr, fifth edition (Köln: Carl Heymanns Verlag, 2010), p. 492.

169 Grainger, "Broadcasting, Co-Regulation and the Public Good, 1999 Spry Memorial Lecture," p. 53; Mark Cole, "Die (Massen-)Medien im Überblick," in *Handbuch Medienrecht, Recht der elektronischen Massenmedien*, ed. Dieter Dörr, Johannes Kreile and Mark Cole, second edition (Frankfurt am Main: Verlag Recht und Wirtschaft, 2010), p. 7.

170 Tony Ballard, "Broadcasting," in *Media Law and Practice*, ed. David Goldberg, Gavin Sutter and Ian Walden, (Oxford: Oxford University Press, 2009), p. 304; see also Grainger, "Broadcasting, Co-Regulation and the Public Good, 1999 Spry Memorial Lecture," pp. 2, 16.

171 Lord Annan, Parliament of the United Kingdom, Report of the Committee on the Future of Broadcasting, 1977, p. 26 quoted in Grainger, "Broadcasting, Co-Regulation and the Public Good, 1999 Spry Memorial Lecture," p. 20.

comments, thereby enhancing the medium's widespread impact.[172] Some of the characteristics of broadcasting are enhanced by offering audiovisual media services. An audiovisual service available on-demand over the Internet may potentially be consumed or retrieved from all over the world (unless geo-blocking is used to restrict access to a certain territory), which multiplies the reach of audiovisual programmes. If content that violates the rights of third parties (e.g. their reputation and private life) or material that is defined as illegal in a jurisdiction is transmitted, great harm can be done. To tame the broadcast and audiovisual services industry and to control its "potential power over public opinion," states have imposed limits on the activities of service providers via regulation.[173]

Accordingly, such regulation aims at enhancing plurality[174] and availability of audiovisual media (including radio) as well as promoting "cultural and linguistic diversity"[175] through such media. It also aims at protecting consumers, particularly vulnerable groups of the population such as minors, the elderly, the disabled, and national minorities.[176] It is intended to further the quality of programmes and the impartiality and objectivity of news and to strengthen democracy, the freedom of expression, and the right to receive information.[177] It is also intended to prevent or sanction speech (e.g. hate speech) that violates the very pillars upon which democracy and the peaceful and respectful cohabitation of people rests.

---

172 Schüller-Keber,"Rundfunkfreiheit," p. 491; Kempermann, *Content-Regulierung in konvergierenden Medien*, p. 198.

173 Lord Annan, Parliament of the United Kingdom, Report of the Committee on the Future of Broadcasting, 1977, p. 26 quoted in Grainger, "Broadcasting, Co-Regulation and the Public Good, 1999 Spry Memorial Lecture," p. 20.

174 On the importance of pluralism and plurality of opinions in a democratic society, see generally Kristoff M. Ritlewski, *Pluralismus als Strukturprinzip im Rundfunk*, Anforderungen aus dem Funktionsauftrag und Regelungen zur Sicherung in Deutschland und Polen (Frankfurt am Main: Peter Lang, 2009).

175 Christopher Marsden, "Co-Regulation in European Media and Internet Sectors," *Multimedia und Recht*, 2005, p. 3; Eve Salomon, *Guidelines for Broadcasting Regulation*, second edition (London: Commonwealth Broadcastingn Association, 2008), pp. 12, 14, http://unesdoc.unesco.org/images/0018/001832/183285e.pdf (accessed 17.5.2014).

176 Marsden, "Co-Regulation in European Media and Internet Sectors," p. 3.

177 Salomon, *Guidelines for Broadcasting Regulation*, p. 12, 2.10; Schüller-Keber, "Rundfunkfreiheit," p. 490.

Such regulation, adopted in the public interest, is still necessary.[178] Although today's channels and services have proliferated, thereby multiplying the potential sources of information available to the public, continuing maintenance of certain (albeit more liberal) programme standards remains justified.[179] Some even argue that viewers expect the same or similar traditional broadcast regulatory standards for the Internet or at least for on-demand audiovisual media services provided online.[180]

A more-objective ground motivating state involvement in broadcast transmission had always been the scarcity of the one resource it required, namely, a finite number of radio frequencies.[181] Thus, allocation of this finite resource, owned by the state in the interest of the public, appeared justified. By granting licenses to use a particular part of the radio spectrum that were contingent on certain public-interest obligations and were only valid for a specified period of time, the state administers that finite resource. Some states granted such licenses for free (often on a first-come, first-served basis) while others used a public-tendering procedure in which

---

178 Grainger, "Broadcasting, Co-Regulation and the Public Good, 1999 Spry Memorial Lecture," p. 45.

179 Schüller-Keber, "Rundfunkfreiheit," p. 491.

180 Ballard, "Broadcasting," p. 305. The British regulator Ofcom has conducted research into viewer's perspectives above all, their expectations about the level of regulation applicable to different kinds of audiovisual services. It found in a study of 2012 that viewers had high expectations of the level of regulating on-demand services and catch-up TV, see Ipsos MORI, "Protecting Audiences in a Converged World, Deliberative Research Report of 25.1.2012," 2012, pp. 20–23, http://stakeholders.ofcom.org.uk/binaries/research/tv-research/946687/Protecting-audiences.pdf (accessed 25.5.2014); see also related Ofcom research Essential Research, "The Regulation of Video-On-Demand: Consumer Views on What Makes Audiovisual services 'TV-like' – a Qualitative Research Report," December 2009, http://stakeholders.ofcom.org.uk/binaries/research/tv-research/vod.pdf (accessed 25.5.2014); Essential Research, "On-Demand Services: Understanding Consumer Choices, A Research Report for Ofcom," October 2012, http://stakeholders.ofcom.org.uk/binaries/broadcast/tv-ops/vod/Research_Report.pdf (accessed 25.5.2014).

181 Ballard, "Broadcasting," p. 303; Dyson and Humphreys, "Deregulating Broadcasting: The West European Experience," pp. 137, 141; Grainger, "Broadcasting, Co-Regulation and the Public Good, 1999 Spry Memorial Lecture," pp. 2, 11; Salomon, *Guidelines for Broadcasting Regulation*, p. 11; Schüller-Keber, "Rundfunkfreiheit," p. 491; Pierre Trudel, "Internet Risks Management and Paradigm Shifts in the Regulation of the Audiovisual Industry," *Quaderns Del CAC 37* XIV, no. 2 (2011): p. 8.

potential service providers competed for a particular frequency.[182] With the advent of satellite television and then digital[183] compression technologies, however, television channels have mushroomed across Europe, resulting in a purported abundance of available frequencies and "increased choice, interactive options [and] high-definition television".[184]As a consequence, continued reliance on the underlying scarcity rationale has been called into question.[185] Yet, Grainger argues that the spectrum remains a public resource so that "its use must be for a public benefit".[186] Although spectrum is less scarce than it was thirty years ago, its availability remains, by its very nature, limited.[187] Hence, the initial rationale, although perhaps weakened by technological advances in transmission techniques, still maintains its validity. It may no longer be a convincing, stand-alone rationale, but when read in light of the 'democratic function' of television, it justifies state intervention in form of regulation.

### *C. Regulation by the European Union*

Starting in the mid-1980s, the European Union began to regulate cross-border broadcasting as a service. The CJEU laid the basis for the EU's involvement which led to the adoption of a Directive, an instrument of Secondary Union law. This Directive illustrates the balancing exercise that has been conducted by the EU legislature. Through successive revisions, the subject matter of the Directive has expanded and today encompasses

---

182 Salomon, *Guidelines for Broadcasting Regulation*, para. 2.6, p. 11.

183 Within the European Union, the Commission suggested in 2005 that the transition from analogue to digital broadcasting be accomplished by the end of 2010 concerning certain Member States or 2012 respectively. See European Commission, "Communication from the Commission to the Council, the European Parliament, the European Economic and Social Committee and the Committee of the Regions on Accelerating the Transition from Analogue to Digital Broadcasting, COM(2005) 204 Final," May 24, 2005, para. 5, p. 9.

184 Grainger, "Broadcasting, Co-Regulation and the Public Good, 1999 Spry Memorial Lecture," p. 16; James Bennett and Niki Strange, eds., *Television as Digital Media* (Durham and London: Duke University Press, 2011), p. 3.

185 Ballard, "Broadcasting," p. 304.

186 Grainger, "Broadcasting, Co-Regulation and the Public Good, 1999 Spry Memorial Lecture," p. 44.

187 Salomon, *Guidelines for Broadcasting Regulation*, p. 11; Schüller-Keber, "Rundfunkfreiheit," p. 491.

audiovisual media services. This enlargement is an expression of the convergence between different kinds of (media) services. The following section thus traces the genesis of the Directive expounding the motives pursued by the EU.

## I. The rationale for regulating the EU audiovisual media services market

Regulation of broadcasting and on-demand audiovisual media services by the European Union is rooted in starkly different motives than those traditionally invoked by states, which is primarily explained by the *sui generis* character of the EU – a construct with supranational and intergovernmental elements. As such, the Union can only regulate a matter if it has received an express mandate from the Member States. The principle of conferral (or attributed competence)[188] thus sets the limits of Union competence and actions. Pursuant to Art. 5 (2) TEU,

> "the Union shall act only within the limits of the competences conferred upon it by the Member States in the Treaties to attain the objectives set out therein. Competences not conferred upon the Union in the Treaties remain with the Member States".

Hence, all actions taken by the Union must be firmly based on "lawmaking competences", dispositions included in the Treaties that allow it to govern a certain matter in a certain way (either exclusively or in parallel with the Member States).[189] In addition to the specific legal bases set out in the Treaties, Art. 352 TFEU provides a general competence to take appropriate measures to attain the objectives of the Treaties. In exercising its attributed competences, including its Art. 352 TFEU competence, the Union must conform to the principles of subsidiarity and proportionality set out in Art. 5 (3) and (4) TEU in conjunction with the Second Protocol on the application of the principles of subsidiarity and proportionality. Art. 5 (3) TEU provides, in relevant part, that, when acting in areas for which it does not have exclusive competence:

188 Hofmann, Rowe, and Türk, *Administrative Law and Policy of the European Union*, p. 117.

189 Hofmann, Rowe and Türk, *Administrative Law and Policy of the European Union*, p. 117.

> "the Union shall act only if and in so far as the objectives of the proposed action cannot be sufficiently achieved by the Member States ... but can rather, by reason of the scale or effects of the proposed action, be better achieved at Union level".[190]

Art. 5 (4) TEU further obligates the Union, when taking any action, not to "exceed what is necessary to achieve the objectives of the Treaties".[191] As a corollary of the attribution of competences, Member States committed to cooperate loyally in the execution of Union policies. The principle of sincere cooperation[192] finds expression in the second and third sentences of Art. 4 (3) TEU:

> "The Member States shall take any appropriate measure, general or particular, to ensure fulfilment of the obligations arising out of the Treaties or resulting from the acts of the institutions of the Union. The Member States shall facilitate the achievement of the Union's tasks and refrain from any measure which could jeopardise the attainment of the Union's objectives".

Accordingly, the Member States are obliged to cooperate in good faith and act in the interest of the Union. This duty of loyalty covers the enforcement[193] of the Court's jurisprudence and the implementation of Secondary Union Law, particularly Directives that, in contrast to Regulations, are not directly applicable and, thus, need to be transferred into national legal orders.[194] Enforcement at the national level intended to comply with Secondary-Union-Law instruments is guided by the principles of equivalence and effectiveness.[195] The former implies that any infringement of Union law is prosecuted and sanctioned in a manner equivalent to an infringement of national law, while the latter ensures that enforcement is neither

---

190 Hofmann, Rowe and Türk, *Administrative Law and Policy of the European Union*, p. 125.

191 Hofmann, Rowe and Türk, *Administrative Law and Policy of the European Union*, p. 129.

192 Hofmann, Rowe and Türk, *Administrative Law and Policy of the European Union*, p. 134.

193 Hofmann, Rowe and Türk, *Administrative Law and Policy of the European Union*, p. 690 et seq.

194 Art. 288 TFEU. See also Eleftheria Neframi, "The Duty of Loyalty: Rethinking its Scope through its Application in the Field of EU External Relations," *Common Market Law Review* 47 (2010): p. 325.

195 Hofmann, Rowe and Türk, *Administrative Law and Policy of the European Union*, pp. 691, 692.

made "virtually impossible" nor "excessively difficult".[196] Moreover, Neframi contends that the principle of sincere cooperation incorporates the principle of effectiveness or, more specifically, the "effective protection of rights stemming from Union rules".[197] The principle of effectiveness, thus, requires Member States to take all necessary measures to ensure the accomplishment of Treaty objectives and to abstain from any measures endangering or undermining them.[198] Thus, the principle of sincere cooperation as a constitutive element of the Union's legal order determines the relationship between the Union and its Member States and is significant with regards to the regulation of an area, such as audiovisual media services, which is grounded in cultural and social aspects and is characterised by national particularities, perceptions, and attitudes.[199]

At the Union level, regulation of broadcasting and audiovisual media services was inextricably intertwined with economic considerations and the need to create a common market that allowed for cross-border circulation and, hence, enhanced competition. The European Commission, relying on Art. 56 TFEU, which lays down the free movement of services, initiated its regulatory activity in response to the Court's jurisprudence during the 1970s and early 1980s, which served as the motor of integration in this policy field. In two landmark cases, one in 1974 and the other in 1980, the Court clarified the nature of broadcasting and broadcast advertising.[200]

The Court's 1974 *Sacchi*[201] decision involved criminal proceedings against Mr. Sacchi because he refused to pay the license fee required un-

---

196 Case 68/88 *Commission of the European Communities v Hellenic Republic*, Judgment of 21.9.1989, EU:C:1989:339, paras. 24, 25; case C-261/95 *Rosalba Palmisani v Istituto nazionale della previdenza sociale (INPS)*, Judgment of 10.7.1997, EU:C:1997:351, para. 27. See also Hofmann, Rowe and Türk, *Administrative Law and Policy of the European Union*, p. 692.

197 Neframi, "The Duty of Loyalty," p. 326.

198 Neframi, "The Duty of Loyalty," pp. 330, 331.

199 Neframi suggests that the principle of sincere cooperation is a "fondement identitaire de l'Union européenne" Eleftheria Neframi, "Le principe de coopération loyale comme fondement identitaire de l'Union européenne," *Revue de l'Union européenne*, no. 556 (March 2012): p. 201.

200 Alison Harcourt, *The European Union and the Regulation of Media Markets* (Manchester and New York: Manchester University Press, 2005), pp. 24, 25; Alison Harcourt, "Institution-Driven Competition: The Regulation of Cross-Border Broadcasting in the EU," *Journal of Public Policy* 27, no. 3 (2007): p. 305; Harrison and Woods, *European Broadcasting Law and Policy*, pp. 68, 93, 94.

201 Case 155/73 *Giuseppe Sacchi*, Judgment of 3.4.1974, EU:C:1974:40.

der Italian law for the television receivers used to relay television programmes over cable. The Court held that "the transmission of television signals, including those in the nature of advertisements, comes, as such, within the rules of the Treaty relating to services".[202] In contrast, it held that "trade in material, sound recordings, films, apparatus and other products used for the diffusion of television signals are subject to the rules relating to freedom of movement for goods".[203] Similarly, the Court confirmed its finding in *Debauve*[204] who was accused of violating a provision of the Belgian law prohibiting the inclusion of advertising in programmes retransmitted from foreign providers. Mr. Debauve (as representative of Coditel) and two other individuals of another cable television distributer (Mr. Denuit and Mr. Lohest of the *Association Liégeoise d'Électricité*) had refused to blot out the advertisements included in foreign programmes retransmitted in Belgium in violation of Belgium's advertising ban. Such non-compliance had become common practice in Belgium and was tolerated by the Belgian authorities until several consumer associations complained about the violations in 1979.[205] Relying on its ruling in *Sacchi*, the

202 Case 155/73 *Sacchi*, para. 7. See also opinion of Advocate General Reischl delivered on 20.3.1974 in case 155/73 *Giuseppe Sacchi*, EU:C:1974:22, para. II, 1, cc) and II, 2, a). The same is true for dissemination via satellites, see case C-17/00 *François De Coster v Collège des bourgmestre et échevins de Watermael-Boitsfort*, Judgment of 29.11.2001, EU:C:2001:651, paras. 28, 31.

203 Case 155/73 *Sacchi*, para. 8.

204 Case 52/79 *Procureur du Roi v Marc J. V. C. Debauve and others*, Judgment of 18.3.1980, EU:C:1980:83.

205 Case 52/79 *Debauve*, para. 5; for a more detailed description of the facts, see the opinion of Advocate General Warner delivered on 13.12.1979 in cases 52/79 *Debauve and 62/79 SA Compagnie générale pour la diffusion de la télévision, Coditel, and others v Ciné Vog Films and others*, Judgment of 18.3.1980, EU:C:1979:291. Case 62/79 is of minor relevance in this context as it focused on the exercise of an exclusive right for a feature film: in that case, a Belgian cinematographic film distribution company bought a license for a particular film valid for the Belgian market. When said film was broadcast in Germany, Coditel picked up the signal and broadcast the film in Belgium by cable television. Ciné Vog alleged Coditel infringed its license. The Court skipped the first preliminary question formulated by the Belgian court (which inquired about the transnational nature of the services involved) holding that Ciné Vog was entitled to copyright protection against a cable television provider established in the same country relaying the protected work. The Court noted that the freedom to provide services does not restrict intellectual property rights guaranteed by national law. See case 62/79 *Coditel*, paras. 15, 18.

Court made clear that the transmission of advertisements by cable television falls under the freedom to provide services guaranteed by the Treaty.[206] With respect to the conformity of the Belgian ban on advertising with then-Community law, the Court found:

> "in the absence of any approximation of national laws and taking into account the considerations of general interest underlying the restrictive rules of this area, the application of the laws in question cannot be regarded as a restriction upon freedom to provide services so long as those laws treat all such services identically".[207]

Indeed, the Court highlighted that regulation of television advertising was "subject to widely divergent systems of law in the various Member States" and that it remained their prerogative in the absence of the harmonisation thereof at the Community level.[208] The Court's repeated reference to the lack of approximation of laws hinted at the possible need to coordinate the rules governing television advertising.[209]

Interestingly, the Commission, in its submissions in the case elaborated on the appropriateness of applying freedom-to-provide-services protections to a situation that was wholly internal to one Member State; it asserted that such a reading of a rule such as the Belgian ban could adversely affect the conclusion of contracts outside its territory and, thus, impede the freedom to provide services.[210] Still, the Commission was mindful that "the problem is to decide whether, in a common market, each Member

---

206 In case 352/85 *Bond van Adverteerders and others v The Netherlands State*, Judgment of 26.4.1986, EU:C:1988:196, para. 14, the Court clarified that the transmission of programmes in the form of advertisements involves "at least two separate services [within the meaning of the Treaty]. The first is provided by the cable network operators (…) to the broadcasters (…) and consists of relaying to network subscribers the television programmes sent to them by the broadcaster. The second is provided by the broadcasters (…) to advertisers (…) by broadcasting advertisements which the advertisers have prepared especially for the public in the Member State where the programmes are received".

207 Case 52/79 *Debauve*, para. 13.

208 Case 52/79 *Debauve*, para. 15.

209 Case 52/79 *Debauve*, paras. 13, 15.

210 Case 52/79 *Debauve*, submissions of the Commission, ECR 1980, p. 849. By the same token, Advocate General Warner claimed that the Belgian rule had negative repercussions on the provision of transnational services and, therefore, was contrary to Community law. See opinion of Advocate General Warner, delivered on 13.12.1979, EU:C:1979:291, p. 872, 876, 877.

State must or must not "recognise" the laws of the others".[211] It is against this background that the Commission's subsequent activities need to be examined: it took steps to progressively move toward the establishment of a common market for broadcasting. One of the milestones in that progression was the publication of its Green Paper on the establishment of the common market for broadcasting of June 1984.[212]

## II. The genesis of the Directive

This section traces the evolution of the Directive, from the 1989 Television Without Frontiers Directive to the 1997 revision and the reform in 2007 leading to the Audiovisual Media Services Directive that is still in effect today but is currently undergoing another more far-reaching revision.

### 1. From the 1984 Green Paper to the 1989 Television Without Frontiers Directive

Developments at the Community level in the 1980s occurred in parallel with, and were influenced by, those of the Council of Europe, as will be discussed below.[213] One point should, nevertheless, be emphasised here. While the legal act adopted at the then-Community level essentially furthered the economic integration of its Member States because it was anchored in one of the four economic freedoms, the instrument issued by the

211 Case 52/79 *Debauve*, submissions of the Commission, EU:C:1979:291.

212 European Commission, "Green Paper on the Establishment of the Common Market for Broadcasting, Especially by Satellite and Cable, COM(84) 300 Final," June 14, 1984. The Green Paper is not accessible online but was provided on the basis of Art. 15 (3) TFEU in conjunction with Regulation (EC) 1049/2001 of the European Parliament and of the Council of 30 May 2001 regarding public access to European Parliament, Council and Commission document, OJ L 145 of 31.5.2001, p. 43.

213 See recital 8 TWFD 1989 which explicitly refers to the Council of Europe's Convention on Transfrontier Television. See also Mark Cole, "Europäisches Medienrecht," in *Europäisches und Internationales Medienrecht*, ed. Udo Fink, Mark Cole and Tobias Keber, (Heidelberg: C. F. Müller Verlag, 2008), para. 60, p. 47; Kogler, *TV (On-Demand)*, pp. 6–8.

Council of Europe was deeply influenced by the safeguard of the fundamental right to freedom of expression as stipulated by Art. 10 ECHR.

While the Commission acknowledged the dual nature of broadcasting and other audiovisual media services,[214] meaning their economic and cultural importance, the Union has only limited competence in matters of culture,[215] as Art. 167 (5) TFEU specifically "exclude[s] any harmonisation of the laws and regulations of the Member States". This provision was, however, only integrated in 1992 by the Treaty of Maastricht and, therefore, was non-existent at the time the Directive was adopted.[216] Under the Treaty establishing the European Economic Community, culture was a matter to be governed exclusively by the Member States; the Commission was only competent to regulate economic aspects arising from the free movement of services as defined by the Court. Nevertheless, certain rules, particularly those promoting European works and independent productions, have unequivocal cultural repercussions leading to the "beginnings of a positive cultural policy" for the Union that, nevertheless, sprung forth out of the Union's goals of ensuring free movement of services and eras-

214 Peter Humphreys, "The Principle Axes of the European Union's Audiovisual Policy," in *Communication and Cultural Policies in Europe*, ed. Alonso Moragas i Spa (Barcelona: Generalitat de Catalunya: Collecio Lexicon, 2008), p. 152. See for instance part 2, p. 23 et seq. of the Commission Green Paper on a Common Market for Broadcasting of 1984 or recital 14 of the Commission's proposal for a Council Directive on the coordination of certain provisions laid down by law, regulation or administrative action in Member States concerning the pursuit of broadcasting activities, OJ of 17.7.1986, C 179, p. 4.

215 On the Union's cultural policy related to audiovisual media services, see Mira Burri-Nenova, "The New Audiovisual Media Services Directive: Television without Frontieris, Television without Cultural Diversity," *Common Market Law Review* 14 (2007): pp. 1689–1725; Mira Burri-Nenova, "Cultural Diversity and the EC Audiovisual Media Services Directive," Working Paper No 2009/9 (2009); Rachel Craufurd Smith, "From Heritage Conservation to European Identiy: Article 151 EC and the Multi-Faceted Nature of Community Cultural Policy," *European Law Review* 32, no. 1 (2007): pp. 48–69; Evangelia Psychogiopoulou, "The Cultural Mainstreaming Clause of Article 151 (4) EC: Protection and Promotion of Cultural Diversity or Hidden Cultural Agenda?," *European Law Journal* 12, no. 5 (2006): pp. 575–92.

216 Michaela Seifert, "Fundamentals of Community Law and Policies (Including Funding Programmes) Governing the Content Industry," in *Regulatingn Content – European Regulatory Framework for the Media and Related Creative Sectors*, ed. Michael Holoubek, Dragana Damjanovic and Matthias Traimer, (The Netherlands: Kluwer Law International, 2006), pp. 42–45.

ing distortions to competition.[217] The Green Paper of 1984 was a document of more than 300 pages and it investigated both the economic aspects of television and radio broadcasting as well as its cultural and social implications. Interestingly, the Commission underscored the positive role of television in "developing and nurturing awareness of the rich variety of Europe's common cultural and historical heritage" thereby fostering a "European identity".[218] According to the Commission, cross-border transmission of (national) programmes would increase the number of sources of information available and would generally facilitate mutual understanding of the peoples profiting from European integration.[219] To this end, the Commission regarded the removal of obstacles within the European market as a protective measure offsetting the prevalence of American productions, which were (and still are) popular in the Member States.[220] Regarding the economic value of broadcasting, the Commission pointed out that this would have network effects on content providers, programme financing, advertising markets, and even the communications and space industry.[221] After the Green Paper first established the dual nature of broadcasting, the Commission undertook a comprehensive assessment of the then-existing Treaty provisions governing services in line with the Court's definitions from the case law mentioned above.[222] The Green Paper hinted at the issues that would later receive more in-depth attention in the Commission's proposal for a Council Directive coordinating certain provisions concerning the pursuit of broadcasting activities, which was published in April 1986.[223] The final Directive was eventually adopted in October 1989

---

217 Harrison and Woods, *European Broadcasting Law and Policy*, p. 100.

218 European Commission, "Green Paper on a Common Market for Broadcasting," p. 28.

219 European Commission, "Green Paper on a Common Market for Broadcasting," pp. 29, 32.

220 European Commission, "Green Paper on a Common Market for Broadcasting," p. 33.

221 European Commission, "Green Paper on a Common Market for Broadcasting," p. 37 et seq.

222 European Commission, "Green Paper on a Common Market for Broadcasting," p. 105 et seq.

223 Commission, Proposal for a Council Directive on the coordination of certain provisions laid down by law, regulation or administrative action in Member States concerning the pursuit of broadcasting activities, OJ of 17.7.1986, C 179, p. 4.

and specifically referred to television broadcasting.[224] The significant lapse of time between the Commission's initial proposal and the publication of the 1989 Directive reflects the intensity and intricacy of the Community institutions' debates and underscores the perpetual struggle between the economic and cultural aspects inherent in broadcasting.

The political compromise reflected in the 1989 version of the Directive is proof of the significance of broadcasting in modern societies and the sensitivity they have regarding its regulation. Up to now, the 1989 Television without Frontiers Directive (the TWFD) represents one building block in an integrated and dynamic market for audiovisual media services in which such services are exchanged across borders (to the extent that social and cultural barriers, such as linguistic barriers, allow). The TWFD's recitals established the Community's competence to act in this field and its motives for harmonising the rules relating thereto. The 1989 TWFD essentially aimed at creating a common television broadcasting market by abolishing "obstacles to freedom of movement for services" and reducing distortions to competition.[225] Nonetheless, recital 15 TWFD hinted at its broader purpose: "facilitating the pursuit of the professional activities concerned, and, more generally, the free movement of information and ideas within the Community",[226] which was also reflected in its recital 30's emphasis on the importance of (and need for) coordinated cross-border rules to "make it easier for persons and industries producing programmes having a cultural objective to take up and pursue their activities".[227] Both recitals were retained in the final version of the TWFD. Likewise, it stressed the link between its protections and the distribution of television

224 Council Directive 89/552/EEC of 3 October 1989 on the coordination of certain provisions laid down by law, regulation or administrative action in Member States concerning the pursuit of television broadcasting activities, OJ of 17.10.1989, L 298, p. 23, hereinafter referred to as TWFD of 1989.

225 Recital 6 of the TWFD of 1989. Interestingly, in the initial proposal of 1986, the Commission firstly referred to advertising as being covered by the free movement of services while only subsequently referring to "the broadcasting of *other* messages". This may underpin the economic rationale underlying the Commission's approach as the "liberalization of this service [advertising] helps to promote trade in goods and services". Recitals 11, 12 of the Commission's proposal of 1986.

226 Recital 15 of the TWFD of 1989. Compare to recital 23 of the Commission's proposal of 1986.

227 Recital 22 of the TWFD of 1989.

services as a "specific manifestation in Community law of a more general principle, namely the freedom of expression as enshrined in" Art. 10 (1) ECHR.[228] Moreover, through its preamble, the TWFD clarified that the kind of harmonisation it sought represented only the "minimum rules needed to guarantee freedom of transmission in broadcasting".[229] It follows that the TWFD only established the minimum level of protection to be afforded by the Member States (as opposed to full harmonisation that exhaustively regulated the subject matter) in their national legal orders by means of transposition. Art. 3 TWFD, on the other hand, expressly recognised the Member States right to adopt "more detailed or stricter rules in the areas covered by this Directive", meaning that the Member States were free to apply more restrictive or more protective measures to broadcasters established solely within their territory. Finally, Art. 8 TWFD, when read in conjunction with its recital 29, reiterates the right to be more restrictive with respect to the protection of languages, particularly those spoken by a national minority. Although subsequent revisions of the TWFD would eliminate Art. 8 (while retaining a reference to it in the preamble),[230] the provision could easily be regarded as superfluous in light of all Member States' general right to adopt more detailed rules.

The areas coordinated by the TWFD included: the promotion and distribution of European works; television advertising and sponsorship; the protection of minors; and the right of reply. Accordingly, Member States were to oblige broadcasters to reserve a "majority proportion of their transmission time" to European works as defined by Art. 6 TWFD and dedicate a certain percentage of their transmission time or, alternatively, programming budget to European works created by independent producers.[231] With respect to television advertising, Art. 10 TWFD set forth general standards to ensure the separation between editorial and commercial content (i.e. the principle of separation) and the easy recognition of advertis-

228 Recitals 16-18 of the Commission's proposal of 1986 and recital 12 of the TWFD of 1989.

229 Recital 17 of the TWFD of 1989.

230 Recital 78 AVMSD of 2010.

231 Arts. 4 (1) and 5 of the TWFD of 1989. The initial 1986 proposal of the Commission was more specific with regards to the quotas for European works. Pursuant to Art. 2 thereof, broadcasters were to reserve "at least 30 percent of their programming time" to such works and were to "progressively" increase such proportion to 60 percent within the three years following the date of entry into force of the proposed directive.

ing (i.e. the principle of identification). In addition to regulating the content of advertising in its Arts. 12 and 16 and determining the products and services that could not be advertised in its Arts. 13 through 15 TWFD, the TWFD also established limits on the insertion and frequency of advertising though its Arts. 11 and 18. Content restrictions and other requirements were also imposed on sponsored programmes by its Art. 17. Furthermore, the protection of minors from unsuitable programmes as well as the prohibition of incitement to hatred constituted other essential elements as set forth in its Art. 22. Finally, the TWFD included, in its Art. 23, a rule ensuring the right of reply for persons whose "legitimate interest, in particular reputation and good name, have been damaged by an assertion of incorrect facts in a television programme" that was not included in the Commission's original proposal.

Strikingly, the Commission's initial 1986 proposal included a chapter entitled 'Copyright' that, if incorporated in the final directive, would have ensured the protection of copyrighted programmes retransmitted by cable in other Member States. To this end, Art. 17 of that initial 1986 proposal provided for "contractual agreements between right-owners and cable operators" and the possibility for cable operators to be subject to "civil and penal sanctions" if no agreement had been reached or statutory license supplied. Where retransmission of a broadcast was prevented due to a failure to obtain such an agreement, the initial proposal's Art. 18 set out an arbitration mechanism in which the cable operator could notify the Member State in which the holder of the copyright was established, and that Member State was obliged to allocate a statutory license within a period of two years. Art. 19 further specified that the statutory license secured "equitable remuneration for the holders of copyright and related rights" on the basis of certain criteria enumerated in its second paragraph. The initial proposal's draft provisions with regards to copyright were intentionally eliminated from the TWFD because a sector-specific approach (restricted to broadcasting) was considered inadequate and contrary to the interests of both the rights holders and consumers.[232] Like television broadcasting, the Treaty then in force did not contain any express legal basis for harmoniz-

232 See the Opinion of the Economic and Social Committee on the proposal for a Council Directive on the coordination of certain provisions laid down by law, regulation or administrative action in Member States concerning the pursuit of broadcasting activities, OJ of 31.8.1987, C 232, p. 29, para. 2.26.

ing copyright such that the Community's competence was contested.[233] Hence, most copyright *acquis* derive from the Commission's use of its general law-making competence, first laid down in Art. 100a TEC/95 TEC (now Art. 114 TFEU) and Art. 235 TEC/308 TEC (now Art. 352 TFEU) to foster the functioning of the internal market. Due to its close ties to the TWFD, the subsequent 1993 Directive concerning copyright and related rights applicable to satellite broadcasting and cable retransmission[234] was primarily grounded on the freedom of establishment and the freedom to provide services guaranteed by the Treaty. That 1993 Directive, a spinoff from the rejected copyright chapter of the initial 1986 proposal, constituted one of the first Community instruments to harmonise certain aspects of copyright, thereby supplying "the missing element"[235] needed by the 1989 TWFD.[236]

Most importantly, the TWFD introduced several definitions that established the Directive's material scope of application. This canon of definitions in the TWFD was gradually expanded by subsequent revisions, as will become apparent below. Art. 1 (a) TWFD stated that television broadcasting:

---

233 Since the Lisbon Treaty's entry into force, Art. 118 (1) TFEU explicitly allows for "the creation of European intellectual property rights to provide uniform protection of intellectual property rights throughout the Union and for the setting up of cenetralised Union-wide authorisation, coordination and supervision arrangements". Justine Pila, "Intellectual Property as a Case Study in Europeanization: Methodological Themes and Context," in *The Europeanization of Intellectual Property Law, Towards a European Legal Methodology*, ed. Ansgar Ohly and Justine Pila, (Oxford: Oxford University Press, 2013), pp. 3–23; Bernd Justin Jütte, "A New Era in European Intellectual Property Law, European Judiciaries for Intellectual Property – Is Copyright Next?," *Revista Română de Drept* 4 (2015): pp. 64–79.

234 Council Directive 93/83/EEC of 27 September 1993 on the coordination of certain rules concerning copyright and rights related to copyright applicable to satellite broadcasting and cable retransmission, OJ of 6.10.1993, L 248, p. 15.

235 Press Release of the European Commission, Directive on coordination of certain rules concerning copyright and rights related to copyright applicable to satellite broadcasting and cable retransmission, IP/93/803 of 28.9.1993, available at http://europa.eu/rapid/press-release_IP-93-803_en.htm?locale=en (accessed 6.5.2014).

236 Bernt Hugenholtz, "Is Harmonization a Good Thing? The Case of the Copyright Acquis," in *The Europeanization of Intellectual Property Law, Towards a European Legal Methodology*, ed. Ohly and Pila, (Oxford: Oxford University Press, 2013), p. 59.

> "means the initial transmission by wire or over the air, including that by satellite, in unencoded or encoded form, of television programmes intended for reception by the public. It includes the communication of programmes between undertakings with a view to their being relayed to the public. It does not include communication services providing items of information or other messages on individual demand such as telecopying, electronic data banks and other similar services".

In contrast to the initial 1986 Commission proposal, which was otherwise couched in similar terms, the term broadcasting does not cover radio services.[237] Interestingly, the initial proposal distinguished between "internal broadcasts" and "cross-frontier broadcasts", the former referring to initial diffusion of programmes within a Member State including those exclusively intended for reception in another Member State, and the latter implying transmissions intended only for an internal audience but which could nevertheless be received in other Member States (e.g. due to satellite footprint) or relays of programmes in other Member States. The proposal's differentiation was not subsequently adopted as determining jurisdiction was problematic and it did not provide a clear-cut framework in light of overlapping and complex broadcasting concepts.[238]

It is also interesting to note that Art. 1 (a) TWFD exempted communications offered on individual request from its scope. While the TWFD's successor-in-interest, the AVMSD, excluded on-demand audiovisual media services from that exemption, other individually requested services, like databases still remain outside the AVMSD's scope. The TWFD's definition stressed the mass media character of broadcasting by reference to the indeterminate expression "the public" and clarified that it covered both the initial transmission and all subsequent retransmissions of a programme.[239]

What was, perhaps, the most fundamental element of the legal framework for broadcasting was already embedded in the TWFD.[240] To reduce barriers to providing cross-border broadcast services and to facilitate a

---

237 Art. 21 (1) of the Commission's proposal of 1986.

238 Oliver Castendyk and Lorna Woods, "Article 1 TWFD (Definitions)," in *European Media Law*, ed. Castendyk, Dommering and Scheuer, (The Netherlands: Kluwer Law International, 2008), para. 15, p. 276.

239 Castendyk and Woods, "Art. 1 TWFD," paras. 38, 39, p. 284.

240 Cole, "Europäisches Medienrecht," para. 61, p. 49; Kurt Faßbender, "Zu Inhalt und Grenzen des rundfunkrechtlichen Sendestaatsprinzips," *Archiv für Presserecht* 6 (2006): p. 505.

common broadcasting market, the country of origin principle (also known as the principle of home country control and the "one-stop shop" principle)[241] was introduced pursuant to which the Member State with jurisdiction over a broadcaster was determined. In accordance with Art. 2 (1) TWFD, the Member State under whose jurisdiction a broadcaster fell was obliged to ensure the latter's compliance with the law. No further checks or reviews could be enacted by Member States to which a programme was also transmitted. In other words, the Member State "from which the broadcast emanate[d]"[242] bore responsibility for the broadcaster's lawful dissemination of the broadcast programme within the Community. A broadcast was typically found to have emanated from the place of establishment of the broadcaster even though the TWFD was silent on this matter. It just specified that a broadcaster, "while not being under the jurisdiction of any Member State," could be regarded as being under its jurisdiction by making use of a "frequency or a satellite capacity granted by, or a satellite uplink situated" in that Member State.[243] Due to the practical difficulties inherent in that formulation (i.e. multiple responsible jurisdictions or no responsible jurisdiction),[244] the country of origin principle was subsequently refined by the Court in the mid-1990s to include a number of additional criteria to aid in determining the responsible jurisdiction.[245]

---

241 Harrison and Woods, *European Broadcasting Law and Policy*, p. 173.

242 Mark Cole, "The Country of Origin Principle – from State Sovereignty under Public International Law to Inclusion in the Audiovisual Media Services Directive of the European Union," in *Europäische Integration und Globalisierung, Festschrift zum 60-Jährigen Bestehen des Europa-Instituts*, ed. Werner Meng, Georg Ress and Torsten Stein, vol. 84, Schriften des Europa-Instituts der Universität Des Saarlandes- Rechtswissenschaft (Baden-Baden: Nomos, 2011), p. 118.

243 Art. 2 (1) second indent of the TWFD of 1989.

244 Cole, "The Country of Origin Principle," pp. 119, 120.

245 See generally, case C-221/89, *The Queen vs. Secretary of State for Transport, ex parte Factortame Ltd a.o.*, Judgment of 25.7.1991, EU:C:1991:320, para. 20. More specifically, regarding the broadcasting sector, in case C-222/94 *Commission of the European Communities v United Kingdom of Great Britain and Northern Ireland*, Judgment of 10.9.1995, EU:C:1996:314, the CJEU found that "a Member State' s jurisdiction *ratione personae* over a broadcaster can be based only on the broadcaster' s connection to that State' s legal system, which in substance overlaps with the concept of establishment as used in the first paragraph of Article 59 of the EC Treaty, the wording of which presupposes that the supplier and the recipient of a service are "established" in two different Member States". It also held that the criterion of establishment implied "the place where decisions concerning programme policy are taken and the programmes to be broadcast are

As a corollary to the country of origin principle and the regulatory floor created by the 1989 TWFD throughout the Member States, Art. 2 (2) TWFD guaranteed the free flow of information across the Community. Nevertheless, temporary derogations from the general rule of free transmission were permissible under certain precisely defined conditions. Although such derogations have, to date, had "limited practical effect",[246] its mere existence has counteracted concerns about the Member States entering into a "race to the bottom"[247] in which each would undercut the others by designing liberal legal frameworks to attract broadcasting business.[248] In reality, the country of origin principle has served as a model for other areas of law harmonised by the Union, such as Art. 3 (1) of the E-Commerce Directive (ECD) of 2000.[249] At the same time, the set of rules contained in the TWFD allowed Member States to emphasise more protective

---

finally put together" in order to avoid the problem of "double control", paras. 42, 58. Confirmed in cases C-56/96 *VT4 v Vlaamse Gemeenschap*, Judgment of 5.6.1997, EU:C:1997:284, paras. 17, 18; C-11/95 *Commission of the European Communities v Kingdom of Belgium*, Judgment of 10.9.1996, EU:C:1996:316, paras. 18, 19; joined cases C-34-36/95 *Konsumentombudsmannen v De Agostini, Förlag AB and TV-Shop I Sverige AB*, Judgment of 9.7.1997, EU:C:1997:344, para. 29. Strikingly, Art. 1 (1) of the Commission's proposal of the TWFD of 1986 was clearer on this issue requiring that "each Member State shall ensure that all internal broadcasts originating on its territory comply with its law".

246 Cole, "The Country of Origin Principle," p. 121.

247 Cole, "The Country of Origin Principle," p. 121; Faßbender, "Zu Inhalt und Grenzen des rundfunkrechtlichen Sendestaatsprinzips," p. 507; Harrison and Woods, *European Broadcasting Law and Policy*, p. 173 et seq.; Anna Herold, "Country of Origin Principle in the EU Market for Audiovisual Media Services: Consumer's Friend or Foe?," *Journal of Consumer Policy* 31, no. 1 (2008): p. 6.

248 In similar vein, Member States may take action against a broadcaster circumventing its internal legislation (so-called forum shopping) in accordance with Art. 4 (2) (b) AVMSD of 2010. The need for anti-circumvention measures was also recognised by recital 19 of the TwFD of 1997, see Herold, "Country of Origin Principle in the EU Market for Audiovisual Media Services: Consumer's Friend or Foe?," p. 7; Julia Hörnle, "Country of Origin Regulation in Cross Border Media: One Step beyond the Freedom to Provde Services?," *International & Comparative Law Quarterly* 54, no. 1 (2005): p. 117.

249 Directive 2000/31/EC of the European Parliament and of the Council of 8 June 2000 on certain legal aspects of information society services, in particular electronic commerce, in the Internal Market ('Directive on electronic commerce'), OJ of 17.7.2000, L 178, p. 1. See also Hörnle, Julia, "Country of Origin Regulation in Cross Border Media," p. 108; Kramer, Thorsten, *Das sekundärrechtliche Herkunftslandprinzip als Regelungstechnik des Binnenmarktes* (Berlin: Freie

standards exceeding the minimum threshold of coordination achieved at the Community level.[250] The compromise negotiated under the umbrella of the TWFD has generally proven sustainable. The core of the rules adopted in 1989 has been retained, albeit successively modified to adapt to a changing media landscape.

## 2. First revision: the 1997 TWFD

The need for the first revision of the TWFD was indisputable due to the rapid technological changes in the broadcasting industry, particularly the growth of satellite transmission and digitalisation.[251] As a result of those advances, the structure of the market for broadcasting transformed, creating a much larger number of (commercial) channels and new forms of television programming, like paid access to specialised television channels through subscriptions (pay-TV), and new forms of advertising, like television programmes dedicated to consumers shopping at home via television offerings (often referred to as 'television home-shopping' and later abbreviated to 'teleshopping').[252] The general societal move toward internationalisation and globalisation also affected the industry.[253] In light of the dynamic nature of the industry, the Commission sought to shape a coherent European audiovisual policy in the early- and mid-1990s. Several of the instruments it adopted, such as the MEDIA programme,[254] the Green Pa-

Universität Berlin, 2006), p. 147, http://www.diss.fu-berlin.de/diss/servlets/MCRFileNodeServlet/FUDISS_derivate_000000002712/?hosts= (accessed 20.4.2013).

250 Hörnle, "Country of Origin Regulation in Cross Border Media," p. 118.

251 Proposal amending Council Directive 89/552/EEC, paras. 5, 1, pp. 8, 26.

252 Proposal amending Council Directive 89/552/EEC, para. 2, p. 13, paras. 2.4.4-2.4.5, pp. 41, 42. See also European Commission, "Green Paper on Strategy Options to Strengthen the European Programme Industry in the Context of the Audiovisual Policy of the European Union, COM(94) 96 Final," June 4, 1994, p. 53.

253 European Commission, "Green Paper on a Common Market for Broadcasting," p. 54.

254 Council Decision 90/685/EEC of 21 December 1990 concerning the implementation of an action programme to promote the development of the European audiovisual industry (MEDIA) 1991-1995, OJ of 31.12.1990, L 380, p. 37.

per on pluralism and media concentration[255] and, of course, the Green Paper entitled "Strategy options to strengthen the European programme industry in the context of the audiovisual policy of the European Union"[256] (the 1994 Strategy Green Paper) clearly indicated its commitment to establishing that policy. The 1994 Strategy Green Paper evaluated the competitiveness of the European programme industry on the international stage and aimed at launching a more intensive debate about measures that could overcome a fragmented market and strengthen the industry while "help[ing] European culture to flourish and create jobs in Europe".[257] To this end, "the liberalisation of services and the removal of obstacles to the single market [was the Commission's] first objective".[258] In parallel with the developments in the television sector, the Commission promoted the growth of the so-called information society by setting the stage for coordination of certain aspects of the regulatory frameworks applicable to telecommunications, intellectual property rights, and the concentration of media markets by publishing its action plan on "Europe's way to the information society".[259]

Art. 26 TWFD, which required regular assessments of the Directive's application, facilitated subsequent adjustments in response to developments in the broadcasting sector. Together with its first report on the application of the TWFD, covering a period of five years and published in May 1995, the Commission took the opportunity to publish a proposal that included a number of amendments in light of those developments (the 1995

255 European Commission, "Green Paper, Pluralism and Media Concentration in the Internal Market, An Assessment of the Need for Community Action, COM(92) 480 Final," December 23, 1992.

256 Commission of the European Communities, Green Paper, Strategy options to strengthen the European programme industry in the context of the audiovisual policy of the European Union, COM(94) 96 final, 6.4.1994.

257 European Commission, "Green Paper on Strengthening the European Programme Industry," p. 53.

258 European Commission, "Green Paper on Strengthening the European Programme Industry," p. 55.

259 European Commission, "Communication from the Commission to the Council and the European Parliament and to the Economic and Social Committee and the Committee of Regions, Europe's Way to the Information Society, An Action Plan, COM(94) 347 Final," July 19, 1994, pp. 2, 3, 5, 7. The E-Commerce Directive 2000/31/EC regulating certain legal aspects of information society services, among many other initiatives, arose from said Communication.

Proposal).[260] It maintained that there was an overall "consensus on the essential value of the [TWFD]", finding that it had served as a reliable and "stable legal framework" that upheld the balance struck between the different rights and interests of the stakeholders involved.[261] Hence, its 1995 Proposal was not designed to be a complete overhaul thereof; rather, the 1995 Proposal's scope was limited to the essential points of law that had proved problematic as implemented and applied at the national level. Broadly speaking, the Commission intended to clarify the concept of jurisdiction to better identify the applicable law and thereby enhance legal certainty.[262] It also intended to make the application of the rules on European works more effective by clarifying not only the monitoring mechanisms to be employed by Member States, but also the precise obligations incumbent on broadcasters after taking into account market developments such as the ever-increasing amount of teleshopping.[263]

Before analysing the precise modifications proposed in the 1995 Proposal, it is worth noting two of the Commission's underlying assumptions when drafting it. First, when defining the role of the TWFD in the broader information society, the Commission alluded to the need to keep regulation technology-neutral, a concept that would be further developed in the context of the AVMSD.[264] Moreover, because technological progress was expected to continue in both unprecedented and unpredictable ways, the Commission emphasised that any regulation needed to target the broadcast's content regardless of its "mode of transmission".[265] Designing a regulatory structure for broadcasting content that remained independent of its transmission technology has been a sustainable solution. Secondly, the Commission expressly opposed an expansion of the TWFD's scope of application to "new point-to-point services", a category of services that offer on-demand transmission, due to the "specific nature of the problems they

260 Commission of the European Communities, Report on application of Directive 89/552/EEC and Proposal for a European Parliament and Council Directive amending Council Directive 89/552/EEC on the coordination of certain provisions laid down by law, regulation or administrative action in Member States concerning the pursuit of television broadcasting activities, COM(95) 86 final of 31.5.1995.

261 Proposal amending Council Directive 89/552/EEC, para. 1, pp. 25-26.

262 Proposal amending Council Directive 89/552/EEC, para. 3.1.1, p. 15.

263 Proposal amending Council Directive 89/552/EEC, para. 1, p. 26.

264 Proposal amending Council Directive 89/552/EEC, para. 4, pp. 7, 8.

265 Proposal amending Council Directive 89/552/EEC, para. 4, pp. 7, 8.

present".[266] Rather, it characterised "newer" services, like "pay-per-view" and "near-video-on-demand",[267] as mass communication and, thus, covered by the concept of broadcasting as defined in the TWFD and stated its intent to devise a regulatory framework for so-called information society services. The uncertainties accompanying these novel services prompted the Commission to suggest that further research should be conducted to properly construct the Community's response.[268] The Commission's deliberate and resolute decision to constrain regulatory action under the TWFD to television broadcasting (interpreted broadly) foreshadows the recurring discussions about media convergence and the emergence of on-demand audiovisual media services accessible to large proportions of the public. The basis for the distinction of conventional and more dynamic forms of television (leading to forms that only remotely resemble television) was, and still remains, a controversial aspect of the Union's regulatory model.

Two years after the 1995 Proposal, a revised version of the TWFD (the TWFD 1997)[269] was published, which, among other things, reworked the criteria previously used to determine which Member State had jurisdiction in order to further enhance legal certainty and the stability of the regulatory regime in response to continuing growth in the number of channels and in satellite transmissions.[270] In line with the Court's relevant case law, the principle criterion continued to be the broadcaster's place of establishment, so Art. 2 (3) TWFD 1997 outlined a "series of practical criteria"[271] for determining where that place might be, such as the broadcaster's "head office", or the place where "editorial decisions on programme schedules" were taken, or, the place where a "significant part of the [broadcaster's] workforce" operated, or the place "where it first began broadcasting (...)

266 Proposal amending Council Directive 89/552/EEC, para. 1, p. 25.

267 Proposal amending Council Directive 89/552/EEC, para. 1, p. 25. The question of whether near-video-on-demand services fell under the scope of the TWFD was affirmed by the Court of Justice in case C-89/04 *Mediakabel BV v Commissariaat voor de Media*, Judgment of 2.6.2005, EU:C:2005:348, paras. 39, 41.

268 Proposal amending Council Directive 89/552/EEC, para. 1, p. 26.

269 Directive 97/37/EC of the European Parliament and of the Council of 30 June 1997 amending Council Directive 89/552/EEC on the coordination of certain provisions laid down by law, regulation or administrative action in Member States concerning the pursuit of television broadcasting activities, OJ of 30.7.1997, L 202, p. 60.

270 Recital 13 TWFD of 1997.

271 Recital 12 TWFD of 1997.

provided that [the broadcaster] maintain[ed] a stable and effective link with the economy of that Member State".[272] If the application of those criteria did not result in an unequivocal determination of jurisdiction, that failure would trigger application of the "technical criteria" stipulated in Art. 2 (4) TWFD 1997.[273] And, if that still did not unequivocally result in a jurisdiction, Art. 2 (5) 1997 TWFD provided a final fall-back: the concept of "establishment" within the meaning of Art. 52 TEC (now Art. 56 TFEU) was to be applied. The logic of this hierarchical cascade of rather vague criteria, especially its new Art. 2 (5) was criticised.[274] Still, Art. 1 (b) TWFD 1997 defined the term "broadcaster" to mean a person "who has editorial responsibility for the composition of schedules (…) and who transmits them or has them transmitted by third parties". Together, these two new provisions strengthened the country of origin principle and provided feasible points of reference for determining jurisdiction in a particular market. Nevertheless, recital 14 TWFD 1997 reiterated that the Court had held that Member States were permitted to take measures against broadcasters who chose their place of establishment in an effort to evade legislation that would have applied if they had not settled in a different Member State. Hence, the concept of circumvention – first recognised by the Court and then acknowledged, but not expressly stated, in the text of the TWFD 1997 – was already taking shape and would further crystallise in the AVMSD.

The TWFD 1997 also introduced a rule for designated events that purported to "protect the right to information and to ensure wide access by the public to television coverage of (...) events of major importance for society".[275] As pay-per-view services proliferated, it was feared that certain events, which were of social significance and which were traditionally

---

272 On the interpretation of the criteria determining jurisdiction, see Egbert Dommering, "Article 2 TWFD (Country of Origin Principle/Jurisdiction)," in *European Media Law*, ed. Castendyk, Dommering and Scheuer, (The Netherlands: Kluwer Law International, 2008), paras. 21–46, pp. 347–53.

273 Dommering, "Art. 2 TWFD," para. 63, p. 357.

274 Dommering, "Art. 2 TWFD," para. 63, p. 357; Harrison and Woods, *European Broadcasting Law and Policy*, pp. 185–87.

275 Recital 18 TWFD of 1997. On the rule on listed events, see generally Mark Cole, "Der Fußball auf der Liste und im Free-TV – noch immer ein Entscheidungsprivileg der Mitgliedstaaten," *Europäische Zeitschrift für Wirtschaftsrecht*, November 2011, pp. 425–28; Harrison and Woods, *European Broadcasting Law and Policy*, pp. 266–89; Katrien Lefever, Hannes Cannie and Peggy Valcke, "Watching Live

covered extensively on free television (e.g. the Olympic Games or the football World Cup)[276] would no longer be accessible to large segments of the population who could not afford pay-per-view subscriptions. The business model of pay-TV services essentially hinged on the provision of exclusive content (e.g. popular national sports or series) that attracted large audiences. In order to reconcile the interests of broadcasters and rights holders, on the one hand, and viewers, on the other hand, Art. 3a (1) TWFD 1997 allowed Member States to draw up a list of designated events "of major importance for [its] society". These designated events could not be broadcast on exclusive basis on its territory but instead had to be made available on free television. Art. 3a TWFD 1997 also outlined procedural aspects.[277] Any measures proposed by a Member State was to be notified to the Commission so that the Commission could verify their compatibility with Union law after consulting the Contact Committee established pursuant to Art. 23a TWFD 1997 and publish the measures to be taken by the Member State in the Union's Official Journal. Publication would trigger mutual recognition by other Member States, which were obliged to ensure that broadcasters under their jurisdiction did not "exercise [their] exclusive rights (...) in such a way that a substantial proportion of the public in an-

Sport on Television: A Human Right? The Right to Information and the List of Major Events Regime," *European Human Rights Law Review*, no. 4 (2010): pp. 396–407; Alexander Scheuer and Max Schoenthal, "Article 3a TWFD (Major Events)," in *European Media Law*, ed. Castendyk, Dommering and Scheuer (The Netherlands: Kluwer Law International, 2008); Max Schoenthal, "Major Events and Reporting Rights," in *Major Events and Reporting Rights*, ed. Susanne Nikoltchev, IRIS Plus (Strasbourg: European Audiovisual Observatory, 2006), pp. 2–8.

276 Recital 18 TWFD of 1997.

277 In its *Infront* decision, the Court of First Instance (now the General Court) held that a letter from the Commission notifying a Member State (in this case the United Kingdom) of the compatibility of its list with Union law constituted an act that could be challenged in Union courts by natural or legal persons via an annulment action pursuant to Art. 230 TEC (now Art. 263 TFEU). Accordingly, the General Court found the Commission's internal decision-making rules applied, and since the rules on collegiate procedure had been disregarded, an essential procedural requirement had been infringed such that the Commission's decision had to be annulled. The ruling was approved by the CJEU on appeal. Cases T-33/01, *Infront WM AG v Commission of the European Communities*, Judgment of 15.12.2005, EU:T:2005:461; confirmed by C-125/06 P *Commission of the European Communities v Infront WM AG*, Judgment of 13.3.2008, EU:C:2008:159.

other Member State is deprived of the possibility of following events which are designated by that other Member State". Measures taken by several Member States pursuant to Art. 3a TWFD 1997 were subject to review by the European courts in 2011 and 2013.[278] These rulings demonstrated the limited power of review retained by the Commission under Art. 3a TWFD 1997 and inversely acknowledged that the Member States retained a large margin of discretion in designating such measures. Yet, such discretion is not unlimited; Member States must still justify their designation of events and the measures taken.[279]

Like the 1989 TWFD, the TWFD 1997 devoted a great deal of attention to revising the quota rules on European works. Nevertheless, despite the Commission's suggestion, in its 1995 Proposal, to substantially clarify the broadcaster's obligations and establish a greater level of coordination,[280] the TWFD 1997 made only minimal changes, primarily related to the definition of "European works". Nevertheless, several TWFD 1997 recitals reinforced the on-going significance of those quota rules. On the one hand, its promotion of European works served cultural ends explicitly recognised in Art. 128 (4) TEC (now Art. 167 (4) TFEU), which was inserted

---

278 The series of cases concerned Commission decisions that found the Belgian and British lists of major events compatible with Union law. FIFA and UEFA, as the exclusive holders of rights to the World Cup and EURO, had initiated proceedings alleging that national lists that included all matches of those tournaments violated, among other things, the freedom to provide services and the right to establishment (Art. 43, 49 TEC, now Art. 49, 56 TFEU) and their property rights. The General Court rejected such allegations, instead confirming the Member States' exercise of discretion in designating major events. The CJEU, to which FIFA and UEFA appealed, found that the General Court erred when it found that the Commission could not override the Member States' designation. However, this error did not invalidate the judgement. Cases T-385/07 *Fédération Internationale de Football Association (FIFA) v European Commission*, Judgment of 7.2.2011, ECR:T:2011:42; T-55/08 *Union des associations européennes de football (UEFA) v European Commission*, Judgment of 7.2.2011, EU:T:2011:43; T-68/08 *Fédération Internationale de Football Association (FIFA) v European Commission*, Judgment of 7.2.2011, EU:T:2011:44. The CJEU upheld the findings of the General Court in 2013 in cases C-204/11P *FIFA v European Commission*, Judgment of 18.7.2013, EU:C:2013:477; C-201/11P *UEFA v European Commission*, Judgment of 18.7.2013, EU:C:2013:519; C-205/11P *FIFA v European Commission*, Judgment of 18.7.2013, EU:C:2013:478.

279 C-204/11P *FIFA v Commission*, paras. 40, 41; C-201/11P *UEFA v Commission*, para. 31; C-205/11 *FIFA v Commission*, para. 42.

280 Arts. 4-6 of the Commission proposal of 1995.

by the Maastricht Treaty.[281] On the other hand, it also pursued economic goals, especially improved "competitiveness of the [European] programme industry".[282] The fact that the quota rules were not extensively modified hinted at the delicate political compromise that had been reached in 1989 between the quota system's proponents (e.g. France and Spain) and opponents (e.g. Germany), which could not, just a few years later, be fundamentally renegotiated: Recital 30 TWFD 1997 reflected that continuing compromise by acknowledging that "the proportions of European works must be achieved taking economic realities into account".

The TWFD 1997 also extended the rules on television advertising to teleshopping (which was characterised as an "economically important activity for operators as a whole and a genuine outlet for goods and services within the Community")[283] and added specific provisions to account for teleshopping windows and channels exclusively dedicated to teleshopping.[284] With regard to the protection of minors, Art. 22 TWFD 1997 reinforced the distinction between programmes that were "likely to impair the physical, mental or moral development of minors" and those that "might seriously impair" them.[285] Programmes of the latter category were not to be broadcast at all, while programmes in the former category could only be broadcast under certain circumstances and then only if clearly marked as such.[286] Interestingly, recital 42 TWFD 1997 required the Commission, "in liaison with competent Member State authorities" to consider the advantages and disadvantages of the desirability of measures like filtering mechanisms, rating systems, awareness-raising and education. The need for and scope of such protective measures would remain pertinent before, during, and after the AVMSD was adopted. In short, the TWFD 1997 represented an adaptation of the existing regulatory framework to a changing broadcasting sector; more dramatic transformations in that sector, however, ultimately required far more extensive modifications, necessitating its complete overhaul, the result of which was the AVMSD.

---

281 Recital 25 TWFD of 1997.

282 Recital 28 TWFD of 1997.

283 Recital 36 TWFD of 1997.

284 Arts. 10-20 TWFD of 1997.

285 Art. 22 TWFD of 1997 no longer included the rule on prohibition of incitement to hatred which was incorporated in a separate provision (Art. 22a TWFD of 1997).

286 Art. 22 (3) TWFD of 1997.

## 3. Second revision: the 2007 Audiovisual Media Services Directive

### a) Developments prior to the adoption of the AVMSD

Shortly after the TWFD 1997 was enacted, a pressing need for still more adaptations became obvious in light of media convergence brought about by the emergence and growth of the Internet. By the end of 1997, the Commission had already published a Green Paper on the convergence of the telecommunications, media and information technology sectors,[287] intended to stimulate debate about a horizontal approach to regulation as opposed to the vertical, sector-specific approach that has been pursued to date, to the extent different sectors became integrated in the European common market. Pursuant to that 1997 Green Paper, the term "convergence" implied "the ability of different network platforms to carry essentially similar kinds of services, or the coming together of consumer devices such as the telephone, television and personal computer".[288] The Commission extensively analysed market developments and the impact of perceived convergences in an attempt to identify regulatory challenges and to raise questions about future regulatory models. To this end, the Commission acknowledged that the vertical strategies to regulation in place provided a "high degree of certainty for most market actors," but that economic trends and technological progress pointed to a "single regulatory model for all sectors within a converged environment, based on common principles, but perhaps maintaining certain distinct elements focused on the specific services offered".[289] To date, no such cross-sector horizontal approach to regulation has been implemented. Nevertheless, the discussions in 1997, albeit broader in scope, appear to mirror the current debate regarding the audiovisual media services sector.

The Commission's 1997 Green Paper exposed the complexities of designing an appropriate and effective regulatory framework. While many of the key industries in that sector continued to merge, the regulatory objec-

287 European Commission, "Green Paper on the Convergence of the Telecommunications, Media and Information Technology Sectors, and the Implications for Regulation, Towards an Information Society Approach, COM(97) 623," March 12, 1997.

288 European Commission, "Green Paper on Convergence and the Implications for Regulation," p. 1.

289 European Commission, "Green Paper on Convergence and the Implications for Regulation," p. 30.

tives related to them remained diverse and based on fundamentally different rationales.[290] In contrast to the telecommunications market for example, the broadcasting sector had traditionally been the "bearer of social, cultural and ethical values within our society".[291] In addition, convergence has not always progressed uniformly across these sectors, such that different intensities and speed made "full convergence" impossible.[292] The obvious reluctance by the Commission to carve out an entirely new regulatory framework that applied uniformly across different media could be explained by economic uncertainties as to the kinds of products and services consumers would, eventually, accept. Member States were also reluctant to establish a "converged" supra-regulatory regime, as they feared it would be accompanied by a transfer of (new) competences to the Union.

Despite the debate spurred by the 1997 Green Paper, eight more years would pass before the TWFD 1997 was fundamentally reformed. In the meantime, the Court's case law, as well as the Commission's 2004 Communication on new forms of advertising,[293] interpreted the existing TWFD 1997 rules in light of enhanced convergence, newly emerged services, and other market developments. The judgment in *Mediakabel*[294] illustrates the adaptations thereof brought about by the Court. Mediakabel, a Dutch service provider, offered a subscription service using a decoder with a smart card, called Mr Zap, which allowed its subscribers to order, on a pay-per-view basis, films from the catalogue of another offer called Filmtime. The Dutch media regulator classified the service as television broadcasting, which required a license. Mediakabel questioned that classification, arguing that its Filmtime offerings were only provided to subscribers on request and, therefore, constituted an information society service. The Court rejected Mediakabel's characterisation, holding that the Filmtime service fell under the concept of television broadcasting within the meaning of the

290 European Commission, "Green Paper on Convergence and the Implications for Regulation," p. 5.

291 European Commission, "Green Paper on Convergence and the Implications for Regulation," p. 28.

292 European Commission, "Green Paper on Convergence and the Implications for Regulation," p. 33.

293 European Commission, "Commission Interpretative Communication on Certain Aspects of the Provisions on Televised Advertising in the 'Television without Frontiers' Directive, OJ of 28.4.2004, C 102, p. 2," n.d.

294 Case C-89/04 *Mediakabel*.

TWFD 1997.[295] In spite of the limited number of addressees (i.e. only subscribers of the additional pay-per-view service), the programmes were "selected by the broadcaster and [were] broadcast at times set by the broadcaster". In contrast, genuine on-demand services are available whenever the subscriber wants to view them. Furthermore, the Court classified the Filmtime offer as "near-video on-demand", which was provided on a "'point to multipoint' [*sic*] basis".[296] Later, during the negotiations of the AVMSD, the distinction between traditional forms of broadcasting and more "interactive" and, thus, hybrid services offered on demand would become a central point of discussion during the negotiations of the AVMSD.

The Court also addressed another subject, one that had already kicked up some dust during the negotiations surrounding the adoption of the TWFD 1997 and had already been linked to the question of jurisdiction: circumvention.[297] Although recital 14 of the TWFD 1997 recognised such "behaviour", no rule regarding it was included in the substantive part of the TWFD 1997.[298] Nevertheless, even prior to the TWFD's adoption, the Court followed its *Van Binsbergen*[299] reasoning, by confirming, in its *TV10* judgment, the Member States' right to

295 Case C-89/04 *Mediakabel*, para. 32.

296 To delineate the scope of application of the TWFD and distinguish broadcasting from information society services, the Court looked to Directive 98/34/EC of the European Parliament and of the Council of 22 June 1998 laying down a procedure for the provision of information in the field of technical standards and regulations and of rules on Information society services, OJ of 21.7.1998, L 204, p. 37. Its Art. 1 (2), when read in conjunction with its Annex V, defines the concept of information society services. Specifically, para. 3 (a) of Annex V refers to "television broadcasting services (including near-video on-demand)" as being excluded from the concept of information society services. See case C-89/04 *Mediakabel*, paras. 39, 41.

297 Tarlach McGonagle and Ad Van Loon, "Jurisdiction over Broadcasters in Europe, Report on a Round-Table Discussion," in *Jurisdiction over Broadcasters in Europe*, ed. Susanne Nikoltchev, IRIS Special (Strasbourg: European Audiovisual Observatory, 2002), pp. 8–10; Susanne Nikoltchev, "Right of Intervention to Address Abuses of the Fundamental Freedoms, The Role of the Case-Law," in *Regulating the New Media Landscape. A Directive for Audiovisual Media Services without Frontiers*, Schriftenreihe des Instituts für Europäisches Medienrecht (EMR) (Baden-Baden: Nomos, 2008), p. 29.

298 Harrison and Woods, *European Broadcasting Law and Policy*, pp. 182, 183.

299 Case 33/74 *Van Binsbergen v Bedrifsvereniging voor de Metallnijverheid*, Judgment of 3.12.1974, EU:C:1974:131.

> "take measures to prevent the exercise by a person providing services whose activity is wholly or principally directed towards its territory of the freedoms guaranteed by the Treaty for the purpose of avoiding the rules which could be applicable to him if he were established within that State".[300]

The *TV10* case concerned a broadcaster, established in Luxembourg, transmitting its programmes, via satellite, to the Netherlands. Since the programmes and advertisements were primarily directed at a Dutch audience, the Dutch regulator equated the broadcaster to domestic service providers, thereby obliging TV10 to adhere to stricter programme standards than other 'foreign' broadcasters. The stricter standards were justified by a cultural policy pursued by Dutch media law.[301] TV10 contested that status. First, the Court confirmed that Member States are entitled to counter service provider action designed to circumvent stricter national rules, thereby derogating from the country of origin principle *stricto sensu*. Yet, a different line of Court reasoning stressed that the "Treaty does not prohibit an undertaking from exercising the freedom to provide services if it does not offer services in the Member State in which it is established".[302] Thus, a service provider's quest to establish itself in the most favourable regulatory environment within the Union is lawful, as long as the provider did not deliberately do so to evade more burdensome obligations across the border. Obviously, locating the exact line between a permissible use of the freedoms enshrined in the Treaties and an illegal abuse of such freedoms would be difficult and would depend on a case-by-case factual assessment. To avoid that, the Commission and the Member States were able, in the subsequently adopted AVMSD discussed below, to create a specific procedure intended to make things simpler and easier.

---

300 Case C-23/93 TV 10 *SA v Commissariaat voor de Media*, Judgment of 5.10.1994, EU:C:1994:362, para. 20.

301 As to the lawfulness of the maintenance of pluralism as a cultural policy objective in the general interest pursued by national media laws, see cases C-288/89 *Collectieve Antennevoorziening Gouda v Commissariaat voor de Media*, Judgment of 25.7.1991, EU:C:1991:323, paras. 22, 23, C-353/89 *Commission v Netherlands*, Judgment of 25.7.1991, EU:C:1991:325, paras. 3, 29, 30, C-148/91 *Veronica Omroep Organisatie v Commissariaat voor de Media*, Judgment of 3.2.1993, EU:C:1993:45, para. 9.

302 Cases C-56/96 *VT4 Ltd v Vlaamse Gemeenschap*, Judgment of 5.6.1997, EU:C:1997:284, para. 22, C-212/97 *Centros v Erhvervs-og Selskabsstyrelsen*, Judgment of 9.3.1999, EU:C:1999:126, para. 27.

Prior to the adoption of the AVMSD, the Court was also called upon to review Member State provisions regulating advertising and to clarify their application in practice. In two different cases involving the concept of "television advertising", the Court held that indirect advertising – in the form of hoardings (or billboards) bearing advertisements – visible on the viewer's television screen during a sports event was not covered by the TWFD 1997.[303] Similarly, just before the AVMSD was adopted, the Court ruled on the distinction between teleshopping and television advertising.[304]

As discussed above, the Court was also asked to address whether the frequency of advertising interruptions during and between audiovisual works should use the gross or net principle.[305] In *ARD v Pro Sieben* the Court confirmed that Art. 11 of the 1997 TWFD stipulated the gross principle from which Member States could derogate by adopting stricter or more detailed rules.[306] The Court was asked to further clarify the same provision in *RTL v NML;*[307] it was asked to construe the meaning of the term (television) "series". In contrast to feature-length films, the Court found that a series can easily be followed with "less sustained concentration on the part of the television audience".[308] Hence, series (like serials, light entertainment programmes, and documentaries) profit from lighter regulation, which translates into more frequent advertising breaks. The Court pointed out that, essentially, the concept of a "series" hinged on

---

303 Cases C-429/02 *Bacardi France SAS v Télévision francaise 1 (TF1) and Others*, Judgment of 13.7.2004, EU:C:2004:432, paras. 27, 28, C-262/02 *Commission of the European Communities v French Republic (Loi Evin)*, Judgment of 13.7.2004, EU:C:2004:431, paras. 28, 29.

304 Case C-195/06 *Kommunikationsbehörde Austria (KommAustria) v Österreichischer Rundfunk (ORF)*, Judgment of 18.10.2007, EU:C:2007:613, paras. 37, 47.

305 On the net principle, see Dieter Dörr, "Das Nettoprinzip für die Unterbrechung von Spiel- und Fernsehfilmen durch Werbung und das europäische Medienrecht," *Zeitschrift für Urheber- und Medienrecht* 38, no. 6 (1994): pp. 342–51.

306 Case C-6/98 *ARD and PRO Sieben*, paras. 33, 43. The case concerned a preliminary question that had been referred to the Court prior to the entry into force of the TWFD of 1997 and, thus, had to be interpreted under the TWFD of 1989. Still, the amendments enacted in 1997 were minor (mostly linguistic) and did not alter the substance of the provision.

307 Case C-245/01 *RTL Television GmbH v Niedersächsische Landesmedienanstalt für Privaten Rundfunk (NML)*, Judgment of 23.10.2003, EU:C:2003:580.

308 Case C-245/01 *RTL v NML*, para. 107.

"links of substance, that is to say, common elements which relate to the content of the films concerned".[309]

The uncertainties revolving around the application of the TWFD 1997 advertising rules were further amplified by technical advancements in the broadcasting market and innovative forms of promotion, such as split-screen advertising.[310] In 2004, in response to obvious need to provide additional guidance, the Commission published a Communication intended to clarify the scope of certain provisions of the TWFD 1997.[311] It drew inspiration from the opinions and recommendations published by the Council of Europe's Standing Committee on Transfrontier Television.[312] The Communication, though non-binding, signaled a move towards a more comprehensive reform of the TWFD 1997, (discussions of which had already begun).[313] Although such reform – through the AVMSD – was ultimately delayed, that 2004 Communication represented a (relatively) swift reaction by the Commission[314] to changes in the industry and thereby alleviated some of the (political) pressure (at least in the short term) for such

309 Case C-245/01 *RTL v NML*, para. 105. Such "common elements" included, for example, "the development of the same story or the reappearance of one or more characters", para. 107.

310 Kogler, *TV (On-Demand)*, p. 11.

311 European Commission, "Interpretative Communication on Television Advertising," para. 6.

312 Opinion no. 4 (1995) on certain provisions on advertising and sponsorship; Opinion no. 6 (1995) on the legal framework for "infomercials"; Opinion no. 7 (1996) on the application of the convention to advertising transmitted via teletext services; Recommendation (97) 1 concerning the use of virtual advertising notably during the broadcast of sports events; Opinion no. 9 (2002) on split-screen advertising. The opinions and recommendation adopted by the Standing Committee on Transfrontier Television are available at http://www.coe.int/t/dghl/standardsetting/media/T-TT/T-TT(2006)012rev_en.asp#TopOfPage (accessed 11.12.2013).

313 See in this respect European Commission, "Communication from the Commission to the Council, the European Parliament, the Economic and Social Committee and the Committee of the Regions on Principles and Guidelines for the Community's Audiovisual Policy in the Digital Age, COM(99) 657 Final," December 14, 1999; European Commission, "Communication from the Commission to the Council, the European Parliament, the European Economic and Social Committee and the Committee of the Regions, The Future of European Regulatory Audiovisual Policy, COM(2003) 784 Final, 15.12.2003," December 15, 2003.

314 European Commission, "Communication on the Future European Regulatory Audiovisual Policy," para. 4, p. 24.

reform.[315] In its Communication, the Commission clarified that the advertising rules set out in the TWFD 1997, especially the principle of separation of editorial and commercial content and the maximum hourly limit on advertising, applied to new advertising formats, like mini-spots (a highly shortened advertising spot) and telepromotions (spots of advertising within game shows).[316] Above all, the Communication made clear that the use of split-screen and virtual advertising[317] were to be regarded as television advertising compatible with the TWFD 1997 provided that they otherwise adhered to its principal standards.[318] Further, it stated that the TWFD 1997 was applicable to interactive advertising, so long as the viewer had not entered the "interactive environment", which was characterised as a service provided on individual demand.[319] Interestingly, the Communication differentiated between, on the one hand, teleshopping and surreptitious advertising, the latter was prohibited by the 1997 TWFD, and, on the other, "lawful references to goods, services, brands or names of economic operators" (so-called product placements) within programmes, on the basis of the "undue prominence" criterion.[320] Although somewhat blurry, that particular distinction was carried forward into the AVMSD's regulatory framework.[321]

---

315 Cole, Mark, "Europäisches Medienrecht," para. 75, p. 59; Kogler, *TV (on Demand)*, p. 11.

316 European Commission, "Interpretative Communication on Television Advertising," paras. 21, 26, 29.

317 On split screen and interactive forms of advertising, see Holznagel, Bernd and Stenner, Daniel, "Die Zulässigkeit neuer Werbeformen, Von Splitscreentechnik zu den neuen interaktiven Werbestrategien im Fernsehen," *Zeitschrift für Urheber- und Medienrecht*, 2004, pp. 617–26.

318 European Commission, "Interpretative Communication on Television Advertising," paras. 45, 49, 50, 51, 67.

319 European Commission, "Interpretative Communication on Television Advertising," paras. 58, 65.

320 European Commission, "Interpretative Communication on Television Advertising," paras. 32–33; see also Kogler, *TV (On-Demand)*, p. 11.

321 Christina Angelopoulos, "Product Placement in European Audiovisual Productions," in *Product Placement*, ed. Susanne Nikoltchev, IRIS Plus 3/2010 (Strasbourg: European Audiovisual Observatory, 2010), pp. 19, 20; Oliver Castendyk, "Werbeintegration im TV-Programm – wann sind Themen Placements Schleichwerbung oder Sponsoring?," *Zeitschrift für Urheber- und Medienrecht*, 2005, pp. 857–65; Jean-Éric De Cockborne and Emmanuel Joly, "Le placement de produit dans l'Union européenne," *Gazette du Palais*, no. 131 (2008); Georgis Gounalakis and Christoph Wege, "Product Placement und Schleichwerbungsver-

In short, this subsection has briefly recounted several aspects of the most significant developments in the broadcasting sector and its regulation prior to the AVSMD. First, both the Court and the Commission have shaped the Union's audiovisual policy since its inception. The Court's jurisprudence has served market integration, particularly in its early phase, by providing guidance based on the fundamental freedoms guaranteed by the Treaties. Second, the market for audiovisual services has been, and continues to be, a rapidly changing, volatile and heterogeneous market to which regulators (including the Commission) are obliged to respond in a way that does not stifle, but rather enables and promotes innovation and creativity, while simultaneously providing a stable regulatory environment in which undertakings are willing to invest. The AVMSD reflects these tensions as regulation struggles to keep up with market developments.

#### b) The AVMSD and its scope of application

The adoption of the AVMSD was preceded by extensive negotiations between stakeholders and civil society, Member States and their national regulatory authorities (NRAs). The Commission organised two separate public consultations on the subject of audiovisual media services regulation (the first in April and June 2003 and the second in September 2005), through which the Commission received more than 340 written submissions.[322] During the early years of the new millennium, the Commission also commissioned a number of independent studies on different aspects

---

bot – Widersprüche im neuen Fernsehrichtlinien-Entwurf," *Kommunikation und Recht*, no. 3 (2006): pp. 97–101; Moritz Holzgraefe, *Werbeintegration in Fernsehsendungen und Videospielen, Product Placement und verwandte Formen im Spiegel des Medien- und Wettbewerbsrechts*, ed. Wolfgang Hoffmann-Riem, Materialien zur interdisziplinären Medienforschung 64 (Baden-Baden: Nomos, 2010), p. 124 et seq.; Rani Mallick, *Product-Placement in den Massenmedien, Rechtstatsachen und Rechtsgrundlagen*, ed. Wolfgang Hoffmann-Riem, Materialien zur interdisziplinären Medienforschung 63 (Baden-Baden: Nomos, 2009); Rolf Platho, "Die Systematik von Schleichwerbung und Produktplazierung und ihre Verfehlung in der AVMD-Richtlinie," *Multimedia und Recht* 11, no. 9 (2008): pp. 584–86.

322 The contributions to the consultations of 2003 and 2005 are respectively available at http://ec.europa.eu/avpolicy/reg/history/consult/consultation_2003/contributions/index_en.htm, http://ec.europa.eu/avpolicy/reg/history/consult/consultation_2005/contributions/index_en.htm (websites accessed 23.11.2012).

of the sector's existing regulatory framework and meetings of the focus groups and Contact Committee equally discussed questions about the future regulation of audiovisual media services.[323] A few months after the most prominent of those meetings and discussions, the Major Audiovisual Conference held in Liverpool, England in September 2005,[324] the Commission published, in December 2005, its proposed Audiovisual Media Services Directive (the 2005 Proposal).[325] The Audiovisual Media Services Directive was eventually adopted in December 2007 (the AVMSD) but was later codified, in March 2010, for the sake of readability and clarity.[326] The title of the Directive was even altered to accommodate the expansion of its scope of application to video on-demand services.

The AVMSD's concept of an audiovisual media service encompasses both linear (broadcasting) and non-linear (on-demand) audiovisual media services. The Commission's 2005 Proposal called attention to the fact that

---

323 See for instance the study on co-regulation measures in the media sector or the study on the impact of control measures on the televisual advertising markets in European Union Member States or the study on the impact of measures concerning the promotion of the distribution and production of TV programmes which are available at http://ec.europa.eu/avpolicy/info_centre/library/studies/index_en.htm#finalised (accessed 23.11.2012).

324 See http://ec.europa.eu/avpolicy/reg/history/consult/liverpool_2005/index_en.htm (accessed 23.11.2012).

325 European Commission, "Proposal for a Directive of the European Parliament and of the Council Amending Council Directive 89/552/EEC on the Coordination of Certain Provisions Laid down by Law, Regulation or Administrative Action in Member States Concerning the Pursuit of Television Broadcasting Activities, COM(2005) 646 Final, 13.12.2005," December 13, 2005.

326 Recital 1 AVMSD. All citations of provisions and recitals refer to the numbering as set out in the codified version of the AVMSD. Directive 2007/65/EC of the European Parliament and of the Council of 11 December 2007 amending Council Directive 89/552/EEC on the coordination of certain provisions laid down by law, regulation or administrative action in Member States concerning the pursuit of television broadcasting activities, OJ of 18.12.2007, L 332, p. 27, as codified by Directive 2010/13/EU of the European Parliament and of the Council of 10 March 2010 on the coordination of certain provisions laid down by law, regulation or administrative action in Member States concerning the provision of audiovisual media services (Audiovisual Media Services Directive), codified version, OJ of 15.4.2010, L 95, p. 1. See, Corrigendum to Directive 2010/13/EU of the European Parliament and of the Council of 10 March 2010 on the coordination of certain provisions laid down by law, regulation or administrative action in Member States concerning the provision of audiovisual media services, OJ of 6.10.2010, L 263, p. 15.

traditional broadcasting services "increasingly [competed] with other linear services on other platforms and non-linear (on-demand) services that offer the same or similar audiovisual media content, but are subject to a different regulatory environment".[327] Recital 24 AVMSD also stresses that the similarity of services offered "would lead the user reasonably to expect regulatory protection within the scope of this Directive", thus the underlying rationale for extending the scope of the Directive was to establish a level playing field for providers delivering comparable content to traditional broadcasts.[328] The definitions of the services regulated are technologically neutral,[329] a concept derived from the Commission's Communication of 1999[330] but which had already been alluded to in its 1995 Proposal.[331] Accordingly, the mode of transmission – be it satellite, cable, or the Internet – is immaterial to a transmission's classification as a regulated activity subject to the AVMSD. Hence, for purposes of the AVMSD, an audiovisual media service is defined as

> "a service as defined by Articles 56 and 57 of the [TFEU] which is under the editorial responsibility of a media service provider and the principal purpose of which is the provision of programmes, in order to inform, entertain or educate, to the general public by electronic communications networks". [332]

---

327 AVMSD proposal of 2005, para. 1, p. 2. See also recital 24 AVMSD which states that "it is characteristic of on-demand audiovisual media services that they are 'television-like', i.e. that they compete for the same audience".

328 AVMSD proposal of 2005, para. 1, p. 2. See also recital 10 AVMSD.

329 AVMSD proposal of 2005, paras. 2, 5, pp. 5, 10.

330 Commission Communication on Principles and guidelines for the Community's audiovisual policy in the digital age, para. 3, p. 10.

331 TWFD proposal of 1995, para. 4, pp. 7, 8.

332 Recitals 21- 29 AVMSD give guidance on the meaning of certain elements of the definition of an audiovisual media service set out in Art. 1 (1) (a) AVMSD. Art. 1 (1) (a) (i) AVMSD. See also Mark Cole, "The European Legal Framework for on-Demand Services: What Directive for Which Services?," in *The Regulation of on-Demand Audiovisual Services: Chaos or Coherence?*, ed. Susanne Nikoltchev, IRIS Special (Strasbourg: European Audiovisual Observatory, 2011), pp. 36–40; Francisco Cabrera Blázquez, "On-Demand Services: Made in the Likeness of TV?," in *What Is an on-Demand Service?*, ed. Susanne Nikoltchev, IRIS Plus 4/2013 (Strasbourg: European Audiovisual Observatory, 2013), pp. 7–27.

The meaning of electronic communications networks is construed pursuant to Art. 2 (a) of the Framework Directive[333] and, thus, encompasses a wide span of transmission techniques. Apart from broadcasting and on-demand services, the concept of "audiovisual media services" also covers audiovisual commercial communication, the new term for all forms of advertising.[334] Furthermore, the AVMSD uses a graduated approach[335] to regulation implying that "different levels of regulation, and levels of detail in regulatory requirements, will apply to different electronic media".[336] More specifically, linear services are regulated more heavily than non-linear services. This two-tier system establishes a "basic tier of coordinated rules"[337] applicable to all audiovisual media services as well as a subset of more stringent rules that only applies to television broadcasting. The more intensive interference with the provision of broadcasting services is motivated by the greater impact television has on public opinion and the lesser degree of control the viewer can exercise. Linear audiovisual media services imply simultaneous viewing of a programme by a mass audience (point to multi- point) on the basis of a programme schedule determined by the broadcaster.[338] By contrast, non-linear services are offered at the request of the user, at his/her convenience, from a catalogue of choices presented by the service provider.[339] Thus, in case of linear services, the viewer is obliged to conform to the broadcaster's programme grid whereas he/she determines the date and time of viewing when using non-linear services. This distinction has been criticised by academia for being artificial

333 Directive 2002/21/EC of the European Parliament and of the Council of 7 March 2002 on a common regulatory framework for electronic communications networks and services, OJ of 24.4.2002, L 108, p. 33.

334 Art. 1 (1) (h) AVMSD in conjunction with Art. 1 (1) (i) – (m) AVMSD and Art. 1 (1) (a) (ii) AVMSD.

335 Commission Communication on Principles and guidelines for the Community's audiovisual policy in the digital age, para. 3 (3), p. 12.

336 Peggy Valcke and David Stevens, "Graduated Regulation of 'Regulatable' Content and the European Audiovisual Media Services Directive, One Small Step for the Industry and One Giant Leap for the Legislator?," *Telematics and Informatics* 24 (2007): p. 291.

337 Recital 11 AVMSD.

338 Art. 1 (1) (e) AVMSD. Recital 30 AVMSD clarifies that "quasi-simultaneous viewing" is covered by the definition of broadcasting.

339 Art. 1 (1) (g) AVMSD.

and impractical especially from the perspective of the user.[340] Whether the user watches a live stream of a basketball game on the Internet, catches up on the highlights of the game on the team's website, or views a programme offering highlights coverage of the day in sports on television, he/she is unaware of the legal classifications of these individual services and, hence, the implications arising from such categorisation. Besides, the presumption of active on-demand users and passive television viewers appears over-simplistic. Some users may well consume on-demand services in a passive manner whereas others may watch television more actively by frequently swapping channels to avoid advertising breaks or by recording their favourite series to watch at a later time. In short, the user is interested in content regardless of the way such content is marketed, presented, or delivered. Much of that criticism may be particularly apropos in connec-

340 Monica Arino, "Content Regulation and New Media: A Case Study of Online Video Portals," *Communications & Strategies* 66, no. 2 (2007): pp. 117, 123; Monica Arino and Carles Llorens, "Back to the Future: New Media, Same Principles? Convergence Regulation Re-Visited," in *The European Union and the Culture Industries, Regulation and the Public Interest*, ed. David Ward, (Hampshire: Ashgate, 2008), p. 137 et seq.; Camille Bonenfant-Jeanneney and Séverine Fautrelle, "La Révision de la Directive "Télévision sans Frontrières » : Une Adaptation du Cadre Réglementaire Européen aux Evolutions du Paysage Audiovisuel," in *Télévision sans Frontières: Une Adaptation du Cadre Réglementaire Européen aux Evolutions du Paysage Audiovisuel* (Strasbourg: European Audiovisual Observatory, 2008), p. 4; Andreas Breitschaft, "Evaluating the Linear/non-Linear Divide – Are There Any Better Factors for the Future Regulation of Audiovisual Media Content?," *Entertainment Law Review* 20, no. 8 (2009): p. 292; Stephen Ridgway, "The Audiovisual Media Services Directive – What Does It Mean, Is It Necessary and What Are the Challenges to Its Implementation?," *Computer and Telecommunications Law Review* 14, no. 4 (2008): p. 110; Jutta Stender-Vorwachs, "Die Revision der Fernsehrichtlinie, Ist die Revision eine Reform?," *Zeitschrift für Urheber- und Medienrecht*, 2006, pp. 366, 367; Peggy Valcke et al., "Audiovisual Media Services in the EU, Next Generation Approach or Old Wine in New Barrels?," *Communications & Strategies* 7, no. 3 (2008): pp. 111, 112; Valcke and Stevens, "Graduated Regulation of 'Regulatable' Content and the AVMSD," pp. 297–300; Nico Van Eijk, "Scope of Application of the Modernised Directive," in *Regulating the New Media Landscape. A Directive for Audiovisual Media Services without Frontiers*, Schriftenreihe des Instituts für Europäisches Medienrecht (EMR) 36 (Baden-Baden: Nomos, 2008), pp. 22, 23; On the changing role of the user in a converged media environment, see Natali Helberger, "From Eyeball to Creator: Toying with Audience Empowerment in the Audiovisual Media Service Directive," *Entertainment Law Review* 6 (2008): pp. 128–37.

tion with hybrid or co-existing services,[341] which constitute borderline cases between linear and non-linear services.

Nevertheless, the two-tiered approach to regulation that was supported by a majority of stakeholders[342] during the consultation process necessitates an internal distinction between conventional television broadcasts and new, on-demand services.[343] Those same stakeholders agreed that a more comprehensive horizontal approach to regulation (as contemplated by the Commission's 1997 Green Paper on Convergence) was premature and would represent too great a leap away from the traditional (heavy-handed) way of regulating the broadcasting sector. The AVMSD, thus, lowered the intensity of regulation for broadcasting by liberalising certain rules contained in the TWFD 1997 (such as the rules on advertising) while simultaneously raising the level of regulation for on-demand services (some of which may have been unregulated prior to its adoption). From the Commission's perspective, the two-step regulatory scheme left room for adaptations needed to accommodate the ongoing transformations of the market; most of those involved in the AVMSD discussions expected demand for non-linear services to increase exponentially over the years following its adoption, pushing the focus of any such regulation towards on-demand services. However, at the time of this writing, it appears that the market for audiovisual media services (not to mention the users' viewing habits) is far more fragmented and heterogeneous across all age groups than anticipated, necessitating a more fundamental rethinking of how best to regulate it. At the moment, correctly applying the AVMSD's vague and problematic distinctions between linear and non-linear services and between, more generally, audiovisual media services and information society services is likely to constitute one of the most fundamental, but most difficult, tasks the NRAs must perform on a day-to-day basis, and the consist-

---

341 Remy Chavannes and Oliver Castendyk, "Article 1 AVMSD (Definitions)," in *European Media Law*, ed. Castendyk, Dommering and Scheuer, (The Netherlands: Kluwer Law International, 2008), paras. 101–23, pp. 831–37.

342 AVMSD proposal of 2005, para. 2, p. 5. See also the Commission Issue Paper for the Liverpool Audiovisual Conference of Group No 1 on Rules applicable to Audiovisual Content Services, July 2005, para. 1.1, p. 2.

343 On the excessive focus on the linear/non-linear distinction and an alternative interpretation of deficiencies of the Directive, see Michael Dizon, "Looking beyond the Linear/non-Linear Horizon: Content Regulation in the Converging Multilayered Contours of the European Audiovisual Media Landscape," *Entertainment Law Review* 21, no. 5 (2010): pp. 185–91.

ent and fair application of those distinctions is absolutely essential for service providers.

c) The substantive changes brought by the AVMSD

This section briefly touches upon the most important changes brought by the AVMSD in order to give an overview of its entire legal framework. With respect to its general provisions, the AVMSD retains the establishment criteria originally enumerated in the TWFD 1997[344] and a reinforced principle of free flow of information.[345] It still allows Member States to provisionally derogate from normally applicable rules to stop the free transmission of an on-demand audiovisual media service; the procedure for doing so is outlined in Art. 3 (4) AVMSD, which involves the Member State having jurisdiction as well as the Commission and resembles the derogation rule applicable to broadcasting.[346] More importantly, the Court's case law on the Member States' margin to manoeuvre in case of

---

344 Art. 2 (2)-(6) AVMSD.

345 The Court of Justice underscored the country of origin principle in case C-244-245/10 *Mesopotamia Broadcast A/S METV and Roy TV A/S v Germany*, Judgment of 22.9.2011, EU:C:2011:607. The case concerned a Danish broadcaster transmitting programmes mainly in the Kurdish language via satellite to Europe and the Middle East. The German Federal Interior Ministry took the view that the activities of the broadcaster promoted the Kurdistan Workers Party (PKK) and violated the "principle of international understanding" within the meaning of the German Law of Associations (Vereinsgesetz) and prohibited them. The Court clarified that the principle of international understanding could be included in the concept of "incitement to hatred on grounds of race, sex, religion or nationality" as outlined by Art. 22a TwFD (now Art. 6 AVMSD) (paras. 39-46). Yet, it made clear that it was for the Member State in which the broadcaster was legally established (Denmark) to check compliance with the rules of the Directive (para. 48). Thus, the German authorities could only prohibit the activities of the Danish broadcaster in so far as they fell within the Vereinsgesetzt (e.g. the production of broadcasts or the public screening of the broadcaster's programmes) and could not prohibit retransmission per se of its programmes in Germany (paras. 50, 53). Thus, Germany was obliged to guarantee the "reception and private use" of the broadcaster's programmes (para. 52). For a more detailed discussion, see Mark Cole, "Note d'observation, 'Roj TV' entre ordre public et principe du pays d'origine," *Revue du Droit des Technologies de l'Information* 47 (2012): pp. 50–61.

346 Art. 3 (2), (3) AVMSD.

circumvention is now codified in Art. 4 (2)-(5) AVMSD, which sets out precise conditions for the adoption of countervailing measures and the procedure to be followed.[347] The basic tier of rules includes a provision that guarantees the viewers have easy, direct, and permanent access to a minimum amount of information identifying the service provider, such as its name, geographical address, mailing address, or website.[348] This so-called transparency obligation allows a service provider to be found and may even indicate its connection to a specific Member State, which may hint at its place of establishment for jurisdictional purposes.[349] At the instigation of the European Parliament, the AVMSD added a new provision improving access to audiovisual media services for hearing- and visually-impaired persons.[350] Recital 46 AVMSD, for example, suggests that improved accessibility could be accomplished through "sign language, subtitling, audio-description and easily understandable menu navigation". The TWFD's rules prohibiting incitement to hatred[351] and establishing the release windows for rights exploitation[352] were only amended to accommodate the AVMSD's extended scope.

The AVMSD also added new provisions addressing commercial communications, sponsorship, and product placement to the base tier of the two-tiered regulatory framework. In that regard, Art. 9 AVMSD details qualitative rules relating to all types of audiovisual commercial communication, which is defined in Art. 1 (1) (h) AVMSD, in a purported effort to reinforce general advertising standards, such as the identification of commercial content (as opposed to editorial content), the truthfulness of pro-

347 On the interpretation of Art. 4 AVMSD, see Egbert Dommering, Alexander Scheuer and Thorsten Ader, "Article 3 AVMSD (Stricter Rules/Measures against Abuse/ Compliance/ Co- and Self-Regulation/ Relation to the E-Commerce Directie," in *European Media Law*, ed. Castendyk, Dommering and Scheuer, (Kluwer Law International, 2008), paras. 6–12, pp. 860–62.

348 Art. 5 AVMSD.

349 Egbert Dommering and Remy Chavannes, "Article 3a AVMSD (Identification of Providers)," in *European Media Law*, ed. Castendyk, Dommering and Scheuer, (The Netherlands: Kluwer Law International, 2008), para. 3, p. 869.

350 Art. 7 AVMSD. See Draft European Parliament Legislative Resolution on the proposal for a directive of the European Parliament and of the Council amending Council Directive 89/552/EEC on the coordination of certain provisions laid down by law, regulation or administrative action in Member States concerning the pursuit of television broadcasting activities, 23.11.2006, Art. 3hc.

351 Art. 6 AVMSD.

352 Art. 8 AVMSD.

motional content, and the general prohibition of advertising certain products and services.[353] Moreover, Art. 10 AVMSD outlines the requirements that sponsored programmes have to fulfil, while Art. 11 AVMSD sets forth a rather complex rule on product placement.[354] Although Art. 11 (2) AVMSD lays down a general ban on product placement, Art. 11 (3) AVMSD establishes a virtually automatic exception to that ban, thereby allowing product placement in certain types of audiovisual programmes or in cases where production props or prizes provided by third parties have only an insignificant value.[355] The "significant-value test" is crucial to the evaluation of potential product placements and is anchored in recital 91 AVMSD. Interestingly, the Art. 11 (3) AVMSD exception automatically applies *unless* a Member State opts out. To the extent a permitted product placement is inserted, certain requirements, which are reminiscent of those applicable to sponsored programmes, must still be respected. These qualifications ensure, among other things, that editorial content remains unaffected by the inclusion of such product placement or sponsorship credit and that viewers are informed of their existence.[356] Since product place-

---

353 Kathrin Böttcher et al., "Article 3e (Principles and Standards for Audiovisual Commercial Communications)," in *European Media Law*, ed. Castendyk, Dommering and Scheuer, (The Netherlands: Kluwer Law International, 2008), paras. 2–38, pp. 892–902; Cole, "Europäisches Medienrecht," paras. 91–93, pp. 68–70; Agnes Granchet-Valentin and Emmanuel Derieux, *Droit des Médias*, 6th ed., Droit Français, Européen et International (Paris: LGDJ, 2010), para. 3481, p. 1037.

354 On product placement, see generally Angelopoulos, "Product Placement in European Audiovisual Productions"; Oliver Castendyk, "Article 3g AVMSD (Product Placement)," in *European Media Law*, ed. Castendyk, Dommering and Scheuer (The Netherlands: Kluwer Law International, 2008), pp. 907–18; Jean-Éric De Cockborne and Emmanuel Joly, "Le placement de produit dans l'Union européenne"; Georgis Gounalakis and Christoph Wege, "Product Placement und Schleichwerbungsverbot – Widersprüche im neuen Fernsehrichtlinien-Entwurf," pp. 97–101; Leitgelb, *Product-Placement*; Mallick, *Product-Placement in den Massenmedien, Rechtstatsachen und Rechtsgrundlagen*; Müller-Rüster, *Product Placement im Fernsehen, Die Legalisierung programmintegrierter Werbung im Lichte der deutschen und europäischen Kommunikationsgrundrechte*; Kai Glockzin, "Product Placement im Fernsehen, Abschied vom strikten Trennungsgebot zwischen redaktionellem Inhalt und Werbung," *Multimedia und Recht*, 2010, pp. 161–66.

355 See also recital 92 AVMSD.

356 See recital 93 AVMSD. See also Art. 10 (1) (a)-(c) and Art. 11 (3) (a)-(d) AVMSD.

ment is "built into the action of a programme",[357] "undue prominence"[358] must not be accorded to the relevant product or service. Although the Directive itself does not define the concept of "undue prominence", the Commission's 2004 interpretative communication on advertising indicates that "the undue nature may result from the recurring presence of the brand, good or service in question or from the manner in which it is presented and appears".[359] Still, the imprecise formulations contained in these provisions imply that Member States and their NRAs have a great deal of discretion when monitoring compliance with the AVMSD's conditions.

Two other provisions apply solely to on-demand services; they mirror provisions for broadcasting even though the obligations imposed on broadcasters are less stringent. Art. 12 AVMSD ensures minors are protected when interacting with on-demand services by requiring any content that "might seriously impair the physical, mental or moral development of minors" only be "made available in such a way as to ensure that minors will not normally hear or see" it.[360] Recital 60 AVMSD mentions some of the technical means that might be employed to prevent children from viewing unsuitable material, such as: personal identification numbers (PIN

---

357 Recital 91 AVMSD.

358 Art. 11 (3) (d) AVMSD.

359 European Commission, "Interpretative Communication on Television Advertising," para. 33.

360 On the protection of minors in on-demand services, see generally Federica Casarosa, "Children Protection Online: Uneasy Steps towards a Balance between Risks and Freedoms," *European Journal of Legal Studies*, 2010, http://www.ejls.eu/6/79UK.htm (accessed 13.6.2012); Oliver Füg, "Content Ratings Harmonization and the Protection of Minors in the European Information Society," in *The European Union and the Culture Industries, Regulation and the Public Interest*, ed. David Ward, (Hampshire: Ashgate, 2008), pp. 165–86; Oliver Füg, "Save the Children: The Protection of Minors in the Information Society and the Audiovisual Media Services Directive," *Journal of Consumer Policy* 31 (2008): pp. 45–61; Eva Lievens, *Protecting Children in the Digital Era, The Use of Alternative Regulatory Instruments*, pp. 345–51; Alexander Scheuer and Cristina Bachmeier, "The Protection of Minors in the Case of New (Non-Linear) Media, European Legal Rules and Their National Transposition and Application," in *Protection of Minors and Audiovisual Content on-Demand*, ed. Susanne Nikoltchev, IRIS Plus 6/2012 (Strasbourg: European Audiovisual Observatory, 2012), pp. 7–27; Alexander Scheuer, "Additional Youth Protection Measures in the European Union- Filters, Children's Networks, Media Literacy," in *Protection of Minors and Audiovisual Content On-Demand*, IRIS Plus 6/2012 (Strasbourg: European Audiovisual Observatory, 2012), pp. 41–48.

codes), filtering systems, and labelling.[361] In contrast to the absolute ban on inappropriate content in broadcasts (i.e. content that can "seriously" damage minors, such as pornography or gratuitous violence),[362] there is no such absolute prohibition for on-demand services. In a similar vein, the rule on promotion of European works in on-demand services laid down in Art. 13 AVMSD is lighter than its broadcast counterpart,[363] even though it uses similarly vague language: on-demand service providers are encouraged to further, "where practicable and by appropriate means [,] the production of and access to European works".[364] Art. 13 AVMSD further suggests that "such promotion could relate, inter alia, to the financial contribution made by such services to the production and rights acquisition (...) or to the share and/or prominence of European works in the catalogue" the service provider offers.

Whereas the rules on listed events[365] and European works [366] were transferred from the TWFD without major changes, a new provision was introduced concerning the right to short news reports.[367] Art. 15 AVMSD complements Art. 14 AVMSD highlighting both, the freedom of expression and the right to receive information.[368] Hence, Art. 15 AVMSD contributes to a pluralistic society based on a variety of sources covering news-worthy events and developments. In fact, the right to short news reports was enshrined in Art. 9 of the Convention on Transfrontier Televi-

361 See Recommendation of the European Parliament and of the Council of 20 December 2006 on the protection of minors and human dignity and on the right of reply in relation to the competitiveness of the European audiovisual and on-line information services industry, OJ of 27.12.2006, L 378, p. 72.

362 Art. 27 (1) AVMSD.

363 Arts. 16-18 AVMSD.

364 On the promotion of European works in on-demand services, see generally Pascal Kamina, "Promouvoir les oeuvres européennes dans les services à la demande, Incitations à l'action de la part des législateurs, des régulateurs et de l'industrie," in Susanne Nikoltchev, ed., "Video On-Demand and the Promotion of European Works", IRIS Special (Strasbourg: European Audiovisual Observatory, 2009), pp. 77-84.

365 Art. 14 AVMSD.

366 Arts. 16-18 AVMSD.

367 European Commission, "Communication on the Future European Regulatory Audiovisual Policy," para. 3.3, p. 16. See also the European Commission working paper of Focus Group No 3 on the right to information and the right to short extracts, October 2004, available at http://ec.europa.eu/avpolicy/docs/reg/modernisation/focus_groups/fg3_extracts_en.pdf (accessed 13.2.2013).

368 Recital 55 AVMSD.

sion of 1989 from which the Commission drew inspiration, even though it worded the right much less precisely. In essence, broadcasters holding exclusive rights to cover an "event of high interest to the public"[369] are obliged to grant other broadcasters established in the Union access thereto for the purpose of producing short extracts to be diffused during general news programmes.[370] Typically, the broadcaster is allowed to "freely choose short extracts from the transmitting broadcaster's signal", as long as the source is identified during the programme.[371] Other means of access, such as physical access to the site where the relevant event takes place must be "fair, reasonable and non-discriminatory".[372] Art. 15 (as Art. 14) AVMSD is at the nexus of the different rights and interests of rights holders, broadcasters and viewers. On the one hand, rights holders have invested in the acquisition of rights that privilege them to transmit certain content on exclusive basis. Broadcasters, on the other hand, are interested in covering important societal events and developments in their news programmes in order to offer viewers up-to-date information. Art. 15 AVMSD attempts to reconcile these opposing interests by striking a balance, which is illustrated, for example, by the fact that potential compensation arrangements made between the rights holder and the broadcaster wishing to gain access "shall not exceed the additional costs directly incurred in providing access".[373] The validity of Art. 15 (6) AVMSD in light of Art. 16 (freedom to conduct business) and 17 (right to property) of the EU's Charter of Fundamental Rights (CFR) was confirmed by the Court in case *Sky Österreich* as discussed above.[374]

Although the TWFD's central provisions and principles were retained in the AVMSD,[375] rules on television advertising and teleshopping were liberalised to give more flexibility to insert advertising during pro-

369 Art. 15 (1) AVMSD.

370 Peter Matzneller, "Short Reporting Rights in Europe: European Legal Rules and their National Transposition and Application," pp. 14–23; Claudia Wildmann, *Das Europäische Kurzberichterstattungsrecht im Lichte der Richtlinie über audiovisuelle Mediendienste*, pp. 41–60.

371 Art. 15 (3) AVMSD.

372 Art. 15 (4) AVMSD.

373 Art. 15 (6) AVMSD.

374 Case C-283/11 *Sky Österreich*.

375 The central rules are considered to be the principles of separation and identification (Art. 19 AVMSD), the rule on insertion of advertising (Art. 20 (1) AVMSD), and the rules banning advertising for certain goods or services (Art. 21 AVMSD

grammes.[376] While the TWFD's hourly limit of 20 percent for advertising was left intact, its daily limit was discarded.[377] In 2013, the Court upheld a national law that stipulated stricter thresholds, which were in line with Art. 4 (1) AVMSD, but applied different hourly limits to free-to-air broadcasters as opposed to pay-TV operators.[378] In addition, the AVMSD also omitted the TWFD's maximum number of teleshopping windows (each could be a minimum of 15 minutes).[379] The final substantive provisions of the AVMSD, which relate to the protection of minors[380] and the right to reply in television programmes,[381] are similar to those of the TWFD1997.

This short description demonstrates that the AVMSD represents a shift in the Union's approach to audiovisual material. While the backbone of the Union's rules applicable to broadcasting were only moderately changed, the scope of those rules has now been extended to on-demand services. Regulation has thereby become "more" horizontal, treating "TV-like" services offered on an individual basis like traditional television services. Yet, due to continuous, unhampered market developments resulting in even greater convergence of media, the concepts stipulated in the Directive have already been, and increasingly continue to be challenged.

---

on teleshopping for medicinal products) and allowing advertising under certain conditions (Art. 22 AVMSD on alcoholic beverages) as well as the rule limiting advertising time (Art. 23 AVMSD).

376 Art. 20 (2) AVMSD no longer stipulates that a certain time span has to pass before the next advertising break.

377 Art. 23 AVMSD.

378 Case C-234/12 *Sky Italia srl v Autorità per le Garanzie nelle Comunicazioni (AGCOM)*, Judgment of 18.7.2013, EU:C:2013:496. For free-to-air broadcasters, the threshold was set at 18 percent whereas pay-TV operators were limited to 14 percent of advertising per hour. Sky Italia, a pay-TV operator established in Italy, alleged that the different limits were contrary to the principle of equal treatment. The Court found that pay-TV operators could be regarded as being in an objectively different situation than free-to-air broadcasters, due to (a) their economic situation (pay TV operators generate income mainly from subscription whereas free-to-air broadcasters are predominantly financed by advertising) and (b) their direct commercial relationship with viewers (paras. 20, 21). Thus, the Court held the Italian regulation to be in compliance with Union law as required by Art. 4 (1) AVMSD (para. 23).

379 Art. 24 AVMSD.

380 Art. 27 AVMSD.

381 Art. 28 AVMSD.

### d) Another revision in light of media convergence

Not long after its adoption in 2007, discussions about the AVMSD's fate resumed in light of further technological advances that included hybrid and converged services. The preamble of the AVMSD already gives guidance on the intensity of regulation applicable to services encompassing both linear and non-linear elements: Recital 27 AVMSD states that a programme offered on television and as an on-demand service by the same service provider must meet the standards applicable to broadcasting; when linear and non-linear services are offered simultaneously "but are clearly separate services",[382] the AVMSD applies to each service respectively. If, however, the service is mixed together, the tier of regulation applicable to television prevails and the provider must observe its stricter rules.[383] Recital 22 AVMSD, however, specifies that offers in which "any audiovisual content is merely incidental to the service and is not its principal purpose" do not fall under the Directive and enumerates a number of examples such as gambling, on-line games, and search engines that are not covered by the AVMSD. In addition, recital 21 AVMSD highlights that the AVMSD regulates services that are in competition with television broadcasting and, thus, exempts "private websites and services consisting of the provision or distribution of audiovisual content generated by private users for the purposes of sharing and exchange within communities of interest". This rather awkward formulation was intended to exclude user-generated content (UGC) that is up-loaded to social networking sites like Facebook and YouTube and other video-sharing platforms. At the time the AVMSD was adopted, many already feared that the Internet, the epitome of freedom and innovation, would be regulated and, consequently, stifled. In an attempt to allay that fear and counter concerns expressed by representatives of the printed press (e.g. newspaper publishers), recital 28 AVMSD clarifies that electronic versions of newspapers and magazines remain outside its scope; it implies a strict separation between the two sectors.[384] Moreover, with a view to information society services governed by the ECD, Art. 4 (8) AVMSD specifies that the AVMSD trumps the ECD in the event of a conflict between the two. Unfortunately, this conflict resolution rule does not clarify which regulatory regime applies to services that com-

382 Recital 27 AVMSD.

383 Cole, "The EU Legal Framework for On-Demand Services," p. 38.

384 Cole, "The EU Legal Framework for On-Demand Services," p. 38.

prise elements of both audiovisual media services and information society services. Although a great number of its recitals, in addition to Art. 4 (8) AVMSD, attempt to delineate its precise scope of application, it seems that different types of content (be they text-based, audiovisual, or user-generated) and, thus, different media have continued to converge, such that the formerly clear-cut boundaries among printed press, broadcasting, and Internet services have blurred, which challenges the existing concepts upon which the Union's regulatory frameworks are built.

One striking example of this development is so-called Connected TV, which allows simultaneous viewing of both television and Internet services on the same screen.[385] The viewer may enter an interactive Internet environment while simultaneously watching a programme on TV. The user may consult detailed statistics about his favourite football player while watching him play or she may simultaneously purchase a pair of shoes her favourite actor is wearing in the movie she is watching. Currently, most TV device manufacturers enable Internet access via applications – commonly known as "apps" – listed in a catalogue on their platforms.[386] A few, it appears, even provide web browsers with which the viewer can surf the entire World Wide Web. The platforms are, moreover, closed, proprietary systems (intended to tie customers to the manufacturer's own services and products) and their content often varies depending on their customers' geographic location and the rights they have obtained for them. The dominant producers of TV sets are either American or Asian (e.g. Samsung, LG, Sony or Panasonic) and include global players like Google and Apple, which have forcefully pushed into the traditional broadcasting market.[387]

385 Kogler, *TV (On-Demand)*, p. 60; Alexander Scheuer, "Convergent Devices, Platforms and Services for Audiovisual Media, Challenges set by Connected TV for the EU Legislative Framework," in *Converged Media: Same Content, Different Laws?*, ed. Susanne Nikoltchev, IRIS Plus 3/2013 (Strasbourg: European Audiovisual Observatory, 2013), pp. 7–9.

386 Sebastian Artymiak, "Introduction to Different Forms of On-Demand Audiovisual Services," in *The Regulation of On-Demand Audiovisual Services: Chaos or Coherence?*, ed. Susanne Nikoltchev, IRIS Special (Strasbourg: European Audiovisual Observatory, 2011), p. 33, 43; Cole, "The EU Legal Framework for On-Demand Services," pp. 43, 44.

387 Artymiak, "Introduction to Different Forms of On-Demand Audiovisual Services," p. 33.

Connected TV, thus, has enormous potential to innovative business models and alter consumers' viewing habits; it also fundamentally muddles the current regulatory structures, which rely on a differentiated approach that regulates different content types in different ways. While media service providers are obliged to meet minimum standards to protect minors, such protection may be undermined by freely accessible, online pornographic content offered by a service provider located outside the EU. Similar disparities exist when rules relating to audiovisual commercial communications exist for audiovisual media services but do not exist for commercial communications found on websites. A level-playing field is, thus, necessary to rectify these regulatory differences. Further, Connected TV has implications for other areas of law, like IT and telecommunications by raising questions about standards like HbbTV and their interoperability as well as data protection by bringing to the fore questions about personal data collection for the purpose of, among other things, personalised advertising and services.

The Commission, as well as the European Parliament, are both well aware of the legal issues revolving around Connected TV. In April 2013, the Commission published a Green Paper preparing for a fully converged audiovisual world.[388] That 2013 Green Paper tracked the economic growth of the market for audiovisual media services that gradually moved online.[389] On the one hand, the Commission's Green Paper embraced the economic potential and the possibilities for innovative business models that such convergence demonstrated.[390] On the other hand, it recognised the inherent deficiencies of an internal market that was still fragmented because of cultural and linguistic barriers and its susceptibility to international competition, especially from the USA.[391] Notwithstanding private-sector attempts at creating a European brand (like Euro news) and common formats (like series) "which are increasingly traded within Europe", the Commission acknowledged that existing markets for audiovisual me-

388 European Commission, "Green Paper Preparing for a Converged Audiovisual World.".

389 European Commission, "Green Paper Preparing for a Converged Audiovisual World," paras. 2, p. 4.

390 European Commission, "Green Paper Preparing for a Converged Audiovisual World," para. 2, pp. 4, 5.

391 European Commission, "Green Paper Preparing for a Converged Audiovisual World," para. 2.1, p. 5.

dia services remain national and predominantly targeted at national or local audiences. The 2013 Green Paper formulated twenty-seven questions relating to different topics addressed to stakeholders, who were invited to submit comments until September 2013.[392] Next to the questions of standard-setting to ensure interoperability of portals and services and of infrastructure,[393] the 2013 Green Paper focused on "values", a section that elaborated on the future regulatory framework for audiovisual media services. It follows that the Commission also reflected on the AVMSD's scope of application (particularly its distinction between linear and non-linear audiovisual media services) and how best to meet the purported market distortions between providers falling inside and outside that scope.[394]

By the same token, the Commission examined the effects of convergence on media freedom and pluralism; it cautioned that citizens might not necessarily be empowered to the extent that platform providers functioned as gatekeepers limiting access to content or making content difficult to find due to the vast amount of material offered.[395] In addition, the Commission brought out other concerns associated with Connected TV: the controversial aspects of commercial communication, the protection of minors, and the accessibility of the services to persons with disabilities. It questioned the effectiveness of the AVMSD's rules in response to commercial overlays and unsuitable material freely accessible on the Internet.[396] Although its substance may appear relatively meagre, the 2013 Green Paper was, nonetheless, insightful. The Commission sought broad public input on all of the questions raised in the 2013 Green Paper on which to base a broader, more comprehensive, and more relevant regula-

---

392 The contributions to the consultation on the Green Paper Preparing for a fully converged audiovisual world are available at http://ec.europa.eu/digital-agenda/en/news/consultation-green-paper-preparing-fully-converged-audiovisual-world-growth-creation-and-values (accessed 19.8.2014).

393 European Commission, "Green Paper Preparing for a Converged Audiovisual World," para. 2.3-2.4, pp. 9, 10.

394 European Commission, "Green Paper Preparing for a Converged Audiovisual World," para. 3.1, p. 11; see also Bernd Holznagel, "Grünbuch Konvergenz der Medien 2013, Verpasste Chance oder gangbarer Weg aus dem Globalisierungsdilemma?," *Multimedia und Recht*, 2014, p. 21.

395 European Commission, "Green Paper Preparing for a Converged Audiovisual World," para. 3.2, p. 13.

396 European Commission, "Green Paper Preparing for a Converged Audiovisual World," para. 3.2, p. 13.

tory framework. To that end, the 2013 Green Paper was a success because it posed the right questions, even though the Commission was still a long way away from modifying the existing EU *acquis*. Rather, the Green Paper emphasised that the future regulation of audiovisual media services could no longer be addressed in an insular manner; its effects on other areas of Union law, such as data protection, telecommunication and intellectual property law (all of which are or have been undergoing a comprehensive review) need to be taken into account.

The Connected TV market, though on the rise, is still in its start-up phase during which a number of business models are likely to assert themselves on the market. While the market is in flux, it would be premature to design a network of intersecting, detailed rules that might prove detrimental to some or all of the market's evolving economic developments. While many stakeholders participated in the Commission's Green Paper consultation, their comments did not paint a uniform picture and diverged on the level of regulation the stakeholders supported. Some, of course, argued for broadcasting deregulation to level the playing field for linear and non-linear services, while others argued that the new market players be regulated in the same way as the broadcasters with whom they compete. As the 2013 Green Paper consultation did not result in any obvious consensus, it was even more difficult for the Commission to design a new approach to achieve it. Moreover, political events, such as the European elections held in May 2014, as well as the inauguration of a new Commission, put a stop to any immediate modification of the AVMSD or other regulatory instruments. Yet, it is blatantly clear that many of the central regulatory concepts laid down in the AVMSD are unable to cope with the continual convergence of media such that its review is now indispensable. Nevertheless, the AVMSD, it seems, will remain, for the foreseeable future, at the heart of the Union's media policies; fortunately, the Union does not appear to be suffering from a mass exodus of service providers because of that.

The Commission's struggle to find a way forward amidst current insecurities was made evident by its decision to establish, in February 2014, the European Regulators Group for Audiovisual Media Services (ERGA), which was first convened in March 2014 (ERGA Decision).[397] Composed of delegates from the NRAs and a representative of the Commission, ER-

397 Commission Decision of 3.2.2014 on establishing the European Regulators Group for Audiovisual Media Services, C(2014)462 final (hereinafter Decision on ERGA). In 2003, the establishment of such a group was already contemplated

GA was established to assist and advise the Commission on all matters falling within the Commission's competence: first and foremost, it is to be a forum for "exchange[s] of experience and good practice as to the application of [the] regulatory framework for audiovisual media services".[398] Strikingly, ERGA functions side by side with the Contact Committee, comprising Member States' representatives,[399] which is intended to help facilitate the implementation and application of the AVMSD and discuss "any development[s] arising in the sector on which an exchange of views appears useful". The duplicative mandates of these bodies could lead to counterproductive competition between them. What can, nonetheless, be deduced from the creation of ERGA is that the Commission is looking to the NRA to help frame the Union's response to the current legal conundrums, which could lead to greater consensus among the Member States and a more uniform application of the AVMSD in the absence of more up-to-date European rules.

The European Parliament (EP) issued two reports in reaction to the 2013 Green Paper, the first in June 2013 and the second in January 2014.[400] Both reports were prepared by its Committee on Culture and Education (CULT) and pointed out the challenges associated with Connected TV, focusing on the cultural potential of the audiovisual sector. The June 2013 Report stressed the on-going need to regulate both broadcasting and on-demand services due to their "outstanding importance for society and democracy as vectors of identities, values and opinions".[401] Yet, that Report questioned the validity and effectiveness of the AVMSD's two-tier regulatory approach in the context of Connected TV, which the Report suggested could "result in unequal competitive conditions and unacceptable discrepancies in the protection of users".[402] Although the committee generally found a differentiated regulatory scheme workable, it argued that the AVMSD's linear/non-linear distinction should be replaced by a distinc-

---

by the Commission in its Communication on the Future of European regulatory audiovisual policy, para. 3.8, p. 22.

398 European Commission, "Decision on ERGA", Sec. 2 (c).

399 See Art. 29 AVMSD.

400 European Parliament, Report on Connected TV (2012/2300(INI)), Committee on Culture and Education, Rapporteur: Petra Kammerevert, 10.6.2013. European Parliament, Report on Preparing for a fully converged audiovisual world (2013/2180(INI)), Rapportuer: Sabine Verheyen, 28.1.2014.

401 European Parliament, Report on Connected TV, p. 5.

402 European Parliament, Report on Connected TV, p. 6.

tion based on new criteria that highlights the "potential socio-political impact of services and specific features of that impact, particularly their relevance to opinion-forming and to diversity of opinion, as well as on the basis of editorial responsibility".[403] The second Report dated January 2014 contained like findings and arguments; it encouraged the Commission to reconsider the linearity criterion.[404] Nevertheless, the 2014 Report favoured a broader, so-called value-chain approach intended to "reflect the connections between the generation, processing, distribution and presentation of content and should take the form of a horizontal legal framework at European level".[405] To this end, the 2014 Report recommended discarding the AVMSD's rules, particularly its broadcast advertising rules.[406] In addition, it suggested building on and specifying the notion of platform providers, which it argued should go beyond the simple act of making technical capacities available to encompass content portals.[407] Because access to platforms and content findability on any particular device are predominantly controlled by the manufacturers of such devices and search engines, it questioned whether general competition law rules could ever suffice and suggested that sector-specific legislation might be better suited to the task.[408]

Both the 2013 and 2014 Reports identified similar pertinent issues requiring regulatory oversight: net neutrality; platform and services interoperability; audiovisual content integrity; and access to, and "findability" of content of public value on platforms.[409] Nevertheless, they appear to have diverged in their respective assessments of the need for rules based on the

403 European Parliament, Report on Connected TV, p. 7.

404 European Parliament, Report on Preparing for a fully converged audiovisual world, paras. 47, 48, p. 9.

405 European Parliament, Report on Preparing for a fully converged audiovisual world, Explanatory statement, p. 13. The report likewise calls for a "horizontal, cross-media legal framework", para. 5, p. 5.

406 European Parliament, Report on Preparing for a fully converged audiovisual world, para. 18, p. 6, para. 49, p. 9.

407 European Parliament, Report on Preparing for a fully converged audiovisual world, para. 13, p. 6, Explanatory statement, p. 13.

408 Bernd Holznagel, "Grünbuch Konvergenz der Medien 2013, Verpasste Chance oder gangbarer Weg aus dem Globalisierungsdilemma?," p. 23.

409 European Parliament, Report on Connected TV, p. 7, para. 2, p. 9, paras. 29, 31, p. 10, paras. L, M, p. 6, para. 34, p. 11. European Parliament, Report on Preparing for a fully converged audiovisual world, paras. 6, 9-11, pp. 5, 6, para. 39, p. 8, para. 53, p. 10.

"must-be-found" principle, which implies prominence for specific, socially and culturally relevant general interest content. The 2013 Report unambiguously favoured rules that grant "privileged status" to public-service broadcasters and other providers that "help to promote objectives in the public interest".[410] Such objectives, the 2013 Report suggested, may relate to voluntary compliance with more-detailed advertising rules or promotional measures furthering the distribution and production of European works or content accessible to minorities (e.g. subtitling).[411] The 2013 Report also called on the Commission to devise other "incentive schemes" to guarantee quality programmes and a plurality of opinion.[412] The 2014 Report, on the other hand, questioned the effectiveness and enforceability of that same "must-be-found" principle.[413] Indeed, Connected TV offers a plethora of content in unprecedented quantities and its users have the means to retrieve such content by using navigation systems, EPGs, and search engines. Yet, the 2014 Report acknowledged that searching for and finding content on converged devices is made more difficult due to the "appization" of content, which implies that users increasingly rely on "applications".[414] Thus, the 2014 Report reckoned that the Union's future regulatory action should aim to ensure visibility of general interest content by way of user-friendly, transparent modes of navigation.[415]

The Reports (and, to some extent, the 2013 Green Paper to which they responded) make unequivocally clear that one of the underlying rationales for regulating audiovisual media services remains valid, albeit in an attenuated form. Spectrum scarcity is no longer the pressing concern evoked by the Commission in its 1997 Green Paper.[416] However, the other democracy-enhancing rationale – that is, the rational that recognises the paramount importance of television and television-like services (regardless of the cri-

---

410 European Parliament, Report on Connected TV, Explanatory statement, pp. 14, 15.

411 European Parliament, Report on Connected TV, Explanatory statement, p. 15.

412 European Parliament, Report on Connected TV, Explanatory statement, p. 15.

413 European Parliament, Report on Preparing for a fully converged audiovisual world, Explanatory statement, p. 13.

414 European Parliament, Report on Preparing for a fully converged audiovisual world, para. 15, p. 6, Explanatory statement, p. 12.

415 European Parliament, Report on Preparing for a fully converged audiovisual world, Explanatory statement, p. 13.

416 European Commission, "Green Paper on Convergence and the Implications for Regulation," p. 20.

teria used to define them) in enabling freedom of expression and the receipt of information and, thereby, facilitating public opinion-making and the exchange of views – is more than sufficient to justify continuing regulatory interference with the market in order to ensure that public-interest objectives are protected. Murray and Scott hint at such risks when noting that "new and unpredictable configurations of power are among the hallmarks of the new media".[417] From Connected TV may emerge powerful economic actors who could abuse their special status to discriminate against other operators and content providers with devastating effect on the promotion of public values. Thus, Union regulation must protect the public interest, and must serve as its primary motivation which, in turn, will be fostered by internal market considerations at the Union level. Interestingly, the Commission's 2013 Green Paper and the EP's Reports, referred to co- and self-regulation as complementary regulatory strategies that could address at least some of the challenges raised by the ubiquitous nature of the Internet.[418]

At the end of November 2014, only 10 months after the EP's 2014 Report was published and just about one month after the new Juncker Commission came into power, the Council of the European Union adopted conclusions on the European audiovisual policy in the digital era. Those conclusions highlighted two important, interconnected elements that the Council apparently believed to be prerequisites for creating a genuine "digital single market". First, it called on the Commission to undertake an "urgent review" of the AVMSD and submit its proposal regarding needed changes "as soon as possible".[419] Second, the Council emphasised that the

---

417 Andrew Murray and Colin Scott, "Controlling the New Media: Hybrid Responses to New Forms of Power," *The Modern Law Review* 65, no. 4 (2002): p. 516.

418 European Commission, "Green Paper on Convergence and the Implications for Regulation," p. 12 European Parliament, Report on Connected TV, para. 21, p. 9.

419 In carrying out its review of the AVMSD, the Commission assessed, among others, whether to uphold the distinction between linear and non-linear audiovisual media services, how a level playing field of all stakeholders can be accomplished and how minors can be adequately protected. Council of the European Union, "Council Conclusions on European Audiovisual Policy in the Digital Era. Education, Youth, Culture and Sport Council Meeting of 25 November 2014," 2014, pp. 1, 5, http://www.consilium.europa.eu/uedocs/cms_data/docs/pressdata/en/educ/145950.pdf (accessed 4.12.2014); Council of the European Union, "Press Release of 3349th Council Meeting on Education, Youth, Culture and Sport of 25 November 2014," 2014, p. 8, http://www.consilium.europa.eu/uedocs/cms_data/docs/pressdata/en/educ/145953.pdf (accessed 4.12.2014).

Commission's work on modernising the European legal framework for copyright needed to continue. The Council also highlighted the twin objectives pursued by the Union's audiovisual policy: "creating sustainable growth and jobs and fostering cultural and linguistic diversity".[420] These two, sometimes-incompatible goals – strengthening the European economy and fostering cultural diversity – have been at the heart of the EU's media policies and, according to the Council, must continue to define the parameters of the Union's involvement in the field. As a result of the Council's urging, the Commission flagged the AVMSD for its Regulatory Fitness and Performance programme (REFIT) under its Better Regulation agenda; the Commission will attempt to make regulation "lighter, simpler and less costly".[421] As part of any REFIT exercise, the Commission makes a retrospective assessment of the relevant regulatory instrument's effectiveness and then a forward-looking assessment of the need for future legislative initiatives; that second assessment includes stakeholder consultations regarding potential new legislation or changes to existing legal acts. With the respect to the AVMSD's REFIT process, the Commission launched a three-months consultation in mid-2015[422] and published its proposal for a revised AVMSD in May 2016. The proposal will be discussed in the sixth chapter.

## D. *"Regulation" by the Council of Europe*

### I. The 1989 Convention on Transfrontier Television

The Council of Europe (CoE), an international organisation unrelated to the European Union, was founded in 1949 and had, at the time of this writing, forty-seven Contracting States. In 1989, the CoE successfully brokered the adoption of the Convention on Transfer Television (CTT), among its Contracting States, addressing broadcasting across borders. In

420 Council of the European Union, "Council Conclusions on European Audiovisual Policy in the Digital Era," p. 1.

421 European Commission, Better Regulation, REFIT, available at http://ec.europa.eu/smart-regulation/refit/index_en.htm (accessed 2.6.2015).

422 The contributions to the public consultation are available at https://ec.europa.eu/digital-single-market/en/news/contributions-and-preliminary-trends-public-consultation-audiovisual-media-services-avmsd (accessed 15.11.2015).

contrast to the European Union's TWFD and AVMSD, which constitute instruments of Secondary Union law, the CoE's legal tools are governed by public international law and are only binding on those Contracting States after their ratification of the relevant document. Thus, the CTT, which was negotiated prior to the adoption of the TWFD 1989, was signed in March 1989, but only entered into force on 1 May 1993.[423] The CTT's underlying rationale resembled that of the TWFD 1989, though its objectives were different. Technological developments in the early 1980s, particularly satellite television transmission, profoundly changed the nature of broadcasting. Coverage that had previously been confined to regional or, at best, national zones, now extended across country borders and even beyond the CoE's geographic contours.[424] In addition, those new modes of transmission enabled a greater number of channels and, by enhancing competition, offered consumers increased choice.[425] While the Community's motives for adopting the TWFD principally focused on broadcasting's economic character and its potential, the CoE stressed broadcasting's crucial role (especially public service broadcasting)[426] in "the free formation of opinions and the development of culture" in accordance with the freedom of expression and information set forth in Art. 10 ECHR.[427] Due to the "magnitude and complexity of [those] developments", the CoE's Contracting States believed a common response to be inevitable.[428] As its Explanatory Report admitted, the TWFD was limited to "common basic stan-

423 European Convention on Transfrontier Television, Strasbourg, 5.V.1989, Text amended according to the provisions of the Protocol (ETS No. 171) which entered into force on 1 March 2002. Pursuant to its Art. 29 (2), the CTT could only enter into force after the seventh ratification (of which at least five had to be made by members of the Council of Europe, as it was open for ratification by non-members of the Council of Europe. The first states to ratify the CTT were Cyprus, Italy, Malta, Poland, San Marino, Switzerland, and the United Kingdom. The Holy See, not being a member of the Council of Europe, ratified the Convention in May 1993. See Udo Fink, "Medienfreiheiten im Rahmen des Europarates," in *Europäisches und Internationales Medienrecht*, ed. Fink, Cole and Keber, (Heidelberg: C. F. Müller Verlag, 2008), paras. 270–80, pp. 181–87.

424 European Convention on Transfrontier Television, Explanatory Report as amended by the provisions of the Protocol (ETS No. 171), paras. 21-23.

425 European Convention on Transfrontier Television, Explanatory Report, para. 24.

426 European Convention on Transfrontier Television, Explanatory Report, para. 25.

427 European Convention on Transfrontier Television, Explanatory Report, para. 24 and Preamble, recitals 3, 5.

428 European Convention on Transfrontier Television, Explanatory Report, para. 26.

dard[s]" leaving intact "domestic broadcasting policies and arrangements of the Parties".[429] Thus, the CTT only harmonised those "crucial aspects" of transfrontier television that impacted the "protection of certain individual rights", the maintenance of "programme standards", "advertising", and "sponsorship".[430] Like the TWFD, using home-country control, the CTT purported to guarantee the free transmission of broadcasts adhering to the programme standards outlined therein while permitting signatories of the Convention to apply stricter standards within their territories.[431]

Following the adoption of the TWFD 1997, the CTT was amended to align with the updated TWFD to maintain consistency between the two instruments and "in the interest of legal certainty"[432] for broadcasters established within EU Member States that were also CTT signatories.[433] Interestingly, the CoE also discussed extending the Convention's scope of application to "communication services operating on individual demand," but concluded that such extension was premature in light of the then-"embryonic stage of development"[434] of on-demand services. After overcoming France's objection thereto,[435] the amending protocol to the CTT finally entered into force in March 2002.[436]

In general, the key provisions of the TWFD 1997 were reflected in the CTT of 2002;[437] thus, this work will only briefly discuss those provisions that are specific to the CTT. With regard to its general programme stan-

429 European Convention on Transfrontier Television, Explanatory Report, para. 30.

430 European Convention on Transfrontier Television, Explanatory Report, para. 33.

431 European Convention on Transfrontier Television, Explanatory Report, paras. 32, 33. Arts. 4, 28 CTT.

432 European Convention on Transfrontier Television, Explanatory Report, para. 39. In its 1997 TWFD proposal, the Commission had highlighted the fact that "some of the amendments to the Directive proposed by the Commission (…) [would] increase the disparities" between the then-Community instrument and the CTT and expressed a desire for the two texts to "be as compatible as possible". Above all, the Commission advocated that "the Community accede to the Convention", as made possible by Art. 29 (1) of the Convention, para. 3.1, pp. 43-45.

433 European Convention on Transfrontier Television, Explanatory Report, paras. 39, 40.

434 European Convention on Transfrontier Television, Explanatory Report, para. 42.

435 Kogler, *TV (On-Demand)*, 10.

436 All references to provisions contained in the CTT are made with respect to the numbering of the CTT.

437 On the freedom of reception and retransmission, see for instance Art. 4 CTT (confer Art. 3 (1) AVMSD), Art. 5 on jurisdiction (confer Art. 2 AVMSD), Art. 7 (2) CTT on the protection of minors (which is less comprehensive than Art. 27

dards, Art. 7 (1) CTT requires "all items of programme services (...) shall respect the dignity of the human being and the fundamental rights of others"; its second sentence goes on to clarify that programmes "shall not (a) be indecent and in particular contain pornography; [and] (b) give undue prominence to violence or be likely to incite to racial hatred". In contrast to Art. 6 AVMSD, which prohibits incitement to hatred in audiovisual media services, the CTT rule seems broader and more attuned to its inherent rights-based approach, although its pornographic or violent material prohibitions are reminiscent of Art. 27 (1) AVMSD's protection of minors, which is, however, more detailed. Art. 7 (3) CTT, which states that "news fairly presents facts and events and encourages the free formation of opinion," is one expression of that approach. More importantly, however, the Art. 10*bis* CTT, reinforces its cultural objectives, such as promoting access to news reports, major events, and European works through the Contracting States' commitment to media pluralism; but, it is only a general commitment, "without (...) imposing any specific obligations".[438] The CTT relies on a Standing Committee[439] composed of representatives of the Contracting States;[440] it is charged with applying the CTT and developing recommendations and opinions to facilitate interpretation of its rules. The Standing Committee may also have a role to play in settling disputes arising from the CTT.[441] In that way, the Standing Committee's role is similar to that of the European Commission, as it monitors the application of the AVMSD by the Member States. The Standing Committee, however, is an inter-governmental body only convened on an ad hoc basis (notwithstanding its name) and its powers and functions (especially its enforcement powers) are limited when compared to those of the European Commission, which is a supranational EU institution endowed with extensive powers.

---

AVMSD), Art. 8 CTT on the right of reply (which is less specific than Art. 28 AVMSD), Art. 9 CTT on the right to short news reports (which is less precise than Art. 15 AVMSD), Art. 9bis CTT on access to major events (confer Art. 14 AVMSD), Art. 10 CTT on the promotion of European works (confer Art. 16 AVMSD), Arts. 12-15 CTT on advertising standards (confer Arts. 19, 20, 22, 23 AVMSD), Art. 24 CTT on violations of the CTT (confer Art. 3 (2), (3) AVMSD), Art. 24bis CTT on abuse (confer Art. 4 (2) AVMSD).

438 European Convention on Transfrontier Television, Explanatory Report, para. 204.

439 Arts. 20-22 CTT.

440 The Standing Committee includes representatives of states not party to the CTT. These representatives have observer status according to Art. 20 (3) CTT.

441 Art. 25 (2), (3) CTT.

The CTT, in recognition of the overlap between it and EU law, incorporates a specific conflict rule: Art. 27 (1) CTT provides that

> "parties which are members of the European Community shall apply Community rules and shall not therefore apply the rules arising from this Convention except in so far as there is no Community rules governing the particular subject concerned".

Thus, in the event of a conflict between the two instruments, the AVMSD prevails for all EU Member States, and the obligations arising out of the CTT are set aside. Where the AVMSD is silent, however, the Convention is still applicable.[442] This is an appropriate mechanism to capture the unique nature of Union law and the supra-national character of the Union.

The CTT, its Standing Committee's opinions and recommendations, together with the case law of the ECtHR have become a source of inspiration for the EU legislature and judiciary, both of which have referred to them on numerous occasions.[443] In fact, the TWFD and the CTT had become closely intertwined and each influenced the other; but that was before the failure to align the CTT with the AVMSD.

## II. A Failed reform: the draft Convention on Transfrontier Audiovisual Media Services

Not long after the up-dated CTT of 2002 entered into force, calls were made to further revise it in light of the European Commission's proposal for the AVMSD. In 2003, Grünwald published his report on "possible options for [its] review"[444] and, in the summer of 2009, a draft of a newly titled "European Convention on Transfrontier Audiovisual Media Services" (Draft CTAVMS), intended to replace the CTT, was presented to

442 Fink, "Medienfreiheiten im Rahmen des Europarates," para. 280, p. 187.

443 See for instance case C-6/98 *ARD and Pro Sieben*, paras. 22, 24; European Commission, "Interpretative Communication on Television Advertising," para. 19 and opinion of Advocate General Bot delivered on 5.5.2011 in joined cases C-244, 245/10 *Mesopotamia Broadcast and Roj TV*, EU:C:2011:284, para. 74.

444 European Convention on Transfrontier Television, Standing Committee on Transfrontier Television, Final report by Dr. Andreas Grünwald, 24.4.2003, available at http://www.coe.int/t/dghl/standardsetting/media/T-TT/T-TT(2003)002_en.pdf (accessed 23.11.2014).

the CoE's Committee of Ministers.[445] The stated objective for its modification was to "bring the Convention into line with the reality of broadcasting" resulting from ongoing media convergence, which had fundamentally altered the broadcasting landscape.[446] To accomplish this objective, the Draft CTAVMS sought to align itself to the AVMSD to ensure their coherence.[447] As a result, its scope, like that of the AVMSD, was broadened to encompass on-demand services that were "television-like, addressing the same audience as television broadcast and offering similar types of programmes by similar means of access".[448] Provisions of the draft explanatory report to the Draft CTAVMS replicated recital 24 AVMSD. Moreover, the Draft CTAVMS adopted a graduated regulatory approach similar to that adopted by the AVMSD, by establishing more liberal rules for on-demand service.[449] In the end, the bulk of the changes incorporated in the Draft CTAVMS coordinated with the AVMSD; so much so, that in certain places the Draft CTAVMS reproduced phrases from the AVMSD.[450] Nonetheless, the Draft CTAVMS retained and enhanced the CTT's particularities, demonstrated by its more-detailed dedication to media pluralism and media content diversity intended to promote "full transparency of ownership of media service providers" as well as to define the key ele-

445 European Convention on Transfrontier Television, Standing Committee of Transfrontier Television, Draft explanatory report to the revised European Convention on Transfrontier Television updated following the consultation on 25-27 February 2009, 11./12.6.2009, available at http://www.coe.int/t/dghl/standard setting/media /T-TT/T-TT_2009_009_enpercent20Preliminarypercent20Draftpercent20Explpercent20Reppercent20ECTT.pdf (accessed 23.11.2014). Draft second protocol amending the European Convention on Transfrontier Television and its Explanatory report, 24.9.2009, available at http://www.coe.int/t/dghl/standardsetting/media/T-TT/T-TT_2009_007FIN_enpercent20secondpercent20protocolpercent20amendment.pdf (accessed 23.11.2014).

446 Draft explanatory report to the revised European Convention on Transfrontier Television, para. 44.

447 Draft explanatory report to the revised European Convention on Transfrontier Television, paras. 70, 74.

448 Draft explanatory report to the revised European Convention on Transfrontier Television, para. 70.

449 Draft explanatory report to the revised European Convention on Transfrontier Television, paras. 71, 72.

450 See for instance Arts. 2 (d), (e), (l)-(o), 5, 7, 9, 15 (1), (3), 17, 19, 21draft CTAVMS.

ments of "a [broadcaster's] public service mission".[451] Its draft explanatory report, however, assured that the Draft CTAVMS, if adopted, would only apply to audiovisual media services that were "transfrontier in character",[452] while the minimums established by the AVMSD were applicable internally.

The CoE's review of the Draft CTAVMS, however, came to an abrupt halt after an unexpected intervention by the European Commission.[453] In a letter dated 23 October 2009 from Commissioner Viviane Reding to the responsible national ministers of the EU Member States, the Commission voiced its objection to the purported competence of EU Member States to ratify any version of CTAVMS due to the Union's exclusive external competence in fields already coordinated by Union law, including audiovisual media services via the AVMSD.[454] To buttress its position, the Commission relied on the "implied-powers doctrine"[455] enunciated in the Court's 1971 *AETR*[456] decision and reinforced in its 2002 *Open Skies*[457] decision. Pursuant to that doctrine, the Commission argued, the Member States

451 Art. 12 draft CTAVMS and draft explanatory report to the revised European Convention on Transfrontier Television, paras. 270-273.

452 Draft explanatory report to the revised European Convention on Transfrontier Television, para. 78.

453 For a detailed account of the developments see Daithí Mac Síthigh, "Death of a Convention: Competition between the Council of Europe and European Union in the Regulation of Broadcasting," *Edinburgh School of Law Research Paper Series 2013/26*, 2013, http://papers.ssrn.com/sol3/papers.cfm?abstract_id=2282769 (accessed 23.11.2014).

454 Udo Fink, Tobias Keber and Przemyslaw Roguski, "Die Zukunft der Medienregulierung im Europarat," *Zeitschrift für Urheber- und Medienrecht*, 2011, pp. 293–95; Kogler, *TV (On-Demand)*, pp. 20–24.

455 On the doctrine of implied powers, see Craig and De Búrca, *EU Law, Text, Cases, and Materials*, pp. 307–18; Piet Eeckhout, *External Relations of the European Union, Legal and Constitutional Foundations* (Oxford: Oxford University Press, 2004), pp. 58–100; Fink, Keber and Roguski, "Die Zukunft der Medienregulierung im Europarat," pp. 293–95; Mac Síthigh, "Death of a Convention," pp. 6–8.

456 Case 22/70 *Commission of the European Communities v Council of the European Communities, European Agreement on Road Transport (AETR)*, Judgment of 31.3.1971, EU:C:1971:32, paras. 16-18, 22, which jurisprudence has been codified by Art. 3 (2) TFEU in conjunction with 216 (1) TFEU by the Treaty of Lisbon.

457 Cases C-466/98 *Commission of the European Communities v United Kingdom of Great Britain and Northern Ireland*, Judgment of 5.11.2002, EU:C:2002:624, C-467/98 *Commission of the European Communities v. Kingdom of Denmark*,

were not authorised to conclude international agreements that "might affect or alter the scope of 'internal' [Union] rules"[458] even if there is no contradiction between the Member States' international commitments and the Union's rules;[459] rather, once the Union has acted in a particular field and "complete harmonisation has been achieved in a given area",[460] its powers are to be regarded as exclusive, both internally (law-making within the Union) and externally (conclusion of international agreements).[461] The Commission's position was reiterated in a second letter, dated 10 December 2010, from Commissioner Neelie Kroes (Reding's successor) to the CoE's Secretary General, in which the Commission made clear that its Member States were not allowed, pursuant to EU law, to individually sign the (final) CTAVMS[462] and, perhaps even more importantly, the Union did not intend to accede to a final version of the Draft CTAVMS as it would restrict the Union's flexibility regarding future amendments to the AVMSD.[463] The Commission further threatened its Member States, stating that it would consider opening an infringement procedure against them pursuant to Art. 260 TFEU if they continued along that path. The Commission's surprisingly sharp remarks had never before been officially expressed.

---

Judgment of 5.11.2002, EU:C:2002:625, C-468/98 *Commission of the European Communities v Kingdom of Sweden*, Judgment of 5.11.2002, EU:C:2002:626, C-469/98 *Commission of the European Communities v Republic of Finland*, Judgment of 5.11.2002, EU:C:2002:627, C-471/98 *Commission of the European Communities v Kingdom of Belgium*, Judgment of 5.11.2002, EU:C:2002:628, C-472/98 *Commission of the European Communities v Grand Duchy of Luxembourg*, Judgment of 5.11.2002, EU:C:2002:629, C-475/98 *Commission of the European Communities v Republic of Austria*, Judgment of 5.11.2002, EU:C:2002:630, C-476/98 *Commission of the European Communities v Federal Republic of Germany*, Judgment of 5.11.2002, EU:C:2002:631.

458 Eeckhout, *External Relations of the European Union, Legal and Constitutional Foundations*, p. 63.

459 Opinion of the Court of 19 March 1993, Convention N° 170 of the International Labour Organization concerning safety in the use of chemicals at work, Opinion 2/91, ECR 1993, p. I-1061, paras. 25, 26.

460 Opinion of the Court of 15 November 1994, Competence of the Community to conclude international agreements concerning services and the protection of intellectual property, Opinion 1/94, ECR 1994, p. I-5267, para. 96.

461 Eeckhout, *External Relations of the European Union, Legal and Constitutional Foundations*, p. 64.

462 Kogler, *TV (On-Demand)*, p. 20.

463 Mac Síthigh, "Death of a Convention," pp. 10, 20.

Shortly thereafter, in January 2011, the CoE's review of the Draft CTAVMS was discontinued and, at the time of this writing, it had yet to be resumed.[464] Consequently, the inconsistencies between the two legal orders endure and have even been aggravated by the Union's adoption of the AVMSD.[465] Notable differences subsist between the CTT and the AVMSD in, for example, their scope of application, which affects, in turn, other rules, such as the protection of minors and the exploitation of rights in case of on-demand services, and the regulatory scheme (or lack thereof) for audiovisual commercial communications, especially product placement.[466] In its September 2011 Recommendation, the CoE's Committee of Ministers recognised that "developments in information and communication technologies and their application to mass communication have led to significant changes in the media ecosystem" that demands a new, broader conception of media services encompassing all relevant actors.[467] The appendix to that Recommendation sets out the criteria for identifying media and furnishes guidance on the standards that are to be applied in a graduated manner to different forms of media. The criteria refer to the "intent to act as media", the "purpose and underlying objectives of media", "editorial control", "professional standards", "outreach and dissemination" and "public expectation",[468] but they are neither exhaustive nor cumulative. Nor are they equally relevant; their application must take into account the "service provider's own characteristics and idiosyncrasy as well as [its]

---

464 Kogler, *TV (On-Demand)*, p. 19. In September 2014, the CoE's Committee of Ministers responded to the Parliamentary Assembly's Recommendation and Resolution of January 2014 urging it to resume work on an amended CTT. In its reply, the Committee of Ministers mentioned the EU's exclusive external competence for most aspects regulated by the CTT and the fact that the EU had expressly declined to become a member of any revised CTT. The Committee of Ministers declared that this "deadlock" was "regrettable" and that, due to the circumstances, it had not allocated resources to either continue to negotiate an up-dated CTT or to draft a new legal instrument. See Parliamentary Assembly, Resolution 1978 (2014) of 31.1.2014, and Recommendation 2036 (2014) of 31.1.2014; see Committee of Ministers Reply, Doc. 13605 of 23.9.2014.

465 Kogler, *TV (On-Demand)*, p. 24.

466 Fink, Keber and Roguski, "Die Zukunft der Medienregulierung im Europarat," pp. 299, 300; Kogler, *TV (On-Demand)*, pp. 25–29.

467 Recommendation CM/Rec(2011)7 of the Committee of Ministers to member states on a new notion of media, adopted by the Committee of Ministers on 21.9.2011 at the 1121st meeting of the Ministers' Deputies, paras. 5, 7.

468 Recommendation CM/Rec(2011)7, Appendix, paras. 16-55.

maturing process as media".[469] The standards established by the Recommendation, on the other hand, relate to "right, privileges and prerogatives", "media pluralism and diversity of content" and "media responsibilities".[470] The Recommendation underlines that "despite the changes in its ecosystem, the role of media in a democratic society [...] has not changed" and that media are of paramount importance as a "tool for freedom of expression".[471]

Against this backdrop, the need to modernise the CTT gained new impetus in January 2014 by initiatives within the CoE's Parliamentary Assembly.[472] Those initiative reports emphasised that thirteen of its thirty-three Contracting States were not members of the EU and they would benefit from a revised legal framework addressed to pressing issues in a "constantly changing media environment".[473] By the same token, they argued that the European Union would profit from standards applicable beyond its geographic boundaries in the CoE's "pan-European ambit", which would ultimately "help to ensure that [the EU's] AVMS regulations are not undermined by non-EU member States".[474] The reports indicated several avenues for resolving the then-current impasse between the two bodies.[475] One such approach included the CoE designing a new (framework) convention concentrating on its "core competences" such as "democracy, human rights and the rule of law" governing issues such as media pluralism, the role of public service broadcasting, and the independence of regulatory

469 Recommendation CM/Rec(2011)7, Appendix, paras. 10-12.

470 Recommendation CM/Rec(2011)7, Appendix, paras. 50-98.

471 Recommendation CM/Rec(2011)7, paras. 1, 7. The need to preserve the "essential role of media in the digital age" was once again underscored by the Council of Europe Conference of Ministers responsible for Media and Information Society, Freedom of expression and democracy in the digital age, Opportunities, rights, responsibilities, Belgrade 7.-8.11.2013. See the Steering Committee on Media and Information Society, background paper.

472 Revision of the European Convention on Transfrontier Television, Committee on Legal Affairs and Human Rights, Rapporteur James Clappison, Doc. 13383 of 10.1.2014, Committee on Culture, Science, Education and Media, Rapporteur Roger Gale, Doc. 13406 of 24.1.2014.

473 Revision of the European Convention on Transfrontier Television, report by Clappison, draft resolution, para. 3.

474 Revision of the European Convention on Transfrontier Television, report by Clappison, para. 44.

475 Revision of the European Convention on Transfrontier Television, report by Clappison, paras. 37-41.

authorities.[476] Building on elements deemed to be outside the scope of Union law was, however, thought to be an "unstable starting point because the European Union's agenda could – and most likely will – evolve over time [to include] traditional Council of Europe field[s] of activity".[477] Rather, the initiative reports appeared to give priority to the resumption of the talks on possible options for revising the CTT or adopting other legal instruments by establishing, with the help of the EU, those aspects of audiovisual media services regulation that fall outside the scope of the EU's exclusive competence.[478] Indeed, standard setting by the CoE could help resolve some of the ongoing enforcement issues that NRAs currently face with respect to the identification or classification of media and the protection of minors, provided that important international actors participate in such standard setting and ultimately ratify any future convention or similar instrument.

---

476 Pursuant to Art. 15 (a) of the Statute of the Council of Europe, the Committee of Ministers is authorised to conclude conventions, but the development of "framework conventions" is not contemplated by the Statute and few examples of such conventions exist (cf. Framework Convention for the Protection of National Minorities of February 1995). Unlike ordinary conventions, framework conventions purport to only establish general objectives to which the parties are committed; their provisions are not directly applicable and leave parties a great deal of discretion regarding their implementation, which could include general policies by the government. See explanatory report of the Framework Convention for the Protection of National Minorities, paras. 11-13. See also Revision of the European Convention on Transfrontier Television, report by Clappison, paras. 37, 40.

477 Revision of the European Convention on Transfrontier Television, report by Clappison, para. 38. On media pluralism, see, Art. 11 (2) CFR, independent report from the High-Level Group on Media Freedom and Pluralism of January 2013, a public consultation on this report closed in July 2013, Council conclusions and of the representatives of the Governments of the Member States, meeting within the Council, on media freedom and pluralism in the digital environment of November 2013. On the role of public service broadcasting, see Protocol no 32 on the system of public broadcasting in the Member States, annexed to the EC Treaty by the Treaty of Amsterdam, OJ of 10.11.1997, C 340, now Protocol no 29, OJ of 26.10.2012, C 326, p. 312. On the independence of national regulatory authorities for the media the consultation of July 2013, see contributions available at https://ec.europa.eu/digital-agenda/en/news/public-consultation-independence-audiovisual-regulatory-bodies-read-contributions (accessed 23.11.2014.).

478 Revision of the European Convention on Transfrontier Television, report by Clappison, draft resolution, para. 5.

# Chapter 2. Regulatory models

> "From the middle of the twentieth century until the 1980s, governments were accustomed to media systems organised on a national scale, amenable to top-down regulatory control by the state and recognised for their central role in underpinning social cohesion and national identity".[479]

During this period, "large portions of a national media system" were owned by the state itself.[480] In a globalised networked society, the role of states is, however, diminishing.[481] Today, the number of actors, be they public or private, national, regional or international, that influence public policy, has augmented. This is proliferated by the global and ubiquitous nature of the Internet. In order to keep up with new realities, states have shifted power "downwards as functions of the state are performed through regulation rather than through legislation".[482] The dispersion of power from the centre to more decentralised places or actors, often described as a shift from government to governance,[483] goes even further. States devise new regulatory models to react more flexibly and dynamically to rapidly changing circumstances. Importantly, the AVMSD promotes co- and self-regulation as alternatives to state regulation.[484] Although co- and self-regulation are increasingly used they are flawed with the lack of democratic guarantees and other problems. Thus, an *ex ante* balancing exercise is required by Member States wishing to revert to such regulatory models. Democratic safeguards will have to be built in the system to ensure that

---

479 Peter Lunt and Sonia Livingstone, *Media Regulation, Governance and the Interests of Citizens and Consumers* (London: Sage Publications, 2012), p. 2.

480 Lunt and Livingstone, *Media Regulation, Governance and the Interests of Citizens and Consumers*, p. 2.

481 Lunt and Livingstone, *Media Regulation, Governance and the Interests of Citizens and Consumers*, p. 1.

482 Lunt and Livingstone, *Media Regulation, Governance and the Interests of Citizens and Consumers*, p. 5.

483 Lunt and Livingstone are quoting Jessop's The State and the Contradictions of the Knowledge-driven Economy", in: "Knowledge, Space, Economy" by Daniels Bryson and Pollard Henry, published in 2000. Lunt and Livingstone, *Media Regulation, Governance and the Interests of Citizens and Consumers*, p. 5.

484 Art. 4 (7) AVMSD in conjunction with recital 44 AVMSD.

implicated rights are respected. This study endeavours to contribute to the current debate about regulatory models, their strengths and weaknesses.

This chapter serves as an introduction, clarifying key terms used in this study. In a first part, it defines the concept of regulation and sketches theories of regulation that explain why regulation is used. The second part of this chapter maps models of regulation including state regulation, co- and self-regulation. In the absence of detailed definitions, this chapter provides an understanding of these concepts, including their advantages and disadvantages. It underscores the significance of alternative regulatory strategies (co- and self-regulation); particularly for regulating rapidly transforming sectors such as the audiovisual media services market. Therefore, the final section of this chapter discusses co- and self-regulation in a European context, focusing on how they are employed by the AVMSD.

## *A. The concept of regulation and the reasons for regulating*

The question "what is regulation" is posited more generally in the debate about the role of the state in contemporary societies.[485] From the rise of the "regulatory state"[486] and the shift towards a "post-regulatory state",[487] regulation is tightly interwoven with democratic, legitimate and participatory rule-making and just enforcement. The following section examines the questions of what regulation is and why states regulate.

### I. Conceptualising regulation

The term regulation is broad and elusive and has conventionally been associated with the state and the way it manages its tasks and ensures observance, on its territory, of the norms it has established. The state encom-

485 Hans Bredow Institut and Institut für Europäisches Medienrecht, eds., "Final Report, Study on Co-Regulation Measures in the Media Sector, Study for the European Commission," June 2006, p. 11, http://ec.europa.eu/avpolicy/docs/library/studies/coregul/final_rep_en.pdf (accessed 28.11.2014).

486 Giandomenico Majone, "The Rise of the Regulatory State in Europe," *West European Politics* 17, no. 3 (1994): pp. 77–101.

487 Colin Scott, "Regulation in the Age of Governance: The Rise of the Post-Regulatory State, National Europe Centre Paper No. 100," June 6, 2003, https://digitalcollections.anu.edu.au/bitstream/1885/41716/3/scott1.pdf (accessed 29.11.2014).

passes the government and its executive bodies in the form of regulatory authorities. These act as intermediaries between the government and the industry. Latzer et al. highlight the significance of regulatory authorities, conflating them as the "fourth branch of government"[488] due to their independence and expertise. In 1985, Selznick formulated an influential definition viewing regulation as "sustained and focused control exercised by a public agency over activities that are valued by a community".[489] This presupposes "public recognition that the regulated activity is worthwhile in itself and therefore needs protection as well as control".[490] Selznick further posits that regulation is continuous and evolving ("sustained") as it involves not only law-making but also the supervision of the application and implementation of the rules prescribed as well as their assessment and adaptation to changing circumstances. Directed to the promotion of certain "values" or "selected activities" of (sectors of) the industry, regulation is ideally "focused".[491] Selznick's definition of regulation entails several aspects which were adopted by subsequent scholars reflecting particular strands or theories as outlined below. Ogus emphasises the "directive function" of regulation implying "the idea of control by a superior", the state, compelling individuals to behave in certain ways.[492]

Similarly but less forcefully, Latzer et al. refer to the purposeful steering of behaviour in order to solve political problems.[493] This is consistent with Harlow and Rawlings concept of "red light" which emphasises the aspect of control and the need to balance the powers (to restrain the executive by a strong and independent judiciary) while the "green light theory" is less sceptical of the administrative expansion of government and the state taking control.[494] Against this background, regulation may restrict undesirable behaviour or activities deemed as inappropriate or it may be

---

488 Latzer et al., *Selbst- und Ko-Regulierung im Mediamatiksektor*, p. 63.

489 Philip Selznick, "Focusing Organisational Research on Regulation," in *Regulatory Policy and the Social Sciences*, ed. Roger Noll, (Berkeley: University of California Press, 1985), p. 363.

490 Selznick, "Focusing Organisational Research on Regulation," p. 363.

491 Selznick, "Focusing Organisational Research on Regulation," p. 364.

492 Anthony Ogus, *Regulation: Legal Form and Economic Theory* (Oxford: Hart Publishing, 1994), p. 2.

493 Latzer et al., *Selbst- und Ko-Regulierung im Mediamatiksektor*, p. 30.

494 Carol Harlow and Richard Rawlings, *Law and Administration*, third edition (Cambridge: Cambridge University Press, 2009), pp. 25, 31, 37.

enabling and stimulating conduct perceived of as positive.[495] To give credit to the numerous perceptions of regulation, Baldwin and Lodge suggest that it appears in different forms. "As a specific set of commands", regulation refers to a "binding set of rules" which are applied "by a body devoted to this purpose".[496] More broadly, regulation is regarded "as deliberate state influence" on society and the market.[497] Even more generally, regulation may cover "all forms of social or economic influence" not restricted to state action.[498] This interpretation of regulation also takes into account non-state actors such as self-regulators, trade unions, organisations, corporations and other institutions or bodies affecting behaviour in a multi-layered governance scheme.

In a similar vein, Lessig points to four interdependent constraints which regulate an individual. These are the market, law, norms and architecture.[499] The novel and most interesting constraint is architecture, which on the Internet implies the "software and hardware that make cyberspace what it is".[500] Briefly, Lessig refers to the technology, or code, which regulates individual's access to cyberspace and which can be regulated by governments. Many scholars have henceforth stressed the relevance of code as an element of regulation.[501] Thus, in this study, the notion of regulation is sketched broadly including the activities and measures of public as well as private bodies controlling (certain) behaviour. The control of behaviour inevitably leads to regulatory choices, trade-offs between different (opposing) objectives. The exact balance will affect the interests of those regulated; it may be beneficial to some but may also be un-

495 Robert Baldwin, Martin Cave and Martin Lodge, *Understanding Regulation. Theory, Strategy, and Practice*, second edition (Oxford: Oxford University Press, 2012), p. 3.

496 Baldwin, Cave and Lodge, *Understanding Regulation*, p. 3.

497 Baldwin, Cave and Lodge, *Understanding Regulation*, p. 3.

498 Baldwin, Cave and Lodge, *Understanding Regulation*, p. 3.

499 Lawrence Lessig, *Code Version 2.0* (New York: Basic Books, 2006), p. 123.

500 Lessig, *Code Version 2.0*, p. 124.

501 Antonios Broumas, "Governing Media through Technology. The Empowerment Perspective," in *Routledge Handbook of Media Law*, ed. Monroe E. Price, Stefaan Verhulst and Libby Morgan (London and New York: Routledge, 2013), pp. 419–38; Burri, "Controlling New Media (without the Law)," in *Routledge Handbook of Media Law* (London and New York: Routledge, 2013), pp. 327–42; Katzenbach, "Media Governance and Technology," pp. 399–418; critically Viktor Mayer-Schönberger, "Demystifying Lessig," *Wisconsin Law Review*, 2008, pp. 713–46; Murray and Scott, "Controlling the New Media," pp. 502–6.

favourable for others. Thus, regulation and its effects inherently have social implications.

## II. Theories of regulation

The definitional dilemma of what regulation is, is further complicated by the question of why states regulate. Regulation is commonly justified by different theories which are briefly discussed. The first strand, which can further be sub-divided, is "interest-based". According to the public interest theory, regulation serves to protect objectives in the public interest.[502] Regulatory bodies thus act "as benevolent agents for the public interest".[503] Regulation is made necessary, so it is argued, because the market as such fails to deliver results in the public interest.[504] The market failure explanation (or normative theory according to Majone)[505] is essentially an economic rationale, where the uncontrolled and unregulated market is not competitive due to monopolistic (or oligopolistic) structures (leading to higher prices and lower output) or negative externalities which constitute spillovers of the production process like waste or other costs affecting third parties.[506] The lack of information (summarised as information asymmetries) by regulators about precise market conditions and the behaviour and interests of consumers may also impinge on competition and thus counter the public interest.[507] Critiques of this theory question the uniformity and consistency of the conception of the public interest.[508] Indeed, *the* public interest may be composed of different contradictory and clashing interests and the search for *the* public interest may be susceptible

---

502 Baldwin, Cave and Lodge, *Understanding Regulation*, pp. 40, 41; Stephan Breyer, *Regulation and Its Reform* (United States of America: Harvard University Press, 1982), p. 15; Latzer et al., *Selbst- und Ko-Regulierung im Mediamatiksektor*, p. 31.

503 Baldwin, Cave and Lodge, *Understanding Regulation*, p. 41.

504 Baldwin, Cave and Lodge, *Understanding Regulation*, pp. 15–21; Latzer et al., *Selbst- und Ko-Regulierung im Mediamatiksektor*, p. 31; Ogus, *Regulation: Legal Form and Economic Theory*, pp. 29–41.

505 Majone, "The Rise of the Regulatory State in Europe," pp. 81, 82.

506 Baldwin, Cave and Lodge, *Understanding Regulation*, p. 18; Breyer, *Regulation and Its Reform*, p. 22.

507 Baldwin, Cave and Lodge, *Understanding Regulation*, pp. 18, 19; Ogus, *Regulation: Legal Form and Economic Theory*, pp. 38–41.

508 Baldwin, Cave and Lodge, *Understanding Regulation*, p. 41.

to "capture" [509] either by the industry (where the regulator is influenced by the most powerful market participants or other groups lobbying for a certain regulatory outcome) or by its own account (where the regulator pursues its own agenda).[510] In addition, Prosser, drawing on the writings of Durkheim advances a more social understanding of the public interest underlining that regulation purports to protect certain rights or maintain social solidarity.[511] According to Prosser, proponents of the market failure approach consider "regulation (...) as second best".[512] Yet, Prosser claims that other, social and moral values (particularly the provision of public services by the state) constitute an explanation for regulation and should be considered alongside economic considerations.[513] He essentially proposes that regulation be based on a core set of values, the individual mix of which be chosen on case by case basis.[514]

The second strand of the interest-based theory considers regulation as being "driven by the particularistic concerns of interest groups".[515] At the heart of the Chicago school of thought (also called positive theory) is the

509 Baldwin, Cave and Lodge, *Understanding Regulation*, p. 43. The notion of "capture" goes back to George Stigler's The Theory of Economic Regulation published in 1971 in the Bell Journal of Economics and Management Science, Vol. 2, No. 1, pp. 3-21; Ogus, *Regulation: Legal Form and Economic Theory*, pp. 57, 58; interestingly, Gibbons points out that regulatory authorities inevitably have to have close ties with the industry and the "policy community" at the national and European levels and submits that "viewpoint capture may be a greater risk than industry capture". See Thomas Gibbons, "'Club Government' and Independence in Media Regulation," in *Routledge Handbook of Media Law*, ed. Monroe, Verhulst and Morgan (London and New York: Routledge, 2013), p. 56.

510 Baldwin, Cave and Lodge, *Understanding Regulation*, p. 42.

511 Tony Prosser, "Regulation and Social Solidarity," *Journal of Law and Society* 33, no. 3 (2006): p. 364.

512 Prosser, "Regulation and Social Solidarity," p. 366; see also Breyer, *Regulation and Its Reform*, p. 16; the reason for considering "regulation (.) as second best" is because "market allocation" will be preferred where the market functions fully and no market failures have materialised. See Prosser, "Regulation and Social Solidarity," pp. 366, 369.

513 Ogus also indicates non-economic goals of regulation like "distributional justice", "paternalism" and "community values". Ogus, *Regulation: Legal Form and Economic Theory*, pp. 46–54; see also Prosser, "Regulation and Social Solidarity," pp. 381–83, 385.

514 Prosser, "Regulation and Social Solidarity," pp. 383, 385.

515 Baldwin, Cave and Lodge, *Understanding Regulation*, p. 43; see also Latzer et al., *Selbst- und Ko-Regulierung im Mediamatiksektor*, p. 32.

fact that market participants strive to maximise their utility (wealth) by pursuing their self-interest.[516] Hence, regulation is primarily influenced by and beneficial to a powerful, concerted industry, which is capable of mobilising its members to "capture" the regulator, while the interests of unorganised, diffused groups of society (like consumers) tend to be overlooked in the regulatory output.[517] The interest group theory brings self-interested behaviour to the fore but neglects the relevance of other factors like ideological and emotional perspectives, moral outlooks and attitudes and policy objectives.[518] These, especially the importance of overarching ideas as well as "the wider intellectual and political climate",[519] are taken into account by other theories.

The interest-group theory furthermore emphasises that the ideas and perception of society and about society form the institutions and regulatory responses of competent authorities.[520] Similarly, a group of scholars highlights the importance of institutions and the way they shape the regulatory setting and policies.[521] Understanding institutional structures and contexts, external as well as internal, is considered essential to understanding the "rules of the game" and foreseeing regulatory action and improving regulatory outcomes.[522] Within the institutional school of thought, the network theory has become very popular in recent years.[523] It relates to the notion of governance, which implies that the state no longer acts solely within the "regulatory space", but that the demands of globalisation and

---

516 In contrast to the Chicago school, the Virginia school of political economy stresses the political gains expected by regulators or legislators, above all, votes in future elections and ideological considerations. See Baldwin, Cave and Lodge, *Understanding Regulation*, pp. 43–46; on "positive theory", see Majone, "The Rise of the Regulatory State in Europe," pp. 81, 82; Ogus, *Regulation: Legal Form and Economic Theory*, p. 71.

517 Baldwin, Cave and Lodge, *Understanding Regulation*, p. 44.

518 Baldwin, Cave and Lodge, *Understanding Regulation*, p. 46.

519 Baldwin, Cave and Lodge, *Understanding Regulation*, p. 50.

520 Baldwin, Cave and Lodge, *Understanding Regulation*, p. 50.

521 Baldwin, Cave and Lodge, *Understanding Regulation*, p. 53; Latzer et al., *Selbst- und Ko-Regulierung im Mediamatiksektor*, p. 32.

522 Latzer et al., *Selbst- und Ko-Regulierung im Mediamatiksektor*, p. 32.

523 See in general Claudia Padovani and Elena Pavan, "Actors and Interactions in Global Communication Governance: The Heuristic Potential of a Network Approach," in *The Handbook of Global Media and Communication Policy*, ed. Robin Mansell and Marc Raboy, (West Sussex, United Kingdom: Wiley-Blackwell, 2011), pp. 541–63.

international standard-setting and especially European integration have prompted it to disperse its power and diversify its regulatory instruments (including self- and co-regulation), establishing and cooperating with plenty of regulatory bodies and agencies.[524] The governance approach takes into account the myriad of interactions between public and private bodies, between government, the industry and citizens as well as the "heterogeneity" and "pluralisation of actors" in a multi-layered, "multi-stakeholder" system.[525] It follows that the "communications structures of contemporary societies" have become "increasingly complex, dynamic and diverse".[526] Consequently, the role of the state, which previously monopolised the administration and regulation of society, has been diminished leading to "smaller government".[527] In this context, Black has coined the expression "decentered" regulation.[528] "Decentring" refers not only to the (external) role and position of governments within a regulatory arena, it equally refers to the (internal) fragmentation of political processes and the distribution of regulatory tasks to various bodies.[529] It follows that "governments are constrained in their actions, and (...) are as much acted upon as they are actors".[530] In terms of regulatory models, the "decentred" state takes recourse to co- and above all self-regulation to account for a complex regulatory environment. On the contrary, the "centred" state retains primary responsibility for regulation, employing traditional command- and control tools. The types of regulation are thus explained below.

---

524 Baldwin, Cave and Lodge, *Understanding Regulation*, pp. 63, 64.

525 Katzenbach, "Media Governance and Technology," p. 401; Latzer et al., *Selbst- und Ko-Regulierung im Mediamatiksektor*, p. 34; on "multi-stakeholderism" in a global context, see Bart Cammaerts, "Power Dynamics in Multi-Stakeholder Policy Processes and Intra-Civil Society Networking," in *The Handbook of Global Media and Communication Policy*, ed. Robin Mansell and Marc Raboy, (West Sussex, United Kingdom: Wiley-Blackwell, 2011), pp. 131–46.

526 Katzenbach, "Media Governance and Technology," p. 400.

527 Darren Sinclair, "Self-Regulation versus Command and Control? Beyond False Dichotomies," *Law & Policy* 19, no. 4 (1997): p. 530.

528 Julia Black, "Decentring Regulation: Understanding the Role of Regulation and Self-Regulation in a 'Post-Regulatory' World," *Current Legal Problems* 54, no. 1 (2001): pp. 103–46; Julia Black, "Critical Reflections on Regulation," *Australian Journal of Legal Philosophy* 27 (2002): pp. 1–36; Dimity Kingsford Smith, "What Is Regulation? A Reply to Julia Black," *Australian Journal of Legal Philosophy* 27 (2002): pp. 37–46.

529 Black, "Decentring Regulation," pp. 103, 104.

530 Black, "Decentring Regulation," p. 104.

## B. Models of regulation

### I. State regulation

Traditionally, regulation has been the prerogative of the state that has exercised its authority directly and in a top down manner. In this respect, the expression command and control regulation is frequently employed.[531] To command means to order or rule. This element is reflected in the setting of binding standards. To control means to oversee and have power over the compliance of the subjects of regulation with the pre-determined standards. To this end, states have recourse to the instrument of criminal law to sanction violations of the standards and inappropriate behaviour.[532] Whether criminal law penalties or rather "quasi-criminal" sanctions, which at their heart have a civil law nature are imposed is contingent upon national legal frameworks.[533] According to Sinclair, the "theory of deterrence" constitutes the underlying rationale of the regulatory system.[534] In order to avoid (heavy) sanctions, industry stakeholders are induced to observe the standards prescribed by the state.[535] This description draws a rather negative picture of state regulation: the industry acts because the alternative would be worse. Black, however, notes that command and control regulation is "more a caricature than an accurate description of the operation of any particular regulatory system".[536] It nevertheless reinforces the presumption that the state alone is in a position to regulate and "has the capacity to command and control, to be the only commander and con-

531 Baldwin, Cave and Lodge, *Understanding Regulation*, p. 106; Black, "Decentring Regulation," p. 105; Wolfgang Schulz and Thorsten Held, "Regulated Self-Regulation as a Form of Modern Government, Study Commissioned by the German Federal Commissioner for Cultural and Media Affairs, Interim Report (October 2001)," ed. Hans-Bredow-Institut, October 2001, p. 6, http://www.hans-bredow-institut.de/webfm_send/38 (accessed 4.12.2014).

532 Baldwin, Cave and Lodge, *Understanding Regulation*, p. 106; Black, "Decentring Regulation," p. 105; Ogus, *Regulation: Legal Form and Economic Theory*, pp. 79–81; Sinclair speaks of "negative sanctions" instead of sanctions prescribed by criminal law. See Sinclair, "Self-Regulation versus Command and Control," p. 534.

533 Ogus, *Regulation: Legal Form and Economic Theory*, pp. 79, 80.

534 Sinclair, "Self-Regulation versus Command and Control," p. 534.

535 Sinclair, "Self-Regulation versus Command and Control," p. 534.

536 Black, "Decentring Regulation," p. 105.

troller, and to be potentially effective in commanding and controlling".[537] Black therefore refers to the term "centred regulation", which is contrasted to "decentred regulation", as mentioned above.

Furthermore, the notion of the state is, however, ambiguous. On their continuum, Latzer et al. distinguish between state regulation in the narrow sense and state regulation in the wider sense.[538] While the former comprises "the classic sovereign tasks (legislative, executive and judiciary)", the latter implies the creation of "sovereign institutions that carry out sovereign tasks, but act at a distance to sovereignty, because they are not subject to instructions or are subject to a loose context of instructions".[539] Similarly, Prosser refers to a "public authority gaining its legitimacy from the political process [that] issues orders to companies or individuals requiring them to meet public policy goals".[540] Sinclair also marks the two possibilities as pertaining to state regulation: either the state acts directly (by legislative tools) or indirectly (by "delegated authority").[541] In the field of audiovisual media, such institutions are commonly referred to as national regulatory authorities (NRAs) that have been vested with a specific mandate pre-determined by government. Typically, governments adopt a legal act that specifies the exact modalities of the delegation and the powers of the authority. NRAs thus exercise executive tasks in place of the state. The construction of NRAs essentially constitutes a balancing exercise between the guarantee for independence of the authority and the necessary attachments to the state (resource allocation and funding by the state budget). In this study, the term state regulation encompasses regulation performed by NRAs. Lievens, Valcke and Valgaeren thus offer an inclusive conception of regulation. Departing from the keywords command and control, they deduce common elements of the definitions and find that "the state performs all regulatory tasks: creation, implementation and monitoring, and enforcement".[542]

---

537 Black, "Decentring Regulation," p. 106.

538 Michael Latzer et al., "Regulation Remixed: Institutional Change through Self and Co-Regulation in the Mediamatics Sector," *Communications & Strategies* 50, no. 2 (2003): p. 135.

539 Latzer et al., "Regulation Remixed," p. 135.

540 Tony Prosser, "Self-Regulation, Co-Regulation and the Audio-Visual Media Services Directive," *Journal of Consumer Policy* 31, no. 1 (2008): p. 100.

541 Sinclair, "Self-Regulation versus Command and Control," p. 534.

542 Eva Lievens, Peggy Valcke and Pieter Jan Valgaeren, "State of the Art on Regulatory Trends in Media. Identifying Whether, What, How and Who to Regulate in

State regulation has traditionally been associated with a number of benefits, but it has also more recently been criticised for various drawbacks. On the one hand, state regulation is enshrined in the democratic decision-making process and legitimated by popular elections. It is regarded as beneficial to society, as pursuing the public interest. On the other hand, state regulation is considered as "costly and inefficient" and as discouraging innovation.[543] In addition, an information asymmetry is identified to the detriment of governments (or their regulators) so that regulation is accused of being misguided and inappropriate.[544] Moreover, a system entirely based on deterrence appears too one-dimensional leading to "motivation failure" of industry stakeholders, thereby stifling progressive market dynamics and to "implementation failure" causing discrepancies between regulatory objectives and their implementation.[545] These deficiencies next to other factors have put increasing strain on state-centred regulation in the past decade. The expansion of any kind of activity across countries due to improved communications and transportation technologies and the proliferation of ideas like market liberalisation have multiplied linkages and interdependencies between previously isolated states.[546] Regional integration like the construction of the European Union has facilitated cross-border activities.

Succinctly, regulation has become more complex[547] and is shifting: A shift from command and control regulation to alternative models of regu-

Social Media," December 2011, p. 17, http://emsoc.be/wp-content/uploads/2012/01/State-of-the-art-on-regulatory-trends-in-media.Identifying-whether-what-how-and-who-to-regulate-in-social-media.pdf (accessed 4.12.2014).

543 Sinclair, "Self-Regulation versus Command and Control," p. 530; Lievens, Valcke and Valgaeren, "State of the Art on Regulatory Trends in Media," p. 18.

544 Black, "Decentring Regulation," p. 106; Schulz and Held speak of a "knowledge gap" in this context Schulz and Held, "Regulated Self-Regulation," p. 10.

545 Black, "Decentring Regulation," p. 106; Schulz and Held, "Regulated Self-Regulation," p. 10.

546 Just and Latzer, "Self- and Co-Regulation in the Mediamatics Sector," p. 39.

547 Black, "Decentring Regulation," p. 109; Hans Bredow Institut and Europäisches Institut für Medienrecht, "Study on Co-Regulation Measures in the Media Sector, Study for the European Commission", pp. 13,14.

lation[548], a shift from government regulation to media governance,[549] a shift from the "positive/interventionist state" to the "regulatory state",[550] a shift from "vertical to horizontal regulation",[551]or a transfer of "some of the regulatory responsibility from governments to suppliers to consumers and citizens"[552]. What is relevant here is that states have been required to adapt their regulatory systems to improve their responsiveness and flexibility.[553] As a result, regulatory strategies have become "hybrid (…), multi-faceted (…), and indirect".[554] State regulation no longer is the final result of the equation; it has become a variable next to other regulatory instruments. Today, the regulatory toolkit ("instrument mix",[555] "remix"[556] or "cocktail"[557]) is diverse and presupposes interaction and above all, "cooperation between state and non-state actors".[558] In spite of increasing diversification of regulatory models, Katzenbach indicates that statutory law remains the "regulative 'pillar'".[559] Thus, the state retains a pivotal role in the regulatory process, albeit as a "lean state" characterised by a "transformed statehood".[560] This, however, necessitates, on part of states, the ca-

548 Lievens and Valcke, "Regulatory Trends in a Social Media Context," p. 558; Lievens, Valcke and Valgaeren, "State of the Art on Regulatory Trends in Media," pp. 6, 16.

549 Manuel Puppis, "Media Governance as a Horizontal Extension of Media Regulation: The Importance of Self- and Co-Regulation," *Communications* 32, no. 3 (2007): p. 331; Latzer et al., "Regulation Remixed," p. 127; Latzer et al., *Selbst- und Ko-Regulierung im Mediamatiksektor*, p. 34; Hans Bredow Institut and Institut für Europäisches Medienrecht, "Final Report, Study on Co-Regulation Measures in the Media Sector, Study for the European Commission," pp. 15, 16.

550 Latzer et al., "Regulation Remixed," p. 130.

551 Just and Latzer, "Self- and Co-Regulation in the Mediamatics Sector," p. 40.

552 Lievens and Valcke, "Regulatory Trends in a Social Media Context," p. 570.

553 Price and Verhulst, "Self-Regulation on the Internet," p. 57.

554 Black, "Decentring Regulation," p. 111.

555 Black, "Decentring Regulation," pp. 113, 124.

556 Just and Latzer, "Self- and Co-Regulation in the Mediamatics Sector," p. 55.

557 Prosser, "Self-Regulation, Co-Regulation and the AVMSD," pp. 101, 102, 106.

558 Hans Bredow Institut and Europäisches Institut für Medienrecht, "Study on Co-Regulation Measures in the Media Sector, Study for the European Commission," pp. 13, 14.

559 Katzenbach, "Media Governance and Technology," p. 402.

560 Just and Latzer, "Self- and Co-Regulation in the Mediamatics Sector," pp. 42, 55.

pacities to change and become "dynamic, fertile landscapes and remain open, flexible and engaged agents".[561]

## II. Alternative regulatory strategies

The following section is devoted to co- and self-regulation as alternatives to state regulation. Due to the engagement and participation of non-state actors, the nature of regulation is classified as bottom up. On account of the attention these models have received in the field of media law, it predominantly focuses on these two and will only tangentially touch upon other types of regulation like risk-based or principles-based regulation. Co-regulation and above all, self-regulation are "not new phenomena" and are not unique to the field of media and communications law.[562] They have gained momentum during the past fifteen years and are increasingly used today.[563] In the broadcasting sector, Canada (in the late 1980s) and Australia (in the early 1990s) can be regarded as pioneers having turned towards such models, which have been emulated internationally.[564] Against the background of an increasing regulatory mix of instruments, co- and self-regulation do not substitute state regulation but supplement it.[565] State regulation and co- and self-regulation are not mutually exclusive but their use is contingent on the national circumstances and the regulatory objectives. Generally, co- and self-regulation are considered valuable regulatory responses where markets rapidly evolve and regulation thus needs to be fast and flexible.[566] In such cases, co- and self-regulation are more effective and less expensive than heavy-handed state intervention. The following section conceptualises co- and self-regulation before outlining the advantages and disadvantages of each model. In doing so, it takes into account the AVMSD's relevant recitals and provisions.

561 Raboy and Mawani, "Are States Still Important? Reflections on the Nexus between National and Global Media and Communication Policy," p. 357.

562 Latzer et al., "Regulation Remixed," pp. 130, 138.

563 Marsden, "Co-Regulation in European Media and Internet Sectors," p. 6.

564 Grainger, "Broadcasting, Co-Regulation and the Public Good, 1999 Spry Memorial Lecture," pp. 26, 32.

565 Lievens, Valcke and Valgaeren, "State of the Art on Regulatory Trends in Media," p. 21.

566 Marsden, "Co-Regulation in European Media and Internet Sectors," p. 3.

## 1. Self-regulation

### a) Conceptualising self-regulation

The origins of self-regulation as a form of regulation may be traced to the US, where it has been widely used in diverse sectors of the economy.[567] In Europe, too, it has traditionally been employed in the press sector to reinforce the independence of the press from undue government influences.[568] Besides, the regulation of advertising on television has traditionally been prone to self-regulatory mechanisms.[569] Nonetheless, self-regulation has suffered from a rather negative connotation, which is strongly connected to the disadvantages associated with this form of regulation. As Black acknowledges, "self-regulation usually comes with a policy health warning attached".[570] In addition, self-regulation is often perceived of as pre-empting state regulation.[571] This means that state regulation (like a Damocles sword) is used, where self-regulatory initiatives have failed to produce satisfactory results. Self-regulation will thus remain in the "shadow of the law".[572] Still, in an increasingly globalised, thus international and interconnected environment, conventional state regulation has come under pressure by, for instance, jurisdictional questions or overlapping and multi-facetted policy objectives. Against this background, self-regulation has also gained new momentum in the field of European media law by the adoption of the EU AVMSD in 2007 which explicitly encourages Member States to resort to co- and self-regulation. The advent of the Internet, its ubiquity and changeable, international nature have similarly heralded the significance of alternative regulatory models.[573]

---

567 Just and Latzer, "Self- and Co-Regulation in the Mediamatics Sector," p. 50.

568 Latzer et al., "Regulation Remixed," p. 138; Lievens and Valcke, "Regulatory Trends in a Social Media Context," p. 562.

569 Neil Gunningham and Joseph Rees, "Industry Self-Regulation: An Institutional Perspective," *Law & Policy* 19, no. 4 (1997): p. 364; Lievens, Valcke and Valgaeren, "State of the Art on Regulatory Trends in Media," p. 25.

570 Black, "Decentring Regulation," p. 114.

571 Baldwin, Cave and Lodge, *Understanding Regulation*, p. 138; Just and Latzer, "Self- and Co-Regulation in the Mediamatics Sector," p. 49; Latzer et al., "Regulation Remixed," p. 143; Marsden, "Co-Regulation in European Media and Internet Sectors," p. 4.

572 Sinclair, "Self-Regulation versus Command and Control," p. 536.

573 On regulatory models and the Internet, see for instance Price and Verhulst, "Self-Regulation on the Internet," pp. 57–78; Pamela Samuelson, "Five Challenges for

The concept of self-regulation is, however, difficult to delineate[574] and as Price and Verhulst emphasise "almost always a misnomer".[575] In its broadest sense, it implies regulation by private actors, namely the subjects of regulation. In this respect, Gunningham and Rees distinguish between "individual self-regulation", where a single economic actor (e.g. an undertaking) regulates itself and "self-regulation by groups", where a number of economic actors of a particular industry branch regulate themselves.[576] More particularly, the industry or a specific sector thereof voluntarily establish rules, which regulate a certain activity, a perceived risk or stimulate a certain conduct. Two issues emerge from this conceptualisation. First, the form of decision-making, i.e. whether an institution is created that is tasked to draw up standards on behalf of "the industry". Palzer, for instance, assumes the setting up of "bodies [which] draw up their own regulations in order to achieve certain objectives and take full responsibility for monitoring compliance with those regulations".[577] In order to achieve a sufficient level of cooperation amongst companies, self-regulation requires a degree of coordination, be it in the form of common institutions

---

Regulating the Global Information Society," in *Regulating the Global Information Society*, ed. Christopher Marsden, (London: Routledge, 2000), pp. 316–30; Nico Van Eijk and Tom Van Engers, "Duties of Care on the Internet, Paper Presented at the Telecommunications Policy Research Conference, September 23-25, 2011," 2011, http://dare.uva.nl/document/483341 (accessed 2.11.2014); more generally, see Christopher Marsden, ed., *Regulating the Global Information Society* (London: Routledge, 2000); Chris Reed, *Making Laws for Cyberspace* (Oxford: Oxford University Press, 2012); Diane Rowland, Uta Kohl and Charlesworth, eds., *Information Technology Law*, 4th edition (London: Routledge, 2012).

574 Angela Campbell, "Self-Regulation and the Media," *Federal Communications Law Journal* 51, no. 3 (1999): p. 714; Lievens, Valcke and Valgaeren, "State of the Art on Regulatory Trends in Media," pp. 27, 28; Sinclair, "Self-Regulation versus Command and Control," p. 532; Ogus, *Regulation: Legal Form and Economic Theory*, p. 108; Price and Verhulst, "Self-Regulation on the Internet," p. 58.

575 Price and Verhulst, "Self-Regulation on the Internet," p. 58.

576 Gunningham and Rees, "Industry Self-Regulation," p. 364; see also Just and Latzer, "Self- and Co-Regulation in the Mediamatics Sector," p. 44; Price and Verhulst, "Self-Regulation on the Internet," p. 64.

577 Carmen Palzer, "Co-Regulation of the Media in Europe," in *Co-Regulation of the Media in Europe: European Provisions for the Establishment of Co-Regulation Frameworks*, ed. Susanne Nikoltchev, IRIS Plus 6/2002 (Strasbourg: European Audiovisual Observatory, 2002), p. 2.

or alternative, lose mechanisms. The second issue concerns the (legal) nature of the output produced by the institutional framework, i.e. whether uniform standards are negotiated and whether these are binding and for whom. Puppis posits that "private actors formulate and enforce rules and sanction non-compliance directed towards their own industry" whereby he implies that a set of binding rules is laid down and enforced against negligent companies.[578] Baldwin, Cave and Lodge clarify that the rules may either be binding and thus valid for all participating companies (not necessarily the entire industry though) or non-binding in which case their observance is voluntary.[579]

The dilemmas of conceptualising self-regulation is overcome by Lievens, Valcke and Valgaeren, who claim that a rigid definition is irrelevant and instead rely on two cumulative elements: first, "a group of actors create, implement and enforce rules" and second, "there is minimal involvement of government".[580] The first component is reminiscent of Campbell's notion of self-regulation which appears to adequately capture the diversities of self-regulatory models.[581] Accordingly, the industry takes over one or more functions of regulation, which are "legislation", "enforcement" or "adjudication".[582] "Legislation" means the drawing up and enactment of common rules, "enforcement" implies their application, for example, by means of monitoring and finally "adjudication" is the mechanism whereby violations are prosecuted and punished.[583] The second component of Lieven's, Valcke's and Valgaeren's notion of self-regulation relates to the state's role. Most scholars seem to consent that there is

578 Puppis, "The Importance of Self- and Co-Regulation," p. 332; similarly, see Schulz and Held, "Regulated Self-Regulation," p. 6.

579 Baldwin, Cave and Lodge, *Understanding Regulation*, pp. 139, 141; on voluntary participation, see Palzer, "Co-Regulation of the Media in Europe," p. 2.

580 Lievens, Valcke and Valgaeren, "State of the Art on Regulatory Trends in Media," p. 28.

581 It is posited that the conjunction "and" employed in the formulation "create, implement and enforce rules" does not exclusively refer to self-regulation in a strict sense, that is, where a self-regulatory body is charged with all three tasks. This becomes evident when reading the quotation in context and in particular in light of the second element ("minimal involvement of government").

582 Campbell, "Self-Regulation and the Media," p. 715; see also Michael Latzer, Natascha Just and Florian Saurwein, "Self- and Co-Regulation. Evidence, Legitimacy and Governance Choice," in *Routledge Handbook of Media Law*, ed. Price, Verhulst and Morgan (London and New York: Routledge, 2013), p. 376.

583 Campbell, "Self-Regulation and the Media," p. 715.

a role for the state to play in self-regulation, albeit a marginal one.[584] Schulz and Held, however, constrain the concept of self-regulation to "private arrangements" which are made "without any interference by the state".[585] Yet, self-regulation rarely occurs in its purest form or literal meaning. More frequently, certain links exist between the industry and the state, their specificities varying from one country to another and from one industry to another.[586] Latzer et al. encounter these various manifestations and semantic complexities of self-regulation by the construction of a continuum.[587] The continuum represents a scale where the end points are defined as "ideal-type models of pure state regulation (…) and pure self-regulation by industry".[588] By the same token, Price and Verhulst sketch a "continuum along which regulation is more or less formalised" highlighting three distinct forms of regulation: "government organisation, industry self-organisation, and market organisation".[589] While the former represents the most formalised approach, the latter is the least formal. The authors do, however, clarify that these forms are not isolated but overlap and in certain policy fields even complement each other.[590]

In a similar vein, Price and Verhulst generally distinguish between "enforced (or coerced) self-regulation", where self-regulation pre-empts state regulation, and "voluntary self-regulation", where self-regulation is the result of "a civic culture in which the government co-operates with industry".[591] More specifically, Price and Verhulst differentiate further between mandated and sanctioned self-regulation. With respect to the former, the state sets the general framework within which industry "is virtually required […] to formulate and enforce norms".[592] The latter constitutes a

584 Campbell, "Self-Regulation and the Media," p. 715; Just and Latzer, "Self- and Co-Regulation in the Mediamatics Sector," p. 42; Lievens, Valcke and Valgaeren, "State of the Art on Regulatory Trends in Media," p. 28; Price and Verhulst, "Self-Regulation on the Internet," p. 58.

585 Schulz and Held, "Regulated Self-Regulation," p. 6.

586 Baldwin, Cave and Lodge, *Understanding Regulation*, p. 138; Price and Verhulst, "Self-Regulation on the Internet," p. 58.

587 Latzer et al., "Regulation Remixed," pp. 134–36; Latzer, Just and Saurwein, "Self- and Co-Regulation. Evidence, Legitimacy and Governance Choice," p. 377.

588 Latzer et al., "Regulation Remixed," p. 134.

589 Price and Verhulst, "Self-Regulation on the Internet," p. 59.

590 Price and Verhulst, "Self-Regulation on the Internet," p. 59.

591 Price and Verhulst, "Self-Regulation on the Internet," p. 65.

592 Price and Verhulst, "Self-Regulation on the Internet," p. 65.

model within which the industry determines certain rules that are subsequently approved by the state.[593] The classification proposed by Price and Verhulst may be translated into a continuum according to Latzer et al. whereby the intervention by the state lessens from sanctioned self-regulation (which requires government approval), mandated self-regulation (which operates in a framework set by government), enforced self-regulation (where government action is threatened) to voluntary self-regulation (lacking "active state involvement").[594] In fact, where self-regulation preempts state regulation, the existence of a lurking government (or a "heavy stick in the background") is considered beneficial to the success of self-regulation.[595] Whatever the denominations, the bottom line in this discussion remains to be the involvement (in whatever form and scope) of the state in self-regulation. Moreover, these different models, however nuanced and overlapping they may be in reality, may aggravate or alleviate the costs and benefits of self-regulation in practice as is shown below.

b) Advantages of self-regulation

Self-regulation is commonly associated with a number of advantages.[596] It is generally conceived of as being less costly than heavy-handed government regulation, albeit not altogether gratuitous.[597] For self-regulation to be successful, undertakings need to invest into the self-regulatory scheme by providing their resources and facilities, sharing knowledge, time and personnel. Thus, self-regulation constitutes a real alternative to government regulation if its costs are decisively lower than those of government

593 Price and Verhulst, "Self-Regulation on the Internet," p. 65.

594 Price and Verhulst, "Self-Regulation on the Internet," p. 65.

595 Schulz and Held, "Regulated Self-Regulation," p. 22; Campbell, "Self-Regulation and the Media," p. 758.

596 For a bulletin list of advantages and disadvantages see Latzer, Just and Saurwein, "Self- and Co-Regulation. Evidence, Legitimacy and Governance Choice," p. 375.

597 Campbell, "Self-Regulation and the Media," p. 715; Gunningham and Rees, "Industry Self-Regulation," p. 366; Latzer et al., *Selbst- und Ko-Regulierung im Mediamatiksektor*, pp. 48, 49; Lievens, Valcke and Valgaeren, "State of the Art on Regulatory Trends in Media," p. 29; Anthony, *Regulation: Legal Form and Economic Theory*, p. 107; Puppis, "The Importance of Self- and Co-Regulation," p. 332; Price and Verhulst, "Self-Regulation on the Internet," p. 63.

regulation. In terms of the rules or codes negotiated by industry participants, self-regulation may lead to "more practicable standards".[598] On account of its experience and expertise,[599] which accord the industry an "information lead" over governments,[600] the former is better placed to find suitable solutions "tailored to the needs identified"[601] by undertakings. This is especially true in areas where governments grapple with defining policy objectives for certain (controversial) phenomena or market developments. [602] Above all, the response offered by the industry is often more rapid and flexible and thus more effective.[603] The decision-making and standard-setting process of self-regulatory systems is speedy in comparison to the formalised, rigid and lengthy legislation-making at the state level. This allows the industry to promptly adapt to a specific problem. In the media and communications sector, which is characterised by continuous technological changes, this capacity is especially valuable.

Furthermore, self-regulatory models can have positive effects. The more undertakings participate, the more "peer pressure" is generated and public expectations rise.[604] A self-regulatory model, which is carried by a great majority of the industry, also "enhance[s] credibility of the industry in the eyes of the consumer, making the industry, or part of it, appear responsible and trustworthy".[605]Additionally, self-regulation increases incentives for compliance, not least due to the peer pressure that is creat-

598 Gunningham and Rees, "Industry Self-Regulation," p. 366.

599 Baldwin, Cave and Lodge, *Understanding Regulation*, p. 139; Black, "Decentring Regulation," p. 115; Latzer et al., *Selbst- und Ko-Regulierung im Mediamatiksektor*, p. 48; Lievens, Valcke and Valgaeren, "State of the Art on Regulatory Trends in Media," p. 29; Price and Verhulst, "Self-Regulation on the Internet," p. 64, Anthony, *Regulation: Legal Form and Economic Theory*, p. 107; Puppis, "The Importance of Self- and Co-Regulation," p. 332.

600 Campbell, "Self-Regulation and the Media," p. 715.

601 Lievens, Valcke and Valgaeren, "State of the Art on Regulatory Trends in Media," p. 29.

602 Price and Verhulst, "Self-Regulation on the Internet," p. 64.

603 Black, "Decentring Regulation," p. 115; Campbell, "Self-Regulation and the Media," p. 715; Gunningham and Rees, "Industry Self-Regulation," p. 366; Latzer et al., *Selbst- und Ko-Regulierung im Mediamatiksektor*, p. 48; Lievens, Valcke and Valgaeren, "State of the Art on Regulatory Trends in Media," p. 29; Price and Verhulst, "Self-Regulation on the Internet," p. 64; Puppis, "The Importance of Self- and Co-Regulation," p. 332.

604 Lievens and Valcke, "Regulatory Trends in a Social Media Context," p. 563; Price and Verhulst, "Self-Regulation on the Internet," p. 63.

605 Price and Verhulst, "Self-Regulation on the Internet," p. 71.

ed.[606] Naturally, undertakings are more willing to obey the rules they have themselves established and perceive of as just and feasible than follow the (more intrusive) rules crafted by a legislator that is detached from daily business and the specificities of a certain industry or branch thereof. Basically, undertakings may be more inclined to respect self-regulatory initiatives due to the trust they have in the 'institution of self-regulation' and the ensuing suitability of the envisaged measures.[607]

#### c) Disadvantages of self-regulation

The shortcomings of self-regulation primarily relate to and stem from its informal and "self-serving" nature.[608] Since the industry enjoys considerable leeway in formulating policy objectives and setting universal standards, it is said to succumb to its own interests and consequently and, more importantly, lose sight of the public interest. The prioritisation of the private interest over the public interest undermines the purpose (the achievement of a public policy goal) of regulation and its effectiveness. It is also worth noting that *the* private interest may in fact be a diverse and competitive collection of private interest*s* that may be dominated by a handful of powerful undertakings with plenty of resources and capital. Thus, the self-regulatory process may in fact be biased in favour of the interests of large enterprises at the expense of small and medium sized companies.[609] Against this background, self-regulation may facilitate anti-competitive behaviour and the emergence of cartels.[610] Generally, "regula-

606 Black, "Decentring Regulation," p. 115; Campbell, "Self-Regulation and the Media," p. 715; Latzer et al., *Selbst- und Ko-Regulierung im Mediamatiksektor*, p. 48; Lievens, Valcke and Valgaeren, "State of the Art on Regulatory Trends in Media," p. 29; Price and Verhulst, "Self-Regulation on the Internet," p. 75.

607 Baldwin, Cave and Lodge, *Understanding Regulation*, p. 140.

608 Black, "Decentring Regulation," p. 115.

609 Latzer et al., *Selbst- und Ko-Regulierung im Mediamatiksektor*, p. 50; Just and Latzer, "Self- and Co-Regulation in the Mediamatics Sector," p. 46.

610 Campbell, "Self-Regulation and the Media," p. 718; Latzer et al., *Selbst- und Ko-Regulierung im Mediamatiksektor*, p. 50; Lievens, Valcke and Valgaeren, "State of the Art on Regulatory Trends in Media," p. 30.

tory capture" is exacerbated where external oversight of the self-regulatory mechanism is insufficient or non-existent.[611]

A further (albeit secondary) deficiency defines the relationship between a government and a self-regulatory scheme. An argument in favour of self-regulation is the fact that the industry constitutes a hub of knowledge and expertise. If self-regulation is preferred to government regulation, these information asymmetries are further reinforced at the expense of government.[612] This superiority in terms of intangible assets will only be enhanced, thereby leaving government literally "in the dark". In the media and communications industry, which heavily relies on rapidly developing technologies, it is important that knowledge gaps are avoided in order to adequately protect citizens and ensure the freedom of expression and the right to receive information.

Another weakness of self-regulation relates to the output of the system, which is often not "compulsory enough" and thus, not more than "symbolic policy".[613] Due to the voluntarism inherent in the system, the standards are laid down in a race to the bottom,[614] eventually settling at the lowest common denominator of the participants. This is especially true in cases where self-regulation pre-empts government regulation and private actors agree upon standards to forego more intrusive actions by the state.[615] In addition, not only the setting of standards but also their subsequent application and enforcement (especially by imposing sanctions if any such sanctioning mechanism exists at all) are considered to be weak.[616] This may be explained by the voluntary and informal nature of the scheme that may prompt certain actors to lean back and profit from the investment of

---

611 Baldwin, Cave and Lodge, *Understanding Regulation*, p. 142; Campbell, "Self-Regulation and the Media," p. 717; Gunningham and Rees, "Industry Self-Regulation," p. 366; Latzer et al., *Selbst- und Ko-Regulierung im Mediamatiksektor*, p. 50; Lievens, Valcke and Valgaeren, "State of the Art on Regulatory Trends in Media," p. 31; Puppis, "The Importance of Self- and Co-Regulation," p. 333.

612 Latzer et al., *Selbst- und Ko-Regulierung im Mediamatiksektor*, p. 51.

613 Puppis, "The Importance of Self- and Co-Regulation," p. 333; Latzer et al., *Selbst- und Ko-Regulierung im Mediamatiksektor*, p. 50; Just and Latzer, "Self- and Co-Regulation in the Mediamatics Sector," p. 46.

614 Latzer et al., *Selbst- und Ko-Regulierung im Mediamatiksektor*, p. 50.

615 Latzer et al., *Selbst- und Ko-Regulierung im Mediamatiksektor*, p. 50; Price and Verhulst, "Self-Regulation on the Internet," p. 64.

616 Black, "Decentring Regulation," p. 115; Campbell, "Self-Regulation and the Media," p. 718; Lievens, Valcke and Valgaeren, "State of the Art on Regulatory Trends in Media," p. 30.

more active actors, which basically sponsor their passive counterparts. Such free riders may indeed only invest what is necessary to avoid condemnation or persecution by fellow actors so that the burden of the self-regulatory regime is unevenly distributed, a situation which might jeopardise the whole system if taken to its extremes.[617]

A major point of criticism of self-regulation is its lack of "democratic quality" or in other words, the existence of a "democratic deficit".[618] The underlying question is whether self-regulation and its deliverables (e.g. uniform standards), which operate "outside the line of hierarchical control or oversight by the central administration"[619] can be removed from all authority as they are "not accountable to the body politic".[620] In contrast to government regulation, which is grounded in popular sovereignty, self-regulation cannot claim to be legitimised by general elections and broad popular consent. Quite the opposite, self-regulation is detached from ordinary political processes and acceptance by the people and as a result lacks legitimacy.[621] Similarly, the capacity to hold self-regulatory actors accountable for their actions seems difficult.[622] A government is held accountable by different actors, not least by the public through the device of elections or the possibility to test legislative proposals before constitutional courts. The industry, on the contrary, is not answerable to the same extent, so that the question of external control and monitoring arises. Additionally, the modes of how the self-regulatory system works, particularly

617 Black, "Decentring Regulation," p. 115; Campbell, "Self-Regulation and the Media," p. 718; Latzer et al., *Selbst- und Ko-Regulierung im Mediamatiksektor*, p. 50; Price and Verhulst, "Self-Regulation on the Internet," p. 63.

618 Latzer et al., *Selbst- und Ko-Regulierung im Mediamatiksektor*, p. 51; Robert Baldwin and Julia Black, "Really Responsive Regulation," in *LSE Law, Society and Economy Working Paper*, 2007, p. 141; Lievens and Valcke, "Regulatory Trends in a Social Media Context," p. 563.

619 Majone, "The Rise of the Regulatory State in Europe," p. 83.

620 Ogus, *Regulation: Legal Form and Economic Theory*, p. 108.

621 Latzer, Just and Saurwein, "Self- and Co-Regulation. Evidence, Legitimacy and Governance Choice," pp. 382–84; Puppis, "The Importance of Self- and Co-Regulation," p. 333.

622 Baldwin, Cave and Lodge, *Understanding Regulation*, p. 142; Lievens, Valcke and Valgaeren, "State of the Art on Regulatory Trends in Media," p. 31; Ogus, *Regulation: Legal Form and Economic Theory*, p. 111.

its internal procedures may lack transparency or fairness.[623] Access rights by third parties to such procedures, for instance, may not be accounted for. Hence, certain groups of the population who would have a valid stake (because, for example, their interests are affected) in the self-regulatory process are left out. On the one hand, it is precisely the lack of formalism and institutionalism that allows for increased flexibility and promptness of the regulatory response. On the other hand, they may insufficiently guarantee the protection of fundamental rights like due process rights and acts as a bar to the public's involvement.[624] In this respect, Price and Verhulst underscore that "private censorship can [even] be more coercive and sweeping than its public form".[625] It follows that the intensity of the "democratic deficit" is thus contingent upon the precise institutional design and other mechanisms that may act as a safety net.

#### d) Remedies

The disadvantages self-regulation may entail may be cushioned or even overcome by "success factors" that may be built into the framework of the self-regulatory system. [626] Latzer at al. underline that, *inter alia*, "operational objectives and clearly defined responsibilities" guide the industry with respect to the concrete (public) aims pursued.[627] By shaping the mandate of the industry and voicing expectations, the risk of consensus at the lowest level (which translates into weak standards) could be alleviated. Moreover, Latzer et al. also advocate for "transparent regulatory processes and measurable results". The outcome or output of self-regulation should be "measurable" implying the identification of deliverables and their assessment in view of the pre-determined objectives. Accordingly, the process whereby standards are formulated should be transparent to accommodate the positions of all stakeholders. In particular, Price and Verhulst

623 Latzer et al., *Selbst- und Ko-Regulierung im Mediamatiksektor*, p. 50; Lievens, Valcke and Valgaeren, "State of the Art on Regulatory Trends in Media," p. 30; Baldwin, Cave and Lodge, *Understanding Regulation*, p. 145.

624 Lievens and Valcke, "Regulatory Trends in a Social Media Context," pp. 563, 574.

625 Price and Verhulst, "Self-Regulation on the Internet," pp. 63, 64.

626 Latzer et al., "Regulation Remixed," p. 145.

627 Latzer et al., "Regulation Remixed," p. 145; see also Campbell, "Self-Regulation and the Media," p. 761.

stress that the public (especially those predominantly affected) should be actively involved in all stages of the regulatory process.[628] This would not only enhance the democratic quality of self-regulation, it would also contribute to a more compulsory system in which the industry is monitored more closely. The monitoring of the industry, according to Latzer et al. should be effectuated by "periodical reviews and external control" conducted by both, the public and the government.[629] Control is not only enhanced by more effective monitoring but also, as McGonagle points out, by "responsiveness of complaints and appeals systems"[630] or more generally, by fair process guarantees.[631] The more responsive and transparent procedural rules are, the more control may be exercised by the general public and the less partisan the industry may become.

These are just several factors that influence the effective functioning of a self-regulatory scheme. They may also adversely affect the positive characteristics of self-regulation. The more safeguards (protecting fundamental rights for instance) are erected, the more flexibility is compromised and regulation is slowed down. The exact interplay between these (positive and negative) factors and their causality cannot be determined *in abstracto* but the necessary trade-offs depend on the characteristics of the industry and the regulatory setting of each country. Price and Verhulst argue that self-regulation is most effective when the interests of the industry and the government coincide and both engage in a continuous dialogue.[632] In brief, the full potential of self-regulation can only materialise in an atmosphere of cooperation rather than confrontation of the industry and the government.

---

628 Price and Verhulst, "Self-Regulation on the Internet," p. 64.

629 Latzer et al., "Regulation Remixed," p. 145; on the need for "effective monitoring and compliance mechanisms", see also Tarlach McGonagle, "Co-Regulation of the Media in Europe: The Potential for Practice of an Intangible Idea," ed. European Audiovisual Observatory, *IRIS plus 2002-10*, 2002, p. 7.

630 McGonagle, "Co-Regulation of the Media in Europe," p. 7.

631 Campbell, "Self-Regulation and the Media," p. 761.

632 Price and Verhulst, "Self-Regulation on the Internet," pp. 67, 68.

## 2. Co-regulation

### a) Conceptualising co-regulation

Alongside self-regulation, co-regulation has gained importance as a regulatory strategy. Similar to self-regulation, "there is no universally acceptable recipe for successful co-regulation".[633] This quote by Marsden stresses that there is no one-size-fits-all co-regulatory system but that each system needs to be carefully designed and adapted to national conditions and specificities. Nonetheless, some scholars reckon that co-regulation remedies the disadvantages of self-regulation, while at the same time preserving the latter's benefits.[634] By calling it a "middle road"[635] other scholars have expressed similar optimism about the effectiveness of co-regulation combining positive elements of both, state regulation as well as self-regulation.[636] The conceptualisation of co-regulation, like that of self-regulation is rather problematic. Not only is the notion of co-regulation vague, but different terms have been used inconsistently such as "regulated self-regulation",[637] "audited self-regulation",[638] "two-tired regulation"[639] or "sponsored regulation".[640] The former two reinforce the link with self-regulation, whereas the latter two are primarily coupled with conventional state regulation. Evidently, links to either of the two forms of regulation cannot be negated. Lievens, Valcke and Valgaeren underscore that it is unclear "where self-regulation ends and co-regulation starts".[641] Due to vary-

---

633 Marsden, "Co-Regulation in European Media and Internet Sectors," p. 6.

634 Black, "Decentring Regulation," p. 115; Erkki Liikanen, "Co-Regulation: A Modern Approach to Regulation" (Meeting of Association of the European Mechanical, Electrical, Electronic and Metalworking Industries (Orgalime) Council, Brussels, May 4, 2000), http://europa.eu/rapid/press-release_SPEECH-00-162_en.htm (accessed 13.12.2014).

635 Schulz and Held, "Regulated Self-Regulation," p. 5; Marsden, "Co-Regulation in European Media and Internet Sectors," p. 4.

636 See also Prosser, "Self-Regulation, Co-Regulation and the AVMSD," p. 106.

637 Schulz and Held, "Regulated Self-Regulation.".

638 Campbell, "Self-Regulation and the Media," p. 719.

639 Latzer et al., *Selbst- und Ko-Regulierung im Mediamatiksektor*, p. 39.

640 Hans Bredow Institut and Institut für Europäisches Medienrecht, "Final Report, Study on Co-Regulation Measures in the Media Sector, Study for the European Commission," p. 11; Palzer, "Co-Regulation of the Media in Europe," p. 2.

641 Lievens, Valcke and Valgaeren, "State of the Art on Regulatory Trends in Media," p. 40.

ing degrees of "involvement and participation of the different actors", not only is an exact demarcation between self- and co-regulation difficult, the distinction between state and co-regulation is likewise blurry.[642] Hence, Prosser draws up "a continuum between different regulatory regimes with varying degrees of public and private input".[643] By the same token, Latzer et al. refer to a "continuum", which represents a fluid transition between the two opposing ends of state regulation and self-regulation as stated above.[644] Similarly, Marsden alludes to the two extremes, taking recourse to a negative definition stating that "co-regulation is neither state command-and-control regulation in its bureaucratic central or IRA (Independent Regulatory Agency) specialised functions, but is also not "pure" self-regulation as observed in industry-led standard setting".[645]

More specifically, co-regulation is considered as "self-regulation with public oversight or ratified by the state".[646] Schulz and Held also take self-regulation as a starting point adding that it "is supported by traditional, imperative instruments".[647] In their study of 2001, they apply a broad definition of co-regulation defining it as "self-regulation that fits in with a legal framework or has a basis laid down in law".[648] Other academics outline more detailed definitions. According to Puppis, co-regulation entails "the formulation and enforcement of rules and the sanctioning of non-compliance by private actors who are mandated to do so and who work together with the state".[649] As Palzer highlights, there are different ways in which private regulation is integrated into a state structure: first, the state invokes

642 Lievens, Valcke and Valgaeren, "State of the Art on Regulatory Trends in Media," p. 40; Just and Latzer, "Self- and Co-Regulation in the Mediamatics Sector," p. 49; Latzer et al., *Selbst- und Ko-Regulierung im Mediamatiksektor*, p. 37; McGonagle, "Co-Regulation of the Media in Europe," p. 2; Gunningham and Rees, "Industry Self-Regulation," p. 366; Palzer, "Co-Regulation of the Media in Europe," p. 2.

643 Prosser, "Self-Regulation, Co-Regulation and the AVMSD," p. 101.

644 Latzer et al., "Regulation Remixed," pp. 134–36; Latzer, Just and Saurwein, "Self- and Co-Regulation. Evidence, Legitimacy and Governance Choice," p. 377.

645 Marsden, "Co-Regulation in European Media and Internet Sectors," p. 4.

646 Just and Latzer, "Self- and Co-Regulation in the Mediamatics Sector," p. 44.

647 Schulz and Held, "Regulated Self-Regulation," p. 6.

648 Schulz and Held, "Regulated Self-Regulation," p. 7; on the requirement of a "legal basis", see also Just and Latzer, "Self- and Co-Regulation in the Mediamatics Sector," p. 44.

649 Puppis, "The Importance of Self- and Co-Regulation," p. 332.

a legal basis to set up a framework for the functioning of a co-regulatory body and second, the state may incorporate an existing self-regulatory scheme or body into its framework.[650] This differentiation is also forwarded by Just and Latzer who refer to top down and bottom up co-regulation in this respect.[651] Palzer's first option corresponds to the top down approach to co-regulation as the state establishes the regulatory structure *ex ante* including means of enforcement and supervision. The second of Palzer's options equates to bottom up co-regulation as "private agreements are transformed into legally binding rules and/or self-regulatory arrangements are institutionalised by means of legal authority".[652]

In sum, it appears that the bottom line of co-regulation is a relation of "institutionalised" cooperation between the industry and the state, the latter of which is more strongly integrated in the regulatory task as in a self-regulatory model.[653] Institutionalised cooperation implies the establishment of some kind of legal framework (either *ex ante* or *ex post* to the existence of self-regulatory arrangements) by the state in which regulatory activities take place.[654] This also ties in with the shift in the role of the state from the "sovereign state" to the "corporate bargaining state" as pointed out by Schulz and Held.[655] They underscore that regulation no longer occurs in a vacuum in which the state is autonomous. On the contrary, regulation happens on a multi-layered playing field in which the state has assumed the position of an umpire who "moderate[s] and mediate[s] rather than control[s]".[656]

### b) Advantages and disadvantages of co-regulation

The advantages and disadvantages of co-regulation correspond *grosso modo* to the benefits and risks associated with self-regulation. Yet, in contrast to self-regulation, which is located on one end of the regulatory spectrum, the advantages and disadvantages of co-regulation are softened as co-regu-

650 Palzer, "Co-Regulation of the Media in Europe," p. 2.
651 Just and Latzer, "Self- and Co-Regulation in the Mediamatics Sector," p. 49.
652 Just and Latzer, "Self- and Co-Regulation in the Mediamatics Sector," p. 49.
653 Just and Latzer, "Self- and Co-Regulation in the Mediamatics Sector," p. 44.
654 Schulz and Held, "Regulated Self-Regulation," p. 6.
655 Schulz and Held, "Regulated Self-Regulation," p. 6.
656 Schulz and Held, "Regulated Self-Regulation," p. 6.

lation occupies the middle ground of the continuum. Because it is independent of the usual slow-moving administrative process of the state apparatus, co-regulation is faster and more reactive than traditional state regulation.[657] Disadvantages of self-regulation like regulatory capture and information asymmetries may be mitigated by co-regulation. A co-regulatory body could be more independent of partisan interests of the industry and could thus potentially formulate and enforce higher standards. Assuming that a co-regulatory body disposes of greater expertise and knowledge about the industry than the government, the imbalances in this respect could be corrected. Similarly, the integration of a co-regulatory body in the state structure would strengthen the "democratic quality" of regulation, enhance legal certainty, legitimacy of regulatory actions and accountability of regulators.[658] To what extent policies and standards are set openly and in transparent manner and engage or "empower" the public depends on the specific regulatory setting.[659] Prosser, who is generally a proponent of co-regulation, is mindful of the risk that co-regulation might offer the "worst of both worlds" (meaning self-regulation and state regulation).[660] Prosser thereby underpins that a co-regulatory framework has to be carefully designed in order to avoid the drawbacks and failures identified above. He also highlights the uniqueness of every co-regulatory system and the domestic specificities which inevitably will have to be taken into account.

Furthermore, "success factors" proposed by Latzer et al. as outlined above may counter the disadvantages of co-regulation.[661] The determination of workable objectives as well as the necessity for regular (internal and external) reviews of the progress achieved appear valuable in the context of co-regulation.[662] In respect of audiovisual media, Puppis suggests

---

657 Just and Latzer, "Self- and Co-Regulation in the Mediamatics Sector," p. 45; Latzer et al., "Regulation Remixed," p. 142; Marsden, "Co-Regulation in European Media and Internet Sectors," p. 6.

658 Latzer et al., *Selbst- und Ko-Regulierung im Mediamatiksektor*, p. 51; Lievens, Valcke and Valgaeren, "State of the Art on Regulatory Trends in Media," p. 43.

659 Lievens and Valcke, "Regulatory Trends in a Social Media Context," pp. 567, 568; on user empowerment in relation to audiovisual media services, see generally Helberger, "From Eyeball to Creator: Toying with Audience Empowerment in the Audiovisual Media Service Directive," pp. 128–37.

660 Prosser, "Self-Regulation, Co-Regulation and the AVMSD," p. 103.

661 Latzer et al., "Regulation Remixed," p. 145.

662 Latzer et al., "Regulation Remixed," p. 145.

that co-regulation (as well as self-regulation) is an adequate tool to regulate content.[663] More specifically, the study undertaken by the German Hans Bredow Institut of 2006, examining a great number of European and international co-regulatory systems, identifies two objectives of broadcast regulation suitable for co-regulation: the protection of minors and advertising.[664] Both concern the regulation of content and in particular the advertising industry has traditionally had a high level of self-commitment.[665] On the one hand, the protection of minors constitutes an important public interest justifying state involvement. On the other hand, the classification of content adequate for children of different age groups appears to be a function that governments are willing to "outsource" to co-regulatory bodies. Thus, co-regulation should not simply be viewed as an artificial construction of elements of self-regulation and state regulation but has indeed proven to be a valuable and workable regulatory strategy in practice.

### 3. Regulatory choice

In contrast to intrusive heavy-handed state regulation, co- and self-regulation represent "'lighter' forms of regulation".[666] In spite of many positive attributes, it has become apparent that co- and self-regulation are neither preordain to succeed nor can they be regarded as a panacea. [667] A multitude of factors may play into the regulatory game and influence its outcome. Thus, regulatory decisions are contingent on the context in which they are implanted and the object of regulation.[668] They ultimately depend on the modalities of their design and the acceptance by the public

663 Puppis, "The Importance of Self- and Co-Regulation," p. 334.

664 Hans Bredow Institut and Europäisches Institut für Medienrecht, "Study on Co-Regulation Measures in the Media Sector, Study for the European Commission," p. 123.

665 Hans Bredow Institut and Europäisches Institut für Medienrecht, "Study on Co-Regulation Measures in the Media Sector, Study for the European Commission," p. 123.

666 McGonagle, "Co-Regulation of the Media in Europe," p. 2.

667 Marsden, "Co-Regulation in European Media and Internet Sectors," p. 6.

668 McGonagle, "Co-Regulation of the Media in Europe," pp. 3, 7; Prosser, "Self-Regulation, Co-Regulation and the AVMSD," p. 105; Puppis, "The Importance of Self- and Co-Regulation," p. 334; Schulz and Held, "Regulated Self-Regulation," pp. 22, 28.

as well as the industry. Naturally, the structure of the market and the "attitudes" of individual companies are pertinent, above all whether "big players" support or undermine regulatory efforts and whether a "culture of cooperation" prevails.[669] The concordance of interests and objectives of the state and the industry will foster regulation by alternative means.[670] Incentives to cooperate are indispensable as are guarantees of fundamental values like transparency, accountability and legitimacy.[671]

Due to the multi-faceted and detailed nature of audiovisual media policies, the question of which regulatory model to apply is not a compulsive either/or decision but rather a question of which "cocktail"[672] or "mix"[673] of complementary modes of regulation are considered most adequate. Which mode of regulation is to be used in which situation or field can only be determined on case by case analysis. Latzer at al. nonetheless offer some indication arguing that the "regulatory choice depends crucially on the intensity of intervention of the intended measure, i.e. the greater a regulatory measure encroaches upon an individual's basic rights the more urgent is its democratic legitimacy".[674] It follows that state regulation is preferable where fundamental rights are affected and alternative forms of regulation are more appropriate where the interference with fundamental rights is marginal or less severe. For these reasons, co-regulation which provides for democratic guarantees (at least on an abstract level) is considered suitable for the regulation of advertising content and the protection of minors in audiovisual media.[675] Moreover, Latzer, Just and Sauerwein propose a more specific set of criteria to evaluate, *ex ante* and *ex post*, the suitability of co- and self-regulation.[676] These entail "performance criteria" as well as "enabling contextual factors" and "institutional/organisa-

669 Schulz and Held, "Regulated Self-Regulation," pp. 24, 28.

670 Schulz and Held, "Regulated Self-Regulation," p. 22.

671 Hans Bredow Institut and Institut für Europäisches Medienrecht, "Final Report, Study on Co-Regulation Measures in the Media Sector, Study for the European Commission," p. 179.

672 Prosser, "Self-Regulation, Co-Regulation and the AVMSD," p. 112.

673 Latzer et al., "Regulation Remixed," pp. 143, 151.

674 Latzer et al., "Regulation Remixed," p. 148.

675 Hans Bredow Institut and Institut für Europäisches Medienrecht, "Final Report, Study on Co-Regulation Measures in the Media Sector, Study for the European Commission," p. 123.

676 Latzer, Just and Saurwein, "Self- and Co-Regulation. Evidence, Legitimacy and Governance Choice," p. 389.

tional success factors". "Performance criteria" relate not only to the activities and measures as such but also include the attitudes and perceptions towards the regulatory scheme. Contextual factors relate to the characteristics of the market and the industry while institutional factors cover the design and structure of the scheme. The former are exogenous factors which are difficult to modify, whereas the latter are endogenous and can more easily be altered by adjusting the organisational setting.[677] In brief, there is no recipe for which regulatory strategies will be successful; rather such strategies have to be adjusted to the respective circumstances and settings in each country.

### 4. Co- and self-regulation as policy instruments of the European Union

Since the adoption of the White Paper on the Internal Market of 1985[678] and the Single European Act of 1986, the EU has actively promoted the use of new regulatory forms (co and self-regulation as well as soft law instruments) as an alternative to legislation (i.e. EU Secondary Law). The initiatives primarily served to counter the population's distrust in the European integration process, thereby alleviating the democratic deficit. They are intrinsically linked to the efforts of the Union to strengthen the principle of proportionality and subsidiarity which were laid down in Art. 5 TEC (now Art. 5 (3) and (4) TEU) and underpinned by the Protocol annexed to the Treaty of Amsterdam.[679] In accordance with these principles, the EU attempted to reduce formal top down legislation by its institutions and to augment the engagement by the broader public and the regulated industries.[680] A first glimpse of such attempts can be witnessed by the 1998 Council Recommendation that promoted self-regulatory frameworks for the protection of minors and human dignity in the audiovisual and in-

677 Latzer, Just and Saurwein, "Self- and Co-Regulation. Evidence, Legitimacy and Governance Choice," p. 388.

678 European Commission, "White Paper from the Commission to the European Council, Completing the Internal Market, COM(85) 310 Final," June 14, 1985.

679 Linda Senden, "Soft Law, Self-Regulation and Co-Regulation in European Law: Where Do They Meet?," *Electronic Journal of Comparative Law* 9, no. 1 (2005): p. 9.

680 Lievens, Valcke and Valgaeren, "State of the Art on Regulatory Trends in Media," p. 8; Palzer, "Co-Regulation of the Media in Europe," p. 3; Senden, "Soft Law, Self-Regulation and Co-Regulation in European Law," p. 9.

formation services industry.[681] At the beginning of the new millennium, the Commission extensively lobbied for a change in regulatory culture highlighting the significance of co- and self-regulation.[682] These efforts culminated in the publication of a White Paper on European Governance in 2001[683] which was followed by an Action Plan in 2002 aimed at "simplifying and improving the regulatory environment".[684] The White Paper called for a combination of policy instruments including self-regulation and above all, co-regulation.[685] According to the Commission, co-regulation leads to higher levels of compliance and "wider ownership of the policies in question by involving those most affected by implementing rules in their preparation and enforcement"[686]. These benefits help to bring the Union closer to its citizens. However, where rules are to be applied uniformly or where "fundamental rights or major political choices" are at stake, co-regulation does not constitute an appropriate regulatory response in the Commission's opinion. Rather, co-regulation is permissible where it "clearly adds value and serves the general interest".[687]

Moreover, co-regulation entails a legislative framework that sets the general objectives and conditions of regulation. This requirement is underlined by the Commission's 2002 Action Plan setting out a general framework for co-regulation. Essentially, the Union legislator (the European Parliament, EP and the Council) acting on the Commission's proposal is to

---

681 Council Recommendation 98/560/EC of 24 September 1998 on the development of the competitiveness of the European audiovisual and information services industry by promoting national frameworks aimed at achieving a comparable and effective level of protection of minors and human dignity, OJ of 7.10.1998, L 270, pp. 48-55.

682 See Speech by Erkki Liikanen, Co-Regulation: a modern approach to regulation, 4.5.2000, Speech/00/162, available at http://europa.eu/rapid/press-release_SPEECH-00-162_en.htm (accessed 3.12.2014) Speech by Erkki Liikanen, Better Regulation: From Principles to Practice, 6.2.2001, Speech/01/57, available at http://europa.eu/rapid/press-release_SPEECH-01-57_en.htm (accessed 3.12.2014.).

683 European Commission, "European Governance, A White Paper, COM(2001) 428 Final," July 25, 2001.

684 European Commission, "Communication from the Commission, Action Plan 'Simplifying and Improving the Regulatory Environment', 5.6.2002, COM(2002) 278 Final".

685 European Commission, "White Paper on European Governance," p. 20.

686 European Commission, "White Paper on European Governance," p. 20.

687 European Commission, "White Paper on European Governance," p. 21.

determine the exact modalities and the shape of co-regulation. Interestingly, the parties involved in the regulation must be "considered [by the European institutions] to be representative, organised and responsible".[688] On the one hand, this ensures that interested parties are competent to act and act in the general interest. On the other hand, the criteria are ambiguous and subject to interpretation by the institutions. In addition, the requirement for formal legislative action also serves to draw a distinction between co- and self-regulation.[689] By contrast, self-regulation "concerns a large number of practices, common rules, codes of conduct and voluntary agreements which economic actors, social players, NGOs and organised groups establish themselves on a voluntary basis in order to regulate and organise their activities".[690] This appears to be a broad understanding of self-regulation, making possible industry action in different forms and shapes. The 2003 Interinstitutional Agreement on "Better Law-Making" outlines specific definitions of co- and self-regulation and the Commission's 2005 Communication on "Better Regulation for Growth and Jobs" acknowledges the role of co- and self-regulation as regulatory instruments as integral parts of the European regulatory culture.[691] These two instruments have received special attention in the AVMSD, the key legal act whereby the Union regulates the market for audiovisual media services.

## 5. Co- and self-regulation promoted by the AVMSD

The AVMSD explicitly refers to co- and self-regulation in one of its substantive provisions and one of its recitals as demonstrated above. In view of other European level initiatives referred to above of improving regulatory outcomes and reducing regulatory failures to strengthen the internal

688 European Commission, "Communication on Simplifying the Regulatory Environment," p. 13.

689 European Commission, "Communication on Simplifying the Regulatory Environment," p. 11.

690 European Commission, "Communication on Simplifying the Regulatory Environment," p. 11.

691 European Commission, "Communication from the Commission to the European Parliament, the Council, the European Economic and Social Committee and the Committee of the Regions, A Renewed EU Strategy 2011-14 for Corporate Social Responsibility, COM(2011) 681 Final," October 25, 2011, para. 4.3, pp. 9, 10.

market, the Commission was instrumental in advocating for the inclusion of such regulatory methods in the AVMSD. In its 2005 proposal for an amended Directive, the Commission relied on responses by stakeholders assessing co- and self-regulation as suitable instruments in the field of advertising and the protection of minors in audiovisual media.[692] The Commission also considered that the proportionality principle was well served by encouraging implementation of the Directive by such types of regulation.[693] This is explained by the fact that alternative forms of regulation are considered less burdensome and intrusive to the interests and rights of those regulated so that regulation does not "exceed what is necessary to achieve the objectives".[694]

Thus, Art. 4 (7) AVMSD provides that "Member States shall encourage co-regulation and/or self- regulatory regimes at national level in the fields coordinated by this Directive to the extent permitted by their legal systems. These regimes shall be such that they are broadly accepted by the main stakeholders in the Member States concerned and provide for effective enforcement". In conjunction with recital 44 AVMSD, the first sentence of Art. 4 (7) pays tribute to "different legal traditions of (…) Member States", which may or may not foster alternative forms of regulation.[695] Art. 4 (7) AVMSD as well as recital 44 AVMSD are worded softly, "encourage[ing]" recourse to co- and self-regulation. Member States' discretion to set up or continue successful domestic schemes is highlighted once again by the last sentence of recital 44 AVMSD. It is also implicitly expressed by its inclusion in Art. 4 AVMSD, a general provision which stipulates the right of Member States to adopt more detailed or stricter rules in the Directive's coordinated fields. Since the Directive merely sets out a minimum harmonisation, which does not exhaustively regulate an issue, Member States remain free to prescribe stricter standards in their territory provided that these conform to Union law. It follows that paragraph 7 of Art. 4 AVMSD is to be read in light of the general provision allowing Member States some leeway with respect to the implementation of the Directive in national law. Paragraphs (2) to (5) of Art. 4 AVMSD lay down the conditions and procedure to be followed in case of circumvention by a broadcaster of the more detailed rules applicable in a Member State. Fur-

692 European Commission, "AVMSD Proposal of 2005," pp. 5, 9.

693 European Commission, "AVMSD Proposal of 2005," p. 9.

694 Article 5 (4) TEU.

695 Recital 44 AVMSD.

thermore, paragraph (6) of Art. 4 AVMSD sets forth Member States' responsibility to "ensure, within the framework of their *legislation*, that media service providers under their jurisdiction effectively comply with the provisions of this Directive". This general obligation stems from Union law as such, notably Art. 288 TFEU in conjunction with the principles of sincere cooperation, subsidiary and proportionality, making the insertion of this paragraph superfluous. Nonetheless, when jointly reading paragraphs (6) and (7) of Art. 4 AVMSD, the Union legislator underscores that transposition may, where appropriate, take the form of "legislation" as well as "co-regulation and/or self-regulatory regimes". The significance of the assessment of the "appropriate regulatory approach" is further underlined by recital 44 AVMSD which also accentuates the "high level of consumer protection" achieved by co- and self-regulation.

Moreover, the second sentence of Art. 4 (7) AVMSD defines the conditions for co- and self-regulation which were already contained in the Commission's 2005 proposal.[696] The first element "acceptance" implies that the regulatory scheme is supported by the main stakeholders and is thus legitimated. Yet, many questions arise as to the meaning of the terms "acceptance" or "main stakeholders".[697] It is unclear who is considered a stakeholder (under which conditions) and whether and how acceptance is measured. The vagueness of these expressions has in fact repercussions on the "practicability and uniform implementation of these requirements".[698] The second element underpins the effectiveness of the scheme in applying and enforcing its rules. In this regard, recital 44 AVMSD seems to suggest that acceptance of a co- or self-regulatory system, implying "active support of the service providers", is a precondition for it to function effectively. It is true that the effectiveness of co- and above all self-regulation are contingent on the participation and support by the industry. Yet, the review of the literature above also appears to consider indispensable some form of control materialising in *ex post* monitoring and a precisely defined relationship between the state and the regulatory body. In addition, the effectiveness of co- and self-regulation is enhanced by installing guarantees such as transparency, participation by a large number of stakeholders and due process rights.[699]

696 European Commission, "AVMSD Proposal of 2005," p. 9.
697 Dommering, Scheuer and Ader, "Arts. 3-4 AVMSD," para. 11, pp. 862–63.
698 Dommering, Scheuer and Ader, "Arts. 3-4 AVMSD," para. 11, pp. 862–63.
699 Dommering, Scheuer and Ader, "Arts. 3-4 AVMSD," para. 12, p. 863.

While the substantive part of the Directive merely refers to co- and self-regulation (without providing detailed definitions) as a form of regulation, recital 44 AVMSD is very comprehensive and above all, more specific. In the first place, it refers to the Commission's 2005 Communication on "Better Regulation for Growth and Jobs in the European Union",[700] which in turn relies on the definitions set out in the 2003 Interinstitutional Agreement on Better Law-Making.[701] The Interinstitutional Agreement aims at improving "the quality of law-making" by promoting general principles as well as values like "simplicity, clarity and consistency".[702] The context in which these definitions have been adopted is a European one taking into account the *sui generis* of the Union and its institutions as opposed to the definitions presented above, which are conceptualised from a nation-state perspective. Additionally, models of co- and self-regulation are to respect criteria like "transparency" and "representativeness" and are to constitute "added value for the general interest".[703] The Interinstitutional Agreement also lays down conditions for the use of alternative methods of regulation by way of negation. Thus, co- and self-regulation are excluded, where "fundamental rights or important political options are at stake", or where harmonisation and thus the uniform application of Union law is required.[704] Harmonisation and more profound integration are especially desirable in relation to the internal market, the functioning of which also depends upon competition law. It follows that co- and self-regulation, in spite of being "swift and flexible" are favoured in situations where the interference with fundamental rights is minimal and where the economic roots of the Union are not significantly affected.[705]

---

700 European Commission, "Communication from the Commission to the Council and the European Parliament. Better Regulation for Growth and Jobs in the European Union, COM(2005) 97 Final," March 16, 2005, para. 2, p. 4.

701 European Parliament, Council, Commission, "Inter-Institutional Agreement on Better Lawmaking" (OJ C 321, December 31, 2003).

702 European Parliament, Council, Commission, "Inter-Institutional Agreement on Better Lawmaking," para. 2.

703 European Parliament, Council, Commission, "Inter-Institutional Agreement on Better Lawmaking," para. 17.

704 European Parliament, Council, Commission, "Inter-Institutional Agreement on Better Lawmaking," para. 17.

705 European Parliament, Council, Commission, "Inter-Institutional Agreement on Better Lawmaking," para. 17.

More concretely, self-regulation implies "the possibility for economic operators, the social partners, non-governmental organisations or associations to adopt amongst themselves and for themselves common guidelines at European level (particularly codes of practice or sectoral agreements)" by virtue of para. 18 of the Interinstitutional Agreement.[706] In addition, self-regulation constitutes "a voluntary initiative" that does not require prior activities by the Union's institutions.[707] Contrary to the Commission's proposal, recital 44 AVMSD no longer refers to the Interinstitutional Agreement's definitions.[708] The EP in its first reading as well as the Council had removed this reference in their positions and reinforced the "legal traditions" of Member States.[709] Strikingly, the final definition of self-regulation inserted in the Directive reiterates the essential elements as outlined in the Interinstitutional Agreement, albeit acknowledging different national approaches.

Above all, recital 44 AVMSD makes abundantly clear that self-regulation does not replace state regulation but rather constitutes a "complement to the legislative and judicial and/or administrative mechanisms in place" in the Member States.[710] Such evident opposition to self-regulation as an independent form of regulation is, however, not expressed with regards to co-regulation. The Directive thus considers legislation (including subsequent judicial and administrative enforcement) as the most adequate form of implementation.[711] This, it may be argued, appears to adversely affect the truthfulness of the encouragement to co- and self-regulation as included in recital 44 AVMSD and Art. 4 (7) AVMSD. The watering down of this recommendation may also be explained by the negotiations be-

---

706 European Parliament, Council, Commission, "Inter-Institutional Agreement on Better Lawmaking," para. 22.

707 European Parliament, Council, Commission, "Inter-Institutional Agreement on Better Lawmaking," para. 22.

708 Prosser, "Self-Regulation, Co-Regulation and the AVMSD," pp. 108, 109.

709 European Parliament, "Draft European Parliament Legislative Resolution on the Proposal for a Directive of the European Parliament and of the Council Amending Council Directive 89/552/EEC on the Coordination of Certain Provisions Laid down by Law, Regulation or Administrative Action in Member States Concerning the Pursuit of Television Broadcasting Activities," November 23, 2006, recital 25 (amendment 36) and 25 A (new) (amendment 37).

710 See also European Commission, "Communication on Principles and Guidelines for the Community's Audiovisual Policy in the Digital Age," para. 3 (5), p. 13.

711 Dommering, Scheuer and Ader, "Arts. 3-4 AVMSD," para. 9, p. 862.

tween the EU institutions leading to the adoption of the AVMSD. While the Commission's initial proposal was silent on this point, the EP seems to have pushed for the specifications which clarify the relation between state regulation and self-regulation.[712] Nonetheless, self-regulation represents an option in the "regulatory portfolio". Whether recital 44 AVMSD and Art. 4 (7) AVMSD *oblige* Member States to "thoroughly assess whether co- or self-regulation" are realistic is questionable.[713] The soft wording of recital 44 AVMSD ("this Directive *encourages* the use of co-regulation and self-regulation") and above all Art. 4 (7) AVMSD ("Member States *shall encourage* co-regulation and/or self-regulatory regimes") do not point at a mandatory assessment but rather leave the taking of such considerations to Member States.

With respect to co-regulation, the Interinstitutional Agreement refers to a "mechanism whereby a Community legislative act entrusts the attainment of the objectives defined by the legislative authority to parties which are recognised in the field (such as economic operators, social partners, non-governmental organisations, or associations)".[714] The Interinstitutional Agreement thus recognises that a particular objective as outlined by the public authority (in this case the Union legislature) is achieved by non-governmental actors. By analogy, the concept of co-regulation implies the establishment by a legislature of a common objective in the general interest that is transposed practically by agents other than the legislature. Prosser rightly argues that the definitions of both, co- and self-regulation as stipulated by the Interinstitutional Agreement and outlined in the Commission's proposal are "highly restrictive".[715] He posits that they are crouched from a top down perspective and consequently do not entail

712 European Parliament, "European Parliament Draft Legislative Resolution on the Commission's Proposal Amending the TWFD," recital 25 (amendment 36); European Parliament, "European Parliament Legislative Resolution on the Proposal for a Directive of the European Parliament and of the Council Amending Council Directive 89/552/EEC on the Coordination of Certain Provisions Laid down by Law, Regulation or Administrative Action in Member States Concerning the Pursuit of Television Broadcasting Activities," December 13, 2006, recitals 38, 39.

713 Dommering, Scheuer and Ader, "Arts. 3-4 AVMSD," para. 10, p. 862.

714 European Parliament, Council, Commission, "Inter-Institutional Agreement on Better Lawmaking," para. 18.

715 Prosser, "Self-Regulation, Co-Regulation and the AVMSD," p. 107.

regulatory initiatives developing "bottom-up".[716] By the same token, the restrictiveness of the concepts results in insufficient leeway for regulatory bodies and lack of clarity as regards issues like enforcement or sanctioning.[717]

During the negotiations, the EP had demonstrated its opposition by drafting its own definition of co-regulation. Recital 39 of the EP's position after the first reading provides that

> "the generic term "co-regulation" covers regulatory instruments which are based on cooperation between State bodies and self-regulating bodies, and vary widely in terms of their designations and structures at national level. The actual form which such instruments take reflects the specific tradition of media regulation in the individual Member States. What co-regulation systems have in common is that tasks and objectives which were originally the preserve of the State are achieved in cooperation with the players affected by regulation. It is for the participants themselves, designated or authorised by the State, to guarantee the achievement of the regulatory objective. In every case the systems are founded on a State legal framework which lays down instructions as to content, organisation and procedures. On this basis, the interested parties create further criteria, rules and instruments, compliance with which they themselves monitor (…)".[718]

This amendment is proof of the difficulty of conceptualising co-regulation which necessarily develops under different national circumstances.[719] Yet, the EP relies on common characteristics of co-regulatory models like a relationship of cooperation between the industry and the state and the existence of a legal framework detailing the structure and design of the prospective authority. The EP's intention to specify the concept of co-regulation is noteworthy. Nevertheless, the wording of the amendment is almost too precise and exclusive.[720] It strips the definition of the flexibility

716 Prosser, "Self-Regulation, Co-Regulation and the AVMSD," p. 107.

717 Prosser, "Self-Regulation, Co-Regulation and the AVMSD," p. 107.

718 European Parliament, "European Parliament Legislative Resolution on the Commission's Proposal Amending the TWFD", recital 39.

719 In 2003, the Commission already cautioned about the risks that conceptual differences between Member States could lead to "re-fragmentation of markets" with negative implications for the internal market. See European Commission, "Communication on the Future European Regulatory Audiovisual Policy," para. 3.10, p. 23.

720 Recital 39 of the European Parliament's position suggests, for instance that co-regulation is always ("in any case") encompassed by a state legal structure which, furthermore, "lays down instructions as to content, organisation and procedures". The wording of this recital appears too absolute and thus exclusive.

and thus appears to undermine the "generic" nature of the term which allows its application in different national contexts. The EP's amendment was rejected by the Commission in its modified proposal of March 2007. Besides the inadequacy of the formulations, Prosser indicates that the Hans-Bredow-Institute's study on co-regulation in the media sector published in 2006 has influenced the discussions towards more open definitions.[721] Recital 44 AVMSD indeed does not lay down a precise definition, something that Prosser supports, but specifies that co-regulation provides "a legal link between self-regulation and the national legislator".[722] It is noted that the AVMSD as such does not prescribe co-regulation (or self-regulation) to be employed in a particular field but leaves the choice of regulatory instruments to Member States. Such instruction would also jar with the characteristics of a Directive as an instrument of Secondary Union Law. Still, the AVMSD stresses that co-regulation "should allow for the possibility of State intervention in the event of its objectives not being met". Hence, state regulation is considered as a safety net, a fallback mechanism (or "legal back-stop")[723] should co-regulation fail.

### 6. Other alternative regulatory strategies

While discussions on alternative regulatory models in the media sector have centred on co- and self-regulation, the potential of other alternative strategies like risk-based[724] or principles-based regulation is increasingly being fathomed.[725] These should be regarded as complementary methods of regulation. Instead of securing compliance by deterrence, overarching

---

721 Hans Bredow Institut and Europäisches Institut für Medienrecht, "Study on Co-Regulation Measures in the Media Sector, Study for the European Commission"; Prosser, "Self-Regulation, Co-Regulation and the AVMSD," p. 109.

722 Dommering, Scheuer and Ader, "Arts. 3-4 AVMSD," para. 9, p. 862; Prosser, "Self-Regulation, Co-Regulation and the AVMSD," p. 111.

723 Dommering, Scheuer and Ader, "Arts. 3-4 AVMSD," p. 863 para. 12.

724 On risk-based regulation, see Pierre Trudel, "Internet Risks Management and Paradigm Shifts," pp. 5–10; Peggy Valcke, "Risk-Based Regulation in the Media Sector: The Way Forward to Advance the Media Pluralism Debate in Europe?" (ICRI Working Paper 2/2011, 2011), http://papers.ssrn.com/sol3/papers.cfm?abstract_id=1898133 (accessed 14.12.2014); Peggy Valcke, "Challenges of Regulating Media Pluralism in the European Union: The Potential of Risk-Based Regulation," *Quaderns Del CAC 38* XV, no. 1 (June 2012): pp. 25–35.

725 Valcke, "The Potential of Risk-Based Regulation," p. 28.

'values' (whether risks in one or principles in the other) are identified.[726] Risk-based regulation primarily aims at controlling risks.[727] Typical elements of risk-based regulation are a "risk-scoring system" established by the regulator, and a link between the scoring mechanism and the allocation of resources.[728] The scoring system allows for rational and transparent appraisal of the regulatees' conduct for instance by means of a "traffic light" warning system (or more sophisticated systems) based on certain pre-defined thresholds.[729] Accordingly, regulators will principally intervene, where market participants depict high risks.[730] On account of the numerical assessment of risks and the "more calculative and formalised approach", risk-based regulation is regarded as efficient, "cost-effective and controllable".[731] Yet, the detection and identification of risks and their translation into numerical values and thresholds, which represent regulatory priorities, is a complex and inherently subjective matter dependent upon discretionary value judgments.[732] Due to the disadvantages of risk-based regulation, Baldwin, Cave and Lodge suggest that it should not be viewed as "a free-standing and technical guide to regulatory intervention but as a particular way to construct the regulatory agenda and as a control strategy that has to be combined with other control strategies".[733]

In addition, principles-based regulation relies on the establishment of general principles (rather than specific rules) that embody regulatory objectives.[734] The regulated businesses thus enjoy some discretion with regards to the form and means they employ with a view to the serving of the principles.[735] Principles-based regulation is different from traditional state regulation as the state does not dictate behaviour by setting precise rules (although in reality, the principles are accompanied by guidance in the

---

726 Baldwin, Cave and Lodge, *Understanding Regulation*, p. 281.

727 Carol Harlow and Richard Rawlings, *Law and Administration*, p. 269; Trudel, Pierre, "Internet Risks Management and Paradigm Shifts," p. 7.

728 Baldwin, Cave and Lodge, *Understanding Regulation*, p. 282.

729 Baldwin, Cave and Lodge, *Understanding Regulation*, p. 282.

730 Baldwin, Cave and Lodge, *Understanding Regulation*, p. 282.

731 Harlow and Rawlings, *Law and Administration*, p. 269; Baldwin, Cave and Lodge, *Understanding Regulation*, p. 292.

732 Baldwin, Cave and Lodge, *Understanding Regulation*, p. 292.

733 Baldwin, Cave and Lodge, *Understanding Regulation*, p. 295.

734 Baldwin, Cave and Lodge, *Understanding Regulation*, p. 302.

735 Baldwin, Cave and Lodge, *Understanding Regulation*, p. 302.

form of written statements or rules).[736] Instead, the state provides a general framework within which the industry is allowed to operate. As Baldwin, Cave and Lodge argue, this approach is reminiscent to the "delegation of control".[737] Due to the absence of formal rules, principles-based regulation constitutes a flexible, "outcome-oriented" regulatory model.[738] In its ideal form, the principles set out by the regulator guarantee "some durability in a rapidly changing market environment".[739] However, the appeal of principles-based regulation has faded after the financial crisis starkly revealed that it was in fact "light touch regulation that placed too much reliance on firms themselves to behave responsibly".[740] Not only is the formulation of principles difficult but also their enforcement.[741] Regulators are required to incite compliance by the regulated companies and clearly communicate desired outcomes.[742] It follows that the principles-based model is essentially built on good faith and mutual trust,[743] values which may rapidly be jeopardised in light of rational economic decisions. Principles are nonetheless important as a basis for regulation. As overarching and enduring values like transparency or accountability, they may serve to reinforce the democratic quality of regulation.[744] By the same token, "smart regu-

736 Baldwin, Cave and Lodge, *Understanding Regulation*, pp. 302, 303; Black distinguishes between "formal" and "substantive" principles-based regulation. The former specifically refers to regulation "at the level of the rulebook" where detailed and precise rules are formulated. See Julia Black, "The Rise, Fall and Fate of Principles Based Regulation" (LSE Law, Society and Economy Working Papers 17/2010, 2010), p. 5, http://papers.ssrn.com/sol3/papers.cfm?abstract_id=1712862&download=yes (accessed 15.3.2015).

737 Baldwin, Cave and Lodge, *Understanding Regulation*, p. 303.

738 Black, "The Rise, Fall and Fate of Principles-Based Regulation," p. 3.

739 Julia Black, "Forms and Paradoxes of Principles-Based Regulation," *Capital Markets Law Journal* 3, no. 4 (2008): p. 426.

740 Black, "The Rise, Fall and Fate of Principles-Based Regulation," p. 3; see also Baldwin, Cave and Lodge, *Understanding Regulation*, p. 302.

741 Black, "Forms and Paradoxes of Principles-Based Regulation," p. 446; Baldwin, Cave and Lodge, *Understanding Regulation*, p. 304.

742 Baldwin, Cave and Lodge, *Understanding Regulation*, p. 304; Black, "Forms and Paradoxes of Principles-Based Regulation," p. 447.

743 Baldwin, Cave and Lodge, *Understanding Regulation*, p. 305.

744 Black, "The Rise, Fall and Fate of Principles-Based Regulation," p. 20; see for instance the principle of low interventionism or the principle of empowerment suggested by Neil Gunningham and Darren Sinclair, "Integrative Regulation: A Principle-Based Approach to Environmental Policy," *Law & Social Inquiry*, 1999, pp. 863, 876.

lation",[745] "better regulation", "responsive regulation"[746] and "really responsive regulation"[747] are catchphrases denoting other methods of regulation specifically aiming at improving enforcement of regulatory objectives. Enforcement problems have also been encountered by the advocacy for (*ex ante*) impact assessments and (*ex post*) monitoring and evaluation.[748]

This chapter provided an overview of the concepts of regulation, notably co- and self-regulation, that are pertinent to this study. On the basis of these concepts, the next chapter examines the regulatory framework of the media in the UK, Germany and France.

---

745 Gunningham and Sinclair, "Designing Smart Regulation," in *Smart Regulation: Designing Environmental Policy*, ed. Neil Gunningham and Peter Grabosky, (Oxford: Clarendon Press, Oxford University Press, 1998).

746 Ian Ayres and John Braithwaite, *Responsive Regulation: Transcending the Deregulation Debate*, Oxford Socio-Legal Studies (New York: Oxford University Press, 1992).

747 Baldwin and Black, "Really Responsive Regulation.".

748 On impact assessments, see Baldwin, Cave and Lodge, *Understanding Regulation*, pp. 315–37.

# Chapter 3. The national media authorities of the UK, Germany and France

In the EU Member States, many different bodies are involved in the regulation of audiovisual media services. As discussed in the first chapter, the most common organisational form of regulation is national regulatory authorities (NRAs) that are independent of the state apparatus.[749] NRAs have "almost become a natural institutional form for regulatory governance".[750] NRAs monitor industry's compliance with relevant legislation, thereby acting as guardians of the public interest. These bodies are deeply embedded in the socio-cultural, economic and political national contexts. Tracing their evolution is important to understanding the goals pursued by their establishment. To regulate audiovisual media services, NRAs are equipped with pre-defined competences and manage their tasks under a legal framework. Although the AVMSD only makes a passing reference to NRAs' independence,[751] it is crucial that they achieve a high degree of independence and are free from undue interference, in particular by political and economic interests.[752] The relationship between NRAs and state institutions is especially sensitive as the latter define the general framework within which regulators operate and determine the parameters of such operation, including the scope of NRAs' mandate or remit, their powers, institutional structure and their funding. Similarly, NRAs are vulnerable to the industry which may "capture" the regulator and undermine the public interest. Thus, NRAs' independence is crucial to allow for impartial decision-making. Apart from being independent, it is also important that

749 See EPRA, About Regulatory Authorities, available at http://www.epra.org/articles/about-regulatory-authorities (accessed 3.7.2016).

750 Kristina Irion and Roxana Radu, "Delegation to Independent Regulatory Authorities in the Media Sector: A Paradigm Shift through the Lens of Regulatory Theory," in *The Independence of the Media and Its Regulatory Agencies, Shedding New Light on Formal and Actual Independence against the National Context*, ed. Wolfgang Schulz, Peggy Valcke and Kristina Irion (Bristol, UK and Chicago, USA: Intellect, 2013), p. 15.

751 Art. 30 AVMSD.

752 Majone, "The Rise of the Regulatory State in Europe," p. 84.

NRAs are accountable to the public and function as transparently as possible.

This study concentrates on the regulators of the UK, Germany and France because they represent different models or approaches to regulating media. As products of the respective national environments, the British, German and French regulatory bodies also have different "perceptions" or "mind-sets" on the regulation of audiovisual media services. The British regulatory framework is geared towards the market in a liberal manner that has been defined by some as "aggressively 'deregulatory' pro-market".[753] A co-regulatory scheme for on-demand audiovisual media services existed for five years but was ended on account of media convergence. The German regulatory framework is based on the federal organisation of the state. German federalism has led to the creation of numerous regulatory bodies that have to cooperate on a federal level. The freedom of broadcasting and its independence from the state have generally formed the German regulatory culture. To protect minors in audiovisual media services, a system of regulated self-regulation has been established that allows for self-regulation under a framework defined by the state. By contrast, the regulatory structure in France is centralised and focuses on a single NRA. French identity and culture have been in the centre of media policies. The countries have also been selected due to their importance for the digital single market. Almost half of all TV channels licensed in the EU in 2015 were established in the UK, Germany and France and the same kind of concentration can be found in the market for on-demand audiovisual media services.[754] In addition, Connected TV take up is among the highest in these countries.[755] Apart from their economic weight, the British, German and French regulatory authorities have furthermore been very active in shaping the implementation of the AVMSD

753 Humphreys, "The Principle Axes of the European Union's Audiovisual Policy," p. 152.

754 Schneeberger and Fontaine, "Linear and On-Demand Services in Europe 2015," pp. 8, 31.

755 European Audiovisual Observatory, ed., "Annex – On-Demand Audiovisual Markets in the European Union, Final Report," 2014, para. 1.2, figure 10, p. 12, https://ec.europa.eu/digital-agenda/en/news/demand-audiovisual-markets-european-union-smart-20120028 (accessed 2.9.2014).

in their respective Member States and have been front-runners or "European trendsetters" in responding to pressing regulatory issues.[756]

To understand how media policies are devised and shaped at the national level and which actors play what role in this process, it is indispensable to examine the national legal frameworks with a particular focus on regulatory structures. National particularities, specificities and sensitivities are inherent in the legal landscapes that are gradually being recalibrated to different phenomena of the media sector, brought about by media convergence. This chapter thus looks at the regulatory frameworks in the UK, Germany and France. It sketches the national contexts in which regulatory authorities are established and function. In the UK, liberal and market-oriented thinking has shaped the design of the regulatory scheme, whereas in Germany and France, constitutional protections have played a major role. The *raison d'être* of the regulatory authorities is therefore not the same in the three countries. Highlighting differences and similarities is a prerequisite to understanding regulators approaches to implementing the AVMSD, both, in terms of regulatory strategies as well as content standards. This chapter therefore examines the NRAs competent to regulate audiovisual media services, more particularly, the areas analysed in the fourth and fifth chapters of this study (i.e. regulation of on-demand audiovisual media services and protection of minors in such services). It traces the genesis of NRAs, examines the national legal sources and looks at their composition, funding and competences. This chapter deals with the concrete design of NRAs in the UK, Germany and France and it sheds light on Member States' regulatory strategies accommodating media convergence and fast-paced media markets.

## A. The UK media authorities

> "The thinking that has occurred in the United Kingdom about the role of broadcasting and the way in which governments need to deal with it from a regulatory point of view has (…) been critically influential in many countries".[757]

756 Dieter Brockmeyer, *EuroReg 2011: From Connected TV to Coherent Media, A Conference by Germany's "Die Medienanstalten" and LPR Hessen, Documentation*, Schriftenreihe der Landesmedienanstalten 48 (Berlin: Vistas, 2012), p. 53.

757 Grainger, "Broadcasting, Co-Regulation and the Public Good, 1999 Spry Memorial Lecture," p. 16.

In a speech in 1999, Gareth Grainger, former Deputy Chairman of the Australian Broadcasting Authority[758] underlined the UK's pioneering role for broadcast regulation, in particular referring to the creation of public service broadcasting and the protection of the public interest. Likewise, in the age of convergence, the UK's regulatory framework continues to set an example for many countries, its structure and approach being emulated worldwide. In addition to its exemplary function, the UK is home to a multitude of service providers, be it broadcasters (roughly 850 in 2016) or providers of video-on-demand (VOD) services (approximately 175 in 2016).[759] On an international scale, the British media market is significant as many services directed to third countries are licensed or notified in the UK, such as Arabic, Asian, Turkish or US-American channels.[760] Some providers also target other EU Member States. For the purpose of regulation, such services are considered to be established in the UK and the relevant British legislation consequently applies. The attractiveness of the British market finds expression in the revenue of GBP 60.2 billion generated in 2013 by the communications sector (encompassing telecoms, TV, radio and postal services), the television industry generating GBP 12.9 billion.[761] The market for VOD services is growing rapidly and more and more viewers watch VOD services.[762] Interestingly, the penetration of

758 The Australian Broadcasting Authority has been subsumed by the Australian Communications and Media Authority which is itself a converged regulator established by virtue of the Australian Communications and Media Authority Act 2005. See Australian Communications and Media Authority (ACMA), Corporate, Organisational structure, available at http://www.acma.gov.au/theACMA/About/Corporate/Structure-and-contacts/organisational-structure-acma (accessed 25.9.2014). The Australian Communications and Media Authority Act 2005 is available at http://www.comlaw.gov.au/Details/C2005A00044 (accessed 25.9.2014).

759 See European Audiovisual Observatory, Mavise database, United Kingdom, available at http://mavise.obs.coe.int/country?id=14 (accessed 1.10.2016).

760 Daithi Mac Sithigh, "Co-Regulation, Video-on-Demand and the Legal Status of Audio-Visual Media," *International Journal of Digital Television* 2, no. 1 (2011): p. 51.

761 Ofcom, "The Communications Market Report," July 8, 2014, paras. 1.3.1, 2.1.1, pp. 25, 131, http://stakeholders.ofcom.org.uk/binaries/research/cmr/cmr14/2014_UK_CMR.pdf (accessed 9.10.2014).

762 The time spent watching VOD services accounted for 8 percent of total viewing time (69 percent watch live TV and 16 percent watch TV on conferred basis) and in 2013, half of all British adults consumed at least one VOD service. See Ofcom, "Market Report 2013," para. 2.1.4, p. 145.

Connected TVs which connect to the Internet is gradually increasing. In the first quarter of 2014, 12 percent of UK homes were equipped with such a device and almost 40 percent of UK households had Internet-enabled set-top boxes.[763] Although many viewers are still oblivious to the Internet functions of their television device, consumers are progressively more active on the Internet through their television screens.[764] These figures illustrate the market potential of the British communications industry, especially its broadcast and VOD sector. At the basis of this flourishing industry is a strong regulatory framework which combines different characteristics of regulatory models as outlined above.

Thus, the following section sketches the competent UK regulatory authorities for the media. Even though a converged regulator has been established, several other bodies are involved in the regulation of broadcast and on-demand services. This is due to the fact that the statutory regulator has externalised certain regulatory tasks to specialised bodies. The creation of a converged regulator for the British communications industry and subsequent delegation to other bodies was effectuated under the New Labour Government (1997-2010) headed by Prime Minster Blair (1997-2007) who was succeeded in office by Prime Minster Brown (2007-2010). The New Labour Government acknowledged the implications arising from globalised and inter-connected markets realising the potential of a nascent yet burgeoning communications market. Thus, media policy was a priority for the government in order to boost the knowledge and information society.[765] New Labour enacted sweeping social reforms in the 1990s building on a "strong yet decentralised state".[766] Against this background, Ofcom, the UK's converged regulator is a "prominent child of New Labour"[767] even if it was not the first of its kind (Ofcom was modelled upon the Financial Services Authority).[768] The move towards one unified and integrated regulator aimed at enhancing regulatory effectiveness and coher-

763 Ofcom, "Market Report 2013," para. 2.1.3, p. 131.

764 Ofcom, "Market Report 2013," para. 2.1.3, p. 132.

765 Lunt and Livingstone, *Media Regulation, Governance and the Interests of Citizens and Consumers*, p. 26.

766 Lunt and Livingstone, *Media Regulation, Governance and the Interests of Citizens and Consumers*, p. 4.

767 Lunt and Livingstone, *Media Regulation, Governance and the Interests of Citizens and Consumers*, p. 11.

768 Lunt and Livingstone, *Media Regulation, Governance and the Interests of Citizens and Consumers*, p. 29.

ence of policies. By the same token, the trends towards deregulation and decentralisation are reflected in the reliance on co-regulation. However, the Coalition Government which came to power in 2010 under Prime Minister David Cameron has had a different outlook emphasising "the small state",[769] backtracking from the wide dispersion of powers to non-governmental organisations (so-called quangos), redistributing power to the citizens (the "big society").[770] This change of track (or "bonfire of quangos" as it was called)[771] was motivated by the lack of accountability and transparency of such public bodies which was met by returning final control to ministers.[772] The changing political landscape has impacted the regulatory authorities, particularly Ofcom.

## I. Fundamental rights protection in the UK

In contrast to Germany and France, the UK does not have a written constitution enshrining fundamental rights in a bill of rights or comparable form. Fundamental rights are nonetheless directly applicable in the UK by virtue of the Human Rights Act of 1998 (HRA), which entered into force in October 2000 and incorporates the ECHR.[773] As a result, the hitherto uncertain status of rights that developed under common law have been formally guaranteed and protected under this legislation. The HRA obliges UK courts to take into account relevant ECtHR jurisprudence and any legislation "must be read and given effect in a way which is compatible" with the

769 Lunt and Livingstone, *Media Regulation, Governance and the Interests of Citizens and Consumers*, p. 4.

770 Lunt and Livingstone, *Media Regulation, Governance and the Interests of Citizens and Consumers*, p. 177.

771 Polly Curtis, "Government Scraps 192 Quangos," *The Guardian*, October 14, 2010 http://www.theguardian.com/politics/2010/oct/14/government-to-reveal-which-quangos-will-be-scrapped?guni=Graphic:in%20body%20link (accessed 17.9.2014).

772 Lunt and Livingstone, *Media Regulation, Governance and the Interests of Citizens and Consumers*, p. 178.

773 Sec. 1 (1) (a) Human Rights Act. See also Eric Barendt, "Freedom of Expression in the United Kingdom under the Human Rights Act 1998," *Indiana Law Journal* 84, no. 3 (2009): p. 851; Catherine Elliott and Frances Quinn, *English Legal System*, tenth edition (Essex: Pearson, 2009), p. 320.

ECHR.[774] The HRA's impact is, however, limited as judges do not have the power to declare legislation that is incompatible with the ECHR unconstitutional.[775] The principle of parliamentary sovereignty, which implies that the UK Parliament is the supreme legal authority which can adopt and repeal laws, remains unaffected.[776] As opposed to Germany and France, where the freedom of expression is constitutionally entrenched, the development of the UK's legal framework regulating broadcasting and on-demand audiovisual media services is detached from this right as is shown below.

## II. Legal sources

In December 2000, the British government announced its agenda for the communications sector in a White Paper entitled "A new future for Communications" presented to Parliament by the Secretary of State for Trade and Industry and the Secretary of State for Culture, Media and Sport.[777] As the title suggests, government planned a fundamental reform that would include the drafting of a distinct legal act which would govern the regulation of telecommunications *and* media as well as the establishment of a *single* regulator. The overhaul was pursued under the headline of making the UK "home to the most dynamic and competitive communica-

774 Sec. 2, 3 Human Rights Act. See also Barendt, "Freedom of Expression in the United Kingdom under the Human Rights Act 1998," p. 851; Elliott and Quinn, *English Legal System*, pp. 320–22.

775 Elliott and Quinn, *English Legal System*, p. 324.

776 For a detailed discussion of parliamentary sovereignty, see Albert Dicey Venn, *Introduction to the Study of the Law of the Constitution*, eight edition (London: Macmillan, 1915), pp. 3–104; Elliott and Quinn, *English Legal System*, p. 324, UK Parliament, Parliamentary Sovereignty, available at https://www.parliament.uk/about/how/role/sovereignty/ (accessed 3.5.2015).

777 The White Paper of 2000 can be traced back to the Green Paper published in 1998 entitled "Regulating Communications" in which the British government set out its visions in a rapidly evolving and technology-driven communications market. In contrast to the White Paper of 2000, the Green Paper of 1998 favoured incremental and less profound changes to the communications sector. See Lunt and Livingstone, *Media Regulation, Governance and the Interests of Citizens and Consumers*, p. 44.

tions market in the world".[778] Government was acutely aware of the knitting together of the telecommunications and broadcasting sectors: "the regulation of content and infrastructure [have become] so intertwined so as to be indistinguishable from each other".[779] In government's view, convergence of industries, made inevitable a radical overhaul of the legislative and regulatory framework.

A converged regulator would be the logical extension of converged legislation. As a result, the Communications Act (CA), a voluminous piece of legislation, was adopted in 2003 receiving royal assent on 17 July. In fact, the CA had a dual purpose: first, to revise existing statutes with a view to adjusting them to the demands of a converged environment and second, to comply with obligations arising from European Union law by implementing the EU's telecommunications package, aimed at enhancing competition in and the competitiveness of the telecommunications sector.[780] As a key characteristic, regulation was intended to be "technology-neutral" so

---

778 Doyle and Vick quote p. 10 of the White Paper on a new future for communications. See Gillian Doyle and Douglas Vick, "The Communications Act 2003: A New Regulatory Framework in the UK," *Convergence: The International Journal of Research into New Media Technologies* 11, no. 3 (2005): p. 86.

779 Weinstein, "The Medium Is the Message," p. 165.

780 The telecoms package includes the following EU Directives and Decision of 2002: Directive 2002/19/EC of the European Parliament and of the Council of 7 March 2002 on access to, and interconnection of, electronic communications networks and associated facilities (Access Directive), OJ of 24.4.2002, L 108, pp. 7-20; Directive 2002/20/EC of the European Parliament and of the Council of 7 March 2002 on the authorisation of electronic communications networks and services (Authorisation Directive), OJ of 24.4.2002, L 108, pp. 21-32; Directive 2002/21/EC of the European Parliament and of the Council of 7 March 2002 on a common regulatory framework for electronic communications networks and services ("Framework Directive"), OJ of 24.4.2002, L 108, pp. 33-50; Directive 2002/22/EC of the European Parliament and of the Council of 7 March 2002 on universal service and users' rights relating to electronic communications networks and services (Universal Service Directive), OJ of 24.4.2002, L 108, pp. 51-77; Directive 2002/58/EC of the European Parliament and of the Council of 12 July 2002 concerning the processing of personal data and the protection of privacy in the electronic communications sector (Directive on privacy and electronic communications), OJ of 31.7.2002, L 201, pp. 37-47; Decision No 676/2002/EC of the European Parliament and of the Council of 7 March 2002 on a regulatory framework for radio spectrum policy in the European Community (Radio Spectrum Decision), OJ of 24.4.2002, L 108, pp. 1-6. The "telecoms package" was amended in 2009 by Directive 2009/140/EC of the European Parliament and of the Council of 25 November 2009, OJ of 18.12.2009, L 337, pp.

as to seamlessly accommodate future technological developments.[781] The British government heralded the CA as "light touch regulation" reinforcing deregulatory tendencies and the trust in market forces.[782] The birth of a converged regulator was thus essentially motivated by economic reasons as the existing regulatory framework was not considered apt to meet the needs of a converging communications industry.[783] Interestingly, the original CA excluded services transmitted over the Internet, while at the EU level, the UK lobbied for restricting the scope of application of the AVMSD during the negotiations in the Council.[784] Since the scope of application of the Directive was opened to services diffused over the Internet,[785] the CA was consequently amended by means of two regulations of 2009 and 2010, which implemented the AVMSD in the UK. On the one hand, the CA signalled a radical departure from previous heavy-handed regulation towards liberal, laissez-faire thinking. On the other hand, it created a powerful regulator risking the potential seizure and monopolisation of certain aspects of regulation, gradually turning light legislation into tight regulation.[786] So far, Ofcom has been able to refute this criticism.

---

37-69. It is currently undergoing another reform aimed at modernising it. See also Mike Feintuck and Mike Varney, *Media Regulation, Public Interest and the Law*, second edition (Edinburgh: Edinburgh University Press, 2006), pp. 154, 162; Alexander Roßnagel, Thomas Kleist and Alexander Scheuer, *Die Reform der Regulierung elektronischer Medien in Europa*, Schriftenreihe Medienforschung der Landesanstalt für Medien Nordrhein-Westfalen 53 (Düsseldorf: Vistas, 2007), p. 278.

781 Crane, "Communications Reglator OFCOM," p. 37.

782 James Curran and Jean Seaton, *Power without Responsibility, The Press, Broadcasting and New Media in Britain*, sixth edition (London and New York: Routledge, 2003), p. 388; Feintuck and Varney, *Media Regulation, Public Interest and the Law*, p. 154.

783 Doyle and Vick, "The Communications Act 2003," p. 90.

784 Mac Sithigh, "Co-Regulation, VOD and the Legal Status of Audio-Visual Media Services," p. 56.

785 Daithi Mac Sithigh, "Convergence, The Impact of Broadcast Regulation on Telecommunications," in *Telecommunications Law and Regulation*, ed. Ian Walden, fourth edition (Oxford: Oxford University Press, 2012), p. 664.

786 Crane, "Communications Reglator OFCOM," p. 37.

## III. The UK regulatory framework for the media

The following section sketches the UK's regulatory framework for the media, in particular the creation of Ofcom, a converged regulator, and ATVOD, a co-regulator for on-demand services that exercised its delegated functions for five years.

### 1. The Office of Communications

#### a) The creation of the "super-regulator" Ofcom

For more than one and a half years, the Office of Communications (Ofcom) solely existed on paper before it was up and running. While its legal basis, the Office of Communications Act (OCA) received royal assent on 19 March 2002, Ofcom was only given a pair of running shoes on 29 December 2003.[787] The transitory period of more than one and a half years between its statutory creation and the actual commencement of its activities is proof of the intensive remodelling of the regulatory framework in the UK at the turn of the new millennium. In fact, the trimming of several regulatory bodies and their consolidation into one necessitated a preliminary phase for cooperation and structural reform. In addition, the OCA merely installed the new regulator but refrained from conferring any powers on Ofcom. The delegation of functions was eventually accomplished by the CA.[788] Rather than being the result of a crisis, Ofcom constitutes a "creature of convergence" and a product of the "digital revolution".[789] Due to its vast amount of functions relating to both, the regulation of content and infrastructure, it has been characterised as a "super-regulator".[790]

---

787 The Ofcom Chief Executive called it the "vesting day" Stephen Carter, "Address by Ofcom Chief Executive" (Royal Television Society Cambridge Convention, Cambridge, September 19, 2003), http://media.ofcom.org.uk/speeches/2003/royal-television-society-cambridge-convention-friday-19-september-2003/ (accessed 25.6.2013).

788 See Office of Communications Act 2002, Explanatory Notes, paras. 13, 14, 26.

789 Weinstein, "The Medium is the Message," p. 165; Carter, "Address by Ofcom Chief Executive.".

790 Crane, "Communications Reglator OFCOM," p. 37; Craufurd Smith et al., "The Independence of the UK and Finnish NRAs," p. 313; Stephanie Liston, "OFCOM – the Perfect Dish or a Recipe for Disaster?," *Entertainment Law Review* 14, no.

This denotation seems pithy but nonetheless captures the enormousness of Ofcom in contrast to prior regulators.[791]

More specifically, Ofcom absorbed five sector-specific regulatory bodies, namely the Broadcasting Standards Commission, the Director General of Telecommunications, the Independent Television Commission, the Radio Authority and the Secretary of State regulating the Radiocommunications Agency.[792] Hence, Ofcom is in charge of the regulation of telecommunications, broadcasting and new media services, radio, communications networks, spectrum management and certain aspects of competition law.[793] In 2011, the postal service's regulator Postcomm was also merged

2 (2003): p. 19; Weinstein refers to Ofcom as a "super-size regulator", a "super-agency" or a "supra-regulator". See Weinstein, "The Medium is the Message," pp. 161, 171.

791 Gibbons posits that "Ofcom is the sum of its predecessors and that gives it considerable authority", Gibbons, "'Club Government' and Independence in Media Regulation," p. 53.

792 See the Ofcom, Regulator Archives, available at http://www.ofcom.org.uk/website/regulator-archives/ (accessed 2.9.2014). See also Office of Communications Act 2002, Explanatory Notes, para. 3.

793 In the field of competition law, Ofcom shares responsibility with the Office of Fair Trading (OFT) which is the primary regulator. In the communications industry, Ofcom is entitled to conduct market investigations, to advice the OFT on newspaper mergers and bring enforcement actions jointly with the OFT. Stuart Weinstein, "OFCOM, Information-Convergence and the Never Ending Drizzle of Electric Rain," *International Journal of Communications Law and Policy*, no. 8 (2004 2003): pp. 34–37; Doyle and Vick, "The Communications Act 2003," pp. 83–85; Smartt, *Media and Entertainment Law*, p. 425. The Coalition Government headed by Prime Minister Cameron had announced to cut red tape and make administration more efficient by curbing the powers of a great number of national regulatory bodies (quangos) including the fusion of some and the transferal of power from the regulator to the government. With regards to Ofcom, its policy setting role was considered especially critical by the Coalition Government which intended to return some functions to the Secretary of State for Culture, Olympics, Media and Sport (SoS). To this end, an order was drafted in 2013 which would have modified Ofcom's public service remit (by modifying Sec. 264 CA) by granting the SoS the power to determine whether a review of public service broadcasters should be carried out. The Public Bodies Order 2013 is available at http://www.legislation.gov.uk/ukdsi/2013/9780111101919/introduction (accessed 18.9.2014). It was argued that this change would remove "the rigidity of when these reviews have to happen, and [would] ensure that when they do they will be timely, and of relevant scope". See Eplanatory Memorandum to Order 2013, available at https://www.gov.uk/government/uploads/system/uploads/attachment_data/file/224604/130717_Explanatory_document__Final__1707__6_.p

with Ofcom. The construction of just one regulatory body acting as the umbrella aimed at furthering a coherent and consistent regulatory approach in light of media convergence. Yet, Weinstein opines that "Parliament has posited in Ofcom the responsibility for administering and developing the electronic 'nervous system' for Britain".[794] At its outset, skepticism about this giant squid Ofcom and mistrust towards its powers was palpable. It was argued that a range of regulators (as opposed to a unified regulator) was beneficial for the purpose of defending independence and resisting capture and political pressure.[795] Dispersing regulatory power according to communications sectors was considered necessary for the pursuit of social and cultural goals that otherwise could be sacrificed too easily for economic goals.[796] With a view to broadcast regulation, there was "great concern that this authority of Ofcom [would] be misused so as to direct licence holders to produce certain kinds of content in favour of others".[797]

Similarly, the drafting of a Broadcast Code, with which Ofcom was charged, appeared to some scholars as a "political minefield" due to the sensitive decisions which the regulator would inevitably have to make.[798]

---

df (accessed 18.9.2014). After a public outcry over the trimming of Ofcom's powers, the Government announced in February 2014 that it would withdraw the draft Ofcom Order. See "Government drops plans to reduce television powers of media regulator Ofcom, the Independent of 24.2.2014, available at http://www.independent.co.uk/news/media/government-drops-plans-to-reduce-television-powers-of-media-regulator-ofcom-9148778.html (accessed 18.9.2014) after the House of Lords communications committee chaired by Lord Inglewood recommended in a report submitted at the beginning of February 2014 that Ofcom should retain powers to regulate media plurality issues including its drafting of periodical reviews. See Select Committee on Communications, 1st report of session 2013-14, Media plurality, published 4.2.2014, paras. 196, 200, available at http://www.publications.parliament.uk/pa/ld201314/ldselect/ldcomm/120/120.pdf (accessed 18.9.2014), see also Sweney, Mark, "Ofcom should have final say on media takeovers, say peers", in The Guardian of 4.2.2014, available at http://www.theguardian.com/media/2014/feb/04/ofcom-final-say-media-takeovers-peers (accessed 18.9.2014). Still, Government is convinced that modifications remain necessary and is fathoming out what it could do.

794 Weinstein, "Information-Convergence and OFCOM," p. 2.

795 Crane, "Communications Reglator OFCOM," p. 38.

796 Doyle and Vick, "The Communications Act 2003," p. 91.

797 Weinstein, "The Medium Is the Message," p. 168; see also Feintuck and Varney, *Media Regulation, Public Interest and the Law*, p. 158.

798 Sec. 3 (2) (f) CA. See also Weinstein, "The Medium is the Message," p. 169.

In the field of competition law, a sinister picture was painted of "an all-singing, all-dancing supra-regulator [which] evokes images of Ofcom SWAT teams launching dawn raids, powerful individuals controlling the entire media and communications industry exercising sweeping powers of investigation and enforcement under the competition legislation, blocking mergers at will, unanswerable to Parliament".[799] In spite of all this doom-mongering, Ofcom gradually gained the respect of the industry as well as the public and has turned into a role model "converged" regulator which is imitated across Europe.[800]

b) Functions

By virtue of Sec. 2 (1) CA, the functions of previous regulators are transferred to Ofcom. These are outlined in schedule 1 attached to the CA and include, inter alia, the licensing of broadcast services and the enforcement of requirements of fairness and privacy in broadcasting.[801] In carrying out its functions, Ofcom's general duties are twofold: first, "to further the interests of citizens in relation to communications matters" and second, "to further the interests of consumers in relevant markets, where appropriate by promoting competition".[802] Apart from consumer's interests in "choice, price, quality of service and value for money", Ofcom is to pursue policies in the public interest taking into account cultural objectives like media pluralism and diversity.[803] Ofcom's first Chief Executive Stephen Carter

799 Liston, "OFCOM – the Perfect Dish or a Recipe for Disaster?," p. 23.
800 Craufurd Smith et al., "The Independence of the UK and Finnish NRAs," pp. 297, 307; Weinstein, "The Medium Is the Message," p. 162.
801 Sec. 3 and 13 of Schedule 1 of the CA.
802 Sec. 3 (1) (a) and (b) CA.
803 Sec. 3 (5) CA. The provision stipulating Ofcom's general duties, above all, the explicit mentioning of the protection of citizens' interest, were subject to intense discussions before the CA was adopted. While the government introduced the term "customer" in the bill of May 2002, Lord Puttnam (in his report of 2002) and other public interest groups insisted on the explicit inclusion of the term "citizen" in the bill. For a chronology of events see Lunt and Livingstone, *Media Regulation, Governance and the Interests of Citizens and Consumers*, pp. 45–58; for the report see David Puttnam, "Joint Committee on Draft Communications Bill, Report" (House of Lords, House of Commons, July 25, 2002), http://www.publications.parliament.uk/pa/jt200102/jtselect/jtcom/169/16901.htm (accessed 8.9.2014); see also Doyle and Vick, "The Communications Act 2003," p. 77.

in a speech at the Royal Television Society Cambridge Convention in September 2003 stated that "it is this interlinked interest of the citizen-consumer that will be the benchmark against which Ofcom's decisions will be checked".[804] This two-fold obligation to serve the citizen as well as the consumer has been criticised. Craufurt Smith is unbelieving noting that "these interests at time coincide but at others conflict, thereby projecting Ofcom into a contested policy arena".[805] Where these duties clash, Ofcom will unavoidably have to prioritise one over the other. According to Lunt and Livingstone, Ofcom has been disproportionately committed to serving consumers while lacking a coherent approach towards furthering citizens' interests.[806] The relatively clear framework to protect consumers (ensure quality of services for adequate prices) marks a sharp contrast to the ambiguities surrounding the notion of the "citizen". According to Lunt and Livingstone, Ofcom itself "gives the impression of being more comfortable dealing with consumer than with citizenship issues".[807] Whether or not the criticism, in its depth, is justified, cannot be elaborated in full in this study.

804 Carter, "Address by Ofcom Chief Executive.".

805 Craufurd Smith et al., "The Independence of the UK and Finnish NRAs," p. 308; similarly, Lunt and Livingstone, *Media Regulation, Governance and the Interests of Citizens and Consumers*, pp. 115, 180.

806 Lunt and Livingstone, *Media Regulation, Governance and the Interests of Citizens and Consumers*, p. 62; the consumer/citizen discrepancy is best exemplified by an Ofcom consultation on Citizens, Communications and Convergence and the subsequent (rather meagre) statement by Ofcom of 2010 which proposed a distinct "citizen" toolkit for future policy appraisals conducted by Ofcom managers, see Ofcom, "Citizens, Communications and Convergence, Discussion Paper," November 7, 2008, http://stakeholders.ofcom.org.uk/binaries/consultations/citizens/summary/discussionpaper.pdf (accessed 8.9.2014); Ofcom, "Citizens, Communications and Convergence, A Summary of Stakeholder Responses, and Our next Steps," June 4, 2010, paras. 4.34, 5.2, pp. 11, 13, http://stakeholders.ofcom.org.uk/binaries/consultations/citizens/statement/Citizen_Statement.pdf (accessed 8.9.2014); similar criticism is voiced by Doyle and Vick who evaluate Ofcom's review of the PSB landscape and find that Ofcom's Phase 1 report published in April 2004 "chime[s] closely with the blueprint laid out for it by the Government via the Communications Act 2003". Doyle and Vick, "The Communications Act 2003," p. 91.

807 Lunt and Livingstone, *Media Regulation, Governance and the Interests of Citizens and Consumers*, pp. 44–62; Gibbons agrees that when Ofcom was established, a high proportion of its staff appeared to have an economics background, thus reflecting "a "consumer" rather than a "citizen" perspective", leading to concerns that it was not sufficiently committed to the public interest goals within its remit". Gibbons however takes a more positive stance arguing that today, Ofcom

What is highlighted in this section is the evident discrepancy between the dual statutory responsibilities of Ofcom and the market approach that the regulator has endorsed since its inception.

More specifically, Ofcom is to secure, among others, the "availability (…) of a wide range of television (…) services (…) of high quality and calculated to appeal to a variety of tastes and interests", as well as the "maintenance of a sufficient plurality of providers of different television (…) services".[808] In addition, the regulator is to apply and enforce specific standards which, inter alia, protect certain values like fairness and privacy and protect the public from offensive and harmful content.[809] In relation to non-linear audiovisual media services, the CA's initial scope of application did not cover VOD services. Subsequent to two amending regulations of 2009 and 2010, Ofcom acquired powers to regulate VOD services. The amendments were integrated in a new part 4A entitled "On-demand programme services".

Interestingly, in performing its duties, Ofcom may have recourse to alternative forms of regulation and consider the "desirability of promoting and facilitating the development and use of effective forms of self-regulation".[810] Co-regulation is not mentioned in this context. Yet, when taking into account the principle that regulatory action will only be taken where appropriate[811] and the requirement that Ofcom review its activities and "roll back"[812] regulation where unnecessary costs are incurred,[813] self- and also co- regulation represent less intrusive means of regulation.[814] In fact, Ofcom has committed to reducing the red tape of regulation by making it more efficient.[815] To this end, Ofcom has developed into a research hub,

---

has a "more balanced approach". See Gibbons, "'Club Government' and Independence in Media Regulation," p. 54 et seq.

808 Sec. 3 (2) (c), (d) CA.

809 Sec. 3 (2) (e), (f) CA.

810 Sec. 3 (4) (c) CA.

811 Sec. 3 (3) (a) CA.

812 Franklin, Bob, ed., *British Television Policy: A Reader* (London: Routledge, 2001), p. 174.

813 Sec. 6 (1) CA.

814 Roßnagel, Kleist and Scheuer even speak of a continuing trend to delegation of regulatory tasks. See Roßnagel, Kleist and Scheuer, *Die Reform der Regulierung elektronischer Medien in Europa*, p. 280.

815 Lunt and Livingstone, *Media Regulation, Governance and the Interests of Citizens and Consumers*, p. 68.

producing enormous volumes of research, conducting *ex ante* impact assessments and large-scale public consultations.[816] Hence, the CA with its "programme of deregulatory 'reform'" has allowed Ofcom to take recourse to alternative forms of regulation. [817]

### c) Composition and funding

Ofcom was set up as a body corporate under the OCA.[818] Sec. 1 (9) OCA safeguards its independence from the state.[819] In view of Ofcom's concrete composition, the OCA remains imprecise, stipulating that the Secretary of State for Culture, Media and Sport (SoS) determines the precise number of members (executive and non-executive), appointing a chairman from Ofcom's members.[820] The OCA nonetheless clarifies that there is a majority of non-executive members.[821] The selection of Ofcom's members follows a process regulated by the Commissioner for Public Appointments (so-called Nolan processes) that is based on a public call for applications and

---

816 Lunt and Livingstone, *Media Regulation, Governance and the Interests of Citizens and Consumers*, pp. 69, 78,80. While admitting that Ofcom has established an innovative approach which relies on extensive investments in scientific evidence and research, Lunt and Livingstone are also critical about its limits. They note that not all public interest groups are resourced to participate in Ofcom's consultations or refute its evidence.

817 Doyle and Vick, "The Communications Act 2003," p. 86.

818 Sec. 1 (1) OCA.

819 For more information on the independence of UK regulators, see Hans Bredow Institut für Medienforschung et al., "INDIREG, Indicators for Independence and Efficient Functioning of Audiovisual Media Services Regulatory Bodies for the Purpose of Enforcing the Rules in the AVMS Directive, Study Conducted on Behalf of the European Commission, Final Report," February 2011, pp. 292–96, http://ec.europa.eu/archives/information_society/avpolicy/docs/library/studies/regulators/final_report.pdf; see also Michael Begg, "INDIREG Annex II Country Tables, United Kingdom," February 2011, http://www.indireg.eu/wp-content/uploads/Annex_II-_CountryTables_UK.pdf; the INDIREG findings are up-dated in a new AVMS RADAR study of 2015, see Mark Cole et al., "Update on Recent Changes and Developments in Member States and Candidate Countries That Are Relevant for the Analysis of Independence and Efficient Functioning of Audiovisual Media Services Regulatory Bodies (SMART 2013/0083)," 2015, http://publications.europa.eu/en/publication-detail/-/publication/b6e4a837-8775-11e5-b8b7-01aa75ed71a1/language-en (all websites accessed 4.9.2016).

820 Sec. 1 (3), (4) OCA.

821 Sec. 1 (6) (b) OCA.

open competition. Today, the Ofcom board comprises 9 members[822] including Chairman Dame Patricia Hodgson, who was appointed in April 2014 to serve a three year term and Sharon White, who took over as Chief Executive from Ed Richards in March 2015.[823] Apart from Sharon White, the board consists of two further executive members.[824]

In general, the board provides "strategic direction", setting the agenda and oversees the fulfilment of Ofcom's statutory duties.[825] According to the Board Procedures laid down by Ofcom, the quorum is five board members (including the Chairman or Deputy Chairman) provided that a majority of non-executive board members is present.[826] Decisions of the board are generally taken by consensus. If members do not agree, a vote will be taken. In case of a tied vote, the Chairman has the decisive vote.[827] The Board has delegated the fulfilment of certain statutory missions to other committees and boards that act under precisely defined terms.[828] Ofcom's twin duties pursuant to the CA are replicated in two bodies,[829] the Content Board and the Consumer Panel which was renamed the Communications Consumer Panel in 2008.[830] The latter is a peculiarly hybrid body as it operates externally offering advice on consumer-related policy

---

822 Para. 1 of the Ofcom Board Procedures specifies that the maximum number of board members is 10. See Ofcom, Board Procedures, available at http://www.ofcom.org.uk/about/how-ofcom-is-run/ofcom-board/board-procedures/ (accessed 2.9.2014).

823 See Ofcom Members, available at http://www.ofcom.org.uk/about/how-ofcom-is-run/ofcom-board/members/ (accessed 2.9.2014).

824 When Ofcom was established, the composition of its board was subject to public debate criticising the recruitment of "superstars" from the private sector who allegedly lacked experience and knowledge about the management of bureaucratic bodies. See "Off Target at Ofcom, The Media Regulator Needs Fewer Luvvies and More Sense," *The Times*, February 2, 2004.

825 Ofcom, Functions and Role, available at http://www.ofcom.org.uk/about/how-ofcom-is-run/ofcom-board/function-and-role/ (accessed 2.9.2014).

826 Ofcom, Board Procedures, para. 5.

827 Ofcom, Board Procedures, para. 12.

828 Ofcom, "The Office of Communications, Annual Report and Accounts for the Period 1 April 2013 to 31 March 2014," July 2014, pp. 50, 51, http://www.ofcom.org.uk/files/2014/07/annrep1314.pdf (accessed 4.9.2014).

829 Sec. 12 (1) and 16 (2) CA.

830 The Coalition Government (composed of Conservative Party and the Liberal Democrats elected in 2010) headed by Prime Minister Cameron proposed to subsume several consumer panels including the Communications Consumer Panel in the umbrella organisation Citizens Advice (see http://www.citizensadvice.org.uk

aspects, while being funded by the regulator.[831] The Content Board represents the citizens' interests in content-related matters as reflected in broadcast standards, a realm expressly withdrawn from the remit of the Communications Consumer Panel.[832] In total, Ofcom had 795 employees as at the end of March 2016.[833]

As a result of the economic crisis and the British government's subsequent efforts to curtail public spending, Ofcom underwent a significant reorganisation in 2011 following the Expenditure Review Project which began in 2010.[834] Accordingly, internal processes were rationalised and made more efficient, staff made redundant and certain projects were discontinued. Ofcom's 2015/2016 budget is fixed at GBP 114 million (the Treasury sets the overall level of spending), which is a reduction in expenditure by roughly 30 percent compared to its 2010/2011 budget.[835] Ofcom is funded mainly by fees levied on service providers[836] and it receives a modest contribution by the state.[837] In 2015/2016 Ofcom collected GBP 270 million for the state budget generated from licensing services and imposing fines on negligent providers.[838] These figures demonstrate the sheer size and massiveness of Ofcom, which is contingent on the state of

---

/, accessed 3.10.2013) to provide for one unified voice representing consumer interests. So far, the Communications Consumer Panel continues to exist (see http://www.communicationsconsumerpanel.org.uk/index.php, accessed 13.10.2013) and no statutory instrument has been adopted to amend Sec. 16 (2) CA, the legal basis of the Panel. See also Lunt and Livingstone, *Media Regulation, Governance and the Interests of Citizens and Consumers*, pp. 75–76, 81–82.

831 Lunt and Livingstone, *Media Regulation, Governance and the Interests of Citizens and Consumers*, p. 75.

832 Sec. 16 (5) CA.

833 Ofcom, "The Office of Communications, Annual Report and Accounts for the Period 1 April 2015 to 31 March 2016," July 2016, p. 82, http://www.ofcom.org.uk/content/about/annual-reports-plans/annual-reports/annual-report-15-16/Ofcom_Annual_Report_2015-2016.pdf (accessed 2.8.2016).

834 Ofcom reorganisation, available at http://www.ofcom.org.uk/about/ofcom-reorganisation/ (accessed 4.9.2014). See also Sweney, Mark, 2011, Ofcom to cut 170 jobs and reduce budget by 28.2 percent over four years, the Guardian, available at http://www.theguardian.com/media/2010/oct/21/ofcom-job-losses-spending-review (accessed 4.9.2014).

835 Ofcom, "Annual Report 2015/2016," pp. 11, 42.

836 Sec. 38 and 347 CA. See also OCA Explanatory Notes, para. 26.

837 Begg, "INDIREG Country Tables UK," p. 22, table 25; Craufurd Smith et al., "The Independence of the UK and Finnish NRAs," p. 311.

838 Ofcom, "Annual Report 2015/2016," p. 42.

the public purse. In sum, Ofcom has established considerable standing during the first roughly ten years of its activities. It has acquired a "powerful position in the UK communications market [that] has enabled it to act both as referee and influential policy entrepreneur" underlined by its evidence-based approach and extensive consultations and collaborations with stakeholders.[839] Above all, it "has created a new, more open, accountable and egalitarian environment in which policy issues can be debated within society".[840] Still, the balancing exercise Ofcom is required to carry out, reconciling public interest objectives with economic imperatives, remains a defining feature of its existence.

d) Broadcast regulation

In light of Ofcom's new regulatory approach, Ofcom's Chief Executive Stephen Carter foreshadowed in 2003 that

> "in broadcasting, we will seek to umpire or police where necessary or required, but to facilitate where possible. (...) Regulation in broadcasting has historically been to stop things going wrong and no doubt there will be policing to be done. But Ofcom should be oxygen rather than the fire extinguisher. Importantly, independent of Government, our aim will be to serve the audience's interest and to help secure a flourishing communications industry".[841]

This mission statement echoes Ofcom's general duties of promoting the availability and plurality of content broadcast on UK television as stipulated by the CA.[842] In addition, broadcast regulation also encompasses the establishment of standards pursuant to Sec. 319 CA which are contained in the Ofcom Broadcasting Code (Ofcom Code or Code).[843] The Ofcom Code is generally applicable to all radio and television programme services, except for the BBC, the UK's public service broadcaster (PSB) which is subject to special rules and oversight. As it is tasked with the regulation of content, the Ofcom Content Board is primarily responsible

839 Craufurd Smith et al., "The Independence of the UK and Finnish NRAs," p. 312.
840 Craufurd Smith et al., "The Independence of the UK and Finnish NRAs," p. 312.
841 Carter, "Address by Ofcom Chief Executive.".
842 Sec. 3 (2) (e), (f) CA.
843 The Ofcom Broadcasting Code, May 2016, available at http://stakeholders.ofcom.org.uk/binaries/broadcast/code-may16/Ofcom_Broadcast_Code_May_2016.pdf (accessed 3.6.2016).

for devising the Code.[844] After a mandatory[845] consultation from July to October 2004, the Ofcom Code was originally adopted in May 2005 and repeatedly modified thereafter.[846] The most recent version of 9 May 2016 consists of ten sections which can be structured according to three themes: Sec. 1-6 lay down standards, Sec. 7-8 concern fairness and privacy and Sec. 9 and 10 regulate commercial matters.[847]

In assessing compliance with the Code, Ofcom considers the context in which the material is aired.[848] In more detail, the protection of minors is ensured by "appropriate scheduling" and respect for the watershed times, meaning that before specified times, unsuitable content is prohibited.[849] Generally, offensive material (e.g. material which glorifies violent or anti-social behaviour)[850] or content which incites the commitment of crimes is impermissible.[851] Broadcasters are furthermore required to responsibly broadcast religious programmes and exercise due impartiality and accuracy in relation to news programmes.[852] The requirement of objective coverage is especially pertinent during times of election and referendums.[853] With a view to the persons or organisations affected by specific programmes, broadcasters are obliged to ensure that these are treated fairly and that contributors have, for instance, consented to being included in a programme.[854] In addition, the privacy of persons is protected, including the procurement of material that is subsequently screened.[855] Finally, when commercial references such as product placement or sponsorship credits are included in programmes, transparency requirements apply and

844 Lunt and Livingstone, *Media Regulation, Governance and the Interests of Citizens and Consumers*, p. 81.

845 Sec. 324 CA.

846 Feintuck and Varney, *Media Regulation, Public Interest and the Law*, p. 186.

847 Mac Sithigh, "Convergence, The Impact of Broadcast Regulation on Telecommunications," p. 676.

848 Ofcom, How to use the Code, March 2013, p. 5, available at http://stakeholders.ofcom.org.uk/binaries/broadcast/831190/howtousethecode.pdf (accessed 17.9.2014).

849 Sec. 1 of the Ofcom Code (Protecting the Under-Eighteens).

850 Sec. 2 of the Ofcom Code (Harm and Offense).

851 Sec. 3 of the Ofcom Code (Crime).

852 Sec. 4 of the Ofcom Code (Religion), Sec. 5 of the Ofcom Code (Due Impartiality and Due Accuracy and Undue Prominence of Views and Opinions).

853 Sec. 6 of the Ofcom Code (Elections and Referendums).

854 Sec. 7 of the Ofcom Code (Fairness).

855 Sec. 8 the Ofcom Code (Privacy).

broadcaster's independence is protected.[856] In setting these standards, Ofcom took into account the criteria outlined in Sec. 319 (4) CA which include, among others, "the degree of harm or offence", "the likely size and composition of the potential audience" as well as "the likely expectation[s] of the audience".

To fulfil its obligations pursuant to Sec. 319 (2) CA, Ofcom has adopted several other Codes apart from the Broadcasting Code. Above all, the Code on the Scheduling of Television Advertising regulates the quantity of advertising and transposes the advertising rules contained in the AVMSD.[857] The Code on Sports and Other Listed and Designated Events guarantees the coverage, live or deferred, of important (sports) events on free TV, thereby implementing Art. 14 AVMSD.[858] Moreover, in order to enhance the accessibility of programmes by persons suffering from a visual or hearing disability, the Code on Television Access Services sets out detailed requirements on sign language, subtitling and audio description in line with Art. 7 AVMSD.[859]

Complaints about alleged violations of the Codes can be brought by the public[860] or be initiated by Ofcom.[861] Viewers alleging misconduct may

---

856 Sec. 9 of the Ofcom Code (Commercial References in Television Programming). Sec. 10 of the Ofcom Code lays out similar transparency requirements for radio programmes.

857 See Ofcom Code on the scheduling of television advertising, updated 20.12.2010, available at http://stakeholders.ofcom.org.uk/binaries/broadcast/other-codes/tacode.pdf (accessed 17.9.2014).

858 See Ofcom Code on Sports and Other Listed and Designated Events, 4.7.2014, available at http://stakeholders.ofcom.org.uk/binaries/broadcast/other-codes/ofcom_code_on_sport.pdf (accessed 17.9.2014).

859 See Ofcom Code on Television Access Services, published 18.12.2012, available at http://stakeholders.ofcom.org.uk/binaries/broadcast/other-codes/tv-access-services-2013.pdf (accessed 17.9.2014).

860 See Ofcom Procedures for investigating breaches of content standards for television and radio, published 1.6.2011, available at http://stakeholders.ofcom.org.uk/binaries/broadcast/guidance/june2011/breaches-content-standards.pdf, (accessed 17.9.2014), see also Ofcom TV & Radio complaints, Advice and Complaints, available at http://consumers.ofcom.org.uk/complain/tv-and-radio-complaints/ (accessed 17.9.2014).

861 Mac Sithigh, "Convergence, The Impact of Broadcast Regulation on Telecommunications," p. 677.

submit a complaint form (available on Ofcom's website)[862] within 20 working days of the broadcast of the relevant programme.[863] On the basis of a copy of the programme at issue (which Ofcom may ask of broadcasters), Ofcom makes an initial assessment within 15 working days.[864] Where Ofcom finds that a complaint is substantiated, an in-depth investigation is carried out typically involving representations by the broadcaster.[865] Ofcom prepares a preliminary view subject to change in light of additional material provided by the broadcaster or third parties. Its final decisions as well as the outcomes of initial assessments are published fortnightly in the Broadcast Bulletin.[866] Ofcom determines whether the broadcaster is in breach or not in breach or whether the matter has been resolved. In general, judicial review of Ofcom decisions concerning procedural issues is before the High Court.[867] Where Ofcom holds that a matter raises severe issues under the Codes and the broadcaster acted "seriously, deliberately, repeatedly, or recklessly", it may consider the imposition of statutory sanctions.[868]

The sanctions include "a decision to issue a direction not to repeat a programme or advertisement, issue a direction to broadcast a correction or a statement of Ofcom's findings [broadcast in a form and at a time determined by Ofcom], impose a financial penalty, shorten or suspend a licence and/or revoke a licence".[869] Financial penalties are determined in accordance with Sec. 392 CA in conjunction with Ofcom's Penalty Guidelines[870] and may reach GBP 250,000 or 5 percent of broadcasters qualify-

862 The complaint forms concerning the content of television or radio programmes are available at http://consumers.ofcom.org.uk/complain/tv-and-radio-complaints/a-programme-I-saw-or-heard/ (accessed 17.9.2014).

863 Sec. 1.13 of the Ofcom Procedures for investigating breaches.

864 Sec. 1.18-1.21 of the Ofcom Procedures for investigating breaches.

865 Sec. 1.22 of the Ofcom Procedures for investigating breaches.

866 Sec. 1.20, 1.30 of the Ofcom Procedures for investigating breaches.

867 Begg, "INDIREG Country Tables UK," sec. 32, pp. 28, 29.

868 See Ofcom Procedures for the consideration of statutory sanctions in breaches of broadcast licences, Sec. 1.15, available at http://stakeholders.ofcom.org.uk/binaries/broadcast/guidance/proceduresjuly2013/Procedures_for_consideration.pdf (accessed 17.9.2014).

869 Sec. 1.11 of the Ofcom Procedures for the consideration of statutory sanctions. See also Mac Sithigh, "Convergence, The Impact of Broadcast Regulation on Telecommunications," p. 678.

870 Ofcom Penalty Guidelines, published 13.6.2011, available at http://www.ofcom.org.uk/files/2010/06/penguid.pdf (accessed 17.9.2014).

ing revenue whichever is greater.[871] Sanction decisions are published on Ofcom's website and a summary is included in the Broadcast Bulletin.[872] In the period of 2013/2014, Ofcom imposed financial penalties on nine broadcasters collecting a total of GBP 317,500.[873] Two broadcasters, Al Ehya Digital Television Limited and DM Digital Television Limited were fined respectively GBP 85,000 which amounted to the highest sanctions imposed in this period. In general, the graduated catalogue of sanctions at Ofcom's disposal appears adequate to react to broadcaster's misconduct. It gives Ofcom, who bears the burden of proof, effective and deterring instruments ranging from warnings (or directions) to more painful measures affecting broadcaster's finances or standing and reputation within British society.

## 2. The Authority for Television On-Demand

### a) The UK Government: paving the way for co-regulation of VOD services

The CA's liberal and deregulatory *raison d'être* foreshadowed the British government's approach to the implementation of the AVMSD. When transposition of the Directive was prepared, the government headed by Labour Prime Minister Gordon Brown announced its intention to construct a co-regulatory system for the regulation of non-linear audiovisual media services. Under the aegis of the Department for Culture, Media and Sport (DCMS) a three-month consultation took place in mid-2008 enquiring stakeholders about their views on the most appropriate regulatory arrangements.[874] The consultation also encompassed questions about the notion of a VOD service and its scope of application, the regulation of product placement, the regulation of third country satellite channels using an

871 Sec. 1.11 of the Ofcom Procedures for the consideration of statutory sanctions.

872 Sec. 1.29 of the Ofcom Procedures for the consideration of statutory sanctions.

873 Ofcom, "Annual Report 2013/2014," p. 120.

874 Department for Culture, Media and Sport, "The Audiovisual Media Services Directive, Consultation on Proposals for Implementation in the United Kingdom," July 2008, http://webarchive.nationalarchives.gov.uk/20100407120701/http://www.culture.gov.uk/images/consultations/AVMS_Consultation_Document.pdf (accessed 17.9.2014).

uplink situated in the UK and wider competition law aspects.[875] With regards to the type of regulation, the British government laid down its position in detail, revealing a clear preference for co-regulation. Quoting recital 44 AVMSD in conjunction with Art. 4 (7) AVMSD, the British government posited that the transposition of the Directive into the national legal order necessitated either state intervention or the establishment of a co-regulatory scheme.[876] The involvement of the industry in setting the standards and enforcing them militated in favour of co-regulation.[877] It followed that "there would need to be legislation which allowed either the Government or Ofcom, as the national regulator, to intervene- but only if strictly necessary, and as a last resort- in order to ensure that the content standards required by the Directive were met. However, for the most part, the scheme would be expected to operate independently, with little if any intervention by Government or Ofcom".[878]

In general, the consultation distinguished between the regulation of programme content and the regulation of advertising, both of which should be pursued by co-regulatory means. This study focuses on the regulation of VOD services and the establishment of ATVOD. The CA did not cover VOD services, which remained unregulated by statutory tools until the 2009 and 2010 amendments implementing the AVMSD. Nonetheless, several self-regulatory bodies existed enforcing their codes of practice on providers who would voluntarily abide by them. At that time, content regulation was undertaken by two self-regulatory bodies, the Association for Television On-Demand (ATVOD) and the Independent Mobile Classification Body (IMCB). Importantly, the British government considered that self-regulatory standards could not simply be extended to the whole sector but required a more comprehensive recalibration of the legal framework to meet the objectives prescribed by the Directive.[879] In addition, advertising in VOD services as other forms of non-broadcast advertising

875 For a full list of the 47 questions, see Department for Culture, Media and Sport, "DCMS Consultation on the Implementation of the AVMSD," pp. 81–84 (part 6).

876 Department for Culture, Media and Sport, "DCMS Consultation on the Implementation of the AVMSD," para. 4, p. 21.

877 Department for Culture, Media and Sport, "DCMS Consultation on the Implementation of the AVMSD," para. 5, p. 21.

878 Department for Culture, Media and Sport, "DCMS Consultation on the Implementation of the AVMSD," para. 5, p. 21.

879 Department for Culture, Media and Sport, "DCMS Consultation on the Implementation of the AVMSD," p. 41.

were overseen by the Committee of Advertising Practice (CAP), a self-regulatory body under the auspices of the Advertising Standards Authority (ASA). With respect to content regulation,[880] the British government proposed three models.[881] Firstly, the government would directly assign powers to the responsible co-regulatory authority.[882] Yet, the British government acknowledged the inflexibility of government to respond to system failure or other ensuing problems, submitting that Ofcom would be better positioned to find flexible and effective solutions.[883] Secondly, Ofcom would be empowered to delegate functions to the co-regulatory institution.[884] This model would reflect the successful co-regulatory scheme in

880 In view of commercial messages, the UK government outlined four options for the future regulatory framework. First, the ASA would continue to regulate advertising in VOD services, thereby acting as a "one stop shop for all public complaints and concerns about advertising in the UK". Second, advertising matters could be covered by the body responsible for the regulation of programme content. This would promote this body as a "one-stop-shop or shops for all aspects of video-on-demand services" but it would also undermine the ASA. Third, government considered the setting up of another regulatory body admitting that the introduction of yet another regulator "would not seem to offer any particular benefit". Fourth, the government contemplated that the body responsible for the regulation of content could further delegate this aspect. Yet, government was aware of the "potentially clumsy and lengthy process" and clearly expressed its support for the ASA as the tried flagship being in charge. The differentiation between the regulation of advertising and the regulation of programme content had proven successful for broadcast and radio and was regarded as similarly promising for other media. See Department for Culture, Media and Sport, "DCMS Consultation on the Implementation of the AVMSD," paras. 29–31, pp. 31-32.

881 Preceding the government's proposal, several requirements for the co-regulatory structure were enumerated such as "transparency to the public and to industry", "incentives for video-on-demand providers to participate in the scheme", "incentives for video-on-demand providers to comply with the rules", "flexibility and future proofing" and "complaints handling, appeals and enforcement" some of which are regarded as necessary safeguards for effective and fair co-regulation (see above). Department for Culture, Media and Sport, "DCMS Consultation on the Implementation of the AVMSD," paras. 9, 11–19, pp. 22-23.

882 Department for Culture, Media and Sport, "DCMS Consultation on the Implementation of the AVMSD," para. 24, p. 24.

883 Department for Culture, Media and Sport, "DCMS Consultation on the Implementation of the AVMSD," para. 30, p. 25.

884 Department for Culture, Media and Sport, "DCMS Consultation on the Implementation of the AVMSD," para. 31, p. 25.

place for the regulation of broadcast advertising.[885] Thirdly, the government proposed that Ofcom itself be mandated to regulate VOD services.[886] However, "there would be a downside for the video-on-demand industry, which would have no part in the ownership or operation of the arrangements. The UK would have turned its back on the effective self-regulatory arrangements in this area that have been pioneered by ATVOD and the IMCB".[887] Thus, the British government unequivocally expressed its support for Ofcom being in charge of delegating regulation of VOD services to a co-regulatory body.[888]

In March 2009, the British government published a summary of the 59 responses to the consultation.[889] A majority of respondents expressed broad support for the government's preferred approaches.[890] Therefore, Secretary of State for Culture, Media and Sport Andy Burnham announced

---

885 Department for Culture, Media and Sport, "DCMS Consultation on the Implementation of the AVMSD," para. 34, p. 25.

886 Department for Culture, Media and Sport, "DCMS Consultation on the Implementation of the AVMSD," para. 37, p. 26.

887 Department for Culture, Media and Sport, "DCMS Consultation on the Implementation of the AVMSD," para. 41, p. 26.

888 Department for Culture, Media and Sport, "DCMS Consultation on the Implementation of the AVMSD," para. 44, p. 27.

889 Department for Culture, Media and Sport, "Consultation on Proposals for the Implementation of the EU Audiovisual Media Services Directive in the United Kingdom, Summary of Responses," March 2009, http://webarchive.nationalarchives.gov.uk/20100407120701/http://www.culture.gov.uk/images/publications/summary_report.pdf (accessed 2.2.2013).

890 Interestingly, some stakeholders urged the government to give reasons why it had excluded self-regulation from the outset as a means to implement the Directive. Indeed, the UK government appeared to have neglected self-regulation on the sole grounds of recital 44 AVMSD which states that "while self-regulation might be a complementary method of implementing certain provisions of this Directive, it should not constitute a substitute for the obligations of the national legislator". Self-regulation is thus considered insufficient to implement and enforce the standards contained in the Directive. Most respondents to the consultation agreed with the British government that Ofcom was to retain backstop powers even if the co-regulator was to be responsible for the drafting, interpretation and monitoring of the rules. See Department for Culture, Media and Sport, "DCMS Summary of Responses to the Consultation on the Implementation of the AVMSD," paras. 5, 17, 20, 22, pp. 18–22; it is also interesting to note that in its response to the DCMS consultation of 2008, the BBFC argued that it should play a significant role in the regulation of VOD services arguing that regulation of non-linear services was more akin to the regulation of DVD rental and retail rather than the

on 11 March 2009 that Ofcom would be accorded powers to delegate the regulation of certain aspects of content provision to a co-regulatory body.[891] Ofcom would also be given powers to mandate the ASA for the regulation of advertising in VOD services including those types of commercials featured within programmes.

b) Ofcom: setting the starting block for co-regulation of VOD services

In response to the government's initiatives, Ofcom launched a further 6 weeks consultation in mid-September 2009 which concerned primarily two issues, namely the scope of VOD regulation and the design of the co-regulatory framework for "VOD editorial services [content regulation] and VOD advertising".[892] In this chapter, focus is laid on exploring the reasons and motives for co-regulation. In the document accompanying the consultation, Ofcom suggested that ATVOD be designated to regulate VOD editorial services and that ASA be designated to regulate VOD advertising.[893] Interestingly, self-regulation as an instrument of implementing the AVMSD was rejected from the outset. Referring to recital 44 AVMSD, which regards self-regulation as complementary to state involvement, Ofcom argued that "at a minimum, the AVMS Directive provides for a co-regulatory system in which the VOD industry takes responsibility for en-

regulation of broadcasting. Accordingly, consumers experienced "a virtual shop" and expected a similar level of regulation than that applicable to DVD or video rental stores. BBFC, "Department of Culture, Media and Sport Public Consultation on Implementing the EU Audiovisual Media Services Directive, The Response of the British Board of Film Classification," 2008, paras. 37, 62, 63, pp. 15, 22, http://webarchive.nationalarchives.gov.uk/20100407120701/http://www.culture.gov.uk/images/publications/BBFC.pdf (accessed 27.8.2014); see also Mac Sithigh, Daithi, "Co-Regulation, VOD and the Legal Status of Audio-Visual Media Status of," p. 61.

891 Written Ministerial Statements, Wednesday 11 March 2009, Column 15-18 WS, available at http://www.publications.parliament.uk/pa/cm200809/cmhansrd/cm090311/wmstext/90311m0001.htm#09031164000108 (accessed 28.7.2014).

892 Ofcom, "Proposals for the Regulation of Video on Demand Services, Consultation," September 14, 2009, http://stakeholders.ofcom.org.uk/binaries/consultations/vod/summary/vod.pdf (accessed 28.7.2014).

893 Ofcom, "Consultation for the Regulation of VOD Services," paras. 1.12, 1.17, pp. 2, 3.

suring content standards underpinned by statutory powers".[894] The voluntary nature of a self-regulatory scheme was viewed by Ofcom as insufficient to conform to the requirements of Union law. Co-regulation, by contrast, was firmly rooted in legislation and was thus preferable to exclusive regulation by industry.[895] In practice, Ofcom, though delegating regulatory tasks to an external authority, would be ultimately responsible as the competent public body and held accountable for the well functioning of the entire co-regulatory structure.[896] This arrangement would grant Ofcom backstop powers so that it could step in whenever the co-regulatory body would lose sight of the public interest.

Ofcom conducted an assessment of ATVOD's appropriateness in line with the statutory requirements (which came to be)[897] outlined in Sec. 368B (9) (a) – (e) CA as well as a series of criteria set out in its Principles for Analysing Self- and Co-regulation developed in 2004 and revised in 2008.[898] Several major UK VOD providers were members of ATVOD,

894 Ofcom, "Consultation for the Regulation of VOD Services," para. 5.8, p. 36.

895 For an overview of different forms of regulation, see figure 5 of Ofcom, "Consultation for the Regulation of VOD Services," para. 5.9, pp. 36-37.

896 Ofcom, "Consultation for the Regulation of VOD Services," para. 5.12, p. 37; Ofcom would retain regulatory powers for VOD services only in case an appropriate co-regulatory body could not be found, para. 5.13, p. 37.

897 Sec. 368B was inserted in the CA by means of a regulation of November 2009 which entered into force on 19 December 2009. Ofcom's consultation preceded the coming into force of the regulation and thus the introduction of Sec. 368B. In its consultation of September 2009, Ofcom therefore refers to the statutory criteria as stipulated in the proposed regulations which would only become binding by mid-December 2009. The 2009 regulations were supplemented by regulations of February 2010 detailing among others the notification system and the fees to be paid by VOD providers. These regulations came into force on 18 March 2010.

898 Ofcom's Principles for Analysing Self- and Co-regulation set out certain analytical steps which Ofcom follows in evaluating the potential role and use of self- and co-regulation in areas which Ofcom may be mandated to regulate. Ofcom clarified that it will apply these steps and criteria on a case-by-case basis taking into account the evolutionary nature of the market structure and changing consumer habits and interests (paras. 3.4-3.7, p. 14; paras. 4.2, 4.3, p. 18). Ofcom's assessment would proceed in two phases. First, a set of five questions would inquire about the appropriateness of self- and co-regulation (e.g. asking about whether a collective interest of the industry could be identified and whether that interest could be aligned with the interest of the public, para. 3.18, p. 16). Second, a number of good practice (or institutional) criteria including such values like "public awareness", "transparency", "enforcement measures" "system or re-

which was set up in 2003.[899] ATVOD's board comprised a representative of each member in addition to two independent board members. Service providers adhered to a code of practice enforced by ATVOD.[900] In order to meet the statutory conditions, ATVOD would remodel from a self-regulatory initiative to a responsible co-regulatory body.[901] This would imply, in particular, changes to its governing structure (especially the composition of its board and role of its chair and chief executive) to guarantee its independence of the industry and the modification of its code of practice to reflect the AVMSD's rules.[902] Although the documentation of the transformation of ATVOD from a self-regulatory to a co-regulatory body seems vast, there is, in fact, little known about the VOD Editorial Steering Group (VESG) which was incremental in developing the co-regulatory scheme.[903] At that time, the VESG was chaired by Antony Walker, the head of the Broadband Stakeholder Group,[904] an organisation founded in 2001 which today represents stakeholders across the media value-chain such as broadcasters, VOD providers, platform operators, internet service providers and mobile network operators, and advices the UK government

dress" would be considered to design the self- or co-regulatory regime (para. 4.25, p. 22). The Ofcom Principles demonstrate that Ofcom is acutely aware of the benefits and drawbacks of alternative forms of regulation as outlined above and attempts to mitigate potential disadvantages by broad stakeholder involvement and the prior analysis of the appropriateness of such forms of regulation on the basis of a set of uniform but sufficiently broad criteria and questions. See Ofcom, "Identifying Appropriate Regulatory Solutions: Principles for Analysing Self- and Co-Regulation, Statement," October 12, 2008, http://stakeholders.ofcom.org.uk/binaries/consultations/coregulation/statement/statement.pdf (accessed 30.7.2014).

899 Christopher Marsden, *Internet Co-Regulation, European Law, Regulatory Governance and Legitimacy in Cyberspace* (Cambridge: Cambridge University Press, 2011), p. 147.

900 Before being designated as a co-regulator, ATVOD had at its disposal a number of graduated sanctions like requiring the service provider to remedy the alleged violation, to require the service provider to reimburse the costs, to warn service providers or fine them. Ofcom, "Consultation for the Regulation of VOD Services," para. 3.8.1, p. 95, Annex 7.

901 Ofcom, "Consultation for the Regulation of VOD Services," para. 5.24, pp. 40, 41.

902 Ofcom, "Consultation for the Regulation of VOD Services," para. 5.31, p. 43.

903 Mac Sithigh, "Co-Regulation, VOD and the Legal Status of Audio-Visual Media Services," p. 55.

904 See http://www.broadbanduk.org/ (accessed 30.7.2014).

on broadband issues.[905] Furthermore, the system would be financed by a flat fee for notification for new services.[906] The fees would be collected and administered by Ofcom.

Besides Sec. 368B, Ofcom also tested whether ATVOD's proposal would be in line with its own principles for analysing co- and self-regulation. It noted that the industry had a collective interest in the active participation in the regulation of VOD services by the establishment of a co-regulatory system.[907] Ofcom posited that attempts at free-riding or circumvention by service providers would be minimal.[908] Transparency, as a criterion of best practice would be enhanced by ATVOD's publication of the details concerning its composition and complaints handling procedures as well as its investigations of services.[909] In addition, Ofcom would carry out regular reviews and audits in order to evaluate the system's effectiveness.[910]

In its statement of December 2009, Ofcom presented the results of the consultation and its decision to designate ATVOD (and ASA).[911] In general, the industry pledged overwhelming support for the ATVOD proposal.[912] Importantly, Ofcom reiterated the reasons for selecting a co-regula-

---

905 Ofcom, "Consultation for the Regulation of VOD Services," para. 5.22, p.40.

906 Ofcom estimated that approximately 150 services would be notied. Thus, the flat fee would amount to GBP 2,000 – 2,500 for each service. Ofcom, "Consultation for the Regulation of VOD Services," paras. 5.27, 5.31, pp. 42, 43 see also para. 4.3, p. 102, Annex 7.

907 Ofcom, "Consultation for the Regulation of VOD Services," para. 5.33, p. 44.

908 Ofcom, "Consultation for the Regulation of VOD Services," para. 5.33, p. 44.

909 Ofcom, "Consultation for the Regulation of VOD Services," paras. 5.34, p. 45.

910 Ofcom, "Consultation for the Regulation of VOD Services," paras. 5.17, 5.34, pp. 38, 45.

911 Ofcom, The regulation of video-on-demand services, 18.12.2009, http://stakeholders.ofcom.org.uk/binaries/consultations/vod/statement/vodstatement.pdf. (accessed 5.8.2014).

912 Out of the 22 contributions to the consultation, eight fully agreed with the ATVOD proposal, a large group of respondents suggested (minor) modifications while only two respondents rejected the ATVOD proposal in its entirety. Of these two, one respondent preferred Ofcom to retain regulatory powers for VOD services and the other submitted that the ATVOD proposal did not grant ATVOD sufficient enforcement powers and it was afraid that this would result in very "light touch" or even no regulation at all. See Ofcom, "The Regulation of Video on Demand Services, Statement," December 18, 2009, paras. 4.19, 4.20, p. 51, http://stakeholders.ofcom.org.uk/binaries/consultations/vod/statement/vodstatement.pdf (accessed 5.8.2014).

tory framework, stressing the "evident benefits" for the industry like "ownership and commitment", "reputation of VOD industry" and high levels of compliance from which consumers would profit.[913] Concerning the scope of functions which Ofcom would designate to ATVOD, Ofcom underlined that it intended to "designate the widest possible range of such powers and duties to the co-regulator" to establish ATVOD as a one-stop-shop for the editorial side of the regulation of VOD services.[914] This mandate would entail the regulation of product placement.[915] Ofcom would be ultimately accountable, a fact which is underpinned by Ofcom keeping its statutory sanctioning powers. In sum, extensive discussions between Ofcom and industry stakeholders preceded the formation of the co-regulatory framework that has an editorial and an advertising arm, both of which are operated and managed by different regulatory authorities. This study concentrates on ATVOD and the regulation of non-linear services. Ofcom conducted a comprehensive prior assessment of the requirements of the regulatory regime and repeatedly justified the appropriateness of co-regulation. This process of elaboration was transparent, allowing for a veritable exchange of viewpoints.

#### c) ATVOD: from self- to co-regulator for VOD services

In the midst of the discussions about the CA's drafting, the Association for Television On- Demand (the Association) emerged as a self-regulatory body in 2002/2003. At that time, ATVOD represented the VOD industry and acted as its mouthpiece campaigning for the exclusion of VOD services from the CA's material scope.[916] ATVOD was based on a member-

913 Ofcom, "Statement on the Regulation of VOD Services," para. 4.23, p. 53.

914 In its statement, Ofcom negated that it should retain the power to implement Art. 7 (access to VOD services of visually or hearing impaired people), Art. 9 (2) (codes of conduct concerning the promotion of inappropriate food or drinks high in fat, salt or sugar [HFSS] in commercial communications) and Art. 13 AVMSD (promotion of European works in VOD services) as suggested by some respondents to the consultation. Ofcom, "Statement on the Regulation of VOD Services," pp. 58–62.

915 Ofcom, "Statement on the Regulation of VOD Services," para. 5.21, p. 67.

916 Mac Sithigh, "Co-Regulation, VOD and the Legal Status of Audio-Visual Media Status of," p. 56; Craufurd Smith et al., "The Independence of the UK and Finnish NRAs," p. 309.

ship system to which several big UK providers such as BT, Channel 4 and Virgin Media had subscribed. Members of the Association committed to compliance with a code of practice which was enforced by the Association by means of a progressive system of sanctions which were, however, never applied in practice.[917] The Association's transformation into a co-regulator by spring 2010 was not as easy as its name change (henceforth Authority) suggests. Mac Sithigh remarks that "it is not an obvious situation of a self-regulatory system being co-opted or incorporated into the statutory system, but a more awkward transition between what we could call ATVOD 1.0 and ATVOD 2.0".[918] Indubitably, the changes, which the Association made, above all to its governing structure and the difficult task of elaboration common rules and guidance clarifying provider's statutory duties.

In September 2010, the Authority for Television On-Demand (ATVOD) began operating as a co-regulator subsequent to being designated by Ofcom in March 2010 for a (renewable) period of 10 years.[919] ATVOD was set up as a private company limited by guarantee pursuant to Sec. 3 (3) of the Companies Act of 2006.[920] According to the designation, ATVOD's remit encompassed the administration of the notifications required of providers offering a VOD service including the collection of fees as well as the supervision of providers' obligations set out in Sec. 368C (1) – (3) CA which implement Arts. 5, 7 and 13 AVMSD.[921] To this end, ATVOD was endowed with the power to devise procedures for notification and de-

917 Ofcom, "Consultation for the Regulation of VOD Services," paras. 5.20, 5.21, pp. 39, 40; Marsden, *Internet Co-Regulation*, p. 147.

918 Mac Sithigh, "Co-Regulation, VOD and the Legal Status of Audio-Visual Media Status of," p. 57; Marsden refers to a "potemkin regulator" in relation ATVOD's existence as a self-regulatory body. See Marsden, *Internet Co-Regulation*, p. 147.

919 Mac Sithigh, "Convergence, The Impact of Broadcast Regulation on Telecommunications," p. 680; Ofcom, "Designation pursuant to Section 368B of the Communications Act 2003 of Functions to the Association for Television On-Demand in Relation to the Regulation of On-Demand Programme Services," 2010.

920 ATVOD, "Articles of Association of ATVOD," June 22, 2011; Marsden, *Internet Co-Regulation*, p. 147.

921 Art. 5 AVMSD prescribes the obligation to make easily accessible certain information about the service provider like his name, mail address or website. Art. 7 AVMSD requires service providers to make gradually accessible VOD services to persons suffering from a visual or hearing disability. Art. 13 AVMSD encourages service providers to promote access to and production of European works in VOD services. Ofcom, "ATVOD Designation of 2010," sec. 5.

termine the meaning of the terms "on-demand programme service", "service provider" and "programme".[922] Moreover, ATVOD was expected to draw up Rules accompanied by non-binding interpretative Guidance to ensure compliance by service providers with the duties laid down in the CA including the prohibition of transmission of harmful content and the requirements for sponsored programmes and those containing product placement.[923] Where ATVOD found that a service provider had infringed the requirement of prior notification or had contravened the relevant rules outlined in the CA, it issued an enforcement notification, whereas Ofcom remained competent to impose financial penalties in line with Sec. 368J CA.[924] Although ATVOD had to refer any case for application of statutory sanctions to Ofcom, it nevertheless had at its disposal several sanctioning mechanisms such as requiring negligent providers to publish a statement on their website or suspending a VOD service.[925] A review of the initial designation of 2010 led to minor modifications and an amended designation of September 2012.[926] By virtue of the amended designation, Ofcom was entitled to revise ATVOD's mandate in view of market developments.[927] Importantly, service providers were entitled to appeal ATVOD's determinations before Ofcom.[928] In line with specific procedures, service providers could contest ATVOD's findings on what constitutes an on-demand service (scope determinations) within 20 working days of ATVOD's

922 Ofcom, "ATVOD Designation of 2010," sec. 6 (i), (ii).

923 These obligations reflect Arts. 6, 10, 11 and 12 AVMSD. See Ofcom, "ATVOD Designation of 2010," sec. 6 (iv) (b)-(e), (v).

924 Ofcom, "ATVOD Designation of 2010" sec. 6 (viii) in conjunction with sec. 368BB (1) (a) CA and sec. 6 (xi).

925 Ofcom, "ATVOD Designation of 2010," sec. 6 (xii); see also Mac Sithigh, Daithi, "Convergence, The Impact of Broadcast Regulation on Telecommunications," p. 681.

926 Ofcom, "The Amended Designation Dated 14 September 2012, Designation pursuant to Section 368B of the Communications Act 2003 of Functions to the Association for Television On-Demand in Relation to the Regulation of On-Demand Programme Services," 2012. A formal review of the original designation of March 2010 was required by virtue of sec. 13.

927 Ofcom, "Amended ATVOD Designation," sec. 13.

928 Ofcom, "ATVOD Designation of 2010" Sec. 7 (iii), (xvii); see also ATVOD, "Procedure for Determining Breaches of ATVOD Rules Relating to VOD Services," December 19, 2013, para. 44 et seq.

decision.[929] During the course of the appeal procedure, the enforcement action was stayed until publication of Ofcom's decision.[930] The appeal decisions were regularly prepared by two senior executive members who may request further information from the service provider, any directly affected third party or ATVOD.[931] The procedures did not set out a strict deadline for Ofcom to draw up its decision. Nonetheless Ofcom would "aim to complete appeals within 60 working days from the date it receives a full request for an appeal".[932] This time period might be exceeded in individual cases depending on the circumstances underlying the case.[933]

With regards to its institutional structure, ATVOD was headed by Chief Executive Officer (CEO) Pete Johnson. ATVOD was managed by a Board which comprised five independent and four non-independent members, the CEO not being part of the Board.[934] Interestingly, ATVOD's Articles of Association did not stipulate a precise number of Board members which was consequently variable but required that the number of independent members be greater than the number of non-independent members.[935] The Board was chaired by one of the independent members, who was supported by an independent Deputy Chair. The non-independent Board members were mostly affiliated with the broadcast industry like BSkyB, Channel 4 or NBCUniversal.[936] This composition ensured ATVOD's independence

---

929 Ofcom, "Procedures for the Handling of Appeals of ATVOD Decisions in Relation to What Constitutes an On-Demand Programme Service," January 10, 2013, para. 1.8, http://stakeholders.ofcom.org.uk/broadcasting/tv/video-on-demand/ (accessed 28.8.2014).

930 Ofcom, "Procedures for Handling Appeals of ATVOD Scope Determinations," para. 1.13.

931 Ofcom, "Procedures for Handling Appeals of ATVOD Scope Determinations," paras. 1.6, 1.15.

932 Ofcom, "Procedures for Handling Appeals of ATVOD Scope Determinations," para. 1.23.

933 Ofcom, "Procedures for Handling Appeals of ATVOD Scope Determinations," para. 1.23.

934 Craufurd Smith et al., "The Independence of the UK and Finnish NRAs," p. 309.

935 Art. 20 (1) ATVOD, "Articles of Association.".

936 The amended designation of 2012 removed, inter alia, ATVOD's duty to consult Ofcom prior to issuing an enforcement notification in case of contravention of the notification requirement. ATVOD, "Register of Interests," May 22, 2014.

from the government as well as from the industry.[937] This was bolstered by the fact that two members or one third of the total number of members (whichever was greater) constituted the quorum to take decisions provided that independent members were in the majority.[938] Nonetheless, ATVOD had retained close ties with the VOD sector. This cooperation was institutionalised by the Industry Forum to which ATVOD was accountable. In fact, ATVOD sought the Industry Forum's views on a quarterly basis and consulted it in relation to any envisaged modifications to the funding system and ATVOD's scope guidance.[939] The industry thus seemed to have a significant hold on ATVOD and there was no similarly formal mechanism which would engage the general public in regular intervals. The Industry Forum might be regarded as a relic of ATVOD's self-regulatory roots, highlighting the difficult transition from a self- to a co-regulator. Yet, ATVOD's Articles of Association did not specify to what extent ATVOD was required to take note of the Industry Forum's discussions and findings. Rather than reproaching ATVOD with one-sidedness, the Industry Forum served as a channel for dialogue and exchange of viewpoints necessary in a field of law that has been undergoing unrivalled changes and that has been dominated by technical aspects requiring expertise. In addition, ATVOD's practice in many areas appeared to reflect a balanced approach, which mediated between the preservation of public interest objectives and stakeholder interests.

ATVOD was financed by fees levied on providers for each VOD service.[940] The funding of ATVOD had already been an aspect intensely discussed during Ofcom's consultation in 2009 when Ofcom considered a flat fee appropriate and pragmatic in spite of opposition from small-scale

937 The ATVOD Code of Conduct for Members of January 2013 specifies that especially independent members take their decisions in an impartial manner accounting for the public interests pursued by regulation. This is particularly crucial for future employment options or other financial interests. The ATVOD Code of Conduct permits non-independent members of the Board to be closely associated with industry stakeholders including paid employment provided that any conflict of interests is declared and discussed according to internal procedures. ATVOD, "Code of Conduct for Members, Edition 1.2," January 2013, paras. 2, 9.

938 ATVOD, "Articles of Association," para. 27 (2).

939 ATVOD, "Articles of Association," p. Art. 6; see also Craufurd Smith et al., "The Independence of the UK and Finnish NRAs," p. 311.

940 Craufurd Smith et al., "The Independence of the UK and Finnish NRAs," p. 312.

providers.[941] Prior to every new regulatory year (running from April until March), ATVOD in conjunction with Ofcom, which had to approve ATVOD's budget, consulted on the parameters and amount of fees. After the initial funding period of March 2010 to April 2011 when a flat fee of GBP 2,900 was applied,[942] discussions commenced at the end of 2011 in the ATVOD Industry Forum on a fairer and more cost-reflective fee structure.[943] In its second year (covering the period of April 2011 to March 2012), ATVOD set out differential rates contingent on provider's annual turnover (so-called three band fee structure).[944] Distinguishing between two rates levied on large-scale commercial operators[945] and a concessionary rate applied to non-commercial, commercial micro-scale and commer-

941 Ofcom, "Consultation for the Regulation of VOD Services," para. 5.31, p. 43; Ofcom and ATVOD, "Regulatory Fees for Video on Demand Services for the Period up to 31 March 2011, Joint Statement," June 17, 2010, pp. 50, 51; Ofcom, "Statement on the Regulation of VOD Services," paras. 4.15, 4.32, pp. 50, 55, 56.

942 ATVOD had invited stakeholders to submit their views on the possibility of concessionary regulatory fees for small-scale service providers but received only limited contributions from the industry. It thus concluded that the introduction of lower tariffs next to the regular amount was not necessary. Nonetheless, ATVOD would make an individual assessment in case of small-scale providers who could provide evidence that they were facing "genuine difficulties" in paying the established fee. ATVOD and Ofcom, "Joint Statement by ATVOD and Ofcom on the Possibility of Concessionary Regulatory Fees for Small-Scale Vide on Demand Services for the Period up to 31 March 2011," December 11, 2010, paras. 13–17, pp. 5, 6.

943 Interestingly, a fee based on audience size and measurements such as the number of programmes or the number of minutes viewed was debated but eventually rejected due to the difficulties of generating and monitoring such audience data (which, above all, would have adversely affected small providers) and its verification by ATVOD. See for instance ATVOD, "Minutes of the Second Meeting of the ATVOD/Industry Forum Fees Working Party," October 10, 2011, p. 2; ATVOD, "Minutes of the Third Meeting of the ATVOD/Industry Forum Fees Working Party," April 11, 2011, p. 2; ATVOD, "Minutes of the Fourth Meeting of the ATVOD/Industry Forum Fees Working Party," December 14, 2014, p. 4.

944 Craufurd Smith et al., "The Independence of the UK and Finnish NRAs," p. 312; Mac Sithigh, Daithi, "Convergence, The Impact of Broadcast Regulation on Telecommunications," p. 685.

945 In fact, the standard rates applicable to commercial operators distinguish between a super A rate for providers whose annual revenue exceeds GBP 25.9 million, an A rate levied on providers with an annual turnover of more than GBP 6.5 million and a B rate applicable to providers with an annual revenue of not more than GBP 6.5 million.

cial small-scale providers,[946] ATVOD accounted for providers of different scales. Throughout the five years (from April 2011 until the end of March 2015), the fees gradually decreased slightly for providers notifying their first service. Providers with multiple notified services were permitted to band their services and a group cap was applied at GBP 25,000.[947] In its first year of operation, its budget amounted to approximately GBP 450,000, while its estimate for the period of 2014/2015 was GPD 510,000.[948] In its first year, 154 services were notified[949] while in its fourth year, the number of notified services had grown, amounting to more than 460 providers in mid-2016.[950]

d) Termination of ATVOD's co-regulatory role

In spite of the renewed designation of ATVOD in September 2012 for a period of ten years, Ofcom announced the abrupt end of the co-regulatory scheme on 14 October 2015.[951] From January 2016 Ofcom has taken "sole responsibility"[952] for regulating VOD services.[953] Following an internal

946 The concessionary rates distinguish between non-commercial rates applicable to registered charities, community interest companies or other not-for-profit companies, commercial micro-scale rates applicable to providers with a yearly turnover of less than GBP 50,000 and commercial small-scale rates which apply to providers who have an annual turnover of less than GBP 100,000.

947 Services can be grouped when provided by "entities which are wholly owned by the same parent company". See for instance ATVOD, "2014-2015 Fee Tariff, Regulatory Fees for Providers of On-Demand Programme Services for the Period 1 April 2014 – 31 March 2015," June 13, 2014, p. 5.

948 ATVOD, "Statement on Regulatory Fees for On-Demand Programme Services for the Period 1 April 2011 to 31 March 2012 ('Year Two')," June 28, 2011, paras. 4.4, 4.5, p. 31; ATVOD, "Statement on Regulatory Fees for On-Demand Programme Services for the Period 1 April 2014 to 31 March 2015," June 13, 2014, para. 4.18, p. 14.

949 ATVOD, "Annual Report 2010/11," September 30, 2011, p. 6.

950 See European Audiovisual Observatory, Mavise database, United Kingdom, available at http://mavise.obs.coe.int/country?id=14 (accessed 1.10.2016).

951 Ofcom, "Ofcom Brings Regulation of 'Video-On-Demand' In-House," October 14, 2015, http://media.ofcom.org.uk/news/2015/1520333/ (accessed 3.11.2015).

952 Ofcom, "Ofcom Brings Regulation of 'Video-On-Demand' In-House.".

953 The author is thankful to Professor Dr. Julia Hörnle and Robin Foster for sharing their views in relation to the termination of the co-regulatory scheme in an email exchange dated 15 and 16 December 2015. From the correspondence, it emerged

review, which has not been made public, Ofcom decided that it would be more efficient to reduce the number of regulatory bodies in order to "create operational efficiencies" and decrease administrative costs.[954] Above all, "in light of the increasing convergence of linear services and on-demand programme services (…) and the need for a comprehensive solution to the future of content regulation (…) having a separate organisation carrying out this aspect of Ofcom's work is no longer the most effective way of delivering this part of our remit".[955] In its press release, Ofcom recognised that "ATVOD has played an important, effective role in regulating on-demand TV" for nearly six years.[956] Both regulators pledged close collaboration to ease the transition from co-regulation to "mono-regulation".

At first glance, the explanations given in the press statements of Ofcom and ATVOD to discontinue the co-regulatory scheme seem reasonable. First, media convergence is progressing rapidly and the boundaries between broadcast and VOD services are vanishing. Consumer perceptions seem to become more pronounced expecting similar levels of protection for linear and non-linear services available on the same device (e.g. TV set). It seems reasonable that convergence of services is followed by convergence of regulation. In the early years of the new millennium, Ofcom was precisely established as a super-regulator to account for such convergence. Nonetheless, Ofcom decided to delegate the regulation of VOD services in 2010, reverting to an existing industry body that was transformed into a proper co-regulator. It can be deduced from ATVOD's press statement quoting from Ofcom's review that the level of convergence has progressed to a point where it tipped the balance to the detriment of the co-regulatory model. The sudden termination of the co-regulatory scheme at this particular moment is surprising. It seems to be entirely based on market research and does not follow from any prior revision of the substantive provisions, for instance as a consequence of a revised AVMSD at the EU level. It remains to be seen whether Ofcom as a large regulator will respond as swiftly and efficiently to developments in the VOD market as

---

that ATVOD board members were first notified about the review and the possibility of a change in June 2015. After several meetings between ATVOD and Ofcom, the latter made its decision known in October. ATVOD members have not had access to Ofcom's review.

954 Ofcom, "Ofcom Brings Regulation of 'Video-On-Demand' In-House.".

955 ATVOD, "ATVOD Responds to Ofcom Review Decision," October 14, 2015.

956 Ofcom, "Ofcom Brings Regulation of 'Video-On-Demand' In-House.".

ATVOD and can establish similarly good channels and dialogue on various levels with the industry.

Second, Ofcom referred to the high costs (not necessarily but certainly also financial) of entertaining a co-regulatory framework. On objective grounds, the shift from two bodies to one appears to save costs. Yet, ATVOD appeared to be a lean and cost-effective regulator with limited resources (staffing and funding). With an annual budget of roughly half a million GBP and three to four permanent staff, ATVOD did not seem to absorb huge amounts of money. ATVOD operated and functioned on its own while in the future, Ofcom will have to spend money on the unit that deals with VOD issues. In the absence of concrete evidence regarding cost savings, it is difficult to see the (financial) benefits advocated by Ofcom. Reading between the lines of Ofcom's statement, it may refer to administrative costs or inefficiencies which resulted, among others, from inconsistent approaches of the co-regulator and its parent-regulator. These materialised above all in differences regarding the scope of ATVOD's remit (i.e. the notion of on-demand programme services). As will be shown below, service providers challenged a great number of ATVOD determinations and lengthy appeal procedures were instigated before Ofcom. It seems that the option of appeal to Ofcom created incentives for service providers who knowingly delayed the decision-making process. These reveal fundamental discrepancies in regulatory approaches between ATVOD and Ofcom that seemingly could not be overcome. Such administrative costs, however, are not entirely to blame on ATVOD as cases got literally stuck within Ofcom. It remains to be seen whether Ofcom will be as active and fast as ATVOD and how the appeal mechanism will be structured.

Regrettably, little information about this fundamental change of the regulatory structures has entered the public domain. This is striking as previous reviews of the co-regulatory scheme (especially when ATVOD was installed as a co-regulator) are publicly available. This rather atypical absence of transparency lends itself to speculations about ulterior motives, which Ofcom may have pursued, by discontinuing the co-regulatory scheme. ATVOD seemed to have the support of the industry and established a reputation as an efficient co-regulator in spite of criticism surrounding its attempt to regulate sub-sites of online newspapers (see chapter four). As VOD services are becoming more relevant for increasingly large parts of the UK public, Ofcom may have craved for taking back the power it once outsourced. Possibly, the review of the BBC's Charter and the demands for a separate regulator to oversee the UK's most important public service broadcaster may have played into Ofcom's decision.[957] The supervision of the BBC, currently exercised by the BBC Trust, entails its catalogue of VOD services (BBC iPlayer). If Ofcom were to oversee the BBC,[958] it would certainly want to make sure that such mandate includes VOD services and not risk sharing responsibility with a co-regulator active in the same field. So Ofcom's move to internalise the regulation of VOD services may have been a first step, or a pretext, to ensure its position in case it would be asked to take on a bigger role in the future regulation of the BBC.

e) Future regulation of VOD services by Ofcom

In mid-December 2015, Ofcom published a number of documents which set out its approach towards the regulation of VOD services. In order to ease the transition from co-regulation to regulation by a sole regulator and enhance continuity and predictability, Ofcom substantially retained ATVOD's previous rules and guidance on who needs to notify and established interim rules of procedure which closely resembled those previously in place.[959] In a statement on the "future regulation of on-demand programme services", Ofcom underpinned that it was not gaining any new powers but that it now exercised sole responsibility over ODPS while previously, it had shared such powers with its co-regulator ATVOD.[960] It jus-

957 The BBC's Charter runs until the end of 2016. The UK government currently reviews the Charter. In May 2016, the government published a white paper on the BBC's future entitled "A BBC for the future: a broadcaster of distinction", available at https://www.gov.uk/government/uploads/system/uploads/attachment_data/file/524863/DCMS_A_BBC_for_the_future_linked_rev 1.pdf. The response of the BBC Trust is available at http://www.bbc.co.uk/bbctrust/news/press_releases/2016/charter_review. On the BBC's Charter review, see also http://futureoftv.org.uk/report/ (all websites accessed 1.10.2016).

958 On the possibility for Ofcom to oversee the BBC, see Peter Lunt and Sonia Livingstone, "Is the BBC Safe in Ofcom's Hands?," *LSE Blog*, June 22, 2016, http://blogs.lse.ac.uk/mediapolicyproject/2016/06/22/is-the-bbc-safe-in-ofcoms-hands/ (accessed 4.8.2016).

959 See Ofcom, Rules and Guidance, Procedures and Notifications, available at http://stakeholders.ofcom.org.uk/broadcasting/on-demand/rules-guidance/ (accessed 18.1.2016).

960 Ofcom, "Future Regulation of On-Demand Programme Services, Statement and Consultation," December 18, 2015, paras. 1.6, 2.2, pp. 2, 5, http://stakeholders.of

tified the move away from co-regulation by the "growing convergence" between television broadcast and on-demand audiovisual media services as recognised by recital 10 AVMSD.[961] This was best illustrated, according to Ofcom, by the dissemination of similar or identical content (offered as catch-up thus previously broadcast on TV) and by the fact that the largest ODPS providers established in the UK also owned a broadcast license.[962] Ofcom nonetheless acknowledged that there was less overlap regarding small scale ODPS providers, which were not necessarily broadcast licensees.[963]

Regarding procedures, Ofcom published interim breach procedures[964] and up-dated the procedures for consideration of statutory sanctions[965] and made clear that future procedures should be in line with existing procedures applicable to broadcasters. In this respect, Ofcom announced a consultation on two aspects running until 1 March 2016, first regarding procedures for investigating breaches of rules for ODPS providers and second regarding fees.[966] Given the nature of ODPS, Ofcom emphasised that there was a need to craft more flexible rules and expedite the procedures (in comparison with those applicable to broadcasting)[967] especially where the incriminated material would continue to be available to the public.[968] In contrast to ATVOD, Ofcom also noted that it would not separate issues

com.org.uk/binaries/consultations/vod_procedures/summary/Future_regulation_of_on-demand_programme_services.pdf (accessed 18.1.2016).

961 Ofcom, "Future Regulation of VOD Services," para. 3.3, p. 8.

962 Ofcom, "Future Regulation of VOD Services," para. 3.4, p. 8.

963 Ofcom, "Future Regulation of VOD Services," para. 3.6, p. 8.

964 Ofcom, "Interim Breach Procedures for Investigating Breaches of Rules for On-Demand Programme Services," December 18, 2015, http://stakeholders.ofcom.org.uk/binaries/broadcast/on-demand/rules-guidance/interim_procedures.pdf (accessed 18.1.2016).

965 Ofcom, "Procedures for the Consideration of Statutory Sanctions Arising in the Context of On-Demand Programme Services," December 18, 2015, http://stakeholders.ofcom.org.uk/binaries/broadcast/on-demand/rules-guidance/Revised_sanctions_procedures.pdf (accessed 18.1.2016).

966 Ofcom, "Future Regulation of VOD Services," paras. 3, 4 pp. 8-14.

967 The draft procedures set forth an expedited procedure which would allow for the bypassing of service provider's internal complaints processes and would shorten the deadlines for representations by the concerned provider. Adherence to the urgent procedure would be a case-by-case decision by Ofcom which would be communicated to the service provider. Ofcom, "Future Regulation of VOD Services," p. 30.

968 Ofcom, "Future Regulation of VOD Services," paras. 3.8 (a), 3.9, pp. 9, 10.

of scope from any other breaches of the "editorial rules" (such as the prohibition to incite hatred or to harm under eighteens)[969] but that it would investigate the scope and substantive issues in parallel unless Ofcom was faced with a particularly complex case that warranted derogation from the rule.[970] Ofcom's decisions would be subject to judicial review before the High Court.[971] While ATVOD was primarily funded by the industry, Ofcom outlined three options in its consultation, two of which would not involve the charging of fees while the third option would require only larger service providers to pay a fee.[972] Ofcom clearly argued in favour of abandoning the fee structure. It submitted that it would carry out the task of regulating ODPS at substantially lower costs than ATVOD and did not want to set up a parallel system replicating the licensing regime for broadcasters.[973] As a result, Ofcom adopted up-dated procedures for investigating breaches by VOD providers and for considering imposition of statutory sanctions.[974] More importantly, it issued rules and guidance for ODPS providers in late May 2016 and published a notification form on its website.[975]

---

969 On the differentiation between administrative and editorial content rules, see Ofcom, "Future Regulation of VOD Services," p. 22.

970 Ofcom, "Future Regulation of VOD Services," para. 3.9 (e), pp. 10, 29.

971 In contrast to the draft procedures, the interim breach procedures provide for an internal review by a senior staff of Ofcom not involved in the initial decision. The reason for the lack of any internal review mechanism is the alignment of procedures between broadcasting and ODPS and the necessity for "prompt resolution" of disputes. Ofcom, "Future Regulation of VOD Services," para. 3.8 (f), p. 10; Ofcom, "Interim Breach Procedures for VOD Services," paras. 47–49, pp. 11-12.

972 Ofcom, "Future Regulation of VOD Services," para. 4.1, p. 11.

973 Ofcom, "Future Regulation of VOD Services," para. 4.11, p. 12.

974 Ofcom, "Procedures for Investigating Breaches of Rules for On-Demand Programme Services," April 1, 2016, http://stakeholders.ofcom.org.uk/binaries/broadcast/on-demand/rules-guidance/procedures-investigating-breaches.pdf (accessed 5.5.2016); Ofcom, "Sanctioning Procedures.".

975 Ofcom, "Rules & Guidance, Statutory Rules and Non-Binding Guidance for Providers of On-Demand Programme Services (ODPS)," January 1, 2016, http://stakeholders.ofcom.org.uk/binaries/broadcast/on-demand/rules-guidance/rules_and_guidance.pdf; Ofcom, "Notification Form for On-Demand Programme Service Providers," 2016, http://stakeholders.ofcom.org.uk/binaries/broadcast/on-demand/notification.rtf; see also Ofcom, "How to Notify, Guidance Notes on How to Notify an on Demand Programme Service to Ofcom," December 18, 2015, http://

### 3. Other regulatory bodies

Two further "'niche' regulatory bodies",[976] namely the British Board of Film Classification (BBFC) and the Internet Watch Foundation (IWF) are additionally briefly mentioned here in view of their roles in implementing specific rules of the AVMSD in the UK. The BBFC, founded in 1912 as the British Board of Film Censors, the oldest regulator and one of the "most trusted and highly regarded" bodies in the UK.[977] It is a non-governmental body which classifies films (in accordance with the Cinemas Act of 1985 and the Licensing Act of 2003) and video works (under the Video Recordings Act of 1984 and 2010) prior to their release. The classifications imply that content is deemed suitable for certain age groups. The BBFC, being independent of government and the industry, is funded by the fees it charges for its services (contingent on the running time of the works to be classified).[978] While the decisions of the BBFC are binding for video works, local authorities can override the BBFC's classifications for films intended for theatrical release in cinemas.[979] The BBFC's classifications have been extended to online content (so-called digital age ratings) under a voluntary scheme to which service providers like iTunes, Microsoft and Netflix have subscribed.[980] Likewise, the BBFC provides classifications for content accessed on mobile networks in a self-regulatory partnership with the mobile industry.[981] The use of BBFC age ratings in digital media reflects the BBFC's high standing as well as the trust of the British population in this body to deliver appropriate classifications. The BBFC's age ratings represent public opinion and public morality and

---

stakeholders.ofcom.org.uk/binaries/broadcast/on-demand/rules-guidance/How_to_Notify.pdf (all websites accessed 18.1.2016).

976 Mac Sithigh, "Co-Regulation, VOD and the Legal Status of Audio-Visual Media Services," p. 51.

977 Smartt, *Media and Entertainment Law*, p. 440.

978 See BBFC, Who we are, available at http://bbfc.co.uk/about-bbfc (accessed 25.9.2014).

979 See BBFC, Legislation, Film Licensing and The Video Recordings Act, available at http://www.bbfc.co.uk/education-resources/student-guide/legislation/film-licensing and http://www.bbfc.co.uk/education-resources/student-guide/legislation/video-recordings-act (websites accessed 25.9.2014).

980 See BBFC, Digital Age Ratings, available at http://bbfc.co.uk/what-classification/digital-age-ratings (accessed 25.9.2014).

981 BBFC, Mobile Content, available at http://bbfc.co.uk/what-classification/mobile-content (accessed 25.9.2014).

are subject to regular reviews including public consultations. In establishing the age categories, the BBFC is mindful of two guiding principles namely the protection of minors and other vulnerable groups from harmful or unsuitable content and the empowerment of consumers to make informed viewing decisions.[982]

There are six categories of age ratings ranging from "U" which stands for "Universal" implying suitable material for viewers older than four years, to "PG" which means "Parental Guidance" denoting films, which are generally suitable for all age groups but certain scenes may require parental guidance, to age groups 12A and 12, 15, 18 and R18, the latter being restricted to sexually explicit works, which can only be shown in licensed cinemas or shops.[983] In making its decisions, the BBFC takes into account criteria such as the context, theme, tone and impact of the work as well as the promotion of drugs, depictions of criminal activities, the use of language and the portrayal of nudity as well as sexual activity.[984] Although the classification of audiovisual services is not explicitly governed by the AVMSD, it is considered an appropriate means whereby the protection of minors is safeguarded in line with Arts. 12 and 27 AVMSD.[985]

Furthermore, the IWF, established in 1996, is pertinent to the protection of minors, combating child sexual abuse content disseminated on the Internet. Being self-regulated, Internet service providers, mobile operators, content providers, trade associations and financial sector organisations among others have joined the IWF as members.[986] The IWF cooperates with law enforcement agencies on an international scale and is backed by the EU.[987] In fact, the IWF is partly funded by the EU Safer Internet Programme and partly by membership fees. Most importantly, it operates hotlines for the reporting of criminal content to which the public has accidentally been exposed. Once reported to the IWF, ISPs are notified to take-down the relevant material according to a procedure in line with the

982 BBFC, "BBFC Guidelines, Age Ratings You Trust," 2014, p. 3, http://bbfc.co.uk/sites/default/files/attachments/BBFC%20Classification%20Guidelines%202014_0.pdf (accessed 25.9.2014).

983 BBFC, "BBFC Guidelines, Age Ratings You Trust," pp. 15–24.

984 BBFC, "BBFC Guidelines, Age Ratings You Trust," pp. 4–7.

985 Recital 60 AVMSD explicitly mentions labeling especially of on-demand audiovisual media services to ensure the protection of minors.

986 See IWF, Members, available at https://www.iwf.org.uk/members (accessed 26.9.2014).

987 Smartt, *Media and Entertainment Law*, p. 435.

ECD.[988] Since 2004, the IWF has provided a list of web pages (which is regularly up-dated) featuring child pornography content to its members and other companies that can filter or block access to them.[989] To a certain extent, the IWF's remit touches on ATVOD's mandate to protect children in VOD services. While the IWF receives complaints about and tracks down content that is illegal under UK criminal law (pursuant to the Protection of Children Act 1978 as amended by the Sexual Offences Act 2003), ATVOD is concerned with legal content considered unsuitable for minors but available for adults aged over 18.

In conclusion, the British regulatory framework in its current form is a rather young construct. New Labour's innovative approach at the beginning of the new millennium resulted in a fundamental overhaul of legislation which was accompanied by an equally profound reorganisation of the regulatory landscape. To meet the demands of convergence, a massive statute, the CA was adopted covering the entire communications industry. Simulating the CA's scope and securing coherence of objectives and application of standards across media platforms and services is the key regulatory authority Ofcom. Its creation and structure reflect the thinking of the incumbent government and its preference for light touch regulation. When Ofcom's construction was debated, controversies ensued about whose interests Ofcom was to defend first and foremost. A compromise was reached empowering Ofcom to secure the interests of citizens *and* consumers. The awkward and conflicting distinction between citizens and consumers sits at the heart of Ofcom's existence and the regulator has been reproached at times for having favoured the economic over the public interest. Regardless of this duality, Ofcom, though being *the* key regulator on the communications market, is surrounded by other regulatory bodies. Commenting on the complex threads of the British regulatory net, Craufurd Smith notes that "the plethora of regulators responsible for different types of media content has led to a complex system of regulation in

---

988 See IWF Code of Practice for notice and takedown of UK hosted content, available at https://www.iwf.org.uk/members/member-policies/funding-council/code-of-practice (accessed 26.9.2014).

989 Edwards is especially critical of the lack of transparency with respect to the blocklist and its impact on free speech. See Edwards, Lilian, "Pornography, Censorship and the Internet," in *Law and the Internet*, ed. Edwards, Lilian and Waelde, Charlotte, third edition (Oxford and Portland, Oregon: Hart Publishing, 2009), pp. 653, 652–58; see also Smartt, *Media and Entertainment Law*, p. 437.

need of rationalisation".[990] Owing to the statutory duty to actively promote co- and self-regulatory arrangements, Ofcom delegated certain clearly delimited tasks to other bodies. In the context of the implementation of the AVMSD in the UK, three such transfers of functions have occurred in the form of co-regulation. In 2010, ATVOD was charged to regulate certain aspects of non-linear services. The ASA oversees commercial communications in VOD services. Together, these bodies have shaped the regulation of linear and non-linear audiovisual media services as will be shown subsequently. Their internal organisation and general outlook are therefore crucial to understand the policy priorities they have set and the manner in which they have approached new developments.

## *B. The German media authorities*

German law applies a tripartite structure with respect to the media and communications industry. In particular, the German legal order distinguishes between broadcasting, telemedia (on-demand audiovisual media services) and telecommunications, regulation of which is motivated by different reasons.[991] As a result, regulation differentiates according to the type of service and applies a specific set of rules to each respective genre.[992] The underlying rationale for the regulation of telecommunications has been to foster a functioning market characterised by effective competition.[993] The regulation of broadcasting (and to a certain but lesser extent the regulation of telemedia) rests on different footing. Since broadcasts are considered to have a far-reaching impact on public opinion formation, the *leitmotif* of broadcast regulation has been to secure plurality and diversity of opinion.[994] In 2016, almost 400 free-to-air commercial channels were established in Germany, most of them transmitted on state,

---

990 Craufurd Smith et al., "The Independence of the UK and Finnish NRAs," p. 297.

991 Roßnagel, Kleist and Scheuer, *Die Reform der Regulierung elektronischer Medien in Europa*, p. 91.

992 Roßnagel, Kleist and Scheuer, *Die Reform der Regulierung elektronischer Medien in Europa*, p. 91.

993 Roßnagel, Kleist and Scheuer, *Die Reform der Regulierung elektronischer Medien in Europa*, p. 92.

994 Roßnagel, Kleist and Scheuer, *Die Reform der Regulierung elektronischer Medien in Europa*, p. 91.

regional or local level.[995] Broadcasters disseminating programmes nationwide expected an annual turnover of EUR 9 billion in 2015.[996] In contrast to the sophisticated TV market, the market for telemedia is still nascent justifying more lenient standards of transparency and labelling.[997] In early 2016, more than 280 providers of VOD services were established in Germany and more than 450 services were available to the German public.[998] Overall turnover of VOD in 2013 was EUR 163 million. Rapid growth is projected for the coming years, almost tripling current figures by 2018.[999] Similarly, the take-up of Connected TVs as well as online consumption of content is growing. In early 2016, approximately 30 percent of German households owned a Connected TV and it is interesting to note that such TVs are actually connected to the Internet in almost 12 percent of households.[1000]

Another feature of the German legal order is its federal structure, which is especially significant in the context of media regulation. The *Grundgesetz* (GG, Basic Law) prescribes the distribution of competence between the *Bund* (federal level) and the *Länder* (states). The constituents are autonomous and enjoy a state-like character with sole responsibility for their tasks and competencies.[1001] As a general rule, the 16 German states are competent to legislate and regulate an issue unless explicit competence has been conferred to the federal level.[1002] The GG is silent on broadcast-

---

995 ALM GbR, ed., *Jahrbuch 2015/2016, Privater Rundfunk und Telemedien* (Berlin: Vistas, 2016), p. 64, http://www.die-medienanstalten.de/fileadmin/Download/Publikationen/ALM-Jahrbuch/Jahrbuch_2016/Jahrbuch_2015-2016.pdf (accessed 26.8.2016).

996 ALM GbR, *Jahrbuch 2015/2016*, p. 68.

997 Roßnagel, Kleist and Scheuer, *Die Reform der Regulierung elektronischer Medien in Europa*, p. 91.

998 See Mavise database, country Germany, available at http://mavise.obs.coe.int/country?id=2 (accessed 1.10.2016).

999 By 2018, turnover is expected to rise to around 450 million Euros, see European Audiovisual Observatory, "Final Report VoD Markets in the EU," para. 8.2.2, p. 131 (accessed 26.8.2016).

1000 ALM GbR, *Jahrbuch 2015/2016*, p. 43.

1001 Hubertus Gersdorf, "Begrenzte Aufsicht und einfache Aufsichtsstrukturen," in *Neuordnung des Medienrechts, Neuer rechtlicher Rahmen für eine konvergente Technik?*, ed. Alexander Roßnagel, Schriftenreihe des Instituts für Europäisches Medienrecht (EMR) 30 (Baden-Baden: Nomos, 2005), p. 109.

1002 Art. 30 GG in conjunction with Art. 70 (1) GG. See also Roßnagel, Kleist and Scheuer, *Die Reform der Regulierung elektronischer Medien in Europa*, p. 96.

ing, which is consequently regulated at the state level.[1003] Nonetheless, the federal level has exclusive power in matters of telecommunications ser-

1003 The question of competence was not only a contentious issue internally (i.e. between the federal level and the states) but also externally (vis-à-vis international organisations). The participation of Germany in the Council raised the question which organ (federal level or the states) would take part in the legislative process at the EU level. Legal proceedings were initiated juxtaposing the federal government to the states in a so-called Bund-Länder-Streit pursuant to Art. 93 (1) No. 3 GG. Interestingly, the case concerned the transposition of the 1989 TWFD, the predecessor to the AVMSD in Germany. When the Commission tabled a proposal in April 1986, the German states expressed general reservations. They posited that the EU (EC at the time) lacked the competence to act in matters of cultural policy and that the competence to harmonise the provision of services was insufficient. The most controversial issue in this respect was the quota rules. The government, however, by reference to the entry into force of the Single European Act and the case law of the Court of Justice, had voted for the Directive as the quota rules were regarded as a political objective rather than binding provisions (which was affirmed in a joint declaration by the Commission and the Council). In March 1995, the BVerfG held that the government would represent the interests of Germany at the negotiations of EU institutions once the EU had claimed competence to act. Even if competence was attributed to the states in accordance with the GG, it was for the federal level to represent the rights of the states towards the EU acting as their agent (Sachwalter). The states could not directly exercise their competence vis-à-vis European institutions. If they doubted the competence of the EU to adopt acts of Secondary Union law, the states would be dependent on the government to act as their agent and preserve their rights. In doing so, the government was obliged to respect procedural guarantees flowing from Art. 70 (1) GG in conjunction with Art. 24 (1) GG and the unwritten principle of bundesfreundliches Verhalten and its corollary, the principle of Bundestreue (loyal cooperation). It followed that the government and the states were required to cooperate closely in preparing legal acts elaborated at the EU level. As a consequence, the government reported regularly on the progress of the EU legislative procedure in the Bundesrat, the Upper House of the German Parliament representing the Länder. The BVerfG found that the government had not infringed the rights of the states during the legislative process leading to the adoption of the TWFD with the exception of the inclusion of the quota rules. The government had not achieved the deletion of the quota rules from the final text of the Directive and contented itself with a mere declaration. While the government insisted that the quota rules were non-binding, the BVerfG was doubtful and referred to the submissions of the Commission representative during the oral proceedings. It followed that by agreeing to the quota rules, the government violated the rights of the Länder as the former did not inform the states about the concrete result of the negotiations and had not coordinated the course of action with the states. See BVerfG, Judgment of 22.3.1995, 2 BvG 1/89. For a detailed analysis of the judgment and the

vices and certain aspects of commerce and trade.[1004] Thus, repeated turf wars about competence ensued, which were resolved by the *Bundesverfassungsgericht* (BVerfG, Federal Constitutional Court).[1005] In its decision of 1961,[1006] the BVerfG clarified that the provision of broadcasting constituted a public task that is fulfilled by the states (in the alternative, it would become a state-run task which was not authorised by the GG).[1007] The German states are thus competent to guarantee the freedom to disseminate broadcasts, while the federal level is empowered to regulate the technical aspects of distribution and the management of frequencies.[1008] This separation came under pressure when the Telemedia Act was drafted as will be shown below.

---

implications for federal states of the EU's competence to adopt legal acts, see Jörg Gerkrath, "L'arrêt du Bundesverfassungsgericht du 22 mars 1995 sur la directive 'télévision sans frontières', Les difficultés de la répartition des compétences entre trois niveaux de législation," *Revue trimetrielle de droit européen* 31, no. 3 (1995): pp. 539–59. This case may explain the general unease of Germany with regards to the quota rules which are considered to be an interference with the editorial freedom of service providers (Programmautonomie). Art. 4 TWFD (now Art. 16 AVMSD) was integrated in the German legal order in 1991 (now Art. 6 RStV). The wording of the German provision is, however, less specific. The RStV is, moreover, silent about the promotion of European works created by producers who are independent of broadcasters (Art. 17 AVMSD).

1004 Arts. 73 (1) 5. and 7. GG.

1005 Roßnagel, Kleist and Scheuer, *Die Reform der Regulierung elektronischer Medien in Europa*, p. 96.

1006 The case concerned a controversial federal law which established a public service broadcaster (the Deutschland-Fernsehen-GmbH) with its head office in Cologne. In spite of reservations on part of the states, the government had unilaterally decided to introduce federal legislation in 1960. The initial capital of the company was held in part by the Federal Republic and in part by Justice Minister Schäffer who represented the German states. Since no state was willing to participate in the company, Justice Minsiter Schäffer transferred his assets to the Federal Republic which consequentially wholly owned the broadcaster. The states of Hamburg and Hessen challenged the creation of the broadcaster on grounds of competence (Art. 30 GG in conjunction with Art. 73 (1) 7. GG and Art. 87 (3) GG) and basic rights (Art. 5 (1) GG). The BVerfG found that the foundation of the Deutschland-Fernsehen GmbH contravened the Basic Law, above all Art. 5 GG as the company was entirely controlled by and became an instrument of the state.

1007 BVerfG, Judgement of 18.2.1961, 2 BvG 1 u. 2/60, para. 138.

1008 BVerfG, Judgement of 18.2.1961, 2 BvG 1 u. 2/60, paras. 81, 84-85.

What is more, broadcast regulation (especially the development of public service broadcasting) has been characterised by a repulsion of heavy-handed state intervention since the 1950s. The current media landscape (especially with respect to broadcasting) has its origins in the post-war period and was heavily influenced by the Allied forces, which occupied the Germany at that time.[1009] In taking account of the experiences of the Weimar Republic (in which the provision of radio services was centralised) and the Nationalist Socialist regime, both of which exploited the reach and impact of broadcasts (and above all, radio which was more widespread than television) for propagandistic purposes,[1010] the legal framework establishing PSB was designed to curb state influence and ensure the independent dissemination of broadcasts and the independence of supervisory bodies from the state.[1011] This approach was endorsed with regards to the introduction of commercial broadcasting in 1984 and it has since left an indelible mark on the regulatory framework of Germany.[1012] What is more, the BVerfG has upheld this value and has been crucial for today's regulatory structure.

## I. The role of constitutional law and the Federal Constitutional Court's jurisprudence

To a large extent, media law in Germany has been determined by constitutional law and the BVerfG's jurisprudence.[1013] By virtue of the first sen-

1009 Valérie Schüller-Keber, "Die Kommunikationsfreiheiten in der Verfassung," in *Handbuch Medienrecht, Recht der elektronischen Massenmedien*, ed. Dieter Dörr, Johannes Kreile and Mark Cole, second edition (Frankfurt am Main: Verlag Recht und Wirtschaft, 2010), para. 129, p. 84.

1010 Dieter Dörr, "Grundsätze der Medienregulierung," in *Handbuch Medienrecht, Recht der elektronischen Massenmedien*, ed. Dörr, Kreile and Cole, second edition (Frankfurt am Main: Verlag Recht und Wirtschaft, 2010), para. 6, p. 162; Schüller-Keber, "Die Kommunikationsfreiheiten in der Verfassung," para. 127, p. 83.

1011 Schüller-Keber, "Die Kommunikationsfreiheiten in der Verfassung," para. 129, p. 84.

1012 BverfG, Judgement of 16.6.1981, 1 BvL 89/78.

1013 Dörr, "Grundsätze der Medienregulierung," para. 10, p. 164; Bernd Holznagel, Dieter Dörr and Doris Hildebrand, *Elektronische Medien, Entwicklung und Regulierungsbedarf* (München: Franz Vahlen, 2008), p. 172; Sebastian Müller and Christian Gusy, "Media Policy in Germany: Main Features and Current Issues,"

tence of Art. 5 (1) GG, the freedom of expression and the right to information are protected as basic rights.[1014] Pursuant to the second sentence of Art. 5 (1) GG the freedom of the press as well as the freedom of reporting by means of broadcasts and films are guaranteed. Against the background of the Weimar Republic and the totalitarian and inhuman Third Reich, the BVerfG has championed the right to freedom of expression and has prescribed high hurdles for the legislature when intervening with this right. In this respect, the BVerfG has also bolstered free media and a pluralist society.[1015] Above all, in 1958, the BVerfG handed down its landmark decision in the *Lüth* case in which it reinforced the basic right to freedom of expression as "absolutely essential to a free and democratic state or-

in *Understanding Media Policies, A European Perspective*, ed. Evangelia Psychogiopoulou (United Kingdom: Palgrave Macmillan, 2012), p. 119; Roßnagel, Kleist and Scheuer, *Die Reform der Regulierung elektronischer Medien in Europa*, p. 146; Schüller-Keber, "Die Kommunikationsfreiheiten in der Verfassung," para. 130, p. 85; for a concise overview of the case law of the BVerfG concerning the freedom of broadcasting, see *Medienrecht*, 5th ed., Lexikon für Wissenschaft und Praxis (Köln: Carl Heymann, 2010), pp. 555–61; Rolf Schwartmann, "Rundfunkrechtliche Grundlagen," in *Praxishandbuch Medien-, IT- und Urheberrecht*, ed. Rolf Schwartmann, third edition (Heidelberg: C. F. Müller Verlag, 2014), paras. 31–41, pp. 57-61.

1014 Schüller-Keber, "Die Kommunikationsfreiheiten in der Verfassung," paras. 132–36, pp. 86–88.

1015 Schüller-Keber, "Die Kommunikationsfreiheiten in der Verfassung," para. 125, p. 81.

der".[1016] Relying on U.S. Supreme Court Justice Cardozo,[1017] the BVerfG remarked that the right to freedom of expression is "constituent of this free and democratic state order" and is "the basis of freedom itself, 'the matrix, the indispensable condition of nearly every other form of freedom'".[1018] The BVerfG thereby recognised the significance of the freedom of expression, its founding capacity and inextricable link to democracy.[1019] It follows that the state is required to ensure that its people can form opinions on the basis of diverse sources. The right to information thus constitutes a necessary complement to the freedom of expression.[1020] By the same token, the freedom of the press and the freedom of reporting by means of broadcasts are essential for a flourishing democracy in line with the second sentence of Art. 5 (1) GG.

From the scarce wording of this provision, the BVerfG, in a series of cases, derived several general principles, which are still valid today.[1021] These were initially formulated with respect to public service broadcasting and expanded to commercial broadcasting in the 1980s. From the outset,

1016 BVerfG, Judgement of 15.1.1958, 1 BvR 400/51, para. 31. In this case, journalist Erich Lüth (Director of the State Press Office in Hamburg) called for the boycott of the film entitled "Unsterbliche Geliebte" (Immortal Lover) produced by Veit Harlan at the opening of the film festival "German Film Week" in 1950 (which he repeated in an open letter). Lüth criticised the selection of this film director who had become well-known in the Third Reich for his anti-Semitic and national-socialist feature- film "Jud Süß" which was commissioned by the Nationalist Socialist Party for reasons of propaganda. The two film production companies Domnick-Film-Produktion GmbH and Herzog-Film GmbH obtained injunctions prohibiting Mr. Lüth firstly, to call on theatre managers and film distributors not to programme the film "Unsterbliche Geliebte" and secondly, to call on the German public not to view said film. The Landgericht Hamburg (district court of Hamburg) considered that Mr. Lüth's statements violated public morals and constituted an unethical and immoral call for boycott. The BVerfG, however, found that the Landgericht Hamburg had not sufficiently valued the basic right to freedom of expression as guaranteed by the first sentence of Art. 5 (1) GG.

1017 Mr. Justice Cardozo delivered the opinion of the U.S. Supreme Court in Palko v. State of Connecticut, 302 U.S. 319 (1937).

1018 BVerfG, Judgement of 15.1.1958, 1 BvR 400/51, para. 31.

1019 Schüller-Keber, "Die Kommunikationsfreiheiten in der Verfassung," para. 134, p. 87.

1020 Schüller-Keber, "Die Kommunikationsfreiheiten in der Verfassung," para. 135, p. 88.

1021 Schüller-Keber, "Die Kommunikationsfreiheiten in der Verfassung," para. 140, p. 90.

the BVerfG highlighted the mass media character of broadcasting[1022] which thus constitutes an "eminent factor of public opinion formation", contributing to public opinion and opinion formation.[1023] The Court thus constructed a strong bond between the freedom to disseminate broadcasts and the freedom of expression. The former not only complements the latter freedom, it is above all a constituting feature for a democratic basic order by ensuring the free formation of opinions.[1024] As opposed to the printed press, which encompasses a high number of independent and diverse (in terms of political and ideological stances) press products competing for readership, the broadcasting sector of the 1960s only consisted of few players due to the high costs associated with the provision of broadcasts and technical constraints, namely spectrum scarcity.[1025] This "*Sondersituation*"[1026] (special situation) of broadcasting according to the BVerfG, justifies that precautions are taken to safeguard the values enshrined in Art. 5 GG including the institutional freedom of broadcasting. Due to its reach and impact, the Court opined that broadcasting was of such significance for a democratic society that it could not be left unregulated.[1027] Instead, the public should be responsible for organising broadcasting and such organisation should be independent and free from any partisan influence, be it of the state or any powerful societal group.[1028] In this context, the BVerfG has coined the term "positive order" implying that the state has to ensure a diversity of opinions (the breadth and scope thereof) is represented.[1029] The positive order also purports to further the principle of independence or in other words, it prevents misuse and con-

---

1022 BVerfG, Judgement of 27.7.1971, 2 BvF 1/68, 2 BvR 702/68, para. 29; BVerfG, Judgement of 5.6.1973, 1 BvR 536/72, para. 48.

1023 BVerfG, Judgement of 18.2.1961, 2 BvG 1 u. 2/60, para. 183.

1024 Müller and Gusy refer to the "democratic function" of media. See Müller and Gusy, "Media Policy in Germany"; see also Roßnagel, Kleist and Scheuer, *Die Reform der Regulierung elektronischer Medien in Europa*, p. 97.

1025 BVerfG, Judgement of 18.2.1961, 2 BvG 1 u. 2/60, para. 184.

1026 BVerfG, Judgement of 18.2.1961, 2 BvG 1 u. 2/60, para. 184.

1027 BVerfG, Judgement of 27.7.1971, 2 BvF 1/68, 2 BvR 702/68, para. 29; BVerfG, Judgement of 16.6.1981, 1 BvL 89/78, para. 94.

1028 BVerfG, Judgement of 18.2.1961, 2 BvG 1 u. 2/60, para. 184; BVerfG, Judgement of 27.7.1971, 2 BvF 1/68, 2 BvR 702/68, para. 33.

1029 BVerfG, Judgement of 16.6.1981, 1 BvL 89/78, para. 88. In this case, the BVerfG was asked to assess the constitutionality of the rules on private broadcasting contained in the media law of the Saarland. As the first state, the Saarland had permitted the organisation of private broadcasting in its media law. More con-

trol of broadcasting by politics and the state.[1030] The state's influence on providers is thus constrained to a precisely confined area of supervision.[1031] By the same token, the BVerfG clarified that the need for a legal framework persisted even in the wake of technological progress, particularly digitalisation which solves the problem of spectrum scarcity.[1032]

In the 1980s, the BVerfG laid the ground for the introduction of private broadcasting.[1033] It confirmed that a dual order of PSB and commercial broadcasting was permissible pursuant to the Basic Law but required an explicit decision by the legislature.[1034] The Court found that the same rationale for regulating public service broadcasting was valid for commercial TV.[1035] Nonetheless, differences could be made. In a dual order, it was imperative that the "*Grundversorgung*" (basic supply)[1036] be provided by

---

cretely, the subject of the case was the refusal by the state government of the application for a license by the "Freie Rundfunkaktiengesellschaft in Gründung". The BVerfG declared the Saarland media law unconstitutional as it violated the freedom of expression as set out in Art. 5 GG. In more detail, see Dörr, "Grundsätze der Medienregulierung," para. 1, p. 160; Roßnagel, Kleist and Scheuer, *Die Reform der Regulierung elektronischer Medien in Europa*, pp. 98, 99.

1030 Schüller-Keber, "Die Kommunikationsfreiheiten in der Verfassung," para. 154, p. 96.

1031 Schüller-Keber, "Die Kommunikationsfreiheiten in der Verfassung," para. 154, p. 96.

1032 BVerfG, Judgement of 16.6.1981, 1 BvL 89/78, para. 93.

1033 Art. 111a (2) of the Bavarian state constitution prescribes that broadcasting can only be provided by a public body (i.e. the Bayrische Landeszentrale für neue Medien, BLM). The BLM is de facto comparable to other state media authorities and the situation for service providers is similar as in other states. See Wiebke Baars, *Kooperation und Kommunikation durch Landesmedienanstalten, Eine Analyse ihres Aufgaben- und Funktionsbereichs*, Materialien zur interdisziplinären Medienforschung 35 (Baden-Baden: Nomos, 1999), pp. 101, 102.

1034 BverfG, Judgement of 4.11.1986, 1 BvF 1/84, para. 102. On the basis of the 1981 decision of the BVerfG, several German states adopted laws regulating private broadcasting. Several members of Parliament introduced a complaint before the BVerfG against the law of Niedersachsen (Lower Saxony). The BVerfG held that several provisions did not conform to the Constitution such as the rules concerning supervision, the application procedure for licenses and the provisions preventing dominant opinion power.

1035 BVerfG, Judgement of 16.6.1981, 1 BvL 89/78, paras. 97, 98.

1036 The term Grundversorgung (basic supply) was further specified in BverfG, Judgement of 24.3.1987, 1 BvR 147, 478/86, para. 81. Two public service

public broadcasters.[1037] Only if public service broadcasters provided a comprehensive programme (entertainment, education and information), which covered the whole range of social life and reflected cultural diversity, and which was directed to the entire population and accessible to all, standards applicable to commercial broadcasting regarding the scope of their programme offer and the representation of diverse and balanced public opinions could be lower.[1038] The fact that commercial broadcasting is financed by selling airtime for advertising[1039] was considered as a valid reason why the overall offer of such providers was lacking. Commercial broadcasters nonetheless are required to ensure a minimum level of objectivity, impartiality and balanced coverage.[1040] As a result, the liberties of commercial broadcasters essentially hinge on the fulfillment by public broadcasters of their public service remit.[1041] What is more, the legislature is to aspire to the highest level of balanced coverage of diverse opinions in establishing the legal framework for private broadcasting.[1042] Interestingly, the BVerfG clarified in this context that the term broadcasting within the meaning of the second sentence of Art. 5 (1) GG had to be interpreted dynamically accounting for the changing environment and circumstances. The term could not be tied to a specific kind of technology (which, on the contrary, would rapidly be superseded) but instead encompassed television-like communications services.[1043] The BVerfG thereby paved the way

---

broadcasters, the Süddeutscher Rundfunk and the Südwestfunk initiated proceedings against parts of the media law of Baden-Württemberg arguing that several provisions of the law violated their freedom to disseminate broadcasts. The BVerfG found that it was not in conformity with the Basic Law (GG), in particular Art. 5 (1) GG to exclude public service broadcasters from the provision of certain programmes and television-like services. However, the Court accepted, among others, the prohibition for regional and local public service broadcasters to screen advertising and the introduction of specific license requirements for subscribers or on-demand users of paid TV.

1037 Roßnagel, Kleist and Scheuer, *Die Reform der Regulierung elektronischer Medien in Europa*, p. 99.

1038 BverfG, Judgement of 4.11.1986, 1 BvF 1/84, para. 105. See also Schüller-Keber, "Die Kommunikationsfreiheiten in der Verfassung," para. 156, p. 97.

1039 Müller and Gusy, "Media Policy in Germany," p. 118.

1040 Schüller-Keber, "Die Kommunikationsfreiheiten in der Verfassung," para. 156, p. 97.

1041 Schüller-Keber, "Die Kommunikationsfreiheiten in der Verfassung," para. 156, p. 97.

1042 BverfG, Judgement of 4.11.1986, 1 BvF 1/84, para. 105.

1043 BverfG, Judgement of 24.3.1987, 1 BvR 147, 478/86, para. 132.

for an expanded and more flexible constitutional notion of broadcasting which has been defined in the absence of a technology criterion. This approach is reminiscent of the EU's AVMSD, which equally refrains from technological specifications in the definitions. Importantly, the notion of broadcasting in a constitutional sense is broader than the concept applied in relevant legislation[1044] and is contingent on three elements: it is destined to the general public, disseminated by communications networks and constitutes a performance suitable for public opinion forming.[1045]

With respect to the regulation of broadcasting and its supervision, neither Art. 5 GG nor the BVerfG prescribe a certain type of regulatory model. Yet, adherence to the principle of independence or distance from the state ("*Gebot der Staatsferne*")[1046] is of utmost importance. Furthermore, regulatory oversight must be fully operative and effective.[1047] It can further be derived from the jurisprudence of the BVerfG that the legislature may freely determine the regulatory structure, be it internally pluralistic ("*innenpluralistisch*") or externally pluralistic ("*außenpluralistisch*").[1048] The internally pluralistic model (which is applicable to PSB), may be characterised as a form of self-regulation.[1049] More concretely, all political, societal and ideological groups of the public are represented in the internal bodies (frequently called councils) of the broadcasters. These councils constitute the primary control mechanism.[1050] By contrast, the repre-

---

1044 Schüller-Keber, "Die Kommunikationsfreiheiten in der Verfassung," paras. 146, 148, pp. 92, 93.

1045 Schüller-Keber, "Die Kommunikationsfreiheiten in der Verfassung," para. 150, p. 93. The criterion of „Darbietung" is further specified by the criteria Breitenwirkung (wide-spread impact), Aktualität (relevance to the present) and Suggestivkraft (power of suggestion). See BVerfG, Judgement of 22.2.1994, 1 BvL 30/88, para. 140; Schwartmann, "Rundfunkrechtliche Grundlagen," para. 17, pp. 51–52.

1046 BVerfG, Judgement of 4.11.1986, 1 BvF 1/84, para. 171. See also Malzanini, "Aufsichtsgremien," in *Medienrecht, Lexikon für Praxis und Wissenschaft*, ed. Peter Schiwy, Walter Schütz and Dieter Dörr, fifth edition (Köln: Carl Heymanns Verlag, 2010), p. 20; Müller and Gusy, "Media Policy in Germany," p. 119; Schwartmann, "Rundfunkrechtliche Grundlagen," para. 47, p. 63.

1047 Baars, *Kooperation und Kommunikation durch Landesmedienanstalten*, p. 99.

1048 BVerfG, Judgement of 16.6.1981, 1 BvL 89/78, paras. 99, 100. See also Frank Götz, "Rundfunkorganisationsrecht," in *Medienrecht, Lexikon für Praxis und Wissenschaft*, ed. Schiwy, Schütz and Dörr, fourth edition (Köln: Carl Heymanns Verlag, 2010), pp. 505, 507.

1049 Malzanini, "Aufsichtsgremien," p. 20.

1050 Götz, "Rundfunkorganisationsrecht," p. 505.

sentation of society and supervision of programmes are carried out by external agencies in the externally pluralistic model. The core activity, namely programme production and provision are externalised, being the responsibility of private broadcasters.[1051] The media authorities serve a coordinating function by licensing diverse broadcasters with different profiles (programme offers) to establish a varied and coordinated overall programme.[1052] In Germany, there are 14[1053] state media authorities (*Landesmedienanstalten, LMA*), which are responsible for the allocation of licenses and the supervision of commercial providers.[1054] To achieve a plural and balanced offer of programmes, the media authorities are required to cooperate and coordinate with each other, whereby they contribute to the realisation of the freedom of broadcasting.[1055]

## II. Legal sources

The German legal order generally differentiates between broadcasting, which is subject to the *Rundfunkstaatsvertrag*[1056] (RStV, Interstate Broadcasting Treaty) and telemedia services, which are governed by the *Teleme-*

---

1051 Baars, *Kooperation und Kommunikation durch Landesmedienanstalten*, p. 100.

1052 Baars, *Kooperation und Kommunikation durch Landesmedienanstalten*, p. 101.

1053 Due to administrative reasons, the states of Berlin/Brandenburg and Hamburg/Schleswig Holstein share a media authority. See also Pierre-Francois Docquir, Sebastian Müller and Christian Gusy, "Does the Complexity of Institutional Structures in Federal States Influence the Independence of AVM Regulatory Authorities? A Review of the Cases of Germany and Belgium," in *The Independence of the Media and Its Regulatory Agencies, Shedding New Light on Formal and Actual Independence against the National Context*, ed. Schulz, Valcke and Irion (Bristol, UK and Chicago, USA: Intellect, 2013), p. 274; Dörr, "Grundsätze der Medienregulierung," para. 103, p. 213.

1054 Hans Hege, "Landesmediengesetze," in *Medienrecht, Lexikon für Praxis und Wissenschaft*, ed. Schiwy, Schütz and Dörr, fifth edition (Köln: Carl Heymanns Verlag, 2010), p. 328.

1055 Baars, *Kooperation und Kommunikation durch Landesmedienanstalten*, p. 101.

1056 A German version of the Interstate Broadcasting Treaty (in the version of its 15th amendment) is available at http://www.die-medienanstalten.de/fileadmin/Download/Rechtsgrundlagen/Gesetze_aktuell/15_RStV_01-01-2013.pdf (accessed 4.11.2014). An English version can be retrieved from http://wwwen.uni.lu/recherche/fdef/droit_des_medias/audiovisual_media_services_directive/national_execution_measures/germany (accessed 4.11.2014).

*diengesetz*[1057] (TMG, Telemedia Act). While the former is regulated by the states which jointly set out rules in an interstate agreement that is implemented in each state, the latter is regulated by the federal level. After extensive negotiations and repeated failed attempts in the early and mid-1980s,[1058] the RStV was first signed by all minister-presidents in April 1987 and has since been amended 18 times.[1059] Due to the difficulties of reaching consensus among all German states and the fundamental framework it lays down for the provision of cross-state broadcasting, it has been heralded as the "basic law for broadcasting".[1060] Thus, the RStV regulates commercial and PSB, sets out programme standards, licensing and access requirements, rules on data protection and administrative offences. Interestingly, the RStV prescribes certain rules for telemedia services such as information requirements, the right of reply, rules on data protection as well as commercial communication. Compliance with the specific provisions included in the RStV is overseen by the competent state authorities as determined by state law.[1061] This set of rules was introduced in the RStV by virtue of the 9th amendment which entered into force

---

1057 A German version of the Telemedia Act is available at http://www.gesetze-im-internet.de/tmg/index.html (accessed 3.11.2014). An English version can be retrieved from http://wwwen.uni.lu/recherche/fdef/droit_des_medias/audiovisual_media_services_directive/national_execution_measures/germany (accessed 3.11.2014).

1058 For a detailed historical account of the development of the RStV, see Reinhard Hartstein et al., "Entstehungsgeschichte," in *Rundfunkstaatsvertrag, Kommentar*, Loose-leaf commentary (Köln: Rehm, n.d.), B1, paras. 1-75.

1059 A German version of the 18th RStV that entered into force on 1 January 2016 is available at http://www.die-medienanstalten.de/fileadmin/Download/Rechtsgrundlagen/Gesetze_aktuell/RStV_18.pdf (accessed 1.10.2016). An English version can be retrieved from http://www.die-medienanstalten.de/fileadmin/Download/Rechtsgrundlagen/Gesetze_aktuell/15_RStV_english_01-01-2013.pdf (accessed 1.10.2016).

1060 Reinhard Hartstein et al., "Rechtsgrundlagen des Rundfunks," in *Rundfunkstaatsvertrag, Kommentar*, Loose-leaf commentary (Köln: Rehm, n.d.), B 3, para. 2.

1061 Art. 59 (2) RStV. The competent state authorities are either media authorities (LMA) or a department of the state government or regional council or district authority. For a detailed list of competent state authorities, see Christian Volkmann, "§ 59 Aufsicht," in *Recht der elektronischen Medien*, ed. Gerald Spindler and Fabian Schuster, second edition (München: C. H. Beck, 2011), para. 33; see also Dörr, "Grundsätze der Medienregulierung," para. 110, p. 216; Malzanini, "Aufsichtsgremien," p. 23.

on first of March 2007 and purports to regulate content-related matters of the provision of (press- and television-like) telemedia services, whereas the federal level, in the TMG, which entered into force on the same day, covers the economic aspects thereof as well as data protection requirements.[1062]

More specifically, the TMG of 2007 resolved quarrels which had been smouldering for more than a decade between the states and the federal level about competence over (albeit gradually growing and thus more significant) a "niche" matter located "between" the firm axes of broadcasting and telecommunications.[1063] When Germany had adopted a widely imitated modern cyber- law in the late 1990s, it had found a provisional solution attributing competence to regulate services addressed to the general public (so-called media services) to the states, while according to the federal level the competence to regulate services intended for individual communication (so-called tele services).[1064] Consequently two distinct laws with partially overlapping provisions were adopted.[1065] This confusing and artificially constructed differentiation between media services and tele services

1062 Marc Oliver Brock and Michael Schmittmann, "Telemedienrecht," in *Praxishandbuch Medien-, IT- und Urheberrecht*, ed. Rolf Schwartmann, third edition (Heidelberg: C. F. Müller Verlag, 2014), para. 10, p. 325; Reinhard Hartstein et al., "§ 36 RStV Zuständigkeiten, Aufgaben," in *Rundfunkstaatsvertrag, Kommentar*, Looseleaf commenatry (Köln: Rehm, n.d.), p. B5, para. 1; Tobias Keber, "Internet- und Telemedienrecht," in *Handbuch Medienrecht, Recht der elektronischen Massenmedien*, ed. Dörr, Kreile and Cole, second edition (Frankfurt am Main: Verlag Recht und Wirtschaft, 2010), para. 41, p. 520; Johannes Kreile, "Telemedien," in *Medienrecht, Lexikon für Praxis und Wissenschaft*, ed. Schiwy, Schütz and Dörr, fifth edition (Köln: Carl Heymanns Verlag, 2010), p. 617; Roßnagel, "Das Telemediengesetz, Neuordnung für Informations- und Kommunikationsdienste," *Neue Zeitschrift für Verwaltungsrecht*, 2007, p. 743; see also Eckpunkte zur Fortentwicklung der nationalen Medienordnung, 2.11.2005, available at http://www.bundesregierung.de/Content/DE/Artikel/BKM/2005-11-02-eckpunkte-zur-fortentwicklung-der-nationalen-medienordnung.html;jsessionid=F2F84F06C9B21894D3BE78C0E644E1A5.s3t2 (accessed 4.11.2014).

1063 Art. 73 No. 9 GG (industrial property rights, copyrights and publishing) and Art. 74 (1) No. 1 (civil law, criminal law [.]) and No. 11 GG (the law relating to economic matters. See also Roßnagel, "Das Telemediengesetz," p. 743.

1064 Roßnagel, Kleist and Scheuer, *Die Reform der Regulierung elektronischer Medien in Europa*, p. 95.

1065 Volker Kitz, "Das neue Recht der elektronischen Medien in Deutschland- sein Charme, seine Fallstricke," *Zeitschrift für Europarechtliche Studien*, 2007, p. 369; Stephan Ory, "Differenzierte Regelung für Rundfunk, Medien- und Teledi-

was abandoned by the TMG, which is applicable to telemedia (services).[1066] In fact, the term "telemedia", a cross-breeding between "tele services" and "media services", was first employed in the law protecting minors in the media (*Jugendmedienschutz-Staatsvertrag*, JMStV, Interstate Broadcasting Treaty on the Protection of Minors) of 2003[1067] and was subsequently applied in the specific law, the TMG. The distribution of competence between the content and economic side of the service remained controversial to the last.[1068] The TMG purports to transpose the rules stipulated in the EU's ECD.[1069] These had previously been outlined in the two separate acts on tele services and media services. The TMG is applicable to telemedia services which, broadly speaking, constitute information and communications services provided on-demand. It specifies the scope of application by negatively distinguishing it from telecommunications services (and similar services)[1070] and broadcasting.[1071] The content requirements for telemedia services within the meaning of audiovisual media services as defined by the AVMSD are laid down in the RStV, while the economic aspects are prescribed by the TMG. The TMG thus sets out

---

enste," in *Neuordnung des Medienrechts, Neuer rechtlicher Rahmen für eine konvergente Technik?*, ed. Alexander Roßnagel, Schriftenreihe des Instituts für Europäischens Medienrecht (EMR) 30 (Baden-Baden: Nomos, 2005), p. 68; Roßnagel, "Das Telemediengesetz," p. 743.

1066 Roßnagel, "Das Telemediengesetz," p. 743.

1067 Mark Cole, "Jugendmedienschutz," in *Handbuch Medienrecht, Recht der elektronischen Massenmedien*, ed. Dörr, Kreile and Cole, second edition (Frankfurt am Main: Verlag Recht und Wirtschaft, 2010), para. 8, p. 305; Kitz, "Das neue Recht der elektronischen Medien," p. 369.

1068 Kitz, "Das neue Recht der elektronischen Medien," p. 369.

1069 Roßnagel, "Das Telemediengesetz," p. 743.

1070 Telecommunications services within the meaning of the Telekommunikationsgesetz (TKG, Telecommunications Act) constitute services transmitting signals over telecommunications networks. If content is provided in parallel to the technical infrastructure, the TMG is applicable, too. For a more detailed differentiation between telecommunications services and telemedia services and the consequences of these classifications, see Keber, "Internet- und Telemedienrecht," para. 44, p. 520; Kitz, "Das neue Recht der elektronischen Medien," p. 369; Roßnagel, "Das Telemediengesetz," p. 745.

1071 Art. 1 (1) TMG. On the scope of application of the TMG, see Thomas Hoeren, "Das Telemediengesetz," *Neue Juristische Wochenschrift*, 2007, p. 802; Keber, "Internet- und Telemedienrecht," paras. 432–48, pp. 520–23; Kitz, "Das neue Recht der elektronischen Medien," pp. 369–72; Kreile, "Telemedien," pp. 617–21; Roßnagel, "Das Telemediengesetz," pp. 744–46.

the country of origin principle and entails rules on freedom of access, transparency of services, responsibility of providers and data protection.[1072] The TMG was amended in 2010 to implement the AVMSD, especially the rules applicable to on-demand services.[1073] It expressly exempts telemedia service providers from licensing or notification.[1074]

Furthermore, the protection of minors online and offline is regulated by two specific acts that entered into force on 1 April 2003. The separation results from the particularities of the German federal system. The disputes over competence between the states and the federal level[1075] were settled by a cooperation agreement between the states in charge of the protection of minors in all kinds of media (telemedia and broadcast) and the federal level regulating all non-media related aspects including offline media such as films, writings, picture and sound carriers in the *Jugendschutzgesetz*[1076] (JuSchG, Protection of Young Persons Act). The provisions contained in the JuSchG relating to the protection of young people in the context of media are relevant to the analysis conducted in the fifth chapter of this study, entailing, for instance, the question of labelling. Moreover, the German states adopted the *Jugendmedienschutz-Staatsvertrag* (JMStV, Interstate Treaty for the Protection of Minors),[1077] which constituted a comprehensive reform package in order to react to the deficiencies of previous legislation caused by technological developments.[1078]

---

1072 Keber, "Internet- und Telemedienrecht," para. 42, p. 520.

1073 Keber, "Internet- und Telemedienrecht," para. 51, p. 525.

1074 Art. 4 TMG in conjunction with Art. 54 (1) RStV.

1075 The federal level relied on the concurrent legislative powers, above all Art. 74 (1) No. 7 (public welfare) and No. 11 (the law relating to economic matters). See also Dorit Bosch, *Die "Regulierte Selbstregulierung" im Jugendmedienschutz-Staatsvertrag, Eine Bewertung des neuen Aufsichtsmodells anhand verfassungs- und europarechtlicher Vorgaben*, Studien zum deutschen und europäischen Medienrecht 22 (Frankfurt am Main: Peter Lang, 2006), pp. 28–31; Christine Langenfeld, "Die Neuordnung des Jugendschutzes im Internet," *Multimedia und Recht*, 2003, p. 305; Rupert Stettner, "Der neue Jugendmedienschutz-Staatsvertrag – eine Problemsicht," *Zeitschrift für Urheber- und Medienrecht*, 2003, pp. 428–29.

1076 A German and English version of the Protection of Young Persons Act are available at http://www.kjm-online.de/recht/gesetze-und-staatsvertraege/jugendschutzgesetz-juschg.html (accessed 5.11.2014).

1077 A German and English version of the Interstate Treaty for the Protection of Minors are available at http://www.kjm-online.de/recht/gesetze-und-staatsvertraege/jugendmedienschutz-staatsvertrag-jmstv.html (accessed 5.11.2014).

1078 Cole, "Jugendmedienschutz," para. 6, p. 304.

Above all, the JMStV expands protection, which had only been rudimentary beforehand, establishing a genuine legal framework for the Internet.[1079] On the basis of the rules previously contained in the RStV, the JMStV establishes a coherent level of protection of minors and human dignity in view of all information and communications services. For this reason, the federal level withdrew from regulating the protection of minors in tele services so that the states could form a consistent framework by referring to the newly crafted term "telemedia".[1080] The primary objectives of the JMStV are the safeguarding of human dignity in programmes as well as the protection of minors from unsuitable content. To this end, the JMStV distinguishes and classifies content according to the level of harm caused to children and specifies what kinds of measures providers of such content are required to take. It also affects the regulatory structure, above all by introducing the so-called system of "regulated self-regulation" and establishing the *Kommission für Jugendmedienschutz* (KJM, Commission for the Protection of Minors) as a centralised regulatory authority overseeing commercial broadcasting and content disseminated on the Internet. On the basis of an evaluation conducted five years after the JMStV's adoption,[1081] several amendments were proposed to strengthen the existing regulatory

---

1079 Murad Erdemir, "Die Kommission für Jugendmedienschutz der Landesmedienanstalten – Ein zentrales Aufsichtsorgan für Rundfunk und Telemedien," *Recht der Jugend und des Bildungswesens* 3 (2006): p. 298; Stettner, "Der neue JMStV," p. 425.

1080 Roland Bornemann, "Der Jugendmedienschutz-Staatsvertrag der Länder," *Neue Juristische Wochenschrift*, 2003, p. 787; Bosch, *Die "Regulierte Selbstregulierung" im JMStV*, p. 51; Roßnagel, Kleist and Scheuer, *Die Reform der Regulierung elektronischer Medien in Europa*, p. 127; Stettner, "Der neue JMStV," p. 428. The official statement of reasons attached to the Interstate Treaty (amtliche Begründung) refers to a restructuring of competence between the federal level and the states. The states may thus use the margin of discretion opened by the withdrawal of the federal level to set out consistent youth protection standards. The official statement of reasons is available at http://www.kjm-online.de/fileadmin/Download_KJM/Recht/Amtliche_Begruendung_zum_JMStV_korrigiert.pdf (accessed 6.11.2014).

1081 See official statement of reasons (amtliche Begründung), p. 3. Since the lawmakers of the JMStV scheduled an evaluation of the law in advance, Bosch and Stettner point out that the character of the JMStV was essentially experimental. As a result, the law is subject to rectifications and improvements after pre-determined assessment periods. See Bosch, *Die "Regulierte Selbstregulierung" im JMStV*, p. 66; Stettner, "Der neue JMStV," p. 432.

structures and respond to progressive convergence of media.[1082] The introduction of a voluntary system of age classification for telemedia services was controversially discussed and presumably one of the reasons why the draft JMStV was not adopted.[1083] Although all minister-presidents of the states had signed the draft JMStV, the reform process was halted as the state parliament of North Rhine-Westphalia voted against the modifications in December 2010. A modest reform took place in 2016 with the adoption of the 19th treaty amending the RStV, which entered into force in October 2016.

In brief, the above list of sector-specific legal acts is proof of a very delicate political balance between the states and the federal level. The RStV constitutes the relevant legislation governing broadcasting and television-like on-demand services. It is complemented by the TMG that sets out economic aspects of the regulation of telemedia and on-demand audiovisual media services. The protection of minors in audiovisual media services is "outsourced" to the JMStV, which is enforced by an innovative system of "regulated self-regulation". The following section sheds light on the regulatory regimes prescribed by the RStV and JMStV and their supervisory authorities.[1084]

---

1082 For an overview of the proposed modifications in the draft JMStV of 2010, see Karsten Altenhain, "Die Neuregelung des JMStV insbesondere im Hinblick auf Computerspiele und Filme," *BPJM-Aktuell* 4 (2010): pp. 5–16; Birgit Braml and Kristina Hopf, "Der neue Jugendmedienschutz-Staatsvertrag, Fort- oder Rückschritt für den Jugendmedienschutz?," *Zeitschrift für Urheber- und Medienrecht*, 2010, pp. 645–55; Kristina Hopf, "Der Jugendmedienschutz-Staatsvertrag. Die Novelle ist tot, es lebe die Novelle – die umstrittenen Regelungen auf einen Blick," *Kommunikation und Recht* 1 (2011): pp. 6–11; Verena Weigand, "Der novellierte Jugendmedienschutz-Staatsvertrag, Konsequenzen für die Arbeit der KJM," *JMS Report* 4 (2010): pp. 2–4.

1083 Hopf, "Der JMStV. Die Novelle ist tot, es lebe die Novelle," p. 6.

1084 This study focuses on the activities of national regulatory authorities. Thus, it covers the regulatory framework pursuant to the TMG only to the extent that the provision of telemedia services (within the meaning of the AVMSD) is overseen by state media authorities. In some states, notably Bavaria, Baden-Württemberg, Mecklenburg-West Pomerania, Lower Saxony, Saxony, North Rhine-Westphalia and Rhineland-Palatinate the provision of telemedia services is overseen by bodies or departments of state governments. Kunisch criticises such regulatory structures for their proximity to the state violating the principles established by the BVerfG in its jurisprudence concerning Art. 5 GG. See Kasper Kunisch, "Verfassungswidrige Telemedienaufsicht durch Regierungsstellen, Aufsicht

## III. State media authorities

### 1. Functions

Almost every German state has a state media authority (LMA) which is an institution under public law.[1085] The states of Berlin/Brandenburg and Hamburg/Schleswig Holstein respectively share one authority.[1086] The legal bases are set out in the state media laws. Essentially, LMA are public service bodies serving the general interest without being integrated into the state apparatus.[1087] The influence of the state on the LMA is discernible (the state monitors the activities of the LMA) but constrained to a minimum as required by the BVerfG's jurisprudence.[1088] LMA principally serve two main aims: first, they are to develop and further commercial broadcasting and second, they are to defend the public interest. Initially, the contradictory nature of the dual functions was criticised.[1089] Likewise, LMA were reproached for their identification and solidarity with the interests and positions of their supervised subjects.[1090] Informal correspondence and cooperation between LMA and service providers was regarded as proof of an inefficient regulatory regime.[1091] Nonetheless, the "policy of the raised eyebrow" has gradually gained acceptance. Cooperation between service providers and regulatory bodies has come to be considered an indispensable regulatory tool and is constitutionally legitimate.[1092] More specifically, LMA are responsible for the licensing of providers as well as the supervision of licensed providers. With regards to providers of-

---

über Internetdienste im Schutzbereich der Rundfunkfreiheit," *Multimedia und Recht*, 2011, pp. 796–99.

1085 Müller and Gusy, "Media Policy in Germany," p. 121.

1086 Doris Brocker, "Privater Rundfunk," in *Praxishandbuch Medien-, IT- und Urheberrecht*, ed. Rolf Schwartmann, third edition (Heidelberg: C. F. Müller Verlag, 2014), para. 9, p. 123; Docquir, Pierre-Francois, Müller, and Gusy, "Complexity of Institutional Structures in Federal States," p. 274; Dörr, "Grundsätze der Medienregulierung," para. 103, p. 213.

1087 Dörr, "Grundsätze der Medienregulierung," para. 103, p. 213.

1088 Dörr, "Grundsätze der Medienregulierung," para. 102, p. 212.

1089 Baars, *Kooperation und Kommunikation durch Landesmedienanstalten*, p. 25.

1090 Baars, *Kooperation und Kommunikation durch Landesmedienanstalten*, p. 25.

1091 Baars, *Kooperation und Kommunikation durch Landesmedienanstalten*, pp. 26, 27.

1092 Baars, *Kooperation und Kommunikation durch Landesmedienanstalten*, pp. 25, 28, 169, 187.

fering their services across states, the LMA of that state is competent that granted the license. This *ex post* control of compliance with the legal requirements stipulated in the RStV (as mirrored in the state media laws) is carried out by spot checks and complaints initiated by the public.[1093] In addition, LMA are committed to promoting programme production and distribution as well as media education and literacy.[1094] Importantly, LMA's functions as outlined by state media laws are crouched in general terms, attributing substantial leeway to regulators to specify the legal provisions.[1095] Briefly, LMA fulfil all the functions necessary for the preparation, safeguarding and enforcing of the objectives stipulated in the law.[1096]

To be decisive and efficient, LMA have several instruments at their disposal to sanction breaches of the law which constitute administrative offences. The sanctions depend, among others, on the type of rule that was infringed and the gravity and duration of the infringement. Hence, LMA may determine a breach of law[1097] or they may order providers to disseminate a notice.[1098] In addition, fines may be imposed as prescribed by state media laws. With respect to commercial broadcasters providing national services, the maximum fine constitutes EUR 500,000.[1099] Financial sanctions, which are tied to the economic success of providers, have a strong deterring effect.[1100] Above all, the suspension,[1101] or revocation[1102] of licenses by LMA may have serious consequences for providers. Similarly, state media authorities may sanction violations by blocking an offer tem-

---

1093 Stefan Sporn, *Die Ländermedienanstalt, Zur Zukunft der Aufsicht über den privaten Rundfunk in Deutschland und Europa*, ed. Dieter Dörr, Studien zum deutschen und europäischen Medienrecht 11 (Frankfurt am Main: Peter Lang, 2001), p. 14; Malzanini, "Aufsichtsgremien," p. 22.

1094 Malzanini, "Aufsichtsgremien," p. 22.

1095 For a detailed analysis of the tasks of state media authorities and their margin of discretion, see Baars, *Kooperation und Kommunikation durch Landesmedienanstalten*, pp. 164–89.

1096 Baars, *Kooperation und Kommunikation durch Landesmedienanstalten*, p. 188.

1097 Baars, *Kooperation und Kommunikation durch Landesmedienanstalten*, p. 152.

1098 Art. 49 (4) RStV concerning national broadcasters. See also Eva Wagner, "Aufsichtsmittel im dualen Rundfunksystem – Ungerechtfertigte Ungleichbehandlung?," *Zeitschrift für Urheber- und Medienrecht*, 2013, p. 851.

1099 Art. 49 (2) RStV Wagner, "Aufsichtsmittel im dualen Rundfunksystem," p. 851.

1100 Wagner, "Aufsichtsmittel im dualen Rundfunksystem," p. 856.

1101 Baars, *Kooperation und Kommunikation durch Landesmedienanstalten*, p. 152; Wagner, "Aufsichtsmittel im dualen Rundfunksystem," p. 851.

1102 Wagner, "Aufsichtsmittel im dualen Rundfunksystem," p. 851.

porarily or completely barring it.[1103] Such sanctions are mechanisms of last resort and will have to be employed proportionally. In sum, LMA are given a broad mandate by state legislation to oversee the provision of broadcasting and (depending on the state) telemedia services. As such, they are in an area of tension: on the one hand, they are required to regulate the actors of the media sector, curbing if necessary individual behaviour and on the other hand, they are to act as the guardian of the public interest by enabling and furthering media pluralism.[1104] If at all and how LMA have solved such conflicts will be explored in chapters four and five examining certain rules derived from the AVMSD.

## 2. Composition and funding

An expression of their independence from the state is LMA's right to self-administration.[1105] LMA are thus permitted to determine their institutional design and internal organisation.[1106] Typically, LMA are composed of two bodies: an assembly (assembly model) or council (council model) and an executive organ (president or director).[1107] The main regulatory body is either the assembly or the council.[1108] Representatives of the social groups relevant to a state are dispatched to an assembly that constitutes a pluralis-

---

1103 Art. 59 (3) RStV.

1104 Wagner, "Aufsichtsmittel im dualen Rundfunksystem," p. 852.

1105 ALM GbR, ed., *Jahrbuch 2013/2014, Landesmedienanstalten und privater Rundfunk in Deutschland* (Berlin: Vistas, 2014), p. 336, http://www.die-medienanstalten.de/fileadmin/Download/Publikationen/ALM-Jahrbuch/Jahrbuch_2014/Jahrbuch_2013-14_Druckversion.pdf (accessed 4.6.2015); Baars, *Kooperation und Kommunikation durch Landesmedienanstalten*, p. 117; Docquir, Müller and Gusy, "Complexity of Institutional Structures in Federal States," p. 259; Sporn, *Die Ländermedienanstalt*, p. 7.

1106 Helge Rossen-Stadtfeld, "Grenzen der Staatsaufsicht im Bereich des kommerziellen Rundfunks," *Zeitschrift für Urheber- und Medienrecht*, 2008, p. 5; on to the right to self-administration of public service broadcasting, see Georgios Gounalakis, "Funktionsauftrag und anstaltliches Selbstverwaltungsrecht," *Archiv für Presserecht, Zeitschrift für Medien- und Kommunikationsrecht* 5 (2003): pp. 395–405.

1107 Docquir, Müller and Gusy, "Complexity of Institutional Structures in Federal States," p. 259; Dörr, "Grundsätze der Medienregulierung," para. 104, p. 213; Malzanini, "Aufsichtsgremien," p. 22; Sporn, *Die Ländermedienanstalt*, p. 8.

1108 Malzanini, "Aufsichtsgremien," p. 22.

tic body comprising members of state parliament, the government, interest groups, associations and organisations.[1109] In contrast to assemblies, which are ordinarily big in numbers,[1110] a council comprises a small group of independent persons elected by state parliaments on account of their expertise and experience in the media sector.[1111] Although councils are usually smaller and allegedly more efficient bodies, the deficiency of this model is that it seemingly enhances the influence of the state by the appointment and election of the experts.[1112] The assembly model is more wide-spread.[1113] For the most part, the state media laws specify the exact details of the composition and competencies of the individual bodies and committees.

LMA are financed by the fees charged for licensing and other activities. The most significant source of financing is, however, a portion of the *Rundfunkbeitrag,* which constitutes the broadcasting charge levied on all households to finance public service broadcasting. Given the factual connection (i.e. the provision of broadcasting), such means of funding are permissible.[1114] Pursuant to Art. 10 (1) *Rundfunkfinanzierungsstaatsvertrag* (RFinStV, Interstate Treaty on the Financing of Broadcasting currently in the version of the 16th amendment which entered into force on 1 April

1109 Dörr, "Grundsätze der Medienregulierung," para. 104, pp. 213, 214; Stefan Sporn, "Auf dem Weg zur 'Ländermedienanstalt', Entwicklung, Stand und Perspektive der Aufsicht über den privaten Rundfunk und die Telemedien," *Kommunikation und Recht* 4 (2009): p. 238.

1110 Wolfgang Schulz and Thorsten Held, "§ 1 JMStV Zweck des Staatsvertrages," in *Beck'scher Kommentar zum Rundfunkrecht*, ed. Werner Hahn and Thomas Vesting, third edition (München: C.H. Beck, 2012), p. 35.

1111 Dörr, "Grundsätze der Medienregulierung," para. 104, p. 214; Hege, "Landesmediengesetze," p. 337.

1112 Schulz and Held, "§ 1 JMStV Zweck des Staatsvertrages," p. 36.

1113 Brocker, "Privater Rundfunk," para. 9, p. 124; Docquir, Müller and Gusy, "Complexity of Institutional Structures in Federal States," p. 259; a council is established in the media authorities of Berlin/Brandenburg and less pronounced in Hamburg/Schlewsig-Holstein and in Saxony, a hybrid model is deployed. The terms assembly and council are used inter-changeably in some states so that on face value, a media council (Medienrat) is constructed which nonetheless constitutes an assembly representing societal groups and influences. See ALM GbR, *Jahrbuch 2013/2014*, pp. 358–441.

1114 Michael Kühn, "§ 10, 11 RFinStV," in *Beck'scher Kommentar zum Rundfunkrecht*, ed. Werner Hahn and Thomas Vesting, third edition (München: C. H. Beck, 2012), para. 1.

2015), the share accorded to LMA is 1.8989 percent.[1115] From the total amount, each LMA receives an annual basic amount of EUR 511,290 and in addition, a share corresponding to the contribution to the broadcasting charge.[1116] As a result, populous states my profit (25 times more) from larger shares but this advantage is offset by the basic amount, which exceeds what some LMAs would be able to claim according to the broadcasting charge.[1117] The budget of the Bavarian authority for 2016, for instance, is estimated at approximately EUR 29.8 million (of which EUR 23.7 million are allotted from the broadcasting charge).[1118] Bavaria is not only a populous state; it has attracted more than 100 commercial broadcasters and contributes to more than 50 percent of all revenues generated in the German broadcasting sector.[1119] Furthermore, the budget of the media authority of North Rhine Palatine is calculated at approximately EUR 20.5 million (of which about EUR 17.1 million stem from the broadcasting charge), whereas the income of the Saarland media authority is only around EUR 2.7 million (of which EUR 2.2 million are financed by the broadcasting charge) and the budget of the Bremen LMA is about EUR 1.7 million (of which roughly EUR 1.6 million are financed through

---

1115 Docquir, Müller and Gusy, "Complexity of Institutional Structures in Federal States," p. 260; Reinhard Hartstein et al., "§ 40 Finanzierung besonderer Aufgaben," in *Rundfunkstaatsvertrag, Kommentar*, Looseleaf commenatry (Köln: Rehm, n.d.), para. 38; Kühn, "§ 10, 11 RFinStV," para. 1; Sporn, "Auf dem Weg zur 'Ländermedienanstalt,'" p. 238.

1116 Interestingly, Art. 10 (2) RFinStV encouraged the fusion of state media authorities by outlining financial incentives. Accordingly, the merging state media authorities would continue to receive their individual basic amounts in full for three years and gradually decreasing parts thereof until the eighth year of their consolidation. Yet, the intended effects of the provision failed to materialise. The state media authorities of Bremen and North Rhine Westphalia had a possible fusion appraised by the latter's state audit office which considered that merging the bodies would be financially unsound and thus advised against it. The only genuine fusion occurred between the state media authorities of Hamburg and Schlewig-Holstein in 2007 while the state of Brandenburg refrained from establishing a state media authority after the re-unification of Germany and instead the state media authority of Berlin was expanded. See Kühn, "§ 10, 11 RFinStV," paras. 6–8.

1117 Kühn, "§ 10, 11 RFinStV," paras. 4, 5.

1118 ALM GbR, *Jahrbuch 2015/2016*, p. 228.

1119 Bayrische Landeszentrale für neue Medien, Aktuelle Daten & Fakten zum Medienstandort Bayern, available at http://www.blm.de/de/medienstandort/aktuelle_daten_fakten.cfm (accessed 20.11.2014).

the broadcasting charge).[1120] These figures reveal the differences between LMA's (financial) capacities and equipment.

Moreover, the means are distributed by each state authority in charge of the administration of the broadcasting charge.[1121] Interestingly, a Protocol was annexed to the RFinStV in 2000 which abandoned the automatism between the augmentation of the shares accorded to LMA and the increase in broadcasting charges as of 2005 and instead capped the share at roughly 2 percent.[1122] The proportion is evaluated periodically and the states may jointly "opt-in" to an increase of charges.[1123] The funds are to be used by LMA in line with the tasks enumerated in Art. 40 RStV, i.e. for licensing and supervisory tasks and the promotion of public access channels. The return of excess funds to PSB's budget is mandatory.[1124] The current system of financing has been heavily criticised as the payment of a flat rate is neither in line with demand nor with the tasks of LMA and above all, does not encourage LMA to actually save money or administer resources more economically.[1125] In addition, the huge costs of the decentralised model with its 14 state media authorities have been underscored. Therefore, Sporn has, among others, advanced the proposal for a *Ländermedienanstalt* (media authority of the states), which would bundle the tasks and competencies for services offered on a nation-wide basis.[1126] The potential for savings generated by this consolidation is enormous. Yet, the "structural complexity" of the regulatory framework has further been reinforced by the establishment of several bodies that deal with cross-border (national) issues.[1127]

---

1120 ALM GbR, *Jahrbuch 2015/2016*, pp. 236, 256, 264.

1121 Kühn, "§ 10, 11 RFinStV," para. 11. State legislatures may withhold parts of the share and not allocate the total amount to LMA by virtue of Art. 40 (2) RStV. See Docquir, Müller and Gusy, "Complexity of Institutional Structures in Federal States," p. 261.

1122 Hartstein et al., "§ 40 Finanzierung besonderer Aufgaben," para. 7c; Kühn, "§ 10, 11 RFinStV," para. 2.

1123 Hartstein et al., "§ 40 Finanzierung besonderer Aufgaben," para. 7c; Kühn, "§ 10, 11 RFinStV," para. 2.

1124 Art. 40 (3) RStV. See Sporn, "Auf dem Weg zur 'Ländermedienanstalt,'" p. 241. According to Sporn, LMA are permitted by state media laws to build up reserves for the fulfillment of their tasks in the future.

1125 Sporn, "Auf dem Weg zur 'Ländermedienanstalt,'" p. 241.

1126 Sporn, "Auf dem Weg zur 'Ländermedienanstalt,'" pp. 241–42.

1127 Sporn, "Auf dem Weg zur 'Ländermedienanstalt,'" p. 240.

### 3. Supra-state bodies

In recent years, a shift in LMA's role has been identified. Due to digitalisation technologies, the original objectives of LMA (to ensure a diverse offer of programmes in the light of spectrum scarcity) have evolved. In a similar vein, decentralised regulatory models are likely to reinforce competition of states and may lead to forum shopping and a raise to the bottom (regarding programme standards for example).[1128] To counter these phenomena, uniform procedures and uniform assessments of programmes become necessary in order to ensure equal treatment of providers.[1129] The need for LMA to cooperate across state borders and jointly on a national level was palpable not least with respect to providers operating nationwide and culminated in the construction of several cross-state or supra-state authorities, which has arguably caused a loss of influence of LMA.[1130] With the tenth amendment to the RStV, which entered into force in September 2008, the reform brought forth the establishment (or reorganisation) of bodies with special competence for a pre-defined subject matter.[1131] These "*Wanderorgane*"[1132] (moving organs) or "virtual *Ländermedienanstalt*"[1133] serve the respective media authorities for which their decisions are binding.[1134] As a result, the *Kommission zur Zulassung und*

---

1128 Schulz and Held, "§ 1 JMStV Zweck des Staatsvertrages," para. 32.

1129 Brocker, "Privater Rundfunk," para. 10, pp. 5, 124; Schulz and Held, "§ 1 JMStV Zweck des Staatsvertrages," para. 31.

1130 The "federal" organs are established under the umbrella of the Arbeitsgemeinschaft der Landesmedienanstalten (ALM), see Brocker, "Privater Rundfunk," para. 11, pp. 5, 125; see also the ALM's Statute available at http://www.die-medienanstalten.de/fileadmin/Download/Rechtsgrundlagen/Satzungen/ALM-Statut_20.11.2013.pdf (accessed 22 November 2014); Hege, "Landesmediengesetze," p. 337; Schulz and Held, "§ 1 JMStV Zweck des Staatsvertrages," para. 30.

1131 Andreas Grünwald, "§ 36 RStV Zuständigkeiten, Aufgaben," in *Recht der elektronischen Medien*, ed. Gerald Spindler and Fabian Schuster, third edition (München: C. H. Beck, 2015), para. 1.

1132 Christoph Gröpl, "Die Reform der Medienkontrolle durch den Zehnten Rundfunkänderungsstaatsvertrag, Anforderungen an eine vertragsgemäße Umsetzung durch die Landesmedienanstalten," *Zeitschrift für Urheber- und Medienrecht*, 2009, p. 23; Jens Prütting, "Das Prinzip der regulierten Selbstregulierung im Jugendmedienschutz," *Kommunikation und Recht* 12 (2013): p. 778.

1133 Schulz and Held, "§ 1 JMStV Zweck des Staatsvertrages," para. 8.

1134 Gröpl, "Die Reform der Medienkontrolle durch den 10. RÄStV," p. 23; Schulz and Held, "§ 1 JMStV Zweck des Staatsvertrages," para. 8; Wolfgang Thaenert, "Nochmals zur Reform der Medienkontrolle durch den Zehnten Rund-

*Aufsicht* (Commission on Licensing and Supervision, ZAK) was created and the *Kommission zur Ermittlung der Konzentration im Medienbereich* (Commission on Concentration in the Media, KEK) was restructured.[1135] The ZAK comprises one representative of each state media authority, typically the executive organs (i.e. the president or director).[1136] It is competent to act in all matters regarding licensing (including decisions to withdraw or revoke a license) and supervision of national broadcasters as well as the regulation of platforms.[1137] The ZAK's creation primarily purported to "reduce competition among state media authorities", to enhance cooperation and "presumably prevent single interest decisions by one of the state media authorities".[1138]

Similarly, the KEK is comparable to a specialised competition authority overseeing the level of concentration in the media market with a view to securing and furthering plurality. When the KEK was established in the late 1990s, it was made up of six experts. These were complemented by six representatives of state media authorities.[1139] Furthermore, the protection of minors is ensured by the KJM which was established in 2003 and is subject to a more detailed discussion below. In addition, the representatives of the internal bodies of the state media authorities also meet in dif-

---

funkänderungsstaatsvertrag," *Zeitschrift für Urheber- und Medienrecht*, 2009, p. 133.

1135 For an overview on the modifications brought about by the tenth amendment to the RStV, see Brocker, "Privater Rundfunk," paras. 12–18, pp. 5, 125–27; Gröpl, "Die Reform der Medienkontrolle durch den 10. RÄStV," pp. 21–29; Kristoff Ritlewski, "Pluralismussicherung im 10. Rundfunkänderungsstaatsvertrag, Ein Beitrag zur Dogmatik der Pluralismussicherung," *Zeitschrift für Urheber- und Medienrecht*, 2008, pp. 403–10; Thaenert, "Nochmals zur Reform der Medienkontrolle durch den 10. RÄStV," pp. 131–35.

1136 Art. 35 (3) RStV.

1137 Art. 36 (2) RStV. See also Docquir, Müller and Gusy, "Complexity of Institutional Structures in Federal States," p. 260; Dörr, "Grundsätze der Medienregulierung," para. 106, p. 214; Hartstein et al., "§ 40 Finanzierung besonderer Aufgaben," paras. 1, 7; Ritlewski, "Pluralismussicherung im 10. RÄStV," p. 407.

1138 Docquir, Müller and Gusy, "Complexity of Institutional Structures in Federal States," p. 269.

1139 Gröpl, "Die Reform der Medienkontrolle durch den 10. RÄStV," p. 23; Ritlewski, "Pluralismussicherung im 10. RÄStV," p. 409; Thaenert, "Nochmals zur Reform der Medienkontrolle durch den 10. RÄStV," p. 133.

ferent constellations.[1140] To underline the increased cooperation at federal level, Art. 35 (7) RStV prescribes the setting up of a joint management office which was inaugurated in Berlin in 2013.[1141] The office constitutes the organisational umbrella and thus a single point of reference and support for the various bodies operating on the federal and state levels to foster country-wide cooperation and networking. The complexities of the German regulatory regime flow from the concise presentation above.[1142] Indubitably, this (almost incomprehensible) structure can partially be explained by the federal nature of the country but it may be sensible to ask whether such regulatory constructions do not actually inhibit innovation or slow down regulation. By contrast, in the field of the protection of minors, the German system relies on a more flexible framework of regulated self-regulation.

## IV. Regulated self-regulation of the protection of minors in audiovisual media

This part outlines the German co-regulatory framework for the protection of minors, examining the various bodies and their respective roles and the manner in which they interact with each other.

### 1. The legal framework: background and rationale

The protection of minors in audiovisual media constitutes an overarching societal objective of constitutional rank imposing a positive obligation on

1140 The directors of the state media authorities unite in the Direktorenkonferenz der Landesmedienanstalten (DLM) while the chairpersons of the decision-taking councils and assemblies gather in the Gremienvorsitzendenkonferenz (GVK). The GVK was revalued by the tenth revision of the RStV and is responsible for determining the selection of providers for scarce transmission capacities and platforms. It also participates in the principal developments and fundamental decision-making. See Grünwald, "§ 36 RStV Zuständigkeiten, Aufgaben," para. 5, on the composition of the GVK, see Art. 35 (4) RStV and on its competencies see Art. 36 (3) RStV.

1141 On the construction of the joint management office, see Gröpl, "Die Reform der Medienkontrolle durch den 10. RÄStV," pp. 21–29.

1142 Sporn, "Auf dem Weg zur 'Ländermedienanstalt,'" p. 240.

the state.[1143] By virtue of Art. 2 (1) GG in conjunction with Art. 1 (1) GG and Art. 5 (2) GG it is mandatory for the state to ensure the free development of one's personality. Similarly, Art. 6 (2) GG stipulates the right of parents for care and upbringing of their children.[1144] With regards to, among others, the dissemination of pornographic or sexually explicit content as well as programmes featuring extreme violence, these values markedly clash with the freedom of expression and the freedom to broadcast as outlined in Art. 5 (2) GG as well as the occupational freedom enshrined in Art. 12 GG.[1145] Due to these inherent conflicts at constitutional level requiring delicate compromising, a co-regulatory model often referred to in German literature as "regulated self-regulation" was introduced in 2003.[1146] At this time, the regulatory approach was altered as it was considered that the state could no longer satisfactorily fulfil its functions by traditional imperative and sovereign regulatory instruments.[1147] This was the result of the dynamism, volatility and speed of innovation caused by revolutionary economic and technological developments as well as rapidly changing social cultural values and perceptions. The pursuit of the traditional regulatory strategy in form of rigid norms and rule-setting (which could quickly become obsolete) was regarded as inadequate and

---

1143 Mark Cole, "Der Dualismus von Selbstkontrolle und Aufsicht im Jugendmedienschutz, Zum Verhältnis von FSF und KJM im System der 'regulierten Selbstregulierung' – Eine Untersuchung aus Anlass des Konflikts um Schönheitsoperationen im Fernsehprogramm," *Zeitschrift für Urheber- und Medienrecht*, 2005, p. 464; Helge Rossen-Stadtfeld, "Die Konzeption Regulierter Selbstregulation und ihre Ausprägung im Jugendmedienschutz," *Archiv für Presserecht, Zeitschrift für Medien- und Kommunikationsrecht* 3 (2004): p. 6.

1144 Bosch, *Die "Regulierte Selbstregulierung" im JMStV*, pp. 86–118; Cole, "Der Dualismus von Selbstkontrolle und Aufsicht im Jugendmedienschutz," p. 463; Erdemir, "Die Kommission für Jugendmedienschutz," pp. 285–86; Rossen-Stadtfeld, "Die Konzeption Regulierter Selbstregulation," pp. 6–7; Christian Von Coelln, "Jugendmedienschutz zwischen staatlichem Schutzauftrag und Zensurverbot," in *Jugendmedienschutz im Informationszeitalter*, ed. Nikolaus Bosch and Stefan Leible, Bayreuther Studien zum Wirtschafts- und Medienrecht 6 (Sipplingen: Jenaer Wissenschaftliche Verlagsgesellschaft, 2012), p. 46; Sabine Frank, "Selbstkontrolle im Internet," in *Positionen zum Jugendmedienschutz in Deutschland, Eine Textsammlung*, KJM Schriftenreihe 1 (Berlin: Vistas, 2009), p. 43.

1145 Erdemir, "Die Kommission für Jugendmedienschutz," p. 286; Rossen-Stadtfeld, "Die Konzeption Regulierter Selbstregulation," p. 7.

1146 Bosch, *Die "Regulierte Selbstregulierung" im JMStV*, p. 77.

1147 Bosch, *Die "Regulierte Selbstregulierung" im JMStV*, p. 76.

the need for an elastic framework with flexible elements became apparent.[1148] In order to master the sheer masses of offers, a self-regulatory component was reinforced.[1149]

Thus, the novel scheme improved *ex ante* control by enhancing the responsibility of providers for self-control and recognised organisations of voluntary self-regulation (*Einrichtung der Freiwilligen Selbstkontrolle*),[1150] which operate in a legal framework prescribed by the state.[1151] Hence, the state can retreat to the extent that the self-regulatory bodies possess more expertise to take decisions.[1152] What is more, the state can retake regulatory action in case the scheme functions inadequately.[1153] Arguably, responsibility and compliant behaviour by economic actors are increased and so equally is the effectiveness of the entire system.[1154] In addition, the 2003 reform aimed at modernising the legal framework and above all establishing coherent standards across all types of information and communications media.[1155] In light of increased cross-media commercialisation of programmes and changing user behaviour and habits, the

---

1148 Bosch, *Die "Regulierte Selbstregulierung" im JMStV*, p. 77.

1149 Reinhard Hartstein et al., "Entstehungsgeschichte – JMStV," in *Rundfunkstaatsvertrag, Kommentar*, Loose-leaf commentary (Köln: Rehm, n.d.), C2, II., para. 9.

1150 Malzanini, "Aufsichtsgremien," p. 23; Sonja Schwendner, "Die Zusammenarbeit mit Einrichtungen der Freiwilligen Selbstkontrolle," in *Positionen zum Jugendmedienschutz in Deutschland, Eine Textsammlung*, KJM Schriftenreihe 1 (Berlin: Vistas, 2009), p. 90.

1151 Cole, "Jugendmedienschutz," para. 47, p. 326; Mark Cole, "Das Zusammenwirken von Selbstkontrolle und hoheitlicher Kontrolle im Jugendmedienschutz," *Recht der Jugend und des Bildungswesens* 3 (2006): p. 307; Frank, "Selbstkontrolle im Internet," p. 38.

1152 Cole, "Das Zusammenwirken von Selbstkontrolle und hoheitlicher Kontrolle im Jugendmedienschutz," p. 301.

1153 Cole, "Das Zusammenwirken von Selbstkontrolle und hoheitlicher Kontrolle im Jugendmedienschutz," p. 301.

1154 Cole, "Das Zusammenwirken von Selbstkontrolle und hoheitlicher Kontrolle im Jugendmedienschutz," p. 301; for a discussion of the advantages and disadvantages of co-regulation in general, see chapter 1 and more specifically with respect to the German regulatory model for the protection of minors Cole, "Jugendmedienschutz," paras. 48–49, p. 327.

1155 Cole, "Jugendmedienschutz," para. 6, p. 304.

JMStV ensures consistent protection of minors in (both public and private)[1156] broadcasting and telemedia services.[1157]

The adoption of the JMStV (and the JuSchuG at the federal level) was prepared for a couple of years. In 2000, several meetings took place between the state ministers responsible for the protection of minors and the federal level. A draft law was prepared on the basis of the cornerstones agreed upon in February 2000.[1158] This draft law, in particular questions about the inclusion of PSB, the strengthening of voluntary self-control and the regulatory framework were discussed amongst stakeholders in August 2001. Industry representatives like PSB, commercial broadcasters, state media authorities, self-regulatory organisations and associations were invited and heard.[1159] This draft was, however, heavily criticised for the lack of precision of key terminology, the insufficient respect for the particularities of broadcasting and the lack of clarity with regards to the regulatory regime.[1160] A new attempt was ventured by what came to be called the "Usedom draft" (as it was initiated at a meeting of the offices of the minister presidents and senates on the island Usedom). The drafters highlighted two aspects: first, due to the enormous amounts of programmes, exclusive supervision by the state was impossible to realise on the Internet. Second, *ex ante* control in case of broadcasting was considered indispensable, but could be effectuated by means of self-regulation provided that the independence of self-regulatory bodies was guaranteed and providers participating in the scheme would be exonerated in some way.[1161] Once the text was finalised in May 2002, stakeholders were once more consulted in June

1156 The substantive rules set out in the JMStV are applicable to public service broadcasters, too. Compliance with the rules is overseen internally by broadcasters. See Erdemir, "Die Kommission für Jugendmedienschutz," p. 289.

1157 Erdemir, "Die Kommission für Jugendmedienschutz," p. 285; see also Deutscher Bundestag, Gesetzentwurf der Fraktionen der SPD und BÜNDNIS 90/DIE GRÜNEN, Entwurf eines Jugendschutzgesetzes, Drucksache 14/9013 of 13.4.2002, p. 26-27, available at http://fsf.de/data/user/Dokumente/Downloads/bt_drucksache_14_9013.pdf (accessed 28.11.2014); Hartstein et al., "Entstehungsgeschichte – JMStV", C2, II., paras. 9, 12.

1158 Hartstein et al., "Entstehungsgeschichte – JMStV", C2, II., para. 15.

1159 Hartstein et al., "Entstehungsgeschichte – JMStV", C2, II., 4.2, para. 21.

1160 Hartstein et al., "Entstehungsgeschichte – JMStV", C2, II., 4.3, para. 22.

1161 Hartstein et al., "Entstehungsgeschichte – JMStV", C2, III., 1., para. 24.

2002.[1162] The echo was predominantly positive even if a certain degree of mistrust towards self-regulation and scepticism about its effectiveness was voiced. While providers questioned the benefits of joining an organisation of voluntary self-regulation, the state media authorities criticised the expansion of the latter's powers and demanded effective (*ex post*) oversight including sanctioning mechanisms.[1163] The text was again modified to accommodate stakeholders' positions, and the law was adopted in September 2002.

## 2. The regulatory bodies for the protection of minors

### a) The Commission for the Protection of Minors

The JMStV did not only foster pre-existing self-regulatory initiatives, it also established a central supervisory body in charge of services disseminated nationally.[1164] As a quasi-federal organ, the KJM is jointly funded by the state media authorities. Its tasks are enumerated in Art. 16 (1) JMStV and include first and foremost the supervision of the application of the rules outlined in the JMStV to ensure compliance with the law. In addition, the KJM decides, among others, upon the certification of organisations of voluntary self-regulation, the scheduling of programmes, the assessment of encryption and blocking technology and the certification of technical systems.[1165] The state media authorities (in case of broadcasting) and jugendschutz.net, the joint organisation of all states for the protection of minors (in case of tele media services) examine the programmes prior

1162 A detailed list of participants of the hearing is included in Hartstein et al., "Entstehungsgeschichte – JMStV", C2, III., 3., para. 29; for a detailed account of stakeholders' positions, see Hartstein et al., "Entstehungsgeschichte – JMStV", C2, II., 3.1, paras. 30-49.

1163 Hartstein et al., "Entstehungsgeschichte – JMStV", C2, III., 3.2, para. 31 and V., 2. para. 67.

1164 Erdemir, "Die Kommission für Jugendmedienschutz," p. 285; Schwartmann, "Rundfunkrechtliche Grundlagen," para. 56, pp. 7, 200.

1165 In May 2013, the KJM certified the technical systems of JusProg and Deutsche Telekom. See KJM, Jugendschutzprogramme, available at http://www.kjm-online.de/telemedien/jugendschutzprogramme.html (accessed 2.12.2014); Erdemir, "Die Kommission für Jugendmedienschutz," p. 291; Frank, "Selbstkontrolle im Internet," p. 45.

to their transmission. Jugendschutz.net is "organisationally linked to the KJM" and supports the latter in the fulfilment of its tasks, notably monitoring telemedia services.[1166] If an initial suspicion is found, the case is referred to the KJM which investigates and assesses the programme after having heard the respective provider. During the proceedings, the KJM may request further information or access to content from the provider.[1167]

The decisions of the KJM including potential sanctions are subsequently enforced by the state media authorities. Hence, the KJM serves the competent LMA pursuant to Art. 14 (2) JMStV in conjunction with Art. 17 (1) JMStV.[1168] The KJM typically takes unanimous decisions through examining boards headed by at least one KJM member.[1169] During the first decade of its existence, the KJM examined approximately 6,100 complaints and requests: 1,000 in relation to broadcasts and more than 1,400 in relation to telemedia services.[1170] Between March 2013 and February 2015, the KJM was concerned with 106 broadcasting cases (most of which concerned sexual depictions in different contexts) of which around 90 have been assessed and about 57 were found to be violations of the JMStV.[1171] In the same reference period, the KJM handled 313 cases of alleged infringements, the majority of which concerned telemedia services depicting erotic or pornographic content.[1172] The KJM took decisions in more than 180 of these cases, finding that in about 72 cases providers had infringed the JMStV.[1173] In more than half of the cases, the proceedings

1166 Art. 18 (1) and (2) JMStV.

1167 Art. 21 JMStV.

1168 Bosch, *Die "Regulierte Selbstregulierung" im JMStV*, p. 63; Cole, "Jugendmedienschutz," para. 51, p. 328; Erdemir, "Die Kommission für Jugendmedienschutz," pp. 288–89; Wolf-Dieter Ring, "Jugendschutz im Spannungsfeld zwischen Selbstregulierung der Medien und staatlicher Medienkontrolle," *Archiv für Presserecht, Zeitschrift für Medien- und Kommunikationsrecht* 3 (2004): p. 10; Schwartmann, "Rundfunkrechtliche Grundlagen," para. 56, pp. 7, 200. In case of potential criminal content, the case is forwarded to the public prosecutor.

1169 Art. 14 (5) JMStV.

1170 KJM, "Sechster Tätigkeitsbericht über die Durchführung der Bestimmungen des Jugendmedienschutz-Staatsvertrag gem. § 17 Abs. 3 JMStV in der Zeit vom März 2013 – Februar 2015," May 2015, pp. 17, 24, http://www.kjm-online.de/fileadmin/Download_KJM/Service/Berichte/Sechster_Taetigkeitsbericht_der_KJM.pdf (accessed 6.7.2015).

1171 KJM, "Sixth activities report," p. 17.

1172 KJM, "Sixth activities report," p. 26.

1173 KJM, "Sixth activities report," pp. 26–27.

could be ended following the KJM's decision.[1174] The figures demonstrate a marked difference between broadcasting and telemedia services and are proof of a growth of problematic content on the Internet.

In order to effectively enforce the standards of the JMStV, the KJM may punish violations acting as the extended arm of the competent state media authority.[1175] The catalogue of sanctions set forth in the JMStV entails both, criminal and administrative sanctions.[1176] A provider is criminally liable for intentionally disseminating broadcasts "evidently suited to seriously impair the development" of minors as well as telemedia services of such kind not limited to closed user groups. A prison sentence of up to one year or a fine may be imposed by the state media authority.[1177] Moreover, the JMStV enumerates administrative offences including fines of up to EUR 500,000. Providers may additionally be required to transmit or make accessible the decisions of the regulatory bodies.[1178] The decisions of the regulatory authorities are subject to judicial review and providers may challenge them before the Federal Administrative Court.[1179]

Furthermore, the institutional structure of the KJM is different from most state media authorities and it does not, so one could presume, consist of one member representing each state media authority. In contrast to the plural composition of LMA, the KJM is composed of 12 experts of which 6 members are delegated by directors of state media authorities, 4 members are delegated by the supreme state youth authorities charged with the protection of minors and 2 members are moreover delegated by the supreme federal authority for the protection of minors.[1180] Given the technical complexity of the subject matter, expertise and experience are rele-

1174 KJM, "Sixth activities report," p. 27.

1175 Interestingly, the decisive criterion to determine competence in accordance with Art. 24 (4) JMStV is the authority which issued the license of a broadcaster and in case of providers of telemedia services (which need not acquire a license nor do they have to notify their services) the location of the "office, seat or residence, or, failing that, [the] permanent domicile.".

1176 Arts. 23, 24 JMStV.

1177 In case of negligent behaviour, the prison sentence is reduced to six months or a fine pursuant to the second sentence of Art. 23 JMStV.

1178 Art. 24 (6) JMStV.

1179 Art. 22 JMStV.

1180 Art. 14 (3) JMStV. See Bosch, *Die "Regulierte Selbstregulierung" im JMStV*, p. 305; Cole, "Der Dualismus von Selbstkontrolle und Aufsicht im Jugendmedienschutz," p. 466; Cole, "Jugendmedienschutz," para. 52, p. 328; Erdemir, "Die Kommission für Jugendmedienschutz," p. 288; Ring, "Jugendschutz im Span-

vant qualifications of KJM members, who hold their office for five years.[1181] To minimise the extensive state influence at the organisational level, the JMStV explicitly safeguards the KJM's independence and sets forth incompatibility rules for its members.[1182] Yet, the KJM does not act in an insular area but instead regularly exchanges and coordinates with stakeholders and other regulatory bodies like organisations of voluntary self-regulation and appointees for the protection of minors.[1183] Broadcasters offering services beyond one German state and commercial providers of telemedia services accessible to the general public (with *de minimis* exceptions)[1184] as well as providers of search engines are required to have an appointee who gives advice to the provider and serves as a point of contact for users. As such, appointees are at the nexus of involved stakeholders and thus contribute to the effective functioning of the co-regulatory framework.[1185]

### b) Organisations of voluntary self-regulation

Organisations of voluntary self-regulation are principal actors in the regulatory landscape for the protection of minors in audiovisual media.[1186] They constitute industry boards that monitor compliance with the rules

---

nungsfeld," p. 10; Schwartmann, "Rundfunkrechtliche Grundlagen," para. 57, p. 200.

1181 Ring, "Jugendschutz im Spannungsfeld," p. 10.

1182 Art. 14 (4) and (6) JMStV. See Rossen-Stadtfeld, "Die Konzeption Regulierter Selbstregulation," p. 8.

1183 Art. 7 JMStV.

1184 Art. 7 (2) JMStV exempts providers of telemedia "employing less than 50 members of staff or dealing with less than 10 million verified visits per average month of a given year if they have joined an organisation of voluntary self-regulation. The same applies to broadcasters that do not transmit their programmes nationally.

1185 Erdemir, "Die Kommission für Jugendmedienschutz," p. 295; In more detail see Reinhard Hartstein et al., "§ 7 JMStV Jugendschutzbeauftragte," in *Jugendmedienschutz-Staatsvertrag, RStV Kommentar*, Looseleaf commenatry (Köln: Rehm, n.d.); Oliver Knöfel, "Der Rechtsanwalt als Jugendschutzbeauftragter für Telemedien," *Multimedia und Recht*, 2005, pp. 816–20; Marc Liesching, "§ 7 JMStV Jugendschutzbeauftragte," in *Beck'scher Online-Kommentar zum JMStV*, 13th ed. (C.H. Beck, 2014).

1186 Due to the distribution of competence, the federal level regulates the protection of minors in offline media by the JuschG. More specifically, the JuschG applies

contained in the JMStV (possibly including their own codes and guidelines) by affiliated service providers and assess programmes submitted by providers prior to their dissemination. Such self-regulatory bodies existed

---

to films or games produced for cinemas or contained in data media such as DVDs, Blu-rays, VHS as defined by Art. 1 (2) JuschG. The JuschG also relies on a system of regulated self-regulation in order to effectively guarantee the protection of minors. Yet, the influence of the supreme state youth authorities (Oberste Landesjugendbehörden) is much more intensive than in case of the KJM. The oldest and best known organisation of voluntary self-regulation in this field constitutes the Freiwillige Selbstkontrolle der Filmwirtschaft (FSK) which has existed since 1949 under the umbrella of the Spitzenorganisation der Filmwirtschaft e.V. (SPIO) and has been responsible for labeling and age ratings since 1984. The FSK performs tasks delegated by state authorities by virtue of Art. 14 (6) JuschG. It is a pluralistic body composed of representatives of the film industry, representatives of the federal and state levels and representatives of the church and other youth associations. Importantly, representatives of the state are directly involved in the decision-making process. Similarly, the Unterhaltungssoftware Selbstkontrolle (USK) has been established to cater for the games industry. The self-regulatory bodies of the JuschG and JMStV do not operate in isolated vacuums. When programmes previously broadcast on TV are distributed on data media or when programmes disseminated on data media are subsequently screened on TV, the voluntary organisations of self-regulation respect the labels and classifications previously attained. This is especially relevant today when content originally produced as "offline" media is increasingly made available "online". Providers of telemedia services are required by virtue of Art. 12 JMStV to use the existing labeling of recorded video cassettes and other data media if content is largely identical. Thus, the FSK and USK are implicitly recognised by Art. 19 (4) JMStV. Interestingly, the FSK has provided a website (fsk.online) which assesses whole websites and consults on protection of minors on the Internet. Thereby, the two models of self-regulation under the JuschG on the one hand and the JMStV on the other hand appear to converge on regulatory grounds. Nonetheless, the laws clearly differentiate between protection of minors in offline and online media and the state supervision in case of offline media is stronger, resulting in a system which is less self-regulated as its denomination might suggest. See Cole, "Jugendmedienschutz," paras. 65–68, pp. 336–37; Hans Bredow Institut and Institut für Europäisches Medienrecht, "Final Report, Study on Co-Regulation Measures in the Media Sector, Study for the European Commission," pp. 57–59; Wolfgang Reißer, *Verfassungsrechtliche Anforderungen an die Medienkontrolle im Bereich Jugend- und Erwachsenenschutz*, Nomos Universitätsschriften 742 (Baden-Baden: Nomos, 2011), p. 199; Inken Witt, *Regulierte Selbstregulierung am Beispiel des Jugendmedienschutzstaatsvertrages*, Nomos Universitätsschriften 573 (Baden-Baden: Nomos, 2008), pp. 163–65, 300; see also FSK, Mitwirkung der Länder, available at https://www.fsk.de/?seitid=472&tid=473 (accessed 5.2.2015).

previously but their role was substantially reinforced by the 2003 reform that integrated them into the regulatory scheme.[1187] Such integration was accomplished by requiring the organisations to apply for certification to be granted by the KJM, which acts as a "quasi-MOT".[1188] The formal recognition by the KJM purports to ensure a high level of protection and is contingent on several criteria outlined in the JMStV. Thus, an organisation is certified provided that its independence and competence can be safeguarded, it is adequately resourced, it draws up instructions to guide decision-making, procedural rules are put in place guaranteeing, *inter alia*, the review of its decisions.[1189] The KJM awards the certification for four years and may even revoke it if the criteria are no longer met or if the practice of the organisation of voluntary self-regulation is contrary to the provisions stipulated in the JMStV.[1190] The temporal restriction of the certification serves as "preventive control" and the possibility to revoke the certification constitutes a "repressive" instrument at the disposal of the KJM.[1191] So far, two organisations have been certified, for broadcasting, the *Freiwillige Selbstkontrolle Fernsehen* (FSF)[1192] in 2003 and for telemedia ser-

---

1187 Hartstein et al., "Entstehungsgeschichte – JMStV", C2, II., 1.1, para. 10.

1188 Cole, "Der Dualismus von Selbstkontrolle und Aufsicht im Jugendmedienschutz," p. 462.

1189 Art. 19 (2) JMStV. See Bosch, *Die "Regulierte Selbstregulierung" im JMStV*, pp. 64, 319–39; Cole, "Das Zusammenwirken von Selbstkontrolle und hoheitlicher Kontrolle im Jugendmedienschutz," p. 305; Erdemir, "Die Kommission für Jugendmedienschutz," p. 291; Ring, "Jugendschutz im Spannungsfeld," p. 13; Alexander Scheuer, "Das neue System des Jugendmedienschutzes aus der Sicht der Selbstkontrolleinrichtungen," *Recht der Jugend und des Bildungswesens* 3 (2006): p. 310; Schulz and Held, "§ 1 JMStV Zweck des Staatsvertrages," paras. 26, 29; Schwendner, "Die Zusammenarbeit mit Einrichtungen der Freiwilligen Selbstkontrolle," pp. 90–91.

1190 Art. 16 (2) in conjunction with Art. 19 (4) JMStV. See Erdemir, "Die Kommission für Jugendmedienschutz," p. 291.

1191 Bosch, *Die "Regulierte Selbstregulierung" im JMStV*, pp. 315, 317, 339.

1192 See in more detail Thomas Groß, "Selbstregulierung im medienrechtlichen Jugendschutz am Beispiel der Freiwilligen Selbstkontrolle Fernsehen," *Neue Zeitschrift für Verwaltungsrecht*, 2004, pp. 1393–99; Joachim Von Gottberg, "Die Freiwillige Selbstkontrolle Fernsehen," in *Positionen zum Jugendmedienschutz in Deutschland, Eine Textsammlung*, KJM Schriftenreihe 1 (Berlin: Vistas, 2009), pp. 51–70; Cole, "Jugendmedienschutz," para. 60, pp. 331–32.

vices, the *Freiwillige Selbstkontrolle Multimedia-Diensteanbieter* (FSM)[1193] in 2005.[1194]

The rationale and simultaneously the incentive for service providers to join an organisation of voluntary self-regulation are to forego regulatory measures enforced by the KJM. In a certain way, such organisations act as a shield for service providers,[1195] who are rewarded for their engagement in self-regulatory bodies.[1196] The reform of the JMStV essentially built on a revaluation of self-regulation and the enhancement of service providers' responsibility to present their programmes to an organisation of voluntary self-organisation, which subsequently evaluates the content on the basis of the JMStV.[1197] It is in the interest of service providers to take autonomous decisions free from state interference and in case of conformant behaviour be protected from bad publicity and sanctions.[1198] In general, the self-regulatory bodies merely handle content, which impairs the development of minors and not extremely harmful or illegal content.[1199] Self-regulatory bodies, thus, bear the main regulatory burden and enforce the JMStV on a

1193 On the tasks of the FSM, see Von Coelln, "Jugendmedienschutz zwischen staatlichem Schutzauftrag und Zensurverbot," pp. 79–83; in general see Cole, "Jugendmedienschutz," para. 61, p. 332; Erdemir, "Die Kommission für Jugendmedienschutz," p. 291; Frank, "Selbstkontrolle im Internet," pp. 71–89.

1194 On the cooperation between the FSF and FSM with the KJM, see Schwendner, "Die Zusammenarbeit mit Einrichtungen der Freiwilligen Selbstkontrolle," pp. 94–104.

1195 Scheuer, "Das neue System des Jugendmedienschutzes aus der Sicht der Selbstkontrolleinrichtungen," p. 312.

1196 Erdemir, "Die Kommission für Jugendmedienschutz," p. 291; Scheuer, "Das neue System des Jugendmedienschutzes aus der Sicht der Selbstkontrolleinrichtungen," p. 312; Cole, "Jugendmedienschutz," paras. 62–64, pp. 332–35.

1197 Art. 20 (3), (5) JMStV. See Erdemir, "Die Kommission für Jugendmedienschutz," p. 290; Prütting, "Das Prinzip der regulierten Selbstregulierung im Jugendmedienschutz," p. 777.

1198 Prütting, "Das Prinzip der regulierten Selbstregulierung im Jugendmedienschutz," p. 777.

1199 The indexing or listing of audiovisual media (covered by the JMStV) or films (falling under the JuschG) with a severely damaging impact on minors' development is conducted by the Bundesprüfstelle für jugendgefährdende Medien (BPjM, Federal Review Board for Publications Harmful to Young Persons) according to Art. 17 JuschG. Art. 19 JuschG sets out the composition of the BPjM and Art. 18 JuschG outlines the type of content which is considered extremely harmful. Services and programmes listed cannot be disseminated pursuant to Art. 4 (1) No. 11 and 4 (2) No. 2 and 4 (3) JMStV and Art. 15 JuschG. On the procedure of indexing, see Reißer, *Verfassungsrechtliche Anforderungen an die*

day-to-day basis.[1200] Providers having undergone this *ex ante* scrutiny are privileged in so far as the KJM is obliged to accept the decision of the self-regulatory body unless the latter has exceeded its scope of discretion-with its decision, or lack thereof.[1201] As a result, the KJM's supervision of decisions by self-regulatory bodies is reduced to the review of misuse or reasonableness in cases of grave errors or misjudgement.[1202] This reflects a procedural law approach.[1203] The scope self-regulatory organisations' margin of discretion is still ambiguous.[1204]

Likewise, the question when exactly the KJM can interfere remains open. Scheuer argues that there should be room for the development of an autonomous practice of self-regulatory bodies.[1205] In a similar vein, Cole points out that a certain leeway of self-regulatory bodies is significant to allow their members to rely on them and consider them as a substitution

---

*Medienkontrolle im Bereich Jugend- und Erwachsenenschutz*, pp. 147–61; see also Cole, "Jugendmedienschutz," paras. 66–67, p. 336; Witt, *Regulierte Selbstregulierung am Beispiel des Jugendmedienschutzstaatsvertrages*, pp. 231–35.

1200 Scheuer, "Das neue System des Jugendmedienschutzes aus der Sicht der Selbstkontrolleinrichtungen," p. 310.

1201 Art. 20 (3) JMStV. See Erdemir, "Die Kommission für Jugendmedienschutz," p. 290; Ring, "Jugendschutz im Spannungsfeld," p. 13; Bosch, *Die "Regulierte Selbstregulierung" im JMStV*, p. 65; Cole, "Der Dualismus von Selbstkontrolle und Aufsicht im Jugendmedienschutz," p. 467.

1202 The official statement of reasons grants organisations of voluntary self-regulation a margin of discretion which is subject to limited review and examination by the state authority, p. 2. The official statement of reasons (amtliche Begründung) is available at http://www.kjm-online.de/fileadmin/Download_KJM/Recht/Amtliche_Begruendung_zum_JMStV_korrigiert.pdf (accessed 26.11.2014). See also Scheuer, "Das neue System des Jugendmedienschutzes aus der Sicht der Selbstkontrolleinrichtungen," pp. 308–18; Erdemir, "Die Kommission für Jugendmedienschutz," p. 290.

1203 Cole, "Das Zusammenwirken von Selbstkontrolle und hoheitlicher Kontrolle im Jugendmedienschutz," p. 305; Hartstein et al., "Entstehungsgeschichte – JMStV", C2, V., 2.2, para. 69; Scheuer, "Das neue System des Jugendmedienschutzes aus der Sicht der Selbstkontrolleinrichtungen," p. 314.

1204 Bosch, *Die "Regulierte Selbstregulierung" im JMStV*, pp. 343–57; Cole, "Der Dualismus von Selbstkontrolle und Aufsicht im Jugendmedienschutz," pp. 469–70; Scheuer, "Das neue System des Jugendmedienschutzes aus der Sicht der Selbstkontrolleinrichtungen," pp. 314–16; Schwartmann, "Rundfunkrechtliche Grundlagen," para. 63, pp. 7, 203.

1205 Scheuer, "Das neue System des Jugendmedienschutzes aus der Sicht der Selbstkontrolleinrichtungen," p. 314.

for state involvement.[1206] From this perspective, granting a reasonable room to manoeuvre constitutes a prerequisite for the effective functioning of the regulatory system as a whole. In addition, Art. 8 (2) JMStV provides for scheduling restrictions which may be taken by both, the KJM or the self-regulatory bodies. Nonetheless, the freedom of self-regulatory bodies is not absolute and the KJM reserves the right to intervene as it has demonstrated in case of entertainment programmes showing cosmetic operations.[1207] Although the KJM's course of action in this specific case was disputed before a court, it can reasonably be assumed that the KJM has a general monitoring obligation that includes possible correction or ramification of self-regulatory organisations' measures.[1208] Thus, the final decision making is incumbent on the KJM in conjunction with the state media

---

1206 Cole, "Das Zusammenwirken von Selbstkontrolle und hoheitlicher Kontrolle im Jugendmedienschutz," p. 302.

1207 Cole, "Das Zusammenwirken von Selbstkontrolle und Hoheitlicher Kontrolle Im Jugendmedienschutz," pp. 305, 306; see in more detail Cole, "Der Dualismus von Selbstkontrolle Und Aufsicht Im Jugendmedienschutz, Zum Verhältnis von FSF Und KJM Im System Der 'Regulierten Selbstregulierung' – Eine Untersuchung Aus Anlass Des Konflikts Um Schönheitsoperationen Im Fernsehprogramm," pp. 471– 472; Kristina Hopf and Birgit Braml, "Das Verhältnis Der KJM Zur FSF Anhand Einer Kritischen Würdigung Der Entscheidung Des VG Berlin Vom 6.7.2006," *Zeitschrift Für Urheber- Und Medienrecht*, 2007, pp. 23–30.

1208 In 2004, the music channel MTV promoted its show "I want a famous face" in Germany. The programme presented adolescents who had their faces altered by a cosmetic surgeon to imitate the appearance of their popular idols and other celebrities. The whole process was recorded and marketed as reality TV. The channel presented three episodes of the programme to the FSF which considered that their transmission even during the day was permissible. The KJM, by contrast, decided that programmes featuring cosmetic surgery were unsuitable for minors and impaired their development within the meaning of Art. 5 (1) JMStV. Hence, the KJM clarified that such programmes could only be broadcast after 11 p.m. In its decision, the KJM indicated that the FSF had exceeded its margin of appreciation. The KJM's decision was made public in form of a press release. Consequently, the FSF brought an action before the Verwaltungsgericht Berlin (Administrative Court) against the KJM's press release alleging disregard of the position of self-control and assertion of incorrect facts. In its judgement of 6 July 2006, the VG Berlin found that the assertion of the KJM contained in the press release was unlawful and that the KJM was not entitled to take such a general decision in such a form and in case of an authoritative rule-making intention would have had to issue guidelines in line with the second sentence of Art. 16 No. 2 JMStV in conjunction with Art. 8 JMStV (VG Berlin, Judgement

authorities.[1209] This interpretation reinforces the underlying rationale of

---

of 6.7.2006, 27 A 236.04, paras. 49, 52-54). Even after this ruling, the relationship between the KJM and the FSF or other organisations of voluntary self-regulation is still unclear. The judgement has been heavily criticised by Hopf and Braml for its ignorance of the system of regulated self-regulation. Accordingly, the KJM is entitled to take fundamental decisions in the context of its public relations work in order to inform the public and stimulate public debate about new programme formats (p. 27). By referring to Art. 19 (2) JMStV, Hopf and Braml also point out that the KJM takes precedence regarding preventive measures to protect minors (p. 28). They further opine that the court erroneously assumed that the KJM and the FSF act in parallel. Notwithstanding the strengthening of the self-regulatory element, Hopf and Braml derive a hierarchy from the JMStV with the KJM at its apex (p. 29). See Kristina Hopf and Birgit Braml, "Das Verhältnis der KJM zur FSF anhand einer kritischen Würdigung der Entscheidung des VG Berlin vom 6.7.2006," *Zeitschrift für Urheber- und Medienrecht*, 2007, pp. 23–30. Similarly, in a case about the show Super-Nanny broadcast on RTL Germany, the VG Hannover clarified that in matters of human dignity, the KJM was entitled to take a final decision (ex post) even if the broadcaster had submitted the programme to a certified organisation of voluntary self-regulation which had permitted the dissemination of said programme. The show the Super-Nanny presented a pedagogue who visited families in order to give assistance with parenting and education of children ("coaching format"). It was screened on a weekly basis at 8:15 p.m. in the evenings. The show at issue portrayed a single mother who repeatedly and brutally beat her children aged three, four and seven. RTL also broadcast a trailer ("teaser") containing several violent scenes before 8 p.m. (before the relevant watershed). The programme itself repeatedly depicted various violent acts by the mother towards, in particular, her four year old son. After its transmission, the KJM decided to initiate proceedings against RTL arguing that the programme was illegal pursuant to the first sentence of Art. 4 (1) No. 8 JMStV by violating human dignity of the minors presented in the show. In its decision of 8 July 2014, the VG Hannover confirmed that the KJM was mandated to take such decisions in cases of alleged contraventions of Art. 4 (1) JMStV. The blocking effect by virtue of Art. 20 (3) JMStV giving priority to self-regulatory bodies was not applicable in relation to violations of human dignity. Due to the special protection accorded to human dignity under Art. 1 of the German Grundgesetz (Basic Law), the KJM as an organ of the state is obliged to protect human dignity and take positive action. In cases concerning human dignity, self-regulatory bodies did not have a margin of discretion attributed to them according to Art. 20 (3) JMStV. The court was convinced that the salacious and sensational presentation of the beatings was humiliating and that the children were being degraded and turned into objects. The court found that the children could not fully understand nor freely decide about their participation in the show but instead were exploited for the commercial objectives of the broadcaster (aiming for high viewing figures and thus more income). RTL did not appeal the decision for fear of bad publicity. Succinctly, the court clarified what is expressly stipulated in Art. 20 (5) JMStV applicable to a

the system of regulatory self-regulation, which relies on the industry to bear the main regulatory burden under the auspices of a framework established by the state and enforced by an expert body engaged in effective monitoring. In general, the German approach, which was developed at a crucial time when national as well as European decision makers increasingly looked towards alternative models of regulation, was positively received in many European states. Above all, it has been praised as a "milestone of contemporary youth protection".[1210]

In conclusion, the German regulatory framework for audiovisual media services is a complex web of legal sources and actors including private and state entities.[1211] Importantly, regulation of the media sector has been profoundly influenced by the case law of the BVerfG, which sought to expand the protection accorded to the freedom of broadcasting to new media services pursuant to Art. 5 (2) GG. Thus, all aspects of the provision of audiovisual media services are inherently linked to the German Basic Law that requires observance of this constitutional right and possibly its balancing with other constitutional rights. The BVerfG has also laid the foundation for the design of the regulatory structure, above all, the need for a positive state intervention and the independence of regulatory authorities from the state. These values are recurrent themes and are taken into account whenever the regulatory model or the substantive provisions of the laws are changed.

Another significant factor contributing to the "structural complexity" of the German legal framework is federalism.[1212] Due to the ambivalent distribution of competence in the German Basic Law, there had been frequent quarrels over what entity, either the federal level or the states was entitled to regulate an issue. The negotiations between the federal level and the states, which preceded legislation, were time-consuming and resulted in

---

telemedia provider, namely that alleged infringements of Art. 4 (1) JMStV are to be assessed by the KJM thereby demarcating the limits of the involvement and powers of organisations of voluntary self-regulation. See VG Hannover, Judgement of 8.7.2014, 7 A 4679/12, paras. 59-66.

1209 Cole, "Das Zusammenwirken von Selbstkontrolle und hoheitlicher Kontrolle im Jugendmedienschutz," p. 307.

1210 Ring, "Jugendschutz im Spannungsfeld," p. 14; similarly but phrased more prudently Cole, "Der Dualismus von Selbstkontrolle und Aufsicht im Jugendmedienschutz," p. 307.

1211 Müller and Gusy, "Media Policy in Germany," pp. 116, 118.

1212 Sporn, "Auf dem Weg zur 'Ländermedienanstalt,'" p. 240.

sector-specific laws. The main legal acts, the RStV and TMG uphold the traditional distinction between broadcasting and telemedia services. To a certain extent, the fragmentation of competence and legal acts was counteracted by reforms aimed at introducing common, coherent standards across audiovisual media. The JMStV is a prime example of such consolidation.

With regards to supervision, there are 14 state media authorities that monitor compliance with the RStV, the TMG (with the exception of states in which oversight of telemedia services is conducted by state bodies) and the JMStV and enforce their standards. As neither broadcasts nor telemedia services can be stopped at state borders, it is vital that LMA coordinate at the national level. To this end, several regulatory bodies have been created to centralise decision-making. Thus, regulatory oversight is primarily executed by traditional delegation of powers from the state to regulatory authorities for the media. In the area of protection of minors, Germany has crafted a co-regulatory structure. Under the telling concept of regulated self-regulation, self-control of service providers has been encouraged, bolstering organisations of voluntary self-regulation. These ensure adherence of its members to the legal standards outlined in the JMStV. Hence, regulatory responsibility is shared between the state (the states drawing up provisions contained in the law) and the industry. Even if the internal complexities have not been diminished, the co-regulatory scheme has been maintained for more than a decade, which is proof of its appropriateness in this particular field.

## *C. The French media authority*

In France, the evolution of the regulatory framework for audiovisual media is closely tied to the political sphere. An anecdote of the mid-1980s serves to underpin this peculiar relationship and the government's influence on economic operators and decision-makers. During the licensing process of the first French commercial broadcaster in 1985, the ruling Socialist party and President Miterrand faced up to a defeat in the upcoming parliamentary elections. In order to swing the electorate on its side, President Miterrand endeavored to grant the license to a company that suited him and supported his politics. The license was granted to La Cinq, a broadcaster in the hands of two French industrials with close relations to

President Miterrand.[1213] The quarrel over power in the early and mid-1980s left substantial traces on the legislative as well as regulatory arrangements for audiovisual media services. During the Socialist President Miterrand's term of office from 1981 to 1995, Minister Presidents of the different political camps alternated in government. These changes directly related to the organisation of the audiovisual landscape. While consent had been achieved in the early 1980s on the type of legislation building on a dual broadcasting system and the freedom of communication, the regulatory scheme took three attempts following in rapid succession to construct a regulatory authority in the late 1980s that proved durable, competent and independent. Since the late 1980s, a time of "veritable revolution",[1214] political parties have agreed on the values underlying legislation and the principal structures of the regulatory model.[1215]

In this respect, two values, which represent the cornerstones of the regulatory system, should be highlighted. Firstly, the cultural aspect is very visible in French media policies. Cultural identity and French cultural heritage are actively promoted to secure a pluralistic and diverse media landscape. Secondly, the independence of the national regulator has been a contentious issue, especially at the birth of today's national regulator, the *Conseil supérieur de l'audiovisuel* (CSA). The closeness between political elites and the regulatory authority has today been broken up thanks to repeated improvements to the authority's institutional organisation. The values of independence and pluralism also recur in the relevant legislation. In addition, the primary French law relevant for the media encompasses audiovisual media services, linear and non-linear as well as commercial and public service media. Its scope is thus much wider than the rules stipulated in the AVMSD. Yet, a division has been maintained, albeit provisionally abandoned in the mid-1980s, between telecommunications and media regulation. This separation is reflected in the competencies of the French regulatory authority. In general, the French apply a relatively centralised form of regulation, which centres on a single body, the CSA. Nonetheless, in the field of advertising, a self-regulatory body, the *Au-*

---

1213 Bernd Holznagel, *Rundfunkrecht in Europa, Auf dem Weg zu einem Gemeinrecht europäischer Rundfunkordnungen* (Tübingen: Mohr Siebeck, 1996), p. 40.

1214 Pascal Kamina, *JurisClasseur Propriété littéraire et artistique, Cadre administratif, Communication audiovisuelle* (JurisClasseur, 2014), para. 3.

1215 Holznagel, *Rundfunkrecht in Europa*, p. 46.

*torité de regulation professionnelle de la publicité*[1216] supplements the CSA by administering a pre-clearance scheme for commercial communi-

1216 Since the 1930s, the advertising industry in France has been self-regulated across media platforms including press products, radio services, broadcasting and electronic communications. To this effect, a private body (the Office de Communication des Annonces) was set up in 1935 to promote loyal, truthful and sound advertising. In 1953, it was renamed as the Bureau de verification de la publicité (Office of verification of advertisements, BVP) before it became the Autorité de regulation professioinnelle de la publicité (Authority for the professional regulation of advertising, ARPP) in 2008 (see http://www.arpp-pub.org/, accessed 22.1.2015). The ARPP is administered by advertisers, advertising agencies and the media, the three professions implicated in the production and diffusion of advertising campaigns. It represents more than 1,000 companies thereby supervising about 80 percent of all advertisements published in France. In the absence of any public funding, the ARPP is entirely financed by the industry, through remuneration for certain of its services and above all, yearly membership fees of about EUR 2,500. Its annual budget amounts to approximately EUR 3 million. In line with its key principles, the ARPP ensures that advertisements are fair, genuine and sound. The ARPP thus operates under a broad legal framework encompassing laws on protection of consumers, public health, the environment (e.g. concerning the advertising of weapons and munitions, electronic cigarettes or games of chance) and other sector-specific media laws (audiovisual, printed press or radio services). It has established a code of ethics comprising several recommendations (the code of ethics is available at http://www.arpp-pub.org/Regles-en-vigueur.html, accessed 26.1.2015), that interpret and clarify the rules contained in the various legal texts. The recommendations are elaborated by the administrative body of the ARPP after consultation of stakeholders. The ARPP regulates all types of advertisements distributed on all kinds of media outlets. With respect to advertisements included in linear and non-linear audiovisual media services, it is necessary that the content of advertisements is examined before their broadcast. By a CSA decision of 1990, clearance of advertisements broadcast on TV became obligatory in advance of publication. See CSA, Décision No. 90-182 du 19 juin 1990 relative à l'exercice du contrôle du Conseil supérieur de l'audiovisuel sur les messages publicitaires diffusés par les sociétés de radio et de télévision, Official Journal No. 145 of 24.6.1990, p. 7350. While its predecessor, the CNCL had itself carried out an assessment of the advertisements prior to their transmission, the CSA in the early 1990s favoured a self-regulatory model and encouraged the engagement and participation of the industry. In a decision of 1992, it determined that it would henceforth solely exercise ex post control of advertisements broadcast on TV. See CSA, Décision n° 92-1133 du 22 décembre 1992 relative à l'exercice du contrôle du Conseil supérieur de l'audiovisuel sur les messages publicitaires diffusées par les sociétés de radio et de télévision, Official Journal No. 34 of 10.2.1993, p. 2260. By contrast, such pre-clearance is not required for commercial communication in VOD services which may nonetheless submit their adver-

cations featured in audiovisual media services. Its remit covers advertisements depicted in all kinds of media including the press and radio. This study, while acknowledging the existence of the self-regulatory scheme for advertising, focuses on other issues, such as the notion of an on-demand audiovisual media service and the protection of minors in such services. The CSA has sole competence to regulate these fields. In the following, a general overview is provided of the French legal and regulatory framework.

## I. Protection of the freedom of communication by the French Constitutional Council

Although the French Constitution is silent on the right to freedom of expression, this important right is implicitly safeguarded as a constitutional

---

tisements for evaluation and comments by the ARPP. The ARPP will issue advice to VOD providers. In general, the ARPP becomes active prior to transmission of advertisements, whereas the CSA monitors compliance with the advertising standards set out in the LLC and the relevant decrees only a posteriori. The ARPP's decisions are, however, not binding upon the CSA. By the same token, the recommendations of the ARPP are not mandatory for the CSA which may still take them into account according to Art. 14 LLC. Although the ARPP's decision does not bar the CSA from initiating any legal action against the broadcaster after the advertisement was screened, it nonetheless allows the service provider to estimate the risks and avert prosecution. The cases in which the CSA intervenes have become rare, underpinning the trust the CSA has established in the self-regulatory body. Even though the ARPP acts a priori, it may establish a breach of its rules once the advertisement has been broadcast. Similarly, third persons (e.g. viewers) may submit a complaint to the jury de déontologie publicitaire (JDP) that decides on the validity and substance of the complaint. In contrast to the CSA, the ARPP/JDP's sanctioning powers are rather limited. Its decisions are published on its website and in cases of serious and grave contraventions, are accompanied by a press release which explicitly refers to the name of the provider. This has the effect of discrediting the provider publicly. There is an internal appeal procedure against the decision of the JDP. The ARPP, albeit fulfilling a broad range of tasks, is rather weak in terms of enforcement. Lacking any effective sanctioning tools, its activities remain rather symbolic. On the ARPP, see generally Daniel Poinsot, "Publicité commerciale à la télévision: le rôle du BVP," *Légicom* 16, no. 1 (1998): pp. 75–81; Christophe Haquet, *JurisClasseur Communication,Publicité audiovisuelle* (JurisClasseur, 2011), p. I, B; Eric Andrieu and Oriane Droulers, "Le jury de déontologie publicitaire," *Légipresse* 271 (2010): pp. 57–60.

right. In a series of cases in the 1970s and 1980s concerning the constitutionality of several laws, the *Conseil constitutionnel* (Constitutional Council) accorded constitutional protection to fundamental rights contained in the *Déclaration des droits de l'homme et du citoyen* of 1789 (Declaration of the Rights of Man and of the Citizen, Declaration). On account of the general reference to the Declaration in the Constitution's preamble, the *Conseil constitutionnel* carved out the doctrine on the Declaration's binding nature. Thus, in a case concerning the freedom of association of 1971, the *Conseil constitutionnel* postulated that the Declaration has a binding force and is of constitutional value.[1217] The constitutional rank of the right to freedom of expression as outlined in Art. 11 Declaration consequently derives from this jurisprudence.[1218] More specifically, when the *Conseil constitutionnel* was asked to review the broadcasting laws and their numerous alterations in the 1980s,[1219] it held in 1982 that the freedom of communication was inherent in the freedom of expression and thus enshrined in the Constitution.[1220] In its case law on the freedom of expres-

---

1217 The French Constitution underlines that "Le peuple français proclame solennellement son attachement aux Droits de l'Homme et aux principes de la souveraineté nationale tels qu'ils ont été définis par la Déclaration de 1789 (.)". ["The French people solemnly proclaim their attachment to the Rights of Man and the principles of national sovereignty as defined by the Declaration of 1789 (.)"]. Confer also Cour constitutionnel, Judgement of 16.7.1971, Decision n° 71-44 DC, Official Journal of 18.7.1971, p. 7114, para. 2 (FR:CC:1971:71.44.DC). See also Stéphane Davy and François Hurard, *Lamy Droit des Médias et de la Communication, La télévision: évolution législative*, ed. Pierre Sirinelli, Christian Gavalda and Lionel Costes, 2014, paras. 321–51; Holznagel, *Rundfunkrecht in Europa*, p. 105.

1218 Holznagel, *Rundfunkrecht in Europa*, p. 105; François Jongen, *La police de l'audiovisuel, Analyse comparée de la régulation de la radio et de la télévision en Europe* (Brussels: Bruylant, 1994), p. 27.

1219 See in particular Cour constitutionnel, Judgement of 27.7.1982, Decision n °82-141 DC, Official Journal of 29.7.1982, p. 2422 (FR:CC:1982:82.141.DC), Cour constitutionnel, Judgement of 25.7.1984, Decision n°84-176 DC, Official Journal of 28.7.1984, p. 2492 (FR:CC:1984:84.176.DC), Cour constitutionnel, Judgement of 18.9.1986, Decision n°86-217 DC, Official Journal of 19.9.1986, p. 11294 (FR:CC:1986:86.217.DC), Cour constitutionnel, Judgement of 17.1.1989, Decision n°88-248 DC, Official Journal of 18.1.1989, p. 754 (FR:CC:1989:88.248.DC.).

1220 Cour constitutionnel, Judgement of 27.7.1982, Decision n°82-141 DC, Official Journal of 29.7.1982, p. 2422 (FR:CC:1982:82.141.DC), paras. 3, 5. See also Kamina, *Communication audiovisuelle*, para. 23, I.

sion and the freedom of communication, the *Conseil constitutionnel* underlined the limits to the rights and the need for reconciliation of values of equal constitutional rank. Hence, the freedom of communication may be restricted for reasons of public order, the freedoms of others or the maintenance of pluralism.[1221] The preservation of a pluralistic and diverse media landscape, as set forth by the *Conseil constitutionnel* in a case of 1986 on the new law on freedom of communication, has become a principle value henceforth protected by the court and policy makers.[1222] In spite of a considerable margin of discretion enjoyed by law-makers when designing the regulatory framework for the media,[1223] the effects and influence on pluralism have to be taken into account.[1224] In aforementioned decision of 1986, the *Conseil consitutionnel* also found that the enforcement of the freedom of communication presupposes an independent regulatory authority.[1225] Although a regulatory authority competent for broadcast regulation had been established in 1982, this decision paved the way for further reforms culminating in the creation of the CSA in 1989. In brief, the judicature in France set the basis for constitutional protection of the freedom of expression and the freedom of communication. It emphasised the balancing act to be undertaken by the legislature and highlighted the significance of protecting pluralism. By its review, the *Conseil constitutionnel* has played an important role in constructing the general legal framework even

---

1221 Cour constitutionnel, Judgement of 27.7.1982, Decision n°82-141 DC, Official Journal of 29.7.1982, p. 2422 (FR:CC:1982:82.141.DC), para. 5; Judgement of 18.9.1986, Decision n°86-217 DC, Official Journal of 19.9.1986, p. 11294 (FR:CC:1986:86.217.DC), paras. 8-9. See also Davy and Hurard, *Lamy Droit des Médias et de la Communication*, paras. 321–52; Diane de Bellescize and Laurence Franceschini, *Droit de la communication*, second edition (Paris: Presses Universitaires de France, 2011), p. 143; Holznagel, *Rundfunkrecht in Europa*, p. 106; Kamina, *Communication audiovisuelle*, para. 23, I.

1222 Cour constitutionnel, Judgement of 18.9.1986, Decision n°86-217 DC, Official Journal of 19.9.1986, p. 11294 (FR:CC:1986:86.217.DC), para. 11.

1223 Holznagel, *Rundfunkrecht in Europa*, p. 108.

1224 Cour constitutionnel, Judgement of 18.9.1986, Decision n°86-217 DC, Official Journal of 19.9.1986, p. 11294 (FR:CC:1986:86.217.DC), paras. 11-12. See also de Bellescize and Franceschini, *Droit de la communication*, p. 30; Holznagel, *Rundfunkrecht in Europa*, pp. 106, 108; on law-makers margin of discretion, see Holznagel, *Rundfunkrecht in Europa*, p. 108.

1225 Davy and Hurard, *Lamy Droit des Médias et de la Communication*, paras. 321–52.

if the details were determined by the legislature in its numerous amendments of the legal sources.

## II. Legal sources

The following section outlines the legal sources of France, examining the most important legislation, the LLC and its accompanying Decree.

### 1. Ordinary legislation

In the early 1980s, the French legal framework for the media was modified profoundly. The *Loi du 29 juillet 1982 sur la communication audiovisuelle* (Law of 29 July 1982 on Audiovisual Communication, LCA)[1226] constitutes the first expression of the willingness of French policy makers to open the, to date, closed market and abolish the state monopoly of broadcasting.[1227] This paradigm shift was precipitated by a recommendation by a commission presided by Moinot in 1981, thus without intervention by the judiciary.[1228] The LCA contained two essential innovations. Firstly, Art. 1 LCA set out the freedom of audiovisual communication ("*la communication audiovisuelle est libre*").[1229] This explicit postulation underlines the spirit of liberalisation underlying the reform process. Against this background, several private channels were founded including the first French pay TV operator Canal+ in 1983.[1230] Secondly, the law promotes the independence of the audiovisual sector from the political sphere by the

---

1226 Loi n°82-652 du 29 juillet 1982 sur la communication audiovisuelle, Official Journal of 30.7.1982, p. 2431.

1227 In this respect Chevallier refers to "la volonté d'ouverture" in Jacques Chevallier, "Le nouveau statut de la liberté de communication," *L'actualité juridique: Droit administratif*, 1987, p. 59; de Bellescize and Franceschini, *Droit de la communication*, p. 20.

1228 Pierre Moinot, "Pour une reforme de l'audiovisuel, Rapport au Premier ministre de la Commission de réflexion et d'orientation," September 30, 1981; Holznagel, *Rundfunkrecht in Europa*, p. 38; Charles Debbasch, Hervé Isar and Xavier Agostinellig, *Droit de la communication, Audiovisuel – Presse – Internet*, first edition (Paris: Dalloz, 2002), para. 66, p. 66.

1229 Chevallier, "Le nouveau statut de la liberté de communication," p. 59.

1230 Chevallier, "Le nouveau statut de la liberté de communication," p. 60; Debbasch, Isar and Agostinellig, *Droit de la communication, Audiovisuel – Presse –*

creation of a regulatory authority, the *Haute Autorité de la communication audiovisuelle* (High Authority for Communication, HACA) that acts as an intermediary.[1231] Nonetheless, the government harvested essential powers such as the determination of providers' *cahier de charges,* the book of obligations attached to licenses.[1232] The relations and power struggles between on the one hand the state attempting to hold on to its prerogatives and on the other hand a regulatory body wishing to assert itself and achieve a standing with the industry it regulates were only just emerging after the LCA's adoption.

In 1986, the legislative framework was fundamentally overhauled. In line with a global process of liberalisation and privatisation (affecting not only the broadcasting sector),[1233] the LCA was abrogated by the *Loi du 30 septembre 1986 relative à la liberté de communication* (Law of 30 September 1986 on Freedom of Communication, LLC).[1234] Inspired by the Bredin report of May 1985, the LLC continued the trends initiated by the LCA promoting three aspects: independence, transparency and competition.[1235] As mentioned below in more detail, the disengagement of the state was further effectuated by the construction of a new regulator replacing the HACA.[1236] Above all, the dual broadcasting system of public and private operators was maintained and strengthened. The LLC contains rules that entice competition between public and private broadcasters guarding certain equilibrium.[1237] A strong sign of the rise of private broadcasters at that time was the privatisation of the previously public broad-

---

*Internet*, para. 73, p. 73; de Bellescize and Franceschini, *Droit de la communication*, pp. 21–22; Holznagel, *Rundfunkrecht in Europa*, pp. 39–40.

1231 Chevallier, "Le nouveau statut de la liberté de communication," pp. 59–60; Debbasch, Isar and Agostinellig, *Droit de la communication, Audiovisuel – Presse – Internet*, para. 68, p. 69.

1232 Debbasch, Isar and Agostinellig, *Droit de la communication, Audiovisuel – Presse – Internet*, para. 69, p. 69; de Bellescize and Franceschini, *Droit de la communication*, p. 21.

1233 Debbasch, Isar and Agostinellig, *Droit de la communication, Audiovisuel – Presse – Internet*, para. 71, pp. 71–72.

1234 Loi n°86-1067 du 30 septembre 1986 relative à la liberté de communication, Official Journal of 1.10.1986, p. 11755.

1235 Chevallier, "Le nouveau statut de la liberté de communication," p. 63.

1236 Chevallier, "Le nouveau statut de la liberté de communication," p. 61.

1237 Chevallier, "Le nouveau statut de la liberté de communication," pp. 59, 63.

caster TF1.[1238] This transfer profoundly changed the French broadcasting landscape.[1239] Succinctly, the LLC has proven a durable compromise. Even though it has been amended multiple times, the LLC constitutes the cornerstone of the French legal order and is still in force today.[1240] Such amendments would not question the underlying legislation but rather adapt parts of the law to changes and developments of the industry.[1241]

Interestingly, Art. 1 LLC still protects the freedom of communication. According to settled case law, which has been codified in Art. 1 LLC, this right is not absolute but may be limited by, *inter alia*, the respect of human dignity, the rights and properties of others, the pluralism of opinions, the protection of minors and adolescents, the protection of public order and the national security.[1242] As a corollary to the freedom of communication, the freedom of reception is safeguarded by Art. 3 LLC, introduced in 2004.[1243] The LLC covers both, private and public audio (radio services) as well as audiovisual media services. In addition, the LLC specifies the structure and organisation of the regulatory authority. It also prescribes, among others, the licensing regime applicable to broadcasters and the obligations imposed on media service providers, such as content rules.

Importantly, the LLC was amended in 2009.[1244] The modifications served a two-fold purpose. Firstly, the AVMSD was transposed in the

1238 Debbasch, Isar and Agostinellig, *Droit de la communication, Audiovisuel – Presse – Internet*, para. 71, p. 71; de Bellescize and Franceschini, *Droit de la communication*, p. 22; Jean Morange, "Le Conseil supérieur de l'audiovisuel," *Revue française de droit administratif* 5, no. 2 (1989): p. 235.

1239 Debbasch, Isar and Agostinellig, *Droit de la communication, Audiovisuel – Presse – Internet*, para. 73, p. 73.

1240 Debbasch, Isar and Agostinellig, *Droit de la communication, Audiovisuel – Presse – Internet*, para. 71, p. 72; de Bellescize and Franceschini, *Droit de la communication*, p. 23.

1241 Debbasch, Isar and Agostinellig, *Droit de la communication, Audiovisuel – Presse – Internet*, para. 71, p. 72.

1242 Art. 1 LLC stipulates that "*La communication au public par voie électronique est libre*".

1243 Art. 3 LLC reads as follows: "Le secret des choix faits par les personnes parmi les services de communications électroniques et parmi les programmes offerts par ceux-ci ne peut être levé sans leur accord." See also Kamina, *Communication audiovisuelle*, para. 24, I.

1244 Loi n°2009-258 du 5 mars 2009 relative à la communication audiovisuelle et au nouveau service public de la télévision, Official Journal of 7.3.2009, p. 4321. On the same day, another law was adopted pertaining to the appointment of Presidents of France Télévisions and Radio France. Confer *Loi du 5 mars 2009*

French legal order. Above all, the LLC's scope of application was enlarged to cover on-demand audiovisual media services defined in Art. 2 LLC. Consequently, the CSA is tasked with the oversight of such services that have to be notified to the CSA.[1245] Secondly, the PSB scheme was revised due to political considerations.[1246] Preceding the adoption of the law in 2009, the *Conseil constitutionnel* reviewed the constitutionality of some provisions concerning the reform of PSB.[1247]

## 2. Decrees

In addition to legislative acts, a number of legal acts (decrees) have been issued by the executive branch to detail the rules contained in the LLC. In the section below, reference is made to the most relevant decrees that specify some of the rules contained in the AVMSD which are examined in

---

*relative à la nomination des présidents des sociétés France Télévisions et Radio France et de la société en charge de l'audiovisuel extérieur de la France*, Official Journal of 7.3.2009, p. 4321. This law was also subject to constitutional review by the Conseil constitutionnel. Confer Cour constitutionnel, Judgement of 3 March 2009, Decision No. 2009-576, Official Journal of 7.3.2009, p. 4336 (FR:CC:2009:2009.576.DC).

1245 Art. 33-1 LLC. By derogation, notification is not required in line with Art. 33-1 II. LLC for on-demand services not using a frequency distributed by the CSA and disposing of an annual budget of less than EUR 150,000.

1246 Emmanuel Derieux, "Réforme de l'audiovisuel. – À propos des lois du 5 mars 2009," *La Semaine Juridique Entreprise et Affaires* 12 (2009); Christophe Haquet, "Loi n° 2009-258 du 5 mars 2009 relative à la communication audiovisuelle et au nouveau service public de la télévision," *Communication Commerce électronique* 4 (2009).

1247 In its decision, the Conseil constitutionnel found constitutional the regrouping of France Télévisions and the gradual suppression of advertising on French public service channels. The lack of resources resulting from the prohibition to transmit advertising has been offset by a financial compensation by the state. Confer Conseil constitutionnel, Judgement of 3 March 2009, Decision No. 2009-577 DC, Official Journal of 7.3.2009, p. 4336 (FR:CC:2009:2009.577.DC). See also Davy and Hurard, *Lamy Droit des Médias et de la Communication*, paras. 321–52; Derieux, "Réforme de l'audiovisuel"; Haquet, "Loi n° 2009-258 du 5 mars 2009 relative à la communication audiovisuelle et au nouveau service public de la télévision.".

the course of this study.[1248] By virtue of the amended LLC, the government prepared a decree that set forth more precise rules applicable to on-demand audiovisual media services (VOD). Following two public consultations in April 2009[1249] and March 2010,[1250] the *Décret du 12 novembre 2010 relatif aux services de médias audiovisuels à la demande*[1251] (Decree of 12 November 2010 on audiovisual media services on demand, SMAD Decree) was adopted in the fall of 2010. The government sought the views and positions of the public and in particular industry stakeholders in order to find a balance between the freedoms pertaining to a burgeoning market for VOD services and the protection of fundamental values such as pluralism and diversity of expressions. In October 2010, the CSA gave a negative opinion on the SMAD Decree criticising the disproportionate nature of the obligations (in particular with respect to the provisions outlining financial contributions to the production and promotion of European and French audiovisual works) incumbent on service providers.[1252] The CSA posited that the draft decree did not take into account the economic realities and argued that the strict standards proposed in the draft decree would penalise providers established in France vis-à-vis providers located in other EU Member States.[1253] Thus, the draft decree risked placing French providers at a competitive disadvantage and made delocalisation to other

1248 For an overview of all the decrees taken in view of executing the LLC, see the website of the CSA, available at http://csa.fr/Espace-juridique/Decrets-et-arretes (accessed 22.1.2015).

1249 Ministère de la culture et de la communication, "Consultation publique sur les dispotitions applicables aux services de médias audiovisuels à la demande," April 2009, http://www.culturecommunication.gouv.fr/Politiques-ministerielles/Audiovisuel/Archives-2009/Consultation-publique-sur-les-dispositions-applicables-aux-services-de-medias-audiovisuels-a-la-demande (accessed 22.1.2015).

1250 Ministère de la culture et de la communication, "Consultation publique sur le projet de décret relatif aux services de médias audiovisuels à la demande," March 2010, http://www.culturecommunication.gouv.fr/Politiques-ministerielles/Audiovisuel/Archives-2010/Consultation-publique-sur-le-projet-de-decret-relatif-aux-services-de-medias-audiovisuels-a-la-demande (accessed 22.1.2015).

1251 Décret n° 2010-1379 du 12 novembre 2010 relatif aux services de médias audiovisuels à la demande, Official Journal No. 264 of 14.11.2010, p. 20315.

1252 CSA, "Avis n° 2010-22 du 27 septembre 2010 sur un projet de décret relatif aux services de médias audiovisuels à la demande, Official Journal No. 264 of 14.11.2010, p. 70," 2010, http://www.csa.fr/Espace-Presse/Communiques-de-presse/Decret-relatif-aux-services-de-medias-audiovisuels-SMAD-le-CSA-emet-un-avis-defavorable (accessed 22.1.2015).

1253 CSA, "Avis sur un projet de décret relatif aux SMA," p. 1.

(less severely regulated) countries probable.[1254] Hence, the CSA suggested, inter alia, alleviating providers' burden by introducing progressive standards (contingent on providers' net annual turnover) in relation to the promotion of European and French audiovisual works.[1255] It furthermore reinforced the significance of the principle of identification and the need for adequate information of users with respect to commercial communications.[1256] In its opinion, the CSA highlighted the need for a more flexible framework for VOD services based on their characteristics. It emphasised that a blunt reproduction of the standards applicable to broadcasting would curb innovation and stifle the distribution of original formats as well as the experimentation with pioneering services. In view of the critical opinion of the CSA, the government substantially modified the decree before it entered into force.[1257]

Importantly, the decree is currently subject to a revision process. In line with Art. 22 SMAD Decree, the CSA published a report on the application of the SMAD Decree in November 2013 in which it advanced several amendments to provisions applicable to VOD services contained in both, the LLC and the SMAD Decree.[1258] In its report, the CSA generally advocated a relaxation of the obligations imposed on VOD service providers with a view to strengthening their competiveness. In this respect, the CSA underlined the need for clarification of the scope of application of the SMAD Decree and simplification of the rules contained therein, notably with respect to the promotion of European and French audiovisual works.[1259] The public was consulted on the CSA's proposals in June

1254 CSA, "Avis sur un projet de décret relatif aux SMA," p. 1.

1255 CSA, "Avis sur un projet de décret relatif aux SMA," para. I.-II., pp. 1-3.

1256 CSA, "Avis sur un projet de décret relatif aux SMA," para. III., p. 3.

1257 In accordance with Art. 9 in conjunction with Art. 27 and Art. 33-2 LLC, the CSA is consulted in view of draft laws and other statutory acts. By the letter of the law, the CSA's opinion is advisory only.

1258 CSA, "Rapport au Gouvernement sur l'application du décret n° 2010-1379 du 12 novembre 2010 relatif aux services de médias audiovisuels à la demande (SMAD)," December 2013, http://csa.fr/Etudes-et-publications/Les-autres-rapports/Rapport-au-Gouvernement-sur-l-application-du-decret-n-2010-1379-du-12-novembre-2010-relatif-aux-services-de-medias-audiovisuels-a-la-demande-SMAD (accessed 22.1.2015). The proposals of the CSA are summarized on p. 61.

1259 CSA, "Rapport sur l'application du décret relatif aux SMA," p. 37 et seq.

2014.[1260] It seems unlikely that the government will act upon the CSA's proposals before a revised AVMSD is adopted at the EU level.

Besides the SMAD Decree, the *Décret du 27 mars 1992 (...) fixant les principes généraux définissant les obligations des éditeurs de services en matière de publicité, de parrainage et de télé-achat*[1261] (Decree of 27 March 1992 on the general principles defining the obligations of broadcasters concerning advertising, sponsorship and teleshopping) sets out the rules on certain types of television advertising. The SMAD Decree extends the obligations in matters of commercial communications to on-demand service providers.[1262] By the same token, the SMAD Decree specifies the measures with respect to the promotion and production of European and French works. For the broadcasting sector, these are outlined in the *Décret du 17 janvier 1990 (...) fixant les principles généraux concernat la diffusion des œuvres cinématographiques et audiovisuelles par les éditeurs de services de télévision*[1263] (Decree of 17 January 1990 on the general principles concerning the transmission of cinematographic and audiovisual works by television broadcasters). Succinctly, the French legal framework applicable to audiovisual media services comprises several governmental decrees that execute rules contained in the law, the LLC. The LLC was conceived in the mid-1980s, when it was a deliberate decision of policy makers to liberalise the market and establish a dual broadcasting order. Adopted in 1986, the LLC, albeit undergoing several revi-

1260 Ministère de la culture et de la communication, "Consultation publique sur l'adaptation du décret relatif aux services de médias audiovisuels à la demande," June 2014, http://www.culturecommunication.gouv.fr/Politiques-ministerielles/Audiovisuel/Actualites/Consultation-publique-sur-l-adaptation-du-decret-relatif-aux-services-de-medias-audiovisuels-a-la-demande (accessed 22.1.2015).

1261 Décret n°92-280 du 27 mars 1992 pris pour l'application des articles 27 et 33 de la loi n° 86-1067 du 30 septembre 1986 et fixant les principes généraux définissant les obligations des éditeurs de services en matière de publicité, de parrainage et de télé-achat, Official Journal No. 75 of 28.3.1992. For a complete list of decrees regulating different aspects of advertising and commercial communication, see CSA, Décrets et arêtes relatives à la publicité, available at http://csa.fr/Espace-juridique/Decrets-et-arretes/Decrets-et-arretes-relatifs-a-la-publicite (accessed 22.1.2015).

1262 Arts. 14-18 SMAD Decree.

1263 Décret n°90-66 du 17 janvier 1990 pris pour l'application de la loi n° 86-1067 du 30 septembre 1986 et fixant les principes généraux concernant la diffusion des oeuvres cinématographiques et audiovisuelles par les éditeurs de services de télévision, Official Journal No. 15 of 18.1.1990, p. 757.

sions, has been retained until today. Only three years after the LLC came into force, the regulatory authority, the CSA, was created, which is still in place today.

## III. The French regulatory framework

This part deals with the French regulatory framework for audiovisual media services and the evolution of an independent regulatory authority, the CSA that today regulates the French audiovisual media services market.

### 1. The genesis of an independent regulator

Historically, the genesis of the CSA is tightly interwoven with its two predecessors; the HACA established in 1982 and the *Commission nationale pour la communication et les libertés* (National Commission for Communication and Freedoms, CNCL) constructed in 1986 due to a change in the majority ratio of the *Assemblée Nationale* (French Parliament).[1264] Within seven years, two regulatory authorities had been worn out and a third had been established. The failure of the first two regulators underscores the French legislature's incapacity to adjust the regulatory framework to the technological innovations of a constantly changing sector.[1265] From the outset, the brutal replacement of the HACA for political reasons constituted a black mark against the CNCL's name.[1266] The attempt to enhance the CNCL's independence largely backfired. Although its composition was enlarged and designed more pluralistically than that of its predecessor,[1267] the process of designation of its members was heavily politicised and

1264 Davy and Hurard, *Lamy Droit des Médias et de la Communication*, paras. 321-38; de Bellescize and Franceschini, *Droit de la communication*, pp. 149–51; Derieux and Granchet, *Droit des médias, Droit francais, européen et international*, para. 570, p. 190; Kamina, *Communication audiovisuelle*, p. 35; Didier Truchet, *JurisClasseur Administratif, Communication audiovisuelle, Régulation et secteur public* (JurisClasseur, 2014), paras. 7–8.

1265 Jacques Chevallier, "De la CNCL, au Conseil superieur de l'audiovisuel," *L'actualité juridique: Droit administratif*, 1989, p. 59.

1266 Chevallier, "De la CNCL, au Conseil superieur de l'audiovisuel," p. 60.

1267 Chevallier, "Le nouveau statut de la liberté de communication," p. 78.

favoured those in power.[1268] In addition, its first series of decisions did nothing to dissolve the distrust displayed towards it.[1269] Scandals about bribery of its members dominated public debate.[1270] During its brief period of existence, the CNCL was also isolated from the industry on the one hand and from policy makers on the other hand. It lacked the stage to explain its decisions and make itself heard.[1271] With the re-election of François Mitterrand as President of the French Republic and the majority of the Socialists in the *Assemblée Nationale* led by Minister President Rocard, the end of the CNCL dawned.[1272] Preceding the construction of the CSA was a wide-ranging consultation of stakeholders, which was prepared and guided by a committee of seven experts in the summer of 1988.[1273] The statement of reasons of the draft law establishing the CSA unequivocally stated the primary objective which was to establish a new independent regulatory authority capable of adjusting to the evolutions of the audiovisual world; an effective authority that guarantees pluralism, transparency and the cohesion of the audiovisual value chain.[1274]

The capacity to adjust to the dynamic and evolutionary nature of the audiovisual market and the independence of the regulator were regarded as crucial components for the effective safeguarding of pluralism, transparency and the cohesion of the audiovisual regime. Referring to lessons learnt from the past, a comprehensive overhaul of the entire legal framework was rejected in 1988 in favour of the (exclusive) reorganisation of the regulatory authority, which was regarded as the "keystone of the sys-

1268 Chevallier, "De la CNCL, au Conseil superieur de l'audiovisuel," p. 60; Morange, "Le Conseil supérieur de l'audiovisuel," p. 239.

1269 Chevallier, "De la CNCL, au Conseil superieur de l'audiovisuel," pp. 60–61.

1270 Holznagel, *Rundfunkrecht in Europa*, p. 42.

1271 Chevallier, "De la CNCL, au Conseil superieur de l'audiovisuel," p. 67.

1272 Chevallier, "De la CNCL, au Conseil superieur de l'audiovisuel," p. 64; Holznagel, *Rundfunkrecht in Europa*, p. 42; Morange, "Le Conseil supérieur de l'audiovisuel," p. 236.

1273 Chevallier, "De la CNCL, au Conseil superieur de l'audiovisuel," p. 64; Morange, "Le Conseil supérieur de l'audiovisuel," p. 236.

1274 Sénat, "Projet de loi modifiant la loi n° 86-1067 du 30 septembre 1986 relative à la liberté de communication," December 10, 1988, p. 2, http://www.senat.fr/leg/1988-1989/i1988_1989_0027.pdf; see also Morange, "Le Conseil supérieur de l'audiovisuel," p. 237.

tem".[1275] The first stumbling block came, however, in the form of a review by the *Conseil constitutionnel* to the constitutionality of the amending law pursuant to Art. 61 of the French Constitution. In its decision of 17 January 1989, the *Conseil constitutionnel* declared parts of the amending law unconstitutional.[1276] More specifically, the provisions preventing concentration in the industry were held to contravene the Constitution.[1277] Yet, the court confirmed that delegation of delimited regulatory powers to administrative bodies for the execution of laws was in line with Art. 21 of the Constitution (which confers upon the Prime Minister the prerogative to implement legislation) as well as settled case law on this matter.[1278] Similarly, the sanctioning powers of the CSA conformed to Art. 34 of the Con-

---

1275 Sénat, "Projet de loi modifiant la loi n° 86-1067 du 30 septembre 1986 relative à la liberté de communication," p. 2; see also Chevallier, "Le nouveau statut de la liberté de communication," p. 75 et seq.

1276 The anti-concentration rules, for example, were declared unconstitutional. They were, however, modified to meet constitutional demands and were integrated in the LLC by an amending law of November 1986 (Loi n°86-1210 du 27 novembre 1986 completant la Loi n°86-897 du 1 août 1986 portant reforme du regime juridique de la presse et la Loi n°86-1067 du 30 Septembre 1986 relative à la liberté de communication, Official Journal of 28.11.1986, p. 14297). Confer Conseil constitutionnel, Judgement of 17.1.1989, Decision n° 88-248 DC, Official Journal of 18.1.1989, p. 754 (FR:CC:1989:88.248.DC). Confer Constitution du 4 octobre 1958. An English version is available at the website of the Conseil constitutionnel under http://www.conseil-constitutionnel.fr/conseil-constitutionnel/english/constitution/constitution-of-4-october-1958.25742.html (accessed 17.12.2014). See also de Bellescize and Franceschini, *Droit de la communication*, pp. 145–46; Chevallier, "De la CNCL, au Conseil superieur de l'audiovisuel," p. 65; Bruno Genevois, "Le Conseil constitutionnel et la définition des pouvoirs du Conseil supérieur de l'audiovisuel," *Revue française de droit administratif* 5, no. 2 (1989): pp. 215–34.

1277 Conseil constitutionnel, Judgement of 17.1.1989, Decision n° 88-248 DC, paras. 31-37. The anti-concentration rules were modified to meet constitutional demands and were integrated in the LLC by an amending law of November 1986 (Loi n°86-1210 du 27 novembre 1986 completant la Loi n°86-897 du 1 août 1986 portant reforme du regime juridique de la presse et la Loi n°86-1067 du 30 Septembre 1986 relative à la liberté de communication, Official Journal of 28.11.1986, p. 14297). See also de Bellescize and Franceschini, *Droit de la communication*.

1278 In 1986, the Conseil constitutionnel held that the conferral of power to the CNCL was constitutional. See Cour constitutionnel, Judgement of 18.9.1986, Decision n° 86-217 DC, Official Journal of 19.9.1986, p. 11294 (FR:CC:1986:86.217.DC). See also Genevois, "Le Conseil constitutionnel et la définition des pouvoirs du Conseil supérieur de l'audiovisuel," p. 217.

stitution, in particular the separation of powers as well as the freedom of expression as guaranteed by the ECHR on account of the statutory prescription of, inter alia procedural guarantees and the limits to the imposition of fines in the amending law.[1279] Still, the *Conseil constitutionnel* found that the competencies envisaged by the amending law regarding the regulation of advertising were too broad and hence unconstitutional.[1280]

Thus, the *Conseil constitutionnel* reversed the trend towards delegation of wide powers to an independent administrative authority.[1281] Instead, the scope of functions of the regulator was confined even if the judgement acknowledged the need for the CSA to be endowed with wider sanctioning powers in comparison with previous regulators.[1282] Hence, the *Loi du 17 janvier 1989 modifiant la loi du 30 septembre 1986 relative à la liberté de communication* (Law of 17 January 1989 modifying the Law of 30 December 1986 on the Freedom of Communication, amending law 1989)[1283] entered into force the same day as the court's decision, except for the parts identified as unconstitutional. Morange assesses the LLC in its version of 1989 as a "mature text" which integrates the "lessons learnt from past experience".[1284] So far, the LLC has indubitably proven to be a solid "basis of a durable compromise".[1285]

---

1279 Conseil constitutionnel, Judgement of 17.1.1989, Decision n° 88-248 DC, paras. 38, 42. See also Genevois, "Le Conseil constitutionnel et la définition des pouvoirs du Conseil supérieur de l'audiovisuel," pp. 220–28; Debbasch, Isar, and Agostinellig, *Droit de la communication, Audiovisuel – Presse – Internet*, para. 122, p. 103; de Bellescize and Franceschini, *Droit de la communication*, pp. 145–46; Holznagel, *Rundfunkrecht in Europa*, p. 108; Morange, "Le Conseil supérieur de l'audiovisuel," pp. 244–45.

1280 Conseil constitutionnel, Judgement of 17.1.1989, Decision n° 88-248 DC, para. 16.

1281 Truchet, *Communication audiovisuelle, Régulation et secteur public*, 2014, para. 74, IV.

1282 Genevois, "Le Conseil constitutionnel et la définition des pouvoirs du Conseil supérieur de l'audiovisuel," p. 228.

1283 Loi n°89-25 du 17 janvier 1989 modifiant la loi du 30 septembre 1986 relative à la liberté de communication, Official Journal of 18.1.1989, p.728.

1284 Morange, "Le Conseil supérieur de l'audiovisuel," p. 247.

1285 Chevallier, "De la CNCL, au Conseil superieur de l'audiovisuel," p. 76.

## 2. Functions

The tasks and competencies of the CSA are set forth in Art. 3-1 LLC.[1286] Accordingly, its general mission is to ensure the exercise of the freedom of audiovisual communication in accordance with the law. To this end, the CSA oversees both, the public[1287] and private sectors of audiovisual media. What is more, Art. 3-1 LLC enumerates several more specific tasks. Thus, the CSA is to guarantee equal treatment and the independence and impartiality of the public sector. It is to further free competition and establish non-discriminatory relations between publishers and distributors of services. The CSA also promotes the quality and diversity of programmes, furthers the development, production and creation of primarily national audiovisual works and defends the French language and culture.[1288] To this end, the law highlights values like diversity and plurality of programmes, equality of sexes and the protection of the environment as well as public health.[1289] In contrast to its predecessor, the CNCL, the CSA's tasks and responsibilities with regards to the audiovisual sector have increased. At the same time, the CSA's overall regulatory remit has deflated. While the CNCL also regulated the telecommunications sector,[1290] this function has been exercised by the Minister competent for post, telegraph and telephone. Due to a lack of knowledge and expertise of the CNCL regarding the domestic telecommunications market, the initial regulatory separation between telecommunications and audiovisual media was re-

1286 Debbasch, Isar and Agostinellig, *Droit de la communication, Audiovisuel – Presse – Internet*, para. 148, p. 114; de Bellescize and Franceschini, *Droit de la communication*, p. 142; Truchet, *Communication audiovisuelle, Régulation et secteur public*, 2014, p. 67, IV.

1287 With regards to public service media, the CSA nominates, for instance, five independent members of the administrative council of France Télévisions (No. 3 of Art. 47-1 LLC) and four independent members of Radio France (No.3 of Art. 47-2 LLC). Moreover, the CSA gives an opinion on the elaboration of the cahier des charges (book of obligations) incumbent on public service media (Art. 48 LLC) and attributes their frequencies (Art. 26 II LLC). See also Debbasch, Isar, and Agostinellig, *Droit de la communication, Audiovisuel – Presse – Internet*, paras. 154–65, pp. 116–20.

1288 Art. 3-1 LLC.

1289 Art. 3-1 LLC.

1290 Chevallier, "Le nouveau statut de la liberté de communication," pp. 75–76.

stored in 1989.[1291] In a transitory period, the CSA continued to regulate the telecommunications industry until new legislation was adopted.[1292] The differentiation between the regulation of telecommunications on the one hand and audiovisual media on the other hand implies distinct regulatory rationales, objectives and approaches. In a similar vein, detailed knowledge and know-how of the industry and its economic actors are required for regulators to exercise their mandates effectively. In France, these differences were considered as substantial hurdles for any more global regulation by a single entity.

In practice, one of the most important tasks carried out by the CSA is the administration of the licensing system for broadcasting services, which relies on a system of authorisation and conventions introduced by the law of 1989.[1293] Too often, the HACA and CNCL were powerless against service providers not adhering to the promises they made during the licensing process. The novel contractual framework intended to remedy this lack of enforcement, enhancing compliance with the conditions attached to licenses.[1294] The French legal order generally differentiates licensing on the basis of technical modes of transmission, like analogue terrestrial, digital terrestrial, cable or satellite.[1295] Still, the licensing process for each technology is similar. Typically, after a call for tender[1296] and selection of suitable providers, the CSA and the provider sign a convention,[1297] which stipu-

---

1291 Roßnagel, Kleist and Scheuer, *Die Reform der Regulierung elektronischer Medien in Europa*, p. 222.

1292 Sénat, "Projet de loi modifiant la loi n° 86-1067 du 30 septembre 1986 relative à la liberté de communication," p. 5; Chevallier, "De la CNCL, au Conseil superieur de l'audiovisuel," pp. 71–72; Morange, "Le Conseil supérieur de l'audiovisuel," p. 248.

1293 Sénat, "Projet de loi modifiant la loi n° 86-1067 du 30 septembre 1986 relative à la liberté de communication," p. 4; see also Chevallier, "De la CNCL, au Conseil superieur de l'audiovisuel," p. 74.

1294 Holznagel, *Rundfunkrecht in Europa*, p. 45.

1295 See in more detail Debbasch, Isar, and Agostinellig, *Droit de la communication, Audiovisuel – Presse – Internet*, paras. 184–219, pp. 126–43.

1296 Art. 30-1 LLC. See also Kamina, *Communication audiovisuelle*, para. 78, IV.

1297 Derieux and Granchet, *Droit des médias, Droit francais, européen et international*, para. 600, p. 196; Roßnagel, Kleist and Scheuer, *Die Reform der Regulierung elektronischer Medien in Europa*, p. 225; for a more detailed overview of the procedural aspects of the convention concluded between the CSA and the service provider, see Didier Truchet, *JurisClasseur Administratif, Communication audiovisuelle, Secteur privé* (JurisClasseur, 2014), paras. 14–40, II.

lates the obligations of providers as well as sanctions, which the CSA may impose in case of violation.[1298] The convention essentially defines a list of conditions, which has become a sort of catalogue common to all providers.[1299] Licenses commonly do not exceed 10 years[1300] and may be renewed twice for five years respectively, each without a new call for tender.[1301] Once the convention is signed, the CSA provides an authorisation for the use of the frequency (conditions attached) and sets a deadline for use of such. Providers of on-demand audiovisual media services have been required to notify their services since 2013.

In addition, the CSA enjoys significant consultative powers. It gives opinions on draft decrees applying the LLC, publishes annual reports addressed to the President, government and Parliament in which it may propose legislative or regulatory changes. In a similar vein, the CSA communicates among others an information bulletin to the President of the Parliament and heads of parties represented in Parliament.[1302] This regular interaction with the political institutions was considered important to give a voice to the CSA in the political arena and enhance its influence.[1303] Importantly, the CSA may address recommendations to providers and opera-

---

1298 Art. 27, 28 LLC. See also Truchet, *Communication audiovisuelle, Régulation et secteur public*, 2014, paras. 5–8, I.

1299 Kamina, *Communication audiovisuelle*, para. 79, IV.; Truchet, *Communication audiovisuelle, Régulation et secteur public*, 2014, para. 10, I.

1300 Art. 28-1 I LLC. See also Kamina, *Communication audiovisuelle*, para. 80, IV.; Roßnagel, Kleist, and Scheuer, *Die Reform der Regulierung elektronischer Medien in Europa*, p. 226.

1301 Art. 28-1- I LLC. See also Holznagel, *Rundfunkrecht in Europa*, p. 239; Kamina, *Communication audiovisuelle*, para. 80., IV. In exceptional cases provided for by Art. 28-1 I No. 1-5 LLC, the license is not renewed by the CSA. With regards to analog and digital television, licenses will only be renewed once for 5 years pursuant to Art. 30 and 30-1- LLC.

1302 Derieux and Granchet, *Droit des médias, Droit francais, européen et international*, para. 619, p. 202; Debbasch, Isar and Agostinellig, *Droit de la communication, Audiovisuel – Presse – Internet*, paras. 113–14, pp. 98–100; Truchet, *Communication audiovisuelle, Régulation et secteur public*, 2014, para. 73, IV.

1303 Chevallier, "De la CNCL, au Conseil superieur de l'audiovisuel," p. 67; Derieux and Granchet, *Droit des médias, Droit francais, européen et international*, para. 621, pp. 202–3; Kamina, *Communication audiovisuelle*, paras. 52–53, II; Morange, "Le Conseil supérieur de l'audiovisuel," p. 247; Truchet, *Communication audiovisuelle, Régulation et secteur public*, 2014, paras. 71–72, IV.

tors, specifying or clarifying a regulatory issue.[1304] In the area of competition law, the CSA monitors compliance with the rules on ownership of cross-media or same media outlets. The LLC sets out several complex provisions distinguishing by service (radio or broadcasting), transmission mode (analogue or digital) and area of coverage (national or regional/ local).[1305] The rules aim at protecting the pluralism of the French media landscape. With regards to anti-competitive practices used by providers of audiovisual media, the CSA cooperates with the *Autorité de la concurrence* (Competition Authority) providing the latter with opinions.[1306]

In order to effectively carry out its functions, the CSA is equipped with a number of administrative sanctions. By the same token, criminal sanctions may be imposed according to the *Code de procedure pénale* (Code of criminal procedure).[1307] While past regulators were endowed with certain (administrative) sanctioning powers, such instruments were expanded by the law of 1989 to enhance the effectiveness of the regulator.[1308] Today, the CSA enjoys a large margin of discretion in the application of the ad-

1304 Derieux and Granchet, *Droit des médias, Droit francais, européen et international*, para. 618, p. 202; Kamina, *Communication audiovisuelle*, para. 51, II.

1305 Art. 41 – 41-2-1 LLC. See in more detail Debbasch, Isar, and Agostinellig, *Droit de la communication, Audiovisuel – Presse – Internet*, paras. 224–39, pp. 145-151.

1306 Davy and Hurard, *Lamy Droit des Médias et de la Communication*, pp. 321–40; Art. 17 LLC. See also Kamina, *Communication audiovisuelle*, paras. 100–104, IV.; Debbasch, Isar, and Agostinellig, *Droit de la communication, Audiovisuel – Presse – Internet*, paras. 240–42, pp. 151-152; for a more detailed overview of the competition rules applicable to the media sector, see Jean-Jacques Biolay, *JurisClasseur Concurrence – Consommation, Application des règles de concurrence aux médias* (JurisClasseur, 2014); on the distribution of competencies between the competition authority and the CSA, see Didier Théophile and Étienne Renaudeau, "Les relations entre le Conseil de la concurrence, l'ARCEP, la CRE et le CSA: Coopération ou concurrence?," *Concurrences* 3 (2008): pp. 67–75.

1307 On the imposition of criminal sanctions stipulated by Arts. 74-79 LLC, see in more detail Debbasch, Isar, and Agostinellig, *Droit de la communication, Audiovisuel – Presse – Internet*, paras. 131–36, pp. 106-110.

1308 The possibility for the CSA to suspend programmes, reduce the duration of the authorisation and the application of pecuniary sanctions were introduced in 1989. See Sénat, "Projet de loi modifiant la loi n° 86-1067 du 30 septembre 1986 relative à la liberté de communication," p. 6; Chevallier, "De la CNCL, au Conseil superieur de l'audiovisuel," p. 75.

ministrative penalties postulated by No. 1-4 of Art. 42-1 LLC.[1309] Before sanctions are imposed, the CSA addresses a letter of formal notice to the holder of the authorisation and asks for observance of the legal obligations.[1310] If the provider does not conform, the CSA may impose a penalty. It may suspend a programme or parts thereof or prohibit certain types of advertising for the period of one month or more.[1311] The CSA may reduce the duration of the authorisation or convention by a maximum of one year[1312] or, in more serious cases, withdrawn completely or cancelled unilaterally[1313]. Moreover, pecuniary sanctions may be pronounced possibly in addition to the suspension of the distribution of a service or programme.[1314] In France, the amount of fines is contingent on operators' turnover. Taking into account the gravity of the breach as well as the advantages resulting from the breach, the fines cannot exceed three percent of providers' turnover excluding tax calculated on the basis of the past twelve months.[1315] In case of recidivism, the amount of the fine may be increased to a maximum of five percent.[1316] The money collected is recovered by the state budget.[1317]

Moreover, in special cases, i.e. when the conditions under which the original authorisation was granted have substantially altered (like for in-

1309 Chevallier, "De la CNCL, au Conseil superieur de l'audiovisuel," p. 75; de Bellescize and Franceschini, *Droit de la communication*, p. 156; Kamina, *Communication audiovisuelle*, para. 54, II.; Truchet, *Communication audiovisuelle, Régulation et secteur public*, 2014, para. 51, II.

1310 Art. 42 LLC. See also Debbasch, Isar and Agostinellig, *Droit de la communication, Audiovisuel – Presse – Internet*, para. 123, p. 103; de Bellescize and Franceschini, *Droit de la communication*, p. 155; Derieux and Granchet, *Droit des médias, Droit francais, européen et international*, para. 604, p. 199; Truchet, *Communication audiovisuelle, Régulation et secteur public*, 2014, para. 49, II.

1311 No. 1 of Art. 42-1 LLC. See also Debbasch, Isar and Agostinellig, *Droit de la communication, Audiovisuel – Presse – Internet*, para. 124, pp. 103-104.

1312 No. 2 of Art. 42-1 LLC. See also Debbasch, Isar and Agostinellig, *Droit de la communication, Audiovisuel – Presse – Internet*, para. 125, p. 104.

1313 No. 4 of Art. 42-1 LLC. See also Debbasch, Isar and Agostinellig, *Droit de la communication, Audiovisuel – Presse – Internet*, para. 127, p. 104.

1314 No. 3 of Art. 42-1 LLC. See also Debbasch, Isar and Agostinellig, *Droit de la communication, Audiovisuel – Presse – Internet*, para. 126, p. 104. The sanctions imposed by the CSA in case of a breach of contractual obligations pursuant to Art. 28 LLC resemble those outlined in Art. 42-1 No. 1-4 LLC.

1315 Art. 42-2 LLC.

1316 Art. 42-2 LLC.

1317 Art. 42-2 LLC.

stance fundamental changes to the composition of share capital, management organs or the sources of funding), the CSA may revoke an authorisation without prior letter of formal notice.[1318] In all cases of breach of duty, the CSA may order the dissemination of a communication during the programmes of the negligent provider under its conditions.[1319] The procedure for imposition of sanctions was revised in the aftermath of the ECtHR judgement in case *Dubus SA v France*[1320] of 2009. The ECtHR found that the mixing of the functions of prosecution, investigation and adjudication of the French Banking Commission violated Art. 6 (1) ECHR, which enshrines the right to fair trial.[1321] In response to the judgement, the French legislature reformed several administrative bodies endowed with sanctioning powers including the CSA (to which the case applied by analogy), underpinning the distinction between the different tasks and procedural phases. The *Loi du 15 novembre 2013 relative à l'indépendance de l'audiovisuel public*[1322] (Law of 15 November 2013 on the independence of the audiovisual public, amending law 2013) fostered the CSA's independence and impartiality with regards to the exercise of its sanctioning powers. Accordingly, an independent *rapporteur* was appointed by the *Conseil d'Etat* (State Council) pertaining to the administrative jurisdictions.[1323] The *rapporteur* initiates the proceedings (either by its own motion or alternatively upon request of the CSA) and investigates the case, ultimately notifying the service provider if there is sufficient evidence of the latter's miscon-

---

1318 Art. 42-3 LLC. See also Kamina, *Communication audiovisuelle*, para. 54, II.

1319 Art. 42-4 LLC. See also Debbasch, Isar and Agostinellig, *Droit de la communication, Audiovisuel – Presse – Internet*, para. 128, p. 105; Kamina, *Communication audiovisuelle*, para. 54, II.

1320 ECtHR, *Dubus SA v France*, Judgement of 11.9.2009, Application no. 5242/04. See also Hubert Delzangles, "Un vent d'impartialité souffle encore sur le droit de la régulation," *Actualité juridique Droit administratif* 18 (2014): p. 1022; Truchet, *Communication audiovisuelle, Régulation et secteur public*, 2014, para. 55, II.

1321 ECtHR, *Dubus SA v France*, Judgement of 11.9.2009, Application no. 5242/04, paras. 54, 60-61.

1322 Loi n° 2013-1028 du 15 novembre 2013 relative à l'indépendance de l'audiovisuel public, Official Journal of 16.11.2013, p. 18622.

1323 Art. 42-7 LLC. See also Delzangles, "Un vent d'impartialité souffle encore sur le droit de la régulation," p. 1025.

duct. The file is then submitted to the CSA for pronunciation of a sanction.[1324] The novel model of the *rapporteur* as it has been deployed by the *Autorité de la concurrence* was approved by the *Conseil constitutionnel* in 2012 as ensuring a sufficient level of independence.[1325]

Finally, Debbasch et al. point out that the CSA is not under the tutelage of any administrative control. In their view the lack of any appeal procedure enhances the CSA's independence.[1326] All administrative acts adopted by the CSA (including in particular its sanctioning decisions) are moreover subject to judicial review before the *Conseil d'État.*[1327] Moreover, all deliberations, decisions (which must be motivated) and opinions of the CSA are published in the *Journal official* (official journal)[1328] enhancing accountability and transparency. The requirement to guarantee the independence of the regulatory authority is equally significant with regards to the internal organisation and operation of the CSA as will be demonstrated below.

### 3. Composition and funding

Pursuant to Art. 3-1 LLC, the CSA is an independent public body endowed with legal personality.[1329] Its independence is explicitly safeguarded by the law to underpin the significance of this value, which is acknowl-

---

1324 No. 6 of Art. 42-7 LLC. See also Laurence Franceschini, "Les points clés de la loi du 15 novembre 2013 'relative à l'indépendance de l'audiovisuel public,'" *Revue Lamy de Droit de l'Immatériel*, no. 101 (2014): p. 39.

1325 Cour constitutionnelle, Judgement of 12.10.2012, Decision n° 2012-280 QPC, Official Journal of 1.10.2012, para. 18, p. 16031(FR:CC:2012:2012.280.QPC). See also Delzangles, "Un vent d'impartialité souffle encore sur le droit de la régulation," p. 1023; Franceschini, "Les points clés de la loi du 15 novembre 2013 'relative à l'indépendance de l'audiovisuel public,'" p. 39.

1326 Debbasch, Isar, and Agostinellig, *Droit de la communication, Audiovisuel – Presse – Internet*, para. 137, p. 110.

1327 Truchet, *Communication audiovisuelle, Régulation et secteur public*, 2014, para. 69, IV.; on the procedure before the Conseil d'État, see in more detail Dominique Maillard Desgrées du Loû, *JurisClasseur Justice administrative, Référé en matière de communication audiovisuelle* (JurisClasseur, 2014).

1328 Kamina, *Communication audiovisuelle*, para. 54, II.; Truchet, *Communication audiovisuelle, Régulation et secteur public*, 2014, para. 82, IV.

1329 This amendment was only adopted by the law of 15 November 2013.

edged also by political decision-makers.[1330] In addition, the CSA having legal personality enhances its independence and additionally implies budgetary autonomy.[1331] With respect to funding, the CSA proposes an annual budget necessary for the fulfilment of its mandate. These funds flow solely from the overall state budget.[1332] In 2015, the CSA's budget amounted to approximately EUR 38 million, 36 percent of which the CSA attributed to the fulfilment of its statutory missions.[1333] In this respect, more than 1400 judicial proceedings were initiated and handled by the CSA in 2015.[1334] Due to austerity measures of the French government, the CSA operates under a tight budget aiming at making savings where possible. For a period of ten years, the CSA's budget gradually augmented from roughly EUR 31 million in 2000 to about EUR 35 million in 2009, with a major increase to EUR 39 million in 2010.[1335] For the past years however, funds have been stable below 39 million.[1336] In 2015, the CSA employed about 300 persons.[1337] The actual council, apparently, is much smaller.

Importantly, the composition of the CSA was recently modified by the amending law of 2013. Since 1st of January 2014, it is composed of seven

---

1330 Chevallier, "De la CNCL, au Conseil superieur de l'audiovisuel," p. 66; Debbasch, Isar, and Agostinellig, *Droit de la communication, Audiovisuel – Presse – Internet*, para. 107, p. 95.

1331 Franceschini, "Les points clés de la loi du 15 novembre 2013 'relative à l'indépendance de l'audiovisuel public,'" p. 38; Kamina, *Communication audiovisuelle*, para. 35, II; see also Chevallier, "De la CNCL, au Conseil superieur de l'audiovisuel," p. 67.

1332 Debbasch, Isar and Agostinellig, *Droit de la communication, Audiovisuel – Presse – Internet*, para. 147, p. 113; Derieux and Granchet, *Droit des médias, Droit francais, européen et international*, para. 584, p. 193; Kamina, *Communication audiovisuelle*, para. 40, II.

1333 CSA, "Rapport Annuel 2015," April 4, 2016, pp. 148–49, http://www.csa.fr/content/download/216245/580039/file/Rapport_annuel_2015.pdf (accessed 6.5.2016).

1334 CSA, "Rapport Annuel 2015," p. 149.

1335 CSA, "Rapport Annuel 2010," August 9, 2011, p. 61, http://csa.fr/Etudes-et-publications/Les-rapports-annuels-du-CSA/CSA-Rapport-annuel-2010 (accessed 6.5.2016).

1336 CSA, "Rapport Annuel 2012," May 28, 2013, p. 197, http://csa.fr/Etudes-et-publications/Les-rapports-annuels-du-CSA/CSA-Rapport-annuel-2012; CSA, "Rapport Annuel 2011," December 6, 2012, p. 32, http://csa.fr/Etudes-et-publications/Les-rapports-annuels-du-CSA/CSA-Rapport-annuel-2011; CSA, "Rapport Annuel 2010," p. 61 (all reports accessed 6.5.2016).

1337 CSA, "Rapport Annuel 2015," p. 151.

members, three of whom are appointed by the President of the *Assemblée nationale* (National Assembly) and three by the President of the *Sénat* (Senate). Moreover, the President of the Republic appoints the President of the CSA.[1338] The members hold their offices, which are neither reversible nor renewable, for six years.[1339] Every two years, three members (except for its President) are exchanged in a pre-determined rotating system.[1340] Four members have to be present to reach the quorum. Decisions are taken by simple majority voting, giving the President a prevailing vote in case of a tie.[1341] Furthermore, Art. 5 LLC sets out incompatibility rules, which are supplemented by a code of ethics.[1342] Further details about the organisation of the CSA are outlined in its internal regulation of 1989 which was repealed by a decree of 2014.[1343] The reform of the CSA aimed at curtailing the powers of the French President exerting influence on the

---

1338 Art. 4 LLC. See also Davy and Hurard, *Lamy Droit des Médias et de la Communication*, paras. 321–39; Franceschini, "Les points clés de la loi du 15 novembre 2013 'relative à l'indépendance de l'audiovisuel public,'" p. 38; Kamina, *Communication audiovisuelle*, para. 37, II; Truchet, *Communication audiovisuelle, Régulation et secteur public*, 2014, para. 64, IV.

1339 Debbasch, Isar, and Agostinellig, *Droit de la communication, Audiovisuel – Presse – Internet*, para. 139, p. 11; Truchet, *Communication audiovisuelle, Régulation et secteur public*, 2014, p. 64, IV.

1340 Art. 4 LLC. See also Davy and Hurard, *Lamy Droit des Médias et de la Communication*, paras. 321–39; Debbasch, Isar and Agostinellig, *Droit de la communication, Audiovisuel – Presse – Internet*, para. 139, p. 111; Derieux and Granchet, *Droit des médias, Droit francais, européen et international*, paras. 576–77, p. 191; Kamina, *Communication audiovisuelle*, para. 37, I.; Truchet, *Communication audiovisuelle, Régulation et secteur public*, 2014, p. 64, IV.

1341 Art. 4 LLC. See also Kamina, *Communication audiovisuelle*, para. 38, I.

1342 CSA, "Code de déontologie applicable aux membres du Conseil," April 2, 2003, http://csa.fr/Le-CSA/Presentation-du-Conseil/Code-de-deontologie-applicable-aux-membres-du-Conseil (accessed 3.8.2014); Davy and Hurard, *Lamy Droit des Médias et de la Communication*, paras. 321–39; Debbasch, Isar and Agostinellig, *Droit de la communication, Audiovisuel – Presse – Internet*, paras. 141–44, pp. 111-112; Derieux and Granchet, *Droit des médias, Droit francais, européen et international*, para. 579, p. 192; Kamina, *Communication audiovisuelle*, para. 39, I.

1343 Décret n°89-518 du 26 juillet 1989 relatif à l'organisation et au fonctionnement du Conseil supérieur de l'audiovisuel; Décret n° 2014-382 du 28 mars 2014 relatif à l'organisation et au fonctionnement du Conseil supérieur de l'audiovisuel, JORF n° 76 of 30.3.2014, p. 6193. See also Debbasch, Isar and Agostinellig, *Droit de la communication, Audiovisuel – Presse – Internet*, para. 145, pp. 112-113.

regulator's personnel. In addition, the procedure for nomination was altered to enhance the involvement of the opposition in the French Parliament.[1344]

Originally, the composition of the CSA was modelled upon the structure of the *Conseil constitutionnel* comprising nine members of whom the President of France, the President of the French Parliament and the President of the Senate respectively appointed three.[1345] This particular design had already been deployed for the HACA and was considered adequate for the CSA until the end of 2013. The structural resemblance between the CSA and HACA was a deliberate decision in view of the defects of the CNCL's composition.[1346] The latter's internal dissensions were primarily imputed to its large and heterogeneous composition.[1347] The inclusion of magistrates contributed to the politicisation of the CNCL rather than its objectivity.[1348] Thus, when devising the composition of the CSA, the primary objective had been to safeguard its internal cohesion and encourage its members to take decisions collectively and in solidarity in order to enhance its credibility and avoid the rifts and conflicts that shook the CNCL.[1349] From this genesis, it can be deduced that securing the independence of the CSA has been a primary concern of policy makers. In this respect, Chevallier points out that there is no ideal composition laid down by law to ensure independence of the regulator. What is more important is

1344 Assemblée nationale, "Projet de loi relatif à l'indépendance de l'audiovisuel public, Exposé des motifs," May 6, 2013.

1345 Debbasch, Isar and Agostinellig, *Droit de la communication, Audiovisuel – Presse – Internet*, para. 138, p. 110; Derieux and Granchet, *Droit des médias, Droit francais, européen et international*, para. 573, p. 191; Holznagel, *Rundfunkrecht in Europa*, p. 45; Truchet, *Communication audiovisuelle, Régulation et secteur public*, 2014, para. 63, IV.

1346 Chevallier, "De la CNCL, au Conseil superieur de l'audiovisuel," p. 65; Debbasch, Isar and Agostinellig, *Droit de la communication, Audiovisuel – Presse – Internet*, para. 138, p. 110; Derieux and Granchet, *Droit des médias, Droit francais, européen et international*, para. 573, p. 191; Davy and Hurard, *Lamy Droit des Médias et de la Communication*, paras. 321–27, 321–39; Morange, "Le Conseil supérieur de l'audiovisuel," p. 238.

1347 Sénat, "Projet de loi modifiant la loi n° 86-1067 du 30 septembre 1986 relative à la liberté de communication," p. 3; Chevallier, "De la CNCL, au Conseil superieur de l'audiovisuel," p. 67; Morange, "Le Conseil supérieur de l'audiovisuel," p. 239.

1348 Chevallier, "De la CNCL, au Conseil superieur de l'audiovisuel," pp. 67–68; Morange, "Le Conseil supérieur de l'audiovisuel," p. 239.

1349 Chevallier, "De la CNCL, au Conseil superieur de l'audiovisuel," p. 70.

that the regulator acquires its own identity by "conquering the independence", which was not previously foreseen by the letter of the law, thereby going beyond legal guarantees.[1350] Holznagel consents that the CSA, in spite of its initial proximity to the Socialist government, has succeeded in building a cross-party reputation.[1351]

In brief, the French regulatory structure is relatively centralised with the CSA as the principal regulator. Set up in the late 1980s, the CSA has regulated the market for audio- and audiovisual media services including private and public service media. It has functioned under the LLC, which was drafted in the mid-1980s, and has since been amended to adapt to technological progress and developments at the EU level necessitating the transposition of Secondary Union Law. To date, only in the field of advertising, a self-regulatory mechanism has been set up under the aegis of the ARPP. Although the ARPP has elaborated some recommendations that touch on issues regulated by the AVMSD, this study investigates different aspects of the AVMSD's application and enforcement at the national level, notably the interpretation of the notion of an on-demand audiovisual media service and the protection of minors in such services.

## D. Summary

In sum, this chapter provides an overview of the British, German and French regulatory frameworks for audiovisual media services. It highlights the different regulatory models employed in the three countries. In the UK, a powerful converged regulator has been established that temporarily delegated the regulation of VOD services to a co-regulator. The end of the co-regulatory scheme was motivated by media convergence and the need to apply common rules to linear and non-linear services. In Germany, the regulatory framework is more complex given the federal structure of the state. While the state media authorities are competent to regulate audiovisual media services, coordination is accomplished by several bodies established at the federal (supra-state) level. Due to the constitutional constraints inherent in federalist Germany, a one-stop-shop or converged reg-

1350 Chevallier, "De la CNCL, au Conseil superieur de l'audiovisuel," p. 69.
1351 Holznagel, *Rundfunkrecht in Europa*, p. 45.

ulator like the UK's Ofcom has been inconceivable in Germany.[1352] Still, media convergence has prompted the creation of an innovative co-regulatory regime for the protection of minors that relies on organisations of voluntary self-regulation, which are integrated in a legal framework and ultimately monitored by the regulatory authority, the KJM. This co-regulatory scheme has functioned effectively for more than a decade and is an example of the success of alternative regulatory forms. In France, regulation is centralised in one regulatory authority that has a broad mandate for regulating audiovisual media services, linear and non-linear. While the distinction between regulating audiovisual media services and telecommunications is upheld in Germany and France, the British regulatory authority is responsible for both sectors. Owing to the concentration on a central regulatory body, the use of alternative regulatory strategies in France is limited to the advertising sector.

It is interesting to note that the mandates of the key regulatory authorities in the three countries refer to values which may potentially conflict. In the UK, Ofcom, underpinned by a liberal market-oriented approach, has faced the citizen-consumer paradox. In Germany, NRA's independence and the maintenance of media pluralism and diversity have been primary objectives. In a similar vein, the French regulator promotes pluralism and the linguistic and cultural diversity of the country by encouraging the production and distribution of French and European works. Hence, the NRAs seem to oscillate between cultural and economic objectives and have had to mediate between the two. This tension, inherent in the regulation of audiovisual media services, is furthermore illustrated by the analysis conducted in the fourth and fifth chapters of this study which look at NRAs' measures taken to implement certain provisions of the AVMSD.

1352 Gersdorf, "Begrenzte Aufsicht und einfache Aufsichtsstrukturen," p. 108; Thaenert, "Nochmals zur Reform der Medienkontrolle durch den 10. RÄStV," p. 132.

# Chapter 4. The UK, German and French regulators' approaches to the notion of an on-demand audiovisual media service

## *A. The material scope of application of the AVMSD*

A lot of scholarly attention has focused on the AVMSD's (material and territorial) scope of application. One of the important novelties brought about when it was adopted in 2007 was the extension of its scope from previously broadcasting to all kinds of audiovisual media services including on-demand (non-linear) services. Many Member States have reproduced the exact formulations in their national laws transposing the AVMSD.[1353] Some have even included guidance from the Directive's preamble to clarify the meaning of these key terms denoting scope.[1354] It follows that the definitions of an audiovisual media service and that of an on-demand service are complex, relying on a range of criteria and NRAs have since struggled with their application in practice.[1355] This is why this research includes a case study on scope. The question of whether a service is within or outside of scope of AVMS-regulation is crucial, not least for service providers which have to abide by the relevant rules. It is therefore the starting point for NRAs' assessments on the nature of service. Uncer-

1353 See for instance the national execution measures of Austria, Belgium, Bulgaria, Cyprus, Greece, Hungary, Ireland, Luxembourg, Latvia, Malta, Romania and Spain, available in English at http://wwwen.uni.lu/recherche/fdef/droit_des_medias/audiovisual_media_services_directive/national_execution_measures and also on the EAO's AVMS Database available at http://avmsd.obs.coe.int/cgi-bin/search.php (both websites accessed 15.3.2016).

1354 See for instance the national execution measures of Bulgaria, France, Italy and Slovenia.

1355 See for instance Irini Katsirea, "Electronic Press: 'Press-Like' or 'Television-Like'?," *International Journal of Law and Information Technology*, 2015, pp. 1–23; Jenny Metzdorf, "The Implementation of the Audiovisual Media Services Directive by National Regulatory Authorities – National Responses to Regulatory Challenges," *Journal of Intellectual Property, Information Technology and Electronic Commerce Law* 5, no. 2 (2014): paras. 6–11, pp. 90–92, http://www.jipitec.eu/issues/jipitec-5-2-2014/3998 (accessed 15.3.2015); Peggy Valcke and Jef Ausloos, "What If Television Becomes Just an App?" (accessed 10.1.2014).

tainties surrounding the criteria composing an (on-demand) audiovisual media service have adverse effects for legal certainty and ultimately, for service providers operating in a fluid environment. NRAs are thus interested in clarifying the precise meaning of these concepts and have, in many countries, issued guidance in this respect.

The following chapter therefore examines how the notion of an on-demand audiovisual media service is transposed in the national legal orders of the UK, Germany and France, and, moreover, how it is interpreted and applied by the respective NRAs. These have been very active in shaping the definition attempting to bring enhanced clarity on its application. Before delving into a detailed analysis of national executive measures, the most important terms as defined by the AVMSD are briefly recapitulated, with references to relevant case law, in particular, the case of *New Media Online* decided in October 2015 which raised questions of the Directive's scope in relation to online newspapers. Regulators' measures are then scrutinised per country in order to place these in the national context and allow for detailed analysis of these. The three sub-sections dealing with the UK, German and French regulators are similarly structured. They first present the legal provisions transposing the AVMSD before examining regulators' measures encompassing their practice, specific guidance documents as well as research or other policy papers that indicate regulators' perspectives on the concept of an (on-demand) audiovisual media service. The final section compares regulators' measures, identifying differences and similarities. On the basis of this comparison, the sixth chapter deduces best practices and discusses issues pertinent for the Directive's review. This chapter shows how regulators have attempted to adapt the AVMSD's criteria to media convergence and changing market conditions and highlights the problems they have faced in this respect.

### I. Linear and non-linear audiovisual media services

The notion of an on-demand audiovisual media service is defined in Art. 1 (1) (g) AVMSD as a service

> "provided by a media service provider for the viewing of programmes at the moment chosen by the user and at his individual request on the basis of a catalogue of programmes selected by the media service provider."

The definition can be divided into the following elements: (i) viewing takes place at the moment chosen by the user (ii) at their individual request (iii) on the basis of a catalogue of programmes (iv) selected by the media service provider. It is the user who initiates the transmission of the programme by choosing it from a catalogue fed by the service provider. An on-demand or non-linear audiovisual media service is a type of audiovisual media service. Therefore, the definition of an on-demand service is intrinsically linked to the definition of an audiovisual media service and they jointly determine the material scope of application of the AVMSD. While the notion of an audiovisual media service serves as an umbrella catching all services to which the AVMSD applies, the notion of an on-demand service is more specific and delimits the scope of application "at the bottom end", i.e. delineating services within and services outside of its scope. Services which offer audiovisual material but which are not classified as non-linear remain unaffected by the obligations contained in the AVMSD.

Similarly, television broadcasts or linear audiovisual media services demarcate the scope of application towards the upper end.[1356] A more strin-

---

1356 A few months before the Commission published its proposal on the amendment of the TWFD, the CJEU decided on a preliminary reference by the Dutch Raad van State on the interpretation of the term "television broadcasting" (differentiating it from the concept of an information society service within the meaning of the E-Commerce Directive), in particular, the classification of what is called "near-video on-demand". The CJEU pointed out that a service such as Filmtime provided by Mediakabel constituted television broadcasting (para. 35). Although subscribers were handed an individual key by which the service was activated, the offering was intended for viewing by the general public. The keys triggered the broadcast in unencoded form of the programmes which were simultaneously screened to all subscribers (para. 38). The list of films as well as the times at which they were broadcast were, moreover, determined by the service provider (para. 38). The CJEU posited that a service which was "not commanded individually by an isolated recipient who has free choice of programmes in an interactive setting (.) must be considered to be a near-video on-demand service, provided on a 'point to multipoint' basis" (para. 39). Strikingly, in its characterisation of near-video on-demand, the CJEU referred to the indicative list of services not covered by the definition of an information society service included in Annex V to Directive 98/34/EC (as amended by Directive 98/48/EC) as well as to the Explanatory Report accompanying the CTT (para. 41). It stressed that the "determining criterion" of the definition of television broadcasting was whether the programmes were "intended for reception by the public" (para. 42). Importantly, the CJEU noted that "priority should be given to the standpoint of the service provider in the assessment" (para. 42). The service

gent tier of rules is applicable to linear services.[1357] These are defined by Art. 1 (1) (e) AVMSD as a service "provided by a media service provider for simultaneous viewing of programmes on the basis of a programme schedule". In contrast to programmes offered on-demand, television broadcasts are disseminated for simultaneous viewing along a schedule of programmes. The viewer can neither control nor influence the start of the transmission of programmes which is, instead, determined by the service provider who arranges the programmes in a sequential order. The term "schedule" can be juxtaposed to the term "catalogue" in which programmes are assembled or aggregated and from which the user can select the programme he or she is interested in. It follows that tuning into a programme (at the time it starts) or switching to another channel are the only means whereby viewers "control" linear emissions. The level of control individual viewers have is thus considerably limited in comparison to on-demand services. This difference has been the justification for the introduction of different tiers of regulation as outlined in the first chapter. In a converged media environment, the boundary between linear and non-linear services becomes increasingly blurred and the legal differentiation appears all the more artificial – especially from a user perspective.[1358]

Furthermore, an understanding of the notion of audiovisual media service is essential when analysing the Directive's scope. Art. 1 (1) (a) outlines three types of audiovisual media services: first, television broadcasts, second, on-demand audiovisual media services and, third, audiovisual commercial communications. While the notions of television broadcasts and on-demand audiovisual media services are pertinent to this study, it will not examine in detail the national implementations of the notion of audiovisual commercial communication as set out in Art. 1 (1) (h)

---

Filmtime would thus have to adhere to the content standards (e.g. promotion of European works) laid down in the TWFD and transposed in the Dutch legal order. In this context, the CJEU pointed out that the inquiry into the nature of the service did not have to take into account possible negative implications from characterisation as a broadcast for the service provider (para. 49). See case C-89/04 *Mediakabel BV v Commissariaat voor de Media*, Judgment of 2.6.2005, EU:C:2005:348.

1357 On the graduated approach to regulation adopted by the AVMSD, see for example Valcke, and Stevens, "Graduated Regulation of 'Regulatable' Content and the AVMSD," pp. 285–302.

1358 Dizon, "Looking beyond the Linear/non-Linear Horizon," pp. 185, 191; Van Eijk, "Scope of Application of the Modernised Directive," p. 23.

AVMSD. Pursuant to Art. 1 (1) (a) AVMSD, an audiovisual media service means:

> "(i) a service as defined by Articles 56 and 57 of the Treaty on the Functioning of the European Union which is under the editorial responsibility of a media service provider and the principal purpose of which is the provision of programmes, in order to inform, entertain or educate, to the general public by electronic communications networks within the meaning of point (a) of Article 2 of Directive 2002/21/EC. Such an audiovisual media service is either a television broadcast as defined in point (e) of this paragraph or an on-demand audiovisual media service as defined in point (g) of this paragraph;
> (ii) audiovisual commercial communication"

Thus, the definition consists of several cumulative[1359] criteria which can be summarised as (i) a service within the meaning of the Treaty (ii) under the editorial responsibility of a provider (iii) with the principal purpose of providing audiovisual programmes (iv) to the general public (v) by electronic communications networks.[1360]

The term "editorial responsibility" is further specified in Art. 1 (1) (c) implying

> "the exercise of effective control both over the selection of the programmes and over their organisation either in a chronological schedule, in the case of television broadcasts, or in a catalogue, in the case of on-demand audiovisual media services. Editorial responsibility does not necessarily imply any legal liability under national law for the content or the services provided".[1361]

---

1359 See recital 29 AVMSD.

1360 Castendyk and Woods, "Art. 1 TWFD," paras. 24–49, pp. 812-818; Cole, "The EU Legal Framework for on-Demand Services," pp. 35–45; Michael Kogler, "Fernsehähnliches TV-On Demand, Was ist (k)ein 'Audiovisueller Mediendienst auf Abruf'?," *Medien und Recht* 4 (2011): pp. 229–37; Valcke, et al., "The EU Regulatory Framework Applicable to Broadcasting," in *Telecommunications, Broadcasting and the Internet, EU Competition Law & Regulation*, ed. Laurent Garzaniti and Matthew O'Regan, third edition (London: Sweet & Maxwell, 2010), paras. 2.22-2.41; Valcke and Ausloos, "What If Television Becomes Just an App?".

1361 In 2009, the regulatory authority of the French Community of Belgium, the Conseil supérieur de l'audiovisuel (CSA-Be) referred a preliminary ruling on the interpretation of Art. 1 (1) (c), more precisely the concepts of "supplier" and of "effective control both over the selection of the programmes and over their organisation". The CJEU, however, dismissed the case on formal grounds as the CSA-Be lacked the quality of a court or tribunal within the meaning of Union law and was thus not competent to refer questions for preliminary ruling in accordance with Art. 234 TEC (Art. 267 TFEU). The outcome of the case, had it

In other words, the person who controls the selection and organisation of programmes bears the editorial responsibility and is considered as the service provider by virtue of the AVMSD.[1362] This is reiterated in a somewhat circular manner with the definition of "media service provider" contained in Art. 1 (1) (d) AVMSD. With respect to video-sharing sites or connected TVs, the tasks of selecting and organising content are frequently carried out by different actors who consequently exercise different editorial roles and different degrees of editorial responsibility.

Another notion firmly rooted in the broadcasting era and which is being challenged today is that of "programme". By virtue of Art. 1 (1) (b), a programme is defined as

> "a set of moving images with or without sound constituting an individual item within a schedule or a catalogue established by a media service provider and the form and content of which are comparable to the form and content of television broadcasting."

The second part of the definition consists of a non-exhaustive list of examples of programmes, such as "feature-length films, sports events, situation comedies, documentaries, children's programmes and original drama". The Directive requires a "dynamic interpretation" of the notion of "programme" and will thus apply to new formats.[1363]

## II. The guidance contained in the preamble of the AVMSD

A considerable number of non-binding recitals detail the material scope of application of the Directive and specify the criteria which constitute an audiovisual media service. This striking fact shows that the criteria used to

---

been admissible, would have been interesting and could have given precious guidance on the notion of editorial responsibility. On the notion of editorial responsibility and its relation to legal liability, see also Chavannes, Remy and Castendyk, Oliver, "Art. 1 AVMSD," para. 74, p. 825; Raf Schoefs, "Connected TV: Editorial Responsibility in a Converged Media Environment," *Auteurs & Media* 5 (2014): p. 348.

1362 For a more comprehensive discussion, see Wolfgang Schulz, *Editorial Responsibility*, IRIS Special (Strasbourg: European Audiovisual Observatory, 2008); Remy Chavannes and Oliver Castendyk, "Art. 1 AVMSD," paras. 63–80, pp. 822–27; on the notion of editorial responsibility in a converging media eco-system, see Schoefs, "Connected TV and Editorial Responsibility," pp. 348–55.

1363 Recital 24 AVMSD.

define key notions are fluid and difficult to grasp in a rapidly changing environment. Although non-binding in nature, these recitals have indeed served an integral function for the conceptualisation and contextualisation of the definitions and substantive provisions. Above all, the CJEU has made frequent references to the Directive's preamble in its jurisprudence.[1364]

Recitals 21 to 29 AVMSD are instrumental in specifying the notion of an audiovisual media service. Accordingly, the Directive is applicable to audiovisual media services which are "mass media, that is, which are intended for reception by, and which could have a clear impact on, a significant proportion of the general public".[1365] This is an important caveat which implicitly exempts from the Directive's scope such services which, due to their small scale or very limited offer, cannot be considered as being addressed to the general public. Thus, non-economic activities which are "not in competition with television broadcasting" do not fall under the AVMSD such as "private websites and services" (including email)[1366] and social networking sites or other forums to which users turn to for sharing and exchanging information.[1367]

Moreover, services for which providing programmes is not the principal purpose are equally excluded. This is, for instance, the case when entities "merely transmit programmes" for which they do not have editorial responsibility.[1368] The principal purpose criterion is not satisfied where "audiovisual content is merely incidental to the service" such as "websites that contain audiovisual elements only in an ancillary manner".[1369] While the Directive applies to "text-based services" such as sub-titling or electronic programme guides (EPGs) which accompany programmes, it does

1364 See for example the recent cases C-281/09 *European Commission v Kingdom of Spain*, Judgment of 24.11.2011, EU:C:2011:767, paras. 44, 46; C-283/11 *Sky Österreich GmbH v Österreichischer Rundfunk*, Judgement of 22.1.2013, EU:C:2013:28, para. 51; C-234/12 *Sky Italia Srl v Autorità per le Garanzie nelle Comunicazioni*, Judgment of 18.7.2013, EU:C:2013:496, para. 13; C-314/14 *Sanoma Media Finland Oy/Nelonen Media, Helsinki*, Judgment of 17.2.2016, EU:C:2016:89, paras. 31-32, 34.

1365 Recital 21 AVMSD.

1366 Recital 22 AVMSD.

1367 Recital 21 AVMSD.

1368 Recital 26 AVMSD.

1369 Recital 22 AVMSD.

not apply to "stand-alone text-based services".[1370] Similarly, "electronic versions of newspapers and magazines" are not affected by the AVMSD.[1371] Thus, the relevant recital 28, as will be shown below, is controversial and its interpretation differs throughout many EU Member States. In some Member States, websites or sub-sites of online newspapers fall under AVMS-type regulation while in others, such approaches have explicitly been rejected by national regulators.

Furthermore, recital 24 AVMSD clarifies the relation between linear and non-linear services underlining that "it is characteristic of on-demand audiovisual media services that they are 'television-like', i.e. that they compete for the same audience as television broadcasts, and the nature and the means of access to the service would lead the user reasonably to expect regulatory protection within the scope of this Directive".[1372] The formulation "TV-like" has become a buzzword to delineate the material scope of the AVMSD implying competition for the same audience and similar user expectations regarding the expected level of protection.[1373] Recital 27 AVMSD lists examples of linear services ("analogue and digital television, live streaming, webcasting and near-video-on-demand") and non-linear services ("video-on-demand", VOD).[1374]

### III. The interpretation of recital 28 AVMSD: the case of New Media Online

In 2014, a case on the scope of application of the AVMSD was referred to the CJEU for the first time. The case of *New Media Online* put the growing convergence of the press sector in the spotlight, particularly its online activities providing audiovisual media services. As Katsirea observes, "newspapers are not just 'news' printed on 'paper', but are also understood as news content available on websites carrying videos that are reminiscent of television. A notable development of recent times has been the exponential increase of video content available on newspaper websites, of-

1370 Recital 23 AVMSD.
1371 Recital 28 AVMSD.
1372 Recital 24 AVMSD.
1373 For a concise overview, see Cabrera Blázquez, "On-Demand Services: Made in the Likeness of TV?," pp. 7–27.
1374 Recital 27 AVMSD.

ten produced by major newspapers as well as news agencies such as United Press International, Reuters and the AP, which were once specialised in print only".[1375]

Today, electronic versions of newspapers and magazines no longer replicate the material published in print form but are edited for online consumption and seek to enhance consumers' experience. The progressive convergence of the press and the audiovisual market on the Internet will have serious repercussions on the "historically disparate regulation of the two sectors".[1376] While the press has been subject to self-regulation, a much more extensive and burdensome regulatory regime has applied to audiovisual media services due to their enhanced impact on public opinion formation. Recital 28 AVMSD is a relic of such times. If today the press ventures into the territory traditionally occupied by broadcasters, this will raise the question of fairness to apply similar rules to similar kinds of activities.

The Austrian media regulator, KommAustria, pursued such an approach when it characterised the video section of the website of the daily newspaper *Tiroler Tageszeitung* (TT) as an on-demand audiovisual media service.[1377] The company New Media Online operates the TT under the domain http://www.tt.com. Apart from written articles which are organised

1375 Katsirea, "Electronic Press: 'Press-Like' or 'Television-Like'?," p. 1.

1376 Katsirea, "Electronic Press: 'Press-Like' or 'Television-Like'?," p. 1.

1377 In the case *Sotiris Papasavvas* decided on 11 September 2014, the CJEU held that the website of the daily Cypriot newspaper constituted an information society service within the meaning of the E-Commerce Directive. The applicant had initiated an action for damages in defamation proceedings regarding articles published on the two websites of the national newspaper. The CJEU clarified that the concept of "service" did not only cover those activities remunerated by those who receive them but implied remuneration generated by advertisements included on the websites (para. 30). In addition, the CJEU made clear that a newspaper publishing company could not be considered an intermediary service provider and would not be exempt from liability pursuant to Art. 12 to 14 E-Commerce Directive as it had "in principle, knowledge about the information which it posts and exercises control over that information" (para. 45). Although this case does not explicitly touch on the AVMSD's scope of application, it nonetheless is significant as it underpins the CJEU's wide interpretation of the term "service" within the meaning of Art. 57 TFEU. In addition, it demonstrates that online newspapers, viewed in their entirety, are commonly considered as information society services and are thus caught by the E-Commerce Directive. See C-291/13 *Sotiris Papasavvas v O Fileleftheros Dimosia Etaireia Ltd and Others*, Judgment of 11 September 2014, EU:C:2014:2209.

in different categories, the website also contains a video section entitled "Video" which featured more than 300 videos. At the relevant time, the videos were edited and varied in length from 30 seconds to several minutes.[1378] In October 2012, the KommAustria took its decision on account of the independent function which the video subdomain of the website performed.[1379]

New Media Online appealed to the Austrian Bundekommunikationssenat (BKS) which in December 2013 confirmed KommAustria's analysis, above all, with regards to the independent function test. The BKS held that the video section of the TT constituted a "consumable offer" ("*konsumierbares Angebot*") which users could use independently and regardless of its being embedded in the website's complete offer.[1380] New Media Online appealed the decision of the BKS before the Austrian *Verwaltungsgerichtshof* (Supreme Administrative Court, VGH), which, in June 2014, decided to stay proceedings and refer two questions to the CJEU.[1381] The first question concerned the notion of "programme" as defined in Art. 1 (1) (b) AVMSD, in particular whether short clips showing local news, sports or other entertainment are comparable to programmes typically featured on TV such as "feature-length films, sports events, situation comedies, documentaries, children's programmes and original drama" as enumerated in Art. 1 (1) (b) AVMSD. The second referred question asked whether a particular section of the website of an online newspaper could be extracted from the global offer of the provider for the purpose of the principal purpose assessment pursuant to Art. 1 (1) (a) (i) AVMSD.

### 1. Advocate General Szpunar's assertion that "we all know what a horse is"

In his opinion delivered on 1 July 2015, Advocate General (AG) Szpunar went beyond the preliminary questions and presented an interesting view

1378 KommAustria, "Bescheid KOA 1.950/12-048," September 10, 2012, para. 2, pp. 3–5.

1379 KommAustria, "Order Tiroler Tageszeitung," para. 4.4.2, p. 11.

1380 Bundeskommunikationssenat, "Entscheidung GZ 611.191/0005-BKS/2012," December 13, 2012, para. 10, p. 5.

1381 Verwaltungsgerichtshof, "Beschluss Zl. 2013/03/0012, C-347/14," June 26, 2014.

of the AVMSD, considerably diminishing its role in, and impact on, today's converging media environment. Presuming that everyone is capable of intuitively defining an audiovisual media service in the same way as everyone knows what a horse is, AG Szpunar nonetheless admitted that apart from an approximate explanation, it was difficult to formulate a specific and concrete notion based on unambiguous and precise legal terms.[1382] In his introduction, the AG rightly pinpointed the conundrum brought by applying rules stemming from analogue times to a borderless, ubiquitous and digital Internet.[1383] This observation set the tone of the opinion in which AG Szpunar interpreted the current provisions of the AVMSD strictly, while calling for their adjustment by the EU legislature. What is more, the AG noted that the expansion of the Directive's scope of application to audiovisual media services was necessary due to technological progress, the emergence of new services and a gradual shift in users' behaviour as well as their expectations.[1384] He underlined that a graduated approach to regulation had been adopted and as a result, a core body of rules were applicable to "traditional television", while on-demand audiovisual media services were subject to a lighter set of rules.[1385] The AG gleaned from the Directive's history that the rules concerning non-linear services constituted "merely a derivative of the rules on linear services, that is to say television".[1386]

This finding shaped AG Szpunar's interpretation of the notion of audiovisual media service which he interpreted narrowly, focussing essentially on television broadcasting. He criticised the approach taken by the Austrian regulator arguing that it was the intention of the Union legislature to extend regulation only to those services which are "in *direct* competition with television broadcasting".[1387] He also posited that the interpretation advanced by KommAustria (and the BKS for that matter) would include in the scope of application of the AVMSD "a large number of persons who operate websites with audiovisual content but the basic purpose of whose

1382 Opinion of Advocate General Szpunar delivered on 1 June 2015 in case C-347/14 *New Media Online GmbH*, EU:C:2015:434, para. 1.
1383 Opinion of AG Szpunar in case C-347/14 *New Media Online*, paras. 2, 22-24. In para. 23 of the opinion, AG Szpunar refers to an "Internetisation".
1384 Opinion of AG Szpunar in case C-347/14 *New Media Online*, para. 18.
1385 Opinion of AG Szpunar in case C-347/14 *New Media Online*, para. 20.
1386 Opinion of AG Szpunar in case C-347/14 *New Media Online*, para. 21.
1387 Opinion of AG Szpunar in case C-347/14 *New Media Online*, para. 29.

activity is not to offer audiovisual services".[1388] Such excessive broadening of the scope might also, according to the AG, put a strain on the capacities of national regulatory authorities to monitor the activities of service providers and enforce the law at the national level.[1389] In addition, the AG argued that the Austrian reading of the Directive would make its application "dependent on the architecture of the specific website".[1390] Accordingly, content aggregated in a catalogue of a website would be subject to regulation, whereas the same content would not fall under the scope if it were scattered across different areas of the website (e.g. sub-sites). By contrast, the AG considered that the accumulation of content in a catalogue merely constituted "a particular technical solution which should not affect the application of the Directive".[1391] While the Austrian authorities relied on a literal interpretation of the Directive, the AG considered that such an approach would neither be compatible with the intention of the EU legislature, nor in line with the objective and purpose of the Directive. It followed that the Directive's material scope of application should be "determined by the nature of the service and not the architecture of the Internet portal on which [audiovisual content] is offered".[1392] Importantly, AG Szpunar proposed a narrow interpretation of the notion of audiovisual media services, covering only those services explicitly referred to by the Directive.[1393]

One by one, the AG examined the audiovisual media service criteria as stipulated by Art. 1 (1) (a) (i) AVMSD. With respect to the notion of service, the AG noted that today many websites were indirectly financed by advertisements and "branded channels" on "YouTube-like" platforms were becoming more frequent so that the "dividing line" between user-generated content and professional content was becoming less clear-cut.[1394] The AG confirmed that the online news portal offered by the *Tiroler Tageszeitung* should be considered as an economic activity and thus constituted a service within the meaning of the TFEU. He also affirmed that the website was addressed and available to the general public and provid-

1388 Opinion of AG Szpunar in case C-347/14 *New Media Online*, para. 30.
1389 Opinion of AG Szpunar in case C-347/14 *New Media Online*, para. 31.
1390 Opinion of AG Szpunar in case C-347/14 *New Media Online*, para. 32.
1391 Opinion of AG Szpunar in case C-347/14 *New Media Online*, para. 32.
1392 Opinion of AG Szpunar in case C-347/14 *New Media Online*, paras. 32-33, 42.
1393 Opinion of AG Szpunar in case C-347/14 *New Media Online*, para. 37.
1394 Opinion of AG Szpunar in case C-347/14 *New Media Online*, para. 39.

ed informational, entertainment or educational programmes by electronic communications networks.[1395] The AG considered that the fact that Art. 1 (1) (b) AVMSD defined the notion of programme in relation to television broadcasting underscored the EU legislature's intention to restrict the scope of the Directive.[1396] Furthermore, although the criterion of editorial responsibility was not decisive in the case at hand, the AG made the interesting remark that it was "intended *merely* to distinguish providers of content from persons supplying a data transfer service (such as the providers of cable television networks or Internet connections)".[1397]

In relation to the element of principal purpose, AG Szpunar reiterated his criticism of the Austrian regulators' approach arguing that partitioning the website would necessarily result in finding that the principal purpose test was met. This would, however, erode the meaning of the principal purpose criterion and make the application of the Directive contingent on the structure and design of the website.[1398] Similarly, the AG opined that the concept of catalogue as appears in the definition of an on-demand audiovisual media service in Art. 1 (1) (g) AVMSD should not be excessively emphasised. To the AG, the existence of a catalogue was inherent to the provision of a non-linear service. Conversely, the existence of a catalogue *alone* did not imply the existence of an on-demand audiovisual media service.[1399]

To further shed light on the object and purpose of the Directive as well as on the intentions of the legislature, AG Szpunar examined the preamble of the Directive, in particular recitals 24 and 28 AVMSD. He found that the expression "television-like" as set out in the 24th recital primarily served to level the playing field between linear and non-linear services. Consequently, "the television-like nature of non-linear services must be treated strictly" and the Directive could not apply to "new phenomena connected with the spread of the Internet (…) such as the emergence of multimedia websites".[1400] He moreover rejected the formulation that non-linear services "compete for the same audience" as television broadcasting stating that television broadcasts offered "very diverse content intended in

1395 Opinion of AG Szpunar in case C-347/14 *New Media Online*, paras. 40, 43.
1396 Opinion of AG Szpunar in case C-347/14 *New Media Online*, para. 43.
1397 Opinion of AG Szpunar in case C-347/14 *New Media Online*, para. 41.
1398 Opinion of AG Szpunar in case C-347/14 *New Media Online*, para. 42.
1399 Opinion of AG Szpunar in case C-347/14 *New Media Online*, para. 45.
1400 Opinion of AG Szpunar in case C-347/14 *New Media Online*, para. 47.

principle for every conceivable audience, satisfying their need for information, entertainment and education".[1401] Interestingly, the dynamic interpretation of the concept of "programme" as prescribed by recital 24 AVMSD, was in the AG's opinion, equally considered as restricting the scope of application of the Directive to "the basic regulatory subject-matter (…) which is linear services".[1402] Thus, AG Szpunar warned that making non-linear services a separate regulatory subject-matter would "make it necessary to include an ever-increasing number of types of audiovisual content which may have nothing in common with linear television broadcasting".[1403]

To bolster this reading, the AG referred to recital 28 AVMSD which expressly exempts electronic versions of newspapers and magazines from the AVMSD. He remarked that nowadays the online publication of paper versions of newspapers and magazines was dropping and instead "Internet information portals" were on the rise which offered different forms of content including text-based as well as audiovisual material.[1404] He stressed that such portals commonly shared some characteristics and were offered not only by publishers of newspapers and magazines but also by providers of television and radio services.[1405] Thus, different treatment based on the mere fact that a portal was operated by a newspaper publisher was unfounded. From this line of argumentation, the AG derived the legislature's intention to exclude from the Directive "all kinds of Internet information portals which are multimedia in nature, that is to say contain audiovisual content among other things".[1406]

As a result, the AG found that the website of the *Tiroler Tageszeitung* in its entirety did not constitute an audiovisual media service. Instead, the AG classified the portal as "an entirely new phenomenon" which lacked any material link to television broadcasting constituting the core subject matter of the Directive.[1407] In addition, the AG also disapproved of the dismantling of the website and the examination by regulators of a specific section thereof which primarily offered audiovisual content in a cata-

1401 Opinion of AG Szpunar in case C-347/14 *New Media Online*, para. 47.
1402 Opinion of AG Szpunar in case C-347/14 *New Media Online*, para. 48.
1403 Opinion of AG Szpunar in case C-347/14 *New Media Online*, para. 48.
1404 Opinion of AG Szpunar in case C-347/14 *New Media Online*, para. 49.
1405 Opinion of AG Szpunar in case C-347/14 *New Media Online*, para. 49.
1406 Opinion of AG Szpunar in case C-347/14 *New Media Online*, para. 49.
1407 Opinion of AG Szpunar in case C-347/14 *New Media Online*, para. 55.

logue.[1408] Such separation undermined the very nature of multimedia services comprising a "combination of different forms of communication – word, image and sound".[1409] Finally, the AG remarked that his interpretation of the term audiovisual media service was based on the current wording of the Directive and encouraged the Union's legislature to adapt its provisions to the Internet in the course of its refit exercise.

The opinion of AG Szpunar represents a rather conservative and one-dimensional interpretation of the Directive placing excessive weight on the historical genesis of the legal instrument, and above all, the intentions of the EU legislature. While the AG's assessment of the general technological context and the resulting deficiencies of the AVMSD are adequate, the conclusions he draws through his interpretation of key notions are difficult to align with the general aim of establishing a "level playing-field and a true European market for audiovisual media services" as postulated by recital 10 AVMSD. One nonetheless has to agree with the AG's observation that contrary to what its founders had hoped, the AVMSD did not "prove to be 'future-proof'".[1410] This is reflected not least by the ongoing reform of the Directive, as well as the Commission's general action plan as outlined in its Digital Single Market (DSM) Strategy.[1411] Although the AG pledged to give the provisions of the Directive "correct meaning in the current, rapidly changing, Internet reality",[1412] he did not analyse the definitions in light of media convergence and the emergence of new services. Instead, he considerably narrowed the Directive's scope of application to television broadcasting and those services "which are in *direct* competition with television, that is to say those offering the *same* content in a non-linear form".[1413]

It is true that the shape of the AVMSD owes a lot to its historical predecessor, the TWFD. The latter had a narrower scope while the AVMSD encompasses all audiovisual media services. The graduated approach introduced by the AVMSD took into account the different levels of market penetration, the different levels of control as well as the different expectations and behaviour by users in relation to linear and non-linear services. To this

1408 Opinion of AG Szpunar in case C-347/14 *New Media Online*, para. 55.
1409 Opinion of AG Szpunar in case C-347/14 *New Media Online*, para. 55.
1410 Opinion of AG Szpunar in case C-347/14 *New Media Online*, para. 34.
1411 European Commission, "Communication on a Digital Single Market Strategy.".
1412 Opinion of AG Szpunar in case C-347/14 *New Media Online*, para. 34.
1413 Opinion of AG Szpunar in case C-347/14 *New Media Online*, para. 52.

extent, the "lighter touch" rules applicable to on-demand audiovisual media services were modelled upon those applicable to broadcasting. However, the statement by AG Szpunar that the provisions concerning non-linear services were "merely a derivative of the rules on linear services"[1414] which constituted the "basic subject-matter"[1415] of regulation is misleading. He posits a firm border and, what is more, a hierarchy between two distinct regulatory matters in spite of his allegations that "non-linear services should not become a separate regulatory subject-matter" of the Directive.[1416] This is not to deny a close link between the rules for linear and non-linear services, with those of the latter originating from the former, but rather to question the AG's pre-occupation with the legislative history of the AVMSD. Such a restrictive reading of the Directive calls into question the "continued relevance of the Directive in a converged multimedia world".[1417]

Furthermore, AG Szpunar's interpretation of recitals 24 and 28 AVMSD is not entirely convincing. Recital 24 AVMSD requires that two aspects be investigated to appraise the TV-likeness of a service: first, competition for the same audience and second, similar user expectations of regulatory protection. While the AG refrained from any reference to user expectations, he read the recital as an expression of the "legislature's [primary] concern" to prevent distortions of competition between linear and non-linear services.[1418] The economic rationale is certainly visible in the preamble of the Directive. However, the phrase "competition for the same audience" not only means the dissemination of very diverse content addressed to "every conceivable audience"[1419] but also reaching those viewers who would otherwise turn to another service. In other words, recital 24 AVMSD implies the fight for users' eyeballs and attention. In this respect, new services (however defined and whatever their function) may indeed compete for the audience which would have previously been satisfied by watching television. Thus, the AG's mechanical exclusion of all "new

1414 Opinion of AG Szpunar in case C-347/14 *New Media Online*, para. 21.
1415 Opinion of AG Szpunar in case C-347/14 *New Media Online*, para. 48.
1416 Opinion of AG Szpunar in case C-347/14 *New Media Online*, para. 48.
1417 Michael Wagner, Legal Case Note: Does audiovisual regulation stop at the Internet?, 7.7.2015, available at https://www3.ebu.ch/contents/news/2015/07/legal-case-note-does-audiovisual.html (accessed 25.1.2016).
1418 Opinion of AG Szpunar in case C-347/14 *New Media Online*, para. 47.
1419 Opinion of AG Szpunar in case C-347/14 *New Media Online*, para. 47.

phenomena connected with the spread of the Internet" appears too limited.[1420] Likewise, the AG's reference to the "dynamic interpretation of the term 'programme'" contained in recital 24 AVMSD cannot be considered particularly "dynamic" when it is chained to television broadcasting and a strict reading of this concept.[1421]

In a similar vein, AG Szpunar's reading of recital 28 AVMSD seems flawed. It is doubtful whether the Union legislature when drafting the Directive in 2005 intended to exempt "all kinds of Internet information portals" from its scope.[1422] Above all, it can be questioned whether a "multimedia Internet portal is the current form of what the legislature, when working on the AVMSD, could still describe as the 'electronic version of newspapers or magazines'".[1423] The "anachronistic" wording of the 28th recital would rather seem to suggest that an exception for the paper versions of newspapers and magazines once published online should be carved out.[1424] Such an exception was aimed at protecting the printed press and the written word as its prerogative. When the Directive was drawn up and adopted in the years 2005-2007, the state of media convergence was rudimentary and not comparable to today's level of convergence. It is thus argued that by recital 28 AVMSD the Union legislature sought to solely exempt the printed versions of online newspapers and magazines primarily composed of text-based material rather than preclude the Directive's application to any multimedia portal or part thereof.

Interestingly, the AG does not attribute any particular significance to the notion of "catalogue" as contained in the definition on an on-demand service. He criticised the Austrian regulator's allegedly heavy reliance on this notion which would result in triggering the application of the Directive according to technical requirements composing the "architecture" of the website.[1425] The representation of the Austrian regulator's approach in the instant case seems too simplified and does not seem to give justice to the comprehensive analysis of the online version of the *Tiroler*

1420 Opinion of AG Szpunar in case C-347/14 *New Media Online*, para. 47.
1421 Opinion of AG Szpunar in case C-347/14 *New Media Online*, para. 48.
1422 Opinion of AG Szpunar in case C-347/14 *New Media Online*, para. 49.
1423 Opinion of AG Szpunar in case C-347/14 *New Media Online*, para. 55.
1424 Opinion of AG Szpunar in case C-347/14 *New Media Online*, para. 54.
1425 Opinion of AG Szpunar in case C-347/14 *New Media Online*, paras. 32, 42, 45, 55.

*Tageszeitung* including its self-standing and independent function.[1426] The notion of "catalogue" is one of the decisive criteria defining an on-demand service and it appears appropriate to examine whether content is collated and aggregated in a special section which represents a catalogue of viewing options. The AG nonetheless made a reasonable point that application of the Directive should not be contingent on the form and structure of the website – which would be too fluid a criterion. Succinctly, the delineation of the Directive's scope as forwarded by AG Szpunar seems unreasonably strict in light of the fast pace of technological progress. A reason for his unwillingness to go beyond the formulations of the provisions in their literal sense may be the exercise of self-restraint of the Union judiciary. He unambiguously identified the need for revising the AVMSD. Rather than developing the current rules by way of dynamic interpretation, in the final paragraph of his opinion AG Szpunar implicitly encouraged the Union legislature to act. In this respect, the AG's assessment is welcomed.

### 2. The CJEU's decision that a newspaper sub-site may fall under the AVMSD

In its decision of 21 October 2015,[1427] the CJEU did not follow AG Szpunar but instead held that a sub-site of an online newspaper compiling audiovisual material could be subjected to the rules outlined in the AVMSD. With regards to the interpretation of the term "programme" (first preliminary question), the CJEU pointed out that the comparison required by Art. 1 (1) (b) AVMSD did not entail comparing "the complete compilation of short videos" aggregated on the newspaper's website to "a complete schedule or a catalogue" but rather necessitated a comparison of individual items.[1428] The Court furthermore underlined that the AVMSD did not specify a minimum duration of programmes which could be of long, medium or short length.[1429] In addition, the Court found that the clips dis-

1426 More precisely, KommAustria pointed out that the sub-domain offering videos constituted a self-standing part of the website which could be used and consumed independently of the other content made available on the website. KommAustria, "Order Tiroler Tageszeitung," para. 4.4.2, p. 11.

1427 Case C-347/14 *New Media Online GmbH v Bundeskommunikationssenat*, Judgment of 21.10.2015, EU:C:2015:709.

1428 Case C-347/14 *New Media Online,* para. 19.

1429 Case C-347/14 *New Media Online,* para. 20.

seminated in the video section of the website of New Media Online were aimed at a mass audience and thus likely to have a clear impact on the public within the meaning of recital 21 AVMSD.[1430] The service provider's catalogue offered different modes of navigation, allowing for selection of videos by category ("heading") and by most watched or most recent videos. In this respect, the Court observed, the catalogue of the TT resembled those typically put in place by providers of non-linear services, which were regulated by the AVMSD.[1431] Above all, the CJEU underlined, referring to recitals 10, 21 and 24 AVMSD that the Directive aimed at ensuring a "competitive media landscape" and fair competition between market players competing for the same audience.[1432] Since a large proportion of the videos featured on the website of the TT were in fact produced by the regional broadcaster *Tirol TV,* the Court found that they did indeed compete for the same audience as broadcasts screened on TV.[1433] This was equally valid, according to the Court, with respect to videos not produced by broadcasters as they appealed to audiences targeted by "music channels, sports channels and entertainment programmes".[1434] It followed from the Court's analysis that Art. 1 (1) (b) AVMSD should be considered as including "videos of short duration consisting of local news bulletins, sports and entertainment clips".[1435]

The second part of the judgment is devoted to the interpretation of the notion of principal purpose as set forth in Art. 1 (1) (a) (i) AVMSD (second preliminary question). The Court noted that a service offering audiovisual material will only enter the AVMSD's scope of application if the audiovisual elements are *not* incidental or complementary to the text-based material. This stemmed from recitals 22 and 28 AVMSD and was reflected by the decision of the Austrian regulator to classify only a part of the service as a non-linear service rather than the entire website.[1436] It is significant that the Court highlighted the incompatibility with recital 28 AVMSD to "systematically" exclude all kinds of audiovisual services "solely on the grounds that the operator of the website of which that ser-

1430 Case C-347/14 *New Media Online,* para. 21.
1431 Case C-347/14 *New Media Online,* para. 21.
1432 Case C-347/14 *New Media Online,* para. 22.
1433 Case C-347/14 *New Media Online,* para. 23.
1434 Case C-347/14 *New Media Online,* para. 23.
1435 Case C-347/14 *New Media Online,* para. 24.
1436 Case C-347/14 *New Media Online,* paras. 26-27.

vice is part [was] a publishing company of an online newspaper".[1437] An automatic and all-encompassing exemption for online newspapers would fail to account for the myriad of services and their specific multimedia design. Instead, in the Court's opinion, an assessment of the principal purpose of the relevant service should be carried out on a "case-by-case basis".[1438] The assessment should not, however, relate to *all* the activities and services offered by the relevant operator which potentially were undertaken in different fields or markets.[1439] The CJEU unambiguously made clear that the principal purpose of a website did not "depend on whether the website concerned, considered in its entirety, [was] related to the principal activity of an undertaking or an activity, which, for that undertaking, [was] ancillary".[1440] The principal purpose criterion instead called for an examination of the "service at issue, in itself and regardless of the framework in which it [was] offered".[1441]

Moreover, the referring court was to determine whether the "form and content" of the video sub-domain was "independent" of the sub-domains of the written articles. This would not be the case if the written articles were "indissociably complementary to the journalistic activity of that publisher, in particular as a result of the links between the audiovisual offer and the offer in text form".[1442] The Court also commented on the design of the website arguing that it was irrelevant whether the audiovisual offer was presented on the home page ("in the principal domain") or in a sub-domain.[1443] Regardless of the discretion attributed to the referring court, the CJEU conducted a preliminary assessment finding that an overwhelming majority of videos were not connected to press articles and that the videos could be accessed and consumed on their own.[1444] These factors "tend[ed]" to support the view that the audiovisual service comprising the video section of the website was sufficiently independent from the "journalistic activity" of the newspaper publisher and thus constituted a distinct service falling under the AVMSD's scope.[1445] In sum, the principal pur-

1437 Case C-347/14 *New Media Online,* para. 28.
1438 Case C-347/14 *New Media Online,* para. 29.
1439 Case C-347/14 *New Media Online,* para. 30.
1440 Case C-347/14 *New Media Online,* para. 31.
1441 Case C-347/14 *New Media Online,* para. 33.
1442 Case C-347/14 *New Media Online,* para. 34.
1443 Case C-347/14 *New Media Online,* para. 35.
1444 Case C-347/14 *New Media Online,* para. 36.
1445 Case C-347/14 *New Media Online,* para. 36.

pose test implied an assessment of whether the "content and form" of the audiovisual content was "independent of that of the journalistic activity of the operator of the website (…) and [was] not merely an indissociable complement to that activity, in particular as a result of the links between the audiovisual offer and the offer in text form".[1446]

The Court's ruling is likely to have been received with great relief in Austria and other EU Member States which have classified individual sections of newspaper websites as non-linear audiovisual media services as shown below. In contrast to AG Szpunar, the CJEU offered a refreshingly pragmatic and realistic outlook on the AVMSD and its scope of application, acknowledging the continued significance of the Directive as the backbone of the EU legal framework for audiovisual media. Like the AG, the Court relied upon the Directive's preamble to distil its purpose and objective. Like the AG, the Court identified the Directive's underlying rationale as preserving undistorted competition and establishing a level playing field. While AG Szpunar referred to competition between linear and non-linear audiovisual media services, the CJEU took a more expansive perspective on the meaning of competition in converging media markets. According to the Court, the Directive provides protection to audiovisual media service providers against unfair competition by operators that catalogue or compile videos in the same manner as providers of on-demand audiovisual media services. The Court's interpretation of the notion of "programme" seems reasonable in light of recital 24 AVMSD. The AVMSD does not specify the length of programmes shown on TV and the lack of any minimum duration is an expression of the diversity of programmes which may have very different durations depending, among other criteria, on their genre. The Court underlined that short form content competed for the same audience as television broadcasts. This clear statement was made by reference to the second sentence of Art. 1 (1) (b) AVMSD, which enumerates examples of programmes of rather long or medium length. Given the content of the clips (news bulletins, sports and entertainment), the Court was satisfied that they appealed to the same audience as comparable programmes on TV. This assessment seems realistic and is likely to be backed by market research, especially consumption patterns of younger audiences.

---

1446 Case C-347/14 *New Media Online,* para. 37.

What is more, the interpretation of recital 28 AVMSD by the Court is welcomed and marks a stark contrast to the AG's understanding. While the AG accorded prevalence to the Union's intention to carve out an exemption for all types of hybrid services, the CJEU was careful not to give carte blanche to one category of services or service providers. It held that no audiovisual service should be excluded simply because it is offered by a publisher rather than a service provider, pointing out that operators of websites might use the multimedia nature of their portal to avoid coming under the scope of application of the AVMSD. On this point, the CJEU and the AG, who claimed that circumvention would not occur, diverge again.[1447] Although no direct evidence was brought forth in front of the Court here, "jurisdiction shopping" is a well-known phenomenon of the audiovisual media services market to which one could add "regulation shopping".[1448] There is evidence of the ease with which operators of websites change location and alter their jurisdictions (confer the UK cases of *Playboy* and *Vice Video* examined below) as well as their speedy adaptation to the practices of national regulators in designing their services. On this latter point it seems that the CJEU and AG Szpunar converge. The CJEU is certainly mindful of the rapidity with which the design or architecture of a website can be altered. Similarly, the AG reiterates that the specific architecture of a portal should not trigger regulation.[1449]

What are we then left with? A reasonable ruling of the CJEU which clarifies some pressing issues regarding the scope of the AVMSD. Namely, the notion of "programme" is not defined in relation to minimum length but encompasses short clips for information, education or entertain-

1447 Compare Case C-347/14 *New Media Online,* para. 29 and Opinion of AG Szpunar in case C-347/14 *New Media Online*, para. 57.

1448 On jurisdiction under the TWFD, see the earlier case law such as cases C-148/91 *Veronica Omroep Organisatie v Commissariaat voor de Media*, Judgment of 3.2.1993, EU:C:1993:45; C-23/93 *TV 10 SA v Commissariaat voor de Media*, Judgment of 5.10.1994, EU:C:1994:362; C-11/95 *Commission of the European Communities v Kingdom of Belgium*, Judgment of 10.9.1996, EU:C:1996:316; C-56/96 *VT4 Ltd v Vlaamse Gemeenschap*, Judgment of 5.6.1997, EU:C:1997:284. As a result, Art. 4 (2) (b) was inserted in the AVMSD which gives Member States that consider that a broadcaster has circumvented the rules applicable in its territory the possibility to regulate that particular provider after having contacted the Member State where the broadcaster claims to be established.

1449 Compare Case C-347/14 *New Media Online,* para. 35 and Opinion of AG Szpunar in case C-347/14 *New Media Online*, paras. 32 and 42.

ment. Furthermore, online newspapers may be subjected to regulation pursuant to the AVMSD if a part of the website (typically the video section) satisfies the criteria of an audiovisual media service. Consequently, a multimedia portal may comprise different services including audiovisual services. To determine whether an audiovisual service constitutes an audiovisual *media* service by virtue of the Directive, its principal purpose must be the provision of programmes. The principal purpose test requires moreover an "individualised approach" which examines the main aim of the relevant service regardless of any other (online) activities of the provider.[1450] More concretely, the criterion of principal purpose implies that the service is independent of the other (e.g. journalistic) activities of the provider and is "not merely an indissociable complement to that activity".[1451] The ties between the audiovisual content and other material are indicative of the complementarity of the activity in question. In other words, can the videos be accessed and made sense of without the support of written articles?

The question is whether the Court's guidance in this case is sufficiently precise to be applied by NRAs investigating in similar cases of hybrid or multimedia services and whether it provides a foreseeable standard for industry. It is doubtful whether the formula "indissociably complementary" is much clearer than the wording of recital 22 which refers to exemptions for services where the audiovisual content is "merely incidental", such as websites which contain "audiovisual elements only in an ancillary manner". The existence of links between audiovisual and text-based material is equally vague as it does not specify the nature of such links. The fact that the videos "can be accessed and watched regardless of whether the articles (…) [were] consulted" seems a relatively low hurdle.[1452] Interestingly, in specifying the criterion of principal purpose, the CJEU only referred to part of the submissions of the parties advanced during the hearing of 22 April 2015. The Commission then had proposed several factors for the principal purpose test. Aside from the question of whether the offer was self-standing (which is mirrored in the CJEU's formulation "independent"), the Commission suggested to analyse whether the sub-domain had its own business model. In its representations, New Media Online had raised the same point and had suggested taking into consideration the be-

1450 Case C-347/14 *New Media Online,* para. 30.
1451 Case C-347/14 *New Media Online,* paras. 34, 37.
1452 Case C-347/14 *New Media Online,* para. 36.

haviour and interests of users. The Commission had considered it useful to look at the number and type of advertisements featured on the sub-site collating videos in comparison to other parts of the website. Yet, the Court did not include considerations of the business model in the principal purpose test and instead focussed on the function of the audiovisual service. To this end, the outcome and analysis resemble KommAustria's original findings concerning the website of the TT.

## *B. The notion of an on-demand programme service in the UK*

The transposition of the AVMSD in the UK was accompanied by the establishment of a new co-regulator, ATVOD, which was put in charge of the regulation of certain aspects of on-demand audiovisual media services as discussed in the third chapter. Its remit included, above all, the specification of the definition of what constituted an on-demand service. When ATVOD's mandate was established in early 2010, there was uncertainty about its scope and the precise meaning of non-linear services which would be henceforth subjected to content standards.[1453] It was particularly uncertain how ATVOD would interpret the statutory definition [of on-demand services] in light of accelerating convergence of the broadcast market with the printed press and the mobile phone sector.[1454] The early practice of ATVOD is especially illustrative of how it grappled with the blurring boundaries between media outlets. The delineation of the statutory definition was likewise shaped by Ofcom which had retained backstop powers and thus got involved at the appeal stage. Through numerous appeal decisions, Ofcom developed several sets of criteria which specified certain key aspects of the definition of an on-demand service. These were deployed by ATVOD in its subsequent practice and above all, were codified in its guidance notes on who needs to notify. In 2016 Ofcom withdrew the delegation of powers and has since been the sole regulator relying extensively on previous ATVOD guidance.

The following section briefly outlines the statutory definition of an on-demand service, before assessing the measures of the UK regulatory au-

---

1453 Mac Sithigh, "Co-Regulation, VOD and the Legal Status of Audio-Visual Media Services of," p. 58.

1454 Mac Sithigh, "Co-Regulation, VOD and the Legal Status of Audio-Visual Media Services of," pp. 58, 59.

thorities. To this end, Ofcom's research initiatives are presented before extracts of the vast body of ATVOD's and Ofcom's practice are analysed. The cases chosen for analysis cover a great majority of issues; the regulators' early practice is almost comprehensively examined, while several subsequent cases have been ommitted due to their resemblance with earlier cases. Finally, ATVOD's guidance notes, which were reviewed by Ofcom in early 2016, are discussed as they give an overview of the status quo.

## I. The legal definition of an on-demand programme service

In the UK, the AVMSD was transposed by means of the Audiovisual Media Services Regulations of 2009, 2010 and 2014 which modified the CA. When examining the meaning of an on-demand audiovisual media service the first two statutory instruments are most relevant.[1455] While the regulation of 2009 introduced the definition of an on-demand programme service (ODPS) and stipulated content standards, the regulation of 2010 notably established the structures for the administration of such services by the regulator (e.g. the requirements to advance notification and to pay a fee). The definition of an ODPS is set forth in Sec. 368A which reads:

> "(1) For the purposes of this Act, a service is an 'on-demand programme service' if—
> (a) its principal purpose is the provision of programmes the form and content of which are comparable to the form and content of programmes normally included in television programme services;
> (b) access to it is on-demand;
> (c) there is a person who has editorial responsibility for it;
> (d) it is made available by that person for use by members of the public; and
> (e) that person is under the jurisdiction of the United Kingdom for the purposes of the Audiovisual Media Services Directive.
> (2) Access to a service is on-demand if—
> (a) the service enables the user to view, at a time chosen by the user, programmes selected by the user from among the programmes included in the service; and

1455 The Audiovisual Media Services Regulation of 2014 transposes Art. 12 AVMSD and is therefore relevant for the analysis conducted in chapter 5 on the protection of minors in non-linear services.

(b) the programmes viewed by the user are received by the user by means of an electronic communications network (whether before or after the user has selected which programmes to view).
(3) For the purposes of subsection (2)(a), the fact that a programme may be viewed only within a period specified by the provider of the service does not prevent the time at which it is viewed being one chosen by the user.
(4) A person has editorial responsibility for a service if that person has general control—
(a) over what programmes are included in the range of programmes offered to users; and
(b) over the manner in which the programmes are organised in that range; and the person need not have control of the content of individual programmes or of the broadcasting or distribution of the service (and see section 368R(6)).
(5) If an on-demand programme service ("the main service") offers users access to a relevant ancillary service, the relevant ancillary service is to be treated for the purposes of this Part as a part of the main service.
(6) In subsection (5), "relevant ancillary service" means a service or facility that consists of or gives access to assistance for disabled people in relation to some or all of the programmes included in the main service.
(7) In this section "assistance for disabled people" has the same meaning as in Part 3."[1456]

Once a service falls within the scope of the statutory definition, the provider is required to notify the service, pursuant to Sec. 368BA CA to the appropriate regulatory body (previously ATVOD, now Ofcom) prior to launching its activities.[1457] In addition, Sec. 368NA CA permits the levying of a fee for the provision of ODPS. While ATVOD deployed this discretion and set up a fee structure which was reviewed annually, Ofcom, at the end of 2016, had refrained from introducing a fee structure as discussed in the third chapter.[1458] The statutory definition outlined in Sec. 368A CA manifests a compound structure encompassing elements of the definitions contained in the AVMSD, notably the definitions of audiovisual media service (Art. 1 (1) (a) AVMSD), programme (Art. 1 (1) (b) AVMSD), editorial responsibility (Art. 1 (1) (c) AVMSD) and an on-demand audiovisual media service (Art. 1 (1) (g) AVMSD). Sub-Sec. 1 (a)

1456 The Audiovisual Media Services Regulations 2009.

1457 On advance notification, confer also Rules 1-3 of ATVOD's guidance ATVOD, "Rules & Guidance, Statutory Rules and Non-Binding Guidance for Providers of On-Demand Programme Services (ODPS), Edition 3," May 5, 2015; see also Ofcom, "Rules and Guidance for Providers of ODPS" (accessed 7.7.2016).

1458 On the payment of a fee, confer Rule 4 ATVOD, "Rules and Guidance for Providers of ODPS.".

and 1 (c) of Sec. 368A CA have proven particularly difficult to apply in practice.[1459] Several cases litigated before the UK regulators have necessitated the interpretation of key notions like "principal purpose" and "editorial responsibility". This has resulted in key terms stemming from the AVMSD being specified and adapted to different contexts. In addition, Ofcom considered it conducive to study developments in users' behaviour and attitudes towards new services to obtain practical insights. The most pertinent studies will briefly be mentioned.

## II. Ofcom's research into audience attitudes

In tandem with the process of transposing the AVMSD in the UK, Ofcom commissioned research into consumer opinion about the distinguishing features of on-demand services.[1460] On account of the expansion of its mandate brought about by the regulation of non-linear services in 2009, Ofcom launched an enquiry about consumers' understanding of what constitutes a non-linear service and what regulatory expectations were attached to this characterisation. This conceptualisation of consumer attitudes and perceptions would help it to demarcate its regulatory remit entailing TV-like on-demand services. To this end, the qualitative research report which was presented in December 2009 identified several drivers considered by consumers to make services more or less TV-like on the basis of a range of sample audiovisual content contained in non-linear services.[1461] From interviews with consumers and discussions in focus groups, the following factors were identified as contributing to the "TV-

---

1459 Sub-Sec. 1 (c) in conjunction with sub-Sec. 4 of Sec. 368A CA detail the notion of editorial responsibility.

1460 In 2015, Ofcom published another report which looked into the attitudes and use of media by adults. This report covered various media including TV, radio, mobile phones, games and the Internet and enquired about the level of media literacy. To this end, this report is more comprehensive than the research carried out in 2009 and 2012 which specifically investigated about the way viewers dealt with on-demand services. Ofcom, "Report on Adults' Media Use and Attitudes" (Ofcom, May 2015), http://stakeholders.ofcom.org.uk/market-data-research/other/research-publications/adults/media-lit-10years/ (accessed 27.7.2015).

1461 Essential Research, "The Regulation of Video-On-Demand: Consumer Views on What Makes Audiovisual Services 'TV-Like' – a Qualitative Research Report," December 2009, http://stakeholders.ofcom.org.uk/binaries/research/tv-research/vod.pdf (accessed 27.5.2015). For an overview of the examples tested, see

likeness" of a service: the fact that the content was previously broadcast on TV, professional or high-quality production values, the intended target audience was mainstream, the programme title was well known, the producer was a professional or reputable person, the format of the content was feature-length and included full programmes, the service provider or its brand were well known and appealed to a mainstream audience, presentation of the content was professional and well-structured and there was "no micro payment required at the point of viewing".[1462] On the contrary, users considered as largely irrelevant factors such as the purpose of the programme, its genre and other technical characteristics (e.g. whether content was downloaded or streamed).[1463]

In 2012, Ofcom again commissioned Essential Research to carry out an assessment into consumers' rationales for selecting a specific service. In comparison with the research conducted in 2009, the focus of this study, published in October of 2012, shifted slightly towards determining whether a VOD service was a "reasonable substitute" for watching linear TV.[1464] The study took into account the paradigm outlined in recital 24 AVMSD referring to competition between services and consumers' expectations about regulatory protection. The factors on which consumers based their choices and determined whether a service was considered to be a competing alternative for watching TV included "the purpose of the service", "the look and feel of the service", "the frequency with which content is refreshed", "who controls what is watched", the "effort expended to find the service", the "viewing experience", "the length of content", the "volume of content", the "perceived quality of content" and "where the content originated".[1465] In general, three types of factors were distinguished: those relating to the service itself, the viewing experience and the

---

p. 27. For a detailed discussion of consumer views on these examples, see pp. 36-45.

1462 Essential Research, "Research on On-Demand Services and Consumer Views on 'TV-Likeness,'" p. 31. For a more detailed explanation of the drivers of TV-like, see pp. 31-34.

1463 Essential Research, "Research on On-Demand Services and Consumer Views on 'TV-Likeness,'" p. 31.

1464 Essential Research, "On-Demand Services: Understanding Consumer Choices. A Research Report for Ofcom," October 2012, http://stakeholders.ofcom.org.uk/binaries/broadcast/tv-ops/vod/Research_Report.pdf (accessed 27.5.2015).

1465 Essential Research, "Research on On-Demand Services and Consumer Choices," pp. 33–38.

characteristics of the content disseminated.[1466] As a result, a spectrum of non-linear services illustrative of their wide array was drawn up showing services considered as close substitutes on the one end (like content on SkyGo, 4OD or the BBC iPlayer) and services not considered as replacing the TV experience on the other (the latter included videos on the Guardian's website, user-generated content on YouTube or Fosters).[1467] Significantly, the study recognised that consumer views on one and the same service could vary widely due to other (contextual) factors. Very personal factors, like "the role of age, lifestage and device ownership [implying 'technological savviness']", consumers' mood (whether users wanted to relax, seek entertainment or be creatively engaged with other users), the context (whether alone at home or in other settings) and the type of content (what genre the content pertained to) could impact on the selection process.[1468]

Another study published in December 2014 is noteworthy as it examined consumers' expectations vis-à-vis current protection standards of audiovisual content across different platforms and devices as well as consumers' views on the adequacy of means employed to protect vulnerable audiences.[1469] Overall the study found that participants had a "very limited understanding of the current regulatory landscape" and in particular, "very little awareness (...) of ATVOD and its role in the regulation of on-demand content".[1470] When analysing the perceived importance of regulation, the

---

1466 Essential Research, "Research on On-Demand Services and Consumer Choices," p. 38.

1467 Essential Research, "Research on On-Demand Services and Consumer Choices," pp. 6, 68. For consumer views on the different examples, see pp. 40-66.

1468 Essential Research, "Research on On-Demand Services and Consumer Choices," pp. 17–20.

1469 Kantar Media, "Protecting Audiences in an Online World, Deliberative Research Report," April 12, 2014, http://stakeholders.ofcom.org.uk/market-data-research/other/tv-research/protecting-audiences-online-world/. In addition, Ofcom surveys consumer attitudes (e.g. the Media Tracker) to broadcasting and their experiences on a regular basis, see Ofcom, "UK Audience Attitudes to the Broadcast Media," July 5, 2013, http://stakeholders.ofcom.org.uk/market-data-research/other/tv-research/attitudes-broadcast-media/ (accessed 6.5.2015); Ofcom, "The Consumer Experience of 2014," January 28, 2015, http://stakeholders.ofcom.org.uk/market-data-research/market-data/consumer-experience-reports/consumer-experience-14/ (all websites accessed 6.5.2015).

1470 Kantar Media, "Research on Views of Protection for Audiovisual Content," para. 4.3, p. 26.

study revealed that users expected a high level of regulation of TV broadcasting due to the public nature of the television set which sits in an open area of the household, the living room, and is shared by all family members. Users' expectations can be explained by the passive manner in which television broadcasts are consumed as well as potential exposure of vulnerable family members to harmful content.[1471] Catch-up services were considered to be regulated to the same extent as TV broadcasts because the content had previously been screened on TV.[1472] With regards to on-demand services, older participants to the study and less technologically-apt participants associated a similar level of regulation as that for catch-up services. The more technologically-savvy recognised that on-demand services enhanced individual control and "active decision-making" and thus considered it should not be subject to the same regulatory standards as TV.[1473] Consumer attitudes markedly diverged with respect to regulatory models regarding content distributed on the Internet. While some highlighted the importance of individual freedoms (like the freedom of expression and information) placing responsibility for protection on service providers, others underlined the need to protect minors and other sensitive audience groups placing their trust in public bodies like regulatory authorities.[1474] Users appeared to agree on the difficulty of establishing an effective regulatory framework on the Internet.[1475] Broadly speaking, the current forms of regulation, especially limitations on a provider's freedom to conduct their economic activity for reasons of public interest (such as the protection of minors) seem to overlap with consumer's expectations.

Succinctly, Ofcom's reliance on quantitative research sends a positive signal by demonstrating the regulator's willingness to fulfil its statutory duty in line with market realities defined by consumer behaviour and attitudes. Ofcom's engagement with the wider public (represented by these "snapshot" studies), allows regulation to remain close to the mindset of

---

1471 Kantar Media, "Research on Views of Protection for Audiovisual Content," para. 6.3, p. 33.

1472 Kantar Media, "Research on Views of Protection for Audiovisual Content," para. 6.3, p. 34.

1473 Kantar Media, "Research on Views of Protection for Audiovisual Content," para. 6.3, p. 35.

1474 Kantar Media, "Research on Views of Protection for Audiovisual Content," para. 6.3, pp. 36–38.

1475 Kantar Media, "Research on Views of Protection for Audiovisual Content," para. 6.3, p. 38.

the average user, who can in turn identify with and understand the regulator's practice.[1476] By the same token, Ofcom's consideration of consumers is presumably valued by service providers as it reflects the users' intentions in seeking a particular service and the manner in which they use it. The renewal of the study in 2012 with its slightly different outlook was necessitated by the rapid development of the market and the increasingly unwieldy plethora of new services and business models. Between 2009 and 2012, the landscape had evolved and more and more users were familiar with VOD services and particularly appreciated the flexibility in terms of viewing options.[1477] What is more, Ofcom is aware of the deficiencies of the studies inherent in quantitative research methods, above all, their limits in terms of scale, scope and the representativeness of findings. In its appeal decisions, Ofcom therefore refers to the research as a complementary argument to strengthen its interpretation of the nature of a service in appeal proceedings as is demonstrated below.

### III. The practices of ATVOD and Ofcom

In the UK, the interpretation of the statutory definition of an ODPS has evolved with the practices of the UK regulators. To this end, the cases adjudicated before ATVOD and Ofcom constitute the primary source for the meaning of an ODPS. It should be noted that after ATVOD's inauguration as co-regulator in 2010, the bulk of practice steadily increased. However, since January 2016 when the co-regulatory scheme came to an end, only a few cases have been instigated (predominantly upon complaint by the public). The following are some of the most important and trend-setting cases, which in spite of the shift away from a co-regulatory model retain

---

1476 Hasebrink argues that the design of today's regulatory framework for the media has become increasingly complex and thus requires innovative approaches which ensure users' involvement in regulatory processes. In this context, he calls for an expanded notion of users as citizens and not just consumers and underlines the importance of their involvement in regulatory processes (e.g. by complaints about programmes, participation in boards or councils of regulators). See Uwe Hasebrink, "Giving the Audience a Voice: The Role of Research in Making Media Regulation More Responsive to the Needs of the Audience," *Journal of Information Policy* 1 (2011): pp. 321–36.

1477 Essential Research, "Research on On-Demand Services and Consumer Choices," pp. 21–26.

their relevance today as they find expression in Ofcom's guidance documents. ATVOD's early practice is almost entirely covered, whereas determinations in its 4th and 5th year are examined to the entent that they raise new issues.

### 1. Principal purpose test

Pursuant to Sec. 368A (1) (a) CA, the principal purpose of an ODPS is the provision of programmes. This requirement originates from Art. 1 (1) (a) (i) AVMSD which defines the generic term "audiovisual media service", be it linear or non-linear. The integration of the notion of principal purpose in the CA highlights its significance for differentiating between services covered by ATVOD's/now Ofcom's remit and those falling outside the regulatory regime for ODPS. The principal purpose implies a service providing audiovisual programmes as its primary aim. Identifying the principal purpose may be complex as providers' intentions about the kind of service may conflict with regulators' perceptions of what is actually offered. How the UK regulators, above all, Ofcom have shaped the interpretation of the concept of principal purpose is demonstrated below with the decisions in *Viva TV Music*, *Sun Video*, *Everton TV*, *The Business Channel* and *Vice Video*.

#### a) A part of a media outlet may constitute an ODPS: Viva TV Music

In its determination concerning the Viva TV Music service of 18 March 2011, ATVOD pointed out that a service could be composed of several distinct services, each of which required notification.[1478] MTV's notification of its service to ATVOD prompted an investigation into one of its channels, or more precisely, its Viva TV website. ATVOD contended that the music section of the Viva website which predominantly aggregated music videos constituted an on-demand service. In its decision of 22 February 2012, Ofcom agreed with ATVOD in substance but substituted ATVOD's determination by its own decision in order to outline more

1478 ATVOD, "Determination That the Provider of the Service Named Viva TV Music Has Contravened Sec. 368BA and Sec. 368D (3) (ZA) of the Communications Act," March 18, 2011.

clearly the regulator's reasoning.[1479] Ofcom focused on the first limbs of the statutory test, examining whether the principle purpose was the provision of TV-like programmes, taking into account the criteria it had established in The *Sun Video* appeal. In that context, Ofcom had clarified that a single website may host several self-standing services with different principal purposes. In this respect Ofcom noted that the AVMSD did not support a "narrow interpretation whereby diverse services would be deemed to share a single principal purpose merely by reason of sharing a domain name".[1480]

It would indeed be ill-suited to capture diverse services offered through one outlet (e.g. a website) under the umbrella of a single principal purpose (the identification of which may be a complex endeavour in and of itself). Where the different purposes of services are so dissimilar and varied as in the MTV example, such services are reasonably considered to be independent of each other. The line remains, however, blurred when determining whether one service, or element thereof, is ancillary to another (e.g. electronic versions of newspapers) and should thus be subsumed in this service or whether it represents a service in its own right with a sufficiently autonomous principal purpose. In *Viva TV Music*, Ofcom agreed with ATVOD that the "breadth, completeness and independence of the audiovisual material" was such that the music section of Viva TV's website constituted an on-demand service in its own right.[1481] This case thus makes clear that a website may comprise numerous services, each of which with a different principal purpose. It reflects economic realities and is therefore a pragmatic decision. MTV was thus obliged to notify to ATVOD the music section of its Viva TV website as an ODPS.

### b) Criteria indicative of principal purpose: Sun Video

In the first half of 2011, ATVOD carried out investigations into the video sections of a number of UK newspapers (including the Guardian, the Fi-

---

1479 Ofcom, "Appeal by MTV Networks Europe against a Notice of Determination by ATVOD That the Provider of the Service Viva TV Music Has Contravened Section 368BA of the Communications Act 2003," February 22, 2012, para. 4, p. 1.

1480 Ofcom, "Appeal Decision Viva TV Music," para. 50, p. 13.

1481 Ofcom, "Appeal Decision Viva TV Music," para. 52, p. 13.

nancial Times and the Independent). This in itself is remarkable as the press sector in the UK is self-regulated.[1482] Due to media convergence and the need to remain competitive, the printed press has ventured out into the Internet, providing additional products online. Previously, online versions of newspapers and magazines replicated the design and structure of their printed counterpart. Increasingly, though, audiovisual content and additional interactive functionality is offered on such websites.[1483] In seven cases, ATVOD found that the video section of the online versions of newspapers constituted ODPS and that service providers had failed to notify them as such.[1484] ATVOD was convinced that the principal purpose of the video sections was the provision of audiovisual content which was aggregated in a separate section of the website. Thus, the video sections were marketed as "consumer destination[s] in [their] own right, and the programmes provided (…) [could] be viewed, enjoyed and made sense of

---

1482 Interestingly, the Press Complaints Commission (PCC), the UK's body administering the self-regulatory system of the press issued a guidance note in 2007 "on the extension of the PCC's remit to include editorial audio-visual material on newspaper and magazine websites". Accordingly, the PCC will only become active provided that "the editor of the newspaper or magazine is responsible for [editorial audiovisual material] and could reasonably have been expected both to exercise editorial control over it and apply the terms of the Code". A second requirement for the PCC's involvement is that the relevant material "was not pre-edited to conform to the on-line or off-line standards of another media regulatory body". Importantly, in the aftermath of the phone-hacking scandal implicating the News of the World and the subsequent Leveson Inquiry into the culture, practice and ethics of the press, the PCC closed in September 2014 and was replaced by the Independent Press Standards Organisation (IPSO). The IPSO does not seem to have issued similar guidance on audiovisual content on press outlets. The guidance note of the PCC is available at http://www.pcc.org.uk/faqs.html#faq2_14. The PCC's (few) adjudications concerning edited audiovisual material are listed under http://www.pcc.org.uk/advanced_search.html?page=1&num=10&publication=x&decision=x&audio=1&keywords= (all websites accessed 6.5.2015).

1483 Ivar Erdal John, "Repurposing of Content in Multi-Platform News Production, Towards a Typology of Cross-Media Journalism," *Journalism Practice* 3, no. 2 (2009): p. 184; Katsirea, "Electronic Press: 'Press-Like' or 'Television-Like'?," pp. 1–2.

1484 More precisely, ATVOD determined that the video sections of the online newspapers of The Sun, The Sunday Times, the News of the World, the Telegraph, the Guardian, the Financial Times and the Independent constituted non-linear services and should have been notified as such.

without reference to the newspaper offering".[1485] ATVOD also considered that the videos were sufficiently independent of the text-based material and could be consumed and understood without reference to the written articles.[1486] The newspaper publishers contested ATVOD's findings before Ofcom. The first case decided was the *Sun Video* case in December 2011, and it served as precedent for future cases. In contrast to ATVOD, Ofcom held that the video section of The Sun's website did not fall under the scope of application of Sec. 368A CA and was not to be regarded as an ODPS.[1487] It set aside ATVOD's determination, upholding News Group's appeal.

---

1485 See for instance ATVOD, "Determination That the Provider of the Service Named Sun Video Has Contravened Sec. 368BA of the Communications Act," November 2, 2011.

1486 See for instance ATVOD, "Scope Determination Sun Video.".

1487 Ofcom, "Appeal by News Group Newspapers Limited against a Notice of Determination by ATVOD That the Provider of the Service Sun Video Has Contravened Section 368BA of the Communications Act 2003," December 21, 2011; NRAs of other EU Member States have also struggled with the convergence of the formerly distinct sectors of the online press and broadcasting. Interestingly, in several EU Member States, NRAs have classified the video sections of websites of online newspapers and magazines as on-demand audiovisual media services. This marks a stark contrast to Ofcom's practice in the UK. In July 2012, for instance, the Slovakian regulator determined after reconsideration of its earlier position in April 2010 that the service tvsme provided by the publisher of the sme newspaper constituted an on-demand service and thus fell within its regulatory ambit. This change of position occured when the tvsme service was made available on connected TV exclusively offering audiovisual material. See Juraj Polak, "TVSME Considered on-Demand Audiovisual Media Service," ed. European Audiovisual Observatory, *IRIS Merlin Newsletter* 9, no. 1 (2012): p. 38; in Sweden, the Swedish regulator published in October 2012 four decisions en bloc deciding that the web TV services (24HD Play by Helsingborgs Dagblad Nya Media AB, Aftonbladet Web TV by Aftonblad Hierta AB, DN Web TV by AB Dagens Nyheter and Norran TV by Norra Västerbotten Tidnings AB) of four online newspapers were non-linear services governed pursuant to the Radio and Television Act which transposes the AVMSD in Sweden. See Erik Ullberg and Michael Plogell, "Radio and Televisions Act Applies to Newspapers' Web TV Services," ed. European Audiovisual Observatory, *IRIS Merlin Newsletter* 1, no. 1 (2013): p. 35; similarly, at the end of 2012, the Belgian regulator of the Flemish Community, the Vlaamse Regulator voor de Media (VRM) held that Het 60 seconden Journaal provided by De Persgroep on its website Het Laatste Nieuws was a non-linear audiovisual media service and urged the provider to notify the service. VRM did not take a formal decision but informal correspondence between the regulator and the provider took place. The relevant

In Ofcom's decision, the interpretation of the principal purpose concept

---

service constituted a newscast which was made available on a section of the website. The newscast lasted 60 seconds, was up-dated several times per day and reported on current affairs. VRM considered that the material was prepared editorially and was addressed to the general public under a separate title. In addition, VRM saw the services' economic nature fulfilled by the showing of an advertising spot at the beginning of each video. The fact that the newscast was not linked to or accompanied the written articles proved, according to VRM, its self-standing character. VRM's interpretation especially of the TV-likeness of the audiovisual material included on the online newspaper as well as the notion of "programme" is noticeably different from Ofcom's approach. Subsequent to the oral proceedings, De Persgroep notified the service which has been discontinued in April 2013. Detailed information about this case was obtained through email correspondence with the VRM in May 2015, for which the author is very thankful. See also Geneviève de Bueger, "Comparative Document on Supervising VOD Services: Best Practices and Methodology" (EPRA, December 20, 2013), p. 6, http://www.epra.org/attachments/vilnius-plenary-session-1-supervising-vod-services-final-comparative-document; in Austria, the case of the Tiroler Tageszeitung (TT) received much public attention and was even litigated before the CJEU as discussed above (case C-347/14). In October 2012, KommAustria had characterised the video section of the TT as an on-demand service on account of the independent function which this part of the website performed. To this effect, KommAustria's approach differs considerably from Ofcom's which has devised a qualitative approach entailing a non-exhaustive list of criteria. See Katsirea, "Electronic Press: 'Press-Like' or 'Television-Like'?," pp. 9–11, 14, 18; a second case concerning the TV broadcaster oe24TV how the Austrian NRAs classify services. The original dispute concerned the right to short news reports by virtue of Art. 5 Fernseh-Exklusivrechtegesetz (FERG) which transposes Art. 15 AVMSD. In its decision of February 2012, KommAustria had granted oe24TV the right to report on the Austrian football league in the form of brief extracts, the material of which was to be made available by Sky Österreich, holder of the exclusive rights. KommAustria set forth several conditions for the exercise of the right to short news reports. In this context, the question arose whether oe24TV could make the short reports available online as on-demand services after they had been broadcast on TV as stipulated by Art. 5 (5) FERG (Art. 15 (5) AVMSD). The broadcaster had notified the video section of its website www.oe24.tv as an on-demand service. In addition, Oe24TV operates a website under www.österreich.at which essentially constitutes the electronic version of the daily newspaper entitled "Österreich" which collates videos in a separate sub-website. KommAustria considered that the fact pattern of this service was commensurable to the case of TT which was brought to the CJEU. Thus, the question on the use of the short reports on the websites of Oe24tV was suspended. See KommAustria, "Bescheid KOA 3.800/15-009," December 2, 2015. In its second decision of February 2016, the regulator confirmed that the video section oe24.at/video constituted an on-demand audiovisual media service which served an independent function separate from the online newspaper, in

took centre stage.[1488] The regulator took the opportunity to formulate several criteria to guide the future application and enforcement of the principal purpose test by ATVOD, with the simultaneous intention of enhancing legal certainty for providers of mixed (i.e. audiovisual and text-based) content. In a preliminary observation, Ofcom reprimanded ATVOD for having neglected to examine the service in its entirety. According to Ofcom, ATVOD had placed too much emphasis on the video section, unduly isolating it from the whole offer for the purposes of its analysis.[1489] Moreover, Ofcom retrieved additional evidence from The Sun's website, a process which does not normally pertain to its appellate functions and which demonstrates the significance of the decision as well as its relevance for future practice.[1490] Before examining The Sun's website, Ofcom set out its understanding of and approach to the statutory definition. It reiterated that all conditions stipulated in Sec. 368A (1) CA would have to be met cumulatively and it highlighted the key aspects of sub-paragraph (a) addressing principal purpose and comparability.[1491] According to Ofcom, the principal purpose part entailed the question whether

> "a. any of the audio-visual material comprises something that in its own right is a 'service' whose 'principal purpose' is the provision of that material, or
> "b. is ancillary to the provision of some other service."[1492]

In order to answer part (a) of the question, Ofcom outlined several characteristics which would be indicative that a service's principal purpose was

---

spite of the short, or very short duration of videos. KommAustria underlined that the majority of videos had already been broadcast on TV and that there were no or only very few links to the text-based material offered in different sections of the website. See KommAustria, "Bescheid KOA 3.800/15-020", February 11, 2016.

1488 News Group merely disputed the correct application of the principal purpose test and submitted that the video section did not primarily provide TV-like programmes. It accepted that the remaining statutory criteria set out in Sec. 368A (1) CA were satisfied. Ofcom, "Appeal Decision Sun Video," para. 21, p. 7.

1489 Ofcom, "Appeal Decision Sun Video," paras. 5, 48, 94–96, pp. 2, 16, 29-30.

1490 Ofcom, "Appeal Decision Sun Video," paras. 6, 34, pp. 2, 10. Thus, Ofcom looked at material provided at the time of ATVOD's determination (prior to February 2011) and at material offered when it took its decision (prior to December 2011) outlining two positions which negate the classification as a non-linear audiovisual service.

1491 Ofcom, "Appeal Decision Sun Video," paras. 67, 70, p. 23.

1492 Ofcom, "Appeal Decision Sun Video," para. 72, p. 24.

the provision of audiovisual programmes.[1493] Hence, such a service would likely have its own homepage, the audiovisual material would be catalogued in a discrete section of the website, the audiovisual material would be "presented or styled (and marketed) as a television channel", the amount of audiovisual material would be "of substantial duration and/or comprise complete programmes" which are independent of other content provided.[1494] There would also be a great number of access and content links between the audiovisual material and other content. Where audiovisual content is provided alongside written material, "(i) the balance of the material is more likely significantly to lean towards the audiovisual, (ii) the written material is brief and/or merely an introduction to, or summary of, the audio visual material and (iii) the audio visual material is the primary means of conveying to users the information sought to be conveyed".[1495] Finally, an overall assessment (or "step back" test) revealed that the audio visual material "cannot be said to be integrated into, nor ancillary to, another service".[1496] No single criterion is determinative on its own but all characteristics are weighted equally and examined together.[1497] Ofcom indicated that the list was non-exhaustive and provided a general framework for the analysis rather than a "checklist exercise".[1498]

By applying the criteria, Ofcom concluded that the principal purpose of The Sun's website was not the provision of audiovisual programmes.[1499] It noted *inter alia* that the videos lacked independence and merely supplemented the written articles. Without the accompanying articles, most videos could not be fully understood and enjoyed by users, while the opposite was true for the text-based material.[1500] Ofcom considered that the

---

1493 Ofcom, "Appeal Decision Sun Video," para. 90, pp. 27-29.

1494 Ofcom, "Appeal Decision Sun Video," para. 90a.-90d., pp. 27-28.

1495 Ofcom, "Appeal Decision Sun Video," para. 90g., pp. 28–29; Katsirea distinguishes between formal (access via own homepage, style and presentation as TV channel) and substantive criteria (duration of audiovisual material, its independence and its prominence compared to the written material). See Katsirea, "Electronic Press: 'Press-Like' or 'Television-Like'?," pp. 11, 13, 17.

1496 Katsirea, "Electronic Press: 'Press-Like' or 'Television-Like'?," p. 17; Ofcom, "Appeal Decision Sun Video," para. 90h., p. 29.

1497 Ofcom, "Appeal Decision Sun Video," paras. 82–83, p. 26.

1498 Ofcom, "Appeal Decision Sun Video," para. 82, p. 26.

1499 For a summary of the application of the criteria to the material examined at the time of Ofcom's decision ("current" material provided by the Sun), see Ofcom, "Appeal Decision Sun Video," para. 158, p. 41.

1500 Ofcom, "Appeal Decision Sun Video," paras. 151–53, pp. 40-41.

audiovisual material on The Sun's website was "more likely integrated into, and an ancillary part of, an electronic version of The Sun newspaper".[1501] In addition, Ofcom conducted an assessment under the AVMSD.[1502] In this context, it specifically referred to recitals 21 and 24 AVMSD, which underpin competition aspects and users' expectations. Ofcom posited that it was improbable for users to consider The Sun's website as a substitute for linear television. In a similar vein, it was of the opinion that users did not expect the same level of regulatory protection as afforded under the AVMSD when surfing the website at issue.[1503]

Although Ofcom reversed ATVOD's analysis, it repeatedly stressed that its decision did not amount to a "blanket exclusion" of all online newspapers and magazines from the scope of Sec. 368A CA.[1504] This enabled Ofcom to retain flexibility and as a corollary, it advocated for a dynamic interpretation of the statutory conditions (above all, the principal purpose part). To this end, Ofcom was mindful of the fact that the design and content of online services evolve rapidly and the balance could potentially tip towards making them more TV-like.[1505] Ofcom also clarified that it fell to service providers to regularly review whether they were providing a nonlinear service.[1506]

It is important to note that the changes to The Sun's website over the course of the investigation period, which spanned roughly a year, are remarkable. Ofcom took note in its decision of the alterations to the web-

---

1501 Ofcom, "Appeal Decision Sun Video," para. 159, p. 42.

1502 Ofcom, "Appeal Decision Sun Video," paras. 169–80, pp. 43-45.

1503 Ofcom, "Appeal Decision Sun Video," para. 179, p. 45.

1504 Ofcom, "Appeal Decision Sun Video," paras. 78, 183, 186, pp. 25, 46-47; see also Valcke and Ausloos, "What If Television Becomes Just an App?," p. 16. In the Everton TV decision, Ofcom equally warned that "audiovisual material not presently within the scope of regulation, could, (.) in future be so." Ofcom, "Appeal by Everton Football Club against a Notice of Determination by ATVOD That the Service Everton TV Has Contravened Section 368D (3) (ZA) of the Communications Act 2003," June 26, 2013, para. 124, p. 32; see also Lowde, Shaun and Wells, Orlando, "ATVOD Determined to Do Better," *Computer and Telecommunications Law Review* 18, no. 4 (2012): para. 102, p. 104.

1505 Ofcom, "Appeal Decision Sun Video," paras. 183, 186, pp. 46-47.

1506 Ofcom, "Appeal Decision Sun Video," para. 185, p. 46; see also Ofcom, "Appeal Decision Everton TV," para. 125, p. 32; Ofcom, "Appeal by The Business Channel.TV against a Notice of Determination by ATVOD That the Service The Business Channel Has Contravened Sections 368BA and 368D (3) (ZA) of the Communications Act 2003," January 18, 2013, para. 19, p. 5.

site's design and structure which were carried out between ATVOD's determination and the start of the appeal proceedings.[1507] Over that period, it appears that the website and especially the video section became less TV-like and more press-like.[1508] This is a frequent phenomenon and demonstrates providers' responses to regulatory practice. The fact that Ofcom upheld its right to regulate online press products under Sec. 368A CA induced providers to ensure that they escaped the more stringent and burdensome regulatory regime applicable to on-demand audiovisual media services and remained sufficiently dissimilar from linear television.

As an aside, it is noted that ATVOD withdrew its determinations regarding the video sections of other online newspapers and magazines on the day of publication of Ofcom's decision. It is questionable whether ATVOD actually reviewed its determinations in the light of the criteria set forth by Ofcom. The fact that ATVOD withdrew all of its determinations appears to indicate a radical shift in its policy. ATVOD's conduct may also be explained by the fact that its activities at the time were immensely unpopular with service providers who had criticised its approach.[1509] Ofcom's decision put a damper on ATVOD's understanding of its regulatory remit. As is elaborated below in more detail, Ofcom's decision in the *Sun Video* case reinforces its liberal approach to its mission, as stipulated in Sec. 3 (1) CA.[1510]

#### c) Necessity of an overall assessment: Everton TV

Similar to the *Sun Video* case, the *Everton TV* is a borderline case in which ATVOD determined that a sub-section on the website of the Everton foot-

---

1507 Ofcom, "Appeal Decision Sun Video," para. 103, p. 31; this is also reflected in the fact that Ofcom took two positions, one examining the material at the time of ATVOD's determination (the "earlier" position) and one examining the material at the time of its decision (the "current" position). See paras. 101-168.

1508 See several images of The Sun website included in Annex 1.

1509 Pimlott, Nick and Lewis, David, "Regulation of Video On-Demand Services Following the 'Sun Video' appeal," *Entertainment Law Review* 23, no. 3 (2012): p. 67.

1510 Jenny Metzdorf, "Regulierung der Elektronischen Presse in Großbritannien? Ein Anwendungsbeispiel zum Erwägungsgrund 28 der AVMD-RL," ed. Jürgen Taeger, *Law as a Service, Recht Im Internet- Und Cloud-Zeitalter*, Tagungsband Herbstakademie, 2013, p. 511.

ball club entitled "Everton TV" constituted an ODPS. ATVOD's determination issued in April 2012 was subsequently reversed by Ofcom in its appeal decision of June 2013.[1511] ATVOD was of the opinion that the audiovisual material which was collated in a separate section of the website "serve[d] a distinct purpose in providing a full range of stand-alone audiovisual material".[1512] ATVOD also considered that the form and content of the audiovisual material offered was comparable to the programmes included on the TV channels of other Premier League clubs.[1513] Ofcom, however, overturned ATVOD's opinion arguing that although ATVOD had carried out an assessment of the whole of what was provided, it had drawn incorrect conclusions from the facts.[1514] Ofcom found, after careful examination, that the football club's website functioned as an "online magazine or fanzine, or information service, comprising a mixture of written, visual and audiovisual content".[1515] The section denominated "Everton TV" was integrated into this service, playing an ancillary and complementary role. This finding was supported by the application of the characteristics elaborated in *Sun Video*.[1516] Among others, Ofcom pointed out that the "Everton TV" section did not possess its own homepage and was furthermore similar in layout, structure and design to the homepage of the service.[1517] Although the service provider catalogued the audiovisual material (a characteristic making it more TV-like), the videos could also be found in other sections of the website, notably the "News" section, and contained cross-links as well as links to other types of content (e.g. articles, graphics).[1518] While Ofcom acknowledged that the use of the term "TV" as the title of the subsection was indicative of the material having the required principal purpose, it nevertheless took the view that the "label 'Everton TV' [was] not indicative of a service having a sufficiently strong and distinct charac-

---

1511 ATVOD, "Determination That the Provider of the Service Named Everton TV Has Contravened Sec. 368D (3) (ZA) of the Communications Act," November 4, 2012; Ofcom, "Appeal Decision Everton TV.".

1512 ATVOD, "Scope Determination Everton TV.".

1513 ATVOD, "Scope Determination Everton TV". On the aspect of comparability in the Everton TV case, see below.

1514 Ofcom, "Appeal Decision Everton TV," paras. 29, 48, pp. 11, 16.

1515 Ofcom, "Appeal Decision Everton TV," para. 54b., p. 18.

1516 Ofcom, "Appeal Decision Everton TV," paras. 51–90, pp. 17-25.

1517 Ofcom, "Appeal Decision Everton TV," para. 56, p. 18.

1518 Ofcom, "Appeal Decision Everton TV," paras. 60–61, p. 19.

ter as a service in its own right".[1519] Ofcom also underlined that the duration of the majority of the audiovisual material was short (approximately 5 minutes) and lacked independence as it was linked to articles that provided more detailed information.[1520]

Throughout the decision, Ofcom struggled with the classification of the service. It frequently admitted that one or the other characteristics from the *Sun Video* decision was satisfied and that "in a number of respects, the appellant came close to providing a service with the principal purpose of providing audiovisual material".[1521] Ofcom agreed with ATVOD that "within the Everton TV section, [the balance of audiovisual and written material] leant significantly towards the audiovisual material".[1522] Yet the overall review showed that videos were also included in other sections of the website and a substantial amount of other content was provided including written articles, podcasts, user comments, ticket sales and merchandising.[1523] Interestingly, ATVOD argued during the appeal proceedings that Ofcom placed too much emphasis on the assessment of the whole website, especially the "News" section.[1524] Ofcom countered ATVOD's submission holding that a balanced and overall evaluation of the entire service was required.[1525]

The two cases of *Sun Video* and *Everton TV* are crucial to the interpretation of the principal purpose prong of the definition of an ODPS. Ofcom's list, in *Sun Video,* of characteristics for determining the principal purpose of a service pursuant to Sec. 368A (1) CA facilitates future assessments in similar cases. Katsirea, however, doubts its usefulness and is sceptical as to the benefit it brings to the industry. In her opinion, the criteria are subjective, too broad and lead to ambiguity.[1526] It is true that the criteria Ofcom elaborated need to be applied on a case-by-case basis and

1519 Ofcom, "Appeal Decision Everton TV," para. 63, p. 20.

1520 The aspect of duration of the audiovisual material was picked up again by Ofcom when examining the comparability part. See Ofcom, "Appeal Decision Everton TV," para. 93, p. 26.

1521 Ofcom, "Appeal Decision Everton TV," para. 90, p. 25.

1522 Ofcom, "Appeal Decision Everton TV," para. 86, p. 24.

1523 Ofcom, "Appeal Decision Everton TV," para. 87, p. 24.

1524 Ofcom, "Appeal Decision Everton TV," para. 115, p. 30.

1525 Ofcom, "Appeal Decision Everton TV," paras. 116–17, p. 31.

1526 Katsirea, "Electronic Press: 'Press-Like' or 'Television-Like'?," pp. 20–22.

preclude any over-hasty decision making.[1527] On the one hand, they clarify the meaning of one of the essential notions of the statutory definition, at least in the abstract. On the other hand, application of the criteria in individual cases, as demonstrated in *Everton TV,* remains a complex exercise. What is more, in the two cases, Ofcom strongly insists on the necessity of a global analysis of the service (rather than considering the video sections in isolation). This approach seems to increase regulators' flexibility and in turn to decrease legal certainty.

It is, to put it bluntly, an easy way out for the regulator in cases where many of the characteristics indicative of principal purpose point towards the service being TV-like, but for some ulterior, possibly political, motive such services should not fall under ATVOD's/now Ofcom's regulatory remit. The trend towards presentation and embedding of audiovisual material is strongly associated with media convergence and there are surely good reasons why fan websites of football clubs or online newspapers and magazines should not be regulated to the same extent as "proper" non-linear audiovisual media services. However, Ofcom has made clear that all content offered by a service is included in the analysis and unless providers were to ignore Ofcom's warning and alter the design in such a way as to make it more TV-like, it seems unlikely that in the future electronic versions of newspapers or any kind of "fanzines" would be covered by Sec. 368A CA. On the contrary, providers of online newspapers in the UK have, for instance, taken measures to ensure that their websites resemble the "traditional" print media.

#### d) Prominence of TV-like programmes: The Business Channel

In January 2013 Ofcom upheld ATVOD's determination of April 2011 concerning *The Business Channel*, a website which provides business documentaries and other programmes reporting on economic developments and topical issues. ATVOD had found that the *Business Channel* offered audiovisual material akin to television programmes in different parts of its

1527 Pimlott, Nick and Lewis, "Regulation of Video on Demand Services Following the 'Sun Video' appeal," p. 68.

website.[1528] Ofcom approved of ATVOD's assessment, highlighting that "despite (…) commercial links, the provision of audiovisual content (including authoritative long form documentary content (…) dominated the service in terms of the layout, navigation and design of the site as a whole".[1529] The videos and programmes (denoted as such) were furthermore "presented prominently on the home page" and for Ofcom the prominence of audiovisual material of long duration substantiated the comparability part: it acknowledged that the amount of short material was considerable but the provision of longer programmes which were presented and marketed prominently was more significant.[1530] In addition, some of the programmes which were made available on the website had previously been broadcast on TV and were thus offered as "watch again".[1531] They also contained features of programmes broadcast on TV such as the complete coverage of a particular subject and an episode structure.[1532]

Interestingly, the appellant argued that its service was not in competition with linear services due to the "modest volume of content, (…) modest viewing figures" and relative infrequency of updating of the audiovisual material.[1533] Ofcom, however, clarified that the question of potential competition should be interpreted in light of recital 21 AVMSD which states that the AVMSD applies to mass media with the exception of services of a primarily non-economic nature. To Ofcom, recital 21 AVMSD did not set forth a specific benchmark, excess of which would trigger regulation.[1534] Hence, the question about viewing figures was irrelevant in determining whether a service was in competition with its linear counterparts.

1528 ATVOD, "Determination That the Provider of the Service Named The Business Channel Has Contravened Sec. 368BA and Sec. 368D (3) (ZA) of the Communications Act," April 26, 2011.

1529 Ofcom, "Appeal Decision The Business Channel," para. 26, p. 7.

1530 Ofcom, "Appeal Decision The Business Channel," paras. 26, 33–24, pp. 7-8.

1531 Ofcom, "Appeal Decision The Business Channel," para. 40, p. 10.

1532 Ofcom, "Appeal Decision The Business Channel," para. 36, p. 9.

1533 Ofcom, "Appeal Decision The Business Channel," para. 49, p. 12.

1534 Ofcom, "Appeal Decision The Business Channel," paras. 50–51, pp. 12-13.

### e) Online magazines: Vice Video

Apart from online newspapers, ATVOD analysed several websites comprising online versions of magazines.[1535] An interesting case touching on the notion of principal purpose is *Vice Video,* a sub-section of the website of Vice, an online magazine which successfully targets young adults between 20 and 30 years of age with provocative, borderline and immersive journalism reported from trouble spots all over the world.[1536] Today, printed copies of the magazine only account for approximately five percent of Vice's annual turnover.[1537] Its programmes have been purchased by long-established broadcasters like HBO in the US, ZDF and Spiegel TV in Germany and SRF in Switzerland.[1538] Far from being brief, shaky amateur videos, Vice's documentaries are professionally made and of high quali-

---

1535 In February 2011, ATVOD had classified the sub-section titled Elle TV of the online version of the magazine Elle as a non-linear service falling under its purview. ATVOD had opined that the sub-section promoted as Elle TV was a "consumer destination in its own right" and could be separated from the remaining offering of an online magazine. The provider of the magazine had submitted that the service purported to "augment, expand and publicise" its offering. The audiovisual material was of brief duration (on average three minutes long) and was embedded in text-based material and served to provide additional information. ATVOD's line of argumentation is reminiscent of the determinations in Sun Video and other online newspapers taken at that time. The legal assessment is brief and very imprecise. Not surprisingly, this determination was withdrawn following Ofcom's appeal decision in Sun Video. It is very likely that ATVOD's determination would not have sustained scrutiny by Ofcom. ATVOD, "Determination That the Provider of the Service Named Elle TV Has Contravened Sec. 368BA of the Communications Act," November 2, 2011.

1536 Since the more than twenty years of its creation Vice, having been founded in 1994 in Canada, has become more than a gratuitous magazine laid out in hip bars, shops and other trendy places. Vice has turned into a media conglomerate entailing a music label, a publishing house, an event management agency, a film production company, an advertising agency, an advertising network as well as a pub (located at London East End). Martin Hitz, "'Vice' liebt das Wilde und Waghalsige," *Neue Zürcher Zeitung*, June 24, 2014, sec. Feuilleton, http://www.nzz.ch/feuilleton/medien/vice-liebt-das-wilde-und-waghalsige-1.18328580 (accessed 13.12.2014); Christoph Scheuermann, "Angriff der 'Vice'-Macher," *Der Spiegel*, 2013, 14 edition, sec. Medien, p. 73.

1537 Hitz, "'Vice' liebt das Wilde und Waghalsige"; Scheuermann, "Angriff der 'Vice'-Macher," p. 73.

1538 Hitz, "'Vice' liebt das Wilde und Waghalsige"; Scheuermann, "Angriff der 'Vice'-Macher," p. 73.

ty.[1539]Against this background, ATVOD published its determination in August 2013. The determination is especially pertinent to this chapter as it represents a borderline case, even more so than the *Sun Video* litigation in 2011. ATVOD's analysis in this case appears to be more thorough and detailed than in other cases, raising the issue of scope. This is apparent in the detailed description of the service made available under the outlet Vice Video as well as by distinguishing Vice Video from previous relevant appeal decisions of Ofcom.

In its determination, ATVOD focused on the video section of the website which was accessible through the "video" tab (subsequently renamed "watch") on Vice's homepage. According to ATVOD, this sub-site "is a pocket of TV-like territory which constitutes a service in its own right".[1540] In its description of the service, ATVOD highlighted the limited number of access links between the video section and other generic sections of the website.[1541] Although audiovisual material was presented in other sub-sections, it was not embedded in these but instead the user was taken to the video section when clicking on them.[1542] Conversely, videos which were embedded in text-based material were not made available in the video section. ATVOD thus considered that a distinction could be drawn between the video section and other audiovisual content dispersed

1539 In 2013, Vice was nominated for an Emmy for 'Outstanding Documentary or Nonfiction Series' and received two additional nominations in 2014 for 'Outstanding Cinematography for Nonfiction Programming' for the programme titled "Greenland Is Melting/Bonded Labor" and for 'Outstanding Sound Editing for Nonfiction Programming' for the programme "Terrorist University/ Armageddon Now". It won an Emmy in the category of 'Outstanding Informational Series or Special'. Vice Staff, 'Vice' on HBO just got nominated for three emmys, 10.7.2014, available at http://www.vice.com/read/vice-on-hbo-just-got-nominated-for-three-emmys. In March 2015, Vice announced a major deal with HBO concerning the expansion of its news programmes. See Vice News, Vice and HBO enter major deal to expand news programming, 26.3.2015, available at https://news.vice.com/article/vice-and-hbo-enter-major-deal-to-expand-news-programming (all websites accessed 21.4.2015).

1540 Strikingly, the reference to "a pocket of TV-like territory" recurrs in ATVOD's determination. See ATVOD, "Summary of Determination That the Provider of Vice (Video) Is in Breach of ATVOD Rules 1 & 4 and Thereby Has Contravened Sec. 368BA and Sec. 368D (3) (ZA) of the Coomunications Act," August 14, 2013, pp. 3, 6.

1541 ATVOD, "Scope Determination Vice Video," p. 3.

1542 ATVOD, "Scope Determination Vice Video," p. 3.

throughout the rest of the site.[1543] In addition, ATVOD referred to the Vice YouTube channel[1544] indicating that the latter encompassed "much of the

1543 ATVOD, "Scope Determination Vice Video," p. 3.

1544 ATVOD instigated several proceedings against providers of services hosted by Youtube. In May 2011, it considered that the service entitled Top Gear, a motoring magazine provided by BBC Worldwide constituted an on-demand service. ATVOD conceded that the programmes provided were of relatively short duration (between two and eight minutes). Although such programmes were not in the majority on TV channels, such formats were nonetheless included, albeit to a lesser degree ("one in every thirty programmes on the five main channels"). See ATVOD, "Determination That the Provider of the Service Named Top Gear YouTube Has Contravened Sec. 368BA and Sec. 368D (3) (ZA) of the Communications Act," March 5, 2011; BBC Worldwide successfully appealed against ATVOD's assessment arguing that the clips made available on Youtube Top Gear were short and served as "tasters" to promote the Top Gear magazine on linear TV. Moreover, the clips were offered without any links and quality editing, lacked credits and were of low quality. The service provider submitted that there was a difference in consumption patterns between the clips on Youtube and television programmes. While the former were designed to be viewed "on the move" or during brief breaks on smaller, mobile devices with lower resolution, TV programmes were of high quality and watched passively "in comfort on the large screen" (para. 19 d, p. 6). In the appeal decision, the principal purpose part of the statutory definition stipulated in Sec. 368A (1) (a) CA was not contentious. Ofcom considered that this requirement was met (para. 39, p. 11), focussing instead on the comparability prong. With regards to the duration of the videos, Ofcom acknowledged that programmes of up to ten minutes in length were disseminated on TV but emphasized that such were typical of genres like cartoons or adult entertainment and not common for motoring or other magazine style formats (para. 41, p. 11). Ofcom stated that there was no coherent editing or complete narrative that linked individual videos which rather appeared as an unrelated collection so that users would have to rely on written text to make sense of the audiovisual material (para. 42, p. 11). The lack of comparability was not disputed by the reliance on playlists which grouped clips according to specific subject matter. Ofcom posited that the playlists did not provide an overarching and coherent link which would form a single programme and highlighted that the individual pieces began and ended abruptly lacking any consistent editing such as voiceover, graphics or studio based scenes to construct a complete narrative (para. 44, p. 12). Ofcom admitted that the quality of the videos was reminiscent of the quality of TV programmes (para. 45, p. 12). On the contrary, the videos did not contain any opening or closing credits making the audiovisual material less TV-like (para. 46, p. 12-13). On overall assessment, Ofcom concluded that the videos offered on the Youtube Top Gear site, albeit possessing some of the characteristics of TV programmes (notably being of quality) were primarily presented "as disjointed short clips" and thus not comparable to the form and content of programmes featured on TV (para. 47, p.

same material as is provided in the video section". Lacking "any signifi-

13). This finding was underpinned by the research Ofcom commissioned into users' behaviour and attitudes. According to the study, the service "tended not to be perceived [by users] as a reasonable substitute for linear TV" (p. 46). Ofcom therefore followed the views of consumers holding that Top Gear on Youtube would not function as a substitute for similar TV programmes (para. 50, p. 13). Interestingly, one of the participants of the study noted that "Top Gear is TV – it's on TV – but on Youtube, it's just clips that you're choosing, so it would be a poor substitute for the real thing" (p. 46). This statement may be a good summary of users' perspectives that seem to perceive audiovisual content on Youtube predominantly as a website rather than television. Importantly, in its appeal decision in Top Gear Ofcom clarified that it was for the service provider to evaluate on a continuous basis whether its service fell under the statutory definition or not (para. 61, p. 16). Thus, Ofcom took account of the fact that the services (including the one at issue) rapidly changed and could evolve from being less TV-like to becoming TV-like. By the same token, Ofcom turned down ATVOD's determination in BBC Food on Youtube on essentially similar grounds as discussed above. ATVOD's determination and Ofcom's appeal decisions were published at the same dates as those in the case of Top Gear. In the case concerning the Guardian Youtube Channel, ATVOD withdrew its determination of June 2011 in light of Ofcom's appeal decision in Sun Video. See Ofcom, "Appeal by BBC Worldwide against a Notice of Determination by ATVOD That the Service Top Gear YouTube Has Contravened Sections 368BA and 368D (3) (ZA) of the Communications Act 2003," January 18, 2013; in April 2014, ATVOD held that the service of the British newspaper UK Column offered on Youtube constituted a non-linear service within the meaning of Sec. 368BA CA. The co-regulator considered that the videos including "interviews, news style programmes and studio based discussions about topical issues" were similar to programmes broadcast on TV. The videos appeared to be professionally produced featuring titles on the screen as well as credits (p. 3). ATVOD was furthermore convinced that the principal purpose of the service was the provision of programmes. Being promoted as "UKC TV", audiovisual content was presented prominently on the homepage while text-based material merely accompanied the videos serving an ancillary function (p. 4). Interestingly, the service provider had claimed that the service was a "non-commercial 'hobby' enterprise" and as such did not form an economic activity, consequently falling outside the scope of Sec. 368BA CA. ATVOD made clear that the term "economic" was interpreted broadly and noted that the UK Clumn Youtube site did not contain user-generated content "posted by a private individual" but was instead "part of the promotional apparatus for the UK Column publications" (p. 5). See ATVOD, "Determination That the Provider of The UK Column Is in Breach of ATVOD's Rules 1 & 4 and Thereby Has Contravened Sec. 368BA and Sec. 368D (3) (ZA) of the Communications Act," April 24, 2014; in the aftermath of its determination, ATVOD released a statement on 3 July 2014 in response to several enquiries about its enforcement action in this case. In its statement, ATVOD underlined that it did neither order the removal of content from the

cant broader context" such as accompanying text articles or the typical Vice branding and presentation of videos, ATVOD concluded that the Vice service provided on the YouTube platform unequivocally constituted an ODPS. Yet, the determination solely concerned the Vice website video section, not its YouTube accessory.

When applying the statutory criteria, ATVOD undertook a detailed analysis of the principal purpose part in line with Sec. 368A (1) (a) CA. It indicated that the video section referred to expressions like "shows", "series", "episodes" and "trailers" which are commonly associated with television broadcasting.[1545] Because the offer included programmes previously screened on HBO, ATVOD deduced that users expected regulatory protection.[1546] It argued that some videos were of substantial duration of more than ten minutes on average and possessed typical features of television programmes, such as a complete narrative, credits and the use of music.[1547] In this context, ATVOD distinguished the Vice Video outlet from Ofcom's *Sun Video* and *Everton* appeal decisions, emphasising that the audiovisual material on Vice Video constituted a "distinct consumer offering" with an "independent identity" brought about by the prominence of audiovisual material aggregated in a separate section and its TV-like branding.[1548] With regards to the comparability test, ATVOD held that the videos closely resembled programmes disseminated on TV due to their considerable length and the inclusion of characteristics typical of TV programmes.[1549] In line with recital 24 AVMSD, ATVOD stressed that over-

---

Youtube site nor the closure of the service. It clarified that as a result of its determination, the service provider was required to notify its service, pay a fee and comply with the content standards outlined in the CA. The publication of an explanatory note by ATVOD may signal the complexities of the regulatory framework for audiovisual media services as well as the public's lack of awareness of the precise body of applicable rules. The subjugation of previously unregulated subsections of websites under the regulatory umbrella for audiovisual media may also be a sensitive topic which is hastily connected to censorship and intrusive state interference in matters of freedom of speech. ATVOD's statement is thus helpful in raising public awareness of the co-regulators mandate and enhancing transparency of the reasons for the adjudication. See ATVOD, "Statement on UK Column," March 7, 2014.

1545 ATVOD, "Scope Determination Vice Video," p. 5.

1546 ATVOD, "Scope Determination Vice Video," p. 5.

1547 ATVOD, "Scope Determination Vice Video," p. 5.

1548 ATVOD, "Scope Determination Vice Video," pp. 5–6.

1549 ATVOD, "Scope Determination Vice Video," p. 6.

all Vice Video competed for the same audience as providers of linear channels due to the close resemblance with "broadcast genres (documentary, travel, feature films) in terms of subject matter, structure [and] production quality".[1550]

The long-awaited appeal decision by Ofcom was rendered in July 2015 and turned out to be a disappointment in view of specifying the principal purpose test.[1551] While the appellant submitted evidence that it did not meet the criteria of principal purpose and comparability,[1552] the main focus of the case shifted towards the question of jurisdiction, more particularly the question of whether Vice UK had editorial responsibility for the service or rather its US-based parent company Vice Media Inc. did, as argued by the appellant.[1553] In the absence of any contractual wording to determine which entity had editorial control, Ofcom resorted to examining the practice of the parties involved.[1554] Ofcom recognised that editorial roles differed for text material and video content and that the entity with editorial responsibility for the video tab was Vice Media Inc. established in the USA.[1555] While the written material produced in the US was adapted to UK tastes, almost all video material published on the website originated in the USA. In line with Art. 2 (3) (c) AVMSD, Ofcom had to determine whether a "significant part of the workforce [located in the UK was] involved in the pursuit of the audiovisual media service activity". Ofcom observed that "decisions relating to the audiovisual media service were

1550 ATVOD, "Scope Determination Vice Video," p. 7.

1551 Ofcom, "Appeal by Vice UK Limited against a Notice of Determination by ATVOD That the Service Vice (Video) Has Contravened Sections 368BA and 368D (3) (ZA) of the Communications Act 2003," July 21, 2015.

1552 Ofcom, "Appeal Decision Vice Video," paras. 44–45, pp. 12-15.

1553 Ofcom, "Appeal Decision Vice Video," paras. 50–59, pp. 16-19.

1554 Ofcom inquired about contractual terms. The appellant pointed out that no contract had been concluded between two companies pertaining to the same group. The appellant provided some job descriptions but underlined that "the company had a strong cultural element from the US parent where job descriptions (and contracts) were less formalised". See Ofcom, "Appeal Decision Vice Video," para. 58, p. 19.

1555 Ofcom, "Appeal Decision Vice Video," para. 84, p. 24. With regards to text material, the UK branch of the company enjoyed greater discretion in matters of editorial control. However, the US team also held a significant share of responsibility for the text material. See para. 85, p. 24.

made in both the US and the UK".[1556] It clarified however that this did not involve a significant part of the workforce in the UK, neither quantitatively (18 out of 192 employees) nor qualitatively (decision-making powers in the UK were considerably constrained by the general control held by the US head office).[1557]

In response to ATVOD's complaint that Ofcom should have remitted the decision back to ATVOD in view of the new evidence provided by the appellant at the appeal stage, Ofcom referred to the significant lapse of time since ATVOD's original determination. In the interest of "bringing the matter to a prompt conclusion, limiting further cost", Ofcom decided to quash ATVOD's determination and substitute its decision for ATVOD's.[1558] Interestingly, at the end of its decision Ofcom alluded to the interpretation of the statutory requirement of principal purpose. It stated that "it was necessary to look at the offering provided by the website as a whole: the written content and the audiovisual material on the Vice.com website".[1559] Ofcom acknowledged that ATVOD had not had access to all the necessary information to properly appraise "all of the material at Vice.com, outside the Vice (Video) tab".[1560] Ofcom consented that for future scope determinations, evidence of actual consumer behaviour which indicated how users "access, view and use the audiovisual material on the site in question" was *a* (though not the sole) useful source to make a thorough assessment.[1561] It emerges from the appeal decision in *Vice Video* that Ofcom takes recital 28 AVMSD seriously, which it expressly cited.

---

1556 Ofcom, "Appeal Decision Vice Video," para. 91, p. 25. ATVOD in fact noted an inconsistency in the wording of Ofcom's preliminary view communicated to it and the appellant at an earlier stage. Ofcom had referred to "the production of audiovisual material" rather than "the pursuit of the audiovisual media service activity" as prescribed by Art. 2 (3) (c) AVMSD. Ofcom remarked that the latter formulation covered a broader range of activities related to the provision of audiovisual media services and the appellant was asked to correct previous submissions. See paras. 73-78, p. 22-23.

1557 Ofcom, "Appeal Decision Vice Video," para. 92, p. 26.

1558 Ofcom, "Appeal Decision Vice Video," para. 83, p. 24. Still, Ofcom "recognized the importance of full information being supplied by service providers to ATVOD in the first instance and agreed [with ATVOD] that, in a case where it appeared that information had been held back or an appellant had not engaged, this may well be a reason to remit back.".

1559 Ofcom, "Appeal Decision Vice Video," para. 97, p. 26.

1560 Ofcom, "Appeal Decision Vice Video," para. 97, p. 27.

1561 Ofcom, "Appeal Decision Vice Video," para. 99, p. 27.

The principal purpose test thus requires a broad examination of the myriad of content provided on the whole website even if audiovisual material is aggregated in a separate section.

## 2. Comparability test

In tandem with the principal purpose test, Sec. 368A (1) (a) CA requires that the programmes provided are commensurable in form and content to programmes screened on linear TV. The formulation of the statute replicates the wording of Art. 1 (1) (b) AVMSD defining the term programme. The following section analyses the decisions in *Demand Adult* and *Climax 3 Uncut*, *Channel Flip*, *BBC Food on You Tube* and *Everton TV,* thus shedding light on the UK regulators' approach to interpreting the second prong of Sec. 368A (1) (a) CA.

### a) Comparable, not identical programmes: Demand Adult and Climax3 Uncut

One of the first conclusive cases of the comparability test arose with regards to two services, *Demand Adult* and *Climax 3 Uncut,* provided by Playboy TV UK Limited. In two determinations, of September and December 2010, which were identical in substance, ATVOD postulated that the material offered on the websites of the two services was comparable to the form and content normally included in television broadcasts.[1562] Interestingly, Playboy TV had argued that the type of content made available on the websites was typically considered as "hardcore porn", i.e. material which was commonly classified by the BBFC as R18, the sale of which was permitted solely in licensed sex shops.[1563] The service provider asserted that since such programmes were banned from UK TV, the material

1562 ATVOD, "Determination That the Provider of the Service Named Demand Adult Has Contravened Sec. 368BA of the Communications Act," September 24, 2010; ATVOD, "Determination That the Provider of the Service Named Climax 3 Uncut Has Contravened Sec. 368BA of the Communications Act," December 21, 2010.

1563 Playboy TV UK Limited did not make any representations concerning its service "Demand Adult" in proceedings before ATVOD but the line of argumentation can nonetheless be extended to both cases as is shown by Playboy TV's

it offered was essentially different and not at all TV-like. Playboy TV also claimed that in line with recital 24 AVMSD, there was no competition for the same audience between the "soft content shown on UK TV" and the "hardcore" nature provided on its websites.[1564] This rather creative line of argumentation was quashed by ATVOD which acknowledged that the material offered by Playboy TV "[might] be more explicit" than programmes aired on UK TV but was nonetheless comparable to such.[1565] By the same token, ATVOD dared a look across borders pointing out that the kind of material provided was comparable to "adult" content disseminated in many linear services of "other EU jurisdictions".[1566]

ATVOD's determinations were appealed and Ofcom published its appeal decisions in May 2011. These are sufficiently similar to be analysed jointly. The heart of the matter revolved around the interpretation of the comparability prong of the statutory test pursuant to Sec. 368A (1) (a) CA. Ofcom underlined that the CA merely required the programmes to be "comparable but not identical".[1567] Hence, the test implies a comparison of the type of programmes "normally included in the range of television programmes" rather than a specific format or programme.[1568] The fact that the material offered by Playboy TV on its websites was "stronger and more explicit" was irrelevant as long as such kinds of pornographic programmes were generally provided on TV. [1569] The degree of sexuality, be

submissions during the appeal procedure regarding the "Demand Adult" service before Ofcom. See ATVOD, "Scope Determination Climax 3 Uncut.".

1564 ATVOD, "Scope Determination Demand Adult"; ATVOD, "Scope Determination Climax 3 Uncut.".

1565 This part of ATVOD's determination is identically worded in both determinations ATVOD, "Scope Determination Climax 3 Uncut"; ATVOD, "Scope Determination Demand Adult.".

1566 ATVOD, "Scope Determination Climax 3 Uncut"; ATVOD, "Scope Determination Demand Adult.".

1567 Ofcom, "Appeal by Playboy TV against a Notice of Determination by ATVOD That the Provider of the Service Climax 3 Uncut Has Contravened Section 368-BA of the Communications Act 2003," May 13, 2011, p. 8; Ofcom, "Appeal by Playboy TV against a Notice of Determination by ATVOD That the Provider of the Service Demand Adult Has Contravened Section 368BA of the Communications Act 2003," May 13, 2011, p. 7.

1568 Ofcom, "Appeal Decision Climax 3 Uncut," pp. 9–10; Ofcom, "Appeal Decision Demand Adult," pp. 8–9.

1569 Ofcom, "Appeal Decision Climax 3 Uncut," p. 9; Ofcom, "Appeal Decision Demand Adult," p. 8.

it soft porn or hardcore, was irrelevant. Ofcom also explicated the rationale behind its approach, outlining that too strict a comparability test (as proposed by Playboy TV) could lead service providers to evade regulation by "maximising the extremity (e.g. in sex/violence) of [their] video content".[1570] Opening the door for this type of circumvention by providers would undermine the very essence of the AVMSD and the levels of protection afforded there under. Moreover, Ofcom agreed with ATVOD that viewers consuming material characterised as soft porn might also be interested and attracted by the services offered by Playboy TV.[1571] It was thus reasonable to conclude that *Demand Adult* and *Climax 3 Uncut* competed for the same audience as comparable linear services, thereby satisfying the conditions set by recital 24 AVMSD.

Linked to this finding is Ofcom's reference to the "means of access" of a service. It remarked that the graduated system of regulation introduced by the AVMSD (and thus by the CA) led users to expect "at least [a] base level of" regulatory protection in the online realm rather than no protection at all.[1572] Ofcom's interpretation of the comparability test appears adequate, especially with respect to the dynamic development of programme types recognised in recital 24 AVMSD. The AVMSD's scope of application would be considerably restricted (and falsely so) if it related only to those programmes actually and previously aired on TV. Hence, Ofcom correctly underpinned the meaning of the term "comparable". Still, it is striking that both regulators referred to similar formats screened on TV in other EU Member States to stress competition for the same audience.[1573] In spite of the differences in classification of pornographic material across the EU, the conclusion drawn from this brief comparison appears reasonable, namely that non-linear service providers of pornographic content are in competition with linear service providers offering similar (albeit softer) sexualised material.

---

1570 Ofcom, "Appeal Decision Climax 3 Uncut," p. 9; Ofcom, "Appeal Decision Demand Adult," p. 9.

1571 Ofcom, "Appeal Decision Climax 3 Uncut," p. 10; Ofcom, "Appeal Decision Demand Adult," p. 10.

1572 Ofcom, "Appeal Decision Climax 3 Uncut," p. 11; Ofcom, "Appeal Decision Demand Adult," p. 11.

1573 ATVOD, "Scope Determination Climax 3 Uncut"; ATVOD, "Scope Determination Demand Adult"; Ofcom, "Appeal Decision Climax 3 Uncut," p. 10.

b) Duration of programmes: Channel Flip and BBC Food Worldwide on YouTube

In the two cases *Channel Flip* and *BBC Food Worldwide on YouTube,* decided by ATVOD at the end of April and beginning of May 2011, the comparability part of the statutory test was the most crucial point. While Channel Flip featured light entertainment material, notably comedy content, the BBC's Food channel on YouTube presented extracts of cooking shows as well as recipe sections. ATVOD determined that Channel Flip and the BBC's Food channel on YouTube constituted ODPS within the meaning of the CA.[1574] The service providers appealed this classification before Ofcom which published its decisions more than one and a half years later, in December 2012 and January 2013 respectively, upholding the appeals.[1575] In both cases, the principal purpose as being the provision of audiovisual material was undisputed. With regards to the comparability test, Ofcom outlined certain factors which were indicative that the form and content of the service were comparable to television broadcasting. Ofcom examined the duration of the audiovisual material, noting the short length of the majority of "clips", in contrast with the longer duration of similar programme genres aired on TV.[1576] Both, ATVOD and Ofcom were careful not to indicate a specific duration which would make audiovisual material "comparable" to television programmes. Such a quantitative limit would be unnecessarily rigid and would not take into account the dynamics of market developments in programme formats. It would also give providers ample room to evade regulatory burdens by permitting

1574 ATVOD, "Determination That the Provider of the Service Named Channel Flip Has Contravened Sec. 368BA and Sec. 368D (3) (ZA) of the Communications Act," April 26, 2011; ATVOD, "Determination That the Provider of the Service Named BBC Food Youtube Has Contravened Sec. 368BA and Sec. 368D (3) (ZA) of the Communications Act," March 5, 2011, http://www.atvod.co.uk/complaints/determinations/2011-determinations/bbc-food-youtube (accessed 16.6.2015).

1575 Ofcom, "Appeal by Channel Flip Media Limited against a Notice of Determination by ATVOD That the Service Channel Flip Has Contravened Section 368BA of the Communications Act 2003," December 14, 2012; Ofcom, "Appeal by BBC Worldwide Limited against a Notice of Determination by ATVOD That the Service BBC Food YouTube Has Contravened Sections 368BA and 368D (3) (ZA) of the Communications Act 2003," January 18, 2013.

1576 Ofcom, "Appeal Decision Channel Flip," para. 59, pp. 15–16; Ofcom, "Appeal Decision BBC Food YouTube," para. 41, p. 11.

them to design clips and videos in such a way so as to remain (just) under the time limit. Instead, the comparability test pursuant to the CA implies, inter alia, a comparison between the duration of the audiovisual material provided and the duration of the equivalent programme type or genre on TV.

In the *BBC Food channel* decision, Ofcom additionally referred to the fact that the extracts taken from the cooking programmes were "devoid of the original surrounding programme context, and were frequently disjointed".[1577] The incompleteness of videos (which were abruptly ended before preparation of the final dish) and the absence of links between individual clips were furthermore indicative of the lack of comparability.[1578] Although the BBC Food channel on YouTube contained material grouped in playlists according to themes, these were pre-determined by the BBC and "did not function to link elements in the manner of a coherent longer format piece of content".[1579] By merely stringing clips together, the playlists lacked uniform voiceover, graphics and narrative.[1580] Ofcom considered that the incoherence and incompleteness of the individual items collected in a playlist were uncharacteristic of programmes broadcast on TV. Moreover, the videos lacked production elements typical of linear broadcasts such as opening and closing credits.[1581] Interestingly, in the appeal proceedings the BBC had argued that the clips on its YouTube Food channel were intended to be "shared through social media and viewed on devices (such as smart phones and tablets) which have smaller screens and lower resolution".[1582] The intended consumption pattern thus contrasted with programmes screened on TV where viewers could lean back "in comfort" to watch programmes "on a large screen".[1583] Ofcom did not fully accept the BBC's argument and merely remarked that quality was not a pertinent criterion for the comparability test.[1584] Indeed, to make the intention of service providers indicative of TV-likeness of audiovisual material would be trumps in the hands of service providers, as the criterion would be too

1577 Ofcom, "Appeal Decision BBC Food YouTube," para. 43, p. 12.
1578 Ofcom, "Appeal Decision BBC Food YouTube," paras. 43–44, p. 12.
1579 Ofcom, "Appeal Decision BBC Food YouTube," para. 45, p. 12.
1580 Ofcom, "Appeal Decision BBC Food YouTube," para. 45, p. 12.
1581 Ofcom, "Appeal Decision BBC Food YouTube," para. 47, p. 13.
1582 Ofcom, "Appeal Decision BBC Food YouTube," para. 19d., p. 6.
1583 Ofcom, "Appeal Decision BBC Food YouTube," para. 19d., p. 6.
1584 Ofcom, "Appeal Decision BBC Food YouTube," paras. 48–49, pp. 13-14.

subjective. Thus, Ofcom focussed on much more objective factors in determining comparability with linear services.

In its *Channel Flip* decision, Ofcom underlined that the comparability test entailed an analysis of the whole range of material provided to avoid bias, and not just certain isolated examples with a particular resemblance to broadcasts.[1585] Strikingly, Ofcom referred to its 2009 and in particular its 2012 research into consumer perspectives, attitudes and behaviour towards different kinds of services.[1586] As noted above, the study drew up a "spectrum of comparability (between those highly comparable with linear television and those not closely comparable) based on ten different factors" derived from interviews and discussion groups with users.[1587] Since Channel Flip was included in the list of examples users had tested and experienced, Ofcom substantially relied on the findings of the study in its *Channel Flip* decision. Users had considered Channel Flip to be less TV-like and positioned the service at the "lower end of the spectrum of comparability with linear television".[1588] Due to the "'look and feel' of the website", i.e. relatively low quality of the content,[1589] its brevity, simple graphics, camera work and the characters involved, users did not associate Channel Flip with television broadcasting.[1590] The readiness with which Ofcom embraced users' perspectives about Channel Flip is striking.[1591] In fact, the decision in *Channel Flip* appears to be based in large parts on the research commissioned by Ofcom. While it would have been implausible for Ofcom to contradict users' attitudes, Ofcom could have undertaken a more comprehensive analysis of the service itself. Ofcom's approach of taking users' perspectives into account should generally be welcomed but

1585 Ofcom, "Appeal Decision Channel Flip," para. 63, p. 16.

1586 Essential Research, "Research on On-Demand Services and Consumer Views on 'TV-Likeness'" (accessed 9.3.2015); Essential Research, "Research on On-Demand Services and Consumer Choices" (accessed 9.3.2015).

1587 Ofcom, "Appeal Decision Channel Flip," para. 45, p. 12; Ofcom, "Appeal Decision BBC Food YouTube," para. 55, p. 15.

1588 Ofcom, "Appeal Decision Channel Flip," para. 48, p. 13.

1589 Ofcom did not define it as "amateur" content but considered that the "material appeared to be professionally made but on a limited budget". See Ofcom, "Appeal Decision Channel Flip," para. 34, p. 8.

1590 Ofcom, "Appeal Decision Channel Flip," para. 48, p. 13.

1591 Like in Channel Flip, Ofcom relied on research it had commissioned into user behaviour in its appeal decision in Everton FC, albeit to a lesser extent. See Ofcom, "Appeal Decision Everton TV," paras. 107–14, pp. 29-30.

the inherent limits of qualitative research (which merely provides a "snap shot" as Ofcom itself admitted)[1592] need to be offset by a thorough analysis by the regulator – which Ofcom carried out in the decision concerning the BBC's Food channel.

### c) Criteria indicative of comparability: Everton TV

Similar to the line of argumentation used in *Viva TV Music* (concerning music programmes)[1593] and *Channel Flip* (regarding comedy), in *Everton TV* Ofcom underlined that comparability would not be satisfied if videos (only) featured the highlights of football club matches. In its appeal decision, Ofcom considered that such videos commonly "comprised only one element of what would usually comprise a sports bulletin or sports magazine show".[1594] In contrast to sports programmes or programmes covering sports events, the items represented incomplete and incoherent short reports lacking an overarching connection.[1595] They were thus not typical of programmes of the sports genre aired on TV and, according to Ofcom, showed significant differences to programmes broadcast on the channels of some of the football clubs (e.g. MUTV or LFCTV).[1596] Ofcom posited that the material disseminated by Everton FC was best characterised as

1592 Ofcom, "Appeal Decision Channel Flip," para. 46, p. 12.

1593 Ofcom, "Appeal Decision Viva TV Music". In its appeal decision in Viva TV Music, Ofcom emphasized that the comparability part implied a "comparison between services" (para. 55). Thus, reliance on individual examples of videos is insufficient to distil that the form and content of the audiovisual material provided is reminiscent of TV programmes (para. 55). Ofcom agreed with ATVOD that the music videos provided on the music section of the website of Viva TV were the same kind of videos shown on linear TV (para. 56). While ATVOD had traced (a little artificially) the plot of the videos, Ofcom considered that the description of the narrative in case of music videos was not particularly useful (paras. 57-58) and instead pointed out that "rolling promotional music videos are an established genre" on linear TV (para. 59). Even though channels commonly do not list individual videos in their EPGs, the bundling of such videos "sometimes linked by a loose theme or genre (.) in the form of "charts" implies their quality as programmes (para. 59); confer also ATVOD's determination ATVOD, "Scope Determination Viva TV Music.".

1594 Ofcom, "Appeal Decision Everton TV," para. 95, p. 26.

1595 Ofcom, "Appeal Decision Everton TV," paras. 95–96, p. 26.

1596 Ofcom, "Appeal Decision Everton TV," para. 97, p. 27.

"sports related news and highlights" and did not constitute "programmes" within the meaning of the AVMSD.[1597] Importantly, it summarised the features it examined to determine comparability. Drawing from its assessment in *Channel Flip*, it concentrated on the "duration of audiovisual items, the use of opening and closing credits, any narrative structure and the production values".[1598]

### 3. Principal purpose and comparability applied to websites offering adult material

#### a) Frankie and Friends

In 2013 and 2014 ATVOD instigated an increasing number of proceedings against providers of websites offering adult material. With respect to the same service, ATVOD determined in a number of cases violations of scope (rules 1 and 4 of ATVOD's guidance document) as well as breaches of the rules on protection of minors (rule 11 of ATVOD's guidance).[1599] In this chapter, focus is placed on scope, and in particular the interpretation of the two-prong test encompassing principal purpose and comparability. ATVOD's determination concerning the service Frankie and Friends provided by Harry Barrett is interesting because it illustrates that ATVOD (and Ofcom for that matter) continued to enforce the statutory rules even if changes had been made to the service prior to the publication of ATVOD's determination. In this specific case, ATVOD determined in August 2013 that the offer of Frankie and Friends had constituted an ODPS in April 2013 (when ATVOD gathered evidence) even though it no longer

---

1597 Ofcom, "Appeal Decision Everton TV," para. 104, p. 28.

1598 Ofcom, "Appeal Decision Everton TV," para. 39, p. 14.

1599 See for instance ATVOD determinations in respect of the following services: Belted by Beauty (9.7.2013), the UK Institution (9.7.2013), Jessica Pressley (23.7.2013), Absolute Cruelty (2.8.2013), CFNM (2.8.2013), CMNM (2.8.2013), The Casting Room (2.8.2013), Bitch Slapped (8.8.2013), Young Dommes (9.8.2013), Mistress Whiplash (6.12.2013), Bra Busters of Britain (11.3.2014), Hardglam (25.4.2014), One Stop Porno Shop (25.4.2014), Facesitting Mistress (25.4.2014), Extreme Movie Pass (21.7.2014), Scottxxx (22.10.2014), SheBang TV (26.11.2014). Upon receipt of several 2014 determinations, many providers initiated changes to their services and/or remedied the shortcomings identified by ATVOD by notifying the service and paying the fee.

fell under ATVOD's remit as of July 2013, when modifications were effectuated by the provider.[1600] Hence, ATVOD took measures against a provider that had allegedly infringed statutory provisions at a certain point in the past [but had in the meantime ceased the infringing activity]. Whether Ofcom will continue along this line is doubtful in view of its refusal to investigate "historic" cases, i.e. where the complaint was not initiated promptly and the material was no longer available to the general public.[1601]

The service provider, however, disputed ATVOD's authority in April 2013 and appealed to Ofcom arguing that it mainly provided photographic content. In its appeal decision of August 2014, Ofcom agreed with ATVOD emphasising the "strong thematic links between the photographic material and the video material" and the way the material was accessed by users and presented on one "main homepage".[1602] Ofcom followed its habitual approach, applying the criteria it had outlined in its *Sun Video* and *Viva TV Music* decisions. The regulator highlighted that the service was hosted on one homepage from which users could enter both the photographic and video galleries.[1603] Although the two kinds of material were in separate catalogues, the style (headings had the same font, colour and size) and branding of the sub-sites were identical to that of the homepage.[1604]The videos were self-contained and could be consumed without accompanying material so that users could enjoy a "standalone viewing experience".[1605] Ofcom also rejected the provider's argument that the photographic content entailing about 12,000 stills was more prominent than the 79 videos included in its offer, postulating that the videos "were clearly one of the primary means by which the website offered a service to users".[1606] Emphasising that the prominence or significance of a certain

1600 ATVOD, "Summary of Determination That the Provider of Frankie and Friends Is in Breach of ATVOD Rules 1 & 4 and Thereby Has Contravened Sec. 368BA and Sec. 368D (3) (ZA) of the Coomunications Act," September 8, 2013, p. 4.

1601 Ofcom, "Future Regulation of VOD Services," para. 3.8d, p. 9.

1602 Ofcom, "Appeal by Harry Barrett against a Notice of Determination by ATVOD That the Provider of the service 'Frankie and Friends' has Contravened Sections 368BA and 368D (3) (ZA) of the Communications Act," August 14, 2014, para. 23, p. 8.

1603 Ofcom, "Appeal Decision Frankie and Friends," para. 47, p. 16.

1604 Ofcom, "Appeal Decision Frankie and Friends," paras. 48–49, pp. 16-17.

1605 Ofcom, "Appeal Decision Frankie and Friends," para. 50, p. 17.

1606 Ofcom, "Appeal Decision Frankie and Friends," para. 52, p. 18.

kind of material is not exclusively evaluated on the basis of quantity,[1607] it found that on balance, the service made equally available two types of material which were connected by a strong thematic link.[1608]

With regards to the comparability test of the statutory provision, Ofcom posited that the content provided was adult material comparable to the programmes broadcast on TV for the "primary purpose of sexual arousal or stimulation" which are permitted late at night or are shown on linear subscription services.[1609] By reference to its *Channel Flip* decision, Ofcom pointed out that duration (the majority of videos on the "Frankie and Friends" website were shorter than typical programmes broadcast on TV) was not the sole factor to consider when assessing comparability.[1610] Instead, it established many parallels between linear programmes and those provided by Harry Barrett, such as the development of a plot, the use of props and other elements, camera techniques and a professional production, all of which contributed to enhancing the viewer's experience.[1611] What is more, Ofcom interestingly compared the videos of the Frankie and Friends service to the programme entitled "XXX First Timers" aired on Playboy TV on 24 September 2013 at 10 p.m. noting the similarity in fictional narratives, staging and custom.[1612] Ofcom concluded that the service appealed to an audience interested in adult content screened on linear TV.[1613]

While the comparability part of Ofcom's analysis is understandable especially in light of earlier decisions, the principal purpose part appears made-up or at least less solidly argued than previous cases with the same focus. The question of prominence seems especially difficult. Ofcom opined that the two types of material, photographic and audiovisual were equally provided to users, without one type of content taking precedence over the other.[1614] While it is reasonable to take into account different factors to evaluate prominence, one of which is volume, it nonetheless seems insufficient for the audiovisual material to be "*one* of the primary means

1607 Ofcom, "Appeal Decision Frankie and Friends," para. 52, p. 18.
1608 Ofcom, "Appeal Decision Frankie and Friends," paras. 52–53, pp. 18-19.
1609 Ofcom, "Appeal Decision Frankie and Friends," para. 57, p. 20.
1610 Ofcom, "Appeal Decision Frankie and Friends," para. 62, p. 21.
1611 Ofcom, "Appeal Decision Frankie and Friends," paras. 65–67, p. 22.
1612 Ofcom, "Appeal Decision Frankie and Friends," paras. 60, 64, pp. 20–22.
1613 Ofcom, "Appeal Decision Frankie and Friends," para. 69, p. 22.
1614 Ofcom, "Appeal Decision Frankie and Friends," para. 52, p. 18.

by which the website offered a service to users".[1615] Should not, in order to affirm the principal purpose test, the provision of audiovisual material be *the* primary means whereby content is transmitted? Ofcom however placed the audiovisual material on the same footing as the photographic material, stating that users "had a choice of equal value in terms of accessing the information that is sought to be conveyed between the audiovisual and non-audiovisual material available".[1616] This formulation seems to water down the principal purpose test making it difficult for providers to assess whether they are within scope or outside.

This aspect is furthermore linked to a question during the appeal proceedings as to whether the website hosted two distinct services, i.e. one comprising photographic images and the other comprising video material. ATVOD was concerned that such a distinction could impact its second determination regarding rule 11 which purports to protect minors in non-linear services.[1617] Ofcom only touched on this issue tangentially by repeatedly noting that there was a "strong thematic connection between the two bodies of content on the site".[1618] However, Ofcom's finding that the audiovisual and non-audiovisual material constituted two main means of consumption on a par with each other could indicate the existence of two distinct services. Such interpretation would in turn have called into question ATVOD's determination that the entire material offered breached rule 11. Read in this light, Ofcom gave the impression that it recognised ATVOD's concerns and decided accordingly. The Frankie and Friends case illustrates the difficulty of applying Ofcom's criteria in practice. Surprisingly, ATVOD in its determination did not follow the criteria in detail and only briefly evaluated the services' principal purpose.

#### b) Urban Chick Supremacy Cell

In a similar vein, ATVOD determined that the service named The Urban Chick Supremacy Cell (UCSC) constituted an ODPS at a specific point in time (19-20 August 2013) and which the service provider had failed to notify. In a relatively comprehensive 9-page determination, noting that the

1615 Ofcom, "Appeal Decision Frankie and Friends," para. 52, p. 18.
1616 Ofcom, "Appeal Decision Frankie and Friends," para. 52, p. 18.
1617 Ofcom, "Appeal Decision Frankie and Friends," para. 21, p. 7.
1618 Ofcom, "Appeal Decision Frankie and Friends," paras. 23, 53, pp. 8, 19.

service had changed during its internal decision-making process, ATVOD consented that it no longer was a non-linear service within the meaning of Sec. 368A CA due to the removal of video content. The service provider had classified its service as "an art project" (more particularly, "an example of relational art") which aimed to provoke and push the boundaries of conventional erotic attitudes and perceptions.[1619] Denying that the principal purpose of the service was the provision of programmes, the service provider argued that the videos were "merely a means to an end, that of 'showcasing artistic talent'".[1620] Interestingly, the provider submitted that it was not covered by ATVOD's remit as it could not be characterised as mass media "intended for reception by, and (…) [with] a clear impact on, a significant proportion of the general public" as set forth by recital 21 AVMSD.[1621] ATVOD, however, confirmed the comparability of programmes with those normally screened on TV by reference to Ofcom's appeal decisions in *Demand Adult* and *Climax 3 Uncut*. Essentially, ATVOD considered that the "strong adult fetish programmes" under investigation were similar to "milder 'adult' fetish programmes" such as the "Lara series" ("Lara world of uniforms/nylon") broadcast on Television X.[1622]

What is more, ATVOD found that the audiovisual material "featured heavily on the home page", although stills and blogs were also made available.[1623] Users would benefit from the videos only upon subscription to the service. In response to the provider's arguments, ATVOD pointed out that any service was "a means to an end (financial, artistic, etc…)" and that exemption from regulation could not be granted merely on grounds that the service was intended as an art project.[1624] According to ATVOD

---

1619 ATVOD, "Determination That the Provider of 'The Urban Chick Supremacy Cell' is in Breach of ATVOD's Rules 1 & 4 and Thereby Has Contravened Sec. 368BA and Sec. 368D (3) (ZA) of the Communications Act," June 1, 2014, para. 4.4, 6.1, pp. 2-3.

1620 ATVOD, "Scope Determination The Urban Chick Supremacy Cell," para. 6.1., p. 3.

1621 ATVOD, "Scope Determination The Urban Chick Supremacy Cell," para. 6.1., p. 4.

1622 ATVOD, "Scope Determination The Urban Chick Supremacy Cell," para. 8.2, p. 6.

1623 ATVOD, "Scope Determination The Urban Chick Supremacy Cell," para. 8.2, p. 6.

1624 ATVOD, "Scope Determination The Urban Chick Supremacy Cell," para. 8.2, p. 7.

the service functioned as a non-linear service from the user's standpoint. With regards to the notion of mass media in light of recital 21 AVMSD, ATVOD stressed the various forms broadcasting could take and highlighted the fact that it could also cater to very small communities covering, for instance, "minority sports and hobbies" or "certain political or religious broadcasts".[1625] Interestingly, ATVOD held that "a relatively small audience may nevertheless be considered to constitute a not insignificant proportion of the general public".[1626] By marginally altering the formulation contained in recital 21 AVMSD (not insignificant instead of significant), ATVOD gave it a slightly different touch. Indeed, ATVOD also underlined the fact that the service was "*capable* of being accessed by a much larger audience than may choose to access it at a given time and therefore could have a clear impact on a greater proportion of the general public than it has reached to date".[1627]

In the appeal decision of August 2014, Ofcom disagreed with ATVOD on the grounds that the material on offer lacked comparability with TV-like programmes.[1628] Ofcom nonetheless found that the principal purpose of the website was the provision of audiovisual material. While the layout of the homepage, the absence of any reliable navigation or filtering tools and the unstructured way in which audiovisual material was catalogued (other than uploaded chronologically) worked against the service falling under the scope of Sec. 368A CA, Ofcom presented evidence in favour of the principal purpose being the provision of audiovisual material. In particular, Ofcom emphasised that a promotional claim advertising "over 10 hours of relentless, no mercy Hard Edge, high resolution Femdom Videos" was indicative of a service fulfilling the principal purpose pursuant to Sec. 368A (1) (a) CA.[1629] Indeed, the large number of clips pointed towards a "significant offering" in support of a service with the required principal

1625 ATVOD, "Scope Determination The Urban Chick Supremacy Cell," para. 8.3, p. 9.

1626 ATVOD, "Scope Determination The Urban Chick Supremacy Cell," para. 8.3, p. 9.

1627 ATVOD, "Scope Determination The Urban Chick Supremacy Cell," para. 8.3, p. 9.

1628 Ofcom, "Appeal by Itziar Bilbao Urrutia against a Notice of Determination by ATVOD That the Provider of the service 'The Urban Chick Supremacy Cell' has Contravened Sections 368BA and 368D (3) (ZA) of the Communications Act Whilst Operating an ODPS," August 14, 2014.

1629 Ofcom, "Appeal Decision The Urban Chick Supremacy Cell," para. 46, p. 15.

purpose.[1630] The amount of audiovisual content as well as the manner in which it was promoted was decisive for Ofcom.[1631]

In a second step, Ofcom denied the comparability part. In line with previous appeal decisions, it considered the duration of the material provided by UCSC, averaging roughly eight minutes, to be "broadly consistent and comparable" with adult content broadcast on TV.[1632] Yet, the paucity of credits (in spite of the UCSC logo which was featured at the end of the videos) and the isolation of clips which were taken from one fetish session made them less TV-like.[1633] In addition, Ofcom underlined that the narrative of many videos was different from TV programmes, comparing them to an experimental video which lacked any coherent conceit.[1634] The obviously low production budget and unprofessional equipment with which the videos were filmed also differentiated the UCSC website content from professionally made programmes on TV.[1635] In the final stage of the comparability test, Ofcom compared the clips of UCSC to material on linear broadcast services referring to ATVOD's example of "Lara's world of uniforms" and additionally referring to programmes broadcast on the TV channel XXCESS. It found that the lack of script and the lack of complete narrative differentiated UCSC's material from the programmes of linear service providers.[1636] Further, Ofcom stressed that the viewing experience on UCSC was different, requiring users to "manually select another video upon the conclusion of the one they were viewing".[1637]

With respect to the appellant's reference to recital 21 AVMSD and the question of competition between services as well as regulatory expectations, Ofcom noted that a "market definition and a precise assessment of competition between services in a market" similar to competition law was

---

1630 Ofcom, "Appeal Decision The Urban Chick Supremacy Cell," paras. 47, 49, p. 15.

1631 Ofcom, "Appeal Decision The Urban Chick Supremacy Cell," para. 51, p. 16.

1632 Ofcom, "Appeal Decision The Urban Chick Supremacy Cell," para. 55, pp. 17–18.

1633 Ofcom, "Appeal Decision The Urban Chick Supremacy Cell," paras. 57, 58, p. 18.

1634 Ofcom, "Appeal Decision The Urban Chick Supremacy Cell," para. 59, pp. 18–19.

1635 Ofcom, "Appeal Decision The Urban Chick Supremacy Cell," para. 60, p. 19.

1636 Ofcom, "Appeal Decision The Urban Chick Supremacy Cell," paras. 62–66, pp. 19-20.

1637 Ofcom, "Appeal Decision The Urban Chick Supremacy Cell," para. 61, p. 19.

not necessary for the purposes of determining scope.[1638] In its assessment, it considered the following three questions initially set out in its *Sun Video* appeal decision:

> "a. Would a user wanting to watch programmes normally included in linear television programme services have considered, or consider, audiovisual material on the Service as amongst his competing options?
> b. when viewing such material, would the user have considered, or consider, himself to be watching a programme service competing with linear television programme services?; and
> c. when doing so, would that user have expected or expect, what he is viewing to be regulated as television programmes, in the ways provided under the Directive?"[1639]

Ofcom did not consider that users interested in watching linear programmes would turn to UCSC as an alternative (question a).[1640] It emphasised that the means of navigating the UCSC service were essentially web-like and held that users would consequently not consider that they were watching a television programme (question b).[1641] Moreover, Ofcom acknowledged that the service appealed to a niche audience which was very limited and was not in competition with linear services due to its "small user base and turnover". It concluded that users would not reasonably expect regulation to the same extent as for linear services (question c).[1642]

c) Daisy Rock UK

In October and November 2014, ATVOD qualified the offers of Daisy Rock UK and Candy Girl Productions as non-linear services pursuant to Sec. 368A (1) CA. Both determinations were scrutinised by Ofcom on appeal. Similar to UCSC, Daisy Rock UK is a small-scale provider with 16 active members (registered at the time of the determination) and monthly

---

1638 Ofcom, "Appeal Decision The Urban Chick Supremacy Cell," para. 72, p. 22.
1639 Ofcom, "Appeal Decision Sun Video," para. 176, p. 44; Ofcom, "Appeal Decision The Urban Chick Supremacy Cell," para. 72, p. 22.
1640 Ofcom, "Appeal Decision The Urban Chick Supremacy Cell," para. 73, p. 22.
1641 Ofcom, "Appeal Decision The Urban Chick Supremacy Cell," para. 74, pp. 22–23.
1642 Ofcom, "Appeal Decision The Urban Chick Supremacy Cell," para. 75, p. 23.

traffic of a couple of thousand visitors.[1643] The provider declared that it made a monthly profit of about GBP 250.[1644] Regardless of this low user base, ATVOD considered that the videos resembled TV programmes broadcast on typical adult channels. Picking up Ofcom's point in the *UC-SC* appeal decision, ATVOD referred to the broad notion of broadcasting which encompasses programmes specifically catering to particular groups of society and appealing to minority interests.[1645] ATVOD also pointed out that the service was in principle accessible to a greater audience and could thus have a clear impact on the general public.[1646]

Furthermore, the similarity of the service to broadcasts was reinforced by the duration of the programmes (lasting on average between 20 and 30 minutes), the inclusion of typical TV features such as titles, credits, music, high production values and the language employed on the homepage referring to "movies" or "HD".[1647] Such characteristics differentiated this case from that of UCSC which generally offered audiovisual material of low production quality. With regards to the principal purpose, ATVOD found that the volume of videos provided on the homepage was substantial and permitted a standalone user experience.[1648] The material was moreover catalogued and easy to navigate.[1649] To buttress its assessment, ATVOD referred to the providers' promotional claim (as suggested by Ofcom in its *UCSC* appeal decision) marketed as "exclusive content, with newly produced full movies and thousands of hours of home footage of me Daisy Rock UK in raw hard-core action".[1650]

Almost a year later, Ofcom backed ATVOD's decision, holding that Daisy Rock UK was subject to VOD regulation.[1651] Ofcom proceeded in

---

1643 ATVOD, "Determination That the Provider of Daisy Rock UK Is in Breach of ATVOD's Rules 1 & 4 and Thereby Has Contravened Sec. 368BA and Sec. 368D (3) (ZA) of the Communications Act," November 26, 2014, para. 7.2, p. 3.

1644 ATVOD, "Scope Determination Daisy Rock UK," para. 7.2, p. 3.

1645 ATVOD, "Scope Determination Daisy Rock UK," para. 9.3, p. 4.

1646 ATVOD, "Scope Determination Daisy Rock UK," para. 9.3, p. 5.

1647 ATVOD, "Scope Determination Daisy Rock UK," para. 9.3, p. 4.

1648 ATVOD, "Scope Determination Daisy Rock UK," para. 9.3, p. 5.

1649 ATVOD, "Scope Determination Daisy Rock UK," para. 9.3, p. 5.

1650 ATVOD, "Scope Determination Daisy Rock UK," para. 9.3, p. 5.

1651 Ofcom, "Appeal by Brightonrock Communications Limited against a Notice of Determination by ATVOD That the Provider of the service 'Daisy Rock UK' has Contravened Sections 368BA and 368D (3) (ZA) of the Communications Act," September 17, 2015.

several steps, analysing the service's principal purpose according to the criteria established in *Sun Video*.[1652] It found that the homepage contained substantial amounts of video content which were presented as the primary user destination and promoted as such. The non-audiovisual material (text and still images) was not prominent and was considered insignificant in comparison to audiovisual content.[1653] On balance, Ofcom considered the 92 videos (in contrast to approximately 2500 photos) as a considerable offer of audiovisual material which was intended to be "the primary means by which the site offered a service to users".[1654] Moreover, all the videos were catalogued and accessible via thematic tabs and "comprised complete programmes that could be understood and watched fully on their own, rather than 'bite sized' extracts of longer programmes or material needing access to supporting material, such as text, to understand sufficiently".[1655] In relation to the comparability test, Ofcom referred to its *Channel Flip* decision and pointed out that short form content was characteristic of certain genres such as adult content. It held that an average duration of about 20 minutes was "broadly consistent and comparable" with programmes broadcast on TV.[1656] In addition, the videos made available featured typical elements of linear services such as titles and end credits, "relatively professional lighting techniques" and complete narratives.[1657]

Having concluded that the service fulfilled the required principal purpose and was comparable to TV broadcasting, Ofcom embarked on a noteworthy assessment of recitals 21 and 24 AVMSD in response to the provider's allegations that the service as a fan-club for Daisy was not in competition with linear channels and did not qualify as mass media due to its low membership (10) and turnover (GBP 300 in November 2014).[1658] The provider claimed that its service was so niche that it was essentially

1652 In the following, a summary of the analysis regarding principal purpose and comparability is given and focus is laid on the most noteworthy findings. This necessarily means that not every individual criterion of the principal purpose and comparability tests is commented on.
1653 Ofcom, "Appeal Decision Daisy Rock," para. 42, p. 10.
1654 Ofcom, "Appeal Decision Daisy Rock," para. 49, p. 12.
1655 Ofcom, "Appeal Decision Daisy Rock," paras. 43, 46, p. 11.
1656 Ofcom, "Appeal Decision Daisy Rock," paras. 57–58, p. 14.
1657 Ofcom, "Appeal Decision Daisy Rock," paras. 59–63, pp. 14-15.
1658 Ofcom, "Appeal Decision Daisy Rock," paras. 22–25, 29 pp. 6–7; in the appeal proceedings, the provider of Daisy Rock referred to the turnover threshold of EUR 100,000 set out by the Italian regulator AGCOM. See AGCOM, "Delibera

non-economic in nature.[1659] Ofcom, however, disagreed and made clear that recital 24 AVMSD implied "a measure of specific competition for the attention of viewers and advertisers".[1660] It concluded that "Daisy Rock was a competitive option" for a user interested in consuming adult content normally aired on TV and that users would expect a similar level of protection as for TV programmes.[1661] With respect to recital 21 AVMSD and the mass media character of the service, Ofcom distinguished *Daisy Rock* from *UCSC*. The material provided by UCSC did not meet the comparability test and the service was based on a "blogging" template which was reminiscent of a navigation tool typically used online.[1662] By contrast, the material offered on the Daisy Rock website was considered "mainstream adult content" and could be accessed "more like a television service".[1663]

Moreover, Ofcom clearly rejected the appellant's argument regarding low turnover. It stressed that low turnover could be indicative of a relatively new service or a service which has not been "marketed effectively to potential viewers".[1664] Above all, such evidence does not mean that the service is not "capable of competing with the same audience as television broadcasts" and thus is not intended for reception by the general public.[1665] In brief, the service was openly accessible to the public and not "merely to a closed community of like-minded individuals".[1666] Ofcom's line seems justified in view of a lack of statutory provisions exempting services with a low turnover. It is certainly true that membership and turnover can grow rapidly once the service becomes more popular. Yet, to speak of mass media in relation to a service with ten members appears exaggerated. This approach could stifle small-sized enterprises and be an obstacle to their development. The reason Ofcom upheld ATVOD's determination may also be linked to the type of content offered by Daisy Rock:

---

n. 607/10/CONS Regolamento in materia di fornitura di servizi di media audiovisivi a richiesta ai sensi dell'articolo 22-bis del Testo unico dei servizi di media audiovisivi e radiofonici," 2010, p. 6; see also Machet, "Content Regulation and New Media," pp. 3, 9 (accessed 35.3.2013).

1659 Ofcom, "Appeal Decision Daisy Rock," para. 23, p. 6.

1660 Ofcom, "Appeal Decision Daisy Rock," para. 68, p. 16.

1661 Ofcom, "Appeal Decision Daisy Rock," paras. 70–71, p. 17.

1662 Ofcom, "Appeal Decision Daisy Rock," para. 74, p. 18.

1663 Ofcom, "Appeal Decision Daisy Rock," paras. 75–76, p. 18.

1664 Ofcom, "Appeal Decision Daisy Rock," para. 30, p. 8.

1665 Ofcom, "Appeal Decision Daisy Rock," paras. 30, 78, pp. 8, 19.

1666 Ofcom, "Appeal Decision Daisy Rock," para. 78, p. 19.

adult material harmful to minors. Thus, this case illustrates that ATVOD and Ofcom take the protection of minors seriously and include in their regulatory remit small-scale providers which are, in theory, "capable" of competing with TV broadcasters.

d) Candy Girl Productions

ATVOD also investigated Candy Girl Productions, which is reminiscent of *UCSC* and (a little less so) *Daisy Rock UK*. Candy Girl Productions provides its service through various outlets. According to the provider, it is an interactive "fan site" which links to different sub-pages ("'satellite' home pages") presenting the models and actresses from the clips. Customers get acquainted with the performers and interact with them via blogs, forums or chat rooms.[1667] In response to ATVOD's inquiry, the provider argued that the videos were not comparable to programmes normally broadcast on TV due to their low quality and short duration (on average 3-5 minutes long).[1668] ATVOD, however, posited that the short length of the videos resembled the duration of programmes on adult channels like XXXCESS.[1669] It disagreed with the provider on the quality of the clips finding that they featured "relatively professional lighting techniques, staging and costumes, to create a TV like experience".[1670] In contrast to the content on UCSC, the videos portrayed complete narratives.[1671] The service provider claimed that it did not fall under Sec. 368A (1) (a) CA stating, above all, that less than one percent of the material offered was of audiovisual character, whereas the bulk of material constituted still photographs.[1672] In order to refute that argument, ATVOD pointed out that the balance of material was just one among many factors to assess the principal purpose of a service and thus not determinative on its own.[1673] While

1667 ATVOD, "Determination That the Provider of Candy Girl Productions Is in Breach of ATVOD's Rules 1 & 4 and Thereby Has Contravened Sec. 368BA and Sec. 368D (3) (ZA) of the Communications Act," October 22, 2014, para. 7.2, pp. 3–4.
1668 ATVOD, "Scope Determination Candy Girl Productions," para. 7.2, p. 3.
1669 ATVOD, "Scope Determination Candy Girl Productions," para. 9.3, p. 4.
1670 ATVOD, "Scope Determination Candy Girl Productions," para. 9.3, p. 5.
1671 ATVOD, "Scope Determination Candy Girl Productions," para. 9.3, p. 5.
1672 ATVOD, "Scope Determination Candy Girl Productions," para. 7.2, p. 3.
1673 ATVOD, "Scope Determination Candy Girl Productions," para. 9.3, p. 6.

ATVOD acknowledged the significant amount of non-audiovisual material, it found that the "video offering [was] substantial and significant with both the central sites and the 'satellite' home pages featuring video material prominently".[1674] Similar to its determination in UCSC, ATVOD determined that consumption of videos was the primary benefit of subscription.[1675] With respect to the presentation of the audiovisual content, ATVOD stressed that the videos were catalogued under the "videos" tab and could thus easily be found.[1676]

In June 2016, more than one and a half years later, Ofcom rejected ATVOD's assessment on appeal, considering that the service Candy Girl Productions lacked the required principal purpose and therefore was not an ODPS.[1677] Ofcom found that the service Candy Girl Productions, in fact, consisted of two distinct services, Candy Girl Pass and All Teens World, which it analysed separately.[1678] For both services, the principal purpose test was the crucial element. As has been established practice, Ofcom applied the characteristics it identified in the *Sun Video* decision.[1679] With regards to Candy Girl Pass, Ofcom noted that the homepage, pre and post the pay wall, was a destination for both, photographic as well as audiovisual material featuring the models who "were the main theme of the website and the purpose of the website was to provide different media content for these models".[1680] Interestingly, the regulator did not accept the appellant's arguments the "fan" aspects of the site were the primary features of the service underlining that the store, blog, chats and forum were inactive.[1681]

Furthermore, the cataloguing and accessing as well as the presentation and styling of the service were such that they equally depicted images and videos. Neither form was considered to be ancillary but they both were

1674 ATVOD, "Scope Determination Candy Girl Productions," para. 9.3, p. 5.
1675 ATVOD, "Scope Determination Candy Girl Productions," para. 9.3, p. 6.
1676 ATVOD, "Scope Determination Candy Girl Productions," para. 9.3, p. 6.
1677 Ofcom, "Appeal by Laura Jenkins against a Notice of Determination That the Provider of the services 'Candy Girl Pass' and 'All Teens World' has Contravened Sec. 368BA and Sec. 368(3)(ZA) CA" (Broadcast and On Demand Bulletin, Issue 306, June 6, 2016).
1678 Ofcom, "Appeal Candy Girl Productions," para. 31, pp. 35–36.
1679 Ofcom, "Appeal Candy Girl Productions," para. 34, p. 36.
1680 Ofcom, "Appeal Candy Girl Productions," para. 35, p. 36.
1681 Ofcom, "Appeal Candy Girl Productions," paras. 43, 56, pp. 37, 39.

complementary.[1682] The same was true for content and access links which led Ofcom to conclude that the service "was offering different types of content in an integrated fashion and both photographic and audiovisual content could be accessed depending on user preference and navigation of the website".[1683] Yet, the videos were self-contained, portraying a complete, albeit short narrative (of an average duration of 4 minutes) which "offered a stand-alone entertainment experience".[1684] The audiovisual content was, however, materially different from the photographic material (i.e. the images did not replicate scenes of the video footage).[1685] On balance, Ofcom agreed with ATVOD that the video content was a substantial offering but pointed out that it was made alongside a substantial offering of photographic content, both of which were regularly up-dated.[1686] Ofcom did not find evidence that the videos were the primary means of communication.[1687] It acknowledged that they were a "key purpose of the service" but stressed that the stills were equally important.[1688]

In a similar vein, Ofcom decided that the service All Teens World did not fulfil the principal purpose test. In contrast to Candy Girl Pass, this service did not present a significant offering of audiovisual content.[1689] About 40 videos contrasted sharply to approximately 26,000 stills.[1690] Videos were also not available for a number of models and they were, moreover, not refreshed.[1691] Due to the lack of audiovisual material, Ofcom considered that users looking for such content were unlikely to turn to the All Teens World website.[1692] As in previous decisions, Ofcom referred to recital 24 AVMSD and, in particular clarified the notion of competition. It made clear that the AVMSD aimed to establish "a measure of fair competition for those (…) who provide similar services and who, in doing so, provide a measure of specific competition for the attention of

1682 Ofcom, "Appeal Candy Girl Productions," paras. 46–47, pp. 37-38.
1683 Ofcom, "Appeal Candy Girl Productions," para. 50, p. 38.
1684 Ofcom, "Appeal Candy Girl Productions," para. 48, p. 38.
1685 Ofcom, "Appeal Candy Girl Productions," para. 51, p. 38.
1686 Ofcom, "Appeal Candy Girl Productions," para. 52, pp. 38–39.
1687 Ofcom, "Appeal Candy Girl Productions," para. 53, p. 39.
1688 Ofcom, "Appeal Candy Girl Productions," paras. 57–58, p. 39.
1689 Ofcom, "Appeal Candy Girl Productions," paras. 79, 84, 87, pp. 42–43.
1690 Ofcom, "Appeal Candy Girl Productions," para. 84, p. 43.
1691 Ofcom, "Appeal Candy Girl Productions," paras. 85–87, p. 43.
1692 Ofcom, "Appeal Candy Girl Productions," para. 90, p. 43.

viewers and advertisers".[1693] Ofcom classified the two services as web-based portals which provided sexually explicit images and, in the case of Candy Girl Pass, stills as well as audiovisual material.[1694] Thus, users of such websites did not expect AVMS-type regulation.

Succinctly, the two services Candy Girl and Daisy Rock appear to share certain characteristics with UCSC. Daisy Rock is a small-scale service with a limited number of subscribers, viewership and turnover, factors which indicate that the service does not compete for the same audience as linear channels. Nonetheless, it features a promotional claim similar to UCSC and its videos are more stringently catalogued and more easily accessible to users. Candy Girl Productions appears to be different than other adult content websites in that it emphasises interaction between its models and the end-users. It would probably be too far-fetched to qualify it as an art project (a defense which seemed to be accounted for by Ofcom in its *UCSC* appeal decision) but it nonetheless can be differentiated from the presentation and branding of websites like Demand Adult or Playboy TV which prominently display a substantial volume of audiovisual content.

#### e) Panties Pulled Down

Another related case concerned the Panties Pulled Down service, provided by Frank Hollins. ATVOD determined in February 2015 that the service constituted an ODPS for which the provider had failed to notify and pay a fee.[1695] In spite of the short duration of the videos and the lack of credits to cast and crew, ATVOD considered that the videos were comparable to TV-like programmes typically shown on adult TV channels such as XXXCESS.[1696] In addition, ATVOD argued that the principal purpose of the service was the provision of TV-like material because the videos were "a principal benefit of a subscription to the service, representing a greater time commitment on the part of the user".[1697] It recognised that still im-

1693 Ofcom, "Appeal Candy Girl Productions," para. 66, p. 40.

1694 Ofcom, "Appeal Candy Girl Productions," paras. 68, 90, pp. 41, 43–44.

1695 ATVOD, "Determination That the Provider of 'Panties Pulled Down' was in Breach of ATVOD's Rules 1 & 4 and Thereby Has Contravened Sec. 368BA and 368D (3) (ZA) of the Communications Act," February 26, 2015.

1696 ATVOD, "Determination Panties Pulled Down," para. 9.3, p. 3.

1697 ATVOD, "Determination Panties Pulled Down," para. 9.3, p. 4.

ages were offered alongside audiovisual content, both of which were tied by "strong thematic links".[1698] Yet, ATVOD pointed out that a search facility was available only in relation to "movies" (and not for "photos") and that a search yielded the substantial amount of approximately 400 videos.[1699] Since the remaining statutory elements were undisputed, ATVOD categorised the service as an ODPS, a categorisation challenged by the service provider.

On appeal, Ofcom found in favour of the service provider, quashing ATVOD's determination. The appeal decision, published in May 2016, is interesting as it takes into account the CJEU's ruling in *New Media Online*. During the appeal procedure, the service provider had argued that it was primarily non-economic and was intended to raise interest in "glamour photography with the purposes of sharing and exchange within communities of interest".[1700] Importantly, the service did not fulfil the principal purpose test.[1701] This was supported by the limited amount of audiovisual content made available on the website in comparison to other types of material.[1702] In addition, the provider stressed the length of the videos of, on average, nine minutes, and the fact that these treated more or less identical topics lacking a plot, a script, credits or music.[1703] ATVOD, on the other hand, questioned the consistency of Ofcom's decisions, referring in particular to its decision in *Frankie and Friends* where the service was found to be an ODPS.[1704] ATVOD was convinced that the Panties Pulled Down service was similar to the Frankie and Friends service and expressed concerns that different outcomes in the two cases could create uncertainty.[1705] In addition, ATVOD submitted that Ofcom's approach risked creating a loophole for providers of adult content that would merely have

1698 ATVOD, "Determination Panties Pulled Down," para. 9.3, p. 4.
1699 ATVOD, "Determination Panties Pulled Down," para. 9.3, p. 4.
1700 Ofcom, "Appeal by Frank Hollins against a Notice of Determination That the Provider of the service 'Panties Pulled Down' has Contravened Sec. 368BA and 368D (3) (ZA) of the Communications Act" (Broadcast and On Demand Bulletin, Issue 304, May 9, 2016), para. 24d, p. 81.
1701 Ofcom, "Appeal Decision Panties Pulled Down," para. 24, pp. 80–81.
1702 Ofcom, "Appeal Decision Panties Pulled Down," para. 24a, p. 80.
1703 Ofcom, "Appeal Decision Panties Pulled Down," para. 24b, p. 80.
1704 Ofcom, "Appeal Decision Panties Pulled Down," para. 28, p. 81.
1705 Ofcom, "Appeal Decision Panties Pulled Down," paras. 28–30, pp. 81–82.

to ensure that a considerable number of still images, with equal prominence, was offered alongside audiovisual material.[1706]

In its decision, Ofcom focussed on the principal purpose part and appraised the service on the basis of the criteria it had outlined in *Sun Video*. It highlighted the fact that the audiovisual material was neither promoted independently nor was it presented more prominently than the photographic content.[1707] Both types of material were also displayed in parallel on the homepage as well as the sub-pages of the service. Typically, users would access content through the model's pages which featured stills and linked to videos or contained embedded videos.[1708] Ofcom noted that the "degree of integration between the photographic and video content" was stronger than in the Frankie and Friends service where the videos were collated in a standalone section of the website and appeared nowhere else.[1709] In addition, there were no "navigational links" between the audiovisual and non-audiovisual material on the Frankie and Friends website so that a user wishing to access videos would always have to return to the landing page of the service. By contrast, the Panties Pulled Down website simultaneously offered audiovisual and non-audiovisual material on every subsite.[1710]

Furthermore, Ofcom admitted that the videos, in spite of their relatively short duration, were TV-like. They were self-contained and possessed a "basic but complete narrative structure depicting a sexual act until the point of its completion".[1711] The lack of an auto-play function was not determinative on its own.[1712] Ofcom found that the videos could be viewed and understood independently of other material.[1713] The stills did not depict scenes taken from the videos but portrayed similar, though not identical sexual acts.[1714] However, Ofcom stressed that users would have "to navigate to an individual video through an individual model or through a rating awarded by users of the service".[1715] Hence, a user could ordinarily

1706 Ofcom, "Appeal Decision Panties Pulled Down," para. 32, p. 82.
1707 Ofcom, "Appeal Decision Panties Pulled Down," para. 41, pp. 83–84.
1708 Ofcom, "Appeal Decision Panties Pulled Down," para. 43, p. 84.
1709 Ofcom, "Appeal Decision Panties Pulled Down," para. 46, pp. 84–85.
1710 Ofcom, "Appeal Decision Panties Pulled Down," para. 46, p. 85.
1711 Ofcom, "Appeal Decision Panties Pulled Down," para. 47, p. 85.
1712 Ofcom, "Appeal Decision Panties Pulled Down," para. 48, p. 85.
1713 Ofcom, "Appeal Decision Panties Pulled Down," para. 50, p. 86.
1714 Ofcom, "Appeal Decision Panties Pulled Down," para. 49, p. 85.
1715 Ofcom, "Appeal Decision Panties Pulled Down," para. 50, p. 86.

select from a broad range of audiovisual *and* photographic material, both of which were presented equally, without according either one more prominence.[1716] Ofcom therefore considered that "it would be difficult in practice for a user of the website to navigate through the website to view the video content independently of the photographic content".[1717] Given the close links between the types of content disseminated on the website, Ofcom concluded that the audiovisual and photographic material were complementary.[1718] In addition, Ofcom stressed that there was "no threshold" which would mark the point at which a service became an ODPS.[1719] It acknowledged that 400 videos constituted "a substantial offering" which stood next to "a substantial offering of photographic content", both of which were regularly refreshed.[1720]

On overall balance, Ofcom recognised though, that the case "was finely balanced" and several factors spoke in favour of an ODPS with the required principal purpose.[1721] Yet, when assessing the video content in the context of the service as a whole, Ofcom found that it was "not given greater prominence" than the photographic content. Both kinds of material were "distributed evenly" alongside each other and were integrated by "clear links".[1722] Since the types of content were complementary, the video content constituted "one integrated element of the overall offering".[1723] Thus, it did not fulfil an independent function and was not distinct from other content.[1724] This assessment, according to Ofcom though ATVOD disagreed, was in line with the CJEU's judgment in *New Media Online*. The regulator notably referred to the CJEU's requirement of a "substantive approach" in determining whether a service was an ODPS. It also mentioned paragraph 34 of the ruling which exempts from the scope of the AVMSD a service which is "indissociably complementary to the journalistic activity of [a] publisher, in particular as a result of the links between the audiovisual offer and the offer in text form".[1725] Due to the

1716 Ofcom, "Appeal Decision Panties Pulled Down," para. 50, p. 86.
1717 Ofcom, "Appeal Decision Panties Pulled Down," para. 50, p. 86.
1718 Ofcom, "Appeal Decision Panties Pulled Down," para. 50, p. 86.
1719 Ofcom, "Appeal Decision Panties Pulled Down," para. 51, p. 86.
1720 Ofcom, "Appeal Decision Panties Pulled Down," para. 51, p. 86.
1721 Ofcom, "Appeal Decision Panties Pulled Down," para. 54, pp. 86–87.
1722 Ofcom, "Appeal Decision Panties Pulled Down," para. 55, p. 87.
1723 Ofcom, "Appeal Decision Panties Pulled Down," para. 56, p. 87.
1724 Ofcom, "Appeal Decision Panties Pulled Down," para. 56, p. 87.
1725 Ofcom, "Appeal Decision Panties Pulled Down," para. 59, p. 87.

"clear links" between the audiovisual and non-audiovisual material on the Panties Pulled Down service, Ofcom considered that its decision was consistent with the jurisprudence of the CJEU.[1726] Finally, Ofcom acknowledged, in regard to recitals 21 and 24 AVMSD the low membership and low turnover of the service but stressed that these factors did not mean that the service could not be in competition with broadcasting.[1727] On the contrary, Ofcom submitted that the service was capable of reaching a large audience and could thus have a clear impact on a significant proportion of the general public. It therefore considered that the service was an economic activity.[1728] However, Ofcom doubted that the service was in direct competition with adult content screened on TV.[1729] It characterised the service as a "web-based portal for accessing both photographic and/or video content of an adult nature depending on the user's preferences".[1730] It was therefore unlikely that users would expect the same level of regulatory protection as for television broadcasts.[1731] It is interesting to note that Ofcom allayed ATVOD's fear that providers of adult content could easily escape regulation under the CA by including a substantial amount of still images in their services. Ofcom remarked that "websites vary aesthetically – in design, presentation and also in navigation".[1732] It assured ATVOD that any service would be subject to a case-by-case assessment which would take into account all the criteria established in relation to the principal purpose and comparability test.[1733]

In general, the case of *Panties Pulled Down* demonstrates a considerable depth of analysis carried out by Ofcom. The regulator meticulously appraises every aspect of the service in light of the criteria set forth in the *Sun Video* appeal decision. On the one hand, it demonstrates the sincerity and seriousness with which Ofcom fulfils its regulatory function. It is also an expression of the variety of online services characterised by an even greater number of specific qualities and peculiarities. Ofcom's detailed investigation shows that these characteristics are important and can be de-

1726 Ofcom, "Appeal Decision Panties Pulled Down," para. 60, pp. 87–88.
1727 Ofcom, "Appeal Decision Panties Pulled Down," para. 69, p. 89.
1728 Ofcom, "Appeal Decision Panties Pulled Down," para. 69, p. 89.
1729 Ofcom, "Appeal Decision Panties Pulled Down," para. 73, p. 89.
1730 Ofcom, "Appeal Decision Panties Pulled Down," para. 74, p. 89.
1731 Ofcom, "Appeal Decision Panties Pulled Down," para. 74, p. 89.
1732 Ofcom, "Appeal Decision Panties Pulled Down," para. 75, pp. 89–90.
1733 Ofcom, "Appeal Decision Panties Pulled Down," para. 75, pp. 89–90.

cisive in practice for determining the applicable level of regulation. On the other hand, ATVOD's concern about inconsistencies and uncertainties of Ofcom's decision-making does not seem entirely unjustified. What singles out the present case may only hinge on one specific criterion. In *Frankie and Friends*, for instance, Ofcom found that audiovisual material was offered on the same level as photographic material, both of which were catalogued in specific sections of the website. In contrast, the Panties Pulled Down service presented the two types of content alongside each other and did not collate one type in one specific place of the website. The difference in structure had repercussions on the way users accessed and navigated the material: with the catalogue in *Frankie and Friends* and via the individual models' profiles in *Panties Pulled Down*. In the latter case, Ofcom underlined that the user was given a choice between a wide range of photographic as well as audiovisual content, neither of which was attributed greater importance or prominence.

This argument is not very convincing as most websites nowadays contain various types of material such as text-based, photographic and audiovisual, from which the user may select the content he or she is interested in or finds most appealing. Ofcom's assessment therefore seems to centre on the question whether the audiovisual material fulfils an independent function. Due to the apparent links and the complementary nature, Ofcom concluded that the audiovisual material was not independent and thus did not constitute an ODPS. The assessment takes into account recent CJEU case law and it is unclear whether this caused Ofcom to shift its analysis and attribute greater importance to the criterion of "independence" or whether this criterion was coincidentally decisive in the *Panties Pulled Down* case.

### 4. The appropriateness of Ofcom's criteria regarding comparability and principal purpose

The criteria which Ofcom has developed to facilitate both the principal purpose test and the comparability test, take into account the variety of non-linear services and the wide array of business models. They have the flexibility to apply to a service under investigation and allow the regulators to take note of particularities pertaining to the service itself or developments in the sector. The criteria construed for the comparability test appear reasonable and reflect typical characteristics of TV programmes such as professionally made longer-format programmes including opening or closing credits, uniform voice-over, the use of music and staging. Above all, the existence of a narrative spanning the entire programme is a significant element of linear programmes, distinguishing them from short, incomplete and disjointed clips. It seems reasonable and in line with recital 21 AVMSD to exempt from regulation any small-scale provider of a website who makes available brief (possibly self-made) clips. The earlier set of cases from *Channel Flip* to *Viva TV Music* and *Everton TV* seem homogenous and consistent, giving clear indications to service providers. Yet, later cases such as *UCSC*, *Daisy Rock UK* and *Candy Girl Productions* suggest less clear-cut outcomes. The criteria themselves are qualitative in nature. The longer duration of programmes is evidently reminiscent of television broadcasting. Yet, Ofcom refrains from specifying an exact length (understandably so) which would clearly set apart short clips from television programmes. On the one hand, regulators retain some flexibility in adapting the criteria to new business models and new types of services. On the other hand, a grey zone will remain at the brink of each criterion (e.g. the shorter a video becomes), and will adversely affect legal certainty. This oscillating state is facilitated, among others, by the underlying trend of media convergence which seems to clash with any possibility of an exhaustive list of TV-like characteristics. It is thus for the regulators to reduce the grey zone surrounding the criteria through a coherent body of practice.

With respect to the principal purpose test, ATVOD did not appear to precisely follow Ofcom's framework. Tellingly, ATVOD neither enumerated nor appraised the whole range of criteria (with the exception of its determination in *Vice Video*) outlined by Ofcom. The absence of any uniform analytical pattern underlying ATVOD's determinations resembles cherry-picking rather than a systematic approach. ATVOD also turned around the two-prong statutory test by virtue of Sec. 368A (1) (a) CA in that it first assessed comparability and only in a second step moved on to the principal purpose part. While the order could be considered negligible, a major defect in the application of these criteria is their lack of foreseeability and clarity.

Even now that Ofcom has regained its regulatory powers over VOD services, the test essentially remains a very subjective exercise which is contingent on the regulators' interpretation. Ofcom has refrained from establishing an internal hierarchy of criteria, attributing equal weighting to each factor. Repeatedly, Ofcom has reiterated that none of the criteria are determinative on their own but that they are at best indicative of a service falling under the statutory definition of Sec. 368A (1) (a) CA. Ofcom has not signalled that it will affirm the TV-like quality of a service merely on the basis of it adhering to a *majority* of indicators. Such a quantitative approach does not appear to be favoured nor employed by Ofcom. Rather, the regulator conducts an assessment, carefully weighing each indicator individually before analysing all indicators jointly. So the most pertinent question is this: when will the "'tipping point' [be] reached at which the video elements are no longer ancillary but become the principal purpose of the overall service"?[1734] The answer is far from simple and may even bear the risk of over- or under-regulation, as Katsirea remarks.[1735] Ofcom's qualitative approach, albeit recognising the uniqueness of each service and fact pattern of a particular adjudication, is, however, highly uncertain and disadvantageous for those primarily affected by regulation. Katsirea points out that "Ofcom's holistic approach makes it hard to predict the mixture that would bring a hybrid service within the scope of regulation".[1736]

Cases ranging from *Sun Video* to *Vice Video* also highlight the fundamental differences between ATVOD and Ofcom. While ATVOD seemed to follow the letter of the law in a "strict regulatory approach",[1737] Ofcom has pursued a liberal, market-oriented agenda in line with its statutory mandate.[1738] ATVOD was still new to the game when the *Sun Video* appeal decision was rendered and sought to delineate its remit, and potentially to even expand it.[1739] Its genesis from self-regulator to co-regulator may have influenced its actions which in retrospect appear as seeking to protect the core industry of VOD providers (offering "classical type" non-linear services like catch-up or pay per view) which entered into flux when providers of online newspapers and magazines began integrating increasing quantities of audiovisual content into their websites and which for their part are facing increasing competition from Internet services expand-

1734 Katsirea, "Electronic Press: 'Press-Like' or 'Television-Like'?," p. 21.
1735 Katsirea, "Electronic Press: 'Press-Like' or 'Television-Like'?," p. 22.
1736 Katsirea, "Electronic Press: 'Press-Like' or 'Television-Like'?," p. 21.
1737 Katsirea, "Electronic Press: 'Press-Like' or 'Television-Like'?," p. 20.
1738 Metzdorf, "Regulierung Der Elektronischen Presse in Großbritannien? Ein Anwendungsbeispiel Zum Erwägungsgrund 28 Der AVMD-RL," p. 511.
1739 Katsirea posits, however that ATVOD's "decision was not simply a mistake made by a co-regulator still in its infancy" but that "it was a perfectly defensible position, reflecting a belief in the need for more regulation of the online press". See Katsirea, "Electronic Press: 'Press-Like' or 'Television-Like'?," p. 20.

ing into the audiovisual realm (such as YouTube[1740] or other social networking sites like Twitter or Facebook). This was in stark contrast to the direction taken by Ofcom, as the UK communications regulator seems to have been mindful of the concerns of the press about being subordinated to regulation. Against the background of the phone-hacking scandal in 2011 which implicated the News of the World and triggered the 2012 Leveson inquiry into the "Culture, Practice and Ethics of the Press",[1741] the press sector in the UK has been in a deuce of a stir. Any indications of the expansion of broadcast regulation (or its lesser counterpart applicable to on-demand services) to the press sector would have met with fundamental opposition.[1742] Ofcom gives the impression of having taken a policy decision to prevent ATVOD from extending its regulatory arm towards providers of online newspapers and magazines. If one were to take it to extremes, the reliance on a range of criteria to determine principal purpose offers Ofcom a pragmatic instrument whereby it could always deny TV-likeness of a service. Admittedly, this does not give justice to Ofcom's thorough assessments of the nature of services and the fulfilment of its statutory duty. Moreover, Ofcom does not operate in a legal vacuum and its decisions are subject to public scrutiny and to a great extent dictated by the vague and ambivalent wording of the AVMSD, encompassing the substantive provisions as well as relevant recitals.

Finally, an observation may be made regarding the length of the proceedings before UK regulators when the co-regulatory scheme was in place, especially the appeal stage. In a number of cases covered in this

---

1740 Limor Peer and Thomas Ksiazek, "Youtube and the Challenge to Journalism, New Standards for News Videos Online," *Journalism Studies* 12, no. 1 (2011): p. 47.

1741 The Leveson Inquiry, see http://webarchive.nationalarchives.gov.uk/20140122145147/http:/www.levesoninquiry.org.uk/. The report by Leveson published on 29.11.2012 entitled "An inquiry into the culture, practices and ethics of the press" is available at http://webarchive.nationalarchives.gov.uk/20140122145147/http://www.official-documents.gov.uk/document/hc1213/hc07/0780/0780.asp (all websites accessed 29.4.2015).

1742 This is underlined by the number of submissions by representatives of the press sector to ATVOD's modified scope guidance which heavily opposed any expansion of ATVOD's powers to online newspapers and magazines. See ATVOD, "Statement on the Adoption of New Guidance on the Scope of the Regulations Relating to Video On-Demand Services," May 2, 2014, p. paras. 3.9-3.15, 4.9-4.17, pp. 7-9, 12-14; see also Katsirea, "Electronic Press: 'Press-Like' or 'Television-Like'?," p. 8.

chapter, Ofcom took an exceedingly long time (between one and one and a half years) before rendering its decision.[1743] Although the procedures for handling appeals of ATVOD's determinations do not refer to a strict time frame, Ofcom committed to managing a case within 60 days.[1744] This caused serious time lags between ATVOD's determination and Ofcom's review on appeal. During this time, service providers were left in limbo, uncertain about the legal nature of their service. And in a number of cases, service providers used this time to modify their services in such a way that they would unmistakably escape the scope of ATVOD's powers or alternatively comply with the content standards for non-linear services (e.g. protection of minors). When the co-regulatory regime was ended, Ofcom committed to expediting procedures and its revised breach procedures illustrate this commitment.[1745]

### 5. Editorial responsibility

By virtue of Sec. 368A (1) (c) CA, an ODPS is provided if a person can be identified as bearing editorial responsibility. Pursuant to sub-Sec. (4), the notion of editorial control implies general control over the selection and organisation of programmes. To this end, the person who is editorially responsible is not required to have control over individual programmes. The following section sketches the cases of *Viacom channels content on Virgin Media*, *BBCW on Mediaset* and *Viacom channels on Sky Anytime* to shed light on the regulators' understanding of editorial responsibility. These are cases in which broadcasters cooperated with providers of portals to offer their TV programmes on-demand.

---

1743 The appeal proceedings in *Everton TV* and *Frankie and Friends* took approximately one year, in the case of *Channel Flip* a year and a half. In the *Vice Video* case, Ofcom took almost two years to decide on appeal. The considerable delay in this case may be explained by the fact that the Austrian case *New Media Online* was referred to the CJEU for preliminary ruling in July 2014 (C-347/14) requesting interpretation of Art. 1 (1) (a) and (b) AVMSD.

1744 Ofcom, "Procedures for Handling Appeals of ATVOD Scope Determinations," para. 1.23.

1745 Ofcom, "ODPS Procedures for Investigating Breaches".

### a) Analysis of contractual terms allocating editorial responsibility: Viacom channels content on Virgin Media

In three essentially identical determinations in July 2011, ATVOD found that it was not the content aggregator or the platform provider Virgin Media which was editorially responsible for Nickelodeon, Comedy Central and MTV content (Viacom channels) but that editorial responsibility lay with the individual service providers.[1746] To this end, ATVOD examined the contracts between Virgin Media and the three content providers which explicitly allocated editorial responsibility to the latter. ATVOD affirmed that the content providers selected the programmes (providing an "avails list") from which Virgin Media was entitled to select individual items. With regards to the organisation of programmes, ATVOD acknowledged that, in parallel to the content providers, Virgin Media executed a degree of responsibility through branding but that the content providers supplied the marketing, promotional materials as well as the metadata accompanying the programmes (e.g. viewing information to be included in EPGs). Nickelodeon, Comedy Central and MTV appealed to Ofcom which upheld ATVOD's determinations in a joint decision of January 2012.[1747] Ofcom clarified that only one person could have editorial control by virtue of Sec. 368R (5) CA read in conjunction with Sec. 368A (1) (c) and (4) CA.[1748] Yet, it did point out that it was "conceivable that more than one party [had] a role in determining the range of programmes offered and the orga-

1746 ATVOD, "Determination That Nickelodeon UK Ltd Is the Provider of the On Demand Programme Service Nickelodeon Content on Virgin Media," June 7, 2011; ATVOD, "Determination That Paramount UK Partnership, Trading as Comedy Central Is the Provider of the On Demand Programme Service Comedy Central Content on Virgin Media," June 7, 2011; ATVOD, "Determination That MTV Networks Europe Is the Provider of the On Demand Programme Service MTV Content on Virgin Media," June 7, 2011.

1747 Ofcom, "Appeal by (1) Nickelodeon UK Limited (in Relation to Nickelodeon Content on Virgin Mary); (2) Paramount (UK) Partnership (in Relation to Comedy Central Content on Virgin Media); and (3) MTV Networks Europe (in Relation to MTV Content on Virgin Media) against a Notice of Determination by ATVOD That the Services Have Contravened Section 368BA of the Communications Act 2003," January 18, 2012.

1748 Ofcom, "Appeal Decision Viacom Channels Content on Virgin Media," para. 35, p. 9.

nisation within that range".[1749] In order to settle any ambiguities, Ofcom approved ATVOD's approach of examining the contractual relations between the parties as primary evidence.[1750] Ofcom even encouraged service providers to resort to "clear contractual wording" to allocate editorial responsibility.[1751] Except for cases where contractual clauses had been designed to allocate editorial control "where it plainly [did] not lie", one could assume that the parties' intention was reflected in the agreement they concluded and that "their relationship should operate as clearly stated on the face of the contract".[1752] Since the three content providers had not provided "strong and compelling evidence" that the wording of the contract countered the parties' intentions, Ofcom considered their contracts as decisive for the purpose of determining editorial responsibility.[1753] Consequently, Ofcom held that both, the content providers as well as Virgin Media played a role in the selection of programmes.[1754] The three content providers established lists of programmes from which Virgin Media could select specific items.[1755]

With respect to the organisation of the programmes, Virgin Media arranged the content it gathered from different providers in a consistent and uniform manner on its platform.[1756] Nonetheless, the data that allowed Virgin Media to organise the material was provided by the content providers.[1757] In addition, the source of the programmes was clearly indicated and content providers were referenced in the overall catalogue (a

---

1749 Ofcom, "Appeal Decision Viacom Channels Content on Virgin Media," para. 35, p. 9.
1750 Ofcom, "Appeal Decision Viacom Channels Content on Virgin Media," para. 35, p. 9.
1751 Ofcom, "Appeal Decision Viacom Channels Content on Virgin Media," para. 35, p. 9.
1752 Ofcom, "Appeal Decision Viacom Channels Content on Virgin Media," para. 37, p. 9.
1753 Ofcom, "Appeal Decision Viacom Channels Content on Virgin Media," para. 40, p. 10.
1754 Ofcom, "Appeal Decision Viacom Channels Content on Virgin Media," para. 41a., p. 10.
1755 Ofcom, "Appeal Decision Viacom Channels Content on Virgin Media," para. 41a., p. 10.
1756 Ofcom, "Appeal Decision Viacom Channels Content on Virgin Media," para. 40b., p. 10.
1757 Ofcom, "Appeal Decision Viacom Channels Content on Virgin Media," para. 40b., p. 10.

search function by content provider was included).[1758] Thus, Ofcom consented that the content providers rather than the platform provider bore unfettered editorial responsibility. While assignment of editorial control seemed a relatively straightforward matter in *Nickelodeon/Comedy Central/MTV content on Virgin Media* due to the express formulations in the contract, the later cases are more complex. Ofcom specified in subsequent decisions concerning *BBC Worldwide on Mediaset (BBCW on Mediaset)* and the *Viacom Channel providers' content on the Sky Anytime platform (Viacom channels on Sky Anytime)* that the practice and conduct of the parties should be assessed if the provisions of the contract were ambivalent.[1759]

#### b) Analysis of other contractual terms and parties' conduct: BBCW on Mediaset and Viacom channels on Sky Anytime

In *BBCW on Mediaset,* ATVOD opined in a determination of May 2011 that according to several of the contract's provisions, BBCW bore editorial control over the selection of BBCW programmes on the Italian Mediaset platform.[1760] ATVOD rejected BBCW's assertion that in practice Mediaset organised the programmes, referring to the "clear facility in the contract for BBCW to have final say over the organisation of its content".[1761] Ofcom, however, overruled ATVOD on appeal finding in a decision dated April 2012 that BBCW did not have general control within the meaning of Sec. 368A (1) (c) CA. Ofcom distinguished between "(1) editorial responsibility for a service, based on general control from an editorial perspec-

---

1758 Ofcom, "Appeal Decision Viacom Channels Content on Virgin Media," para. 40b., p. 10.

1759 Ofcom, "Appeal by BBC Worldwide against a Notice of Determination by ATVOD That the Service BBC Worldwide on Mediaset Has Contravened Section 368BA of the Communications Act 2003," April 27, 2012, para. 32, p. 11; Ofcom, "Appeal by BSKYB against a Notice of Determination by ATVOD That the Service Viacom Channel Providers' on the Sky Anytime Platform Has Contravened Sections 368BA and 368D (3) (ZA) of the Communications Act 2003," December 7, 2012, para. 39, p. 19.

1760 ATVOD, "Determination That the Provider of the Service Named BBC Worldwide on Mediaset Has Contravened Sec. 368BA and Sec. 368D (3) (ZA) of the Communications Act," 05 2011.

1761 ATVOD, "Scope Determination BBC Worldwide on Mediaset.".

tive over what programmes are actually included in a range of programmes offered to users and the way they are organised in that range; and (2) control of the content of individual programmes".[1762] Ofcom found that BBCW provided a collection of non-linear programmes which Mediaset was entitled to include in whole, in part or not at all in the service.[1763] Ofcom posited that Mediaset generally organised the content it selected from the material provided by BBCW.[1764] It distilled this finding from several provisions of the contract noting that both parties intended for Mediaset to have "more of the kind of general control" referred to in Sec. 368A (1) (c) CA.[1765] This was supported by the fact that it was Mediaset which had notified its service where it was established, i.e. to the Italian regulator AGCOM and thus assumed editorial responsibility.[1766]

Similarly, in *Viacom channels on Sky Anytime* ATVOD had determined in January 2012 that Sky "on balance" had "a greater degree of control" and thus held editorial responsibility for the content made available by Nickelodeon, Comedy Central and MTV.[1767] The careful phrasing by ATVOD and the reference to a "finely balanced decision" reveal the complexities of precisely allocating editorial responsibility and seem to signal the co-regulator's unease with its own determination. According to ATVOD, Sky controlled the selection of programmes and determined what to include in the service.[1768] Although ATVOD acknowledged that Sky's position in this respect was constrained by technical considerations of platform capacity.[1769] With regards to the organisation of programmes, ATVOD recognised that the Viacom channels provided the relevant metadata. Yet, by looking at the agreement between Sky and the Viacom channels, ATVOD concluded that Sky had control over the marketing and pre-

1762 Ofcom, "Appeal Decision BBC Worldwide on Mediaset," para. 42b., p. 15.
1763 Ofcom, "Appeal Decision BBC Worldwide on Mediaset," para. 43, p. 16.
1764 Ofcom, "Appeal Decision BBC Worldwide on Mediaset," para. 43, p. 16.
1765 Ofcom, "Appeal Decision BBC Worldwide on Mediaset," paras. 44, 46, p. 16.
1766 Ofcom, "Appeal Decision BBC Worldwide on Mediaset," para. 50, p. 18.
1767 ATVOD, "Determination That the Provider of the Service Named Viacom Channel Providers' Content on the Sky Anytime Platform Has Contravened Sec. 368BA and Sec. 368D (3) (ZA) of the Communications Act," January 23, 2012.
1768 ATVOD, "Scope Determination Viacom Channel Providers' Content on the Sky Anytime Platform," para. 5.4.
1769 ATVOD, "Scope Determination Viacom Channel Providers' Content on the Sky Anytime Platform," para. 5.5.

sentation of each channel on the Sky Anytime platform.[1770] This was bolstered by the fact that the "Anytime" branding (e.g. logo) was depicted prominently in comparison to the display of the channel information.[1771] Importantly, this determination was handed down before Ofcom clarified the interpretation of the notion of editorial responsibility in its appeal decision in the *BBCW on Mediaset* case. For this reason Ofcom decided on appeal to quash the initial determination and remit it back to ATVOD for reconsideration in light of the approach outlined in the *Viacom channels on Virgin Media* and *BBCW on Mediaset* decisions.[1772] At the beginning of October 2012, ATVOD published three similarly worded determinations applying Ofcom's approach.[1773] In the absence of any contractual wording expressly addressing editorial responsibility, ATVOD turned to other clauses of the agreement which specified the parties' intention in this regard.[1774] For ATVOD, the provisions assigned editorial responsibility to the Viacom channels.[1775] Since they provided sufficient proof, it was not necessary for ATVOD to look at the parties' practice or at other evidence. Notwithstanding, ATVOD answered the question of whether the parties had allocated editorial responsibility "where it plainly [did] not lie in reali-

1770 ATVOD, "Scope Determination Viacom Channel Providers' Content on the Sky Anytime Platform," para. 5.11.

1771 ATVOD, "Scope Determination Viacom Channel Providers' Content on the Sky Anytime Platform," para. 5.13.

1772 Ofcom, "Appeal Decision Viacom Channel Providers' on the Sky Anytime Platform," paras. 32, 45, pp. 16–21.

1773 ATVOD, "Determination That Nickelodeon UK Ltd Is the Provider of the On-Demand Programme Service Nickelodeon on Sky Anytime," March 10, 2012; ATVOD, "Determination That Paramount UK Partnership Trading as Comedy Central Is the Provider of the On-Demand Programme Service Comedy Central on Sky Anytime," March 10, 2012; ATVOD, "Determination That MTV Networks Europe Is the Provider of the On-Demand Programme Service MTV on Sky Anytime," March 10, 2012.

1774 ATVOD, "Scope Determination Nickelodeon Content on Sky Anytime," paras. 5.7-5.8; ATVOD, "Scope Determination Comedy Central Content on Sky Anytime," paras. 5.7-5.8; ATVOD, "Scope Determination MTV Content on Sky Anytime," paras. 5.7-5.8.

1775 ATVOD, "Scope Determination Nickelodeon Content on Sky Anytime," para. 5.9; ATVOD, "Scope Determination Comedy Central Content on Sky Anytime," para. 5.9; ATVOD, "Scope Determination MTV Content on Sky Anytime," para. 5.9.

ty" in the negative.[1776] Although ATVOD's second assessment in its determinations of October 2012 appears very succinct, it is consistent with Ofcom's approach.

Interestingly, the tone of Ofcom's decision is amicable, almost forgiving, explaining that ATVOD could not have taken Ofcom's approach into account as the latter's appeal decision in *BBCW on Mediaset* was only published in the aftermath of ATVOD's analysis of the case.[1777] Consequently, Ofcom did not substitute its decision for that of ATVOD as it had done on previous occasions but instead trusted that ATVOD, as the appropriate co-regulatory body at the material time, had reconsidered its assessment in light of the specifications made by Ofcom in the meantime. The result of ATVOD's second assessment is therefore not surprising given the hints Ofcom had dropped in the appeal decision.[1778] Although Ofcom refrained from correcting ATVOD's initial position, it is unquestionable that Ofcom considered the Viacom channel providers as bearing editorial responsibility by virtue of certain contractual clauses.[1779] And when ATVOD evaluated the matter for a second time, it was with a clear outcome in mind. Strikingly, ATVOD did not pinpoint the contractual provisions which underline its assessment but only abstractly referred to "other clauses in the Agreement".[1780] In the interest of clarity and transparency, it would have been preferable to specifically mention the concrete wording of said provisions.

---

1776 ATVOD, "Scope Determination Nickelodeon Content on Sky Anytime," para. 5.10; ATVOD, "Scope Determination Comedy Central Content on Sky Anytime," para. 5.10; ATVOD, "Scope Determination MTV Content on Sky Anytime," para. 5.10.

1777 Ofcom, "Appeal Decision Viacom Channel Providers' on the Sky Anytime Platform", see in particular para. 5, p. 2, para. 32, p. 16, para. 41, p. 20.

1778 Ofcom, "Appeal Decision Viacom Channel Providers' on the Sky Anytime Platform," para. 40, p. 20.

1779 Ofcom, "Appeal Decision Viacom Channel Providers' on the Sky Anytime Platform," paras. 40–41, p. 20.

1780 Ofcom, "Appeal Decision Top Gear YouTube," para. 32, p. 11; ATVOD, "Scope Determination Comedy Central Content on Sky Anytime," para. 5.8; ATVOD, "Scope Determination Nickelodeon Content on Sky Anytime," para. 5.8; ATVOD, "Scope Determination MTV Content on Sky Anytime," para. 5.8.

### c) Appropriateness of Ofcom's criteria regarding editorial responsibility

Through the various cases discussed above, a step-by-step test to assign editorial responsibility has crystallised. This schema originally constructed by Ofcom in its appeal decisions has been reproduced in ATVOD's/now Ofcom's guidance. Thus, the first step is to identify parties' intentions, by considering "whether there is contractual wording which expressly contemplates editorial responsibility".[1781] "In the absence of [such] wording", at a second stage, "other terms of any relevant contract (and as to the intentions they disclose)" are examined.[1782] If editorial responsibility still cannot be unequivocally attributed, the parties' "agreed conduct and practice"[1783] are examined in third place, and in a last step, "other evidence of the position in practice" is considered.[1784] In general, the assessment of contractual clauses seems a good starting point to determine the person with editorial responsibility. It seems unrealistic that parties to an agreement would deliberately wrongly attribute editorial responsibility. This would frustrate the relationship of trust between contractual parties and might even destroy the very reasons for entering into a contract as the interests of a party might no longer be sufficiently safeguarded. It cannot, however, be totally ruled out that both parties could gain from falsely allocating editorial responsibility. Thus, the gradual approach outlined by Ofcom appears reasonable. Yet, with every step of the analysis, the regulators dispose of a greater margin of discretion. Economic operators having the foresight to address the issue of editorial responsibility by unambiguous contractual formulations may be well served by this approach. The inclusion of the test in ATVOD's guidance may also incentivise providers to

1781 Ofcom, "Appeal Decision Top Gear YouTube," para. 32, p. 11; ATVOD, "Guidance on Who Needs to Notify, Application and Scope of the Regulations for Video on Demand (VOD) Services, Edition 4.0," May 2, 2014, para. 4.4a, p. 12; Ofcom, "Who Needs to Notify, Guidance Notes on Who Needs to Notify an on-Demand Programme Service to Ofcom," December 18, 2015, para. 4.4, p. 12, http://stakeholders.ofcom.org.uk/binaries/broadcast/on-demand/rules-guidance/Guidance_on_who_needs_to_notify.pdf (accessed 13.1.2016).

1782 ATVOD, "Guidance on Who Needs to Notify," para. 4.4d, p. 13; Ofcom, "Guidance on Notification Requirement," para. 4.4, p. 12.

1783 ATVOD, "Guidance on Who Needs to Notify," para. 4.4c, p. 13; Ofcom, "Guidance on Notification Requirement," para. 4.4, p. 12.

1784 ATVOD, "Guidance on Who Needs to Notify," para. 4.4d, p. 13; Ofcom, "Guidance on Notification Requirement," para. 4.4, p. 12.

clarify editorial responsibility contractually. To assume that all operators would settle the issue in this manner would, however, fall short of reality. The interpretation of contractual wording which only implicitly allocates editorial responsibility is less straight forward. Finally, the analysis of the conduct habitually exposed by parties to the dispute appears even more ambivalent and open to subjectivity. Future cases might give indications as to how to apply the third and fourth steps in practice. In spite of Ofcom's clear guidance as to the objects to be assessed, the notion of editorial responsibility remains blurry in the absence of any direct or indirect contractual references.

## IV. The guidance by the UK regulators

This section details the UK regulators' guidance in relation to the concept of an ODPS. ATVOD's guidance is still valid and has been integrated in Ofcom's guidance notes.

### 1. ATVOD guidance on who needs to notify

As co-regulator for non-linear services, ATVOD drew up a document on "guidance on who needs to notify" (scope guidance).[1785] The scope guidance interpreted the statutory requirements stipulated in Sec. 368A (1) CA which defines an ODPS. Following a public consultation between mid-September and mid-December 2013, the scope guidance was adopted on 5 February 2014, after ATVOD had also consulted with Ofcom. Accompanying the scope guidance, ATVOD published a statement in which it summarised the contributions of the eleven stakeholders that had participated as well as ATVOD's response.[1786] In general, the scope guidance was, to a great extent, derived from relevant appeal decisions taken by Ofcom. It

1785 In parallel to guidance specific to scope, ATVOD issued guidance on the statutory requirements applicable to ODPS. Confer ATVOD, "Rules and Guidance for Providers of ODPS.".

1786 Interestingly, five (almost half of the) representations were submitted by providers affiliated to newspapers and magazines (including publishers like the Telegraph or the Guardian and trade associations) demonstrating that the question of whether or not online versions of newspapers or magazines are regulated by ATVOD is of crucial concern to the printed press. In response to these

mirrored the outcome of the cases adjudicated and explicated the essential points for stakeholders. The scope guidance in a way "codified" the regulators' practice and outlined ATVOD's approach when investigating services raising concerns under scope. To this effect, the scope guidance enhanced transparency of ATVOD's conduct of its evaluations and how it was likely to interpret the statutory rules.[1787] It was also beneficial for service providers who sought explanations in order to determine the precise nature of their service. Nonetheless, the scope guidance remained non-binding and it was for service providers to consider whether they were within or outside of scope.[1788] ATVOD made clear that either the entire offering or a part thereof might constitute an ODPS, so that in fact one media outlet (e.g. a website) might host several services which could be regulated differently.[1789]

The cumulative criteria defining an ODPS were "interpreted purposively in line with the [AVMSD]",[1790] in short, services offering primarily audiovisual material which was television-like (not identical to television programmes).[1791] ATVOD retained the order of analysis as in its determinations, focussing firstly on the comparability test and secondly on the principal purpose test. It thereby derogated from the schema applied by Ofcom. The factors which increased TV-likeness were the insertion of opening and closing titles or credit sequences (structuring content in dif-

representations, ATVOD clarified that it did not intend to expand regulation into the realm of the online press. It reiterated the most important findings of Ofcom in Sun Video and pointed out that Ofcom had not ruled out that a service which also provided an online newspaper or magazine could fall under ATVOD's remit. As a result, ATVOD modified the proposed new scope guidance by expressly including the statement on electronic versions of newspapers and magazines (para. 3.11 of scope guidance) which it had omitted in the draft scope guidance. See ATVOD, "Statement on Scope Guidance," paras. 3.9-3.15, 4.9-4-17, pp. 7-9, 12-14.

1787 ATVOD, "Guidance on Who Needs to Notify," para. 1.1, p. 3. In order to facilitate provider's self- assessment, the scope guidance contains a flowchart of the individual steps of the analysis and several examples of non-linear services (pp. 4-5).

1788 ATVOD, "Guidance on Who Needs to Notify," paras. 1.2-1.3, p. 3.

1789 ATVOD, "Guidance on Who Needs to Notify," para. 2.5, pp. 5–6.

1790 Particular weight is attributed to recital 24 AVMSD in this context. ATVOD, "Guidance on Who Needs to Notify," para. 3.2, p. 7. The scope guidance also clarifies that the notion of "economic activity" is interpreted broadly in light of the AVMSD (para. 2.4, pp.5-6).

1791 ATVOD, "Guidance on Who Needs to Notify," paras. 3.4-3.6, p. 7.

ferent programmes with "separate identity"), the use of "presenters, voiceover, commentary and/or captions", provision of complete, self-contained programmes based on a "dramatic conceit and/or a narrative arc to convey an idea, analogy or theme, to have a structure of acts and scenes in which a story, theme or sustained purpose is maintained and conveyed and within which there are dramatic or narrative developments", "longer-format programmes" or the use of playlist options and the inclusion of advertisements or programmes previously broadcast on TV.[1792]

Furthermore, ATVOD outlined a list of non-cumulative and non-exhaustive criteria, none of which were determinative on their own but had to be appraised together. Factors indicative of principal purpose were the existence of a "point of entry that is styled as providing, and in practice does provide, a service with its own independent identity", the aggregation of audiovisual material in a distinct area "presented as a catalogue of viewing options which could exist as a coherent consumer offering if removed from the broader service", content links between audiovisual material and other content, the prominence of the audiovisual material in terms of "branding and structure" as well as "presentation and organisation" and the high volume of audiovisual content in terms of "absolute numbers and viewing time" (considering whether the audiovisual material constituted "the key benefit of a subscription").[1793] Moreover, if the video content were consumed separately in order to "receive the information, education or entertainment" ("which content is the primary means of conveying the information sought to be conveyed?") or if the audiovisual material was provided on a stand-alone basis (taking into account the "duration, completeness and independence of the video material and the proportion it comprises"), it was more likely that the offering would satisfy the principal purpose test. In view of the great number of adjudications concerning online newspapers and magazines and the responses of publishers and trade unions to the consultation preceding the revised scope guidance, the scope guidance made express reference to such services. ATVOD underlined that they might be caught by Sec. 368A CA in spite of recital 28 AVMSD denying their TV-like quality. To this end, ATVOD distinguished between "an online newspaper offering video reports which supplement and sit alongside text based news stories" and would fall outside of

1792 ATVOD, "Guidance on Who Needs to Notify," para. 3.9, p. 8.
1793 ATVOD, "Guidance on Who Needs to Notify," para. 3.11, p. 9.

ATVOD's remit and "an online newspaper giving over a distinct section of its website to TV like programmes which have no clear and direct link to the broader 'newspaper' offering and which could exist as a stand-alone service" which could be caught by the statutory definition of an ODPS.[1794] This reflects Ofcom's appeal decisions notably in *Sun Video*.

The scope guidance further explained the statutory requirement outlined in Sec. 368A (1) (b) CA and further refined in its sub-section (2) that access to the service was on-demand.[1795] ATVOD indicated that the service was transmitted over electronic communications networks encompassing the "selection, downloading and viewing of a movie via the internet".[1796] It was irrelevant whether content was streamed, downloaded for rental purposes or downloaded for purchase.[1797] In addition, the scope guidance contained extensive explanations on the requirement that a person had editorial responsibility pursuant to Sec. 368A (1) (c) CA. ATVOD stressed that *one* person had to exercise editorial responsibility. In the absence of any person bearing such responsibility, the service was not qualified as an on-demand programme service.[1798] Editorial responsibility might also be split between different parties (for instance in case of an aggregated service)[1799] each of which might have "some editorial role".[1800] Importantly, Sec. 368A (1) (c) CA required that one party is identified who bears editorial responsibility within the meaning of the CA. This provision underlay the presumption that the service characterised as "mass media"[1801] was made available to the general public in line with Sec. 368A (1) (d) CA.[1802] The notion of mass media encompassed the dissemination of "highly specialised or non-mainstream" material targeting small groups (e.g. minority

1794 ATVOD, "Guidance on Who Needs to Notify," para. 3.13, p. 10.

1795 ATVOD, "Guidance on Who Needs to Notify," para. 3.14, p. 10.

1796 ATVOD, "Guidance on Who Needs to Notify," para. 3.16, p. 10.

1797 ATVOD, "Guidance on Who Needs to Notify," para. 3.17, p. 10. To ATVOD, programmes streamed in linear fashion including those deploying a pause or live restart function are subject to the rules for broadcasting (para. 3.19, p. 10).

1798 ATVOD, "Guidance on Who Needs to Notify," para. 3.21, p. 11.

1799 ATVOD, "Guidance on Who Needs to Notify," para. 3.23, p. 11.

1800 ATVOD, "Guidance on Who Needs to Notify," para. 4.3, p. 12. Content providers may be considered to have editorial responsibility even if a third party is involved in distributing the service (e.g. via a platform) (para. 3.27, p. 11-12).

1801 This characterisation may be distilled from recital 21 AVMSD. ATVOD, "Guidance on Who Needs to Notify," para. 3.25, p. 11.

1802 The notion of making available to the general public includes subscription-based services. ATVOD, "Guidance on Who Needs to Notify," para. 3.24, p. 11.

sports or pornographic content).[1803] To determine the reach of a service, it was considered whether the service was "capable of being seen by, and having a clear impact on, a significant proportion of the general public".[1804] By virtue of Sec. 368A (4) (a) and (b) CA editorial control implied the exercise of general control over the selection of programmes and their organisation. On the basis of Ofcom's appeal decisions, in particular in *BBCW on Mediaset* and *Viacom channels on Sky Anytime* from which the wording was literally transferred to the scope guidance, ATVOD applied a phased approach for determining the identity of the person with editorial responsibility. What is more, ATVOD clearly warned service providers not to use contractual clauses to attribute editorial responsibility "where it plainly does not lie in reality".[1805]

The scope guidance additionally referred to situations where numerous parties were involved, stating that a person may have editorial responsibility for a service without necessarily having control over individual programmes or the distribution of a service.[1806] What is more, general control over the selection of programmes was defined as "decision-making on which individual programmes [were] included in the service and not on the choice of whole 'channels' of content".[1807] Accordingly, general control over the organisation of programmes implied control over "the relevant viewing information provided alongside the on-demand programme" such as a summary of the programme, additional information to rate and classify programmes or apply other content warnings.[1808] In this respect, the scope guidance referred to a platform operator for illustration purposes and clarified that it was not sufficient that a person decided on the "design, branding or look and feel of the catalogue" or the provision of technical measures (e.g. restrictions on sexually explicit content).[1809] Similarly, in case of a content aggregator that makes available several services, various providers of content could retain editorial control over their service or al-

1803 ATVOD, "Guidance on Who Needs to Notify," para. 3.25, p. 11.

1804 ATVOD, "Guidance on Who Needs to Notify," para. 3.25, p. 11.

1805 ATVOD, "Guidance on Who Needs to Notify," para. 4.5, p. 13.

1806 ATVOD, "Guidance on Who Needs to Notify," para. 4.6a, p. 13. See also Sec. 368A (4) (b) CA.

1807 ATVOD, "Guidance on Who Needs to Notify," para. 4.6b, p. 13.

1808 ATVOD, "Guidance on Who Needs to Notify," para. 4.6c, p. 13. It is, however, not sufficient to identify the provider of metadata for the purpose of attributing general control over the organisation of programmes.

1809 ATVOD, "Guidance on Who Needs to Notify," para. 4.6d, pp. 13–14.

ternatively, the content aggregator was responsible for all (or only a part of the) services it groups together.[1810]

With regards to the final statutory requirement, Sec. 368A (1) (e) CA specified that the "person [was] under the jurisdiction of the [UK] for the purposes of the [AVMSD]". This provision explicitly referred to the AVMSD, more specifically the criteria to determining jurisdiction set out in Art. 2 AVMSD.[1811] If the provider deemed all statutory requirements to be fulfilled, the service would have to be notified in advance of its provision.[1812] ATVOD noted that providers offering audiovisual content through multiple outlets might make a "single overarching notification" and consequently be treated as providing one service.[1813] Conversely, providers might make several notifications with respect to one service rather than grouping them under one notification if the content was "aimed at two or more distinct audiences".[1814] What is more, a new notification was required if the nature of the service as originally notified was fundamentally altered (e.g. by making available programmes of new genres).[1815]

### 2. Ofcom guidance on VOD regulation

In December 2015, Ofcom published its guidance notes on who needs to notify an ODPS, which closely resemble ATVOD's scope guidance of February 2014.[1816] This is not surprising given Ofcom's confirmation of the continued validity of the ATVOD guidance and interpretation of the statutory rules, thus providing continuity and legal certainty to non-linear service providers.[1817] Most formulations, especially those used to specify the meaning of comparability, principal purpose and editorial responsibility were materially the same or even identical. Two clarifications were nonetheless striking and stem from Ofcom's latest practice. In relation to

---

1810 ATVOD, "Guidance on Who Needs to Notify," para. 4.6e, p. 13.
1811 ATVOD, "Guidance on Who Needs to Notify," para. 5.3, p. 15.
1812 ATVOD, "Guidance on Who Needs to Notify," para. 6.1, p. 15.
1813 ATVOD, "Guidance on Who Needs to Notify," para. 6.2, p. 15.
1814 ATVOD, "Guidance on Who Needs to Notify," para. 6.5, p. 16.
1815 ATVOD, "Guidance on Who Needs to Notify," para. 6.7, p. 16.
1816 Ofcom, "Guidance on Notification Requirement," para. 1.2, p. 2; Ofcom, "Future Regulation of VOD Services," para. 2.7, p.6.
1817 Ofcom, "Guidance on Notification Requirement," para. 1.2, p. 2; Ofcom, "Future Regulation of VOD Services," para. 2.6, p. 5.

the economic nature of a service, Ofcom points out that "the number of subscribers and revenue may be relevant, low figures for either does not necessarily imply a service is 'non-economic'".[1818] With respect to electronic versions of newspapers, Ofcom notes that a factual assessment will have to be made in any case and that the mere connection with "a newspaper or magazine brand will not necessarily take a service out of scope".[1819] These remarks reflect Ofcom's appeal decisions and solely serve to bring more clarity to guidance issued previously. In addition, Ofcom made available new guidance notes on how to notify an ODPS.[1820] These set out practical indications intended to assist service providers in the notification process. It follows that providers are required to notify an ODPS at least ten days before service launch. Ofcom offers providers the possibility to discuss informally whether the service constitutes an ODPS or falls outside the statutory definition but underlines that it is the responsibility of the service provider to comply with the obligations arising from the CA.[1821] In the notification form which was published alongside the guidance on Ofcom's website,[1822] service providers have to include information about the person providing the service as well as the service itself.[1823] In addition, the jurisdiction of the service provider is to be determined in line with Art. 2 AVMSD.[1824] The information required by Ofcom is more detailed than the notification form drawn up by the French CSA.

In the absence of a tie to UK jurisdiction, Ofcom requires evidence by the service provider of their establishment in another country/EU Member State (e.g. notification in that country or proof of compliance with national law).[1825] It is not clear whether Ofcom solely addresses providers located

1818 Ofcom, "Guidance on Notification Requirement," para. 2.4b, p. 4.

1819 Ofcom, "Guidance on Notification Requirement," para. 3.11, pp. 8–9.

1820 Ofcom, "How to Notify, Guidance Notes on How to Notify an On-Demand Programme Service to Ofcom," December 18, 2015, http://stakeholders.ofcom.org.uk/binaries/broadcast/on-demand/rules-guidance/How_to_Notify.pdf (accessed 18.1.2016).

1821 Ofcom, "How to Notify," December 18, 2015, paras. 11–12, p. 5.

1822 The notification form is available at http://stakeholders.ofcom.org.uk/binaries/broadcast/on-demand/notification.rtf (accessed 18.1.2016).

1823 Ofcom, "How to Notify," December 18, 2015, paras. 21–23, 28–32, pp. 6–7. See also sec. 2 and sec. 4 of the notification form.

1824 Ofcom, "How to Notify," December 18, 2015, paras. 24–27, 6. See also sec. 3 of the notification form.

1825 Ofcom, "How to Notify," December 18, 2015, para. 26, p. 6.

in another EU Member State (rather than in a third country). The request for evidence may have evolved in light of Ofcom's experiences with service providers migrating to other non-European jurisdictions and may equally apply to providers (primarily) located in North America.

## V. Ofcom's reply to the Commission consultation on "A media framework for the 21st century"

Ofcom's reply to the Commission's consultation on the revision of the AVMSD sketches out the future regulatory model Ofcom envisages.[1826] In its reply, Ofcom recognises changing market conditions, referring above all to the increasing availability of on-demand audiovisual media services accompanied by the increasing use of such services, especially by younger audiences (e.g. 11-15 year olds).[1827] Notwithstanding these pressures, Ofcom notes that the broadcast industry, in particular the advertising market, has been robust.[1828] Referring to audience research concerning consumer attitudes and expectations in relation to audiovisual content, Ofcom argues that consumers expect a coherent regulatory framework with respect to TV, catch-up and on-demand audiovisual media services. By contrast, consumers understand that such TV-like content is different from "Internet content" and thus it should be treated differently.[1829] As a result, Ofcom carves out a distinction between a "TV-like space" where consumers expect regulatory protection and an "Internet space" where the expectations as to the level of protection are substantially lower and consumers' responsibility consequently higher.[1830] It associates "non-TV-like" material such as user-generated content with "Internet content".[1831] Ofcom is thus convinced that "the extent to which today's on-demand industry is an off-

1826 Ofcom, "Consultation on Directive 2010/13/EU on Audiovisual Media Services (AVMSD), A Media Framework for the 21st Century," September 2015, http://ec.europa.eu/newsroom/dae/document.cfm?doc_id=11230 (accessed 15.12.2015).
1827 Ofcom, "Reply AVMSD Consultation," p. 9.
1828 Ofcom, "Reply AVMSD Consultation," p. 9.
1829 Ofcom, "Reply AVMSD Consultation," p. 9.
1830 Ofcom, "Reply AVMSD Consultation," p. 9.
1831 Ofcom, "Reply AVMSD Consultation," p. 9.

shoot of the broadcast television industry" speaks in favour of maintaining the current legal framework.[1832]

With regards to the material scope of the AVMSD, the most pertinent aspect of the reply for this chapter, Ofcom expresses overall support for a status quo as laid down in the Directive. It considers that the scope of the Directive remains effective and the notion of "TV-like" services is sufficiently broad and flexible to accommodate new types of services. In this context, it relies on the criteria developed through its practice.[1833] Ofcom is, however, mindful of the differences in interpretation existing between Member States.[1834] In order to achieve a homogeneous application of the Directive across the EU, it calls on the Commission, in consultation with ERGA and the industry, to draw up EU-level guidance.[1835] Furthermore, Ofcom rejects an extension of the Directive's scope to intermediaries and platforms on account of their lack of editorial responsibility over audiovisual content.[1836] Rather, Ofcom considers that their role in the audiovisual value chain should be assessed separately, in the Commission's consultation regarding online platforms and intermediaries running (almost in parallel to the AVMSD consultation) from October to December 2015.[1837] Ofcom contends that such actors should not be subjected to regulation under the AVMSD because any extension of that type of regulation would "cut across" the responsibilities of media service providers and thus blur the "locus of responsibility".[1838] In addition, Ofcom is of the opinion that search engines, platforms, intermediaries and other content hosts like YouTube, "none of which exercise editorial control over content" are not

1832 Ofcom, "Reply AVMSD Consultation," p. 10.

1833 Ofcom refers to its appeal decisions in which it details the principal purpose text. It also explicitly refers to its appeal decisions in cases Channel Flip and Urban Chick Supremacy Cell in relation to the "TV-like programmes criterion". See Ofcom, "Reply AVMSD Consultation," pp. 8, 11.

1834 Ofcom refers to hybrid services such as online newspapers which offer considerable amounts of audiovisual content next to written material or photographs. See Ofcom, "Reply AVMSD Consultation," p. 11.

1835 Ofcom, "Reply AVMSD Consultation," pp. 10–11.

1836 Ofcom, "Reply AVMSD Consultation," pp. 11–12.

1837 European Commission, "Consultation on the Regulatory Environment for Platforms, Online Intermediaries, Data and Cloud Computing and the Collaborative Economy," December 2015, https://ec.europa.eu/eusurvey/runner/Platforms/ (accessed 15.12.2015).

1838 Ofcom, "Reply AVMSD Consultation," pp. 11–12.

in competition with audiovisual media service providers.[1839] Yet, Ofcom does acknowledge that such actors are not, *per se*, exempt from regulation and that the objectives of such regulation could be similar to those upon which the AVMSD is built. It nonetheless reiterates that any kind of future regulatory scheme should reflect specific roles and responsibilities.[1840]

Interestingly, there is a certain elusiveness about Ofcom's answer regarding the appropriateness of the graduated approach to regulation. On the one hand, Ofcom admits that the boundaries between linear and non-linear services are blurring and that audiences expect a consistent level of protection across all kinds of TV-like content. In this respect it calls for a levelling up of the rules on the protection of minors and the right of reply and highlights the importance of the prohibition of incitement to hatred.[1841] On the other hand, Ofcom is in favour of maintaining the current rules on commercial communications including the quantitative restrictions on television advertising.[1842] Succinctly, Ofcom seems to abandon the linear/non-linear distinction in certain fields (notably for the protection of minors), calling for "minimum standards provided by the Directive [which] (…) apply equally across linear and on-demand services".[1843] These EU-level minimum standards should be stronger than those currently in place. At the same time, the modified European framework should maintain Member States' flexibility to pursue public policy objectives and "protect audiences in their territories as they feel appropriate" (e.g. quantitative limits on television advertising).[1844] The lack of clarity of Ofcom's position in this regard is proof of the difficulty of designing a coherent regulatory framework which applies consistently across all audiovisual media services.

## VI. Summary

In sum, the UK regulatory authorities ATVOD and Ofcom have undertaken numerous measures to clarify the notion of ODPS. Aside from research

---

1839 Ofcom, "Reply AVMSD Consultation," p. 12.
1840 Ofcom, "Reply AVMSD Consultation," p. 12.
1841 Ofcom, "Reply AVMSD Consultation," p. 25.
1842 Ofcom, "Reply AVMSD Consultation," pp. 21–25.
1843 Ofcom, "Reply AVMSD Consultation," p. 26.
1844 Ofcom, "Reply AVMSD Consultation," p. 26.

into audience attitudes and behaviour, a body of practice has emerged and is codified in the non-binding guidance to service providers. This guidance sets forth the non-exhaustive criteria comprising key notions of the definition of an ODPS by virtue of the CA. Even though the guidance is expressly non-binding, it becomes quasi-binding on providers as UK regulators use it as a basis to assess the nature of a service and do not seem to deviate from it. While ATVOD attempted to ensure rigorous enforcement of the rules applicable to non-linear services, Ofcom's approach seems to have been guided by a more liberal understanding of the legal framework as well as market considerations. These discrepancies may have been one reason (although not publicly acknowledged) for Ofcom to take back responsibility for the regulation of ODPS and put an end to ATVOD's role as co-regulator. 2016 has seen Ofcom carrying on in light of ATVOD's achievements. Since then, Ofcom has not carried out extensive scope investigations but rather concentrated on closing several appeal decisions still pending from ATVOD's co-regulatory term. In contrast to ATVOD's pro-active investigations into many kinds of services, Ofcom appears to rely more substantially on public complaints, which at the time of this writing do not appear to have been lodged.

## C. *The notion of telemedia services in Germany*

In Germany, the notion of telemedia is intertwined with the definition of broadcasting. This is because, unlike in France and the UK, there is no registration or notification requirement for providers of telemedia. In addition, telemedia are only defined negatively, by differentiation from broadcasting and telecommunications. For this reason, the most pertinent issue in Germany is the distinction between broadcasting, for which a license is required, and telemedia, for which no such requirement exists. The notion of broadcasting generally covers audio services (radio) and audiovisual services. A differentiation can be made between the constitutional meaning of broadcasting and its meaning according to the legislation in force (notably the RStV). The constitutional meaning is wider in scope so as to encompass within the protection under Art. 5 GG all kinds of media services including telemedia. By contrast, the concept of broadcasting stemming from the RStV exempts telemedia which are subject to a more liberal set of rules outlined in the RStV in conjunction with the TMG. In addition, the distribution of competences between the federal and state levels has led to the adoption of two legal acts as explained in the third chapter, the RStV (negotiated as an interstate treaty between the German *Länder*) and the TMG (at the federal level). While the RStV contains rules regarding the content of telemedia, the TMG regulates the economic aspects of the distribution of telemedia. In practice, having two separate instruments has led to complex situations, in particular, questions of differentiation, as outlined below. This legal scheme which seems appropriate in theory has led to complex questions of differentiation in practice as will be demonstrated below.[1845] This study examines the content of telemedia and thus focusses on the RStV as the main legal source. Before analysing the practice of state media authorities, the meaning of broadcasting and telemedia services according to the RStV are set out with reference to relevant academic literature.

## I. The notion of broadcasting in ordinary legislation

The following section looks at the concept of broadcasting as set out in the German legislation. It is of fundamental importance to the German legal order as the notion of on-demand audiovisual media services, or telemedia services, is defined by reference to it.

### 1. The legal definition of broadcasting

Art. 2 (1) RStV defines broadcasting as

> "a linear information and communication service; it means the provision and transmission of offers for the general public or simultaneous reception in moving images or sound along a schedule, using electromagnetic oscillations. The term includes offers which are transmitted in encrypted form or can be received against special payment."

This notion was considerably reformulated in June 2009 by the 12th amendment to the RStV which aimed at aligning the RStV with the AVMSD. While the previous definition of broadcasting corresponded to

---

1845 Brock and Schmittmann, "Telemedienrecht," para. 40, p. 337.

the constitutional meaning carved out by the BVerfG in its jurisprudence,[1846] the notion changed as a result of the transposition of the AVMSD. This was due to the fact that a key element of the constitutional definition took into account the impact of a media on the general public and thus its relevance for public opinion formation (so-called *Meinungsbildungsrelevanz*). By abandoning the criterion of performance (*Darbietung)* which encompassed the "relevance for public opinion formation test", the definition of broadcasting became content neutral.[1847] Instead, the RStV introduced the criterion of "linearity" to reflect the wording of Art. 1 (1) (e) AVMSD defining television broadcasting.[1848]

The struggle stemming from this transformation is clearly illustrated by the German *Länder*'s (the competent legislature in this case) choice to retain implicitly the criterion of *Darbietung*. The official statement of reasons (*amtliche Begründung*) to the 12[th] amendment of the RStV suggests that the relevance of a particular service for public opinion formation[1849] is appraised in the context of the criterion of general public (*Allgemein-*

---

1846 Reinhard Hartstein et al., "§ 2 RStV Begriffsbestimmungen," in *Rundfunkstaatsvertrag, Kommentar*, Looseleaf commenatry (Köln: Rehm, n.d.), para. 12; Bernd Holznagel, "RStV § 2 Begriffsbestimmungen," in *Recht der elektronischen Medien*, ed. Gerald Spindler and Fabian Schuster, third edition (München: C. H. Beck, 2015), para. 13.

1847 Jan Baier, "Zulassungspflicht für Web-TV? Maßgebliche Kriterien im Lichte des Rundfunkbegriffs," *Computer und Recht* 12 (2008): p. 775; Brock and Schmittmann, "Telemedienrecht," para. 21, p. 329; Hartstein et al., "§ 2 RStV Begriffsbestimmungen," para. 19; Holznagel, "RStV § 2 Begriffsbestimmungen," para. 13; Eva-Maria Michel, "Senden als konstitutiver Bestandteil des Rundfunkbegriffs? Der Rundfunkbegriff im Lichte neuerer europarechtlicher Entwicklungen," *Zeitschrift für Urheber- und Medienrecht*, 2009, p. 457.

1848 Brock and Schmittmann, "Telemedienrecht," para. 19, p. 328; Hartstein et al., "§ 2 RStV Begriffsbestimmungen," paras. 18–19.

1849 The relevance of a service for public opinion formation is assessed according to the criteria of Breitenwirkung (wide-spread impact), Aktualität (relevance to the present) and Suggestivkraft (power of suggestion) as developed by the BVerfG in its jurisprudence on Art. 5 (1) GG.

*heit*)[1850] and thus still pertinent in the classification of media services.[1851] The apparent contradiction[1852] between the wording of the RStV and the official statement of reasons accompanying its 12th amendment sits uneasily with the AVMSD. Yet, it can be argued that even the AVMSD implicitly recognises the relevance of audiovisual media services for public opinion formation. Art. 1 (1) (a) (i) AVMSD refers to services which "inform, entertain or educate" the general public. What is more, recital 21 AVMSD clarifies that the Directive covers mass media, meaning "intended for reception by, and which could have *a clear impact* on, a significant proportion of the general public".[1853] In spite of this attempt to reconcile the German and European Union legal orders, the importance held by the criterion of *Meinungsbildungsrelevanz* in the RStV where it is one of the core elements defining broadcasting is in stark contrast to the importance accorded by the AVMSD, where it is only implicitly embedded in a non-binding recital.[1854]

---

1850 Brock and Schmittmann posit that the relevance for public opinion formation constitutes an unwritten criterion and does not relate to the analysis of the criterion of general public. See Brock and Schmittmann, "Telemedienrecht," para. 29, p. 333.

1851 The official statement of reasons (amtliche Begründung) to the 12th amendment of the interstate treaty is published in Hartstein et al., *Rundfunkstaatsvertrag, Kommentar*, sec. 2.10, see in particular B No. 3; Brock and Schmittmann, "Telemedienrecht," para. 21, p. 329; Hartstein et al., "§ 2 RStV Begriffsbestimmungen," paras. 13, 19; Holznagel, "RStV § 2 Begriffsbestimmungen," para. 22; Michel, "Senden als Bestandteil des Rundfunkbegriffs?," p. 457; Raimund Schütz, "Rundfunkbegriff: Neutralität der Inhalte oder der Übertragung? Konvergenz und Innovation," *Multimedia und Recht*, 2009, p. 229.

1852 Brock and Schmittmann, "Telemedienrecht," para. 21, p. 329; Hartstein et al., "§ 2 RStV Begriffsbestimmungen," para. 19; Schütz, "Rundfunkbegriff," p. 230.

1853 Baier, "Zulassungspflicht für Web-TV? Maßgebliche Kriterien im Lichte des Rundfunkbegriffs," p. 774; Michel, "Senden als Bestandteil des Rundfunkbegriffs?," p. 458; Schütz, "Rundfunkbegriff," p. 232.

1854 Michel illustrates that this difference in meaning might result in different classifications of the same service as demonstrated with regards to pay-per view or near-video-on-demand offers. The classification of teleshopping was disputed, too. Originally, it was classified as telemedia pursuant to the fourth sentence of Art. 2 (1) RStV. When the AVMSD was transposed into the German legal order, this sentence was omitted by the 12th amendment of the Interstate Treaty. See Michel, "Senden als Bestandteil des Rundfunkbegriffs?," pp. 458–59; see also Brock and Schmittmann, "Telemedienrecht," paras. 22–23, pp. 329–30; the classification of teleshopping as a linear service requiring a license was confirmed in a case decided by the Landesanstalt für Medien Nordrhein-Westfalen in Jan-

With the adoption of the 12th amendment to the RStV, broadcasting is defined by three criteria. Firstly, broadcasting constitutes a "linear information and communication service". Linearity is further specified by two aspects newly integrated in the provision.[1855] It implies the "simultaneous reception in moving images or sound along a schedule". Hence, the concept of linearity is not contingent on the type of content transmitted and its relevance for public opinion.[1856] Simultaneous reception commonly means point-to-multipoint communication and serves to delineate broadcasting from telemedia consumed on-demand.[1857] The meaning of the term schedule adopted literally from Art. 1 (1) (e) AVMSD has been debated in German academic writing. Generally, it means that programmes are sorted according to a pre-determined chronological order[1858] determined on the basis of an editorial plan, and a viewer cannot influence the selection and arrangement of individual programmes within the schedule.[1859] In this respect, the construction of the schedule is linked to the activity of the service provider who is assumed to have editorial responsibility within the

---

uary 2010 by virtue of the third sentence of Art. 20 (2) RStV. The name of the service and other confidential information was blackened in the decision so that the name "ABC" only stands as a placeholder. Bayerische Landeszentrale für neue Medien, "Bescheid C," August 2, 2011.

1855 Roland Bornemann, "Der Sendeplan im Rundfunkrecht," *Zeitschrift für Urheber- und Medienrecht*, no. 11 (2013): p. 848.

1856 Hartstein et al., "§ 2 RStV Begriffsbestimmungen," para. 21.

1857 Hartstein et al., "§ 2 RStV Begriffsbestimmungen," para. 21; by contrast, Schulz posits that poin-to-multi-point communication is not constitutive for linearity of a service. See Wolfgang Schulz, "RStV § 2 Begriffsbestimmungen," in *Beck'scher Kommentar zum Rundfunkrecht*, ed. Werner Hahn and Thomas Vesting, third edition (München: C. H. Beck, 2012), para. 42a; Bornemann clarifies that from a technical point of view it is irrelevant whether a point-to-multi-point connection (e.g. broadcasting via a classical distribution network) is operated or rather many simultaneous single connections exist (e.g. broadcasting via mobile telephony or the Internet). See Bornemann, "Der Sendeplan im Rundfunkrecht," p. 848; Brock and Schmittmann, "Telemedienrecht," para. 24, p. 330.

1858 Hartstein et al., "§ 2 RStV Begriffsbestimmungen," para. 22; Mario Martini, "Rundfunk und presseähnliche Telemedien, Begriffsbestimmungen," in *Informations- und Medienrecht, Kommentar*, ed. Hubertus Gersdorf and Boris Paal (München: C. H. Beck, 2014), para. 5, p. 217.

1859 Bornemann, "Der Sendeplan im Rundfunkrecht," p. 848; Martini, "Rundfunk und presseähnliche Telemedien, Begriffsbestimmungen," para. 6b, p. 218.

meaning of Art. 1 (1) (c) AVMSD.[1860] The RStV like the AVMSD are silent on the number of programmes required to establish a schedule. A single programme broadcast at a certain time or repeated in a loop does not seem to be sufficient to form a schedule. This interpretation seems to be supported by the fact that a Google Hangout of Chancellor Merkel which was publicly disseminated via Google+ in April 2013 was not considered as broadcasting due to the absence of a schedule.[1861] Martini argues that a schedule entails at least two subsequently transmitted programmes.[1862] Others are mindful of the length of programmes noting that a case-by-case analysis of units containing several programmes, albeit of short duration, is required.[1863] It follows that there is no uniform meaning of the term schedule, corresponding to the term catalogue which is used in the context of non-linear services.[1864]

The second criterion is not new and stems from the wording "offers directed at the general public" (*Allgemeinheit*). This criterion reflects the mass communication character of broadcasting and the intention of providers to address their services to the general public. More precisely, the exact number of recipients is irrelevant as long as the offer is directed at an indeterminate number of addressees.[1865] Hence, the number of viewers who actually watch the programme is not decisive but rather the num-

1860 Bornemann, "Der Sendeplan im Rundfunkrecht," p. 848; Holznagel, "RStV § 2 Begriffsbestimmungen," para. 17; Schulz, "Rundfunkrecht," 2012, para. 42b.

1861 Martini, "Rundfunk und presseähnliche Telemedien, Begriffsbestimmungen," para. 6b.

1862 Martini, "Rundfunk und presseähnliche Telemedien, Begriffsbestimmungen," para. 5, p. 217; by contrast, Bornemann points out that the wording of Art. 2 (2) No. 1 RStV which defines the term "programme" is ambiguous (more ambiguous than Art. 1 (1) (e) AVMSD). By reference to recital 27 AVMSD, he remarks that the AVMSD applies to single programmes (which are also offered as on-demand services by the same provider). Interestingly, he also asks whether the term "catalogue" requires the aggregation of more than one programme. See Bornemann, "Der Sendeplan im Rundfunkrecht," p. 849.

1863 Holznagel, "RStV § 2 Begriffsbestimmungen," para. 18; Schulz, "Rundfunkrecht," 2012, para. 42c.

1864 Art. 58 (3) RStV refers to a catalogue of content rather than a catalogue of programmes as set out in Art. 1 (1) (g) AVMSD which defines an on-demand audiovisual media service. Interestingly, Bornemann asks whether the term "catalogue" requires the aggregation of more than one programme. See Bornemann, "Der Sendeplan im Rundfunkrecht," p. 849.

1865 Holznagel, "RStV § 2 Begriffsbestimmungen," para. 19; Schulz, "Rundfunkrecht," 2012, para. 43.

ber of potential viewers.[1866] The general public criterion is interpreted broadly as including services directed at small niche audiences.[1867] In addition, encrypted offers are expressly regarded as broadcasting by virtue of the second sentence of Art. 2 (1) RStV. Such (pay TV) services based on conditional access are open for all customers who are willing to pay the subscription fees.[1868] By contrast, the general public criterion is not fulfilled by services like business TV which are tailored to members of a group who are identified or identifiable in advance due to common characteristics and a particular relationship (e.g. employment) with the provider.[1869]

The third characteristic of broadcasting is its transmission using electromagnetic oscillations. Although this criterion is technical, it is technology-neutral as promoted by the AVMSD. It encompasses broadcasting by any analogue as well as digital transmission technique and implies successfully overcoming the spatial distance between the sender and the recipient.[1870] This criterion is the least important element of the definition of broadcasting and serves to differentiate broadcasting from the printed press.[1871]

### 2. Exemptions from the notion of broadcasting

It is important to note that the RStV also enumerates offers which do not constitute broadcasting but which are telemedia. Some of these telemedia might be subject to the rules outlined in chapter VI RStV applicable to

1866 Hartstein et al., "§ 2 RStV Begriffsbestimmungen," para. 13; Holznagel, "RStV § 2 Begriffsbestimmungen," para. 19.

1867 Brock and Schmittmann, "Telemedienrecht," para. 26, p. 332.

1868 Holznagel, "RStV § 2 Begriffsbestimmungen," para. 29; Schulz, "Rundfunkrecht," 2012, para. 50; see also Direktorenkonferenz der Landesmedienanstalten, "Drittes Strukturpapier zur Unterscheidung von Rundfunk und Mediendiensten" (Die Medienanstalten, June 11, 2003), para. 3.3.4, p. 16.

1869 Brock and Schmittmann, "Telemedienrecht," para. 26, p. 332; Hartstein et al., "§ 2 RStV Begriffsbestimmungen," para. 13; Holznagel, "RStV § 2 Begriffsbestimmungen," para. 20.

1870 The transmission of an event (e.g. a football match) on a large public screen (public viewing) next to the stadium is not covered by the definition of broadcasting. See Hartstein et al., "§ 2 RStV Begriffsbestimmungen," para. 14; Holznagel, "RStV § 2 Begriffsbestimmungen," paras. 26–27.

1871 Schulz, "Rundfunkrecht," 2012, para. 49.

telemedia within the meaning of the AVMSD, while others might be solely governed by the TMG.[1872] It is Art. 2 (3) RStV which exempts from the notion of broadcasting services which

> "1. are offered to fewer than 500 potential users for simultaneous reception in any case,
> 2. are destined for the immediate reproduction from reception equipment storage media,
> 3. exclusively serve personal or family purposes,
> 4. are not journalistic edited offers, or
> 5. consist of programmes which are each activated against individual payment."

The first exemption referring to less than 500 potential users highlights that the services lack the mass media character (or the *Breitenwirkung* in constitutional terms)[1873] and are not offered to the general public.[1874] Baier remarks that this is a condition difficult to prove in practice.[1875] Still, there seems to be consensus that the exception outlined in number 1 of Art. 2 (3) RStV constitutes a *de minimis* rule rather than a rigid and strictly enforced limit.[1876] The formulation "in any case" grants some leeway to the ZAK and the respective state media authority to derogate on a case-by-case basis, taking into account the relevance for and the impact of the service on public opinion.[1877] Similarly, this wording allows for the "up-grading" of the offer to broadcasting if the user base grows beyond the speci-

---

1872 Roland Bornemann, "Der 'Verbreitensbegriff' bei Pornografie in audiovisuellen Mediendiensten, Straferweiternd im Internet und strafverkürzend im Runfdunk?," *Multimedia und Recht*, 2012, p. 125.

1873 Brock and Schmittmann, "Telemedienrecht," para. 17, p. 327; Holznagel, "RStV § 2 Begriffsbestimmungen," para. 21.

1874 Brock and Schmittmann, "Telemedienrecht," paras. 26–27, pp. 331-332; Hartstein et al., "§ 2 RStV Begriffsbestimmungen," para. 24; Holznagel, "RStV § 2 Begriffsbestimmungen," para. 21.

1875 Baier, "Zulassungspflicht für Web-TV? Maßgebliche Kriterien im Lichte des Rundfunkbegriffs," p. 775; Schulz opines that the threshold of 500 does not refer to individual users but relates to typical media outlets used by end-users of a certain technology. See Schulz, "Rundfunkrecht," 2012, para. 52.

1876 See para. B No. 3 of the official statement of reasons to the 12th amendment of the interstate treaty published in Hartstein et al., *Rundfunkstaatsvertrag, Kommentar*, sec. 2.10; Martini, "Rundfunk und presseähnliche Telemedien, Begriffsbestimmungen," para. 12, p. 219.

1877 Brock and Schmittmann, "Telemedienrecht," para. 27, p. 332; Hartstein et al., "§ 2 RStV Begriffsbestimmungen," para. 25; Peter Matzneller, "Rechtsrahmen der Werbung für Webradios," *Archiv für Presserecht, Zeitschrift für Medien-*

fied threshold of 500.[1878] In a similar vein, offers which are intended for private consumption and thus not directed at the general public are exempted by virtue of the third exception.

The second exception refers to technical forms of transmission similar to video on-demand services. While the user choses the time of consumption, the transmission of the content is determined by the provider of the service or network operator. If however such offers are diffused "along a schedule" they could be considered as near-video-on-demand which, further to the CJEU decision in *Mediakabel* of 2005 and since underpinned by recital 27 AVMSD, is regarded as broadcasting.

Moreover, audiovisual content which has not been journalistically edited is not considered as broadcasting according to exception number 4 of Art. 2 (3) RStV. The adjective "journalistically edited" is also employed with respect to telemedia and is discussed in more detail below. This exception purports to exempt services which merely transmit raw data such as webcams that simply stream images.[1879] The final exception (number 5) covers individual programmes available in un-encoded form upon payment. The rationale behind this exception was to allow for the transmission of pornographic programmes which, if classified as broadcasting, would have been *per se* impermissible by virtue of the JMStV.[1880] Regardless of the linearity of the transmission of such offers, they are considered akin to on-demand services. Succinctly, numbers 1, 3 and 5 of Art. 2 (3) RStV imply services not addressed to the general public and they are therefore excluded from the definition of broadcasting; numbers 2 and 4 cover services lacking relevance for the formation of public opinion that is inherent to broadcasting.[1881]

---

*und Kommunikationsrecht* 4 (2013): p. 298; Schulz, "Rundfunkrecht," 2012, para. 52.

1878 Brock and Schmittmann, "Telemedienrecht," para. 27, p. 332.

1879 Brock and Schmittmann, "Telemedienrecht," para. 28, pp. 332–33; Hartstein et al., "§ 2 RStV Begriffsbestimmungen," para. 27; Martini, "Rundfunk und presseähnliche Telemedien, Begriffsbestimmungen," para. 15, p. 220; Schulz, "Rundfunkrecht," 2012, para. 57.

1880 See the first sentence of Art. 4 (2) No. 1 JMStV Hartstein et al., "§ 2 RStV Begriffsbestimmungen," para. 28.

1881 Brock and Schmittmann, "Telemedienrecht," para. 30, p. 333.

## II. The legal definition of telemedia services

Telemedia services are the German expression for on-demand audiovisual media services. This part specifies the concept of telemedia services which is only negatively defined by German legislation and outlines various other notions of telemedia-related services set out in the RStV.

### 1. Telemedia services: between broadcasting and telecommunications services

The term telemedia was integrated in the RStV in its 9th amendment. In parallel to the modified RStV, the TMG also entered into force at the federal level in March 2007. For harmonisation purposes, both acts adopted the same definition of telemedia. According to the official statement of reasons annexed to the 9th amendment of the RStV, a simplification of the legal framework was sought by consolidating the distinctly regulated notions of tele services and media services into the single notion of telemedia.[1882] The third sentence of Art. 2 (1) RStV[1883] negatively defines telemedia as meaning

> "all electronic information and communications services, as far as they are not telecommunications services pursuant to Article 3 no. 24 of the Telecommunications Act, which consist entirely in the conveyance of signals across telecommunications networks or telecommunications-supported services pursuant to Article 3 no. 25 of the Telecommunications Act, or broadcasting pursuant to sentences (1) and (2)."

The definition refers to the generic terminology of electronic information and communications service which encompasses broadcasting, telemedia and telecommunications services.[1884] Broadcasting is similarly defined in

---

1882 The official statement of reasons (amtliche Begründung) to the 9th amendment of the interstate treaty is published in Hartstein et al., *Rundfunkstaatsvertrag, Kommentar*, sec. 2.7, in particular B number 4.

1883 See also the first sentence of Art. 1(1) TMG. This study refers to the definition of telemedia contained in the RStV unless expressly indicated otherwise. Since this study is concerned with the content of telemedia, the RStV serves as the main legal source.

1884 See the official statement of reasons accompanying the 9th amendment to the interstate treaty published in Hartstein et al., *Rundfunkstaatsvertrag, Kommentar*, sec. 2.7, see in particular B No. 4.

Art. 2 (1) RStV by reference to information and communications service, albeit replacing the general term "electronic" by the more specific term "linear". Telemedia are thus not defined independently but by distinction to broadcasting on the one hand and telecommunications services on the other.[1885] The official statement of reasons attached to the 9$^{th}$ amendment of the RStV clarifies that telemedia cover a broad range of economic activities.[1886] It enumerates examples of telemedia, including online retail services (such as news groups, chat rooms, electronic press, teletext), Internet search engines, or commercial distribution of information via promotional emails. Pursuant to the official statement of reasons, VOD is considered telemedia provided that the offer does not constitute broadcasting within the meaning of the AVMSD.[1887]

As the differentiation between broadcasting and telemedia is analysed in detail in this study, only a brief explanation of the meaning of telecommunications services will be provided here. The definition clarifies that telemedia are to be distinguished form both telecommunications networks and telecommunications-supported services. Previously, it was unclear whether telecommunications-supported services constituted tele services (purely technical services) or media services (transporting content).[1888] If the services exclusively or predominantly transmit signals within telecommunications networks, they are governed by the *Telekommunikationsgesetz* (TKG), which regulates the technical infrastructure.[1889] If, however,

1885 Roland Bornemann, "Zur Telemedienordnung," *Recht der Jugend und des Bildungswesens* 2 (2013): p. 125; Brock and Schmittmann, "Telemedienrecht," para. 13, p. 326; Hartstein et al., "§ 2 RStV Begriffsbestimmungen," paras. 31–32.

1886 See the official statement of reasons accompanying the 9th amendment to the interstate treaty published in Hartstein et al., *Rundfunkstaatsvertrag, Kommentar*, sec. 2.7, see in particular B No. 4.

1887 See the official statement of reasons accompanying the 9th amendment to the interstate treaty published in Hartstein et al., *Rundfunkstaatsvertrag, Kommentar*, para. 2.7, see in particular B No. 4.

1888 See the official statement of reasons accompanying the 9th amendment to the interstate treaty published in Hartstein et al., *Rundfunkstaatsvertrag, Kommentar*, sec. 2.7, see in particular B No. 4.

1889 Rotraud Gitter, "Telemediengesetz, Anwendungsbereich," in *Beck'scher Kommentar zum Recht der Telemediendienste*, ed. Alexander Roßnagel (München: C. H. Beck, 2013), paras. 34–35, p. 45; Hartstein et al., "§ 2 RStV Begriffsbestimmungen," para. 32; Holznagel, "RStV § 2 Begriffsbestimmungen," para. 50;

the content is the primary service, the TMG applies (possibly in conjunction with the RStV).[1890]

In order to give impetus to and foster the dynamic development of telemedia, no license or registration is required, as stipulated by Art. 54 (1) RStV.[1891] And in accordance with the graduated approach underlying the AVMSD, section VI RStV[1892] outlines content requirements for telemedia which correspond to on-demand audiovisual media services by virtue of Art. 1 (1) (g) AVMSD. The RStV is thus *lex specialis* to the TMG.[1893] The RStV introduces several types of telemedia which are examined below, and the classification of a service has practical consequences for the kind and intensity of rules applicable.

### 2. Different forms of telemedia services

The RStV outlines several forms of telemedia which are examined below. Some of these are expressly defined in Art. 2 (2) RStV whereas others are referred to in the substantive provisions of the RStV, notably its sixth section.

#### a) Programme-related telemedia services

Art. 2 (2) No. 19 RStV defines "programme-related telemedia" as

> "offers for the analysis of contents of a specific programme including background information, as far as recourse is made to the materials and sources used for the programme in question and as far as these offers enhance and support the content and the topic of the programme, without, however, already presenting an independent new or modified offer pursuant to Article 11 f (3)."

Programme-related telemedia are relevant in the context of PSB and the scope of their public service mission. This type of telemedia does not need

Mario Martini, "Medienwirtschaft, Telemediengesetz, Anwendungsbereich," in *Informations- und Medienrecht, Kommentar*, ed. Gersdorf and Paal (München: C. H. Beck, 2014), paras. 11–14, pp. 1482–83.

1890 Brock and Schmittmann, "Telemedienrecht," para. 39, p. 336.

1891 Hartstein et al., "§ 54 RStV Allgemeine Bestimmungen," para. 2.

1892 See Arts. 54- 60 RStV.

1893 Brock and Schmittmann, "Telemedienrecht," para. 13, p. 326.

to pass the three-step test[1894] set forth in Art. 11d (2) No. 3 and 11f RStV. Conversely, telemedia not related to programmes are only permissible if they comply with the three-step test. Importantly, the telemedia covered by Art. 2 (2) No. 19 RStV are not only linked to the programmes broadcast on TV, they mirror a concrete broadcast which has been edited (e.g. by providing background information). The audiovisual material previously broadcast is used or re-used in the telemedia, or reference is made to the original broadcast. Hence, the topic and content of the telemedia accompany or reinforce the initial broadcast.[1895] Telemedia are not considered programme-related if they are self-standing or provide a modified offer.[1896]

### b) Press-type offers

In a similar vein, Art. 2 (2) No. 20 RStV defines "press-type offers" as

> "not only electronic editions of print media, but all journalistic edited offers which correspond to newspapers or magazines in their design and content".

This definition encompasses not only (literally speaking) copies of newspapers or magazines which have been modified for publication on mobile devices but also includes offers which are equivalent in content and form.[1897] Press-type offers serve as substitutes for newspapers or magazines and are characterised by their text-based focus.[1898] In line with the 9th amendment's official statement of reasons, digital newspaper offerings constitute telemedia. The definition of press-type offers is relevant for public service broadcasting because PSB are prohibited, by virtue of Art. 11 (2) No. 3 RStV, to distribute press-type offers by means of telemedia. This prohibition represents the demarcation between broadcasting and

1894 On the three-step test, see Reinhard Hartstein et al., "§ 11f Telemedienkonzepte," paras. 16–53, VI.

1895 Hartstein et al., "§ 2 RStV Begriffsbestimmungen," para. 61; Holznagel, "RStV § 2 Begriffsbestimmungen," para. 95.

1896 Hartstein et al., "§ 2 RStV Begriffsbestimmungen," para. 61; Holznagel, "RStV § 2 Begriffsbestimmungen," para. 95.

1897 Hartstein et al., "§ 2 RStV Begriffsbestimmungen," para. 62; Holznagel, "RStV § 2 Begriffsbestimmungen," para. 96; Martini, "Rundfunk und presseähnliche Telemedien, Begriffsbestimmungen," para. 65, pp. 230–31.

1898 Martini, "Rundfunk und presseähnliche Telemedien, Begriffsbestimmungen," para. 65, pp. 230–31.

the press. PSB are not allowed to distribute offers which are almost indistinguishable from press products. Their telemedia are to be designed in form and content as TV-like rather than press-like.[1899] Yet today, the distinction between TV-like and press-like content is becoming watered down as media amalgamate and services entail different forms of editorial content which compete against each other.[1900] In addition, to distinguish between press-type offers defined in Art. 2 (2) No. 20 RStV and journalistically edited offers which do not correspond to newspapers or magazines but which "completely or partially reproduce text or visual contents of periodical print media" as stipulated in Art. 54 (2) RStV is practically impossible.[1901] Yet, the use of different terminology can be explained by the special context within which the term press-type offers is used. This is further explained when examining the jurisprudence on the *Tagesschau* app.

#### c) Comparable telemedia services

The term "comparable telemedia" is employed in the context of platform regulation. The definition of platform provider is set forth in Art. 2 (2) No. 13 RStV and in Art. 50 dealing with transmission capacities of platforms. Comparable telemedia are defined as "telemedia directed at the general public". Hence, such telemedia are comparable to broadcasting and are services targeting the general public. Hartstein et al. point out that most telemedia fulfil the requirement of being addressed to the general public.[1902] Thus, this broad expression is used specifically in relation to platforms, which have only been regulated by the RStV since its 10th amendment adopted in 2008.[1903]

1899 Martini, "Rundfunk und presseähnliche Telemedien, Begriffsbestimmungen," para. 67, p. 231.
1900 Martini, "Rundfunk und presseähnliche Telemedien, Begriffsbestimmungen," para. 66, p. 231.
1901 Martini, "Rundfunk und presseähnliche Telemedien, Begriffsbestimmungen," para. 66, p. 231.
1902 Hartstein et al., "§ 2 RStV Begriffsbestimmungen," para. 50.
1903 Hartstein et al., "§ 2 RStV Begriffsbestimmungen," para. 49.

### d) TV-like telemedia services

The expression "TV-like telemedia" was integrated in the RStV by its 13th amendment, which came into force in April 2010 and was aimed at transposing Art. 9-11 AVMSD, which prescribe standards for audiovisual commercial communications.[1904] Interestingly, the heading of Art. 58 refers to TV-like telemedia while the body of the provision, in its third paragraph, refers to

> "telemedia including contents which are television-like in their form and content and which are provided by a provider for individual on-demand retrieval at a time determined by the user and form a catalogue of contents stipulated by the provider (audiovisual on-demand media services)".

Thus, Art. 58 (3) RStV reproduces the main elements of the definition of a non-linear service as stipulated by Art. 1 (1) (g) AVMSD and is also reminiscent of recital 24 AVMSD. The official statement of reasons of the 13th amendment of the RStV highlights that the term TV-like telemedia is to be interpreted in conformity with the AVMSD, in particular implying services which "compete for the same audience as television broadcasts, and the nature and the means of access to the service would lead the user to reasonably expect regulatory protection".[1905]

---

1904 In parallel to the modifications of the RStV, the TMG was first amended in May 2010 when Art. 2 No. 6 TMG was introduced to define the term on-demand audiovisual media service which was derived from the AVMSD. The definition contained in the TMG resembles the definition of Art. 58 (3) RStV and it is further referred to in the definition of service provider set out in Art. 2 No. 1 TMG and the rule outlining the country of origin principle in Art. 2a TMG. According to Martini, the term TV-like telemedia constitutes a "mixtum compositum" between broadcasting and classical telemedia. It denotes non-linear services which are TV-like, thus have a mass media character and a considerable impact on the general public. See Martini, "Rundfunk und presseähnliche Telemedien, Begriffsbestimmungen," para. 30, 1494 and para. 38, p. 1495 see also; Rotraud Gitter, "Telemediengesetz, Begriffsbestimmungen," in *Beck'scher Kommentar zum Recht der Telemediendienste*, ed. Roßnagel (München: C. H. Beck, 2013), para. 30, p. 57.

1905 Recital 24 AVMSD.

e) Telemedia services providing journalistically edited offers

Finally, several provisions, in particular those contained in section VI of the RStV refer to "telemedia providing journalistically edited offers". According to Art. 54 (2) RStV, these imply telemedia which "in particular (…) completely or partially reproduce texts or visual contents of periodical print media" prior to distribution. The objective and purpose of the rule contained in Art. 54 RStV is to extend the journalistic standards of the press to telemedia. This presupposes that telemedia within the meaning of Art. 54 RStV are offered with the aim of contributing to public opinion formation.[1906] Due to their similarity with press products, such telemedia must conform to "press-like" requirements laid down in Art. 54 et seq RStV.[1907] Rather than providing an exhaustive list, (given the use of "in particular") periodical print media are mentioned by way of illustration.[1908] Conversely, online versions of newspapers or magazines constitute, as a general rule, journalistically edited offers.[1909] The concept of journalistically edited offers, however, is not defined by the RStV. The terms journalistically and edited are to be read cumulatively and are inherently interwoven.[1910] Nonetheless, a content-related function, entailing the purpose of the publication and its relevance for society[1911] can be distinguished from the formal function[1912] which implies the design and editing

1906 Christian Weiner and Christoph Schmelz, "Die elektronische Presse und andere neue Kommunikationsformen im neuen rechtlichen Regulierungsrahmen," *Kommunikation und Recht*, no. 10 (2006): p. 457.

1907 Brock and Schmittmann, "Telemedienrecht," para. 40, p. 337; Keber, "Internet- und Telemedienrecht," para. 47, p. 522.

1908 Weiner and Schmelz, "Die elektronische Presse im neuen rechtlichen Regulierungsrahmen," p. 457.

1909 Brock and Schmittmann, "Telemedienrecht," para. 42, p. 339; Wolfgang Lent, "Elektronische Presse zwischen E-Zines, Blogs und Wikis. Was sind Telemedien mit journalistisch-redaktionell gestalteten Angeboten?," *Zeitschrift für Urheber- und Medienrecht*, 2013, pp. 918–19.

1910 Lent, "Was sind Telemedien mit journalistisch-redaktionell gestalteten Angeboten?," p. 915.

1911 Brock and Schmittmann, "Telemedienrecht," para. 42, p. 338; Weiner and Schmelz, "Die elektronische Presse im neuen rechtlichen Regulierungsrahmen," p. 457.

1912 Brock and Schmittmann, "Telemedienrecht," para. 41, p. 338; Weiner and Schmelz, "Die elektronische Presse im neuen rechtlichen Regulierungsrahmen," p. 457.

of the content. Moreover, the formal function primarily relates to the term "edited" and means the selection, revision, arrangement and commenting of content. What is more, the process of making such offers available to the public displays a certain level of organisation and continuity.[1913] Reporting is thus done regularly.[1914] By contrast, the mere transmission of data without human intervention is not covered by the notion of journalistically edited offers, and neither is the automatic enumeration of content or offers aggregated by software, nor a string or transmission of unedited information.[1915] Hence, a minimum level of intellectual examination of a topic is needed.[1916]

Interestingly, Lent relies on the criteria of universality, topicality, periodicity and public disclosure derived from classical media studies to approach online journalism, asserting that journalistic offers encompass a variety of content (universality) including content directed at small niche groups. The criterion of universality serves to differentiate journalistic offers from private and entrepreneurial telemedia which express personal opinions or advance promotional messages and commercial aims.[1917] The topics reported on, in journalistic offers, typically relate to news or current affairs. The criterion of topicality is interpreted widely, covering events which are not relevant to the present day.[1918] Furthermore, the perpetual updating of the offer, which does not necessarily follow a specific pattern (daily, weekly, monthly), is characteristic of journalistic offers. New content is provided on a continuous rather than sporadic basis.[1919] Finally, this content is made available to the public. Lent acknowledges that the disclo-

1913 Brock and Schmittmann, "Telemedienrecht," para. 42, p. 338; Lent, "Was sind Telemedien mit journalistisch-redaktionell gestalteten Angeboten?," pp. 915–16; Matzneller, "Rechtsrahmen der Werbung für Webradios," p. 298; Rahvar, *Die Zukunft des deutschen Presserechts*, p. 48.

1914 Brock and Schmittmann, "Telemedienrecht," para. 42, p. 339.

1915 Brock and Schmittmann, "Telemedienrecht," para. 42, p. 338; Lent, "Was sind Telemedien mit journalistisch-redaktionell gestalteten Angeboten?," p. 917.

1916 Weiner and Schmelz, "Die elektronische Presse im neuen rechtlichen Regulierungsrahmen," p. 457.

1917 Lent, "Was sind Telemedien mit journalistisch-redaktionell gestalteten Angeboten?," p. 915. For a more detailed distinction between private telemedia and entrepreneurial telemedia, see pp. 917-918.

1918 Lent, "Was sind Telemedien mit journalistisch-redaktionell gestalteten Angeboten?," p. 916.

1919 Lent, "Was sind Telemedien mit journalistisch-redaktionell gestalteten Angeboten?," p. 916.

sure of content to the public is typically fulfilled by offers distributed online, as fast-moving and immediate publication of information is inherent in the nature of the Internet.[1920] He nonetheless posits that low reception of an offer may be indicative of it lacking the required journalistic relevance for the formation of public opinion.[1921]

It emerges from the discussion above that though the contours of the notion of telemedia providing journalistically edited offers have been established, the exact meaning of this term remains ambivalent. Similarly, the question of how to classify hybrid services, of which journalistically edited telemedia are a part, has not been resolved in the RStV. It stems from the information obligations laid down in the second sentence of Art. 55 (2) RStV that a service may consist of several services including telemedia offering journalistically edited content.[1922] In the German academic literature an analysis of the service from the perspective of the user is advocated by Weiner and Schmelz who opine that it is the core activity of the actual service or website which is to be examined.[1923] Lent posits that the whole offer is classified as journalistically edited if regular reporting is the principal purpose and other offerings or services are ancillary.[1924] Rahvar remarks that the whole offer may not imply a full web presence (e.g. www.zeit.de) but may, in fact, concentrate on part of a service which constitutes a single, self-contained and self-standing offer.[1925] Lent is of the opinion that an author's' column of a digital newspaper cannot be considered as a distinct service.[1926] The question of what parts of a service are "worthy" of being considered self-standing and thus classified as telemedia (with journalistically edited offers) will continue to be hotly

1920 See also Rahvar, *Die Zukunft des deutschen Presserechts*, p. 63.

1921 Lent, "Was sind Telemedien mit journalistisch-redaktionell gestalteten Angeboten?," p. 916; Rahvar, *Die Zukunft des deutschen Presserechts*, p. 48.

1922 Lent, "Was sind Telemedien mit journalistisch-redaktionell gestalteten Angeboten?," p. 915; Weiner and Schmelz, "Die elektronische Presse im neuen rechtlichen Regulierungsrahmen," p. 458.

1923 Weiner and Schmelz, "Die elektronische Presse im neuen rechtlichen Regulierungsrahmen," p. 458.

1924 Lent, "Was sind Telemedien mit journalistisch-redaktionell gestalteten Angeboten?," p. 919.

1925 Rahvar, *Die Zukunft des deutschen Presserechts*, p. 61.

1926 Wolfgang Lent, "Rundfunk und presseähnliche Telemedien, Allgemeine Bestimmungen," in *Informations- und Medienrecht, Kommentar*, ed. Gersdorf and Paal (München: C. H. Beck, 2014), para. 3, p. 561.

debated. A hint of how to approach the classification of TV-like versus press-like telemedia is given by the recent jurisprudence concerning the apps of German PSB ARD, as examined below.

To sum up, the RStV employs the term telemedia in a complex and inconsistent manner which is difficult to comprehend, not least for service providers.[1927] At first glance, the amended RStV and TMG did away with the complicated distinction between tele services (previously regulated by a federal law) and media services (formerly regulated by the *Länder* in an interstate treaty). Upon closer inspection however, the rationale behind the differentiation has been revived in the context of delimiting telemedia (without journalistically edited offers) governed by the TMG and telemedia (with journalistically edited offers) covered by the RStV.[1928]

## III. The practice of the state media authorities based on a confirmation of non-objection

This section looks at several cases that have been lodged before the German state media authorities in a special type of procedure. These are all the decisions which several regulators have accepted to provide for scientific inspection.

### 1. Purpose and procedure

It has been demonstrated above that the meaning of telemedia firmly rests upon a demarcation from telecommunications and, more importantly for this study, broadcasting. This distinction also finds expression in procedural terms. While commercial broadcasters require a license pursuant to Art. 20 (1) RStV and to broadcast without is an administrative offense,[1929] provision of telemedia is not subjected to any form of licensing or registration, by virtue of Art. 54 (1) RStV. Thus, the question of whether a service is defined as broadcasting or telemedia is crucial from the outset.

1927 Kitz, "Das neue Recht der elektronischen Medien," p. 371.

1928 Hoeren, "Das Telemediengesetz," p. 806; Martini, "Medienwirtschaft, Telemediengesetz, Anwendungsbereich," paras. 29–30, pp. 1486–87; Rahvar, *Die Zukunft des deutschen Presserechts*, p. 53.

1929 See Art. 49 (1) No. 17 RStV.

Art. 20 (2) RStV sets out procedures for two cases: first, where a provider has not applied for a license – if the competent state media authority becomes aware of this, it may bring the matter to the ZAK's attention. If the ZAK subsequently finds (by unanimous vote) that the service does in fact constitute broadcasting, the provider is required to immediately apply for a license from the competent state media authority or, alternatively, to modify the service in such a manner that it cannot be classified as broadcasting.[1930] Schulz points out that the wording "if and as far as" contained in Art. 20 (2) RStV implies that partitioning an overall offer into telemedia on the one hand and a broadcasting service on the other is possible provided that the two are self-standing, clearly distinct and not overlapping.[1931]

Interestingly, providers may refer to the competent state media authority for confirmation (so-called *Unbedenklichkeitsbescheinigung*)[1932] that the service does not constitute broadcasting pursuant to the third sentence of Art. 20 (2) RStV.[1933] This provision purports to enhance legal certainty and safeguards providers from being faced with a sanctioning procedure for providing broadcasting services without a license. This confirmation by means of an official declaration issued by the state media authority sig-

1930 Reinhard Hartstein et al., "§ 20 RStV Zulassung," in *Jugendmedienschutz-Staatsvertrag, RStV Kommentar*, Looseleaf commenatry (Köln: Rehm, n.d.), para. 14; Wolfgang Schulz, "RStV § 20 Zulassung," in *Beck'scher Kommentar zum Rundfunkrecht*, ed. Werner Hahn and Thomas Vesting, third edition (München: C. H. Beck, 2012), paras. 59, 91.

1931 Schulz, "Rundfunkrecht," 2012, paras. 72–75.

1932 Brock and Schmittmann, "Telemedienrecht," para. 36, p. 335; Schulz, "Rundfunkrecht," 2012, para. 98.

1933 At the state level, media authorities are more commonly contacted by service providers to discuss the launch of a project in advance (and determine which set of rules would be applicable) or the modification of an existing service to clearly fit into the category of broadcasting or telemedia. Being classified as a broadcaster, and thus acquriring a license, may be beneficial to providers when approaching content providers or advertising agencies. In Bavaria, for instance, the football club FC Bayern München was required to request a license for its web TV offer from the state media authority, the BLM. Due to nation-wide implications of the service, the issue was debated in the ZAK. The ZAK held that the service, which included game summaries as well as press conferences, constituted broadcasting within the meaning of the RStV. It pointed out that the programmes were edited and not just transmitted without commentary. Similar web offerings of other German football clubs such as the VfB Stuttgart, Borussia Dortmund and the Hamburger Sport-Verein also required a broadcast license. See Brock and Schmittmann, "Telemedienrecht," paras. 32, 33, p. 334.

nifies that the provider does not need to apply for a broadcasting license.[1934] Yet, the confirmation is not a *carte blanche* for the service provider. In accordance with the second sentence of Art. 20 (2) RStV, the competent state media authority may revise the decision as the service develops and categorise it as broadcasting.[1935] Consequently, the service provider would be required to apply for a license or alternatively design its service in such a way to qualify as telemedia. This "*Rückholklausel*" in fact, hangs like a "Sword of Damocles" over the heads of service providers.[1936] Nonetheless, such decision requires a unanimous vote by the ZAK which represents a high hurdle in practice.[1937] As can be inferred from the joint annual reports of the state media authorities of the past five years, few providers have taken the opportunity of having the nature of their service assessed in accordance with the third sentence of Art. 20 (2) RStV. In spite of the small number of such procedures, the *Unbedenklichkeitsbescheinigung* remains the instrument used by state media authorities to specify the notion of telemedia, differentiating it from broadcasting. The following section assesses some of the decisions taken by state media authorities. Such decisions are typically not disclosed to the public (they are only referred to *in abstracto* in the joint annual reports) and not all state media authorities have granted access to the relevant documents as requested. In addition, several decisions have been anonymised due to data protection considerations.

### 2. Cases of confirmations of non-objection

#### a) A motorway service: Tank & Rast

In May 2012, the *Landeszentrale für Medien und Kommunikation Rheinland-Pfalz* (LMK) informed the service provider *Tank & Rast GmbH* of a

1934 Hartstein et al., "§ 20 RStV Zulassung," para. 14a, III.

1935 Brock and Schmittmann, "Telemedienrecht," para. 37, p. 336.

1936 Brock and Schmittmann, "Telemedienrecht," para. 37, p. 336.

1937 According to the official statement of reasons to the 9th amendment of the Interstate Treaty, the requirement of unanimity was enshrined in order to guarantee uniform interpretation of legal provisions. See Schulz, "Rundfunkrecht," 2012, para. 91; Brock and Schmittmann remark that a state media authority which considers itself competent may act on its own initiative under Art. 49 (1) No. 17 RStV. See Brock and Schmittmann, "Telemedienrecht," para. 38, p. 336.

decision of the ZAK concerning its system of in-store advertising. *Tank & Rast GmbH* had applied to have the content from the screens across its motorway service areas evaluated. The material was audiovisual (excluding sound) and included advertising as well as weather and news and was presented as scrolling text. The material amounted to two minutes in length and was transmitted in a loop, its exact composition was contingent on the availability of the material at the national or regional level. The LMK first observed that the relevant material, in particular advertisements (e.g. Mars), contained moving images which were identical to those featured on TV. In addition, it contended that the provider offered a linear information and communication service, by virtue of Art. 2 (1) RStV. In this context, it posited that the criterion of linearity prescribed by the RStV merely served to delineate linear from non-linear services offered on-demand. Consequently, the criterion of linearity did not equate to the element of "simultaneous reception". More concretely, the offer of *Tank & Rast* drew on a stock of videos transmitted to a central server which then fed into "playout-PCs" of the individual service areas. Each "playout PC" generated content for individual screens within the service areas so that the content differed from screen to screen or service area to service area. In addition, the tenant of the service area could further individualise the material presented on the screens. Due to the lack of simultaneous transmission and the differentiated content featured across screens and service areas, the service was not considered as broadcasting. Above all, the service was offered to fewer than 500 potential viewers for simultaneous reception and was thus covered by the exception outlined in Art. 2 (3) No. 1 RStV.

#### b) A spiritual thematic channel: Schoenstatt-tv

In June 2010, the LMK decided to grant a broadcast license for national TV to the *Schoenstatt-tv GmbH.*[1938] The service, a thematic channel directed at members of the spiritual Schoenstatt movement was to be exclusively transmitted on the Internet under the domain www.schoenstatt-tv.de . The offer predominantly comprised live transmissions of holy masses

1938 Landeszentrale für Medien und Kommunikation Rheinland-Pfalz, "Bescheid Schoenstatt-tv GmbH," June 22, 2010.

taking place in the town of Schoenstatt twice per month. In addition, coverage of occasional events (such as special masses or other events of the Schoenstatt movement) was also planned. The transmissions would be in German, English, Spanish and Portuguese and would be available on-demand when no live coverage was taking place.[1939] The service would be financed by sponsors and donations and the programmes would be edited by members of the Schoenstatt movement in their honorary capacity. Thus, the service would operate on a small budget targeting a small group of religious followers. Still, the ZAK decided that the service should not be exempted from broadcast regulation. In particular, it pointed out that the programmes would be simultaneously accessible to more than 500 potential users.[1940] Schoenstatt-tv was thus allocated a license to operate its service.

c) Adult material: between near-video-on-demand and video-on-demand

The *Bayerische Landeszentrale für neue Medien* (BLM) decided in August 2011[1941] on the classification of a service offering pornographic feature films in a closed user group. The KJM had already determined that the age verification system complied with the JMStV.[1942] The offer comprised three digital feeds which were grouped according to topics (comparable to "channels") and available on individual demand. The films were featured at the transmission time determined by the provider. In total, about 12 films per feed were shown on a daily basis including re-plays. Users had to pay for each individual content item. To make the offer more attractive, the provider intended to introduce a system of "bundled tickets" whereby users could select the first film for EUR 6 and subsequently choose two films from the two other feeds for EUR 2.[1943] According to the provider, such bundling was not comparable to "zapping" implying multiple activations of several films in parallel.[1944] In case of "zapping",

1939 Landeszentrale für Medien und Kommunikation Rheinland-Pfalz, "Bescheid Schoenstatt-tv GmbH," para. III, 1.b, p. 4.
1940 Landeszentrale für Medien und Kommunikation Rheinland-Pfalz, "Bescheid Schoenstatt-tv GmbH," para. III, 2., p. 5.
1941 Bayerische Landeszentrale für neue Medien, "Bescheid C.".
1942 Bayerische Landeszentrale für neue Medien, "Bescheid C," para. I, p. 2.
1943 Bayerische Landeszentrale für neue Medien, "Bescheid C," para. I, p. 3.
1944 Bayerische Landeszentrale für neue Medien, "Bescheid C," para. I, p. 3.

one film was ordered, while all the remaining content available at the same time, was accessible to the user. By contrast, in this instance the user selected and activated each film with individual codes.[1945] In line with the amended third structural paper of 2009 on the differentiation between broadcasting and media services, the BLM made clear that near-video-on-demand services do constitute broadcasting.[1946] Nonetheless, it stressed that the exception set forth in Art. 2 (3) No. 5 RStV, even when interpreted restrictively, covered single films which were activated individually. There the system of pay-per-view applied to an individual film rather than to a certain time window (e.g. two hours or longer). As a result, the BLM classified the service as telemedia which did not require a broadcast license.[1947] The BLM retained this approach in December 2011 with respect to another service of the same provider entailing a 24 hour on-demand offer.[1948] The BLM emphasised that the provider had structured and marketed its service in compliance with the exception outlined in Art. 2 (3) No. 5 RStV. The service which allowed for multiple individual on-demand accesses (including the option of buying tickets at a discount or bundle tickets) correspondeded exactly to the case envisaged by the law and thus did not constitute broadcasting.

The BLM's assessment in the two orders seems consistent with the jurisprudence of the CJEU in the *Mediakabel* case of 2005.[1949] This case concerned a Dutch provider who offered its "Mr. Zap" subscribers an additional service called "Filmtime" which showed feature-length films upon additional payment. The time of broadcast was determined by the provider. The CJEU emphasised that a "pay-per-view service even one which [was] accessible to a limited number of subscribers, but which comprise[d] only programmes selected by the broadcaster and [was] broadcast at times set by the broadcaster, cannot be regarded as being provided on individual demand".[1950] The Court noted that the programmes were transmitted simultaneously to an "indeterminate number of potential television

1945 Bayerische Landeszentrale für neue Medien, "Bescheid C," para. I, p. 3.
1946 See below for an in-depth analysis of the third structural paper and its amendments by the state media authorities.
1947 Bayerische Landeszentrale für neue Medien, "Bescheid C," para. II., p. 4.
1948 Bayerische Landeszentrale für neue Medien, "Bescheid E," January 12, 2011.
1949 Case C-89/04, *Mediakabel BV v Commissariaat voor de Media*, Judgement of 4 June 2004, EU:C:2005:348.
1950 Case C-89/04, *Mediakabel*, para. 32.

viewers" regardless of the means required to encode the images.[1951] In contrast to near-video-on-demand, the CJEU clarified that an on-demand service was "commanded individually by an isolated recipient who has free choice of programmes in an interactive setting".[1952]

d) Service featured in department stores: In-store TV

In two cases decided in December 2009 and February 2011 respectively, shop owners applied to the BLM regarding their in-store TV concepts. One shop owner planned to show still and moving images in several departments of its stores located across Germany. The content was principally characterised as advertising[1953] and included the following categories: introduction of new technologies, trends and innovation, entertainment programmes including music videos as well as music and film trailers, social talk (gossip with stars or prominent figures) and local weather, store-specific information like opening hours and services, local offers and local TV spots.[1954] The exact percentage of each content category was established by market research and thus differed for each individual department of the respective stores.[1955] The store or department manager selected the programmes from an online library, adding specific local content to fixed programme items (e.g. social talk, weather forecasts).[1956] The programme lasted 30-45 minutes and was repeated on a daily basis between 14 and 20 times.[1957]

---

1951 Case C-89/04, *Mediakabel*, paras. 29, 33.

1952 Case C-89/04, *Mediakabel*, para. 39.

1953 The question of whether the service which mainly featured advertising could be classified as a self-promotional channel is negligible to this study. When the application was filed, self-promotional channels were exempted from the notion of broadcasting by virtue of Art. 2 (3) No. 6 RStV. This provision was subsequently repealed by the 13th amendment of the RStV to bring German legislation in line with the AVMSD. The BLM held in this respect that the service did not qualify as a self-promotional channel and was not covered by No. 6 as it contained elements of entertainment in addition to self-promotion. See Bayerische Landeszentrale für neue Medien, "Bescheid D," December 15, 2009, para. II, p. 5.

1954 Bayerische Landeszentrale für neue Medien, "Bescheid D," para. I, p. 2.

1955 Bayerische Landeszentrale für neue Medien, "Bescheid D," para. I, p. 2.

1956 Bayerische Landeszentrale für neue Medien, "Bescheid D," para. I, pp. 2–3.

1957 Bayerische Landeszentrale für neue Medien, "Bescheid D," para. I, p.3.

In its order of 2009, the BLM detailed the notion of "simultaneous reception in moving images or sound along a schedule" as set forth in Art. 2 (1) RStV. It highlighted that the transmission of content in individual stores was different in terms of content and timing. The BLM distinguished two phases. First, a pre-determined concept was produced centrally for each department,[1958] according to which the percentages of the content categories were determined, based on the type of department. In addition, an online library assembling material pertaining to the respective content blocks was made accessible. Some material was selected centrally and its inclusion in the overall programme mix was made mandatory.[1959] The second stage took place at the local level with the complete selection of programme items.[1960] Store managers completed the pre-selected items with local content adapted to local marketing strategies. There was no simultaneous reception as the service was merely available to customers present in the respective store departments and was not intended for parallel viewing by the public.[1961] The BLM pointed out that a viewer would consider the service as a bundling of different programmes specific to individual departments.[1962] Due to the inherent differences, the service was not viewed simultaneously on different devices by the public.[1963] It thus did not constitute broadcasting within the meaning of the first sentence of Art. 2 (1) RStV. The reference to the viewer's perspective is striking but supports the assessment of the BLM.

In a similar vein, the BLM outlined the criteria "schedule" and "simultaneous reception" in an order of early 2011. The provider intended to offer moving images, primarily films showing landscape, animals or nature on the screens in its stores, and in particular in the department for electrical appliances to demonstrate the viewing quality of its television sets.[1964] Advertising breaks were inserted between individual programmes. Throughout all stores, the programmes were neither disseminated simultaneously nor did all stores show the same programmes. Local content (including advertising spots or reference to opening hours) was included by

1958 Bayerische Landeszentrale für neue Medien, "Bescheid D," para. II, p. 4.
1959 Bayerische Landeszentrale für neue Medien, "Bescheid D," para. II, p. 4.
1960 Bayerische Landeszentrale für neue Medien, "Bescheid D," para. II, p. 5.
1961 Bayerische Landeszentrale für neue Medien, "Bescheid D," para. II, p. 5.
1962 Bayerische Landeszentrale für neue Medien, "Bescheid D," para. II, p. 5.
1963 Bayerische Landeszentrale für neue Medien, "Bescheid D," para. II, p. 5.
1964 Bayerische Landeszentrale für neue Medien, "Bescheid C," para. I, p. 2.

decision of the relevant managers.[1965] The content to be shown in a particular store was transmitted by download, independent of other content packages.[1966] The BLM opined that it was of secondary importance whether the content was disseminated according to a schedule. The order of items was determined centrally, in advance, so that a film was followed by advertisements. The decision to add local content was, however, taken at a decentralised level.[1967] It was therefore in the hands of a local manager to organise the content and customise it in line with the overall guidelines.[1968] Moreover, the content packages were not provided for simultaneous viewing. The BLM pointed out that the material disseminated was different from store to store and that local managers decided on the start of the programmes in each store. The programmes were thus not transmitted simultaneously. As a result, the service was classified as telemedia.[1969]

The points raised by the two cases regarding in-store TV are reminiscent of the question of who bears editorial responsibility for the service as a whole or for particular parts thereof. Thorough discussions were held in the UK and France whereas the BLM does not indulge in a detailed assessment regarding (the distribution of) editorial responsibility in the two orders. It can nonetheless be implicitly derived from the BLM's decision that it considered that the local manager operating at the de-centralised level was primarily responsible for the selection of content. Yet, the BLM also acknowledged the role of the provider at the central level, be it the distribution of content categories and the selection of fixed programme items in the order of 2009 or the organisation of the content according to a grid alternating between films and advertising in the order or 2011. Given the specific nature of the assessment conducted by the BLM pursuant to the third sentence of Art. 20 (2) RStV, the interpretation of the terms "simultaneous reception" and "schedule" seem to require, albeit implicitly, the examination of editorial responsibility.

1965 Bayerische Landeszentrale für neue Medien, "Bescheid C," para. I, p. 2.
1966 Bayerische Landeszentrale für neue Medien, "Bescheid C," para. I, p. 2.
1967 Bayerische Landeszentrale für neue Medien, "Bescheid C," para. II, p. 3.
1968 Bayerische Landeszentrale für neue Medien, "Bescheid C," para. II, p. 3.
1969 Bayerische Landeszentrale für neue Medien, "Bescheid C," para. II, p. 3.

### e) Animated series: TV channel on games console

In August 2011, the BLM received an application by a producer and provider of game consoles and video games. In order to enhance the popularity of one of the characters of a video game, the provider intended to offer a "TV channel" which featured two (alternatively three) episodes of the animated series broadcast on TV. The episodes were available around the clock for one or two weeks. The service was construed for about 6 months and would show approximately 50 episodes in total.[1970] The user could choose the programme from among the episodes offered. In its order, the BLM found that the criterion of "linearity" was not satisfied. The programmes were not intended for simultaneous reception as the episodes were accessible on-demand.[1971] Similar to online libraries, each user could authorise the download individually.[1972] The service was thus classified as telemedia. Contrary to the applicant's argument, the BLM pointed out that the users of the game console could not be defined as a closed group, and the programmes were instead offered to the general public.[1973] This case is clear cut in terms of the criterion of "linearity". The more interesting questions alluded to at the end of the BLM's order were unfortunately not dealt with and the BLM was under no obligation to consider these aspects as the service already lacked the criterion of "linearity". Regarding the applicant's claims that the service was not provided along a schedule and did not comprise journalistically edited content, the BLM did not take a stand but did express doubts.[1974] The particularly interesting question is whether the criterion of schedule is met when two (alternatively three) episodes are made available. Presuming linearity, one could argue that two items would be the minimum threshold for constituting a schedule as some kind of order would have to be established (e.g. which episode preceded the other). In case of three or more components, the decision concerning the arrangement of content is likely to become more complex and involve numerous considerations (e.g. audience interests, habits and loyalties). Thus, the

1970 Bayerische Landeszentrale für neue Medien, "Bescheid F," August 16, 2011, para. I, p. 2.
1971 Bayerische Landeszentrale für neue Medien, "Bescheid F," para. II, p. 3.
1972 Bayerische Landeszentrale für neue Medien, "Bescheid F," para. II, p. 3.
1973 Bayerische Landeszentrale für neue Medien, "Bescheid F," para. II, p. 3.
1974 Bayerische Landeszentrale für neue Medien, "Bescheid F," para. II, p. 3.

more items a linear service entails, the more likely the criterion of schedule is fulfilled.

#### f) Live streams offered to a maximum of 100 users: PR agency service

In September 2013, the BLM issued an order declaring that a PR agency offering webcasts to a limited number of users, and at most 100, did not constitute broadcasting.[1975] Two weeks prior to the transmission, the provider invited customers by email to follow a live stream on its website. Users had to register and in turn received a personalised link whereby they could access the webcast.[1976] Due to bandwidth limitations, the webcast was accessible to a maximum of 100 potential users for simultaneous reception.[1977] By reference to the technical safeguards put in place by the provider, the BLM confirmed that the service was covered by the exception prescribed by Art. 2 (3) No. 5 RStV, and such examination is unquestionable.[1978] By restricting the number of live streams to a maximum of 100 (well below the *de minimis* of 500 of No. 5 of Art. 2 (3) RStV), the service can be considered as available to a closed group, which is different from and insignificant to the general public. Interestingly, the BLM alluded to an issue not further specified by the order. It implicitly asked whether the customers of the PR agency who collaborated in the creation of the journalistically edited content bore a share of the editorial responsibility.[1979] Due to the irrelevance of this question for the specific assessment conducted by the BLM, no further details as to the collaboration between the PR agency and its customers or their respective roles in the selection and organisation of the webcasts are laid down in the order. Nonetheless, the BLM did not exclude shared responsibility by customers.

---

1975 Bayerische Landeszentrale für neue Medien, "Bescheid G," September 24, 2013.

1976 Bayerische Landeszentrale für neue Medien, "Bescheid G," para. I, p. 2.

1977 Bayerische Landeszentrale für neue Medien, "Bescheid G," para. I, p. 2.

1978 Bayerische Landeszentrale für neue Medien, "Bescheid G," para. II, p. 3.

1979 Bayerische Landeszentrale für neue Medien, "Bescheid G," para. II, p. 3.

g) Storage of "pushed content" on the hard disks of TV receivers: pay-per-view service

Another provider applied for confirmation that its service would not raise objections under the broadcasting law in 2009, and with a slightly modified service in 2011.[1980] In both instances, the service was qualified, by virtue of the broadcasting exception in Art. 2 (3) No. 2 RStV, as an offer "destined for the immediate reproduction from reception equipment storage media". In 2009, the service constituted a pilot project to develop a VOD system based on the business model of pay TV.[1981] From 2011, the provider offered packages of content upon subscription, including content available on a pay-per-view basis. The technical details had not been altered and the service could still only be received by means of a special receiver which contained a hard disk. The viewer could use half of the capacity for recording content while the other half was used to store between 30 and 40 items of "push content".[1982] These included, in particular, pre-selected films and entertainment programmes. The data were compressed and sent to the user's receivers in small packages. Inside the devices, the data packages were assembled on the hard disk using a special software.[1983] After initial storage of the content, individual films were replaced on a weekly basis.[1984]

The BLM clarified that the service was not considered as broadcasting due to the immediate reproduction from storage media. It made clear that the legislature exempted certain services from the notion of broadcasting which were akin to VOD offers in their effect.[1985] This exception covered individual "push services" which were accessed at a time chosen by the user even if the technical point of transmission (i.e. storage on the media)

1980 Bayerische Landeszentrale für neue Medien, "Bescheid I," September 11, 2009; Bayerische Landeszentrale für neue Medien, "Bescheid H," March 11, 2011.

1981 Bayerische Landeszentrale für neue Medien, "Bescheid I," para. I, p. 2.

1982 Bayerische Landeszentrale für neue Medien, "Bescheid I," para. II, p. 3; Bayerische Landeszentrale für neue Medien, "Bescheid H," para. I, p. 2.

1983 Bayerische Landeszentrale für neue Medien, "Bescheid I," para. I, p. 2.

1984 Bayerische Landeszentrale für neue Medien, "Bescheid I," para. I, p. 2.

1985 Bayerische Landeszentrale für neue Medien, "Bescheid I," para. II, p. 4; Bayerische Landeszentrale für neue Medien, "Bescheid H," para. II, p. 3.

was determined by the provider.[1986] This case is a perfect illustration of the exception and it appears reasonable to refer to reception by the user rather than the technical making available by the provider when interpreting the term "simultaneous reception". Notwithstanding the examination under the exemption, the BLM made an interesting observation in its order of 2009 regarding the criterion of "schedule". It took the view that the service relied on a kind of schedule as the provider determined the order in which the programmes were stored on the hard disk.[1987] In addition, the provider determined the uploading and deletion of programmes on the storage media and thus had a clear editorial function. The BLM considered that in general the provider exercised continued control over the content, even if the degree of control was less than in case of a typical broadcasting schedule.[1988] These remarks are interesting as they specify the criterion of "schedule" as set forth in the RStV and are closely linked to the criterion of "editorial control" as prescribed by the AVMSD.

## IV. Public service broadcasting and the prohibition of press-type telemedia services not related to programmes

Special rules are applicable to public service broadcasters in Germany. One of these rules deals with the provision of press-type telemedia services that has been subject to interpretationi by German courts. The following section looks at the case law specifying the meaning of press-type telemedia.

### 1. The provision of telemedia services by public service broadcasters

The following sub-section concentrates on the interpretation of the term "press-type telemedia" in an attempt to apply the concept, by analogy, to TV-like telemedia. The decision pertaining to the *Tagesschau* app is rendered in a specific context: public service media (PSM). Broadly speak-

1986 The BLM referred to a "Zeitsouveräne", implying that access was on-demand. See Bayerische Landeszentrale für neue Medien, "Bescheid I," para. I, p. 3; Bayerische Landeszentrale für neue Medien, "Bescheid H," para. II, p. 3.

1987 Bayerische Landeszentrale für neue Medien, "Bescheid I," para. II, p. 4.

1988 Bayerische Landeszentrale für neue Medien, "Bescheid I," para. II, p. 4.

ing, PSM are entrusted by states to fulfill a remit defined at the national level and encompassing the provision of a diverse and pluralistic programme offer. PSM contribute to unbiased opinion formation of citizens and are thereby essential actors for the democratic process.[1989] In order to maintain a balanced offer of services in the market (including press products), the RStV sets out certain safeguards. As discussed above, PSM are permitted to provide telemedia as long as they are related to their programmes.[1990] By contrast, "press-type offers" not related to programmes are prohibited.[1991] This ban serves to protect the press from unimpeded expansion of PSM activities into the press's realm.[1992] Freedom of the press is protected by the constitutional order just as freedom of broadcasting.[1993]

In addition, a three-step test will be carried out in relation to new offers or modifications of existing telemedia.[1994] This test comprises, among others, an assessment of the extent to which the new offer satisfies the "democratic, social and cultural needs of society", the degree to which the new offer "contributes to editorial competition in a qualitative manner" and an estimate of the financial implications of the new offer.[1995] Above all, the test assesses the implications of the new offer on existing services as well as its impact on the market.[1996] The review of a new telemedia is conducted internally, by the competent broadcasting councils and subsequently verified by the authority in charge of legal supervision.[1997] This is a further idiosyncrasy of the regulatory framework in Germany allowing

1989 See also Art. 11 RStV which sets forth that "under their remit, the public service broadcasting corporations are to act as a medium and factor in the process of the formation of free individual and public opinion through the production and transmission of their offers, thereby serving the democratic, social and cultural needs of society.".

1990 See Art. 11d (2) 2. and 3. RStV.

1991 See last sentence of Art. 11d (2) 3. RStV.

1992 Hartstein et al., "§ 11d Telemedien," para. 15, IV, 1.4.

1993 See also LG Köln, Judgement of 27.9.2012, 31 O 360/11, para. 94.

1994 See Art. 11f RStV, in particular its fourth paragraph. On the three-step test, see Hartstein et al., "§ 11f Telemedienkonzepte," paras. 16–53, VI.

1995 See Art. 11f (4) 1.-3. RStV.

1996 See last sub-paragraph of Art. 11f (4) RStV.

1997 See first sentence of Art. 11f (7) RStV. See also Karl-Eberhard Hain, "Medienmarkt im Wandel: Technische Konvergenz und Anbieterkonkurrenz als Herausforderung an Verfassungsrecht und Regulierung," *Archiv für Presserecht, Zeitschrift für Medien- und Kommunikationsrecht* 4 (2012): p. 322; Hartstein et al., "§ 11f Telemedienkonzepte," paras. 49–53, VIII.

for "internal self-regulation" of PSM in contrast to arm's-length regulation by state authorities of commercial providers.[1998]

Due to the rapidly transforming market triggered by media convergence and increasing audience fragmentation, PSM have struggled to reach all audiences and appropriately fulfil their remit. Likewise, other market actors, including commercial broadcasters as well as newspaper publishers (and the press in general) face fierce competition (not least from overseas) for the limited attention of consumers. All market participants attempt to diversify their offers and reach audiences on all devices, online and offline.[1999] As a result, offers become increasingly hybrid entailing a combination of audio/audiovisual and other content.[2000] However PSM have a particular role in society and operate under an architecture set by the state. They are funded by public money and are thus accountable to the public. The question that arises (and which deserves more in-depth analysis than this study can achieve) is what kind of online activities and services are covered by the legal remit of PSM.[2001] Conversely, what services are press-like and thus prohibited for PSM.

---

1998 Dörr, "Grundsätze der Medienregulierung," paras. 90–101, III.; Wagner, "Aufsichtsmittel im dualen Rundfunksystem," pp. 850–57.

1999 Rahvar, *Die Zukunft des deutschen Presserechts*, p. 20.

2000 Lent, "Was sind Telemedien mit journalistisch-redaktionell gestalteten Angeboten?," p. 914; Rahvar, *Die Zukunft des deutschen Presserechts*, p. 60.

2001 See for instance the legal opinion on the differentiation between the freedom to broadcast and the press freedom of Hans-Jürgen Papier and Meinhard Schröder, "Rechtsgutachten zur Abgrenzung der Rundfunk- und Pressefreiheit zur Auslegung des Begriffs der „Presseähnlichkeit" und Anwendung des Verbots nicht sendungsbezogener presseähnlicher Angebote gemäß § 11 d Abs. 2 Nr. 3 Hs. 3 RStV," 2010; see also Stephan Ory, "Nur die Tagesschau wäre ein bisschen wenig," *Kommunikation und Recht* 3 (2011): p. 1 who is sceptical of the results of the legal opinion and provides a short overview of the interests at stake; regarding the online activities (heute app) of the German public service broadcaster ZDF see Karin Schmidtmann, "Die neue 'heute'- App des ZDF – ein presseähnliches Angebot?," *Zeitschrift für Urheber- und Medienrecht*, 2013, pp. 536–41; more generally on online activities of PSM, see Mario Martini, "Auch im Internet in der ersten Reihe? – Online Aktivitäten öffentlich-rechtlicher Rundfunkanstalten im Spannungsfeld zwischen Funktionsauftrag und europäischem Wirtschaftsrecht," *Deutsches Verwaltungsblatt* 13 (2008): pp. 1477–85; Hain, "Medienmarkt im Wandel: Technische Konvergenz und Anbieterkonkurrenz als Herausforderung an Verfassungsrecht und Regulierung," p. 321 et seq.

## 2. The Tagesschau app jurisprudence

### a) The decision of the Cologne District Court

In the particular case of the *Tagesschau* app, a group of 11 newspaper publishers, who also offered online newspapers and press products, collectively brought a complaint before the *Landgericht Köln* (Cologne District Court, *LG Köln*) alleging unfair competition by the PSB ARD.[2002] Most online services of the applicants were also available in the form of an app and were thus in direct competition with the *Tagesschau* app. In its decision of September 2013,[2003] the *LG Köln* examined a particular version of the app dated 15 June 2011.

Firstly, the court confirmed that the *Tagesschau* app was subject to the three-step test carried out in relation to the telemedia *Tagesschau.de* which was approved in August 2010.[2004] The telemedia as well as the app constituted a single offer and the app made it (technically) possible to consume the offer on mobile devices, such as smartphones and tablets. The app did not constitute a self-standing offer as it served to supplement the website accessible at tagesschau.de.[2005] The court clarified that the development of an app for mobile use had been considered in the original assessment (along the three steps).[2006] Hence, the *LG Köln* rejected a blanket restriction of the app as such.

Although the concept of the telemedia comprising the Tagesschau app was permissible, the court found that the design of the offer at a specific time could be subject to review by the courts. In a second step, it thus examined the concrete version of the app of 15 June 2011. This particular aspect is more pertinent to the present study, i.e., the interpretation of the

---

2002 The ARD is the *Arbeitsgemeinschaft der öffentlich rechtlichen Rundfunkanstalten der Bundesrepublik Deutschland*, a union of nine regional public service broadcasters and the international channel *Deutsche Welle*. All „broadcasters“ provide radio services, broadcasting and telemedia services. Within the ARD, the regional broadcaster *Norddeutscher Rundfunk* (NDR) is in charge of the implementation of the Tagesschau app and thus also a defendant next to the ARD.

2003 See LG Köln, Judgement of 27.9.2012, 31 O 360/11.

2004 See LG Köln, Judgement of 27.9.2012, 31 O 360/11, para. 89.

2005 Martini, "Rundfunk und presseähnliche Telemedien, Begriffsbestimmungen," para. 68, p. 231.

2006 See LG Köln, Judgement of 27.9.2012, 31 O 360/11, para. 91.

notion of "press-type offers" in accordance with Art. 11d (2) 3. RStV. What is more, the rationale and interpretation of the notion of "press-type offers" may be indicative of the concept of "TV-like telemedia" as prescribed by the RStV and more generally, the principal purpose test outlined in the AVMSD. The *LG Köln* made clear that an appraisal of the whole offer rather than individual items was necessary to determine whether it was press-like.[2007] Such an assessment would have to be made from the perspective of the user, asking whether the latter would consider the offer as a substitute for press products.[2008] The court found that the version of the app it examined was press-like and declared it as inadmissible.[2009]

The *LG Köln* highlighted two aspects. First, in order to determine the "press-likeness" of an offer, the offer at issue should be compared to conventional/typical print media.[2010] By contrast, apps or electronic offers aggregating content do not serve as suitable standards for comparison. The court deduced this rationale from the legislature's intention, in particular the definition of press-type offers pursuant to Art. 2 (2) No. 20 RStV. As examined above, this provision refers to "electronic editions of print media" as well as "all journalistically edited offers which correspond to newspapers or magazines in their design and content".[2011] This implies that PSM are prohibited from offering text-based services including those focussing, in content and form, on texts.[2012] Second, the court pointed out that an offer was press-like when it substituted reading of the press in the sense of newspapers and magazines.[2013] Press-like did not imply *full* substitution of the one (newspaper/magazine) by the other (*Tagesschau* app) but entailed a similar breadth and scope of information common to press products, in particular the level of detail provided.[2014] On the contrary, criteria such as interactive elements, links to other audio or audiovisual ele-

2007 See LG Köln, Judgement of 27.9.2012, 31 O 360/11, para. 95.

2008 See LG Köln, Judgement of 27.9.2012, 31 O 360/11, para. 95.

2009 See LG Köln, Judgement of 27.9.2012, 31 O 360/11, para. 96. See also Martini, "Rundfunk und presseähnliche Telemedien, Begriffsbestimmungen," para. 68, p. 231.

2010 See LG Köln, Judgement of 27.9.2012, 31 O 360/11, para. 96. The German formulation refers to „herkömmliche typische Printmedien".

2011 See LG Köln, Judgement of 27.9.2012, 31 O 360/11, para. 99.

2012 See LG Köln, Judgement of 27.9.2012, 31 O 360/11, para. 100.

2013 See LG Köln, Judgement of 27.9.2012, 31 O 360/11, para. 101.

2014 See LG Köln, Judgement of 27.9.2012, 31 O 360/11, para. 101.

ments or the written version of audiovisual items are irrelevant for a user's consideration of the offer as substitutable to press products.[2015] An important criterion is, however, the user's perception of the material in relation to the programmes of the provider. The court posited that the user was able to recognise programme-related offers within the meaning of Art. 2 (2) No. 19 RStV. Such content demonstrates a clear link to and is complementary to specific programmes. It can thus not be qualified as a self-standing offer and, consequently, does not substitute press products.[2016] The court thus concluded that the individual items which were capable of replacing press products prevailed when considering the offer as a whole. Of particular relevance were the detailed text-based presentations (for example about strikes in Greece) which exhaustively covered current affairs in numerous items linking to other related topics (for instance the Greek austerity scheme and further financial aid by European partners).[2017] In this respect the court underlined the visual dominance of press-like text-based items which lacked discernible reference to programmes. This finding was not called into question by the apparent (numeric) sum of audio and audiovisual elements as claimed by the defendant.[2018]

#### b) The Tagesschau app on appeal

##### (aa) The first decision of the Cologne Appeal Court

On appeal, ARD challenged the court's capacity to examine the particular version of the Tagesschau app, arguing that it had been approved by the German authorities (*Niedersächsische Staatskanzlei,* state chancellery of Lower Saxony) as part of the telemedia concept Tagesschau.de. The publishers, in turn, submitted that the *Tagesschau* app constituted a self-standing offer and was not legitimised by the three-step test carried out in relation to *Tagesschau*.de. Due to the press-like nature of the app, they demanded that ARD refrain from disseminating it. On 20 December 2013, the *Oberlandesgericht Köln* (Cologne Appeal Court, *OLG Köln*) ruled that the *Tagesschau* app was identical in terms of content to the service offered

2015 See LG Köln, Judgement of 27.9.2012, 31 O 360/11, para. 102.
2016 See LG Köln, Judgement of 27.9.2012, 31 O 360/11, para. 103.
2017 See LG Köln, Judgement of 27.9.2012, 31 O 360/11, para. 106.
2018 See LG Köln, Judgement of 27.9.2012, 31 O 360/11, para. 108.

at *Tagesschau*.de.[2019] As a result, the court was bound by the assessment of the German authorities involved in the three-step test (i.e. state chancellery and broadcasting council).[2020] A new examination by the court would, in fact, call into question the authorities' assessment and undermine the very procedure of the three-step test.[2021] Importantly, the assessment by virtue of the three-step test encompassed not only the concept of telemedia as such but also its practical implementation including individual offers such as the *Tagesschau* app.[2022] Moreover, the potential press-likeness of the offer was already examined during the procedure. The authorities and institutions involved had declared the offer, considered in its entirety, as not press-like regardless of the press-likeness of individual contributions.[2023] Although the court refrained from evaluating the similarity with press-type offers in the concrete case, it agreed with the approach taken by the *LG Köln*.[2024] Accordingly, an appraisal would have to take into account all types of content accessible by the app.[2025] Due to the fundamental nature of the rules contained in the RStV, the *OLG Köln* admitted an appeal before the *Bundesgerichtshof* (Federal Court of Justice, *BGH*).

2019 OLG Köln, Judgement of 20 December 2013, 6 U 188/12, paras. 41-42.

2020 OLG Köln, Judgement of 20 December 2013, 6 U 188/12, paras. 43-52. In this part of the judgement, the OLG Köln discusses the procedure of the three-step test and the legal nature of the assessment conducted by the state chancellery of Lower Saxony. The OLG Köln emphasised that the state chancellery of Lower Saxony had examined the telemedia concept, above all its compliance with the RStV and that its letter of August 2010 constituted an administrative act binding on the broadcasting council of the ARD (paras. 47, 52). In the event that the letter would not qualify as a formal administrative act, the assessment of the state chancellery would nonetheless have a comparable effect by legitimising the telemedia concept (para. 51). The court reiterated that the state chancellery in an *ex ante* test had examined the telemedia concept in great detail including, above all, its conformity with the RStV (para. 52). The broadcasting council was thus bound by the result of the assessment by the state chancellery (para. 52).

2021 OLG Köln, Judgement of 20 December 2013, 6 U 188/12, para. 63.

2022 OLG Köln, Judgement of 20 December 2013, 6 U 188/12, para. 55.

2023 OLG Köln, Judgement of 20 December 2013, 6 U 188/12, paras. 58, 60-61.

2024 OLG Köln, Judgement of 20 December 2013, 6 U 188/12, para. 64.

2025 OLG Köln, Judgement of 20 December 2013, 6 U 188/12, para. 57.

### (bb) The decision of the Federal Court of Justice

In April 2015, the *BGH* agreed with the OLG Köln that the procedure of the three-step test had been properly carried out and that the content of the app corresponded to the telemedia concept developed for *Tagesschau*.de.[2026] In contrast to the *OLG Köln*, the *BGH* held that the assessment in the context of the three-step test did evaluate the compliance of the *Tagesschau* app with the RStV's rules prohibiting PSM to distribute press-type offers.[2027] The BGH underlined that the "permission"[2028] given by the German authorities for the telemedia concept did encompass the concrete implementation of the offer.[2029] The court underlined that the telemedia concept would certainly set out guidelines for the design of the offer,[2030] however telemedia concept defined abstractly could not ensure that the provisions of the RStV were respected by a concrete offer (such as the *Tagesschau* app).[2031]

Importantly, the *BGH* clarified that Art. 11d (2) No. 3 RStV required the assessment of the entire telemedia service to determine its press-type character regardless of individual items which could themselves be considered press-like.[2032] The court also stressed that the prohibition to disseminate press-type offers was constrained to content that was not specifically related to programmes (conversely, PSM are allowed to distribute

---

2026 BGH, Judgement of 30.4.2015, I ZR 13/14, paras. 40-41, 43.

2027 BGH, Judgement of 30.4.2015, I ZR 13/14, paras. 33, 45.

2028 The *BGH* pointed out that the letter of the state chancellery of Lower Saxony addressed to the ARD did not constitute an administrative act as it did neither contain a decision nor reasons thereof. It consequently examined the legal nature of the letter in light of the rules outlined in the RStV. See BGH, Judgement of 30.4.2015, I ZR 13/14, para. 37.

2029 BGH, Judgement of 30.4.2015, I ZR 13/14, paras. 47-48.

2030 BGH, Judgement of 30.4.2015, I ZR 13/14, para. 50.

2031 BGH, Judgement of 30.4.2015, I ZR 13/14, paras. 50-51.

2032 In the context of the application for suspension of the app, the *BGH* made also clear that Art. 11 (2) No. 3 RStV constituted a rule which regulates both, market entry (of PSM on the market for telemedia) as well as the conduct of providers on the market (limiting the activities of PSM on the market for telemedia). The court acknowledged that telemedia activities of PSM had economic repercussions on the press sector and thus infringed the freedom of the press as guaranteed by the second sentence of Art. 5 (1) GG. The *BGH* considered, however, that the RStV set appropriate limits and thus ensured the core of the freedom of the press. See BGH, Judgement of 30.4.2015, I ZR 13/14, paras. 58-59, 61, 66.

press-type offers provided these are programme-related).[2033] As a result, the BGH qualified its original statement, positing that only those allegedly press-type offers un-related to programmes would have to be examined.[2034] Due to the mandatory reference to programmes, items lacking a link to programmes could easily be identified and subsequently assessed as to their similarity with press products.[2035] The yardstick for such a comparison, as already decided by the *LG* and *OLG Köln* would be the printed versions of newspapers and magazines rather than the online offers of publishers.[2036] According to the *BGH*, newspapers and magazines typically comprise mainly written material, alongside still pictures.[2037] In sum, an offer is press-like if the text-based material prevails.[2038] It is striking that the *BGH* forcefully rejected the decision of the first instance court to take into account the substitutability (based on the scope of information provided) of the offer from the perspective of the user.[2039] Instead, it underpinned that within their remit (including telemedia not related to programmes) PSM were allowed to comprehensively cover current events reported on in newspapers and magazines.[2040] The BGH thus referred the question concerning the press-likeness of the *Tagesschau* app back to the OLG.

#### c) The second decision of the Cologne Appeal Court

On 30 September 2016, the OLG Köln decided that the Tagesschau app dated 15 June 2011 was press-like and thus impermissible.[2041] In applying the BGH's decision on appeal, the court assessed the overall offer of content unrelated to programmes. It found that the sites the user first accesses (e.g. the homepage or sub-sites providing overviews of the material included in the outlet) mainly consisted exclusively of text and stills which

2033 BGH, Judgement of 30.4.2015, I ZR 13/14, para. 62.
2034 BGH, Judgement of 30.4.2015, I ZR 13/14, para. 62.
2035 BGH, Judgement of 30.4.2015, I ZR 13/14, para. 62.
2036 BGH, Judgement of 30.4.2015, I ZR 13/14, para. 64.
2037 BGH, Judgement of 30.4.2015, I ZR 13/14, para. 65.
2038 BGH, Judgement of 30.4.2015, I ZR 13/14, para. 65.
2039 BGH, Judgement of 30.4.2015, I ZR 13/14, para. 65.
2040 BGH, Judgement of 30.4.2015, I ZR 13/14, para. 65.
2041 OLG Köln, Judgement of 30.9.2016, 6 U 188/12.

mostly referred to text-based material, sometimes including stills.[2042] In addition, the design of other sub-sites was similar and pre-dominantly featured self-contained news reports in written form, often illustrated by stills.[2043] The court pointed out that the majority of material consisted of self-standing news articles which could be understood and made sense of on their own.[2044] If audiovisual material was offered, it served to supplement the written texts. This ancillary function of audiovisual content was reinforced by the structure of the sub-sites which mainly featured the videos below the articles. Even where the videos were presented in between parts of the text, which were separated by sub-titles, the articles did not encourage users to consume the videos. The content was structured in a manner that the user would not necessarily become aware of additional (audiovisual) material.[2045]

The court concluded that generally text-based material and stills were the pre-dominant means of communication which concerned not only the structure of the app but also the presentation of individual items and should therefore be qualified as press-like.[2046] It underlined that only in four cases (on the homepage), the videos were equally prominent than the written articles and that only in exceptional cases, audiovisual content constituted the principal means of communication with users. The OLG thus implemented the BGH's guideline, focussing on the overall presentation of the material and the share of text-based versus audiovisual content. The OLG's assessment of whether a certain type of content was self-standing is reminiscent of the independent function test which follows from the CJEU's *New Media Online* decision and which is also part of Ofcom's principal purpose criteria.

### 3. From "press-like" to "TV-like"?

The *Tagesschau* app case has provided valuable insights into the interpretation of the notion "press-type offer" as set out in the RStV. Although the courts have interpreted this notion in a particular context, i.e. the remit of

2042 OLG Köln, Judgement of 30.9.2016, 6 U 188/12, para. 70.
2043 OLG Köln, Judgement of 30.9.2016, 6 U 188/12, paras. 78-110.
2044 OLG Köln, Judgement of 30.9.2016, 6 U 188/12, para. 76.
2045 OLG Köln, Judgement of 30.9.2016, 6 U 188/12, para. 76.
2046 OLG Köln, Judgement of 30.9.2016, 6 U 188/12, para. 111.

PSM, it may be applied by analogy to the notion of "TV-like". It stems from the jurisprudence that a service must be assessed as a whole. The specificity introduced by the *BGH* to (only) evaluate the *ensemble* of press-type offers *not related* to programmes does not seem relevant in a context other than PSM-related, i.e. when differentiating TV-like telemedia from other telemedia not covered by the RStV. It follows that all components of a service are examined as a unified offer. The separation of the components comprising the service and subsequent focus on particular elements are not acceptable. The benchmark for the comparison appears to be (typical) television broadcasts as screened on TV. By contrast, hybrid services mixing elements (TV-like and not) do not seem a suitable comparator for the assessment. Broadcasts are typically audiovisual in nature and consist predominantly of moving images, with or without sound, which are structured in programmes or other items. Conversely, services that primarily rely on written or other kinds of material do not appear to be TV-like. Interestingly, a service's capacity to substitute another should be immaterial and the user's perspective is of no relevance for the classification as TV-like. Thus, it seems that only the dominance or prevalence of audiovisual elements would be significant for the TV-like nature of a service. It is questionable whether this rather abstract criterion is helpful in practice.

## V. The guidance by the state media authorities

The part below examines the guidance provided by the German state media authorities, including their position papers.

### 1. The third structural paper

The 14 media authorities in Germany have jointly published several documents which give indications about the interpretation of the term telemedia, its distinction from broadcasting and its application in a converged landscape. The first decisive document is the third structural paper on the difference between broadcasting and media services issued by the *Direktorenkonferenz* (Conference of Directors of the media authorities, DLM) in November 2003.[2047] Although the third structural paper was drawn up under a legal framework which is now outdated, it nonetheless gives useful insights on the meaning of the term broadcasting and thus contributes to clarifying the line of demarcation with the concept of telemedia. What is more, the third structural paper does not specifically elaborate on the notion of telemedia (a term which was only integrated in the amended JMStV) but instead sheds light on the distinction between broadcasting and media services as regulated by the *Staatsvertrag über Mediendienste* (Interstate Treaty on media services, MDStV). According to the media authorities, the single appropriate criterion for a systematic distinction between broadcasting and media services is the criterion of *Darbietung,* which implies the impact of a service (or rather the content thereof) on public opinion formation (*Meinungsbildungsrelevanz*).[2048] The media authorities acknowledged that media services could have an impact on society and thus be of relevance for the general public, but highlighted that broadcasting, due to its *Breitenwirkung*, *Aktualität* and *Suggestivkraft,*[2049] exerted a more significant influence on the general public.[2050]

By reference to the constitutional meaning of broadcasting, the media authorities deduced that the term was to be interpreted dynamically, purporting to protect its essential function, i.e. the defence against the exertion of influence in the process of public opinion formation.[2051] It follows that broadcasting exhibits certain non-exhaustive characteristics which the media authorities pinned down in their third structural paper. They highlighted that a service may lack certain characteristics or represent one characteristic more strongly than another but still be categorised as broad-

---

2047 Direktorenkonferenz der Landesmedienanstalten, "Third Structural Paper.".

2048 Direktorenkonferenz der Landesmedienanstalten, "Third Structural Paper," para. 2.2, p. 5.

2049 The media authorities reinforce the importance of broadcasting for the general public by reference to the constitutional characteristics of Breitenwirkung, Aktualität and Suggestivkraft as couched by the BVerfG in its jurisprudence on Art. 5 (1) GG. The media authorities also clarify that broadcasting is to be defined dynamically so as to maintain its protective function under the GG. Direktorenkonferenz der Landesmedienanstalten, "Third Structural Paper," para. 2.3, pp. 6–7.

2050 Direktorenkonferenz der Landesmedienanstalten, "Third Structural Paper," para. 2.2, p. 5.

2051 Direktorenkonferenz der Landesmedienanstalten, "Third Structural Paper," para. 2.4.1, p. 7.

casting. The more characteristics a service displayed, the more likely its classification as broadcasting.[2052] The underlying *leitmotif* of the list of characteristics was the potential to influence individual and public opinion formation. Thus, a conclusive assessment of the nature of the service was to be taken on the basis of this *leitmotif*.

The media authorities enumerated five characteristics of services which were typical of TV broadcasting ("*rundfunktypisch*"). The first characteristic was the potential of the content to influence the formation of public opinion to which it linked how effective the disseminated content was.[2053] The rationale behind this characteristic was that the more frequent references were made to the general public and to community life, the more communication among recipients of the content would ensue, the higher the potential to influence the formation of public opinion. Secondly, broadcasting was characterised by its editorial design implying a structural sequence of content items which were knit together in such a way as to maintain the attention of the recipient.[2054] This comprised an assessment of whether the content was selected and edited for transmission. Interestingly, the media authorities underlined that the more events were covered live (rather than on deferred basis), the higher the potential to influence public opinion formation.[2055] The third characteristic reinforced the "power of moving images" resulting from the combination of sound and images inherent in broadcasting. Hence, broadcasting and TV-like services presented content in a realistic and authentic manner.[2056] The fourth characteristic of TV-like services related to their reach and their actual use. It was posited that the more society "talks to itself", the more influence could be exerted on society. The possibilities of reception by a potential audience was decisive rather than the actual number of users.[2057] The fifth

2052 Direktorenkonferenz der Landesmedienanstalten, "Third Structural Paper," para. 2.4.1, p. 8.
2053 Direktorenkonferenz der Landesmedienanstalten, "Third Structural Paper," para. 2.4.2, p. 9.
2054 Direktorenkonferenz der Landesmedienanstalten, "Third Structural Paper," para. 2.4.2, pp. 9–10.
2055 Direktorenkonferenz der Landesmedienanstalten, "Third Structural Paper," para. 2.4.2, pp. 9–10.
2056 Direktorenkonferenz der Landesmedienanstalten, "Third Structural Paper," para. 2.4.2, p. 10.
2057 Direktorenkonferenz der Landesmedienanstalten, "Third Structural Paper," para. 2.4.2, p. 10.

characteristic stressed the low interactivity of broadcasting and the simple usage of the TV set. The media authorities argued that the simpler the operation of the device, the more frequent it would be used and the higher the potential to influence the viewer. In contrast to a passive user with a diminished level of concentration (due to the ease of using a TV), a user actively seeking information was less prone to subtle methods of manipulation.[2058]

The third structural paper also specified that self-standing parts of a service might be classified as broadcasting and thus required a license in line with the first sentence of Art. 20 (2) RStV.[2059] The formula "if and as far as" (in German "*soweit*") presupposed that the individual parts of the service could be clearly separated and thus subjected to different regulatory regimes. Still, licensing only parts of a service could not be motivated by a goal of circumventing the stricter rules applicable to broadcasting. In addition, the media authorities clarified that a broadcasting service might contain elements which were classified as a media service. Nonetheless, the whole offer would be governed by broadcast regulation.[2060]

The enumeration of characteristics in lieu of definite criteria seems to reflect an innovative approach which allows for a flexible adaptation of the characteristics to future developments. To a certain extent, these characteristics can be transferred to the distinction between broadcasting and telemedia. Broadcasting is associated with and legally defined by the simultaneous reception of content. On the contrary, telemedia are provided on-demand. This difference is enshrined in the RStV. It is also true that (even today) broadcasting constitutes the medium with the biggest potential to reach a mass audience and influence public opinion. Yet, popular telemedia may exceptionally (and in the future more regularly) reach similar levels of usage. This is reinforced by the legal definition of broadcasting contained in the RStV which no longer expressly refers to the relevance of the service for public opinion formation. Similarly, the level of interactivity serves as an appropriate trait to delineate broadcasting and

2058 Direktorenkonferenz der Landesmedienanstalten, "Third Structural Paper," para. 2.4.2, p. 10.

2059 Brock and Schmittmann, "Telemedienrecht," para. 32, p. 334; Schulz, "Rundfunkrecht," 2012, paras. 72, 74; Direktorenkonferenz der Landesmedienanstalten, "Third Structural Paper," para. 3.1, p. 11.

2060 Direktorenkonferenz der Landesmedienanstalten, "Third Structural Paper," para. 3.1, p. 11.

telemedia when interpreted in light of the AVMSD. The distinction between linear and non-linear services is based on the level of control assumed by the user and juxtaposes the passive television viewer with the active user of on-demand services.[2061] Still, the ease and comfort with which a service is used no longer provides a suitable line of differentiation. Technology has evolved to a point where it is easily managed by a great proportion of the general public and the consumption of telemedia does not seriously challenge those interested in watching them. Moreover, characteristics such as the editorial design of content delivered or the realistic depiction of events no longer exclusively apply to broadcasts but also apply to telemedia which are professionally produced (unless they are user-generated). Succinctly, the characteristics recognised in the third structural paper of the media authorities are still typical of broadcasting (*"rundfunktypisch"*) but they seem to have lost their sharpness in view of the blurring distinction between broadcasting and telemedia. As media convergence progresses, these characteristics will become even more blurry.

2. Revising the third structural paper

With the entry into force of the 9th amendment of the RStV and of the TMG in March 2007, the third structural paper was revised to take into account the increasingly wide-spread provision of broadcasting over the Internet (IP-TV).[2062] With the Internet as *the* new distribution medium, the DLM formulated several general principles in a decision of June 2007 which further developed the ideas laid down in the 2003 third structural paper. At the outset of their decision, the media authorities stressed that the differentiation between broadcasting and telemedia continued to be made along the criterion of *Meinungsbildungsrelevanz*.[2063] Furthermore, live streaming (dissemination of content online in parallel to broadcast transmission) and webcasting (exclusive dissemination of content on the Internet) were considered as forms of broadcasting, whereas a wide array

2061 See recital 58 AVMSD.

2062 Direktorenkonferenz der Landesmedienanstalten, "Überarbeitung des dritten Strukturpapiers/ Internet-Radio und IP-TV" (Die Medienanstalten, June 27, 2007).

2063 Direktorenkonferenz der Landesmedienanstalten, "First revision of Third Structural Paper," para. 1.2, p. 4.

of economic activities constituted telemedia as enumerated in the official statement of reason accompanying the 9th amendment of the RStV.[2064] In this respect, on-demand services were generally regarded as telemedia.[2065] The media authorities acknowledged that the problems of categorising content as either broadcasting or telemedia, both of which were equally directed at the general public, remained even under the modified legal framework.[2066] Yet, they posited that the Internet as the underlying distribution technology did not affect the characterisation as broadcasting of streaming services.[2067] In addition, an exemption from the notion of broadcasting was formulated for a service addressed to less than 500 users, which was subsequently integrated in the RStV with its 12th amendment.[2068]

Following the 12th amendment of the RStV, in November 2009, the ZAK deliberated over the further revision of the third structural paper. It clarified that the criteria *Breitenwirkung*, *Aktualität* and *Suggestivkraft* did not stem from an unwritten criterion but were immanent in the evaluation of the exemptions outlined in Art. 2 (3) RStV, above all, numbers 4 and 5 (i.e. services that are not journalistically edited offers and those consisting of programmes activated against individual payment).[2069] The exception contained in number 5 of Art. 2 (3) RStV was to be interpreted narrowly. Near-video-on-demand was thus to be regarded as broadcasting in line with the AVMSD, notably its 27th recital. While two or more hours of programmes or a particular time window activated against payment would not be caught by the exemption of Art. 2 (3) No. 5 RStV, the distribution of a single programme would fall thereunder.[2070] The scope of the revisions of

2064 Direktorenkonferenz der Landesmedienanstalten, "First revision of Third Structural Paper," para. 1.2, p. 4.

2065 Direktorenkonferenz der Landesmedienanstalten, "First revision of Third Structural Paper," para. 2, p. 8.

2066 Direktorenkonferenz der Landesmedienanstalten, "First revision of Third Structural Paper," para. 1.2, p. 5.

2067 Direktorenkonferenz der Landesmedienanstalten, "First revision of Third Structural Paper," para. 2, p. 6.

2068 Direktorenkonferenz der Landesmedienanstalten, "First revision of Third Structural Paper," para. 2, p. 6.

2069 Kommission für Zulasung und Aufsicht, "Überarbeitung des dritten Strukturpapiers der Landesmedienanstalten zur Abgrenzung von Rundfunk und Mediendiensten," November 17, 2009, para. 1.1, p. 1.

2070 Kommission für Zulasung und Aufsicht, "Second revision of Third Structural Paper," para. 1.4, p. 1 and para. A 4, p. 3.

the third structural paper in 2007 and 2009 were rather meagre and an all-encompassing revision which would mirror the changes in the legal framework did not take place. Rather, a piecemeal approach was taken to clarify certain points which required immediate interpretation. To a certain degree, this may be explained by the uncertainties of the market for telemedia which translated into uncertainties regarding the exact meaning of this concept. Nonetheless, a more forward-looking explanation of the effects of the changes implemented after the third structural paper would have been desirable.

### 3. Positions on Connected TV and the Commission's Green Book on Convergence

Two further documents drawn up by the media authorities in 2013 may be consulted to understand the regulatory approach of the German media authorities and clarify the notions of broadcasting and telemedia in the context of connected or hybrid services. In February 2013, the DLM produced a position paper on Connected TV.[2071] Apart from issues relating to advertising, the protection of minors, platform regulation and signal integrity, the licensing aspect was developed. In this respect, the media authorities agreed that the differentiation between broadcasting and telemedia was to be upheld.[2072] Constitutional reasons argued in favour of licensing for broadcasting, whereas telemedia could be offered free of licenses or any other form of registration. It was suggested that the obligation to acquire a license would be based primarily on the impact and reach of a service as well as its relevance for the formation of public opinion.[2073] What is more, a graduated licensing and notification scheme was proposed. The so-called traffic-light concept would only oblige providers of those services which were especially relevant to apply for a license. Under a certain threshold, a

---

2071 Direktorenkonferenz der Landesmedienanstalten, "Positionspapier Connected TV" (Die Medienanstalten, February 19, 2013), http://www.die-medienanstalten.de/service/positionen.html (accessed 25.2.2013).

2072 Direktorenkonferenz der Landesmedienanstalten, "Positionspapier Connected TV," para. 4, p. 5.

2073 Direktorenkonferenz der Landesmedienanstalten, "Positionspapier Connected TV," para. 4, p. 5.

notification system would be installed for broadcasts.[2074] The position paper of February 2013 signals the dissatisfaction of the German authorities with the content-neutral definition of broadcasting and their desire to return to the criterion of *Meinungsbildungsrelevanz* which the AVMSD had made redundant. However no such initiatives to modify the licensing scheme have been taken at legislative level yet.

Moreover, the joint response of the media authorities to the Commission's Green Paper entitled "Preparing for a fully converged audiovisual world" gives interesting indications as to the design of the future regulatory system for audiovisual media services.[2075] In their statement, the media authorities underlined the necessity for regulating audiovisual media services due to their significance for democracy, the perception of reality, culture and society in general.[2076] It was argued that audiovisual media services have retained this status in a converged media environment. Hence, a regulatory differentiation between broadcasting on the one hand and on-demand services on the other hand is still justified today.[2077] Except for some minor modifications (such as abandoning the quantitative rules for advertising screened on TV), the graduated approach established by the AVMSD is still considered valid today.[2078] Nonetheless, the media authorities advocated for the alignment of regulatory approaches in the

2074 Direktorenkonferenz der Landesmedienanstalten, "Positionspapier Connected TV," para. 4, p. 6.

2075 Die Medienanstalten, "Stellungnahme der Medienanstalten zum 'Grünbuch der Europäischen Kommission,'" August 29, 2013, http://www.die-medienanstalten.de/service/positionen.html (accessed 1.12.2015).

2076 Die Medienanstalten, "Stellungnahme der Medienanstalten zum 'Grünbuch der Europäischen Kommission,'" p. 11.

2077 Die Medienanstalten, "Stellungnahme der Medienanstalten zum 'Grünbuch der Europäischen Kommission,'" p. 11; see also the response of the Media Commission of the media authority of North Rhine-Westphalia which stresses the maintenance of the regulatory framework for audiovisual media in the context of Connected TV. It reprimands that the creation of a level playing field should not be accompanied with excessive deregulation. In this context, the Media Commission underlines the importance of Member States' sovereignty and militates against European wide supervision under the aegis of the Commission. Medienkommission der Landesanstalt für Medien NRW, "Stellungnahme der nordrhein-westfälischen Medienkommission der Landesanstalt für Medien NRW (LfM)," March 9, 2013, pp. 1–2, http://www.lfm-nrw.de/fileadmin/lfm-nrw/Aktuelles_Startseite/Gruenbuch_Stellungnahme_MK.pdf (accessed 1.12.2015).

2078 Die Medienanstalten, "Stellungnahme der Medienanstalten zum 'Grünbuch der Europäischen Kommission,'" pp. 11, 19.

long run for services offering content that is relevant for the formation of public opinion.[2079] In addition, the media authorities call for the regulation of platforms at the European level, as an instrument to expand European values to, above all, US-based companies.[2080] The dominance and success of US players in the fight for "European eyeballs" is tied to their size, their financial power, and the ability to create an eco-system of vertically integrated companies spanning all levels of the value chain thereby generating positive network effects and locking users in their worlds. [2081] Thus, the media authorities posited that the AVMSD's scope should be extended to operators of platforms following the German regulation of platforms set out in Art. 52 RStV et seq.[2082] An important aim to be promoted by the regulation of platforms is the open, unimpeded, non-discriminatory and free access to portals or platforms. Hence, all those offering content directed at the general public should be able to make their service available on portals.[2083] In their response to the Commission's Green Paper, the media authorities once again highlighted the need to take into account the nature of the content and its potential to influence public opinion when constructing a future regulatory framework for audiovisual media. This presupposes that the importance of telemedia or on-demand services for the general public steadily grows to a point where they could replace broadcasting, as suggested by recital 69 AVMSD. By the same token, the media authorities called for for the regulation of certain platforms to eliminate regulatory gaps and put European providers on equal footing, at least factually.

---

2079 In the case of broadcasting, such potential to influence public opinion is presumed. See Die Medienanstalten, "Stellungnahme der Medienanstalten zum 'Grünbuch der Europäischen Kommission,'" p. 11.

2080 Die Medienanstalten, "Stellungnahme der Medienanstalten zum 'Grünbuch der Europäischen Kommission,'" pp. 2–3, 12.

2081 Die Medienanstalten, "Stellungnahme der Medienanstalten zum 'Grünbuch der Europäischen Kommission,'" pp. 2, 4, 14.

2082 Die Medienanstalten, "Stellungnahme der Medienanstalten zum 'Grünbuch der Europäischen Kommission,'" p. 12.

2083 Die Medienanstalten, "Stellungnahme der Medienanstalten zum 'Grünbuch der Europäischen Kommission,'" p. 15.

### 4. The checklist for the provision of Web-TV

2014 saw the publication of a checklist for the provision of web-TV by the media authorities. The checklist comprises six questions (of which the last will not be examined here, as it informs providers of the possibility to contact the competent state media authority for further discussions). The handful of questions serve as guidelines for service providers to appraise the nature of their offer and determine whether a license is required, in sum, a self-assessment mechanism for content providers. The first question asks whether the offer is transmitted live or whether the provider determines at least the start of the programme. A live transmission means that the relevant event can only be watched simultaneously by the public. When the user cannot determine the start of the programme, it is transmitted in a linear way. By contrast, on-demand services are typically regarded as telemedia.[2084] The second question inquires about the size of the potential target group, reiterating the exemption set forth in Art. 2 (3) No. 1 RStV. If the offer is directed to fewer than 500 users for simultaneous reception, it does not constitute broadcasting. In line with the official statement of reasons of the 12$^{th}$ amendment of the RStV, the checklist refers to the number of users who could actually consume the offer. As this is difficult to apply in practice, the media authorities advise providers in case of doubt to clarify whether the network (e.g. the server) actually has the capacity for 500 simultaneous accesses.[2085]

The third question asks about the nature of the content. Content that has not been journalistically edited implies that the service does not constitute broadcasting. As an illustration, reference is made to the transmission of un-edited images such as uncommented live-cam transmissions.[2086] The fourth question also relates to the specific content of a service and the frequency of dissemination. It makes clear that the more comprehensive and differentiated an offer, the more likely it will qualify as broadcasting. Similarly, the more an offer is planned in advance and distributed regularly, the more TV-like it is. By contrast, the notion of broadcasting does not

---

2084 Die Medienanstalten, "Checkliste der Medienanstalten für Veranstalter von Web-TV," September 24, 2014, para. 1, p. 1, http://www.die-medienanstalten.de / (accessed 2.12.2015).

2085 Die Medienanstalten, "Checkliste Web-TV," para. 2, p. 1.

2086 Die Medienanstalten, "Checkliste Web-TV," para. 3, p. 2.

cover single or sporadic disseminations of content.[2087] The fifth question acts as a catch-all and asks "are you (still) doing YouTube or do you provide a broadcasting service requiring licensing?".[2088] The media authorities acknowledge that the differentiation between broadcasting and telemedia is more complex if different forms of communication converge (e.g. if google hangouts are regularly made available or offered as live streams, if content is collected in catch-up services). Here, case-by-case assessments are required and should take into account, in particular, whether a commercial purpose is pursued by the offer or the provider acts in commercial capacity.[2089]

In general, the initiative of drawing up a checklist as guidance for providers to self-classify their services is laudable. The short questions help the industry form a first impression about the kind of service offered. This is especially useful if the relevant service displays characteristics which are clearly "TV-like" or clearly "un-TV-like". The self-assessment, however, becomes more difficult if the service does not fall into the obvious categories of traditional broadcasting on the one hand or YouTube on the other, especially due to the vagueness of the language employed in the checklist and the lack of context given to individual questions. Question four, for instance, is formulated ambivalently by referring to ambiguous phrases such as "the more comprehensive", "the more differentiated", "the more regular". The references to a "one-off" or "sporadic" transmission of an offer in the next sentence do not help in the clarification of the characteristics of more nuanced services. In addition, the formulation in question 1 seems awkward or at least unclear. From the wording, one could imagine that a differentiation is made between live transmissions and linear transmissions. One can only infer from the explanatory paragraph that the term "live" implies linear because the user himself cannot influence the start of the programme. In addition, the general statement that on-demand services are telemedia is not further specified. Moreover, question 3 seems to convey a simplistic impression of the legal provisions prescribed by the RStV. It stipulates that offers lacking any kind of journalistically edited design do not constitute broadcasting. Yet, the more problematic distinction between journalistically edited telemedia and broadcasting is sidestepped. The reason for the vagueness may, in fact, be the limited purpose

2087 Die Medienanstalten, "Checkliste Web-TV," para. 4, p. 2.
2088 Die Medienanstalten, "Checkliste Web-TV," para. 5, p. 2.
2089 Die Medienanstalten, "Checkliste Web-TV," para. 5, p. 2.

of the checklist which merely intends to give providers a few indications to assess whether they require a license.

## VI. The state media authorities' reply to the Commission consultation on "A media framework for the 21st century"

The German state media authorities (in the form of the DLM) clarified their position regarding the revision of the AVMSD in their reply to the Commission's consultation in the summer of 2015.[2090] Focus here is on the viewpoints regarding the AVMSD's material scope of application.[2091] The reply was supplemented by a position paper published in late June 2015 which gives additional indications regarding the regulatory framework envisaged by the state media authorities.[2092] The DLM insists that *ex ante* regulation of audiovisual content which has the potential to impact public opinion formation, democracy and the perception of society, is still necessary and relevant.[2093] Yet, the current regulatory framework needs to adapt to the transformations of the market, changing modes of distribution, production, exploitation and use of audiovisual content as well as the emergence of innovative forms of content and new actors.[2094] The DLM thus calls for removing the criterion "TV-like" as the trigger for regu-

---

2090 Direktorenkonferenz der Landesmedienanstalten, "Antwort der DLM auf die Konsultation der Kommission zur AVMD-RL, Eine Mediengesetzgebung für das 21. Jahrhundert," September 2015, www.die-medienanstalten.de/fileadmin/Download/Positionen/Europa/Antwort_der_DLM_auf_die_Konsultation_der_Kommission_zur_AVMD-RL_-_Eine_Mediengesetzgebung_f%C3%BCr_das_21._Jahrhundert_web.pdf (accessed 2.12.2015), hereinafter Reply AVMSD Consultation.

2091 See questions 1.1 of the Commission's questionnaire.

2092 Direktorenkonferenz der Landesmedienanstalten, "Stellungnahme der DLM zur Revision der AVMD-Richtlinie," September 6, 2015, www.die-medienanstalten.de/fileadmin/Download/Positionen/Gemeinsame_Positionen/Stellungnahme_der_DLM_zur_Revision_der_AVMD-RL_f%C3%BCr_die_Bund-L%C3%A4nder-Kommission_27Juli2015.pdf (accessed 2.12.2015), hereinafter Position on the revision of the AVMSD.

2093 Direktorenkonferenz der Landesmedienanstalten, "Reply AVMSD Consultation," p. 8.

2094 Direktorenkonferenz der Landesmedienanstalten, "Reply AVMSD Consultation," p. 8.

lation.[2095] It notes that broadcasters and on-demand providers increasingly face competition from "short form content" (i.e. short videos) disseminated on hosting platforms (like YouTube) or included in online newspapers and magazines. In order to achieve a level playing field and fair competition, the DLM proposes to revise the criteria which make up an audiovisual media service.[2096] It posits that the criterion of "principal purpose" should be interpreted to include single websites as self-standing services, provided that they exclusively or predominantly offer audiovisual material.[2097] Similarly, online newspapers or magazines should be covered by the AVMSD in so far as the audiovisual material constitutes "a significant part" of the overall offer.[2098] In order to enhance legal certainty regarding the differentiation between audiovisual and non-audiovisual services, the DLM suggests two additional criteria. The criterion of journalistically edited content could be crafted to imply that certain offers are important for public communication.[2099] The criterion of reach or relevance for the audience (based on market data and audience research) could signify the importance for public opinion formation and serve as a benchmark to exclude less relevant (small-scale) services from the regulatory realm.[2100]

Furthermore, the DLM is in favour of retaining a graduated approach to regulation, albeit in a different manner. It suggests outlining a basic set of rules for all audiovisual media services at the EU level. The existing rules on protection of minors and human dignity should be strengthened.[2101] In addition, another layer of rules should be designed to regulate audiovisual

---

2095 Direktorenkonferenz der Landesmedienanstalten, "Reply AVMSD Consultation," p. 8.

2096 Direktorenkonferenz der Landesmedienanstalten, "Reply AVMSD Consultation," pp. 9–10.

2097 Direktorenkonferenz der Landesmedienanstalten, "Reply AVMSD Consultation," p. 9.

2098 Direktorenkonferenz der Landesmedienanstalten, "Reply AVMSD Consultation," p. 9.

2099 Direktorenkonferenz der Landesmedienanstalten, "Position on the revision of the AVMSD," p. 5.

2100 Direktorenkonferenz der Landesmedienanstalten, "Position on the revision of the AVMSD," p. 5.

2101 Direktorenkonferenz der Landesmedienanstalten, "Reply AVMSD Consultation," p. 9; Direktorenkonferenz der Landesmedienanstalten, "Position on the revision of the AVMSD," p. 4.

platforms.[2102] The rationale for regulating platforms is their increasingly strong role as gatekeepers, operating between content providers and users.[2103] In this position, they control access to their platforms; they aggregate (audiovisual) content and provide user interfaces and other navigation tools. Such operators, in particular those with considerable market share and power, thus manage large parts of the audiovisual value chain. In order to ensure user's access to a plurality of content of their choice, audiovisual platforms should be regulated under the umbrella of the AVMSD. To this end, a separate set of rules should be introduced covering, for instance, non-discriminatory access, findability of ("quality") content, secondary responsibility for protection of minors and signal integrity.[2104]

Apart from these platform-specific provisions, a solid tier of provisions applicable to all audiovisual media services should be established at the EU level. In addition, Member States could regulate certain services more extensively at the national level. Such enhanced standards could, for instance apply to services providing public value content. The national framework could also be incentive-driven, thereby rewarding voluntary compliance with stricter standards.[2105] The DLM notes that the criterion of linearity is no longer appropriate to delimit different services because both linear and non-linear services are presented on the same screen.[2106] By contrast, the criterion of schedule could be used to distinguish between audiovisual services covered by the basic (European) rules and those services relevant for stricter (national) rules.[2107]

---

2102 Direktorenkonferenz der Landesmedienanstalten, "Reply AVMSD Consultation," p. 9; Direktorenkonferenz der Landesmedienanstalten, "Position on the revision of the AVMSD," p. 4.

2103 Direktorenkonferenz der Landesmedienanstalten, "Reply AVMSD Consultation," p. 9; Direktorenkonferenz der Landesmedienanstalten, "Position on the revision of the AVMSD," p. 2.

2104 Direktorenkonferenz der Landesmedienanstalten, "Reply AVMSD Consultation," pp. 9–10; Direktorenkonferenz der Landesmedienanstalten, "Position on the revision of the AVMSD," p. 2.

2105 Direktorenkonferenz der Landesmedienanstalten, "Reply AVMSD Consultation," pp. 9–10; Direktorenkonferenz der Landesmedienanstalten, "Position on the revision of the AVMSD," p. 4.

2106 Direktorenkonferenz der Landesmedienanstalten, "Position on the revision of the AVMSD," p. 4.

2107 Direktorenkonferenz der Landesmedienanstalten, "Position on the revision of the AVMSD," p. 5.

## VII. Summary

In essence, the meaning of the term telemedia is interpreted in the German legal order by reference to its differentiation from broadcasting. The need to determine whether a service constitutes broadcasting arises from the obligation to acquire a license for linear services. By contrast, telemedia can be distributed free from any registration. The transposition of the definitions of linear and non-linear audiovisual media services within the meaning of Art. 1 (1) (a) (i) AVMSD in conjunction with Art. 1(1) (e) and 1 (1) (g) AVMSD has led to considerable problems in light of the constitutional meaning of broadcasting as interpreted by the BVerfG. The suppression of the criterion of *Darbietung* in the RStV which necessitated an assessment of the impact of a service and its relevance for the formation of public opinion by an institution independent of the state (i.e. the competent media authority) has led to the conceptualisation of broadcasting along technical criteria. In particular, the German media authorities seem to struggle with the classification of services which are transmitted in linear fashion (hence technically constitute broadcasting) but which evidently are not mass media, and thus have a low impact on and a low importance for the population. According to the RStV, such services would have to be categorised as broadcasting if the grounds of exception by virtue of Art. 2 (3) RStV do not apply. In practice, the media authorities stay away from such services, possibly to avoid public outcries alleging over-regulation.

Similarly, the question of differentiation between telemedia and online press products is merely debated theoretically and media authorities remain silent on this point. The underlying problem seems to be the aim pursued by regulation. The AVMSD differentiates between linear and non-linear services to apply a different set of rules to different types of content (advertising, content unsuitable for minors, content of European origin or content of significant importance for society). The RStV distinguishes between broadcasting and telemedia to determine whether a license is needed. Only in a second step does the categorisation result in application of a graduated regulatory scheme. As stipulated in recital 19 AVMSD, the Directive does not, however, affect national systems of licensing or requirements of authorisation. The AVMSD was drawn up for a different purpose and the consequent transposition of the AVMSD to the German legal order has revealed uncertainties about whether to follow an interpretation in conformity with Union law while simultaneously ignoring the jurisprudence of the BVerfG. Alternatively, the re-introduction of the criterion of *Meinungsbildungsrelevanz* in the RStV would excessively expand, if not purposely misread, the definitions prescribed by the AVMSD. This dilemma seems impenetrable for media authorities and might be the reason for their reluctance to disclose previous decisions.[2108]

### D. The notion of an on-demand audiovisual media service in France

Compared to the UK and Germany, the concept of on-demand audiovisual media service in France seems to resemble most closely the definition set out in the AVMSD. This is illustrated first and foremost by the definition prescribed by the LLC and the CSA's practice which is geared towards establishing a level playing field among operators for the purpose of investing in original (national) content and promoting French cultural heritage. Similar to the UK, providers are required to notify non-linear services to the CSA prior to starting their activities. This allows the regulator to better monitor compliance by the industry of the requirements stemming from the LLC and in this respect, the CSA has investigated in the nature of some services. It has also given guidance in several policy documents regarding the criteria composing an on-demand audiovisual media service. Importantly, the French regulator has been a fore-runner with regards to Connected TV and has taken several initiatives aimed at understanding this phenomenon and its implications for the audiovisual media services market. It is interesting to note that media convergence has led to discussions in France on the regulatory framework, in particular, the possibility to establish a converged regulator or to introduce co-regulation in conjunction with extending the CSA's mandate to regulate all kinds of audiovisual content disseminated on the Internet. This section thus outlines the legal definition of an on-demand audiovisual media service and it looks at the practical cases that have arisen in France. It also examines several policy documents to extract the meaning of the definitional criteria. The final part deals with the CSA's activities in relation to Connected TV and the broader reflections on the French regulatory framework.

2108 Some media authorities, notably the BLM, the LMK and the LfM have made available their decisions. This level of transparency is highly appreciated and the author is sincerely thankful for the follow-up in-depth discussions with representatives of these media authorities.

## I. The notion of an on-demand audiovisual media service in ordinary legislation

This part examines the concept of an on-demand audiovisual media service as defined by the French law and accompanying Decree.

### 1. The legal definition of an on-demand audiovisual media service

In France, the definition of an on-demand audiovisual media is set out in the sixth paragraph of Art. 2 LLC. This paragraph was inserted by a 2009 law transposing several provisions of the AVMSD.[2109] Accordingly,

> "one considers as on-demand audiovisual media service, any communication service to the public by electronic means allowing users to view programmes at the time they have chosen and at their request, from a catalogue of programmes; the selection and the organisation of which are controlled by the provider of these services."

In contrast to the German "telemedia service" and UK "on-demand programme service", the LLC retains the terminology stipulated in the AVMSD. The definition comprises elements associated with the criteria prescribed by Art. 1 (1) (a) AVMSD such as "any communication service", "to the public" and "by electronic means". These *general* criteria are supplemented by criteria *specific* to non-linear services such as the viewing of "programmes at the time" chosen by users and "at their request"; a "catalogue of programmes"; and the service provider having control over the "selection and organisation" of programmes. Interestingly, the French language version of the LLC does not reproduce the term "*fournisseur*" (provider) of the AVMSD but instead refers to "*editeur*" which is used synonymously. The term "*editeur*" is reminiscent of the broadcast vocabulary and underpins the editorial function of the natural or legal person providing the service. In addition, Art. 2-1 LLC defines the "*distributeur*" (distributor) as a person having contractual relationships with providers of services (*editeurs*) or other distributors in order to put together an offer of audiovisual communication available to the general public by electronic communications networks. It follows that the service

2109 Loi n° 2009-258 du 5 mars 2009 relative à la communication audiovisuelle et au nouveau service public de la télévision, JORF n°0056 of 7.3.2009, p. 4321.

provider offers the content whereas the distributor bundles content from various service providers and operators to disseminate it to the consumer.

Importantly, the sixth paragraph of Art. 2 LLC exempts certain services from the definition of an on-demand audiovisual media service. Three of these five exemptions are drawn expressly from recitals 21 and 22 AVMSD. They include services where audiovisual content is merely incidental (recital 22 AVMSD), services which do not entail an economic activity, and services consisting of the provision or distribution of audiovisual content generated by private users for the purposes of sharing and exchange within communities of interest (recital 21 AVMSD). In addition, services which ensure the storage of audiovisual signals for the purpose of making available a service and those where the audiovisual content is selected and organised by third parties do not constitute on-demand services within the meaning of Art. 2 LLC. The last sentence of Art. 2 (6) LLC, furthermore makes clear that "an offer comprising an on-demand audiovisual media service and another service not covered by this definition is regulated under the LLC only with respect to the part constituting an on-demand service." This implies that a service may be composed of different elements of which each component may fall under different regulatory regimes.

### 2. The Decree on on-demand audiovisual media services

The material rules applicable to on-demand services are laid down in the LLC and the *Décret du 12 novembre 2010 relatif aux services de médias audiovisuels à la demande* (Decree on on-demand audiovisual media services, SMAD Decree).[2110] The SMAD Decree exclusively governs non-linear services by distinguishing three such forms, namely catch-up television (*télévision de rattrapage*), subscription services (*vidéo à la demande par abonnement*) and other VOD services free of charge or pay per view (*vidéo à la demande à l'acte*). Importantly, while the LLC refers to catch-up services in two distinct provisions, the SMAD Decree merges them into one genuine legal category.[2111] Pursuant to Art. 1 SMAD Decree, non-linear services are defined as services offering programmes previously

---

2110 Décret n° 2010-1379 du 12 novembre 2010 relatif aux services de médias audiovisuels à la demande, JORF n° 264 of 14.11.2010, p. 20315.

2111 Machet, "Content Regulation and New Media," p. 8.

transmitted on TV, for a limited time period and upon individual request. Two criteria are thus essential: First, prior transmission as a linear service and second, limited duration of the distribution of the service.[2112] As a result, all services which are made available for an unlimited duration are excluded *a priori*.[2113] Yet, it is not clear whether the first criterion means that programmes must be offered in their entirety. According to the CSA, the current wording implies that extracts of programmes previously disseminated on TV are covered by the notion of catch-up television.[2114] The CSA has conducted various studies into the markets of the different non-linear services. Besides a study on VOD business models commissioned by the CSA in 2011, the regulator published a detailed study on the French market of catch-up TV in February 2015.[2115]

The SMAD Decree entered into force on 1st January 2011 and details the obligations imposed on service providers contributing to the French audiovisual market, depending on the nature of their service.[2116] The first

2112 CSA, "Rapport sur l'application du décret relatif aux SMA," p. 33 (accessed 23.5.2014).

2113 CSA, "Rapport sur l'application du décret relatif aux SMA," p. 33.

2114 CSA, "Rapport sur l'application du décret relatif aux SMA," p. 33.

2115 Sophie Girieud and Gilles Fontaine, "Etude sur les modèles économiques des services de médias audiovisuels à la demande actifs sur le marché français," June 2011, http://www.csa.fr/content/download/18055/322463/file/etude_csa_smad_juillet_2011a.pdf; CSA, "La télévision de rattrapage: une pratique installée, une économie en devenir," February 13, 2015, http://www.csa.fr/content/download/201366/533023/file/%C3%89tude%20sur%20le%20march%C3%A9%20de%20la%20TVR_CSA_02-2015.pdf; confer also the study carried out by the French Ministry of Culture and Communication on the on-demand audiovisual media services offered by television broadcasters Ministre de la Culture et de la Communication, "Le coût, la valorisation et l'évolution des usages de l'offre gratuite des SMADs des éditeurs de services de télévision," June 2015, http://www.culturecommunication.gouv.fr/content/download/121766/1357492/version/2/file/Etude%20SMAD%20DGMIC%20rapport%20final.pdf (all websites accessed 4.1.2016).

2116 See in particular Arts. 3-5 SMAD Decree regarding the financial contributions of service providers. On the application and enforcement of the substantive rules of the SMAD Decree see CSA, "Bilan de l'activité et du respect des obligations des Services de Médias à la Demande en 2012," May 2014, http://www.csa.fr/content/download/51787/499153/file/Bilan%20des%20d%C3%A9clarations.pdf; CSA, "Bilan de l'activité et du respect des obligations des Services de Médias à la Demande en 2013," February 2015, http://www.csa.fr/content/download/202544/536524/file/Bilan%20SMAD%202013%20version%20publiable.pdf (websites accessed 4.1.2016).

two chapters set out the mechanisms to promote the production and distribution of French and European works, including financial contributions and shares (quotas). The third chapter prescribes rules regarding advertising, sponsorship and teleshopping and the fourth chapter lays down final provisions such as reporting obligations and amendments of other decrees. Importantly, the SMAD Decree has been subject to an extensive review. In April 2013, the CSA launched a public consultation on the application of the SMAD Decree in line with Art. 22 SMAD Decree.[2117] The questions focussed on the application and enforcement of the rules promoting national and European works. The CSA received 19 stakeholder responses including from eight providers of on-demand audiovisual media services, among them Canal+, France Télévisions, M6 and Orange.[2118] The contributions of stakeholders served as a source in the CSA's report[2119] which was submitted to the French government in November 2013. In this report, the CSA calls for simplification of the legal framework and alleviation of the obligations imposed on non-linear service providers. Its proposals regarding the categorisation of services and the challenges to classify them are discussed below.[2120] In June 2014, the French Ministry of Culture and Communication consulted stakeholders on the adaptation of the SMAD

2117 See CSA, Consultation publique portant sur l'application du décret du 12 novembre 2010 relatif aux SMAD, 30.4.2013, available at http://www.csa.fr/Services-interactifs/Services-de-medias-audiovisuels-a-la-demande-SMAD/Consultation-publique-sur-l-application-du-decret-du-12-novembre-2010-relatif-aux-SMAD/Consultation-publique-portant-sur-l-application-du-decret-du-12-novembre-2010-relatif-aux-SMAD (accessed 4.1.2016).

2118 The CSA produced a summary of the contributions of stakeholders. This summary is made public in annex 4 of the report together with the list of stakeholders. See CSA, "Rapport sur l'application du décret relatif aux SMA," Annex 4, 133 et seq.; for a summary of the CSA's main positions, see CSA, "Rapport Annuel 2013," December 3, 2014, p. 149, http://csa.fr/Etudes-et-publications/Les-rapports-annuels-du-CSA/CSA-Rapport-annuel-2013 (accessed 4.1.2016).

2119 CSA, "Rapport sur l'application du décret relatif aux SMA," p. 37.

2120 This study concentrates on the CSA's proposals regarding the scope of application of the SMAD Decree, in particular the classification as catch-up TV, subscription VOD or pay-per view VOD. It excludes all proposals concerning the substantive provisions of the SMAD Decree, such as the proposal to establish uniform threholds for all types of non-linear services or the suggestion to integrate all revenues generated by catch-up services in the contribution of linear services. CSA, "Rapport sur l'application du décret relatif aux SMA," p. 37 et seq.

Decree, notably on the CSA's proposals as outlined in its report.[2121] To date, the government has not introduced any legislative changes and it is unlikely that these will be made before the review of the AVMSD at the EU level has not yet been concluded.

3. Notification of on-demand audiovisual media services

When the AVMSD was transposed in 2009 and 2010, the LLC did not prescribe any form of registration for providers of non-linear services established in France. As a result, the CSA's remit was expanded to include all kinds of audiovisual communications including on-demand services.[2122] In its annual report of 2012, the CSA noted that it had encountered vast practical difficulties in the application and enforcement of the LLC and the SMAD Decree regarding on-demand services. In a market characterised by unprecedented growth, the identification of service providers as a prerequisite for their regulation by the CSA constituted a difficult task which was inherently incomplete.[2123] The CSA pointed out that the standards stipulated by relevant legislation risked becoming ineffective as service providers fell off the regulatory radar.[2124] The regulator therefore proposed to amend the LLC and introduce an obligation of prior declaration or notification before the CSA.[2125] The same request is reiterated in the CSA's report of November 2013 on the application of the SMAD Decree.[2126] In this report, the CSA noted that it deemed it unnecessary to introduce a notification scheme when the AVMSD was transposed in 2008. At that time, a light touch approach was pursued which established rules for non-linear services. According to the CSA, the obligations set out in the SMAD Decree, however, justify prior notification and facilitate the regulator's control of relevant providers.[2127]

2121 The consultation also takes into account the modifications of the LLC as proposed by the CSA. Ministère de la Culture et de la Communication, "Consultation publique sur les dispotitions applicables aux SMA," June 2014 (accessed 5.1.2016).
2122 Art. 3-1 LLC.
2123 CSA, "Rapport Annuel 2012," pp. 18, 25, 32–33.
2124 CSA, "Rapport Annuel 2012," pp. 18, 25, 32–33.
2125 CSA, "Rapport Annuel 2012," pp. 18, 25, 32–33.
2126 CSA, "Rapport Annuel 2013," p. 37.
2127 CSA, "Rapport Annuel 2013," pp. 37–38.

Consequently, Art. 33-1 II and III LLC were modified by a law of November 2013 to set forth an *ex ante* notification requirement.[2128] In its 2013 annual report, following the introduction of the notification procedure, the CSA underlined that this requirement has greatly facilitated the stock-keeping exercise of the CSA and thus its duty to supervise relevant providers.[2129] In the same report, the CSA called for the expansion of criminal sanctions to providers failing to notify their service(s).[2130] This would give the CSA a more effective hold on providers and ensure better enforcement of the LLC. To date, Art. 78 LLC (only) sanctions the disrespect of the registration of television and radio services as well as the failure to communicate any changes. It has not yet been modified as envisaged by the CSA.[2131] Moreover, the CSA recently announced that the notification procedure would be simplified and rationalised.[2132] In May 2015 it therefore launched an online registration form. Providers registering as natural persons have to provide their name, address, telephone number and email address. Providers registering as legal persons have to indicate the name of their undertaking, its judicial form, date and number of registration as well as the commercial register entry. In addition, information (identical to the data required of natural persons) about a contact person

2128 Loi n° 2013-1028 du 15 novembre 2013 relative à l'indépendance de l'audiovisuel public, JORF n° 266 of 16.11.2013, p. 18622.

2129 CSA, "Rapport Annuel 2013," p. 16.

2130 CSA, "Rapport Annuel 2013," p. 56.

2131 For the changes to the wording of Art. 78 LLC proposed by the CSA see CSA, "Rapport Annuel 2013," pp. 56–57. The French legislature may follow suit arguing that failure to notify a non-linear service is comparable to failure to license a linear service. This would reinforce the significance and role of non-linear services for the French society and culture and put them on equal footing with television services. It may on the contrary consider criminal sanctions too intrusive as the requirement to notify a non-linear service is less important than the registration of television and radio services which use and compete for scarce resources such as spectrum as technical infrastructure. Given the technological progress and the reduction of capacity problems on the Internet, this argument may be undermined (or at least under attack).

2132 See the press release by the CSA, "Le CSA lance un formulaire de déclaration en ligne pour les services de médias audiovisuels à la demande," May 22, 2015, http://www.csa.fr/Espace-Presse/Communiques-de-presse/Le-CSA-lance-un-formulaire-de-declaration-en-ligne-pour-les-services-de-medias-audiovisuels-a-la-demande; see also CSA, "Rapport Annuel 2014," 04 2015, p. 85, http://www.csa.fr/Etudes-et-publications/Les-rapports-annuels-du-CSA/CSA-Rapport-annuel-2014 (all websites accessed 6.1.2016).

must be provided, including the name of the director responsible for the publication. Following online registration, providers gain access to an account which allows them to change the data submitted at any moment.[2133] The online form, its design as well as the information it requests are very simple and straightforward. This mechanism symbolises the CSA's willingness to avoid administrative burdens for service providers at the notification stage.

## II. The practice of the CSA

The CSA has shaped the interpretation of the notion of an on-demand audiovisual media service by its practice. It inspected in particular three different types of services: first, video sections included in the websites of providers of radio services, second, certain YouTube channels, and third, services offering the downloading of programmes. These inspections have helped specify the elements composing an on-demand audiovisual media service, notably the concept of principal purpose. The following section thus examines all relevant cases on the basis of press releases and information included in annual reports or other policy documents.

### 1. Video section of websites of radio providers

In May 2013, the CSA qualified the video sections of several websites offered by radio providers as on-demand audiovisual media services within the meaning of Art. 2 LLC. In so doing, the CSA specified the notion of principal purpose with regards to websites offering mixed types of content through a single media outlet. Importantly, the part of the website considered as non-linear constituted a catalogue of videos of radio shows which had previously been filmed and subsequently been made available, as well as music clips. The providers of the radio services argued that the audiovisual content was secondary to the audio material (radio podcasts) and served a complementary function. The videos were, moreover, a by-prod-

2133 See explanation provided on the website of the CSA under http://www.csa.fr/Services-interactifs/Services-de-medias-audiovisuels-a-la-demande-SMAD. The notification can be made under http://www.csa.fr/Services-en-ligne/Formulaire-de-declaration-SMAD (all websites accessed 23.12.2015).

uct of the radio transmissions and were of low quality due to low production costs and the use of a fixed camera. In addition, the radio service providers claimed that the majority of videos which featured recordings of radio shows were not TV-like.[2134] The CSA, however, posited that the video sections constituted a coherent offer which existed independently of the radio service. It also considered that the videos could be watched independently from other content made available on the same website.[2135] The regulator concluded that the video catalogues constituted non-linear services and admonished the service providers to respect the relevant obligations arising from the LLC. The cases are reminiscent of the practice of the UK regulators regarding online newspapers and magazines. While Ofcom negated the existence of an on-demand audiovisual media service in the latter case, the CSA affirmed the same for video catalogues on the websites of radio providers.

The criteria the CSA employs focus on the nature of the offer as being self-standing, coherent and independent. These are also used by ATVOD and Ofcom, though they refer to other criteria as well. Strikingly, the CSA's assessment of the concept of principal purpose is commensurable with the independent function test used by the Austrian regulators in the *New Media Online* case. Similarly, in July 2014, the CSA distinguished between different services offered on a single portal for the purposes of the SMAD Decree. According to the CSA, the service provider made available catch-up TV as well as video-on-demand free of charge. As the service provider did not comply with the obligations laid down in the French legislation, the CSA addressed a warning (*mise en garde*) to the provider.[2136] It follows from the two cases above that the CSA accepts that a single website may be composed of different kinds of services which may in turn be subject to different sets of rules or even governed by different regulatory instruments.

---

2134 CSA, "Consultation sur la directive 2010/13/EU relative aux services de médias audiovisuels (directive SMA), Un cadre pour les médias au 21e siècle," September 2015, pp. 12–13, http://ec.europa.eu/newsroom/dae/document.cfm?action=display&doc_id=12036 (accessed 8.2.2016), hereinafter Reply AVMSD Consultation.

2135 CSA, Qualification juridique des vidéos en libre accès sur les sites Internet des radios, 26.6.2013, available at http://www.csa.fr/Espace-juridique/Decisions-du-CSA/Qualification-juridique-des-videos-en-libre-acces-sur-les-sites-Internet-des-radios (accessed 8.2.2016).

2136 CSA, "Rapport Annuel 2014," p. 86.

### 2. YouTube channels

In 2012, several French broadcasters launched their own YouTube channels. These were co-financed by YouTube and presented content specifically produced for YouTube in a professional manner. Given their commercial nature, the CSA classified the 13 channels as on-demand audiovisual media services. Several service providers contested the decision of the CSA stating that the principal business activity was not the distribution of audiovisual material but the provision of online media or online press products. They also argued that the criterion of editorial responsibility was not met as the content was managed by pre-determined algorithms.[2137] The decision of the CSA appears to focus on the commercial character of the YouTube channels that makes them stand in sharp contrast to user-generated content intended for exchanges within communities of interest and similar forums. Such non-professional or private content is exempt from the AVMSD pursuant to its 21st recital. In addition, the cases demonstrate the CSA's approach towards video-sharing platforms and their mass media character.[2138] In the absence of further information on the subject, the CSA's interpretation of the notion of editorial responsibility cannot be assessed.

### 3. Services offering downloads of programmes

Another interesting case concerning a service making available downloads of programmes arose in 2013. Apart from on-demand access to individual programmes via IPTV, the service *DisneyTek* made possible the acquisition of audiovisual content through downloads. The consumer could either view a programme online or purchase a digital copy. The service provider considered that this activity constituted trade in dematerialised DVDs and solely fell under the regime of the E-Commerce Directive. The CSA submitted a question about the legal qualification of the service to the Commission, which responded by letter dated 27 March 2013 that a service

2137 CSA, "Reply AVMSD Consultation," p. 13.

2138 See also CSA, "Contribution sur l'adaptation de la régulation audiovisuelle," January 24, 2013, p. 27, www.csa.fr/content/download/29369/393286/file/Contribution%20adaptation%20r%C3%A9gulation%20Janvier%202013.pdf (accessed 8.2.2016).

like *DisneyTek* could be subject to both the AVMSD and the E-Commerce Directive. The Commission clarified that the payment method as well as the fact that the consumer acquired copies of programmes were of no pertinence for the classification of the service.[2139] The CSA thus applied both regulatory frameworks.[2140]

## III. The guidance by the CSA

In contrast to the UK regulators, the CSA has not drawn up a uniform guidance document which specifies the interpretation and application of the legal provisions set forth in the relevant French legislation. Yet, similar to the German state media authorities, the CSA provides explanations in several policy documents regarding individual criteria of the legal definition of audiovisual media services generally, and of on-demand audiovisual media services specifically. These are examined below to extract relevant guidelines as per criterion. The policy documents are not legally enforceable and merely serve as reference point for the analysis.

### 1. Typology of services

In its report on the application of the SMAD Decree published at the end of 2013, the CSA considered opportune to simplify the typology of non-linear services. The SMAD Decree distinguishes between catch-up services, subscription services and other VOD services, for example, offering programmes per view. The CSA proposed to reduce the number of types to catch-up and on-demand services (merging subscription services and other VOD services).[2141] Referring to hybrid or "mixed services", the CSA found that many providers offer different types of services simultaneously or develop new business models which do not fit the established

2139 CSA, "Rapport Annuel 2013," p. 30; CSA, "Reply AVMSD Consultation," p. 14.

2140 Art. 4 (8) AVMSD envisages a service which features characteristics of both, audiovisual media services and information society services. It specifies that in case of conflict, the rules of the AVMSD prevail over those of the E-Commerce Directive.

2141 CSA, "Rapport sur l'application du décret relatif aux SMA," p. 40.

legal categories.[2142] In response to reservations expressed by several stakeholders during the preceding public consultation, the CSA made clear that the differentiation of subscription and other VOD services and release windows was maintained and did not affect the typology of services defined by the SMAD Decree. For the CSA, simplification was inevitable, in the long run, by abandoning the distinction between subscription and other non-linear services.[2143] Even if part of the French industry was opposed to the CSA's proposal, it is evident that the current differentiation between non-linear services offered upon subscription and in other manners (e.g pay-per-view) is artificial and does not reflect market realities where providers combine various business models and apply them in parallel.

2. Editorial responsibility

Some indications regarding the notion of editorial responsibility may be inferred from the declaratory form of 2012. This was drawn up to validate the observance of the rules on the production and promotion of French and European works. The document took the form of a questionnaire comprising numerous tables and some explanations. Providers were expected to fill out the form and submit it to the CSA for reporting purposes. With respect to the "quota" obligations included in providers' catalogues and their prominence on the home page, the CSA provided a brief explanation of the notion of editorial responsibility in view of several actors taking part in the editorial process. The regulator first reiterated that it is the service provider who had editorial responsibility for the selection and organisation of programmes by virtue of the LLC.[2144] This is particularly relevant when the provider considers that a distributor exercises an editorial role (for instance regarding the design of the provider's catalogue or home page) and which restricts the provider's editorial responsibility. Importantly, it fell on the provider to ensure compliance with the LLC, notably by contractual

2142 CSA, "Rapport sur l'application du décret relatif aux SMA," p. 32.

2143 CSA, "Rapport sur l'application du décret relatif aux SMA," p. 40.

2144 CSA, "Déclaration pour l'année 2012 au titre du décret SMAD," 2013, p. 10, www.csa.fr/content/download/37263/444477/file/Questionnaire%20-%20D%C3%A9cret%20Smad%20-%20Exercice%202012%20-%20word.docx (accessed 10.2.2016).

means.[2145] Reliance on contracts to specify who has editorial responsibility is reminiscent of the UK regulators' practice. Whether this means that the CSA would accept a contract separating the editorial roles of providers and distributors, and thus hold each accountable for compliance to the LLC is unclear. It appears that the CSA established a default position in line with the wording of Art. 2 LLC, making the service provider bear (the entire) editorial responsibility in all cases (of shared responsibility). As a result, the service provider was liable for any violation of the LLC. This reading of Art. 2 LLC places the service provider at the centre. This is certainly in line with the AVMSD which does not apply to operators that merely transmit audiovisual media services. Yet, one may question whether the CSA's literal interpretation of the definition of an on-demand service is still appropriate in light of the increasingly bigger role of distributors and their influence on the selection and organisation of programmes.

This consideration is reflected in the CSA's report on the application of the SMAD Decree of November 2013 in which the regulator acknowledged distributors' strong editorial roles, for example with IPTV where the provider is bound by constraints imposed by the distributor, e.g., the size of the catalogue or the configuration of the home page.[2146] Due to the extensive editorial intervention of distributors, the CSA recognised that doubts about the person bearing editorial responsibility within the meaning of the LEM and SMAD Decree may arise.[2147] Similarly uncertain might be a situation in which a provider offers a service to a second party who takes and distributes it under his own name, such as the service created by Filmoline and commercialised by Orange under the label *Livebox Star*.[2148] The CSA specified that it considers the party that commercialises the service as the one being editorially responsible.[2149] In view of such developments and an increasing blurring of the editorial tasks of providers and distributors, the CSA underlined that the essence of the notion constitutes the *control* of the selection and organisation of the catalogue.[2150] In practice, the CSA admitted that the distribution of editorial tasks may take different forms. Both actors might jointly exercise tasks of the editorial

2145 CSA, "Questionnaire SMAD Decree," p. 10.
2146 CSA, "Rapport sur l'application du décret relatif aux SMA," p. 28.
2147 CSA, "Rapport sur l'application du décret relatif aux SMA," p. 28.
2148 CSA, "Rapport sur l'application du décret relatif aux SMA," p. 29.
2149 CSA, "Rapport sur l'application du décret relatif aux SMA," p. 30.
2150 CSA, "Rapport sur l'application du décret relatif aux SMA," p. 29.

process (the provider, for example selecting the content and the distributor organising the audiovisual material on the home page and the catalogue) or one party might be solely responsible for the selection and organisation of content.[2151] Yet, the regulator stressed that the notion of "co-diffusion" or "co-publishing" (*coédition*) was not legally recognised. The CSA nonetheless demonstrated its willingness to consider concepts of shared or split editorial responsibility for the purpose of respecting the obligations set out in the SMAD Decree.[2152]

However only one party bears editorial responsibility for the purpose of the LLC. Thus, as the law currently stands, the decisive question is, who *controls* the two activities of selecting and organising programmes in a catalogue regardless of who selects or organises the catalogue in practice.[2153] The CSA noted that the actual distribution of tasks could be found in the contract concluded between provider and distributor. Consequently, the person who was endowed with editorial responsibility within the meaning of the LEM was to be designated by said contract.[2154] The CSA inferred from the wording of the sixth paragraph of Art. 2 LLC, the obligation to specify in a contract the person bearing editorial responsibility for the purpose of adhering to the rules on promotion and distribution of audiovisual works. In the absence of any other more specific provision, this reading by the CSA appears very expansive. On the one hand, attributing editorial responsibility by contractual arrangements seems like a straightforward and inexpensive solution, at least on paper. A standard clause could be drawn up and easily integrated into a contract. On the other hand, in practice it may be difficult or even impossible to reach agreement due to discrepancies between a provider and a distributor regarding their respective roles. Furthermore, this raises the question of whether the duty to insert a clause delimiting editorial responsibility imposed by the CSA interferes with the parties' contractual freedom. This would necessitate an in-depth analysis of the freedom to contract under French civil law. Without entering into such discussion, it can be said that such interference with the freedom to contract appears minor and does not affect the essence of the freedom. It is also unclear whether the lack of such a contractual clause could lead to an administrative sanction by the regulator. In the ab-

2151 CSA, "Rapport sur l'application du décret relatif aux SMA," p. 29.
2152 CSA, "Rapport sur l'application du décret relatif aux SMA," pp. 29–30.
2153 CSA, "Rapport sur l'application du décret relatif aux SMA," p. 29.
2154 CSA, "Rapport sur l'application du décret relatif aux SMA," p. 29.

sence of any concrete legal disposition, such a legal consequence of the failure to designate who is editorially responsible seems to go too far.

## 3. Connected TV

### a) Four principles of Connected TV

In 2011 and 2012, the CSA assumed a pioneering role among European regulatory authorities in view of the dawning phenomenon of Connected TV.[2155] It organised a series of gatherings, engaging a wide range of stakeholders including, among others, content producers, device manufacturers, broadcasters, on-demand service providers, regulators, consumer associations and civil society. The objective of the meetings was to share knowledge about and better understand the emergence of connected TV and its impact on the audiovisual sector. The CSA understands Connected TV in a broad sense encompassing all connected devices which allow the reception of audiovisual content or the transmission of elements connected to content (e.g. social networks, contextual information) regardless of the network used to access the service.[2156] Thus, consumption of audiovisual programmes is "de-linearised" (*délinéarisée*) leading to a co-existence of television and Internet on the television screen.[2157]Accordingly, the Internet constitutes a new source of content for television viewers.[2158] The amalgamation of different sources of communication which are treated differently in legal terms presents an unprecedented challenge to regula-

2155 At this time, the French government also took a keen interest in the emergence of Connected TV. The Ministry of Culture and Communication and the Ministry of Industry, Energy and the Digital Economy jointly commissioned a report written by five independent experts. See Takis Candilis et al., "La télévision connectée, Rapport au ministre de la culture et de la communication et au ministre chargé de l'industrie de l'energie et de l'economie numérique," November 2011, http://www.culturecommunication.gouv.fr/content/download/20480/174705/version/1/file/Lien%20vers%20le%20rapport%20sur%20la%20t%C3%A9l%C3%A9vision%20connect%C3%A9e.pdf (accessed 10.2.2016).

2156 This definition stems from an article written by the legal director of the CSA. See Elisabeth Mauboussin, "Accompagner l'arrivée de la télévision connectée," *Juris art etc. 2*, May 2013, p. 22.

2157 Mauboussin, "Accompagner l'arrivée de la télévision connectée," p. 22.

2158 Mauboussin, "Accompagner l'arrivée de la télévision connectée," p. 22.

tors.[2159] It requires that the image on the screen be dissected into components which are legally classified and assigned to specific laws or which fall outside the scope of current legislation and are thus un-regulated. However, the user or television viewer will most likely perceive them as an inseparable image.[2160]

The first output of the forums was presented at a press conference in December 2011 by the President of the CSA, Mr. Michel Boyon. Mr. Boyon presented four general principles, stressing that the penetration of connected TV sets in France was growing and that it was estimated that by 2014 the quasi-totality of television devices sold would be connected TVs.[2161] He pointed out that considerably fewer viewers actually connected their TV to the Internet and used its "connected functions". At this point in the development of connected TV, it was difficult to estimate its impact on, for instance, the behaviour of viewers, the financing of productions, the economy of the audiovisual sector as a whole and the respect of fundamental values shared by all EU Member States. Mr. Boyon underlined that the Internet was not a competitor of TV but a supplement, in so far as the Internet ensured wider exposure of audiovisual programmes and thus presented an opportunity to better recoup investments. Yet, he also referred to challenges for the protection of consumers, particularly minors, pluralism, the fight against racism and anti-Semitism, against violence and all kinds of incitement to hatred. In this respect, Mr. Boyon outlined the risk that broadcasters' could be passed over and their role be diminished given the fact that producers could disseminate their content directly on platforms and other networks. This would deprive television channels of their content and could have direct repercussions on the French audiovisual market which is contingent on the welfare of its broadcasters to finance the production and development of audiovisual (and cinematographic) works.

When it came to the design of the regulatory framework, Mr. Boyon warned not to recoil from regulation (just because the object of regulation

2159 Mauboussin, "Accompagner l'arrivée de la télévision connectée," p. 23.

2160 Mauboussin, "Accompagner l'arrivée de la télévision connectée," p. 24.

2161 CSA, Présentation des travaux de la Commission de suivi des usages de la télévision connectée, available at http://www.csa.fr/Espace-Presse/Conferences-de-presse/Presentation-des-travaux-de-la-Commission-de-suivi-des-usages-de-la-television-connectee (accessed 7.1.2015).

was complex)[2162] and highlighted the need to adapt the current rules, in collaboration with the industry. He set forth four general principles as cornerstones of the CSA's approach to Connected TV.[2163] Firstly, the respect of fundamental values, above all, the protection of minors, human dignity and pluralism would justify regulation. Secondly, to achieve a fair and level playing field, some actors would have to be relieved of current obligations. Such re-shifting of regulatory burdens would have to be done carefully so as not to adversely affect the interests of creators and producers. Thirdly, support for the production and development of audiovisual works would be maintained and would have to include all parties generating revenue from the exploitation of audiovisual works.[2164] Fourthly, the CSA would resort to other models of regulation to regulate the Internet. As a result, a co-regulatory scheme would be drawn up, involving industry. The primary aim would be to guarantee viewers' freedoms in a "connected" audiovisual world. At the end of his presentation, Mr. Boyon announced the creation of a *Commission de suivi des usages de la TV connectée* (Commission monitoring the usage of connected TV, CTV Commission) to be established as a "think tank".[2165] This CTV Commission, headed by CSA Member Emmanuel Gabla, institutionalised the dialogue with stakeholders and has served as a forum for discussion and elaboration of recommendations and best practices since its official inauguration in February 2012.[2166] Five working groups composed of numerous stakeholders and chaired by independent experts were created. The topics covered are

2162 Similarly, Mauboussin stresses that the Internet is not a "law-less" space. See Mauboussin, "Accompagner l'arrivée de la télévision connectée," p. 24.

2163 Michel Boyon, Quatres principes pour la télévision connectée, 2011, http://www.csa.fr/content/download/20069/334608/file/HD_forum_discours_boyon.mp3; see also a summary of the four general principles CSA, "Les principes fondateurs et les 14 propositions de la Commission de suivi des usages de la télévision connectée," May 12, 2012, p. 2, www.csa.fr/content/download/27118/374848/file/dossierdepresseCommission%20TV%20connect%C3%A9e051212.pdf (all websites accessed 7.1.2016).

2164 See also Pascal Rogard, "Moderniser la réglementation," *Juris art etc. 2*, May 2013, p. 29.

2165 Mauboussin, "Accompagner l'arrivée de la télévision connectée," p. 22.

2166 CSA, "Rapport Annuel 2012," p. 177.

(i) economy and competition, (ii) the financing of content, (iii) technology, (iv) vulnerable viewers and profiling, and (v) new advertising formats.[2167]

b) Fourteen proposals regarding Connected TV

At the end of 2012, the CTV Commission formulated 14 proposals along four broad strands which foster the emergence of a fair and sustainable architecture for Connected TV.[2168] While the user is at the heart of the considerations of the CTV Commission,[2169] it also concentrates on encouraging innovation and ensuring adequate remuneration of producers and creators. The first section underlines that technology is at the service of the consumer, allowing the latter to benefit as much as possible from connected services and terminal equipment. More concretely, it advocates for technical conditions and standards to be set up at the European level to ensure inter-operability; terminal equipment should be long-lived and designed in a way to accommodate technical progress and technology should make possible the processing and transfer of data linked to audiovisual programmes.[2170]

The second theme addresses fair competition among all actors (regardless of their place of establishment) for the benefit of consumers and content creators. A fair tax regime which removes current competitive discrepancies and ensures the effectiveness of the financing mechanism for audiovisual works should be adopted.[2171] A code of best practices regarding fair competition should be elaborated.[2172] The third and most compre-

2167 CSA, "La synthèse des travaux des cinq groupes de réflexion," May 12, 2012, www.csa.fr/content/download/27118/374852/file/fichesconf51212%20%5BMode%20de%20compatibilit%C3%A9%5D.pdf (accessed 7.1.2016).

2168 CSA, "General principles and 14 proposals concerning connected TV," p. 2–4; An English version of the 14 proposals is available at http://www.csa.fr/content/download/27118/374856/file/14%20propositions%20CSA%20du%205%20d%C3%A9cembre%202012%20anglais.pdf (accessed 6.1.2016).

2169 Mauboussin, "Accompagner l'arrivée de la télévision connectée," p. 24.

2170 CSA, "General principles and 14 proposals concerning connected TV," p. 2, propositions number 1-3.

2171 See also the contribution by Rogard who refers to numerous defects of the current system such as the ease with which companies can de-locate and benefit from tax havens. See Rogard, "Moderniser la réglementation," pp. 28–29.

2172 CSA, "General principles and 14 proposals concerning connected TV," p. 3, propositions number 4-5.

hensive issue reinforces the central role of the consumer and the need to shape future changes along consumers' interests and behaviour. The CTV Commission suggests reviewing all aspects of the legal framework touching on Connected TV. Current standards for the protection of minors should be extended, through co-regulation, to Connected TV. With regards to advertising inserted into new services, certain principles should be strengthened while some rules should be simplified. General recommendations and best practices concerning the processing of personal data should be set out in conjunction with the competent regulatory bodies and organisations. Users should also be better informed about the referencing of content by means of a portal. In this respect, the possibility of privileging access to the homepage of services contributing to the creation of audiovisual works should be examined and more generally, research should be conducted to adapt current obligations.[2173] Similarly, the final proposal stresses the need to gain more insights into the phenomenon of Connected TV and proposes the establishment of a permanent observatory.[2174]

The CTV Commission and its working groups continue their work today. Interestingly, in February 2013, the CSA under the auspices of its *Commission de réflexion prospective sur l'audiovisuel* published a first set of findings in view of "Social TV".[2175] The term Social TV implies the possibility for users to interact with audiovisual content featured on a (Connected TV), for instance by posting comments (or tweets), liking content, voting or participating in games. Typically, the notion of Social TV encapsulates services offered by social networks like Facebook, Twitter, Myspace and Google+. Social TV thus enriches the experience of linear television through interactive elements. In its publication, the CSA traces the emergence of Social TV in France, outlines opportunities and threats and also presents an estimate of costs and revenues for broadcasters. For the CSA, Social TV constitutes a concrete illustration of the transformation of the audiovisual market brought about by Connected TV. Its interest

2173 CSA, "General principles and 14 proposals concerning connected TV," p. 3, propositions number 6-13.

2174 CSA, "General principles and 14 proposals concerning connected TV," p. 4, proposition number 14.

2175 CSA, "Premier approache de la Télévision Sociale," February 2013, www.csa.fr /content/download/30546/422747/file/Commission%20prospective%20-%20TV %20sociale.pdf (accessed 12.1.2016); see also CSA, "Rapport Annuel 2013," pp. 150–51; for the copyright aspect of Social TV, see Eléonore Scaramozzino, "TV connectée, réglementation déconnectée," *Juris art etc. 2*, May 2013, p. 20.

in Connected TV and other phenomena intrinsically linked thereto is laudable. The consultation and involvement of a large number of stakeholders is important for the acceptance of the regulatory framework and its future reforms. It seems fair for the CSA to require all players of the audiovisual value chain who draw an advantage from the exploitation of audiovisual content to contribute to the production of audiovisual works. The "follow-the-money" approach will put an end to the alleged "free-riding" of operators distributing or hosting audiovisual material. It should bring about a more just system for safeguarding plurality and diversity of audiovisual productions. By advocating this change, the CSA has sided with traditional players established on the French market (e.g. broadcasters) in order to protect them from (US) competition.[2176] While there may be good reasons to expand regulation to new players, such protectionist tendencies seem to be part of the French regulator's DNA, which, admittedly, is mandated by law to ensure the pluralism of media.

## IV. The CSA's reply to the Commission consultation on "A media framework for the 21st century"

This section of the chapter analyses the CSA's reply to the Commission's 2015 consultation on the revision of the AVMSD.

### 1. General context

At the outset of its reply, the CSA flags current market developments and trends. It highlights the fact that audiovisual content accounts for a significant amount of Internet traffic and thus acts as a "motor" of online consumption.[2177] Business models are increasingly geared towards providing

2176 There had been serious concerns about the arrival of Netflix in France. Netflix was available on the Android Box of Bouygues Telecom as of September 2014. In parallel, Paris Tech carried out a study on the impact of Netflix on the French audiovisual sector with a view to the obligation to finance audiovisual works. Arthur Kanengieser, "Après Netflix, Sensibilité des obligations de production de la télévision à la pénétration de la SVOD" (Chaire Paris Tech d'Economie des Médias et des Marques, September 1, 2014), http://www.cerna.mines-paristech.fr/images/stories/media/apres_netflix.pdf (accessed 12.1.2016).

2177 CSA, "Reply AVMSD Consultation," p. 7.

audiovisual content and become more professional. This development is amplified by the widespread availability and constant technical improvement of connected devices.[2178] According to the CSA, there are certain Internet actors which predominantly build their business models on audiovisual content and which typically have an unprecedented worldwide rate of growth and are vertically integrated.[2179] This "silo" approach bears potential risks for the financing of audiovisual content, for fair competition, access to content, the protection of personal data and cultural diversity.[2180] The CSA underlines the guarantee to respect certain fundamental values in an era of convergence and calls for the contribution from every player which gains revenue from the exploitation or distribution of audiovisual content.[2181] These are players which "squeeze" themselves between service providers (both, linear and non-linear) and consumers.[2182] In this respect, the CSA provides an extensive list of all kinds of intermediaries such as Internet access providers, content sharing platforms, device manufacturers, editors of user interfaces, social networks, as well as operators of search and recommendation tools.[2183] The CSA calls for the current regulatory inequalities stemming from the fact that some fall in and some fall out of the scope of the AVMSD to be eliminated. Thus, the CSA proposes two inter-connected lines of reform for the EU legal framework for audiovisual media services: first, an adaptation of the AVMSD to the transforming market, in particular a clarification of its material scope, and second, an extension of its material scope to platforms and intermediaries.[2184]

### 2. Minor adjustments to the criteria delineating scope

In relation to the material scope of the AVMSD, the CSA comments on the different criteria which delineate the scope of application of the Directive. It points out that the concept of editorial responsibility as stipulated

2178 CSA, "Reply AVMSD Consultation," p. 7.
2179 CSA, "Reply AVMSD Consultation," p. 7.
2180 CSA, "Reply AVMSD Consultation," p. 7.
2181 CSA, "Reply AVMSD Consultation," p. 7.
2182 CSA, "Reply AVMSD Consultation," p. 7.
2183 CSA, "Reply AVMSD Consultation," p. 7.
2184 CSA, "Reply AVMSD Consultation," pp. 7, 11, 14–15.

by the AVMSD rests on the audiovisual media service provider. Yet today, certain actors intervene in the editorial process without being qualified as providers within the meaning of the Directive.[2185] Such intervention occurs for instance with the selection of programmes which feature on the home page or home screen, or by organising the offer and determining the number of programmes made available, or the titles of the categories or tabs according to which content is structured. For this reason, the CSA suggests to expand the notion of editorial responsibility to cover all actors involved in the editorial process (i.e. the organisation and selection of programmes).[2186] This would weaken or even eliminate the privileges of host providers by virtue of the *Loi du 21 juin pour la confiance dans l'économie numérique*[2187] which transposes the E-Commerce Directive in France.[2188] Acknowledging that different actors from time to time share editorial responsibility, and thus editorial responsibility cannot be clearly attributed, the CSA supports the establishment of a graduated responsibility scheme based, for example, on the nature of the content or the type of provider.[2189]

Moreover, the CSA puts forward a qualitative reading of the notion of principal purpose criterion and a quantitative reading of the notion "incidental". [2190] As a result, a service may be offering mostly audiovisual programmes in terms of content but its principal purpose may be the publishing of newspaper articles. The CSA also calls for more clarity between the notions "incidental" and "ancillary" as set out in the 22nd recital of the AVMSD. It explains that the French law does not reproduce the principal purpose criterion and relies on a quantitative approach (i.e. taking into account the number of programmes available and the number of categories/ tabs dedicated to audiovisual content).[2191] Referring to the *New Media Online* case, the CSA differentiates between a service including, among other kinds of content, audiovisual material in an ancillary manner (falling outside the scope of the AVMSD) and a service comprising a catalogue of

2185 CSA, "Reply AVMSD Consultation," p. 8.
2186 CSA, "Reply AVMSD Consultation," p. 8.
2187 Loi n° 2004-575 du 21 juin 2004 pour la confiance dans l'économie numérique, JORF n° 143 of 22.6.2004, p. 11168.
2188 Scaramozzino, "TV connectée, réglementation déconnectée," p. 18.
2189 CSA, "Reply AVMSD Consultation," p. 8.
2190 CSA, "Reply AVMSD Consultation," p. 8.
2191 CSA, "Reply AVMSD Consultation," p. 8.

videos structured as an independent and self-standing offer (being subject to the AVMSD).[2192] According to the CSA, this ruling is reflected in a provision of the French law stipulating that a part of a website may constitute an audiovisual communication and thus be regulated as an audiovisual media service. With regards to the notion of mass media as prescribed by recital 21 AVMSD, the CSA is convinced of its relevance. It nonetheless draws attention to the difficulty of applying it in practice, for example when examining the mass media character of a platform vis-à-vis the mass media character of every service offered on the platform. The CSA posits that both the platform and the service should be mass media for regulation to take effect.[2193]

Regarding the notion of on-demand audiovisual media services, the CSA offers some interesting insights. It questions the qualification of services by virtue of the "lean back" functionality referring to playlists or other tools which continuously show audiovisual content (sometimes in a loop). The CSA opines that such services should still be classified as non-linear provided that the playlist is activated by the user and at the moment in time chosen by the latter.[2194] Moreover, the CSA admits that it has encountered difficulties in applying the notion of "catalogue", especially the questions of whether a catalogue requires a minimum number of programmes and whether a catalogue may include editorial elements between programmes. The regulator also underlines that the criterion of "catalogue" alone is insufficient to classify a service as on-demand.[2195] Interestingly, the CSA expresses support for the criterion of "TV-like" which is absent from the French law. The criterion takes into account not only the form of the service and its programmes but also its position within the audiovisual landscape. According to the CSA, the notion of "TV-like" excludes programmes which are addressed to a different audience than those targeted by broadcast media. Yet, broadcast media may take inspiration from new providers or operators of content to develop new formats directed at different audiences. Due to this uncertainty, the CSA calls for specification of this concept in light of regulator's practice.[2196]

---

2192 CSA, "Reply AVMSD Consultation," pp. 8–9.
2193 CSA, "Reply AVMSD Consultation," p. 9.
2194 CSA, "Reply AVMSD Consultation," p. 10.
2195 CSA, "Reply AVMSD Consultation," p. 10.
2196 CSA, "Reply AVMSD Consultation," p. 10.

### 3. The case for platform regulation under the AVMSD

Furthermore, the CSA submits that the cross-border (or rather borderless) character of the distribution of audiovisual content and the growing importance of intermediaries[2197] for the respect of fundamental principles like pluralism of media, diversity, competition and the protection of minors speak in favour of introducing rules applicable to platforms into the AVMSD.[2198] The audiovisual value chain is becoming increasingly dense and complex and more space is occupied by important intermediaries.[2199] This development may have important repercussions on the financing of creative content or the respect of fundamental values. It may also create competition distortions between those currently subject to regulation (under the AVMSD) and those falling outside.[2200] Even if platforms and intermediaries generate massive revenues from the distribution and exploitation of content, they currently do not contribute to audiovisual productions.[2201] This lack of contribution runs counter the virtuous cycle of in-

---

2197 Prior to the AVMSD consultation, the CSA pointed to the heterogeneity of the sector of audiovisual media services and noted the emergence and perpetual rise of intermediaries in several policy documents. See CSA, "Rapport sur l'application du décret relatif aux SMA," pp. 53–54; CSA, "Réponse à la consultation publique de la Commission européenne sur le Livre vert: 'Se préparer à un monde audiovisuel totalement convergent : croissance, création et valeurs,'" September 25, 2013, pp. 3–6, 11–12, 22–27, www.csa.fr/%20csa/content/download/41934/471929/file/R%C3%A9ponse%20CSA%20LV%20finale.pdf (accessed 15.5.2015); while in the policy documents published in 2013, the CSA advocated the inclusion of the notion of "distributors" in the AVMSD, it proposed the introduction of the notion of "platforms" as a new legal category in its annual report of 2014. The term platform is wider than the term distributor. See CSA, "Rapport Annuel 2013," p. 19 et seq.; CSA, "Rapport Annuel 2014," pp. 21, 84.

2198 CSA, "Reply AVMSD Consultation," p. 11.

2199 In its 2013 report on the SMAD Decree, the CSA stressed that video-sharing platforms increasingly disseminate professional content (such as genuine thematic channels on YouTube) next to user-generated content. According to the CSA, the boundaries between publishers (providers of audiovisual services) and distributors are blurring. Operators of such platforms increasingly exercise (certain) editorial functions but are excluded from the scope of application of audiovisual regulation. The CSA thus demands an in-depth analysis of the role of platform operators and distributors with a view to determining their legal status. See CSA, "Rapport sur l'application du décret relatif aux SMA," pp. 53–54.

2200 CSA, "Reply AVMSD Consultation," p. 11.

2201 CSA, "Reply AVMSD Consultation," p. 11.

vestments in audiovisual productions and gradually risks having a negative effect on the diversity of content.[2202]

In addition, the CSA warns against the powerful means of intervention of intermediaries and platforms in a "big data" environment. It refers to personalisation and recommendation tools which could have a "perverse effect" by offering the user more of the same (the so-called "filter bubble effect"),[2203] trapping them in their conventional tastes and interests and preventing them from being curious and discovering new content.[2204] The CSA reiterates that diversity and plurality of content is at risk. In this context, the notion of platforms should be construed broadly, in order to include all actors who place themselves between content and consumer.[2205] The CSA notes that these actors occupy a fundamental position in the market and exert great influence on the functioning of the digital ecosystem, in particular access to content.[2206] Considering intermediaries who go beyond the passive storage of content, the CSA is sceptical whether the current dichotomy between content providers and those merely hosting content can be upheld.[2207] Hence, digital platforms should be defined broadly to ensure that actors which emerge in the future as "gatekeepers" will be covered by the regulation. [2208] A revised AVMSD should therefore cover operators which distribute content, video sharing platforms which

---

2202 CSA, "Reply AVMSD Consultation," p. 11.

2203 For a short explanation of the filter bubble effect, see for instance Robin Foster and Tom Broughton, "PSB Prominence in a Converged Media World," December 21, 2012, p. 22, downloads.bbc.co.uk/aboutthebbc/insidethebbc/howwework/reports/pdf/bbc_psb_prominence.pdf (accessed 15.1.2016); For more extensive reading, see Eli Pariser, *The Filter Bubble: What the Internet Is Hiding from You* (London: Penguin Press, 2011).

2204 CSA, "Reply AVMSD Consultation," p. 12.

2205 CSA, "Reply AVMSD Consultation," p. 11.

2206 CSA, "Reply AVMSD Consultation," p. 15.

2207 CSA, "Reply AVMSD Consultation," p. 11.

2208 CSA, "Reply AVMSD Consultation," p. 11; in its response to the Commission's Green Paper, the CSA underlines that video-sharing platforms are in competition with audiovisual media service providers and that competitive pressures of the former on the latter will augment further. It therefore proposes to expand regulation to distributors of audiovisual services. This notion could be introduced in the AVMSD and construed in line with Art. 2 LLC. It should cover device manufacturers which provide audiovisual media services as well as operators of application stores. The CSA also draws attention to the role of search engines, in particular, the practices of Google. See CSA, "Reply to Commission Green Book," pp. 25–27; see also CSA, "Rapport Annuel 2013," p. 149.

offer professional content, manufacturers of terminal equipment, operators of app stores and interfaces (which may promote certain services to the detriment of others) as well as search engines (which determine the order in which services – legal or illegal appear).[2209] In this context, the CSA urges caution in particular with respect to vertically integrated companies. At the end of September 2016, the CSA published a study that assessed in-depth the business model of digital platforms, their role in converging media markets and their interaction with other players in the audiovisual value chain.[2210] The study found that digital platforms have a far-reaching impact on the audiovisual market. With respect to the regulation of digital platforms, the study highlighted ten issues for possible regulatory intervention including ensuring non-discriminatory access to platforms, content referencing (by algorithms), uniformisation of content (so-called "filter-bubble effect"), advertising, promotion of values and content financing.[2211]

## V. The French regulatory framework in the future

The final section of this part's chapter is devoted to current discussions in France about possible changes to the regulatory framework.

---

2209 CSA, "Reply AVMSD Consultation," p. 15; see also the Lescure report in which an extension of the notion of distributors to Internet access providers, manufacturers of terminal equipment and devices and managers of app stores is discussed. Pierre Lescure, "Mission 'Acte II de l'exception culturelle': Contribution aux politiques culturelles à l'ère numérique," May 2013, pp. 160–61, http://www.culturecommunication.gouv.fr/var/culture/storage/culture_mag/rapport_lescure/index.htm#/1 (accessed 20.1.2016).

2210 CSA, "Plateformes et accès aux contenus audiovisuels, Quels enjeux concurrentiels et de régulation?," September 23, 2016, http://www.csa.fr/content/download/223681/597947/file/CSA-Etude_plateformes_%202016.pdf (accessed 20.1.2016).

2211 CSA, "Plateformes et accès aux contenus audiovisuels," paras. 3.1-3.10, pp. 78–90.

1. Incentive-based regulation

Interestingly, the CSA reflects on the introduction of a regulatory scheme based on incentives (*régime de conventionnement*) in its 2013 report on the SMAD Decree.[2212] In this context, the CSA refers to the *Lescure* report, a voluminous review of French audiovisual policy commissioned by the French government and published in May 2013, which proposes, *inter alia*, a balanced scheme based on two components: voluntary commitments and benefits/advantages.[2213] During the consultation carried out by the CSA, several stakeholders expressed support for an optional scheme. This would allow the CSA to negotiate stricter standards with service providers, beyond the rules prescribed by the SMAD Decree, in return for specific advantages. The voluntary commitments would mainly consist in raising providers' contribution to the development and production of audiovisual works. Possible advantages or benefits, as suggested by the *Lescure* report, could be easier access to aids or other subsidies, facilitating access to consumers (e.g. by ensuring non-discriminatory access to platforms of distributors) or audiovisual works (e.g. by reducing media release windows).[2214] In line with the *Lescure* report the CSA considers that the presence and distribution of services adhering to the voluntary scheme (*service conventionné)* might also be enhanced by a mechanism of "must-distribute". [2215] Such a mechanism would, according to the CSA, ensure fair, reasonable and non-discriminatory access to platforms and other networks of services supporting the public interest (including PSM). In addition to facilitating access, privileged referencing of such services to ensure greater visibility could also be foreseen.[2216] The CSA's considerations for a complementary voluntary level of regulation based on incentivising providers are still in an embryonic state. They would, if implemented, necessitate a fundamental overhaul of the French legal framework, a fact that

---

2212 CSA, "Rapport sur l'application du décret relatif aux SMA," pp. 55–56.

2213 Lescure, "Report on cultural policy in the Internet era," sec. fiche A-9, p. 150–154, in particular proposition number 17.

2214 Lescure, "Report on cultural policy in the Internet era," pp. 153–54; CSA, "Rapport sur l'application du décret relatif aux SMA," p. 55.

2215 Lescure, "Report on cultural policy in the Internet era," sec. fiche A-10, pp. 157, 162–163, in particular proposition number 19; CSA, "Rapport sur l'application du décret relatif aux SMA," pp. 56–57.

2216 Lescure, "Report on cultural policy in the Internet era," pp. 164–65; CSA, "Rapport sur l'application du décret relatif aux SMA," p. 57.

the CSA has acknowledged. Nonetheless, the 2013 report signals the regulator's willingness to contemplate new approaches which go beyond traditional regulatory models.

## 2. Possible changes to the regulatory framework

### a) Convergence of regulators

In the summer of 2012, the French government launched a reflection process on the adaptation of audiovisual regulation and the question of convergence of regulators. Within half a year, the CSA submitted two contributions. The first response of October 2012 focussed strictly on institutional aspects of the regulatory framework while the second response, of January 2013, included an analysis of legal provisions as well as proposals for reform.[2217] In both contributions, the CSA underlined the need to reform the regulatory scheme in light of the profound transformations that are shaking the sector.[2218]

With respect to the institutional question, the government has contemplated a merger of regulatory authorities, notably the regulators for audiovisual communication (CSA) and the regulator in charge of electronic communications and postal services (*L'Autorité de Régulation des Communications Electroniques et des Postes*, ARCEP).[2219] The CSA outlined

2217 CSA, "Contribution à la réflexion sur l'évolution de la régulation de l'audiovisuel et des communications électroniques," October 30, 2012, http://www.csa.fr/es/content/download/25048/367928/file/Contribution+CSA+r%C3%A9gulation+audiovisuel+-+Octobre+2012+prot%C3%A9g%C3%A9.pdf (accessed 10.1.2016); CSA, "Reply to government consultation on the adaptation of audiovisual regulation.".

2218 CSA, "Reply to government consultation on the evolution of audiovisual regulation," p. 16; CSA, "Reply to government consultation on the adaptation of audiovisual regulation," pp. 7–19.

2219 The French government also considerd the consolidation of further regulators like the Haute Autorité pour la diffusion des oeuvres et la protection des droits sur internet (HADOPI). Regarding a potential fusion between the CSA and HADOPI, the CSA notes that the Lescure report (not published at the time) would elaborate this question and that the commonalities between the two authorities were quasi inexistant (with the exception of the issue of the private copy). See CSA, "Reply to government consultation on the evolution of audiovisual regulation," pp. 12–13.

two options for merging the CSA and the ARCEP. Firstly, it proposes a consolidation in two phases. In a first step, the two authorities would be maintained while a common body or instance endowed with decision-making powers could be set up. This new instance would comprise members of the two regulators. Whenever a subject of common interest was raised (such as spectrum management), the new instance would be called upon to take a decision.[2220] In a second step, a unique regulatory authority consisting of two units would be established, one unit would be competent to regulate content and pluralism, the other would regulate the infrastructure and the networks, and both would be chaired by the same person. In addition, each unit could involve members of the other unit in a consultative capacity and they could sit in one formation to address common subjects.[2221]

The second option presented by the CSA would entail the creation of a single institution with only one unit.[2222] This would be a more radical reconstruction of the regulatory framework and, the CSA presumed, would encounter strong opposition. Considering that option 2 would be premature and could risk subordinating cultural objectives to market and competition considerations, unsurprisingly the CSA pronounced in favour of option 1.[2223] This would guarantee a more independent regulation of audiovisual communications. Depending on the concrete design of the two units, the CSA could continue to exist in (more or less) its current form. This would enhance continuity of practice and ease the transition from two regulators to a single one. This could, however, be only a symbolic move if the separation of the two units persisted internally and no regular exchanges were organised. In the absence of a concrete proposal of a converged regulator amalgamating the CSA and ARCEP, the impact and effects are difficult to foresee. So far, the French government has refrained from taking any further action in this respect. This discussion nonetheless shows the effects of media convergence on the organisation of regulatory

2220 CSA, "Reply to government consultation on the evolution of audiovisual regulation," p. 14.

2221 CSA, "Reply to government consultation on the evolution of audiovisual regulation," p. 14.

2222 CSA, "Reply to government consultation on the evolution of audiovisual regulation," p. 15.

2223 CSA, "Reply to government consultation on the evolution of audiovisual regulation," p. 15.

bodies and the pressure it exerts on national regulatory bodies to converge or at least institutionalise regular exchanges.

b) Co-regulation of audiovisual content distributed online

The CSA's first contribution to the government's inquiry is supplemented by a second one submitted in January 2013 which is more comprehensive and tackles more substantive questions on the reform of the French audiovisual sector.[2224] At the outset of its publication, the CSA pointed to the general context and the need to anchor the forthcoming law within the strong political ambition of furthering a fruitful digital revolution, favouring access to quality content and protecting the general public.[2225] The CSA proposed several modifications to the existing regulatory framework. Mainly, an adaptation of the substantive rules to the changes within the audiovisual sector as well as the extension of its own scope of intervention, accompanied by the introduction of a co-regulatory scheme.[2226] In this respect, the CSA advocated an expansion of its competences to online video sites covering *all* audiovisual content disseminated online.[2227] This would imply that the CSA would be responsible for regulating services explicitly exempt from the current AVMSD (and correspondingly the LLC), such as video-sharing portals offering user-generated content.[2228] The co-regulatory scheme would rely on two components: first, the establishment of general principles by the CSA (such as the development of a voluntary labelling system) and second, self-regulation by service providers and operators of platforms in cooperation with family associations.[2229] The regulator would monitor the effective functioning of the co-regulatory

---

2224 CSA, "Reply to government consultation on the adaptation of audiovisual regulation," p. 5.

2225 CSA, "Reply to government consultation on the adaptation of audiovisual regulation," p. 6.

2226 CSA, "Reply to government consultation on the adaptation of audiovisual regulation," p. 24.

2227 CSA, "Reply to government consultation on the adaptation of audiovisual regulation," pp. 26–27.

2228 CSA, "Reply to government consultation on the adaptation of audiovisual regulation," p. 27.

2229 CSA, "Reply to government consultation on the adaptation of audiovisual regulation," p. 27.

scheme.[2230] Action could primarily be taken for the protection of minors, the respect of human dignity and the prohibition of incitement to hatred, three areas enshrined in Art. 15 LLC.[2231]

The introduction of a co-regulatory scheme appears reasonable for online audiovisual content that does not qualify as an audiovisual media service. Such a regulatory model is less intrusive than top-down regulation stemming from the CSA itself. It would give industry and other stakeholders an important voice and could legitimise the extension of the regulator's competences in areas not (yet) coordinated at the EU level. The proposal by the CSA is, however, very imprecise and the legal nature of co-regulation in general, as well as the general principles drawn up by the CSA, are unclear. To date, the competences of the CSA have not been enlarged. It continues to regulate audiovisual communication within the meaning of Art. 2 LLC but does not have a hold on *other* audiovisual content which does not qualify as such. A co-regulatory scheme in which the CSA outlines principles which are further refined by the industry itself has also not been developed. The French government's inaction, both in view of convergence of regulators and co-regulation may be attributed to the volatile and fluctuating state of the market. The government might consider the necessity for further research and evidence before taking concrete steps. In addition, the current review of the AVMSD is likely to have halted any such initiatives and it seems improbable that the French government will act before a revised AVMSD has been adopted.

## VI. Summary

In sum, the notion of on-demand audiovisual media service in France is interpreted in light of the respect and promotion of cultural diversity which is constitutionally guaranteed. The French regulator is predominantly concerned with adapting the obligations concerning the financing of audiovisual and cinematographic production to current market realities. This context sets the scene for the CSA's activities and practice. The SMAD Decree constitutes a first illustration of the adjustment of the

2230 CSA, "Reply to government consultation on the adaptation of audiovisual regulation," p. 27.

2231 CSA, "Reply to government consultation on the adaptation of audiovisual regulation," p. 28.

French legal framework.[2232] It is a strong signal that the cultural objectives of French audiovisual policy are extended to VOD providers operating on the Internet. This objective is made more difficult by the emergence of new(er) players which target (among others) the French public but are established outside of France/the EU. So far, these are not covered by the obligations incumbent on broadcasters and providers of on-demand services. Yet, the CSA has repeatedly stressed its support for subjecting online platforms to European regulation in order to put an end to "cultural dumping".[2233]

## *E. Comparing the UK, German and French regulators' approaches to the notion of an on-demand audiovisual media service*

The three regulators examined in this study have been very active in shaping their respective regulatory environments. The question of scope, more particularly the question of what constitutes an (on-demand) audiovisual media service is one of fundamental significance because that is what triggers a specific regulatory regime, and one that is much more burdensome for providers in comparison to the obligations stemming from the E-Commerce Directive for example. Since the national legal orders combine elements pertaining to the notions of an audiovisual media service and an on-demand audiovisual media service as set out in Art. 1 (1) (a) (i) and Art. 1 (1) (g) AVMSD, the specifications consequently relate to both of these concepts. In the UK, a bulk of cases has emerged from the examination of numerous services. Through regulators' analysis, a practice has developed incrementally. It relies on criteria which specify the key terms contained in the CA as transposed from the AVMSD. In France and Germany, fewer cases have been decided by the regulators which have mainly been active through guidelines and position papers. The CSA and, to a lesser extent,

2232 Rogard, "Moderniser la réglementation," p. 29; see also CSA, "Reply to government consultation on the adaptation of audiovisual regulation," p. 26.

2233 Rogard, "Moderniser la réglementation," p. 29; in contrast, Flourens, a Google employee, outlines how Google contributes to cultural objectives arguing that YouTube is an important vector for the emergence of original content creators. See Cordelia Flourens, "L'innovation au soutien de la création selon Google," *Juris art etc. 2*, May 2013, pp. 34–35.

the German media authorities have set a particular focus on the phenomenon of connected TV.

In France, the regulator has led an open dialogue engaging all stakeholders to participate in the formulation of core principles. A key outcome has been the recognition to re-shift regulatory burdens and to include all parties deriving revenue from the distribution of audiovisual content into the delicate scheme supporting audiovisual productions. In Germany, the media authorities have struggled to adjust the legal framework to the requirements of the AVMSD. While the boundaries between TV-like telemedia (corresponding to on-demand audiovisual media services) and other telemedia remain blurry, the distinction between broadcasting and TV-like telemedia has been specified through orders of several state media authorities. Overall, however, it appears that the unease of German regulators regarding the definitions of broadcasting and on-demand services is greatest among the regulators scrutinised here. This is indubitably the reason why the DLM, representing the 14 German state media authorities, pushes for more fundamental changes of the AVMSD than its UK and French counterparts. The following section summarises the positions taken by the three regulators with regards to the notion of editorial responsibility and principal purpose, crucial elements of the definition of on-demand audiovisual media services. It also outlines their perspectives on the reform of the AVMSD and commences by some general observations. On the basis of this condensed overview, best practices are extracted and suggestions are made for a future EU regulatory framework for audiovisual media services, as presented in the sixth chapter.

## I. General observations

The comparison of the measures taken by national regulatory authorities in the UK, Germany and France is made difficult by several factors. While there has been a notification requirement for service providers established in France (since 2013) and the UK, there is no such obligation in Germany where the RStV explicitly makes possible the provision of non-linear services without registration or other comparable administrative act. Thus, state media authorities are primarily interested in identifying broadcasters for the purpose of allocating licenses (which are also required in the UK and France). Below the threshold of what constitutes broadcasting, state media authorities have no particular obligation (other than the general task of supervision) and seemingly no particular motivation to proactively classify services and differentiate between journalistically edited or TV-like telemedia and other telemedia or services not subject to content standards. To this end, Germany as a subject of analysis stands apart from France and the UK.

What is also different in Germany and makes the delineation what constitutes an on-demand audiovisual media service so difficult is the fact that telemedia services are only defined by reference to other services and neither the RStV nor the TMG stipulate a positive definition of telemedia services. These are instead defined in relation to broadcasting as the "upper limit" and telecommunications services as the "lower limit". The orders of state media authorities examined above, purport to investigate whether a service constitutes broadcasting (and thus requires a license) or whether it does not raise any objections and is thus exempt from registration. Most of the orders relate to express exceptions from the notion of broadcasting laid down in the RStV. The RStV, moreover, introduces several concepts of telemedia services contingent on providers (e.g. PSM) so that the overarching legal framework is incoherent and heterogeneous, owing to successive amendments of the interstate treaty.

While the concept of broadcasting as developed by the jurisprudence of the German BVerfG is the main issue in Germany, the CSA is engrossed in the guarantee of pluralism. Its actions are geared towards recalibrating the regulatory framework and achieving a just participation of all market players in the financing of audiovisual (and cinematographic) works. The identification of on-demand audiovisual media services is important to secure contributions to the virtuous cycle of audiovisual production which, according to the CSA, is seriously at risk in an era of convergence. In contrast to the German and French regulators that appear to operate through a particularly visible lens, the UK regulators do not, at first glance, expose a similarly strong "ideology". Yet, they (strictly speaking Ofcom) seem to be similarly "branded" by their statutory mission. Ofcom has pursued a liberal market approach promoting competition and a "hands off" policy which it imposed on ATVOD. The UK's historically close ties to the US market, with which it shares the same language and close cultural relations, may be one reason for Ofcom's reluctance to regulate "new players" often located in the US. Service providers established in the UK may benefit from privileged cooperation agreements with US companies which could backtrack in view of the threat of EU regulation. It follows that every regulator is subject to, and thus predetermined by, the particular national context within which it is established. For this reason the present study briefly outlined national regulatory schemes in the third chapter. These paradigms constitute the regulators' very fabric which they defend in every policy arena and which in turn has to be taken into account when examining regulators' interpretations of the notion of an on-demand audiovisual media service.

## II. Specifications of some elements of an on-demand audiovisual media service

### 1. TV-like

In Germany and the UK, different positions seem to have crystallised regarding the interpretation of the notion of "TV-like". Recital 24 AVMSD refers to competition for the same audience. Ofcom has conducted extensive research into audience attitudes and users' consumption patterns. It also takes users' perspectives into account when appraising the nature of an audiovisual service. Above all, Ofcom puts itself into users' shoes by asking whether the user would substitute the time spent watching TV for the audiovisual service under consideration. In sum, Ofcom examines, from a user perspective, whether the audiovisual service is an alternative to TV broadcasting. What is relevant to Ofcom is whether the service is *capable* of competing for the same audience and *capable* of reaching the general public. This is the reason why Ofcom is careful not to exempt small-scale providers or those with a low user base/membership or turnover. New services starting off on a small-scale may have the potential to develop and become "bigger". Similarly, small-scale services may cater for niche audiences and appeal to minority tastes just like specialised TV channels.

In sharp contrast to Ofcom, the notion of competition in Germany has been narrowed down by the BGH which rejected the substitutability argument (in relation to press-like offers) as inappropriate. Instead, the benchmark for comparison would be the conventional or analogue form of the media in question (e.g. television broadcasting). With regards to the online press, the BGH referred to a similar breadth and scope of information which the service must offer in relation to its analogue counterpart. And contrary to Ofcom, the BGH posited that interactive elements or links between the audiovisual and text-based material were irrelevant for the assessment.

While in the UK, no minimum threshold has been established below which regulation would not take effect, the RStV in Germany stipulates several *de minimis* exceptions. These exceptions are, however, stipulated in relation to broadcasting. An audiovisual service which meets an exception thus constitutes a telemedia service. Nonetheless, the state media authorities highlight in their orders the mass media character of services falling under broadcast regulation, in particular their relevance for public opinion formation. In specifying the notion of "mass media", the regulatory authorities consider irrelevant the exact number of recipients, provided that the service is addressed to an indeterminate number of potential viewers, including services built on small budgets or addressed to niche audiences. This is reminiscent of Ofcom's approach relying on the general capacity of a service to reach the public and the number of *potential* users rather than its *actual* user base. Yet, the derogation prescribed by the RStV which exempts services addressed to less than 500 users from the definition of broadcasting relates to the number of actual users as is mirrored in the orders of the state media authorities.

2. Principal purpose

The regulators of the UK, Germany and France have dealt with the notion of principal purpose to varying degrees. All regulators seem to share the position that one media outlet (e.g. a website) may comprise multiple services. In order to trigger regulation under the AVMSD as transposed into national law, the audiovisual service must constitute a coherent offer distinct from the other parts of the same outlet. It must fulfil an independent function or have an independent identity, in other words, be self-standing. Ofcom has, above all, stressed the need for a "step-back test" or "sense check" which entails a global and balanced assessment of *all* the material made available through the particular media outlet under investigation, rather than a focussed analysis of the audiovisual content only. The same approach is reflected in the case law concerning the prohibition of press-type offers by PSM in Germany. Importantly, the regulators consent that a purely quantitative assessment of the principal purpose would be insufficient.

The CSA, however, has noted that a quantitative interpretation of principal purpose was not precluded by the LLC which does not reproduce this notion. In addition, the French regulator considers that the term "incidental" could be interpreted quantitatively. Yet, it appears as if the CSA would not classify an audiovisual service as an audiovisual media service exclusively on the basis of quantitative criteria.

In contrast to the regulators in France and Germany, Ofcom has drawn up comprehensive guidance on the notion of principal purpose. Although the guidance is non-binding in nature, it gains a quasi-binding character through its application by the regulators. More precisely, this guidance takes the form of a non-exhaustive list of criteria to which Ofcom (and ATVOD until the end of 2015) have referred, such as the presentation, branding and structure of the audiovisual material or the links between the audiovisual content and other material. Ofcom also takes into account the significance of the audiovisual material examining the "quantity and proportion" as well as the "relevance" of the audiovisual service for the user. In so far as Ofcom looks at the number of videos, a quantitative element is included in the list of criteria. Similarly, the jurisprudence before the German courts seems to suggest that an on-demand service exclusively or predominantly offers audiovisual material or offers a significant part of audiovisual material. This formula is less refined than in the UK but corresponds to some of the Ofcom criteria, especially those regarding the prominence and significance of audiovisual material.

### 3. Comparability

Closely linked to the notion of principal purpose is the issue of comparability which is inherent to the concept of "programme". In the UK, Ofcom has established criteria for comparability or similarity of audiovisual content with programmes screened on TV. As for the principal purpose criteria, the list of factors is non-exhaustive and no individual criterion is determinative on its own. Criteria which are indicative of such comparability are, *inter alia*, the use of opening and closing titles, of presenters, voiceover, commentators and the completeness of programmes based on a narrative. By contrast, incomplete clips lacking a coherent whole or overarching connection are not typical of broadcasts. Neither are playlists which merely string such clips together. Moreover, Ofcom refrains from specifying a particular length for programmes but emphasises that long-form programming is generally typical of TV programmes. Yet, the regulator also confirms that short-form content may meet the comparability test as it is characteristic of certain programme genres, such as music videos, comedy or sexually explicit content broadcast on TV. From the practice of the UK regulatory authorities, it can be inferred that videos of duration of eight to ten minutes are considered TV-like.

No such concrete measures have been taken by the regulatory authorities in France and Germany. Nonetheless, the aspect of comparability finds expression in the formulation "journalistic edited offers" as contained in the German RStV. This notion, which is also closely associated with the concept of "editorial responsibility", implies that audiovisual content has been edited for publication. A wholly unedited string of data, such as a playlist on a video-sharing site, does not fall under this concept. In this respect, the German interpretation of a "simple" playlist mechanism in which the platform host does not (or only to a very minimal degree) exert any influence on the selection of videos matches the UK regulators' understanding of such a tool.

The CSA has qualified so-called "branded channels" on YouTube as on-demand audiovisual media services in spite of the use of algorithms and playlists. To the CSA, it was the commercial nature of the services which was decisive and brought them under the regulatory regime for audiovisual media services. Ofcom also classified YouTube channels of professional broadcasters as non-linear services within the meaning of the CA.

### 4. Editorial responsibility

Aside from the criterion of principal purpose, NRAs have detailed the notion of editorial responsibility. While ATVOD and Ofcom in the UK, and the CSA in France have expressly examined this concept, it has not been a major concern in Germany. There some hints can be derived from the orders of the state media authorities, in particular from the formalisation of the term "schedule".

The positions taken by Ofcom (in its appeal decisions) and the CSA are strikingly similar to the extent that they examine contractual clauses to determine editorial responsibility. Through its practice, Ofcom has devised a four-step test in which it (and ATVOD until December 2015) would look for any explicit contractual wording before examining implicit formulations contained in the agreement. The UK regulator would subsequently analyse the parties' conduct as agreed outside of formal contracts and finally, any other evidence relevant for the parties' conduct in practice. It stems from its guidance that only one person bears editorial responsibility within the meaning of the CA and that service providers are encouraged to settle this issue contractually. In a similar vein, the CSA has made clear that the LLC does not provide for the concept of shared or split editorial responsibility. Conversely, the CSA negates the existence of an on-demand audiovisual media service if a third party organises and selects the programmes. Importantly, the French regulator has carved out from the LLC's definition of an audiovisual media service an obligation to designate the person with editorial responsibility in a contract. It follows from several of its policy documents that the CSA presumes that the service provider (in the sense of the *editeur*) rather than the operator of a website, portal or other infrastructure holds editorial responsibility for the purpose of the law. While this reflected the distribution of functions at the time the AVMSD was adopted, it is no longer as clear-cut today. The fact that platform operators and other intermediaries increasingly take on editorial roles is certainly recognised by the CSA.

Both Ofcom and the CSA consider that regulatory supervision is facilitated by the identification of the provider bearing editorial responsibility in the contracts defining the business relationship between producers, content providers and operators of infrastructure. In France, providers and other market participants are obliged to specify the person with editorial responsibility, whereas in the UK providers are encouraged by the regulator to resolve this issue in advance. The CSA's approach to extract an obligation from the LLC appears to be more interventionist and illustrative of top-down regulation. It is questionable to what extent the CSA's strict approach interferes with the activities and rights of service providers and other economic actors, in particular their contractual freedoms. The discretionary approach pursued by Ofcom, in particular its (secondary) reliance on parties' conduct and practice appears more reasonable.

What becomes apparent is that regulatory authorities are facing growing difficulties in identifying the person with editorial responsibility. This demonstrates the inadequacy of the notion of editorial responsibility (and the definition of audiovisual media service provider for that matter) as set forth in the AVMSD. It is also an expression or consequence of media convergence and the emergence of new actors taking part in the editorial process. For NRAs the oversight of compliance with national rules becomes more complicated so that they increasingly rely on market participants themselves for the attribution of roles to which different responsibilities are attached.

Overall, the crucial question which emerges from the discussion on the notion of on-demand audiovisual media services is whether an audiovisual service could be qualified differently by the three regulators studied here. There is no easy answer to this question except for the evasive reply that it would depend on the specific characteristics of the service. All regulators apply a case-by-case analysis which is certainly the most appropriate method. It seems as if different categorisations of similar services have not had an adverse effect on the overall offer of on-demand services available in the three countries which appears to continue to grow. Moreover, the guidance produced by ATVOD and Ofcom is the most comprehensive and detailed. Yet, the reliance on criteria which are inherently subjective may, in certain circumstances, have a reverse effect on legal certainty, notably from the perspective of service providers. The contradicting results of ATVOD and Ofcom are an expression of the difficulty to coherently interpret the guidance. If one were to give a tentative answer to the above question, it could read as follows: On a spectrum where the middle would represent a "typical" on-demand audiovisual media service comprising the "typical" elements, it seems as thought all regulators would classify the service as non-linear. On the edges of the spectrum, however, where a service comprised some "typical", some "atypical" elements or some which were novel and did not fit into established categories, regulators' assessments might diverge.

This is not least to the different core areas of regulation which regulators have actively constructed or have passively been subjected to. Since the notification requirement has been introduced in the UK and France, the rules applicable to non-linear services have been effectively enforced. Protection of pluralism and support for a vibrant audiovisual sector is preponderant in France and has been one of the main aims of the CSA. In contrast to Ofcom and the German media authorities, the CSA might more readily impose AVMS-style regulation on "new" services. In the UK, an active and dedicated co-regulator has promoted and shaped the rules for non-linear services. In its five years of existence, ATVOD rigorously enforced the CA and did not shy away from controversial decisions (such as its attempt to regulate video sections of online newspapers or magazines). In its first year as sole regulator, Ofcom has not shown the same rigor as ATVOD. This may be explained by the on-going transition from co-regulation or by the fact that the most controversial questions had been resolved during ATVOD's co-regulatory term resulting in clear guidance which is known to the industry. Ofcom's withdrawing from detailed regulatory oversight may also be explained by its "traditional" liberal approach. In Germany, the classification of non-linear services is more opaque due to the decentralised way in which the law is applied in this federal country and, above all, due to the importance of the notion of broadcasting for the entire legal order. Since no form of registration is needed, state media authorities typically do not have to take difficult decisions on the nature of a service (unless it constitutes broadcasting). In sum, the classification of a service as non-linear by the UK, German and French regulatory authorities is contingent on too many factors to give a simple answer.

### III. Regulators' outlook on the AVMSD's revision

The Commission, in revising the AVMSD has led a dialogue with stakeholders, launching a consultation in mid-2015. Perspectives of the UK, German and French regulators on the future EU regulatory framework can be gleaned from their replies to this consultation. These perspectives are nourished from the measures (e.g. activities and practice) they have taken in view of implementing and applying the AVMSD at the national level and their general position and role in the national regulatory arena. While the UK regulator is in favour of maintaining the status quo with minor modifications, the French and German regulators call for more profound changes to the AVMSD.

Regarding the material scope of application, Ofcom posits that the AVMSD is still effective and the notion of "TV-like" grants a sufficient level of flexibility to accommodate future phenomena under the framework applicable to audiovisual media services. Ofcom perceives fundamental differences (not least in consumer expectations) between what it calls a "TV-like space" (encompassing TV, catch-up and VOD services) and an "Internet space" and is in favour of maintaining different baskets of regulation. It nonetheless recognises the need for a coordinated and harmonious interpretation of the notion "TV-like" across the EU and proposes that guidance should be drawn up to specify the term at the EU level, involving the Commission, ERGA as well as the industry.

Though the notion of "TV-like" is absent from the French LLC, the CSA nonetheless supports its inclusion in a revised AVMSD. The DLM however advocate deleting it altogether. Furthermore, the German media authorities posit that the current criteria of an audiovisual media service should be rethought (above all the principal purpose element) and that two additional criteria be introduced. The revised definition should specify that audiovisual media services are journalistically edited offers and that they have a particular reach or relevance for the audience, measured on the basis of audience research and market data. These additional criteria reflect the definition of broadcasting in Germany. For the CSA, it is essential that the notion of editorial responsibility be expanded to encompass all actors involved in the editorial process, thereby widening the scope of application to platforms and other actors operating in the value chain and exercising similar levels of editorial control over audiovisual content.

With respect to differentiating linear and non-linear services, regulators' perspectives seem to diverge. Ofcom generally demonstrates support for maintaining the distinction, albeit it is sympathetic to dissolving the graduated scheme in *some* respects regulated by the AVMSD. The CSA is in favour of a graduated regulatory regime based on the type of offer or the service provider. However it is unclear whether the present divide between linear and non-linear services should be maintained in its entirety or whether, similar to Ofcom, it should only be given up in *certain* areas. By contrast, the German DLM expressly calls for abandoning this distinction while upholding a graduated approach to regulation vis-à-vis the new subject matter of regulation, i.e. platforms.

The regulation of platforms is also controversial. While Ofcom argues that platforms and intermediaries do not exercise editorial responsibility and are, moreover, not in competition with broadcasting, the CSA and the DLM are aligned in their demand to introduce platform regulation under the umbrella of the AVMSD. Both regulators forcefully argue that service providers of linear and non-linear services face increasing competition from platforms and other actors such as publishers of online newspapers that typically provide short form audiovisual content. These actors, which are currently exempt from the scope of application of the AVMSD, are thus in a preferential position as compared to service providers subject to the AVMSD. Yet, they exert influence on the distribution of audiovisual material, thereby affecting diversity and plurality of content. This line of argumentation is particularly prominent in the CSA's reply. The CSA has been the guardian of pluralism at the national level and in order to capture all actors which have a role in the editorial process, the regulator promotes a broad understanding of the notion of platforms. It also considers that the future regulatory scheme could be incentive-driven and encourage service providers and other operators to commit to higher levels of contributions for audiovisual production in return for specific advantages.

In a similar vein, the DLM submits that a basic tier of rules should apply to all audiovisual media services. Member States should be free to introduce stricter standards for certain services (e.g. PSM) or incentivise service providers to voluntarily comply with stricter standards at the national level. In addition, a second tier of provisions should be applicable to platforms. Possible policy objectives to be pursued could include non-discriminatory access, findability of quality content or secondary responsibility for the protection of minors. Hence, a graduated regulatory model would still exist, albeit in modified form. Regulators' proposals are discussed more in-depth in the sixth chapter.

# Chapter 5. The UK, German and French regulators' approaches to the protection of minors in on-demand audiovisual media services

For decades, the protection of minors in audiovisual media services has been a concern of policy makers at various levels. In the EU Member States, the protection of minors, if not guaranteed constitutionally, constitutes a fundamental societal value. In relation to the dissemination of audiovisual media services, there seems to be consensus that the state should actively design a legal framework which bans illegal content and protects children under the age of 18 from age-inappropriate content. Yet, this regulatory claim is not absolute as it may collide with other fundamental rights and values, especially the freedom of expression, which also encompasses the right to receive information. At the nexus of this issue is thus an inherent tension between the demands of the right to freely express oneself and receive the kind of (legal) content one desires, and the need to ensure the protection of minors.

Today, this balancing exercise has become more complex on account of different factors. Above all, the Internet has facilitated the distribution of an unwieldy multitude of content, harmful to different degrees or, at worst, illegal under national criminal law. The global and ubiquitous nature of the Internet makes it difficult for individual states to assert jurisdiction and regulate content under their umbrella.[2234] A great number of providers of inappropriate content are located outside the EU so that the internal market rationale based on the country of origin principle, is undermined. As a result, Member States struggle to identify providers and enforce national content standards.[2235] In addition, consumption patterns of media types are changing. Ever younger children access content on the go. Mobile devices can no longer be monitored by parents or guardians as efficiently as the

2234 Stettner, "Der neue JMStV," p. 426.

2235 ATVOD, "Response to the European Commission Green Paper 'Preparing for a Fully Converged Audiovisual World: Growth, Creation and Values'" (European Commission, September 27, 2013), para. 4.8, p. 13, http://ec.europa.eu/newsroom/dae/document.cfm?doc_id=3979 (accessed 27.12.2015).

TV of the central living room.[2236] Today, minors indulge in more individualised forms of communication which increasingly escape their parents' watchful eyes.[2237] Phenomena like cyberbullying and grooming, sexting and revenge porn have emerged.[2238]

The Commission and Member States alike seem to pursue the same goals and strategies. Many initiatives at the EU level[2239] are mirrored at the national level and vice versa. In general, illegal content is intercepted,[2240] while age-inappropriate content is permissible, provided that it is restricted to adults. Art. 12 AVMSD, in contrast to Art. 27 (1) AVMSD,

---

2236 Daniel Hajok and Gregor Schwarz, "Technischer Jugendmedienschutz bei digitalen Medien, Ein Überblick zu anbieter- und nutzerseitigen Schutzmöglichkeiten," *JMS-Report* 4 (2014): p. 1; Friedemann Schindler, "Technische Möglichkeiten des Jugendschutzes im Internet," in *Positionen zum Jugendmedienschutz in Deutschland, Eine Textsammlung*, KJM Schriftenreihe 1 (Berlin: Vistas, 2009), p. 124.

2237 Thomas Günter and Friedemann Schindler, "Technische Möglichkeiten des Jugendschutzes im Internet," *Recht der Jugend und des Bildungswesens*, no. 3 (2006): p. 350.

2238 Grooming means that a person establishes a relationship of trust to a minor for the purpose of sexual abuse or exploitation. Sexting implies sexually explicit communication between two persons, primarily by sending and receiving messages via mobile phones. Revenge porn is when a person discloses private sexual photos or videos with the intent to cause distress to another person (former partner). On bullying and sexting in social networks, see Eva Lievens, "Bullying and Sexting in Social Networks: Protecting Minors from Criminal Acts or Empowering Minors to Cope with Risky Behaviour?," *International Journal Crime, Law & Justice* 42, no. 3 (2014): 251–70; on German and US responses to sexting, see Sandra Schmitz and Lawrence Siry, "Teenage Folly or Child Abuse? State Responses to 'Sexting' by Minors in the US and Germany," *Policy & Internet* 3, no. 2 (2011).

2239 European Commission Safer Internet Action Plan. On the genesis of the safer Internet programmes, see in more detail Eva Lievens, *Protecting Children in the Digital Era, The Use of Alternative Regulatory Instruments*, pp. 122–35; see also European Commission, "Communication from the Commission to the Council, the European Parliament, the European Economic and Social Committee and the Committee of the Regions on a European Strategy for a Better Internet for Children, COM(2012) 196 Final," May 2, 2012. This strategy promotes a safe online environment by the production of "high quality content" for children and the wider use of parental controls as well as age ratings. It also aims at empowering parents as well as children by enhancing levels of media literacy and raising awareness of the pitfalls of the Internet.

2240 On the different strategies of removing illegal content, see Karel Demeyer, Eva Lievens and Jos Dumortier, "Blocking or Removing Illegal Content: Analysis

permits the transmission of on-demand services containing seriously harmful material under certain conditions. Thus, the object of this research is content which "might seriously impair" the development of minors and not content which is illegal *per se*. This chapter examines the measures taken by the British, German and French regulators in view of implementing and enforcing Art. 12 AVMSD as transposed into the respective national legal orders. The two most pertinent questions are thus what kind of material is considered seriously harmful and what kinds of controls are required by service providers to ensure the protection of under 18-year-olds. Due to cultural implications and national sensitivities as well as the EU's lack of competence, classifications and age ratings of material included in audiovisual media services are not harmonised across the EU. The nature of the material considered to have serious detrimental effects on minors may thus differ in the three countries investigated. Similarly, the AVMSD leaves Member States a margin of discretion with respect to the measures, technical or otherwise, whereby the protection of minors is safeguarded in on-demand services. The filtering of unsuitable content is, for example, a wide-spread method. However, this method and other techniques raise not only questions of efficiency but, more importantly, of the compatibility with fundamental rights, above all, the freedom of expression. After a short introduction of the substantive rule set forth in Art. 12 AVMSD, this chapter examines the approaches of the UK, German and French regulators to protecting minors looking at their practice, guidance and other pertinent policy documents.

## *A. The protection of minors by the European Union*

The rights of the child are protected by Art. 24 CFR which provides in its first paragraph that, "children shall have the right to such protection and care as is necessary for their well-being. They may express their views freely." Art. 24 (2) CFR further stipulates that "in all actions relating to children, whether taken by public authorities or private institutions, the child's best interests must be a primary consideration". The wording of Art. 24 (1) and (2) CFR is unambiguously strong and reflects the impor-

---

from a Technical and Legal Perspective," *Policy & Internet* 4, no. 3–4 (2012): pp. 1–23.

tance of the protection of minors for the overall legal framework. Even prior to the adoption of the Charter, the European institutions had issued various instruments and taken numerous actions aimed at the twin objectives of protecting minors and human dignity.[2241] In the mid-1990s, when the Internet developed into a mass media, the Commission had placed the protection of minors high on its agenda. Simultaneously, it published a Communication on illegal and harmful content on the Internet as well as a Green Paper on the protection of minors and human dignity in audiovisual and information services.[2242] Both documents highlighted the need for reconciliation of public interest objectives such as the protection of minors with the free flow of information and the emergence of new services.[2243] They also set out technical instruments whereby the protection of minors could be realised including parental control software such as filtering technology as well as European rating systems as a response to US standards.[2244] Two years later, in 1998, the Council elaborated a recommendation on the development of the competitiveness of the European audiovisual and information services industry by promoting national frameworks aimed at achieving a comparable and effective level of protection of minors and human dignity.[2245] This recommendation was up-dated in

2241 Human dignity is protected by Art. 1 CFR which provides that "human dignity is inviolable. It must be respected and protected".

2242 European Commission, "Communication from the Commission to the Council, the European Parliament, the Economic and Social Committee and the Committee of the Regions on Illegal and Harmful Content on Othe Internet. COM(96) 487 Final," October 16, 1996; European Commission, "Green Paper on the Protection of Minors and Human Dignity in Audiovisual and Information Services, COM(96) 483 Final," October 16, 1996.

2243 European Commission, "Communication on Illegal and Harmful Content on the Internet," p. 4; European Commission, "Green Paper on the Protection of Minors and Human Dignity," p. 3; see also Lievens, *Protecting Children in the Digital Era, The Use of Alternative Regulatory Instruments*, pp. 90, 94.

2244 European Commission, "Communication on Illegal and Harmful Content on the Internet," pp. 19–24; European Commission, "Green Paper on the Protection of Minors and Human Dignity," pp. 18–20.

2245 "Council Recommendation 98/560/EC on the Development of the Competitiveness of the European Audiovisual and Information Services Industry by Promoting National Frameworks Aimed at Achieving a Comparable and Effective Level of Protection of Minors and Human Dignity, OJ of 7.10.1998, L 270, P. 48-55," September 24, 1998.

2006.[2246] The 2006 recommendation is addressed to the Member States and the industry, the latter of which is encouraged, among others, to "develop positive measures for the benefit of minors (…) while avoiding potentially harmful content".[2247] The importance of media literacy is underscored by the recommendation which also proposed possible actions in this regard.[2248]

Another expression of the Commission's commitment to the protection of minors constitutes the 2003 Communication on the future of European regulatory audiovisual policy in which the need for a distinct and encompassing regulatory policy in the audiovisual sector to safeguard certain public interests like cultural diversity, media pluralism and above all, the protection of minors was reinforced.[2249] This is reflected in recital 59 AVMSD which states that "the availability of harmful content in audiovisual media services is a concern for legislators, the media industry and parents". Consequently, recital 59 AVMSD recognises the need for "rules protecting the physical, mental and moral development of minors (...) in all audiovisual media services". At the same time, the AVMSD takes into account the fundamental right to freedom of expression which should be "carefully balanced" with the measures taken in view of the protection of minors. Importantly, recital 62 AVMSD clarifies that no "prior verification of audiovisual media services by public bodies" is necessary to implement the rules relating to the protection of minors as stipulated in the Directive.

From its inception, the protection of minors has been enshrined in the Directive as a fundamental public value or "general public interest" objective.[2250] Today, the AVMSD protects minors in different contexts. Recital

---

2246 "European Parliament and of the Council Recommendation 2006/952/EC on the Protection of Minors and Human Dignity and on the Right of Reply in Relation to the Competitiveness of the European Audiovisual and Online Information Services Industry, OJ of 27.12.2006, L 378, P. 72-77," December 20, 2006; On the genesis of the recommendation, see in more detail Lievens, *Protecting Children in the Digital Era, The Use of Alternative Regulatory Instruments*, pp. 101–22.

2247 "European Parliament and Council Recommendation 2006/952/EC on the Protection of Minors and Human Dignity," para. II 1.

2248 "European Parliament and Council Recommendation 2006/952/EC on the Protection of Minors and Human Dignity", Annex II.

2249 European Commission, "Communication on the Future European Regulatory Audiovisual Policy," p. 3.

2250 See recitals 41 and 104 AVMSD.

59 AVMSD underlines the necessity for introducing legislation to protect minors in all types of audiovisual media services (including commercial communications) and acknowledges that "there will be new challenges in "connection with new platforms and new products". The rules on commercial communications, for instance, set out specific provisions which recognise the vulnerability of minors as they act as market participants and consumers (even before they acquire the legal capacity to contract under national law).[2251] Above all, Arts. 12 and 27 AVMSD prescribe standards for the protection of minors from unsuitable material contained in audiovisual media services. They are in line with the two-tier approach of the Directive stipulating stricter rules for television broadcasts in comparison to on-demand services. Importantly, violations of the rules concerning the protection of minors may result in the restriction of retransmissions of audiovisual media services pursuant to Art. 3 (2) for linear and 3 (4) (a) (i) AVMSD for non-linear services. The derogation from the free flow of information in case of serious contraventions of the rules regarding the protection of minors is an expression of the importance of the latter. Apart from the substantive rules, the AVMSD underpins the significance of media literacy and media education in order to raise children as responsible and independent persons and the role of legislatures, the media industry as well as parents in this respect.[2252] Positive measures like the support for the production and transmission of age-appropriate content are an indispensable element in today's media policies.

## I. The protection of minors in linear audiovisual media services: Art. 27 AVMSD

Art. 27 AVMSD, albeit in less detailed form, was already included in the 1989 TWFD. In its current form it exclusively applies to television broadcasting and differentiates between programmes which "might seriously impair the physical, mental or moral development of minors" and programmes which "are likely" to have such a detrimental effect on minors. The former are banned from television and include "in particular programmes that involve pornography or gratuitous violence". The Directive

2251 See for instance Art. 9 (1) (g) and 9 (2), last sentence of Art. 11 3., second sentence of Art. 20 (2), Art. 22 (a) AVMSD.

2252 See recitals 47 and 59 AVMSD.

is silent on the meaning of the terms "pornography" and "gratuitous violence" which are thus interpreted in accordance with national law and practice. The notion of pornography could be read in light of Directive 2011/92/EU on combating the sexual abuse and sexual exploitation of children and child pornography.[2253] It may be derived from Art. 2 (c) of that Directive, that pornography implies "sexually explicit conduct" or a "depiction of sexual organs (…) for primarily sexual purposes". Furthermore, the term "gratuitous violence" commonly encompasses scenes which focus to an unreasonable degree on violence.[2254] However, the ban stipulated in Art. 27 (1) AVMSD does not extend to (realistic) representations of violent acts or war during non-fictional programmes (e.g. news programmes or documentaries).[2255] Member States retain the prerogative to delineate the precise contours of each concept.

Moreover, programmes including material which is likely to have an adverse effect on minors is permissible provided that "it is ensured, by selecting the time of the broadcast or by any technical measure, that minors in the area of transmission will not normally hear or see such broadcasts".[2256] Typically, Member States set forth national watershed rules which establish certain blocks of time during which content considered harmful to a particular age group is impermissible. In addition, broadcasters may implement technical measures such as the use of PIN codes or other access restrictions to obstruct minors from viewing such programmes. In case of unencoded broadcasts of unsuitable material, viewers have to be adequately informed by an "acoustic warning" or a "visual symbol" featured throughout the entire duration of the programme.[2257] This provision serves to inform under-age viewers that the following programme may cause distress or anxiety but also adult viewers who may more easily assert parental responsibilities.

---

2253 Directive 2011/92/EU of the European Parliament and of the Council of 13.12.2011 on combating the sexual abuse and sexual exploitation of children and child pornography, and replacing Council Framework Decision 2004/68/JHA, OJ of 17.12.2011, L 335, pp. 1-14.

2254 Jörg Ukrow, "Article 22 TWFD (Protection of Minors)," in *European Media Law*, ed. Oliver Castendyk, Egbert Dommering, and Alexander Scheuer (The Netherlands: Kluwer Law International, 2008), para. 17, p. 712.

2255 Ukrow, "Art. 22 TWFD," para. 17, p. 712.

2256 Art. 27 (2) AVMSD.

2257 Art. 27 (3) AVMSD.

## II. The protection of minors in non-linear audiovisual media services: Art. 12 AVMSD

In 2007, when the Directive was revised, Art. 27 AVMSD was complemented by a rule applicable to on-demand audiovisual media services.[2258] Accordingly,

> "on-demand audiovisual media services provided by media service providers (…) which might seriously impair the physical, mental or moral development of minors are only made available in such a way as to ensure that minors will not normally hear or see [them]".

The (technical) means whereby protection may be accomplished are enumerated (non-exhaustively) in recital 60 AVMSD which refers to personal identification numbers (PIN codes), filtering systems and labelling.[2259] What is more, the 2006 recommendation on the protection of minors and human dignity encouraged industry actions such as "systematically providing users with an effective, updatable and easy-to-use filtering system when they subscribe to an access provider" or "offering access to services specifically intended for children which are equipped with automatic filtering systems operated by access providers and mobile telephone operators".[2260] In addition, the recommendation encouraged providers to regularly supply descriptions of the content they offer in order to classify and assess such content. In this respect, the 2006 recommendation also underscored the significance of self-regulatory initiatives which must be backed by "continuous dialogue between national and European legislators, regulatory authorities, industries, associations, citizens and civil society".[2261]

---

2258 See in more detail Füg, "Save the Children: The Protection of Minors in the Information Society and the Audiovisual Media Services Directive," p. 45; Scheuer and Bachmeier, "The Protection of Minors in New (Non-Linear) Media," pp. 7–27.

2259 See in more detail Scheuer, "Additional Youth Protection Measures in the EU," pp. 41–48.

2260 "European Parliament and Council Recommendation 2006/952/EC on the Protection of Minors and Human Dignity", Annex 3, p. 7.

2261 "European Parliament and Council Recommendation 2006/952/EC on the Protection of Minors and Human Dignity," recital 12 in conjunction with para. I 4 (a); see also Christina Angelopoulos et al., "Study on Fundamental Rights Limitations for Online Enforcement through Self-Regulation," ed. Institute for Information Law (IViR), 2016, http://www.ivir.nl/publicaties/download/1796 (accessed 20.3.2016).

In contrast to the provision concerning broadcasting, Art. 12 AVMSD merely refers to material "which might seriously impair" the development of minors. It nonetheless employs the same vague language as Art. 27 AVMSD. Interestingly, Art. 12 AVMSD lacks the reference to "pornography or gratuitous violence".[2262] Yet, one could infer from the identical formulation employed in both rules that pornographic and blatantly violent content constitute material seriously impairing children's development within the meaning of Art. 12 AVMSD. The graduated scheme is, moreover, illustrated by the fact that seriously harmful material is prohibited on television, while providers of on-demand services may disseminate it provided that "minors will not normally hear or see" it.[2263] During the co-decision procedure leading to the adoption of the AVMSD, the European Parliament had lobbied for a horizontal rule which would have encouraged the establishment of a "Community-wide labelling, assessment and filtering system".[2264] This far-reaching amendment was rejected by the Council and the Commission and demonstrates the sensitive nature of the subject matter. Instead, the provision is construed in a manner which leaves ample room for Member States to manoeuvre thereby respecting diverging national cultures, social norms and perceptions.

## *B. The protection of minors in on-demand programme services in the UK*

### I. The transposition of Art. 12 AVMSD in Sec. 368E (2) CA

In the United Kingdom, the Audiovisual Media Services Regulations of 2009 transposed Art. 12 AVMSD by inserting Sec. 368E (2) CA in the Communications Act (CA). This provision was again modified in 2014. Sec. 368E CA regulates "harmful material" and contains the prohibition of

2262 Nonetheless, all service providers (of linear and non-linear services) are subject to a ban on the distribution of child pornography as recognized by Council Framework Decision 2004/68/JHA of 22 December 2003 on combating the sexual exploitation of children and child pornography. See also recital 61 AVMSD.

2263 Interestingly, the Commission, in its proposal of 2005 had set out an outright ban of seriously harmful content in on-demand services, mirroring the rule concerning broadcasting (now Art. 27 [1] AVMSD). See European Commission, "2005 AVMSD Proposal" Art. 3d.

2264 European Parliament, "European Parliament Legislative Resolution on the Commission's Proposal Amending the TWFD". Art. 3d (1) AVMSD.

incitement to hatred in on-demand services apart from the rule on protection of minors in such services. The initial wording of subsection (2) largely corresponded to Art. 12 AVMSD prescribing that

> "if an [ODPS] contains material which might seriously impair the physical, mental or moral development of persons under the age of 18, the material must be made available in a manner which secures that such persons will not normally see or hear it".

The key phrases of the Directive were replicated by the national legal order. The content targeted by the rule was classified as "material which might seriously impair the physical, mental or moral development" of children. The availability of such material was restricted to prevent minors from seeing or hearing it. Furthermore, Sec. 368E (2) CA 2003 specified the addressee of the rule, namely under 18s while the Directive refers to the generic term "minors".

2014 saw the amendment of Sec. 368E (2) CA by virtue of the Audiovisual Media Services Regulations 2014 which came into effect on 1 December 2014. It stipulates that

> "(2) An on-demand programme service must not contain any prohibited material.
> (3) "Prohibited material" means—
> (a) a video work which the video works authority has determined for the purposes of the 1984 Act not to be suitable for a classification certificate to be issued in respect of it, or
> (b) material whose nature is such that it is reasonable to expect that, if the material were contained in a video work submitted to the video works authority for a classification certificate, the video works authority would determine for those purposes that the video work was not suitable for a classification certificate to be issued in respect of it.
> (4) An on-demand programme service must not contain any specially restricted material unless the material is made available in a manner which secures that persons under the age of 18 will not normally see or hear it.
> (5) "Specially restricted material" means—
> (a) a video work in respect of which the video works authority has issued a R18 classification certificate,
> (b)material whose nature is such that it is reasonable to expect that, if the material were contained in a video work submitted to the video works authority for a classification certificate, the video works authority would issue a R18 classification certificate, or
> (c) other material that might seriously impair the physical, mental or moral development of persons under the age of 18".

As will be shown below, this modification was brought about by the practice of ATVOD and Ofcom which both had lobbied for legislative adjustments.[2265] The 2014 statutory instrument introduces a differentiation between "prohibited material" and "specifically restricted material" contained in ODPS. It details the nature of the material as well as the legal consequence attached to it. While prohibited material is banned in ODPS, specifically restricted material may be included in ODPS under certain circumstances. Prohibited material is defined as a programme ("video work") which has been refused a classification certificate by the BBCF or for which it is reasonable to believe that such a certificate would have been refused.[2266] In its guidance, the BBFC clarifies that only as a "last resort" and in order to prevent irreparable harm to viewers the video work will be refused a certificate. This could be the case where there is "sustained focus on sexual or sadistic violence".[2267] Before refusing the dissemination of a work, the BBFC considers alternative measures of intervention such as cuts. Similarly, material which is in violation of UK criminal law, including obscene content pursuant to the Obscene Publications Act of 1959, is unacceptable.[2268] This study does not however, examine material which is

2265 ATVOD, "For Adults Only? Underage Access to Online Porn, A Research Report by the Authority for Television On Demand ('ATVOD')," March 28, 2014, para. 6, pp.21–22.

2266 Sec. 368E (3) (a) and (b) CA.

2267 BBFC, "BBFC Guidelines, Age Ratings You Trust," p. 28.

2268 The Obscene Publications Act 1959 stipulates in Sec. 1 (1) the test of obscenity. Accordingly, material is obscene if it tends to "deprave and corrupt persons who are likely, having regard to all relevant circumstances, to read, see or hear the matter contained or embodied in it". The Obscene Publications Act is available at http://www.legislation.gov.uk/ukpga/Eliz2/7-8/66/contents (accessed 9.2.2016).The Crown Prosecution Service has published guidance on the meaning of obscenity under http://www.cps.gov.uk/legal/l_to_o/obscene_publications/ (accessed 10.2.2016). This guidance sets forth that "where children are likely to access material of a degree of sexual explicitness equivalent to what is available to those aged 18 and above in a licensed sex shop, that material may be considered to be obscene and subject to prosecution. This applies to material which is not behind a suitable payment barrier or other accepted means of age verification, for example, material on the front page of pornography websites and non-commercial, user-generated material which is likely to be accessed by children and meets the threshold. See R v Perrin, [2002] EWCA Crim 747." Yet, no recent prosecution has been launched under this guidance, a fact which ATVOD highlighted in its submissions to the CMS committee inquiry into online safety (p. 9). On the regulation and classification of obscene material in the UK, see Lawrence Siry, *Knowing It When It Is Seen: The Polemic of the Regu-*

illegal but focuses on legal audiovisual content which may be provided in the form of an ODPS is subject to restrictions in the public interest.

Hence, specifically restricted material may be included in ODPS provided that it is ensured that "persons under the age of 18 will not normally see or hear it". Thus, this content category may be disseminated with restrictions or safeguards. Specifically restricted content implies a programme ("video work") which has been classified as R18 by the BBFC or which would reasonably have been classified as R18. ATVOD had referred to the classification R18 in its guidance.[2269] In determining the nature of the material, in particular in case a classification certificate was not expressly issued, the guidelines of the BBFC are to be taken into account.[2270] According to the BBFC, R18 material implies "explicit works of consenting sex or strong fetish material involving adults".[2271] The distribution of works classified as R18 is limited to persons of age and registered places: films can only be shown in specially licensed cinemas and video works/DVDs can only be supplied by specially licensed sex shops.

In addition, "other material that might seriously impair the physical, mental or moral development of persons under the age of 18" is equally regarded as specifically restricted content pursuant to Sec. 368E (5) (c) CA. This clause is formulated openly and seems to constitute a catch-all phrase which accords considerable leeway to the regulatory authorities in the interpretation and application of this clause. It is unclear to what extent it may catch harmful material under the threshold of R18. Still, it reflects the wording of the former statutory provision as adopted in 2009 and moreover corresponds to the vague language of Art. 12 AVMSD. Due to the introduction of an absolute prohibition of certain material in ODPS, the structure of Sec. 368E appears to have become more aligned with Art. 27 AVMSD applicable to television broadcasting. Since its amendment in 2014, the statutory provision has become more detailed in pinpointing the type of material which is considered inappropriate in the UK. Nonetheless, it does not specify the means whereby specifically restricted material may be supplied. It also leaves a margin of discretion to regula-

*lation of Sexualized Speech in the United States and Europe*, vol. 6, Luxemburger Juristische Studien – Luxembourg Legal Studies (Baden-Baden: Nomos, 2015).

2269 Sec. 368E (5) (a) and (b) CA.

2270 Sec. 368E (6) in conjunction with Sec. 368E (3) (b) and (5) (b) CA.

2271 BBFC, "BBFC Guidelines, Age Ratings You Trust," p. 24.

tors in determining whether audiovisual content can reasonably be assumed to have been classified as R18. ATVOD has therefore drawn up detailed guidance about the meaning and application of Sec. 368E (2)-(5) CA which is outlined below.

## II. The measures taken by the UK regulators ATVOD and Ofcom

This part examines ATVOD's guidance that has been integrated in Ofcom's guidance notes after the co-regulator seized to exist. It also looks at ATVOD's practice that fed into the guidance by highlighting the most important decisions. While ATVOD's early practice is almost entirely covered, the analysis of cases in 2014/2015 is less comprehensive due to similar case facts and findings.

### 1. ATVOD rules and guidance

In 2011, the UK government and regulators agreed to pursue a precautionary approach regarding the protection of minors in VOD services. Ofcom had produced a report on behalf of the government which had made clear that it was infeasible to attain conclusive evidence of the harm to children caused by pornographic content due to the ethical considerations such studies would entail (i.e. systematically exposing minors to sexual content in order to measure the effects). Inversely, it could equally not be established conclusively that there was no harm and thus no risk at all.[2272] Given the scientific uncertainties and the fact that potential harm to minors could not be confidentially excluded, a precautionary approach was justified in Ofcom's opinion.[2273] ATVOD shared Ofcom's position which was reflected in several policy documents as well as its guidance discussed below.[2274] In a letter of August 2011, Minister for Culture, Communications

2272 Ofcom, "Sexually Explicit Material and Video-On-Demand Services, A Report to DCMS by Ofcom," August 4, 2011, para. 3.37, p. 20, http://stakeholders.ofcom.org.uk/binaries/internet/explicit-material-vod.pdf (accessed 25.3.2016).

2273 Ofcom, "Sexually Explicit Material and VOD Services," paras. 6.9-6.10, p. 46.

2274 Ofcom, "Sexually Explicit Material and VOD Services," para. 7.22, pp. 53-54; see also ATVOD, "Report on Underage Access to Online Porn," paras. 3, 6, pp. 9, 22.

and Creative Industries Ed Vaizey officially backed Ofcom's approach.[2275] Ofcom furthermore recommended that government amend legislation by specifically restricting R18 material in VOD services and prohibiting material which was stronger than R18.[2276] Likewise, ATVOD pursued the same tactics calling for legislative clarifications. At the end of 2014, the CA was modified accordingly.

In order to explain its interpretation of legal provisions and give guidance on the practical application of the statutory requirements, ATVOD published rules and guidance which it last up-dated in May 2015. The 14 rules reproduced the provisions contained in the CA applicable to ODPS (excluding the rules regarding commercial communications). A violation of the rules equated to a violation of the corresponding provision set forth in the CA. The ATVOD rules were complemented by non-binding guidance as an "aid to interpretation".[2277] The protection of minors from harmful content was ensured by rules 11 and 14.[2278] As of 1 January 2016, Ofcom has been the sole regulator for on-demand services. It replaced ATVOD's rules and guidance in January 2016 and up-dated these in May 2016. The relevant rules and guidance notes are identical, in substance, to those elaborated by ATVOD.[2279] Rule 11 of the guidance notes concerns specifically restricted material under Sec. 368E (4) and (5) CA while rule 11 regulates prohibited material pursuant to Sec. 368E (2) and (3) CA. The former is in the focus of this study.

The guidance accompanying rule 11 makes clear that R18, R18-equivalent and any other material which might seriously affect minors pertains to the "specifically restricted" category of material. Rule 11 is applicable to

---

2275 Ed Vaizey, "Sexually Explicit Material and Video-On-Demand Services," August 3, 2011, http://webarchive.nationalarchives.gov.uk/20121204113822/http://www.culture.gov.uk/images/publications/EVletter-to-ed-richards-3aug2011pdf.pdf (accessed 25.3.2016).

2276 Ofcom, "Sexually Explicit Material and VOD Services," para. 7.21, p. 53.

2277 ATVOD, "Rules and Guidance for Providers of ODPS," p. 4 (accessed 27.3.2016).

2278 Previous editions of the ATVOD rules and guidance did not include rule 11 (prohibited material) which was only inserted in the CA by the Audiovisual Media Services Regulation of 2014 which took effect on 1 December 2014.

2279 Ofcom, "Rules and Guidance, Statutory Rules and Non-Binding Guidance for Providers of On-Demand Programme Services," May 20, 2016, stakeholders.ofcom.org.uk/binaries/broadcast/on-demand/rules-guidance/rules_and_guidance.pdf (accessed 20.6.2016).

the entirety of material on the service, be it audiovisual or not (still images). By reference to the BBFC's classification guidance, R18 material includes "pornographic works, primarily for explicit works of consenting sex or strong fetish material involving adults".[2280] The CA does not require prior classification by the BBFC of audiovisual content provided on an ODPS but the competent regulator will apply the BBFC's guidelines in determining the nature of the material. It results from the classification as R18 or R18-equivalent that such content cannot be freely supplied in a non-linear service. Instead, the guidance requires that access to such content is controlled by means of an "effective content access control (CAC) system which verifies that the user is aged 18 or over at the point of registration or access".[2281] Importantly, the guidance unequivocally makes clear that age must be effectively checked when the user subscribes or gains access to the service. It is not necessary that age be verified each time the user enters or returns to a service. Hence, for repeated use of a service, "mandatory security controls" in form of PIN codes or passwords are sufficient provided that the user's age was effectively verified at one point. [2282] The permissible technical tools set out by the guidance include; "confirmation of credit card ownership or other form of payment where mandatory proof that the holder is 18 or over is required prior to issue; a reputable personal digital identity management service which uses checks on an independent and reliable database, such as the electoral roll or other comparable proof of account ownership which effectively verifies age, for example, possession and ownership of an effectively age-verified mobile phone". [2283]

By contrast, confirmation of ownership of a card where the holder is not required to be of age (e.g. debit, solo, or electron card) is inadequate. Interestingly, Ofcom accepts age verification by means of a mobile phone. More precisely the "SIM card [holder] rather than the physical handset" must have presented proof of his identity and age to the mobile phone operator. The CAC system in this case must provide evidence that the holder of the SIM card is the one accessing the content.[2284] Compliance with rule

2280 Ofcom, "Rules and Guidance for Providers of ODPS," p. 12; BBFC, "BBFC Guidelines, Age Ratings You Trust," p. 24.
2281 Ofcom, "Rules and Guidance for Providers of ODPS," p. 11.
2282 Ofcom, "Rules and Guidance for Providers of ODPS," p. 11.
2283 Ofcom, "Rules and Guidance for Providers of ODPS," p. 11.
2284 Ofcom, "Rules and Guidance for Providers of ODPS," p. 11.

11 and thus the existence of effective controls verifying user's age fall on the provider who bears editorial responsibility for the service.

In addition, Rule 11 spells out the prohibition of material which was or would have been refused a classification by the BBFC. The guidance thus focuses on the type of material banned in ODPS and sets out a non-exhaustive list of examples of content which might be prohibited. Broadly, these are three types of categories of content: firstly, "material in breach of the criminal law"; secondly, "material which risks harm to individuals, or, through their behaviour, to society" and thirdly, "material in pornographic works". [2285] These examples evidently borrow from the BBFC's guidelines but appear to be more detailed in the description of the unsuitable material.

In sum, ATVOD and Ofcom (as of 2016) have given detailed guidance on the controls to be put in place regarding unsuitable but legal content. It is crucial for the regulators that the providers effectively verify user's age and take successive measures to restrict harmful content to adults. The technical tools available to providers seem to be reasonable and well defined. In view of the type of material susceptible to be classified as R18, the guidance only refers to the BBFC's guidelines without further specifying the type of material considered R18-equivalent and the type of material considered as otherwise impairing for minors. Still, the guidance pertaining to rule 11 on prohibited material may be helpful in drawing a line between unsuitable content which is legal in contrast to illegal material. The practice of ATVOD further sheds light on the interpretation of this rule.

## 2. ATVOD's practice protecting minors in ODPS

As Ofcom's co-regulator ATVOD took numerous determinations to ensure observance of rule 11. It also engaged directly with the industry and, starting in January 2012, invited service providers to a series of seminars to raise awareness about the statutory obligations flowing from rule 11. Its practice and other activities clearly demonstrate that ATVOD had made the protection of minors from unsuitable content a priority. Under the co-regulatory scheme, Ofcom's role in shaping regulatory practice was limi-

2285 Ofcom, "Rules and Guidance for Providers of ODPS," p. 29.

ted to the imposition of statutory sanctions. In contrast to issues relating to scope, providers, who had been served an ATVOD determination, could not stage an appeal before Ofcom.[2286] Service providers could only request an internal review of ATVOD's determinations. Between 2010 and 2015, only three providers applied for such review, an insignificant number judging by the sheer amount of rule 11 determinations. The following section provides an overview of ATVOD's practice and highlights the most pertinent problems ATVOD encountered in enforcing rule 11.

### a) ATVOD's first determination: Bootybox TV

The first case that arose under rule 11 was instigated by a public complaint. A parent had complained to ATVOD in June 2011 that his son had watched pornographic videos on Bootybox TV and three similar online services. ATVOD conducted detailed inspections of the websites and established that only the Bootybox TV service fell under UK jurisdiction. It thus issued a determination on 9 December 2011 in which it found that the provider had infringed rule 11.[2287] ATVOD first examined the nature of the content which was offered for free and upon payment. By reference to Ofcom's appeal decisions in matters of scope, ATVOD concluded that R18 level material was considered TV-like.[2288] It posited that the audiovisual material contained on the websites constituted "programmes" which "appeared to be 'R18' level sex works (…) and featured explicit sight of clearly unsimulated sexual activity".[2289] ATVOD characterised the videos as TV-like "episodes of particular series (…) each episode ('scene') of which had its own opening sequence, on-screen series title and opening credits" in spite of their misleading description as "scenes".[2290] These are some of the criteria of the comparability test of Sec. 368A CA which Ofcom would later establish in its *Channel Flip* and *Everton TV* appeal decisions. Moreover, ATVOD remarked that some of the material available

2286 Sec. 6 (ii) of 2014 Designation permitted appeal proceedings before Ofcom only in matters of scope.
2287 ATVOD, "Determination That the Provider of the On-Demand Programme Service 'bootybox.tv' was in Breach of Rule 11," December 9, 2011.
2288 See for instance Ofcom, "Appeal Decision Climax 3 Uncut"; Ofcom, "Appeal Decision Demand Adult.".
2289 ATVOD, "Rule 11 Determination Bootybox TV," p. 4.
2290 ATVOD, "Rule 11 Determination Bootybox TV," p. 5.

upon subscription was stronger than R18 and could be regarded as surpassing this category.[2291] ATVOD was thus satisfied that the content offered by the provider was seriously harmful within the meaning of the CA.

ATVOD then looked at the existence of effective CAC systems. It distinguished between pornographic content which was offered with and without payment. Any user could freely access sexually explicit trailers and other promotional videos as well as hardcore porn images shown on the homepage. ATVOD made clear that any kind of material including still images which were provided by an ODPS were subject to the statutory requirements.[2292] It considered that a warning and links upon which users could "enter" or "leave" the service did not constitute an effective CAC system.[2293] In the absence of any prior controls, minors could directly access R18-equivalent content which was contrary to rule 11.[2294] A second breach was established in relation to material for which a subscription was needed. Payments could be made using the services of CCBill and Epoch which allowed payment by debit card as well as credit card. In addition, Epoch provided an option to use "UKash" which relied on vouchers which could be purchased from different retailers, not all of which verified users' age reliably.[2295] It followed that the payment systems did not effectively verify age and thus failed to prevent minors from accessing sexually explicit content. ATVOD concluded that the provider had infringed rule 11 twice and ordered the latter to rectify the situation. It is interesting to note that throughout the following years as co-regulator, ATVOD retained the structure of its rule 11 determinations adopted in *Bootybox TV*.

---

2291 ATVOD, "Rule 11 Determination Bootybox TV," p. 4.

2292 ATVOD, "Rule 11 Determination Bootybox TV," p. 5.

2293 The warning read as follows: "This site contains sexually explicit material. The sexually explicit material I am viewing is for my own personal use and I will not expose minors to the material. I desire to receive/ view sexually explicit material. I believe that as an adult it is my inalienable right to receive/ view sexually explicit material." See ATVOD, "Rule 11 Determination Bootybox TV," pp. 4–5.

2294 ATVOD, "Rule 11 Determination Bootybox TV," pp. 6, 7.

2295 Interestingly, in order to determine whether the service "UKash" effectively controlled age, ATVOD examined the frequently asked questions as published on the UKash website. See ATVOD, "Rule 11 Determination Bootybox TV," pp. 5–6.

### b) No violations: Frankie Boyle and Mr. Woodcock

In February 2011 and March 2012, ATVOD rejected two complaints determining that two programmes featured on 4OD, the ODPS of Channel 4 Television did not violate rule 11.[2296] In 2011, a user had complained that an episode of the comedy series Frankie Boyle Tramadol Nights was highly offensive to disabled people. ATVOD explored whether the programme raised issues under rule 11. It found that the episode contained sexual references as well as explicit statements about persons with disabilities. Nonetheless, ATVOD did not consider that the statutory test was met, underlining that legislation prescribed the "might seriously impair" test which did not forbid the provision of all types of unsuitable content. The co-regulator furthermore stressed that the "attitudes expressed, and the manner in which they [were] expressed, while objectionable to some viewers, [were] not intended to be taken seriously and [were] unlikely to have a significant impact on the beliefs, attitudes, well-being or behaviour of under 18s".[2297]

In a similar vein, the inclusion of the feature film Mr. Woodcock in 4OD's catalogue in 2012 prompted a complaint by a viewer. ATVOD acknowledged that the viewer had suffered distress while watching the programme but underlined that it was not "empowered to enforce any standards in relation to content which might cause offence and distress *per se*, or to exercise any restraint over the provision of such material on demand".[2298] It further noted that the BBFC had accorded a classification of "12" to the film (whereas 4OD had given the film the classification "15" in its EPG) emphasising the programme's humorous nature. Consequently, ATVOD stated that the programme did not "condone or trivialise psychological or physical abuse". It explained that the statutory test was not "whether even a vulnerable minor who has been abused would be further victimised or distressed by the film. It [was] whether development of per-

2296 ATVOD, "Determination on a Complaint That the On-Demand Programme Service 4OD Included Unsuitable or Harmful Content (Frankie Boyle Tramadol Nights Series)," February 3, 2011; ATVOD, "Determination on a Complaint That the On-Demand Programme Service 4OD Included Unsuitable or Harmful Content (Mr. Woodcock)," March 29, 2012.

2297 ATVOD, "No Breach of Rule 11 Determination Frankie Boyle," p. 3.

2298 ATVOD, "No Breach of Rule 11 Determination Mr Woodcock," p. 2.

sons under 18 would be seriously impaired".[2299] In both cases, 4OD had voluntarily provided additional information about the respective programmes in addition to warnings that the content could be considered as highly offensive and could cause distress to individual viewers. These two cases highlight that ATVOD conducted a careful appraisal of the potential of the programme to cause serious harm to under 18s.

With respect to 4OD's two programmes, ATVOD rightly pointed at the nature of the material which was comedic. While there are different degrees of comedy and different levels of humour (some of which may be hurtful to some viewers), ATVOD stressed that the programmes were not meant to be taken seriously. The hurdle of the statutory test takes into account the right to freedom of expression of those producing controversial programmes and those consuming them. Any measure that would restrict the dissemination of audiovisual material invariably has consequences for the rights and freedoms of others. While ATVOD could not react in relation to material which any individual user might have found appalling, it could only restrict the distribution of programmes which were seriously harmful to minors in general.

#### c) Serious violations: Playboy TV and Demand Adult

##### (aa) ATVOD determines that the service provider breaches rule 11

2012 saw ATVOD's first major initiative in monitoring compliance with rule 11. ATVOD led a number of investigations and published 15 determinations in July 2012, some of which concerned services of the same provider.[2300] Two of the providers reprimanded by ATVOD, Playboy TV and Strictly Broadband, were subsequently fined by Ofcom for non-compliance with rule 11. The *Playboy TV* and *Demand Adult* determinations

2299 ATVOD, "No Breach of Rule 11 Determination Mr Woodcock," p. 3.

2300 See ATVOD determinations of 2 July 2012 in cases Black Vixen, Porn Pass, English Milf, Paul Raymond, Rosewoodxxx, Sexy UK Pornstars, Splat Bukkake, Strictly Broadband, UK Porn Party, UK Pussy Talk, UK Vixens. The majority of the services offered free-to-view as well as paid content including audiovisual and non-audiovisual material (stills) qualified as R18 level sex works. The payment processing systems allowed for payments by debit card and some even made possible payment by phone (such as Sexy UK Pornstars, Splat Bukkake, UK Porn Party or Rosewoodxxx).

issued to the service provider Playboy TV UK/Benelux Ltd (Playboy) are representative of ATVOD's practice at the material time and are examined jointly below. Where appropriate, reference is also made to the proceedings regarding Strictly Broadband. The two services Playboy TV and Demand Adult were very similar in the type of content disseminated, the design, branding and management of the service. Both services offered adult content and used the same payment methods. The only difference was the fact that the Demand Adult service also contained free access to some of the material apart from paid access (in the form of pay-per-view or subscription). The two determinations are thus similarly worded, even identical for most parts. ATVOD began by analysing the nature of the content provided on the two websites, positing that the videos "appeared to resemble television programmes on adult linear services", thus were considered TV-like.[2301] It also found that the content "appeared to be 'R18' level sex works (hardcore works) the primary purpose of which [was] sexual arousal or stimulation".[2302] In line with its precautionary approach,[2303] ATVOD qualified R18-equivalent material as seriously harmful material for the purposes of the CA and established that rule 11 was applicable.

It subsequently turned to examine the manner in which access was granted. In case of the Demand Adult service, users could freely access stills "containing hardcore images".[2304] ATVOD made clear that the wording of Sec. 368E (2) CA (now Sec. 368E (4) CA) referred to "*material* which might seriously impair" children. The term "material" was broader in scope than, for instance, the notion of "programme". Its use in the legislation implied that *any* type of unsuitable content (audiovisual and non-audiovisual) included in an ODPS was subject to rule 11.[2305] Due to the lack of any age verification system, minors could easily access the materi-

2301 ATVOD, "Determination That the Provider of the On-Demand Programme Service 'Demand Adult' was in Breach of Rule 11," February 7, 2012, p. 4; ATVOD, "Determination That the Provider of the On-Demand Programme Service 'playboytv.co.uk' was in Breach of Rule 11," February 7, 2012, p. 4; see also ATVOD, "Determination That the Provider of the On-Demand Programme Service 'Strictly Broadband' was in Breach of Rule 11," July 2, 2012, pp. 4–5.

2302 ATVOD, "Rule 11 Determination Demand Adult," p. 4; ATVOD, "Rule 11 Determination Playboy TV," p. 4.

2303 ATVOD, "Rule 11 Determination Demand Adult," p. 4; ATVOD, "Rule 11 Determination Playboy TV," p. 4.

2304 ATVOD, "Rule 11 Determination Demand Adult," p. 5.

2305 ATVOD, "Rule 11 Determination Demand Adult," p. 5.

al. ATVOD pointed out that a warning[2306] as well as links to confirm age stating "Enter. I am over 18" or "Exit if you are under 18" (which were also placed on the website of the Playboy TV service) did not constitute an effective age verification system. In relation to paid content provided on both websites, ATVOD noted that the payment methods of Pay Wizard and CC Bill could process debit card payments and bank transfers (in case of CC Bill's "Direct Pay"). CC Bill's credit card option could also process payments by debit card.[2307] The service provider had argued that debit cards were the preferred method of payments in many EU countries and that reliable technical tools for age verification were not supported in many jurisdictions. ATVOD was unsympathetic to this argument underscoring that it was "not the responsibility of the regulator to find technical solutions for commercial service providers".[2308]

Likewise, users of the service Strictly Broadband could pay by debit card as well as by mobile phone, via SMS. ATVOD equally criticised the payment methods which allowed any young person to access the services "without being challenged by any further age verification process".[2309] Hence, ATVOD concluded that the payment systems used by the service

2306 The warning read „This site contains sexually explicit adult material intended for individuals 18 years of age or older and of legal age to view sexually explicit material as determined by the local and national laws of the region in which you reside. If you are not 18; If adult material offends you; Or if you are accessing this site from any country or locale where adult material is specifically prohibited by law, do not enter this site." ATVOD, "Rule 11 Determination Demand Adult," p. 4.

2307 ATVOD, "Rule 11 Determination Demand Adult," p. 5; ATVOD, "Rule 11 Determination Playboy TV," pp. 4–5. Strictly Broadband had relied on the Surf and Pay service which could process debit card payments. In addition, users could make a payment by mobile phone, via SMS. ATVOD thus found that the payment systems did not effectively verify the age of users. See ATVOD, "Rule 11 Determination Strictly Broadband," p. 5.

2308 ATVOD, "Rule 11 Determination Demand Adult," p. 7; ATVOD, "Rule 11 Determination Playboy TV," p. 6. The provider of the Rosewoodxxx had argued that the installation of an effective CAC system was too burdensome and infeasible for a small-scale provider which would have to close done due to the ensuing costs. In its determination, ATVOD did not accept the claim that a CAC system "not practicable, as other service providers [had] found satisfactory solutions." See ATVOD, "Determination That the Provider of the on Demand Programme Service 'www.rosewoodnnn.com' is in Breach of Rule 11," July 2, 2011, p. 7.

2309 ATVOD, "Rule 11 Determination Strictly Broadband," p. 5.

providers did not effectively verify age and did not appropriately restrict access solely to adults as the paywalls could easily be circumvented by under 18s.[2310] ATVOD also did not accept Playboy's claim that it was "in the process of transferring editorial responsibility" for the two services to Canada.[2311] The co-regulator clarified that the breach of rule 11 occurred at the time when the provider was indubitably under UK jurisdiction. In parallel proceedings analysed below, ATVOD and Ofcom dealt with the question whether Playboy had in fact re-located to Canada.

(bb) The imposition of heavy fines by Ofcom

During the summer of 2012, ATVOD conducted several investigations to verify compliance with rule 11. Each time, it found that the provider had not remedied the breach and set a deadline until which the provider was asked to conform to the statutory requirements. In mid-August, the co-regulator referred three cases to Ofcom considering that the continued violations merited the imposition of a statutory sanction pursuant to Sec. 368J.[2312] In December 2012, Strictly Broadband was fined GBP 60,000 for non-compliance with rule 11 and in January 2013, Ofcom imposed a fine of total GBP 100,000 on Playboy (comprising GBP 65,000 in relation to the service Demand Adult and GBP 35,000 concerning the service Playboy TV).[2313] In the three cases, the violation of rule 11 had continued

2310 ATVOD, "Rule 11 Determination Demand Adult," pp. 6, 7; ATVOD, "Rule 11 Determination Playboy TV," pp. 5, 6; ATVOD, "Rule 11 Determination Strictly Broadband," pp. 5–6.

2311 ATVOD, "Rule 11 Determination Demand Adult," p. 7; ATVOD, "Rule 11 Determination Playboy TV," p. 6. Strictly Broadband also raised this argument alleging that it was in the process of re-locating outside the UK. ATVOD however pointed out that the provider had not given any evidence to bolster its allegation. See ATVOD, "Rule 11 Determination Strictly Broadband," p. 6.

2312 Ofcom, "Sanction Decision for the Provision of the On-Demand Programme Service 'Demand Adult,'" January 16, 2013, paras. 9–12, p. 3; Ofcom, "Sanction Decision for the Provision of the On- Demand Programme Service 'playboytv.co.uk,'" January 16, 2013, paras. 9–12, p. 3.

2313 Ofcom, "Sanction Decision Demand Adult," para. 108, p. 16; Ofcom, "Sanction Decision Playboy TV," para. 102, p. 15. According to Sec. 368J (1) CA, the maximum level of the financial penalty may not exceed five per cent of the provider's qualifying revenue or GBP 250,000, whichever is greater. When cal-

for a period of roughly two months. Because the Strictly Broadband and Demand Adult services featured adult content for free and upon payment, the amount of the fines reflected that providers had committed two breaches.[2314] The Playboy sanctioning decisions are in the focus of the analysis below as they are more detailed and thus give a more comprehensive overview of the different interests at stake.

The service provider contested the sanctions on five grounds.[2315] Firstly, it challenged Ofcom's power to impose a penalty which Ofcom rejected by reference to the relevant provisions of the CA.[2316] Secondly, the service provider submitted that the announcement of its re-location to a non-UK jurisdiction would pre-empt any sanctioning measures by the regulators, claiming that its legitimate expectations would otherwise be undermined.[2317] Ofcom underlined that the provider was punished for its failure to comply with the statutory requirements during a time period when the services were unambiguously "in scope".[2318] The sanctions did not take into account the period following the service provider's declaration on 24 July 2012 that the transfer of its activities was under way.[2319] Thirdly,

culating the fines, Ofcom remarked that "at present there is no reliable or easily verifiable method of measuring the revenue or profit associated with a particular ODPS" (para. 94, p. 14 in Demand Adult; para. 88, p. 13 in Playboy TV and para. 49, p. 9 in Strictly Broadband). It concluded that the highest fine it could apply was thus GBP 250,000. In determining the fines, Ofcom took into account the proportionality of the sanction (by reference to the provider's annual turnover: GBP 12,687,000 in 2010 for Playboy TV UK/Benelux and GBP 616,566 in 2010 for Strictly Broadband) and the fact that the penalty should serve as a deterrent and encourage providers to respect the statutory rules.

2314 Ofcom, "Sanction Decision Demand Adult," para. 9, p. 3; Ofcom, "Sanction Decision Strictly Broadband," para. 36, p. 7.

2315 Strictly Broadband did not submit any representations to Ofcom other than the statement that the provider intended to move editorial responsibility outside the UK. In October 2012, the provider informed Ofcom that it had entered liquidation. The service had been sold to an American company. Ofcom, "Sanction Decision Strictly Broadband," paras. 12, 43 pp. 3–9.

2316 Ofcom, "Sanction Decision Demand Adult," paras. 37–47, pp. 7-8; Ofcom, "Sanction Decision Playboy TV," paras. 37–47, pp. 7-8.

2317 Ofcom, "Sanction Decision Demand Adult," paras. 48–55, pp. 8-9; Ofcom, "Sanction Decision Playboy TV," paras. 48–55, pp. 8-9.

2318 Ofcom, "Sanction Decision Demand Adult," para. 50, p. 8; Ofcom, "Sanction Decision Playboy TV," para. 50, p. 8.

2319 Ofcom, "Sanction Decision Demand Adult," para. 53, p. 9; Ofcom, "Sanction Decision Playboy TV," para. 53, p. 8.

Playboy stated that the sanctions were taken in view of and influenced by the fact that the provider had previously pronounced its intention to re-locate to a different jurisdiction.[2320] Ofcom clarified that it understood the provider's move as a "genuine reorganisation within the wider corporate group (…) which [did] not suggest bad faith, an intention to evade scope or to frustrate measures for the protection of children".[2321] Fourthly, the provider denied the violation of the CA, *inter alia* arguing that the Demand Adult website consisted of two distinct parts, one of which encompassed still images and which therefore did not constitute an ODPS.[2322] Ofcom however confirmed ATVOD's interpretation of Sec. 368E (2) CA (today Sec. 368E (4) and (5) CA) emphasising that the "intention and effect of the wording [i.e. 'material'] [was] that all material, whether or not it consist[ed] of moving images, [was] covered if a service [was] an ODPS".[2323] Ofcom moreover pointed out that the website comprised one single service, a finding which was not called into question by the mere fact that certain material was freely accessible while other material was put behind a paywall.[2324] Interestingly, the service provider also argued that the stills shown via the Demand Adult service were included on account of advertising purposes and could thus not be considered as harmful. Yet, Ofcom posited that the primary purpose of the service remained the provision of adult entertainment content for sexual arousal or stimulation.[2325] Fifthly, the seriousness of the breach was disputed by the service provider. Ofcom nonetheless regarded the infringement to be serious, systematic and prolonged.[2326]

2320 Ofcom, "Sanction Decision Demand Adult," para. 56, p. 9; Ofcom, "Sanction Decision Playboy TV," para. 56, p. 9.

2321 Ofcom, "Sanction Decision Demand Adult," para. 57, p. 9; Ofcom, "Sanction Decision Playboy TV," para. 57, p. 9.

2322 Ofcom, "Sanction Decision Demand Adult," para. 59, p. 9.

2323 Ofcom, "Sanction Decision Demand Adult," para. 61, p. 10.

2324 Ofcom, "Sanction Decision Demand Adult," para. 62, p. 10.

2325 Ofcom, "Sanction Decision Demand Adult," paras. 63–64, p. 10.

2326 Ofcom pointed out that the infringement took place over a period of approximately two months. Even at a later point, the provider did not bring the services into compliance. The only reaction from the service provider in response to ATVOD's determination seemed to have been to inform the regulators of its intention to transfer business activities outside UK territory. See Ofcom, "Sanction Decision Demand Adult," paras. 70–79, 90, 100–107, pp. 11–16; Ofcom, "Sanction Decision Playboy TV," paras. 84, 94–191, pp. 12–15.

Furthermore, Ofcom generally bolstered ATVOD's findings and general approach to protecting minors in non-linear services. By reference to the BBFC's guidelines, Ofcom confirmed that the material was R18 level and consequently should have been restricted to adults.[2327] Ofcom underlined that the BBFC's classifications, in particular the R18 category were based on the "potential for harm, including moral harm".[2328] While the provider had accepted the potential for harm, it had stressed that there was "no evidence of a 'significant or substantial degree of harm'".[2329] The regulator, however, opined that "it [was] not necessary (or realistic in the circumstances) (…) to demonstrate that *actual* harm [had] occurred in order to consider a service for sanction, but that there was the *potential* for harm".[2330] It is interesting to note that Ofcom considered the "test for potential harm" to have been met by its assessment of the two services.

The fact that Ofcom re-considered the nature of the material and the access controls may be considered as a form of review of ATVOD's findings (since there was no possibility to appeal ATVOD determinations in matters other than scope). Yet, Ofcom's analysis was similar to ATVOD's and did not go beyond the co-regulator's investigation. What is more, Ofcom supported ATVOD's approach to R18-equivalent material, positing that an "inadequate system" was one that permitted minors to view material which might be seriously impairing.[2331] In fulfilling its mandate prescribed by Sec. 3 CA, Ofcom had special account of the "vulnerability of children" and thus endorsed the precautionary approach adopted by ATVOD (and backed by the government).[2332] In relation to the controls installed by the provider, Ofcom agreed with ATVOD that the payment

2327 Ofcom, "Sanction Decision Demand Adult," paras. 82–83, p. 12; Ofcom, "Sanction Decision Playboy TV," paras. 76–77, p. 11; Ofcom, "Sanction Decision Strictly Broadband," para. 38, pp. 7-8.

2328 Ofcom, "Sanction Decision Demand Adult," para. 87, p. 13; Ofcom, "Sanction Decision Playboy TV," para. 81, p. 12.

2329 Ofcom, "Sanction Decision Demand Adult," para. 98, p. 15; Ofcom, "Sanction Decision Playboy TV," para. 92, p. 14.

2330 Ofcom, "Sanction Decision Demand Adult," para. 99, p. 15; Ofcom, "Sanction Decision Playboy TV," para. 93, p. 14; Ofcom, "Sanction Decision Strictly Broadband," para. 35, p. 7.

2331 Ofcom, "Sanction Decision Demand Adult," para. 99, p. 15; Ofcom, "Sanction Decision Playboy TV," para. 93, p. 14.

2332 Ofcom, "Sanction Decision Demand Adult," para. 85, p. 12; Ofcom, "Sanction Decision Playboy TV," para. 79, p. 11.

methods as well as the warnings and the links to self-verify age were ineffective and did not meet the requirements stipulated in rule 11.[2333]

(cc) Clarifying jurisdiction: Playboy TV and Demand Adult reloaded

In parallel to ATVOD's enquiries into rule 11, the question arose whether the provider Playboy TV UK/Benelux was established in the UK.[2334] This issue which also relates to scope is discussed in this chapter because it is exemplary of the phenomenon of jurisdiction hopping or shopping of providers of controversial content which encroaches on public morals. In a globalised online space, the transfer of business activities from one jurisdiction to another is facilitated. Service providers avoid jurisdictions that impose onerous obligations which are considered as curbing traffic as well as revenue. In addition, "tube sites" have mushroomed which imply websites "which allow users unrestricted free access to large quantities of hardcore pornographic videos which are provided as a "loss leader" on a "try before buy" basis".[2335]

Tube sites attract users by offering sexually explicit content for free and encourage them to subscribe to pay services or to purchase products and services associated with the adult industry. Such outlets are commonly established off-shore and thus are out of reach of UK regulators. In addition, ATVOD was wary of the fact that providers of pornographic content frequently neglected to publish or simply omitted contact details so that it

2333 Ofcom, "Sanction Decision Demand Adult," paras. 88–89, p. 13; Ofcom, "Sanction Decision Playboy TV," paras. 82–83, p. 12.

2334 In the case of Strictly Broadband, the service was sold to an American company and the provider entered liquidation. See Ofcom, "Sanction Decision Strictly Broadband," paras. 12, 43, pp. 3, 9; in another case of March 2013, ATVOD found that the service The Casting Room offered by O & C Entertainment Ltd was no longer operated under UK jurisdiction as editorial responsibility had been transferred to a company established in the Netherlands. See ATVOD, "Summary of Determination That the Provider of the On-Demand Programme Service 'The Casting Room' was in Breach of ATVOD's Rule 11 and Thereby Contravened Sec. 368E (2) CA," March 6, 2013. The scope determination issued on the same day affirmed this finding.

2335 ATVOD, "Report on Underage Access to Online Porn," para. 5, p. 19.

was made excessively difficult for the regulator to identify the provider and determine regulatory competence.[2336]

The two determinations and two appeal decisions in *Playboy TV* and *Demand Adult* in relation to the jurisdiction of the service provider thus add another dimension to the difficulty of enforcing rule 11 on the Internet. In this case more so than in other scope decisions, the aspect of scope is intrinsically linked to the material rule concerning the protection of minors in non-linear services. As can be seen from ATVOD's determination analysed above, the service provider had submitted that it no longer fell under UK jurisdiction and could thus not be sanctioned for non-respect of the statutory obligations arising from the CA. In July 2012, the provider notified ATVOD that the transfer of editorial responsibility from its UK premises to its Canadian head office was completed. Investigating into the place of establishment of the service provider, ATVOD determined in September 2012 that the former remained under UK jurisdiction. Due to the reference to a UK address as the contact information of the provider, the reference to "UK law" in its terms and conditions, domain registration data indicating that the website was registered in America and the lack of any changes in the design and structure of the website, ATVOD posited that, in September 2012, the provider's main location still was the UK.[2337]

---

2336 In its submissions to the inquiry of the parliamentary committee on Culture, Media and Sports about online safety, ATVOD pointed out this difficulty and demanded legislative amendments which would bestow upon the regulator the power to demand information from the person who appears to be the service provider. See ATVOD, "The Culture, Media & Sports Inquiry into Online Safety, Submission from the Authority for Television On-Demand ('ATVOD')," October 3, 2013, paras. 2.8-2.10, p. 8, http://www.publications.parliament.uk/pa/cm201314/cmselect/cmcumeds/729/729vw64.htm (accessed 5.12.2013); similarly, in its reply to the Commission's consultation following the latter's Green Paper on convergence, ATVOD repeated the same concern and called for respective changes of the rules of the AVMSD (i.e. Art. 5 AVMSD). See ATVOD, "Response to Commission Green Paper," para. 4.7, pp. 12-13.

2337 Ofcom, "Appeal by Playboy TV UK/Benelux Limited against a Notice of Determination by ATVOD That It Was the Provider of the service 'Demand Adult' as at 14 September 2012," September 23, 2013, para. 18, p. 5; Ofcom, "Appeal by Playboy TV UK/Benelux Limited against a Notice of Determination by ATVOD That It Was the Provider of the Service 'Playboy TV' as at 14 September 2012," September 23, 2013, para. 17, p. 4.

Playboy appealed to Ofcom which upheld the two appeals in September 2013.[2338] Ofcom had sought more detailed information from the provider, especially regarding the distribution of tasks and allocation of responsibilities between UK and non-UK staff.[2339] From this evidence, Ofcom distilled that there had been a "genuine relocation of responsibility within the corporate group. Key individuals were made redundant in the UK and their responsibilities were taken on by individuals in Canada".[2340] Ofcom was convinced that the most senior staff involved in the editorial process was located in Canada.[2341] It thus agreed with the appellant that the person with editorial responsibility had indeed changed and no longer resided in the UK.[2342] Importantly, Ofcom highlighted the persuasive nature of the evidence and considered that the primary reasons for relocation were "purely commercial and not related to any attempt to evade regulations".[2343] It thus expressly contradicted ATVOD's position. Yet, Ofcom explicitly limited its findings to the points raised in the appeal and did not rule out that two further businesses which were mentioned in the course of the appeal (Manwin Holding SARL and Playboy Plus Entertainment) were located in the UK or another Member State, notably Luxembourg, where the service had not been notified to the competent regulatory authority.[2344]

The case of Playboy demonstrates the difficulty for regulators to determine jurisdiction. ATVOD did not seem to attach credence to Playboy's

---

2338 Ofcom, "Appeal Decision on Jurisdiction Demand Adult"; Ofcom, "Appeal Decision on Jurisdiction Playboy TV.".

2339 Ofcom, "Appeal Decision on Jurisdiction Demand Adult," para. 24, p. 6; para. 33, p. 8; Ofcom, "Appeal Decision on Jurisdiction Playboy TV," para. 23, p. 6; para. 32, p. 7. In light of new evidence, Ofcom interestingly did not remit back the decision to ATVOD but substituted its own decision for ATVOD's determination. This was due to the lapse of time (more than one year) which had passed between ATVOD's initial assessment and Ofcom's final decision in the interest of a "prompt conclusion" and in order to prevent furter costs (para. 38, p. 9 of Demand Adult; para. 37, p. 9 of Playboy TV).

2340 Ofcom, "Appeal Decision on Jurisdiction Demand Adult," para. 32, p. 7; Ofcom, "Appeal Decision on Jurisdiction Playboy TV," para. 31, p. 7.

2341 Ofcom, "Appeal Decision on Jurisdiction Demand Adult," para. 33, p. 8; Ofcom, "Appeal Decision on Jurisdiction Playboy TV," para. 32, pp. 7–8.

2342 Ofcom, "Appeal Decision on Jurisdiction Demand Adult," para. 31, p. 7; Ofcom, "Appeal Decision on Jurisdiction Playboy TV," para. 30, p. 7.

2343 Ofcom, "Appeal Decision on Jurisdiction Demand Adult," paras. 34–35, p. 8; Ofcom, "Appeal Decision on Jurisdiction Playboy TV," paras. 33–34, p. 8.

2344 Ofcom, "Appeal Decision on Jurisdiction Demand Adult," para. 40, pp. 9–10; Ofcom, "Appeal Decision on Jurisdiction Playboy TV," para. 39, p. 9.

contentions that it had altered its business seat but appeared to believe that the provider acted under false pretences in order to avoid the statutory obligations. Ofcom, however, showed that it was necessary to carefully examine the evidence provided and determine upon the value of the evidence alone the provider's establishment.

#### d) Modest fine imposed on a small-scale provider: HardGlam

In contrast to the substantial fines imposed on Playboy and Strictly Broadband, Ofcom fined Mr. James Farey GBP 1,500 for failing to comply with rule 11 in December 2014. The exceptional circumstances of the case and the small scale of the providers' business warranted a small penalty. In April 2014, ATVOD found that the service HardGlam which was made available through 14 different outlets violated rule 11.[2345] ATVOD determined that both, free-to-view as well as subscription material (audiovisual and not) were R18-equivalent or stronger and thus required installation of age controls.[2346] These were either entirely missing as any user could access stills and sample videos without restriction, or did not fulfil the required purpose. The variety of payment methods utilised allowed for debit card payments and payments by post, by SMS or phone (US only), by check (US only) by EU bank account or by Paypal. Although a user is required to be at least 18 to use Paypal according to the latter's terms and conditions, ATVOD pointed out that "no evidence [was] required to prove that a user [was] eighteen or over".[2347] Hence, minors could easily circumvent the paywall which fell short of the statutory requirements. Since the service provider did not take any measures to bring the service in line with rule 11, ATVOD referred the case to Ofcom for consideration of a statutory sanction. Ofcom issued a notice in May and a direction in June 2014 requiring the provider to remove all free-to-view R18-equivalent material

2345 ATVOD, "Determination That the Provider of the On-Demand Programme Service 'HardGlam' was in Breach of ATVOD's Rule 11 and Thereby Contravened Sex. 368E (2) CA," April 25, 2014.

2346 ATVOD, "Rule 11 Determination HardGlam," para. 8.3, pp. 5–6.

2347 ATVOD, "Rule 11 Determination HardGlam," para. 8.4c, p. 7.

from its websites and put into operation an effective CAC system which verifies users' age.[2348]

The service provider reacted in November 2014 arguing that he had been wholly unaware of ATVOD and the legal rules applicable to ODPS. He had dismissed ATVOD's notification as a scam as he had run his business "focusing on niche fetishes (principally women smoking) for nine years without realising compliance with ATVOD rules was required".[2349] In addition, the provider underlined that he operated a "very small business" which had accomplished "very modest sales" during the period of the infringement.[2350] Mr. Farey expressed concerns "about his ability to continue the business were a fine over four figures to be imposed".[2351] He also stated that providers which offered online subscription services faced fierce competition and were placed under pressure by the sheer endless availability of pornographic content circulating on the Internet free of charge.[2352] Moreover, the provider admitted to have falsely relied on payment processors to ensure the protection of minors and had erroneously presumed that these would proactively implement age controls.[2353] In response, Ofcom took a lenient position taking into account the "exceptional personal circumstances" of the case and the provider's collaboration from November.[2354] Importantly, the regulator was "satisfied that the lack of engagement was not part of a strategy to evade regulation and instead represented a genuine lack of appreciation of the seriousness of the situation and the status of ATVOD".[2355] Ofcom furthermore accepted that the provider as a "sole trader" did not have any close links to the adult content industry and thus lacked resources and knowledge about the legal framework.[2356] On the substance, Ofcom fully agreed with ATVOD's findings as outlined in the determination.[2357] With regards to the amount of the fine, Ofcom differentiated this case from earlier sanction decisions in

2348 Ofcom, "Sanction Decision for the Provision of the On-Demand Programme Service 'HardGlam,'" December 11, 2014, paras. 8–10, pp. 3-4.
2349 Ofcom, "Sanction Decision HardGlam," para. 38, p. 8.
2350 Ofcom, "Sanction Decision HardGlam," para. 39, p. 8.
2351 Ofcom, "Sanction Decision HardGlam," paras. 39–40, p. 8.
2352 Ofcom, "Sanction Decision HardGlam," para. 39, p. 8.
2353 Ofcom, "Sanction Decision HardGlam," para. 41, p. 9.
2354 Ofcom, "Sanction Decision HardGlam," para. 42, p. 9.
2355 Ofcom, "Sanction Decision HardGlam," paras. 42, 61, pp. 9, 11.
2356 Ofcom, "Sanction Decision HardGlam," para. 42, p. 9.
2357 Ofcom, "Sanction Decision HardGlam," paras. 71–73, pp. 13-14.

which it had imposed much heavier fines primarily by the "exceptional aspects of the present case" as well as the small scale of the business.[2358] In contrast to, for instance, Playboy, Mr. Farey was not considered a "sophisticated" player on the market.[2359]

The *HardGlam* case illustrates Ofcom's pragmatic market-oriented approach. The cases of *Playboy TV*, *Strictly Broadband* and *HardGlam* seem similar on face value: the providers disseminated a certain proportion of unsuitable material without restriction and did not effectively exclude minors from accessing the full range of content aggregated in their catalogues available on subscription. The infringement committed by Mr. Farey could even be considered more serious as the provider disrespected the legal rules for a period of more than eight months and the material was featured on 14 websites composing the service.[2360] Nonetheless, Ofcom realistically assessed Mr. Farey's standing on the relevant market and gave credence to the provider's lack of understanding of the legal rules and the co-regulatory scheme. In view of ATVOD's collaborative approach actively engaging the industry in numerous information sessions, it is difficult to see, however, how the service provider escaped all these activities. Notwithstanding the ability of the provider to understand the legal requirements, Ofcom rightly took notice of the economic capacities of Mr. Farey which marked a sharp contrast to those of Playboy and Strictly Broadband.

Furthermore, the case helps to explain the business models used by providers of adult entertainment content. Freely available samples or previews of sexually explicit material are offered as honey pots to engage consumers and induce them to sign up for membership at cost. Consequently, compliance with rule 11 is regarded by many "porn providers" as

2358 Ofcom, "Sanction Decision HardGlam," paras. 76, 85, 87–88, 93, 95, pp. 14, 16–17.

2359 Ofcom, "Sanction Decision HardGlam," para. 92, p. 17.

2360 In general, the number of outlets through which a service is made available does not seem indicative of the seriousness of the violation. Interestingly, ATVOD instigated proceedings in mid-2014 against the provider of the service Extreme Movie Pass which comprised 73 websites. The number of outlets is, however, not further discussed by ATVOD's determination of 21 July 2014. This illustrates the dimension individual cases might take. After the provider failed to comply with an enforcement notification of ATVOD, the co-regulator referred the matter to Ofcom for consideration of a statutory sanction. So far, Ofcom has not imposed a penalty.

a burden and as dangerous for business. Interestingly, the managing director of the service Strictly Broadband which was penalised heavily by Ofcom at the end of 2012 had stated that;

> "(...) the requirement to age-verify before even photographic sales can be seen will simply drive most of our customers to sites outside ATVOD's scope. The one company to fully implement these rules to date, [name of company redacted], has seen an 80% fall in new business, and a 28% fall in overall revenue, since they complied. As I'm sure the board will appreciate, few businesses can survive such a decline, especially in the current economic climate".[2361]

This statement makes a causal link between compliance with rule 11 and an immense drop in providers' turnover. The quote also alludes to the problem of jurisdiction shopping exercised by service providers as well as consumers (albeit unconsciously). In order to continue offering "attractive" adult content, providers re-locate outside the UK (the EU) and consumers turn to those websites which fulfil their needs and interests regardless of where they are hosted at no or very low costs. This problem which ATVOD also openly addressed in its policy documents shows the powerlessness of regulators in this global game.

#### e) Barring services: Jessica Pressley and Pleasuring Herself

In mid-2013, ATVOD and Ofcom took robust enforcement action in relation to the two services named Jessica Pressley and Pleasuring Herself. While the latter closed down, the service provider of Jessica Pressley was barred from offering an ODPS in the UK due to its failure to conform to ATVOD's determination. This marked the first time that the statutory sanction to suspend or prohibit a person from exercising the activity of providing an ODPS pursuant to Sec. 368K CA was imposed. Pete Johnson, former Chief Executive of ATVOD, commented in a press release dated 15 November 2013 that "the action taken (...) [was] the first of its kind and demonstrates that the ATVOD rules that apply to UK video on demand services are backed by effective enforcement procedures".[2362]

---

2361 Ofcom, "Sanction Decision Strictly Broadband," para. 38d, p. 8.

2362 ATVOD, News article of 15.11.2013, Pornographer barred from providing video-on-demand service". Following the end of the co-regulatory model, the news article is no longer available online.

ATVOD issued two similar determinations in July and September 2013.[2363]

The two websites of Jessica Pressley and Pleasuring Herself offered free and paid access to sexually explicit material in form of still images as well as videos. On the homepages, users could indulge in a "free tour" which depicted pornographic stills and "previews".[2364] Upon payment, the whole catalogue of videos was made available to members. In line with Ofcom appeal decisions in matters of scope, ATVOD found in a first step that the audiovisual material resembled programmes broadcast on adult channels on linear TV and that they generally had R18 quality.[2365] In a second step, the co-regulator considered that the measures put in place by the two providers to prevent minors from accessing their content were insufficient. Both services included free material which minors could see openly.[2366] ATVOD reiterated that the publication of conditions and a "voluntary declaration" by the user that he or she was of age did not constitute effective controls.[2367] With regards to paid content, ATVOD found that no effective systems to verify age were in place. The payment methods of both services included options to pay by debit card.[2368] In addition, the service Pleasuring Herself allowed for a US online check which appeared to accept payments from US bank accounts which could be held by

2363 Preceding these determinations, ATVOD issued two separate scope determinations finding that the services Jessica Pressley provided by J P Media and the service Pleasuring Herself offered by Mr. S Hilder constituted ODPS within the meaning of Sec. 368A CA.

2364 ATVOD, "Summary of Determination That the Provider of the On-Demand Programme Service 'Jessica Pressley' was in Breach of ATVOD's Rule 11 and Thereby Contravened Sec. 368E (2) CA," July 23, 2013, p. 4; ATVOD, "Summary of Determination That the Provider of the On-Demand Programme Service 'Pleasuring Herself' was in Breach of ATVOD's Rule 11 and Thereby Contravened Sec. 368E (2) CA," September 9, 2013, p. 4.

2365 ATVOD, "Rule 11 Determination Jessica Pressley," p. 4; ATVOD, "Rule 11 Determination Pleasuring Herself," p. 5.

2366 ATVOD, "Rule 11 Determination Jessica Pressley," pp. 5, 6; ATVOD, "Rule 11 Determination Pleasuring Herself," pp. 5, 6.

2367 ATVOD, "Rule 11 Determination Jessica Pressley," p. 5. The conditions read "By proceeding you affirm that you are at least 18 years or older, and that you are voluntarily choosing to view and access such sexually-explicit images and content for your own personal use" (p.4); ATVOD, "Rule 11 Determination Pleasuring Herself," p. 6.

2368 ATVOD, "Rule 11 Determination Jessica Pressley," p. 5; ATVOD, "Rule 11 Determination Pleasuring Herself," pp. 5–6.

persons under the age of 18.[2369] "If they [were] going to offer explicit sex material they must know that their customers are 18, just as they would in the 'offline' world", remarked Pete Johnson in ATVOD's press release. The service providers had thus committed multiple breaches of rule 11 (i.e. in relation to material available for free and against payment). Following an enforcement notification of ATVOD, the service Pleasuring Herself was no longer online.

Due to its disrespect of ATVOD's determination, the service provider of Jessica Pressley was referred to Ofcom for consideration of a statutory sanction in September 2013. On 7 October 2013, Ofcom issued a direction suspending its "right to provide the "Jessica Pressley", or any other, VOD service".[2370] Interestingly, the sanction imposed on the service provider J P Media is harsher than in the *Playboy* and *Strictly Broaband* cases which "merely" received financial penalties. It seems that the chronology of measures taken by ATVOD was similar. ATVOD first established that a breach had occurred. Subsequently an enforcement notification was issued, which stipulated that the provider had not brought the service in line with ATVOD's initial determination. From the description of the programmes, it appears reasonable to assume that the content provided on the Jessica Pressley service was comparable to the material depicted on the two Playboy and the Strictly Broadband services and not necessarily more extreme. All things being equal, the only reason why Ofcom imposed a heavier sanction on J P Media might have been that the *Playboy* and *Strictly Broadband* cases served as precedents. It could be presumed that by mid-2013, the industry had been well aware of the statutory requirements and the need to install effective age controls and paywalls to protect minors. It furthermore gives the impression that the regulators intended to make an example of the *Jessica Pressley* case. In its statement of November 2013, Ofcom underlined that "non co-operation with enforcement by ATVOD or itself in matters concerning the protection of children from harm, [would] be dealt with swiftly".[2371] Likewise, ATVOD referred to the importance of timely and effective enforcement of rule 11. The direc-

2369 ATVOD, "Rule 11 Determination Pleasuring Herself," p. 6.

2370 The direction is directly issued to the service provider and thus not publicly available. See Ofcom, "Ofcom's Enforcement Action against the 'Jessica Pressley' service," November 15, 2013.

2371 Ofcom, "Statement Regarding Jessica Pressley"; see also the quote by an Ofcom spokesman in John Reynolds, "Adult Video-On-Demand Website Closed for

tion had immediate effect and was valid indefinitely. As a result, the service stopped operating the next day.

These two cases illustrate the far-reaching nature of the sanctions imposed by Ofcom and their adverse effect on freedom of expression. It does not only impact the provider's freedom to offer pornographic content but also the user's right to receive such content. Interestingly, another service named Abused Piggy immediately closed in March 2013 after ATVOD had determined a breach of rule 11. The determination is silent on the reasons for the service's sudden closure.[2372] It can thus only be speculated whether it was the fact that ATVOD had established a violation which caused the service to stop operating or any other factors. In general, the examples show the difficult balance regulators have to make between the safeguarding of a public interest and service provider's individual rights and liberties.

#### f) Services brought into compliance: G Spot Productions, Studio 66 TV and The British Institution

In contrast to the cases which resulted in the imposition of statutory sanctions, several service providers closely cooperated with ATVOD in bringing their services in compliance with rule 11.[2373] The services G Spot Productions, Studio 66 TV and The British Institution, for example, offered free (except for Studio 66) as well as paid access to R18 level content in-

Failing to Protect Children," *The Guardian*, November 15, 2013, http://www.theguardian.com/media/2013/nov/15/adult-video-on-demand-site-closed-jessica-pressley (accessed 25.4.2016).

2372 ATVOD, "Determination That the Provider of 'Abused Piggy' was in Breach of ATVOD's Rule 11 and Thereby Contravened Sec. 368E (2) CA," March 25, 2013.

2373 In several cases, service providers simply removed all audiovisual material from their outlets. As a result, the services exclusively offered sexually explicit photographic content and thus no longer constituted ODPS within the meaning of the CA. See ATVOD determinations concerning the services CFNM of 6 March 2013 and Bra Busters of Britain of 13 February 2014. Likewise, ATVOD's determination of 6 January 2014 regarding the Urban Chick Supremacy Cell was withdrawn in August 2014 after a successful appeal to Ofcom which had held that the service was not an ODPS.

cluding stills and videos.[2374] In its initial assessment, ATVOD found fault with the lack of age verification in relation to material provided for free and the absence of an effective CAC system regarding material available upon subscription.[2375] After ATVOD had informed service providers about its initial investigation, the providers contacted ATVOD (in writing and by phone) to discuss necessary changes which providers subsequently implemented. ATVOD then conducted another assessment testing whether seriously impairing content was (still) made available in such a way that minors could see or hear it. The providers of G Spot Productions and the British Institution had removed freely accessible R18-equivalent material from their outlets.[2376] In addition, the payment systems of all providers only accepted credit cards. While G Spot Productions used CCBill EU and The British Institution relied on a method operated by Epoch, the provider of Studio 66 TV used the "Intelligent ID" system to verify the age of users.[2377] This system checked age "against a variety of independent sources including the electoral roll".[2378] The checks were conducted once the user had obtained membership status and at the moment he or she attempted to play a video. If users failed to verify age, they could seek direct contact to the provider by email. ATVOD requested additional information about this process and learnt that the service provider made "a manual check based on driving license or passport number" in this situation.[2379]

2374 ATVOD, "Determination That the Provider of 'G Spot Productions' was in Breach of ATVOD's Rule 11 and Thereby Contravened Sec. 368E (2) CA," March 25, 2013, p. 5; ATVOD, "Determination That the Provider of 'Studio 66 TV' was in Breach of ATVOD's Rule 11 and Thereby Contravened Sec. 368E (2) CA," March 25, 2013, pp. 4–5; ATVOD, "Summary of Determination That the Provider of the On-Demand Programme Service 'The British Institution' was in Breach of ATVOD's Rule 11 and Thereby Contravened Sec. 368E (2) CA," July 9, 2013, pp. 4–5.

2375 ATVOD, "Rule 11 Determination G Spot Productions," p. 6; ATVOD, "Rule 11 Determination Studio 66 TV," p. 5; ATVOD, "Rule 11 Determination The British Institution," p. 6.

2376 ATVOD, "Rule 11 Determination G Spot Productions," p. 7; ATVOD, "Rule 11 Determination The British Institution," p. 7. The service providers continued to offer sexually explicit content for free which, however, did not reach R 18 level according to ATVOD.

2377 ATVOD, "Rule 11 Determination G Spot Productions," p. 8; ATVOD, "Rule 11 Determination The British Institution," p. 7; ATVOD, "Rule 11 Determination Studio 66 TV," pp. 7–8.

2378 ATVOD, "Rule 11 Determination Studio 66 TV," p. 8.

2379 ATVOD, "Rule 11 Determination Studio 66 TV," p. 8.

ATVOD was thus satisfied that the services relied on effective CAC systems and had been brought in line with rule 11. In the three determinations it issued in March and July 2013 respectively, it acknowledged these developments but established that breaches had occurred in the past (i.e. in February and March 2013 respectively).[2380]

ATVOD's findings of that contraventions of rule 11 had been committed which were remedied in the meantime remain without immediate effect for service providers. If, however, ATVOD had found at a later point that the services had been altered in such a way that they no longer conformed to the statutory requirements, the determination that breaches had taken place might have become important in view of the continued enforcement of rule 11 and the possibility to refer the cases to Ofcom for the imposition of statutory sanctions. This is underlined by the fact that ATVOD conducted on-spot checks of services it had investigated in order to ensure effective enforcement of rule 11. The cases also illustrate ATVOD's willingness to engage in a dialogue with the industry. Service providers accepted ATVOD's preliminary findings and were willing to bring their services in full conformity with legal requirements. In 2014, ATVOD remarked that several providers had taken measures to rectify one part of the violation of rule 11 for example by taking down all freely accessible R18-equivalent material from their websites or erecting an effective paywall.[2381] In sharp contrast to other cases examined in this section, these examples reflect a cooperative relation between the co-regulator and service providers.

---

2380 In a similar vein, ATVOD established contraventions of the services Facesitting Mistress for a specified period in January 2014 and the services UKnnnPass and Joybear in April 2015, recognising that the providers had fully complied with rule 11 by the time ATVOD issued its final determination. See ATVOD, "Determination That the Provider of the On-Demand Programme Service 'Facesitting Mistress' Was in Breach of ATVOD's Rule 11 and Thereby Contravened Sec. 368E (2) CA," April 24, 2014; ATVOD, "Determination That the Provider of the On-Demand Programme Service 'UKnnnPass' Was in Breach of ATVOD's Rule 11 and Thereby Contravened Sec. 368E (4) CA," June 22, 2015; ATVOD, "Determination That the Provider of the On-Demand Programme Service 'Joybear' Was in Breach of ATVOD's Rule 11 and Thereby Contravened Sec. 368E (4) CA," June 22, 2015.

2381 See for example ATVOD determinations regarding Speedy Bee and Madam Caramel of 24 March 2014 and the One Stop Porno Shop of 25 April 2014.

### g) Reviews of determinations: Daisy Rock, Panties Pulled Down and Mistress R'eal

In 2015, three ODPS providers made use of their right to request reviews of ATVOD's initial determinations finding breaches of rule 11. Apart from ATVOD's scope determinations which could be appealed to Ofcom, ATVOD's procedures stipulated that providers could request a review by ATVOD of its determinations with regards to content standards. The request had to be filed within ten days of the provider having notice of the determination. An internal review would be conducted by the entire ATVOD board, excluding board member(s) involved in drafting the original determination. In the three cases, the ATVOD board upheld the determinations previously made by (individual) ATVOD executives. The three determinations were reminiscent of those analysed above. ATVOD established violations of rule 11 in view of free-to-view material as well as material available upon subscription.[2382] Service providers had refrained from verifying user's age at all or had failed to put in operation effective age verification mechanisms.

Like the three determinations, the reviews are similar. Service providers challenged the determinations on three grounds. Firstly, they contested the fact that their services were ODPS within the meaning of the CA. In separate determinations, ATVOD had held that the services fell within scope. It noted that the question whether the services constituted ODPS was a matter for Ofcom to decide on appeal. Unless Ofcom was to quash its determinations, the services could be presumed to be ODPS and thus subject to the relevant statutory rules.[2383]

2382 ATVOD, "Determination That the Provider of the On-Demand Programme Service 'Daisy Rock UK' was in Breach of ATVOD's Rule 11 and Thereby Contravened Sec. 368E (4) CA," November 26, 2014; ATVOD, "Determination That the Provider of the On-Demand Programme Service 'Mistress R'eal' was in Breach of ATVOD's Rule 11 and Thereby Contravened Sec. 368E (4) CA," April 20, 2015; ATVOD, "Determination That the Provider of the On-Demand Programme Service 'Panties Pulled Down' was in Breach of ATVOD's Rule 11 and Thereby Contravened Sec. 368E (4) CA," February 28, 2015.

2383 ATVOD, "Review of Rule 11 Determination in Relation to the service 'Daisy Rock UK,'" April 29, 2015, para. 7, p. 2; ATVOD, "Review of Rule 11 Determination in Relation to the service 'Mistress R'eal,'" May 18, 2015, para. 7, p. 2; ATVOD, "Review of Rule 11 Determination in Relation to the service 'Panties Pulled Down,'" April 29, 2015, para. 7, 2. On appeal, Ofcom decided that the service Panties Pulled Down was not an ODPS within the meaning of

Secondly, providers argued that R18 or R18-equivalent material did not constitute material which "might seriously impair" minors under 18. In a surprisingly extensive section (above all, in *Daisy Rock UK*), ATVOD laid down the rationale for its precautionary approach which, it reiterated from its guidance, was bolstered by the government and Ofcom. ATVOD explained that in forming its position, it had relied on several studies which had found a correlation between "exposure to sexually inappropriate material and the development and validation of negative beliefs and ideas".[2384] Acknowledging that there was no conclusive evidence of harm, ATVOD stressed that the *risk* of harm could not be confidentially dismissed and was, moreover, proven by some research.[2385] Therefore, its precautionary approach was justified. In *Daisy Rock UK*, ATVOD referred to the Commission's Communication of 2000 which underlines that "the precautionary principle is relevant only in the event of a potential risk, even if this risk cannot be fully demonstrated or quantified or its effects determined because of the insufficiency or inclusive nature of the scientific data".[2386] ATVOD was thus convinced that "the decision maker can take protective measures despite a full demonstration of risks being present".[2387]

Furthermore, the service providers posited that ATVOD's requirements of age verification went beyond what was necessary. ATVOD highlighted that its age verification policy was in line with those of other organisations protecting children, such as the UK's Gambling Commission.[2388] The co-

---

the CA. As a result, ATVOD's determinations in respect of scope (rules 1 and 4) and the protection of minors (rule 11) have become invalid; see Ofcom, "Appeal Decision Panties Pulled Down"; by contrast, Daisy Rock was considered a service falling under VOD regulation on appeal. See Ofcom, "Appeal Decision Daisy Rock". Ofcom's appeal decisions are discussed in chapter four.

2384 This quote is taken from the Byron Report on Safer Children in a Digital World of 2008, para. 3.39, p. 51, available at http://webarchive.nationalarchives.gov.uk/20101021152907/http://publications.dcsf.gov.uk/default.aspx?PageFunction=productdetails&PageMode=publications&ProductId=DCSF-00334-2008& (accessed 20.2.2016) ATVOD, "Rule 11 Review Daisy Rock UK," para. 9, p. 3.

2385 ATVOD, "Rule 11 Review Daisy Rock UK," paras. 10, 14, pp. 3-4.

2386 European Commission, "Communication from the Commission on the Precautionary Principle (COM (2000)1 Final)," February 2, 2000, para. 5.1; ATVOD, "Rule 11 Review Daisy Rock UK," para. 13, p. 4.

2387 ATVOD, "Rule 11 Review Daisy Rock UK," para. 13, p. 4.

2388 ATVOD, "Rule 11 Review Daisy Rock UK," para. 16, p. 5; ATVOD, "Rule 11 Review Mistress R'eal," para. 13, p. 3; ATVOD, "Rule 11 Review Panties Pulled Down," para. 12, p. 3.

regulator made clear that a splash page warning of adult content was an inappropriate tool to verify age. In addition, ATVOD did not accept that parental control filters offered by ISPs and mobile providers which blocked the services constituted reliable means to "secure that minors will not normally hear or see" specifically restricted material. This was all the more problematic, ATVOD opined, as only 32% of British parents actually used such filters according to Ofcom research.[2389] Interestingly, in its *Daisy Rock UK* review, ATVOD specifically noted that its age verification requirements were in line with Art. 10 ECHR as they were prescribed by law, necessary in a democratic society and proportionate.[2390]

h) Services in breach of rule 14 concerning prohibited material: Dreams of Spanking, The Bondage Mistress, Glasgow Mistress Megara Furie and Mistress R'eal

This section outlines ATVOD's interpretation of rule 14 in relation to prohibited material and serves to distinguish it from rule 11 determinations. On account of the amendment of Sec. 368E CA in late 2014, present legislation expressly bans material which was not granted or would reasonably not be given a classification certificate by the BBFC. In 2015, ATVOD adjudicated four cases *Dreams of Spanking, The Bondage Mistress, Glasgow Mistress Megara Furie* and *Mistress R'eal* which all raised issues in view of both, rules 11 and 14.[2391] The rule 11 determinations in the four cases resemble those analysed above. In appraising the nature of the material contained in each ODPS, ATVOD relied on some examples which were expressly mentioned. It concluded that the material portrayed "explicit sight of clearly un-simulated sexual activity and strong fetish material", including anal and vaginal penetration or oral genital contact.[2392] The sim-

2389 ATVOD, "Rule 11 Review Daisy Rock UK," para. 17, p. 5; ATVOD, "Rule 11 Review Mistress R'eal," para. 13, p. 3; ATVOD, "Rule 11 Review Panties Pulled Down," para. 13, p. 3.

2390 ATVOD, "Rule 11 Review Daisy Rock UK," para. 18, p. 5.

2391 In the cases of Glasgow Mistress Megara Furie, Dreams of Spanking and Mistress R'eal, ATVOD also issued (scope) determinations in relation to rules 1 and 4.

2392 ATVOD, "Determination That the Provider of the On-Demand Programme Service 'Dreams of Spanking' was in Breach of ATVOD's Rule 11 and Thereby Contravened Sec. 368E (4) CA," July 30, 2015, para. 8.3, p. 5; ATVOD, "Deter-

ilarity of the formulations used in the three determinations as well as the conciseness of the description are striking.

In its rule 14 determinations, ATVOD also referred to examples of content which it considered banned, for example sustained kicking to the genitals which started bleeding, cane strokes to the buttocks which caused red marks, whips to a restrained person's back, implied eating of faeces, piercing of the penis or nipples or needles being pushed through genitals as well as different methods of breath restriction (e.g. face sitting) during anal penetration. Such was the kind of material, which "involve[d] the infliction of pain or acts which may cause lasting physical harm, whether real or (in a sexual context) simulated" and was prohibited in accordance with the BBFC's classification guidelines.[2393] ATVOD emphasised that the videos focussed on violence inflicted during sexual intercourse which was reinforced by close ups of markings or bruises as well as statements or questions about a person's injuries. In addition, the restraining of persons and their gagging restricted them from expressing themselves clearly. This was considered to constitute "physical restraint which prevents participants from indicating a withdrawal of consent".[2394]

It appeared as if ATVOD sought specific advice from the BBFC in view of the video depicting the piercing and a clip showing a restrained, whipped and gagged actor. The BBFC confirmed that the material "would

mination That the Provider of the On-Demand Programme Service 'Glasgow Mistress Megara Furie' was in Breach of ATVOD's Rule 11 and Thereby Contravened Sec. 368E (4) CA," April 27, 2015, para. 8.3, p. 5; ATVOD, "Determination That the Provider of the On-Demand Programme Service 'Thebondagemistress.com' was in Breach of ATVOD's Rule 11 and Thereby Contravened Sec. 368E (4) CA," July 30, 2015, para. 8.3, p. 5; ATVOD, "Rule 11 Determination Mistress R'eal," para. 8.3, p. 5.

2393 ATVOD, "Determination That the Provider of the On-Demand Programme Service 'Dreams of Spanking' was in Breach of ATVOD´s Rule 14 and Thereby Contravened Sec. 368E (2) CA," July 30, 2015, para. 8.3, p. 5; ATVOD, "Determination That the Provider of the On-Demand Programme Service 'Thebondagemistress.com' was in Breach of ATVOD's Rule 14 and Thereby Contravened Sec. 368E (2) CA," July 30, 2015, para. 8.3, p. 5; ATVOD, "Determination That the Provider of the On-Demand Programme Service 'Glasgow Mistress Megara Furie' was in Breach of ATVOD's Rule 14 and Thereby Contravened Sec. 368E (2) CA," April 27, 2015, para. 8.3, p. 5; ATVOD, "Determination That the Provider of the On-Demand Programme Service 'Mistress R'eal' was in Breach of ATVOD's Rule 14 and Thereby Contravened Sec. 368E (2) CA," April 20, 2015, para. 8.3, pp. 5–6.

2394 ATVOD, "Rule 14 Determination Mistress R'eal," para. 8.3, p. 5.

not be passed at R18 or any other category".[2395] The remaining videos seemed to have been classified by ATVOD itself pursuant to the BBFC's guidelines. The delineation between restricted and prohibited material seems to run along a fine line between (legal) material which depicts sexual activities and (illegal) material which focuses on the infliction of violence and harm in sexual context. As a result of the two determinations, the two providers had to remove all material considered prohibited from their outlets and had to put in place effective CAC systems to ensure that minors will not normally hear or see specifically restricted material. While the other three services still seem to be operating, the *Glasgow Mistress Megara Furie* service was closed following ATVOD's initial assessment.

i) Critical analysis of ATVOD's practice

The body of practice which developed during ATVOD's role as co-regulator is substantial and shows that ATVOD left an indelible mark on the interpretation of the statutory obligations imposed on service providers in relation to the protection of minors in ODPS. While ATVOD operated initially under a vague statutory formula, its approach spilled over into the national legislation which, today, explicitly requires that R18-equivalent material must be specifically restricted. The fact that the CA was amended on the basis of the regulators' activities (including Ofcom's policy papers) indubitably is a success for ATVOD (and Ofcom) and demonstrates that the position it took was shared by a majority of UK policy makers. Taken at face value, ATVOD's position appears reasonable in light of the standards enforced in relation to the offline distribution of video works. Films classified as R18 by the BBFC may only be shown to adults in licensed cinemas and the supply of such videos or DVDs is only permissible in licensed sex shops and prohibited by mail order. In its determinations, ATVOD thus took on the role of the BBFC and examined the nature of the material by virtue of the latter's classification guidelines. Typically ATVOD would determine that the

> "programmes generally appeared to be R18-equivalent sex works (hard-core works the primary purpose of which [was] sexual arousal or stimulation) e.g.

2395 ATVOD, "Rule 14 Determination The Bondage Mistress," para. 8.4, p. 6; ATVOD, "Rule 14 Determination Mistress R'eal," para. 8.3, pp. 5–6.

> explicit sight of clearly un-simulated sexual activity including anal penetration, oral genital contact and fetish material".

This formulation had entered numerous ATVOD determinations which described the nature of the material in identical terms. Its practice in 2011-2013 lacked references to examples of videos which were supplied by the relevant providers and were only included in its determinations issued in 2014/2015. Even though ATVOD endeavoured to explain in more detail the reasons why it considered that R18-equivalent content was offered, its motivation remained elusive. To a certain extent, the lack of precision may be excused by the fact that ATVOD included screen shots of the relevant material in the annex of its determination. As a general policy, the annexes were not published but only made available to the respective service provider. While this policy might have been in the public interest (and it would have been paradoxical for a regulator to make available copies of R18-equivalent stills), it did not enhance transparency. Furthermore, it is unclear whether the way ATVOD applied the BBFC's guidelines was in conformity with the latter's practice. A more detailed comparative analysis of ATVOD's and the BBFC's "classification" decisions would have to be conducted to shed light on possible differences. It can generally be noted, however, that the application by one regulator of another regulator's guidelines risks discordance in the application of a particular standard in the medium to long run. Still, this approach is expressly legitimised by present legislation.[2396] At the end of ATVOD's co-regulatory term, there appeared to have been some kind of informal exchange between ATVOD and the BBFC as alluded to in some cases. The coordination could have been improved by a more institutionalised collaboration which could have required the BBFC's opinion, for instance. It is likely; however, that the involvement of the BBFC would have delayed ATVOD's decision-making and would have required a clear legal framework for cooperation.

In addition, the cases analysed above shed light on the impact of regulators' practice on the fundamental right of service providers to the freedom of expression. In a majority of cases, service providers were reprimanded by ATVOD to rectify the breaches of rule 11. Some cases concerned the

---

2396 See Sec. 368E (6) CA which stipulates that "in determining whether any material falls within subsection (3)(b) or (5)(b), regard must be had to any guidelines issued by the video works authority as to its policy in relation to the issue of classification certificates.".

imposition of statutory sanctions such as pecuniary penalties and the suspension or barring of services. The imposition of fines may indeed adversely effect the economic situation of providers, and may even become a question of survival for small-scale providers. The fines imposed by Ofcom appear to have been proportionate taking account of economic factors of providers. What is more, the temporary suspension of a service or the total barring of a provider is a serious interference with the fundamental rights of providers. Since its adoption in 2009, this instrument has only been used once. The temporal scope of the sanction, which had indefinite effect as well as its breath, which covered the specific service as well as any further provision of ODPS in the UK, demonstrates the severity of this instrument. This prohibition to exercise a specific economic activity not only prevented the provider from exercising his right to freedom of expression as guaranteed by Art. 11 CFR but also interfered with his right to freely choose an occupation and conduct a business as flowing from Arts. 15 and 16 CFR. However, such rights are not absolute and their exercise may be constrained in the public interest, namely, to secure the protection of minors in ODPS.

On a general note, the procedures set up within the co-regulatory scheme may be criticised. Where fundamental rights are affected, the possibility to apply for review of regulators' decisions is of paramount importance. While Ofcom's sanctioning decisions could be subject to judicial review, the examination of ATVOD's rule 11 determinations was severely limited to an internal review process which did not involve any other independent authority, not least the judiciary. To a certain degree, the lack of independent review was buttressed by the existence of an external review process in relation to scope issues. On account of ATVOD's practice to separate issues of scope from any other material aspects (like the protection of minors), providers would have had to challenge ATVOD's determinations on grounds of scope in order to accomplish withdrawal of a rule 11 determination through the backdoor. In such a case, a rule 11 determination would not have been reviewed but would have hinged on the provider being within scope or not. If providers refrained from contesting a scope determination, the only alternative to achieve some kind of review would have been to continue violating national legislation until the case would have been referred to Ofcom for consideration of statutory sanctions. That, obviously, would not have been a solution. This brief analysis shows the importance of fair and direct procedures within a co-regulatory framework. It is crucial that providers are able to directly challenge decisions which may have a profound effect on the exercise of their fundamental rights.

### 3. Other policy documents

#### a) Ofcom's research

Although Ofcom's role in the practical enforcement of Sec. 368E CA was limited under the co-regulatory scheme, it approved of ATVOD's approach and additionally conducted research to better understand the multitude of factors which impact the protection of minors. Next to research into audience's attitudes on the general level of protection accorded online,[2397] Ofcom specifically looked into Internet safety measures from two angles: first, from the perspective of parents[2398] and second, from the perspective of Internet service providers (ISPs). The report about "strategies of parental protection for children online" built upon earlier research exploring children's use and understanding of media.[2399] It also examined "parental mediation strategies" which encompassed the use of technical tools such as filters, PIN codes/passwords, safe search (a filter which blocks unsuitable images from a list of search results), regular conversations about managing online risks, rules or restrictions concerning online

2397 Ipsos MORI, "Protecting Audiences in a Converged World, Deliberative Research Report of 25.1.2012"; Kantar Media, "Research on Views of Protection for Audiovisual Content". The majority of participants of the study considered, for instance, that age-confirmation screens were a "poor substitute for the broadcast TV watershed and were easily abused." (p. 35).

2398 In order to assist parents in understanding content standards across different media, ParentPort was set up in 2011 by the UK's regulators including ATVOD, Ofcom, the BBFC and the ASA. The website constitutes an information portal and facilitates complaints making and handling. It also offers tips and advice to parents for keeping children safe online. For more information, see http://www.parentport.org.uk/ (accessed 25.2.2016).

2399 Ofcom, "Report on Internet Safety Measures, Strategies of Parental Protection for Children Online," January 15, 2014, http://stakeholders.ofcom.org.uk/internet/internet-safety-measures/; Ofcom, "Children and Parents: Media Use and Attitudes Report," October 2014, http://stakeholders.ofcom.org.uk/binaries/research/media-literacy/media-use-attitudes-14/Childrens_2014_Report.pdf (all websites accessed 25.2.2016).

activities and supervision.[2400] Most parents use a combination of strategies. As reliance on technical tools alone was found to be extremely rare (1 percent of parents of 5-15 year olds).[2401] Ofcom tested parents' awareness and use of several specific technical tools like content filters (in the form of network level filters or parental control software set up on a particular device or those built into the device by the manufacturer), PINs/ passwords, safe search, YouTube safety mode (which filters inappropriate content), other kinds of software.[2402]

The three tools of which parents were most aware were also those most frequently used: PINs/passwords (31 percent of 5-15s), network level filters by ISPs (21 percent) and parental control software installed on a particular device (20 percent).[2403] When asked about the reasons for the lack of technical tools at their homes, two in five parents of 5-15s responded that they regularly talked to their child and had trust in the child's online capacities.[2404] Additional research previously carried out by Ofcom also highlighted parents' "reluctance or inability (…) to engage with technology" and their lack of knowledge or indifference ("due to the challenges of managing day to day life") towards online risks for minors.[2405] In general, Ofcom's quantitative analysis of parents' awareness of technical tools, their take up and confidence thereof is valuable and contributes to an understanding of the practical application of the legal rules protecting minors on the Internet. The research demonstrates that technical tools are not a "silver bullet solution" due to their intrinsic deficiencies and, more importantly, due to the very limited use by parents. The protection of minors in ODPS must therefore be based on broader footing, involving, above all, the industry.

---

2400 Ofcom, "Report on Internet Safety Measures, Strategies of Parental Protection for Children Online," January 12, 2015, para. 7.5, p. 49, http://stakeholders.ofcom.org.uk/internet/internet-safety-2015 (accessed 25.2.2016).

2401 Ofcom, "Report on Internet Safety Measures: Parental Protection (2)," paras. 7.7-7.9, p. 49.

2402 Ofcom, "Report on Internet Safety Measures: Parental Protection (2)," para. 7.56, p. 62.

2403 Ofcom, "Report on Internet Safety Measures: Parental Protection (2)," para. 7.61, p. 63.

2404 Ofcom, "Report on Internet Safety Measures: Parental Protection (2)," para. 9.7, p. 79.

2405 Ofcom, "Report on Internet Safety Measures: Parental Protection (2)," para. 9.10, p. 81.

This collaborative dialogue with the industry is reflected in Ofcom's report on voluntary measures taken by ISPs. The report goes back to the government's agreement with BT,[2406] Sky, TalkTalk and Virgin Media, the UK's four largest ISPs to introduce family-friendly network filtering services by the end of 2013. This initiative followed a parliamentary inquiry into online child protection in 2012[2407] and a speech by Prime Minister (PM) Cameron on 22 July 2013 about "cracking down on online pornography and making the Internet safer for children". PM Cameron expressed serious concerns about "the fact that many children are viewing online pornography and other damaging material at a very early age and that the nature of that pornography is so extreme it is distorting their view of sex and relationships."[2408]

In response to this "cultural challenge" the PM announced a far-reaching industry initiative which would enable the installation of "family-friendly filters" which could be switched on by default whenever cus-

---

2406 As the first UK ISP, BT had voluntarily put in place filters to block all content considered illegal under UK law (predominantly child sexual abuse content). The filters (so-called Cleanfeed) became operative in 2004 and were based on the Internet Watch Foundation's (IWF) blacklist. The IWF drew up good practice guidance for blocking which aim at enhancing transparency and minimising over-blocking and latency issues. See IWF Blocking: Good Practice, available at https://www.iwf.org.uk/members/member-policies/url-list/blocking-good-practice (accessed 13.3.2016).
The initiative was heavily criticised by the Guardian as "the first mass censorship of the web attempted in a Western democracy." See The Guardian, BT puts block on child porn sites, 6.6.2004, available at http://www.theguardian.com/technology/2004/jun/06/childrensservices.childprotection. BT promotes the Cleanfeed filters as "built-in security" on their website, see http://www.globalservices.bt.com/uk/en/products/internet_connect_uk. (all websites accessed 13.3.2016).

2407 The report found that many children have access to online pornography which they "stumble upon" accidentally or seek deliberately. Increased exposure to ever more violent pornography has an impact on the body image and sexual behaviour of minors and increasingly leads to relationship difficulties (pp. 12-13). The report called on the government to monitor more strictly the roll out of network level filters ("Active Choice") (pp. 16-17). See Claire Perry, "Independent Inquiry into Online Child Protection, Findings and Recommendations," April 2012.

2408 Speech by Prime Minister David Cameron on 22 July 2014, The internet and pornography: Prime Minister calls for action, available at https://www.gov.uk/government/speeches/the-internet-and-pornography-prime-minister-calls-for-action (accessed 20.2.2016).

tomers set up new Internet accounts or changed providers. In its report, Ofcom outlined the measures ISPs put in place. Refraining from assessing the efficacy of the filters as such, Ofcom merely noted that "over-blocking has been found low".[2409] It nonetheless pointed out that the filters required constant technical improvement and called upon ISPs to contain possibilities of circumvention.[2410]

Ofcom confirmed that the government's policy had successfully been implemented by the four ISPs. It found that the filters operated at network level and covered all devices using the household's Internet connection.[2411] The filters applied different editorial categories (supplied by third party providers) such as crime, violence, nudity, pornography, sexual education. These could be customised and filtering levels could be adjusted (e.g. strict, moderate, light).[2412] Importantly, customers were faced with "an unavoidable choice" whether to turn on the filters when first installing the broadband connection.[2413] In practice, customers received a prompt on the starting screen which informed them about the availability of the filters. Above all, the notifications were designed in such a way that the filters were pre-ticked, requiring customers to tick the No box if they wanted to turn the filters off.[2414] While take up of the filters operating at network level was slow (under 10 percent in most cases, except for 36 percent

2409 Ofcom, "Report on Internet Safety Measures, Internet Service Providers: Network Level Filtering Measures," July 22, 2014, p. 2, http://stakeholders.ofcom.org.uk/internet/internet-safety-2; see also Cybion Srl and Stiftung Digitale Chancen, "Benchmarking of Parental Control Tools for the Online Protection of Children SIP-Bench II," 2011, p. 29, https://ec.europa.eu/digital-agenda/en/news/benchmarking-study-parental-control-tools-latest-findings; see also the up-dated results Cybion Srl and Stiftung Digitale Chancen, "Benchmarking of Parental Control Tools for the Online Protection of Children SIP-Bench II," 2013, p. 15, http://sipbench.eu/phase7.cfm/secid.7 (all websites accessed 10.2.2016).

2410 Ofcom, "Report on Internet Safety Measures: ISPs," paras. 5.9-5.10, p. 22; possibilities to circumvent the filters (including a google-plug in entitled "Go Away Cameron" which used a proxy server) were reported. See Jörg Weinrich, "Jugendschutz in Großbritannien: Erfolgreiche Einführung von Netzanschlussfiltern," *JMS-Report*, no. 5 (2014): p. 3.

2411 Ofcom, "Report on Internet Safety Measures: ISPs," para. 2.2, p. 4.

2412 Ofcom, "Report on Internet Safety Measures: ISPs," para. 2.21, p. 7.

2413 Ofcom, "Report on Internet Safety Measures: ISPs," para. 3.5, p. 11.

2414 Ofcom, "Report on Internet Safety Measures: ISPs," paras. 1.13, 3.5, pp. 2, 11.

measured by TalkTalk), a great number of existing customers chose to activate the filters via their account settings.[2415]

In general, pre-selected filters raise a set of complex issues regarding the freedom of expression and do not enable citizens to have an actual choice to install filtering techniques at their homes. The fact that users have to engage with the prompt and cannot continue the installation process if no decision on filters is taken seems overly strict even if it raises awareness for such tools. The right to privacy also appears affected if users have to take action to de-activate the filters and self-identify as porn consumers. ISPs become powerful gatekeepers holding valuable information about the use of filters or lack thereof. It follows that the installation and advancement of filters (aimed at reducing their error rates) is only one piece in the puzzle of ensuring that minors are adequately protected from harmful content. The proactive involvement of the industry, notably ISPs, is of great significance in this respect.

### b) ATVOD's research report

Starting in 2012/2013, ATVOD prioritised the fight against hardcore pornographic material freely available online. It issued a series of determinations and found more than 30 providers established in the UK in violation of the statutory requirements.[2416] The sanctions ranged from notifications and warnings to more onerous penalties such as fines and, in extreme cases, even the barring of a service provider by Ofcom which had retained backstop sanctioning powers. Thereby, ATVOD gave the impression of a rigorous regulator that was backed by an effective sanctioning system jointly enforced by ATVOD and Ofcom.[2417] In March 2014, ATVOD published a research report entitled "For Adults Only? Underage Access to Online Porn" in which it set forth its recommendations for future regula-

---

2415 Ofcom, "Report on Internet Safety Measures: ISPs," para. 3.31, p. 18.

2416 The number of media outlets found to be in breach of rule 11 was substantially higher.

2417 The impression of a rigorous regulator was reiterated in its report so as to reinforce ATVOD's self-characterisation. See, for instance the phrases "robust action" (para. 2, p. 7), "tough and targeted action", "vigorous action" (para. 3, p. 9) or "robust action" (para. 6, p. 22); ATVOD, "Report on Underage Access to Online Porn.".

tory action on the basis of research it had commissioned.[2418] The research was conducted by Nielsen Netview by means of meters installed on personal computers and laptops of survey participants. It found that 1 in 35 children aged 6-11, 1 in 16 children aged 6-15 and 1 in 10 children aged 6-17 "visited an adult website from a PC or laptop in December 2013".[2419] ATVOD repeatedly highlighted the fact that the figures were susceptible to underestimation as they exempted consumption of VOD services by mobile phones, tablets or other devices connecting to the Internet.[2420]

In this respect, it referred to a study on media use and attitudes of children and parents published by Ofcom in October 2013 which demonstrated that children of particular age groups increasingly surfed the Web on devices such as (their own) smart phones, tablets or other devices. With respect to users of age, ATVOD found that almost 10 million UK citizens visited adult websites "at least once" in the given time period and "typically spent 2 ½ hrs on adult websites over 10 visits during [one] month – an average of 15 minutes per visit".[2421] Above all, the "top five" providers of adult websites (xHamster, xVideos, Pornhub, YouPorn and RedTube) had each "over 2m unique UK users in December 2013",[2422] such that ATVOD concluded that the UK constituted a lucrative market for the online adult industry.[2423]

Against this backdrop, ATVOD proposed concrete policy options to ensure that underage users were protected from hardcore pornographic material disseminated online. Apart from the promotion of media education of children and parents alike and the improvement of parental control tools, ATVOD relied on a three-fold strategy which encouraged (i) a clarification of the existing national legal framework, (ii) new legislation concerning the disruption of cash flows from the UK to service providers located in third countries and (iii) amendments to the AVMSD.[2424] Firstly, ATVOD called on the British Government and Parliament to craft more detailed statutory rules which unambiguously identify material comparable to content classified by the BBFC as R18 as constituting material seri-

2418 ATVOD, "Report on Underage Access to Online Porn.".
2419 ATVOD, "Report on Underage Access to Online Porn," para. 5, pp. 15–16.
2420 ATVOD, "Report on Underage Access to Online Porn," para. 5, pp. 14, 15, 16.
2421 ATVOD, "Report on Underage Access to Online Porn," para. 5, p. 18.
2422 ATVOD, "Report on Underage Access to Online Porn," para. 5, p. 18.
2423 ATVOD, "Report on Underage Access to Online Porn," para. 5, p. 18.
2424 ATVOD, "Report on Underage Access to Online Porn," para. 7, p. 24.

ously impairing the development of minors.[2425] This would indeed give more force to the statutory requirements contained in the CA and legitimise ATVOD's precautionary approach. Secondly, ATVOD advocated for legislation which would permit the UK payments industry (including Visa Europe, MasterCard and PayPal) to cut off the funds flowing from UK users to overseas tube sites.[2426] The underlying rationale was that unrestricted hardcore porn sites offered from outside the EU serve as "honey pots" (or "shop windows") which purport to attract users' attention to the primary paid services for which a subscription was required.[2427] This was the way hardcore porn site providers generated their revenues. ATVOD's initiative did not directly affect free adult websites but by "following the money", it would attack their business model by removing the economic basis on which such services depended.[2428] ATVOD was convinced that

> "cutting off that flow of funds to services which allow children to view hardcore porn would provide a powerful incentive for porn websites to put in place effective age verification and access control mechanisms in order to restart the flow of funds from the UK".[2429]

Thirdly, ATVOD suggested modifications to the AVMSD to ensure that all Member States across the EU enforce the standards established in the UK.[2430] Due to the long time span of potential developments at the European level, ATVOD encouraged the Government to "seek agreement on UK-style children protection measures, where these are not already in place" in other Member States.[2431]

In sum, in its research report, ATVOD presented evidence that allegedly forcefully spoke in favour of more comprehensive and detailed legislation which would prohibit the free circulation of hardcore pornographic content on the Internet. ATVOD was careful to explain that "this [was] not censorship" as its action merely targeted "adult content" disseminated by the "adult industry".[2432] It can be distilled from this statement that ATVOD considered that the impact on free speech would be both, propor-

---

2425 ATVOD, "Report on Underage Access to Online Porn," para. 6, pp. 21–22.
2426 ATVOD, "Report on Underage Access to Online Porn," para. 6, p. 23.
2427 ATVOD, "Report on Underage Access to Online Porn," para. 6, p. 23.
2428 ATVOD, "Report on Underage Access to Online Porn," para. 6, p. 23.
2429 ATVOD, "Report on Underage Access to Online Porn," para. 6, p. 23.
2430 ATVOD, "Report on Underage Access to Online Porn," para. 6, p. 22.
2431 ATVOD, "Report on Underage Access to Online Porn," para. 7, p. 24.
2432 ATVOD, "Report on Underage Access to Online Porn," para. 2, p. 8.

tionate and justified in the public interest. Notwithstanding ATVOD's good intentions, it is questionable to what extent the evidence of underage access to adult material provided added-value.[2433] In spite of the large sample of data, the results appear rather imprecise as they were sorted according to rather large age groups (6-11, 6-15, 6-17). The formulations of "large numbers of under 18s" and a "significant number of under 16s and even under 12s" which regularly (once a month) access pornographic material online seem to raise different expectations as those actually presented by ATVOD.[2434] This is not to turn a blind eye on current trends which point at an increasing number of ever younger users accessing content which is ethically questionable and age-inappropriate. Instead, ATVOD's commitment was geared towards lobbying for more detailed legislation which served its interest. Such legislation would empower ATVOD and facilitate enforcement against negligent service providers. In order to gain the attention of the British Government and Parliament, ATVOD was waited on strong language. In the meantime, the UK Government has carried out ATVOD's first policy initiative by adopting the Audiovisual Media Services Regulation 2014. Sec. 368E has been revised and explicitly defines R18 or R18-equivalent material as seriously harmful.

ATVOD's second recommendation which suggested an amendment to the AVMSD could still come into reality. As noted above, the Directive leaves Member States a wide margin of discretion as to the determination of the type of content which is considered unsuitable. ATVOD did not provide any specifications of modifications other than the general statement that "hardcore porn" should be kept "out of reach of children".[2435] Any inclusion of a generic reference to "hardcore pornography" in Art. 12 AVMSD would be prone to interpretation by national regulators and ultimately, national and European courts. The various national classification schemes with respect to programmes broadcast on television are illustrative of cultural and societal differences between Member States which have seemed to persist throughout the lifespan of the Directive. For any more precise amendment of the AVMSD, ATVOD and the UK respectively would have to intensively negotiate in order to obtain the support by a majority of Member States. In addition, a modified version of Art. 12 AVMSD would still hinge upon the effectiveness of national regulatory

2433 ATVOD, "Report on Underage Access to Online Porn," para. 3, p. 12.
2434 ATVOD, "Report on Underage Access to Online Porn," para. 5, p. 14.
2435 ATVOD, "Report on Underage Access to Online Porn," para. 7, p. 24.

frameworks and active authorities as agents of ATVOD. Moreover, ATVOD's initiative of exporting UK standards across the EU (by way of ERGA or EPRA) may also hint at some form of protectionism of ATVOD for the British VOD industry. Since an uneven playing field exists at present within the EU, the uniformity of standards at the level desired by ATVOD would place the UK industry in a better (more competitive) position on the European market than is currently the case. Another particular concern to ATVOD was "tube sites" which were operated from outside the UK and the EU which would be tackled by the prevention of money transfers through the UK payments industry. While this approach appears innovative, it would effectively extend ATVOD's jurisdiction beyond UK borders and thus be heavily disputed and require, above all, a strong legal basis in the CA. Succinctly, the 2014 research report demonstrates that ATVOD became a leading proponent of a more improved level of protection of minors in VOD services. It was also well positioned and well regarded by the industry to which it entertained close connections.

### III. Perspectives of ATVOD and Ofcom on the protection of minors in converging media markets

The refit of the AVMSD has led the British regulators to ponder their measures in light of the European legal framework. Many aspects addressed in its research report of 2014 are echoed in ATVOD's reply to the Commission's Green Paper in 2014. Once again, it highlighted the fact that many service providers of pornographic material took a deliberate decision to establish their business outside the UK to "avoid the need to put in place age verification and access control mechanisms".[2436] Even more worrisome to ATVOD was the fact that "in a converging media world, (…) the greatest threat to minors, in terms of access to inappropriate audiovisual content, comes from online media services operating beyond the jurisdiction on EU Member States".[2437]

In order to grasp these "adult tube sites", ATVOD suggested, as it previously had at the national level, to modify the AVMSD in such a way as to shut off "the flow of funds from customers within the EU to such irre-

2436 ATVOD, "Response to Commission Green Paper," para. 7.6, p. 19.
2437 ATVOD, "Response to Commission Green Paper," para. 7.19, p. 22.

sponsible service providers".[2438] As a result, payments to services affiliated with tube sites should not be processed. By the same token, ATVOD pointed out that it was increasingly difficult for regulators to identify the service provider who might have "an incentive to withhold their identity and/or location" for example by operating a service which was in breach of the statutory requirements.[2439] This was widespread practice in relation to providers supplying sexually explicit content, according to ATVOD. It thus called for the inclusion of rules which would address "those who provide financial hosting or proxy registration services which facilitate the provision of a media service (…) in a manner which obscures the identity of the service provider".[2440] Such third parties could be required to provide information to NRAs which would contribute to the identification of the service provider. Interestingly, ATVOD did not refer to Art. 5 AVMSD transposed by Sec. 368D (2)-(4) CA which requires that service providers publish minimum information which should, routinely, make identification of service providers possible. Similarly, the co-regulator recognised that the "might seriously impair" test was applied differently across the EU and suggested altering the wording of Art. 12 AVMSD to require that hardcore porn material (R18 level) be kept out of reach of children.[2441] Briefly, ATVOD's suggestions in relation to the AVMSD mirrored its policies at the national level. They are proof of the close connection of the two legal orders and the fact that many problems encountered by ATVOD stem not necessarily from imprecise wording of the national legislation but originated in the Directive. The present reform of the AVMSD is an opportunity for NRAs to make their voices heard and lobby for adjustments in their interest.

Ofcom took the first of such opportunities by replying to the Commission's consultation on the AVMSD in 2015. With regards to the provisions aimed at protecting minors, it underlined two aspects of converging media markets: first, enhanced possibilities of children to access plethora of content on multiple devices and second, audience expectations of broadly co-

2438 ATVOD, "Response to Commission Green Paper," para. 7.19, p. 22.

2439 ATVOD, "Response to Commission Green Paper," para. 4.7, pp. 12–13; ATVOD had previously made this proposal; see, for instance, ATVOD, "The Culture, Media & Sports Inquiry into Online Safety, Submission from the Authority for Television On Demand ('ATVOD')," paras. 2.8-2.10, p. 8.

2440 ATVOD, "Response to Commission Green Paper," para. 4.7, pp. 12–13.

2441 ATVOD, "Response to Commission Green Paper," paras. 7.14-7.16, pp. 21–22.

herent regulatory standards across TV, catch-up and ODPS.[2442] It cast light on the deficiencies of the current rules contained in the AVMSD by reference to Rihanna's music video for the song S&M which was considered to be inappropriate to be broadcast before 9 p.m. while it was readily available on the Internet at all times of the day.[2443] The design of Arts. 12 and 27 AVMSD could lead to the same content being available on-demand without restrictions whereas it was screened on TV in compliance with the watershed rules. Ofcom also criticised the wording of the provisions, in particular, the "likely to impair" and "might seriously impair" tests which were "open to interpretation" and could lead to "asymmetries in the application of the minimum standards" across EU Member States.[2444] The regulator thus proposed an alternative structure to the revised AVMSD which "could deliver greater harmonisation without requiring M[ember] S[tates] to change their fundamental approaches to standards or to the range of content permitted on AVMS".[2445]

This approach presupposed abandoning the distinction between linear and non-linear services which would be in line with audience expectations. The future model for the protection of minors would be based on two axes: the severity of the content and the adequacy of the access control. The former covered content suitable for all ages, moderately strong or very strong content (corresponding to R18 level material). The latter implied no control mechanisms, moderate (e.g. after watershed or with age ratings/labels) or strong access controls (e.g. age-verification). In general, protection should be levelled, meaning that, for instance, moderately strong content would be restricted by moderate access controls.[2446] Ofcom envisaged that ERGA could draw up guidance on the types of access restrictions. Significantly, Ofcom acknowledged that its proposal would not eliminate the disparities between the classification of content at the national level but it was positive that "the most problematic content (for example, but not limited to, hardcore pornography) [would be] consistently subject to effective access controls, across the EU".[2447]

2442 Ofcom, "Reply AVMSD Consultation," p. 28.
2443 Ofcom, "Reply AVMSD Consultation," p. 29.
2444 Ofcom, "Reply AVMSD Consultation," p. 29.
2445 Ofcom, "Reply AVMSD Consultation," p. 32.
2446 Ofcom, "Reply AVMSD Consultation," p. 32.
2447 Ofcom, "Reply AVMSD Consultation," p. 33.

The revised rules of the AVMSD should, however, not be expanded to include other content or actors, Ofcom stressed.[2448] The protection of minors on the Internet was a joint endeavour which had to be based on broad societal consensus and action by all stakeholders of the value chain.[2449] The AVMSD with its inherent limits was regarded as one element in a multi-polar policy field. Ofcom cited the industry initiative promoting network level filters by ISPs to draw attention to the role and responsibility of ISPs. Similarly, Ofcom stressed that device manufacturers and platform operators had a stake in furthering technical tools.[2450] Importantly, media literacy was crucial to develop users' "resilience in their media consumption".[2451] The empowerment of users, for example by providing more detailed information about the contentwas essential to tune users' online skills and give them the means to take transparent and well-informed decisions.[2452]

---

2448 Ofcom, "Reply AVMSD Consultation," p. 33.

2449 The government, under the auspices of the UK Council for Child Internet Safety ran a public consultation from February to April 2016 on age verification for pornography. The UKCCIS is an important body purporting to improve child safety on the Internet. It was established following the reports and reviews of Tanya Byron (2008, 2010) and Reg Bailey (2011) and comprises more than 200 organisations drawn from the government, the industry and academia. The Council is chaired by ministers from different government departments. It contributes to forming valuable partnerships between policy makers and the industry and provides a platform for discussion, assisting the government in topical issues of policy making. It has published, for instance, a practical guide for parents and carers whose children use social media and guidance for the industry, encompassing work on social networks, chats or search. For more information see https://www.gov.uk/government/groups/uk-council-for-child-internet-safety-ukccis (accessed 27.2.2016).

2450 Ofcom, "Reply AVMSD Consultation," p. 33.

2451 Ofcom, "Reply AVMSD Consultation," p. 33.

2452 Since 2008, "Good practice principles on audiovisual content information" have been recognised and enforced by leading providers of audiovisual services in the UK like BT, BSkyB, Myspace, Google and Virgin Media. This has been accomplished in cooperation with the Broadband Stakeholder Group, a consultative body to the UK government representing a range of actors like telecoms operators, broadcasters, ISPs, content producers as well as rights holders. The initiative aims at empowering users to make informed choices about the programmes they consume and thus assist parents in selecting appropriate content for their children. For two types of content, namely "content unsuitable for particular age groups" and "content which may cause harm or offence" guidance is offered (paras. 14. and 15 of the principles). While the former implies "inappro-

## IV. Summary

Briefly, the UK regulators, above all, ATVOD during the co-regulatory scheme shaped the interpretation and application of Sec. 368E (2)-(5) CA which transpose Art. 12 AVMSD, resulting in legislative clarifications by late 2014. The number of adjudications instigated by ATVOD on its own motion rather than upon complaint is remarkable and points to an active co-regulator that sought to bring the adult industry in line with statutory requirements. In the UK, the formula "might seriously impair" as stipulated by the Directive (and by national legislation) implies material which has been classified as R18 or for which it is reasonable to expect that such classification would have been accorded if it were included in a video work. In other words, material considered R18-equivalent can only be distributed to adults under certain conditions. This standard which is enforced online appears reasonable in relation to the standard enforced offline. Videos or DVDs of R18 level can only be supplied in places that have acquired a license. It flows from ATVOD's practice in conjunction with the BBFC's classification guidelines that the R18 category typically refers to material which depicts un-simulated sexual activity including anal sex, explicit sight of genitalia and strong fetish scenes.

As a consequence, such content can only be provided to adults and must be kept away from children under the age of 18. It is the responsibility of providers to put in place effective CAC systems which verify the users' age before granting access to R18-equivalent material. In numerous determinations, ATVOD did not accept payment methods which processed payments by debit card, via a bank account as well as systems such as PayPal for which it could not be confidently excluded that under 18s could not use them. By contrast, it permitted paywalls based on credit cards or other mechanisms like payments by phone which effectively verified the

---

priate content", the latter refers to content which causes "harm or offence more generally" by containing inter alia "violence, sex, strong language, upsetting or disturbing themes (which could include drugs, horror, imitable techniques), flashing images". Although these notions are interpreted differently across media outlets, the attempt to enhance content information is laudable in itself. The principles also indicate when and how content information should be given. Since the initiative covers providers of all kinds of media services, the precise means and exact manner in which content information is provided are not unified. For more information see http://audiovisualcontent.org/ (accessed 26.2.2016).

users' age. Since 2016, Ofcom has taken over ATVOD's responsibilities and so far has followed in ATVOD's tracks. Its proposals for a revised Directive take note of ATVOD's experiences and advocate for a more coordinated approach across EU Member States.

## C. *The protection of minors in telemedia services in Germany*

### I. The transposition of Art. 12 AVMSD in Arts. 4 and 5 JMStV

In Germany, the protection of minors is constitutionally guaranteed by Art. 1 (1) GG which protects human dignity in conjunction with Art. 2 (1) GG which stipulates personal freedoms[2453] and Art. 5 (2) GG which sets out the limits to the freedom of expression and the freedom to broadcast.[2454] Art. 5 (2) GG expressly refers to "provisions for the protection of young persons" which may restrict the exercise of the rights prescribed by Art. 5 (1) GG. The BVerfG underlined the importance of the protection of minors and its capacity to function as a limit ("*Schranke*") to the freedom of broadcasting in its early jurisprudence.[2455] The German Basic Law does

---

2453 Art. 2 GG prescribes that
"(1) Every person shall have the right to free development of his personality insofar as he does not violate the rights of others or offend against the constitutional order or the moral law.
(2) Every person shall have the right to life and physical integrity. Freedom of the person shall be inviolable. These rights may be interfered with only pursuant to a law.".

2454 Art. 5 reads as follows
"(1) Every person shall have the right freely to express and disseminate his opinions in speech, writing and pictures, and to inform himself without hindrance from generally accessible sources. Freedom of the press and freedom of reporting by means of broadcasts and films shall be guaranteed. There shall be no censorship.
(2) These rights shall find their limits in the provisions of general laws, in provisions for the protection of young persons, and in the right to personal honour.
(3) Arts and sciences, research and teaching shall be free. The freedom of teaching shall not release any person from allegiance to the constitution.".

2455 BverfG, Judgement of 16.6.1981, 1 BvL 89/78, paras. 107, 117. See also Felix Hertel, "§ 4 JMStV Unzulässige Angebote," in *Beck'scher Kommentar zum Rundfunkrecht*, ed. Werner Hahn and Thomas Vesting, third edition (München: C. H. Beck, 2012), paras. 1–2; Frank Holtmann, *Zur rechtlichen Unterscheidung von Rundfunk und Telemedien bei Hybrid-TV, Unter besonderer Berück-*

not impose a hierarchy of rights. On the contrary, both the freedom to broadcast, on the one hand, and the protection of minors, on the other hand, stand on equal footing. A conflict between them will result in a balancing exercise that must take into account the specificities of individual cases. Neither right is absolute and may be constrained in accordance with the principle of proportionality.[2456] This underlying tension between the freedom to broadcast and the protection of minors is reflected in numerous rules contained in the JMStV,[2457] above all, in Arts. 4 and 5 JMStV[2458] which transpose Arts. 12 and 27 AVMSD. Arts. 4 and 5 JMStV had already been enshrined in the JMStV of 2002 and thus pre-date the AVMSD's adoption.[2459]

This research focuses on the protection of minors in on-demand or telemedia services and hence outlines the relevant national provisions applicable to such services before examining the measures taken by the German regulator(s), notably, the KJM in conjunction with the state media authorities as well as the FSM, a certified self-regulatory body. It examines the detailed guidelines these bodies have drawn up and sketches their perspectives on future regulatory protection.

---

*sichtigung der Werbe- und Jugendschutzregelungen des RStV und JMStV*, vol. 41, Schriften zum Medienrecht (Hamburg: Verlag Dr. Kovac, 2015), p. 151.

2456 Hartstein et al., "Entstehungsgeschichte – JMStV," para. 1.

2457 For a concise overview of the relevant fundamental rights under German law, see Christian Berger, "Jugendschutz im Internet: „Geschlossene Benutzergruppen" nach § 4 Abs. 2 Satz 2 JMStV – Am Beispiel personalausweiskennziffergestützter Altersverifikationssysteme," *Multimedia und Recht*, 2003, pp. 773–78.

2458 Arts. 4 and 5 JMStV correspond to Arts. 14 and 15 JuSchG. The JuSchG is a federal law which regulates the protection of young persons including their protection in relation to data media (i.e. "physical media which carry text, pictures or sound" according to Art. 1 (2) JuSchG). The two laws thereby establish a graduated youth protection. See Felix Hertel, "§ 5 JMStV Entwicklungsbeeinträchtigende Angebote," in *Beck'scher Kommentar zum Rundfunkrecht*, ed. Werner Hahn and Thomas Vesting, third edition (München: C. H. Beck, 2012), paras. 1–2.

2459 The 13th amendment to the Interstate Treaty on Broadcasting and Telemedia of March 2010 modified Art. 6 JMStV concerning the protection of minors in advertising and teleshopping.

1. Illegal content

Art. 4 JMStV outlines content which is illegal and its first paragraph exhaustively lists a detailed catalogue of content which is absolutely banned. The prohibition of impermissible content (which, for instance depicts "propaganda instruments", "glorifies war" or "violates human dignity") is accompanied by references to specific provisions of the German Criminal Code which stand in parallel to the provisions contained in the JMStV. As a result, the dissemination of broadcasts or telemedia which contain content enumerated in Art. 4 (1) JMStV may be prohibited regardless of providers' liability under German criminal law.[2460] Importantly, the total ban encompasses pornographic material which "has as its subject acts of violence, the sexual abuse of children or adolescents or sexual acts of persons involving animals".[2461] This type of pornography, regardless of it being real or simulated/virtual acts (e.g. comics, animated films),[2462] constitutes "hard" or "hardcore" pornography ("*harte Pornografie*") in contrast to "moderate" pornographic material ("*einfache Pornografie*") which is permissible in telemedia services under certain conditions. In order to understand the differences, the notion of hardcore pornography is briefly outlined.

Hardcore pornography covers violent pornography which implies grossly violent behaviour against a person (e.g. abuse, sexual coercion or sexual murder)[2463] including manipulations of parts of the body or genitalia which lead to serious physical or psychological harm or seriously affect a person's integrity.[2464] Yet, consensual sadomasochistic or fetish sexual practices which have become socially acceptable (like cane strokes on the buttocks)[2465] are likely not to be regarded as hardcore pornography to-

2460 Cole, "Jugendmedienschutz," sec. H III, paras. 16-18, pp. 309-310; Murad Erdemir, "§ 4 JMStV Unzulässige Angebote," in *Recht der elektronischen Medien*, ed. Gerald Spindler and Fabian Schuster, third edition (C.H. Beck, 2015), para. 1; Reinhard Hartstein et al., "§ 4 JMStV Unzulässige Angebote," para. 15; Holtmann, *Zur rechtlichen Unterscheidung von Rundfunk und Telemedien bei Hybrid-TV*, p. 153.

2461 Art. 4 (1) No. 10 JMStV.

2462 „Virtual presentations" are expressly prohibited by Art. 4 (1) No. 10 JMStV.

2463 Hartstein et al., "§ 4 JMStV Unzulässige Angebote," para. 47; Hertel, "§ 4 JMStV Unzulässige Angebote," para. 66.

2464 Erdemir, "§ 4 JMStV Unzulässige Angebote," para. 46.

2465 Erdemir, "§ 4 JMStV Unzulässige Angebote," para. 46.

day.[2466] In general, a precise delineation of the notion of hardcore pornography on the basis of such abstract criteria as stipulated by the JMStV is not feasible.[2467] Due to recent social trends tolerating more sexual activities (previously considered as abnormal), the focus of the assessment has shifted to whether these are voluntary and consensual or not and whether the person suffering from excessive violence is made into an object and depicted as such.[2468] The notion of hardcore pornography also covers child pornography which includes sexual abuse of children and adolescents.[2469]

The JMStV differentiates between a child who is defined as a person below the age of 14 and an adolescent, a person over 14 years but below the legal age (i.e. 18 years).[2470] The prohibition to disseminate audiovisual media services depicting child pornography is complemented by the prohibition to present "children or adolescents in unnatural poses" by virtue of Art. 4 (1) No. 9 JMStV. In addition, sodomy is banned in audiovisual media services. This implies bodily contact between a person and an animal[2471] whereby the person must be or appear to be sexually involved, not necessarily to the extent of having sexual intercourse.[2472] The ban on hardcore pornography is motivated by reasons of public order or freedom (purporting to prevent the simulation of such acts), the respect of human dignity as well as the right to sexual self-determination as part of the personality rights flowing from Art. 1 (1) GG in conjunction with Art. 2 (2) GG.[2473]

2466 Erdemir, "§ 4 JMStV Unzulässige Angebote," para. 46; Hartstein et al., "§ 4 JMStV Unzulässige Angebote," para. 47.

2467 Hartstein et al., "§ 4 JMStV Unzulässige Angebote," para. 47.

2468 Hartstein et al., "§ 4 JMStV Unzulässige Angebote," para. 47.

2469 Erdemir, "§ 4 JMStV Unzulässige Angebote," para. 47; Hartstein et al., "§ 4 JMStV Unzulässige Angebote," para. 48.

2470 Art. 3 (1) JMStV.

2471 Erdemir, "§ 4 JMStV Unzulässige Angebote," para. 46; Hartstein et al., "§ 4 JMStV Unzulässige Angebote," para. 49.

2472 Hartstein et al., "§ 4 JMStV Unzulässige Angebote," para. 49.

2473 Erdemir, "§ 4 JMStV Unzulässige Angebote," para. 45.

## 2. Derogation for telemedia services

### a) Nature of the content

While the first paragraph of Art. 4 JMStV postulates an absolute ban of certain material, its second paragraph is pertinent to this study as it specifically relates to the implementation of Art. 12 AVMSD. Art. 4 (2) JMStV states that

> "Without prejudice to any liability under the German Criminal Code, content is furthermore illegal if it is
> 1. Pornographic in any other manner,
> 2. Included in Parts A and C of the List pursuant to Article 18 of the German Protection of Young Persons Act, or is wholly or largely identical in content with any work included in this List,
> 3. Evidently suited to seriously impair the development of children and adolescents or their education into self-responsible and socially competent personalities, taking into account the specific effect of the media via which the content is provided.
>
> In deviation from sentence 1 above, content is legal in telemedia services if the provider has ensured that such content is accessible for adult persons only (closed user group)."

The first sentence lists the type of material which may exceptionally be made available to closed user groups of telemedia services pursuant to the second sentence of Art. 4 (2) JMStV. No derogation for such material broadcast on TV is foreseen so that an absolute ban is maintained in relation to broadcasting.[2474] The nature of the content captured by this rule is explained in broad terms by the JMStV. Hence, pornographic content in the sense of "*einfache Pornografie*" (in contrast to hardcore pornography within the meaning of Art. 4 (1) No. 10 JMStV) may be legally provided in telemedia services. The meaning of moderate pornography is contingent

---

2474 Erdemir, "§ 4 JMStV Unzulässige Angebote," para. 58; Hertel, "§ 4 JMStV Unzulässige Angebote," para. 73; Cole, "Jugendmedienschutz," H III, para. 28, p. 316. Cole notes that the absolute ban of pornographic content applicable to broadcasting has been subject to criticism about a prioritasation of telemedia services. This criticism has been qualified by the fact that individual programmes within a pay-TV offer can be made available on-demand. Consequently, the derogation of Art. 4 (2) JMStV applies to such telemedia services. In this context, Cole stresses that the classification as broadcasting or telemedia is of major impotance.

on its social context and may change over time.[2475] The legislature refrained from enshrining an explicit legal definition in the JMStV (likewise in German criminal law) and left it to courts to develop a definition.[2476]

The definition is derived from a BGH decision of 1969 which was confirmed and further developed by the *Bundesverwaltungsgericht* (BVerwG, Federal Administrative Court).[2477] Accordingly, a presentation is pornographic if it focuses on the portrayal of sexual activities to the exclusion of all human relationships in an exaggerated and obtrusive manner with the primary purpose of sexual arousal.[2478] The notion of moderate pornography is thus based on several criteria.[2479] First, the primary purpose of the presentation, considered objectively and as a whole, is sexual arousal. Second, the focus of the presentation constitutes sexual activities far removed from contextual justifications such as inter-personal relations. Consequently, the person depicted in the presentation is treated as a *replaceable* sexual object. Third, the depiction of sexuality is obtrusive and exaggerated or excessive.

---

2475 Erdemir, "§ 4 JMStV Unzulässige Angebote," para. 66; Holtmann, *Zur rechtlichen Unterscheidung von Rundfunk und Telemedien bei Hybrid-TV*, p. 155; Kristina Hopf, "Rechtliche Grundlagen des Jugendmedienschutz-Staatsvertrags und die Verantwortlichkeit von Chatbetreibern," *Zeitschrift für Urheber- und Medienrecht*, 2008, p. 209.

2476 Erdemir, "§ 4 JMStV Unzulässige Angebote," para. 64; Holtmann, *Zur rechtlichen Unterscheidung von Rundfunk und Telemedien bei Hybrid-TV*, p. 155.

2477 See BGH, Judgment of 22.7.1969 – 1 StR 456/68 and BVerwG, Judgment of 20.2.2002 – 6 C 13/01. See also Erdemir, "§ 4 JMStV Unzulässige Angebote," para. 64.

2478 Translated by the author from the following original wording: *„unter Ausklammerung sonstiger menschlicher Bezüge sexuelle Vorgänge in grob aufdringlicher, anreißerischer Weise in den Vordergrund rücken und ausschließlich oder überwiegend auf die Erregung sexueller Reize abzielen"*. The *Bundesprüfstelle für Jugendgefährdende Medien* (BPjM, Federal Review Board for Media Harmful to Minors) translated the definition of pornography as "a presentation of sexuality that is not connected to any kind of psychologically motivated human relationship and which glorifies sexual satisfaction as the only reason for human existence, accompanied by grossly depicted genitals". See http://www.bundespruefstelle.de/bpjm/Service/english.html (accessed 7.2.2016).

2479 Cole, "Jugendmedienschutz," sec. H III, para. 28, p. 316; Erdemir, "§ 4 JMStV Unzulässige Angebote," para. 65; Hertel, "§ 4 JMStV Unzulässige Angebote," para. 65.

Furthermore, certain indexed offers are illegal pursuant to Art. 4 (2) No. 2 JMStV but may be made available in telemedia services under certain circumstances. This entails material which has been registered by the *Bundesprüfstelle für Jugendgefährdende Medien* (BPjM, Federal Review Board for Media Harmful to Minors) according to Art. 18 JuSchG as having a severely damaging impact on minors. Material which "is evidently suited to seriously impair the development of children and adolescents" is considered illegal unless it is supplied in closed user groups of telemedia services.[2480] Within the structure of the second paragraph of Art. 4 (2) JMStV, the formula contained in No. 3 functions as a catchall clause.[2481] The wording of Art. 4 (2) No. 3 JMStV is broadly comparable to Art. 12 AVMSD. Instead of the phrase "might seriously impair" as used in the Directive, the national clause adds the adjective "evident". This implies that a neutral observer must be able to discern the impairment without detailed assessment in individual cases.[2482] The formulation which moderates the interference with the provider's fundamental rights[2483] seems less strict than Art. 12 AVMSD. Pursuant to the JMStV, the harm caused by the material must be *apparent* whereas the Directive captures content which is *potentially* severely harmful, thereby possibly covering a wider range of unsuitable content. This difference may be crucial in individual cases as providers of audiovisual media services might face heavier restrictions under the Directive. It may on the contrary be argued that Art. 4 (2) JMStV

---

2480 Art. 4 (2) No. 3 JMStV.

2481 Cole, "Jugendmedienschutz," sec. H III, para. 26, p. 315; Hartstein et al., "§ 4 JMStV Unzulässige Angebote," para. 63c; Rolf Schwartmann, "Jugendschutzrecht," in *Praxishandbuch Medien-, IT- und Urheberrecht*, ed. Rolf Schwartmann, third edition (Heidelberg: C. F. Müller Verlag, 2014), para. 22, p. 191; of different opinion is Altenhain who underlines that violations of Art. 4 (2) No. 3 are considered as a criminal act pursuant to Art. 23 while infringements of No. 1 and 2 are sanctioned as administrative offences. See Karsten Altenhain, "§ 4 JMStV Unzulässige Angebote," in *Beck'scher Kommentar zum Recht der Telemediendienste*, ed. Alexander Roßnagel (München: C. H. Beck, 2013), para. 45, p. 349.

2482 Altenhain underlines that the impairment must be discernible for every unbiased person. Altenhain, "§ 4 JMStV Unzulässige Angebote," para. 49, p. 351; Cole, "Jugendmedienschutz," sec. H III, para. 27, p. 315; Hartstein et al., "§ 4 JMStV Unzulässige Angebote," para. 63a; Holtmann, *Zur rechtlichen Unterscheidung von Rundfunk und Telemedien bei Hybrid-TV*, p. 156; Hertel, "§ 4 JMStV Unzulässige Angebote," para. 79.

2483 Cole, "Jugendmedienschutz," sec. H III, para. 27, p. 315.

applies a stricter threshold for determining the nature of the content. The German rule is also more specific or concrete than Art. 12 AVMSD and might thus enhance legal certainty for providers operating under German jurisdiction. Moreover, a serious impairment implies a severe danger of disorientation for minors.[2484] The "specific effect of the media via which the content is provided"[2485] is to be taken into account when evaluating the potential for harm.[2486]

The prohibitions set forth in Art. 4 (2) JMStV aim at protecting minors' right to sexual self-determination encompassing free sexual development as well as the possibility to take a conscious decision about the consumption of pornography (in contrast to being unintentionally confronted with pornography).[2487] It is the prerogative of the legislature to construct the legal framework which meets these objectives.[2488] Only when it can be conclusively excluded by scientific evidence that minors would not be harmed by pornographic content would the legislature overstep its margin or discretion.[2489] An impairment can, however, not reasonably be excluded by the current level of scientific research so that the legislature is free to take measures in this respect.

---

2484 Hartstein et al., "§ 4 JMStV Unzulässige Angebote," para. 63d.

2485 Art. 4 (2) No. 3 JMStV.

2486 Altenhain is critical of this formulation which appears to stipulate an additional criterion which presupposes that the same content might be more or less harmful depending on its distribution as telemedia or data media. As a consequence, the principle that the degree of harm is based solely on the content is abandoned, adding a variable into the equation which is difficult to foresee for providers. See Altenhain, "§ 4 JMStV Unzulässige Angebote," para. 48, p. 351.

2487 Erdemir, "§ 4 JMStV Unzulässige Angebote," para. 62.

2488 Erdemir, "§ 4 JMStV Unzulässige Angebote," para. 62.

2489 BGH, Judgment of 18.9.2007, I ZR 102/05, para. 39 where reference is made to an order of the BVerfG in relation to a pornographic novel entitled "Josefine Mutzenbacher" which had been indexed by the BPjM. The BVerfG confirmed that the German legislature could reasonably assume that writings could have a seriously harmful effects on minors. This assumption was covered by its prerogative to estimate and assess the situation (Einschätzungsprärogative). Due to the scientific uncertainties about the effect of pornographic material on the development of minors, the legislature is authorised to assess the risks and determine whether to take action or not. The BVerfG underlined that the legislature would have acted contrary to the Basic Law if it had overstepped its margin of discretion (i.e. if an impairment of minors would have been excluded by the level of research). See BVerfG, Order of 27.11.1990, 1 BvR 402/87.

### b) Closed user groups

According to the second sentence of Art. 4 (2) JMStV, the dissemination of content listed in the first sentence is legal "if the provider has ensured that such content is accessible for adult persons only" within so-called "closed user groups". Such a closed user group implies a limitable circle of users of age to whom content is supplied.[2490] The rule requires that minors be completely prevented from accessing the kind of material outlined in its first sentence. It is thus not sufficient that it is "made excessively difficult" for minors to consume such content.[2491] In this respect, the wording of Art. 4 (2) JMStV establishes a higher hurdle than Art. 12 AVMSD which *merely* requires that minors "do not normally hear or see" such material. A prerequisite to offering seriously harmful content is the installation of an effective age verification system. In 2003, the KJM, the central supervisory body at the federal level drew up criteria which specified the design of the system to be put in operation by providers. The criteria are further examined below. Importantly, they were approved by the BGH in a judgment of 2007 concerning a provider of age verification systems entitled ueber18.de.[2492] In this case, a competitor had challenged the compatibility of the age verification systems supplied by ueber18.de on

---

2490 Cole, "Jugendmedienschutz," sec. H III, para. 29, p. 316.

2491 Hertel, "§ 4 JMStV Unzulässige Angebote," para. 81; Atenhain is of different opinion arguing that it is neither technically possible to construct a totally closed system nor is it possible for providers to prevent adults from making available the offer to minors. Art. 4 (2) JMStV requires an "effective barrier" taking into account technical savy minors. Altenhain remarks that providers may not rely on minors not committing illegal actions in order to access harmful content. See Altenhain, "§ 4 JMStV Unzulässige Angebote," para. 54, p. 352; para. 57, p. 353.

2492 BGH, Judgment of 18.9.2007, I ZR 102/05. See also Erdemir, "Die Kommission für Jugendmedienschutz," p. 293; Holtmann, *Zur rechtlichen Unterscheidung von Rundfunk und Telemedien bei Hybrid-TV*, p. 158; Hopf, "Rechtliche Grundlagen des Jugendmedienschutz-Staatsvertrags und die Verantwortlichkeit von Chatbetreibern," p. 210; Marc Liesching, "'Sicherstellung' des Erwachsenenzugangs bei pornografischen und sonst jugendgefährdenden Telemedien," *Multimedia und Recht*, 2008, p. 803; Metzdorf, "Jugendmedienschutz in Abrufdiensten – Am Beispiel 'Playboy TV' aus Großbritannien," pp. 687–88.

competition law grounds.[2493] The defendant offered two versions of age verification systems. The first entailed the entry of a number of an identity card (in Germany, the *Personalausweis*) or passport in combination with the zip code of the location where the documents had been issued. The second version build on the information provided in the first and required additionally the name, address and credit card number or account details of the user for the transfer of a small amount of EUR 4.95. The ID or passport numbers were not used to verify whether the user was over 18 years. The provider merely checked whether they complied with the rules concerning the composition of such numbers.[2494]

The BGH upheld the decision of the lower instance court, the *Oberlandesgericht Düsseldorf* (OLG, Appeal court)[2495] which had overturned the

2493 The competitor argued that the provision of an age verificaction system constituted a commercial practice within the meaning of Art. 2 (1) No. 1 of the German *Gesetz gegen den unlauteren Wettbewerb* (UWG, Act Against Unfair Competition) and should be considered "unfair" by virtue of Art. 4 No. 11 UWG. An unofficial English translation of the German *Gesetz gegen den unlauteren Wettbewerb* (Act against Unfair Competition) is available at http://www.gesetze-im-internet.de/englisch_uwg/englisch_uwg.html#UWGengl _000P2, (accessed 16.7.2014).

2494 BGH, Judgment of 18.9.2007, I ZR 102/05, para. 2.

2495 Köhne criticises the judgment of the OLG Düsseldorf. He is doubtful about the power of the state to regulate pornographic content due to the lack of evidence on the dangers of pornography. By reference to the enormous amount of foreign pornographic offers, he argues that the Internet cannot be regulated by national standards. Thus, an isolated assessment of the requirements concerning age verification systems applicable in Germany is unrealistic and disproportionate. On account of the international context, Köhne considers age controls based on ID numbers appropriate. See Michael Köhne, "Jugendmedienschutz durch Alterskontrollen im Internet," *Neue Juristische Wochenschrift*, 2005, pp. 794–95; in a similar vein, Vassilaki is critical of the decision of the OLG. She argues that the notion of "effective barrier" cannot be transferred to the Internet which is inherently borderless. Vassilaki is of the opinion that competition law was used to drive the provider of the AVS out of a lucrative market and that considerations of youth protection were merely used as a pretext. Instead of the restrictive reading of the second sentence of Art. 4 (2) JMStV, she suggests a more differentiated approach depending on the type of offer. The more serious the potential to impair minors, the higher the barriers to access content. In addition, Vassilaki points out that the requirement of a face-to-face control (e.g. postident procedure) deterred today's Internet users who are accustomed to accessing content fast and directly. See Irini Vassilaki, "Strafrechtliche Anforderungen an Al-

decision of the *Landgericht Düsseldorf* (LG, District court).[2496] The BGH confirmed the provider's liability for the service which included the mak-

---

tersverifikationssysteme," *Kommunikation und Recht*, 2006, pp. 211–14; see also Marc Liesching, "Anforderungen an Altersverifikationssysteme, Zugleich eine Replik auf Vassilaki, K&R 2006, 211 ff.," *Kommunikation und Recht*, 2006, pp. 395–97.

2496 The LG Düsseldorf had considered the complaint by the competitor of ueber18.de unfounded. The LG decided that the provision of age verification systems did not affect competition on the market. It furthermore underlined that the concrete requirements for age verification systems were not outlined by the JMStV and posited that the criteria established by the KJM were non-binding. It was not up to the courts in competition law matters to interpret the term "ensure" within the meaning of the second sentence of Art. 4 (2) JMStV and curtail by a general prohibition the leeway which the legislature had expressly left. See LG Düsseldorf, Judgment of 28.7.2004, 12 O 19/04. Marc Liesching criticises the LG's decision as a "misjudgement", "LG Düsseldorf: Altersverifikationssystem ueber18.de, Leitsätze und Anmerkung," *Multimedia und Recht*, 2004, pp. 764–66; in contrast to the LG, the OLG Düsseldorf upheld the complaint underlining that the age verification system did not constitute an "effective barrier" in line with established case law. With respect to the requirement to pay a fee, the OLG stressed that minors could easily obtain a credit card or bank details of parents or other third parties. It argued that minors would normally not reflect on the consequences of their conduct or be confident that the small amount of the fee (EUR 4.95) would not come to their parents' attention. The argument of the defendant that the installation of effective access controls were undermined by the fact that pornographic material was readily made available by foreign providers was not accepted. The OLG underlined that the German legislature was empowered to take measures against providers falling under its jurisdiction even if it could not prevent the dissemination of pornographic content on foreign websites. See OLG Düsseldorf, Judgment of 24.5.2005, I-20 U 143/04. The decision was commented by Marc Liesching, "OLG Düsseldorf: Altersverifikationssystem ueber18.de, Leitsätze und Anmerkung," *Multimedia und Recht*, 2005, pp. 611–15; interestingly, the BVerfG rejected a constitutional complaint by the provider of ueber18.de in October 2009. The complainant contested the prohibition of pornographic content outside of closed user groups on grounds of proportionality. In particular, the complainant argued that the provisions of the JMStV (above all, Art. 4 (2) JMStV) were not suited to protect minors as they could easily consume foreign offers of pornographic material which were made available without restrictions. The BVerfG stressed that adequacy of a law which purports to reach certain aims would be affirmed if the law promotes or supports the said aim. Securing that only adults could view pornographic content did reduce the pornographic material freely available (para. 5). The court also confirmed the margin of discretion of the German legislature (para. 6) which to date was not called into question due to the lack of substantiated evidence on the effects of pornography (para. 7). See BVerfG, Order of 24.9.2009,

ing available (by way of hyperlinks) of a catalogue of adult content on the website ueber18.de accessible via its age verification systems.[2497] In order to establish a uniform level of protection in all types of media, the requirements for access controls in relation to the distribution of pornographic material in other media were to be taken as a yardstick.[2498] According to established case law, an "effective barrier" was required.[2499] An age verification system was considered effective or reliable if it excluded easy and

---

1 BvR 1231/04. See also Erdemir, "§ 4 JMStV Unzulässige Angebote," para. 86.

2497 BGH, Judgment of 18.9.2007, I ZR 102/05, paras. 17, 20-21.

2498 BGH, Judgment of 18.9.2007, I ZR 102/05, para. 23.

2499 BGH, Judgment of 18.9.2007, I ZR 102/05, paras. 24-27. See the case law of the BverwG, Judgment of 20.2.2002, 6 C 13/01 in relation to the dissemination of pornographic material on pay-TV; BGH, Judgment of 22.5.2003, 1 StR 70/03 in relation to a video store for slot machines and BGH, Judgment of 19.7.2007, I ZR 137/04 in relation to the sale of seriously impairing data media on eBay. On the jurisprudence, see also Sibylle Gierschmann, "Was ist eine Geschlossene Benutzergruppe i.S.v. § 4 Abs. 2 Satz 2 JMStV?," in *Jugendmedienschutz im Informationszeitalter*, ed. Nikolaus Bosch and Stefan Leible, Bayreuther Studien zum Wirtschafts- und Medienrecht 6 (Sipplingen: Jenaer Wissenschaftliche Verlagsgesellschaft, 2012), pp. 125–29; in a contribution pre-dating the instant case, Berger disagrees with the meaning of closed user groups as constructed by the BGH. He underlines the specificities of telemedia and argues that the standards applicable to broadcasting (an effective barrier) should not be applied to on-demand services. Berger posits that the legislature expected a reliable age verification system which does not imply that minors are totally excluded from accessing the protected content. The use of ID numbers is thus considered sufficient. Even if a 100 percent secure age verification system could be put in place, it would not prevent minors from accessing pornographic content made available on foreign websites. Berger thus opines that the rule fails to accomplish the aim intended by the legislature. See Christian Berger, "Jugendschutz im Internet: „Geschlossene Benutzergruppen" nach § 4 Abs. 2 Satz 2 JMStV – Am Beispiel personalausweiskennziffergestützter Altersverifikationssysteme," pp. 773–78; in a similar vein, Sellmann is critical of the BGH's approach arguing that there was a fundamental difference between television broadcasting and telemedia. In contrast to the transmission of broadcasts, online offers of pornographic content could not be effectively constrained. Due to the global reach of the Internet, minors could turn to foreign (non-EU) providers who did not face comparable restrictions. Christian Sellmann, "K&R Kommentar," *Kommunikation und Recht*, 2008, p. 367; in contrast (and by way of rejoinder to Berger), Döring and Günter support a strict reading of Art. 4 (2) JMStV. Martin Döring and Thomas Günter, "Jugendmedienschutz: Alterskontrollierte geschlossene Benutzergruppen im Internet gem. § 4 Abs. 2 Satz 2 JMStV," *Multimedia und Recht*, 2004, pp. 231–37.

obvious methods of circumvention.[2500] The BGH underlined that the possibilities of abuse inherent in the medium Internet had to be taken into account in the design of the system.[2501] The age verification system of the defendant did not adhere to these requirements as minors could submit ID numbers of family members, friends or relatives of age. In addition, the payment of a small fee constituted an insufficient barrier as many young persons had a personal account which was not regularly controlled by their parents. [2502] Yet, the BGH also set limits to the level of effectiveness of the system allowing for minors possessing unforeseeable technical skills or having taken exceptional efforts to penetrate the barrier.[2503]

Importantly, the court, in basing itself on the KJM's criteria, required that a personal identification or identification by reliable technical tools (such as by webcam or by reference to biometric characteristics) be carried out. A control mechanism which functioned face-to-face was not necessary.[2504] In addition to a one-off identification, authentication of the user at the point of access to the service was required.[2505] The BGH posited that the two-fold protection comprising the identification and continual authentication of the user which is further detailed below, was reasonable and corresponded to the access controls implemented in case of offline media.[2506] The court concluded that the provider was in breach of Art. 4 (2) JMStV which in turn interfered with the interests of consumers, above all, vulnerable consumers like minors as safeguarded by competition law.[2507] Similarly, the use of an inadequate age verification system had a considerable impact on competition. The BGH pointed to the masses of

2500 BGH, Judgment of 18.9.2007, I ZR 102/05, para. 28. The BGH refers to "*einfache, naheliegende und offensichtliche Umgehunsmöglichkeiten*" which must be prevented.

2501 BGH, Judgment of 18.9.2007, I ZR 102/05, para. 28.

2502 BGH, Judgment of 18.9.2007, I ZR 102/05, paras. 29-30.

2503 BGH, Judgment of 18.9.2007, I ZR 102/05, para. 31.

2504 BGH, Judgment of 18.9.2007, I ZR 102/05, paras. 34-35, 52.

2505 Cole, "Jugendmedienschutz," sec. H III, para. 29, p. 317; Erdemir, "§ 4 JMStV Unzulässige Angebote," para. 79; Hartstein et al., "§ 4 JMStV Unzulässige Angebote," para. 64; Holtmann, *Zur rechtlichen Unterscheidung von Rundfunk und Telemedien bei Hybrid-TV*, p. 158.

2506 BGH, Judgment of 18.9.2007, I ZR 102/05, para. 37. The BGH stressed that adults were not prevented from gaining access but access was only made more difficult.

2507 BGH, Judgment of 18.9.2007, I ZR 102/05, para. 49. See also Hertel, "§ 4 JMStV Unzulässige Angebote," para. 81.

content that was made available on the website of the defendant and underlined that it was in the interest of content providers to have in operation a simple age verification system with low access requirements.[2508] Hence, providers of adequate (i.e. stricter) age verification systems suffered from a competitive disadvantage.[2509] The *uber18.de* case makes clear that it is service provider's responsibility to put into place an adequate age verification system. The BGH took an unambiguous stance on the inadequacy of identification by ID or passport numbers,[2510] thereby confirming the twofold protection mechanism the KJM had developed.[2511] In order to avoid investing into a technical system which does not meet the legal requirements, providers may request an *ex-ante* examination by the KJM.[2512]

### 3. Harmful content

The AVMSD only prescribes rules for on-demand audiovisual media services in relation to content that "might seriously impair" the development of minors, a standard which finds expression in Art. 4 (2) JMStV. What is more, the German law goes beyond the Directive by setting out additional rules applicable to telemedia services. By virtue of Art. 4 (1) AVMSD, Member States are empowered to take more detailed or stricter measures in their territories. Art. 5 JMStV regulates harmful content transmitted in broadcasting and telemedia and thus also transposes Art. 27 AVMSD. Due to this research's focus on the protection of minors in on-demand services, Art. 5 JMStV is discussed in light of this focus leaving aside the specificities of broadcasting.

---

2508 BGH, Judgment of 18.9.2007, I ZR 102/05, para. 51.

2509 BGH, Judgment of 18.9.2007, I ZR 102/05, para. 51.

2510 On the inadequacy of ID or passport numbers as means of age verification, see also KG Berlin (District court), Judgment of 26.4.2004, (5) 1 Ss 436/03 (4/04) in criminal proceedings against a provider of pornographic content (primarily photos) on the Internet. The provider had used the age verification system of ueber18.de. The line of argumentation of the KG Berlin is similar to that of the OLG Düsseldorf and the BGH in the competition law case of *ueber18.de* (i.e. lack of identification of the user; need for an effective barrier).

2511 Karsten Altenhain, "Jugendschutz," in *Multimedia-Recht*, ed. Thomas Hoeren, Ulrich Sieber and Bernd Holznagel, Loose-leaf commentary (München: C. H. Beck, 2015), paras. 65–66.

2512 Altenhain, "Jugendschutz," para. 65.

Art. 5 stipulates:

"(1) Providers transmitting or making accessible content suited to impair the development of children or adolescents into self-responsible and socially competent personalities shall ensure that children or adolescents of the relevant age groups do not normally see or hear such content.
(2) Content is assumed to be suited to impair development as specified in (1) above if it has not been cleared for children or adolescents of the respective age group under the German Protection of Young Persons Act. Sentence 1 shall apply mutatis mutandis to content which is largely identical with the assessed content.
(3) A provider may fulfil his obligation pursuant to (1) above by
1. making access and perception of the content impossible or very difficult for children or adolescents of the respective age group via technical or other means, or
2. scheduling transmission of or access to the content in a manner devised to ensure that children or adolescents of the respective age group do not normally see or hear the content.
(4) If an impairment of the development of children or adolescents as specified in (1) above can be assumed, the provider shall be deemed to fulfil his obligation pursuant to (1) above if he transmits or makes accessible the content during the period 23.00 hours to 06.00 hours only. This shall apply mutatis mutandis for the provision of content made available during the period 22.00 hours to 06.00 hours only if an impairment of the development of children or adolescents under the age of 16 years is to be feared. For films not released for children aged less than 12 years of age pursuant to the German Protection of Young People Act, the well-being of younger children shall be given priority in the scheduling of transmission.
(5) If an impairment on children only as specified in (1) above is to be assumed, the telemedia provider of shall be deemed to fulfil his obligation pursuant to (1) above if the content is transmitted or made available on-demand separately from content aimed at children.
(6) Paragraph (1) above shall not apply to news broadcasts, current affairs broadcasting and similar content available as telemedia to the extent that a justifiable interest in this specific type of presentation or report exists."

Pursuant to Art. 5 JMStV, unsuitable content may be made available to minors of certain age groups provided that it is secured that younger children do not normally hear or see such material.[2513] It follows that harmful content may generally be disseminated, albeit with restrictions.[2514] An

2513 Altenhain, "Jugendschutz," para. 83; Cole, "Jugendmedienschutz," sec. H III, para. 31, p. 318; Hartstein et al., "§ 5 JMStV Entwicklungsbeeinträchtigende Angebote," in *Rundfunkstaatsvertrag, Kommentar*, Looseleaf commenatry (Köln: Rehm, n.d.), para. 2.

2514 Hertel, "§ 5 JMStV Entwicklungsbeeinträchtigende Angebote," para. 1.

overview is given below about the nature of the content tackled by the provision as well as the measures providers are required to take.

a) Nature of the content

The first paragraph of Art. 5 JMStV outlines the standard to assess content.[2515] Content that is "suited to impair" minors' developments into "self-responsible and socially competent personalities" cannot be transmitted freely. The rationale of the provision is to ensure the upbringing of children as an independent and responsible (individual component) as well as a socially competent person (social component).[2516] Importantly, the provision does not aim at imposing upon minors decent convictions in a moral sense ("*anständige Gesinnung*") but strives to further their free development according to the rules and values upon which society is based.[2517] Moreover, the formulation "content suited to impair" is reminiscent of the formula "is likely to impair" as contained in Art. 27 (2) AVMSD. A comparison of the wording seems to yield that the German rule is more concrete owing to the use of the phrase "is suited" in contrast to "is likely". Similar to the differences in formulations regarding Art. 4 (2) JMStV and Art. 12 AVMSD explored above, it might be argued that the Directive's wording potentially covers a greater amount of unsuitable content. This, however, depends on the interpretation of the German provision within the national context.[2518] Both, the Directive as well as Art. 5

---

2515 While the English translation of the JMStV refers to content which is "seriously impairing" in relation to Art. 4 JMStV and content which is "suited to impair" in relation to Art. 5 JMStV, the German version differentiates between „Gefährdung" (Art. 4 JMStV) and "Beeinträchtigung" (Art. 5 JMStV). The remaining formulations of the two provisions are very similar so that the use of the different expressions is confusing, above all as the term "Beeinträchtigung" might imply a more severe effect or detrimental impact upon minors. See Altenhain, "Jugendschutz," para. 83.

2516 Murad Erdemir, "§ 5 JMStV Entwicklungsbeeinträchtigende Angebote," in *Recht der elektronischen Medien*, ed. Gerald Spindler and Fabian Schuster, third edition (C.H. Beck, 2015), para. 5; Hartstein et al., "§ 5 JMStV Entwicklungsbeeinträchtigende Angebote," para. 12; Holtmann, *Zur rechtlichen Unterscheidung von Rundfunk und Telemedien bei Hybrid-TV*, p. 163.

2517 Erdemir, "§ 5 JMStV Entwicklungsbeeinträchtigende Angebote," para. 7.

2518 Altenhain criticises the formulation contained in Art. 5 (1) JMStV as too vague. See Altenhain, "Jugendschutz," para. 85.

(1) JMStV seem to rely on the potential for harm so that there is no requirement to proof the harm caused to minors.[2519]

Commonly, the term impairment implies inhibitions, disorders or harm.[2520] A differentiation is made between physical/bodily harm (e.g. through the duration of a programme, optical and/or acoustic presentation) and psychological/emotional harm (e.g. when minors cannot assimilate or cope cognitively with the content and form of a programme).[2521] Websites of adult content that offer previews free of charge which are "toned down" but combined with lascivious titles such as "horny nymphomaniacs" would, for instance, be susceptible to be regulated under Art. 5 JMStV.[2522] The reference point to appraise the impairment is, however, unclear. Some posit that the assessment should centre on the protection of minors who are *"gefährdungsgeneigt"*, i.e. groups of minors with a specific tendency to endangerment.[2523] Yet, this would distort the overall assessment to the extent that weaker members of the relevant age groups would be dispro-

2519 Erdemir, "§ 5 JMStV Entwicklungsbeeinträchtigende Angebote," para. 2; Hartstein et al., "§ 5 JMStV Entwicklungsbeeinträchtigende Angebote," para. 12.

2520 Erdemir, "§ 5 JMStV Entwicklungsbeeinträchtigende Angebote," para. 5; Schwartmann, "Jugendschutzrecht," para. 25, p. 192.

2521 Erdemir, "§ 5 JMStV Entwicklungsbeeinträchtigende Angebote," para. 7; Altenhain, on the contrary, finds that the aim of the protection of minors is overstretched if an impairment is already affirmed once an offer is too loud or when it is simply too much for minors. He is also critical of the formulation "suited to impair" and underlines the difficulty (due to the vague wording of the law) to establish a meaningful differentiation between seriously harmful (jugendgefährdend within the meaning of Art. 4 JMStV) and impairing (jugendbeeinträchtigend within the meaning of Art. 5 JMStV) content. Altenhain suggests that the assessment pursuant to Art. 5 JMStV should follow the same module as for Art. 4 JMStV. This means that the question whether content is harmful to minors is evaluated on the basis of age groups. If content is not harmful to minors aged 16, it is to be appraised whether it might be harmful to minors aged between 14 and 16. The transmission times of Art. 5 (4) JMStV apply accordingly. See Karsten Altenhain, "§ 5 JMStV Entwicklungsbeeinträchtigende Angebote," in *Beck'scher Kommentar zum Recht der Telemediendienste*, ed. Alexander Roßnagel (München: C. H. Beck, 2013), paras. 6, 9, 13, pp. 361-363.

2522 Erdemir, "§ 5 JMStV Entwicklungsbeeinträchtigende Angebote," para. 1.

2523 Hartstein et al., "§ 5 JMStV Entwicklungsbeeinträchtigende Angebote," paras. 11–12; Holtman favours the inclusion of minors who are "gefährdungsgeneit" as the potential for harm is assessed on the basis of criteria such as the child's social environment, background, education or other social attitudes. See Holtmann, *Zur rechtlichen Unterscheidung von Rundfunk und Telemedien bei Hybrid-TV*, p. 163.

portionately taken into account. Others, with whom the author agrees, argue that the assessment should be based on the "average minor" of each respective age group.[2524]

Furthermore, the second paragraph of Art. 5 JMStV establishes an assumption of impairment by constructing a link between the JuSchG and the JMStV. "Content is assumed to be suited to impair [minors'] development (…) if it has not been cleared for children or adolescents of the respective age group under the [JuSchG]". More concretely, if a film released in the cinema or on a data media (e.g. DVD) was only made available to adolescents over the age of 16, it is presumed that its retransmission in telemedia or on TV is suited to impair minors below 16 years. This assumption also applies to content which is "largely identical" as stipulated by the second sentence of Art. 5 (2) JMStV.[2525] Although Art. 5 (2) JMStV by reference to the JuSchG creates a certain concordance between the two legal instruments; there is still a lack of harmonisation between "online" and "offline" media. If a film was cleared and classified under Art. 14 JuSchG, it can be marketed and distributed on all kinds of media with the respective age label. By contrast, age labels for telemedia and broadcasts which are intended for secondary exploitation on DVDs will require additional age clearings pursuant to the JuSchG.[2526]

---

2524 Confer for instance Erdemir, "§ 5 JMStV Entwicklungsbeeinträchtigende Angebote" who points out that younger and weaker members of the respective age groups should be taken into account but that generally children susceptible to harm should not be the benchmark as this would interfere with the right to information by minors. This seems to be the interpretation given by the Verwaltungsgericht München (VG, administrative court) in a case of 2004 concerning the Freak Show; Cole, "Jugendmedienschutz," pp. 299–337; Schwartmann, "Rundfunkrechtliche Grundlagen," para. 25, p. 192.

2525 Erdemir, "§ 5 JMStV Entwicklungsbeeinträchtigende Angebote," paras. 11–12. Erdemir stresses that cuts of scenes which are considered to have a detrimental effect on children could eliminate the impairment or otherwise alter the age group for which content is cleared. He also underlines that the assumption contained in Art. 5 (2) JMStV may be refuted if the rating dates back more than 15 years. This exception is only applicable to broadcasting by virtue of Art. 9 (1) JMStV; see also Hertel, "§ 5 JMStV Entwicklungsbeeinträchtigende Angebote," para. 10.

2526 Erdemir, "§ 5 JMStV Entwicklungsbeeinträchtigende Angebote," para. 11; Hertel, "§ 5 JMStV Entwicklungsbeeinträchtigende Angebote," para. 8.

b) Service providers' measures to ensure the protection of minors

Service providers bear the responsibility for ensuring that minors "of the relevant age groups do not normally see or hear" content suited to impair their development.[2527] Paragraphs (3)-(5) of Art. 5 JMStV specify different measures that providers are obliged to take. In this respect, Art. 5 (3) JMStV details two options. First, "making access and perception of the content impossible or very difficult for children or adolescents of the respective age group via technical or other means" and second, "scheduling transmission of or access to the content in a manner devised to ensure that children or adolescents of the respective age group do not normally see or hear the content". Technical protection measures play an ever more important role in the diffusion of content on the Internet as this type of content dissemination is not subjected to *ex ante* controls (data media) or licensing (broadcasting) which could account for youth protection.[2528] The demands that are placed on technical measures pursuant to Art. 5 (3) No. 1 JMStV are, however, lower than those applicable for closed user groups so that a face-to-face control is not necessary,[2529] but the age of users must be verified effectively. Hence, access controls which de-code a programme by means of a PIN code/password or which apply the so-called "*Perso-Check*" (verification of ID) are illustrative of such technical measures.[2530]

In addition, certified technical systems for the protection of minors may be installed in accordance with Art. 11 JMStV (so-called *Jugendschutzprogramm,* JSP).[2531] The 19th amendment to the RStV which entered into force on 1 October 2016, amended Art. 11 JMStV. According to Art. 11 (1) JMStV, JSPs are special software that are able to read and

2527 Cole, "Jugendmedienschutz," sec. H III, para. 31, p. 318; Erdemir, "§ 5 JMStV Entwicklungsbeeinträchtigende Angebote," para. 4. The term "provider" is defined in Art. 1 (2) No. 2 as a broadcaster or a telemedia provider.

2528 Schindler, "Technische Möglichkeiten des Jugendschutzes im Internet," p. 123.

2529 Erdemir, "§ 5 JMStV Entwicklungsbeeinträchtigende Angebote," para. 14; Holtmann, *Zur rechtlichen Unterscheidung von Rundfunk und Telemedien bei Hybrid-TV*, p. 164; Schindler, "Technische Möglichkeiten des Jugendschutzes im Internet," p. 127.

2530 Hertel, "§ 5 JMStV Entwicklungsbeeinträchtigende Angebote," para. 18; Schindler, "Technische Möglichkeiten des Jugendschutzes im Internet," p. 127.

2531 Erdemir, "§ 5 JMStV Entwicklungsbeeinträchtigende Angebote," para. 16; Hartstein et al., "§ 5 JMStV Entwicklungsbeeinträchtigende Angebote," para. 17a; Holtmann, *Zur rechtlichen Unterscheidung von Rundfunk und Telemedien bei Hybrid-TV*, pp. 166–67.

recognise age labels used to classify content for particular age groups. Thus, JSPs filter content disseminated online, block access to unsuitable content or assess the potential for harm of a particular content.[2532] They may be installed on individual devices or function at network level (covering all devices connected to the home network).[2533] The blocking of content may be based on keywords or websites or rely on the labelling of websites (page-labelling). In the former two cases (keyword and website blocking), positive or negative lists may be established which either allow access to all content otherwise excluded (blacklist) or only permit access to content included in a list (whitelist).[2534] The option to label websites leaves it to users to set the standards. Content providers classify websites through self-regulation.[2535] These ratings (in the format of age-de.xml) are subsequently recognised by filter software that users may configure ac-

2532 Hartstein et al., "§ 11 JMStV Jugendschutzprogramme," para. 4; Holtmann, *Zur rechtlichen Unterscheidung von Rundfunk und Telemedien bei Hybrid-TV*, p. 167.

2533 Hartstein et al., "§ 11 JMStV Jugendschutzprogramme," para. 4; Hajok and Schwarz refer to protection measures installed at the level of modems or routers which may function on the basis of blacklists. It may be possible to restrict the time spent online via the settings. The authors also look at measures put in place in relation to mobile devices (in particular cell phones) and examine the operation systems Android by Google and iOS by Apple (p. 5). They note that to date, no youth protection app which offers different levels of protection has been invented. See Hajok and Schwarz, "Technischer Jugendmedienschutz bei digitalen Medien," p. 4.

2534 Altenhain, "§ 5 JMStV Entwicklungsbeeinträchtigende Angebote," para. 24, p. 366; Hartstein et al., "§ 11 JMStV Jugendschutzprogramme," paras. 5–6; an example of such a positive measure is the website http://fragfinn.de/kinderliste.html (accessed 11.3.2016). Fragfinn.de is a secure space especially conceived for minors by the FSM. The service is constantly up-dated and offers attractive, child-friendly content including a search engine, different chat rooms, games and riddles. See Hajok and Schwarz, "Technischer Jugendmedienschutz bei digitalen Medien," p. 4; see also Günter and Schindler, "Technische Möglichkeiten des Jugendschutzes im Internet," p. 132.

2535 Art. 12 JMStV obliges providers of telemedia to „provide clear references to any existing labelling" if the content is „wholly or largely identical" to content disseminated on data media. Hence, existing labels under the JuSchG are to be adopted by providers of telemedia and presented in a clear manner to inform users.

cording to their perspectives on harmful material.[2536] Recognition of the labels or age ratings is essential so that content may be differentiated according to age groups.[2537] Art. 11 JMStV promotes the (currently still nascent) development of such JSPs. Hence, these systems have to be expressly certified by a recognised organisation of voluntary self-regulation; certification being valid for three years.[2538] The KJM may determine the assessment criteria in conjunction with the self-regulatory organisation pursuant to Art. 11 (3) JMStV.

Furthermore, No. 2 of Art. 5 (3) JMStV in conjunction with Art. 5 (4) JMStV set out temporal restrictions for the transmission of unsuitable content.[2539] These are equally applicable to on-demand services and broad-

---

2536 Hartstein et al., "§ 11 JMStV Jugendschutzprogramme," para. 4; Hajok and Schwarz, "Technischer Jugendmedienschutz bei digitalen Medien," p. 3; Hartstein et al., "§ 11 JMStV Jugendschutzprogramme," para. 7; Schindler refers to other forms of classification such as third party ratings (e.g. list of indexed content drawn up by the BPjM pursuant to Art. 18 JuSchG). While ratings by experts allegedly was of high quality, it was burdensome and time-consuming and thus, useful only for the assessment of selected content. In addition, Schindler mentions classification of content by users (so-called tagging). Although such tags were subjective and their quality much lower than expert ratings, they might be used more frequently in relation to popular platforms, services or content. Importantly, Schindler remarks that the majority of offers available online could not be grasped by "editorial" labelling but required automated classification mechanisms. In order to rectify incorrect classifications, complaints handling procedures would have to be put in place. See Schindler, "Technische Möglichkeiten des Jugendschutzes im Internet," pp. 122–41.

2537 Art. 11 (3) JMStV. The official statement of reasons of the JMStV refers to the age groups according to Art. 14 (2) JuSchG including no age restriction, 6 years, 12 years, 16 years and 18 years. Since the entry into force of the 19th amendment to the RStV on 1 October 2016, these age groups are now explicitly outlined by Art. 5 (1) JMStV. Liesching notes that different authors posit that JSPs should solely be based on the age groups 14, 16 and 18. See also Marc Liesching, "Jugendschutzprogramme für 'ab 18'-Internetangebote, Rechtliche Beleuchtung und Ausblick," *Multimedia und Recht*, 2013, p. 370; Hartstein et al., "§ 5 JMStV Entwicklungsbeeinträchtigende Angebote," para. 17a; Holtmann, *Zur rechtlichen Unterscheidung von Rundfunk und Telemedien bei Hybrid-TV*, pp. 166–67.

2538 Art. 11 (4) JMStV. Before entry into force of the 19th RStV on 1 October 2016, it was the competent state media authority acting through the KJM that was responsible for certification.

2539 Erdemir, "§ 5 JMStV Entwicklungsbeeinträchtigende Angebote," para. 18; Hertel, "§ 5 JMStV Entwicklungsbeeinträchtigende Angebote," para. 11.

casting. Yet, scheduling requirements are difficult to implement online where content is typically available worldwide and around the clock.[2540] The software used will have to take into account different time zones and recognise the local time where content is accessed.[2541] The fourth paragraph of Art. 5 JMStV specifies the time periods within which unsuitable material may be transmitted (watershed rules). Accordingly, content which is considered harmful to minors under 18 may only be disseminated between 11 p.m. and 6 a.m. Content which is susceptible of having a detrimental effect on minors aged below 16 may exclusively be transmitted between 10 p.m. and 6 a.m. With regards to children of 12 years or younger, no rigid time frame is outlined.[2542] Art. 5 (4) JMStV explicitly requires that "the well-being of younger children shall be given priority in the scheduling of transmission". As a rule of thumb, material deemed to be harmful to younger viewers should be provided after 8 p.m., possibly later depending on the nature of the content in individual cases.[2543] In general, the scheduling restrictions apply to the entire duration of the programme irrespective of individual scenes which might cause the impairment.[2544] If it is feared that certain inappropriate material had a detrimental effect *only*

---

2540 Cole, "Jugendmedienschutz," sec. H III, para. 32, p. 318; Holtmann, *Zur rechtlichen Unterscheidung von Rundfunk und Telemedien bei Hybrid-TV*, p. 170; Altenhain posits that scheduling restrictions may only apply to brodacsting. See Altenhain, "§ 5 JMStV Entwicklungsbeeinträchtigende Angebote," para. 27, p. 367.

2541 Holtmann, *Zur rechtlichen Unterscheidung von Rundfunk und Telemedien bei Hybrid-TV*, p. 170.

2542 Hertel, "§ 5 JMStV Entwicklungsbeeinträchtigende Angebote," para. 14.

2543 Erdemir, "§ 5 JMStV Entwicklungsbeeinträchtigende Angebote," para. 20.

2544 Hertel, "§ 5 JMStV Entwicklungsbeeinträchtigende Angebote," para. 15; Schwartmann, "Jugendschutzrecht," para. 25, p. 192; Erdemir, "§ 5 JMStV Entwicklungsbeeinträchtigende Angebote," para. 23. An interesting question is whether different episodes of a series which have been rated differently are to be regarded as a single programme for the purpose of Art. 5 (4) JMStV. Typically such episodes are transmitted one after the other (e.g. Cliffhanger). Individually, the episodes comply with the scheduling restrictions for the respective age groups. However, the intention of providers is to "hook" minors and "lure them into the forbidden transmission time". Erdemir posits that the aim of the JMStV would be undermined if a provider would market or package the episodes as "one programme" (para. 24). In practice, the intention of the provider to transmit individual episodes or one single programme is, however, difficult to proof.

on *children* defined as minors under the age of 14,[2545] providers of telemedia would be deemed to fulfil their obligations if inappropriate content "is made available on-demand separately from content aimed at children". Thus, Art. 5 (5) JMStV prescribes the principle of separation[2546] and ensures that protected spaces are provided for content specifically designed for children which are separated from other content (i.e. absence of links).[2547] Finally, Art. 5 (6) JMStV stipulates an exception for news and current affairs programmes. Provided a justifiable interest exists in the type of presentation, Art. 5 (1) is not applicable.[2548]

## II. The measures taken by the German regulatory bodies

In the following, the measures taken by the German regulatory bodies are examined including the guidance issued by several bodies and the practice that has developed at the co-regulatory level, analysing the publicly available decisions of the FSM.

---

2545 Erdemir, "§ 5 JMStV Entwicklungsbeeinträchtigende Angebote," para. 25. Erdemir remarks that this provision effectively introduces a new age group (children aged below 14) next to the age groups 12, 16 and 18.

2546 Altenhain, "§ 5 JMStV Entwicklungsbeeinträchtigende Angebote," para. 31, p. 368; Erdemir, "§ 5 JMStV Entwicklungsbeeinträchtigende Angebote," para. 25; Hartstein et al., "§ 5 JMStV Entwicklungsbeeinträchtigende Angebote," paras. 20–22; Hertel, "§ 5 JMStV Entwicklungsbeeinträchtigende Angebote," para. 21.

2547 Erdemir, "§ 5 JMStV Entwicklungsbeeinträchtigende Angebote," para. 25.

2548 See in more detail, Kristina Hopf, "Das Berichterstattungsprivileg des § 5 Absatz 6 JMStV Zeitgeschichtliche bzw. historische Dokumentationen – mit oder ohne fiktionale Elemente – haben die Jugendschutzvorschrift des § 5 Absatz 1 JMStV stets zu beachten," *Zeitschrift für Urheber- und Medienrecht*, 2009, pp. 191–99; Marc Liesching, "Das Darstellungs- und Berichterstattungsprivileg für Sendungen zum politischen Zeitgeschehen nach § 5 Absatz 6 JMStV," *Zeitschrift für Urheber- und Medienrecht*, 2009, pp. 367–74; Erdemir, "§ 5 JMStV Entwicklungsbeeinträchtigende Angebote," paras. 26–27; Hartstein et al., "§ 5 JMStV Entwicklungsbeeinträchtigende Angebote," paras. 23–24; Hertel, "§ 5 JMStV Entwicklungsbeeinträchtigende Angebote," paras. 22–24.

## 1. Joint guidelines of the state media authorities

Less than three years after the adoption of the JMStV, in March 2005, the German state media authorities drew up *Gemeinsame Richtlinien zur Gewährung des Schutzes der Menschenwürde und des Jugendschutzes*, (joint guidelines for the guarantee of the protection of human dignity and young people, *Jugendschutzrichtlinien*, JuSchRiL) which entered into force in June of the same year. The JuSchRiL's preamble makes clear that the guidelines purport to specify the legal provisions of the JMStV by detailing the requirements imposed on providers and outlining concrete instructions.[2549] Their legal status is unclear,[2550] albeit a majority opinion maintains that they are genuine executive measures with binding effect.[2551] This seems plausible as the JuSchRiL are legitimated by express legal bases, i.e. Art. 15 (2) JMStV[2552] in conjunction with Art. 8 (1) and 9 (1) JMStV, the latter two of which concern PSB.[2553] In addition, the guide-

---

2549 Medienanstalten, "Gemeinsame Richtlinien der Landesmedienanstalten zur Gewährleistung des Schutzes der Menschenwürde und des Jugendschutzes," March 8, 2005, para. 1.5, p. 3, http://www.kjm-online.de/fileadmin/Download_KJM/Recht/JuSchRiL.pdf (accessed 20.5.2016).

2550 The case law of the highest administrative court in Bavaria is, for instance, contradictory in relation to guidelines issued by the state media authorities in the area of broadcasting and telemedia. In a judgment of 2009, it considered that the guidelines issued pursuant to Art. 46 RStV in conjunction with Art. 8a RStV specified the legal provisions of the RStV (see BayVGH, Judgment of 28.10.2009, 7 N 09.1377). However, in 2011, it denied any external effect (Außenwirkung) of the JuSchRiL and decided that they merely interpreted the legal provisions of the JMStV (see BayVGH, Judgment of 23.3.2011, 7 BV 09.2517).

2551 Cole, "Der Dualismus von Selbstkontrolle und Aufsicht im Jugendmedienschutz," p. 470; Liesching, "Anforderungen an Altersverifikationssysteme," p. 395; Wolfgang Schulz and Thorsten Held, "§ 15 JMStV Mitwirkung der Gremien der Landesmedienanstalten," in *Beck'scher Kommentar zum Rundfunkrecht*, ed. Werner Hahn and Thomas Vesting, third edition (München: C. H. Beck, 2012), paras. 20–21; in a contribution of 2013, Liesching seems to have changed his opinion and appears to claim that the JuSchRiL are non-binding. Liesching, "Jugendschutzprogramme für 'ab 18'-Internetangebote," pp. 368–71.

2552 The first sentence of Art. 15 (2) JMStV stipulates that "the decision-making committees of the state media authorities which are competent pursuant to the respective state media legislation shall enact concordant statutes and guidelines covering the implementation of this Interstate Treaty".

2553 Bornemann stresses that the scope of discretion of the state media authorities is contingent on the exact formulation of the provision. See Roland Bornemann,

lines are developed on the basis of complicated procedures which involve different institutions and bodies and thus reflect their specialised expertise and experience.[2554] In the following, the relevant guidelines concerning the protection of minors in telemedia are discussed. The preamble to the JuSchRiL underpins that it is the responsibility of providers to guarantee the protection of minors and the respect for human dignity by appraising the nature of the content prior to making it available and putting in place any protection measures, if necessary.[2555]

With regards to illegal content, the JuSchRiL confirm the definition of pornography as established by case law.[2556] The formulation "evidently suited to seriously impair" (No. 3 of Art. 4 (2) JMStV) is considered as a "general clause" with broad meaning. An impairment is "evident" when it can be discerned by an impartial/objective observer.[2557] What is more, the JuSchRiL clarify that the provision of seriously harmful content in line with the second sentence of Art. 4 (2) JMStV in closed user groups is limited to adults. Such closed user groups are protected by two steps.[2558] First, the provider must verify by personal contact that the user is of age. Age verification is considered reliable if it involves a face-to-face identification of a person by official documents (ID or passport).[2559] Second, the provider must ensure that only the person identified in the first step has access to the service by way of authentication. The risk that access data be disclosed or passed on to unauthorised third parties must be prevented or made more difficult.[2560] The two-step mechanism whereby closed user groups are to be constrained to adults is widely accepted in Germany. The BGH, in its ruling in *ueber18.de*, handed down in 2007 (two years after the adoption of the JuSchRiL), generally approved of the two-step method. It nonetheless indicated that technical means of identification which are equivalent to a face-to-face control may also be employed by providers. In this respect, the court took a more liberal approach and demonstrated openness for new technological developments.

---

"Zur Rechtsnatur rundfunkrechtlicher Richtlinien," *Zeitschrift für Urheber- und Medienrecht*, 2012, pp. 90–91.

2554 Bornemann, "Zur Rechtsnatur rundfunkrechtlicher Richtlinien," p. 92.

2555 Medienanstalten, "Jugendschutzrichtlinien," para. 1.1, p. 2.

2556 Medienanstalten, "Jugendschutzrichtlinien," para. 2.3.1, p. 5.

2557 Medienanstalten, "Jugendschutzrichtlinien," para. 2.4.1, p. 5.

2558 Medienanstalten, "Jugendschutzrichtlinien," para. 5.1.1, p. 14.

2559 Medienanstalten, "Jugendschutzrichtlinien," para. 5.1.2, p. 14.

2560 Medienanstalten, "Jugendschutzrichtlinien," para. 5.1.3, p. 15.

Furthermore, the JuSchRiL make clear that Art. 5 (1) JMStV regarding harmful content takes into account not only the integrity of the individual but also the child's personality within its social context.[2561] The benchmark for the assessment constitutes the weaker and less-developed members of the respective age group including an assessment of the effect of the material on specially endangered minors (*gefährdungsgeneigt*).[2562] The particular focus on weaker children rather than the "average minor" is crucial as the threshold for content to be considered harmful becomes lower. As outlined above, providers can attend to their duty by scheduling transmissions so that minors do not normally hear or see the inappropriate material. The JuSchRiL clarify that such scheduling restrictions apply to the entire duration of the material.[2563]

In addition, the JuSchRiL require that offers with a detrimental effect on children under 12 years are only disseminated between 8 p.m. and 6 a.m. In this respect, the JuSchRiL close a gap in the JMStV and specify the vague formulation contained in the last sentence of Art. 5 (4) JMStV.[2564] It is important to note that the JuSchRiL refer to different technical measures whereby providers may comply with their obligations pursuant to Art. 5 JMStV. First, certified systems of closed user groups within the meaning of the second sentence of Art. 4 (2) JMStV may constitute technical measures within the meaning of Art. 5 (3) JMStV.[2565] Second, JSPs that make the consumption of harmful content impossible or excessively difficult may function as technical measures provided they fulfil certain requirements.[2566] Apart from technical effectiveness, JSPs must also be effective in relation to users and their social context. This implies that JSPs are accepted by parents as well as by society and that they are user-friendly and easy to use.[2567]

These requirements have been heavily criticised as contrary to the wording of Art. 11 (1) JMStV which merely stipulates that JSP "allow for

2561 Medienanstalten, "Jugendschutzrichtlinien," para. 3.1.1, p. 6.

2562 Medienanstalten, "Jugendschutzrichtlinien," para. 3.1.2, p. 6.

2563 Medienanstalten, "Jugendschutzrichtlinien," para. 3.2.3, p. 7.

2564 Reference is made to the following sentence of Art. 5 (4) JMStV: "For films not released for children aged less than 12 years of age pursuant to the [JuSchG], *the well-being of younger children shall be given priority* in the scheduling of transmissions".

2565 Medienanstalten, "Jugendschutzrichtlinien," para. 3.4.2, pp. 7–8.

2566 Medienanstalten, "Jugendschutzrichtlinien," para. 5.2.1, p. 15.

2567 Medienanstalten, "Jugendschutzrichtlinien," para. 5.2.2, p. 15.

differentiated access according to age groups".[2568] Liesching argues that it is of no relevance to the *ratio* of Art. 11 JMStV whether and to what extent JSPs are employed by users. Consequently, he posits that the certification of JSPs cannot be made contingent on the number of households where JSPs are actually being used.[2569] In contrast, Braml and Hopf point to the lack of any legal definition of JSPs prior to the 19th amendment of the RStV and the ambivalent wording of Art. 11 JMStV. They indicate that attempts to prescribe more detailed requirements in the JMStV failed in 2010 when the 14th Amendment to the RStV was not adopted.[2570] Since the initial wording of Art. 11 JMStV has been retained; there is a need for state media authorities (and ultimately the KJM) to specify the law.[2571] The KJM, in particular, has a margin of discretion in interpreting the terms stipulated in the RStV (especially, the terms "allow [for differentiated access]" and "in a similar manner").[2572] It is interesting to note that the 19th amendment to the RStV deleted the reference to "fulfil their function in a similar manner" and introduces a legal definition of JSPs. The KJM's leeway seems to have been limited in this respect.

### 2. Guidance drawn up by the Commission for the Protection of Minors

#### a) Criteria for supervision

The *Kriterien für die Aufsicht im Rundfunk und in den Telemedien* (criteria for the supervision of broadcasting and telemedia) published in December 2013 serve as a basis for the examination and assessment of content.[2573]

2568 Liesching, "Jugendschutzprogramme für 'ab 18'-Internetangebote," p. 370.

2569 Liesching thereby criticised the partial certification of two JSPs in February 2012. The initial certification by the KJM excluded the age group "18" which was suspended until June 2013. Liesching opines that the providers of the JSPs had a reasonable claim to full recognition of their JSP by the KJM. See Liesching, "Jugendschutzprogramme für 'ab 18'-Internetangebote," p. 370.

2570 Birgit Braml and Kristina Hopf, "Jugendschutzprogramme, Mehr Schutz für die Jugend oder mehr Sicherheit für den Anbieter?," *Zeitschrift für Urheber- und Medienrecht*, 2012, pp. 362, 364.

2571 Braml and Hopf, "Jugendschutzprogramme," p. 362.

2572 Braml and Hopf, "Jugendschutzprogramme," p. 363.

2573 KJM, "Kriterien für die Aufsicht im Rundfunk und in den Telemedien," December 2013, http://www.kjm-online.de/fileadmin/Download_KJM/Service/Pr%C3

The criteria specify the risks of harm in relation to different types of content and are designed to assist the KJM in conducting a balanced evaluation of the constitutionally protected conflicting fundamental rights on a case-by-case basis. In this respect, the criteria reflect the norms and values of society which are constantly in flux and thus make regular review of the criteria indispensable.[2574] By disclosing and explaining the KJM's approach, the latter also becomes more comprehensible and transparent.[2575] The unit which is being assessed comprises all individual elements of a telemedia (image, text, animation and sound) as well as the overall effect of the whole service offered via one outlet.[2576] This includes all additional windows (pop-ups or pop-unders) and content which is linked on the first level or on deeper link levels if it is apparent from the first level that age-inappropriate content is made accessible to minors.[2577]

The general yardstick for the KJM's assessment is whether an offer disturbs ("*beeinträchtigen*") or endangers ("*gefährden*") the development of minors into self-responsible and socially competent persons. It is thus necessary to determine the relevant age group(s) for which harm is likely to ensue from the relevant content.[2578] The differentiation between "*beeinträchtigen*" and "*gefährden*" which stems from Arts. 4 and 5 JMStV is not reproduced in the English translation of the JMStV which refers to the expressions "suited to impair" (i.e. *beeinträchtigen*) and "suited to seriously impair" (i.e. *gefährden*). According to the KJM, content which is "suited to impair" encompasses inhibitions, disturbances or damage of minors' development including anxiety or psychological destabilisation (individual dimension). In addition, impairment of minors is assumed if the constitutional principles and the fundamental social values (like respect for human dignity, principle of tolerance, protection of marriage and family, as well as democratic principles) are presented in such a way that they are no

%BCfkriterien/Kriterien_KJM_Fassung_Dezember_2013.pdf (accessed 29.6.2016), herinafter JMStV supervision criteria.

2574 KJM, "JMStV supervision criteria," para. A 1, p. 2.

2575 KJM, "JMStV supervision criteria," para. A 1, p. 2.

2576 KJM, "JMStV supervision criteria," para. A 2, p. 3.

2577 KJM, "JMStV supervision criteria," para. A 2, p. 3.

2578 KJM, "JMStV supervision criteria," para. B 1, p. 4.

longer discernible and cannot be assimilated by minors (social dimension).[2579]

By contrast, the formulation "suited to seriously impair" implies a stronger negative effect on the development of minors. Since the JMStV is silent on its precise meaning, the KJM draws inspiration from the JuSchG. Accordingly, this term covers "immoral and brutalising content (...) instigating violence, crime and racism" as well as "presentation in detail of acts of violence, murder and massacre for their own purpose" and material which recommends self-justifying behaviour and vigilantism as the only means to obtain justice.[2580] Furthermore, the KJM outlines several factors which may enhance the potential of harm, distinguishing between recipient-specific and offer-specific factors. The former relate to the social context of the recipient, gender and age.[2581] The latter encompass the extent to which content is realistic, its link to daily life, the extent to which incentives are presented to identify with the actors or find orientation in their behaviour as well as the interactivity of a service.[2582]

It is noteworthy that the KJM details its assessment of violent and sexual content by a list of criteria which are accompanied by questions.[2583] Violence is defined as "physical and psychological or material damage to a person or a thing by subjects, natural catastrophes or accidents".[2584] In assessing the nature of the content, the KJM takes into account the context within which violence is presented, the expectations of recipients regarding the potential of violence and the plot and prevailing mood of an of-

---

2579 KJM, "JMStV supervision criteria," para. B 1, 4. Constitutional principles and fundamental social values include, for instance, respect for human dignity, principle of tolerance, protection of marriage and family or the democratic principle.

2580 See the second sentence of Art. 18 (1) JuSchG.

2581 KJM, "JMStV supervision criteria," para. B 2, pp. 5–7.

2582 KJM, "JMStV supervision criteria," para. B 2, pp. 7–9.

2583 The document also refers to criteria in relation to self-responsibility (Eigenverantwortung) and the ability to live in a community (Gemeinschaftsfähigkeit) as two values of the development of minors which are expressly referred to in Art. 5 (1) JMStV. These include criteria/questions regarding the issues of structural violence, discrimination, ideological, religious and political extremitism, ethical aspects and risk behaviour (para. B 2.3, p. 18-23). In addition, the KJM sets out criteria concerning the protection of minors in advertising and teleshopping (para. B 2.4, p. 24-30). These are not discussed in detail here as they are only of secondary nature for this research. See KJM, "JMStV supervision criteria.".

2584 KJM, "JMStV supervision criteria," para. B 2.1, p. 9.

fer.[2585] In addition, it looks at the forms of violence both, in individual scenes as well as in context appraising the quantity of violent presentations within the overall offer, their quality (i.e. kinds of violence), their relevance for the world of minors as well as the intensity of violence (i.e. the degree of brutality, the degree of detail of the presentation).[2586] What is also taken into consideration is whether the consequences of violence are portrayed (i.e. injuries, pain, anguish or suffering) and the level of suspense (whether suspense is maintained throughout the story or whether it is focussed on individual scenes).[2587] Moreover, the assessment encompasses incentives for recipients to identify with subjects (who exerts violence?) or objects of violence (who is subjected to violence?) leading to legitimisation of violence or inclusion of violent activities in minors' repertoire of actions.[2588] Finally, the KJM evaluates how violence is portrayed within the offer (e.g. whether it is legitimated, whether it is sanctioned or whether it undermines social norms) and how it is stage-managed (e.g. whether violence is presented directly, expressly and in detail or whether it is merely indicated or presented in an artificial and estranging manner by dramaturgical effects or other editorial tools).[2589]

The second pertinent issue is erotic presentations and depictions of sexuality which are defined as "sexual acts or sexual poses associated with the former below the threshold of pornography".[2590] The criteria of sexuality primarily concern offers in which sexuality is dealt with visually and/or verbally (e.g. feature-length films, magazines, talk shows, websites, pop-ups containing advertisements, download of videos, social networks).[2591] Similar to presentations of violence, sexual content is assessed in context. The intention of the presentation is to be taken into account to appraise potential harm. Sexual material may have an educating or informing character or solely serve the sexual stimulation and arousal or

2585 KJM, "JMStV supervision criteria," para. B 2.1, pp. 9–10.
2586 KJM, "JMStV supervision criteria," para. B 2.1, pp. 10–11.
2587 KJM, "JMStV supervision criteria," para. B 2.1, pp. 11–12. In relation to the level of suspense, the KJM points out that minors perceive a film in individual scenes rather than in overall context. This is why the effect of problematic scenes is to be specifically weighted.
2588 KJM, "JMStV supervision criteria," para. B 2.1, pp. 12–13.
2589 KJM, "JMStV supervision criteria," para. B 2.1, p. 14.
2590 KJM, "JMStV supervision criteria," para. B 2.2, p. 15.
2591 KJM, "JMStV supervision criteria," para. B 2.2, p. 15.

users.[2592] Importantly, the KJM outlines content-related characteristics as well as structural characteristics of the presentation of sexuality. Content-related characteristics imply the perspective used to depict sexuality (whether the presentations correspond to the state of development of minors or whether they presuppose a wealth of experience), how promiscuity and prostitution are portrayed (whether they are played down or idealised), which gender roles are represented by the offer (whether stereotypes are upheld, whether one sex is discriminated or shown as servile or presented as sexual partner without own character) and which kind of language is used (whether language is sexualised or vulgar, whether sexist or racial statements are made or whether unusual sexual practices are praised or propagated).[2593]

Above all, the KJM looks at whether sexuality is combined with violence. Offers which contain depictions of spanking (e.g. simulated flogging of students by their teachers) or sexual activities of youthful looking female actresses with multiple male partners including light or indicated violent actions are considered harmful to minors and are typically only permissible in telemedia.[2594] Sadomasochistic offers containing bizarre sexual practices (such as cutting or breath restriction) have similar detrimental effects as minors frequently do not discern their dangerous character.[2595] With regards to the formal presentation of sexuality, the KJM evaluates, *inter alia*, whether it is explicitly portrayed or merely implicitly or whether it is emphasised within the overall offer by the way it is edited (for example whether it is shown in slow-motion or in close-up). In telemedia, such emphasis can be given by pop-ups depicting pixelated sexual images.

Apart from the specifications made in relation to content which may be harmful or seriously harmful, the KJM sets out its interpretation of illegal content, in particular, the notion of pornography. Material which is modestly pornographic within the meaning of Art. 4 (2) No. 1 JMStV may be made accessible in telemedia. The KJM underlines that the notion of pornography by virtue of the JMStV corresponds to the notion of pornography pursuant to German criminal law.[2596] Reciting the definition of

2592 KJM, "JMStV supervision criteria," para. B 2.2, p. 15.
2593 KJM, "JMStV supervision criteria," para. B 2.2, pp. 16–17.
2594 KJM, "JMStV supervision criteria," para. B 2.2, p. 16.
2595 KJM, "JMStV supervision criteria," para. B 2.2, p. 16.
2596 KJM, "JMStV supervision criteria," para. C 2, p. 34.

pornography from established case law (see above), the KJM makes several clarifications. In terms of content, a decpiction is pornographic if its sole purpose is the attainment of pleasure and sexual lust, the reduction to impersonal sexuality as well as the degradation of a person to a replaceable object.[2597] Thus, the KJM investigates whether the fiction conveys an image of an inexhaustible potency and tireless capacity for devotion of the participants who are sex objects available at any time.[2598] Aspects like the constant change of anonymous sex partners and the intention of the presentation for the purpose of sexual arousal are being taken into account by the KJM. Similarly, the KJM assesses whether the depiction exceeds the limits of socially accepted values.[2599] Thus, a violation of human dignity is probable when sexual acts correlate with violent applications.[2600]

In terms of form, pornography means an overly clear and detailed depiction of sexual acts that is conveyed in an unaltered and obtrusive manner.[2601] The proportion of sexual sequences in relation to the overall duration of the offer can be indicative of its pornographic nature.[2602] Thus, the overall tendency of the offer is decisive.[2603] The KJM also considers whether sexual presentations are tied without context or lacking any narrative[2604] and to what extent the camera work contributes to an overly clear and detailed depiction of sexual acts (e.g. by its position, perspective or other settings).[2605] The KJM makes clear that the focus on genitalia (for instance by zooms) is not determinative on its own and it also clarifies that

2597 KJM, "JMStV supervision criteria," para. C 2, p. 34.

2598 KJM, "JMStV supervision criteria," para. C 2, p. 35. The KJM also refers to a "physiologisches Reiz-Reaktionswesen", implying the reduction to a being that only reacts to bodily stimulus.

2599 KJM, "JMStV supervision criteria," para. C 2, p. 35. The KJM acknowledges that social values are subject to change. It nonetheless refers to the existence of a minimum consensus (encompassing, for example fundamental values of the German GG). A presentation is assumed to be pronographic if it contradicts said minimum consensus.

2600 KJM, "JMStV supervision criteria," para. C 2, p. 35.

2601 KJM, "JMStV supervision criteria," para. C 2, p. 34.

2602 KJM, "JMStV supervision criteria," para. C 2, p. 35.

2603 KJM, "JMStV supervision criteria," para. C 2, p. 36.

2604 KJM, "JMStV supervision criteria," para. C 2, p. 36. The KJM outlines a rule of thumb: the less a presentation has a narrative, the more it is pornographic.

2605 KJM, "JMStV supervision criteria," para. C 2, p. 36.

the dominance of coarse language including groans may underline the pornographic tendency of an offer.[2606]

In brief, the criteria outlined by the KJM clarify the latter's method of assessment of content which might raise issues in relation to the protection of minors. These are very comprehensive with regards to the issues they cover as well as detailed with regards to the explanations they provide. To this end, the criteria are a useful tool and make the KJM's assessment more transparent. They are especially valuable with regards to the specifications concerning the notion of pornography. Yet, the criteria are formulated openly so that the KJM principally refrains from taking final positions or making definite statements. This is not surprising as the criteria constitute guidelines which are applied on a case-by-case basis. Nonetheless, more clarity would have been desirable with regards to the distinction *beeinträchtigen/gefährden.* The dichotomy between content which is "suited to impair" and content which is "evidently suited to seriously impair" remains blurry. It can only be implicitly deduced from the criteria and questions what content would fall in which category. This distinction is, however, crucial as it entails different legal consequences depending on the characterisation of content. Hence, content providers must be aware of the slippery slope on which they find themselves. In general, the approach of the KJM is to be welcomed and the criteria should be regularly reviewed.

#### b) Criteria for technical tools to protect minors

##### (aa) Age verification

As a service to providers, the KJM assesses age verification systems (AVS) and other concepts upon request (in a so-called *Positivbewertung*). This collaboration with the industry, was introduced by the 19th amendment to the RStV amending the JMStV and is intended to enhance legal certainty and improve business planning for providers.[2607] Notwithstanding the KJM's assistance, the service or content provider retains sole re-

2606 KJM, "JMStV supervision criteria," para. C 2, pp. 36–37.
2607 Third to fifth sentence of Art. 5 (2) JMStV.

sponsibility for complying with the JMStV.[2608] In order to facilitate the KJM's evaluation of providers' measures and in order to enhance transparency and define standards in light of the current state of technology, the KJM published criteria relating to AVS for closed user groups in September 2014.[2609] This assessment grid, which is subject to periodic refinements, requires a two-step protection measure in line with the JuSchRiL.[2610] It generally distinguishes between modules (partial solution) and concepts (overall solution). Providers may, for instance, select different solutions (which have been positively assessed by the KJM) using the modular principle.[2611] An AVS also constitutes a module, the central element, if used.[2612] In addition, a comprehensive concept (*übergreifendes Konzept*) implies an AVS within the meaning of the second sentence of Art. 4 (2) JMStV which can also be employed as a technical measure pursuant to Art. 5 (3) No. 1 JMStV.[2613]

The criteria are contingent on the kind of access granted to users. Those applicable to one-off access, giving users a so-called one-off key (*Einmalschlüssel*) are lower than those allowing users repeated access (*Generalschlüssel*) granting access to a great amount of different offers which justifies higher access hurdles.[2614] With regards to concepts permitting access once only, the KJM requires that providers verify with great probability that the user has reached the age of majority.[2615] Such verification can be undertaken by means of the electronic ID as included in the new *Personalausweis*.[2616] In addition, an online inspection which identifies the user via a webcam is possible under the condition that the user is recognised

2608 KJM, "Kriterien zur Bewertung von Konzepten für Altersverifikationssysteme," 2014, p. 2, http://www.kjm-online.de/fileadmin/Download_KJM/Telemedien/KJM-AVS-Raster.pdf (accessed 28.7.2015), hereinafter Criteria age verification systems.

2609 KJM, "Criteria age verification systems," p. 3.

2610 KJM, "Criteria age verification systems," p. 1.

2611 KJM, "Criteria age verification systems," p. 2.

2612 KJM, "Criteria age verification systems," p. 3.

2613 KJM, "Criteria age verification systems," p. 3.

2614 KJM, "Criteria age verification systems," p. 5.

2615 This is called Plausibilitätsprüfung. See KJM, "Criteria age verification systems," p. 3.

2616 On the suitability of the electronic ID for purposes of age verification, see Karsten Altenhain, "Altersverifikation mittels des elektronischen Personalausweises," *Kommunikation und Recht*, no. 10 (2009): pp. 619–25. Altenhain posits that the electronic identity card which entails an electronic proof of iden-

by trained staff and the image quality is sufficient.[2617] It must, moreover, be ensured that circumvention methods like playing a film or using a mask are excluded.[2618] If doubts arise about the user's age, for example on account of his or her outward appearance, his or her conduct or statements, the ID document is to be checked from both sides.[2619] However, the mere checking of the ID or passport number ("*Perso-Check*"-procedure) or the presentation of a (certified) copy thereof is insufficient.[2620]

Furthermore, concepts for repeated access rely on two steps. Following a one-off identification, the user receives a master key for all subsequent uses. Thus, a personal identification including a reliable verification of the user's age is crucial as a first step. The KJM requires a face-to-face con-

---

tity introduced in Germany in November 2010 satisfies the criteria of an age verification system under Art. 4 (2) JMStV. He acknowledges the fact that age would not be verified according to a two-stage model but considers that the requirements put in place for the use of the electronic identity card are very strict and do not offer any obvious possibilities of abuse (p. 622). Only when the electronic proof of identity would be easily manipulable would it no longer serve as suitable age verification system (p. 623). Altenhain stresses that new identification technologies should be promoted in view of technology-open regulation (p. 622) and their adequacy as age verification systems should be discussed seriously.

2617 KJM, "Criteria age verification systems," p. 4.

2618 KJM, "Criteria age verification systems," p. 4.

2619 KJM, "Criteria age verification systems," p. 4.

2620 In 2009, the KJM also drew up criteria for technical measures concerning the age groups 16 and 18 in line with Art. 5 (3) No. 1 JMStV. In comparison to the requirements imposed on AVS for closed user groups, these are less detailed. The KJM underlines that age must be convincingly verified on the basis of plausible indicators. The (electronic) provision of the number of an ID or passport (Perso-Check) is generally considered appropriate. If the service is accessed more than once, additional requirements apply such as the delivery of access data by regular mail or temporary codes send by email and the existence of measures to prevent circumvention and abuse by prohibiting parallel use of access data. In addition, auto-complete or auto-login functions of browsers have to be disabled. See KJM, "Kriterien für technische Mittel als Jugendschutzmaßnahme für entwicklungsbeeinträchtigende Inhalte im Bereich des World Wide Web: Stichwort „Personalausweiskennziffernprüfung/„Persocheckverfahren"," 2009, http://www.kjm-online.de/fileadmin/Download_KJM/Rundfunk/Kriterienraster_technische_Mittel.pdf; see also the overview of positively assessed technical measures, see KJM, "Übersicht über positiv bewertete Konzepte für technische Mittel," 2015, http://www.kjm-online.de/fileadmin/Download_KJM/Rundfunk/Uebersicht_technische_Mittel.pdf (all websites accessed 30.3.2016).

trol which comprises the identification in the presence of the user by means of official documents (ID, passport).[2621] This identity check can be carried out at the post office (*Postident* procedure)[2622] or through comparable methods. In contrast to one-off access systems, the KJM generally rejects identification through video transmission unless further security measures have been taken in line with the 2014 circular of the *Bundesanstalt für Finanzdienstleistungsaufsicht* (BaFin, Federal Financial Supervisory Authority).[2623] What is more, reference can be made to previous processes of identification under certain circumstances. This option relates to previously consumed services or previously concluded contracts.[2624] The process of identification encompasses further steps. Following the user's ini-

---

2621 KJM, "Criteria age verification systems," p. 6.

2622 On the legal questions in relation to the Postident procedure, see Mirko Möller, "Rechtsfragen im Zusammenhang mit dem Postident-Verfahren," *Neue Juristische Wochenschrift*, 2005, pp. 1605–9.

2623 The circular specifies the meaning of the formulation "not personally present" as contained in Art. 6 (2) No. 2 GwG (*Gesetz über das Aufspüren von Gewinnen aus schweren Straftagen, Geldwäschegesetz*). The BaFin requires, inter alia, that staff conducting the inspection is appropriately trained and that the conversation between the personnel and the user is recorded. Photos or screenshots have to be created which clearly show the user as well as the front and reverse of the ID document. As proof of identification, the BaFin only accepts identity documents "featuring optical safety features which are equivalent to holographic images". These safety features have to be verified by staff members to determine the authenticity of the document (e.g. requiring the user to tilt the document horizontally or vertically in front of the camera and obliging staff members to check that the document's liminated cover is intact and no image has been glued onto it). The identity process must immediately be cancelled if light conditions or image quality are poor or verbal communication is not possible. Importantly, during the video transmission, the person who is to be identified must "enter online a valid sequence of numbers (TAN) which is specifically produced for this purpose, is centrally generated and is delivered to this person (by email or SMS) and must return this to the staff member electronically. See Bundesanstalt für Finanzdienstleistungsaufsicht, "Rundschreiben 1/2014 (GW) – Verdachtsmeldung Nach §§ 11, 14 GwG," 2014, para. III, available at http://www.bafin.de/SharedDocs/Veroeffentlichungen/DE/Rundschreiben/rs_1401_gw_verwaltungspraxis_vm.html. For an English version of the circular see http://www.bafin.de/SharedDocs/Veroeffentlichungen/EN/Rundschreiben/rs_1401_gw_verwaltungspraxis_vm_en.html (accessed 17.3.2016).

2624 This includes, for instance, contracts concluded for mobile phones or bank accounts or alternatively, the use of communications services like eID (electronic identification function of the German *Personalausweis*) or DE-mail (an e-mail service offered by the German *Post*). See KJM, "Criteria Age Verification Sys-

tial identification, the data of the identified user (including date of birth, name and address) have to be registered and stored.[2625] These data are then processed (online or offline) from the point[2626] where the user was identified to the service provider.[2627] Access to the service can only be granted when the provider of the AVS has received the data which identify the user and has checked the user's age.[2628] If identification took place in advance, access data ought to be sent by registered letter or by similar means which ensure that only the person identified receives the data.[2629]

In a second step, the user must be authenticated before each session (i.e. each time the user accesses the service). Typically, this is ensured by a special password that is individually allocated.[2630] The rationale of authentication is to prevent the multiplication of access data or its passing on to unauthorised third parties.[2631] The KJM outlines two approaches. First, technical measures may be taken that include authentication by means of biometric data (fingerprints or iris recognition) registered in advance,[2632] active (e.g. ID-Chip, SIM card) and passive hardware (e.g. passive chip cards, DVD, CD-ROM),[2633] one-time PINs or through a query of the processor ID of the user's computer.[2634] Apart from technical tools, other

---

tems", p. 6. Importantly, the KJM underlines that the checking of ID or passport number (so-called *Perso-Check*) or (certified) copies thereof are insufficient.

2625 KJM, "Criteria age verification systems," p. 7.

2626 The KJM requires from points where users can be identified that identification procedures are part of their economic activity which is carried out by reliable and trained staff. See KJM, "Criteria age verification systems," p. 7.

2627 The data can either directly be supplied to the service provider or a reference can be forwarded to the latter. See KJM, "Criteria age verification systems," p. 7.

2628 If access data are not personally handed to the user or automatically generated during the process of identification, they are to be delivered subsequently. In this situation, it must be secured that access data are exclusively given to the person identified as of age. See KJM, "Criteria age verification systems," p. 7.

2629 KJM, "Criteria age verification systems," p. 8. The anonymous delivery of access data (by email or bank statements) does not meet the requirements imposed by the KJM.

2630 KJM, "Criteria age verification systems," p. 9.

2631 KJM, "Criteria age verification systems," p. 9.

2632 KJM, "Criteria age verification systems," p. 9.

2633 KJM, "Criteria age verification systems," pp. 9–10. In case of passive hardware (which can only store and not process information), the KJM points out that these require copy protection.

2634 KJM, "Criteria age verification systems," p. 10.

measures may be employed which aim at reducing risks attributed to the sphere of the user. More precisely, the risk of the user forwarding personal access data to non-identified persons is minimised by maximising the user's (pecuniary and immaterial) disadvantages ensuing from such behaviour.[2635] Importantly, the user has to be informed about the consequences in terms of costs and/or in relation to the disclosure of personal data.[2636]

In sum, the KJM specifies in-depth the criteria for closed user groups flowing from the second sentence of Art. 4 (2) JMStV. By requiring a two-step protection scheme that encompasses identification and authentication, the KJM does not deviate from its original approach (adopted when the JMStV entered into force) which has been confirmed by the German courts. The insistence on a strict and rigid[2637] two-step procedure presents high hurdles in practice which may even have a deterring effect.[2638] Since 2003, the KJM has positively assessed 15 modules, 24 concepts and 6 overall concepts.[2639] Liesching is especially critical of the KJM's interpretation of the provision contained in the JMStV. The second sentence of Art. 4 (2) JMStV is ambivalent and merely postulates in an abstract manner that the provider is obliged to *ensure* that seriously harmful content is accessible to adults only.[2640] According to Liesching, a general standard should be formulated removed from the present technical state in order to

2635 KJM, "Criteria age verification systems," p. 11.

2636 The user may, for example be charged huge amounts of money and/or third parties may gain access to the most personal and private areas of life and may unilaterally alter personal data, health data or information on payment transactions. See KJM, "Criteria Age Verification Systems," 11.

2637 Berger, "Jugendschutz im Internet: „Geschlossene Benutzergruppen" nach § 4 Abs. 2 Satz 2 JMStV – Am Beispiel personalausweiskennziffergestützter Altersverifikationssysteme," p. 777; Sellmann, "K&R Kommentar," p. 368.

2638 Holtmann, *Zur rechtlichen Unterscheidung von Rundfunk und Telemedien bei Hybrid-TV*, p. 161; Köhne, "Jugendmedienschutz durch Alterskontrollen im Internet," p. 795; Liesching, "'Sicherstellung' des Erwachsenenzugangs bei pornografischen und sonst jugendgefährdenden Telemedien," p. 804.

2639 KJM, "Übersicht über positiv bewertete Konzepte für geschlossene Benutzergruppen," 2015, http://www.kjm-online.de/fileadmin/Download_KJM/Telemedien/AVS_Uebersicht.pdf; see also the overview of currently six übergreifende Konzepte (comprehensive concepts) which have been assessed positively by the KJM available at http://www.kjm-online.de/telemedien/uebergreifende-konzepte.html (accessed 16.3.2016).

2640 Liesching, "'Sicherstellung' des Erwachsenenzugangs bei pornografischen und sonst jugendgefährdenden Telemedien," p. 807.

accommodate future developments more easily.[2641] Such standards should focus on preventing strategies of abuse, circumvention or manipulations for all relevant processes of the system.[2642] In a similar vein, Sellmann underscores that the impact of the strict requirements for age verification is constrained because minors can access comparable offers hosted on foreign websites without obstruction.[2643] Yet, this argument, which has also been rejected by the German courts, fails to see that the addressees of the rule stipulated by the JMStV are providers located within German jurisdiction. These cannot be given a *carte blanche* in relation to AVS for the sole reason that foreign providers face more lenient requirements.[2644]

#### (bb) Jugendschutzprogramme

While the KJM itself has devised a system of positive assessment for AVS and technical measures, Art. 11 (1) JMStV makes certification of JSPs mandatory. Lacking a precise legal definition of a JSP in the JMStV (before entry into force of the 19th RStV), the KJM drew up criteria in May 2011 that are accompanied by a one-page summary of expectations of providers and measures of May 2013 as well as a short information leaflet for content providers in the form of FAQ of June 2014.[2645] The criteria es-

2641 Liesching, "'Sicherstellung' des Erwachsenenzugangs bei pornografischen und sonst jugendgefährdenden Telemedien," p. 804.

2642 Liesching points out that the two-steps are imprecise and that in fact four different phases can be distinguished: first, identification and verification of age; second, delivery of access data to the user who has been identified as aged over 18; third, granting access to the user and fourth, the prevention of disclosure or multiplication of access data. Interestingly, the KJM alludes to these phases in its assessment grid (p. 6-7). See Liesching, "'Sicherstellung' des Erwachsenenzugangs bei pornografischen und sonst jugendgefährdenden Telemedien," pp. 804–5.

2643 Sellmann, "K&R Kommentar," p. 368.

2644 Döring and Günter, "Alterskontrollierte geschlossene Benutzergruppen," p. 236; Liesching, "Anforderungen an Altersverifikationssysteme," p. 395.

2645 KJM, "Kriterien für die Anerkennung von Jugendschutzprogrammen im Bereich des World Wide Web," May 2011, http://www.kjm-online.de/fileadmin/Download_KJM/Rundfunk/Informationen-fr-JSP-Anbieter_Stand_2011-05-11.pdf; KJM, hereinafter Criteria for JSPs, "Jugendschutzprogramme nach § 11 JMStV, Erwartungen an Anbieter und Maßnahmen der KJM," May 2013, http://www.kjm-online.de/fileadmin/Bilder/Presse/Pressemitteilungen/KJM-PM_04_2013_Jugendschutzprogramme_Anlage.pdf; KJM, "FAQ „Anerkannte Jugendschutzpro-

tablished in 2011 accommodate the experiences from the initial phase of pilot schemes starting with the adoption of the JMStV as well as the evaluation of the JMStV of 2007[2646] and pick up elements discussed during the failed reform of 2010.[2647] Thus, six non-exhaustive criteria are enumerated on the basis of the present state of technology. In light of technological and other developments, the criteria may be adapted or refined.[2648] In addition, the KJM lists the information providers are required to supply to the KJM and gives recommendations in view of certain issues.

The first criterion relates to the autonomy of parents and guardians to install and activate JSPs which allow for differentiated access according to age groups.[2649] By user-autonomy, the KJM understands the possibility for parents to switch off the filters or configure them by adding Internet websites which should either be accessible or blocked.[2650] JSPs should thus be flexibly adjustable to both, the state of development of minors and the style of parenting.[2651] This criterion will be assessed by written documentation (including a detailed description of the JSP and the platforms and operating systems on which it runs) as well as a test installation or license of a JSP which is ready for the market (including an interface for efficiency tests).[2652] As a corollary of user-autonomy, the JSP must be user-friendly in order to encourage more widespread use.[2653] According to the KJM, user-friendliness implies easy handling of the technology by users as well as reasonable costs. Acceptance and use of JSPs on a huge scale will only be realistic if parents' efforts for obtaining, installing, administering and configuring are kept low.[2654] In particular, the KJM examines whether the JSP is fully operative on indicated platforms, whether the filters are kept

---

gramme" für Inhalteanbieter," June 2014, http://www.kjm-online.de/fileadmin/Download_KJM/Rundfunk/FAQ_Jugendschutzprogramme_Inhalteanbieter.pdf (all websites accessed 15.3.2016.

2646 See Hans Bredow Institut, ed., "Analyse des Jugendmedienschutzsystems, Jugendschutzgesetz und Jugendmedienschutz-Staatsvertrag, Endbericht," October 2007, http://www.hans-bredow-institut.de/webfm_send/104 (accessed 15.3.2016).

2647 Braml and Hopf, "Jugendschutzprogramme," p. 365.

2648 KJM, "Criteria for JSPs," p. 1.

2649 KJM, "Criteria for JSPs," p. 1.

2650 KJM, "Criteria for JSPs," p. 1.

2651 Braml and Hopf, "Jugendschutzprogramme," p. 365.

2652 KJM, "Criteria for JSPs," p. 1.

2653 KJM, "Criteria for JSPs," p. 1.

2654 Braml and Hopf, "Jugendschutzprogramme," p. 365.

up-to-date, whether the JSP is easy to manage and to what extent it burdens parents financially.[2655] Above all, the KJM evaluates whether JSPs remain unaffected by simple circumvention strategies employed by minors (for example whether JSPs can be de-installed without passwords or whether they can be de-activated by the task manager).[2656] In this context, the KJM recommends that JSPs are offered free of charge[2657] and that minors should be adequately informed about the blocking of unsuitable content, for instance by using age-appropriate language rather than scolding them.[2658] Moreover, the KJM recommends that the default settings of JSPs should be favourable to parents and allow them to rapidly accomplish an effective level of protection for each age group.[2659] With the adoption of the 19th RStV, the criteria of user-friendly and user-autonomous have been included in Art. 11 (1) JMStV.

Importantly, the KJM requires that JSPs are effective. Since over- and under-blocking are still a reality, JSPs which reliably block 80 percent of unsuitable content are considered effective.[2660] In practice, jugendschutz.net,[2661] an organisation which is linked to the KJM, is tasked with

---

2655 KJM, "Criteria for JSPs," pp. 1–2.

2656 KJM, "Criteria for JSPs," p. 2.

2657 Braml and Hopf, "Jugendschutzprogramme," p. 365.

2658 KJM, "Criteria for JSPs," p. 2.

2659 KJM, "Criteria for JSPs," p. 2.

2660 KJM, "Criteria for JSPs," p. 2; see also Braml and Hopf, "Jugendschutzprogramme," p. 366.

2661 Jugendschutz.net has also supported the KJM in the enforcement of the rules contained in the JMStV. It has taken action against providers of illegal content as prescribed by Art. 4 (1) JMStV (mostly hardcore pornography) by barring the respective host providers from supplying their services. The organisation has also sought contact with the payments industry (Visa, Mastercard) to discuss whether the processing of payments to websites offering illegal content could be stopped. The operators of payment services have reacted positively to the suggestion of jugendschutz.net as they do not want to be associated with illegal activities which are contradictory to their business philosophy and may be damaging to their reputation. In addition, jugendschutz.net has accomplished the deletion of so-called "tasteless-sites" (defined as websites which feature tasteless content ranging from harmless material to material which disrespects human dignity and depicts persons dying or suffering for the purpose of users' entertainment and amusement. This initiative was supported by the self-commitment of access and backbone Internet providers that voluntarily barred providers of such websites. See also Günter and Schindler, "Technische Möglichkeiten des Jugendschutzes im Internet," pp. 342–43.

overseeing and evaluating the effectiveness of certified JSPs.[2662] In its assessment, the KJM takes into account whether content indexed by the BPjM is effectively blocked and whether parents may block material which was not labelled by content providers. Furthermore, JSPs must allow for differentiated access according to age groups pursuant to Art. 11 (1) JMStV. This implies that JSPs correctly analyse age classifications and implement blocking of content according to age groups.[2663] At a minimum, a JSP must recognise the age groups "below 12", "12-16" and "16-18" years and activate appropriate content for all age groups.[2664] In this respect, the KJM recommends that JSPs rely on whitelists (e.g. FragFinn) for minors under 12 years so that all non-classified content is blocked by default. Regarding the age groups 12-16 years and 16 years and older, JSPs should function on the basis of blacklists making available all non-classified content is available by default.[2665]

In addition, JSPs should include simple notification functions for content or offers which were incorrectly blocked or distributed.[2666] Moreover, JSPs must be designed in such a way to adjust to future technological developments.[2667] Providers of JSPs thus are required to continue to develop the technology and annually report on their activities and achievements.[2668] Finally, the KJM posits that protection of minors will only be effectively achieved if JSPs are widespread and widely used by parents.[2669] It thus asks JSP providers to supply concepts about how distribu-

---

2662 See http://www.jugendschutz.net/ (accessed 16.3.2016). See also KJM, "JSP, Expectations and measures"; On the role of jugendschutz.net see Günter and Schindler, "Technische Möglichkeiten des Jugendschutzes im Internet," p. 341; Braml and Hopf, "Jugendschutzprogramme," p. 366.

2663 KJM, "Criteria for JSPs," p. 3.

2664 KJM, "Criteria for JSPs," p. 3; see also Braml and Hopf, "Jugendschutzprogramme," p. 366; the FAQ addressed to content providers are also concerned with labelling. They encourage content providers to voluntarily label their content by using, for instance, label generators (available at FSK Online, USK Online) or questionnaire-based self-classification (available at FSM). The FAQ make clear that content providers benefit from voluntary labelling as as convenient method to comply with the JMStV. KJM, "FAQ JSP.".

2665 KJM, "Criteria for JSPs," pp. 3–4.

2666 KJM, "Criteria for JSPs," p. 4.

2667 KJM, "Criteria for JSPs," p. 4.

2668 KJM, "Criteria for JSPs," p. 4; see also Braml and Hopf, "Jugendschutzprogramme," p. 367.

2669 KJM, "Criteria for JSPs," p. 4.

tion and use of JSPs can be increased.[2670] Beyond its legal mandate, the KJM itself cultivates a regular exchange with providers of certified JSPs and publicly promotes their enhanced use.[2671] These activities of the industry as well as the regulator to raise awareness are essential as public recognition of JSPs is very low. In 2012, a study by Hasebrink, Schröder and Schumacher found that merely 16 percent of parents use JSPs.[2672] Both, the KJM and jugendschutz.net underlined in their annual reports that the filters do not yet live up to their expectations.[2673] Although they appear relatively reliable in relation to the detection of sexualised content, they fail to recognise material containing violence, hatred, self-endangering and other risks.[2674]

To date, the KJM has certified four JSPs, two in February 2012 and two in March 2015.[2675] The small number of certified JSPs may be indicative of the strict requirements imposed on providers of JSPs. The KJM has developed detailed criteria for the assessment of the suitability of youth protection software. These exceed the letter of Art. 11 JMStV but are necessary to ensure that interferences with rights and freedoms of others are

2670 KJM, "Criteria for JSPs," p. 4.

2671 KJM, "JSP, Expectations and measures.".

2672 Uwe Hasebrink, Hermann-Dieter Schröder, and Gerlinde Schumacher, "Kinder- und Jugendmedienschutz aus der Sicht der Eltern," *Media Perspektiven*, no. 1 (2012): pp. 25–26; in a different study, 25 percent of parents indicated that they used JSP at the level of Internet access. Frauenhofer-Institut für Intelligente Analyse- und Informationssysteme (IAIS), ed., "Studie zum technischen Jugendmedienschutz, Möglichkeiten und Grenzen von Verfahren zur Detektion jugendschutzrelevanter Web-Inhalte," 2012, p. 43, http://www.iais.fraunhofer.de/uploads/media/Fraunhofer_Jugendmedienschutz_2013-02-25_01.pdf; see also the two HBI studies on parents' knowledge, expectations and use of youth protection software Stephan Dreyer et al., "Jugendschutzsoftware im Elternhaus: Kenntnisse, Erwartungen und Nutzung, Arbeitspapier Nr. 23," ed. Hans Bredow Institut, January 2012, http://www.hans-bredow-institut.de/webfm_send/639 (all websites accessed 5.3.2016).

2673 KJM, "Sixth activities report," p. 63; jugendschutz.net, "Protection of Minors on the Internet, Annual Report 2014," 2015, p. 13, http://www.jugendschutz.net/fileadmin/download/pdf/Annual-report-2014.pdf (accessed 5.3.2016).

2674 Schindler, "Technische Möglichkeiten des Jugendschutzes im Internet," p. 136.

2675 See the list of certified JSPs at http://www.kjm-online.de/telemedien/jugendschutzprogramme.html (accessed 17.3.2016).

minimised. Most of the criteria appear reasonable,[2676] like the usability of JSPs, their effectiveness and capacity to recognise content targeted at different age groups. Importantly, JSPs must integrate software up-dates to react to technological developments. This is reflected by the amendment to Art. 11 (1) inserted by the 19th RStV which now refers to JSPs as corresponding to the state of technology. Yet, the obligation to design concepts and take measures which increase the spread as well as use of JSPs seem exaggerated. Higher market penetration of JSPs depends on numerous aspects such as media literacy and the social acceptance of filter software, factors that providers of JSPs can only partly influence (if at all). The fact that the four JSPs had initially been certified under certain conditions may be an expression of the difficulty of meeting the criteria. It certainly demonstrates that the KJM is conscious of its responsibility under the JMStV by conducting in-depth and repeated evaluations of the adequacy of JSPs (even if certified).

### 3. The measures taken by the Voluntary Self-Monitoring of Multimedia Service Providers

In parallel to the KJM which supervises compliance with the JMStV acting as the central organ in conjunction with the competent state media authority, several organisations of voluntary self-regulation have been certified.[2677] The *Freiwillige Selbstkontrolle Multimedia Dienste e.V.* (Voluntary Self-Monitoring of Multimedia Service Providers, FSM), a registered non-profit association (*eingetragener Verein*) with more than 40 regular members, among them Deutsche Telekom, Discovery Germany, Google,

2676 The 19th amendment to the RStV entered into force on 1 October 2016, amending, inter alia, the JMStV. Art. 11 JMStV has been modified, setting forth more explicit requirements for JSPs: In addition to differentiated access by age groups (a requirement stipulated currently by Art. 11 (3) JMStV), these would have to be user-friendly and allow for autonomous use by parents and guardians. Moreover, JSPs would have to correspond to the state of technology and be reliable in recognising respective age groups. These requirements mirror the criteria established by the KJM.

2677 On the broadcasting market, the FSF has been certified since 2003. With regards to telemedia, the FSM was accredited in 2004 by the KJM which certified two further organisations in 2011: FSK.online and USK.online. See also Art. 14 (2) JMStV and Art. 16 No. 2 JMStV in conjunction with Art. 19 JMStV.

Facebook, Microsoft Germany, Vodafone, Yahoo and YouNow is committed to the protection of minors in telemedia.[2678] Members of FSM voluntarily subscribe to a code of conduct which sets standards for the protection of minors in various areas, such as search engines, chats, mobile communications, social communities and teletext.[2679] Moreover, the FSM also widely promotes media education for parents and children alike and offers targeted services to both.[2680] It also runs a system of age classification free of charge whereby providers may "calculate" the respective age label on the basis of an online questionnaire.[2681] As detailed in chapter three, members of recognised organisations benefit from a privileged status under the scheme of regulated self-regulation. In case of an offense (other than a breach of Art. 4 (1) JMStV concerning absolutely illegal content), the KJM and the respective state media authority can only initiate legal steps if the self-control body has exceeded "its legal discretionary power with its decision or lack thereof".[2682] The measures taken by the FSM, the oldest registered industry body in Germany, in relation to the protection of minors online are interesting to this study and serve as an illustration of the activities of self-regulatory bodies. The following section is devoted, in particular, to the *Prüfgrundsätze* (assessment principles) elaborated by the FSM in 2011 as well as a selection of publicly accessible decisions issued by the FSM in recent years regarding breaches of Art. 4 (2) and 5 (1) JMStV.

---

2678 FSM, About Us, Members, available in English at http://www.fsm.de/about-us/membership/members (accessed 21.3.2016).

2679 FSM, Voluntary commitments of business, codes of conduct, available in English at http://www.fsm.de/voluntary-commitments (accessed 21.3.2016).

2680 The FSM commissioned, together with other partners, an Internet guide for parents. Confer Guido Bröckling, Cornelia Margraf, and Björn Schreiber, "Internet Guide Für Eltern, Tipps Zur Medienerziehung in Der Familie," ed. FSM, FragFinn, and Kinderhilfswerk, 2015, https://images.dkhw.de/fileadmin/Redaktion/1_Unsere_Arbeit/1_Schwerpunkte/6_Medienkompetenz/6.2_Internet_Guide_fuer_Eltern/Internet_Guide_fuer_Eltern_Deutsches_Kinderhilfswerk.pdf?_ga=1.81945938.514713316.1449478955 (accessed 22.3.2016). The FSM is also involved in the creation and development of the children's platform juki.de and partner to the project fragfinn.de which offers a safe online space for minors including a search engine.

2681 See https://www.altersklassifizierung.de/ (accessed 23.3.2016); see also Hajok and Schwarz, "Technischer Jugendmedienschutz bei digitalen Medien," p. 3.

2682 Art. 20 (5) JMStV.

a) Assessment principles

In order to make its decision-making processes more transparent, the FSM drew up assessment principles which serve as guidelines for the complaints committees in appraising the conformity of an offer with the JMStV.[2683] The assessment principles purport to restrict the margin of discretion granted to complaints committees in order to ensure a coherent practice. In addition, providers may consult complaint committees to secure that their offer is in line with the legal requirements. [2684] Initially, the assessment principles were devised in 2005 by media scientists and lawyers in an inter-disciplinary approach. They were up-dated in 2011 taking into account new insights and developments in law and media. From a legal point of view, they are inspired by the JuSchRiL of the state media authorities and the measures adopted by the KJM, especially the criteria for supervision. The result constitutes a comprehensive document of more than 200 pages including detailed guidance. This section examines pertinent guidance in relation to inappropriate content in the sense of Art. 4 (2) and 5 (1) JMStV. It focusses, in particular, on aspects which go beyond the KJM's criteria.

Similar to the KJM's criteria on supervision, the FSM underlines that the offer under appraisal is to be precisely defined.[2685] The unit or offer which raises issues is to be examined globally and in the exact form as it is presented to the user. Dismembering the offer without considering the overall context within which the content is embedded could lead to biased results.[2686] The FSM's criteria regarding pornographic material pursuant to Art. 4 (2) No. 1 JMStV flow from the jurisprudence of the highest German courts. Similar to the KJM, the FSM stresses that the notion of pornography[2687] is subject to social and cultural changes including paradigm shifts concerning nudity and sexuality.[2688] The FSM outlines several indications for a pornographic offer.[2689] Provided the criteria stemming from the case

---

2683 FSM, "Prüfgrundsätze," 2011, http://www.fsm.de/ueber-uns/veroeffentlichungen/Prfgrundstze_2.Auflage.pdf (accessed 15.3.2016).

2684 FSM, "Prüfgrundsätze", see preface on p. 5.

2685 FSM, "Prüfgrundsätze," para. 5.1-5.10, pp. 81-86.

2686 FSM, "Prüfgrundsätze," p. 81.

2687 See also the guidance on the notion of hardcore pornography (*harte Pornographie*) FSM, "Prüfgrundsätze," paras. 6.10, pp. 108–110.

2688 FSM, "Prüfgrundsätze," para. 7.1, p. 112.

2689 FSM, "Prüfgrundsätze," para. 7.1, pp. 112-114.

law are fulfilled, an offer is pornographic, if, for example, the plot is so weak, trivial and short in comparison to extended and (quantitatively) long passages depicting sexual practices; or if the presentation represents distorted images of male or female sexual conduct such as the tireless sexual devotion of a woman or the inexhaustible potency of a man. In addition, the FSM refers to focussed and accentuated portrayals of sexual organs (as if by a magnifying glass) like close-ups of testicles, the vagina or an erect penis during (oral or anal) sexual intercourse.[2690] The FSM makes clear that the indications are non-exhaustive and that more subtle forms of presentation may be considered pornographic such as "cable versions" of hardcore porn movies which follow the same "narrative" but are less explicit and direct on account of the use of different camera techniques.[2691]

Moreover, content is categorised as pornographic if the presentation is obtrusive and offensive. This may be the case if the camera pauses on the bodies of the actors indulged in sexual activities, if the sexual act which is not shown itself is intensively stage-managed (for example by loud moans or relevant statements), or if close-ups are included zooming on the head of a protagonist, moving rhythmically, while engaged in fellatio.[2692] The FSM notes that pornographic offers may consist of entirely textual or audio descriptions or other visualisations of sexual activities or of a mixture of text, sound and/or image. Thus, the explicit and focussed audiovisual presentation of sexual organs or sexual activities is not a precondition for pornography.[2693] By contrast, the mere textual or visual account of nudity (including genitalia), the mere presentation of sexual activities (including sexual intercourse) and the gratuitous over emphasis on sexual organs (using, in particular, long shots) fall outside the notion of pornography.[2694] The FSM also indicates that the media-specific aspect of the Internet is to be integrated into the assessment in accordance with the last sentence of Art. 4 (2) No. 3 JMStV. As a result, a stricter standard may be applicable to telemedia services which are constantly accessible (in contrast to sched-

2690 FSM, "Prüfgrundsätze," para. 7.1, p. 113.
2691 FSM, "Prüfgrundsätze," para. 7.1, p. 114.
2692 FSM, "Prüfgrundsätze," para. 7.1, p. 114.
2693 FSM, "Prüfgrundsätze," para. 7.1, pp. 114–15.
2694 FSM, "Prüfgrundsätze," para. 7.1, p. 116.

uled broadcasts) and technically superior (regarding the possibilities for users to enlarge or select individual scenes or set bookmarks).[2695]

Furthermore, the FSM specifies the notions "suited to impair" ("*entwicklungsbeeinträchtigend*") as well as "evidently suited to seriously impair" ("*offensichtlich schwer entwicklungsgefährdend*") as stipulated by Art. 4 (2) No. 3 and Art. 5 (1) JMStV. It acknowledges that these are vague legal notions which are interpreted in the context of the values enshrined in the constitution as well as the aims prescribed by the JMStV of educating minors as self-responsible and socially competent personalities.[2696] The FSM stresses the obviousness of the serious impairment by virtue of Art. 4 (2) No. 3 JMStV. Messages which are subtle or concealed are not "evident" within the meaning of this provision.[2697] It follows that the seriousness of the impairment must be discernible for any lay person.[2698] The criteria for seriously harmful content as well as those formulated with regards to content which is suited to impair the development of minors are reminiscent of (albeit more concrete than) the KJM's criteria on supervision and will therefore not be reiterated here.[2699] Interestingly, the FSM applies a more nuanced benchmark (compared to the KJM) regarding the definition of the user group when assessing content pursuant to Art. 5 (1) JMStV.

In general, the FSM takes into account the effects of the content on the "average minor". By derogation, it assesses the offer on the basis of weaker children if it can be deduced from objective criteria and the specificities of the offer that it is being used primarily (above-average) by users that are more easily disturbed by the content. The FSM looks at the content, form of presentation, the way the audience is addressed, the target audience and user base as specificities of the offer.[2700] On the one hand, this approach is more differentiated and allows for a more individualised assessment. On the other hand, the evaluation of the material seems more

---

2695 FSM, "Prüfgrundsätze," para. 7.1, p. 116. The FSM underlines that a decision taken with respect to one media may not be easily transferred to the same service distributed online (para. 9.1.1, p. 127).

2696 FSM, "Prüfgrundsätze," para. 9.1.1, pp. 122–26.

2697 FSM, "Prüfgrundsätze," para. 9.1.2, p. 128.

2698 FSM, "Prüfgrundsätze," para. 9.1.2, pp. 128-129. The FSM points out that the offer need not be assessed from the perspective of a child as these cannot yet decode the impairment.

2699 FSM, "Prüfgrundsätze," paras. 9.2.1-9.2.2, pp. 130-154.

2700 FSM, "Prüfgrundsätze," para. 9.3.1, p. 154.

subjective and less clear-cut, especially from the perspective of the provider. It is unclear at what point weaker members of the respective age group are to be taken as the reference point (when 51/75 percent of these use the offer?); what it means if a child is considered to pertain to the "average" or "weaker" group of the relevant age?; or how and to what extent content and form of the presentation influence the risk group? The assessment matrix of the FSM clarifies that the evaluation concentrates on weaker children if the offer explicitly targets them or if the offer (probably or most probably) is being consumed by a majority of these.[2701]

Furthermore, the assessment principles stipulate the measures which providers may take to design their offers in accordance with the legal requirements. These largely reproduce the measures already discussed in-depth above: AVS for closed user groups, JSPs or other (technical) measures for modestly harmful content.[2702] In brief, the assessment principles established by the FSM are very extensive and at the same time very concrete. Their link to the KJM's criteria on supervision is clearly decipherable. Yet, the clarifications made by the FSM are even more detailed including examples of material likely to be considered (non-) pornographic. To this end, the assessment criteria are a valuable indication to service providers and offer a transparent insight into the method of evaluation by the FSM's complaints panels. The assessment principles, though rich in detail, remain necessarily broad to a certain extent. The complaints committees still dispose of a margin of discretion in appraising the nature of the content.

#### b) Practice

In 2015, the FSM received about 5,450 complaints, an increase of 10 percent in comparison to the previous year.[2703] About 1,000 complaints, about 20 percent of all complaints, concerned pornographic material. Interestingly, complaints about certain types of content have become more numerous such as child pornography, incitement to hatred against parts of the population and content with extreme right-wing tendencies (such as,

2701 FSM, "Prüfgrundsätze," para. 3.2.1, p. 158.
2702 FSM, "Prüfgrundsätze," paras. 10.1–10.2.2, pp. 162–172.
2703 FSM, Statistiken 2015, available at http://www.fsm.de/beschwerdestelle/statistiken (accessed 21.3.2016).

Holocaust denial or content which is directed against the free and democratic order). The public may report content through an online form and the complaints are processed by the FSM's complaints committees.[2704] These comprise three impartial examiners who are appointed by the head of the complaints panel for a two-year term.[2705] The committees take decisions by simple majority and the committee's chairperson has the decisive vote in case of a tie.[2706] The complaints committee may pronounce sanctions in relation to members of the association. These range from a notification (taking the form of disapproval with request for remedy), a warning and an association penalty (fines) to expulsion from the association.[2707] An internal review of decisions addressed to members is provided.[2708] Non-members can merely be sanctioned by notifications.[2709] The provider is then requested to refrain from the current behaviour which is found to be contrary to the JMStV. Importantly, non-compliance with FSM decisions may lead to the referral of the negligent provider to the competent state media authority. The state media authoritiy will again appraise the matter and may even impose sanctions by virtue of the JMStV. Several recent decisions of the FSM against non-members are examined below. The FSM establishes a violation of the rules protecting of minors and orders rectification within a fortnight. The decisions cover the different legal categories of content, ranging from pornographic content (Art. 4 (2) No. 1

2704 FSM, Hotline, Report content, available in English at http://www.fsm.de/hotline/report-content (accessed 21.3.2016).

2705 Membership in the complaints panel is an honorary office. There are 30 members in total that are divided into committees on a rotating basis by the head of the department (Art. 9 complaint rules). Members cannot be involved in decisions concerning their own activities (Art. 12 (2) articles of association). The articles of association dated September 2012 and the complaint rules of April 2014 are available in English at http://www.fsm.de/about-us/documents (accessed 21.3.2016).

2706 The chairperson of each committee is nominated by the committee members themselves. See Art. 10 (1) complaints rules.

2707 See Art. 11 (4) complaints rules. By virtue of Art. 8 (6) articles of association, fines may be imposed of a maximum of EUR 20,000.

2708 See Art. 14 complaints rules. Art. 14 (5) prescribes that examiners involved in the original decision are excluded from reviewing it. In addition, a joint committee may be established by virtue of Art. 15 complaints rules in case a committee indents to derogate from an earlier decision of another committee or in case fundamental issues of relevance to all FSM members are raised.

2709 See Art. 11 (5) complaints rules.

JMStV) to content which is evidently suited to impair minors (Art. 4 (2) No. 3 JMStV) and content which is suited to impair minors (Art. 5 (1) JMStV). They more or less exhaustively cover the FSM's decisions which are publicly available.

(aa) Pornographic content

In 2005, the FSM issued a notification against a provider of various discussion forums in which punters could describe and exchange their sexual experiences with prostitutes.[2710] Access to the forums was possible for different user groups: visitors who did not register had limited but gratuitous access to images, descriptions and some contact data of prostitutes. Extended access to forum contributions, chats was granted free of charge to users who registered by a functioning email. Registered users could also read or place advertisement. Full access was possible at cost. Users were asked to register by indicating their name, address, date of birth, email and telephone number. In addition, a credit card number or, alternatively, banking details were required.[2711]

In analysing the nature of the content, the FSM found that the content disseminated in the forums predominantly aimed at arousing the sexual lust of the user and was thus pornographic within the meaning of Art. 4 (2) No. 1 JMStV. Punters could describe their sexual activities in "epic breadth".[2712] The drastic reports and coarsening of the sexual resulted in

2710 FSM, "Entscheidung Nr. 02095," 2005, https://www.fsm.de/beschwerdestelle/praxisentscheidungen/Entscheidung_PornografieTextform.pdf. See also a decision of the FSM in 2008 in which it determined that a provider of forums allowing for the evaluation of brothels and prostitutes made available on a platform violated Art. 4 (2) No. 1 and 3 JMStV. Users of the forums indulged in exchanges of personal experiences and encounters with prostitues by expressly describing sexual practices. The FSM found that the material (mostly texts and images) depicted the rampant realisation of sexual phantasies and treated women as mere objects of lust (p. 7). The website thus contributed to the unsettling of minors by reinforcing a world view and way of living contrary to recognised social norms and values (p. 8). See FSM, "Entscheidung Nr. 06314," 2008, https://www.fsm.de/beschwerdestelle/praxisentscheidungen/Entscheidung_Bordellbewertungsportal.pdf (all websites accessed 20.3.2016).

2711 FSM, "Entscheidung Nr. 02095," pp. 1–2.

2712 FSM, "Entscheidung Nr. 02095," p. 2.

the degradation of their sex partners to mere, replaceable objects.[2713] The fact that the contributions were solely textual in nature lacking any other kind of visualisation did not undermine the finding that the content was pornographic.[2714] The FSM pointed out that the wording of Art. 4 JMStV did not constrain pornography to specific kinds of depictions and thus covered direct and explicit textual accounts.[2715] According to the FSM, the exclusive and excessive descriptions of unusual sexual practices, using vulgar and brutalised language, and personal preferences in relation to prostitutes amounted to pornographic content.[2716] Such kind of material is only permissible in closed user groups. A part of the content was freely accessible while another part required registration by users. The mere registration by means of email failed to verify the age of users.

Likewise, the mere indication of some existing credit card number or bank account details lacking any proper age verification did not meet the requirements of an AVS. The measures taken by the provider were thus insufficient to protect minors from unsuitable content.[2717] Interestingly, the FSM confirmed that the (host) provider of the forums was responsible for the material made available on the website even if it was the users who posted their contributions. The FSM held that the provider not only stored and made accessible the material but was also liable for the presentation of content once having gained knowledge of its illegal dissemination.[2718]

Similarly, the FSM notified a provider who freely supplied pornographic images as well as textual descriptions in 2006.[2719] On the homepage, photos as well as statements were made with explicit sexual intention. A catalogue of pictures was made accessible on sub-pages showing naked women and men in erotic poses and during different phases of sexual activities. Many photos focussed on genitalia which were broadly pixelated. The fact that pictures were made unrecognisable did not, however, under-

2713 FSM, "Entscheidung Nr. 02095," pp. 2–3.
2714 FSM, "Entscheidung Nr. 02095," p. 3.
2715 FSM, "Entscheidung Nr. 02095," p. 3.
2716 FSM, "Entscheidung Nr. 02095," p. 3. Other material posted in the forums which depicted sexual practices including excrements was considered degrading and hence "evidently suited to impair minors' development" in line with Art. 4 (2) No. 3 JMStV.
2717 FSM, "Entscheidung Nr. 02095," p. 4.
2718 FSM, "Entscheidung Nr. 02095," pp. 4–5; see also Art. 10 TMG.
2719 FSM, "Entscheidung Nr. 04081," 2006, https://www.fsm.de/beschwerdestelle/praxisentscheidungen/Entscheidung_GirlsLinklisten.pdf (accessed 27.3.2016).

mine the general perception of the photos and their statements. Textual explanations to the photos were characterised by obscene and partly brutal language.[2720] In its decision, the FSM discussed whether the homepage was already to be considered pornographic or merely the sub-pages. It remarked that the homepage presented erotic material (images and text) which was at the borderline and only marginally away from being pornographic.[2721] Yet, the overall assessment of the FSM was not called into question as the sub-pages were clearly considered to be pornographic.[2722] This finding was bolstered by the fact that the website was regarded as a medium which "lives on the clicking to integrated sub-pages".[2723]

What was more, the sub-pages featured women in sexually stimulating postures. The FSM considered that the entire website gave the impression that women were mere objects of sexual satisfaction. The minimal or rough pixilation of genitalia and sexual acts did not cover the primary intention and purpose of the pictures. The images gained a pornographic character in combination with the respective textual passages.[2724] According to the FSM, the website as a whole suggested a fictive sexual world where women were traded as readily available commodities. This distorted and incorrect presentation of sexuality was in sharp contrast to reality.[2725] As the material was freely available to minors, the FSM found that the provider offered pornographic content in violation of Art. 4 (2) No. 1 JMStV. By the same token, the FSM took a similar decision in 2009 about a provider who advertised erotic DVDs by showing extracts (images and text) on a website. The photos taken from the films were also pixelated but did not conceal the portrayal of sexual acts. They were accompanied by the title of the film as well as coarse and lascivious explanations. The FSM found that the images in combination with the descriptions were

2720 FSM, "Entscheidung Nr. 04081," p. 3.
2721 FSM, "Entscheidung Nr. 04081," p. 5.
2722 FSM, "Entscheidung Nr. 04081," p. 5.
2723 FSM, "Entscheidung Nr. 04081," p. 6.
2724 FSM, "Entscheidung Nr. 04081," p. 5.
2725 FSM, "Entscheidung Nr. 04081," p. 6. For these reasons, the material was also in breach of Art. 4 (2) No. 3 JMStV concerning content which "is evidently suited to seriously impair" the development of minors.

pornographic and that the provider failed to comply with the JMStV as the material was disseminated without obstruction.[2726]

The FSM handed down another interesting decision in 2009 which illustrates the potential conflict between the protection of minors online and the freedom of arts.[2727] Besides photos and videos, the website at issue contained a great amount of erotic stories of different authors. The texts varied in terms of form encompassing partly lyric and poem-like essays, stories with supposedly autobiographic elements and other, simpler descriptions of sexual experiences and events of all kinds. In general, the texts did not include a narrative or plot going beyond the sexual which was described explicitly and oftentimes drastically.[2728] Several short stories dealt with degrading and violent sexual practices (including human excrements and excessive promiscuity), retrograde role models and described activities with minors.[2729] The FSM determined that the stories fulfilled the requirements of both, Art. 4 (2) No. 1 and 3 and were thus pornographic as well as evidently suited to impair the development of minors.[2730] The FSM equally qualified as pornographic linked offers which contained catalogues of erotic and nude photos predominantly depicting close-ups of female genitalia.[2731] The responsibility of the provider for linked content was confirmed given the identical branding of the catalogue and the original website and the fact that the photos were not labelled as advertisements.[2732] In addition, the FSM found that the short stories and videos available at the second level domain were suited to impair the development of minors aged below 16 in accordance with Art. 5 (1) JMStV.[2733] The provider had not put in place adequate mechanisms to protect minors from pornographic and (seriously) harmful content.

---

2726 FSM, "Entscheidung Nr. 08838," 2009, p. 3, https://www.fsm.de/beschwerdestelle/praxisentscheidungen/Entscheidung_Pornografie_BildTextKombination.pdf (accessed 27.3.2016).

2727 FSM, "Entscheidung Nr. 07933," 2009, https://www.fsm.de/beschwerdestelle/praxisentscheidungen/Entscheidung_erotischeGeschichten.pdf (accessed 27.3.2016).

2728 FSM, "Entscheidung Nr. 07933," pp. 2–3.

2729 FSM, "Entscheidung Nr. 07933," p. 5.

2730 FSM, "Entscheidung Nr. 07933," pp. 4–5.

2731 FSM, "Entscheidung Nr. 07933," p. 6.

2732 FSM, "Entscheidung Nr. 07933," p. 7.

2733 FSM, "Entscheidung Nr. 07933," pp. 7–11.

Interestingly, the FSM took into account the website's clear artistic intention and its claim to constitute a special art project. In the final step of its assessment, it therefore balanced the freedom of art and the protection of minors. By reference to relevant case law on the freedom of art, the FSM considered to what extent the harmful material was embedded in an artistic concept.[2734] The self-regulator found that the numerous self-contained, partly artistic stories which lacked any cross-references did not amount to a work of artistic expression ("*Gesamtkunstwerk*").[2735] The artistic value of the stories was compromised by the explicitness of the descriptions of sexual acts. The stories were, moreover, short and did not appear to be part of a comprehensive artistic concept which would explain the motivation of individual protagonists and detail their personalities.[2736] The FSM also appraised the value of the website for the audience but found no indications that it was regarded as especially valuable.[2737] Thus, the protection of minors was given prevalence in this case.

(bb) Content evidently suited to impair minors

Content evidently suited to impair the development of minors can only be supplied in closed user groups. Art. 4 (2) No. 3 JMStV may cover a wide range of material as shown below. In 2006 and 2008, the FSM issued decisions regarding paedophile material.[2738] The 2006 decision concerned a website dedicated to paedophilia which was administered by an association which promoted the liberalisation of sexual contact between adults and children. To this end, it had published a report as well as a position paper. The FSM found that the report presented children in unnatural poses and was thus absolutely illegal pursuant to Art. 4 (1) No. 9 JMStV and the association was ordered to take it down.[2739] The position paper on "the sexuality between children and adults" was qualified as seriously

2734 FSM, "Entscheidung Nr. 07933," pp. 11–12.
2735 FSM, "Entscheidung Nr. 07933," p. 12.
2736 FSM, "Entscheidung Nr. 07933," p. 12.
2737 FSM, "Entscheidung Nr. 07933," p. 12.
2738 FSM, "Entscheidung Nr. 4099," 2006, http://www.fsm.de/beschwerdestelle/praxisentscheidungen/Entscheidung_pdophilie.pdf; FSM, "Entscheidung Nr. 07213," 2008, https://www.fsm.de/beschwerdestelle/praxisentscheidungen/Entscheidung_Pdophilieforum.pdf (all websites accessed 27.3.2016).
2739 FSM, "Entscheidung Nr. 4099," p. 3.

harmful to minors. It argued that the prohibition of sexual contact between children and adults was based solely on moral grounds ignoring social grounds accounting for the psychological development of minors.[2740] The text also conveyed the image of a responsible paedophile adult who reacted to the wishes and desires of children for sexual contact.[2741] The FSM posited that the position paper was pseudo-scientific from the perspective of minors. Even if the text by its diction, structure and scope was expressly addressed to adults, the FSM considered that it was likely that minors would read it, too. This was especially true for weaker minors finding themselves in an embarrassing situation wishing to obtain further information.[2742] The position paper was said to seriously harm minors' understanding of norms and expectations of behaviour. The FSM acknowledged that the impairment could be less intense for the "average minor" who is less susceptible to external influences. It nonetheless decided that the harm for the group of weaker minors ("*gefährdungsgeneigt*") was obvious enough to presume a violation of Art. 4 (2) No. 3 JMStV.[2743]

In a similar vein, the FSM classified in 2008 a forum entitled "girllover" as material which was obviously seriously inappropriate. The FSM prosecuted the host provider of the German-speaking forum as the domain holder was located in Nigeria.[2744] The forum allowed users to exchange opinions on various subjects. The contributions were partly accessible for everyone and partly available upon registration by email address.[2745] The rules of the forum, enforced by the moderators of the individual forum threads prohibited the up-loading of content which was criminally illegal. Yet, the rules were formulated in such a way that they inhibited any critical and differentiated discussion about paedophilia.[2746] The FSM stressed that the forum was orientated to the needs and perspectives of paedophile men.[2747] As a result, paedophilia was presented as a variety of sexual inclination.[2748] The findings of the FSM are underpinned by several examples which degrade girls to mere sexual objects regardless of

2740 FSM, "Entscheidung Nr. 4099," p. 4.
2741 FSM, "Entscheidung Nr. 4099," p. 4.
2742 FSM, "Entscheidung Nr. 4099," p. 5.
2743 FSM, "Entscheidung Nr. 4099," p. 5.
2744 FSM, "Entscheidung Nr. 07213," p. 2.
2745 FSM, "Entscheidung Nr. 07213," p. 3.
2746 FSM, "Entscheidung Nr. 07213," p. 3.
2747 FSM, "Entscheidung Nr. 07213," p. 3.
2748 FSM, "Entscheidung Nr. 07213," p. 3.

their interests and protection.[2749] In the opinion of the FSM, minors could not cope with and were gravely disorientated by the positions and forum contributions which were presented to them as natural.[2750] The fact that the material was exclusively textual in nature did not affect their classification as seriously harmful content.[2751] Moreover, the provider had failed to put in place an effective AVS and was thus in breach of the JMStV.[2752]

In a similar vein, the FSM notified a host provider of a forum on eating disorders in 2007.[2753] The forum was associated with the Pro Ana/Mia movement and glorified the physical state connected to eating disorders and played down the consequences for health and life of persons affected. The guest book of the website contained plethora of pictures of very slim young women which sometimes were accompanied by text such as "I'm everything that I hate" or "Nothing tastes as good as thin feels".[2754] In other parts of the forum, users were asked to answer questions about their target weight as well as their body-mass-index. Based on the presentation of the forums, the FSM considered that these were primarily directed at adults and adolescents. It pointed out that the website could also raise the curiosity of younger minors who were discontent with the changes of their bodies during puberty or other phases of growth.[2755] The FSM noted that the offer suggested to users that the physical state accomplished by eating disorders was worth striving for, or at least socially acceptable.[2756] The accompanying problems, such as the throwing up of nutrition were presented as criteria to control one's body.[2757] Due to the positive depiction of eating disorders and the lack of an effective AVS, the FSM found that the provider was in breach of Art. 4 (2) No. 3 JMStV.

Furthermore, in 2010, the FSM notified a provider of a zoophilia website which freely discussed erotic or sexual affection towards animals.[2758]

---

2749 FSM, "Entscheidung Nr. 07213," p. 5.
2750 FSM, "Entscheidung Nr. 07213," p. 5.
2751 FSM, "Entscheidung Nr. 07213," p. 6.
2752 FSM, "Entscheidung Nr. 07213," p. 4.
2753 FSM, "Entscheidung Nr. 05259," 2007, http://www.fsm.de/beschwerdestelle/praxisentscheidungen/Entscheidung_Essstrungsforum.pdf (accessed 28.3.2016).
2754 FSM, "Entscheidung Nr. 05259," p. 3.
2755 FSM, "Entscheidung Nr. 05259," p. 3.
2756 FSM, "Entscheidung Nr. 05259," p. 4.
2757 FSM, "Entscheidung Nr. 05259," p. 5.
2758 FSM, "Entscheidung Nr. 10276," 2010, https://www.fsm.de/beschwerdestelle/praxisentscheidungen/Entscheidung_zoophilie.pdf (accessed 28.3.2016).

The website contained mainly textual material of cautious and formal character. It provided information about sexual intercourse with animals, for example by explaining the various possible sexual practices which were anatomically possible and offering recommendations and indications regarding specific sexual practices.[2759] The website also informed about the risks of infection concerning specific illnesses (including warnings and recommendations) and supplied detailed descriptions of sexual organs and copulation of animals (horses and dogs).[2760] Certain material was directly addressed to minors.[2761] The FSM decided that the website could lead to serious disorientation of minors. The provider refrained from employing the term sodomy and consequently referred to zoophilia which was presented as socially acceptable and innocuous.[2762] This image was fostered by the language of the website which was particularly attractive to minors (especially the use of icons) and the blending of detailed medical descriptions of sexual organs of animals as well as their emotions and the resulting possibilities for sexual practices.[2763] The description of illnesses and hygiene served to give the offer a scientific touch.[2764] On overall assessment, the "use" of animals for unusual sexual sensitivities of humans was presented as normal practice of human sexual satisfaction.[2765] Such offers, the FSM pointed out, distress and unsettle minors especially during a phase of sexual orientation.[2766] Due to the lack of measures restricting access to adults, an infringement of the JMStV was established.[2767]

In 2011, the FSM took action against a website of a rap music label which gave an overview of the artistic works of several of its artists.[2768] The website comprised text, audio and (audio)visual material which could be qualified as "ghetto-rap" or "gangster-rap". This genre was characterised by crude, coarse language representing violence and hopelessness of life in metropolitan areas with multi-storey buildings. Themes which

2759 FSM, "Entscheidung Nr. 10276," p. 3.
2760 FSM, "Entscheidung Nr. 10276," p. 3.
2761 FSM, "Entscheidung Nr. 10276," p. 4.
2762 FSM, "Entscheidung Nr. 10276," pp. 5–6.
2763 FSM, "Entscheidung Nr. 10276," p. 6.
2764 FSM, "Entscheidung Nr. 10276," p. 6.
2765 FSM, "Entscheidung Nr. 10276," p. 6.
2766 FSM, "Entscheidung Nr. 10276," p. 7.
2767 FSM, "Entscheidung Nr. 10276," p. 7.
2768 FSM, "Beschwerde Nr. 12418," 2011, https://www.fsm.de/beschwerdestelle/praxisentscheidungen/Entscheidung_gangsterrap.pdf (accessed 28.3.2016).

were typically reflected in these songs were the personal honour, violence, violent fantasies, street fights with knives and guns. The FSM considered that the website was addressed to minors and adolescents.[2769] Strikingly, the FSM's assessment in this case is comprehensive as the self-regulatory body examined whether the material was impermissible pursuant to several sub-paragraphs of Art. 4 (1) JMStV.[2770] The descriptions did not, however, reach the degree required to be classified as illegal content. Still, the FSM found that the material was gravely detrimental to minors and in contradiction to the fundamental order of values enshrined in the German Basic Law.[2771]

Moreover, the texts analysed by the FSM were suited to enhance or at least play down dissocial structures.[2772] The songs "*Schlampe*" and "*Billiges Dreckstück*" represented a patriarchal notion of marriage in which women were considered as possessions over which men exercised power. This included violent forms of sexuality.[2773] Other songs, such as "*Vis a Vis*", "*Hannover -Steintor*", "*Ehre eines Gangsters*" and "*Die Faust*" portrayed violence as an adequate means to solve conflicts. Violence was presented as the optimal or at least an acceptable possibility to achieve glory and as exemplary behaviour.[2774] Some songs conveyed similar impressions about the police (like "*Fick die Polizei*"). The police was generally depicted as the enemy and described by negative attributes. A positive attitude with regard to violence towards the police could also be clearly distilled from the lyrics of the songs.[2775] The FSM concluded that the song texts were seriously harmful[2776] to minors as they were not compatible with prevailing normative and social values.[2777] The FSM rejected the provider's argument that the songs were covered by the freedom of arts. Similar to the decision concerning erotic short stories, it posited that the songs of different musicians did not amount to a coherent piece of art and

2769 FSM, "Beschwerde Nr. 12418," p. 2.
2770 Art. 4 (1) No. 5, 6, 8 JMStV.
2771 FSM, "Beschwerde Nr. 12418," p. 6.
2772 FSM, "Beschwerde Nr. 12418," p. 7.
2773 FSM, "Beschwerde Nr. 12418," p. 6.
2774 FSM, "Beschwerde Nr. 12418," pp. 6–7.
2775 FSM, "Beschwerde Nr. 12418," p. 7.
2776 The FSM also found that the material featured on the website was suited to impair the development of minors by virtue of Art. 5 (1) JMStV. See FSM, "Beschwerde Nr. 12418," pp. 8–10.
2777 FSM, "Beschwerde Nr. 12418," p. 7.

were not embedded in an over-arching artistic concept.[2778] Since no AVS was installed, the provider had violated Art. 4 (2) No. 3 JMStV.

(cc) Content suited to impair minors

The FSM's decisions in relation to content likely to impair minors by virtue of Art. 5 (1) JMStV are similarly diverse as those analysed above and cover all kinds of material. In 2010, the self-regulatory body found a website advertising the services of a woman carrying out typical dominatrix sexual acts in return for remuneration, to be in breach of this provision.[2779] The website presented the dominatrix with a photo and a description of her personal sexual preferences. In the absence of an explicit portrayal of violent sexual practices or other activities typical of dominatrices, the FSM rejected the categorisation of the material under Art. 4 (2) JMStV.[2780] Yet, it classified the material as "*entwicklungsbeeinträchtigend*" as the website promoted a variety of fetish services with unambiguous formulations including dominant behaviour, degradation and the infliction of pain.[2781] At several places, indications were made to the possibility of rape games. In addition, a collection of photos depicted masked and or tied up persons involved in sexual acts.[2782] Due to the presentation of sex as a purchasable good, the FSM considered that the material was suited to impair the development of minors. Minors could get the impression that sexual intercourse was only available on sale and constituted nothing more than a commercial transaction.[2783] The image which was transported by the website grossly diverged from the aims stipulated in the JMStV.[2784]

Interestingly, the FSM referred to the Act on Prostitution which entered into force in 2001 and "normalised the oldest business of the world" in Germany.[2785] Since the adoption of this law, it has been legal for prosti-

2778 FSM, "Beschwerde Nr. 12418," pp. 11–12.
2779 FSM, "Beschwerde Nr. 12057," 2010, http://www.fsm.de/beschwerdestelle/praxisentscheidungen/Entscheidung_12057_dominadienste.pdf (accessed 28.3.2016).
2780 FSM, "Beschwerde Nr. 12057," pp. 3–4.
2781 FSM, "Beschwerde Nr. 12057," p. 4.
2782 FSM, "Beschwerde Nr. 12057," p. 4.
2783 FSM, "Beschwerde Nr. 12057," p. 4.
2784 FSM, "Beschwerde Nr. 12057," p. 5.
2785 FSM, "Beschwerde Nr. 12057," p. 5.

tutes to present themselves in relevant parts of daily newspapers. The FSM pointed out that the presentation by means of a website was comparable to print media.[2786] The potential for harm generated by such advertisements was reasonably assessed under Art. 5 (1) JMStV (rather than Art. 4 JMStV). The FSM considered that minors of 16 years would not be harmed by the website as they had, as a rule, already made sexual experiences and could classify erotic material and offers of prostitution.[2787] It followed that the material would have to be restricted to minors aged below 16 by technical or other tools.[2788]

In another case decided in 2015, the FSM requested that a provider of a freely accessible photo gallery of 20 vulva complied with Art. 5 JMStV.[2789] The majority of photos were accompanied by captions such as "pubic hair can have any colour"; "sometimes inner labia are hardly visible" or "the outer labia can have different sizes". In addition, users had the possibility to comment the photos by 13 pre-defined comments such as "LIKE", "LOL", "SMILE", "FAIL", "SAD", "OMG", "WTF?!" or "BITCH".[2790] The FSM first assessed whether the offer was contrary to Art. 4 (1) JMStV. The question whether the young women presented in the photos had reached the age of majority was the most pertinent in this respect. The provider had, however, assured that the "girls" were over 18 years and it could, moreover, not be determined with sufficient certainty that they had, on the contrary, been minors when the photos were taken.[2791] The FSM also denied the pornographic quality of the material which did not primarily aim at sexual stimulation and arousal.[2792]

Yet, the material was classified under Art. 5 (1) JMStV. The FSM highlighted the language used on the website which was attractive to minors. Above all, the comment buttons allowed sexually connoted admiration but also obvious devaluation. Underneath each photo, the number of comments was shown. The FSM considered that the negative comments could adversely affect the sense of self-esteem of predominantly unstable (weak-

2786 FSM, "Beschwerde Nr. 12057," p. 5.
2787 FSM, "Beschwerde Nr. 12057," p. 6.
2788 FSM, "Beschwerde Nr. 12057," p. 6.
2789 FSM, "Beschwerde Nr. 47707," 2015, http://www.fsm.de/beschwerdestelle/praxisentscheidungen/Entscheidung_Onlinegalerie.pdf (accessed 28.3.2016).
2790 FSM, "Beschwerde Nr. 47707," p. 4.
2791 FSM, "Beschwerde Nr. 47707," p. 5.
2792 FSM, "Beschwerde Nr. 47707," pp. 5–6.

er) minors. They also conveyed the message that certain appearances of genitalia were more or less attractive.[2793] In addition, the website gave the impression that the dissemination of nude images of one's own private parts as well as the comparison thereof was normal. Minors could even share erotic pictures with friends or with the general public.[2794] In taking its decision, the FSM took into account the pedagogical orientation of the website. However, the informative and educative framework was undermined by the fact that the photos could only be tersely commented. The website was thus dominated by poster-like photos.[2795] The provider had put in place measures to protect minors by using the age-de.xml label for the age group 16. The FSM opined that minors aged between 16 and 18 could be impaired by the website so that the provider was required to use the 18 labels to bring its service in conformity with Art. 5 JMStV.[2796]

In another recent example of 2014, the FSM analysed audiovisual material which was the subject of three public complaints. Assessing the videos jointly, the FSM determined that the three videos featuring lightly dressed women struggling to free themselves from gags and shackles was suited to impair the development of minors.[2797] In two videos, two men appeared to have gagged women. One video showed a man hitting the woman on the buttocks and stripping away her bra to roughly touch her breasts. The third video only depicted two women, scantily dressed and tied up. One lay on the bed, one was shown standing, both crying for help. The viewer did not see the faces of the women. All scenes were evidently simulated as the protagonists did not show any signs of fear or anxiety.[2798] The provider had labelled the website as suitable for minors older than 16 years.[2799] In its decision, the FSM first excluded violations of Art. 4 (1) and (2) JMStV, arguing that the material did not reach the required threshold.[2800] The videos did not, above all, show any sexual acts (with the exception of a grip to the breasts of an actress and a blow to her buttocks) and did not

---

2793 FSM, "Beschwerde Nr. 47707," p. 7.
2794 FSM, "Beschwerde Nr. 47707," p. 8.
2795 FSM, "Beschwerde Nr. 47707," p. 8.
2796 FSM, "Beschwerde Nr. 47707," p. 8.
2797 FSM, "Beschwerde Nrn. 43462, 43477, 43478," 2014, http://www.fsm.de/beschwerdestelle/praxisentscheidungen/EntscheidungBondage.pdf (accessed 28.3.2016).
2798 FSM, "Beschwerde Nrn. 43462, 43477, 43478," p. 4.
2799 FSM, "Beschwerde Nrn. 43462, 43477, 43478," p. 4.
2800 FSM, "Beschwerde Nrn. 43462, 43477, 43478," pp. 5–8.

present them in an exaggerated and focussed manner. Although degradation of women was discernible, they did not experience any massive violence which was, moreover, not linked to a sexual context.[2801]

Nonetheless, the FSM emphasised that the women were portrayed in a defenceless state at the mercy of the male actors. The gagging and restraining of the women took away their possibilities to move or speak and reinforced their belittling.[2802] The FSM posited that the videos played down or trivialised the use of violence.[2803] The presentations and thus their impact on viewers were, however, mitigated by the fact that the videos were unprofessionally staged and the protagonists acted discernibly amateurish.[2804] In addition, the clothing of the women purported to make possible voyeuristic shots of the female body which contributed to the absolute subjugation of the women. The FSM noted that such presentations promoted male phantasies of omnipotence and sadistic thoughts.[2805] Thus, the material was considered to be harmful to minors under the age of 18. The provider was requested to rectify the labels used for the website and adjust the technical protection measures.

In sum, the decisions of the FSM examined above demonstrate the variety of content assessed by the certified self-regulator. The FSM has published a selection of its decisions on its website. These are anonymised and appear not to involve members of the FSM. The great bulk of decisions remain, however, unpublished. In the interest of transparency and in order to identify trends in the FSM's practice, it would be desirable that these were accessible on a public database. This would be an additional service of the FSM and require additional capacities, which, at the moment, it might either not have, or may not be willing to invest. The majority of decisions made public in relation to the three categories of material (pornographic, seriously impairing and harmful content) appear to involve predominantly textual or photographic material. This is surprising as the importance and growth of audiovisual material for online services is be-

2801 FSM, "Beschwerde Nrn. 43462, 43477, 43478," pp. 7–8.
2802 FSM, "Beschwerde Nrn. 43462, 43477, 43478," p. 9.
2803 FSM, "Beschwerde Nrn. 43462, 43477, 43478," p. 10.
2804 FSM, "Beschwerde Nrn. 43462, 43477, 43478," p. 9 (see also p. 8). The low quality and poor message of the videos did not justify their exemption on grounds of the freedom of arts (p. 10).
2805 FSM, "Beschwerde Nrn. 43462, 43477, 43478," p. 9.

yond dispute. In this respect, the published decisions may not represent the broader trend.

The FSM's decisions are generally well-reasoned and refer to pertinent case law and academic literature. The FSM is cautious about the sensitive character of its work which may have repercussions on the fundamental right to freedom of expression. For example, in the "gangster-rap" songs, it took into account the supposedly artistic nature of the songs. Its decision was justified as the song texts could not be considered as political commentaries that critically assessed the state of inner city youth, rather they clearly ran counter accepted social norms and public order in promoting violence. The scope of the assessment may vary but typically encompasses more than just one gradation of Art. 4 and 5 JMStV. The FSM thus examines in-depth the nature of the content and evaluates whether the content raises issues. Some complaints committees even justify why the relevant material does not fall under one legal rubric, i.e. why it is not considered illegal. Several decisions also analyse the interaction between the protection of minors and the freedom of arts. A balancing exercise of these conflicting rights is carried out at different extents though.

Strikingly, complaints committees appear to apply different benchmarks in relation to the target audience. The matrix outlined in the FSM's assessment principles does not seem to be applied in practice so that some committees appear to focus on the "average minor" and others base their decisions on unstable minors, i.e. those more easily harmed. To a certain degree, this incoherence is unavoidable due to the large number of complaints filed with the FSM. As noted above, membership in complaints committees is an honorary office and no permanent staff can ensure that decisions are consistent. Hence, decisions necessarily have to be taken in committees which may diverge on individual points. Therefore, it is all the more necessary that committees adhere to the matrix outlined in the FSM's assessment principles. Moreover, the lack of cross-references to the assessment principles may also be pointed out. It would be beneficial and more transparent if exact references would be made in the decisions. These would serve as additional explanations to the generally concise assessments. In general, the FSM is active on many fronts promoting online safety for children. It thereby fulfils an important function as a recognised self-regulatory body within the regulatory scheme in Germany.

### III. Perspectives of the German regulatory bodies on the protection of minors in converging media markets

Against the background of the present revision of the AVMSD, the final section of this part of the chapter examines the perspectives of the German regulatory authorities on the current level of protection and the changes they advocate. As discussed in chapter four, the DLM is in favour of adjusting the rules for all audiovisual media services to a uniform level, thereby eliminating the distinction between linear and non-linear services. This suggestion has repercussions on the substantive rules contained in the AVMSD, above all, on current provisions protecting minors. The DLM highlights the high level of protection established in Germany and consequentially calls for levelling up of regulatory standards.[2806] Thus, protection should be raised to the level currently applicable to broadcasting.[2807] To what extent other inappropriate content disseminated online should be regulated is left blank.[2808] The DLM underlines that online youth protection inevitably has a national and an international dimension. The negotiation of international standards is important to react to the global reach of the Internet. Enhanced cross-border cooperation and solutions are needed as unilateral national concepts are increasingly ineffective.[2809]

In this respect, the DLM advocates the development of common technical tools such as classification standards and technical interfaces.[2810] First

---

2806 Direktorenkonferenz der Landesmedienanstalten, "Reply AVMSD Consultation," pp. 17, 19.

2807 Direktorenkonferenz der Landesmedienanstalten, "Reply AVMSD Consultation," p. 19.

2808 In its position paper of June 2015, the DLM refers to an expansion of the rules to online content (mentioning video platforms and blogs in this respect). It is unclear what kind of content should be captured by the rules. Direktorenkonferenz der Landesmedienanstalten, "Position on the revision of the AVMSD," p. 8.

2809 Direktorenkonferenz der Landesmedienanstalten, "Reply AVMSD Consultation," p. 18.

2810 Direktorenkonferenz der Landesmedienanstalten, "Reply AVMSD Consultation," p. 18; see also Direktorenkonferenz der Landesmedienanstalten, "Position on the revision of the AVMSD," p. 8; see also Andreas Marx, Mark Boots, and Friedemann Schindler, "Perspektiven des technischen Jugendschutzes, Aktuelle Herausforderungen und zukunftsfähige Konzepte," ed. jugendschutz.net, June 2016, http://www.kjm-online.de/fileadmin/Download_KJM/Service/Gutachten/Gutachten_Perspektiven-technischer-Jugendschutz_11.08.16.pdf (accessed 28.3.2016).

and foremost, the DLM envisages European-wide technical measures for age labelling which nonetheless allow for decentralised implementation and adaptation to national specificities and sensitivities.[2811] Pilot projects like "IARC", "Miracle" or "You rate it" are mentioned as positive examples which are to be further promoted.[2812] Succinctly, the DLM supports the creation of a uniform technical framework which allows for flexible adaptations at the national level.[2813] Importantly, the DLM recognises the disparities in national moral concepts and values. To the extent possible and accounting for national particularities, it is open to the harmonisation of definitions of key terms such as "minors", "pornography", "gratuitous violence", "impair" and "seriously impair".[2814]

Another aspect highlighted by the DLM is the inclusion of platform operators in the regulatory framework. It is proposed that platform operators provide user-friendly mechanisms to notify or complain about unsuitable content. In addition, platform operators are to assume secondary responsibility in case the content provider cannot be identified or discovered.[2815] In this context, the DLM suggests that undertakings operating on a global scale are to be incentivised to commit to voluntary standards. Self-regulation is regarded as a valuable regulatory strategy which may mitigate the fast moving nature of the Internet and the rapidity by which content is disseminated.[2816] In spite of the differences in assessment and practice of regulatory authorities, common approaches could be sought in relation to content which is considered illegal (child pornography) around the world.[2817] Finally, the DLM underlines that not all problems can be solved by regulatory intervention; instead, it notes the significance of media edu-

2811 Direktorenkonferenz der Landesmedienanstalten, "Reply AVMSD Consultation," p. 18.

2812 Direktorenkonferenz der Landesmedienanstalten, "Reply AVMSD Consultation," p. 20.

2813 Direktorenkonferenz der Landesmedienanstalten, "Reply AVMSD Consultation," p. 20.

2814 Direktorenkonferenz der Landesmedienanstalten, "Reply AVMSD Consultation," p. 19.

2815 Direktorenkonferenz der Landesmedienanstalten, "Reply AVMSD Consultation," p. 18.

2816 Direktorenkonferenz der Landesmedienanstalten, "Reply AVMSD Consultation," p. 18.

2817 Direktorenkonferenz der Landesmedienanstalten, "Reply AVMSD Consultation," p. 18.

cation and media literacy, aspects which should be enshrined at the EU level.[2818] In line with the precautionary principle, the capacity for children and parents alike to critically view content and to reflect on the personal perception and use of media offers are considered of fundamental importance in today's media environment.[2819]

Apart from the DLM, the KJM offers some insights into the future design of youth protection in online media in its sixth activities report published in 2015. It formulates five themes aimed at improving youth protection at the national and international level.[2820] First, it underscores the need for clear and practical rules. The KJM is critical of the present German legal framework which differentiates according to the type of media (whether online or offline, whether linear or non-linear) and may involve different regulatory bodies which may apply different yardsticks for the assessment of content. Double controls of the same offer and legal uncertainty are the result of a complex regulatory scheme. Thus, the KJM is in favour of consistent regulation on the basis of uniform criteria.[2821] Although the KJM does not refer to the AVMSD, this would imply the abandonment of the linear/non-linear distinction. In addition, the KJM is of the opinion that co-regulatory mechanisms (regulated self-regulation) should be strengthened.[2822] Second, the KJM calls for stepping up efforts in relation to technical measures, especially improving JSPs. This demand is motivated by the fact that parents are increasingly side-tracked and no longer meticulously control their children's use of media as the latter increasingly access content via mobile devices (especially mobile phones). As a corollary of the shift in media use and consumption patterns, minors are confronted more easily with drastic content on the Internet.[2823]

Apart from educating minors, technical solutions are an important tool according to the KJM. Similar to the DLM, the KJM postulates cross-border cooperation, in particular in view of technical standards. Due to the different systems of social norms and values, it is sceptical that uniform

2818 Direktorenkonferenz der Landesmedienanstalten, "Reply AVMSD Consultation," p. 20.
2819 Direktorenkonferenz der Landesmedienanstalten, "Reply AVMSD Consultation," p. 20.
2820 KJM, "Sixth activities report," pp. 63–65.
2821 KJM, "Sixth activities report," p. 63.
2822 KJM, "Sixth activities report," p. 63.
2823 KJM, "Sixth activities report," p. 63.

rules can be established at the EU level. Nonetheless, the elaboration of technical standards and interfaces are realistic.[2824] Third, the KJM underlines that different instruments should be employed for different age groups. The regulatory focus for minors below the age of 14 ("children") should be their protection from unsuitable content. Accordingly, safe online spaces including search engines and "positive content" should be promoted.[2825] With regards to minors between 14 and 18 years ("adolescents"), promotion of self-responsibility and media literacy should be the central concern.[2826] Fourth, the awareness of parents for their responsibility should also be sharpened. In order to support adolescents and allow parents to assume their responsibility, content should be signposted, for instance, by age classifications, labels or other symbols of recognition of information.[2827]

Finally, the KJM stresses that the German regulated self-regulation has been successful and should be bolstered in view of media convergence and the flood of content disseminated on the Internet.[2828] Against this background, the necessity for businesses to assume responsibility is apparent. The KJM considers that the German regulatory framework is adequate but should be simplified.[2829] In brief, the visions of the KJM broadly coincide with those formulated by the DLM in response to the AVMSD consultation. They naturally go beyond considerations of the AVMSD and take into account the national and international contexts. To this end, they help to estimate what kind of amendments to the AVMSD German regulators would accept.

A third policy document authored by the FSM, a certified self-regulatory body, is equally interesting as it explicitly comments on the revision of the AVMSD. The paper was published in June 2015, prior to the Commission's consultation, upon request of the *Beauftragte der Bundesregierung für Kultur und Medien* (Government Commissioner for Culture and Media) as well as the *Bayerische Staatskanzlei* (Bavarian State

2824 KJM, "Sixth activities report," p. 64.
2825 KJM, "Sixth activities report," p. 64.
2826 KJM, "Sixth activities report," p. 65.
2827 KJM, "Sixth activities report," p. 65.
2828 KJM, "Sixth activities report," p. 65.
2829 KJM, "Sixth activities report," p. 65.

Chancellery).[2830] In its position paper, the FSM strongly advocates in favour of abandoning the linear/non-linear distinction which no longer mirrors today's media reality. The kind of technology used to distribute content becomes less and less relevant for users.[2831] Thus, the FSM suggests that the pertinent criterion should be content-related (rather than technology-related). The level of protection should be dependent on the degree of potential harm. Accordingly, Art. 12 AVMSD should, in the future, cover all content which impairs the mental, moral and physical development of minors.[2832]

Furthermore, the FSM generally welcomes a graduated approach which is currently realised by Arts. 12 and 27 AVMSD. The current linguistic discrepancies are to be removed.[2833] Above all, a clear framework is to be devised under the following maxima: the more serious the impairment of minors, the higher the efforts required by providers.[2834] In addition, a revised Art. 6 AVMSD could be expanded to content which is considered illegal pursuant to Art. 4 (1) JMStV.[2835] With respect to child protection software (for example JSPs), the FSM underlines that efforts are needed to sensitise society as a whole. Information campaigns are necessary to raise awareness and offer explanations in view of the multiplicity of devices used in one household and the variations of technical solutions for protecting children of different age groups.[2836] The FSM encourages cooperation of the state, NGOs and undertakings to share knowledge, infrastructure and combine communications channels.[2837] The European legislature should restrain itself and refrain from detailed regulation to permit individual national solutions.[2838]

Similarly, the FSM believes that a revised Directive should not prescribe in too much detail rules on effective age verifications (in relation to

2830 FSM, "Stellungnahme auf Anfrage von BKM und Bayerischer Staatskanzlei zur Revision der Audiovisuellen Mediendienste-Richtlinie," 2015, http://www.fsm.de/ueber-uns/veroeffentlichungen/20150630_FSMStellungnahmezurRevisionderAudiovisuellenMediendiensteRichtlinie.pdf (accessed 29.3.2016).

2831 FSM, "Statement on the revision of the AVMSD," p. 3.

2832 FSM, "Statement on the revision of the AVMSD," p. 4.

2833 FSM, "Statement on the revision of the AVMSD," p. 5.

2834 FSM, "Statement on the revision of the AVMSD," pp. 5–6.

2835 FSM, "Statement on the revision of the AVMSD," p. 5.

2836 FSM, "Statement on the revision of the AVMSD," p. 5.

2837 FSM, "Statement on the revision of the AVMSD," p. 6.

2838 FSM, "Statement on the revision of the AVMSD," pp. 6–7.

seriously harmful content). It should, above all, not refer to a specific procedure or method but remain open for new developments and progressive technologies.[2839] The FSM also stresses that unsuitable content (below the threshold of seriously damaging content) should not require a reliable and effective verification of age.[2840] In addition, the FSM welcomes machine-related labelling of third party content. Providers of professional content would benefit from such labelling and could leave it to parents to configure the software. At the EU level, establishing an obligation for providers to classify and label individual items should be avoided. It should rather be the provider's responsibility whether content is labelled individually or at platform-level.[2841]

Importantly, the FSM currently rejects self-classification in case of user-generated content which could also have negative repercussions on the liability of platform providers. It posits that the notice and take-down approach should be up-held.[2842] The challenge, according to the FSM is to design tools which automatically adapt labels depending on national specificities and content disseminated across platforms and across countries. In this respect, it calls on policy makers to support projects like "Miracle" funded by the EU.[2843] The FSM makes clear that it is too early to introduce detailed rules regarding cross-platform labelling in a modified Directive.[2844] Succinctly, the positions of the German regulatory authorities converge in many respects. The linear/non-linear distinction is considered obsolete and focus is set on the elaboration of technical standards as a complement to promoting media education and media literacy.

## IV. Summary

In sum, the protection of minors in on-demand services is a fundamental value protected by the German legal framework. The provisions contained in the JMStV are stricter and more detailed than Art. 12 AVMSD. The JMStV differentiates between illegal content and legal content which is sub-

2839 FSM, "Statement on the revision of the AVMSD," pp. 7–8.
2840 FSM, "Statement on the revision of the AVMSD," p. 8.
2841 FSM, "Statement on the revision of the AVMSD," p. 9.
2842 FSM, "Statement on the revision of the AVMSD," pp. 9–10.
2843 FSM, "Statement on the revision of the AVMSD," p. 10.
2844 FSM, "Statement on the revision of the AVMSD," p. 10.

ject to restrictions. In line with Art. 12 AVMSD, seriously harmful content may be distributed in closed user groups to an adult audience. This requirement has been further specified by the KJM, the German regulatory authority at the federal level. Not only has the KJM given guidance on the kind of content which is caught by the provisions, it has also clarified the conditions of access for closed user groups. Accordingly, access to considerably detrimental material is only granted after a two-stage process encompassing the identification and authentication of the adult user. This mechanism has been confirmed by German courts.

Furthermore, providers of on-demand services face additional restrictions if they supply unsuitable content within the meaning of Art. 5 JMStV. These are applicable to both, linear and non-linear services and, thus, go beyond the Directive. VOD providers may select different tools, such as temporal restrictions, to block content considered unsuitable for minors of particular age groups. Above all, the JMStV provides for filtering software (JSPs) which could be used for this purpose. The KJM has outlined detailed guidance on the conditions for certification of JSPs. From its activities it emerges that technical youth protection is one important pillar on which the regulatory framework rests. It is necessarily complemented by other pillars promoting media literacy and media education which, in today's fast-paced technology-driven daily life, become more and more important. The commitment of German regulatory bodies to the protection of minors is further illustrated by the measures taken by the FSM, a certified self-regulator. Its in-depth guidance on the manner in which it assesses cases is particularly valuable to shape the meaning of crucial notions such as violence, pornography or sexuality. On an overall level, the measures taken by the German regulatory authorities demonstrate an understanding of the importance of the protection of minors as well as an awareness of the potential conflicts with other values and rights.

## *D. The protection of minors in on-demand audiovisual media services in France*

In France, the protection of minors in on-demand audiovisual media services is recognised as a regulatory objective by the LLC. While the freedom of communication flows from the first sentence of Art. 1 LLC, the second outlines limits to this freedom, explicitly referring, among others, to the protection of children and adolescents. In addition, the protection of minors constitutes a principal task of the CSA. Art. 3-1 (4) LLC, which generally outlines the regulator's mandate, tasks the CSA with the promotion of programmes dedicated to children and adolescents. In addition, Art. 15 LLC which specifically sets forth the rules on the protection of minors in audiovisual communications requires that the CSA ensures "the protection of childhood and youth and the respect for human dignity in the programmes made available" to the public.[2845] For reasons of completeness, reference is also made to the *Loi n° 49-956 sur les publications destinées à la jeunesse* (Law on publications intended for the youth).[2846] This law is applicable to publications which, on account of their character, presentation or aim, appear to be principally directed at children and adolescents. Interestingly, Art. 2 of this law prohibits, *inter alia,* content which presents a danger to minors due to its pornographic character. Complementing these civil law rules are several provisions of the French *Code pénal* (Penal Code) which criminalise the circulation of child pornography and the dissemination of representations having a pornographic or violent character or communications which seriously violate human dignity.[2847] This study concentrates, however, on the provisions set forth by the LLC and their specification through the French regulator for audiovisual media services. To this end, this part of the chapter sketches the legal framework before examining the measures taken by the CSA.

2845 Laurence Franceschini, "Pornographie et télévision," *Légipresse* 197 (2002): p. 166.

2846 *Loi n° 49-956 du 16 juillet 1949 sur les publications destinées à la jeunesse,* JORF 19.7.1949, p. 7006, as amended.

2847 See in particular Art. 227-23 and 227-24 Code pénal (Livre II, Titre II, Chapitre VII, Section 5, entitled « De la mise en péril des mineurs » (Minors in peril)). An English translation of the French Penal Code is available at https://www.legifrance.gouv.fr/Traductions/en-English/Legifrance-translations (accessed 27.4.2016).

## I. The transposition of Art. 12 AVMSD in Art. 15 LCC

When the LLC was aligned with the AVMSD in 2009, Art. 15 LLC was amended with a view to transposing Art. 12 AVMSD. Art. 15 LLC provides[2848] that;

> "[...]
> (2) [The CSA] ensures that programmes which are likely to impair the physical, mental or moral development of minors are not made available to the public by an audiovisual communications service, except where it is ensured by selecting the time or by any technical measure that minors will not normally hear or see them.
> (3) When programmes likely to be harmful to the physical, mental or moral development of minors are made available to the public by television services, the [CSA] shall ensure that they are preceded by a warning to the public and are identified by the presence of a visual symbol throughout their duration. To this end, it shall ensure the implementation of a technical access-control mechanism appropriate for personal mobile television services and the implementation of any means appropriate to the nature of on-demand audiovisual services.

2848 For linguistic reasons, see also the French version of Art. 15 LLC:
"(1) Le [CSA] veille à la protection de l'enfance et de l'adolescence et au respect de la dignité de la personne dans les programmes mis à disposition du public par un service de communication audiovisuelle.
(2) Il veille à ce que des programmes susceptibles de nuire à l'épanouissement physique, mental ou moral des mineurs ne soient pas mis à disposition du public par un service de communication audiovisuelle, sauf lorsqu'il est assuré, par le choix de l'heure de diffusion ou par tout procédé technique approprié, que des mineurs ne sont normalement pas susceptibles de les voir ou de les entendre.
(3) Lorsque des programmes susceptibles de nuire à l'épanouissement physique, mental ou moral des mineurs sont mis à disposition du public par des services de télévision, le conseil veille à ce qu'ils soient précédés d'un avertissement au public et qu'ils soient identifiés par la présence d'un symbole visuel tout au long de leur durée. A cette fin, il veille à la mise en œuvre d'un procédé technique de contrôle d'accès approprié aux services de télévision mobile personnelle ainsi qu'à la mise en œuvre de tout moyen adapté à la nature des services de médias audiovisuels à la demande.
(4) Il veille en outre à ce qu'aucun programme susceptible de nuire gravement à l'épanouissement physique, mental ou moral des mineurs ne soit mis à disposition du public par les services de communication audiovisuelle.
[...]".

(4) It shall also ensure that no programme likely to be seriously harmful to the physical, mental or moral development of minors is made available to the public by audiovisual communication services.
[...]"

At first glance, it can be noted that Art. 15 LLC is more comprehensive than Art. 12 AVMSD. The French provision mirrors, above all, Art. 27 AVMSD which is applicable to broadcasting.[2849] Art. 15 (2) LLC corresponds to Art. 27 (2) AVMSD which concerns content that is "likely to impair" the physical, mental or moral development of minors. Importantly,

---

2849 In December 1998, the European Commission referred France to the European Court of Justice for the country's failure to transpose certain provisions of the TWFD (C-140/99). The procedure was initiated in 1992 under the TWFD of 1989 and continued after the Directive's revision in 1997 as the the complaints by the Commission remained valid. Apart from the issue of jurisdiction, the Commission alleged inadequate transposition of Art. 22 TWFD (now Art. 27 AVMSD) on the protection of minors in television broadcasts. Subsequent to the amendment of Art. 15 LLC in 2000, the infringement procedure was closed and the case removed from the court's register. See European Commission, "The Commission Decides to Make an Application to the Court against France on the 'Television without frontiers' Directive, IP/98/1067," December 7, 1998, http://europa.eu/rapid/press-release_IP-98-1067_en.htm?locale=en; European Commission, "Fourth Report from the Commission to the Council, the European Parliament, the European Economic and Social Committee and the Committee of the Regions, COM(2002) 778 Final," January 6, 2003, para. 2, p. 7, http://eur-lex.europa.eu/legal-content/EN/ALL/?uri=CELEX:52002DC0778; see also Franceschini, "Pornographie et télévision," pp. 165–66; in a communication of 2002, the CSA advocated for the banning of pornographic programmes from French television (in line with the TWFD/AVMSD) and called upon the French legislature to amend Art. 15 LLC by explicitly referring to pornographic and excessively violent programmes. CSA, "Communiqué n° 498, Le CSA préconise la suppression des programmes pornographiques à la télévision," July 2, 2002, http://www.csa.fr/var/ezflow_site/storage/csa/rapport2002/donnees/annexes/A25_IV_communique498.htm. In the same year, MPs Bur, Rivière and Zimmermann tabled an amendment of Art. 15 LLC in the French Parliament. It would have prohibited the dissemination of gratuitous violence and pornographic programmes in radio and television services. By derogation, such content would have been permissible provided that it was ensured by appropriate technical measures, that minors would not normally hear or see it. See Assemblée Nationale, Proposition de Loi visant à protéger les mineurs contre la diffusion de programmes comprenant des scènes de violence gratuite ou de pornographie presentée par MM. Bur, Rivière, Zimmermann, 15.10.2002, available at http://www.assemblee-nationale.fr/12/pdf/propositions/pion0317.pdf (all websites accessed 3.5.2016).

Art. 15 (2) LLC refers to content transmitted by an "audiovisual communications service". Pursuant to Art. 2 (3) LLC, the notion of an audiovisual communications service encompasses television and radio services as well as VOD services. Thus, on-demand providers established in France are required to take measures protecting minors from content which is "likely to impair" minors' development. This is explicitly foreseen by Art. 15 (3) LLC which expressly refers to providers of on-demand audiovisual media services. While broadcasters are obliged to inform their audience of content likely to be harmful by a warning and appropriate labelling, Art. 15 (3) LLC does not stipulate any more detailed obligations for VOD providers. Instead, providers must take "means appropriate to the nature of on-demand audiovisual services". These have been specified by the CSA as will be examined below.

In addition, Art. 15 (4) LLC reproduces Arts. 12 and 27 (1) AVMSD, by prohibiting the dissemination of programmes "likely to be seriously harmful" to minors in audiovisual communications services. However, Art. 15 (4) LLC lacks a reference to programmes involving pornography or gratuitous violence. The notion of "seriously impairing" content is thus not further specified in the French LLC. Interestingly, the French provision also does not copy the formula encapsulated by Art. 12 AVMSD which allows VOD service providers to make seriously detrimental material available "in such a way as to ensure that minors will not normally hear or see" it. On the contrary, Art. 15 (4) LLC seems to bear greater resemblance to Art. 27 (1) AVMSD concerning broadcasts. In comparison with the AVMSD, the French provision appears to ban the transmission, in linear or non-linear form, of all content which is seriously harmful.

This prohibition also emerges from Art. 12 AVMSD in relation to VOD providers. Yet, Art. 12 AVMSD only prohibits the dissemination of gravely harmful material to minors and allows the making available of such material to an adult audience. Thus, from the letter of the law, Art. 15 LLC is stricter than the AVMSD and sets out more detailed requirements. In France, restrictions apply to providers of non-linear services in relation to both types of audiovisual material: that which is likely to impair minors and that which is likely to be seriously impairing. It will be shown below that the French regulator interprets Art. 15 (4) LLC in line with Art. 12 AVMSD by allowing the inclusion of considerably harmful material in VOD services exclusively supplied to persons of age.

## II. The measures taken by the CSA

From its portfolio of activities it can be deduced that the CSA has attributed priority to the protection of minors.[2850] Between 2005 and 2010, the CSA adopted several executive measures in relation to specific aspects of the protection of minors (for example on certain types of fighting contests,[2851] the advertising of programmes or films classified with an age restriction,[2852] on the participation of minors in television broadcasts,[2853] the dissemination of commercial communications promoting operators of games of chance[2854] or the effects of TV on children under three years of

2850 Derieux and Granchet, *Droit des médias, Droit francais, européen et international*, paras. 752–53, pp. 237-238.

2851 CSA, Recommandation n° 2005-8 du 20 décembre 2005 aux éditeurs de services de télévision concernant la retransmission de certains types de combats, JORF 08.01. 2006, n° 7, texte n° 26 (Recommendation No. 2005-8 of 20 December 2005, addressed to providers of television services concerning the broadcasting of certain types of fighting contest). In 2008, the pay-TV operator Canal+ initiated an action for annulment against the CSA's decision which warned it to stop retransmitting fighting contests organised abroad (such as the K-1 World Grand Prix 2006 taking place in Japan) which was contrary to the 2005 Recommendation. The Conseil d'Etat ruled in 2009 that the CSA was competent to adopt the recommendation which prohibited confrontations of great violence which did not have the same level of protection of participants as those organised in France. As a result, the CSA's decision taken in relation to Canal+ was valid. See Conseil d'Etat, Judgment of 18.12.2009, n° 310646 (FR:CESSR:2009:310646.20091218).

2852 CSA, Recommandation n° 2006-6 du 4 juillet 2006 relative à la présentation faite à la télévision d'oeuvres cinématographiques ou audiovisuelles, de jeux vidéo et de services téléphoniques, télématiques ou de sites internet qui font l'objet de restrictions aux mineurs, JORF 5.8.2006, n°36 (Recommendation No. 2006-6 of 4 July 2006 regarding the presentation, on TV of cinematographic and audiovisual works, video games, telephonic and telematic services or Internet sites which are subject to restrictions in view of minors).

2853 CSA, Délibération du 17 avril 2007 relative à l'intervention de mineurs dans le cadre d'émissions de télévision diffusées en métropole et dans les départements d'outre-mer, JORF 20.5.2007, n° 116, text n° 8 (Deliberation of 17 April 2007 concerning the participation of minors in television programmes broadcast in France and in the overseas departments*)*.

2854 CSA, Délibération n° 2010-23 du 18 mai 2010 relative aux conditions de diffusion, par les services de télévision et de radio, des communications commerciales en faveur d'un opérateur de jeux d'argent et de hasard légalement autorisé, JORF 21.5.2010, n° 0116, text n° 90 (Deliberation regarding the conditions for

age[2855]). As a corollary to these activities, minors and young audiences have constituted a target group of the CSA's information campaigns and activities enhancing media literacy.[2856] A working group of the Connected TV Commission was also dedicated to the protection of vulnerable groups of the general public. Under its leadership, an online platform was launched at www.csa.fr/csajeunesse following the Dutch example at www.mediawijzer.net. The platform serves as a space of dialogue between the regulator and the public informing the latter about the CSA's activities and clarifying the legal framework. During the national information campaigns, discussion forums are open for minors and parents alike.

### 1. The deliberation on the protection of young audiences in on-demand audiovisual media services

The key measure taken by the CSA in view of the protection of minors in on-demand services constitutes the *Délibération relative à la protection du*

---

the transmission of commercial communications promoting authorised operators of games of chance on radio and TV).

2855 Délibération n° 2008-85 du 22 juillet 2008 visant à protéger les enfants de moins de trois ans des effets de la télévision, en particulier des services présentés comme spécifiquement conçus pour eux, JORF 20.8.2008, n° 0193, text n° 82 (Deliberation n° 2008-85 of 22 July 2008 aimed at protecting children under the age of three years from the effects of television, in particular services specifically directed at them). This deliberation was subjected to an analysis of its legality by the Conseil d'Etat. The case was brought to the court by the American company Baby First which provided a French channel specifically directed at children which requested the annulment of the CSA's Deliberation. In its decision of May 2010, the Conseil d'Etat decided that the applicant had standing before the court as its programmes were available in France via a satellite operator established in France. On the substance, the court held that the CSA was endowed with a margin of discretion in drawing up executive measures on the basis of information collected from the French Ministry of Health. No manifest error was committed by the CSA during its elaboration. In addition, the court rejected the applicant's argument that the obligation to broadcast a warning violated the principle of equality as it was applicable to all providers of television services in France. The Conseil d'Etat thus rejected the action for annulment and confirmed the legality of the CSA's deliberation. See Conseil d'Etat, Judgment of 26.5.2010, Société Baby First, 5/4 SSR, n° 320863, FR:CESSR:2010:320863:20100526).

2856 CSA, "Reply to government consultation on the adaptation of audiovisual regulation," p. 22 (accessed 5.4.2016).

*jeune public, la déontologie et à l'accessibilité des programmes sur les services de médias audiovisuels à la demande* (Deliberation on the protection of young audiences, the code of conduct and accessibility of programmes in on-demand audiovisual media services, SMAD Deliberation)[2858] adopted in December 2011.[2859] The SMAD Deliberation covers not only the protection of children and adolescents but also encompasses programme standards such as the respect for human dignity, the fight against discrimination as well as honesty and faithfulness of programmes.[2860] It also encourages service providers to make programmes accessible to the hard of hearing and users with visual impairments.[2861] With regards to the protection of minors, the SMAD Deliberation requires that all programmes be classified according to the five categories which

2858 Délibération n° 2011-64 du 20 décembre 2011 relative à la protection du jeune public, la déontologie et à l'accessibilité des programmes sur les services de médias audiovisuels à la demande, JORF of 31.12.2011, n° 0303, p. 143.

2859 The SMAD Deliberation of 2011 is in large parts inspired by the Délibération n° 2014-17 du 5 mars 2014 modifiant la recommandation n° 2005-5 du 7 juin 2005 aux éditeurs de services de télévision concernant la signalétique jeunesse et la classification des programmes, (Deliberation modifying the recommendation no. 2005-5 of 7 June 2005 applicable to providers of television services concerning age ratings and the classification of programmes, hereinafter TV Deliberation), JORF of 9.4.2014, n° 0084, p. 5. The TV Deliberation outlines the five categories of programmes and the conditions under which these may be transmitted on TV prescribing obligations of labelling and scheduling restrictions (Art. 2-5). In contrast to the SMAD Deliberation, programmes are prohibited which disrespect human dignity, i.e. programmes which are devoted to violence and sexual perversions, programmes which are degrading for a human person or lead to his/her self-abasement as well as pornographic programmes stage-managing minors and programmes featuring extreme or gratuitous violence (Art. 3). Importantly, the dissemination of category V programmes is governed by the Recommendation n° 2004-7 du 15 décembre 2004 aux éditeurs et distributeurs de services de télévision diffusant en métropole et dans les départements d'outre-mer des programmes de catégorie V (Recommendation applicable to providers and distributors of television services disseminating category V programmes in France and its overseas departments), JORF 23.12.2004, n°298, p. 61. The Conseil d'Etat confirmed the legality of this recommendation which was challenged by the Association Comité Télévision et Libertes and others. See Conseil d'Etat, Judgment of 17.5.2006, n° 263081 (FR:CESSR:2006:263081.20060517.).

2860 See Art. III. A.-E. SMAD Deliberation.

2861 See Art. IV. SMAD Deliberation.

have been established for broadcasts:[2862] all audiences (category I), programmes harmful to minors below 10 years (category II), 12 years (category III), 16 years (category IV) and 18 years (category V).[2863] The responsibility for classifying content is incumbent on service providers.[2864] In this respect, the SMAD Deliberation details the requirements for content labels which comprise two elements: a label or pictogram which indicates the age group for which the material is considered detrimental (e.g. a round white pictogram showing a black "10" in the middle) as well as a warning message ("*déconseillé aux moins de ... ans*").[2865] The label must be featured in connection with the programme but also in relation to trailers or advertisements. In addition, it may either be shown at the beginning of the programme for a period of five seconds filling the entire screen accompanied by a warning message, or it may be visible through the whole duration of the programme in the bottom right corner provided that the warning message was shown at the start of the programme for at least one minute.[2866]

Furthermore, the SMAD Deliberation sets out conditions for the making available of programmes pertaining to categories I-IV and, separately, for category V programmes. A service provider that offers programmes for all audiences (category I) is required to compile this kind of material in a safe space ("*espace de confiance*").[2867] The SMAD Deliberation thus establishes a clear separation of family-friendly content and content which is subject to restrictions. Images, descriptions, extracts, trailers and advertisements of material classified under categories II to IV may not be in-

2862 In 1996, the CSA drew up the classification scheme ("signalétique jeunesse") which was applicable to all French TV channels as of 2000. In 2002, the scheme was revised and based on age groups. The new rules were formalised in the TV Deliberation of 2005. CSA, "La protection des mineurs à l'heure de la convergence des médias audiovisuels et d'internet," 2012, p. 14, http://www.csa.fr/content/download/20592/342842/file/Protection_des%20_mineurs_et_%20internet.pdf (accessed 5.4.2016); see also Kamina, *Communication audiovisuelle*, para. 139.

2863 See Art. II. SMAD Deliberation.

2864 See Art. II. A. SMAD Deliberation.

2865 See Art. II. A. and B. SMAD Deliberation.

2866 See Art. II. B. SMAD Deliberation.

2867 See Art. II. C. SMAD Deliberation.

cluded in the safe space.[2868] Special rules also apply to programmes classified as unsuitable for minors aged below 16 (category IV). If these are supplied free of charge, they can only be disseminated at certain times (i.e. between 10:30 p.m. and 5 a.m).[2869] No such conditions are in place for the paid transmission of category IV programmes. Interestingly, the CSA explicitly encourages service providers to promote technical tools which restrict access of minors by virtue of their age or the classification of programmes.

Importantly, the SMAD Deliberation stipulates precise conditions for the provision of programmes harmful to under-eighteens (category V).[2870] These can only be marketed as paid offers, i.e. upon subscription or pay-per-view basis.[2871] In addition, offers containing category V programmes may not be provided at more advantageous conditions than offers not comprising such programmes.[2872] Thus, category V programmes as well as their images, descriptions, extracts, trailers and advertisements must be kept in a separate space ("*espace réservé*").[2873] Pursuant to the SMAD Deliberation, the homepage of the service must contain a warning addressed

---

2868 Art. II C. SMAD Deliberation prescribes that images, descriptions, extracts, trailers and advertisements pertaining to programmes of categories I to IV shall take into account the vulnerability and sensitivity of young audiences.

2869 See Art. II. C. SMAD Deliberation.

2870 See Art. II. D. 1.- 6. SMAD Deliberation.

2871 See Art. II. D. 1. SMAD Deliberation.

2872 See Art. II. D. 1. SMAD Deliberation.

2873 See Art. II. D. 2. SMAD Deliberation. The 2004 Recommendation on the dissemination of category V programmes in television broadcasting services stipulates similar requirements as the SMAD Deliberation. Importantly, the preamble to the recommendation motivates the measure by the significant growth in the circulation of category V programmes and the fact that a non-negligible number of minors are exposed to these. The preamble also highlights the negative effects which, according to the CSA, have been proven by several official reports. As a result, the licensing agreement between the regulator and the service provider determines a maximum number of category V programmes which may be transmitted (Art. I. A.). In general, category V programmes may only be scheduled between midnight and 5 a.m. (Art. I. B.). Services containing such programmes may be marketed exclusively as pay-per-view provided that it is ensured that access is limited to adults (Art. I. A.). Interestingly, the Recommendation requires an effective access control system for the digital transmission of category V programmes conforming to six cumulative criteria (Art. II. B. 1.). Firstly, as from the first use, a specific access control must be enabled by default at the level of the decoder. Access to category V programmes must be made im-

to the user indicating the age ratings of the programmes supplied. The message must also indicate the harmfulness of the programmes as well as refer to the criminal sanctions which ensue from their making available to minors.[2874]

An important aspect regarding the provision of category V programmes in on-demand services constitutes technical blocking measures.[2875] The SMAD Deliberation makes clear that access to the separate space of category V programmes is permanently blocked.[2876] The virtual wall is to be activated when the user first accesses the service. More concretely, access is restricted by a personal code comprising, at least, four digits (with the exception of 0000) which are not visible on the screen and automatically deny access after five consecutive fruitless attempts.[2877] The personal code

---

possible ("doit render impossible l'accès") without the activation by a personal code (accompanied by a warning) (Art. II. B. 1. a). Secondly, the access control system must be penetrated before each transmission of category V programmes (Art. II. B. 1. b). Thirdly, the blocking device must be synchronised with the programme and active during its entire duration (Art. II. B. 1. c). Fourthly, the personal code must comprise at least four digits (with the exception of 0000) invisible on the screen (Art. II. B. 1. d) and fifthly, be exclusively employed for that purpose (Art. II. B. 1. e). Sixthly, the subscriber may not disable the blocking mechanism (Art. II. B. 1. f). Furthermore, the user is to be informed about the existence and functioning of the access control system including the necessity to create a personal code and the harm category V programmes may cause to minors (Art. III. A.). Broadcasters are, moreover, required to submit annual reports about the measures taken to prevent minors from accessing adult content (Art. III. B.). A clear concordance can be noted between these criteria and the conditions stipulated for the dissemination of category V programmes included in on-demand services pursuant to the SMAD Deliberation. The criteria stipulated in the Recommendation have been adapted to the specificities of the market for on-demand services. See also Kamina, *Communication audiovisuelle*, para. 138.

2874 See Art. II. D. 3. SMAD Deliberation. By derogation to the labelling requirements pursuant to Art. II B., age ratings may only be shown on the homepage.

2875 See Art. II. D. 4. SMAD Deliberation.

2876 See Art. II. D. 4. a) SMAD Deliberation.

2877 See Art. II. D. 4. b) SMAD Deliberation. It is interesting to note that in 2002, three MPs of the UMP (Union pour un Mouvement Populaire) proposed an amendment of Art. 15 LLC which would have prohibited programmes containing scenes of gratuitous violence or pornography unless they were made available in such a way as to ensure that minors will not normally hear or see them. The provision would have been applicable to radio and television services. As

must be used and configured depending on the nature of the service.[2878] In case of a subscription-based service, the subscriber is to set up the personal code via the service's settings accessible by a general code. Alternatively, the user is to be identified via a payment mechanism (e.g. bank account details, electronic payment identifier). The user is subsequently asked to confirm that he/she is of age (by "*déclaration sur l'honneur*"). A personal code can then be created. The user is to be informed via the screen that a message will be sent to him/her confirming the creation of a personal code. This message is to be addressed to the user by appropriate means (e.g. letter, email, SMS, telephone) encompassing further information about the use and functioning of the blocking device. If a personal code was not set up, access cannot be granted to category V content. Moreover, providers must ensure that the personal code is exclusively used for the reception of category V programmes and that a distinct log in is executed each time the user accesses these.[2879]

Above all, the user may not disable the blocking device him- or herself.[2880] Due to the complexity of the procedure, the SMAD Deliberation stipulates that service providers are to inform users about the existence and functioning of the blocking device. This information is to be accessible permanently and has to be brought to the attention of the user in regular intervals.[2881] It must also remain the free choice of users not to receive category V programmes and the CSA encourages providers to develop techniques which allow the user at any moment not to receive such content.[2882] On a more general level, the SMAD Deliberation attempts to raise awareness of the objective of protecting minors in VOD services. To this

technical measures, the initiative of the MPs aimed at promoting voluntary double decryption ("un système de double cryptage à déverrouillage volontaire") which could be unlocked by adults by using a confidential code. See Assemblée Nationale n° 317, Proposition de loi visant à protéger les mineurs contre la diffusion de programmes comprenant des scènes de violence gratuite ou de pornographie, enregistré le 15.10.2002, available at http://www.assemblee-nationale.fr/12/propositions/pion0317.asp (accessed 4.5.2016).

2878 See Art. II. D. 4. c) SMAD Deliberation.

2879 See Art. II. D. 4. d) and e) SMAD Deliberation.

2880 See Art. II. D. 4. f) SMAD Deliberation.

2881 See Art. II. D. 5. SMAD Deliberation.

2882 See Art. II. D. 6. SMAD Deliberation.

end, service providers are to disseminate annual campaigns to inform users.[2883]

In sum, the French regulator builds on three pillars to foster the protection of minors.[2884] Classification of content according to the five well-known categories is mandatory. Furthermore, providers must put in place systems of access controls of content unsuitable for under-eighteens. Such technical devices block inappropriate material which is only accessible by a procedure specified by the CSA. This procedure entails the creation of a personal code, an electronic declaration of majority as well as information about the configuration and use of this code. Another cornerstone of the CSA's activities constitutes the sensitisation and education of the general public. The extension of the obligation to classify content supplied by on-demand service providers is laudable. Yet, the definition of the nature of the content pertaining to each of the five categories is vague (Art. II. SMAD Deliberation). The descriptions are rudimentary, referring, for instance to "certain scenes susceptible to impair the development of minors below 10 years" or "erotic programmes and programmes of great violence" ("*grande violence*") which are regarded to be harmful to minors under the age of 16. Content which is "pornographic or of highly violent character" ("*très grande violence*") is considered detrimental to under-eighteens. The lack of specifications may make it difficult for service providers to fulfil their responsibility under the SMAD Deliberation. It is also not discernible that the CSA has established a body of practice from which further explanations could be drawn.

It is important to note that the CSA is convinced about the adequacy of a personal code as a means to limit access to adults. The use of the personal code is necessary each time the user accesses the service. On the screen, the entry of the personal code can only be shown in decoded form (presumably showing asterisks or similar symbols for each digit) so that minors cannot see the personal code and thereby obtain access. A four-digit code may, however, be less safe as presumed by the CSA. Minors could, for instance, observe adults when entering the personal code via the smartphone or remote control and deduce the code from their movements. However, the automatic generation of a message informing the user of five failed attempts constitutes a built-in safeguard against minors involved in

2883 See Art. II. E. SMAD Deliberation.

2884 For a concise overview of the measures taken by the CSA, see CSA, "Report on the protection of minors on the Internet," pp. 14–15.

trial and error exercises. The secrecy of the personal code and thus its effectiveness essentially depends on the behaviour and prudence of adults living in the household.

In addition, the identification of the user (non-subscriber) on the basis of account details does not seem to entail a verification of the user's age, nor is it intended as such according to the SMAD Deliberation. It seems that solely the electronic declaration of age serves the purpose of age verification. In contrast to the detailed requirements for the creation and utilisation of the personal code, the CSA refrains from giving further guidance on the process of age verification. It appears that the SMAD Deliberation would allow a simple declaration by electronic means that the user is of age (e.g. ticking a box or clicking a button). While a mere declaration of age is considered insufficient in the UK and Germany, the access control required by the CSA has to be viewed as an *ensemble* of measures including, above all, the creation and use of a personal code. Taken together, these should, under ordinary circumstances, be adequate tools to prevent minors from hearing or seeing adult content.

### 2. Pornographic and violent content

#### a) Vague criteria provided by the CSA

The meaning of the terms "pornography" and "gratuitous violence" are crucial to the application of the SMAD Deliberation and, consequently, the enforcement of Art. 15 LLC. As discussed above, Art. 15 LLC does not expressly refer to the nature of content considered (seriously) harmful. Yet, the classification scheme adopted by the CSA is based on the notions "pornographic programmes" ("*programmes pornographiques*") and "programmes of great violence" ("*programmes de très grande violence*") which are both rated as category V.[2885] Neither the SMAD Deliberation nor its equivalent applicable to television broadcasts further detail these notions. It is striking that the CSA does not further refine the notions and,

2885 In addition to category V, another category of content unsuitable for minors below 16 years refers to sexually explicit and violent content. Category IV programmes are defined as those having an erotic character or featuring violent scenes. Yet, this study focuses on the interpretation of these notions with regards to category V programmes, i.e. those made available to adults.

more importantly, does not seem to doubt the harm caused to minors by such type of material. Instead, the regulator contents itself with referring to studies, such as the Kriegel report on violence on TV of 2002,[2886] which lend support to its own perspective. The Kriegel report defined violence (not extreme violence) as an "unsettling force which prejudices the physical and psychological integrity in order to call into question, for the purposes of domination or destruction, the humanity of the individual".[2887] In addition, the Kriegel report refers to pornography as "a presentation of repeated sexual acts, directed at producing an effect of stimulation". The report further clarifies that pornography constitutes a "spectacle or plot of cumulative sexuality where emotions play a minor role".[2888]

It is not clear, however, to which extent the CSA relies on the definitions proposed by the Kriegel report when enforcing Art. 15 LLC. A taste of how the CSA interprets the crucial expressions "great violence" and "pornography" can be obtained when looking at the conventions (licensing agreements) concluded between the CSA and relevant service providers established in France. The license of the pay-TV operator Canal+ of May 2000, for instance, allowed the service provider to supply cinematographic works which, due to their "obscene character", were reserved to an adult public, provided that certain measures were put in place. By contrast, the dissemination of programmes was prohibited which violated human dignity such as those devoted to "representations of violence and sexual perversions, degrading to the human person or which lead to an abasement of the human person".[2889] A differentiation seems to be made between obscene content (which may be transmitted) and content which surpasses this

---

2886 Blandine Kriegel, "La violence à la télévision. Rapport à M. Jean-Jacques Aillagon, Ministre de la Culture et de la Communication.," 2002; on the adverse effects of violent audiovisual content, see also Sylvia Bréger, "La protection des mineurs sur Internet," *AJ Pénal* 3 (2009): pp. 112–15.

2887 The author translated from the original which reads as follows "la force déréglée qui porte atteinte à l'intégrité physique ou psychique pour mettre en cause dans un but de domination ou de destruction l'humanité de l'individu", see Kriegel, "Rapport sur la violence à la télévision," p. 63.

2888 The author translated from the following original wording: "la présentation d'actes sexuels répétés, destinée à produire un effet d'excitation. Il s'agit du spectacle d'une sexualité cumulative où l'intrigue et les sentiments jouent un très faible rôle", see Kriegel, "Rapport sur la violence à la télévision," p. 64.

2889 Franceschini, "Pornographie et télévision," p. 166. The author refers, in particular, to Art. 16 of the Convention of 29.5.2000 signed by the CSA and Canal+.

threshold by disrespecting the dignity of a person and being degrading. This understanding is reminiscent of the German interpretation which also highlights the fact that a person is degraded and turned into a worthless and replaceable object.

### b) The jusrisprudence of the Conseil d'Etat

In the absence of a positive law definition as well as any publicly available guidance by the CSA, it ultimately falls on the French courts to define these notions in accordance with the concept of morality prevailing at the specific time. The *Conseil d'Etat*, above all, has had the opportunity to judge on this issue in relation to the release of films in French cinemas which is regulated by the *Code du cinéma et de l'image animée* (Code for the Cinema and Animated Images).[2890] Accordingly, film producers apply to the competent Minister, the Minister of Culture and Communications, in order to obtain a "*visa d'exploitation*" (distribution certificate). These certificates are accompanied by classifications which may restrict the distribution of the film according to five categories: no restriction/all audiences, prohibition for minors aged below 12, 16 and 18 years and an absolute prohibition (also referred to as *"X"*). These are similar (though not identical) to the classifications employed for audiovisual media services. For the interpretation of the terms "violence" and "pornography" in the French legal order, the classifications "16", "18" and the total prohibition are interesting. The jurisprudence of the *Conseil d'Etat* in this area, of

2890 See, in particular Art. L-211-1 (partie législative) in conjunction with Art. R. 211-12 (partie réglementaire du code) Code du cinéma et de l'image animée. The French legal framework was fundamentally overhauled in 2009 with a view to modernising and simplifying it. Previously, the distribution of cinematographic works was, inter alia, governed by the Code de l'industrie cinématographique (Code of the Cinematographic Industry) in conjunction with the Décret n°90-174 du 23 février 1990 pris pour l'application des articles 19 à 22 du code de l'industrie cinématographique et relative à la classification des oeuvres cinématographiques, JORF of 25.1.1990, n°48, p. 2450 (Decree concerning the application of Art. 19 to 22 of the Code of the Cinematographic Industry and the classification of cinematographic works).

which only a small selection is examined here, is therefore well suited for the purposes of this study. [2891]

In 2000, the French association Promouvoir, notoriously defending Judaeo-Christian values,[2892] challenged a decision by the Minister of Culture and Communications regarding the film "*Baise-moi*". The Minister, upon opinion of the *commission de classification* (Board of Film Classification),[2893] had accorded a "visa" for its release in French cinemas, classifying the film as suitable for minors older than 16 years. In its decision of June 2000, the *Conseil d'Etat* considered, however, that the film should have been classified by a higher age label and prohibited the showing of the movie to under-eighteens.

The court held that the film "was mostly composed of a succession of scenes of great violence and non-simulated sex". The court also inquired about the intention of the director in making the film and found that the other sequences of the film did not contribute to an intention other than producing a violent and sexually explicit movie. At the time of the decision, the French legal framework did not provide for a certificate restrict-

---

2891 Due to the focus of this study, the case law of the French courts in relation to relevant criminal law provisions, notably Art. 227-23 and 227-24 CP is not discussed. It shall merely be noted that with respect to Art. 227-24 CP, which prohibits the "manufacture, transport, or distribution by whatever means and however supported, of a message bearing a pornographic or violent character or a character seriously violating human dignity", the Tribunal correctionnel de Paris, in 1972, distinguished between an erotic work which glorified the loving gesture and a pornographic work, which, on the contrary, was deprived of the loving ritual and its emotional context, by focussing on the psychological mechanism. The same court defined pornography as a "meticulous representation of violence and sexual perversions" in a case dated 1973. See also Franceschini, "Pornographie et télévision," p. 165.

2892 The association Promouvoir also attacked the classification decisions of other cinematographic works, not included in this study, such as "La Vie d'Adèle" (by Abdellatif Kechiche, initially prohibited for minors younger than 12 years), "Love" (by Gaspar Noé, initially prohibited for minors aged below 16) and "Antichrist" (by Lars von Trier, initially prohibited for minors aged below 16), which were subsequently re-examined by the French Minister of Culture and Communications. See also an article by Sylvie Kerviel entitled: André Bonnet, l'homme derrière l'association Promouvoir, 7.8.2015, available at http://www.lemonde.fr/cinema/article/2015/08/07/de-baise-moi-a-love-blanc-bonnet-et-bonnet-blanc_4715244_3476.html (accessed 2.5.2016).

2893 For more information on the commission de classification, see http://www.cnc.fr/web/en/index (accessed 2.12.2015).

ing the distribution to under-eighteens and the court thus qualified the film as pornographic and inciting to violence which would have implied its inclusion in the list of prohibited movies.[2894] In the aftermath of this case, the lacuna was filled by an amendment of the relevant legal instrument (Decree n° 90-174 was repealed in 2009).[2895] Since 2001, the classification scheme has comprised the categories "16", (the newly introduced) "18" as well as "X".

The film "*Baise-moi*" subsequently received the "18" certificate which prompted the association Promouvoir to again contest the Minister's second decision of 2001. The *Conseil d'Etat*, in its ruling of June 2002 confirmed the decision of the Minister.[2896] Although the movie included scenes of great violence and non-simulated sex (which justified the attribution of the classification "18"), it could not be considered as pornographic or inciting to violence, due to the theme and the manner in which it was stage-managed. An absolute prohibition of the distribution of the film (by its inclusion in the list of indexed films)[2897] was therefore not justified.

Furthermore, the association Promouvoir contested another ministerial decision according a certificate of "16" to the film "*Ken Park*" and asked for its inclusion in the list of prohibited cinematographic works. In February 2004, the *Conseil d'Etat* ruled that the movie, depicting one scene of non-simulated sexual acts and several scenes of violence, did not fulfil the characteristics for being added to the list.[2898] Yet, the court pointed out that this one sexual scene was particularly "raw and explicit" ("*cru et ex-*

---

2894 Conseil d'Etat, Judgment of 30.6.2000, n° 222194; 222195, (FR:CESJS:2000:222194.20000630).

2895 See Décret n°2001-618 du 12 juillet 2001 modifiant le décret n° 90-174 du 23 février 1990 pris pour l'application des articles 19 à 22 du code de l'industrie cinématographique et relatif à la classification des œuvres cinématographiques, JORF of 13.7.2001, n°161, p. 11241, texte n° 28.

2896 Conseil d'Etat, Judgment of 14.6.2002, n° 237910 (FR:CESSR:2002:237910.20020614).

2897 In France, pornographic works of those inciting to violence may be banned and included in the list of prohibited works by an arrêté of the Minister of Culture and Communications. The Board of Film Classification submits an opinion prior to the decision of the Minister. This procedure is regulated by Art. 235ter L et seq. of the General Tax Code as such works are deprived of aids or benefits for audiovisual and cinematographic productions.

2898 Conseil d'Etat, Jugment of 4.2.3004, n°261804 (FR:CESSR:2004:261804.20040204).

*plicit*") and that the movie contained other representations of adults mixing sex and violence. For this reason, the court considered that the Minister had incorrectly applied the 1990 Decree and should have granted an "18" certificate.

Similarly, in 2008 the *Conseil d'Etat* decided about the distribution certificate accorded to the Japanese film entitled "*Quand l'embryon part braconner*" for publication in French cinemas.[2899] The film had received the classification "18" by the Ministry of Culture, restricting the showing of the film to adults. The film production and distribution company Cinéditions contested this classification. The court sided with the Ministry of Culture stating that the film comprised numerous scenes of torture, sadism and great physical and psychological violence. It presented an image of relations between the sexes as being founded on confinement, humiliation and abasement of the female person. Considering that such content was likely to offend the sensitiveness of minors, the court found that the Minister of Culture had not committed an error of assessment. Interestingly, the *Conseil d'Etat* held that the Minister's decision did not interfere with the applicant's right to freedom of expression as guaranteed by Art. 10 ECHR and was compatible with the latter. It highlighted the fact that the legal provisions (including Art. 227-24 CP) were proportionate in that they merely restricted the dissemination of films with a violent or pornographic nature to an adult audience. The regime of prior authorisation (through distribution certificates) did not aim at censuring cinematographic works but was motivated by the protection of minors.[2900] It was accompanied by built-in safeguards which allowed for comprehensive judicial review of the Minister's decisions.[2901]

While some of the cases examined above encompassed both, sexually explicit and violent material, the controversy surrounding the release of the horror movie Saw III sheds light on the interpretation of the term "great violence". The case was lodged in November 2010, three weeks after the release of the film in France, as an urgent procedure by the associa-

2899 Conseil d'Etat, Judgment of 6.10.2008, n° 311017 (FR:CESSR:2008:311017.20081006).

2900 The objective to protect minors is expressly mentioned in Art. L. 211-1 (2) of the Code du cinéma et de l'image animée. See also Marc Le Roy, "De la bonne utilisation de l'interdiction des films aux moins de 18 ans," *Actualité juridique Droit administratif* 10 (2009): p. 546.

2901 Conseil d'Etat, Judgment of 6.10.2008.

tion Promouvoir which aimed at suspending the execution of the decision by the Minister according the film a distribution certificate "16". Due to a change in competence, attributing jurisdiction to the ordinary administrative courts, the *Conseil d'Etat* decided on appeal in June 2015.[2902] While the lower instance courts had confirmed the Minister's decision, the *Conseil d'Etat* found that the film was unsuitable for minors aged below 16 and should have been limited to an adult audience by rating it as "18". In taking this decision, the court took into account the manner in which the controversial scenes were stage-managed (above all, the degree of realism), the effect such scenes were likely to have on viewers (whether the material incited to or trivialised violence) and any other characteristics which allowed viewers to take a critical distance to what they saw. The court underlined that the movie was inappropriate for under-sixteens given the great number of realistic scenes portraying violence amounting to repeated acts of torture and barbarism. The film's violent character was furthermore reinforced by the physical and psychological suffering of victims, who, being trapped by an assassin, were incited to mutilate themselves or others to escape death or save close friends or relatives.[2903]

---

2902 In 2010, the Code de justice administrative was amended by a Decree which revoked the competence of the Conseil d'Etat to rule on administrative decisions in first and last instance (Décret n° 2010-164 du 22 février 2010 relatif aux compétences et au fonctionnement des juridictions administratives, JORF of 23.2.2010, n°0045, p. 3325, texte n° 15). The change took effect as of applications lodged after 1st April 2010. This is the reason why the Conseil d'Etat, initially seized by the association Promouvoir in November 2010, denied competence in December 2010. As a result, the applicant turned to the Paris administrative courts, both of which rejected its application. The case thus reached the Conseil d'Etat on appeal. See the line of cases in chronological order Conseil d'Etat, Judgment of 6.12.2010, n° 344567 (FR:CE-ORD:2010:344567.20101206); Tribunal administrative de Paris, Judgement of 16.12.2011, n° 1021073/7-1; Cour administrative d'appel de Paris, Judgement of 3.7.2013, n° 12PA00838; Conseil d'Etat, Judgment of 1.6.2015, n° 372057 (FR:CESSR:2015:372057:20150601).

2903 The lower administrative courts of Paris had agreed that the film contained numerous scenes of great violence ("très grande violence") such as the subjection of characters to games and the killing of persons under appalling conditions. Interestingly, they considered that the film did not go beyond what would be expected of a film containing gore and slaughter and posited that minors under the age of 16 had a critical stance towards such movies. In opposition to the Conseil d'Etat, the lower courts found that the violent scenes were interrupted by other

Succinctly, the *Conseil d'Etat* has shaped the notions of violence and pornography. With regards to the former, it established certain criteria, such as the presentation of violence and its effects on viewers. These are certainly valuable and help to distinguish categories of content by respective age groups. It remains to be seen whether the criteria serve as precedent and will be used in the future. It also results from the case law that the notion of pornography is associated with the prevalence of scenes showing non-simulated sexual activities which are not justified by an over-arching, socially relevant context (e.g. demonstrating social violence against women). Yet, the inclusion of a scene of non-simulated sex does not necessarily lead to the film being classified as pornographic and banned from French cinema.[2904] Apart from the frequency of pornographic/sexually explicit scenes and their quality or intensity, the court also considers the intention of the author of the work – an analysis which is difficult to undertake for its inherently subjective nature.[2905]

The grading between the different classifications of films remains complex and inevitably entails "grey areas" which make a case-by-case assessment indispensable. Certain general tendencies may nonetheless be deduced from the jurisprudence presented above. A cinematographic work is likely to be prohibited (classification "X") if it includes numerous scenes of non-simulated sexual acts coupled with an intention of the author of the work to produce a pornographic work.[2906] By contrast, a cinematographic film may be distributed under the condition that it is restricted to an adult audience (classification "18") if it contains scenes of non-simulated sexual acts which are raw and explicit ("*cru et explicit*") and a film is likely to receive the classification "16" if there is only one unique and brief scene of non-simulated sexual acts ("*unique et brève*").[2907] It is unclear to what extent the CSA, as the French regulator for audiovisual media services, relies on the *Conseil d'Etat's* jurisprudence in matters of the distribution of

scenes, were not realistic and even displayed a certain form of humour which alleviated the terror caused in spectators.

2904 Le Roy, "De la bonne utilisation de l'interdiction des films aux moins de 18 ans," p. 545.

2905 Le Roy, "De la bonne utilisation de l'interdiction des films aux moins de 18 ans," p. 546.

2906 Le Roy, "De la bonne utilisation de l'interdiction des films aux moins de 18 ans," p. 546.

2907 Le Roy, "De la bonne utilisation de l'interdiction des films aux moins de 18 ans," p. 545.

cinematographic works. The regulator has refrained from adopting concrete definitions of the expressions "excessive violence" and "pornography" which are consequently contingent on the specific time and the particular social context in which they are used. The notions remain vague even if certain indications flow from the jurisprudence of the French courts, in particular, the *Conseil d'Etat*.[2908]

### 3. The CSA's decisions

It follows from the CSA's press releases and annual reports of recent years (notably 2012-2014), that it has been seized by the public or investigated on its own motion in alleged breaches of Art. 15 LLC and the accompanying regulations. Public complaints and inspections by the regulator seem to remain, however, more frequent in relation to programmes broadcast on TV. Nonetheless, the CSA intervened in several cases concerning violations of the rules on protection of minors committed by non-linear service providers. These are discussed below on the basis of publicly available information retrieved from the CSA's website.

#### a) Cases of 2012

The annual report for the year 2012 refers to three cases of non-compliance with the SMAD Deliberation.[2909] The CSA addressed two letters ("*courriel de rappel*") to the catch-up service My TF1 and the VOD provider KZ Play respectively reminding them of their obligations flowing from the SMAD Deliberation. My TF1 had transmitted an advertising spot for a video game classified as "16" (unsuitable for minors below the age of 16) before the dissemination of the animated cartoon "*Barbapapa*" presented in the safe space of the website.[2910] According to the SMAD Delib-

2908 In a judgment of September 2010 concerning the Code général des impôts (General Tax Code), the Conseil d'Etat expressly referred to the "uncertainties which characterise the notion of pornography". See Conseil d'Etat, Judgment of 22.9.2010, n° 341064 (FR:CESSR:2010:341064.20100922).

2909 CSA, "Rapport Annuel 2012," p. 127.

2910 See also CSA, Press release of 3.12.2012, Publicité pour un jeu video déconseillé aux moins de 16 ans : intervention auprès de MyTF1, available at http://www.csa.fr/Espace-juridique/Decisions-du-CSA/Publicite-pour-un-jeu-video-dec

eration, extracts, trailers and advertisements for material subject to age restrictions is prohibited in such parts directed at families. Similarly, the CSA reprimanded KZ Play for having failed to classify extracts of the manga, "No Money", with the appropriate age rating of "16" as the content included several sexually explicit scenes.[2911] In addition, a formal warning ("*mise en garde*") was issued to TVR Direct Star concerning the dissemination of the series "*Enquête très spéciale*" on different "channels" of its service.[2912] The CSA determined several breaches of the SMAD Deliberation. The provider had failed to apply the appropriate classification of "16" and had, moreover, transmitted the material outside the periods specified in the SMAD Deliberation for category IV programmes. The CSA also noted that certain episodes had been under-classified which featured, above all, pornographic content and images of the shooting of a pornographic film. Some of these images, the CSA stressed, would pertain to content of category V (unsuitable for minors under 18 years). In addition, the service provider had made available three extracts of pornographic films which lacked the classification "18" and had promoted two pornographic websites.

b) Cases of 2013

2013 saw two cases of non-compliance with the SMAD Deliberation, as indicated in the CSA's annual report.[2913] These concerned material inappropriate for minors aged below 16 and 18 respectively. The CSA addressed the service providers of FranceTVPluzzVàd, Iminéo and Virgin Méga.fr Vidéo for failure to classify the film "*Les Kaïra*". It also reprimanded the under-classification (as "10") of the same film by Canal Play

onseille-aux-moins-de-16-ans-intervention-aupres-de-MyTF1 (accessed 6.5.2016).

2911 See also CSA, Press release of 3.12.2013, Manga No Money: intervention auprès du service KZ Play, available at http://www.csa.fr/Espace-juridique/Decisions-du-CSA/Manga-No-Money-intervention-aupres-du-service-KZ-Play (accessed 6.5.2016).

2912 See also CSA, Press release of 25.9.2012, Série Enquête très spéciale: Direct Star mise en garde, available at http://www.csa.fr/Espace-juridique/Decisions-du-CSA/Serie-Enquete-tres-speciale-Direct-Star-mise-en-garde (accessed 6.5.2016).

2913 CSA, "Rapport Annuel 2013," p. 80.

VOD, Vidéo à la demande d'Orange, Vidéo Futur and MyTF1 VOD.[2914] Given the crudeness of the language, the inclusion of several scenes of sexual and pornographic character, the regulator underlined that the film, in spite of its humorous tone, had to have been classified as unsuitable for minors under 12 years. Service providers were asked to apply or change the classification accordingly. Another investigation led to a warning being issued to Orange Cinéma Series which had transmitted the pornographic film "*The Last Son: la malediction*" on its catch-up service entitled OCS à la demande.[2915] The film, which was preceded by the pictogram "18", was made available to subscribers without access control. The following day, the service provider informed the CSA that it had rectified the breach, having withdrawn the film from the catalogue and placed in the space reserved for adult content.

c) Cases of 2014

Furthermore, the CSA was involved in six cases in 2014.[2916] The only case which is documented by a press release concerned the "Replay" service supplied by TF1 at Mytf1.fr.[2917] The service provider had featured an advertising message for the horror film "*The Baby*" rated as "12" before the transmission of the animated film "*Les Octonauts*" contained in the safe space of the catch-up service. The CSA reminded TF1, which had infringed the same rule two years before, that content which was age-rated could not be supplied in the safe space where solely material suitable for all audiences was aggregated. In addition, the CSA found that the classifi-

2914 See also CSA, Press release of 9.4.2013, Film Les Kaïra, sous-classifié: intervention auprès de plusieurs services à la demande, available at http://www.csa.fr/Espace-juridique/Decisions-du-CSA/Film-Les-Kaira-sous-classifie-intervention-aupres-de-plusieurs-services-a-la-demande (accessed 6.5.2016).

2915 See also CSA, Press release of 17.7.2013, Diffusion d'un film pornographique sur un SMAD : Orange Cinéma Séries mise en garde, available at http://www.csa.fr/Espace-juridique/Decisions-du-CSA/Diffusion-d-un-film-pornographique-sur-un-SMAD-Orange-Cinema-Series-mise-en-garde (accessed 6.5.2016).

2916 CSA, "Rapport Annuel 2014," p. 32.

2917 See also CSA, Press release of 17.7.2014, Message de promotion d'un film interdit aux moins de 12 ans sur mytf1.fr: intervention auprès de TF1, available at http://www.csa.fr/Espace-juridique/Decisions-du-CSA/Message-de-promotion-d-un-film-interdit-aux-moins-de-12-ans-sur-mytf1.fr-intervention-aupres-de-TF1 (accessed 8.5.2016).

cation of a film distributed by several VOD providers was insufficient and asked the providers to raise the age group for which the material could be made accessible.[2918] Another service provider freely supplied images promoting a VOD service offering category V programmes. These advertisements should have been isolated and only made accessible in a space reserved for adults. The CSA criticised, above all, the lack of technical measures protecting the reserved space.[2919] Moreover, the CSA took action against a broadcaster that had failed to comply with the watershed rules applicable to a category IV programme (not advised for minors less than 16 years). The broadcaster had also included the programme in the catalogue of its catch-up service free of charge. The CSA underlined that programmes with a "16" age label, if they were not provided on a pay-per-view basis, could only be supplied between 10:30 p.m. and 5 a.m. It is interesting to note that the annual report of 2015, published in April 2016, does not mention any further infringements by VOD service providers of the rules protecting minors. It seems as if the CSA, in 2015, only detected breaches in relation to television broadcasters.[2920]

Succinctly, the violations found by the CSA primarily concern the absence of classifications or the existence of incorrect classifications (i.e. where providers under-classified content). In addition, the requirements applicable to special age groups (all audiences or adult content) have been breached repeatedly. The CSA emphasised that in a safe space only content which was suitable for all audiences could be compiled. As a result, content, including advertisements, trailers and extracts of programmes restricted to certain age groups could not be placed in this part of the website. The provision of category IV content (inappropriate for minors younger than 16 years), was subject to transmission restrictions if the material was freely accessible on-demand. Similarly, the CSA pointed out that adult content (category V) including advertisements for pornographic services were to be blocked from minors' view by special technical devices. In general (judging by the relatively small number of decisions taken by the CSA), compliance with the SMAD Deliberation appears high and the industry seems to have accepted the requirements, such as the obligation to classify content or the duty to put in place technical measures restricting access to categories IV and V programmes. The small body of

2918 CSA, "Rapport Annuel 2014," p. 32.
2919 CSA, "Rapport Annuel 2014," p. 32.
2920 CSA, "Rapport Annuel 2015," p. 26.

practice may, conversely, be indicative of the difficulty of enforcing regulatory standards online. Although a notification obligation for VOD providers was introduced in France in late 2013, the CSA has reiterated its difficulty of identifying providers and determining jurisdiction. To this effect, several policy documents are analysed below.

### 4. The debate about systematic blocking of content at the level of access to the Internet

In 2015, the UK debate about systematic blocking of online adult content by Internet access providers spilled over to France. This idea had already been broached in 2005 by the government of UMP Prime Minister Dominique de Villepin. At that time, it was, however, heavily criticised by the public, notably by the association IRIS (*Imaginons un réseau Internet solidaire*). IRIS agreed that the objective to protect minors on the Internet was legitimate but emphasised that it was the sole responsibility of parents, guardians and educators to put in place filtering devices.[2921] The association was also sceptical of the obligation incumbent on Internet providers that would have to operate an automatic system, by default at the level of access to the network and not just a voluntary filtering mechanism active on the personal computer of the customer. Access would have been blocked to illegal content and, more importantly, to legal content considered detrimental or prejudicial to minors' development. Subsequently, an amendment to the *Loi n° 2004-575 du 21 juin 2004 pour la confiance dans l'économie numérique* was tabled by several conservative MPs in 2006. It would have obliged Internet access providers to automatically block access to content which was harmful to minors within the meaning of relevant provisions of the French Penal Code.[2922] Although the amendment, which was narrower in scope than the initial suggestion

2921 See for example an IRIS press release of 16.9.2005, Filtrage automatique des contenus: l'ordre moral s'enhardit, available at http://iris.sgdg.org//info-debat/comm-filtrage0905.html (accessed 6.5.2016).

2922 See the amendment proposed by MPs Gilles, Tian, Diard, Luca, Garraud, Remiller and Mallié, Assemblée Nationale, 20.11.2006, Prévention de la délinquance, available at http://www.assemblee-nationale.fr/12/amendements/3338/333800458.asp (accessed 8.5.2016.).

by the government, would have restricted the blocking to illegal content, it was never adopted.

Roughly ten years later, in July 2015, MP Jean-Jacques Candelier (Gauche démocrate et républicaine-Nord) addressed a parliamentary question to the Minister of Family Laurence Rossignol.[2923] He inquired about how the government intended to protect minors from pornographic content which, due to the emergence of new technologies, was easily accessible, even to the youngest. He suggested, among others, fighting "this nuisance" ("*ce fléau*") by introducing default blocking, as contemplated by UK's Prime Minister Cameron. While the initiative was realised in the UK, the French Minister rejected the proposal. In her response dated September 2015, she highlighted the role of parental controls which currently constituted the "most effective and complete technical solution".[2924] An accord had been concluded in 2005 between the French Ministry of Family and Internet access providers, committing the latter to offer effective and evolutionary parental controls to their customers at no cost. This accord had recently been extended to mobile operators. The Minister underlined that technical protection measures had to be accompanied by actions of awareness-raising of parents, guardians and minors, especially at school.

It is important to note that the Minister pointed out that the government was not opposed to redefining and recalibrating the role of platforms in the future, especially in the context of the withdrawal of illegal content. Interestingly, she also referred to the difficulties the UK had experienced when implementing a system of default blocking operated by Internet access providers. These included technical problems especially for websites hosted abroad, the elaboration of counter-measures to circumvention, the up-dating of the list prohibiting adult content and the choice of criteria for the listing of content. On account of these deficiencies, the French government did not further contemplate the introduction of systematic blocking of adult websites but continued to rely on effective technical devices (such

2923 See Assemblée Nationale, Question n° 85225 de M. Jean-Jacques Candelier, JO of 14.7.2015, p. 5348, available at http://questions.assemblee-nationale.fr/q14/14-85225QE.htm (accessed 4.4.2016).

2924 See Assemblée Nationale, Réponse de Mme Laurence Rossignol, Ministère de Famille, enfance, personnes âgées et autonomie, JO of 8.9.2015, p. 6870, available at http://questions.assemblee-nationale.fr/q14/14-85225QE.htm (accessed 4.4.2016).

as parental controls) as well as preventive measures which promoted sex education, the respect and equality of men and women and the de-construction of stereotypes conveyed by numerous websites. In brief, the chronology of events demonstrates that similar approaches to enhance the protection of minors online are discussed across borders. In France, automatic blocking of adult content has not yet been enshrined in the legal framework, even if the issue has resurfaced several times in recent years. So far, the French governments have privileged less expansive (and what they claim more effective) measures, taking into account the primary responsibility of parents and the importance of educating parents as well as children.

## 5. The CSA's reports on the protection of minors

### a) The 2012 report on the protection of minors in an era of media convergence

In 2012, the CSA was seized by Mrs. Claude Greff, Secretary of State for Family to prepare a report on the protection of minors in light of the convergence between audiovisual media and the Internet. The CSA's report entitled "*La protection des mineurs à l'heure de la convergence des médias audiovisuels et d'internet*", published in March 2012, contained considerations and reflections about current developments as well as a summary of the present legal framework in France. The report was elaborated by the working group of Connected TV dedicated to the protection of vulnerable audiences which was headed by Mrs. Janine Langlois-Glandier. In its report, the CSA sketched the status quo and the technological progress brought about by media convergence. The CSA pointed to the multiplication of screens on which audiovisual content is consumed today.[2925] Minors increasingly used the Internet on various devices, at home or on the go for numerous activities such as school work, research, games, video clips and messaging services.[2926] This did, however, not seem to affect their time spent watching television, which had equally increased throughout the years 2009 to 2011. The increase of content consumption on the Internet did not curb consumption of television content; rather mi-

2925 CSA, "Report on the protection of minors on the Internet," pp. 3–4.
2926 CSA, "Report on the protection of minors on the Internet," p. 4.

nors used different media cumulatively.[2927] As a result, minors were more frequently exposed to violent or pornographic material, often when they least expect it (for example when researching information or surfing on a video-sharing platform).[2928] The CSA underlined the ease with which pornographic videos are distributed online, freely accessible at no cost.[2929]

It also identified a technological gap between parents and their children as the latter master new technologies much faster than the former. In addition, parents and guardians did not always seem to be aware of the dangers the Internet poses for their children and seem to lack the necessary tools and technical skills to effectively protect them. By reference to an EU study, the CSA remarked that parental controls were installed infrequently on computers and were even less rarely used on mobile phones. Instead, parents employed different strategies such as giving advice and providing information about the risks associated with the Internet, formulating rules (such as prohibiting the publication of intimate photos or responding to somebody unknown), accompanying children during their online activities and retrospectively monitoring the content consulted.[2930] Generally, parents and children alike did not possess a sufficient level of media education.[2931] Therefore, the CSA was in favour of the development of a genuine policy promoting media education.[2932]

Furthermore, the CSA posited that the protection of minors was a shared social objective. According to the regulator, psychiatrics consented that exposure to shocking content had a negative impact on the psychological development of minors. The banalisation of pornographic content depicting a mechanic vision of the body and a dehumanised overstatement of sexual performances had direct consequences for minors, in particular for the construction of their sexual identity.[2933] Several studies testified in favour of the harm caused to minors. Interestingly, the CSA referred to scientific consensus and studies *in abstracto* without indicating a source or providing evidence. Furthermore, the regulator delineated the context within which the protection of minors was emotionally debated, opposing

2927 CSA, "Report on the protection of minors on the Internet," p. 5.
2928 CSA, "Report on the protection of minors on the Internet," p. 6.
2929 CSA, "Report on the protection of minors on the Internet," p. 6.
2930 CSA, "Report on the protection of minors on the Internet," p. 7.
2931 CSA, "Report on the protection of minors on the Internet," pp. 6–7.
2932 CSA, "Report on the protection of minors on the Internet," p. 7.
2933 CSA, "Report on the protection of minors on the Internet," p. 8.

proponents of a free Internet and defenders of a regulated Internet.[2934] It emphasised that the protection of minors was oftentimes perceived as a pretext to satisfy the pretentiousness of control of the state over the Internet.[2935] In view of the number of services affected and the international dimension of the network, the CSA considered unrealistic to control the Internet at large.[2936] Hence, the objective was to create a space of freedom respectful of the vulnerability of minors and to give all stakeholders involved a sense of responsibility.[2937]

In another part of the report, the CSA outlined the legal framework for the protection of minors on the Internet and the plethora of activities embarked upon at the European and national level in the context of, above all, the Safer Internet initiative.[2938] The report referred to both sets of rules, electronic communications in line with the ECD as transposed by the *Loi du 21 juin 2004 pour la confiance dans l'économie numérique*,[2939] as well as audiovisual media services within the meaning of the AVMSD and the LLC. In this respect, the CSA highlighted the fragmentation of the legal framework which typically followed a sectoral approach. While the regulation of the Internet was momentarily only assured *a posteriori* by the judiciary, the protection of minors in audiovisual communications within the meaning of the LLC was subject to *ex ante* regulation.[2940] Yet, the CSA made clear that not all content disseminated online was covered by the LLC's scope of application. To the user, the CSA pointed out, the difference was imperceptible between an on-demand audiovisual media service regulated by the LLC and a service containing audiovisual material falling outside its scope, above all, when cohabiting on the same screen.[2941] In view of ensuring the protection of minors on connected devices such as connected TV, the CSA considered that the current legal framework might contain lacunae.[2942]

---

2934 CSA, "Report on the protection of minors on the Internet," p. 8.
2935 CSA, "Report on the protection of minors on the Internet," p. 8.
2936 CSA, "Report on the protection of minors on the Internet," p. 8.
2937 CSA, "Report on the protection of minors on the Internet," p. 8.
2938 CSA, "Report on the protection of minors on the Internet," pp. 9–11.
2939 Loi du 21 juin 2004 pour la confiance dans l'économie numérique, JORF of 22.6.2004, n° 0143, p. 11168 as amended.
2940 CSA, "Report on the protection of minors on the Internet," p. 15.
2941 CSA, "Report on the protection of minors on the Internet," p. 16.
2942 CSA, "Report on the protection of minors on the Internet," p. 16.

Similarly, inconsistencies regarding the classification of content (for cinematographic release or dissemination as an audiovisual media service) might easily arise due to the involvement of different national authorities.[2943] The disparity of rules and heterogeneity of administrative practice lacking common classification standards across all media outlets was incomprehensible for the user, according to the CSA.[2944] This confusion was furthermore enhanced by the fact that content on the Internet was commonly not rated at all.[2945] Yet, on the Internet, the need for minors to navigate through the flood of content readily available by one click was all the more apparent.[2946] It was indispensable to the CSA that guiding principles common to all forms of commercialisation of audiovisual content be elaborated and schemes of protection be globally coordinated.[2947] In the opinion of the CSA, this did not amount to the establishment of strictly identical rules for all media outlets due to the specificities of each media.[2948] Instead, classifications based on age groups should be used horizontally, for all types of content.[2949]

In the final part of its report, the CSA offered some reflections about first, the institutional design of the protection of minors and second, the need to promote media education. Institutionally, the CSA proposed the creation of a national coordinator for the protection of minors.[2950] According to the CSA, this would remedy the absence of regulation on the Internet as well as the incoherence of the level of protection between the sectors "audiovisual" and "Internet". This entity would also serve as a unique reference point for the public as well as stakeholders.[2951] *In concreto*, the CSA suggested coordinating its activities with those taken by the Safer In-

2943 This is especially true with regards to the classification of content intended for cinematographic release, distribution of a film in form of a DVD or other storage media or transmission as an audiovisual media service. While the CSA is charged with the supervision of audiovisual media services, cinematographic works are classified by the Commission de classification des oeuvres cinématographiques, exercising an ex ante control. CSA, "Report on the protection of minors on the Internet," p. 16.

2944 CSA, "Report on the protection of minors on the Internet," p. 17.

2945 CSA, "Report on the protection of minors on the Internet," p. 17.

2946 CSA, "Report on the protection of minors on the Internet," p. 17.

2947 CSA, "Report on the protection of minors on the Internet," p. 18.

2948 CSA, "Report on the protection of minors on the Internet," p. 18.

2949 CSA, "Report on the protection of minors on the Internet," p. 24.

2950 CSA, "Report on the protection of minors on the Internet," p. 18.

2951 CSA, "Report on the protection of minors on the Internet," p. 18.

ternet initiative in France[2952] and seeking collaboration at the European and international level,[2953] in particular with respect to the promotion of common principles for the classification of content disseminated through different media. Importantly, the CSA underlined that the national coordinator should conduct research, draw up recommendations and serve as a point of arbitration.[2954] An urgent topic which the coordinator should approach was the multitude of technical instruments (access controls, parental control software and other filters) used to restrict access of minors to inappropriate content by media service providers and Internet access providers. The use of access restrictions on mobile phones should also be improved.[2955] Finally, the CSA reiterated the importance of media education and media literacy defined by recital 47 AVMSD as "skills, knowledge and understanding that allow consumers to use media effectively and safely".[2956] The CSA relied on the Vincent-Deray report of June 2009 which included fifteen proposals to implement a global project on media education.[2957] Apart from an increased offer of content informing about media education on private and public TV channels, the report also envisaged co-regulatory measures in raising awareness and informing the public about the risks of the Internet and the safe use of media.[2958]

In sum, the reflections of the CSA appear reasonable in light of ever intensifying media convergence and the present legal framework in France. It is especially noteworthy that the CSA took for granted the justification for the protection of minors in audiovisual media. While it recognised the context within which an emotionally loaded discussion takes place, it accepted that there was consistent scientific evidence about the harm caused to minors by exposing them to inappropriate content. This causal link, drawn by the CSA, was, however, not substantiated by reference to any

---

2952 CSA, "Report on the protection of minors on the Internet," p. 19.

2953 CSA, "Report on the protection of minors on the Internet," p. 20.

2954 CSA, "Report on the protection of minors on the Internet," p. 19.

2955 CSA, "Report on the protection of minors on the Internet," pp. 20, 24.

2956 CSA, "Report on the protection of minors on the Internet," p. 21.

2957 Agnès Vincent-Deray, "Commission famille, education aux médias; Rapport à l'attention de Madame Nadine Morano, Secrétaire d'Etat chargée de la Famille et de la Solidarité," 2009, see in particular the 15 recommendations on pp. 15-29.

2958 Vincent-Deray, "Report on media education", see in particular recommendations numbers 6 and 7 on p. 21-23 and recommendations numbers 13 and 14 on pp. 27-29; CSA, "Report on the protection of minors on the Internet," p. 22.

sources, scientific reports or studies, so that the report seems defective in this regard. With respect to the priorities identified by the CSA,[2959] the harmonisation at the national level of rating schemes based on age groups seems indispensable. In the online context, the use of classifications would be beneficial for minors and parents alike who would be empowered to take more informed decisions. It is unclear whether the CSA would prefer an amendment of the law prescribing age classifications for audiovisual content disseminated on the Internet or the establishment of a self-regulatory scheme which incentivises action by service providers. The CSA does, in its report, highlight the possibility and generally seems to be in favour of self-or co-regulation. It remains, however, vague with regards to the concrete design and context within which such regulatory strategies should be employed. Similarly, the objective of implementing a consistent policy enhancing media education is laudable. How exactly this should be accomplished cannot be derived from the CSA's report. Since the report aims at stimulating the debate about the protection of minors on the Internet, it is, to a certain extent, necessarily imprecise. Yet, the CSA does not appear to be overly ambitious in formulating its goals or specifying its approach in more detail. The policy objectives advanced in the report (which, admittedly strives to articulate reflections), thus appear to be of rather "soft" nature.

b) The 2014 report on young persons' media practices and habits

While the 2012 report primarily relied on research conducted at the EU level, the CSA collected its own data two years later on media practices and consumption patterns of 13-24 year olds. In 2014, a report entitled "*Adolescents/Jeunes adultes et médias : Le séquencage des pratiques médias des 13-24 ans*" was published.[2960] In order to better understand minors' use of media on a given day, the regulator interviewed a representative sample of around 10,000 minors in 2008, 2012 and 2013. Minors

2959 For a summary of the priority points identified by the regulator, see CSA, "Report on the protection of minors on the Internet," p. 24.

2960 CSA, "Adolescents/jeunes adultes et médias: Le séquencage des pratiques médias des 13-24 ans," 2014, http://www.csa.fr/content/download/51801/499348/file/Synth%C3%A8se%20jeunes%20et%20m%C3%A9dias%20.pdf (accessed 6.5.2016).

were asked to keep a daily journal indicating which media they used, how much time they spent consuming different media (on the basis of units comprising a quarter of an hour) and in which context.[2961] As a preliminary remark, the CSA flagged the problem of defining "the young" ("*les jeunes*"). It underlined that the notion of "the young" consisted of a great number of heterogeneous age groups, including the very young (3 to 8 years), pre-adolescents (8 to 12 years), minors (12 to 18 years) and young adults (18 to 24 years).[2962] The CSA decided to focus on young audiences[2963] aged between 13 and 24 due to the lack of research attributed to this age group and the fact that minors of this age span acted more independently in comparison to younger audiences and thus attracted the attention of the advertising industry.[2964]

In a first section of the report, the CSA traced the evolution of content directed at young audiences disseminated through various media such as television, radio and the Internet.[2965] It noted an explosion of offers which are accessible through multiple outlets, notably via catch-up or video on-demand services on the Internet. Social networks like Facebook and Twitter or video-sharing platforms like YouTube (which launched thematic channels in France in 2012) and Dailymotion (which entered the French market in 2005) occupy a central role in the life of young persons.[2966] In parallel, the number of devices per family had increased considerably to 6.4 screens on average in 2013.[2967] In comparison to the general public, young audiences spent most of their time watching (music) videos on mobile devices (amounting to more than 11 hours in April 2013, a figure which had more than doubled from 5 hours in February 2012).[2968] Another favourite activity was playing online games, an activity which decreased with age.[2969] In spite of the resilience of TV consumption, young audiences increasingly turned to other devices such as the personal computer

2961 On the methodology of the report, see in more detail CSA, "Report on media in the life of 13-24 year olds," pp. 17–18.
2962 CSA, "Report on media in the life of 13-24 year olds," p. 3.
2963 In this context, the term young audiences implies persons aged between 13 and 24.
2964 CSA, "Report on media in the life of 13-24 year olds," p. 4.
2965 CSA, "Report on media in the life of 13-24 year olds," pp. 4–7.
2966 CSA, "Report on media in the life of 13-24 year olds," p. 6.
2967 CSA, "Report on media in the life of 13-24 year olds," p. 8.
2968 CSA, "Report on media in the life of 13-24 year olds," p. 9.
2969 CSA, "Report on media in the life of 13-24 year olds," p. 9.

to "watch television".[2970] In addition, Internet consumption was also characterised by mobility: 80 percent of users aged between 13 and 24 years used mobile Internet connections.[2971]

Finally, the CSA examined how daily media consumption had changed throughout the reference years of 2008, 2012 and 2013. It found that the daily use of mobile phones by young audiences had doubled representing 43 percent of their total multi-media activities per day.[2972] At the same time, their use of the television and radio had considerably fallen (the decrease in consumption was double the decrease observed for the general public).[2973] With regards to daily consumption patterns, the CSA noted that young audiences tended to listen to the radio in the morning (with a peak between 6 a.m. and 9 a.m.) while the television constituted the primary media after 6 p.m. (with a peak between 8 p.m. and 8:15 p.m.). Young audiences liked to surf the Internet throughout the afternoon and evening, starting at around 2 p.m. until bedtime.[2974] Importantly, the mobile phone was used throughout the entire day by young audiences.[2975] For this reason, the CSA highlighted the necessity for traditional media to be present on and embrace the mobile phone as a "new form of social communication" which was "mass media produced, received and felt individually", a so-called "individual mass media".[2976] The data collected by the CSA in its 2014 report which also referred to several European-wide studies was in line with general trends.

Above all, in the daily life of young audiences the importance of mobile devices (especially the mobile phone) capable of connecting to the Internet was perpetually growing. For this age group, the desire to be constantly connected to the World Wide Web or at least having the possibility to conveniently do so at any moment was preponderant. The CSA's encouragement for traditional media like television and radio to adapt to these consumption habits is noteworthy. By reinforcing the role of mobile phones, it called on content providers to re-invent content production and continue to cater to their audiences taking into account the transforming

2970 CSA, "Report on media in the life of 13-24 year olds," p. 10.
2971 CSA, "Report on media in the life of 13-24 year olds," p. 10.
2972 CSA, "Report on media in the life of 13-24 year olds," p. 11.
2973 CSA, "Report on media in the life of 13-24 year olds," p. 11.
2974 CSA, "Report on media in the life of 13-24 year olds," p. 13.
2975 CSA, "Report on media in the life of 13-24 year olds," p. 14.
2976 CSA, "Report on media in the life of 13-24 year olds," p. 15.

context within which media was consumed by young persons aged between 13 and 24. This wake-up call to traditional media was, however, a gentle one which is, nonetheless, underpinned by convincing data.

## III. Perspectives of the CSA on the protection of minors in converging media markets

In its reply to the Commission's consultation on the revision of the AVMSD in September 2015, the CSA highlights the measures taken to protect minors as a legitimate social objective. In France, a regime of shared responsibility involving distributors and service providers, parents and the regulator has been fostered through the classification of programmes (accompanied by scheduling restrictions or the obligation to block certain types of content), the development of parental controls and the launch of information campaigns.[2977]

More precisely, the French regulator is in favour of maintaining the soft touch approach in relation to VOD services on account of their special nature.[2978] Given the voluntary and active steps to be taken by users of VOD services, the CSA agrees with the European legislature that, in theory, the risk for minors to be confronted by inappropriate content is lower than for television broadcasts. This is all the more true for pay-per-view VOD offers. Against the background of the reports analysed above, this assessment is surprising. It can be challenged especially on grounds of the increased use by minors of mobile Internet connections and the proliferation of freely accessible adult content online. The CSA, at least, acknowledges the convergence of access modes as linear and non-linear services are increasingly made accessible by the same online platforms and the emergence of functionalities aligning the two types of services.[2979] It nonetheless emphasises that the distinction between linear and non-linear services remains pertinent. This is underlined by the expectations of the public which the CSA deduces from the higher number of complaints initiated in relation to TV broadcasts.[2980]

---

2977 CSA, "Reply AVMSD Consultation," p. 26.
2978 CSA, "Reply AVMSD Consultation," p. 25.
2979 CSA, "Reply AVMSD Consultation," p. 25.
2980 CSA, "Reply AVMSD Consultation," p. 25.

The CSA's argument is not backed by evidence about audience expectations and is generally not convincing. What is comprehensible is the CSA's concern that the progressive merging of consumption patterns, leading to the presence of linear and non-linear services on the same screen may result in a lack of understanding by the general public. For this reason, the use of age ratings is regarded as a means to empower the audience to take more informed decisions. Hence, the classification scheme applicable to broadcasting is expanded to VOD services in France.[2981] In practice, this expansion can take two forms. First, given the specificities of each media, the classification obtained for a programme transmitted by an on-demand service is not valid for television services, the broadcaster having to re-consider and re-evaluate the existing classification.[2982] Second, the classification of a particular programme is used coherently across different services; the classification of an on-demand programme being the minimum standard for the dissemination on TV. In France, the CSA is in favour of the alignment of the two systems, using age ratings regardless of the mode of transmission.[2983]

Furthermore, the CSA raises certain issues which it considers problematic under the current regime of the AVMSD. The regulator points out that certain types of audiovisual material, notably content supplied by video-sharing websites, is not covered by the AVMSD as transposed by the French LLC.[2984] As a result, the set of rules purporting to protect minors remains largely segmented hinging on the type of service and the global legal framework seem incomplete to the CSA.[2985] The CSA considers that the role of intermediaries, in particular merits further analysis during the revision process of the AVMSD.[2986] In addition, the CSA remarks that service providers fail to comply with the requirements imposed on the dissemination of adult content (category V programmes) under French law, in particular when they provide their services in different Member States and their jurisdiction can not be easily determined.[2987] This matter came to the fore when the CSA, following public complaints in September 2014, in-

2981 CSA, "Reply AVMSD Consultation," p. 25.
2982 CSA, "Reply AVMSD Consultation," p. 26.
2983 CSA, "Reply AVMSD Consultation," p. 27.
2984 CSA, "Reply AVMSD Consultation," p. 25.
2985 CSA, "Reply AVMSD Consultation," p. 26.
2986 CSA, "Reply AVMSD Consultation," p. 26.
2987 CSA, "Reply AVMSD Consultation," p. 27.

vestigated in the activities of Free, an Internet access provider offering the VOD service MY XXL which specialises in adult content. On MY XXL, the CSA found freely accessible sexually explicit promotional images which violated the SMAD Deliberation. The CSA admits that it encountered difficulties identifying the service provider as well as its country of origin as the latter had substantial ties with the Netherlands.[2988]

This case demonstrates, according to the French regulator, that service providers (European or non-European) profit from the different regulatory levels existing within the EU and encourage economic actors to establish in Member States with more lenient regimes.[2989] As a response to these phenomena, the CSA calls for an enhanced level of harmonisation: harmonisation of technical standards and coordination or certification of technical measures.[2990] It also refers to other possibilities which may be explored during the reform process such as the coordination of classification and labelling systems as well as the elaboration of common definitions of key concepts like "minor", "pornography", "gratuitous violence", "media content likely to impair" or "media content which seriously impairs".[2991] Above all, the CSA expresses its support for the status quo enshrined by the AVMSD. An important exception constitutes the rules concerning the most harmful content which the CSA considers insufficiently protective. Changes to the current regulatory structure are most pertinent in relation to on-demand services containing programmes which are seriously detrimental to minors' development (Art. 12 AVMSD). It is in this context that the CSA advocates a higher level of harmonisation and enhanced coordination of national rules and practices.[2992]

## IV. Summary

In conclusion, the French legal framework outlines a high level of protection of minors in on-demand services. Art. 15 LLC sets out similar standards for content causing various degrees of harm disseminated via linear as well as non-linear services. While Art. 15 LLC is stricter than Art. 12

2988 CSA, "Reply AVMSD Consultation," p. 27.
2989 CSA, "Reply AVMSD Consultation," p. 28.
2990 CSA, "Reply AVMSD Consultation," p. 28.
2991 CSA, "Reply AVMSD Consultation," p. 29.
2992 CSA, "Reply AVMSD Consultation," p. 29.

AVMSD, the former leaves a large margin of discretion to the CSA which has specified the measures on-demand service providers are required to take when transmitting content reserved for an adult audience.[2993] The CSA's key regulatory measure, the SMAD Deliberation of 2011, stipulates the obligation for service providers to classify content and put in place an effective technical barrier which blocks access to seriously harmful content (category V programmes). It results from the CSA's practice that it enforces the SMAD Deliberation and has clarified its rules in individual decisions addressed to defaulting providers. The CSA's decisions take the form of educative and informing letters (rather than statutory sanctions) whereby the regulator intends to enhance the dialogue with the industry. Accompanying these, the CSA has led numerous information and awareness-raising campaigns and has fostered media literacy and media education. Such (soft) measures have been an important additional element in the CSA's policy which generally builds on mutual understanding, education and information.

## *E. Comparing the UK, German and French regulators' approaches to the protection of minors in on-demand services*

### I. General observations

The above assessment of measures taken by the UK, German and French regulatory authorities transposing Art. 12 AVMSD generally demonstrates a great commitment and activism towards the aim of protecting minors. Although Art. 12 AVMSD was transposed in the national legal orders, regulators operate under slightly different legal provisions. In the UK, the national law, which was modified in late 2014, makes a distinction between prohibited material and specifically restricted material. Providers of on-demand services are allowed to supply specifically restricted material (defined as R18 or R18-equivalent) to an adult audience. This rule, which is more detailed, corresponds to Art. 12 AVMSD. In France and Germany, VOD providers face stricter rules. Apart from banning illegal content, restrictions are imposed not only in relation to seriously harmful content but also in relation to harmful content. While in France, the classification of

2993 Franceschini, "Pornographie et télévision," p. 166.

unsuitable content is especially important, the German media law provides for transmission restrictions as well as technical tools to control minors' access to such material.

The focus of the analysis conducted in this chapter lies, however, on programmes or content which is considered to have a considerably negative effect on the development of minors. It is interesting to note that in Germany and the UK, regulatory authorities have tackled the fundamental question about the rationale for regulation of seriously harmful content. Ofcom and ATVOD have repeatedly acknowledged the lack of empirical evidence demonstrating a causal link between minors' behaviour and their exposure to pornographic programmes. Yet, the UK regulators have made clear that it can inversely not be assumed that such programmes are absolutely harmless. They have thus constructed a rationale which justifies regulatory intervention on the basis of the potential or risk of harm. Similarly, German courts have confirmed the prerogative of the legislature in this field which enjoys a margin of discretion to determine that pornographic content is detrimental to minors. This precautionary approach is equally applied in France, where the CSA appears to have been less concerned about the justification for limiting the dissemination of seriously impairing content.

A general remark has to be made with respect to the measures adopted by national regulators. Where possible, the analysis above focussed on the activities of the authorities. In the UK, for example, a great variety of instruments could be examined including ATVOD's practice, its rules and guidance (which Ofcom has adopted at the beginning of 2016) as well as other relevant policy documents. The body of practice which has built up in the UK is proof of a robust enforcement of the rules on the protection of minors. This is reinforced by the imposition of statutory sanctions through Ofcom. The penalties issued by Ofcom mirror its market-oriented approach. In its sanctioning decisions, it took into account the economic position of providers on the relevant market and was mindful of the fact that UK providers face fierce competition from websites and platforms operating globally and oftentimes managed from abroad. It also emerges that collaboration with ATVOD and Ofcom could constitute an extenuating circumstance. In Germany and France, the extraction of regulator's practice was particularly difficult and reference could only be made to publicly available data and information provided upon request. It seems that regulatory authorities in these two countries would favour strategies of collaboration with providers rather than their sanctioning. In order to conduct an in-depth assessment of the impact of the AVMSD (or its successors) and its enforcement at the national level, the timely and full publication of relevant decisions or documents would be desirable.

## II. Content which might seriously impair the development of minors

Due to the vague formulation of Art. 12 AVMSD, Member States enjoy a large margin of discretion regarding the type of content that is considered to be seriously harmful. While the French and German national laws broadly reproduce the formula contained in the Directive, the provision contained in the British law has become more precise following the 2014 amendment. The CA captures material classified as R18 or likely to have been classified under this category. It falls to the regulator for audiovisual media services to apply this standard in accordance with the guidelines issued by the film classification board. Hence, ATVOD has shaped the interpretation of this category of content, commonly referred to in the UK as hardcore pornography. The co-regulator made clear that all kinds of "material", whether text-based, images, audio or audiovisual, included in an on-demand service, is subject to the rule on protection of minors. This is similarly interpreted in France and Germany. It emerges from ATVOD's practice that content is seriously impairing if it depicts un-simulated sexual activities for the sole purpose of sexual arousal. Material is, however, prohibited if it depicts presentations of violent sexual practices involving the restraining of persons. In addition, inflicting pain in a sexual context with the aim to cause lasting physical as well as psychological harm is impermissible, especially if such representations are reinforced by camera techniques focussing on wounds and injuries of victims.

In Germany, the delineation between material which is banned (and therefore illegal) and material which is legal but its transmission restricted seems to be made by an analysis of whether sexual practices are voluntary and consensual or whether a person is victimised and degraded to a mere object. The German legal order generally distinguishes between hardcore pornography (which is impermissible) and moderate pornography. Apart from moderate pornographic content, content which is suited to seriously impair minors' development may be made available in closed user groups. The term (moderate) pornography has been specified by case law and broadly implies the portrayal of sexual activities to the exclusion of all human relationships depicted in an exaggerated and obtrusive manner with the primary purpose of sexual arousal. The KJM as well as a certified self-regulatory body, the FSM, have specified the kind of material which falls under this rule. Above all, their guidance outlines factors the regulators take into account when assessing the material. These are, for instance, the context in which violence/sexuality/pornography are presented, the way these themes are stage-managed, the quantity, quality and intensity of such representations, the likely expectations of users, in particular the relevance of the programmes for minors, and the level of suspense. In order to determine whether material is pornographic, the German regulators look at whether the focus of the depiction is on pleasure and sexual lust (for example by showing an uninterrupted chain of sexual acts without underlying narrative), whether sexual acts are reduced to impersonal acts, whether persons are degraded and depicted as replaceable objects or whether the presentation exceeds socially accepted values. Additionally, the form of the presentation is a significant indicator as camera techniques may be used to provide an overly clear and detailed presentation of sexual acts.

Such criteria, albeit to a more limited extent, also emerge from the jurisprudence of the French courts. Cinematographic content is considered to be inappropriate for under 18s if it depicts a succession of un-simulated sexual acts (possibly combined with violent behaviour) in a raw and explicit manner. An assessment of the content's nature encompasses an analysis of the image conveyed by the presentation and to what extent this image deviates from what is considered socially acceptable (e.g. confinement of a person, humiliation, gender roles portraying the superiority of the male sex). Apart from the intention of the author of the work, the quality, quantity and intensity of controversial scenes is to be weighed. More recent case law on the notion of violence also takes into account the form of the presentation, its stage-management, the degree of realism of the scenes, the effects such content is likely to have on minors as well as other factors which allow users to take a critical distance to the material. It is unclear to what extent the CSA uses the criteria established by the courts. Comparing the three legal frameworks, it is interesting to note that pornographic or sexually explicit content is commonly regarded as seriously harmful to minors. What is more, the definitions flowing from the legal order of the three Member States appear broadly similar implying the presentation of non-simulated sexual acts for the sole purpose of sexual arousal. Yet, the way in which the definitions are applied by national regulators is contingent on national contexts and social as well as cultural perceptions prevailing in the respective Member State.

## III. Making available by appropriate means

Art. 12 AVMSD requires that seriously impairing content is made available to adults only ensuring that minors "do not normally hear or see" such content. The regulators of the UK, Germany and France have highlighted service providers' responsibility in protecting minors. In line with recital 60 AVMSD, which enumerates appropriate means to control access, the national regulators have specified the kind of tools service providers are expected to put in place. Through a great amount of determinations, ATVOD has detailed that UK providers have to put in place a paywall which includes a distinct process whereby age is effectively verified. This requirement is also reflected and further clarified in its rules and guidance which remain valid today. ATVOD accepted the use of credit cards or other payment methods which are reserved for persons over 18 years. Money transfers from bank accounts or payments by debit card have been rejected. Similarly, payment processing services which give no further evidence, except in their terms and conditions, that payments cannot be processed by under 18s, were not regarded as effective controls. In addition, service providers may rely on systems which reputably proof a user's identity including digital identity management systems. The obligations imposed on service providers established in the UK are similar, if not more lenient than in Germany.

The German regulators at the federal and state levels, above all the KJM, have interpreted the legal provision transposing Art. 12 AVMSD strictly. Accordingly, providers of seriously harmful content have to ensure that it is made impossible (and not just excessively difficult) for minors to access such material. The technical infrastructure must also be designed in such a way as to exclude easy and obvious methods of circumvention. Thus, an effective barrier has to be erected which is protected by a two-stage process. This process entails personal identification in a first step and continued authentication in a second step. While UK providers are required to verify age on the basis of an independent piece of evidence (such as a credit card or the electoral roll), providers located in Germany are obliged to verify the user's age by personal contact. More recently, the strict obligation of face-to-face controls has been relaxed and equivalent measures are allowed including identification by electronic means under certain circumstances. In addition and similarly to the UK, identification can take place prior to the use of the service and users may invoke previous identification processes during the conclusion of contracts for bank accounts or mobile phones, for instance. Measures which rely on ID or passport numbers and merely check whether these comply with the rules concerning the composition of such numbers are insufficient. Similar to the UK, the payment of a fee through mechanisms where the user is not required to be of age (e.g. transfer by bank account) are inadequate to protect minors from seriously harmful content. Moreover, the process of authentication, which is also required by the UK and France, is intended to ensure that only the person who was identified as an adult actually has access to the service. This stage is typically enforced by passwords which are individually allocated.

In France, the CSA has attached particular importance to the classification of content disseminated through on-demand services. This obligation extends to all types of content which are classified according to different age groups for which content is considered inappropriate. The classification of content has consequences for its transmission. Programmes rated under category V (unsuitable for under 18s) fulfil the "might seriously impair" test and consequently are to be limited to an adult audience. The CSA has clarified that such services may only be marketed as paid offers and are subject to a permanently active blocking device. To penetrate this "virtual wall", the CSA has specified a procedure which encompasses the creation of a personal code and continued authentication of the user in case of recurring log in. It is doubtful whether this mechanism, which seems to lack an explicit duty imposed on the provider to verify the user's age, would be permissible in Germany and the UK. In both countries, regulators have rejected voluntary declarations of age. It appears as if the requirements elaborated by national regulators are the strictest in Germany, where personal identification of the user is prescribed. This is a rather laborious task for service providers as well as users. The verification of age by means of a reliable source (e.g. credit card ownership), as is practiced in the UK, seems more reasonable and in line with user expectations of gaining direct access to the material desired. What the regulators in the three countries have in common is that access to unsuitable material is perpetually limited to adults who have to undergo repeated authentication by passwords or pin codes.

## IV. Regulators' outlook on the AVMSD's revision

The replies of the UK, German and French regulators to the Commission's consultation on the revision of the AVMSD as well as their recent policy papers indicate what changes should be made to the current EU legal framework, and, in particular, what kinds of improvements should be made to facilitate the cross-border provision of audiovisual media services. With regards to the distinction between linear and non-linear services, Ofcom and the German regulators are in favour of aligning the rules for broadcasting and on-demand services. The regulatory bodies of Germany are especially critical of the categorisation in linear and non-linear services and forcefully lobby for its abandonment. By contrast, Ofcom is generally supportive of the linear/non-linear distinction (see chapter four on scope). It nonetheless proposes a new approach to the protection of minors in audiovisual media services. According to Ofcom's proposal, standards would be based on the severity of content which would have direct repercussions on the choice of access controls. Thus, moderate types of inappropriate content would require moderate access controls. In this context, Ofcom envisages a role for ERGA in drawing up guidance on the nature of the content and the corresponding protection measures. It is interesting to note that the CSA calls for maintaining the status quo and retaining the light touch approach in relation to VOD services. Under the French legal framework, on-demand service providers are required to adhere to stricter rules than those outlined in the Directive. Their obligations are, in fact, similar to those applicable to broadcasters. The CSA may have referred solely to the possibility for VOD providers to transmit seriously harmful content to an adult audience in specifically reserved spaces (a right which is not foreseen for broadcasters by virtue of Art. 27 (1) AVMSD and Art. 15 LLC respectively).

It is furthermore striking that the regulators of the three Member States, albeit to different extents, advocate for the harmonisation or at least coordination of key concepts contained in Art. 12 AVMSD. This is evidence of the lack of clarity of the formulation of this provision. In line with the body of practice which has developed and the modification of the law, Ofcom suggests that the nature of the material caught by the rule is specified as hardcore pornography or R18/R18-equivalent material. The German and French regulatory authorities are less concrete with respect to the wording of the AVMSD. In France, the CSA proposes enhanced cooperation (also at the national level) as well as the coordination of technical and other tools (such as classification schemes) implemented to protect minors. In a similar vein, the German DLM and KJM call for the development of common technical tools such as classification standards and technical interfaces. A uniform technical framework is envisaged which can flexibly be employed by Member States and adapted to national specificities and cultural differences. An issue which is underlined by all regulators is the need to invest in media literacy and media education and develop a genuine policy to this effect, such that it includes incentivising providers to specifically produce content for minors, especially younger children aged under 14. In addition, the responsibility of parents and guardians should be enhanced, for instance, by more wide-spread use of classifications or other sign-posting of content. Activities to this effect would also raise awareness and transparency and would allow consumers of all ages to take more informed decisions.

Furthermore, a concern which is expressly shared by Ofcom and the CSA is the difficulty for regulators to identify service providers and determine their jurisdiction. Both regulators are critical about the phenomenon of "forum shopping" of providers established within, but also and more importantly, outside the EU. Ofcom claims that content providers have good incentives to conceal their identity and escape the radar of European regulators. For this reason, it suggests expanding the AVMSD to those providing financial or registration services to media service providers by obstructing the latter's identity. Providers of such services should be required to supply information to national regulatory authorities to facilitate regulation. In addition, money flows should be cut off to content providers offering freely available pornographic content (or other seriously impairing material) located in third countries. Ofcom (like ATVOD before it) is of the opinion that payments services (such as Visa, MasterCard, etc…) should not process money transfers to services affiliated with operators of such websites. Similar considerations are being made in Germany where closer collaboration with the payments industry is regarded as an option. So far, reflections have focussed on operators supplying illegal content rather than legal but harmful content (as Ofcom seems to suggest).

With regards to the extension of the AVMSD to other actors, the German and French regulators agree that the role of intermediaries and online platforms should be re-considered during the AVMSD's reform. The German media authorities even go a step further in advocating the inclusion of platform operators under the AVMSD and the introduction of a system of secondary responsibility for seriously detrimental content. In parallel, efforts should be stepped up to induce platform operators to submit to voluntary standards regarding prohibited material. Co- and self-regulatory schemes are regarded as valuable instruments to complement state intervention in this field. Ofcom, however, positions itself in sharp contrast to the German and French regulators submitting that no detailed regulation should be imposed on actors such as ISPs or online platforms. In brief, the perspectives and suggestions by the UK, German and French regulatory authorities seem to converge on many aspects, even if fundamental differences remain for certain issues. It nonetheless follows that clarifications to the wording of Art. 12 AVMSD and closer cooperation with respect to the requirements imposed on service providers are considered essential to improve the protection of minors in audiovisual media services in the future.

# Chapter 6. The future regulation of audiovisual media services

At the time of this writing, discussions on the next-generation AVMSD are in full swing. The Commission published its proposal for a revised AVMSD on 25 May 2016 (the 2016 AVMSD proposal)[2994] which is discussed in greater detail below. Suffice it to say, for the moment, that the 2016 AVMSD proposal contains some interesting suggestions and necessary adaptations but it does not go beyond current market realities, lacking a broader vision. Negotiations about the proposed amendments have already started in both the Council and the EP.[2995] The Council is currently engaged in a provision-by-provision assessment of the 2016 AVMSD proposal[2996] and the EP's Committee on Culture and Education (CULT) has

---

2994 European Commission, "Proposal for a Directive of the European Parliament and of the Council Amending Directive 2010/13/EU on the Coordination of Certain Provisions Laid down by Law, Regulation or Administrative Action in Member States Concerning the Provision of Audiovisual Media Services in View of Changing Market Realities, COM(2016) 287 Final," May 25, 2016. A synopsis of the Commission's proposed changes and the AVMSD is available in English, French and German at http://wwwen.uni.lu/recherche/fdef/droit_des_medias/audiovisual_media_services_directive/avmsd_reform_proposal_2016 (accessed 9.15.2016).

2995 On the procedure, see http://eur-lex.europa.eu/legal-content/EN/HIS/?uri=CELEX:52016PC0287&qid=1476021524117 (accessed 10.9.2016). Draft European Parliament Legislative Resolution.

2996 Until the end of 2016, negotiations in the Council were slow-moving as the Slovak Presidency did not seem to attribute high importance to the revision of the AVMSD. It drew up a progress report in late November 2016. In late December 2016, a Presidency compromise text jointly prepared by the Slovak and (incoming) Maltese Council Presidency was made available. In contrast to the European Parliament's co-rapporteur's draft report, the Presidency text proposes less substantial changes and retains the structure of the Directive as proposed by the Commission. Although negotiations are still ongoing at the time of this writing, it seems that the Council supports a modest extension of the Directive's scope, establishing a separate set of rules applicable to VSPs. Interestingly, the Presidency text extends Art. 9(1) outlining certain requirements for audiovisual commercial communications to VSPs, taking in to account the extent to which VSPs market, sell and arrange commercial communications. While the Council agrees with the Commission on a graduated approach, the former differs from the latter in favouring minimum harmonisation. The Council seems to support the Com-

already started drafting a report on the EP's behalf.[2997] Its report, being prepared by two German MEPs, Petra Kammerevert and Sabine Verheyen, is expected in early 2017.[2998]

---

mission's approach to align the rules for broadcasters and on-demand service providers suggesting to move the new rule on content descriptors to Art. 12. It is worth noting that the Presidency text reinforces media literacy, encouraging Member States to draw up policies and design schemes "to develop media literacy skills" in relation to audiovisual media services and requiring VSPs to provide for "effective media literacy measures and tools and [to raise] users' awareness of these measures and tools". In addition, the Presidency is preparing some wording on the protection of citizens from incitement to terrorism as well as complementing the information requirements of media service providers with information about media ownership. .

2997 CULT Draft report on the proposal for a directive of the European Parliament and of the Council amending Directive 2010/13/EU on the coordination of certain provisions laid down by law, regulation or administrative action in Member States concerning the provision of audiovisual media services in view of changing market realities, 5 September 2016, 2016/0151(COD). See also the draft opinion of the Internal Market and Consumer Protection for the Committee of Culture and Education of 21 September 2016 prepared by MEP Emma McClarkin from the European Conservatives and Reformists Group and the draft opinion of the Legal of the Committee on Legal Affairs for the Committee of 14 October 2016 prepared by Daniel Buda from the European People's Party.

2998 The co-rapporteurs represent the two biggest fractions in the European Parliament. Petra Kammerevert is a member of the Group of the Progressive Alliance of Socialists and Democrats and Sabine Verheyen is a member of the Group of the European People's Party. On 8 September 2016, they published their draft report on behalf of the EP's Committee for Culture and Education (CULT). The draft report indicates the willingness of the two rapporteurs to go beyond the Commission's proposal and further extend the normative provisions applicable to VSPs. Accordingly, certain rules should be applicable to all providers covered by the AVMSD (providers of audiovisual media services and VSPs) in order to ensure "a genuine level playing field". These include the protection of minors and the fight against hate speech, the requirement to provide content information (proposed by the Commission), qualitative requirements in relation to audiovisual commercial communications, the protection of cinematographic works and information obligations. While this proposal is certainly interesting and the objective as such should be supported, the effects of the changes should be studied in detail (the merging of provisions concerning the protection of minors and the prohibition of hateful content seems to have the effect of lowering current standards applicable to media service providers). Furthermore, the maximum harmonisation approach would also be abandoned in favour of minimum harmonisation in specified fields, excluding the rules on listed events and short news reports as well as the right of reply. In relation to commercial communica-

To better understand and combat the shortcomings of the existing AVMSD, policy makers must first assess its current implementation and enforcement. This study intends to contribute to that assessment by providing an in-depth analysis of certain specific aspects of the AVMSD as it is being implemented and enforced by certain regulators. Because it is highly likely that any attempt to reform the AVMSD will rely heavily on those regulators' experiences and approaches. Their practices are, and will remain, powerful influences shaping future regulatory instruments. In that regard, this chapter develops best practices as demonstrated by chapter four's case study on scope and chapter five's case study on the protection of minors. For purposes of this chapter, a regulatory measure is considered to be a "best practice" if it – better than any other measure – fulfils three criteria. It must be (1) specific in terms of legal certainty, (2) appropriate in terms of the regulatory burden and (3) effective in terms of enforcement. Thus, this Chapter examines the regulatory strategies and models, as well as content standards, to show how convergence has challenged the current legal framework. Further, on the basis of such best practices, it makes suggestions that acknowledge current deficiencies to aid a future

---

tions, in particular television advertising, the co-rapporteurs are less radical than the Commission aiming at reconciling broadcasters' interests in enhanced flexibility and protecting viewers from excessive advertising. With respect to the promotion of European works in on-demand services, the co-rapporteurs are more ambitious than the Commission, outlining a 30% share of European productions which are to be prominently presented in providers' catalogues. Another striking element of the co-rapporteurs draft report is the introduction of two new provisions in the operative part of the Directive. The first of such provisions recognises Member States prerogative in taking measures to ensure appropriate prominence of general interest content (the Commission had acknowledged this issue in recital 38 of its proposal). The second of these provisions protects the integrity of content which may not be modified without service providers' explicit consent. These are new issues which reflect the concerns of media service providers operating in a converged ecosystem with a growing number of actors that position themselves between users and media service providers. Due to the comprehensive changes proposed by the co-rapporteurs, it is expected that other committee members will introduce further amendments to the draft report. CULT is expected to vote on the report in early 2017. On content integrity, see Lisbeth Hellemans, Eva Lievens, and Peggy Valcke, "Playing Hide-and-Seek? A Legal Perspective on the Complex Distinction between Commercial and Editorial Content in Hybrid Advertising Formats," *The Journal of Policy, Regulation and Strategy for Telecommunications, Information and Media* 17, no. 6 (2015): pp. 19–34.

EU regulatory framework. This chapter then circles back to chapter one which traces the origins of the EU's involvement in the regulation of audiovisual media services and looks at how the future of AVMS regulation builds on the past. In its final section, this Chapter will critically analyse the 2016 AVMSD proposal, testing it against the findings of the case studies.[2999]

## A. Regulatory strategies in converging media markets

This part of the chapter deals with the regulatory strategies employed by the UK, Germany and France. Due to the complexity of each of these three, national regulatory environments, firstly, it distils the essential characteristics of the three regulatory regimes before, secondly, proposing best practices and suggesting the effective use of alternative forms of regulation for the audiovisual media services market. Co-regulation, in particular, is examined as a viable regulatory strategy, provided certain safeguards are put in place. This part of the chapter closes with a reflection on the multi-layered governance structure typical of media markets which underpins the trend towards the Europeanisation of media policies.

### I. The essential characteristics of the regulatory landscapes in the UK, Germany and France

This section outlines the key characteristics of the national regulatory frameworks in the UK, Germany and France.

#### 1. Regulated self-regulation to protect minors in Germany

The three countries examined in this study display a range of regulatory models that are adapted to the general structure of the state. In Germany which is a federal country, media regulation is vested in the local states

2999 By the end of 2016, the positions of the Council and the EP on the 2016 AVMSD proposal are not yet sufficiently evolved to provide comment thereon – the first reading is still on-going – thus, this chapter only discusses the 2016 AVMSD proposal and not any subsequent documentation.

that make up the federation (the *Länder*) which coordinate their policies at the federal level. The absence of such supra-state coordination would seriously impede nation-wide dissemination of audiovisual media services. This coordination is expressed in the negotiation of inter-state treaties which are valid for the whole of Germany or the territory of those *Länder* having ratified the treaty, but is also institutionalised at the federal level through common regulatory bodies that facilitate regulation. Within this delicate balance of power between the *Bund* and the *Länder*, Germany has created an elaborate system of "regulated self-regulation" for the protection of minors which has, since April 2003, functioned successfully. A number of subsequent evaluations of the scheme have led to successive adjustments to the JMStV.[3000]

Germany's co-regulatory system essentially relies on enhancing self-responsibility by service providers which may create or become part of organisations of voluntary self-regulation and which are then formally recognised (certified) by the KJM, Germany's coordinating supervisory body at the federal level. Service providers affiliated with such an organisation are shielded from direct legal action by the KJM, provided that the organisation of voluntary self-organisation has not exceeded its discretionary power set forth in the JMStV. Service providers are, therefore, encouraged to become members of such organisations and adhere to the standards that are rooted in the legal framework of the JMStV and once they have done so, they enjoy an increased level of legal certainty regarding the legality of their offer. They will not fall sudden prey to enforcement actions taken by the KJM. Service providers that choose not to become a member of such a voluntary self-regulatory organisation do not

3000 Before entry into force of the 19th amendment to the RStV amending the JMStV which entered into force on 1 October 2016, a more fundamental reform was discussed in late 2015/early 2016 which aimed at aligning the protection of minors in both online and offline media. Yet, the 19th amendment only makes minor adjustments and a more comprehensive overhaul seems to have been postponed. On the need for more enhanced coordination between the JMStV and the JuSchG, see Mark Cole, "Kontrolle und Aufsicht im Jugendmedienschutz: Einrichtungen und Verfahren nach dem JMStV im Vergleich zum JuSchG, Eine Untersuchung der aktuellen Rechtslage im Blick auf den Novellierungsbedarf," ed. KJM, 2016, http://www.kjm-online.de/fileadmin/Download_KJM/Service/Gutachten/KJM_Verhaeltnis_Selbstkontrolleinrichtungen_und_Anbieter_Gutachten_MDC_2015.pdf (accessed 10.8.2016).

benefit from the latter's protection. In contrast, non-members are subject to direct, primary oversight by the KJM.

Chapter five's analysis demonstrates that Germany's co-regulatory scheme to protect minors in telemedia services functions quite well. In fact, the FSM, a voluntary organisation of self-regulation for multi-media service providers certified in 2004, has become an important actor in the German market, with more than 40 regular members to date, including international companies such as Google, Facebook, Yahoo and Walt Disney. The certification of such self-regulatory bodies which is based on pre-established criteria defined in the applicable law appears reasonable: it is a precondition for their reliable and effective participation in the regulatory scheme. Certification or formal recognition of such bodies ensures that they function efficiently (the internal dimension) and responsibly towards fulfilling the regulatory objective (the external dimension), and it is for this reason that this mechanism is proposed below as a best practice.

## 2. Lessons learnt from the abolition of ATVOD as a co-regulator for VOD services in the UK

The certification mechanism in Germany is similar to the instrument of designation of a co-regulator in the UK. In 2010, Ofcom, the UK's converged communications regulator, designated ATVOD to be the co-regulator for on-demand audiovisual media services in accordance with the criteria enumerated in the CA.[3001] The co-regulation of on-demand services between ATVOD and Ofcom was abruptly terminated after just five years. Although ATVOD's designation was extended in December 2014, Ofcom withdrew ATVOD's functions at the end of 2015. Ofcom has since regulated broadcasting and on-demand services "in-house". Its decision was ostensibly motivated by the high cost of the co-regulatory regime as well as the continued convergence between the two sectors which necessitated, according to Ofcom, a more coherent approach. Even though ATVOD successfully fulfilled its mandate, was respected by all stakeholders and functioned well on a comparably low budget, it seems that it fell victim to

3001 See Sec. 368B (9) CA introduced by the Audiovisual Media Services Regulations of 2009.

several flaws inherent in the UK's co-regulatory structure, for which ATVOD cannot entirely be blamed.

One such deficiency was its mandate: it was too broad and incorporated controversial decisions about the subjects of regulation (i.e. the scope of application of the rules ATVOD monitored). ATVOD was tasked with the regulation of most aspects of the on-demand services, as introduced by the AVMSD and transposed by the CA in 2009 and 2010, except advertising, for which certain elements are, as of this writing, still governed by the UK's Advertising Standards Authority in a co-regulatory regime and by Ofcom with respect to sponsorship and product placement. That broad delegation of powers to ATVOD implied that the latter was obliged to define the nature of the services covered by its remit. In doing so, ATVOD got into conflict with Ofcom as discussed in chapter four. The two bodies had diverging views on how the concept of an ODPS should be construed. In retrospect, it could be argued that decisions about the classification of services and the specification of the concept of an on-demand audiovisual media service were simply too controversial to be delegated to a co-regulator, especially if an appeal was possible to the "real" regulator. It also became apparent that ATVOD and Ofcom took different approaches and were built on different "ideologies". ATVOD did not share Ofcom's liberal, market-oriented approach; rather it attempted to create a level-playing field by including other services in the scope of regulation. Those differences resulted in numerous lengthy and thus costly appeal procedures. Ofcom frequently took over a year to decide a matter on appeal. In the interim period, service providers were left in a state of uncertainty, a situation that is not only unsatisfactory but also damaging to their business. In a rapidly evolving market, in which a multitude of new offers surface every day and services become (un)popular overnight, the regulator needed to act far more quickly to ensure that the service providers operated in a stable legal environment.

Hence, the UK's example shows that a co-regulator is more successful when the two bodies – the regulator and the co-regulator – share a similar outlook and perspective on the relevant market. More importantly, a co-regulator should not be burdened with an overly broad mandate. Instead, it should be endowed with a well-defined, specific and narrow task, such as the oversight of advertising standards or the protection of minors. As the discussion in chapter five highlights, ATVOD was very interested in ensuring an appropriate level of protection for young audiences in VOD services. The protection of minors in audiovisual media services (both on television and in VOD services to ensure consistency) constitutes an area that can reasonably be "outsourced" to a future co-regulator, if Ofcom were to reconsider co-regulation as an alternative regulatory tool.

### 3. Strengthening service providers' self-responsibility in France

In contrast to the UK and Germany, regulation remains very much centralised at the national level in France. This may be explained by the unitary structure of the state which accumulates power within central institutions and regulatory authorities operating at the national level. The CSA is one manifestation of this form of organisation. No co-regulatory initiatives have been taken in France. Self-regulation remains limited to the advertising sector. Notwithstanding these general tendencies, the CSA has recognised the need to strengthen the service provider's self-responsibility. For example, with respect to protecting minors in on-demand audiovisual media services, it relies on service providers to classify their content according to the requirements stipulated in its guidelines in conjunction with the LLC. This obligation is not typically subsumed under the concept of self-regulation, as previously discussed in chapter two. Self-regulation typically implies industry actors joining together to set up (voluntary) codes of conduct or to establish regulatory bodies that steer regulation and monitor members' compliance.

In France, however, regulation is managed from the top down. The CSA retains all the regulatory power and, so far, no joint actions by or with service providers have been taken. Yet, the fact that the CSA has charged service providers with an obligation to classify their content may signal future demands for an enhanced engagement by service providers. In fast-changing markets like the one for audiovisual media services, regulators increasingly design strategies to encourage service providers to act more responsibly and to contribute to the regulatory burden shouldered by regulatory authorities. In France, it appears that the CSA will remain *the* cornerstone of the regulatory structure and will continue to stringently monitor the application of the law, with a particularly keen eye on providers' contribution to audiovisual production and distribution. Providers will, of course, be more supportive of such measures if they get something in return (be it credibility, enhanced reputation, or other, perhaps pecuniary advantages). Thus, incentivising service providers to design their offers in compliance with legal requirements may be one element of any regulatory framework constructed for converging industry sectors.

## II. Best practices and suggestions for regulatory strategies in converging media markets

From the essential characteristics of the national regulatory frameworks outlined above and the analysis conducted in the previous chapters, best practices for regulatory strategies are developed below.

### 1. Characteristics of regulatory instruments used in converging media markets

This research analyses three representative examples of regulatory frameworks that have been established at the national level to regulate audiovisual media services. What is true for the regulatory structures of the UK, Germany and France becomes even more pronounced when looking at the regulatory authorities of the 28 EU Member States. Their regulatory frameworks are diverse and each is adapted to national specificities, national regulatory cultures, and national markets.[3002] As it is the prerogative of Member States to create regulatory authorities in accordance with constitutional traditions, the current diversity in the national regulatory frameworks concretely instituted will continue to exist. Notwithstanding that reality, the question can still be asked whether media convergence requires any one type or model of regulation. This study cannot lend proof to the superiority of one regulatory model over any other for this fast-changing, technology-driven, converged industry sector. Be it a strong, centralised regulator (such as the CSA), a powerful converged regulator with delegating authority (such as Ofcom), or a decentralised system with co-regulatory features (such as that used in Germany), none stands out as the most effective in dealing with media convergence. Still, this research demonstrates that there are, indeed, certain characteristics of regulatory frame-

3002 The adaptability of co-regulation to the national context is also highlighted by ERGA. See ERGA, "Report on the Protection of Minors in a Converged Environment," November 27, 2015, p. 45, http://ec.europa.eu/newsroom/dae/document.cfm?action=display&doc_id=13248 (accessed 2.12.2015).

works that do meet the demands of converged media markets. These characteristics are defined at the meta-level: they are inherently abstract and, thus, must be translated into concrete structures at the national level.

First, it is clear that whatever the regulatory framework, it must be flexible which is an absolute necessity if it has any hope of accommodating the changes that transform the audiovisual media services market at an unprecedented speed. In that regard, it must guarantee that the regulatory framework remains "future-proof". A rigid legal framework, one that is unable to quickly respond to such turbulence, is bound to fail. Even if that turbulence can be initially absorbed, the ever-present pressure will become greater with each disruption, making adjustments to the framework inevitable. Flexibility, thus, must encompass room to manoeuvre, that is room within the overall construction of the legal framework for regulatory bodies to adapt to fulfil their mandate.

A second characteristic is effectiveness.[3003] Regulatory frameworks need to be effective in producing the outcome for which they have been established. If they cannot deliver the intended results, they will not be successful and will need, in all likelihood, to be replaced or modified. Effective functioning of the regulatory body(ies) is(are) only one aspect of the requirement. The other is effective enforcement of the legal requirements.

Two additional characteristics, both linked to effectiveness, are more specific to the overall legal framework for the audiovisual media services market: the regulatory framework must be technology-neutral and have a light touch. Content standards and other legal requirements imposed on service providers must be defined regardless of the technology used to disseminate the audiovisual media services. Such regulation also needs to have a light touch, to take into account the diversity of modes of delivery and consumption of audiovisual content and allow for the emergence of innovative offers. Any heavy-handed, burdensome regulatory regime is likely to stifle innovation and risk an exodus of creativity from the market which requires leeway to experiment and innovate. Light-touch regulation does not imply an absence of detailed legal rules, but refers to their adaptability to the market's state of development and to individual market players. Setting appropriate incentives and engaging the industry in a collabo-

3003 Similarly, ERGA considers that co-regulatory systems are based on an "effective regulatory framework with constitutional guarantees". See ERGA, "Report on the Protection of Minors," p. 45.

rative dialogue would appear to be an inevitable consequence of the need to address the many challenges resulting from media convergence. Moreover, when designing regulatory instruments, the whole value-chain must be taken into account, to prevent any isolated regulation of any part of the value chain.

Co- and self-regulatory schemes lend themselves to a regulatory framework that meets the meta-level characteristics outlined above. Co-regulation, as primarily examined in this study, appears to offer many advantages, especially when there is a lack of support for self-regulation. It is important in that regard that co-regulation is tied to a legal framework defined by national law which legitimises the co-regulator by giving it a clear purpose and objective to pursue. Co-regulation best illustrates a "cooperative approach" between the regulator and the industry, and cooperation seems to be a viable mechanism to close gaps (e.g. in knowledge, compliance, and enforcement) between the regulatory system and those subject to regulation, as long as safeguards are in place to prevent capture of the former by the latter.[3004] In general, co-regulation "is capable of being used more widely in the future and as convergence plays out in a fast-changing arena where statutory regulation is likely to be challenged to keep pace with changing technology and services".[3005]

## 2. Specific proposals for alternative regulatory models in converging media markets

### a) Limiting co-regulation to a specific field of activity

To achieve the meta-level characteristics set forth above, this study's prior analyses offer several suggestions. In both Germany and the UK, co-regulatory schemes were established and continue to exist, with the notable exception of ATVOD. That exception, however, demonstrates that co-regulation is more successful when it is limited to a specific field, such as the protection of minors or commercial communications. In its response to the Commission's Green Paper on convergence, ATVOD posited that "co-regulation could (...) be considered as a viable option in *any area* requiring

3004 ATVOD, "Response to Commission Green Paper," para. 3.4, p. 7.
3005 ATVOD, "Response to Commission Green Paper," para. 3.12, p. 9.

regulation".[3006] This broad statement, it seems, requires at least one qualification: co-regulation is a viable option for *any specifically defined and limited area* requiring regulation. The termination of its co-regulatory role shows that ATVOD's remit was too broad. That remit also concerned an area that was subjected to statutory regulation for the first time which required services to be classified to decide if the particular service fell within the regulatory scheme. The question of what constitutes an on-demand audiovisual media service was, and still is, a controversial task and the legal consequences and implications attached to that classification are enormous when compared to services falling outside of its scope. Normally, that task (i.e. determining the scope of application of a regulation) is left to the regulatory body, not a co-regulatory body, and it appears that it is not a task that should be delegated to the co-regulator. If, however, a co-regulator is given the task, it would have to be backed by a like-minded regulator that would quickly act, on appeal, to resolve conflicts. As a co-regulatory body, ATVOD, for example, functioned efficiently and took its mandate seriously. In matters of scope, however, it did not have sufficient backing from Ofcom which took a different stance in many cases and in addition, frequently delayed the outcome of proceedings, leaving service providers (i.e. those immediately affected by ATVOD's determination and those offering similar services) in a state of flux.[3007]

Nevertheless, the UK's experience with co-regulation in other, more limited fields, such as the classification of films by the BBFC and the regulation of advertising on TV and in VOD services, has been, and continues to be, positive as some of the co-/self- regulatory regimes have been in place for decades. Against this backdrop, co-regulation, as an alternative regulatory form, should be geared towards a specific, well-defined regulatory field in which the regulator and co-regulator share a common understanding.

The 2006 findings of the study by the Hans-Bredow Institut and the Institut für Europäisches Medienrecht which evaluated co- and self-regulatory regimes remain valid. That study found that, while no policy objective was *per se* unsuitable for co-regulation, the protection of minors and advertising-content regulation constituted "especially promising" objec-

3006 ATVOD, "Response to Commission Green Paper," para. 4.11, pp. 13–14.

3007 ERGA also considers that "quick decisions on complaints" are essential requirements for a co-regulatory system. See ERGA, "Report on the Protection of Minors," p. 45.

tives.[3008] It is telling that a study on the effectiveness of co- and self-regulation in the context of the AVMSD from April 2016 also examined a wide range of co- and self-regulatory schemes in relation to these two policy objectives and determined best practices for each after taking into account the stakeholders' acceptance of the schemes and their effectiveness.[3009]

### b) Formal recognition of co-regulation

For a successful co-regulatory scheme, the relationship between the regulator and its co-regulator must be clearly defined. A formal process of recognition detailing the delegation of regulatory tasks to the co-regulator is better done at the national level. In Germany, such recognition takes the form of certification by the regulator whereby, stated simply, self-regulatory bodies are brought into the legal framework and become co-regulatory bodies. The law enumerates the criteria for such certification, including the independence of members, a pluralistic structure, adequate resources, the ability to draft and implement guidelines for committees, and the ability to set out rules of procedure and complaints mechanisms.[3010] The recognition process in the UK requires a similar formal act of designation. To be designated in the UK, co-regulators must be fit and proper bodies with adequate financial resources. The independence of the co-regulator must be ensured as well as its adherence to regulatory principles of transparency, accountability, proportionality, consistency and targetability.[3011]

In both Germany and the UK, the delegation of a task to a co-regulator is periodically reviewed in order to improve the regulatory framework and prevent disintegration of the regulatory task and practices, as well as the

---

3008 Hans Bredow Institut and Institut für Europäisches Medienrecht, "Final Report, Study on Co-Regulation Measures in the Media Sector, Study for the European Commission," para. 4.2.1.3., p. 123.

3009 Panteia and VVA Europe, "Effectiveness of Self- and Co-Regulation in the Context of Implementing the AVMS Directive, A Study Prepared for the European Commission," April 2016, para. 4.3.1, p. 132, https://ec.europa.eu/digital-single-market/en/news/audiovisual-and-media-services-directive-self-and-co-regulation-study (accessed 3.7.2016). For an overview of the national co- and self-regulatory schemes examined, see para. 3.1, pp. 51-54.

3010 Art. 19 JMStV.

3011 Sec. 368B (9) CA.

co-regulators' estrangement from the regulator. Formal recognition of co-regulators contributes to their legitimacy vis-à-vis the industry and sets benchmarks against which the co-regulator's performance can be evaluated and it can be held accountable. It also enhances legal certainty for all stakeholders, an element that is particularly important in Germany's legal framework for the protection of minors.

### 3. Multi-level regulation in converging media markets

As audiovisual media services are cultural and economic goods, they have been, to date, regulated at several policy levels. While media pluralism and media diversity are concerns that have been primarily addressed at the national level, free EU cross-border dissemination of audiovisual media services has been the key objective pursued at the EU level.

Even more broadly, the CoE has also played an important role within EU and non-EU countries but it seems to have lost some of its influence, as it could not conclude a new Convention on the subject due to the Commission's blockage for reasons of the distribution of competence between the EU and its Member States, as discussed in the first chapter.[3012] As a result, its CTT which was last amended in 1998[3013] is outdated, especially in comparison with the AVMSD; a situation which will be further aggravated by an updated AVMSD. Like EU-level legislation which often requires years of hard-fought negotiation before a highly compromised version of the original proposal is finally adopted, the CoE, as a forum to determine media policies, appears to be far too slow-moving to react to the fast-paced developments in the media sector.[3014] Yet, to date, the Commis-

---

3012 On the failure to conclude a new Convention, see for example Fink, Keber and Roguski, "Die Zukunft der Medienregulierung im Europarat," pp. 292–300.

3013 The Protocol amending the CTT of 1989 only entered into force in March 2002.

3014 Perhaps, with the UK's referendum in June 2016 and the likely exit from the EU the CoE may be able to reassert itself as an adequate actor in the field, assuming both the UK, as non-EU country, and the EU are interested in a pan-European framework for audiovisual media services. Yet, by the end of 2016, the UK's ultimate exit from the Union remains uncertain. On Brexit, see Alison J. Harcourt, "How Brexit Might Affect EU Audio-Visual Media Services Policy-Making," *LSE Blog*, May 24, 2016, http://blogs.lse.ac.uk/mediapolicyproject/2016/05/24/how-brexit-might-affect-eu-audio-visual-media-services-policy-making/; John

sion has not manifested any willingness to resolve its quarrel with its Member States over competence and to otherwise engage itself (or allow its Member States to engage) in meaningful negotiations at the CoE level,[3015] it seems unlikely that the CTT negotiations will be revived soon. Nevertheless, with regard to all fundamental rights implications arising out of the provision of audiovisual media services, the CoE retains its crucial role as *the* authority.

Media convergence and the increasingly global business of supplying audiovisual media services may also make it necessary to establish international standards. As national regulation will always suffer from an irreparable enforcement deficit in the global context of the Internet, Bornemann advocates some form of global regulation through international agreements.[3016] Although an AVMSD-style regulation at the international level is unrealistic, international agreements could tackle individual aspects of such services, such as protecting minors from illegal and age-inappropriate content. To be sure, any such initiatives will require strong, global political support and narrow, clearly defined objectives to prevent decades-long negotiations that result in meaningless agreements. The likelihood of successfully concluding such international agreements is quite low.[3017] Before such an international agreement could be concluded, the EU and the US, two major actors on the international stage, would have to

Enser, "After the Vote: What Will Brexit Mean for Film and TV Businesses Operating in the UK?," *LSE Blog*, July 1, 2016, http://blogs.lse.ac.uk/mediapolicyproject/2016/07/01/after-the-vote-what-will-brexit-mean-for-film-and-tv-businesses-operating-in-the-uk/; Ian Begg, "Brexit: Why, What next and How?," *CESifo Forum*, no. 2 (2016): pp. 30–36; ReedSmith, ed., "The Implications of Brexit on the Entertainment and Media Industry," July 2016, https://www.reedsmith.com/files/uploads/alert-attachments/2016/Brexit_-_Client_Briefing_Pack_-_July_2016.pdf (all websites accessed 24.9.2016).

3015 A positive example of the CoE's impact and the importance of its instruments is the CoE's Cybercrime Convention, ETS No. 185 of 2001 that entered into force in July 2004 and that has also been ratified by a number of third countries such as the Argentina, Australia, Canada, Japan, Mexico, South Africa and the US.

3016 Bornemann, "Zur Telemedienordnung," p. 129; see also Mark Cole, "Europäische und globale Regulierungsansätze," in *Medien, Netz und Öffentlichkeit – Impulse für die digitale Gesellschaft*, ed. Jan Marc Eumann, Frauke Gerlach, and Tebea Rößner (Essen: Klartext, 2013), p. 401.

3017 The negotiations of the Transatlantic Trade and Investment Partnership (TTIP) may illustrate the fundamental differences between the EU and US in matters of trade. Although it has been launched, the Privacy Shield (sucessor of the Safe Harbour agreement) which governs transatlantic data flows between the EU and

achieve some measure of consensus which does not seem likely, especially in view of current attempts to negotiate (EU-US or multi-state) trade agreements such as Transatlantic Trade and Investment Partnership (TTIP) and Trade in Services Agreement (TiSA).

Within the European Union, a question arises as to whether all regulation of audiovisual media services will eventually move to the European level. Throughout the European integration process, the Commission has taken over regulation of many policy areas, such as the markets for energy, electricity, and gas, often with the explicit support of the CJEU, by creating European-level agencies to which national regulatory powers have been transferred. A clearly visible regulatory pattern has been pursued by the Commission aimed at the Europeanisation of policy fields. In the field of audiovisual media services, the Commission achieved the approximation of national rules via a Directive founded on the concept of minimum harmonisation. Its choice of legal instrument (i.e. Directive rather than Regulation) tacitly recognises the power struggle between the Commission and the Member States. In this regard, it is important to remember that Art. 167 (5) TFEU precludes harmonisation of cultural matters such that a Directive best seems to reflect that Primary Law requirement. Moreover, the Commission is bound by first, the Treaties which do not confer exclusive competence to regulate the media sector on the EU.[3018] Second, whenever it exercises its shared competence in the area on behalf of the EU, it is obliged to respect the principles of subsidiarity and proportionality.[3019]

Although the legal framework for regulation of audiovisual media services is one of shared competences, such regulation remains an integral part of the Member States' national cultural policies, one that goes to the very heart of each Member State's identity. Hence, any hint that the Commission is considering a move towards full harmonisation is likely to face strong opposition from the Member States. Moreover, as of this writing, the political climate does not favour enhanced integration, due to the many anti-European and Euro-sceptic movements across the EU. Nonetheless,

---

the US, similarly demonstrates such differences and it is questionable whether it will stand renewed review by the courts. See for example Max Schrems, "The Privacy Shield Is a Soft Update of the Safe Harbor," *European Data Protection Review* 2/2016 (2016): pp. 148–50.

3018 Art. 5 (1) – (2) TFEU.

3019 Art. 5 (3) – (4) TFEU.

there have been some tentative steps to Europeanise audiovisual media services regulation, the most prominent of which was the creation of ERGA in early 2014 by issuing the ERGA Decision.[3020]

The preamble of the ERGA Decision makes clear that the Commission's decision to create ERGA was primarily motivated by internal market considerations. "In order to achieve a successful development of an internal market for audiovisual media services notably in view of increased cross-border distribution and the regulatory challenges linked to on-demand services, a coherent application of Directive 2010/13/EU in all Member States is essential. To achieve this goal it is crucial to facilitate a closer and more regular cooperation between the competent independent regulatory bodies of the Member States and the Commission".[3021] Hence ERGA, an "advisory body", provides support to the Commission as it supervises the Member States' implementation of the AVMSD.[3022] The close relationship between the Commission and ERGA is intended to lead, over time, to more uniform and coherent regulatory approaches. Such enhanced cooperation between the Commission and the Member States' independent regulators has been successfully implemented in other EU-law areas, most notably consumer protection,[3023] where "enforcement cooperation networks" have been established.[3024] The Commission's DSM Strategy includes two such entities, the Body of European Regulators in Electronic

3020 European Commission, "Decision on ERGA". See also the Commission's 2016 AVMSD Proposal aimed at elevating ERGA's role.

3021 European Commission, "Decision on ERGA," recital 3.

3022 European Commission, "Decision on ERGA," recital 4.

3023 European Commission, "Decision on ERGA," recital 5.

3024 See for instance the cross-border enforcement and cooperation mechanism for consumer protection laws entitled "Consumer Protection Cooperation" (CPC) which is governed by Regulation (EC) No 2006/2004 of the European Parliament and of the Council of 27 October 2004 on cooperation between national authorities responsible for the enforcement of consumer protection laws, OJ of 9.12.2004, L 364, pp. 1–11. Interestingly, the Commission tabled a proposal in May 2016 (on the same day it published its 2016 AVMSD proposal) to reform the CPC and make it more responsive to and effective in view of challenges associated with the digital single market and online consumer protection. See European Commission, "Proposal for a Regulation of the European Parliament and of the Council on Cooperation between National Authorities Responsible for the Enforcement of Consumer Protection Laws, COM(2016) 283 Final," May 25, 2016.

Communications (BEREC)[3025] for the telecommunications market and the Article 29 Data Protection Working Party (Article 29 WP),[3026] both of which have become important actors in their respective sectors and may have served as an example for ERGA. In contrast to ERGA which was established by a decision unilaterally adopted by the Commission, the legal bases for BEREC and the Article 29 WP are laid down by the applicable regulation or directive.

Interestingly, the Commission's 2005 AVMSD proposal was silent on this issue and it appears that the institutionalisation of cooperation mechanisms was not debated at that time, although the EP expressed a general desire for closer cooperation between national regulators in light of jurisdiction and derogation mechanisms.[3027] The Contact Committee, set up in 1997 pursuant to Art. 23a TWFD which gathers competent representatives of the Member States has since fulfilled a similarly coordinating function. Its impact, however, on either the Commission or European audiovisual media policies has remained limited as it appears that the perceived need for a more formal and intense cooperation between the Commission and the national regulatory bodies has only come to the fore in recent years, due to the "regulatory challenges" posed by on-demand services and the Internet's increasingly global role as a distribution channel for audiovisual media.[3028] Since its inception, ERGA has been very active and has pro-

3025 As part of the 2009 reform telecoms reform package, BEREC was established by Regulation (EC) No 1211/2009 of the European Parliament and of the Council of 25 November 2009 establishing the Body of European Regulators for Electronic Communications (BEREC) and the Office, OJ of 18.12.2009, L 337, pp. 1–10, Art. 1.

3026 The Article 29 Working Party was set up in accordance with Art. 29 of Directive 95/46/EC of the European Parliament and of the Council of 24 October 1995 on the protection of individuals with regard to the processing of personal data and on the free movement of such data, OJ of 23.11.1995, L 281, pp. 31–50. It will be replaced by the European Data Protection Board on 25 May 2018 when the General Data Protection Regulation becomes applicable. In comparison to its predecessor, the new European Data Protection Board is strengthened and has been endowed with more extensive powers. See Regulation (EU) 2016/679 of the European Parliament and of the Council of 27 April 2016 on the protection of natural persons with regard to the processing of personal data and on the free movement of such data, and repealing Directive 95/46/EC, OJ of 4.5.2016, L 119, pp. 1–88, Arts. 68 and 70 in conjunction with recital 139 and Art. 94 (2).

3027 European Parliament, "European Parliament Legislative Resolution on the Commission's Proposal Amending the TWFD.".

3028 European Commission, "Decision on ERGA," recital 3.

duced, particularly in early 2016, reports on issues of paramount importance to the AVMSD revision, such as its material and territorial scope and the protection of minors (see below), and has been outspoken on, *inter alia*, the independence of national regulators and freedom of expression.[3029] The 2016 AVMSD proposal envisages a stronger and more deeply involved ERGA. At the policy-setting stage, for instance, it is expected to identify best practices and, thereby, determine (more) consistent regulatory standards to be applied across the EU (see below). Strikingly, the 2016 AVMSD proposal reiterates the ERGA Decision, highlighting ERGA's new role. Member States, fearing a loss of control, are expected to oppose that new role during the legislative process of the 2016 AVMSD proposal.[3030]

As a result ERGA's creation and subsequent activity within the EU, a non-EU entity, the European Platform of Regulatory Authorities (EPRA), is facing increased competition. EPRA, created in 1995 as a not-for profit association incorporated in France, has a much broader membership. It represents 46 countries and it has built up a rich database of comparative documents on numerous media policy issues.[3031] EPRA is currently rethinking its role and impact on the European market in an effort to avoid duplicating activities performed by other networks, especially ERGA. It appears that it intends to concentrate on activities or tasks that ERGA might not be able to perform or, at least, not perform to the same extent EPRA can.[3032] It remains to be seen whether EPRA can successfully retain its current position or if it will become smaller over time or will shift to other issues as the EU Member States' national regulatory authorities will inevitably be drawn to the forum that is better able to influence the bind-

---

3029 The ERGA work programme, reports, press releases, statements and minutes of its meetings are available at https://ec.europa.eu/digital-single-market/en/audiovisual-regulators (accessed 3.7.2016).

3030 The EP's CULT draft report drawn up in early September also clearly opposes ERGA's stronger involvement and suggests amendments curtailing its position as envisaged by the Commission. The CULT draft report interestingly strengthens the role of the Contact Committee as a counter-balance to ERGA, proposing to enlarge its composition to include four MEPs. See for example AM 82, Art. 29 (1), AM 90 and 91, Art. 30a (a) and (b) of the CULT draft report.

3031 See http://www.epra.org/ (accessed 3.7.2016).

3032 EPRA launched a consultation to set a strategy. See http://www.epra.org/news_items/epra-consults-on-a-draft-three-year-organisational-strategy (accessed 3.7.2016).

ing measures that directly affect them as part of the Union. The Commission, as the centre of power within the EU's DSM, is, and will continue to be, a crucial actor. In monitoring the Member States' application of the current AVMSD and its successor, the Commission will inevitably rely on national regulators (i.e. members of ERGA) for more consistent regulatory solutions. In the long run, national practices are therefore likely to align, in an incremental way.

In brief, audiovisual media services regulation will continue to be implemented at two policy levels, at the European and national levels. Within the EU, primary law recognises the dual nature of audiovisual media services: they are both economic *and* cultural goods. While Member States retain, and vigorously defend, their prerogatives in the cultural sphere, the Commission already pursues common regulatory standards, relying on the internal market rationale, and will continue to Europeanise national media policies in light of ever-converging economies. Its current intention to de-regulate certain aspects of audiovisual media services (as revealed in its 2016 AVMSD proposal) most notably by enhancing flexibility for broadcasters),[3033] will make cooperation among national regulators and the Commission all the more necessary in the future.

## B. Content standards in converging media markets

This section looks at content standards in converging media markets, relying on the findings of the fourth and fifth chapters. It examines which rules can be retained in a converged media market and how existing rules should be modified to remain practicable and feasible amidst media convergence. In its first part, it devises best practices and makes suggestions in relation to the criteria defining an audiovisual media service and the protection of minors in audiovisual media services, while a sub-section on the AVMSD's scope explores the current discussion on the regulation of platforms.

3033 European Commission, "2016 AVMSD Proposal," pp. 10, 12, see also recitals 13, 18 and 19.

## I. Best practices and suggestions in relation to material scope

The following section suggests best practices with respect to the Directive's material scope of application and the concept of an (on-demand) audiovisual media service. Given the Commission's proposal to extend the next-generation AVMSD to VSPs, it also briefly deals with possible regulatory intervention in relation to online platforms.

### 1. Criteria defining an audiovisual media service

Based on chapter four's case study, this subsection identifies best practices that may help guide future regulation. To this end, it examines several criteria incorporated into the definition of an audiovisual media service, including those found in recitals. It also discusses whether such criteria are still relevant and if not, what kind of modifications should be introduced to the next-generation AVMSD. Finally, it briefly analyses platform regulation, with a view toward extending the material scope of the next AVMSD.

#### a) Principal purpose

A service's principal purpose is one criterion used to define an audiovisual media service, one that has been subject to extensive interpretation by national regulatory authorities. It serves to distinguish those audiovisual media services with a principal purpose of providing programmes from other media services, such as online press, social networks, and video-sharing and other digital platforms. As media converge, it will become more and more difficult to make clear-cut distinctions between the different types of media: many websites already contain several services that reflect different legal categories (such as audiovisual media services, information society services, and telecommunications services) to which different legal regimes attach. Hence, the principal purpose criterion for identifying an audiovisual media service will continue to be relevant in the future. It makes clear that only those services that primarily offer audiovisual content (i.e. programmes) will be covered by the next-generation AVMSD. Audiovisual content remains a specific and therefore distinguishing characteristic and justifies different regulatory intervention because convergence has not yet reached a state in which any type of content, regardless of its form, is equally perceived, equally valued and equally consumed by users. Maintaining different standards for different sectors, such as the press, audiovisual media services, and information society services, still seems relevant. In the long term, however, such distinctions will blur and degrade to the point that further refinements will be needed.

The long, slow-moving legislative process at the EU level is likely to become a serious obstacle to such refinement unless the current 2016 AVMSD proposal's de-regulatory approach is reinforced, such that EU-level regulation reverts to simply establishing general rules and principles to be implemented at the national level. However, that reversion risks a lack of uniformity in the application of Union law because national implementation will inevitably diverge. The country of origin principle's success could be undermined as forum shopping, due to the Member States' different regulatory approaches, grows. Although a principles-based approach in an EU instrument would provide more flexibility in coping with technological changes, new uncertainties might also evolve, especially at the implementation level, so that the problem is merely transferred to a different, lower level. Unless the Member States develop detailed rules that conform to common principles, a transfer of power to national executive bodies seems highly likely. In that case, the Commission might well be inclined to create an EU-level regulatory environment (relying on ERGA, or even another newly established agency) that helps to set standards and promotes the exchange of best practices. Even if this scenario is still a long way off and is certainly not the only possible scenario for the European regulatory framework in the long run, there will come a point when it will be vital to decide whether the current approach – detailed rule-setting – is still appropriate.

Because the principal purpose criterion is important and relevant to future regulation, it should be specified in the revised AVMSD in order to enhance legal certainty for providers and facilitate its enforcement by NRAs. A strictly quantitative approach to websites offering diverse content (e.g. counting the number of videos made available by a particular service), is ill-suited to determining the nature of the service(s) offered by those websites. It has already been rejected by the three NRAs investigated in this study. In the *New Media Online* case, the CJEU approved the approach taken by the Austrian regulatory authority which grounded its decision, that a service constituted a coherent offer distinct from other parts of the website, on the service's independence and self-standing nature. According to the Court, the principal purpose of a service implies a service that is independent of, and not merely indissociably complementary to, other activities carried out via the same media outlet and is, above all, determined by the links existing between audiovisual and other material. Although that independence test seems appropriate to determine the principal purpose of a service, it also appears doubtful that, in practice, it will be sufficient to assess *only* the nature of the links to make the determination. As the CJEU in *New Media Online* delegated the detailed assessment of the service to the national court, it can be assumed that the nature of the links is likely to be only one, albeit important, element of the national court's analysis.

From the regulatory practice examined above, it would appear that the criteria originally developed by Ofcom for the principal purpose test constitute a best practice. These entail the presentation, branding, and styling of a service, the compilation of audiovisual material in a catalogue, the way such material is accessed (e.g. through search facilities and navigation menus) and the completeness of videos (including the existence of an auto-play function). Ofcom separately evaluates the independence of audiovisual material, the access links, and the structure of the audiovisual material, including the overall balance (i.e. significance and prominence) of material as well as its relevance.[3034] The Ofcom criteria specifically identify the concept of "principal purpose" and take account of numerous factors that can all contribute to a finding that a service's principal purpose is the provision of programmes and videos. Ofcom has repeatedly highlighted that a service must be assessed within its general context by taking a step back.[3035] The Ofcom list of criteria is not exhaustive and no one factor is determinative on its own, so that different factors may be decisive in different cases.

The problem, however, with the Ofcom criteria is that each of its criterion is inherently subjective and can be interpreted in different ways. Thus, its criteria need to be consistently applied to avoid arbitrary decision-making. Regulators must also provide the rationale for their decisions, so that parties can understand how and why each criterion impacts the designation of a service's principal purpose and the regulator's ultimate finding that a particular service is, or is not, regulated under AVMS

3034 Ofcom, "Appeal Decision Sun Video," para. 90, pp. 27–29.
3035 Ofcom, "Appeal Decision Sun Video," para. 90 h, p. 29.

rules. Rather than trying to cherry-pick from among the many factors, a combination of the *New Media Online* approach and Ofcom's criteria may provide a clearer assessment methodology for regulators. The combination would ground itself on a central question: Is the audiovisual content independent from other material provided on the website (i.e. is it self-standing and dissociable)? That question would be answered by applying Ofcom's criteria. Regulators should use the same criteria for every decision and should justify whether and how any particular criterion should be taken into consideration.

Consistent use of this assessment methodology could provide a greater level of coherence in regulators' decisions and could act as a clear manual for them to follow. Although the principal purpose element of the definition has, in practice, caused some difficulties for NRAs, it is, and will continue to be, an essential element in determining whether or not the AVMSD, as transposed in national law, applies. It will remain relevant to the revised AVMSD which should take into account the Court's *New Media Online* decision as well as Ofcom's list of characteristics indicative of principal purpose. Due to the latter's detailed nature, it may be best to include it in the preamble to the next AVMSD or authorise ERGA to adopt and further define it by issuing guidelines.

#### b) Programme

The notion of a "programme" is another essential element of the definition of an audiovisual media service. It denotes an individual item comprising moving images with or without sound within a schedule or a catalogue.[3036] As the AVMSD suggests a dynamic interpretation of the term,[3037] several NRAs have been regulating short-form content as audiovisual media services including Austria, Flemish-speaking Belgium and Sweden as shown in the fourth chapter. Although it is true that certain programme formats such as music, comedy, and sexually explicit content are typically of short duration, it is difficult to set a minimum duration for videos regulated under the AVMSD and to date, the NRAs have refrained from doing so. But,

3036 Art. 1 (1) (b) AVMSD.
3037 Recital 24 AVMSD.

a grey zone will persist unless a minimum duration is specified. The disadvantage of specifying a minimum length before AVMSD regulation is triggered is, of course, that service providers will, if it is at all profitable, adjust their services to avoid regulation. Hence, short videos (i.e. those lasting a few minutes) rather than brief clips (i.e. those only lasting several seconds) should be subjected to regulation under the AVMSD and this should be clarified in a revised Directive. The dissemination of short-form content is proliferating and it appears that users, especially younger generations, view short-form content as a substitute for long-form programmes.[3038] While the growth in such material is not, by itself, sufficient to justify imposing AVMS-type regulation, it nonetheless points to changing market realities to which regulation must adjust.

The regulatory definition of a programme is also linked to the comparability test that follows from Art. 1 (1) (b) AVMSD: material that has a form and content comparable to the form and content of broadcasts aired on TV, falls within the definition. Here again, Ofcom issued guidance on the comparability test outlining a list of criteria, such as extended duration (about eight to ten minutes), use of titles and credits and the existence of a (complete) narrative structure. The Ofcom criteria also look at the material's production techniques, such as the use of music, presenters/commentators and voiceovers and camera techniques. Moreover, Ofcom considers whether the relevant content is actually broadcast on TV and whether users when consuming the material have a viewing experience typical of TV broadcasts.[3039] Indeed, Ofcom has distilled certain characteristics, unique features that set TV programmes apart from other audiovisual material. While the production of conventional programmes (e.g. feature-length films, documentaries, and series) still remains an important part of the audiovisual media market, audiovisual material is also distributed in a variety of other, innovative forms that are often less structured, less professional, and less oriented toward TV programmes which leads to the in-

3038 Cabrera Blázquez et al., *On-Demand Services and the Material Scope of the AVMSD*, p. 11; ERGA, "Report on Material Jurisdiction," para. 1.2.2 and 1.2.3, pp. 16–17 (accessed 9.1.2016); Bruno Zambardino, Monica Sardelli and Marco Bassini, "AVMSD Refit or Reform? Audio Visual Media Services in the Digital Era" (Institute for Competitiveness (icom), September 2016), pp. 17–20.

3039 Ofcom, "Appeal Decision Everton TV," para. 39, p. 14; see also Ofcom, "Appeal Decision Channel Flip," paras. 45–48, pp. 12–13; Ofcom, "Appeal Decision Top Gear YouTube," paras. 43–47, pp. 12–13.

evitable question that must be posed during the up-coming legislative reform: Should the next-generation AVMSD maintain its current TV-centric approach? Retaining that TV-centric attitude is likely to prevent any substantial enlargement of the next AVMSD's scope of application and would only allow for modest, if any, expansion thereof.

The three regulators studied here are divided on this point.[3040] While the UK's Ofcom argues that a distinct "TV-like space" exists that can be contrasted to an "Internet space",[3041] the German media authorities prefer to abandon the notion of "TV-like" in favour of more forward-looking regulations. The French CSA appears to side with Ofcom, supporting the continued value of the TV-like concept. The need to regulate television broadcasting represents the genesis of the Directive but now it seems rather backwards looking and is no longer helpful in determining whether a new and innovative audiovisual media service should be regulated under the AVMSD. Yet, recital 24 AVMSD remains valid. Accordingly, the AVMSD applies to services that compete with each other. In its decisions, Ofcom relied on that competitive aspect to take account of the users' perspectives (when appropriate and bolstered by market research). Although the CJEU and national courts have been reluctant to refer to user perspectives, it should nevertheless be more frequently included in the NRAs' analysis. Regulators should ask whether (a) the user replaces the time he or she would have otherwise spent watching TV with the time he or she spends using the service under investigation (market data and research will make the NRAs' assessments more precise) and (b) whether the user expects the service under investigation to be subject to the same regulatory protection as he or she receives for TV programmes.

In the UK, recital 24 AVMSD has been interpreted even more broadly, to encompass services that are merely *capable* of competing for the same audience which has led small-scale providers to be covered by AVMS-regulation. It is true that services that start as a small-scale operation, with few users and a small budget, may grow to become well-established and

---

3040 In a similar vein, ERGA does not clearly speak out on this issue in its report on the scope of the AVMSD. It submits that the criterion of "TV-like" constitutes "an anchor" of the current regulatory regime while it may also no longer be "future proof". It thus suggests a solid review of the TV-like criterion during the up-coming reform process. See ERGA, "Report on Material Jurisdiction," pp. 33–34.

3041 Ofcom, "Reply AVMSD Consultation," p. 9.

well-known players in the market and the UK regulators have been careful not to allow such developments to escape regulation. Yet, a question remains as to whether, in the future, regulation should be tied more closely to the mass media aspect of such services, mentioned in recital 21 AVMSD. Some Member States, like Germany and Italy, have established *de minimis* exceptions based on established thresholds tied to the providers' user base, annual turnover and/or audience share.[3042] The audience share criterion is, however, particularly difficult to apply to on-demand services, as it appears that a comparable method of measuring a provider's audience has yet to be developed. While support for *de minimis* exceptions is appropriate, that is not to suggest that thresholds should be defined in the revised AVMSD; rather, the next-generation AVMSD should shift its perspective from micro- to macro-management. Re-calibrating future regulation by concentrating on the mass media aspect of the service would ensure proportionate and targeted regulatory intervention. In short, the next AVMSD should abandon the references to TV-like services, to better facilitate its application to new services that compete with existing audiovisual media services. Moreover, such new, competing services should only be regulated to the extent that they constitute mass media within the meaning of recital 21.

### c) Editorial responsibility

The third criterion, "editorial responsibility", has also received particular attention from the three NRAs studied here, but especially in the UK and France. Editorial responsibility, according to the AVMSD, implies that the provider exercises control over the selection of programmes and their organisation in either a schedule or catalogue.[3043] Determining who actually has editorial responsibility however may prove to be a complex task, espe-

3042 Art. 2 (3) No. 1 RStV. In Italy, the regulatory authority AGCOM has established a threshold of EUR 100,000 annual revenues above which it is presumed that operators are providing services of an economic activity which is comparable and in competition to broadcasters. See Art. 2 of the AGCOM, "Delibera n. 607/10/CONS Regolamento in materia di fornitura di servizi di media audiovisivi a richiesta ai sensi dell'articolo 22-bis del Testo unico dei servizi di media audiovisivi e radiofonici"; see also Machet, "New Services and Scope," p. 7.

3043 Art. 1 (1) (c) AVMSD.

cially when multiple parties are involved.[3044] Nowadays, it is not at all unusual for the functions of programme selection and programme organisation to be performed by different parties: one party pre-selects the content that will be compiled and structured on an online platform or website by a second party.[3045] Nevertheless, the editorial responsibility criterion remains significant and should not be abandoned. It still goes to the very heart of the activity carried out by audiovisual media service providers and helps distinguish them from other operators (e.g. those providing electronic communications infrastructure or those providing e-commerce services). It is, however, necessary that, for the purposes of the AVMSD, one person, whether an individual or a legal entity is identified as *the* person who has such editorial responsibility.

The French CSA requires providers to designate, in a contract, the person with editorial responsibility. Similarly, Ofcom looks at express or implied contractual terms, the actual conduct of the parties, and if necessary other evidence to determine editorial control. Thus, the revised AVMSD should encourage service providers to expressly name the person with editorial responsibility in their contracts or agreements. But if more than one person plays an editorial role and the providers have not expressly identified the editorially responsible person in advance, the appropriate NRA will have to undertake a global, detailed evaluation to find that person which would likely entail a careful analysis of: the level of control exercised by each actor, how active each actor is in fulfilling a specific task, whether and how the actor is able of influencing the orientation of the service and whether a particular actor has a veto power or otherwise decisive say. In sum, editorial responsibility is, and will continue to be a relevant criterion for defining audiovisual media services and should be applied, first, by reference to the express or implied terms of the parties' contracts or agreements. In the absence thereof, a case-by-case analysis is required to identify the person with the greatest level of effective control.

3044 In its report on the material scope of the AVMSD, ERGA also discusses the great number of actors who may be involved in the editorial process. See ERGA, "Report on Material Jurisdiction," pp. 38–39.

3045 Schoefs, "Connected TV and Editorial Responsibility," pp. 353–54.

### d) Possible additional criteria

In their joint reply to the Commission's consultation on a revised AVMSD, the German media authorities in the form of the DLM proposed two additional criteria to be used to decide if a particular service is or is not an audiovisual media service, thereby helping demarcate the Directive's scope. This suggestion was made in a particular context. The DLM is generally critical of the level of detailed regulation being adopted at the EU level. In its statement on the revision of the AVMSD, it proposed limiting common standards to a basic set of rules in the AVMSD which would enhance the Member States' leeway in adopting stricter rules at the national level and/or constructing an incentive-based regulatory scheme.[3046] Departing from a linear/non-linear distinction made at the national level, the DLM suggested a new category of audiovisual media services should be introduced, one comprised of broadcasting and telemedia services. According to the DLM, two further criteria should be added to better define an audiovisual media service: (i) journalistically edited offers and (ii) the service's reach or relevance to the audience.[3047]

The notion of journalistically edited offers which also lacks a uniform understanding stems from the German legal order, as discussed in chapter four. The 2014 report by Kluth/Schulz on convergence and its regulatory implications suggested using that concept to differentiate services that are important for public communication and those that are not.[3048] Again, this suggestion was made in a particular context, namely that of protecting media diversity and pluralism. It reflects the traditional German approach to broadcast regulation which has focussed on the relevance of an offer in forming public opinion, a criterion that has not yet played a role in the AVMSD. The Kluth/Schulz report argued that services may be distinguished on the basis of their value and contribution to public communication.[3049] Those with an added-value for society are worth regulatory pro-

3046 Direktorenkonferenz der Landesmedienanstalten, "Position on the revision of the AVMSD," pp. 4–5.

3047 Direktorenkonferenz der Landesmedienanstalten, "Position on the revision of the AVMSD," pp. 4–5.

3048 Kluth and Schulz, "Arbeitspapier Konvergenz und regulatorische Folgen," pp. 80–83.

3049 Kluth and Schulz, "Arbeitspapier Konvergenz und regulatorische Folgen," p. 82.

tection.[3050] Although the term "journalistically edited" is not specifically defined, it implies a professional selection process regarding topics and agenda, a high degree of organisation and institutionalisation, meaning the topicality and periodicity of such communications and a significant degree of public access and commitment to making content available. Further, it implies asymmetric roles of talking and listening, meaning that those communicating and conveying information are clearly distinguishable from the audience.[3051] It is questionable whether the one-to-one transfer of the propositions by Kluth/Schulz to the AVMSD is appropriate. The logic behind the AVMSD, being an internal market instrument, fundamentally differs from the regulatory aims of the German RStV which primarily aims at protecting media diversity and plurality. The DLM's idea to add a new criterion of journalistically edited offers introduces a qualitative (and moreover very subjective) distinction between offers having a social value and those lacking the potential to contribute to the process of opinion-formation. It is also strongly associated with providing news, current affairs, and other kinds of informative programmes and thus, would be too restrictive in the context of the AVMSD which applies to multiple programme types and genres.

The DLM further believed that the public reach or relevance of a service should be a criterion for determining whether a service is or is not an audiovisual media service. More precisely, the German regulators suggested that thresholds that exempt service providers from the specific regulation applicable to journalistically edited offers should be provided.[3052] The determining factor would be the reach of a service as an indication of its relevance to public-opinion formation. For broadcasting, audience shares could be used to make that determination. The DLM also referred to measurements that assess the use of streaming services by online panels (used, for example, by Nielsen). With regards to on-demand services, however, collecting reliable data is more difficult. Although the reach/relevance criterion was construed within the specific German context, it does reflect the concept of mass media as set forth in recital 21 AVMSD.

3050 Kluth and Schulz, "Arbeitspapier Konvergenz und regulatorische Folgen," p. 83.

3051 Kluth and Schulz, "Arbeitspapier Konvergenz und regulatorische Folgen," p. 83.

3052 Direktorenkonferenz der Landesmedienanstalten, "Position on the revision of the AVMSD," p. 5.

Recital 21 AVMSD makes clear that the audiovisual media services the Directive covers are services which will be seen and heard by the public and that which will have a "clear impact on a significant proportion of the general public". As discussed above, emphasis must be paid to the mass media character of audiovisual media services. Their reach, at least as understood by the DLM, could be one indicator of that character. To conclude, although the DLM's suggested modifications to the existing catalogue of criteria defining audiovisual media services are interesting, they must be carefully analysed. They were, after all, made in a specific context and with a view to reinforcing the importance of relevance to public-opinion formation, a criterion already deeply ingrained in the German broadcasting system. While the idea of journalistically edited offers does not really fit the European legal framework, the concept of reach and relevance to the public (if understood more broadly than just relevance to public-opinion formation) may well be appropriate indicators of the notion of mass media at which regulation should be targeted.

## 2. The regulation of platforms?

The likes of Google, Amazon, and Facebook increasingly penetrate the market for audiovisual media services.[3053] Each has established its diverse online platform, catering to different segments of the population, including video-sharing, search engines, e-commerce, and social networking. Beyond their core business, they have all started to engage in the distribution of audiovisual content. Streaming services, such as Netflix,[3054] Amazon Prime Video, and streaming devices, such as Google's Chromecast and Amazon's Fire TV stick, as well as Connected TV platforms operating on the basis of set-top boxes, such as Android TV (Google TV's successor) and Apple TV, are some of the most prominent examples. Device manufacturers, such as Samsung, LG, and Philips have produced ever-more sophisticated Connected TVs with built-in functions allowing users to access the Internet via their televisions. Not only has the number of online media

3053 Zambardino, Sardelli and Bassini, "AVMSD Refit or Reform?," p. 19; ERGA, "Report on Material Jurisdiction," para. 1.3.5, p. 22–23; para. 1.4, pp. 23–27.

3054 In contrast to Google, Amazon and Facebook, Netflix is an on-demand service provider established in the Netherlands and thus already covered by the AVMSD.

outlets (platforms) on which audiovisual material is provided or shared among users significantly increased, but the infrastructure (device) providers have also been engaging in content distribution. The design of such Connected TV interfaces and their user manuals and navigation systems allow platform operators to exercise control over the content that may be shown on a particular device or platform. These providers and platforms raise many questions – political, socio-cultural, economic, and legal questions – that deserve a more in-depth analysis than can be incorporated in this research. Suffice it to say that prominent discussions about platform regulation are underway. A brief recitation of the most important contributions from regulators, policy makers and academia on the subject are therefore presented below.

a) Regulators' perspectives

During the Commission's public consultation on the revision of the AVMSD running from July to September 2015, many stakeholders called for extending AVMS-type regulation to platform operators due to their powerful market position as content and information gatekeepers. The French CSA and the German media authorities, for similar reasons, argued that the scope of the next AVMSD should be enlarged to cover online platforms. The CSA argued that it is essential that all actors deriving revenues from the dissemination of audiovisual content contribute to the production and distribution of audiovisual works. Today, many platforms pursue a business model that links the consumption of videos or audiovisual material (whether professionally produced or user-generated) to advertisements, thereby replicating the activities of free-to-air broadcasters. Such platforms generate revenue by selling space on their platforms for advertisements. They operate in multiple markets (e.g. the markets for video-sharing and advertising) and benefit from so-called network effects (i.e. the more users the platform has, the more money it may be able to charge for the inclusion of advertisements on its site). Their business model is also data-driven, enabling them to collect and process large amounts of users' data.

In its submissions to the Commission's consultation, the French CSA questioned the current dichotomy between media service providers (regulated by the AVMSD) and host providers (regulated by the ECD), claiming that platform operators no longer passively stock or host content provided by third parties; rather, platforms exercise a degree of editorial control that is comparable to media service providers by organising, indexing, and/or personalising content.[3055] Thus, the CSA suggested that the new regulatory framework should encompass all intermediaries (or "digital platforms") that place themselves between audiovisual media service providers and consumers, including Internet access providers, video-sharing platforms, device manufacturers, social networks and search and recommendation engines.[3056] A broad notion of "digital platforms" should therefore be introduced to the revised AVMSD to ensure that all actors that emerge as gate-keepers are covered by the regulatory framework.[3057] The CSA justified such expanded regulation by looking to the increasingly trans- and cross-border nature of content distribution, the important role played by platforms in the digital ecosystem and the growing importance of intermediaries in safeguarding fundamental values such as pluralism and media diversity, competition and the protection of minors.[3058] The paucity of investment in audiovisual productions was, indeed, the CSA's primary cause for concern which it argued would have serious repercussions on the production of original content and was highly likely to adversely affect content diversity unless regulatory counter-measures were taken.

In a similar vein, the German DLM also favoured an extension of the AVMSD's scope, albeit only to comparable offers that have a similar impact on public-opinion formation, democracy and the general public's perception of media service providers.[3059] In its statement, published in June 2015, about a month before the Commission's public consultation started, the DLM mentioned the need to regulate online newspapers (the ones that solely or predominantly make available audiovisual content) and video-sharing platforms, such as YouTube.[3060] Like the CSA, the DLM highlighted the fact that certain platforms were in increasing competition with

3055 CSA, "Reply AVMSD Consultation," p. 7.
3056 CSA, "Reply AVMSD Consultation," p. 7.
3057 CSA, "Reply AVMSD Consultation," p. 11.
3058 CSA, "Reply AVMSD Consultation," pp. 11, 15.
3059 Direktorenkonferenz der Landesmedienanstalten, "Position on the revision of the AVMSD," p. 2.
3060 Direktorenkonferenz der Landesmedienanstalten, "Position on the revision of the AVMSD," p. 2.

content providers.[3061] Ensuing competitive distortions therefore needed to be evened out. Hence, the DLM called for a new, distinct definition for "audiovisual platforms," to which it suggested a separate set of rules should apply, regulating access, content findability and secondary responsibility for any infringement of the rules protecting minors.[3062] Interestingly, these particular regulatory aims which were not mentioned by the CSA were probably inspired by Germany's existing platform regulation.[3063]

The UK's Ofcom, on the other hand, positioned itself at the opposite end of the regulatory spectrum from the CSA and the DLM, rejecting any kind of platform regulation by the next AVMSD.[3064] It suggested that intermediaries (such as ISPs or search engines) and content hosts (such as YouTube) do not exercise editorial control and thus, do not compete with media service providers.[3065] For Ofcom, video-sharing websites merely provide the infrastructure for third parties to provide their content.[3066] While Ofcom did not reject *per se* the introduction of rules for platforms, it pointed out that any such rules should reflect the role and functions of such operators and thus, should not oblige them to monitor the content they host.[3067] In Ofcom's view, regulation that is imposed on platforms should considerably differ from regulation applicable to media service providers that have editorial responsibility.[3068] In its response to the consultation, Ofcom underscored that any kind of platform regulation should be carefully elaborated and take into account the "openness of the Internet environment, the extent to which it allows the rapid development of new

---

3061 Direktorenkonferenz der Landesmedienanstalten, "Reply AVMSD Consultation," p. 10.
3062 Direktorenkonferenz der Landesmedienanstalten, "Reply AVMSD Consultation," p. 10.
3063 See Arts. 50-53b RStV.
3064 See also Joint letter from the United Kingdom, the Czech Republic, Poland, Luxembourg, Finland, Sweden, Denmark, Estonia, Latvia, Lithuania and Bulgaria to Vice-President Ansip of 4 April 2016. The signatories to this letter favour a light-touch approach to platforms, emphasising the economic potential for the internal market. The letter is available at https://www.gov.uk/government/uploads/system/uploads/attachment_data/file/513402/platforms-letter.pdf (accessed 25.8.2016).
3065 Ofcom, "Reply AVMSD Consultation," p. 12.
3066 Ofcom, "Reply AVMSD Consultation," p. 12.
3067 Ofcom, "Reply AVMSD Consultation," p. 12.
3068 Ofcom, "Reply AVMSD Consultation," p. 11.

and innovative services and in particular how it enables individual citizens to participate in the creation and distribution of content".[3069]

In sum, the three regulatory authorities examined in this study represent different perspectives on the regulation of platforms. While the French regulator, CSA, advocated for a broad and all-inclusive approach to ensure investment in audiovisual productions and the UK regulator, Ofcom, adhering to its liberal market philosophy, was reluctant to regulate platforms within the next AVMSD, the German media authorities took a more targeted approach, arguing that only those platforms that are in competition with media service providers should be subject to regulation. They proposed establishing rules for specific problems, such as guaranteeing free and non-discriminatory access to platforms which they believed would ensure visibility of general interest content and enhance the platforms' responsibility for protecting minors.

#### b) Academic and other contributions to platform regulation

The academic debate has focussed on conceptualising online platforms and examining their effect on different markets to better understand whether regulation is even necessary and if so, what policy objectives it should seek to accomplish and in what form. A study by Van Eijk et al., published in November 2015 developed a framework by which policymakers can analyse the need for regulatory intervention.[3070] Due to the great variety of platform types, the study highlights the need to characterise digital platforms.[3071] On the basis of certain characteristics (such as the revenue model, whether they exploit direct or indirect network effects, whether the platform operator benefits from economies of scale, to what extent there is horizontal or vertical integration in the market or what kinds of products and services are affected), a typology of platforms is established including reseller/distribution, marketplace, social networks and platform of platforms.[3072] The study then identified relevant public policy

3069 Ofcom, "Reply AVMSD Consultation," p. 12.

3070 Nico Van Eijk et al., "Digital Platforms: An Analytical Framework for Identifying and Evaluating Policy Options," November 9, 2015, http://ivir.nl/publicaties/download/1703 (accessed 11.12.2015).

3071 Van Eijk et al., "Policy Options for Digital Platforms," para. 2.2, p. 11.

3072 Van Eijk et al., "Policy Options for Digital Platforms," paras. 2.3-2.5, pp. 11–19.

interests and objectives related to digital platforms, such as sufficient levels of competition (to foster innovation), consumer interests, considerations of improper influence (by the state or by the platforms themselves) and considerations concerning the infrastructure.[3073] Finally, against the existing legal backdrop (e.g. competition law, the AVMSD, the ECD, data protection and copyright law), the study outlined different strategies governments could pursue: they could (1) remove existing regulation, (2) continue to apply existing schemes, (3) reinterpret existing schemes in light of new developments, or (4) design new schemes.[3074] The study can be a useful, practical guide to the platform debate and is very valuable for governments looking at platform regulation. It also stresses the need to conceptualise platforms by their characteristics rather than use predefined platform categories because that approach is more appropriate to "the dynamics and richness of digital platform features than a stable, but necessarily limited, typology".[3075] Moreover, the study reminds governments that they have a variety of regulatory strategies at their disposal to address the concrete policy objectives they identify.

Helberger et al. also made an interesting contribution to the academic debate by examining the extent to which new information intermediaries, such as Facebook and Google, act as gatekeepers. The authors are highly sceptical of the adequacy of existing regulatory tools, such as access obligations, media-ownership rules, due prominence requirements and media diversity, as applied (or not) to these gatekeeper intermediaries.[3076] Interestingly, they claimed that, to date, there is no or no significant evidence of the so-called "filter bubble effect" that is a primary concern for those favouring online platform and intermediary regulation.[3077] The filter bubble effect implies that providing like-minded content which supports, rather than challenges, a person's existing views and attitudes, reduces content diversity and that increasingly personalised or targeted services facilitate such filter bubbles or echo chambers. The authors suggest a more

3073 Van Eijk et al., "Policy Options for Digital Platforms," para. 2.6, pp. 19–23.

3074 Van Eijk et al., "Policy Options for Digital Platforms," paras. 2.8-2.9, pp. 28–38.

3075 Van Eijk et al., "Policy Options for Digital Platforms," para. 4.2, p. 46.

3076 Natali Helberger, Katharin Kleinen-von Königslöw and Rob Van der Noll, "Regulating the New Information Intermediaries as Gatekeepers of Information Diversity," *Info* 17, no. 6 (2015): pp. 50–71.

3077 Helberger, Kleinen-von Königslöw and Van der Noll, "Regulating the New Information Intermediaries," pp. 56–57, 59.

user-centred approach to future regulatory tools, one that takes into account the ability of "the gated" (i.e. the users) to influence their gatekeepers (i.e. the intermediary or platform).[3078] The authors also highlighted the positive role information intermediaries play in promoting content diversity and user exposure thereto. They warned against hasty policy decisions and regulatory interventions that do not take proper account of the nature of intermediaries and platforms.

In Germany, a dedicated group of state- and federal-level representatives (*Arbeitsgruppe*) is currently discussing a comprehensive framework for platforms.[3079] As of this writing, Art. 50 et seq. RStV already regulate platforms. However, the RStV restricts its concept of platform providers to the persons (or entities) who supply the technical infrastructure and collate audiovisual media services and other content provided by third parties.[3080] The reporty by Kluth/Schulz of 2014 is another important contribution to the ongoing debate surrounding platform regulation.[3081] Some of its recommendations may even be valuable beyond Germany's specific legal framework. Like the Van Eijk study, Kluth and Schultz attempted to delineate the concept of platforms, stressing that the delineation must be sufficiently circumscribed and should not cover all communications bottle-

---

3078 Helberger, Kleinen-von Königslöw and Van der Noll, "Regulating the New Information Intermediaries," pp. 63–64.

3079 The final report of the *Bund-Länder Kommission* that includes the suggestions elaborated by the dedicated *Arbeitsgruppe* concludes that regulation of platforms is necessary and draws up certain principles or regulatory objectives (*Eckpunkte*) such as transparency, non-discriminatory access, findability of content relevant for public-opinion formation, signal integrity and must offer. See Bericht der Bund-Länder-Kommission zur Medienkonvergenz, June 2016, pp. 24-29, available at https://www.bundesregierung.de/Content/DE/_Anlagen/BKM/2016/2016-06-14-medienkonvergenz-bericht-blk.pdf?__blob=publicationFile&v=3. See also Die Medienanstalten, "Stellungnahme der Medienanstalten zur Anhörung der Bund-Länder-AG Plattformregulierung," June 25, 2015, www.die-medienanstalten.de/fileadmin/Download/Positionen/Gemeinsame_Positionen/Stellungnahme_der_Medienanstalten_zur_Plattformregulierung_14072015.pdf; Die Medienanstalten, "Positionen der DLM zur Fortentwicklung der Plattformregulierung," March 15, 2016, http://www.die-medienanstalten.de/fileadmin/Download/Positionen/Gemeinsame_Positionen/DLM-Position_Fortentwicklung_der_Plattformregulierung_2016-03-15.pdf (all websites accessed 4.8.2016).

3080 Art. 2 (2) No. 13 RStV.

3081 Kluth and Schulz, "Arbeitspapier Konvergenz und regulatorische Folgen," para. IV, pp. 89–95.

necks.[3082] According to Kluth/Schulz, the concept of a platform should be defined in a technology-neutral way and should take account of the expected risks to desired public interest objectives which, in Germany, relate to access and findability of services.[3083]

From the brief presentation above, it becomes clear that platform regulation is already on the agenda of many Member States. Yet, a number of question marks remain with respect to the kinds of platforms to be regulated, their respective impact on society and the risks they pose to current and future public-policy goals. To better design proportionate regulation of certain of their aspects, such complex questions require more detailed analysis.

#### c) The Commission's Communication on online platforms

##### (aa) Context and objectives

From the discussion above, a guiding principle emerges: platform regulation, if pursued through the new AVMSD, must be carefully measured and apply to only those platforms that compete with audiovisual media services. The Commission, in its 2016 AVMSD proposal, suggests regulating video-sharing platforms (VSPs) and introducing specific rules intended to prohibit hate speech and protect minors. That proposal is analysed in more detail below. It is noteworthy that apart from the public consultation concerning the new AVMSD, the Commission also opened a public consultation, at the end of 2015, on the regulatory environment for online platforms and intermediaries: more than 1,000 stakeholders and more than 10,000 individuals participated therein.[3084] The Commission's

3082 Kluth and Schulz, "Arbeitspapier Konvergenz und regulatorische Folgen," para. IV, pp. 90–91. In a German context, the authors also outline criteria for the definition of platforms, such as the compilation and distribution of offers having a particular impact on society. These criteria would apply to traditional distribution networks as well as virtual platforms.

3083 Kluth and Schulz, "Arbeitspapier Konvergenz und regulatorische Folgen," para. IV, pp. 90–91.

3084 See First brief results published by the Commission under https://ec.europa.eu/digital-single-market/en/news/first-brief-results-public-consultation-regulatory-en

consultation document relied on a broad definition of online platforms[3085] and its questionnaire touched on a range of different topics, such as the ECD's limited liability regime, data protection (especially the data processing by platforms and intermediaries), copyright-related questions on illegal content and legal challenges associated with the collaborative or sharing economy. As a result of the consultation and a subsequent comprehensive assessment, the Commission published a communication on online platforms as part of the DSM Strategy on 25 May 2016, entitled "Online platforms and the Digital Single Market, opportunities and challenges for Europe" (the Platform Communication), the same day it announced its 2016 AVMSD proposal.[3086] In contrast to the detailed regulations set out in the 2016 AVMSD proposal, the Commission's Platform Communication rejected a "one-size-fits-all" approach and instead set out targeted regulations that pursues a principles-based approach in relation to online platforms.[3087]

The Platform Communication acknowledged the diversity of online platforms and the myriad activities they engage in, as well as their growing role in the digital economy and for society at large.[3088] "Online advertising platforms, marketplaces, search engines, social media platforms, communications services, payment systems, and platforms for the collabo-

---

vironment-platforms-online-intermediaries (accessed 31.7.2016). See also European Commission, "Consultation on Platforms and Online Intermediaries.".

3085 The term platform comprises "activities like online advertising platforms, marketplaces, search engines, social media and creative content outlets, application distribution platforms, communications services, payment systems, and platforms for the collaborative economy". See Online Platforms, available at https://ec.europa.eu/digital-single-market/en/online-platforms-digital-single-market (accessed 30.7.2016).

3086 European Commission, "Communication from the Commission to the European Parliament, the Council, the European Economic and Social Committee and the Committee of the Regions on Online Platforms and the Digital Single Market, Opportunities and Challenges for Europe, COM(2016) 288 Final," May 25, 2016; see also European Commission, "Commission Staff Working Document on Online Platforms, Accompanying the document 'Communication on Online Platforms and the Digital Single Market,'" May 25, 2016.

3087 European Commission Press Release of 25.5.2016, Commission updates EU audiovisual rules and presents targeted approach to online platforms, IP/16/1873, available at http://europa.eu/rapid/press-release_IP-16-1873_en.htm (accessed 4.8.2016).

3088 European Commission, "Communication on Online Platforms," para. 2, p. 2.

rative economy" are all subsumed under the term "online platforms"[3089] and the Platform Communication stated that such platforms typically operate in multi-sided markets and benefit from network effects.[3090] Furthermore, it found that online platforms are characterised by "the ability to create and shape new markets" and "facilitate new business ventures and creating new strategic dependencies".[3091] Their business model is based, to a large extent, on collecting, processing and editing large bulks of data.[3092] The Platform Communication went on to say that online platforms positively shape the digital market and "increase consumer choice" by "facilitat[ing] efficiency gains, and act[ing] as a magnet for data-driven innovation".[3093] It also acknowledged the strength of US and Asian operators and therefore, announced an intent to creating market conditions that help such businesses to establish and flourish in the EU.[3094]

(bb) Principles-based approach

To allow online platforms to leverage their potential and foster their "innovation-promoting role", the Commission refrained from describing detailed legal rules for them, preferring instead to rely on existing EU legal instruments in fields such as competition law, consumer protection, data protection and the fundamental freedoms of the internal market.[3095] A balanced regulatory framework for online platforms on the basis of four general principles is elaborated. Its first principle seeks to provide a "level playing field for comparable digital services".[3096] Comparable services in-

3089 European Commission, "Communication on Online Platforms," para. 2, p. 2.
3090 European Commission, "Communication on Online Platforms," para. 2, p. 2.
3091 European Commission, "Communication on Online Platforms," para. 2, pp. 2–3.
3092 European Commission, "Communication on Online Platforms," para. 2, p. 3.
3093 European Commission, "Communication on Online Platforms," para. 2, p. 3.
3094 European Commission, "Communication on Online Platforms," para. 3, p. 3. Vice-President of the Commission Mr. Ansip highlighted that intent when he said that "I want online platforms and the audiovisual and creative sectors to be powerhouses in the digital economy, not weigh them down with unnecessary rules". See European Commission Press Release of 25.5.2016, IP/16/1873, available at http://europa.eu/rapid/press-release_IP-16-1873_en.htm (accessed 30.5.2016).
3095 European Commission, "Communication on Online Platforms," para. 3, p. 5.
3096 European Commission, "Communication on Online Platforms," para. 5 i, p. 6.

clude, for instance, over-the-top communications services which increasingly compete with traditional telecommunications operators but are not subject to any specific regulation.[3097] The Platform Communication also recognised that extending existing regulation to new players implies the need to reconsider its scale and scope.[3098]

The second principle takes account of the growing role online platforms play in content distribution and is directed toward enhancing their responsibility in this respect.[3099] This second principle is expressed by the Commission's proposal to apply rules regarding harmful content and content inciting hatred to VSPs in the next AVMSD.[3100] It also materialised in the Commission's review of the EU copyright package which is intended to ensure fairer remuneration for creators of copy-righted material made available by online platforms.[3101] The Platform Communication also made clear that the Commission will encourage online platforms to voluntarily step up their efforts in the fight against illegal content and collaborate with other stakeholders.[3102] Moreover, due to broad support for the existing intermediary liability regime set out in Arts. 12 through 15 ECD, the Plat-

---

3097 European Commission, "Communication on Online Platforms," para. 5 i, p. 6.

3098 European Commission, "Communication on Online Platforms," para. 5 i, p. 7.

3099 European Commission, "Communication on Online Platforms," para. 5 ii, p. 7.

3100 European Commission, "Communication on Online Platforms," para. 5 ii, p. 8.

3101 European Commission, "Communication on Online Platforms," para. 5 ii, p. 8; see also European Commission, "Proposal for a Directive of the European Parliament and of the Council on Copyright in the Digital Single Market, COM(2016) 593 Final," September 14, 2016; European Commission, "Proposal for a Regulation of the European Parliament and of the Council Laying down Rules on the Exercise of Copyright and Related Rights Applicable to Certain Online Transmissions of Broadcasting Organisations and Retransmissions of Television and Radio Programmes, COM(2016) 594 Final," September 14, 2016.

3102 European Commission, "Communication on Online Platforms," para. 5 ii, 9. An expression of this collaboration is the code of conduct on countering illegal hate speech online, brokered at the end of May 2016 between the Commission and Facebook, Microsoft, Twitter and YouTube. See http://ec.europa.eu/justice/fundamental-rights/files/hate_speech_code_of_conduct_en.pdf. See also the Commission's press release of 31.5.2016, European Commission and IT Companies announce Code of Conduct on illegal online hate speech, IP/16/1937, available at http://europa.eu/rapid/press-release_IP-16-1937_en.htm (all websites accessed 15.6.2016).

form Communication expressed the Commission's intent to refrain from modifying it.[3103]

The third principle emphasises the values of trust, transparency and fairness in the context of the data-intensive and data-driven business model of online platforms.[3104] It acknowledges both sides of the relationship between the consumer, on the one hand and the platform provider, on the other. To build trust and enhance transparency, the Commission also published, on the same day it published the Platform Communication, an updated guidance on the Unfair Commercial Practices Directive (UCPD) and a proposal for a revised Regulation on Consumer Protection Cooperation.[3105] Moreover, the Platform Communication announced that the Commission will undertake a more comprehensive assessment with respect to B2B practices to determine whether additional EU action is required.[3106]

Finally, the Platform Communication's fourth principle purports to maintain open and non-discriminatory access to markets.[3107] This includes data portability as well as free-of-charge access to online platforms and non-discriminatory access to application programme interfaces.[3108] The fourth principle is expressed by the Commission's free flow of data initiative, currently scheduled for late 2016.

---

3103 European Commission, "Communication on Online Platforms," para. 5 ii, pp. 8, 9.

3104 European Commission, "Communication on Online Platforms," para. 5 iii, p. 9.

3105 European Commission, "Communication on Online Platforms," para. 5 iii, pp. 10–11; see also European Commission, "Communication from the Commission to the European Parliament, the Council, the European Economic and Social Committee and the Committee of the Regions on A Comprehensive Approach to Stimulating Cross-Border E-Commerce for Europe's Citizens and Businesses, COM(2016) 320 Final," May 25, 2016; European Commission, "Proposal for a Regulation on Cooperation in Matters of Consumer Protection Laws.".

3106 European Commission, "Communication on Online Platforms," para. 5 iii, pp. 12–13.

3107 European Commission, "Communication on Online Platforms," para. 5 iv, p. 13.

3108 European Commission, "Communication on Online Platforms," para. 5 iv, pp. 13–14; see also European Commission, "Proposal for a Regulation of the European Parliament and of the Council on Ensuring the Cross-Border Portability of Online Content Services in the Internal Market, COM(2015) 627 Final," December 9, 2015.

### (cc) Critical assessment

The Commission's comprehensive assessment which involved an impressively large number of stakeholders and individuals is laudable. Nevertheless, the Platform Communication appears to be little more than a compromise intended to silence a majority of stakeholders. Those calling for regulation to be imposed on online platforms (or on specific types thereof) must content themselves with the four principles outlined in the Platform Communication. Those in favour of a "hands-off" approach must be satisfied by the Commission's choice to only issue a communication, one that emphasises co- and self-regulation, rather than taking a binding legal act. The Commission's choice of legal instrument may have been pre-determined by its expansive and all-encompassing definition of the operators concerned – that is, the online platforms. In that respect, the Platform Communication, except for its self-made claim, does not seem at all "targeted". While its four principles may give an overview of and some insight into the Commission's current and future activities, they do not present a coherent regulatory strategy but rather a haphazard one with many loose ends. In fact, the announced principles represent a very limited expression of values that any future EU legal framework is expected to reflect. The time-frame envisaged by the DSM Strategy is, moreover, very ambitious, requiring the Commission to initiate a large number of different projects in tandem to and conclude them (or, at least get such projects far enough off the ground that they could be concluded) within its five-year term ending in October 2019. Some of these projects, such as the next-generation AVMSD, the copyright acquis, and the telecoms package, constitute major overhauls that require the Commission to have, among other things, a substantial capacity to gather and analyse data (in compliance with Better Regulation principles).

Rather than accommodating all online platforms under one unwieldy large concept, it would have been far more useful if the Commission had followed up on specific types of online platforms; conducting a more in-depth assessment of the legal challenges those specific types of platforms generate, to appraise the need for more targeted EU regulatory intervention. The Commission had, in fact, promised a "problem-driven approach"[3109] that would address specific, clearly identified problems as

3109 European Commission, "Communication on Online Platforms," para. 3, p. 5.

they emerged, but until the end of 2016 it has not given any sign that it is ready to tackle specific platform issues.

In light of the foregoing, it is debatable whether all types of online platforms mentioned in the Platform Communication can, or should, be regulated by one, single legislative or regulatory act. To do so, however, the Commission would have to start by grouping, as far as possible, different types of online platforms together and then evaluate the various effects and impact of each group to prevent inadvertent use of the silo approach (i.e. an over-dissection of the market) which might impinge on needed regulatory flexibility. The Commission could, in that regard, use an approach similar to that which it used for the telecommunications sector. In that way, it could fashion an overarching legal framework to address common characteristics or to outline general principles, such as Platform Communication principles which framework could be fleshed out by other legal instruments that regulate more specific issues if there is evidence of a market failure or a need for supplementary regulation and then those individual regulatory or legislative acts could be revised, giving the Commission a realistic opportunity to react to market or technological developments without questioning its overall regulatory framework.

Alternatively, in the interest of cohesion, any problems associated with certain types of platforms could be regulated through any existing sector-specific EU regulatory instruments. For example, problems arising in online marketplaces could be addressed in the ECD or other consumer protection instruments. The Commission has already used this approach, extracting VSPs from its definition of online platforms and placing them under the AVMSD's purview, as further discussed below. Such an approach, however, would necessitate careful evaluation of the purposes and objectives of any existing legal instruments. If such sector-specific regulations were, however, stretched too far to accommodate particular types of platforms, their purposes and objectives might be blurred or undermined. Certainly, new legislation would also have to be adopted and, as a result, a sector-specific approach might continue without a common umbrella. In short, the Platform Communication represents a first attempt to grasp the role of online platforms and to understand their impact on society. It is doubtful, however, that it will ever have a substantial practical effect but it appears that the Commission never intended it to have such an effect. Nonetheless, the Platform Communication might serve as a basis for more detailed regulatory proposals in the future.

## II. Best practices and suggestions for the protection of minors

Protecting minors from harmful content has been and continues to be a priority for many regulatory authorities. Due to the proliferation of freely accessible, inappropriate content on the Internet and the gradually shifting consumption patterns of young audiences. Because young viewers increasingly turn away from television broadcasting, effectively protecting minors in a converged media environment appears to be a major challenge. Particularly in this coordinated field, the Directive has lagged behind market developments, despite the fact that the heart of its provisions (Arts. 12 and 27 AVMSD) reflects a delicate balancing act between the free flow of all kinds of audiovisual content and the need to protect minors from harmful content. Because of the cultural and social implications of said balancing exercise, the EU's and hence the Commission's role remains limited, given its lack of competence in those areas.[3110] Thus, Member States retain broad discretion when applying the AVMSD at the national level and when interpreting its key terms in accordance with their national traditions, prevailing cultural norms and public morality. Notwithstanding such discretion, a more coordinated EU level approach is desirable, particularly in view of growing cross-border content distribution and heightened competition from global players. The following section presents both best practices for applying Art. 12 AVMSD and reflections on the design of the provisions incorporated in the next-generation AVMSD.

### 1. Seriously harmful content

Art. 12 AVMSD refers to VOD services that "might seriously impair" a minor's physical, mental or moral development which is a necessarily broad formulation that allows Member States a great deal of leeway when applying it in their national context. Seriously harmful content is, more-

3110 Member States' prerogative to take measures to protect children has been recognised by the CJEU in case C-244/06 *Dynamic Medien Vertriebs GmbH v Avides Media AG*, Judgment of 14.2.2008, EU:C:2008:85, paras. 39-41. Importantly, the CJEU further acknowledged that the level of protection may vary from one Member States to another "on the basis of, inter alia, moral or cultural views", and that consequently, "Member States must be recognised as having a definite margin of discretion" (para. 44).

over, a well-established content category, set apart from other categories such as content suitable for all audiences, harmful content and illegal content. Making a differentiation between "harmful" and "seriously harmful" content, both of which can be legally made available in on-demand services so long as adequate safeguards are in place (in contrast to broadcasting where "seriously harmful" content is banned), is and will continue to be justified. Nevertheless, further harmonisation with respect to the meanings of these phrases is likely to prove beneficial to both EU providers and NRAs, particularly with respect to cross-border services. This is especially relevant when such cross-border providers are established in a Member State with a lenient regime but target audiences in another Member State that applies stricter rules. Although Art. 4 (2)–(5) AVMSD provides a derogation from free flow of information in this regard, the provision only applies to broadcasters; no corresponding rule applies to VOD providers. Thus, in the next AVMSD, enhanced coordination of such key terms could prevent, or at least minimise, forum shopping within the EU. Moreover, a more harmonised approach to protecting minors would also enhance legal certainty for all stakeholders. Providers, particularly those simultaneously operating in different markets, might well be encouraged to expand their business beyond one Member State.

When faced with a media outlet that raises issues under Art. 12 AVMSD, as transposed in their respective national legal orders, the UK, German and French regulators currently assess the whole range of material that the media outlet makes available. Today, adult websites typically offer different types of content (e.g. text-based, still images and audiovisual), thus, the regulators' assessments pre-suppose that the media outlet's service, as such, is regulated as an audiovisual media service and is qualified as a substantial offering of audiovisual content.

The UK's approach to defining content offered online that poses a seriously harmful risk to minors seems especially appropriate because it is consistent with the definition of content offered offline. In the UK, seriously harmful content within the meaning of Art. 12 AVMSD is regarded as the equivalent of R18 material. That age-based rating indicates that the relevant content can only be supplied to adults in specifically licensed shops or cinemas, as most content with that rating is pornographic and/or extremely violent. The UK's R18 age rating was originally developed for videos, films and games but has been extended to online media, such that the rationale used in an offline media context (data or carrier media such as video tapes, DVDs, blu-rays, etc…) is likewise applied in an online context, thereby assuring consistency across different media types. The same content, whether distributed online or offline, is subject to the same restrictions intended to protect minors.

It is inexplicable, why different types of restriction should apply depending on the channel of distribution. Unfortunately, in some EU countries, particularly in Germany, achieving appropriate levels of consistency will be difficult, due to the distribution of relevant competences among different state and local entities which is often accompanied by a complicated network of (overlapping) regulatory bodies. Achieving regulatory consistency would require a major overhaul of legal instruments at all levels, an exercise any Member State might be reluctant to undertake. With respect to a revised AVMSD, it might be possible to devise a broad formulation that defines seriously harmful content as content from which minors enjoy the highest level of protection (or, formulated differently, content to which the strictest restrictions apply) in the national legal framework. Such a broad formulation would clarify that Art. 12 AVMSD targets material that, although still permissible in the particular Member State, is but one step away from being prohibited by that Member State. It might also enable an enhanced degree of consistency between the various regulations for different types of media in one Member State.

Unlike Art. 27 (1) AVMSD which expressly refers to "programmes that involve pornography or gratuitous violence" Art. 12 AVMSD is silent on the exact nature of content that "might seriously impair" a minor's physical, mental or moral development. Chapter five's analysis demonstrates that, for most Member States, content considered capable of seriously impairing minors is either pornographic, extremely violent, or both. Despite the lack of any empirical evidence to support the proposition, it still seems appropriate to rely on a precautionary approach, one that restricts (but does not ban) the provision of seriously harmful content to adults. In order to enhance clarity, the next AVMSD should explicitly state that content that is pornographic, gratuitously violent, or both is seriously harmful to minors. It is, however, unclear whether such an express formulation would be approved by the Member States, most notably those with more liberal views (e.g. the Netherlands and the Scandinavian countries).

The extent to which the Commission can provide guidance on the precise meaning of these terms is an entirely different matter. The frequently repeated argument is that the concepts of "pornography" and "gratuitous violence" content are so complex and interpreted so differently across EU Member States, that any attempt to define them at a supra-national level is doomed to fail. In the fifth chapter that examined the measures of the UK, German and French regulators, the concept of pornography has taken a prominent role. In spite of their cultural differences, the concept of pornography in all three Member States boiled down to a single common denominator: the presentation of non-simulated sexual acts for the sole purpose of sexual arousal which means that sexual acts are performed in front of a camera in order to sexually arouse the viewer. This broad understanding of the concept represents the minimum level of consensus among the three Member States studied. Further tests would be required to determine if the same broad understanding is valid for the remaining Member States. Thus, it would appear that conceptualising pornography in the next AVMSD, based on such minimum criteria, would not unnecessarily constrain those Member States that have a definition of pornography that encompasses more elements. Because the new AVMSD would provide a floor, beneath which no Member State could go, rather than a ceiling, Member States would still be able to adopt more detailed or stricter rules in their jurisdictions.

Conceptualising the notion of gratuitous violence, on the other hand, appears somewhat more complicated. The current AVMSD implies that a distinction can be made between *gratuitous* violence which is "seriously harmful" and violence considered "harmful" to minors by national law. Drawing such a distinction can be particularly difficult because what is or is not considered violent or gratuitously violent changes as cultural and social perceptions change.[3111] What was considered *extreme* twenty years ago, may have already become *ordinary* by current standards, and vice versa. The national practices investigated in the fifth chapter primarily dealt with the concept of extreme violence (mainly) in a sexual context. Accordingly, violence is understood as the infliction of lasting physical or psychological harm. Whether such violence is also gratuitous may depend on its presentation which is equally true for any presentation of pornography.

Thus, in conjunction with any attempt to standardise the meaning of the terms "pornography" and "gratuitous violence", the next-generation AVMSD should outline additional indicators to determine the harm caused to minors. The German regulatory bodies have already developed a num-

3111 The notion of pornography is equally contingent on socio-cultural norms and changes over time as moral values evolve.

ber of such indicators which are accompanied by extensive regulatory guidance and the French courts already rely on similar, albeit fewer, indicators. Such indicators might include, for example, the way themes are stage-managed and presented, the quantity, quality and intensity of such representations, the likely expectations of users, in particular, the material's relevance for minors, the level of suspense, the degree of realism of the depictions, the extent to which the representations deviate from socially acceptable behaviour and the intention of the author of the work. These indicators may guide NRAs when carrying out an assessment of the nature of the content provided. They are necessarily subjective, depend on the particular circumstances of the specific case and are likely to be applied differently by different regulators. They would, however, at least provide a common basis to analyse the degree of harm and thus, will likely contribute to a more coherent application of the new AVMSD within the EU. In sum, to protect minors, the "seriously harmful" content category (i.e. pornography and gratuitous violence) should be maintained but the concept, as suggested above, should only be applied to content that meets certain minimum criteria that are, at the same time, clear enough to provide more legal certainty and broad enough to encompass different national interpretations. These minimum criteria, providing a baseline level of protection, could be supplemented by a non-exhaustive list of indicators to help assess the degree of harm posed by the content.

## 2. Restricting access to adults

The second aspect of Art. 12 AVMSD which causes considerable difficulties in practice, is the means employed to limit access to seriously harmful content only to adults. More specifically, Art. 12 AVMSD requires that minors "will not normally hear or see" seriously harmful content. This phrase which is also used in Art. 27 (2) AVMSD applicable to harmful broadcasts is best viewed as a relic from the TWFD era and should be modified. Thus, a reformed Art. 12 in the new AVMSD should simply state that seriously harmful content shall not be made available to minors which would mean that the dissemination of such content is legal but only if access thereto is restricted to adults. The term "minor" should also be defined in the new AVMSD as "a person who has not yet reached the age of majority as defined by national law". Defining the term in relation to the age of majority would be without prejudice to other national definitions, such as child, minor or adolescent. It would make clear that for the purpose of applying the reformed Art. 12 AVMSD, the distinction is made between a minor (under the age of majority) and an adult. In France, Germany, the UK, and many other EU Member States, the age of majority is 18 years of age.

What is more, the current Art. 12 AVMSD leaves it to Member States to determine the kind of measures that are deemed sufficient to restrict access to adults. If the national media laws replicate the wording of Art. 12 AVMSD, it falls on the regulatory authorities to interpret the phrase "will not normally hear or see". As the analysis in chapter five demonstrates, the measures taken by the UK, German and French regulatory authorities have some common features that may serve as best practices in this regard. For each of these countries, Art. 12 AVMSD requires an effective access control composed of two elements: age verification and then authentication prior to every subsequent login. Providers are thus obliged to verify whether the user is actually at least 18 years old. It is not sufficient to permit a user to simply self-declare that he is of age without the provider verifying this declaration. Such controls where users self-declare their age are easily circumvented, thus ineffective and incompatible with Art. 12 AVMSD. It is, of course, impossible to prevent every conceivable kind of circumvention by determined individuals and would put a disproportionate strain on service providers but reasonable age-verification mechanisms should be put in place. The countries require the provider to use a mechanism to verify that a user is older than 18 by providing, for example, reputable proof of the user's identity by way of the user's enrolment in the electoral roll. Thus, acceptable proof should include digital identity-management systems such as new identity card functions that allow citizens to identify themselves in a digital environment and conclude online transactions.

Moreover, as requiring a (physical) face-to-face age verification seems exaggerated and overly burdensome for both the provider and the user, users should be able to rely on forms of identification made prior to using the audiovisual media service, for instance identification accepted for the purpose of opening a bank account, mobile phone subscriptions, and SIM card, etc. This would require the service provider to cooperate with relevant third parties. Another reliable age-verification source could be payment methods reserved to people over 18 years of age, such as credit card ownership but it should only be permitted to the extent that the service provider can demonstrate that its payment service only processes payments made by adults. Such age-verification measures are both reasonable and balanced.

A second layer of control is added by repeated authentication each time the service was accessed which would verify that the same user was accessing the service. The authentication process would oblige already age-verified users to use a self- or provider-generated personal identification number (i.e. a PIN code) or password to access to adult-only content. The French CSA, for example, established detailed requirements including the use of a minimum-length access code or use of an encrypted code whenever the user seeks access. In short, Art. 12 AVMSD should be reformulated to make clear that access to "seriously harmful" audiovisual content is limited to adults and that it is the service providers' obligation to assure that the limitation is respected. Thus, service providers must adopt and implement age-verification measures that verify the age of a user. Moreover, the preamble to the next-generation AVMSD should supply further guidance that suggests that the Directive requires a two-step control that first verifies the user's age and subsequently obliges the user to authenticate his identity via a PIN or password.

## 3. A more holistic approach to protecting minors in the AVMSD

In light of continuing media convergence and the growing penetration of smart devices, the AVMSD's current distinction between linear and non-linear services seems artificial and outdated. Young audiences, in particular, are drawn to clips supplied on mobile devices. In contrast to the days when the family TV set was the focal point of the living room, it is and will continue to become more and more difficult for parents and custodians to monitor children's video consumption. To a lay person, the distinction between broadcasting and on-demand services is incomprehensible. Why should the same kind of content be regulated differently on different platforms or devices? It seems unjustified that a difference in regulatory standards hinges upon the content's mode of distribution or delivery, whether one–to-many or one-to-one communication.[3112] The regulatory

3112 In two of its reports, ERGA discusses the relevance and appropriateness of the distinction between linear and non-linear services. In its report on scope, it suggests that the appropriateness of the linear/non-linear distinction should be assessed for each coordinated field. See ERGA, "Report on Material Jurisdiction,"

authorities studied here disagree on the continued validity of the linear/non-linear distinction. Both the UK's Ofcom and France's CSA broadly support that distinction, although Ofcom seems more willing to give it up in certain areas, notably with respect to the protection of minors. The German state media authorities, on the other hand, are in favour of abandoning the current graduated approach and aligning the rules for on-demand services and broadcasting. The German approach appears inevitable in order to keep up with market developments and provide an effective and consistent level of protection. Whether the linear/non-linear distinction continues to have legitimacy in other fields coordinated by the AVMSD, will briefly be discussed below but in light of the scope of this study, the discussion focusses on the future design of Arts. 12 and 27 in the next AVMSD.

To remain relevant in the ever-converging media ecosystem, the next-generation AVMSD should contain a single set of rules to protect minors in all audiovisual media services. Ofcom's proposed uniform approach could serve as inspiration. In its reply to the Commission consultation on the AVMSD, Ofcom suggested basing the new provision on two inter-related elements: the severity of the harm determines the severity of the access controls. Ofcom suggested two content categories (i.e. moderately strong and very strong content) that correspond to two kinds of access controls (i.e. moderate and strong controls).[3113] It follows that the most harmful content is restricted by the strongest access control. A distinction is made between "harmful" content which would only be subject to moderate control (e.g. watershed rules, age ratings/classifications) and "seriously harmful" content which would be subject to strong controls (e.g. age verification). Adopting Ofcom's proposal in the revised AVMSD would require levelling-up regulation for on-demand services that are, so far, only regulated in connection with seriously harmful content. At the same

---

pp. 41–42; in its report on the protection of minors, a majority of ERGA's members is in favour of establishing one set of rules for all audiovisual media services. This group justifies its approach by audience expectations, technological progress and different consumption patterns and the simultaneous distribution of identical content by different sources (on different platforms or over different devices). An ERGA minority nonetheless holds that the linear/non-linear distinction is still legitimate, effective and up to date due to the more powerful impact of TV on society. See ERGA, "Report on the Protection of Minors," pp. 19–20.

3113 Ofcom, "Reply AVMSD Consultation," p. 32.

time, it would mean liberalising broadcasting regulation, allowing broadcasters to also offer seriously harmful content which is currently banned from TV.[3114] Adopting these modifications in the next-generation AVMSD seems reasonable and fair and would contribute to levelling protection while retaining flexibility for Member States to apply established national standards and existing classification systems.

Further coordination might also be sought at the EU level for appropriate access controls.[3115] Content ratings or classifications which are already used by the CSA in France for content delivered on-demand appears to be an appropriate method of informing users of the nature of the content. Many Member States rely on very detailed national systems that differentiate between various age groups. The Dutch *Kijkwijzer* has, in this regard, received much attention and has already been emulated in many countries.[3116] In addition to age recommendations, it uses easy-to-understand symbols (pictograms) to inform viewers about the nature of the material (e.g. a spider represents fear, a fist represents violence, a syringe represents drug and alcohol abuse and two pairs of feet represent sex).[3117] In a similar vein, the European games industry has developed uniform age ratings that are also supplemented by pictograms.[3118] Classifying content should be made easier and simple ways of sign-posting content (by way of pictograms) should be developed. For example, a system based on traffic-lights could attribute the green light to content appropriate for all audiences, the yellow light to harmful content and the red light to seriously harmful content. That type of system could easily be implemented and applied across the EU, even in parallel with national classifications. Yet, the introduction of uniform EU level age ratings has long been a regulatory taboo. This would, no doubt, require extensive and laborious negotiations

---

3114 Since the Directive is based on minimum harmonisation, Member States might still opt for stricter rules and maintain the current ban for broadcasting.

3115 Ofcom believes that ERGA is well-placed to establish more detailed guidance on the types of access restriction appropriate to the type of harm caused to minors. See Ofcom, "Reply AVMSD Consultation," pp. 32–33.

3116 Madeleine de Cock Buning, "Towards a Future-Proof Framework for the Protection of Minors in European Audiovisual Media," *Utrecht Law Review* 10, no. 5 (2014): p. 15.

3117 See Kijkwijzer Explained, available at http://www.kijkwijzer.nl/about-kijkwijzer (accessed 14.8.2016).

3118 See Pan-European Game Information (PEGI), About PEGI? What do the labels mean?, available at http://www.pegi.info/en/index/id/33/ (accessed 14.8.2016).

and strong political will to coordinate in this field. But, the effort would be immensely beneficial to the industry, to content creators (who can rely on them to better target a certain audience group), to service providers (who can rely on them in organising their schedules and catalogues) and above all, to consumers (that is, the parents and guardians, who can rely on them for clearer and more consistent information about the age-appropriateness of content for their children).

In addition, the technical dimension of youth protection should further be promoted and enhanced cooperation be sought at the EU level.[3119] The German regulatory authorities, in particular, highlighted the need for such coordination based on their experiences that show that existing parental controls, e.g. those that automatically block access to unsuitable content (*Jugendschutzprogramme*) need to be improved to better respect the rights and interests of all parties. A certification process would appear to be useful to ensure compatibility with legal requirements and could also represent a kind of quality label that might help spread their use. In that regard, it is important that any certified tools are accepted by society, that they are easy to use on multiple devices and are adaptable to different consumer interests and are (ideally) free of charge, or at least very affordable. To streamline research and development and achieve higher efficiency levels for parental controls and other technical tools, the German DLM proposed creating a uniform European technical framework that would develop common technical interfaces and classification and labelling standards that would function across platforms and devices.[3120]

While the technical aspect, in particular, demonstrates the complexity of protecting minors across Europe, the need to educate everyone – parents, guardians, and children – remains an ever-challenging goal. As the CSA, among others, stressed, technical advances must be accompanied by measures aimed to enhance media literacy and media education. Children born in the new millennium naturally grow up with the Internet. Even the youngest children (at the age of just 2 or 3) quickly learn how to operate a smartphone or tablet by just watching the adults around them use their

3119 Schindler, "Technische Möglichkeiten des Jugendschutzes im Internet," pp. 140–41; Braml and Hopf, "Jugendschutzprogramme," p. 370; see also Marx, Boots and Schindler, "Perspektiven des technischen Jugendschutzes".

3120 A large majority of ERGA members would also support a more coordinated approach to technical standards. ERGA, "Report on the Protection of Minors," pp. 29–30.

personal devices. Education is the key to fostering responsible use of the World Wide Web while enabling an enjoyable Internet experience. Parents and other custodians who often lack the necessary technical knowledge need to be better informed about available means, and otherwise empowered to take adequate steps, to protect minors in accordance with their personal values and perceptions. Parental responsibility cannot, however, be replaced by state-imposed youth protection.[3121] Particular strategies should therefore be developed to address different segments of the general public.

Another aspect appears significant in developing a more holistic approach to the protection of minors in relation to audiovisual media services. The responsibility to protect minors cannot, and should not solely rest with media service providers. In today's media ecosystem, in which the media service provider does not control the whole value chain, other operators (e.g. platforms, ISPs and device manufacturers) may also influence the distribution of audiovisual material. It would be unjust to place the entire burden of protecting minors on the media service provider. Instead, other actors should promote the protection of minors in accordance with their role in the value chain. In both Germany and the UK, for example, attempts have been made to cooperate with the payments industry. Moreover, it could be envisaged that platforms which host a substantial offering of audiovisual material assume at least secondary responsibility for audiovisual content. To the extent that these actors exercise an editorial role, they should be involved in the protection of minors.[3122] Such responsibility should not, typically, extend to the same degree of responsibility that media service providers must assume (as, at least nominally, platform providers do not have editorial responsibility) but it should go beyond the current level of responsibility (or, more accurately, the lack thereof) prescribed by the ECD. The regulatory measures imposed on these actors

---

3121 Holtmann, *Zur rechtlichen Unterscheidung von Rundfunk und Telemedien bei Hybrid-TV*, p. 161.

3122 ERGA also maps the broad range of actors involved in the creation and distribution of audiovisual content (such as content producers and publishers, content hosts and platforms, ISPs, providers of search and navigation functions and device manufacturers) and considers that their involvement in the protection of minors is crucial in the future. See ERGA, "Report on the Protection of Minors," pp. 46–48.

would have to be finely-tuned and compliance could be enforced by co- or self-regulation.

In conclusion, the current state of the audiovisual market necessitates a more levelled approach to protecting minors by audiovisual media services. A regulatory framework that aligns the standards for broadcasting and on-demand services by establishing two categories of inappropriate content (i.e. harmful and seriously harmful) that are subject to corresponding access controls (i.e. moderate and strong) and that reflect the potential harm caused to minors, would help level the playing field. To implement such a new framework, cooperation at the EU level would have to be reinforced. In that regard, a simplified rating scheme (possibly used on an EU-wide basis) and common technical standards would appear to be the most pressing issues for collaboration. Media literacy and media education cannot be neglected. Finally, to achieve a better level of protection (and possibly relieve the burden on individual operators), developing a more comprehensive legal framework should be considered, one in which all operators drawing advantages from the dissemination of audiovisual content take on their fair share of that responsibility. The actual construction of such a framework would, of course, require a more in-depth legal analysis.

## *C. The Commission's proposal on a revised AVMSD*

As previously mentioned, on 25 May 2016, together with other initiatives relating to the DSM Strategy, the Commission published its 2016 AVMSD proposal for a revised AVMSD.[3123] In view of a fast-moving media landscape, changing consumption as well as distribution patterns and new business models, the Commission expressed its intent to modernise the rules contained in the existing AVMSD.[3124] At the press conference, held on the same date in May 2016, Mr. Oettinger, Commissioner for the Digital Economy and Society said that "the way we watch TV or videos may have changed, but our values don't. With these new rules, we will uphold media pluralism, the independence of audiovisual regulators and will make sure incitement to hatred will have no room on video-sharing platforms".

3123 2016 AVMSD proposal.

3124 See Explanatory Memorandum, para. 1, p. 2 of the 2016 AVMSD proposal.

The following section critically reviews the 2016 AVMSD proposal, commenting on the Commission's amendments in light of the two themes of this study: regulatory strategies and content standards in two different sub-sections. With respect to content standards, it will focus on the aspects examined in the chapters four and five, that is, the proposed material scope of the Directive including its application to VSPs and its proposed modifications concerning the protection of minors. The Commission's proposed changes in other fields coordinated by the reformed AVMSD are briefly reviewed in the final sub-section of this chapter.

## I. Regulatory strategies in the revised AVMSD

This part outlines the regulatory strategies that flow from the Commission's 2016 AVMSD proposal. The proposal underscores the use of co- and self-regulation in converging media markets and it enhances coordination at the EU level through ERGA.

### 1. Reinforcing co- and self-regulation

In general, the Commission's proposed amendments manifest strong support for alternative forms of state regulation. Its 2016 AVMSD proposal expressly mentions co-regulation as an appropriate regulatory regime to implement its Art. 6a (obligation to provide content information) and Art. 28a (rules applicable to VSPs). Similarly, to implement Art. 9 (2) and (4) (inappropriate commercial communications), the 2016 AVMSD proposal also recommends use of co- or self-regulation. The current AVMSD stipulates that co- and self-regulatory systems should be "broadly accepted by the main stakeholders (…) and provide for effective enforcement".[3125] According to the 2016 AVMSD proposal, new Art. 4 (7) furthermore specifies the requirements for such codes, referring to clear and unambiguous objectives, such as "regular, transparent and independent monitoring and evaluation" of the objectives and "effective enforcement" mechanisms (including "appropriate effective and proportionate sanctions").[3126] These

3125 Art. 4 (7) AVMSD.

3126 These requirements are also underscored by recital 7 of the 2016 AVMSD proposal.

may be regarded as useful guidelines for the implementation of national co- and self-regulatory schemes. Formulating clear and precise objectives that delineate the mandate to such co- and self-regulatory bodies is indeed necessary to avoid regulatory overlap or clashes with other regulatory bodies. This also sets the regulatory regime on a strong footing and ensures that it is geared towards fulfilling the identified objectives. The requirements outlined in the 2016 AVMSD proposal's Art. 4 (7) appear appropriate and refine those currently prescribed by the AVMSD. In a sector that is as fast-moving as the media sector, periodic evaluations of the regulatory framework, carried out by independent reviewers, are vital to ensure that the objectives established remain relevant and the regulatory bodies "on track". Similarly, effective enforcement bolstered by a meaningful sanctioning mechanism is crucial to the whole system. Even if the co- or self-regulatory bodies cannot themselves impose sanctions, backstop powers should exist that allow such bodies to refer serious violations to NRAs.

Interestingly, the Commission, for the first time, expressly contemplates the adoption of Union codes of conduct in relation to the provision of content information (proposed Art. 6a) as well as commercial communication for unhealthy food or beverages and alcoholic beverages (proposed Art. 9 (2) and (4)). These Union codes of conduct would be "facilitate[d]" by the Commission which might consult ERGA prior to their publication. ERGA could give an opinion on the draft codes and amend or extend them where appropriate.[3127] Clearly, the Commission believes that these specific areas have the potential for closer coordination at the supra-national level, as they relate to protecting the audience, especially minors, from harmful content (by means of content descriptors) and from inappropriate commercial communications. As several studies have already shown, these areas lend themselves to co- or self-regulatory structures.

The Commission sees the harmonisation or coordination of national laws and practices through regulatory authorities under the auspices of ERGA as a viable method for furthering European integration in the audiovisual sector, as discussed below. But, it is also clear that the Commission recognises that, in spite of the positive effects enhanced cooperation brings (e.g. leading to a more coherent and purportedly effective approach),[3128] it does not come without risk. Questions about the appropriate

3127 See Art. 4 (7) of the 2016 AVMSD proposal.
3128 See recital 12 of the 2016 AVMSD proposal.

authority(ies) competent to monitor and enforce the EU level codes are likely to arise. Or, the Commission might be inclined, in the long run, to see itself as the best-placed authority to oversee compliance, to further empower ERGA or to even establish a new European body or agency and thereby gradually undermine the Member States' sovereignty. Whether the Commission has ulterior motives is pure speculation at this point in time and future Commissions may decide to reverse the current trend towards out-sourcing legislation to regulatory bodies at both, the national and European levels.

## 2. Strengthening the role of the European Regulators Group for Audiovisual Media Services

The 2016 AVMSD proposal, if adopted as initially proposed, would regulate and up-grade ERGA's status. As emphasised above, ERGA was unilaterally established by the Commission in February 2014. In that regard, its proposed recital 36 sets out the Commission's rationale for ERGA, stressing that "ERGA has made a positive contribution towards consistent regulatory practice and has provided high level advice to the Commission on implementation matters". As a consequence, the 2016 AVMSD proposal formally recognises ERGA and reinforces its role. The proposed Art. 30a would essentially re-establish ERGA, replicating much of the wording found in the ERGA Decision. The second paragraph of new Art. 30a addresses ERGA's composition[3129] and the proposed Art. 30a (3) enumerates its tasks. It is interesting to note that the proposed Art. 30a (4) empowers the Commission to adopt ERGA's rules of procedure. This is striking as ERGA adopted its own procedural rules in March 2014.[3130] The fact that the Commission, rather than ERGA itself, would have the power to draw up ERGA's internal rules demonstrates that the former is

3129 Art. 30a (1) of the 2016 AVMSD proposal that corresponds to Art. 4 (1) ERGA Decision.

3130 ERGA Rules of Procedure, March 2014, available at https://ec.europa.eu/digital-single-market/en/audiovisual-regulators (accessed 16.8.2016).

keen to keep a firm grip on the group.[3131] ERGA's tasks broadly correspond to those set out by the ERGA Decision.[3132] It is to assist and advice the Commission in the consistent implementation of the Directive and in any matter relating to the provision of audiovisual media services. ERGA would also serve as a forum for exchanges of experience and best practices by its members which would also support the application of the AVMSD. What is more, upon the Commission's request, ERGA may provide opinions on jurisdictional rules applicable to media service providers, as well as any Union codes of conduct for audience protection, notably minors from harmful content, inappropriate audiovisual commercial communications and video-sharing platforms' obligations.[3133]

As it has in other sectors, such as data protection and telecommunications, the Commission already heavily relies on ERGA, usually as a body that assembles expertise and experience in the application of the AVMSD. Strengthening ERGA through the 2016 AVMSD proposal is just a logical consequence of ERGA's increasing activity over the past two years and its steadily growing visibility gained through its various reports and statements. The consultation of ERGA for the purpose of designing more appropriate regulatory tools is, in this regard, a positive development. Through ERGA, legal instruments supposedly "come closer" to those being regulated. ERGA may also be able to identify weaknesses in existing regulatory instruments which can then be remedied by subsequent revisions. Still, some might criticise any attempt to enhance ERGA's influence on the Commission. As its primary consultant, some are concerned that ERGA might provide the Commission with "biased" input that neglects the views of other stakeholders. Other actors, especially the Member

3131 According to Art. 5 (2) of the ERGA Decision, ERGA was entitled to adopt its rules of procedure "upon the proposal of the Commission services on the basis of the standard rules of procedure adopted by the Commission". ERGA nonetheless had more leeway than it would have under the proposed Art. 30a (4). By contrast, BEREC, the European body comprising electronic communications regulators, is empowered to adopt its rules of procedure without involvement of the Commission. See Art. 4 (10) of Regulation (EC) No 1211/2009 of the European Parliament and of the Council of 25 November 2009 establishing the Body of European Regulators for Electronic Communications (BEREC) and the Office, OJ of 18.12.2009, L 337, p. 1.

3132 See Art. 2 ERGA Decision.

3133 See Art. 2 (5b), 6a (3), 9 (2) and (4), 28a (7)-(8) and recital 37 of the 2016 AVMSD proposal.

States' governments and parliaments may feel left out, or even undermined, with respect to crucial matters, such as national culture and social policy. Thus, due account must be taken to ensure that any rule-making at the EU level reflects a democratic process and accountability of those making the rules. Any transfer of rule-making authority to the executive level must be accompanied by democratic safeguards, such as consultation of all stakeholders, transparency in decision-making and accountability to the public. The Commission's Communication on Better regulation for better results indicates awareness of EU institutions of the lack of transparency and accountability and establishes safeguards in this respect.[3134]

A specific expression of the Commission's awareness may be inferred from Art. 30 of the 2016 AVMSD proposal which introduces certain requirements for independent NRAs.[3135] This modification presaged by the Commission's renewed interest in the national regulators' independence and ERGA's related activities.[3136] Further empowering ERGA seems to go hand in hand with stronger requirements for the independence of NRAs which are already in place for regulators in the field of telecommunications and data protection. Art. 30 AVMSD mentions "independent regulatory bodies" as an aside, whereas proposed Art. 30 guarantees the NRAs' independence. It is interesting to note that the 2016 AVMSD proposal does not define what qualifies as an NRA and that it also uses the term "supervisory body" in its Art. 5 (d). Whether there is a difference between the two (the functions of supervision and regulation are often difficult to separate in practice) and whether the proposed Art. 30 also captures those supervisory bodies, remains to be seen.

Art. 30 of the 2016 AVMSD proposal sets out minimum requirements, similar to those prescribed for regulatory bodies in the telecommunica-

---

3134 European Commission, "Communication from the Commission to the European Parliament, the Council, the European Economic and Social Committee and the Committee of the Regions on Better Regulation for Better Results, An EU Agenda, 19.5.2015, COM(2015) 215 Final," 2015.

3135 These requirements flow from the studies on independence of national regulatory authorities prepared for the Commission. See Hans Bredow Institut für Medienforschung et al., "INDIREG Report"; The INDIREG findings are up-dated in a new AVMS RADAR study of 2015, see Cole et al., "AVMS RADAR Study".

3136 ERGA, "Report on the Independence of National Regulators," 2015, http://ec.europa.eu/newsroom/dae/document.cfm?doc_id=12952 (accessed 27.1.2016).

tions or data protection sector.[3137] Thus, Member States must ensure that NRAs are "legally distinct and functionally independent of any other public or private body". Proposed recital 33 specifies that NRAs should be independent from government, public bodies and the industry to ensure the impartial decision-making. Proposed Art. 30 further clarifies that Member States are free to set up converged regulators, that is to say, regulators "having oversight over different sectors".[3138] Importantly, NRAs must exercise their powers "impartially and transparently" promoting the objectives of the AVMSD.[3139] Proposed Art. 30 further mandates that NRAs cannot seek or take instructions, must be held accountable, must be equipped with adequate enforcement powers and must receive adequate financial and human resources.[3140] Finally, proposed Art. 30 provides that a certain level of protection be afforded to heads or board members being dismissed and that appropriate and effective redress mechanisms, including the right of appeal against a decision of an NRA, are maintained.[3141]

The 2016 AVMSD proposal reflects the Commission's obvious recognition that independent NRAs are an absolute necessity for regulatory success and, for that, it is to be applauded. Independent regulators are paramount to the effective implementation and monitoring of the next-generation AVMSD, as transposed in the Member States. Given the stronger role of ERGA and its members, it is important that adequate safeguards are in place to guarantee a minimum level of independence. Despite the fact that the great majority of European NRAs already appear to enjoy an appropriate degree of independence, developments that can negatively affect an NRA's independence cannot be totally excluded[3142] and it is thus vital that a strong statement in support of that independence be

3137 Compare to Art. 3 in conjunction with recitals 11 and 12 of the Framework Directive and Art. 52-54 in conjunction with recitals 118-121 General Data Protection Regulation.

3138 See Art. 30 (1) of the 2016 AVMSD proposal.

3139 See Art. 30 (2) of the 2016 AVMSD proposal.

3140 See Art. 30 (2), (3), (4) and (6) of the 2016 AVMSD proposal. See also recital 33.

3141 See Art. 30 (5) and (7) of the 2016 AVMSD proposal. See also recitals 33 and 34.

3142 On the controversial Hungarian media law adopted in December 2010, see for instance European Parliament resolution of 10 March 2011 on media law in Hungary, 10.3.2011; Katrin Nyman-Metcalf, "Analysis of the Hungarian Media Legislation," ed. Office of the OSCE Representative on Freedom of the Media,

made at the EU level.[3143] To this end, the requirements proposed by the Commission are adequate and respect the constitutional traditions of the Member States which are ultimately competent for the internal organisation and establishment of their respective regulatory authorities. Although the requirements are numerous, they seem to grant Member States sufficient leeway to implement them in national legal orders. Enshrining the principle of independence in the next-generation AVMSD, by way of detailed requirements, appears legitimate. The provision, especially when read in combination with the proposed Art. 30a which enhances ERGA's role, should be supported.

In sum, if adopted as initially proposed, the 2016 AVMSD proposal would clearly strengthen ERGA and increase its fields of operation. It may be consulted in all fields coordinated by the Directive and would be involved in drafting any Union codes of conduct related to certain fields. The Commission has made clear that it believes such codes are an appropriate tool to avoid disparate national implementation and to ensure uniform application of the Directive's standards. To this end, certain of those coordinated fields would be "Europeanised" through the backdoor – that is to say, it is NRAs that will establish the applicable standards rather than the Member States. Thus, the detailed independence requirements imposed on NRAs can be viewed as an added safeguard, intended to legit-

---

February 2011, http://www.osce.org/fom/75990?download=true (accessed 28.8.2016); On the Polish media law adopted in December 2015, see Walter Berka and Hannes Tretter, "The Polish Interim Broadcasting Act 2015 in the Light of Article 10 ECHR, A Legal Analysis," August 2016, http://www.ebu.ch/files/live/sites/ebu/files/News/2016/10/Berka-Tretter_The%20Polish%20Interim%20Broadcasting%20Act%202015%20in%20the%20light%20of%20article%2010%20ECHR.pdf (accessed 3.10.2016). See also Letter from Council of Europe Secretary General Thorbjørn Jagland to Polish President Andrzej Duda, 5.1.2016, available at https://rm.coe.int/CoERMPublicCommonSearchServices/DisplayDCTMContent?documentId=090000168049a74c (accessed 28.8.2016); Commission press release of 1.6.2016, Commission adopts Rule of Law Opinion on the situation in Poland, IP/16/2015, available at http://europa.eu/rapid/press-release_IP-16-2015_en.htm (accessed 28.8.2016).

3143 On the importance of independent NRAs, see Dirk Voorhoof, Eva Lievens and Peggy Valcke, "Independent Media Regulators: Condition Sine qua Non for Freedom of Expression?," in *The Independence of the Media and Its Regulatory Agencies, Shedding New Light on Formal and Actual Independence against the National Context*, ed. Valcke, Schulz and Irion (Bristol, UK and Chicago, USA: Intellect, 2013), pp. 55–82.

imise ERGA's stronger role. It remains to be seen whether that will be sufficient or whether additional requirements relating to executive rule-making will be needed in the future.

## II. Content standards in the revised AVMSD

In this part, content standards enshrined in the Commission's 2016 AVMSD proposal are examined, focusing on the Directive's scope and the protection of minors in services regulated by the next-generation AVMSD.

### 1. The Directive's material scope of application

#### a) Criteria defining an audiovisual media service

The 2016 AVMSD proposal makes only minor changes to the definition of an audiovisual media service set out in Art. 1 (1) (a) AVMSD. More concretely, its revised definition refers to "the principal purpose of the service or a dissociable section thereof is devoted to providing programmes". The modification clarifies the principal purpose criterion in light of the CJEU's ruling in *New Media Online*. In this case, the CJEU examined whether the video section of a website was independent from its online newspaper, the provider's main activity. In this respect, the 2016 AVMSD proposal codifies the Court's test by asking whether a part of a website is "dissociable". In contrast to recital 28 AVMSD which expressly excludes application of the AVMSD to "electronic versions of newspapers and magazines" proposed recital 3 explicitly includes "stand-alone parts of online newspapers" in its scope. Recital 3 furthermore reiterates the CJEU's formulation stating that "a service should be considered to be merely an indissociable complement to the main activity as a result of the links between the audiovisual offer and the main activity" which the Court apparently saw as the only criterion to assess whether a part of a service can be dissociated from the main activity. The notion of "links" is not specified and it may entail access and navigational links as well as content links.

Moreover, it remains unclear that an assessment *only* of the website's links is appropriate to determine whether a sub-section thereof is actually self-standing. The "look and feel" (branding and styling), cataloguing and structure may be useful indictors, too. Yet, enlarging the number of criteria invariably makes the exercise more subjective, unless these, too, are further refined as discussed above. Similarly, neither the Court nor the 2016 AVMSD proposal expand on the concept of a website's "main activity". For online newspapers and magazines, it might be a relatively straight-forward analysis, but it may be more difficult to determine the "main activity" of a multi-media website, especially as new business models emerge. This will further complicate making a distinction between the particular website's *main* activity and its *other* activities. It follows that the principal purpose criterion has seen some specification. Still, it seems to remain vague, especially when there is no readily identifiable sub-section that compiles all videos in a "typical" catalogue. Thus, the new recital 3 does not go beyond the insights in the CJEU's most recent decision.

Furthermore, the 2016 AVMSD proposal deletes the comparability test from the definition of "programme" in proposed Art. 1 (1) (b). Thus, the benchmark for comparison would no longer be the "form and content of television broadcasting". In a similar vein, the new preamble removes any reference to the notion of "television-like," as described in recital 24 AVMSD. Abandoning the TV-centric approach of the current AVMSD seems appropriate to better adapt the next-generation AVMSD to new market realities. Although the Directive's focus on TV can be explained by its historical roots in the original technology, its pre-occupation with broadcasting has already found its limits in an era of media convergence. If the 2016 AVMSD proposal is adopted as proposed, the notion of a programme would be defined solely by two criteria: a "set of moving images (with or without sound)" and "an individual item (within a schedule or catalogue)". The list of examples would include "videos of short duration". Indeed, the clarification that short videos or clips are considered to be programmes pursuant to the revised AVMSD is useful. Interestingly, the preamble to the 2016 AVMSD proposal does not make reference to recitals 21 and 24 AVMSD which include useful elements determinative of the AVMSD's material scope.[3144] What is more, the 2016 AVMSD pro-

3144 Recital 21 AVMSD stresses that the Directive applies to "mass media, that is which are intended for reception by, and which could have a clear impact on, a significant proportion of the general public". Similarly, recital 24 AVMSD makes clear that "the nature and the means of access to the service would lead the user reasonably to expect regulatory protection". Theoretically, the preamble of the next-generation AVMSD should contain all the recitals of its predecessor (the current AVMSD) as it is an amending Directive.

posal does not offer any other modifications to the definitions set out in Art. 1 (1) AVMSD. Most importantly, the 2016 AVMSD proposal retains, unchanged, the definition of editorial responsibility, a concept that has already been challenged because multiple actors are increasingly involved in the editorial process.[3145] The concept of "effective control" is still ambiguous, especially as the functions of selecting and organising content are not necessarily performed by the same party. Oddly, the Commission chose to maintain the rather ambiguous status quo and, instead, introduce a new set of unique rules for VSPs. While it is true that the type of editorial responsibility these providers assume differs from that of media service providers, it appears that current uncertainties will only be reduced, not completely eliminated.[3146]

#### b) Regulating video-sharing platforms

##### (aa) The Commission's proposal with respect to VSPs

The real novelty of the 2016 AVMSD proposal is its new chapter on VSPs. As reflected in its proposed recital 3, the Commission recognises "new types of content" and "new players" that "gain increasing importance" and "are now well-established" in the market. Thus, the 2016 AVMSD proposal defines VSP service, user-generated video (UG video) and VSP providers. It provides that a VSP service exists when the particular service meets several, cumulative criteria: it must be (a) a service within the meaning of Art. 56 TFEU, (b) made available by electronic communications networks that (c) "consists of the storage of a large amount of programmes or UG videos, for which the video-sharing platform provider does not have editorial responsibility" and (d) which are its principal purpose. Although lacking editorial responsibility, a VSP provider, in turn, determines the "organisation of the stored content (…) including by automatic means or algorithms, in particular by hosting, displaying, tagging and sequencing". Like its definition of an audiovisual media service, the 2016 AVMSD proposal adopts a principal purpose test: the "principal pur-

---

3145 For an overview of the different market players penetrating the audiovisual value chain, see Schoefs, "Connected TV and Editorial Responsibility," p. 349; regarding the splitting of control between various parties, see pp. 353-354.

3146 Schoefs, "Connected TV and Editorial Responsibility," p. 358.

pose of the [VSP] service or a dissociable section thereof is devoted to providing programmes and [UG] videos to the general public, in order to inform, entertain or educate".[3147] The 2016 AVMSD proposal's preamble makes clear that social networks ("social media services") are exempt from its scope of application unless they "provide a service that falls under the definition of a VSP".[3148] Similarly, its proposed recital 3 clarifies that content offered on VSPs may, in itself, constitute an audiovisual media service and it attributes responsibility for compliance with the Directive to the media service provider bearing editorial responsibility. Furthermore, its definition of a UG video is similar to that of a programme. It refers to a "set of moving images with or without sound constituting an individual item that is created and/or uploaded to a VSP by one or more users".[3149] Finally, a VSP provider is the "natural or legal person who provides the VSP service".[3150]

With respect to substantive rules, the 2016 AVMSD proposal, regulates certain aspects, such as the protection of minors and the fight against hate speech in an exhaustive manner, taking a full (or maximum) harmonisation approach that establishes a ceiling from which Member States may not derogate. The Commission defends full harmonisation for reasons of consistency and the prevention of "future fragmentation resulting from national intervention".[3151] It nonetheless refers to the possibility of stricter rules on a voluntary basis.[3152] Proposed recital 26 shows that the Commission is well aware of the popularity of VSPs with minors and the legal challenges that arise from the dissemination and exchange of harmful and hateful content on such platforms. Nonetheless, it stresses that "proportionate rules" must be designed, as most of the content on VSPs is not under the editorial responsibility of VSP providers.[3153] Yet, VSP providers "typically determine the organisation of the content (…) including by automatic means or algorithms".[3154] In so far as they are involved in the dissemination of audiovisual content, the Commission considers that VSP

3147 Art. 1 (1) (aa) (i)-(iv) of the 2016 AVMSD proposal.
3148 See recital 3 of the 2016 AVMSD proposal.
3149 See Art. 1 (1) (ba) of the 2016 AVMSD proposal.
3150 See Art. 1 (1) (da) of the 2016 AVMSD proposal.
3151 See recital 30 of the 2016 AVMSD proposal and p. 5 of the Explanatory Memorandum.
3152 See recital 30 of the 2016 AVMSD proposal.
3153 See recitals 26 and 28 of the 2016 AVMSD proposal.
3154 See recital 28 of the 2016 AVMSD proposal.

providers should assume responsibility in a limited field.[3155] The areas harmonised by the 2016 AVMSD proposal exclude commercial communications which are already subject to the Unfair Commercial Practices Directive[3156] and the liability exemption for illegal information set forth in the ECD.[3157] In addition, nothing in the 2016 AVMSD proposal affects the Member States' freedom to adopt stricter rules regarding illegal content.[3158]

More concretely, proposed Art. 28a (1) requires VSPs to "take appropriate measures" to protect minors from harmful content and protect "all citizens from content containing incitement to violence or hatred". The appropriateness of the VSP's measures is to be appraised on the basis of stated criteria, such as the nature of the content, the harm caused, "the characteristics of the category of persons to be protected as well as the rights and legitimate interests at stake including those of VSP providers and the users having created and/or uploaded the content as well as the public interest".[3159] These criteria are not only useful for VSP providers in establishing adequate tools but they also serve to guide the NRAs when overseeing compliance with these rules.[3160]

Proposed Art. 28a (2) specifies the measures that VSP providers can take which include: defining the concepts of harm and incitement in their terms and conditions of use, establishing reporting mechanisms, whereby unsuitable content may be flagged, providing information about those mechanisms, and implementing age verification systems, parental controls or content-rating systems for users. They must also have procedures to handle complaints and redress mechanisms in place for any disputes that arise between users and VSPs.[3161] Importantly, proposed Art. 28a (3) recommends that the rules applicable to VSPs be implemented through co-regulation. The Commission also envisages a prominent role for ERGA which is expected to promote the exchange of best practices and the devel-

---

3155 See recital 28 of the 2016 AVMSD proposal.

3156 Directive 2005/29/EC of the European Parliament and of the Council of 11 May 2005 concerning unfair business-to-consumer commercial practices in the internal market, OJ of 11.6.2005, L 149, p. 22.

3157 See recitals 27 and 29 of the 2016 AVMSD proposal.

3158 See Art. 28a (5) of the 2016 AVMSD proposal.

3159 See Art. 28 (2) of the 2016 AVMSD proposal.

3160 See Art. 28 (4) of the 2016 AVMSD proposal.

3161 See Art. 28 (6) of the 2016 AVMSD proposal.

opment of Union codes of conduct alongside the Commission.[3162] If the Commission requests it, ERGA might even be involved in drafting those codes of conduct which the Commission would then give "appropriate publicity".[3163]

The 2016 AVMSD proposal's new chapter on VSPs also includes a rule on jurisdiction. Proposed Art. 28b (1) clarifies that a Member State has jurisdiction over the VSP when a parent company, subsidiary, or other entity of the group is established in their territory. This also applies to VSPs that are nominally established outside the EU but which nonetheless have a certain physical presence in the EU market by virtue of the location of the VSP's business units or entities. Like the jurisdictional rule established for media service providers, proposed Art. 28b (1) establishes a hierarchy of these criteria if the parent company, subsidiary, or other entity are located in different Member States. The Member State in which the parent company is established is decisive; in the absence thereof, first the location of the subsidiary and then, lastly, the location of the other entity pertaining to the same group is determinative. If there are several subsidiaries or several other entities established in different Member States, it is up to the VSP provider to designate the competent jurisdiction. To facilitate implementation and monitoring of the Directive's rules, proposed Art. 28b (2) requires Member States to maintain up-to-date records of VSP providers established in their territory that indicate the criterion on which their jurisdiction is based.[3164]

(bb) Critical analysis of the 2016 AVMSD proposal regarding VSPs

Extending the next-generation AVMSD's scope to VSPs is a first step toward ensuring that comparable services are regulated in a similar manner. The importance of VSPs to the dissemination of (live)[3165] audiovisual con-

---

3162 See Art. 28 (7) and (8) of the 2016 AVMSD proposal.

3163 See Art. 28 (8) of the 2016 AVMSD proposal.

3164 See also recital 32 of the 2016 AVMSD proposal.

3165 YouTube, for instance, is increasingly engaged in the provision of live video content. Viewings of live videos grew significantly by 80 percent from 2015 to 2016 and its number of livestreams leapt 130 percent. YouTube's ability to monetise content by advertising is enormous and it has increased new advertising by 30 percent in 2016 compared to the previous year. See Murgia, YouTube live video views grow by 80%, 29 August 2016, available at https://www.ft.com/con

tent and the consequential impact they have on certain parts of the population (in particular, younger audiences) cannot be denied.[3166] Thus, the

tent/26de99fc-6b98-11e6-a0b1-d87a9fea034f. See also Indrek Ibrus and Ulrike Rohn, "Sharing Killed the AVMSD Star: The Impossibility of European Audiovisual Media Regulation in the Era of the Sharing Economy," *Internet Policy Review* 5, no. 2 (2016): p. 6; Facebook has also launched a livestreaming tool similar to Snapchat, Periscope and Meerkat. While it was at first only available to "public figures", who Facebook frequently paid to publish live content through verified pages, it is now rolled out and "ordinary" users are animated to share live videos that are uploaded to users' timeline for catch-up. See https://live.fb.com/about/. The amount of live videos posted has soared between January and June 2016. At the beginning of 2016, approximately 10 percent of the top 500 media publishers posted live videos on Facebook, the percentage has climbed to about 50 percent of publishers six months later. It is also interesting to note that video consumption becomes one of the key user activities on Facebook. In the second quarter of 2016, almost 50 percent of Facebook users of 13 European countries watched a video while almost 70 percent clicked the "like button" and 45 percent messaged a friend. See Media Intelligence Service, "Consumption Trends," 2016, pp. 28–31. Facebook has also tested inserting advertising clips within live broadcasts (co-called mid-roll ad). See Sloane, Facebook Is Testing Mid-Roll Video Ads in Facebook Live, 1.8.2016, available at http://adage.com/article/digital/facebook-testing-mid-roll-video-ads-live-sources/305274/. While the sharing of live videos enables users to participate in and enjoy a new immersive experience, new questions arise regarding compliance with content standards. The Facebook livestreams showing police shootings of black civilians in the US are but one example that raises complex questions of standard-setting for UG live broadcasts as well as Facebook's responsibility for such livestreams. See Reuters, Facebook Live streaming of US police shooting of black man leads to ethical and legal questions, 8.7.2016, available at http://www.telegraph.co.uk/technology/2016/07/07/facebook-live-streaming-of-us-police-shooting-of-black-man-leads/ (all websites accessed 31.8.2016).

3166 In the UK, consumption of short online clips ranks highest among 12 to 15 year olds and is much higher for 6-11 and 16-24 year olds compared to adults aged between 25 and 34 in November 2015. British adolescents aged between16-24 years watched twice as much YouTube and twice as much VOD services than all individuals in 2015. In the EU Member States, young people watch on average only half as much television (01:56 hours in 2014) as the total population (03:53 hours in 2014). In addition, the consumption of video on video-sharing platforms is growing. See Media Intelligence Service, "Consumption Trends," 2015, p. 16; see also Thinkbox, New figures put TV viewing in perspective, March 2016, available at https://www.thinkbox.tv/News-and-opinion/Newsroom/10032016-New-figures-put-TV-viewing-in-perspective (accessed 5.9.2016); Zambardino, Sardelli, and Bassini, "AVMSD Refit or Reform?," pp. 17, 19–20; Cabrera Blázquez et al., *On-Demand Services and the Material Scope of the AVMSD*, p. 11.

Commission is justified in assuming that VSPs compete with media service providers for both user attention and advertising revenue. The conclusion it drew from that assumption, namely the need to regulate VSPs under the AVMSD is well-founded. The definition proposed in the 2016 AVMSD proposal acknowledge that VSP providers do not, themselves, bear editorial responsibility for the content disseminated on their platforms, but also recognise that, even if there is no direct involvement in the conception and production of the audiovisual material, VSPs nonetheless exercise an editorial function by organising it. That task includes compiling content under different themes or, indeed, into different channels (e.g. music, sports, entertainment, "most recent", "most frequently watched", etc.) such that, even if that organisation function is automated by the use of algorithms, it can be reasonably argued that the mere design of the VSP's system constitutes an editorial decision. The extension of the AVMSD's scope to VSPs is proof of the Commission's recognition of the active role of platform providers. Thus, as drafted, the 2016 AVMSD proposal "establishes a bridge" between the AVMSD and the ECD.[3167] Proposed Art. 28 (5) acknowledges and supports the existing liability exemptions set out in Arts. 12 and 15 ECD that apply to purely passive content hosts. In that regard, the Commission clearly recognises that there is a spectrum of actors that ranges from media service providers which bear full editorial responsibility, to VSPs which exercise an editorial role that does not amount to full editorial control, to ISPs which act "in a purely neutral and passive manner".[3168] While the first two types of actors on the spectrum would be considered active providers and thus, covered by the next-generation AVMSD, the last would be passive providers and thus, exempt from liability in accordance with the ECD.

As media markets continue to converge, distinctions along the spectrum of actors that have or do not have editorial responsibility will continue to blur.[3169] At some point in the future, the existing ISP safe harbour will have to be revisited to prevent the bridge between the next-generation AVMSD and the ECD from falling apart. This will force any new regulatory scheme to take a coherent approach to both.[3170] Furthermore, it is characteristic of VSPs to store large amounts of programmes, be they pro-

3167 Zambardino, Sardelli, and Bassini, "AVMSD Refit or Reform?," p. 68.
3168 Zambardino, Sardelli, and Bassini, "AVMSD Refit or Reform?," p. 68.
3169 Zambardino, Sardelli, and Bassini, "AVMSD Refit or Reform?," p. 69.
3170 Zambardino, Sardelli, and Bassini, "AVMSD Refit or Reform?," p. 68.

fessional or UG videos. The storage criterion used in the 2016 AVMSD proposal is reminiscent of the ECD and the current legal framework applicable to ISPs which, in this context, primarily refers to providing the technical infrastructure. Yet, the VSPs' business model is data-driven as providers collect and process massive amounts of personal data to provide recommended and personalised content. Importantly, VSPs business model essentially relies on video consumption financed by advertising through which revenues are generated. Thus, VSPs do not earn income from their storage activity, but rather from offering advertising space on their platforms. Platform users, in turn, accept exposure to advertising as a condition of their access to video content, not the user's ability to store content on the platform: Users use platforms because they want to watch videos and not for the storing of such videos. The 2016 AVMSD proposal does not fully reflect that business model. In order to differentiate and capture the nature of the services provided by VSPs and ISPs, the concept of storage should be further refined.

As mentioned above, the definition of VSPs incorporates a "principal purpose" element which mirrors the principal purpose test set out for audiovisual media services with only one slight adaptation. Whether the principal purpose test is well-suited for delineating the next AVMSD's scope of application in relation to VSPs is debatable. This criterion was originally developed to distinguish between different types of media (i.e. television from the printed press). VSPs, however, have several purposes and, thus, pursue multiple objectives. Reducing VSPs to one "primary" purpose falls short of recognising their multi-purpose and multi-media nature. Proposed recital 3's blanket exclusion of social media services (social networks) is similarly deficient. If social networks become significant players in providing audiovisual content, a scenario that is not altogether unrealistic,[3171] they should be regulated accordingly. It would be paradoxical to exclude any platform that plays an important role in the dissemination of audiovisual content from regulation applicable to such content, only on the basis of labels that may have little or no meaning in the coming years. That is not, of course to suggest that all platforms that provide any access to videos should be regulated. Rather, regulation must be measured and targeted as discussed above but it should never simply exempt certain types of platforms *per se.* Developments in online press outlets which

3171 Consider Facebook's Live above.

were expressly excluded from the scope of the AVMSD by its recital 28 AVMSD should prove instructive in this regard. Nevertheless, to effectively regulate audiovisual media services, including VSPs, it is necessary to draw a line between those platforms fulfilling functions similar to those provided by audiovisual media services and other platforms that do not play a role in informing, entertaining, or educating the general public via audiovisual content. Whether the principal purpose test is an adequate benchmark may be viewed sceptically.

Furthermore, given the differences in editorial control, the application of a graduated approach to regulating VSPs is justified. Establishing a unique set of rules for VSPs that differs from the rules applicable to media service providers appears also feasible politically, in contrast to introducing common rules for all providers regulated by the Directive. The Directive's 2005 reform serves as a precedent in this respect as the inclusion of on-demand services in the Directive's scope was only possible because of the reliance on a two-tier regulatory approach. While the Commission's suggestions as to the intensity of the applicable rules may be supported, the kind of rules applicable to VSPs and the way these are formulated is rather disappointing. The Commission proposes applying a limited set of rules to VSPs. The requirements are essentially reduced to protection from unsuitable content. The 2016 AVMSD proposal suggests that "unsuitable content" means content that impairs a minor's development and content that, regardless of the user's age, incites violence or hatred.[3172]

Interestingly the 2016 AVMSD proposal makes no attempt to bring commercial communications featured on platforms under the umbrella of the next-generation AVMSD, as the Commission apparently believed that the UCPD guarantees a sufficient level of protection. The UCPD applies to business- to- consumer relations and covers commercial practices including commercial communications. Its annex 1 provides that the use of "editorial content in the media to promote a product where a trader has paid for the promotion without making that clear in the content or by images or sounds clearly identifiable by the consumer" is a prohibited misleading practice.[3173] The AVMSD uses a similar principle of identification of commercial communications requiring that commercial communications inserted in audiovisual media services should not be surreptitious or

3172 See Art. 28a (1) of the 2016 AVMSD proposal.
3173 See annex 1 No. 11 UCPD.

otherwise use subliminal techniques which broadly corresponds with the concept of misleading commercial practices adopted in the UCPD.[3174] Yet, Art. 9 AVMSD sets out more specific rules that prohibit certain kinds of content from being included in commercial communications, such as content that prejudices human dignity or incites discrimination.[3175] It also prohibits commercial communications for certain types of products or services, such as cigarettes or medications only available by prescription.[3176] Although similar, it is clear that the levels of protections offered by the AVMSD diverge from that offered by the UCPD. Thus, a strong case can be made for extending the rules on commercial communications applicable to media service providers to VSP providers in the next AVMSD, particularly in view of their heavy reliance on commercial communications in their business model.

The 2016 AVMSD proposal's Art. 28a is formulated in a way that leaves VSP providers a great margin of discretion.[3177] It refers to "appropriate" measures, appropriateness being defined by reference to rather vague criteria, such as the nature of the content, user behaviour and stakeholders' rights and interests.[3178] Moreover, proposed Art. 28a's list of concrete measures to be taken does neither seem to be cumulative nor obliga-

---

3174 Compare Art. 9 (1) (a) and (b) AVMSD with Art. 6 and 7 in conjunction with annex 1 No. 11 UCPD.

3175 See Art. 9 (1) (c) AVMSD.

3176 See. Art. 9 (1) (d) and (f) AVMSD. Special rules also apply to the advertising of alcoholic beverages pursuant to Art. 9 (1) (e) AVMSD.

3177 See Art. 28a (2) of the 2016 AVMSD proposal. Horten is generally critical of the EU's attempts to extend regulation to online intermediaries. She heavily criticises the Commission's proposed legal framework concerning the AVMSD, especially the broad nature in which the provision is drafted and the implications for the freedom of expression. See Monica Horten, "Content 'Responsibility': The Looming Cloud of Uncertainty for Internet Intermediaries," ed. Center for Democracy & Technology, September 2016, p. 14, https://cdt.org/files/2016/09/2016-09-02-Content-Responsibility-FN1-w-pgenbs.pdf; see also Monica Horten, "Liability and Responsibility: New Challenges for Internet Intermediaries," October 20, 2016, http://blogs.lse.ac.uk/mediapolicyproject/2016/10/20/liability-and-responsibility-new-challenges-for-internet-intermediaries/ (all websites accessed 20.10.2016).

3178 ERGA also criticises the vagueness of Art. 28a, in particular the lack of clarity in relation to the criteria to assess the appropriateness of the measures taken by VSPs. See ERGA, "ERGA Opinion on AVMSD Proposals, ERGA (2016)03," October 5, 2016, p. 6, http://ec.europa.eu/newsroom/dae/document.cfm?action=display&doc_id=17994 (accessed 10.10.2016).

tory, but merely exemplary. In addition, it states that co-regulation is the most appropriate regulatory strategy.[3179] Using co-regulation for VSP regulation appears, on the one hand, to be a reasonable solution, as it represents a flexible mechanism that can be adapted to market developments and new circumstances, while also reflecting the fact that VSPs and audiovisual media services, even if they are in competition, are not quite on equal footing because audiovisual media services play a more significant role in the dissemination of audiovisual content. On the other hand, co-regulation is contingent on the involvement and good will of the industry being regulated which, in turn, requires further mechanisms to be put in place to guarantee the effective implementation and enforcement of the rules. In light of the suggestions and reflections outlined above, a co-regulator may be over-burdened by the task of first defining VSP services and then monitoring compliance with the applicable rules to them. Any such co-regulatory system would have to be carefully designed and regularly reviewed to ensure effective application of the Directive's rules at the national level.

What is perhaps even more interesting is that the Commission, in proposing to extend the Directive to VSPs, chose to deviate from its usual minimum harmonisation approach which allows Member States to adopt more restrictive rules and instead decided to prescribe maximum harmonisation. Thus, Member States are bound by the rules established by the Directive which represents a ceiling. That choice is not only inconsistent with the Directive's internal structure, but it also raises new challenges. Minimum harmonisation has permitted Member States to pursue political, socio-cultural and/or economic objectives that might go beyond the AVMSD, while still permitting the free circulation of audiovisual media services with the Union's internal market. It takes into account the dual nature of audiovisual media services as both cultural and economic commodities and thus, aligns with the principles of conferral, subsidiarity and proportionality. Despite the Commission's claim to the contrary,[3180] it seems unlikely that maximum harmonisation, as used for VSPs in the 2016 AVMSD proposal, prevents future regulatory fragmentation. Rather, it is far more likely that implementation and enforcement differences will arise, due to a lack of clear and precise criteria set out in the AVMSD.

---

3179 See Art. 28a (3) of the 2016 AVMSD proposal.

3180 See p. 5 of the Explanatory Memorandum to the 2016 AVMSD proposal.

Another controversial aspect of the 2016 AVMSD proposal's the suggested legal framework for VSPs concerns jurisdiction. It offers Member States the ability to regulate foreign VSP providers by virtue of their EU establishment, either in the form of a parent company, a subsidiary or other group entity which some might view as a welcome step toward ensuring that service providers targeting EU audiences play by EU rules. The terms parent company, subsidiary or group entity are not specified in the AVMSD. Due to the absence of a uniform EU company law these notions would have to be determined in line with national law. A weakness of the rule proposed by the Commission may be the possibility for VSP providers to designate the Member State having jurisdiction in case its various business entities are located in different Member States.[3181] There is no built-in safeguard[3182] that prevents VSP providers from designating the Member State with the most favourable environment and the most lenient (or less active) regulatory authority.

In sum, extending the scope of the next-generation AVMSD to VSPs is justified in light of current technology, new developments and changing consumption patterns. Given the Directive's focus on mass media that disseminates audiovisual content, it seems logical to include VSPs which often offer the exact same content under the same umbrella. Yet, the 2016 AVMSD proposal's definition of VSPs is too narrow and does not adequately capture their true nature. The next-generation AVMSD should adopt a more forward-looking definition of (audiovisual) platforms, one that can endure for at least the next five or ten years.[3183] The way the Commission construes the material scope of the 2016 AVMSD proposal

---

3181 See third sub-paragraph of Art. 28b (1) of the 2016 AVMSD proposal.

3182 Circumvention rules are applicable to broadcasters that direct their programmes "wholly or mostly" to another Member State's territory (confer Art. 4 (2)-(5) AVMSD). Yet, no comparable mechanism exists in relation to VOD services.

3183 Interestingly, during the Commission's consultation on the revision of the AVMSD, the European Broadcasting Union (EBU), a non-profit organisation representing the interests of public service media across Europe, proposed to extend the scope of the AVMSD to "significant audiovisual platforms". The EBU suggested defining audiovisual platform operators as operators "who select or aggregate audiovisual content on a platform for consumers (without taking full editorial responsibility for it, in contrast to media service providers) and/or who provide a user interface to guide viewers. Regulation should be limited to significant operators. Significance should be assessed on the basis of criteria including overall market share, consumption patterns of specific user groups (e.g. young audiences), the extent to which users are "locked in" or the reasons why

could make a second fundamental revision necessary shortly after its adoption. In addition, the substantive rules it proposes to apply to VSPs are limited to a single goal: the fight against unsuitable content. The provision is formulated vaguely and the requirements are overly light. Moreover, its maximum harmonisation is atypical for the AVMSD and its jurisdictional rules which are also quite vague and subject to manipulation by VSPs, complicate matters even further. Taken as a whole, the 2016 AVMSD proposal new chapter on VSPs is a first timid step towards a more comprehensive EU regulatory scheme that is to yet to be shaped in the future. It seems half-hearted in that the Commission has already anticipated a compromise between those who have called for an extension of the Directive's scope to new operators and those who prefer a more liberal regulatory approach, one that leaves ample room for VSP providers to refine and modify their business models. The 2016 AVMSD proposal does not create a visionary, forward-looking legal framework that provides room for future convergence and different business models; rather, the Commission seems engrossed in pragmatic rule-making designed to only address existing problems.[3184] It remains to be seen whether, and to what extent, the 2016 AVMSD proposal's chapter concerning VSPs will be substantially modified during the legislative process. The EP, at least, has already expressed its willingness to regulate a broader range of platforms under the AVMSD in order to "align the rights and obligations of broadcasters with those of other market players by means of a horizontal, cross-media legal framework".[3185]

---

users subscribe to a platform. Importantly, the notion of significance should take into account the potential impact of a platform on public opinion forming. See the EBU's Reply, p. 13, available at https://www.ebu.ch/files/live/sites/ebu/files/News/2015/10/AVMS%20consultation%20-%20EBU%20REPLY%2030%20sept%202015.pdf (accessed 28.8.2016).

3184 Lange, "Vers une révision a minima de la Directive SMA," p. 3.

3185 European Parliament, "European Parliament Resolution on Preparing for a Fully Converged Audiovisual World," December 3, 2014, para. 5.

## 2. The Commission's proposal strengthening the protection of minors

### a) The protection of minors in all audiovisual media services

This study also focusses on the protection of minors in audiovisual media services. In that regard, the Commission's most striking change in the 2016 AVMSD proposal is its decision to align the rules applicable to on-demand services to those that apply to broadcasting. By proposing to delete the existing Art. 27 AVMSD concerning broadcasting, the proposed Art. 12, if adopted as originally proposed in the 2016 AVMSD proposal, will apply – without distinction –to all audiovisual media services. Moreover, it will make a distinction between two types of harmful content: (a) content that "may impair the physical, mental or moral development of minors" and (b) "the most harmful content". These categories of content are reminiscent of the distinction made in Art. 27 AVMSD. The 2016 AVMSD proposal also explicitly classifies gratuitous violence and pornography as "most harmful content". Different consequences attach to the two content categories. Content that may impair minors' development can only be made available "in such a way as to ensure that minors will not normally hear or see" it.[3186] More demanding requirements apply to protect minors from "the most harmful content," which is to be subjected to "the strictest measures". As is presently the case, the degree of harm determines the protective measures that providers must put in place to protect minors, and proposed Art. 12 outlines examples of such measures. Impairing content, on the one hand, should not "normally" be consumed by minors and it requires less rigorous measures which might simply require scheduling 'impairing' programmes when they are less likely to be seen by minors or using age-verification or other technical measures. Restricting "the most harmful content", on the other hand, requires application of the "strictest measures" implying encryption and effective parental controls.[3187]

Proposed Art. 12 has a two-fold effect: first, regulation is levelled up in relation to on-demand services and second, regulation is levelled down in relation to broadcasting. New Art. 12 would require on-demand service providers to take action regarding harmful as well as seriously harmful

3186 See Art. 12 of the 2016 AVMSD proposal.
3187 See Art. 12 of the 2016 AVMSD proposal.

content. Presently, they are only required to protect minors from content that might seriously impair minors' development. Moreover, it would also relax the total ban on seriously harmful content broadcast on TV. The 2016 AVMSD proposal would still permit dissemination of 'the most harmful content' but only under the strictest protection measures. Member States that wish to continue to ban extremely violent or pornographic content on TV for reasons of public morality would still be allowed to adopt stricter or more detailed rules[3188] and even implement a total prohibition at the national level. Due to the country of origin principle, such countries could not, however, block the retransmission of incoming broadcasts by broadcasters established in another Member State containing such content (provided that adequate measures are taken to protect minors).[3189] In general, the 2016 AVMSD proposal appears to strike a reasonable balance. The proliferation of more extreme (e.g. violent and sexually explicit) content on the Internet is a reality, making any attempt at a total ban of such content for all audiovisual media services unfeasible. In fact, the 2016 AVMSD proposal does not call into question the existing four broad content categories: content suitable for all audiences, harmful content, seriously harmful content, and illegal content, while leaving Member States ample room to retain or adopt more differentiated national schemes to protect minors, such as those based on specific age groups.

Nonetheless, the 2016 AVMSD proposal lacks clarity and fails to address existing problems in the original text. For example, content that is to be considered "harmful" or "very harmful" is not specified and is, therefore, left entirely up to the Member States' discretion. Its references to "gratuitous violence" and "pornography" as "the most harmful content" do not add much, either. Unfortunately, as proposed, these "categories" remain just as vague as they currently are when applied in the broadcast context.[3190] The call by many stakeholders, above all, NRAs for clarifica-

---

3188 See Art. 4 (1) of the 2016 AVMSD proposal which explicitly refers to Art. 12.

3189 A Member State which adopted stricter rules could invoke the derogation procedure outlined in Art. 3 AVMSD which would, according to the Commission's proposal also apply to on-demand services (see Art. 3 (2)-(5) of the 2016 AVMSD proposal). The Member State receiving excessively violent or pornographic programmes from a provider established in a different Member State would have to demonstrate that the latter "manifestly, seriously and gravely" infringed Art. 12 (for instance by the lack of appropriate tools to protect minors).

3190 See Art. 27 (1) AVMSD.

tion of key terms thus remains unheard.[3191] Perhaps, this may be explained by the Commission's acute awareness of Member States' desires in this particular field. Rather than suggesting more detailed formulations and responding to existing vagueness, the Commission contented itself with the necessary fusion of two provisions (Arts. 12 and 27 AVMSD) and the replacement of one vague notion ("might seriously impair") with another ("the most harmful content").

In addition, the tools media service providers are required to put in place are already those that are primarily used by the industry today. The Commission seems to believe that scheduling is still only appropriate for broadcasting, even though it is technically possible and frequently used in practice to restrict transmission times for on-demand services, too. Age-verification tools and other technical measures are, of course, appropriate means by which to protect minors from harmful content that can be featured in on-demand services. Yet, the 2016 AVMSD proposal does not specify what kinds of access controls (e.g. identification/age verification and authentication) must be effectuated. Interestingly, its proposed Art. 12 stresses the need for proportional measures that take into account "the potential harm of the programme". This reference is interesting and signals the Commission's recognition of sensitive nature of the area that results in the tension that exists within the regulated field, particularly where conflicting interests are at stake. Proposed recital 39 further supports that interpretation, as it states, in a general manner, that the AVMSD respects the fundamental rights of freedom of expression, freedom to conduct a business, the right to judicial review and the rights of the child as enshrined in the CFR. Thus, for "the most harmful content", proposed Art. 12 recommends content encryption in addition to effective parental controls. Unfortunately, what is to be considered an *effective* parental control and, more generally, what level of protection is required for each type of harmful content, remains unclear. While the Commission's intent is to ensure that minors do not "normally" hear or see programmes that might impair their development, it is unclear whether this very test applies to most harmful content, too. Thus, the modifications proposed by the Commission raise a number of questions with respect to both content categorisation and appropriateness and adequacy of the tools to be used to protect children.

3191 ERGA, "ERGA Opinion on AVMSD Proposal," p. 11.

In sum, the 2016 AVMSD proposal's clear intent to reinforce the protection of minors and the manner in which this aim is pursued – by levelling the regulatory playing field for broadcasting and on-demand video services, is to be applauded. Aligning the standards applicable to broadcasting and on-demand services is a necessary and logical step and differentiating between two types of unsuitable content seems to be in line with current practices, establishing proportionate requirements. But, the 2016 AVMSD proposal could be further refined: for example, as written, several key concepts and definitional terms remain as vague as ever. Many of the problems arising from the application and enforcement of the current Art. 12 AVMSD are left unresolved. Moreover, the technical aspects of the 2016 AVMSD proposal should be made more prominent. Member States must be encouraged to cooperate with the Commission and other stakeholders to develop and implement user-friendly technical tools and to promote best practices. In that regard, ERGA's role should be better defined and strengthened.

b) The requirement to provide content information and the rules applicable to VSPs

In tandem with its attempt to streamline the rules for linear and non-linear audiovisual services, the 2016 AVMSD proposal reflects the Commission's intent to introduce a general duty for media service providers to supply "sufficient information to viewers about content which may impair" minors' development. Its proposed Art. 6a refers to a "system of content descriptors indicating the nature of the content". "Content descriptors" seem to be the Commission's new terminology for content classification and labelling. Proposed recital 9 also clarifies that content descriptors can be "delivered through written, graphical or acoustic means". Interestingly, recital 60 AVMSD which refers to labelling has been removed from the 2016 AVMSD proposal's preamble and proposed Art. 12 no longer contains any reference to age ratings, while Art. 27 (3) AVMSD requires harmful content to be "preceded by an acoustic warning" or be "identified by the presence of a visual symbol throughout [its] duration".

Further, the 2016 AVMSD proposal detaches the service provider's obligation to provide content information from the provision regulating the protection of minors in audiovisual media services and, instead, places it after the rule prohibiting incitement to hatred. This change is odd, as the obligation to provide content descriptors is solely applicable to content considered harmful to minors (and not to any other programmes). Proposed recital 9, however, explains that the content information requirement aims to empower viewers, in particular parents and minors, to make "informed decisions about the content to be watched". Content information provided through content descriptors, in advance of viewing, is an important instrument to enable parents and guardians, as well as minors, to categorise programmes and decide whether or not they are suitable to a particular child's state of development. Content descriptors, thus, enhance transparency and knowledge about content. The question is whether they should not also be used for content the 2016 AVMSD proposal already labels "the most harmful content". It could be argued that the content descriptors themselves could already be classified as most harmful content and would have to abide by the strictest protection measures. Yet, it seems that content descriptors which are themselves harmless could be designed in a useful way. As discussed above, pictograms or traffic light systems could accompany more detailed content information.

In a more horizontal manner, the 2016 AVMSD proposal strengthens the protection of minors by imposing obligations on VSPs. Proposed recital 26 acknowledges the "new challenges" connected with VSPs and underscores that "users – particularly minors – increasingly consume audiovisual content" on such platforms. Thus, the 2016 AVMSD proposal requires VSP providers to take appropriate measures to "protect minors from content which may impair their physical, mental or moral development" pursuant to its proposed Art. 28a (1). Unfortunately, the nature of the content targeted by this rule is "harmful content" rather than "seriously harmful" or "the most harmful content" which are also regulated in audiovisual media services.

Proposed Art. 28a (2) enumerates appropriate measures, such as incorporating the definition of harmful content into the VSPs standard terms and conditions, adopting reporting mechanisms (including the possibility for users to flag inappropriate content), and implementing age verification or parental controls. While the types of measures are certainly useful, the requirements set forth in Art. 28a are, as noted above, quite light and reflect practices that are already in general use.[3192] Because the list of measures does not seem to be either cumulative or exhaustive, proposed Art. 28a facilitates, if not encourages, cherry-picking the least burdensome measures. The requirements are even further watered down by the provision's frequent reference to the appropriateness of any particular measures, such that their ultimate effectiveness can be questioned. That effectiveness will depend, to a large extent, on the good will of the VSPs being regulated and the willingness of the NRAs to adequately assess the appropriateness of the measures a VSP implements and to then enforce meaningful rules.[3193] In order to effectively protect minors on VSPs, Art. 28a will have to be revisited during the co-decision procedure. To summarise, the primary rule regulating protection of minors in audiovisual media services is supplemented by an obligation imposed on all media service providers to provide advance or simultaneous content information and by a limited set of lenient rules applicable to VSPs. To provide an effective level of protection by VSPs, the lenient set of rules must be enhanced.

### III. Proposed changes concerning other fields coordinated by the AVMSD

The Commission's 2016 AVMSD proposal maintains a number of existing provisions, including the rules concerning exclusive rights and shorts

---

3192 The rules proposed by the Commission appear less concrete than those set out in the Code of Conduct on countering illegal hate speech online, brokered between the Commission and leading IT companies like Facebook, Microsoft, Twitter and YouTube at the end of May 2016. Accordingly, signatories of the code of conduct commit themselves to putting in place "clear and effective processes to review notifications regarding illegal hate speech on their services so they can remove or disable access to such content". Notifications are to be promptly reviewed and illegal hate speech is to be removed within 24 hours. The code of conduct also requires its signatories to take measures to educate and raise awareness among users as well as staff.

3193 In its opinion on the 2016 AVMSD Proposal, ERGA stresses that the regulation of VSPs would entail new practical tasks for regulators. It highlighted that the proposed provisions were unclear in several respects, for example, it was not clear how NRAs should assess the appropriateness of measures taken by VSPs (Art. 28a [2]). It also pointed out that NRAs needed to be equipped with information-gathering powers to be able to establish jurisdiction over VSP providers not located in the EU. See ERGA, "ERGA Opinion on AVMSD Proposal," para. 3, pp. 6–7.

news reports in broadcasting, the rules promoting production and distribution of European programmes broadcast on TV, the majority of rules on TV advertising, and the right of reply in TV broadcasts. Thus, it retains the current distinction between linear and non-linear audiovisual media services in most of the fields it coordinates, but also brings an important third kind of service and service provider, VSPs, under its umbrella. As discussed above, the only field for which standards are aligned across audiovisual media services is the protection of minors. The myriad services proposed to be covered by the 2016 AVMSD proposal and the various types of regulation it suggests result in a complex architecture which lacks overall clarity and transparency. It will be seen whether the chapters, for which the Commission advocates the status quo, will be opened up during the legislation-making process but an unwritten rule among EU institutions suggests the contrary.

In addition to the major changes discussed above, the 2016 AVMSD proposal includes some other amendments, the most crucial of which are presented below. These help provide context for the prior, more-detailed discussions that focussed on the main themes of this study. These proposed changes relate to the Directive's geographical scope and jurisdictional rules, its rules on commercial communications and its promotion of European works.

### 1. Geographical scope and the rules on jurisdiction

The 2016 AVMSD proposal's changes to the Directive's geographical scope of application are not as far reaching as those proposed in relation to its material scope. The proposed criteria for determining a provider's place of establishment are simplified. In case a media service provider has its head office in one Member State but takes its editorial decisions in another Member State, the provider is deemed to be established where the "majority of [its] workforce" operates.[3194] This seems to suggest a head count of employees involved in the pursuit of the audiovisual media service activity. Thus, it replaces the notion of "significant part" with a more concrete notion and shortens the current complex hierarchy of options outlined in Art. 2 (3) (b) AVMSD. In the unlikely case in which an identical number

3194 See Art. 2 (3) (b) of the 2016 AVMSD proposal.

of staff is employed in the Member State in which the head office is located and the Member State in which editorial decisions are taken, the provider's ultimate place of establishment is to be determined by reference to the Union law concept of establishment.[3195] Interestingly, the Commission chose to ignore ERGA's call for clarification regarding the concept of the place where a provider's "editorial decisions are taken".[3196] This criterion seems to pose many problems in practice, and is particularly susceptible to manipulation in order to circumvent national rules (e.g. when a media service provider claims that its editorial decisions are taken in the Member State where its head office is located rather than in another Member State in order to remain under the jurisdiction of the former).[3197]

The 2016 AVMSD proposal also proposes introducing a requirement for Member States to keep and communicate to the Commission an up-to-date register of media service providers under their jurisdiction, indicating the criteria on which their jurisdiction is based.[3198] This requirement would certainly facilitate the implementation of the Directive in practice and enhance transparency with respect to the providers' place of establishment. In addition, proposed Art. 2 would allow the Commission to seek ERGA's opinion on jurisdictional disputes arising out of Arts. 3 and 4 AVMSD.[3199]

Furthermore, the 2016 AVMSD proposal aligns the current derogation mechanism for both broadcasting and on-demand services, as outlined in Art. 3 AVMSD which allows Member States to derogate from the principle of free circulation of audiovisual media services if a media service provider has violated either the rule on the prohibition of incitement to hatred or the protection of minors (proposed Arts. 6 and 12).[3200] Other grounds for derogation are prejudices or serious risks to public security or

3195 See Art. 2 (3) (b) and (5) of the 2016 AVMSD proposal.

3196 ERGA, "Scoping Paper on Territorial Jurisdiction in a Convergent Audiovisual World," April 14, 2015, paras. 3.1.3, 3.2.2, 3.3.1, pp. 46, 50, 51–53, http://ec.europa.eu/information_society/newsroom/cf/dae/document.cfm?action=display&doc_id=9387 (accessed 27.4.2015).

3197 ERGA, "Scoping Paper on Territorial Jurisdiction," para. 2.1.1, p. 32.

3198 See Art. 2 (5a) of the 2016 AVMSD proposal.

3199 See Art. 2 (5b) of the 2016 AVMSD proposal.

3200 See Art. 3 (2) (a) of the 2016 AVMSD proposal.

public health.[3201] Ultimately, the list of possible justifications for a derogation is the result of combining the distinct rules applicable to linear and non-linear services currently provided in the AVMSD. The 2016 AVMSD proposal revises the existing notification procedure which appears to make it longer. It is interesting to note that it also expressly obliges Member States to respect the media service providers' rights of defence[3202] and provides for consultation of ERGA in advance of any Commission finding on the compatibility of national measures.[3203] It would still be possible for Member States to accelerate the notification procedure in urgent cases, provided that the Member State explains its reasoning.[3204] While the 2016 AVMSD proposal levels out the derogation mechanism for both linear and non-linear services, its provision concerning circumvention, set out in proposed Art. 4 AVMSD would continue to apply exclusively to broadcasters.[3205] The question is, however, why circumvention rules were not designed for on-demand services. Perhaps the Commission shied away from that task because a simple transposition of the current circumvention rule would not do justice to the nature of on-demand services and would have required a more fundamental change to the provision. Like the derogation

3201 See Art. 3 (2) (b) and (c) of the 2016 AVMSD proposal. With respect to on-demand services, the grounds for derogation are more limited to those currently set out in Art. 3 (4) AVMSD which refers to "public policy, in particular, the prevention, investigation, detection and prosecution of criminal offences, including the protection of minors and the fight against any incitement to hatred (…) and violations of human dignity concerning individual persons" and "the protection of consumers including investors".

3202 See Art. 3 (3) of the 2016 AVMSD proposal.

3203 See Art. 3 (4) of the 2016 AVMSD proposal.

3204 See Art. 3 (6) and (7) of the 2016 AVMSD proposal.

3205 Wagner points out that no "explicit circumvention rules exist for on-demand services". Yet, Art. 3 (4) – (6) AVMSD, which are broadly worded and reflect the provisions of the E-Commerce Directive, are applicable to VOD providers and allow Member States to derogate from the country of origin principle. Although not specifically stipulated, Wagner argues that media pluralism or cultural and linguistic diversity constitute legitimate "policy objectives" within the meaning of Art. 3 (4) (a) (i). In case a VOD provider circumvents stricter national rules aimed at promoting these objectives, Member States could invoke this provision. Michael Wagner, "Revisiting the Country-of-Origin Principle in the AVMS Directive," *Journal of Media Law* 6, no. 2 (2014): p. 289. It is to be highlighted that the grounds for derogating from the country of origin principle would be limited in relation to VOD providers and the "public policy" defense would no longer be available. See Art. 3 (2) (a) – (c) COM proposal.

mechanism, any such circumvention procedure would have to be more demanding for the Member States which would have to "substantiate the grounds" on which the assessment of any "alleged circumvention" is based and duly respect the rights of the defence.[3206] Although the changes to the derogation and circumvention procedures seem appropriate (particularly the reference to providers' rights), the ultimate impact of the proposed amendments can be disputed. The existing mechanisms have already been judged to be too complex and ineffective which may explain the limited number of cases.[3207]

It is significant that the modifications mentioned above are modest and aim to simplify and, at least to a certain extent, align the rules for both linear and non-linear services. The 2016 AVMSD proposal reflects the Commission's decision to avoid the most obvious, but most difficult question (even though it was included in its public consultation): Should non-EU providers targeting EU audiences come under the scope of the AVMSD?[3208] Perhaps that decision is not surprising as ERGA has also refrained from making any concrete proposals regarding the jurisdiction criteria for non-EU providers.[3209] Apart from making some recommendations on ways to address problems identified by NRAs, ERGA advocated non-legislative solutions such as enhanced cooperation, including the exchange of best practices and the creation of a common information system.[3210]

A targeting criterion, however, has some merit, although it would require further clarification. Wagner, for example, suggests making a distinction between the "targeting or differentiation of services for particular national markets/audiences as opposed to the mere accessibility of services for such audiences".[3211] Several factors, such as "the language of the

3206 See Art. 4 (4) of the 2016 AVMSD proposal.

3207 ERGA, "Scoping Paper on Territorial Jurisdiction," para. 2.4.1, pp. 40–41.

3208 Wagner suggests another, more far-reaching alternative to the targeting criterion. Inspired by the approach in the field of data protection (confer Art. 3 (2) GDPR), he suggests considering the "place where the consumer to whom the services are provided is located" as the decisive criterion determining jurisdiction. Wagner, "Revisiting the Country-of-Origin Principle in the AVMS Directive," p. 296.

3209 ERGA, "Scoping Paper on Territorial Jurisdiction," para. 3.3.1, pp. 53–55.

3210 ERGA, "Scoping Paper on Territorial Jurisdiction," para. 3.1, pp. 43–47.

3211 Wagner, "Revisiting the Country-of-Origin Principle in the AVMS Directive," p. 299.

service, the selection of content of particular relevance for a particular country or the presence of commercial communications linked to a particular country" could serve as indicators for a targeting test.[3212] Similar indicators have already been used to assess circumvention. The 2016 AVMSD proposal also incorporates them in connection with the imposition of levies on VOD providers targeting other Member States.[3213]

In its proposal, the Commission, however, clings to the "place of establishment" as its primary criterion for determining jurisdiction. In a globalised online market, in which services can be provided from a distance and the physical place from which content is provided to users becomes more and more irrelevant, it is questionable whether a provider's place of establishment can be a durable or future-proof jurisdictional criterion. In addition to that shortcoming, the 2016 AVSMD Proposal's jurisdictional rules for VSPs contain two other questionable novelties.

Firstly, jurisdiction would hinge on the fact that either a parent company or a subsidiary or another entity pertaining to the providers' group is established in a Member State.[3214] This would include VSP providers established outside the EU that also have a presence in one or more Member States. As mentioned above, in the absence of a harmonised European company law, the Member States would enjoy broad discretion in interpreting the concepts of parent company, subsidiarity and entity which could lead to substantial differences in implementation and enforcement. Secondly, the Commission's proposal allows VSP providers to designate the competent Member State if their business entities are located in more than one Member State.[3215] In theory at least, the risk that VSP providers, particularly non-EU providers, will structure their businesses in such a way as to take advantage of the most lenient forum is palpable. Even if the Commission intends to maximally harmonise the substantive rules applicable to VSPs, it is doubtful even that it would prevent national differences in enforcement and, thus, VSP providers would still have a reason to forum shop. And, if the maximum harmonisation approach is abandoned in favour of minimum harmonisation, that risk of forum shopping would grow exponentially.

3212 Wagner, "Revisiting the Country-of-Origin Principle in the AVMS Directive," p. 299.

3213 See recital 42 AVMSD and recital 23 of the 2016 AVMSD proposal.

3214 See Art. 28b (1) of the 2016 AVMSD proposal.

3215 See Art. 28 (1) third sub-paragraph of the 2016 AVMSD proposal.

In sum, the 2016 AVSMD Proposal's adjustments to the jurisdictional rules would be modest and, at least in relation to audiovisual media services, would not extend the geographical scope of the AVMSD. With respect to VSPs brought under the material scope, jurisdiction would be determined by reference to the VSP's place of establishment: even if reliance on that criterion is coherent within the AVMSD, its suitability as the only relevant criterion is disputable. Finally, the practical effect of allowing VSP providers to designate their "home country" would have to be closely monitored to prevent forum shopping.

## 2. Relaxation of the rules on commercial communications

The 2016 AVSMD Proposal does not alter the qualitative rules concerning commercial communications outlined in Art. 9 (1) AVMSD. Nonetheless, it expands the second paragraph of Art. 9 AVMSD to cover not only inappropriate commercial communications relating to foods and beverages high in salt, sugars or fat but also those relating to alcoholic beverages. It thereby gives new impetus to the development of self- or co-regulatory codes, including Union-wide codes.[3216] In addition, it modifies, but only slightly, the existing provision concerning sponsorship, allowing for promotional references of the sponsor's products or services, while not directly encouraging their purchase.[3217] Above all, the 2016 AVSMD Proposal substantially modifies the existing rule regulating product placement (PP). Its changes would simplify the existing structure set out in Art. 11 AVMSD which would enhance legal certainty, while simultaneously offering more flexibility for the use of this form of commercial communications.[3218] Thus, PP would no longer be generally prohibited, rather, it would be admissible in all audiovisual media services with certain exceptions. These exceptions are clearly outlined in proposed Art. 11 (2) and include "news and current affair programmes, consumer affairs programmes, religious programmes and programmes with a significant children's audience".[3219]

3216 See also recitals 10 and 11 of the 2016 AVMSD proposal.

3217 See Art. 10 (1) (b) and recital 14 of the 2016 AVMSD proposal.

3218 See recital 15 of the 2016 AVMSD proposal and p. 12 of the Explanatory Memorandum.

3219 See also recital 16 of the 2016 AVMSD proposal. .

The 2016 AVSMD Proposal's concept of "programmes with a significant children's audience" which replaces that of "children's programmes" seems broader, covering, for instance, content aimed at families. While the broader concept would expand the protection of minors, the wording is, regrettably, less clear-cut than its predecessor. The term "significant" is ambiguous and thus, subject to interpretation. However, it appears to require that a particular programme must be watched by a certain proportion of children.[3220] The proposed formulation assumes that media service providers, as well as content producers, can know the specificities and composition of the actual (as opposed to target) audience in advance. Moreover, it appears to assume that NRAs, when trying to monitor compliance with this rule, will be able to obtain *ex post* audience measurements that reliably measure the proportion of the audience made up by children. Despite the Commission's obvious good intentions, this particular modification seems to raise a considerable number of difficult questions.

Otherwise, the 2016 AVSMD Proposal generally leaves most of the requirements for programmes containing PP intact. These relate to viewers being informed about the existence of PP and ensuring that service providers' editorial independence is not affected by PP.[3221] Nevertheless, it is interesting to note that it rejects the notion of undue prominence: its proposed recital 17 admits that the undue prominence criterion was difficult to apply in practice and has hampered the use of PP "which, by definition, involves some level of prominent exposure to be able to generate value".[3222] Although that is certainly true, the deletion of the undue prominence criterion altogether could well lead to a story being expressly built around the PP which could negatively affect the service provider's editorial independence. Still, the 2016 AVSMD Proposal's amendments to the existing commercial communications chapter are generally reasonable and, especially in relation to PP, bring about a necessary simplification of the rules, despite the fact that the modifications fail to clarify existing uncertainties and, in at least one case, evoke new ones. Whether the changes will have the expected effect on the take-up of these forms of commercial communications will have to be seen.

3220 Zambardino, Sardelli and Bassini, "AVMSD Refit or Reform?," p. 64.
3221 See also recital 17 of the 2016 AVMSD proposal.
3222 See recital 17 of the 2016 AVMSD proposal.

With respect to advertising aired on TV, the 2016 AVSMD Proposal makes a moderate change to the existing insertion rules which would authorise the insertion of advertising and/or teleshopping every 20 minutes (rather than the existing 30 minutes).[3223] Proposed recital 18 justifies the continued need for insertion regulation by the need to protect the integrity of cinematographic works and feature films that constitute the "specific character of the European television landscape". Importantly, the 2016 AVSMD Proposal shifts away from the current hourly limit to a daily limit to give broadcasters more flexibility to insert advertising "in order to maximise advertisers' demand and viewers' flow".[3224] Accordingly, the proportion of advertising could not exceed 20% between 7 a.m. and 11 p.m.[3225] In addition, the 2016 AVSMD Proposal slightly expands the exceptions for announcements that are not considered as using advertising time. Thus, the calculation of the proportion of advertising excludes announcements made in connection with programmes "from other entities belonging to the same media group".[3226] For example, an announcement by a broadcaster in relation to a programme broadcast on another of its channels would not count as advertising. These changes appear to be an attempt to mitigate the effects of the CJEU's ruling in *Sanoma Finland,* in which the Court strictly construed the advertising rules.[3227] Further, the Commission considers that the current graduated approach used in this

3223 See Art. 20 (2) and recital 18 of the 2016 AVMSD proposal.

3224 See Art. 23 (1) and recital 19 of the 2016 AVMSD proposal. See also p. 12 of the Explanatory Memorandum.

3225 On the liberalisation of the advertising rules, see Rachel Craufurd Smith, "Liberalisation of Advertising & Product Placement Rules in the AVMSD: A Step Too Far?," *LSE Blog*, October 6, 2016, http://blogs.lse.ac.uk/mediapolicyproject/2016/10/06/liberalisation-of-advertising-product-placement-rules-in-the-avmsd-a-step-too-far/ (accessed 10.10.2016). Craufurd Smith strongly criticises the relaxation of advertising standards because it would significantly rebalance "commercial and consumer interests in the AVMSD" to the detriment of the consumer.

3226 See Art. 23 (2) and recital 20 of the 2016 AVMSD proposal.

3227 Case C-314/14 *Sanoma Media Finland Oy- Nelonen Media v Viestintävirasto*, Judgment of 17.2.2016, EU:C:2016:89. The CJEU interpreted Arts. 19 and 23 AVMSD. It held that it was sufficient to separate editorial from commercial content by means of a split screen and broadcasters did not have to cumulatively provide for optical, acoustic and spatial separation (paras. 37, 40). In addition, the Court defined as advertising sponsorship signs which are not broadcast in connection with the sponsored programmes (paras. 47, 50) as well as black seconds which are used to separate individual advertising spots or advertising

field should be retained and that different rules should be maintained for on-demand services and broadcasting. While continuing such distinctions might work for the time being, they will be more difficult to justify as services continue to converge and the simultaneous presentation of different kinds of services on the same screen becomes more prevalent.[3228]

By proposing a daily advertising limit the Commission is arguably implying that strict regulatory standards are no longer necessary or appropriate. Yet, further advertising deregulation may have serious repercussions on the financing of audiovisual productions.[3229] A more detailed examination of its effects would have to be done before making any recommendation on the continued relevance of the existing graduated approach. Nevertheless, what the 2016 AVSMD Proposal's modification do is underscore the need to give media service providers, especially broadcasters, more flexibility in advertising which will likely be, in the end, beneficial to content production.

### 3. Introduction of a quota promoting European works in VOD services

The quota for European works introduced for on-demand service providers in the 2016 AVSMD Proposal was not well received by European and non-European stakeholders alike.[3230] If adopted as written, it would set more concrete and ambitious targets for VOD providers. Past

breaks (paras. 58, 61). As a result, these announcements would have to be included in the calculation of the total amount of advertising.

3228 Zambardino, Sardelli and Bassini, "AVMSD Refit or Reform?," p. 64.

3229 Online advertising is less expensive than advertising on TV. See Cabrera Blázquez et al., *On-Demand Services and the Material Scope of the AVMSD*, pp. 8–9; for a concise overview of the European online advertising market see Christian Grece, "The European Online Advertising Market, A Short Introduction to the European Online Display Advertising Ecosystem," in *New Forms of Commercial Communications in a Converged Audiovisual Sector*, ed. Susanne Nikoltchev, IRIS Special (Strasbourg: European Audiovisual Observatory, 2014), pp. 29–38.

3230 See for instance http://www.bloomberg.com/news/articles/2016-05-25/netflix-amazon-face-minimum-eu-quota-for-european-films-shows; http://www.ft.com/cms/s/0/4798d428-1d19-11e6-b286-cddde55ca122.html#axzz4IpdZhRfG; https://www.euractiv.com/section/digital/news/meps-leading-controversial-bill-question-commissions-netflix-quota/; http://www.bbc.com/news/technology-36378078 (all websites accessed 25.9.2016).

assessments of national implementation of the existing requirements revealed a general lack of effectiveness, especially with respect to monitoring mechanisms.[3231] In an effort to ameliorate those findings, the 2016 AVSMD Proposal requires on-demand providers to reserve “at least 20% share of European works in their catalogue” to ensure their prominence.[3232] Imposing a minimum share requirement is nothing new – broadcasters have been subject to an even higher quota since the adoption of the TWFD.[3233] In addition, financial contributions to the production of European works in the form of either direct investments therein or contributions to national funds may become mandatory for on-demand service providers[3234] Financial obligations may include direct contributions to the production and rights acquisition of European works.[3235] Interestingly, the 2016 AVMSD proposal allows Member States to require contributions by service providers that, although established in other Member States, target audiences in their territories.[3236] Such contributions, however, must only be based on the revenues the service provider earns in the targeted Member State. It also requires the service provider’s home country to take the contributions paid in the targeted Member State into account to determine the relevant contribution.

---

3231 European Commission, “Report from the Commission to the European Parliament, the Council, the European Economic and Social Committee and the Committee of the Regions, First Report on the Application of Articles 13, 16 and 17 of Directive 2010/13/EU for the Period 2009-2010 Promotion of European Works in EU Scheduled and On-Demand Audiovisual Media Services,” September 24, 2012, para. 1.1.3; Lange, “Vers une révision a minima de la Directive SMA,” pp. 12–31.

3232 See Art. 13 (1) of the 2016 AVMSD proposal.

3233 See Arts. 16 and 17 AVMSD.

3234 See Art. 13 (2) of the 2016 AVMSD proposal.

3235 See recital 22 of the 2016 AVMSD proposal.

3236 Schulz and Grothe make clear that this clause represents a derogation from the country of origin principle. More generally, they call for a "more systematic approach" to evaluating the country of origin principle in the field of digital services. They propose categorisation of cases on the basis of (1) the protection of individual consumers, a category that should be broadly construed and (2) cultural exceptions which should be interpreted strictly. Wolfgang Schulz and Thorsten Grothe, “Caution, Loose Cornerstone: The Country of Origin Principle under Pressure,” *LSE Blog*, July 4, 2016, http://blogs.lse.ac.uk/mediapolicyproject/2016/07/04/caution-loose-cornerstone-the-country-of-origin-principle-under-pressure/ (accessed 30.8.2016).

The 2016 AVMSD proposal's concept of "targeting" which is typically used in the context of jurisdiction is new. Proposed recital 22 suggests that Member States can take account of several indicators when deciding if an on-demand service provider that is established in another Member State targets its audience. These include "advertisement or other promotions specifically aiming at customers in its territory, the main language of the service or the existence of content or commercial communications aiming specifically at the audience in the Member State of reception".[3237] The indicators are reminiscent of those set out in recital 42 AVMSD regarding the circumvention rules applicable to broadcasters.[3238] According to Art. 4 (2) (b) AVMSD, the test is whether "a broadcaster under the jurisdiction of another Member State provides a television broadcast which is *wholly or mostly directed towards its territory*". The proposed concept of "targeting" and the existing concept of "wholly or mostly directed" do not seem to be completely congruent though. The new concept seems far broader than the latter, as service providers can now easily target several different markets and audiences at the same time, whereas the older, "wholly or mostly directed" formula presumes that the broadcasts are almost entirely aimed at one particular Member State, one that is not its country of establishment. The imposition of levies in some Member States may counter a uniform approach across the EU which could, in turn, further aggravate existing differences and enhance the risk of forum shopping.[3239]

It is also important to highlight that proposed Art. 13 (5) allows Member States to exempt "providers with a low turnover or low audience or if they are small and micro enterprises" from regulation. They may also waive the requirements where "they would be impracticable or unjustified by reason of the nature or theme of the on-demand audiovisual media services". Proposed Art. 13 (5) mitigates the effect of the 2016 AVMSD proposal's rejection of the current "where practicable and by appropriate means" formula contained in Art. 13 (1) AVMSD. Proposed Art. 13 (1) is much stronger and takes away some degree of the flexibility Member States currently have. The notions of small and micro enterprises are to be

3237 See recital 22 of the 2016 AVMSD proposal.

3238 Interestingly, recital 42 AVMSD is not transferred to the Commission's proposal.

3239 Zambardino, Sardelli and Bassini, "AVMSD Refit or Reform?," p. 72.

interpreted in line with the Commission's recommendation of 2003.[3240] The 2016 AVMSD proposal's exemptions are both reasonable and justified. They would guarantee a higher degree of flexibility for small-scale providers and providers specialising in a particular type of content which might otherwise be over-burdened by or, perhaps, unable to comply with the requirements. Any potential concerns about exempting micro or small enterprises are ameliorated by the fact that if their businesses expand and grow, thereby reaching larger audiences, they will eventually be captured by the rules. The interpretation of the exemption of providers on the basis of the nature or theme of the service lacks clarity and appears far more difficult to apply. Some argue that it creates "a large room for Member States to carve out a safe harbor",[3241] but that risk could be avoided by identifying suitable criteria for such "nature or theme" exemptions in a new recital.

The Commission's rationale for amending Art. 13 in the 2016 AVMSD proposal is to achieve "a more level playing field" and require on-demand providers to invest more heavily in European content.[3242] While promoting the production and distribution of European works is certainly a valid and relevant goal, it is not clear that establishing a fixed quota is the right tool to achieve it. A similar quota system has been applied to broadcasters for a long time but, to date, it has failed to bring strong European players to the force. A recent EAO study shows national productions make up over half of the total number of European works.[3243] For decades, the same questions have been controversially debated by proponents and op-

---

3240 See Commission recommendation of 6 May 2003 concerning the definition of micro, small and medium-sized enterprises, OJ of 20.5.2003, L 124, p. 36. According to Art. 2 of the recommendation's annex, the categories of micro, small and medium-sized enterprises are defined by reference to staff headcount and financial ceilings. Thus, a small enterprise has fewer than 50 employees and an annual turnover and/or balance sheet total not exceeding EUR 10 million and a micro enterprise employs fewer than 10 persons and has an annual turnover and/or balance sheet total not exceeding EUR 2 million.

3241 Zambardino, Sardelli and Bassini, "AVMSD Refit or Reform?," p. 72.

3242 See p. 12 Explanatory Memorandum of the 2016 AVMSD proposal.

3243 *On-Demand Audiovisual Markets in the European Union, Developments 2014 and 2015* (Strasbourg: European Audiovisual Observatory, 2015), pp. 213–16.

ponents of quota systems and have traditionally divided Member States.[3244]

Moreover, the minimum share of 20 percent appears to lack ambition as it represents the status quo for most VOD providers.[3245] More importantly, the 2016 AVMSD provides no guidance as to how to calculate that minimum 20 percent figure. It is questionable whether the proportion should be calculated on the basis of the total number of titles included in the VOD provider's catalogue or on the basis of the total transmission time of these items. Calculation on the basis of titles seems easier, but there is no guidance as to whether each episode of a series, for example, should be counted as separate title or the series, including all its episodes, should count as a single item. The former interpretation would probably be more equitable.[3246]

The concept of "prominence" is equally vague. Although it safeguards against European works being buried invisibly in the providers' catalogues, it is not clear what it entails and how European works must be showcased to ensure sufficient prominence (e.g. a separate European category, a special graphic depiction next to European titles, the first selections available on a catalogue search). On the other hand, the Member States' ability to require on-demand service providers to invest in European content, by contributions to national film funds, appears to be a straight-forward suggestion that is relatively easy to implement. Furthermore, monitoring of the implemented rule is marginally strengthened in that Member States are required to report thereon every two years.[3247] Those national reports will, of course, feed the obligatory Commission as-

---

3244 Lange, "Vers une révision a minima de la Directive SMA," pp. 12–13; Alexander Scheuer, "Are the Guards Stationed at the Right Portals? The Suitability of Regulations on the Promotion of European Works in Non-Linear Audiovisual Media Services," in *Video on Demand and the Promotion of European Works*, ed. Susanne Nikoltchev, IRIS Special (Strasbourg: European Audiovisual Observatory, 2013), pp. 47–51; Tarlach McGonagle, "The Quota Quandary: An Assessment of Articles 4-6 of the Television without Frontiers Directive," in *The European Union and the Culture Industries, Regulation and the Public Interest*, ed. David Ward (United Kingdom: Ashgate Publishing, 2008), pp. 187–212; Irini Katsirea, "Why the European Broadcasting Quota Should Be Abolished," *European Law Review* 28, no. 2 (2003): pp. 190–209.

3245 This was stated during the Commission's press conference of 25 May 2016 announcing the proposal.

3246 ERGA, "ERGA Opinion on AVMSD Proposal," pp. 9–10.

3247 See Art. 13 (3) of the 2016 AVMSD proposal.

sessments which will, in turn, be made available to the EP and Council.[3248]

In general, the aim of ensuring investments in original European content is vital, especially where mainstream (US) content directed at a global audience penetrates markets worldwide.[3249] This contributes to a flourishing European audiovisual production industry and helps to sustain a virtuous cycle. It is also intended to help maintain the diversity of European cultures, including minorities, and thereby enhance media pluralism. It thus appears important to require on-demand service providers, like broadcasters which essentially earn their revenues disseminating audiovisual content, to contribute to achieving these laudable objectives. The means proposed by the Commission may, however, be debatable. Yet, the proposed amendments to Art. 13 AVMSD represent a certain alignment to the rules applicable to broadcasters and thus, any more fundamental alteration would necessitate a consistent approach.

## IV. Summary

To summarise, the 2016 AVMSD proposal constitutes a step in the right direction toward the adopting the overdue, next-generation AVMSD. The extension of the Directive's material scope is necessary to reflect current and anticipated market developments and acknowledge the important role played by VSPs in the dissemination of audiovisual material. Similarly, aligning the rules for the protection of minors in linear and non-linear services is imperative against the background of changing consumption patterns. Its other proposed modifications adopt a more inclusive approach, demanding more commitment by service providers (e.g. promoting European productions) while, at the same time, balancing stricter regulation in some fields with greater flexibility in others (e.g. audiovisual commercial communications).

Nevertheless, the 2016 AVMSD proposal is but the first step. As written, most of the proposed changes are rather modest and do not go beyond codifying the CJEU's case law in relation to current definitions. Thus, it seems that the notion of an audiovisual media service remains as vague

3248 See Art. 13 (4) of the 2016 AVMSD proposal.

3249 Cabrera Blázquez et al., *On-Demand Services and the Material Scope of the AVMSD*, p. 12.

and fluid as it is today. Moreover, the 2016 AVMSD proposal does not appear to provide any real guidance to the NRAs that will be tasked with applying and enforcing the Directive at the national level. In a similar vein, its proposed provision intended to protect minors in media services lacks precision, especially with respect to the measures service providers are required to take. The same criticism can be levied against its attempt to draft normative provisions to be applied to VSPs. These are confined to protecting audiences from so-called unsuitable content (i.e. content harmful to minors and content inciting to hatred and violence) and are formulated in an overly broad manner. Moreover, the 2016 AVMSD proposal, if adopted as written, complicates the general structure of the next-generation AVMSD. It distinguishes between minimum and maximum harmonisation and between graduated regulation in relation to linear versus non-linear and in relation to audiovisual media services versus VSPs. It is, thus, difficult to see how adopting, as written, the 2016 AVMSD proposal can either prevent market distortions or accomplish a uniform level of protection across services that compete with each other.

### *D. Preliminary conclusions*

It is important to consider the criticism of the Commission's 2016 AVMSD proposal that is voiced above in the proper context. One should bear in mind the comprehensive work conducted by the Commission prior to elaborating the proposal: a three-month public consultation in late 2015, which was followed by a detailed impact assessment supported by academic studies and reports. Against this backdrop, the modest revision tabled by the Commission already represents a compromise of stakeholders' interests.

It is interesting that the Commission, with its 2016 AVMSD proposal, seems to have anticipated the possible compromises emerging from the legislative process that is currently unfolding. For example, enlarging the Directive's scope to VSPs on the basis of a graduated approach to regulation (i.e. proposing a separate set of rules applicable to VSPs that differs from the obligations incumbent on media service providers) seems to be a realistic scenario. It mitigates the different positions found in the EP (or at least that of the lead committee, CULT)[3250] generally supporting VSP regulation, and some Member States' reluctance, found in the Council, to introduce these rules in the next-generation AVMSD. In this respect, the Commission's 2016 AVMSD proposal appears as a strategic and politically feasible compromise, even if, in substance, it may be viewed critically. Still, the last revision of the Directive, in 2007, has taught that such compromises quickly become outdated given the speed at which the audiovisual media services market evolves. In addition, the lack of clarity and precision that political compromises inevitably entail has made it necessary for the CJEU (for instance, in the 2005 M*ediakabel* and the 2015 *New Media Online* decisions) to clarify the Directive's key terms and the question of its scope of application. In the meantime, NRAs have developed guidance and, in some Member States, a body of practice at the national level has enhanced legal certainty for service providers. This study therefore recognises the fundamental role played by NRAs in implementing and applying the Directive's rules in practice.

## I. Regulatory strategies in converging media markets

Beyond the current political discussions, how should the future legal framework for audiovisual media services be devised? This study has examined two parameters: first, the type of regulation and second, certain content standards. With respect to the type of regulation, this research studied the regulatory frameworks in three Member States: the UK, Germany and France. Although their regulatory frameworks are very different, some meta-level characteristics and several best practices have been identified in the first part of this chapter. In order to accommodate continuing media convergence, the regulatory framework for audiovisual media services must reflect several meta-level characteristics: they must be flexible, i.e. able to respond to recurring market disruptions, they must be effective, i.e. achieve the pre-determined objective, they must be technology-neutral (or technology-agnostic), i.e. ensure a level playing field and they must have a sufficiently light-touch, so as to unleash the market's potential and encourage innovation, creativity and experimentation. These

3250 See the CULT draft report's proposal to achieve a genuine level playing field for all providers regulated by the AVMSD, in particular Art. -2 to -2f of the draft report.

abstract characteristics should be built-in to the regulatory framework at the EU and national levels.

Co-regulation, as analysed in this study, appears to offer many of these characteristics, provided that the scheme is designed accordingly. Co-regulation, as an alternative to "regular" state regulation, best represents a collaborative approach between the state and industry, where the co-regulator is embedded in a framework defined by the state. The state's involvement ensures that the objectives pursued by regulation take into account stakeholders' rights and interests, including fundamental rights and freedoms. As proposed above, co-regulation should be adequately framed and formalised by a certification or designation. This formal recognition should be based on criteria enshrined in the legal framework, including for example the co-regulator's access to adequate resources, its independence, transparency and accountability. The formal act recognising the co-regulator should also include an obligation to regularly review the scheme to ensure that it continues to comply with the meta-level characteristics.

Generally, all aspects of audiovisual media services regulation can be pursued through co-regulation provided that the co-regulator's mandate is sufficiently precise and stipulates clearly defined objectives. It seems that a limited remit, that does not entail difficult decisions about the scope of regulation, is more successful. Yet, a co-regulator with a broad mandate may be appropriate if it is incorporated in a regulatory structure that allows for swift cooperation with other regulatory bodies (and that share the same outlook on the market that is regulated) and prompt resolution of complaints.

In the absence of co-regulation, service providers' self-responsibility must be strengthened and they must be encouraged to aim for regulatory objectives beyond the legal requirements. Typically, such involvement of service providers is not considered as self-regulation because the industry as such does not regulate itself. Nonetheless, the enhanced involvement of service providers on an individual basis is crucial to alleviate some of the regulatory burden born by NRAs and may even develop in more widespread industry initiatives. Setting up appropriate incentives for providers to comply with certain standards and to take voluntary action beyond what the law requires of them will be decisive. Service providers need to benefit from (or at least to not be disadvantaged by) abiding by voluntary (stricter) rules. There are many ways to devise such a scheme and awarding a quality seal which audiences recognise and trust is just one possibility. What seems important to note is that incentive-based regulation will likely play a more pertinent role in the future to mitigate some of the effects of media convergence.

## II. Content standards in converging media markets

With regard to certain content standards, the second parameter examined in this study, it follows that the key concepts defining an (on-demand) audiovisual media service are still relevant today but require clarification.

Service providers could be encouraged to determine who holds editorial responsibility for the purposes of the AVMSD. According to the CJEU's *New Media Online* judgment, the principal purpose test requires that a service be self-standing and independent from other activities of the same media outlet. The notion of programme must be detached from a broadcasting context and should encompass new, wide-spread forms of presenting content. In addition, best practices that aim at refining these key concepts by a list of indicators or criteria have been identified above. Even if the application of such criteria by NRAs at the national level is unlikely to prevent differences in the implementation by various Member States, they nonetheless enhance legal certainty and common standards, provided that they are applied in a consistent and foreseeable manner. Importantly, the Directive's scope should be re-calibrated to services that are mass media, having a great impact on the general public and which are in competition[3251] with each other. Recital 24 AVMSD continues to be relevant in converged media markets and ensures that regulation remains targeted and proportionate.

Effectively protecting minors in a converging media environment remains a challenging task. Viewing and consumption patterns of minors (under 18) or young audiences (under 25) diverge from those of the remaining population because they are increasingly turning to new forms of audiovisual material that is immediately accessible everywhere. Protecting

3251 The concept of "competition" used throughout this study is interpreted broadly. In determining whether services compete with each other, several factors come into play, including the fast-moving character of media markets, and numerous parameters that define demand and supply-side substitutability such as the user's perspective or advertisers' behaviour, the position of providers in relevant markets (e.g. market shares, lock-in effects) and the services' relevance for and impact on society or its appeal to relevant age groups.

minors on all devices and in different media environments is a complex exercise, one that requires standards that are consistent across, and translatable to, different contexts. The next-generation AVMSD should therefore abandon the existing distinction between broadcasting and on-demand services and apply the same rules for both types of services. These rules should protect minors from harmful and seriously harmful content and require service providers to put in place appropriate measures that are proportionate to the potential harm caused by the respective material. In line with the precautionary principle, the revised Directive should specify that gratuitously violent and pornographic material are seriously harmful to minors' development and should thus not be made available to minors. The conceptualisation of the terms "gratuitous violence" and "pornography" as suggested above would be beneficial to all stakeholders and could lead to more uniform levels of protection across the EU, though socio-cultural differences in interpreting these concepts cannot be prevented. NRAs' interpretation of these terms may also be guided by other indicators, as discussed above, that help determine the harm caused.

Importantly, access to such content should be blocked by a two-step access control that effectively verifies a user's age once and authenticates it each time the service is accessed. In general, more effort should be made to enhance media literacy and empower parents and guardians to take informed decisions about the appropriateness of content for their children. This would require service providers to offer more detailed information about the content they disseminate. This could be done through pictograms or other easily identifiable symbols that could be used uniformly throughout all Member States, possibly on top of national classifications or age labels. Moreover, in order to ensure that pictograms or symbols can be read by all technical infrastructures, coordination of technical standards at the EU level is vital for the protection of minors on all platforms and devices.

Furthermore, the linear/non-linear distinction also appears outdated in other fields coordinated by the Directive. This is because platforms such as Connected TV feature linear services alongside content available on-demand. If linear content is only one of several services offered, it no longer seems appropriate to apply different regulatory regimes. This is especially relevant in light of the emergence of new, hybrid services that are increasingly gaining a foothold in the market, even though traditional or legacy media remain most significant for audiences. It also emerges from the above analysis that the TV-centric approach of the Directive is too narrow to accommodate the fast-paced changes brought about by media convergence. The whole value chain is in a flux and media service providers are increasingly challenged by new actors that are frequently established outside the EU, are vertically integrated and are powerful gate-keepers. An extension of the Directive's scope to certain types of platforms which mainly distribute audiovisual content and thus perform similar functions as media service providers appears justified.

Such an extension could be accomplished by introducing a separate set of less stringent rules than those applicable to media service providers. The graduated regulatory approach, which successfully incorporated on-demand services in the Directive's scope in 2005, appears well-suited for the up-coming revision. A two-tier approach best recognises the likenesses between the services offered by certain types of platforms and media service providers on the one hand and the differences that exist between these two kinds of service providers on the other hand. The differences today are materialised in the criterion of editorial responsibility: while media service providers bear full editorial control over the content they disseminate, certain types of platform operators, such as video-sharing platform providers, merely exercise an editorial function by organising content on their platforms. This editorial role does not, however, amount to editorial responsibility within the meaning of the AVMSD, at least not at this stage. To the extent that they offer similar services, these platforms should be covered by the next-generation AVMSD. The kinds of rules applicable to such platforms should reflect their role and impact on the general public and the public interest objectives pursued by regulation. Such objectives are commercial in nature, including fair competition and a level playing field, as well as cultural, covering media pluralism, cultural diversity, consumer protection and freedom of expression. Above all, protecting minors from inappropriate content appears as one of the primary goals.

To conclude, the effects that the regulatory regime of audiovisual media services has on other areas of regulation will have to be increasingly appraised. Due to media convergence, policy fields that were once separate are converging. They interrelate and overlap which means that adjusting a screw in one area will most certainly have repercussions in other fields, including competition law, data protection, consumer protection, e-Commerce and telecommunications. Thus, taking a 360 degree view,[3252] or in other words, a more holistic approach to regulation drawing from a toolbox of options and taking into account the whole value chain seems vital to ensure a just regulatory framework for audiovisual media services in the future.

3252 Hans Bredow Institut and Institute for Information Law (IViR), eds., "Study on the Future of Audiovisual Regulation, Final Report of the Hermes Project," 2015, http://www.hans-bredow-institut.de/webfm_send/1110 and http://www.ivir.nl/publicaties/download/1643 (accessed 5.12.2015).

# Conclusion

Audiovisual media services regulation is in flux, due in large part, by ever-increasing media convergence. States first regulated broadcast television because of spectrum scarcity: they granted a license to broadcast over a particular frequency subject to the broadcasters' acknowledgement and acceptance of regulations intended to meet social and democratic values. Other audiovisual media services subsequently entering the market have been similarly regulated. Although those early technical limitations have since diminished, if not disappeared, the Member States and now the EU still have, as demonstrated in chapter one, acknowledged a need to regulate such services, arising predominantly from the services' significance in shaping public opinion and the essential democratic role they fulfil. In fact, continued European integration has led to the EU's increasing ability to shape audiovisual media regulation as part of its internal market. While initially economic goals were primarily pursued, other policy objectives have increasingly been taken into account, such as media pluralism and diversity as well as fundamental rights.

The original cornerstone of the EU's media policies was the TWFD, which has since morphed into the AVMSD. The dual nature of audiovisual media services, being both economic and cultural commodities, and the EU's competence (or lack thereof) in these policy fields, has moulded the regulatory instrument the EU employed. Thus, the AVMSD only governs certain aspects of the audiovisual media services provided and it does so only through common (minimum) EU-level rules that must then be implemented at the national level. Member States, on the other hand, retain broad discretion with respect to the concrete means used to attain the EU's regulatory objectives.

Once transposed in the national legal orders, the AVMSD's transposed rules are enforced by NRAs, which are, as discussed in chapters two and three, given their mandates by national legislation that reflects national contexts and specificities. Nevertheless, NRAs, when overseeing compliance with the transposed rules, are acting as important agents of both the national legislatures *and* the EU. The Member States' national regulatory framework may include co- or self-regulatory bodies that can, as conceptualised in chapters two and three, share the regulatory burden and help the NRAs to monitor the audiovisual media industry. All of these national-level regulatory bodies are obliged to interpret and apply the AVMSD's transposed provisions in real time to service providers operating in the ever-converging audiovisual media market, implementing the AVMSD through their practices and guidelines.

This study, therefore, examined the measures taken by the UK, German, and French NRAs with respect to the notion of on-demand audiovisual media services and the protection of minors by such services. Thus, it examined all levels of existing regulation: the EU-level AVMSD, which prescribes the rules; the national legislation that transposes the AVMSD's rules; and, most importantly, the national, executive measures those NRAs use to implement the foregoing. On the basis of those analyses and a comparison of the three NRAs' implementation measures, chapter six distilled best practices and made a number of suggestions as to how the next-generation AVMSD could be better designed to address long-term, rather than immediate, regulatory demands, especially concerning its scope of application.

On a more abstract level, media convergence continues to have significant repercussions on the regulatory strategies Member States have chosen to implement the AVMSD. Thus, chapter three provided an overview of the regulatory models currently in force in the UK, Germany, and France to gain some perspective on the available choices. Apart from top-down state intervention through a central regulatory authority, that overview demonstrated that Member States can choose and have indeed chosen more flexible, adaptable forms of regulation to better adjust to the unprecedented speed of technological progress. It is common knowledge that a legislative process, especially at the EU level, is typically time-consuming and highly contentious (as the different parties pursue their own agendas often entailing conflicting interests) such that the final legislative result reflects a negotiated, not seldom lowest-common-denominator regulatory regime. The reconciliation of diverging interests inherent in the political process exists at the national and the EU levels but it is multiplied within the EU and particularly in the field of audiovisual media where, broadly speaking, the Commission has furthered single market objectives, the EP has traditionally vouched for consumer protection and the Member States in the Council have guarded their prerogatives in cultural matters.

Such a process is, however, antithetical to the fast-paced, dynamic audiovisual service market in which both technological *and* cultural advances can happen in a matter of months, rather than years or decades.

Moreover, the legislative process is typically reactionary, rather than proactive; it does not (and perhaps cannot) anticipate new technological or societal advances, so the legislation does not look forward. Rather, it responds to developments that have already become common practice in the industry and it is certainly possible that the final, negotiated legislation is already under pressure, or worse, obsolete the moment it comes into force. Thus, slow-moving, heavy-handed, from-the-top-down regulatory approaches are unsuitable for a converging media ecosystem. As demonstrated in the second and third chapters, many states revert to more flexible, agile regulatory schemes including co-regulation.

The co-regulatory model, as it existed in the UK and still exists in Germany, allows service providers to assume greater responsibilities in devising pragmatic solutions to the challenges posed by media convergence. The co-regulatory model, which can rely on a single co-regulatory body or multiple co-regulatory bodies, integrates the body(ies) into the Member State's legal framework. That integrated structure has several benefits: it accumulates the industries' collective expertise in the co-regulatory body(ies), leading to industry-relevant standards that, in turn, result in enhanced compliance by the affected service providers. Of course, the relevant NRA or the Member State must remain involved to ensure that the standards respect certain regulatory requirements and are effectively enforced, but any such co- (or self-)regulatory measures must be carefully designed and monitored to prevent its capture by the industry and to guarantee respect of certain values, including due process rights.

To date, there is no perfect model for co- or self-regulation that can simply be implanted in the various Member States; regulatory strategies must still be adapted to the national markets. In Germany, media convergence led to co-regulation to protect minors in audiovisual media services and other content made available via the Internet. The German scheme has been very successful, but its ongoing reform demonstrates that it may be difficult to ensure the same level of protection for minors, regardless of the means used to distribute the content (whether online or offline, whether audiovisual media service or carrier medium). Further media convergence will have even greater global effects on Member States' regulatory frameworks and it will become increasingly difficult to regulate different media types in isolation. Although no longer functioning, the UK example also demonstrated that there can be no 'one-size fits all' solution to co-regulation. Media convergence is not uniform and, thus, may demand merging, rather than separating, regulatory functions to ensure consistent application of common standards, which also shows how tightly regulatory strategies are bound to standard setting. Co- and self-regulation, are promoted in the Commission's proposal for a revised AVMSD, continue to be a valuable regulatory strategy and important part of the Member States' regulatory toolbox.

Interestingly, the Member States have not been the only entities experimenting with new regulatory strategies: the EU institutions have also been quite active, searching for appropriate ways to address the ever-changing audiovisual media industry. Just about two years ago, the Commission created ERGA, a body that unites all of the Member States' NRAs and meets on an ad hoc basis in different constellations; it has been increasingly active and is now quite visible. ERGA is proof that the AVMSD, in its current form, is woefully inadequate in an era of seemingly unstoppable media convergence; for example, it highlights the need – most notably, the Commission's need – to have access to an expert body to better understand the AVMSD's impact on national markets. It also underscores the regrettable vagueness of some of the AVMSD's provisions that lead to different results in different Member States and, inevitably, to the need to coordinate national approaches to regulation. As an amalgam of national regulators convening at the European level, ERGA is not unique: this form of regulatory coordination exists in other areas of EU law, particularly data protection and telecommunications. The creation of EU-level bodies for these markets can be explained by the existence of several common factors, such as the dynamic nature of the regulated market, the complexity of the regulatory framework (including the distribution of competence between the EU and the Member States), and the co-existence of numerous stakeholders with very different interests and their respective rights. ERGA is not a full-fledged European institution or agency, but is, rather, a hybrid body whose status is unclear. It remains to be seen whether the Commission will give ERGA further powers or elevate its role in a revised AVMSD. Its mere existence suggests yet-another move towards the Europeanisation of media policies, a shift that is not expressly authorised by the Treaties.

The impact that media convergence has had on content standards is amply demonstrated by the range of measures taken by the UK, German and French NRAs, analysed in chapters four and five. Converging media services and changing consumption patterns, which are heterogeneous for different age groups, makes it difficult to determine the actual scope of the AVMSD: the criteria used to define an (on-demand) audiovisual media service have blurred, making it difficult to apply them in practice. NRAs' measures show that there are uncertainties about whether a particular service falls within or without the AVMSD's scope. Differences about classifications of services at the national level are the unfortunate-but-logical consequence. Such fragmentation, however, defeats the AVMSD's objectives, which aim to remove obstacles to the free movement of audiovisual media services and to establishing an internal market. Continuing media convergence thus presents particular challenges for the Directive's material scope. Criteria must be found that are both precise and future-proof. They must be precise to ensure legal certainty while capturing the key characteristics of the services regulated by the AVMSD. They must simultaneously be future-proof to accommodate services that are, or become, akin to those covered by the AVMSD. Media convergence has already led to a significant blurring of boundaries between the individual steps in a value chain (such as content production, distribution, and consumption), a chain that is now populated by vastly larger group of actors, some of which are incumbents diversifying their business models and some of which are powerful new players.[3253] It is, thus, vital that the future regulatory framework for audiovisual media services, that is, the next-generation AVMSD, takes account of, or perhaps even anticipates, a constantly changing value chain and does not fence itself off from such developments. Enlarging the Directive's material scope is inevitable as it is the only way to ensure equal treatment of services that perform a similarly relevant democratic function and, hence, have a comparable impact on society.

Protecting minors from unsuitable material is another regulatory field that is similarly challenged by media convergence. Due to the cultural implications (especially the classification of content), the AVMSD is worded in a rather broad way, leaving ample room for the Member States to adopt national rules according to the particular Member States culture and societal norms. In that regard, the UK, German, and French regulatory authorities have adapted the AVMSD's formulations to their respective national contexts. They have, for example, specified the type of content deemed to be seriously harmful to minors and provided detailed requirements for the measures service providers are obliged to put in place to protect them. In doing so, the UK, German, and French regulators seem to rely on similar

3253 ERGA, "Report on Material Jurisdiction," para. 1.4, pp. 23–27.

reasoning despite the fact that, in practice, differences emerge that are, at least partially, explained by cultural differences. While eliminating them entirely, or even just reducing such differences to a minimum, currently appears to be a Herculean, if not impossible, task, doing so in the next-generation AVMSD would be greatly beneficial to establishing a genuine internal market for audiovisual media services within the EU and enhancing the cross-border circulation of audiovisual media services. Designing common approaches to content labelling, as well as technical and other protection measures is absolutely essential to ensure a coherently high-level of protection for young audiences.

Moreover, enforcing national protective measures for minors is made more difficult by media convergence. Harmful and age-inappropriate content that was not available to past generations of minors is now just a click away on the Internet, which demonstrates the limits of regulation in view of the global, ubiquitous nature of the Internet. To effectively enforce measures to protect minors, the next-generation AVMSD must abandon the current distinction between broadcasting and on-demand services in favour of aligned rules and clearer requirements, based on the content of the material rather than the manner in which such content is made available. But, protecting minors from unsuitable materials is not, and never can be, the sole responsibility of media service providers. Instead, a more holistic approach, imposing obligations on other actors deemed to be in competition with media service providers, would be much more effective, such that those other actors should contribute to protecting minors in accordance with their respective role in the audiovisual value chain.

The next-generation AVMSD, being shaped as this work is being written, must strike a balance between highly detailed rule-making on the one end of the spectrum and the broad, flexible requirements that will continue to be effective even as media convergence continues and accelerates, on the other, as neither extreme is a suitable approach to regulating audiovisual media services. Detailed rules are generally burdensome and unresponsive and, thus, are very likely to stifle innovation. Regulation based on broad, loosely defined principles, however, are likely be too vague to be helpful, which will lead Member States (and ultimately NRAs) to fill in the gaps at the national level, which, in turn is very likely to result in fragmented implementation. Solving this conundrum – that is, finding the right balance between those extremes – is one of the most important tasks the Commission, and the other EU institutions, must willingly and conscientiously embrace when negotiating and finally adopting the next generation AVMSD.

# Annexes

*Annex 1*

## *The Sun, Video, 24 September 2012*

**Celebs dazzle on Emmys 2012 red carpet**

Was this the most glamorous TV awards bash ever? Check out the best dressed from this year's do

*24/09/2012 12:05 PM*
*02:04min*

Read full article
TV Biz

**Homeland triumphs at The Emmys 2012**

BRIT Damian Lewis scoops Best Actor gong and terror show wins Best Drama at TV bash in LA

*24/09/2012 10:41 AM*
*02:55min*

Read full article
TV Biz

**Green Day's Billie in foul -mouthed rant**

AMERICAN Idiot star loses his cool after Las Vegas set cut for Usher

*23/09/2012 02:11 PM*
*01:43min*

Read full article
Music Biz

**X Factor judge Tulisa is TV Magazine's cover star**

EXCLUSIVE behind-the-scenes video with pop babe on her photoshoot for Sun mag

*21/09/2012 03:40 PM*
*01:12min*

Read full article
Sun Exclusive

SEE ALL SHOWBIZ VIDEO

THE SUN TODAY

**Celebs dazzle on Emmys 2012 red carpet**

Was this the most glamorous TV awards bash ever? Check out the best dressed from this year's do

*24/09/2012 12:05 PM*
*02:04min*

Read full article
TV Biz

**Celebs complete London Triathlon**

DAVID Hasselhoff, Louie Spence and Nell McAndrew among stars taking part in endurance event

*24/09/2012 11:40 AM*
*02:18min*

Read full article
TV Biz

SUN EXCLUSIVE

**Inside Madagascar's miracle working orphange**

REMOTE island slays newborn twins as a superstition, but hospice does best to rescue as many as possible

*22/09/2012 06:23 PM*
*01:12min*

Read full article
Sun Exclusive

**X Factor judge Tulisa is TV Magazine's cover star**

EXCLUSIVE behind-the-scenes video with pop babe on her photoshoot for Sun mag

*21/09/2012 03:40 PM*
*01:12min*

Read full article
Sun Exclusive

NEWS

SPORT

*The Sun, Homepage, 15 October 2013*

*The Sun, Homepage, 11 March 2015*

Sign In

bargain holiday

PROMOTIONS

membership and as well as the tablet, you'll enjoy the Perks of being a member with £9.50 hols, free days-out, meal deals and much more

PROMOTIONS 23 days ago

**Join Sun+ on a free one month trial**

A whole world of digital entertainment

PROMOTIONS 10 days ago

**Bop Gear: Clarkson suspended for 'punching' producer**

EXCLUSIVE: TOP Gear host Jeremy denies claims he hit a colleague on location, as bosses cancel three shows in current series

TV 2 hours ago

**Madonna Exclusive: Her Madge on sex tapes, Guy & ...David Cameron**

EXCLUSIVE: QUEEN of Pop gives an audience to The Sun's Bizarre column in her only UK newspaper interview - JOIN SUN+ FREE TO READ WHAT SHE HAS TO SAY...

BIZARRE 9 hours ago

*Annex 2*

*The Vice, Homepage, 22 April 2015*

ABOUT ©2015 VICE Media LLC THE VICE CHANNELS UNITED STATES

VICE WATCH SECTIONS PHOTOS MAGAZINE MORE

**The Miraculous Life of El Niño Fidencio**

VICE Mexico Traveled to the Town Espinazo to Watch the Annual Celebration of an Unofficial Saint

READ NOW

Apr 22, 2015 STUFF

Rick Paulas

**Director Jason Woliner Talks About Bob Odenkirk and David Cross's New Netflix Show**

The man behind the camera for such strange, hilarious shows as Chris Elliott's *Eagleheart* and *Comedy Bang Bang* discusses what it's like to work with his heroes.

Apr 22, 2015 FILM

Ryan Britt

**Crying Over the New Star Wars Trailer Makes Total Sense**

From Matthew McConaghey to Twitter nerds, it seems everyone on the internet lost their shit over the new Star Wars trailer.

*The Vice, Watch, Video, 22 April 2015*

ABOUT ©2015 VICE Media LLC THE VICE CHANNELS UNITED STATES

VICE WATCH SECTIONS PHOTOS MAGAZINE MORE

WATCH

FEATURED VIDEO

The Secret History of Cabbage Patch Kids

WATCH NOW

LATEST VIDEOS

Apr 21, 2015 MEXICALIA

20:48

The Miraculous Life of El Niño Fidencio

Niño Fidencio and his legendary healing abilities may not be officially recognized by the Catholic Church, but 40,000 people gather in a small Mexican village each year to celebrate the unofficial saint.

Apr 20, 2015 ELECTION '15

05:51

We Watched London's Weed Fanatics Getting Arrested in Hyde Park for 4/20

The annual celebration doubled as a cannabis legalization rally in the run-up to Election '15.

*The Vice, Watch, Featured Shows, 22 April 2015*

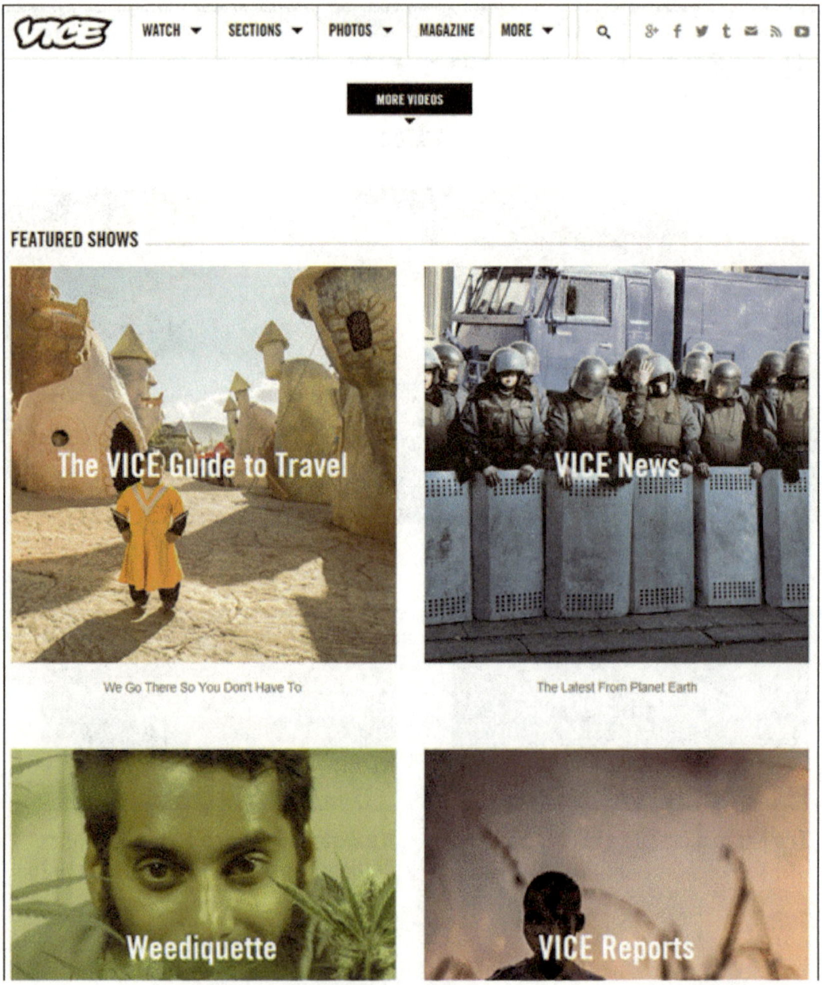

*The Vice, Watch, Series, 22 April 2015*

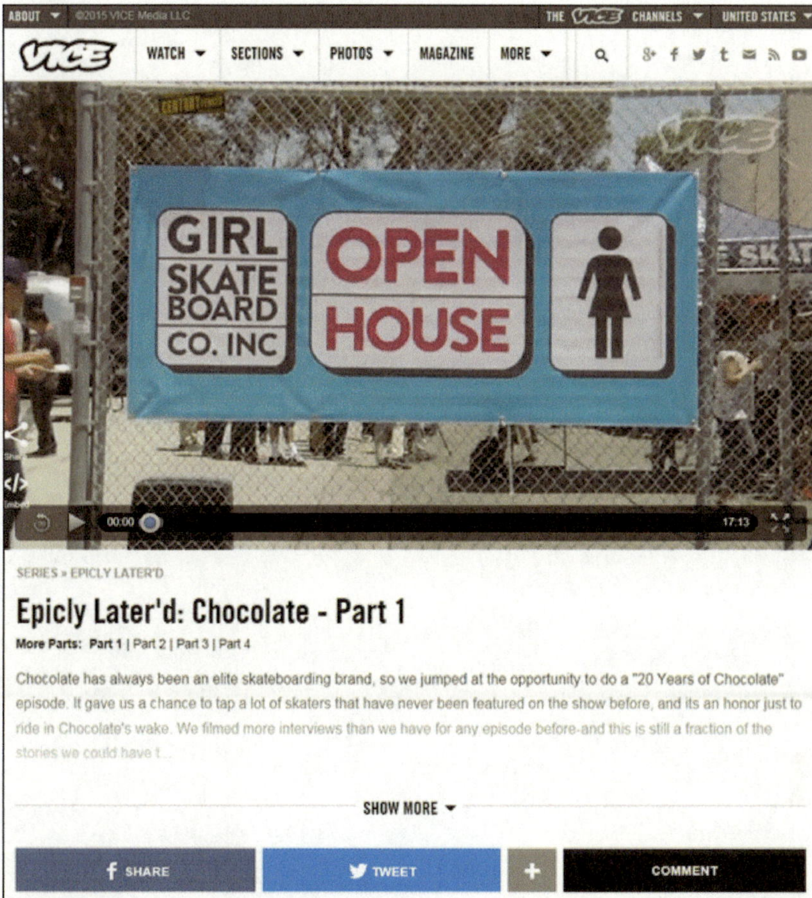
ABOUT ▾ ©2015 VICE Media LLC THE VICE CHANNELS ▾ UNITED STATES ▾

VICE WATCH ▾ SECTIONS ▾ PHOTOS ▾ MAGAZINE MORE ▾

GIRL SKATE BOARD CO. INC OPEN HOUSE

00:00 17:13

SERIES » EPICLY LATER'D

## Epicly Later'd: Chocolate - Part 1

**More Parts: Part 1** | Part 2 | Part 3 | Part 4

Chocolate has always been an elite skateboarding brand, so we jumped at the opportunity to do a "20 Years of Chocolate" episode. It gave us a chance to tap a lot of skaters that have never been featured on the show before, and its an honor just to ride in Chocolate's wake. We filmed more interviews than we have for any episode before-and this is still a fraction of the stories we could have t ...

SHOW MORE ▾

SHARE TWEET + COMMENT

# Bibliography

*Monographs, commentaries and edited volumes*

Ayres, Ian, and John Braithwaite. *Responsive Regulation: Transcending the Deregulation Debate*. Oxford Socio-Legal Studies. New York: Oxford University Press, 1992.

Baars, Wiebke. *Kooperation und Kommunikation durch Landesmedienanstalten, Eine Analyse ihres Aufgaben- und Funktionsbereichs*. Materialien zur interdisziplinären Medienforschung 35. Baden-Baden: Nomos, 1999.

Baldwin, Robert, and Julia Black. "Really Responsive Regulation." In *LSE Law, Society and Economy Working Paper*, 2007.

Baldwin, Robert, Martin Cave, and Martin Lodge. *Understanding Regulation. Theory, Strategy, and Practice*. Second edition. Oxford: Oxford University Press, 2012.

Bennett, James, and Niki Strange. eds. *Television as Digital Media*. Durham and London: Duke University Press, 2011.

Blasi, Martina. *Das Herkunftslandprinzip der Fernseh- und der E-Commerce-Richtlinie, Unter Berücksichtigung des Herkunftslandprinzips auf der Ebene des Primärrechts*. Schriftenreihe zum gewerblichen Rechtsschutz 132. Köln: Carl Heymanns Verlag, 2004.

Bosch, Dorit. *Die "Regulierte Selbstregulierung" im Jugendmedienschutz-Staatsvertrag, Eine Bewertung des neuen Aufsichtsmodells anhand verfassungs- und europarechtlicher Vorgaben*. Studien zum deutschen und europäischen Medienrecht 22. Frankfurt am Main: Peter Lang, 2006.

Breyer, Stephan. *Regulation and Its Reform*. United States of America: Harvard University Press, 1982.

Brockmeyer, Dieter. *EuroReg 2011: From Connected TV to Coherent Media, A Conference by Germany's "Die Medienanstalten"and LPR Hessen, Documentation*. Schriftenreihe Der Landesmedienanstalten 48. Berlin: Vistas, 2012.

Cabrera Blázquez, Francisco, Maja Cappello, Gilles Fontaine, and Sophie Valais. On-Demand Services and the Material Scope of the AVMSD. IRIS Plus 1/2016. Strasbourg: European Audiovisual Observatory, 2016.

Cabrera Blázquez, Francisco, and Amélie Lépinard. eds. Enabling Access to the Media for All. IRIS Plus 3/2014. Strasbourg: European Audiovisual Observatory, 2014.

Cabrera Blázquez, Francisco, Maja Cappello, Laura Ene, Gilles Fontaine, Christian Grece, Martin Kanzler, Kevin Deidre, Agnes Schneeberger, Julio Talavera, and Sophie Valais. Yearbook 2015, Television, Cinema, Video and On-Demand Audiovisual Services - The Pan-European Picture, Key Trends. Edited by European Audiovisual Observatory. Strasbourg, France, 2016.

Cappello, Maja, ed. *New Forms of Commercial Communications in a Converged Audiovisual Sector*. IRIS Special. Strasbourg: European Audiovisual Observatory, 2014.

Chalmers, Damian, Gareth Davies, and Giorgio Monti. *European Union Law*. Second edition. Cambridge: Cambridge University Press, 2010.

Craig, Paul, and Gráinne De Búrca. *EU Law, Text, Cases, and Materials*. Fifth edition. Oxford: Oxford University Press, 2011.

Curran, James, and Jean Seaton. *Power without Responsibility, The Press, Broadcasting and New Media in Britain*. Sixth edition. London and New York: Routledge, 2003.

Davy, Stéphane, and François Hurard. Lamy Droit des Médias et de la Communication, La télévision: évolution législative. Edited by Pierre Sirinelli, Christian Gavalda, and Lionel Costes, 2014.

De Bellescize, Diane, and Laurence Franceschini. *Droit de la communication*. Second edition. Paris: Presses Universitaires de France, 2011.

Debbasch, Charles, Hervé Isar, and Xavier Agostinellig. Droit de la communication, Audiovisucl - Prcssc - Intcrnct. First cdition. Paris: Dalloz, 2002.

Derieux, Emmanuel, and Agnès Granchet-Valentin. Droit Des Médias. 6th ed. Droit Français, Européen et International. Paris: LGDJ, 2010.

Dicey, Albert, Venn. *Introduction to the Study of the Law of the Constitution*. Eight edition. London: Macmillan, 1915.

Eeckhout, Piet. External Relations of the European Union, Legal and Constitutional Foundations. Oxford: Oxford University Press, 2004.

Elliott, Catherine, and Frances Quinn. *English Legal System*. Tenth edition. Essex: Pearson, 2009.

Feintuck, Mike, and Mike Varney. *Media Regulation, Public Interest and the Law*. Second edition. Edinburgh: Edinburgh University Press, 2006.

Fink, Udo, Mark Cole, and Tobias Keber. *Europäisches und Internationales Medienrecht*. Heidelberg: Müller, 2008.

Fontaine, Gilles, and Christian Grece. *On-Demand Audiovisual Markets in the European Union, Developments 2014 and 2015*. Strasbourg: European Audiovisual Observatory, 2015.

Franklin, Bob, ed. British Television Policy: A Reader. London: Routledge, 2001.

Goldberg, David, Gavin Sutter, and Ian Walden, eds. *Media Law and Practice*. Oxford: Oxford University Press, 2009.

Grabosky, Peter, and Gunningham, Neil, eds. *Smart Regulation: Designing Environmental Policy*. Oxford: Clarendon Press, Oxford University Press, 1998.

Gragl, Paul. *The Accession of the European Union to the European Convention on Human Rights*. Oxford: Hart Publishing, 2013.

Harlow, Carol, and Richard Rawlings. *Law and Administration*. Third edition. Cambridge: Cambridge University Press, 2009.

Harrison, Jackie, and Lorna Woods. *European Broadcasting Law and Policy*. Cambridge and New York: Cambridge University Press, 2007.

Hartstein, Reinhard, Wolf-Dieter Ring, Johannes Kreile, Dieter Dörr, Rupert Stettner, Mark Cole, and Eva Wagner. *Rundfunkstaatsvertrag, Kommentar*. Looseleaf commenatry. Köln: Rehm, n.d.

Hofmann, Herwig, Gerard Rowe, and Alexander Türk. *Administrative Law and Policy of the European Union*. Oxford: Oxford University Press, 2011.

Holtmann, Frank. *Zur rechtlichen Unterscheidung von Rundfunk und Telemedien bei Hybrid-TV, Unter besonderer Berücksichtigung der Werbe- und Jugendschutzregelungen des RStV und JMStV*. Vol. 41. Schriften zum Medienrecht. Hamburg: Verlag Dr. Kovac, 2015.

Holzgraefe, Moritz. *Werbeintegration in Fernsehsendungen und Videospielen, Product Placement und verwandte Formen im Spiegel des Medien- und Wettbewerbsrechts*. Edited by Hoffmann-Riem, Wolfgang. Materialien zur interdisziplinären Medienforschung 64. Baden-Baden: Nomos, 2010.

Holznagel, Bernd. *Rundfunkrecht in Europa, Auf dem Weg zu einem Gemeinrecht europäischer Rundfunkordnungen*. Tübingen: Mohr Siebeck, 1996.

Holznagel, Bernd, Dieter Dörr, and Doris Hildebrand. *Elektronische Medien, Entwicklung und Regulierungsbedarf*. München: Franz Vahlen, 2008.

Jongen, François. *La police de l'audiovisuel, Analyse comparée de la régulation de la radio et de la télévision en Europe*. Brussels: Bruylant, 1994.

Kaumanns, Ralf. "Der Smart TV-Markt: Akteure, Strategien, Geschäftsmodelle, in: Die Medienanstalten (Hrsg.), Wie smart ist die Konvergenz? Markt und Nutzung von Connected TV." Edited by Hans Hege and Andreas Hamann. Die Medienanstalten, 2014.

Keller, Perry. *European and International Media Law, Liberal Democracy, Trade, and the New Media*. Oxford: Oxford University Press, 2011.

Kempermann, Philip. *Content-Regulierung in konvergierenden Medien*. Vol. 1. Schriftenreihe der Kölner Forschungsstelle für Medienrecht. Frankfurt am Main: Peter Lang, 2010.

Kogler, Michael R. *TV (On-Demand)*. Europäische Content-Regelungen Für Audiovisuelle Mediendienste. Wien: Manz, 2010.

Kogler, Michael, Matthias Traimer, and Michael Truppe. *Österreichische Rundfunkgesetze, Recht der audiovisuellen Mediendienste und des Hörfunks*. Third edition. Wien: Verlag Medien & Recht, 2011.

Leitgelb, Stephan. *Product-Placement, Verfassungs- und gemeinschaftsrechtliche Bestandsaufnahme vor dem Hintergrund der europäischen Liberalisierung integrativer Werbeformen durch die Richtlininie über Audiovisuelle Mediendienste*. Schriften zum Medienrecht 22. Hamburg: Kovač, 2010.

Lessig, Lawrence. *Code Version 2.0*. New York: Basic Books, 2006.

Lievens, Eva. *Protecting Children in the Digital Era, The Use of Alternative Regulatory Instruments*. International Studies in Human Rights 105. Leiden, Boston: Martinus Nijhoff Publishers, 2010.

Lunt, Peter, and Sonia Livingstone,. *Media Regulation, Governance and the Interests of Citizens and Consumers*. London: Sage Publications, 2012.

Mallick, Rani. *Product-Placement in den Massenmedien, Rechtstatsachen und Rechtsgrundlagen*. Edited by Hoffmann-Riem, Wolfgang. Materialien zur interdisziplinären Medienforschung 63. Baden-Baden: Nomos, 2009.

Marsden, Christopher. *Internet Co-Regulation, European Law, Regulatory Governance and Legitimacy in Cyberspace*. Cambridge: Cambridge University Press, 2011.

Marsden, Christopher, ed. *Regulating the Global Information Society*. London: Routledge, 2000.

Mayer-Schönberger, Viktor. "Demystifying Lessig." *Wisconsin Law Review*, 2008, pp. 713–46.

Monroe, Price, Stefaan Verhulst, and Libby Morgan, eds. *Routledge Handbook of Media Law*. London and New York: Routledge, 2013.

Müller-Rüster, Jannis. *Product Placement im Fernsehen, Die Legalisierung programmintegrierter Werbung im Lichte der deutschen und europäischen Kommunikationsgrundrechte*. Jus Internationale et Europaeum 40. Tübingen: Mohr Siebeck, 2010.

Nicol, Andrew, Gavin Millar, and Andrew Sharland. *Media Law and Human Rights*. Second edition. Oxford: Oxford University Press, 2009.

Nikoltchev, Susanne, ed. *Audiovisual Media Services without Frontiers, Implementing the Rules*. IRIS Special. Strasbourg: European Audiovisual Observatory, 2006.

Nikoltchev, Susanne, ed. *Converged Media: Same Content, Different Laws?* IRIS Plus 3/2013. Strasbourg: European Audiovisual Observatory, 2013.

Nikoltchev, Susanne, ed. *Editorial Responsibility*. IRIS Special. Strasbourg: European Audiovisual Observatory, 2008.

Nikoltchev, Susanne, ed. *Exclusive Rights and Short Reporting*. IRIS Plus 4/2012. Strasbourg: European Audiovisual Observatory, 2012.

Nikoltchev, Susanne, ed. *Jurisdiction over Broadcasters in Europe*. IRIS Special. Strasbourg: European Audiovisual Observatory, 2002.

Nikoltchev, Susanne. *Legal Aspects of Video-On-Demand*. IRIS Special. Strasbourg: European Audiovisual Observatory, 2007.

Nikoltchev, Susanne, ed. *Product Placement*. IRIS Plus 3/2010. Strasbourg: European Audiovisual Observatory, 2010.

Nikoltchev, Susanne, ed. *Protection of Minors and Audiovisual Content on-Demand*. IRIS Plus 6/2012. Strasbourg: European Audiovisual Observatory, 2012.

Nikoltchev, Susanne, ed. *Ready, Set...Go? The Audiovisual Media Services Directive*. IRIS Special. Strasbourg: European Audiovisual Observatory, 2009.

Nikoltchev, Susanne, ed. *The Regulation of On-Demand Audiovisual Services: Chaos or Coherence?* IRIS Special. Strasbourg: European Audiovisual Observatory, 2011.

Nikoltchev, Susanne, ed. *What Is an On-Demand Service?* IRIS Plus 4/2013. Strasbourg: European Audiovisual Observatory, 2013.

Nikoltchev, Susanne, ed. *Video-On-Demand and the Promotion of European Works*. IRIS Special. Strasbourg: European Audiovisual Observatory, 2013.

Ogus, Anthony. *Regulation: Legal Form and Economic Theory*. Oxford: Hart Publishing, 1994.

Pariser, Eli. *The Filter Bubble: What the Internet Is Hiding from You*. London: Penguin Press, 2011.

Rahvar, Zahra. *Die Zukunft des deutschen Presserechts im Lichte konvergierender Medien*. Baden-Baden: Nomos, 2011.

Reed, Chris. *Making Laws for Cyberspace*. Oxford: Oxford University Press, 2012.

Reißer, Wolfgang. *Verfassungsrechtliche Anforderungen an die Medienkontrolle im Bereich Jugend- und Erwachsenenschutz*. Nomos Universitätsschriften 742. Baden-Baden: Nomos, 2011.

Ritlewski, Kristoff. *Pluralismus als Strukturprinzip im Rundfunk*. Anforderungen aus dem Funktionsauftrag und Regelungen zur Sicherung in Deutschland und Polen. Frankfurt am Main: Peter Lang, 2009.

Roßnagel, Alexander, Thomas Kleist, and Alexander Scheuer. *Die Reform der Regulierung elektronischer Medien in Europa*. Schriftenreihe Medienforschung der Landesanstalt für Medien Nordrhein-Westfalen 53. Düsseldorf: Vistas, 2007.

Rowland, Diane, Uta Kohl, and Andrew Charlesworth, eds. *Information Technology Law*. 4th edition. London: Routledge, 2012.

Schoenthal, Max. Von der Fernsehregulierung zur Inhalteregulierung, Die Konzeption der Einstufung von Mediendiensten im Recht der europäischen Gemeinschaft und die "Mediakabel"-Rechtsprechung des Europäischen Gerichtshofes. Schriftenreihe zum Kommunikations- und Medienrecht 12. Hamburg: Verlag Dr. Kovac, 2009.

Siry, Lawrence. *Knowing It When It Is Seen: The Polemic of the Regulation of Sexualized Speech in the United States and Europe*. Vol. 6. Luxemburger Juristische Studien - Luxembourg Legal Studies. Baden-Baden: Nomos, 2015.

Smartt, Ursula. *Media and Entertainment Law*. First edition. Milton Park, Abingdon and Oxon: Routledge, 2011.

Sporn, Stefan. *Die Ländermedienanstalt, Zur Zukunft der Aufsicht über den privaten Rundfunk in Deutschland und Europa*. Edited by Dieter Dörr. Studien zum deutschen und europäischen Medienrecht 11. Frankfurt am Main: Peter Lang, 2001.

Tridimas, Takis. *The General Principles of EU Law*. Second edition. Oxford: Oxford University Press, 2006.

Ward, David, ed. *The European Union and the Culture Industries, Regulation and the Public Interest*. United Kingdom: Ashgate Publishing, 2008.

Wildmann, Claudia. *Das Europäische Kurzberichterstattungsrecht im Lichte der Richtlinie über audiovisuelle Mediendienste*. Schriften zum Medienrecht 28. Hamburg: Kovač, 2011.

Witt, Inken. *Regulierte Selbstregulierung am Beispiel des Jugendmedienschutzstaatsvertrages*. Nomos Universitätsschriften 573. Baden-Baden: Nomos, 2008.

*Journal articles, scientific papers and contributions to edited volumes*

Altenhain, Karsten. "§ 4 JMStV Unzulässige Angebote." In *Beck'scher Kommentar zum Recht der Telemediendienste*, edited by Alexander Roßnagel. München: C. H. Beck, 2013.

Altenhain, Karsten. "§ 5 JMStV Entwicklungsbeeinträchtigende Angebote." In *Beck'scher Kommentar zum Recht der Telemediendienste*, edited by Alexander Roßnagel. München: C. H. Beck, 2013.

Altenhain, Karsten. "Altersverifikation mittels des elektronischen Personalausweises." *Kommunikation und Recht*, no. 10 (2009): pp. 619–25.

Altenhain, Karsten. "Die Neuregelung des JMStV insbesondere im Hinblick auf Computerspiele und Filme." *BPJM-Aktuell* 4 (2010): pp. 5–16.

Altenhain, Karsten. "Jugendschutz." In *Multimedia-Recht*, edited by Thomas Hoeren, Ulrich Sieber, and Bernd Holznagel, Vol. Loose-leaf commentary. München: C. H. Beck, 2015.

Andrieu, Eric, and Oriane Droulers. "Le jury de déontologie publicitaire." *Légipresse* 271 (2010): pp. 57–60.

Angelopoulos, Christina, Annabel Brody, Wouter Hins, Bernt Hugenholtz, Patrick Leerssen, Thomas Margoni, Tarlach McGonagle, Ot van Daalen, and Joris van Hoboken. "Study on Fundamental Rights Limitations for Online Enforcement through Self-Regulation." Edited by Institute for Information Law (IViR), 2016. http://www.ivir.nl/publicaties/download/1796.

Angelopoulos, Christina. "Product Placement in European Audiovisual Productions." In *Product Placement*, edited by Susanne Nikoltchev. IRIS Plus 3/2010. Strasbourg: European Audiovisual Observatory, 2010.

Arino, Monica. "Content Regulation and New Media: A Case Study of Online Video Portals." *Communications & Strategies* 66, no. 2 (2007): pp. 115–35.

Arino, Monica, and Carles Llorens. "Back to the Future: New Media, Same Principles? Convergence Regulation Re-Visited." In *The European Union and the Culture Industries, Regulation and the Public Interest*, edited by David Ward, pp. 125–44. Hampshire: Ashgate, 2008.

Artymiak, Sebastian. "Introduction to Different Forms of on-Demand Audiovisual Services." In *The Regulation of on-Demand Audiovisual Services: Chaos or Coherence?*, edited by Susanne Nikoltchev, pp. 31–34. IRIS Special. Strasbourg: European Audiovisual Observatory, 2011.

Baier, Jan. "Zulassungspflicht für Web-TV? Maßgebliche Kriterien im Lichte des Rundfunkbegriffs." *Computer und Recht* 12 (2008): pp. 769–76.

Baldwin, Robert, and Julia Black. "Really Responsive Regulation." In *LSE Law, Society and Economy Working Paper*, 2007.

Ballard, Tony. "Broadcasting." In *Media Law and Practice*, edited by David Goldberg, Gavin Sutter, and Ian Walden, pp. 299–334. Oxford: Oxford University Press, 2009.

Barata, Joan, Stefaan Verhulst, and Libby Morgan. "The Different Concepts of Free Expression and Its Link with Democracy, the Public Sphere and Other Concepts." In *Routledge Handbook of*, edited by Monroe Price, pp. 125–40. London and New York: Routledge, 2013.

Barendt, Eric. "Freedom of Expression in the United Kingdom under the Human Rights Act 1998." *Indiana Law Journal* 84, no. 3 (2009): pp. 851–66.

Barnard, Catherine, and Jukka Snell. "Free Movement of Legal Persons and the Provision of Services." In *European Union Law*, edited by Catherine Barnard and Steeve Peers, pp. 403–42. Oxford: Oxford University Press, 2014.

Begg, Ian. "Brexit: Why, What next and How?" *CESifo Forum*, no. 2 (2016): pp. 30–36.

Begg, Michael. "INDIREG Annex II Country Tables, United Kingdom," February 2011. http://www.indireg.eu/wp-content/uploads/Annex_II-_CountryTables_UK.pdf.

Berger, Christian. "Jugendschutz im Internet: „Geschlossene Benutzergruppen" nach § 4 Abs. 2 Satz 2 JMStV - Am Beispiel personalausweiskennziffergestützter Altersverifikationssysteme." *Multimedia und Recht*, 2003, pp. 773–78.

Berka, Walter, and Hannes Tretter. "The Polish Interim Broadcasting Act 2015 in the Light of Article 10 ECHR, A Legal Analysis," August 2016. http://www.ebu.ch/files/live/sites/ebu/files/News/2016/10/Berka-Tretter_The%20Polish%20Interim%20Broadcasting%20Act%202015%20in%20the%20light%20of%20article%2010%20ECHR.pdf.

Biolay, Jean-Jacques. *JurisClasseur Concurrence - Consommation, Application des règles de concurrence aux médias*. JurisClasseur, 2014.

Black, Julia. "Decentring Regulation: Understanding the Role of Regulation and Self-Regulation in a 'Post-Regulatory' World." *Current Legal Problems* 54, no. 1 (2001): pp. 103–46.

Black, Julia. "Critical Reflections on Regulation." *Australian Journal of Legal Philosophy* 27 (2002): pp. 1–36.

Black, Julia. "Forms and Paradoxes of Principles-Based Regulation." *Capital Markets Law Journal* 3, no. 4 (2008): pp. 425–57.

Black, Julia. "The Rise, Fall and Fate of Principles Based Regulation." LSE Law, Society and Economy Working Papers 17/2010, 2010. http://papers.ssrn.com/sol3/papers.cfm?abstract_id=1712862&download=yes.

Bonenfant-Jeanneney, Camille, and Fautrelle, Séverine. "La Révision de la Directive "Télévision sans Frontrières" : Une Adaptation du Cadre Réglementaire Européen aux Evolutions du Paysage Audiovisuel." In *Télévision sans Frontières: Une Adaptation du Cadre Réglementaire Européen aux Evolutions du Paysage Audiovisuel*. Strasbourg: European Audiovisual Observatory, 2008.

Bornemann, Roland. "Der Jugendmedienschutz-Staatsvertrag der Länder." *Neue Juristische Wochenschrift*, 2003, pp. 787–91.

Bornemann, Roland. "Der Sendeplan im Rundfunkrecht." *Zeitschrift für Urheber- und Medienrecht*, no. 11 (2013): pp. 845–50.

Bornemann, Roland. "Der 'Verbreitensbegriff' bei Pornografie in audiovisuellen Mediendiensten, Straferweiternd im Internet und strafverkürzend im Runfdunk?" *Multimedia und Recht*, 2012, pp. 157–61.

Bornemann, Roland. "Zur Rechtsnatur rundfunkrechtlicher Richtlinien." *Zeitschrift für Urheber- und Medienrecht*, 2012, pp. 89–92.

Bornemann, Roland. "Zur Telemedienordnung." *Recht der Jugend und des Bildungswesens* 2 (2013): pp. 123–29.

Böttcher, Kathrin, Jan Kabel, Alexander Scheuer, Roberto Mastroianni, Maja Cappello, and Dirk Buschle. "Article 3e (Principles and Standards for Audiovisual Commercial Communications)." In *European Media Law*, edited by Oliver Castendyk, Egbert Dommering, and Alexander Scheuer, pp. 889–903. The Netherlands: Kluwer Law International, 2008.

Boyon, Michel. *Quatres principes pour la télévision connectée*, 2011. http://www.csa.fr/content/download/20069/334608/file/HD_forum_discours_boyon.mp3.

Braman, Sandra. "Where Has Media Policy Gone? Defining the Field in the Twenty-First Century." *Communication Law and Policy* 9, no. 2 (2004): pp. 153–82.

Braml, Birgit, and Kristina Hopf. "Der neue Jugendmedienschutz-Staatsvertrag, Fort- oder Rückschritt für den Jugendmedienschutz?" *Zeitschrift für Urheber- und Medienrecht*, 2010, pp. 645–55.

Braml, Birgit, and Kristina Hopf. "Jugendschutzprogramme, Mehr Schutz für die Jugend oder mehr Sicherheit für den Anbieter?" *Zeitschrift für Urheber- und Medienrecht*, 2012, pp. 361–71.

Bréger, Sylvia. "La protection des mineurs sur Internet." *AJ Pénal* 3 (2009): pp. 112–15.

Breitschaft, Andreas. "Evaluating the Linear/non-Linear Divide – Are There Any Better Factors for the Future Regulation of Audiovisual Media Content?" *Entertainment Law Review* 20, no. 8 (2009): pp. 291–95.

Breyer, Stephan. *Regulation and Its Reform*. United States of America: Harvard University Press, 1982.

Brock, Marc Oliver, and Michael Schmittmann. "Telemedienrecht." In *Praxishandbuch Medien-, IT- und Urheberrecht*, edited by Rolf Schwartmann, Third edition., pp. 321–80. Heidelberg: C. F. Müller Verlag, 2014.

Brocker, Doris. "Privater Rundfunk." In *Praxishandbuch Medien-, IT- und Urheberrecht*, edited by Rolf Schwartmann, Third edition., pp. 119–39. Heidelberg: C. F. Müller Verlag, 2014.

Bröckling, Guido, Cornelia Margraf, and Björn Schreiber. "Internet Guide für Eltern, Tipps zur Medienerziehung in der Familie." Edited by FSM, FragFinn, and Kinderhilfswerk, 2015. https://images.dkhw.de/fileadmin/Redaktion/1_Unsere_Arbeit/1_Schwerpunkte/6_Medienkompetenz/6.2_Internet_Guide_fuer_Eltern/Internet_Guide_fuer_Eltern_Deutsches_Kinderhilfswerk.pdf?_ga=1.81945938.514713316.1449478955.

Brockmeyer, Dieter. *EuroReg 2011: From Connected TV to Coherent Media, A Conference by Germany's "Die Medienanstalten"and LPR Hessen, Documentation*. Schriftenreihe der Landesmedienanstalten 48. Berlin: Vistas, 2012.

Broumas, Antonios. "Governing Media through Technology. The Empowerment Perspective." In *Routledge Handbook of Media Law*, edited by Monroe Price, Stefaan Verhulst, and Libby Morgan, pp. 419–38. London and New York: Routledge, 2013.

Burri, Mira. "Controlling New Media (without the Law)." In *Routledge Handbook of Media Law*, pp. 327–42. London and New York: Routledge, 2013.

Burri-Nenova, Mira. "Cultural Diversity and the EC Audiovisual Media Services Directive," no. Working Paper No 2009/9 (2009).

Burri-Nenova, Mira. "The New Audiovisual Media Services Directive: Television without Frontiers, Television without Cultural Diversity." *Common Market Law Review* 14 (2007): pp. 1689–1725.

Cabrera Blázquez, Francisco. "On-Demand Services: Made in the Likeness of TV?" In *What Is an on-Demand Service?*, edited by Susanne Nikoltchev, pp. 7–27. IRIS Plus 4/2013. Strasbourg: European Audiovisual Observatory, 2013.

Cammaerts, Bart. "Power Dynamics in Multi-Stakeholder Policy Processes and Intra-Civil Society Networking." In *The Handbook of Global Media and Communication Policy*, edited by Robin Mansell, and Marc Raboy, pp. 131–46. West Sussex, United Kingdom: Wiley-Blackwell, 2011.

Campbell, Angela. "Self-Regulation and the Media." *Federal Communications Law Journal* 51, no. 3 (1999): pp. 711–71.

Candela Soriano, Mercedes, and Alexandre Defossez. "La liberté d'expression face à la morale et à la religion: analyse de la jurisprudence de la Cour Européenne des Droit de l'Homme." *Revue trimestrielle des droits de l'homme* 68 (2006): pp. 817–37.

Candilis, Takis, Philippe Levrier, Jérémie Manigne, Martin Rogard, and Marc Tessier. "La télévision connectée, Rapport au ministre de la culture et de la communication et au ministre chargé de l'industrie de l'énergie et de l'économie numérique," November 2011. http://www.culturecommunication.gouv.fr/content/download/20480/174705/version/1/file/Lien%20vers%20le%20rapport%20sur%20la%20t%C3%A9l%C3%A9vision%20connect%C3%A9e.pdf.

Carter, Stephen. "Address by Ofcom Chief Executive." presented at the Royal Television Society Cambridge Convention, Cambridge, September 19, 2003. http://media.ofcom.org.uk/speeches/2003/royal-television-society-cambridge-convention-friday-19-september-2003/.

Casarosa, Federica. "Children Protection Online: Uneasy Steps towards a Balance between Risks and Freedoms." *European Journal of Legal Studies*, 2010. http://www.ejls.eu/6/79UK.htm.

Castendyk, Oliver. "Article 3g AVMSD (Product Placement)." In *European Media Law*, edited by Oliver Castendyk, Egbert Dommering, and Alexander Scheuer, pp. 907–18. The Netherlands: Kluwer Law International, 2008.

Castendyk, Oliver. "Werbeintegration im TV-Programm – wann sind Themen Placements Schleichwerbung oder Sponsoring?" *Zeitschrift für Urheber- und Medienrecht*, 2005, pp. 857–65.

Castendyk, Oliver, and Lorna Woods. "Article 1 TWFD (Definitions)." In *European Media Law*, edited by Oliver Castendyk, Egbert Dommering, and Alexander Scheuer, pp. 267–336. The Netherlands: Kluwer Law International, 2008.

Chavannes, Remy, and Oliver Castendyk. "Article 1 AVMSD (Definitions)." In *European Media Law*, edited by Oliver Castendyk, Egbert Dommering, and Alexander Scheuer, pp. 799–846. The Netherlands: Kluwer Law International, 2008.

Chevallier, Jacques. "De la CNCL, au Conseil supérieur de l'audiovisuel." *L'actualité juridique: Droit administratif*, 1989, pp. 59–81.

Chevallier, Jacques. "Le nouveau statut de la liberté de communication." *L'actualité juridique: Droit administratif*, 1987, pp. 59–79.

Cole, Mark. "Das Zusammenwirken von Selbstkontrolle und hoheitlicher Kontrolle im Jugendmedienschutz." *Recht der Jugend und des Bildungswesens* 3 (2006): pp. 299–307.

Cole, Mark. "Der Dualismus von Selbstkontrolle und Aufsicht im Jugendmedienschutz, Zum Verhältnis von FSF und KJM im System der 'regulierten Selbstregulierung' - Eine Untersuchung aus Anlass des Konflikts um Schönheitsoperationen im Fernsehprogramm." *Zeitschrift für Urheber- und Medienrecht*, 2005, pp. 462–73.

Cole, Mark. "Europäische und globale Regulierungsansätze." In *Medien, Netz und Öffentlichkeit – Impulse für die digitale Gesellschaft*, edited by Jan Marc Eumann, Frauke Gerlach, and Tebea Rößner, pp. 395–405. Essen: Klartext, 2013.

Cole, Mark. "Jugendmedienschutz." In *Handbuch Medienrecht, Recht der elektronischen Massenmedien*, edited by Dieter Dörr, Johannes Kreile, and Mark Cole, Second edition., pp. 299–337. Frankfurt am Main: Verlag Recht und Wirtschaft, 2010.

Cole, Mark. "Kontrolle und Aufsicht im Jugendmedienschutz: Einrichtungen und Verfahren nach dem JMStV im Vergleich zum JuSchG, Eine Untersuchung der aktuellen Rechtslage im Blick auf den Novellierungsbedarf." Edited by KJM, 2016. http://www.kjm-online.de/fileadmin/Download_KJM/Service/Gutachten/KJM_Verhaeltnis_Selbstkontrolleinrichtungen_und_Anbieter_Gutachten_MDC_2015.pdf.

Cole, Mark, Gianna Iacino, Peter Matzneller, Jenny Metzdorf, and Sebastian Schweda. "Update on Recent Changes and Developments in Member States and Candidate Countries That Are Relevant for the Analysis of Independence and Efficient Functioning of Audiovisual Media Services Regulatory Bodies (SMART 2013/0083)," 2015. http://publications.europa.eu/en/publication-detail/-/publication/b6e4a837-8775-11e5-b8b7-01aa75ed71a1/language-en.

Cole, Mark. "Der Fußball auf der Liste und im Free-TV - noch immer ein Entscheidungsprivileg der Mitgliedstaaten." *Europäische Zeitschrift für Wirtschaftsrecht*, November 2011, pp. 425–28.

Cole, Mark. "Die (Massen-)Medien im Überblick." In *Handbuch Medienrecht, Recht der elektronischen Massenmedien*, edited by Dieter Dörr, Johannes Kreile, and Mark Cole, Second edition, pp. 5–8. Frankfurt am Main: Verlag Recht und Wirtschaft, 2010.

Cole, Mark. "Europäisches Medienrecht." In *Europäisches und Internationales Medienrecht*, edited by Udo Fink, Mark Cole, Tobias Keber, pp. 1–148. Heidelberg: C. F. Müller Verlag, 2008.

Cole, Mark. "Note d'observation, 'Roj TV' entre ordre public et principe du pays d'origine." *Revue du Droit des Technologies de l'Information* 47 (2012): pp. 50–61.

Cole, Mark. "The Country of Origin Principle - from State Sovereignty under Public International Law to Inclusion in the Audiovisual Media Services Directive of the European Union." In *Europäische Integration Und Globalisierung, Festschrift Zum 60-Jährigen Bestehen Des Europa-Instituts*, edited by Werner Meng, Georg Ress, and Torsten Stein, pp. 113–30. Schriften des Europa-Instituts der Universität des Saarlandes- Rechtswissenschaft. Baden-Baden: Nomos, 2011.

Cole, Mark. "The European Legal Framework for On-Demand Services: What Directive for Which Services?" In *The Regulation of on-Demand Audiovisual Services: Chaos or Coherence?*, edited by Susanne Nikoltchev, pp. 35–45. IRIS Special. Strasbourg: European Audiovisual Observatory, 2011.

Cole, Mark, and Florian Haus. "Dienstleistungsfreiheit brutto oder netto? Probleme der europäischen Sprachenvielfalt am Beispiel der EG-Fernsehrichtlinie." *Juristische Schulung*, 2001, pp. 435–40.

Crane, Thomas. "OFCOM - a New Order for Communications Regulation or a Bureaucratic Nightmare?" *Computer and Telecommunications Law Review* 9, no. 2 (2003): pp. 37–40.

Craufurd Smith, Rachael, Epp Lauk, Yolande Stolte, and Heikki Kuutti. "The Independence of Media Regulatory Authorities in Finland and the UK: An Assessment." In *The Independence of the Media and Its Regulatory Agencies, Shedding New Light on Formal and Actual Independence against the National Context*, edited by Wolfgang Schulz, Peggy Valcke, and Kristina Irion, pp. 289–332. Bristol, UK and Chicago, USA: Intellect, 2013.

Craufurd Smith, Rachel. "Liberalisation of Advertising & Product Placement Rules in the AVMSD: A Step Too Far?" *LSE Blog*, October 6, 2016. http://blogs.lse.ac.uk/mediapolicyproject/2016/10/06/liberalisation-of-advertising-product-placement-rules-in-the-avmsd-a-step-too-far/.

Craufurd Smith, Rachel. "From Heritage Conservation to European Identiy: Article 151 EC and the Multi-Faceted Nature of Community Cultural Policy." *European Law Review* 32, no. 1 (2007): pp. 48–69.

Cruz Villalón, Pedro. "Rights in Europe: The Crowded House, King's College Papers in European Law, No. 1," 2012. https://www.kcl.ac.uk/law/research/centres/european/research/CELWPEL012012FINAL.pdf.

Curtis, Polly. "Government Scraps 192 Quangos." *The Guardian*. October 14, 2010.

Cybion Srl and Stiftung Digitale Chancen. "Benchmarking of Parental Control Tools for the Online Protection of Children SIP-Bench II," 2011. https://ec.europa.eu/digital-agenda/en/news/benchmarking-study-parental-control-tools-latest-findings.

Cybion Srl and Stiftung Digitale Chancen. "Benchmarking of Parental Control Tools for the Online Protection of Children SIP-Bench II," 2013. http://sipbench.eu/phase7.cfm/secid.7.

de Bueger, Geneviève. "Comparative Document on Supervising VOD Services: Best Practices and Methodology." EPRA, December 20, 2013. http://www.epra.org/attachments/vilnius-plenary-session-1-supervising-vod-services-final-comparative-document.

de Cock Buning, Madeleine. "Towards a Future-Proof Framework for the Protection of Minors in European Audiovisual Media." *Utrecht Law Review* 10, no. 5 (2014): pp. 9–30.

De Cockborne, Jean-Éric, and Joly, Emmanuel. "Le placement de produit dans l'Union européenne." *Gazette du Palais*, no. 131 (2008).

Delzangles, Hubert. "Un vent d'impartialité souffle encore sur le droit de la régulation." *Actualité juridique Droit administratif* 18 (2014): pp. 1021–28.

Demeyer, Karel, Eva Lievens, and Jos Dumortier. "Blocking or Removing Illegal Content: Analysis from a Technical and Legal Perspective." *Policy & Internet* 4, no. 3–4 (2012): pp. 1–23.

Derieux, Emmanuel. "Réforme de l'audiovisuel. - À propos des lois du 5 mars 2009." *La Semaine Juridique Entreprise et Affaires* 12 (2009).

Dizon, Michael, Anthony. "Looking beyond the Linear/non-Linear Horizon: Content Regulation in the Converging Multilayered Contours of the European Audiovisual Media Landscape." *Entertainment Law Review* 21, no. 5 (2010): pp. 185–91.

Docquir, Pierre-Francois, Sebastian Müller, and Christian Gusy. "Does the Complexity of Institutional Structures in Federal States Influence the Independence of AMV Regulatory Authorities? A Review of the Cases of Germany and Belgium." In *The Independence of the Media and Its Regulatory Agencies, Shedding New Light on Formal and Actual Independence against the National Context*, edited by Wolfgang Schulz, Peggy Valcke, and Kristina Irion, pp. 249–83. Bristol, UK and Chicago, USA: Intellect, 2013.

Dommering, Egbert. "Article 2 TWFD (Country of Origin Principle/jurisdiction)." In *European Media Law*, edited by Oliver Castendyk, Egbert Dommering, and Alexander Scheuer, pp. 337–57. The Netherlands: Kluwer Law International, 2008.

Dommering, Egbert, and Remy Chavannes. "Article 3a AVMSD (Identification of Providers)." In *European Media Law*, edited by Oliver Castendyk, Egbert Dommering, and Alexander Scheuer, pp. 869–71. The Netherlands: Kluwer Law International, 2008.

Dommering, Egbert, Alexander Scheuer, and Thorsten Ader. "Article 3 AVMSD (Stricter Rules/Measures against Abuse/ Compliance/ Co- and Self-Regulation/ Relation to the E-Commerce Directie." In *European Media Law*, edited by Castendyk, Oliver, Dommering, Egbert, and Scheuer, Alexander, pp. 860–62, NaN-12. Kluwer Law International, 2008.

Döring, Martin, and Thomas Günter. "Jugendmedienschutz: Alterskontrollierte geschlossene Benutzergruppen im Internet gem. § 4 Abs. 2 Satz 2 JMStV." *Multimedia und Recht*, 2004, pp. 231–37.

Dörr, Dieter. "Grundsätze der Medienregulierung." In *Handbuch Medienrecht, Recht der elektronischen Massenmedien*, edited by Dieter Dörr, Johannes Kreile, and Mark Cole, Second edition., pp. 159–217. Frankfurt am Main: Verlag Recht und Wirtschaft, 2010.

Dörr, Dieter. "Das Nettoprinzip für die Unterbrechung von Spiel- und Fernsehfilmen durch Werbung und das europäische Medienrecht." *Zeitschrift für Urheber- und Medienrecht* 38, no. 6 (1994): pp. 342–51.

Doyle, Gillian, and Douglas Vick. "The Communications Act 2003: A New Regulatory Framework in the UK." *Convergence: The International Journal of Research into New Media Technologies* 11, no. 3 (2005): pp. 75–94.

Dreyer, Stephan, Daniel Hajok, Uwe Hasebrink, and Claudia Lampert. "Jugendschutzsoftware im Elternhaus: Kenntnisse, Erwartungen und Nutzung, Arbeitspapier Nr. 23." Edited by Hans Bredow Institut, January 2012. http://www.hans-bredow-institut.de/webfm_send/639.

Dyson, Kenneth, and Peter Humphreys. "Deregulating Broadcasting: The West European Experience." *European Journal of Political Research* 17 (1989): pp. 137–54.

Edwards, Lilian. "Pornography, Censorship and the Internet." In *Law and the Internet*, edited by Lilian Edwards, and Charlotte Waelde, Third edition., pp. 623–69. Oxford and Portland, Oregon: Hart Publishing, 2009.

Enser, John. "After the Vote: What Will Brexit Mean for Film and TV Businesses Operating in the UK?" *LSE Blog*, July 1, 2016. http://blogs.lse.ac.uk/mediapolicyproject/2016/07/01/after-the-vote-what-will-brexit-mean-for-film-and-tv-businesses-operating-in-the-uk/.

Erdal, Ivar, John. "Repurposing of Content in Multi-Platform News Production, Towards a Typology of Cross-Media Journalism." *Journalism Practice* 3, no. 2 (2009): pp. 178–95.

Erdemir, Murad. "§ 4 JMStV Unzulässige Angebote." In *Recht der elektronischen Medien*, edited by Gerald Spindler and Fabian Schuster, Third edition. C.H. Beck, 2015.

Erdemir, Murad. "§ 5 JMStV Entwicklungsbeeinträchtigende Angebote." In *Recht der elektronischen Medien*, edited by Gerald Spindler and Fabian Schuster, Third edition. C.H. Beck, 2015.

Erdemir, Murad. "Die Kommission für Jugendmedienschutz der Landesmedienanstalten - Ein zentrales Aufsichtsorgan für Rundfunk und Telemedien." *Recht der Jugend und des Bildungswesens* 3 (2006): pp. 285–98.

Essential Research. "On-Demand Services: Understanding Consumer Choices, A Research Report for Ofcom," October 2012. http://stakeholders.ofcom.org.uk/binaries/broadcast/tv-ops/vod/Research_Report.pdf.

Essential Research. "On-Demand Services: Understanding Consumer Choices. A Research Report for Ofcom," October 2012. http://stakeholders.ofcom.org.uk/binaries/broadcast/tv-ops/vod/Research_Report.pdf.

Essential Research. "The Regulation of Video-on-Demand: Consumer Views on What Makes Audiovisual services 'TV-like' - a Qualitative Research Report," December 2009. http://stakeholders.ofcom.org.uk/binaries/research/tv-research/vod.pdf.

Essential Research. "The Regulation of Video-on-Demand: Consumer Views on What Makes Audiovisual services 'TV-Like' - a Qualitative Research Report," December 2009. http://stakeholders.ofcom.org.uk/binaries/research/tv-research/vod.pdf.

European Audiovisual Observatory, ed. "Annex - On-Demand Audiovisual Markets in the European Union, Final Report," 2014. https://ec.europa.eu/digital-agenda/en/news/demand-audiovisual-markets-european-union-smart-20120028.

European Audiovisual Observatory, ed. "On-Demand Audiovisual Markets in the European Union, Final Report," 2014. https://ec.europa.eu/digital-agenda/en/news/demand-audiovisual-markets-european-union-smart-20120028.

Faßbender, Kurt. "Zu Inhalt und Grenzen des rundfunkrechtlichen Sendestaatsprinzips." *Archiv für Presserecht* 6 (2006): pp. 505–12.

Fathaigh, Ronan, and Dirk Voorhoof. "The European Court of Human Rights, Media Freedom and Democracy." In *Routledge Handbook of Media Law*, edited by Monroe Price, Stefaan Verhulst, and Libby Morgan, pp. 107–24. London and New York: Routledge, 2013.

Fink, Udo. "Medienfreiheiten im Rahmen des Europarates." In *Europäisches und Internationales Medienrecht*, edited by Fink, Udo, Cole, Mark, and Keber, Tobias, pp. 161–206. Heidelberg: C. F. Müller Verlag, 2008.

Fink, Udo, Tobias Keber, and Przemyslaw Roguski. "Die Zukunft der Medienregulierung im Europarat." *Zeitschrift für Urheber- und Medienrecht*, 2011, pp. 292–300.

Flourens, Cordelia. "L'innovation au soutien de la création selon Google." *Juris art etc. 2*, May 2013, pp. 31–35.

Foster, Robin, and Tom Broughton. "PSB Prominence in a Converged Media World," December 21, 2012. downloads.bbc.co.uk/aboutthebbc/insidethebbc/howwework/reports/pdf/bbc_psb_prominence.pdf.

Franceschini, Laurence. "Les points clés de la loi du 15 novembre 2013 'relative à l'indépendance de l'audiovisuel public.'" *Revue Lamy de Droit de l'Immatériel*, no. 101 (2014): pp. 38–40.

Franceschini, Laurence. "Pornographie et télévision." *Légipresse* 197 (2002): pp. 163–67.

Frank, Sabine. "Selbstkontrolle im Internet." In *Positionen zum Jugendmedienschutz in Deutschland, Eine Textsammlung*, pp. 71–89. KJM Schriftenreihe 1. Berlin: Vistas, 2009.

Frauenhofer-Institut für Intelligente Analyse- und Informationssysteme (IAIS), ed. "Studie zum technischen Jugendmedienschutz, Möglichkeiten und Grenzen von Verfahren zur Detektion jugendschutzrelevanter Web-Inhalte," 2012. http://www.iais.fraunhofer.de/uploads/media/Fraunhofer_Jugendmedienschutz_2013-02-25_01.pdf.

Füg, Oliver. "Content Ratings Harmonization and the Protection of Minors in the European Information Society." In *The European Union and the Culture Industries, Regulation and the Public Interest*, edited by Ward, David, pp. 165–86. Hampshire: Ashgate, 2008.

Füg, Oliver. "Save the Children: The Protection of Minors in the Information Society and the Audiovisual Media Services Directive." *Journal of Consumer Policy* 31 (2008): pp. 45–61.

Genevois, Bruno. "Le Conseil constitutionnel et la définition des pouvoirs du Conseil supérieur de l'audiovisuel." *Revue française de droit administratif* 5, no. 2 (1989): pp. 215–34.

Gerkrath, Jörg. "En tant que clé de voûte du système de protection des droits fondamentaux de l'Union européenne la Charte demande une application large et décentralisée," 2012.

Gerkrath, Jörg. "L'arrêt du Bundesverfassungsgericht du 22 mars 1995 sur la directive 'télévision sans frontières', Les difficultés de la répartition des compétences entre trois niveaux de législation." *Revue trimetrielle de droit européen* 31, no. 3 (1995): pp. 539–59.

Gersdorf, Hubertus. "Begrenzte Aufsicht und einfache Aufsichtsstrukturen." In *Neuordnung des Medienrechts, Neuer rechtlicher Rahmen für eine konvergente Technik?*, edited by Alexander Roßnagel, pp. 107–14. Schriftenreihe des Instituts für Europäischens Medienrecht (EMR) 30. Baden-Baden: Nomos, 2005.

Gibbons, Thomas. "'Club Government' and Independence in Media Regulation." In *Routledge Handbook of Media Law*, edited by Monroe E. Price, Stefaan Verhulst, and Libby Morgan, pp. 47–64. London and New York: Routledge, 2013.

Gierschmann, Sibylle. "Was ist eine Geschlossene Benutzergruppe i.S.v. § 4 Abs. 2 Satz 2 JMStV?" In *Jugendmedienschutz im Informationszeitalter*, edited by Nikolaus Bosch and Stefan Leible, pp. 121–34. Bayreuther Studien zum Wirtschafts- und Medienrecht 6. Sipplingen: Jenaer Wissenschaftliche Verlagsgesellschaft, 2012.

Girieud, Sophie, and Gilles Fontaine. "Etude sur les modèles économiques des services de médias audiovisuels à la demande actifs sur le marché français," June 2011. http://www.csa.fr/content/download/18055/322463/file/etude_csa_smad_juillet_20 11a.pdf.

Gitter, Rotraud. "Telemediengesetz, Anwendungsbereich." In *Beck'scher Kommentar zum Recht der Telemediendienste*, edited by Alexander Roßnagel, pp. 36–73. München: C. H. Beck, 2013.

Gitter, Rotraud. "Telemediengesetz, Begriffsbestimmungen." In *Beck'scher Kommentar zum Recht der Telemediendienste*, edited by Alexander Roßnagel, pp. 36–73. München: C. H. Beck, 2013.

Glockzin, Kai. "Product Placement im Fernsehen, Abschied vom strikten Trennungsgebot zwischen redaktionellem Inhalt und Werbung." *Multimedia und Recht*, 2010, pp. 161–66.

Godefroid, Patrick, Tobias Keber, Boris Kühnle, and Oliver Zöllner. "Smart TV - ein interdisziplinärer Überblick." *MedienWirtschaft* 3 (2013): pp. 2–12.

Götz, Frank. "Rundfunkorganisationsrecht." In *Medienrecht, Lexikon für Praxis und Wissenschaft*, edited by Peter Schiwy, Walter Schütz, and Dieter Dörr, Fourth edition., pp. 498–510. Köln: Carl Heymanns Verlag, 2010.

Gounalakis, Georgios. "Funktionsauftrag und anstaltliches Selbstverwaltungsrecht." *Archiv für Presserecht, Zeitschrift für Medien- und Kommunikationsrecht* 5 (2003): pp. 395–405.

Gounalakis, Georgis, and Christoph Wege. "Product Placement und Schleichwerbungsverbot - Widersprüche im neuen Fernsehrichtlinien-Entwurf." *Kommunikation und Recht*, no. 3 (2006): pp. 97–101.

Grainger, Gareth. "Broadcasting, Co-Regulation and the Public Good, 1999 Spry Memorial Lecture," October 28, 1999. http://citeseerx.ist.psu.edu/viewdoc/downloa d ;jsessionid=BE2305C10940D3243FF6AB6AA2627117? doi=10.1.1.198.1521&rep=rep1&type=pdf.

Grece, Christian. “The European Online Advertising Market, A Short Introduction to the European Online Display Advertising Ecosystem.” In *New Forms of Commercial Communications in a Converged Audiovisual Sector*, edited by Susanne Nikoltchev, pp. 29–38. IRIS Special. Strasbourg: European Audiovisual Observatory, 2014.

Gröpl, Christoph. “Die Reform der Medienkontrolle durch den Zehnten Rundfunkänderungsstaatsvertrag, Anforderungen an eine vertragsgemäße Umsetzung durch die Landesmedienanstalten.” *Zeitschrift für Urheber- und Medienrecht*, 2009, pp. 21–29.

Groß, Thomas. “Selbstregulierung im medienrechtlichen Jugendschutz am Beispiel der Freiwilligen Selbstkontrolle Fernsehen.” *Neue Zeitschrift für Verwaltungsrecht*, 2004, pp. 1393–99.

Grünwald, Andreas. “§ 36 RStV Zuständigkeiten, Aufgaben.” In *Recht der elektronischen Medien*, edited by Gerald Spindler and Fabian Schuster, Third edition. München: C. H. Beck, 2015.

Gunningham, Neil, and Joseph Rees. “Industry Self-Regulation: An Institutional Perspective.” *Law & Policy* 19, no. 4 (1997): pp. 363–414.

Gunningham, Neil, and Sinclair, Darren. “Designing Smart Regulation.” In *Smart Regulation: Designing Environmental Policy*, edited by Neil Gunningham, and Peter Grabosky. Oxford: Clarendon Press, Oxford University Press, 1998.

Gunningham, Neil, and Darren Sinclair. “Integrative Regulation: A Principle-Based Approach to Environmental Policy.” *Law & Social Inquiry*, 1999, pp. 853–96.

Günter, Thomas, and Friedemann Schindler. “Technische Möglichkeiten des Jugendschutzes im Internet.” *Recht der Jugend und des Bildungswesens*, no. 3 (2006): pp. 341–50.

Hain, Karl-Eberhard. “Medienmarkt im Wandel: Technische Konvergenz und Anbieterkonkurrenz als Herausforderung an Verfassungsrecht und Regulierung.” *Archiv für Presserecht, Zeitschrift für Medien- und Kommunikationsrecht* 4 (2012): pp. 313–28.

Hajok, Daniel, and Gregor Schwarz. “Technischer Jugendmedienschutz bei digitalen Medien, Ein Überblick zu anbieter- und nutzerseitigen Schutzmöglichkeiten.” *JMS-Report* 4 (2014): pp. 2–7.

Hans Bredow Institut, ed. “Analyse des Jugendmedienschutzsystems, Jugendschutzgesetz und Jugendmedienschutz-Staatsvertrag, Endbericht,” October 2007. http://www.hans-bredow-institut.de/webfm_send/104.

Hans Bredow Institut, and Institut für Europäisches Medienrecht. “Study on Co-Regulation Measures in the Media Sector, Study for the European Commission.” Hamburg, Saarbrücken, 2006. http://ec.europa.eu/avpolicy/docs/library/studies/coregul/final_rep_en.pdf.

Hans Bredow Institut für Medienforschung, Interdisciplinary Centre for Law & ICT (ICRI), Katholieke Universiteit Leuven, Center for Media and Communication Studies (CMCS), Central European University, and Cullen International. "INDIREG, Indicators for Independence and Efficient Functioning of Audiovisual Media Services Regulatory Bodies for the Purpose of Enforcing the Rules in the AVMS Directive, Study Conducted on Behalf of the European Commission, Final Report," February 2011. http://ec.europa.eu/archives/information_society/avpolicy/docs/library/studies/regulators/final_report.pdf.

Hans Bredow Institut, and Institut für Europäisches Medienrecht, eds. "Final Report, Study on Co-Regulation Measures in the Media Sector, Study for the European Commission," June 2006. http://ec.europa.eu/avpolicy/docs/library/studies/coregul/final_rep_en.pdf.

Hans Bredow Institut, and Institute for Information Law (IViR), eds. "Study on the Future of Audiovisual Regulation, Final Report of the Hermes Project," 2015. http://www.hans-bredow-institut.de/webfm_send/1110 and http://www.ivir.nl/publicaties/download/1643.

Haquet, Christophe. *JurisClasseur Communication,Publicité audiovisuelle*. JurisClasseur, 2011.

Haquet, Christophe. "Loi n° 2009-258 du 5 mars 2009 relative à la communication audiovisuelle et au nouveau service public de la télévision." *Communication Commerce électronique* 4 (2009).

Harcourt, Alison. "How Brexit Might Affect EU Audio-Visual Media Services Policy-Making." *LSE Blog*, May 24, 2016. http://blogs.lse.ac.uk/mediapolicyproject/2016/05/24/how-brexit-might-affect-eu-audio-visual-media-services-policy-making/.

Harcourt, Alison. "Institution-Driven Competition: The Regulation of Cross-Border Broadcasting in the EU." *Journal of Public Policy* 27, no. 3 (2007): pp. 293–317.

Harcourt, Alison. *The European Union and the Regulation of Media Markets*. Manchester and New York: Manchester University Press, 2005.

Hartstein, Reinhard, Wolf-Dieter Ring, Johannes Kreile, Dieter Dörr, Rupert Stettner, Mark Cole, and Eva Wagner. "§ 2 RStV Begriffsbestimmungen." In *Rundfunkstaatsvertrag, Kommentar*, Looseleaf commenatry. Köln: Rehm, n.d.

Hartstein, Reinhard, Wolf-Dieter Ring, Johannes Kreile, Dieter Dörr, Rupert Stettner, Mark Cole, and Eva Wagner. "§ 4 JMStV Unzulässige Angebote." In *Rundfunkstaatsvertrag, Kommentar*, Looseleaf commenatry. Köln: Rehm, n.d.

Hartstein, Reinhard, Wolf-Dieter Ring, Johannes Kreile, Dieter Dörr, Rupert Stettner, Mark Cole, and Eva Wagner. "§ 5 JMStV Entwicklungsbeeinträchtigende Angebote." In *Rundfunkstaatsvertrag, Kommentar*, Looseleaf commenatry. Köln: Rehm, n.d.

Hartstein, Reinhard, Wolf-Dieter Ring, Johannes Kreile, Dieter Dörr, Rupert Stettner, Mark Cole, and Eva Wagner. "§ 7 JMStV Jugendschutzbeauftragte." In *Jugendmedienschutz-Staatsvertrag, RStV Kommentar*, Looseleaf commenatry. Köln: Rehm, n.d.

Hartstein, Reinhard, Wolf-Dieter Ring, Johannes Kreile, Dieter Dörr, Rupert Stettner, Mark Cole, and Eva Wagner. "§ 11 JMStV Jugendschutzprogramme." In *Jugendmedienschutz-Staatsvertrag, RStV Kommentar*, Looseleaf commenatry. Köln: Rehm, n.d.

Hartstein, Reinhard, Wolf-Dieter Ring, Johannes Kreile, Dieter Dörr, Rupert Stettner, Mark Cole, and Eva Wagner. "§ 11d Telemedien." In *Rundfunkstaatsvertrag, Kommentar*, Looseleaf commenatry. Köln: Rehm, n.d.

Hartstein, Reinhard, Wolf-Dieter Ring, Johannes Kreile, Dieter Dörr, Rupert Stettner, Mark Cole, and Eva Wagner. "§ 11f Telemedienkonzepte." In *Rundfunkstaatsvertrag, Kommentar*, Looseleaf commenatry. Köln: Rehm, n.d.

Hartstein, Reinhard, Wolf-Dieter Ring, Johannes Kreile, Dieter Dörr, Rupert Stettner, Mark Cole, and Eva Wagner. "§ 36 RStV Zuständigkeiten, Aufgaben." In *Rundfunkstaatsvertrag, Kommentar*, Looseleaf commenatry. Köln: Rehm, n.d.

Hartstein, Reinhard, Wolf-Dieter Ring, Johannes Kreile, Dieter Dörr, Rupert Stettner, Mark Cole, and Eva Wagner. "§ 40 Finanzierung besonderer Aufgaben." In *Rundfunkstaatsvertrag, Kommentar*, Looseleaf commenatry. Köln: Rehm, n.d.

Hartstein, Reinhard, Wolf-Dieter Ring, Johannes Kreile, Dieter Dörr, Rupert Stettner, Mark Cole, and Eva Wagner. "§ 54 RStV Allgemeine Bestimmungen." In *Rundfunkstaatsvertrag, Kommentar*, Looseleaf commenatry. Köln: Rehm, n.d.

Hartstein, Reinhard, Wolf-Dieter Ring, Johannes Kreile, Rupert Stettner, Mark Cole, Eva Wagner, and Dieter Dörr. "§ 20 RStV Zulassung." In *Jugendmedienschutz-Staatsvertrag, RStV Kommentar*, Looseleaf commenatry. Köln: Rehm, n.d.

Hartstein, Reinhard, Wolf-Dieter Ring, Johannes Kreile, Rupert Stettner, Mark Cole, Eva Wagner, and Dieter Dörr. "Entstehungsgeschichte." In *Rundfunkstaatsvertrag, Kommentar*, Loose-Leaf commentary. Köln: Rehm, n.d.

Hartstein, Reinhard, Wolf-Dieter Ring, Johannes Kreile, Rupert Stettner, Mark Cole, Eva Wagner, and Dieter Dörr. "Entstehungsgeschichte - JMStV." In *Rundfunkstaatsvertrag, Kommentar*, Loose-Leaf commentary. Köln: Rehm, n.d.

Hartstein, Reinhard, Wolf-Dieter Ring, Johannes Kreile, Rupert Stettner, Mark Cole, Eva Wagner, and Dieter Dörr. "Rechtsgrundlagen des Rundfunks." In *Rundfunkstaatsvertrag, Kommentar*, Loose-Leaf commentary. Köln: Rehm, n.d.

Hasebrink, Uwe. "Giving the Audience a Voice: The Role of Research in Making Media Regulation More Responsive to the Needs of the Audience." *Journal of Information Policy* 1 (2011): pp. 321–36.

Hasebrink, Uwe, Hermann-Dieter Schröder, and Gerlinde Schumacher. "Kinder- und Jugendmedienschutz aus der Sicht der Eltern." *Media Perspektiven*, no. 1 (2012): pp. 18–30.

Hege, Hans. "Landesmediengesetze." In *Medienrecht, Lexikon für Praxis und Wissenschaft*, edited by Peter Schiwy, Walter Schütz, and Dieter Dörr, Fifth edition., pp. 328–38. Köln: Carl Heymanns Verlag, 2010.

Hege, Hans, and Andreas Hamann, eds. "Wie smart ist die Konvergenz? Markt und Nutzung von Connected TV." Die Medienanstalten, 2014. http://www.die-medienanstalten.de/fileadmin/Download/Publikationen/Studie_ConnectedTV.pdf.

Helberger, Natali. "From Eyeball to Creator: Toying with Audience Empowerment in the Audiovisual Media Service Directive." *Entertainment Law Review* 6 (2008): pp. 128–37.

Helberger, Natali, Katharin Kleinen-von Königslöw, and Rob Van der Noll. "Regulating the New Information Intermediaries as Gatekeepers of Information Diversity." *Info* 17, no. 6 (2015): pp. 50–71.

Hellemans, Lisbeth, Eva Lievens, and Peggy Valcke. "Playing Hide-and-Seek? A Legal Perspective on the Complex Distinction between Commercial and Editorial Content in Hybrid Advertising Formats." *The Journal of Policy, Regulation and Strategy for Telecommunications, Information and Media* 17, no. 6 (2015): pp. 19–34.

Herold, Anna. "Country of Origin Principle in the EU Market for Audiovisual Media Services: Consumer's Friend or Foe?" *Journal of Consumer Policy* 31, no. 1 (2008): pp. 5–24.

Hertel, Felix. "§ 4 JMStV Unzulässige Angebote." In *Beck'scher Kommentar zum Rundfunkrecht*, edited by Werner Hahn and Thomas Vesting, Third edition. München: C. H. Beck, 2012.

Hertel, Felix. "§ 5 JMStV Entwicklungsbeeinträchtigende Angebote." In *Beck'scher Kommentar zum Rundfunkrecht*, edited by Werner Hahn and Thomas Vesting, Third edition. München: C. H. Beck, 2012.

Hess, Thomas, and Christian Matt. "Gatekeeper in der digitalen Medienwelt." *MedienWirtschaft* 3 (2012): pp. 48–51.

Hitz, Martin. "'Vice' liebt das Wilde und Waghalsige." *Neue Zürcher Zeitung*. June 24, 2014, sec. Feuilleton. http://www.nzz.ch/feuilleton/medien/vice-liebt-das-wilde-und-waghalsige-1.18328580.

Hoeren, Thomas. "Das Telemediengesetz." *Neue Juristische Wochenschrift*, 2007, pp. 801–6.

Hofmann, Herwig. "General Principles of EU Law and EU Administrative Law." In *European Union Law*, edited by Catherine Barnard and Steeve Peers, pp. 196–225. Oxford: Oxford University Press, 2014.

Hofmann, Herwig, and Bucura Mihaescu. "The Relation between the Charter's Fundamental Rights and the Unwritten General Principles of Law: Good Administration as the Test-Case." *European Constitutional Law Review* 9, no. 1 (2013): pp. 73–101.

Holtmann, Frank. *Zur rechtlichen Unterscheidung von Rundfunk und Telemedien bei Hybrid-TV, Unter besonderer Berücksichtigung der Werbe- und Jugendschutzregelungen des RStV und JMStV*. Vol. 41. Schriften zum Medienrecht. Hamburg: Verlag Dr. Kovac, 2015.

Holzgraefe, Moritz. *Werbeintegration in Fernsehsendungen und Videospielen, Product Placement und verwandte Formen im Spiegel des Medien- und Wettbewerbsrechts*. Edited by Wolfgang Hoffmann-Riem. Materialien zur interdisziplinären Medienforschung 64. Baden-Baden: Nomos, 2010.

Holznagel, Bernd. “RStV § 2 Begriffsbestimmungen.” In *Recht der elektronischen Medien*, edited by Gerald Spindler and Fabian Schuster, Third edition. München: C. H. Beck, 2015.

Holznagel, Bernd. “Grünbuch Konvergenz der Medien 2013, Verpasste Chance oder gangbarer Weg aus dem Globalisierungsdilemma?” *Multimedia und Recht*, 2014, pp. 18–24.

Holznagel, Bernd, and Daniel Stenner. “Die Zulässigkeit neuer Werbeformen, Von Splitscreentechnik zu den neuen interaktiven Werbestrategien im Fernsehen.” *Zeitschrift für Urheber- und Medienrecht*, 2004, pp. 617–26.

Hopf, Kristina. “Das Berichterstattungsprivileg des § 5 Absatz 6 JMStV Zeitgeschichtliche bzw. historische Dokumentationen – mit oder ohne fiktionale Elemente – haben die Jugendschutzvorschrift des § 5 Absatz 1 JMStV stets zu beachten.” *Zeitschrift für Urheber- und Medienrecht*, 2009, pp. 191–99.

Hopf, Kristina. “Der Jugendmedienschutz-Staatsvertrag. Die Novelle ist tot, es lebe die Novelle - die umstrittenen Regelungen auf einen Blick.” *Kommunikation und Recht* 1 (2011): pp. 6–11.

Hopf, Kristina. “Rechtliche Grundlagen des Jugendmedienschutz-Staatsvertrags und die Verantwortlichkeit von Chatbetreibern.” *Zeitschrift für Urheber- und Medienrecht*, 2008, pp. 207–16.

Hopf, Kristina, and Birgit Braml. “Das Verhältnis der KJM zur FSF anhand einer kritischen Würdigung der Entscheidung des VG Berlin vom 6.7.2006.” *Zeitschrift für Urheber- und Medienrecht*, 2007, pp. 23–30.

Hörnle, Julia. “Country of Origin Regulation in Cross Border Media: One Step beyond the Freedom to Provide Services?” *International & Comparative Law Quarterly* 54, no. 1 (2005): pp. 89–126.

Horten, Monica. “Content ‘Responsibility’: The Looming Cloud of Uncertainty for Internet Intermediaries.” Edited by Center for Democracy & Technology, September 2016. https://cdt.org/files/2016/09/2016-09-02-Content-Responsibility-FN1-w-pgenbs.pdf.

Horten, Monica. “Liability and Responsibility: New Challenges for Internet Intermediaries,” October 20, 2016. http://blogs.lse.ac.uk/mediapolicyproject/2016/10/20/liability-and-responsibility-new-challenges-for-internet-intermediaries/.

Hugenholtz, Bernt. “Is Harmonization a Good Thing? The Case of the Copyright Acquis.” In *The Europeanization of Intellectual Property Law, Towards a European Legal Methodology*, edited by Ohly, Ansgar and Pila, Justine, pp. 57–73. Oxford: Oxford University Press, 2013.

Humphreys, Peter. “The Principle Axes of the European Union’s Audiovisual Policy.” In *Communication and Cultural Policies in Europe*, edited by Alonso Moragas i Spa, pp. 151–82. Barcelona: Generalitat de Catalunya: Collecio Lexicon, 2008.

Ibrus, Indrek, and Ulrike Rohn. “Sharing Killed the AVMSD Star: The Impossibility of European Audiovisual Media Regulation in the Era of the Sharing Economy.” *Internet Policy Review* 5, no. 2 (2016): pp. 1–16.

Ipsos MORI. “Protecting Audiences in a Converged World, Deliberative Research Report of 25.1.2012,” 2012. http://stakeholders.ofcom.org.uk/binaries/research/tv-research/946687/Protecting-audiences.pdf.

Irion, Kristina, and Roxana Radu. “Delegation to Independent Regulatory Authorities in the Media Sector: A Paradigm Shift through the Lens of Regulatory Theory.” In *The Independence of the Media and Its Regulatory Agencies, Shedding New Light on Formal and Actual Independence against the National Context*, edited by Wolfgang Schulz, Peggy Valcke, and Kristina Irion, pp. 15–54. Bristol, UK and Chicago, USA: Intellect, 2013.

Just, Natascha, and Michael Latzer. “Self- and Co-Regulation in the Mediamatics Sector: European Community (EC) Strategies and Contributions towards a Transformed Statehood.” *Knowledge, Technology & Policy* 17, no. 2 (2004): pp. 38–62.

Jütte, Bernd, Justin. “A New Era in European Intellectual Property Law, European Judiciaries for Intellectual Property - Is Copyright Next?” *Revista Română de Drept* 4 (2015): pp. 64–79.

Kaitatzi-Whitlock, Sophia. “Changing Media Ontology and the Polity.” In *Nouveaux Écrans, Nouvelle Régulation?*, edited by Pierre-Francois Docquir and Muriel Hanot, pp. 25–54. Brussels: Larcier, 2013.

Kamina, Pascal. *JurisClasseur Propriété littéraire et artistique, Cadre administratif, Communication audiovisuelle*. JurisClasseur, 2014.

Kamina, Pascal. “Promouvoir les œuvres européennes dans les services à la demande, Incitations à l’action de la part des législateurs, des régulateurs et de l’industrie.” In *A vos marques, prêts... partez? La Directive Services de médias audiovisuels*, pp. 77–84. IRIS Special. Strasbourg: European Audiovisual Observatory, 2009.

Kanengieser, Arthur. “Après Netflix, Sensibilité des obligations de production de la télévision à la pénétration de la SVOD.” Chaire Paris Tech d’Economie des Médias et des Marques, September 1, 2014. http://www.cerna.mines-paristech.fr/images/stories/media/apres_netflix.pdf.

Kantar Media. “Protecting Audiences in an Online World, Deliberative Research Report,” April 12, 2014. http://stakeholders.ofcom.org.uk/market-data-research/other/tv-research/protecting-audiences-online-world/.

Katsirea, Irini. “Electronic Press: ‘Press-Like’ or ‘Television-Like’?” *International Journal of Law and Information Technology*, 2015, pp. 1–23.

Katsirea, Irini. “Why the European Broadcasting Quota Should Be Abolished.” *European Law Review* 28, no. 2 (2003): pp. 190–209.

Katzenbach, Christian. “Media Governance and Technology. From ‘code Is Law’ to Governance Constellations.” In *Routledge Handbook of Media Law*, edited by Monroe Price, Stefaan Verhulst, and Libby Morgan, pp. 399–418. London and New York: Routledge, 2013.

Kaumanns, Ralf. “Der Smart TV-Markt: Akteure, Strategien, Geschäftsmodelle, in: Die Medienanstalten (Hrsg.), Wie smart ist die Konvergenz? Markt und Nutzung von Connected TV.” Edited by Hans Hege and Andreas Hamann. Die Medienanstalten, 2014.

Keber, Tobias. "Internet- und Telemedienrecht." In *Handbuch Medienrecht, Recht der elektronischen Massenmedien*, edited by Dieter Dörr, Johannes Kreile, and Mark Cole, Second edition., pp. 493–542. Frankfurt am Main: Verlag Recht und Wirtschaft, 2010.

Kempermann, Philip. *Content-Regulierung in konvergierenden Medien.* Vol. 1. Schriftenreihe der Kölner Forschungsstelle für Medienrecht. Frankfurt am Main: Peter Lang, 2010.

Khan, Daniel-Erasmus, and Dominik Eisenhut. "Dienstleistungen." In *Europäisches Unionsrecht*, edited by Christoph Vedder and Wolff Heintschell von Heinegg, pp. 389–405. Baden-Baden: Nomos, 2012.

Kingsford Smith, Dimity. "What Is Regulation? A Reply to Julia Black." *Australian Journal of Legal Philosophy* 27 (2002): pp. 37–46.

Kitz, Volker. "Das neue Recht der elektronischen Medien in Deutschland- sein Charme, seine Fallstricke." *Zeitschrift für Europarechtliche Studien*, 2007, pp. 368–76.

Kluth, Winfried, and Wolfgang Schulz. "Konvergenz und regulatorische Folgen. Gutachten im Auftrag der Rundfunkkommission der Länder, Arbeitspapier Nr. 30." Hans Bredow Institut, 2014. http://www.hans-bredow-institut.de/webfm_send/1049.

Knöfel, Oliver. "Der Rechtsanwalt als Jugendschutzbeauftragter für Telemedien." *Multimedia und Recht*, 2005, pp. 816–20.

Kogler, Michael. "Fernsehähnliches TV On-Demand, Was ist (k)ein 'Audiovisueller Mediendienst auf Abruf'?" *Medien und Recht* 4 (2011): pp. 229–37.

Kogler, Michael, Matthias Traimer, and Michael Truppe. *Österreichische Rundfunkgesetze, Recht der audiovisuellen Mediendienste und des Hörfunks*. Third edition. Wien: Verlag Medien & Recht, 2011.

Köhne, Michael. "Jugendmedienschutz durch Alterskontrollen im Internet." *Neue Juristische Wochenschrift*, 2005, pp. 794–95.

Kramer, Thorsten. *Das sekundärrechtliche Herkunftslandprinzip als Regelungstechnik des Binnenmarktes*. Berlin: Freie Universität Berlin, 2006. http://www.diss.fu-berlin.de/diss/servlets/MCRFileNodeServlet/FUDISS_derivate_000000002712/?hosts=.

Kreile, Johannes. "Telemedien." In *Medienrecht, Lexikon für Praxis und Wissenschaft*, edited by Peter Schiwy, Walter Schütz, and Dieter Dörr, Fifth edition., pp. 617–26. Köln: Carl Heymanns Verlag, 2010.

Krenc, Frédéric. "La liberté d'expression vaut pour les propos qui 'heurtent, choquent ou inquiètent'. Mais encore?" *Revue trimestrielle des droits de l'homme* 106 (2016): pp. 311–50.

Kriegel, Blandine. "La violence à la télévision. Rapport à M. Jean-Jacques Aillagon, Ministre de la Culture et de la Communication.," 2002.

Kühn, Michael. "§ 10, 11 RFinStV." In *Beck'scher Kommentar zum Rundfunkrecht*, edited by Werner Hahn and Thomas Vesting, Third edition. München: C. H. Beck, 2012.

Kunisch, Kasper. "Verfassungswidrige Telemedienaufsicht durch Regierungsstellen, Aufsicht über Internetdienste im Schutzbereich der Rundfunkfreiheit." *Multimedia und Recht*, 2011, pp. 796–99.

Lange, André. "Vers une révision a minima de la Directive SMA." academia.edu, 2016. https://www.academia.edu/27935361/VERS_UNE_REVISION_A_MINIMA_DE_LA_DIRECTIVE_SMA.

Langenfeld, Christine. "Die Neuordnung des Jugendschutzes im Internet." *Multimedia und Recht*, 2003, pp. 303–10.

Latzer, Michael, Natascha Just, and Florian Saurwein. "Self- and Co-Regulation. Evidence, Legitimacy and Governance Choice." In *Routledge Handbook of Media Law*, edited by Monroe Price, Stefaan Verhulst, and Libby Morgan, pp. 373–97. London and New York: Routledge, 2013.

Latzer, Michael, Natascha Just, Florian Saurwein, and Peter Slominski. "Regulation Remixed: Institutional Change through Self and Co-Regulation in the Mediamatics Sector." *Communications & Strategies* 50, no. 2 (2003): pp. 127–57.

Latzer, Michael, Natascha Just, Florian Saurwein, and Peter Slominski. *Selbst- und Ko-Regulierung im Mediamatiksektor. Alternative Regulierungsformen zwischen Staat und Martk.* Wiesbaden: Westdeutscher Verlag, 2002. http://www.mediachange.ch/media/pdf/publications/Latzer-etal_2002_Selbst--Ko-Regulierung.pdf.

Le Roy, Marc. "De la bonne utilisation de l'interdiction des films aux moins de 18 ans." *Actualité juridique Droit administratif* 10 (2009): pp. 544–46.

Lefever, Katrien, Hannes Cannie, and Peggy Valcke. "Watching Live Sport on Television: A Human Right? The Right to Information and the List of Major Events Regime." *European Human Rights Law Review*, no. 4 (2010): pp. 396–407.

Lent, Wolfgang. "Elektronische Presse zwischen E-Zines, Blogs und Wikis. Was sind Telemedien mit journalistisch-redaktionell gestalteten Angeboten?" *Zeitschrift für Urheber- und Medienrecht*, 2013, pp. 914–20.

Lent, Wolfgang. "Rundfunk und presseähnliche Telemedien, Allgemeine Bestimmungen." In *Informations- und Medienrecht, Kommentar*, edited by Hubertus Gersdorf, and Boris Paal. München: C. H. Beck, 2014.

Lescure, Pierre. "Mission 'Acte II de l'exception culturelle': Contribution aux politiques culturelles à l'ère numérique," May 2013. http://www.culturecommunication.gouv.fr/var/culture/storage/culture_mag/rapport_lescure/index.htm#/1.

Liesching, Marc. "§ 7 JMStV Jugendschutzbeauftragte." In *Beck'scher Online-Kommentar zum JMStV*, 13th ed. C.H. Beck, 2014.

Liesching, Marc. "Anforderungen an Altersverifikationssysteme, Zugleich eine Replik auf Vassilaki, K&R 2006, 211 ff." *Kommunikation und Recht*, 2006, pp. 395–97.

Liesching, Marc. "Das Darstellungs- und Berichterstattungsprivileg für Sendungen zum politischen Zeitgeschehen nach § 5 Absatz 6 JMStV." *Zeitschrift für Urheber- und Medienrecht*, 2009, pp. 367–74.

Liesching, Marc. "Jugendschutzprogramme für 'ab 18'-Internetangebote, Rechtliche Beleuchtung und Ausblick." *Multimedia und Recht*, 2013, pp. 368–71.

Liesching, Marc. "LG Düsseldorf: Altersverifikationssystem ueber18.de, Leitsätze und Anmerkung." *Multimedia und Recht*, 2004, pp. 764–66.

Liesching, Marc. “OLG Düsseldorf: Altersverifikationssystem ueber18.de, Leitsätze und Anmerkung.” *Multimedia und Recht*, 2005, pp. 611–15.

Liesching, Marc. “‘Sicherstellung’ des Erwachsenenzugangs bei pornografischen und sonst jugendgefährdenden Telemedien.” *Multimedia und Recht*, 2008, pp. 802–7.

Lievens, Eva. “Bullying and Sexting in Social Networks: Protecting Minors from Criminal Acts or Empowering Minors to Cope with Risky Behaviour?” *International Journal Crime, Law & Justice* 42, no. 3 (2014): pp. 251–70.

Lievens, Eva, and Peggy Valcke. “Regulatory Trends in a Social Media Context.” In *Routledge Handbook of Media Law*, edited by Monroe Price, Stefaan Verhulst, and Libby Morgan, pp. 557–80. London and New York: Routledge, 2013.

Lievens, Eva, Peggy Valcke, and Pieter Jan Valgaeren. “State of the Art on Regulatory Trends in Media. Identifying Whether, What, How and Who to Regulate in Social Media,” December 2011. http://emsoc.be/wp-content/uploads/2012/01/State-of-the-art-on-regulatory-trends-in-media.Identifying-whether-what-how-and-who-to-regulate-in-social-media.pdf.

Liikanen, Erkki. “Co-Regulation: A Modern Approach to Regulation.” presented at the Meeting of Association of the European Mechanical, Electrical, Electronic and Metalworking Industries (Orgalime) Council, Brussels, May 4, 2000. http://europa.eu/rapid/press-release_SPEECH-00-162_en.htm.

Liston, Stephanie. “OFCOM - the Perfect Dish or a Recipe for Disaster?” *Entertainment Law Review* 14, no. 2 (2003): pp. 19–23.

Lowde, Shaun, and Wells, Orlando. “ATVOD Determined to Do Better.” *Computer and Telecommunications Law Review* 18, no. 4 (2012): pp. 102–4.

Lunt, Peter, and Sonia Livingstone. “Is the BBC Safe in Ofcom’s Hands?” *LSE Blog*, June 22, 2016. http://blogs.lse.ac.uk/mediapolicyproject/2016/06/22/is-the-bbc-safe-in-ofcoms-hands/.

Mac Sithigh, Daithi. “Convergence, The Impact of Broadcast Regulation on Telecommunications.” In *Telecommunications Law and Regulation*, edited by Ian Walden, Fourth edition, pp. 653–700. Oxford: Oxford University Press, 2012.

Mac Sithigh, Daithi. “Co-Regulation, Video-on-Demand and the Legal Status of Audio-Visual Media.” *International Journal of Digital Television* 2, no. 1 (2011): pp. 49–66.

Mac Síthigh, Daithí. “Death of a Convention: Competition between the Council of Europe and European Union in the Regulation of Broadcasting.” *Edinburgh School of Law Research Paper Series 2013/26*, 2013. http://papers.ssrn.com/sol3/papers.cfm?abstract_id=2282769.

Machet, Emmanuelle. “Comparative Background Document on Content Regulation and New Media: Exploring Regulatory Boundaries between Traditional and New Media, 33rd EPRA Meeting.” EPRA, 2011. http://www.epra.org/attachments/ohrid-plenary-1-exploring-regulatory-boundaries-background-document.

Machet, Emmanuelle. “Comparative Background Document on New Media & Regulation: Towards a Paradigm Shift? New Services and Scope: What’s In, What’s out Revisited, 35th EPRA Meeting.” EPRA, 2012. http://www.epra.org/attachments/portoroz-plenary-1-new-services-and-scope-what-s-in-what-s-out-revisited-paper--2.

Machet, Emmanuelle. "Comparative Background Document on The Protection of Minors in a Connected Environment, 37th EPRA Meeting," 2013. http://epra3-production.s3.amazonaws.com/attachments/files/2195/original/protectionofminors_final_publicversion.pdf?1372087443.

Macovei, Monica. *Freedom of Expression, A Guide to the Implementation of Article 10 of the European Convention on Human Rights*. Edited by Directorate General of Human Rights, Council of Europe. Second edition. Human Rights Handbooks 2. Strasbourg, 2004. http://rm.coe.int/CoERMPublicCommonSearchServices/DisplayDCTMContent?documentId=090000168007ff48.

Maillard Desgrées du Loû, Dominique. *JurisClasseur Justice administrative, Référé en matière de communication audiovisuelle*. JurisClasseur, 2014.

Majone, Giandomenico. "The Rise of the Regulatory State in Europe." *West European Politics* 17, no. 3 (1994): pp. 77–101.

Malzanini. "Aufsichtsgremien." In *Medienrecht, Lexikon für Praxis und Wissenschaft*, edited by Peter Schiwy, Walter Schütz, and Dieter Dörr, Fifth edition, pp. 20–24. Köln: Carl Heymanns Verlag, 2010.

Marsden, Christopher. "Co-Regulation in European Media and Internet Sectors." *Multimedia Und Recht*, 2005, pp. 3–7.

Martini, Mario. "Auch im Internet in der ersten Reihe? - Online Aktivitäten öffentlich-rechtlicher Rundfunkanstalten im Spannungsfeld zwischen Funktionsauftrag und europäischem Wirtschaftsrecht." *Deutsches Verwaltungsblatt* 13 (2008): pp. 1477–85.

Martini, Mario. "Medienwirtschaft, Telemediengesetz, Anwendungsbereich." In *Informations- und Medienrecht, Kommentar*, edited by Hubertus Gersdorf, and Boris Paal. München: C. H. Beck, 2014.

Martini, Mario. "Rundfunk und presseähnliche Telemedien, Begriffsbestimmungen." In *Informations- und Medienrecht, Kommentar*, edited by Hubertus Gersdorf, and Boris Paal. München: C. H. Beck, 2014.

Marx, Andreas, Mark Boots, and Friedemann Schindler. "Perspektiven des technischen Jugendschutzes, Aktuelle Herausforderungen und zukunftsfähige Konzepte." Edited by jugendschutz.net, June 2016. http://www.kjm-online.de/fileadmin/Download_KJM/Service/Gutachten/Gutachten_Perspektiven-technischer-Jugendschutz_11.08.16.pdf.

Matzneller, Peter. "Rechtsrahmen der Werbung für Webradios." *Archiv für Presserecht, Zeitschrift für Medien- und Kommunikationsrecht* 4 (2013): pp. 298–304.

Matzneller, Peter. "Short Reporting Rights in Europe: European Legal Rules and Their National Transposition and Application." In *Exclusive Rights and Short Reporting*, edited by Susanne Nikoltchev, pp. 7–24. IRIS Plus 2012/4 4. Strasbourg: European Audiovisual Observatory, 2012.

Mauboussin, Elisabeth. "Accompagner l'arrivée de la télévision connectée." *Juris art etc. 2*, May 2013, pp. 22–26.

Mayer-Schönberger, Viktor. "Demystifying Lessig." *Wisconsin Law Review*, 2008, pp. 713–46.

McGonagle, Tarlach. "The Quota Quandary: An Assessment of Articles 4-6 of the Television without Frontiers Directive." In *The European Union and the Culture Industries, Regulation and the Public Interest*, edited by David Ward, pp. 187–212. United Kingdom: Ashgate Publishing, 2008.

McGonagle, Tarlach. "Co-Regulation of the Media in Europe: The Potential for Practice of an Intangible Idea." Edited by European Audiovisual Observatory. *IRIS plus 2002-10*, 2002, pp. 2–8.

McGonagle, Tarlach, and Ad Van Loon. "Jurisdiction over Broadcasters in Europe, Report on a Round-Table Discussion." In *Jurisdiction over Broadcasters in Europe*, edited by Susanne Nikoltchev. IRIS Special. Strasbourg: European Audiovisual Observatory, 2002.

Media Intelligence Service. "Consumption Trends." Edited by European Broadcasting Union, 2015.

Media Intelligence Service. "Consumption Trends." Edited by European Broadcasting Union, 2016.

Media Intelligence Service. "Market Insights SVOD in Europe." Edited by European Broadcasting Union, June 2016. https://www.ebu.ch/news/2016/06/european-svod-reach-50-mil-2020.

Medienanstalten. "Gemeinsame Richtlinien der Landesmedienanstalten zur Gewährleistung des Schutzes der Menschenwürde und des Jugendschutzes," March 8, 2005. http://www.kjm-online.de/fileadmin/Download_KJM/Recht/JuSchRiL.pdf.

Medienkommission der Landesanstalt für Medien NRW. "Stellungnahme der nordrhein-westfälischen Medienkommission der Landesanstalt für Medien NRW (LfM)," March 9, 2013. http://www.lfm-nrw.de/fileadmin/lfm-nrw/Aktuelles_Startseite/Gruenbuch_Stellungnahme_MK.pdf.

*Medienrecht*. 5th ed. Lexikon für Wissenschaft und Praxis. Köln: Carl Heymann, 2010.

Metzdorf, Jenny. "Regulierung Der Elektronischen Presse in Großbritannien? Ein Anwendungsbeispiel Zum Erwägungsgrund 28 Der AVMD-RL." Edited by Jürgen Taeger. *Law as a Service, Recht Im Internet- Und Cloud-Zeitalter*, Tagungsband Herbstakademie, 2013, pp. 673–92.

Metzdorf, Jenny. "Jugendmedienschutz in Abrufdiensten - Am Beispiel 'Playboy TV' aus Großbritannien." In *Law as a Service (LaaS) - Recht im Internet- und Cloud-Zeitalter, Tagungsband Herbstakademie 2013*, pp. 673–92. Oldenburg: Oldenburger Verlag für Wirtschaft, Informatik und Recht, 2013.

Metzdorf, Jenny. "The Implementation of the Audiovisual Media Services Directive by National Regulatory Authorities - National Responses to Regulatory Challenges." *Journal of Intellectual Property, Information Technology and Electronic Commerce Law* 5, no. 2 (2014). http://www.jipitec.eu/issues/jipitec-5-2-2014/3998.

Michel, Eva-Maria. "Senden als konstitutiver Bestandteil des Rundfunkbegriffs? Der Rundfunkbegriff im Lichte neuerer europarechtlicher Entwicklungen." *Zeitschrift für Urheber- und Medienrecht*, 2009, pp. 453–60.

Mihaescu Evans, Bucura. "The 'gaps' in Protection Stemming from the (Problematic) Coexistence of Fundamental Rights' Sources in the EU Legal Order." *Cahiers de Droit Européen*, no. 1 (2016).

Moinot, Pierre. "Pour une reforme de l'audiovisuel, Rapport au Premier ministre de la Commission de réflexion et d'orientation," September 30, 1981.

Möller, Mirko. "Rechtsfragen im Zusammenhang mit dem Postident-Verfahren." *Neue Juristische Wochenschrift*, 2005, pp. 1605–9.

Monroe, Price, Stefaan Verhulst, and Libby Morgan, eds. *Routledge Handbook of Media Law*. London and New York: Routledge, 2013.

Morange, Jean. "Le Conseil supérieur de l'audiovisuel." *Revue française de droit administratif* 5, no. 2 (1989): pp. 235–50.

Müller, Sebastian, and Christian Gusy. "Media Policy in Germany: Main Features and Current Issues." In *Understanding Media Policies, A European Perspective*, edited by Evangelia Psychogiopoulou. United Kingdom: Palgrave Macmillan, 2012.

Murray, Andrew, and Colin Scott. "Controlling the New Media: Hybrid Responses to New Forms of Power." *The Modern Law Review* 65, no. 4 (2002): pp. 491–516.

Neframi, Eleftheria. "Le principe de coopération loyale comme fondement identitaire de l'Union européenne." *Revue de l'Union européenne*, no. 556 (March 2012): pp. 197–203.

Neframi, Eleftheria. "The Duty of Loyalty: Rethinking Its Scope through Its Application in the Field of EU External Relations." *Common Market Law Review* 47 (2010): pp. 323–59.

Neumann, Karl-Heinz. "Technische und wirtschaftliche Konvergenz." In *Neuordnung des Medienrechts, Neuer rechtlicher Rahmen für eine konvergente Technik?*, edited by Alexander Roßnagel, pp. 29–35. Schriftenreihe des Instituts für Europäischens Medienrecht (EMR) 30. Baden-Baden: Nomos, 2005.

Nikoltchev, Susanne. "Right of Intervention to Address Abuses of the Fundamental Freedoms, The Role of the Case-Law." In *Regulating the New Media Landscape. A Directive for Audiovisual Media Services without Frontiers*, pp. 25–38. Schriftenreihe des Instituts Für Europäisches Medienrecht (EMR). Baden-Baden: Nomos, 2008.

Nyman-Metcalf, Katrin. "Analysis of the Hungarian Media Legislation." Edited by Office of the OSCE Representative on Freedom of the Media, February 2011. http://www.osce.org/fom/75990?download=true.

"Off Target at Ofcom, The Media Regulator Needs Fewer Luvvies and More Sense." *The Times*. February 2, 2004.

Ory, Stephan. "Differenzierte Regelung für Rundfunk, Medien- und Teledienste." In *Neuordnung des Medienrechts, Neuer rechtlicher Rahmen für eine konvergente Technik?*, edited by Alexander Roßnagel, pp. 67–84. Schriftenreihe des Instituts für Europäisches Medienrecht (EMR) 30. Baden-Baden: Nomos, 2005.

Ory, Stephan. "Nur die Tagesschau wäre ein bisschen wenig." *Kommunikation und Recht* 3 (2011): p. Editorial.

Padovani, Claudia, and Elena Pavan. "Actors and Interactions in Global Communication Governance: The Heuristic Potential of a Network Approach." In *The Handbook of Global Media and Communication Policy*, edited by Robin Mansell, and Marc Raboy, pp. 541–63. West Sussex, United Kingdom: Wiley-Blackwell, 2011.

Palzer, Carmen. “Co-Regulation of the Media in Europe.” In *Co-Regulation of the Media in Europe: European Provisions for the Establishment of Co-Regulation Frameworks*, edited by Susanne Nikoltchev, pp. 2–8. IRIS Plus 6/2002. Strasbourg: European Audiovisual Observatory, 2002.

Panteia, and VVA Europe. “Effectiveness of Self- and Co-Regulation in the Context of Implementing the AVMS Directive, A Study Prepared for the European Commission,” April 2016. https://ec.europa.eu/digital-single-market/en/news/audiovisual-and-media-services-directive-self-and-co-regulation-study.

Papier, Hans-Jürgen, and Meinhard Schröder. “Rechtsgutachten zur Abgrenzung der Rundfunk- und Pressefreiheit zur Auslegung des Begriffs der „Presseähnlichkeit“ und Anwendung des Verbots nicht sendungsbezogener presseähnlicher Angebote gemäß § 11 d Abs. 2 Nr. 3 Hs. 3 RStV,” 2010.

Peer, Limor, and Thomas Ksiazek. “Youtube and the Challenge to Journalism, New Standards for News Videos Online.” *Journalism Studies* 12, no. 1 (2011): pp. 45–63.

Perry, Claire. “Independent Inquiry into Online Child Protection, Findings and Recommendations,” April 2012.

Pila, Justine. “Intellectual Property as a Case Study in Europeanization: Methodological Themes and Context.” In *The Europeanization of Intellectual Property Law, Towards a European Legal Methodology*, edited by Ansgar Ohly, and Justine Pila, pp. 3–23. Oxford: Oxford University Press, 2013.

Pimlott, Nick, and David Lewis. “Regulation of Video-On-Demand Services Following the ‘Sun Video’ appeal.” *Entertainment Law Review* 23, no. 3 (2012): pp. 65–68.

Platho, Rolf. “Die Systematik von Schleichwerbung und Produktplazierung und ihre Verfehlung in der AVMD-Richtlinie.” *Multimedia und Recht* 11, no. 9 (2008): pp. 582–88.

Poinsot, Daniel. “Publicité commerciale à la télévision: le rôle du BVP.” *Légicom* 16, no. 1 (1998): pp. 75–81.

Polak, Juraj. “TVSME Considered on-Demand Audiovisual Media Service.” Edited by European Audiovisual Observatory. *IRIS Merlin Newsletter* 9, no. 1 (2012): p. 38.

Price, Monroe, and Stefaan Verhulst. “In Search of the Self, Charting the Course of Self-Regulation on the Internet in a Global Environment.” In *Regulating the Global Information Society*, edited by Christopher Marsden, pp. 57–78. London: Routledge, 2000.

Prosser, Tony. “Self-Regulation, Co-Regulation and the Audio-Visual Media Services Directive.” *Journal of Consumer Policy* 31, no. 1 (2008): pp. 99–113.

Prosser, Tony. “Regulation and Social Solidarity.” *Journal of Law and Society* 33, no. 3 (2006): pp. 364–87.

Prütting, Jens. “Das Prinzip der regulierten Selbstregulierung im Jugendmedienschutz.” *Kommunikation und Recht* 12 (2013): pp. 775–81.

Psychogiopoulou, Evangelia. “The Cultural Mainstreaming Clause of Article 151 (4) EC: Protection and Promotion of Cultural Diversity or Hidden Cultural Agenda?” *European Law Journal* 12, no. 5 (2006): pp. 575–92.

Puppis, Manuel. "Media Governance as a Horizontal Extension of Media Regulation: The Importance of Self- and Co-Regulation." *Communications* 32, no. 3 (2007): pp. 330–36.

Raboy, Marc, and Aysha Mawani. "Are States Still Important? Reflections on the Nexus between National and Global Media and Communication Policy." In *Routledge Handbook of Media Law*, edited by Monroe Price, Stefaan Verhulst, and Libby Morgan, pp. 343–60. London and New York: Routledge, 2013.

ReedSmith, ed. "The Implications of Brexit on the Entertainment and Media Industry," July 2016. https://www.reedsmith.com/files/uploads/alert-attachments/2016/Brexit_-_Client_Briefing_Pack_-_July_2016.pdf.

Reynolds, John. "Adult Video-on-Demand Website Closed for Failing to Protect Children." *The Guardian*, November 15, 2013. http://www.theguardian.com/media/2013/nov/15/adult-video-on-demand-site-closed-jessica-pressley.

Ridgway, Stephen. "The Audiovisual Media Services Directive - What Does It Mean, Is It Necessary and What Are the Challenges to Its Implementation?" *Computer and Telecommunications Law Review* 14, no. 4 (2008): pp. 108–13.

Ring, Wolf-Dieter. "Jugendschutz im Spannungsfeld zwischen Selbstregulierung der Medien und staatlicher Medienkontrolle." *Archiv für Presserecht, Zeitschrift für Medien- und Kommunikationsrecht* 3 (2004): pp. 9–14.

Ritlewski, Kristoff. "Pluralismussicherung im 10. Rundfunkänderungsstaatsvertrag, Ein Beitrag zur Dogmatik der Pluralismussicherung." *Zeitschrift für Urheber- und Medienrecht*, 2008, pp. 403–10.

Rogard, Pascal. "Moderniser la réglementation." *Juris art etc. 2*, May 2013, pp. 27–30.

Rossen-Stadtfeld, Helge. "Die Konzeption Regulierter Selbstregulation und ihre Ausprägung im Jugendmedienschutz." *Archiv für Presserecht, Zeitschrift für Medien- und Kommunikationsrecht* 3 (2004): pp. 1–9.

Rossen-Stadtfeld, Helge. "Grenzen der Staatsaufsicht im Bereich des kommerziellen Rundfunks." *Zeitschrift für Urheber- und Medienrecht*, 2008, pp. 1–10.

Roßnagel, Alexander. "Das Telemediengesetz, Neuordnung für Informations- und Kommunikationsdienste." *Neue Zeitschrift für Verwaltungsrecht*, 2007, pp. 743–48.

Salomon, Eve. *Guidelines for Broadcasting Regulation.* Second edition. London: Commonwealth Broadcastingn Association, 2008. http://unesdoc.unesco.org/images/0018/001832/183285e.pdf.

Samuelson, Pamela. "Five Challenges for Regulating the Global Information Society." In *Regulating the Global Information Society*, edited by Marsden, Christopher T., pp. 316–30. London: Routledge, 2000.

Scaramozzino, Eléonore. "TV connectée, réglementation déconnectée." *Juris art etc. 2*, May 2013, pp. 16–21.

Scheuer, Alexander. "Das neue System des Jugendmedienschutzes aus der Sicht der Selbstkontrolleinrichtungen." *Recht der Jugend und des Bildungswesens* 3 (2006): pp. 308–18.

Scheuer, Alexander. “Additional Youth Protection Measures in the European Union-Filters, Children’s Networks, Media Literacy.” In *Protection of Minors and Audiovisual Content On-Demand*, pp. 41–48. IRIS Plus 6/2012 6. Strasbourg: European Audiovisual Observatory, 2012.

Scheuer, Alexander. “Are the Guards Stationed at the Right Portals? The Suitability of Regulations on the Promotion of European Works in Non-Linear Audiovisual Media Services.” In *Video On-Demand and the Promotion of European Works*, edited by Susanne Nikoltchev, pp. 47–51. IRIS Special. Strasbourg: European Audiovisual Observatory, 2013.

Scheuer, Alexander. “Convergent Devices, Platforms and Services for Audiovisual Media, Challenges Set by Connected TV for the EU Legislative Framework.” In *Converged Media: Same Content, Different Laws?*, edited by Susanne Nikoltchev, pp. 7–22. IRIS Plus 3/2013. Strasbourg: European Audiovisual Observatory, 2013.

Scheuer, Alexander, and Cristina Bachmeier. “The Protection of Minors in the Case of New (Non-Linear) Media, European Legal Rules and Their National Transposition and Application.” In *Protection of Minors and Audiovisual Content on-Demand*, edited by Susanne Nikoltchev, pp. 7–27. IRIS Plus 6/2012. Strasbourg: European Audiovisual Observatory, 2012.

Scheuer, Alexander, and Max Schoenthal. “Article 3a TWFD (Major Events).” In *European Media Law*, edited by Oliver Castendyk, Egbert Dommering, and Alexander Scheuer. The Netherlands: Kluwer Law International, 2008.

Scheuermann, Christoph. “Angriff der ‘Vice’-Macher.” *Der Spiegel*. 2013, 14 edition, sec. Medien.

Schindler, Friedemann. “Technische Möglichkeiten des Jugendschutzes im Internet.” In *Positionen zum Jugendmedienschutz in Deutschland, Eine Textsammlung*, pp. 122–41. KJM Schriftenreihe 1. Berlin: Vistas, 2009.

Schmidtmann, Karin. “Die neue ‘heute’- App des ZDF - ein presseähnliches Angebot?” *Zeitschrift für Urheber- und Medienrecht*, 2013, pp. 536–41.

Schneeberger, Agnes, and Gilles Fontaine. “Linear and on-Demand Services in Europe 2015, Mavise Extra.” Edited by European Audiovisual Observatory, June 2016. http://www.obs.coe.int/documents/205595/264629/MAVISE+EXTRA_TV+and+ODAS+in+Europe+2015.pdf/6f081c35-b205-4cb2-8214-366f7d5bc500.

Schoefs, Raf. “Connected TV: Editorial Responsibility in a Converged Media Environment.” *Auteurs & Media* 5 (2014): pp. 346–59.

Schoenthal, Max. “Major Events and Reporting Rights.” In *Major Events and Reporting Rights*, edited by Susanne Nikoltchev, pp. 2–8. IRIS Plus. Strasbourg: European Audiovisual Observatory, 2006.

Schrems, Max. “The Privacy Shield Is a Soft Update of the Safe Harbor.” *European Data Protection Review* 2/2016 (2016): pp. 148–50.

Schüller-Keber, Valérie. “Die Kommunikationsfreiheiten in der Verfassung.” In *Handbuch Medienrecht, Recht der elektronischen Massenmedien*, edited by Dieter Dörr, Johannes Kreile, and Mark Cole, Second edition., pp. 80–102. Frankfurt am Main: Verlag Recht und Wirtschaft, 2010.

Schüller-Keber, Valérie. "Rundfunkfreiheit." In *Medienrecht, Lexikon für Praxis und Wissenschaft*, edited by Peter Schiwy, Walter Schütz, and Dieter Dörr, Fifth edition., pp. 490–98. Köln: Carl Heymanns Verlag, 2010.

Schulz, Wolfgang. "Eine neue Medienordnung im Zeichen der Konvergenz." In *Neuordnung des Medienrechts, Neuer rechtlicher Rahmen für eine konvergente Technik?*, edited by Alexander Roßnagel, pp. 37–50. Schriftenreihe des Instituts für Europäischens Medienrecht (EMR) 30. Baden-Baden: Nomos, 2005.

Schulz, Wolfgang. "RStV § 2 Begriffsbestimmungen." In *Beck'scher Kommentar zum Rundfunkrecht*, edited by Werner Hahn and Thomas Vesting, Third edition. München: C. H. Beck, 2012.

Schulz, Wolfgang. "RStV § 20 Zulassung." In *Beck'scher Kommentar zum Rundfunkrecht*, edited by Werner Hahn and Thomas Vesting, Third edition. München: C. H. Beck, 2012.

Schulz, Wolfgang, and Thorsten Grothe. "Caution, Loose Cornerstone: The Country of Origin Principle under Pressure." *LSE Blog*, July 4, 2016. http://blogs.lse.ac.uk/mediapolicyproject/2016/07/04/caution-loose-cornerstone-the-country-of-origin-principle-under-pressure/.

Schulz, Wolfgang, and Thorsten Held. "§ 1 JMStV Zweck des Staatsvertrages." In *Beck'scher Kommentar zum Rundfunkrecht*, edited by Werner Hahn and Thomas Vesting, Third edition. München: C.H. Beck, 2012.

Schulz, Wolfgang, and Thorsten Held. "§ 15 JMStV Mitwirkung der Gremien der Landesmedienanstalten." In *Beck'scher Kommentar zum Rundfunkrecht*, edited by Werner Hahn and Thomas Vesting, Third edition. München: C. H. Beck, 2012.

Schulz, Wolfgang, and Held, Thorsten. "Regulated Self-Regulation as a Form of Modern Government, Study Commissioned by the German Federal Commissioner for Cultural and Media Affairs, Interim Report (October 2001)." Edited by Hans-Bredow-Institut, October 2001. http://www.hans-bredow-institut.de/webfm_send/38.

Schulz, Wolfgang. *Editorial Responsibility*. IRIS Special. Strasbourg: European Audiovisual Observatory, 2008.

Schütz, Raimund. "Rundfunkbegriff: Neutralität der Inhalte oder der Übertragung? Konvergenz und Innovation." *Multimedia und Recht*, 2009, pp. 228–32.

Schwartmann, Rolf. "Jugendschutzrecht." In *Praxishandbuch Medien-, IT- und Urheberrecht*, edited by Rolf Schwartmann, Third edition., pp. 183–203. Heidelberg: C. F. Müller Verlag, 2014.

Schwartmann, Rolf. "Rundfunkrechtliche Grundlagen." In *Praxishandbuch Medien-, IT- und Urheberrecht*, edited by Rolf Schwartmann, Third edition., pp. 42–70. Heidelberg: C. F. Müller Verlag, 2014.

Schwendner, Sonja. "Die Zusammenarbeit mit Einrichtungen der Freiwilligen Selbstkontrolle." In *Positionen zum Jugendmedienschutz in Deutschland, Eine Textsammlung*, pp. 90–106. KJM Schriftenreihe 1. Berlin: Vistas, 2009.

Scott, Colin. "Regulation in the Age of Governance: The Rise of the Post-Regulatory State, National Europe Centre Paper No. 100," June 6, 2003. https://digitalcollections.anu.edu.au/bitstream/1885/41716/3/scott1.pdf.

Seifert, Michaela. "Fundamentals of Community Law and Policies (Including Funding Programmes) Governing the Content Industry." In *Regulatingn Content - European Regulatory Framework for the Media and Related Creative Sectors*, edited by Michael Holoubek, Dragana Damjanovic, and Matthias Traimer. The Netherlands: Kluwer Law International, 2006.

Sellmann, Christian. "K&R Kommentar." *Kommunikation und Recht*, 2008, pp. 367–69.

Selznick, Philip. "Focusing Organisational Research on Regulation." In *Regulatory Policy and the Social Sciences*, edited by Roger Noll, pp. 363–67. Berkeley: University of California Press, 1985.

Senden, Linda. "Soft Law, Self-Regulation and Co-Regulation in European Law: Where Do They Meet?" *Electronic Journal of Comparative Law* 9, no. 1 (2005).

Sewczyk, Jürgen, and Holger Wenk. "Mehr als Fernsehen: Smart TV, HbbTV & Co." *Media Perspektiven* 4 (2012): pp. 178–88.

Sinclair, Darren. "Self-Regulation versus Command and Control? Beyond False Dichotomies." *Law & Policy* 19, no. 4 (1997): pp. 529–59.

Sithigh, Daithi. "From Freedom of Speech to the Right to Communicate." In *Routledge Handbook of Media Law*, edited by Monroe Price, Stefaan Verhulst, and Libby Morgan, pp. 175–92. London and New York: Routledge, 2013.

Spaventa, Eleanor. "Fundamental Rights in the European Union." In *European Union Law*, edited by Catherine Barnard and Steeve Peers, pp. 226–54. Oxford: Oxford University Press, 2014.

Sporn, Stefan. "Auf dem Weg zur 'Ländermedienanstalt', Entwicklung, Stand und Perspektive der Aufsicht über den privaten Rundfunk und die Telemedien." *Kommunikation und Recht* 4 (2009): pp. 237–42.

Stender-Vorwachs, Jutta. "Die Revision der Fernsehrichtlinie, Ist die Revision eine Reform?" *Zeitschrift für Urheber- und Medienrecht*, 2006, pp. 362–70.

Stettner, Rupert. "Der neue Jugendmedienschutz-Staatsvertrag - eine Problemsicht." *Zeitschrift für Urheber- und Medienrecht*, 2003, pp. 425–38.

Thaenert, Wolfgang. "Nochmals zur Reform der Medienkontrolle durch den Zehnten Rundfunkänderungsstaatsvertrag." *Zeitschrift für Urheber- und Medienrecht*, 2009, pp. 131–35.

Théophile, Didier, and Étienne Renaudeau. "Les relations entre le Conseil de la concurrence, l'ARCEP, la CRE et le CSA: Coopération ou concurrence?" *Concurrences* 3 (2008): pp. 67–75.

Theurer, Marcus. "Das Ende der Sofakartoffel." *Frankfurter Allgemeine Zeitung*. August 27, 2007, 198 edition.

Truchet, Didier. *JurisClasseur Administratif, Communication audiovisuelle, Régulation et secteur public*. JurisClasseur, 2014.

Truchet, Didier. *JurisClasseur Administratif, Communication audiovisuelle, Secteur privé*. JurisClasseur, 2014.

Trudel, Pierre. "Internet Risks Management and Paradigm Shifts in the Regulation of the Audiovisual Industry." *Quaderns Del CAC 37* XIV, no. 2 (2011): pp. 5–10.

Ukrow, Jörg. "Article 22 TWFD (Protection of Minors)." In *European Media Law*, edited by Oliver Castendyk, Egbert Dommering, and Alexander Scheuer. The Netherlands: Kluwer Law International, 2008.

Ullberg, Erik, and Michael Plogell. "Radio and Televisions Act Applies to Newspapers' Web TV Services." Edited by European Audiovisual Observatory. *IRIS Merlin Newsletter* 1, no. 1 (2013): p. 35.

Vaizey, Ed. "Sexually Explicit Material and Video on Demand Services," August 3, 2011. http://webarchive.nationalarchives.gov.uk/20121204113822/http://www.culture.gov.uk/images/publications/EVletter-to-ed-richards-3aug2011pdf.pdf.

Valcke, Peggy, Dirk Voorhoof, and Eva Lievens. "Independent Media Regulators: Condition Sine qua Non for Freedom of Expression?" In *The Independence of the Media and Its Regulatory Agencies, Shedding New Light on Formal and Actual Independence against the National Context*, edited by Wolfgang Schulz, Peggy Valcke and Kristina Irion, pp. 55–82. Bristol, UK and Chicago, USA: Intellect, 2013.

Valcke, Peggy. "Challenges of Regulating Media Pluralism in the European Union: The Potential of Risk-Based Regulation." *Quaderns Del CAC 38* XV, no. 1 (June 2012): pp. 25–35.

Valcke, Peggy. "Risk-Based Regulation in the Media Sector: The Way Forward to Advance the Media Pluralism Debate in Europe?" ICRI Working Paper 2/2011, 2011. http://papers.ssrn.com/sol3/papers.cfm?abstract_id=1898133.

Valcke, Peggy, and Jef Ausloos. "'What If Television Becomes Just an App?' Re-Conceptualising the Legal Notion of Audiovisual Media Service in the Light of Media Convergence." ICRI Research Paper 17, December 20, 2013. http://papers.ssrn.com/sol3/papers.cfm?abstract_id=2375666.

Valcke, Peggy, Aleksandra Kuczerawy, Katrien Lefever, Eva Lievens, David Stevens, and Evi Werkers. "The EU Regulatory Framework Applicable to Broadcasting." In *Telecommunications, Broadcasting and the Internet, EU Competition Law & Regulation*, edited by Laurent Garzaniti, and Matthew O'Regan, Third edition., pp. 263–330. London: Sweet & Maxwell, 2010.

Valcke, Peggy, and David Stevens. "Graduated Regulation of 'Regulatable' Content and the European Audiovisual Media Services Directive, One Small Step for the Industry and One Giant Leap for the Legislator?" *Telematics and Informatics* 24 (2007): pp. 285–302.

Valcke, Peggy, David Stevens, Eva Lievens, and Evi Werkers. "Audiovisual Media Services in the EU, Next Generation Approach or Old Wine in New Barrels?" *Communications & Strategies* 7, no. 3 (2008): pp. 103–18.

Van Eijk, Nico. "Annotatie bij Hof van Justitie 6 oktober 2015 (C-362/14 *Maximillian Schrems v Data Protection Commissioner*)." *Tijdschrift voor Consumentenrecht en handelspraktijken* 4 (2016): pp. 189–99.

Van Eijk, Nico, Ronan Fahy, Harry Van Til, Pieter Nooren, Hans Stokking, and Hugo Gelevert. "Digital Platforms: An Analytical Framework for Identifying and Evaluating Policy Options," November 9, 2015. http://ivir.nl/publicaties/download/1703.

Van Eijk, Nico. "Scope of Application of the Modernised Directive." In *Regulating the New Media Landscape. A Directive for Audiovisual Media Services without Frontiers*, pp. 21–24. Schriftenreihe des Instituts Für Europäisches Medienrecht (EMR) 36. Baden-Baden: Nomos, 2008.

Van Eijk, Nico, and Tom Van Engers. "Duties of Care on the Internet, Paper Presented at the Telecommunications Policy Research Conference, September 23-25, 2011," 2011. http://dare.uva.nl/document/483341.

Vassilaki, Irini. "Strafrechtliche Anforderungen an Altersverifikationssysteme." *Kommunikation und Recht*, 2006, pp. 211–14.

Vincent-Deray, Agnès. "Commission famille, éducation aux médias; Rapport à l'attention de Madame Nadine Morano, Secrétaire d'Etat chargée de la Famille et de la Solidarité," 2009.

Volkmann, Christian. "§ 59 Aufsicht." In *Recht der elektronischen Medien*, edited by Gerald Spindler and Fabian Schuster, Second edition. München: C. H. Beck, 2011.

Von Coelln, Christian. "Jugendmedienschutz zwischen staatlichem Schutzauftrag und Zensurverbot." In *Jugendmedienschutz im Informationszeitalter*, edited by Nikolaus Bosch and Stefan Leible, pp. 41–64. Bayreuther Studien zum Wirtschafts- und Medienrecht 6. Sipplingen: Jenaer Wissenschaftliche Verlagsgesellschaft, 2012.

Von Gottberg, Joachim. "Die Freiwillige Selbstkontrolle Fernsehen." In *Positionen zum Jugendmedienschutz in Deutschland, Eine Textsammlung*, pp. 51–70. KJM Schriftenreihe 1. Berlin: Vistas, 2009.

Wagner, Eva. "Aufsichtsmittel im dualen Rundfunksystem - Ungerechtfertigte Ungleichbehandlung?" *Zeitschrift für Urheber- und Medienrecht*, 2013, pp. 850–57.

Wagner, Michael. "Revisiting the Country-of-Origin Principle in the AVMS Directive." *Journal of Media Law* 6, no. 2 (2014): pp. 286–304.

Weigand, Verena. "Der novellierte Jugendmedienschutz-Staatsvertrag, Konsequenzen für die Arbeit der KJM." *JMS Report* 4 (2010): pp. 2–4.

Weiner, Christian, and Christoph Schmelz. "Die elektronische Presse und andere neue Kommunikationsformen im neuen rechtlichen Regulierungsrahmen." *Kommunikation und Recht*, no. 10 (2006): pp. 453–60.

Weinrich, Jörg. "Jugendschutz in Großbritannien: Erfolgreiche Einführung von Netzanschlussfiltern." *JMS-Report*, no. 5 (2014): pp. 2–3.

Weinstein, Stuart. "OFCOM, Information-Convergence and the Never Ending Drizzle of Electric Rain." *International Journal of Communications Law and Policy*, no. 8 (2004 2003): pp. 1–39.

Weinstein, Stuart. "The Medium is the Message: The Legal and Policy Implications of the Creation of OFCOM in the Age of Convergence." *Computer and Telecommunications Law Review* 9, no. 6 (2003): pp. 161–73.

Wildmann, Claudia. *Das Europäische Kurzberichterstattungsrecht im Lichte der Richtlinie über audiovisuelle Mediendienste*. Schriften zum Medienrecht 28. Hamburg: Kovač, 2011.

Witt, Inken. *Regulierte Selbstregulierung am Beispiel des Jugendmedienschutzstaatsvertrages*. Nomos Universitätsschriften 573. Baden-Baden: Nomos, 2008.

Woods, Lorna. "Article 11." In *The EU Charter of Fundamental Rights, A Commentary*, edited by Steve Peers, Tamara Hervey, Jeff Kenner, and Angela Ward. United Kingdom: Hart Publishin, 2014.

Wörmann, Michael. "Verhaltensmuster vernetzter TV-Nutzer: Eine ethnografische Studie." Edited by Hans Hege and Andreas Hamann. Die Medienanstalten, 2014.

Zambardino, Bruno, Monica Sardelli, and Marco Bassini. "AVMSD Refit or Reform? Audio Visual Media Services in the Digital Era." Institute for Competitiveness (icom), September 2016.

*Documents by EU institutions and bodies and government material*

Assemblée nationale. "Projet de loi relatif à l'indépendance de l'audiovisuel public, Exposé des motifs," May 6, 2013.

Bundesanstalt für Finanzdienstleistungsaufsicht. "Rundschreiben 1/2014 (GW) - Verdachtsmeldung nach §§ 11, 14 GwG," 2014. http://www.bafin.de/SharedDocs/Veroeffentlichungen/DE/Rundschreiben/rs_1401_gw_verwaltungspraxis_vm.html.

Council of the European Union. "Council Conclusions on European Audiovisual Policy in the Digital Era. Education, Youth, Culture and Sport Council Meeting of 25 November 2014," 2014. http://www.consilium.europa.eu/uedocs/cms_data/docs/pressdata/en/educ/145950.pdf.

Council of the European Union. "Press Release of 3349th Council Meeting on Education, Youth, Culture and Sport of 25 November 2014," 2014. http://www.consilium.europa.eu/uedocs/cms_data/docs/pressdata/en/educ/145953.pdf.

"Council Recommendation 98/560/EC on the Development of the Competitiveness of the European Audiovisual and Information Services Industry by Promoting National Frameworks Aimed at Achieving a Comparable and Effective Level of Protection of Minors and Human Dignity, OJ of 07.10.1998, L 270, P. 48-55," September 24, 1998.

Department for Culture, Media and Sport. "Consultation on Proposals for the Implementation of the EU Audiovisual Media Services Directive in the United Kingdom, Summary of Responses," March 2009. http://webarchive.nationalarchives.gov.uk/20100407120701/http://www.culture.gov.uk/images/publications/summary_report.pdf.

Department for Culture, Media and Sport. "The Audiovisual Media Services Directive, Consultation on Proposals for Implementation in the United Kingdom," July 2008. http://webarchive.nationalarchives.gov.uk/20100407120701/http://www.culture.gov.uk/images/consultations/AVMS_Consultation_Document.pdf.

European Commission. "Commission Interpretative Communication on Certain Aspects of the Provisions on Televised Advertising in the 'Television without frontiers' Directive, OJ of 28.4.2004, C 102, P. 2," n.d.

European Commission. "Commission Staff Working Document, A Digital Single Market Strategy for Europe - Analysis and Evidence, Accompanying the Document Communication from the Commission on A Digital Single Market Strategy for Europe, SWD(2015) 100 Final," June 5, 2015.

European Commission. “Commission Staff Working Document on Online Platforms, Accompanying the document ‘Communication on Online Platforms and the Digital Single Market,’” May 25, 2016.

European Commission. “Communication from the Commission, Action Plan ‘Simplifying and Improving the Regulatory Environment’, 5.6.2002, COM(2002) 278 Final,” May 6, 2002.

European Commission. “Communication from the Commission on the Precautionary Principle (COM (2000)1 Final),” February 2, 2000.

European Commission. “Communication from the Commission to the Council and the European Parliament and to the Economic and Social Committee and the Committee of Regions, Europe’s Way to the Information Society, An Action Plan, COM(94) 347 Final,” July 19, 1994.

European Commission. “Communication from the Commission to the Council and the European Parliament. Better Regulation for Growth and Jobs in the European Union, COM(2005) 97 Final,” March 16, 2005.

European Commission. “Communication from the Commission to the Council, the European Parliament, the Economic and Social Committee and the Committee of the Regions on Illegal and Harmful Content on Othe Internet. COM(96) 487 Final,” October 16, 1996.

European Commission. “Communication from the Commission to the Council, the European Parliament, the Economic and Social Committee and the Committee of the Regions on Principles and Guidelines for the Community’s Audiovisual Policy in the Digital Age, COM(99) 657 Final,” December 14, 1999.

European Commission. “Communication from the Commission to the Council, the European Parliament, the European Economic and Social Committee and the Committee of the Regions on a European Strategy for a Better Internet for Children, COM(2012) 196 Final,” May 2, 2012.

European Commission. “Communication from the Commission to the Council, the European Parliament, the European Economic and Social Committee and the Committee of the Regions on Accelerating the Transition from Analogue to Digital Broadcasting, COM(2005) 204 Final,” May 24, 2005.

European Commission. “Communication from the Commission to the Council, the European Parliament, the European Economic and Social Committee and the Committee of the Regions, The Future of European Regulatory Audiovisual Policy, COM(2003) 784 Final, 15.12.2003,” December 15, 2003.

European Commission. “Communication from the Commission to the European Parliament, the Council, the European Economic and Social Committee and the Committee of the Regions, A Digital Single Market Strategy for Europe, COM(2015) 192 Final,” June 5, 2015.

European Commission. “Communication from the Commission to the European Parliament, the Council, the European Economic and Social Committee and the Committee of the Regions, A Renewed EU Strategy 2011-14 for Corporate Social Responsibility, COM(2011) 681 Final,” October 25, 2011.

European Commission. "Communication from the Commission to the European Parliament, the Council, the European Economic and Social Committee and the Committee of the Regions on A Comprehensive Approach to Stimulating Cross-Border E-Commerce for Europe's Citizens and Businesses, COM(2016) 320 Final," May 25, 2016.

European Commission. "Communication from the Commission to the European Parliament, the Council, the European Economic and Social Committee and the Committee of the Regions on Better Regulation for Better Results, An EU Agenda, 19.05.2015, COM(2015) 215 Final," 2015.

European Commission. "Communication from the Commission to the European Parliament, the Council, the European Economic and Social Committee and the Committee of the Regions on Online Platforms and the Digital Single Market, Opportunities and Challenges for Europe, COM(2016) 288 Final," May 25, 2016.

European Commission. "Consultation on the Regulatory Environment for Platforms, Online Intermediaries, Data and Cloud Computing and the Collaborative Economy," December 2015. https://ec.europa.eu/eusurvey/runner/Platforms/.

European Commission. "Decision of 3.2.2014 on Establishing the European Regulators Group for Audiovisual Media Services, C(2014) 462 Final," February 3, 2014.

European Commission. "European Governance, A White Paper, COM(2001) 428 Final," July 25, 2001.

European Commission. "Fourth Report from the Commission to the Council, the European Parliament, the European Economic and Social Committee and the Committee of the Regions, COM(2002) 778 Final," January 6, 2003. http://eur-lex.europa.eu/legal-content/EN/ALL/?uri=CELEX:52002DC0778.

European Commission. "Green Paper on Strategy Options to Strengthen the European Programme Industry in the Context of the Audiovisual Policy of the European Union, COM(94) 96 Final," June 4, 1994.

European Commission. "Green Paper on the Convergence of the Telecommunications, Media and Information Technology Sectors, and the Implications for Regulation, Towards an Information Society Approach, COM(97) 623," March 12, 1997.

European Commission. "Green Paper on the Establishment of the Common Market for Broadcasting, Especially by Satellite and Cable, COM(84) 300 Final," June 14, 1984.

European Commission. "Green Paper on the Protection of Minors and Human Dignity in Audiovisual and Information Services, COM(96) 483 Final," October 16, 1996.

European Commission. "Green Paper, Pluralism and Media Concentration in the Internal Market, An Assessment of the Need for Community Action, COM(92) 480 Final," December 23, 1992.

European Commission. "Green Paper Preparing for a Fully Converged Audiovisual World: Growth, Creation and Values, COM(2013) 231 Final," April 24, 2013.

European Commission. “Proposal for a Directive of the European Parliament and of the Council Amending Council Directive 89/552/EEC on the Coordination of Certain Provisions Laid down by Law, Regulation or Administrative Action in Member States Concerning the Pursuit of Television Broadcasting Activities, COM(2005) 646 Final, 13.12.2005,” December 13, 2005.

European Commission. “Proposal for a Directive of the European Parliament and of the Council Amending Directive 2010/13/EU on the Coordination of Certain Provisions Laid down by Law, Regulation or Administrative Action in Member States Concerning the Provision of Audiovisual Media Services in View of Changing Market Realities, COM(2016) 287 Final,” May 25, 2016.

European Commission. “Proposal for a Directive of the European Parliament and of the Council on Copyright in the Digital Single Market, COM(2016) 593 Final,” September 14, 2016.

European Commission. “Proposal for a Regulation of the European Parliament and of the Council Laying down Rules on the Exercise of Copyright and Related Rights Applicable to Certain Online Transmissions of Broadcasting Organisations and Retransmissions of Television and Radio Programmes, COM(2016) 594 Final,” September 14, 2016.

European Commission. “Proposal for a Regulation of the European Parliament and of the Council on Cooperation between National Authorities Responsible for the Enforcement of Consumer Protection Laws, COM(2016) 283 Final,” May 25, 2016.

European Commission. “Proposal for a Regulation of the European Parliament and of the Council on Ensuring the Cross-Border Portability of Online Content Services in the Internal Market, COM(2015) 627 Final,” December 9, 2015.

European Commission. “Report from the Commission to the European Parliament, the Council, the European Economic and Social Committee and the Committee of the Regions, First Report on the Application of Articles 13, 16 and 17 of Directive 2010/13/EU for the Period 2009-2010 Promotion of European Works in EU Scheduled and on-Demand Audiovisual Media Services,” September 24, 2012.

European Commission. “Summaries of the Replies to the Public Consultation Launched by the Green Paper ‘Preparing for a Fully Converged Audiovisual World: Growth, Creation and Values,’” 2014. https://ec.europa.eu/digital-agenda/en/news/publication-summaries-green-paper-replies.

European Commission. “The Commission Decides to Make an Application to the Court against France on the ‘Television without frontiers’ Directive, IP/98/1067,” December 7, 1998. http://europa.eu/rapid/press-release_IP-98-1067_en.htm?locale=en.

European Commission. “White Paper from the Commission to the European Council, Completing the Internal Market, COM(85) 310 Final,” June 14, 1985.

European Parliament. “Draft European Parliament Legislative Resolution on the Proposal for a Directive of the European Parliament and of the Council Amending Council Directive 89/552/EEC on the Coordination of Certain Provisions Laid down by Law, Regulation or Administrative Action in Member States Concerning the Pursuit of Television Broadcasting Activities,” November 23, 2006.

European Parliament. "European Parliament Legislative Resolution on the Proposal for a Directive of the European Parliament and of the Council Amending Council Directive 89/552/EEC on the Coordination of Certain Provisions Laid down by Law, Regulation or Administrative Action in Member States Concerning the Pursuit of Television Broadcasting Activities," December 13, 2006.

European Parliament. "European Parliament Resolution on Preparing for a Fully Converged Audiovisual World," December 3, 2014.

"European Parliament and of the Council Recommendation 2006/952/EC on the Protection of Minors and Human Dignity and on the Right of Reply in Relation to the Competitiveness of the European Audiovisual and Online Information Services Industry, OJ of 27.12.2006, L 378, P. 72-77," December 20, 2006.

European Parliament, Council, Commission. "Inter-Institutional Agreement on Better Lawmaking." OJ C 321, December 31, 2003.

European Union Agency for Fundamental Rights. "Freedom to Conduct a Business: Exploring the Dimensions of a Fundamental Right," 2015. http://fra.europa.eu/sites/default/files/fra_uploads/fra-2015-freedom-conduct-business_en.pdf.

Ministère de la culture et de la communication. "Consultation publique sur l'adaptation du décret relatif aux services de médias audiovisuels à la demande," June 2014. http://www.culturecommunication.gouv.fr/Politiques-ministerielles/Audiovisuel/Actualites/Consultation-publique-sur-l-adaptation-du-decret-relatif-aux-services-de-medias-audiovisuels-a-la-demande.

Ministère de la culture et de la communication. "Consultation publique sur le projet de décret relatif aux services de médias audiovisuels à la demande," March 2010. http://www.culturecommunication.gouv.fr/Politiques-ministerielles/Audiovisuel/Archives-2010/Consultation-publique-sur-le-projet-de-decret-relatif-aux-services-de-medias-audiovisuels-a-la-demande.

Ministère de la culture et de la communication. "Consultation publique sur les dispotitions applicables aux services de médias audiovisuels à la demande," April 2009. http://www.culturecommunication.gouv.fr/Politiques-ministerielles/Audiovisuel/Archives-2009/Consultation-publique-sur-les-dispositions-applicables-aux-services-de-medias-audiovisuels-a-la-demande.

Ministre de la Culture et de la Communication. "Le coût, la valorisation et l'évolution des usages de l'offre gratuite des SMADs des éditeurs de services de télévision," June 2015. http://www.culturecommunication.gouv.fr/content/download/121766/1357492/version/2/file/Etude%20SMAD%20DGMIC%20rapport%20final.pdf.

Puttnam, David. "Joint Committee on Draft Communications Bill, Report." House of Lords, House of Commons, July 25, 2002. http://www.publications.parliament.uk/pa/jt200102/jtselect/jtcom/169/16901.htm.

Sénat. "Projet de loi modifiant la loi n° 86-1067 du 30 septembre 1986 relative à la liberté de communication," December 10, 1988. http://www.senat.fr/leg/1988-1989/i1988_1989_0027.pdf.

*Documents of national media authorities*

AGCOM. "Delibera n. 607/10/CONS Regolamento in materia di fornitura di servizi di media audiovisivi a richiesta ai sensi dell'articolo 22-bis del Testo unico dei servizi di media audiovisivi e radiofonici," 2010.

ALM GbR, ed. *Jahrbuch 2013/2014, Landesmedienanstalten und privater Rundfunk in Deutschland*. Berlin: Vistas, 2014. http://www.die-medienanstalten.de/fileadmin/Download/Publikationen/ALM-Jahrbuch/Jahrbuch_2014/Jahrbuch_2013-14_Druckversion.pdf.

ALM GbR, ed. *Jahrbuch 2015/2016, Privater Rundfunk und Telemedien*. Berlin: Vistas, 2016. http://www.die-medienanstalten.de/fileadmin/Download/Publikationen/ALM-Jahrbuch/Jahrbuch_2016/Jahrbuch_2015-2016.pdf.

ATVOD. "2014-2015 Fee Tariff, Regulatory Fees for Providers of On-Demand Programme Services for the Period 1 April 2014 - 31 March 2015," June 13, 2014.

ATVOD. "Annual Report 2010/11," September 30, 2011.

ATVOD. "Articles of Association of ATVOD," June 22, 2011.

ATVOD. "ATVOD Responds to Ofcom Review Decision," October 14, 2015.

ATVOD. "Code of Conduct for Members, Edition 1.2," January 2013.

ATVOD. "Determination on a Complaint That the On-Demand Programme Service 4OD Included Unsuitable or Harmful Content (Frankie Boyle Tramadol Nights Series)," February 3, 2011.

ATVOD. "Determination on a Complaint That the On-Demand Programme Service 4OD Included Unsuitable or Harmful Content (Mr. Woodcock)," March 29, 2012.

ATVOD. "Determination That MTV Networks Europe Is the Provider of the On-Demand Programme Service MTV Content on Virgin Media," June 7, 2011.

ATVOD. "Determination That MTV Networks Europe Is the Provider of the On-Demand Programme Service MTV on Sky Anytime," March 10, 2012.

ATVOD. "Determination That Nickelodeon UK Ltd Is the Provider of the On-Demand Programme Service Nickelodeon Content on Virgin Media," June 7, 2011.

ATVOD. "Determination That Nickelodeon UK Ltd Is the Provider of the On-Demand Programme Service Nickelodeon on Sky Anytime," March 10, 2012.

ATVOD. "Determination That Paramount UK Partnership, Trading as Comedy Central Is the Provider of the On-Demand Programme Service Comedy Central Content on Virgin Media," June 7, 2011.

ATVOD. "Determination That Paramount UK Partnership Trading as Comedy Central Is the Provider of the On-Demand Programme Service Comedy Central on Sky Anytime," March 10, 2012.

ATVOD. "Determination That the Provider of 'Abused Piggy' was in Breach of ATVOD's Rule 11 and Thereby Contravened Sec. 368E (2) CA," March 25, 2013.

ATVOD. "Determination That the Provider of Candy Girl Productions Is in Breach of ATVOD's Rules 1 & 4 and Thereby Has Contravened Sec. 368BA and Sec. 368D (3) (ZA) of the Communications Act," October 22, 2014.

ATVOD. "Determination That the Provider of Daisy Rock UK Is in Breach of ATVOD's Rules 1 & 4 and Thereby Has Contravened Sec. 368BA and Sec. 368D (3) (ZA) of the Communications Act," November 26, 2014.

ATVOD. "Determination That the Provider of 'G Spot Productions' was in Breach of ATVOD´s Rule 11 and Thereby Contravened Sec. 368E (2) CA," March 25, 2013.

ATVOD. "Determination That the Provider of 'Panties Pulled Down' was in Breach of ATVOD's Rules 1 & 4 and Thereby Has Contravened Sec. 368BA and 368D (3) (ZA) of the Communications Act," February 26, 2015.

ATVOD. "Determination That the Provider of 'Studio 66 TV' was in Breach of ATVOD´s Rule 11 and Thereby Contravened Sec. 368E (2) CA," March 25, 2013.

ATVOD. "Determination That the Provider of the on Demand Programme Service 'bootybox.tv' was in Breach of Rule 11," December 9, 2011.

ATVOD. "Determination That the Provider of the On-Demand Programme Service 'Demand Adult' was in Breach of Rule 11," February 7, 2012.

ATVOD. "Determination That the Provider of the On-Demand Programme Service 'Dreams of Spanking' was in Breach of ATVOD´s Rule 14 and Thereby Contravened Sec. 368E (2) CA," July 30, 2015.

ATVOD. "Determination That the Provider of the On-Demand Programme Service 'Dreams of Spanking' was in Breach of ATVOD's Rule 11 and Thereby Contravened Sec. 368E (4) CA," July 30, 2015.

ATVOD. "Determination That the Provider of the On-Demand Programme Service 'Facesitting Mistress' was in Breach of ATVOD's Rule 11 and Thereby Contravened Sec. 368E (2) CA," April 24, 2014.

ATVOD. "Determination That the Provider of the On-Demand Programme Service 'Glasgow Mistress Megara Furie' was in Breach of ATVOD's Rule 11 and Thereby Contravened Sec. 368E (4) CA," April 27, 2015.

ATVOD. "Determination That the Provider of the On-Demand Programme Service 'Glasgow Mistress Megara Furie' was in Breach of ATVOD's Rule 14 and Thereby Contravened Sec. 368E (2) CA," April 27, 2015.

ATVOD. "Determination That the Provider of the On-Demand Programme Service 'HardGlam' was in Breach of ATVOD´s Rule 11 and Thereby Contravened Sex. 368E (2) CA," April 25, 2014.

ATVOD. "Determination That the Provider of the On-Demand Programme Service 'Joybear' was in Breach of ATVOD's Rule 11 and Thereby Contravened Sec. 368E (4) CA," June 22, 2015.

ATVOD. "Determination That the Provider of the On-Demand Programme Service 'playboytv.co.uk' was in Breach of Rule 11," February 7, 2012.

ATVOD. "Determination That the Provider of the On-Demand Programme Service 'Strictly Broadband' was in Breach of Rule 11," July 2, 2012.

ATVOD. "Determination That the Provider of the On-Demand Programme Service 'Thebondagemistress.com' was in Breach of ATVOD's Rule 11 and Thereby Contravened Sec. 368E (4) CA," July 30, 2015.

ATVOD. "Determination That the Provider of the On-Demand Programme Service 'Thebondagemistress.com' was in Breach of ATVOD's Rule 14 and Thereby Contravened Sec. 368E (2) CA," July 30, 2015.

ATVOD. "Determination That the Provider of the On-Demand Programme Service 'UKXXXPass' was in Breach of ATVOD's Rule 11 and Thereby Contravened Sec. 368E (4) CA," June 22, 2015.

ATVOD. "Determination That the Provider of the On-Demand Programme Service 'www.rosewoodxxx.com' is in Breach of Rule 11," July 2, 2011.

ATVOD. "Determination That the Provider of the On-Demand Programme Service 'Daisy Rock UK' was in Breach of ATVOD's Rule 11 and Thereby Contravened Sec. 368E (4) CA," November 26, 2014.

ATVOD. "Determination That the Provider of the On-Demand Programme Service 'Mistress R'eal' was in Breach of ATVOD's Rule 11 and Thereby Contravened Sec. 368E (4) CA," April 20, 2015.

ATVOD. "Determination That the Provider of the On-Demand Programme Service 'Mistress R'eal' was in Breach of ATVOD's Rule 14 and Thereby Contravened Sec. 368E (2) CA," April 20, 2015.

ATVOD. "Determination That the Provider of the On-Demand Programme Service 'Panties Pulled Down' was in Breach of ATVOD's Rule 11 and Thereby Contravened Sec. 368E (4) CA," February 28, 2015.

ATVOD. "Determination That the Provider of the Service Named BBC Food Youtube Has Contravened Sec. 368BA and Sec. 368D (3) (ZA) of the Communications Act," March 5, 2011. http://www.atvod.co.uk/complaints/determinations/2011-determinations/bbc-food-youtube.

ATVOD. "Determination That the Provider of the Service Named BBC Worldwide on Mediaset Has Contravened Sec. 368BA and Sec. 368D (3) (ZA) of the Communications Act," 05 2011.

ATVOD. "Determination That the Provider of the Service Named Channel Flip Has Contravened Sec. 368BA and Sec. 368D (3) (ZA) of the Communications Act," April 26, 2011.

ATVOD. "Determination That the Provider of the Service Named Climax 3 Uncut Has Contravened Sec. 368BA of the Communications Act," December 21, 2010.

ATVOD. "Determination That the Provider of the Service Named Demand Adult Has Contravened Sec. 368BA of the Communications Act," September 24, 2010.

ATVOD. "Determination That the Provider of the Service Named Elle TV Has Contravened Sec. 368BA of the Communications Act," November 2, 2011.

ATVOD. "Determination That the Provider of the Service Named Everton TV Has Contravened Sec. 368D (3) (ZA) of the Communications Act," November 4, 2012.

ATVOD. "Determination That the Provider of the Service Named Sun Video Has Contravened Sec. 368BA of the Communications Act," November 2, 2011.

ATVOD. "Determination That the Provider of the Service Named The Business Channel Has Contravened Sec. 368BA and Sec. 368D (3) (ZA) of the Communications Act," April 26, 2011.

ATVOD. "Determination That the Provider of the Service Named Top Gear YouTube Has Contravened Sec. 368BA and Sec. 368D (3) (ZA) of the Communications Act," March 5, 2011.

ATVOD. "Determination That the Provider of the Service Named Viacom Channel Providers' Content on the Sky Anytime Platform Has Contravened Sec. 368BA and Sec. 368D (3) (ZA) of the Communications Act," January 23, 2012.

ATVOD. "Determination That the Provider of the Service Named Viva TV Music Has Contravened Sec. 368BA and Sec. 368D (3) (ZA) of the Communications Act," March 18, 2011.

ATVOD. "Determination That the Provider of The UK Column Is in Breach of ATVOD's Rules 1 & 4 and Thereby Has Contravened Sec. 368BA and Sec. 368D (3) (ZA) of the Communications Act," April 24, 2014.

ATVOD. "Determination That the Provider of 'The Urban Chick Supremacy Cell' is in Breach of ATVOD's Rules 1 & 4 and Thereby Has Contravened Sec. 368BA and Sec. 368D (3) (ZA) of the Communications Act," June 1, 2014.

ATVOD. "For Adults Only? Underage Access to Online Porn, A Research Report by the Authority for Television On Demand ('ATVOD')," March 28, 2014.

ATVOD. "Guidance on Who Needs to Notify, Application and Scope of the Regulations for Video on Demand (VOD) Services, Edition 4.0," May 2, 2014.

ATVOD. "Minutes of the Fourth Meeting of the ATVOD/Industry Forum Fees Working Party," December 14, 2014.

ATVOD. "Minutes of the Second Meeting of the ATVOD/Industry Forum Fees Working Party," October 10, 2011.

ATVOD. "Minutes of the Third Meeting of the ATVOD/Industry Forum Fees Working Party," April 11, 2011.

ATVOD. "Procedure for Determining Breaches of ATVOD Rules Relating to VOD Services," December 19, 2013.

ATVOD. "Register of Interests," May 22, 2014.

ATVOD. "Response to the European Commission Green Paper 'Preparing for a Fully Converged Audiovisual World: Growth, Creation and Values.'" European Commission, September 27, 2013. http://ec.europa.eu/newsroom/dae/document.cfm?doc_id=3979.

ATVOD. "Review of Rule 11 Determination in Relation to the service 'Daisy Rock UK,'" April 29, 2015.

ATVOD. "Review of Rule 11 Determination in Relation to the service 'Mistress R'eal,'" May 18, 2015.

ATVOD. "Review of Rule 11 Determination in Relation to the service 'Panties Pulled Down,'" April 29, 2015.

ATVOD. "Rules & Guidance, Statutory Rules and Non-Binding Guidance for Providers of On-Demand Programme Services (ODPS), Edition 3," May 5, 2015.

ATVOD. "Statement on Regulatory Fees for On-Demand Programme Services for the Period 1 April 2011 to 31 March 2012 ('Year Two')," June 28, 2011.

ATVOD. "Statement on Regulatory Fees for On-Demand Programme Services for the Period 1 April 2014 to 31 March 2015," June 13, 2014.

ATVOD. "Statement on the Adoption of New Guidance on the Scope of the Regulations Relating to Video on Demand Services," May 2, 2014.

ATVOD. "Statement on UK Column," March 7, 2014.

ATVOD. "Summary of Determination That the Provider of Frankie and Friends Is in Breach of ATVOD Rules 1 & 4 and Thereby Has Contravened Sec. 368BA and Sec. 368D (3) (ZA) of the Coomunications Act," September 8, 2013.

ATVOD. "Summary of Determination That the Provider of the On-Demand Programme Service 'Jessica Pressley' was in Breach of ATVOD's Rule 11 and Thereby Contravened Sec. 368E (2) CA," July 23, 2013.

ATVOD. "Summary of Determination That the Provider of the On-Demand Programme Service 'Pleasuring Herself' was in Breach of ATVOD's Rule 11 and Thereby Contravened Sec. 368E (2) CA," September 9, 2013.

ATVOD. "Summary of Determination That the Provider of the On-Demand Programme Service 'The British Institution' was in Breach of ATVOD's Rule 11 and Thereby Contravened Sec. 368E (2) CA," July 9, 2013.

ATVOD. "Summary of Determination That the Provider of the On-Demand Programme Service 'The Casting Room' was in Breach of ATVOD's Rule 11 and Thereby Contravened Sec. 368E (2) CA," March 6, 2013.

ATVOD. "Summary of Determination That the Provider of Vice (Video) Is in Breach of ATVOD Rules 1 & 4 and Thereby Has Contravened Sec. 368BA and Sec. 368D (3) (ZA) of the Coomunications Act," August 14, 2013.

ATVOD. "The Culture, Media & Sports Inquiry into Online Safety, Submission from the Authority for Television On Demand ('ATVOD')," October 3, 2013. http://www.publications.parliament.uk/pa/cm201314/cmselect/cmcumeds/729/729vw64.htm.

ATVOD, and Ofcom. "Joint Statement by ATVOD and Ofcom on the Possibility of Concessionary Regulatory Fees for Small-Scale Vide on Demand Services for the Period up to 31 March 2011," December 11, 2010.

Bayerische Landeszentrale für neue Medien. "Bescheid C," August 2, 2011.

Bayerische Landeszentrale für neue Medien. "Bescheid D," December 15, 2009.

Bayerische Landeszentrale für neue Medien. "Bescheid E," January 12, 2011.

Bayerische Landeszentrale für neue Medien. "Bescheid F," August 16, 2011.

Bayerische Landeszentrale für neue Medien. "Bescheid G," September 24, 2013.

Bayerische Landeszentrale für neue Medien. "Bescheid H," March 11, 2011.

Bayerische Landeszentrale für neue Medien. "Bescheid I," September 11, 2009.

BBFC. "BBFC Guidelines, Age Ratings You Trust," 2014. http://bbfc.co.uk/sites/default/files/attachments/BBFC%20Classification%20Guidelines%202014_0.pdf.

Bundeskommunikationssenat. "Entscheidung GZ 611.191/0005-BKS/2012," December 13, 2012.

CSA. "Adolescents/jeunes adultes et médias: Le séquençage des pratiques médias des 13-24 ans," 2014. http://www.csa.fr/content/download/51801/499348/file/Synth%C3%A8se%20jeunes%20et%20m%C3%A9dias%20.pdf.

CSA. "Avis n° 2010-22 du 27 septembre 2010 sur un projet de décret relatif aux services de médias audiovisuels à la demande, Official Journal No. 264 of 14.11.2010, p. 70," 2010. http://www.csa.fr/Espace-Presse/Communiques-de-presse/Decret-relatif-aux-services-de-medias-audiovisuels-SMAD-le-CSA-emet-un-avis-defavorable.

CSA. "Bilan de l'activité et du respect des obligations des Services de Médias à la Demande en 2012," May 2014. http://www.csa.fr/content/download/51787/499153/file/Bilan%20des%20d%C3%A9clarations.pdf.

CSA. "Bilan de l'activité et du respect des obligations des Services de Médias à la Demande en 2013," February 2015. http://www.csa.fr/content/download/202544/536524/file/Bilan%20SMAD%202013%20version%20publiable.pdf.

CSA. "Code de déontologie applicable aux membres du Conseil," April 2, 2003. http://csa.fr/Le-CSA/Presentation-du-Conseil/Code-de-deontologie-applicable-aux-membres-du-Conseil.

CSA. "Communiqué n° 498, Le CSA préconise la suppression des programmes pornographiques à la télévision," July 2, 2002. http://www.csa.fr/var/ezflow_site/storage/csa/rapport2002/donnees/annexes/A25_IV_communique498.htm.

CSA. "Consultation sur la directive 2010/13/EU relative aux services de médias audiovisuels (directive SMA), Un cadre pour les médias au 21e siècle," September 2015. http://ec.europa.eu/newsroom/dae/document.cfm?action=display&doc_id=12036.

CSA. "Contribution à la réflexion sur l'évolution de la régulation de l'audiovisuel et des communications électroniques," October 30, 2012. http://www.csa.fr/es/content/download/25048/367928/file/Contribution+CSA+r%C3%A9gulation+audiovisuel+-+Octobre+2012+prot%C3%A9g%C3%A9.pdf.

CSA. "Contribution sur l'adaptation de la régulation audiovisuelle," January 24, 2013. www.csa.fr/content/download/29369/393286/file/Contribution%20adaptation%20r%C3%A9gulation%20Janvier%202013.pdf.

CSA. "Déclaration pour l'année 2012 au titre du décret SMAD," 2013. www.csa.fr/content/download/37263/444477/file/Questionnaire%20-%20D%C3%A9cret%20Smad%20-%20Exercice%202012%20-%20word.docx.

CSA. "La protection des mineurs à l'heure de la convergence des médias audiovisuels et d'internet," 2012. http://www.csa.fr/content/download/20592/342842/file/Protection_des%20_mineurs_et_%20internet.pdf.

CSA. "La synthèse des travaux des cinq groupes de réflexion," May 12, 2012. www.csa.fr/content/download/27118/374852/file/fichesconf51212%20%5BMode%20de%20compatibilit%C3%A9%5D.pdf.

CSA. "La télévision de rattrapage: une pratique installée, une économie en devenir," February 13, 2015. http://www.csa.fr/content/download/201366/533023/file/%C3%89tude%20sur%20le%20march%C3%A9%20de%20la%20TVR_CSA_02-2015.pdf.

CSA. "Le CSA lance un formulaire de déclaration en ligne pour les services de médias audiovisuels à la demande," May 22, 2015. http://www.csa.fr/Espace-Presse/Communiques-de-presse/Le-CSA-lance-un-formulaire-de-declaration-en-ligne-pour-les-services-de-medias-audiovisuels-a-la-demande.

CSA. "Les principes fondateurs et les 14 propositions de la Commission de suivi des usages de la télévision connectée," May 12, 2012. www.csa.fr/content/download/27118/374848/file/dossierdepresseCommission%20TV%20connect%C3%A9e051212.pdf.

CSA. "Plateformes et accès aux contenus audiovisuels, Quels enjeux concurrentiels et de régulation?," September 23, 2016. http://www.csa.fr/content/download/223681/597947/file/CSA-Etude_plateformes_%202016.pdf.

CSA. "Premier approche de la Télévision Sociale," February 2013. www.csa.fr/content/download/30546/422747/file/Commission%20prospective%20-%20TV%20sociale.pdf.

CSA. "Rapport Annuel 2010," August 9, 2011. http://csa.fr/Etudes-et-publications/Les-rapports-annuels-du-CSA/CSA-Rapport-annuel-2010.

CSA. "Rapport Annuel 2011," December 6, 2012. http://csa.fr/Etudes-et-publications/Les-rapports-annuels-du-CSA/CSA-Rapport-annuel-2011.

CSA. "Rapport Annuel 2012," May 28, 2013. http://csa.fr/Etudes-et-publications/Les-rapports-annuels-du-CSA/CSA-Rapport-annuel-2012.

CSA. "Rapport Annuel 2013," December 3, 2014. http://csa.fr/Etudes-et-publications/Les-rapports-annuels-du-CSA/CSA-Rapport-annuel-2013.

CSA. "Rapport Annuel 2014," 04 2015. http://www.csa.fr/Etudes-et-publications/Les-rapports-annuels-du-CSA/CSA-Rapport-annuel-2014.

CSA. "Rapport Annuel 2015," April 4, 2016. http://www.csa.fr/content/download/216245/580039/file/Rapport_annuel_2015.pdf.

CSA. "Rapport au Gouvernement sur l'application du décret n° 2010-1379 du 12 novembre 2010 relatif aux services de médias audiovisuels à la demande (SMAD)," December 2013. http://csa.fr/Etudes-et-publications/Les-autres-rapports/Rapport-au-Gouvernement-sur-l-application-du-decret-n-2010-1379-du-12-novembre-2010-relatif-aux-services-de-medias-audiovisuels-a-la-demande-SMAD.

CSA. "Réponse à la consultation publique de la Commission européenne sur le Livre vert: 'Se préparer à un monde audiovisuel totalement convergent : croissance, création et valeurs,'" September 25, 2013. www.csa.fr/%20csa/content/download/41934/471929/file/R%C3%A9ponse%20CSA%20LV%20finale.pdf.

Die Medienanstalten. "Checkliste der Medienanstalten für Veranstalter von Web-TV," September 24, 2014. http://www.die-medienanstalten.de/.

Die Medienanstalten. "Positionen der DLM zur Fortentwicklung der Plattformregulierung," March 15, 2016. http://www.die-medienanstalten.de/fileadmin/Download/Positionen/Gemeinsame_Positionen/DLM-Position_Fortentwicklung_der_Plattformregulierung_2016-03-15.pdf.

Die Medienanstalten. "Stellungnahme der Medienanstalten zum 'Grünbuch der Europäischen Kommission,'" August 29, 2013. http://www.die-medienanstalten.de/service/positionen.html.

Die Medienanstalten. "Stellungnahme der Medienanstalten zur Anhörung der Bund-Länder-AG Plattformregulierung," June 25, 2015. www.die-medienanstalten.de/fileadmin/Download/Positionen/Gemeinsame_Positionen/Stellungnahme_der_Medienanstalten_zur_Plattformregulierung_14072015.pdf.

Direktorenkonferenz der Landesmedienanstalten. “Antwort der DLM auf die Konsultation der Kommission zur AVMD-RL, Eine Mediengesetzgebung für das 21. Jahrhundert,” September 2015. www.die-medienanstalten.de/fileadmin/Download/Positionen/Europa/Antwort_der_DLM_auf_die_Konsultation_der_Kommission_zur_AVMD-RL_-_Eine_Mediengesetzgebung_f%C3%BCr_das_21._Jahrhundert_web.pdf.

Direktorenkonferenz der Landesmedienanstalten. “Drittes Strukturpapier zur Unterscheidung von Rundfunk und Mediendiensten.” Die Medienanstalten, June 11, 2003.

Direktorenkonferenz der Landesmedienanstalten. “Positionspapier Connected TV.” Die Medienanstalten, February 19, 2013. http://www.die-medienanstalten.de/service/positionen.html.

Direktorenkonferenz der Landesmedienanstalten. “Stellungnahme der DLM zur Revision der AVMD-Richtlinie,” September 6, 2015. www.die-medienanstalten.de/fileadmin/Download/Positionen/Gemeinsame_Positionen/Stellungnahme_der_DLM_zur_Revision_der_AVMD-RL_f%C3%BCr_die_Bund-L%C3%A4nder-Kommission_27Juli2015.pdf.

Direktorenkonferenz der Landesmedienanstalten. “Überarbeitung des dritten Strukturpapiers/ Internet-Radio und IP-TV.” Die Medienanstalten, June 27, 2007.

ERGA. “ERGA Opinion on AVMSD Proposals, ERGA (2016)03,” October 5, 2016. http://ec.europa.eu/newsroom/dae/document.cfm?action=display&doc_id=17994.

ERGA. “Report on Material Jurisdiction in a Converged Environment,” December 18, 2015. http://ec.europa.eu/newsroom/dae/document.cfm?action=display&doc_id=13287.

ERGA. “Report on the Independence of National Regulators,” 2015. http://ec.europa.eu/newsroom/dae/document.cfm?doc_id=12952.

ERGA. “Report on the Protection of Minors in a Converged Environment,” November 27, 2015. http://ec.europa.eu/newsroom/dae/document.cfm?action=display&doc_id=13248.

ERGA. “Scoping Paper on Territorial Jurisdiction in a Convergent Audiovisual World,” April 14, 2015. http://ec.europa.eu/information_society/newsroom/cf/dae/document.cfm?action=display&doc_id=9387.

Essential Research. “On-Demand Services: Understanding Consumer Choices, A Research Report for Ofcom,” October 2012. http://stakeholders.ofcom.org.uk/binaries/broadcast/tv-ops/vod/Research_Report.pdf.

Essential Research. “On-Demand Services: Understanding Consumer Choices. A Research Report for Ofcom,” October 2012. http://stakeholders.ofcom.org.uk/binaries/broadcast/tv-ops/vod/Research_Report.pdf.

Essential Research. “The Regulation of Video-on-Demand: Consumer Views on What Makes Audiovisual services ‘TV-like’ - a Qualitative Research Report,” December 2009. http://stakeholders.ofcom.org.uk/binaries/research/tv-research/vod.pdf.

Essential Research. “The Regulation of Video-on-Demand: Consumer Views on What Makes Audiovisual services ‘TV-Like’ - a Qualitative Research Report,” December 2009. http://stakeholders.ofcom.org.uk/binaries/research/tv-research/vod.pdf.

FSM. “Beschwerde Nr. 12057,” 2010. http://www.fsm.de/beschwerdestelle/praxisentscheidungen/Entscheidung_12057_dominadienste.pdf.

FSM. “Beschwerde Nr. 12418,” 2011. https://www.fsm.de/beschwerdestelle/praxisentscheidungen/Entscheidung_gangsterrap.pdf.

FSM. “Beschwerde Nr. 47707,” 2015. http://www.fsm.de/beschwerdestelle/praxisentscheidungen/Entscheidung_Onlinegalerie.pdf.

FSM. “Beschwerde Nrn. 43462, 43477, 43478,” 2014. http://www.fsm.de/beschwerdestelle/praxisentscheidungen/EntscheidungBondage.pdf.

FSM. “Entscheidung Nr. 02095,” 2005. https://www.fsm.de/beschwerdestelle/praxisentscheidungen/Entscheidung_PornografieTextform.pdf.

FSM. “Entscheidung Nr. 04081,” 2006. https://www.fsm.de/beschwerdestelle/praxisentscheidungen/Entscheidung_GirlsLinklisten.pdf.

FSM. “Entscheidung Nr. 4099,” 2006. http://www.fsm.de/beschwerdestelle/praxisentscheidungen/Entscheidung_pdophilie.pdf.

FSM. “Entscheidung Nr. 05259,” 2007. http://www.fsm.de/beschwerdestelle/praxisentscheidungen/Entscheidung_Essstrungsforum.pdf.

FSM. “Entscheidung Nr. 06314,” 2008. https://www.fsm.de/beschwerdestelle/praxisentscheidungen/Entscheidung_Bordellbewertungsportal.pdf.

FSM. “Entscheidung Nr. 07213,” 2008. https://www.fsm.de/beschwerdestelle/praxisentscheidungen/Entscheidung_Pdophilieforum.pdf.

FSM. “Entscheidung Nr. 07933,” 2009. https://www.fsm.de/beschwerdestelle/praxisentscheidungen/Entscheidung_erotischeGeschichten.pdf.

FSM. “Entscheidung Nr. 08838,” 2009. https://www.fsm.de/beschwerdestelle/praxisentscheidungen/Entscheidung_Pornografie_BildTextKombination.pdf.

FSM. “Entscheidung Nr. 10276,” 2010. https://www.fsm.de/beschwerdestelle/praxisentscheidungen/Entscheidung_zoophilie.pdf.

FSM. “Prüfgrundsätze,” 2011. http://www.fsm.de/ueber-uns/veroeffentlichungen/Prfgrundstze_2.Auflage.pdf.

FSM. “Stellungnahme auf Anfrage von BKM und Bayerischer Staatskanzlei zur Revision der Audiovisuellen Mediendienste-Richtlinie,” 2015. http://www.fsm.de/ueber-uns/veroeffentlichungen/20150630_FSMStellungnahmezurRevisionderAudiovisuellenMediendiensteRichtlinie.pdf.

jugendschutz.net. “Protection of Minors on the Internet, Annual Report 2014,” 2015. http://www.jugendschutz.net/fileadmin/download/pdf/Annual-report-2014.pdf.

KJM. “FAQ „Anerkannte Jugendschutzprogramme“ für Inhalteanbieter,” June 2014. http://www.kjm-online.de/fileadmin/Download_KJM/Rundfunk/FAQ_Jugendschutzprogramme_Inhalteanbieter.pdf.

KJM. “Jugendschutzprogramme nach § 11 JMStV, Erwartungen an Anbieter und Maßnahmen der KJM,” May 2013. http://www.kjm-online.de/fileadmin/Bilder/Presse/Pressemitteilungen/KJM-PM_04_2013_Jugendschutzprogramme_Anlage.pdf.

KJM. “Kriterien für die Anerkennung von Jugendschutzprogrammen im Bereich des World Wide Web,” May 2011. http://www.kjm-online.de/fileadmin/Download_KJM/Rundfunk/Informationen-fr-JSP-Anbieter_Stand_2011-05-11.pdf.

KJM. "Kriterien für die Aufsicht im Rundfunk und in den Telemedien," December 2013. http://www.kjm-online.de/fileadmin/Download_KJM/Service/Pr%C3%BCfkriterien/Kriterien_KJM_Fassung_Dezember_2013.pdf.

KJM. "Kriterien für technische Mittel als Jugendschutzmaßnahme für entwicklungsbeeinträchtigende Inhalte im Bereich des World Wide Web: Stichwort „Personalausweiskennziffernprüfung/„Persocheckverfahren“," 2009. http://www.kjm-online.de/fileadmin/Download_KJM/Rundfunk/Kriterienraster_technische_Mittel.pdf.

KJM. "Kriterien zur Bewertung von Konzepten für Altersverifikationssysteme," 2014. http://www.kjm-online.de/fileadmin/Download_KJM/Telemedien/KJM-AVS-Raster.pdf.

KJM. "Sechster Tätigkeitsbericht über die Durchführung der Bestimmungen des Jugendmedienschutz-Staatsvertrag gem. § 17 Abs. 3 JMStV in der Zeit vom März 2013 - Februar 2015," May 2015. http://www.kjm-online.de/fileadmin/Download_KJM/Service/Berichte/Sechster_Taetigkeitsbericht_der_KJM.pdf.

KJM. "Übersicht über positiv bewertete Konzepte für geschlossene Benutzergruppen," 2015. http://www.kjm-online.de/fileadmin/Download_KJM/Telemedien/AVS_Uebersicht.pdf.

KJM. "Übersicht über positiv bewertete Konzepte für technische Mittel," 2015. http://www.kjm-online.de/fileadmin/Download_KJM/Rundfunk/Uebersicht_technische_Mittel.pdf.

KommAustria. "Bescheid KOA 1.950/12-048," September 10, 2012.

KommAustria. "Bescheid KOA 3.800/15-009," December 2, 2015.

Kommission für Zulassung und Aufsicht. "Überarbeitung des dritten Strukturpapiers der Landesmedienanstalten zur Abgrenzung von Rundfunk und Mediendiensten," November 17, 2009.

Landeszentrale für Medien und Kommunikation Rheinland-Pfalz. "Bescheid Schoenstatt-tv GmbH," June 22, 2010.

Medienanstalten. "Gemeinsame Richtlinien der Landesmedienanstalten zur Gewährleistung des Schutzes der Menschenwürde und des Jugendschutzes," March 8, 2005. http://www.kjm-online.de/fileadmin/Download_KJM/Recht/JuSchRiL.pdf.

Medienkommission der Landesanstalt für Medien NRW. "Stellungnahme der nordrhein-westfälischen Medienkommission der Landesanstalt für Medien NRW (LfM)," March 9, 2013. http://www.lfm-nrw.de/fileadmin/lfm-nrw/Aktuelles_Startseite/Gruenbuch_Stellungnahme_MK.pdf.

Ofcom. "Appeal by (1) Nickelodeon UK Limited (in Relation to Nickelodeon Content on Virgin Mary); (2) Paramount (UK) Partnership (in Relation to Comedy Central Content on Virgin Media); and (3) MTV Networks Europe (in Relation to MTV Content on Virgin Media) against a Notice of Determination by ATVOD That the Services Have Contravened Section 368BA of the Communications Act 2003," January 18, 2012.

Ofcom. "Appeal by BBC Worldwide against a Notice of Determination by ATVOD That the Service BBC Worldwide on Mediaset Has Contravened Section 368BA of the Communications Act 2003," April 27, 2012.

Ofcom. “Appeal by BBC Worldwide against a Notice of Determination by ATVOD That the Service Top Gear YouTube Has Contravened Sections 368BA and 368D (3) (ZA) of the Communications Act 2003,” January 18, 2013.

Ofcom. “Appeal by BBC Worldwide Limited against a Notice of Determination by ATVOD That the Service BBC Food YouTube Has Contravened Sections 368BA and 368D (3) (ZA) of the Communications Act 2003,” January 18, 2013.

Ofcom. “Appeal by Brightonrock Communications Limited against a Notice of Determination by ATVOD That the Provider of the service ‘Daisy Rock UK’ has Contravened Sections 368BA and 368D (3) (ZA) of the Communications Act,” September 17, 2015.

Ofcom. “Appeal by BSKYB against a Notice of Determination by ATVOD That the Service Viacom Channel Providers’ on the Sky Anytime Platform Has Contravened Sections 368BA and 368D (3) (ZA) of the Communications Act 2003,” December 7, 2012.

Ofcom. “Appeal by ChannelFlip Media Limited against a Notice of Determination by ATVOD That the Service Channel Flip Has Contravened Section 368BA of the Communications Act 2003,” December 14, 2012.

Ofcom. “Appeal by Everton Football Club against a Notice of Determination by ATVOD That the Service Everton TV Has Contravened Section 368D (3) (ZA) of the Communications Act 2003,” June 26, 2013.

Ofcom. “Appeal by Frank Hollins against a Notice of Determination That the Provider of the service ‘Panties Pulled Down’ has Contravened Sec. 368BA and 368D (3) (ZA) of the Communications Act.” Broadcast and On Demand Bulletin, Issue 304, May 9, 2016.

Ofcom. “Appeal by Harry Barrett against a Notice of Determination by ATVOD That the Provider of the service ‘Frankie and Friends’ has Contravened Sections 368BA and 368D (3) (ZA) of the Communications Act,” August 14, 2014.

Ofcom. “Appeal by Itziar Bilbao Urrutia against a Notice of Determination by ATVOD That the Provider of the service ‘The Urban Chick Supremacy Cell’ has Contravened Sections 368BA and 368D (3) (ZA) of the Communications Act Whilst Operating an ODPS,” August 14, 2014.

Ofcom. “Appeal by Laura Jenkins against a Notice of Determination That the Provider of the services ‘Candy Girl Pass’ and ‘All Teens World’ has Contravened Sec. 368-BA and Sec. 368(3)(ZA) CA.” Broadcast and On Demand Bulletin, Issue 306, June 6, 2016.

Ofcom. “Appeal by MTV Networks Europe against a Notice of Determination by ATVOD That the Provider of the Service Viva TV Music Has Contravened Section 368BA of the Communications Act 2003,” February 22, 2012.

Ofcom. “Appeal by News Group Newspapers Limited against a Notice of Determination by ATVOD That the Provider of the Service Sun Video Has Contravened Section 368BA of the Communications Act 2003,” December 21, 2011.

Ofcom. “Appeal by Playboy TV against a Notice of Determination by ATVOD That the Provider of the Service Climax 3 Uncut Has Contravened Section 368BA of the Communications Act 2003,” May 13, 2011.

Ofcom. "Appeal by Playboy TV against a Notice of Determination by ATVOD That the Provider of the Service Demand Adult Has Contravened Section 368BA of the Communications Act 2003," May 13, 2011.

Ofcom. "Appeal by Playboy TV UK/Benelux Limited against a Notice of Determination by ATVOD That It Was the Provider of the service 'Demand Adult' as at 14 September 2012," September 23, 2013.

Ofcom. "Appeal by Playboy TV UK/Benelux Limited against a Notice of Determination by ATVOD That It Was the Provider of the service 'Playboy TV' as at 14 September 2012," September 23, 2013.

Ofcom. "Appeal by The Business Channel.TV against a Notice of Determination by ATVOD That the Service The Business Channel Has Contravened Sections 368BA and 368D (3) (ZA) of the Communications Act 2003," January 18, 2013.

Ofcom. "Appeal by Vice UK Limited against a Notice of Determination by ATVOD That the Service Vice (Video) Has Contravened Sections 368BA and 368D (3) (ZA) of the Communications Act 2003," July 21, 2015.

Ofcom. "Children and Parents: Media Use and Attitudes Report," October 2014. http://stakeholders.ofcom.org.uk/binaries/research/media-literacy/media-use-attitudes-14/Childrens_2014_Report.pdf.

Ofcom. "Citizens, Communications and Convergence, A Summary of Stakeholder Responses, and Our next Steps," June 4, 2010. http://stakeholders.ofcom.org.uk/binaries/consultations/citizens/statement/Citizen_Statement.pdf.

Ofcom. "Citizens, Communications and Convergence, Discussion Paper," November 7, 2008. http://stakeholders.ofcom.org.uk/binaries/consultations/citizens/summary/discussionpaper.pdf.

Ofcom. "Consultation on Directive 2010/13/EU on Audiovisual Media Services (AVMSD), A Media Framework for the 21st Century," September 2015. http://ec.europa.eu/newsroom/dae/document.cfm?doc_id=11230.

Ofcom. "Designation pursuant to Section 368B of the Communications Act 2003 of Functions to the Association for Television On-Demand in Relation to the Regulation of On-Demand Programme Services," 2010.

Ofcom. "Future Regulation of on-Demand Programme Services, Statement and Consultation," December 18, 2015. http://stakeholders.ofcom.org.uk/binaries/consultations/vod_procedures/summary/Future_regulation_of_on-demand_programme_services.pdf.

Ofcom. "How to Notify, Guidance Notes on How to Notify an on Demand Programme Service to Ofcom," December 18, 2015. http://stakeholders.ofcom.org.uk/binaries/broadcast/on-demand/rules-guidance/How_to_Notify.pdf.

Ofcom. "How to Notify, Guidance Notes on How to Notify an on-Demand Programme Service to Ofcom," December 18, 2015. http://stakeholders.ofcom.org.uk/binaries/broadcast/on-demand/rules-guidance/How_to_Notify.pdf.

Ofcom. "Identifying Appropriate Regulatory Solutions: Principles for Analysing Self- and Co-Regulation, Statement," October 12, 2008. http://stakeholders.ofcom.org.uk/binaries/consultations/coregulation/statement/statement.pdf.

Ofcom. "Interim Breach Procedures for Investigating Breaches of Rules for on-Demand Programme Services," December 18, 2015. http://stakeholders.ofcom.org.uk/binaries/broadcast/on-demand/rules-guidance/interim_procedures.pdf.

Ofcom. "Notification Form for On-Demand Programme Service Providers," 2016. http://stakeholders.ofcom.org.uk/binaries/broadcast/on-demand/notification.rtf.

Ofcom. "Ofcom Brings Regulation of 'Video-On-Demand' In-House," October 14, 2015. http://media.ofcom.org.uk/news/2015/1520333/.

Ofcom. "Ofcom Response to the European Commission Green Paper 'Preparing for a Fully Converged Audiovisual World: Growth, Creation and Values.'" European Commission, September 27, 2013. http://ec.europa.eu/digital-agenda/en/news/consultation-green-paper-preparing-fully-converged-audiovisual-world-growth-creation-and-values.

Ofcom. "Ofcom's Enforcement Action against the 'Jessica Pressley' service," November 15, 2013.

Ofcom. "Procedures for Investigating Breaches of Rules for on-Demand Programme Services," April 1, 2016. http://stakeholders.ofcom.org.uk/binaries/broadcast/on-demand/rules-guidance/procedures-investigating-breaches.pdf.

Ofcom. "Procedures for the Consideration of Statutory Sanctions Arising in the Context of on-Demand Programme Services," December 18, 2015. http://stakeholders.ofcom.org.uk/binaries/broadcast/on-demand/rules-guidance/Revised_sanctions_procedures.pdf.

Ofcom. "Procedures for the Handling of Appeals of ATVOD Decisions in Relation to What Constitutes an On-Demand Programme Service," January 10, 2013. http://stakeholders.ofcom.org.uk/broadcasting/tv/video-on-demand/.

Ofcom. "Proposals for the Regulation of Video on Demand Services, Consultation," September 14, 2009. http://stakeholders.ofcom.org.uk/binaries/consultations/vod/summary/vod.pdf.

Ofcom. "Report on Adults' Media Use and Attitudes." Ofcom, May 2015. http://stakeholders.ofcom.org.uk/market-data-research/other/research-publications/adults/media-lit-10years/.

Ofcom. "Report on Internet Safety Measures, Internet Service Providers: Network Level Filtering Measures," July 22, 2014. http://stakeholders.ofcom.org.uk/internet/internet-safety-2.

Ofcom. "Report on Internet Safety Measures, Strategies of Parental Protection for Children Online," January 15, 2014. http://stakeholders.ofcom.org.uk/internet/internet-safety-measures/.

Ofcom. "Report on Internet Safety Measures, Strategies of Parental Protection for Children Online," January 12, 2015. http://stakeholders.ofcom.org.uk/internet/internet-safety-2015.

Ofcom. "Rules & Guidance, Statutory Rules and Non-Binding Guidance for Providers of On-Demand Programme Services (ODPS)," January 1, 2016. http://stakeholders.ofcom.org.uk/binaries/broadcast/on-demand/rules-guidance/rules_and_guidance.pdf.

Ofcom. "Rules and Guidance, Statutory Rules and Non-Binding Guidance for Providers of On-Demand Programme Services," May 20, 2016. stakeholders.ofcom.org.uk/binaries/broadcast/on-demand/rules-guidance/rules_and_guidance.pdf.

Ofcom. "Sanction Decision for the Provision of the on Demand Programme service 'Demand Adult,'" January 16, 2013.

Ofcom. "Sanction Decision for the Provision of the on Demand Programme service 'HardGlam,'" December 11, 2014.

Ofcom. "Sanction Decision for the Provision of the on Demand Programme Service 'playboytv.co.uk,'" January 16, 2013.

Ofcom. "Sanction Decision for the Provision of the on Demand Programme service 'Strictly Broadband,'" December 5, 2012.

Ofcom. "Sexually Explicit Material and Video On Demand Services, A Report to DCMS by Ofcom," August 4, 2011. http://stakeholders.ofcom.org.uk/binaries/internet/explicit-material-vod.pdf.

Ofcom. "The Amended Designation Dated 14 September 2012, Designation pursuant to Section 368B of the Communications Act 2003 of Functions to the Association for Television On-Demand in Relation to the Regulation of on-Demand Programme Services," 2012.

Ofcom. "The Communications Market Report," July 8, 2014. http://stakeholders.ofcom.org.uk/binaries/research/cmr/cmr14/2014_UK_CMR.pdf.

Ofcom. "The Consumer Experience of 2014," January 28, 2015. http://stakeholders.ofcom.org.uk/market-data-research/market-data/consumer-experience-reports/consumer-experience-14/.

Ofcom. "The Office of Communications, Annual Report and Accounts for the Period 1 April 2013 to 31 March 2014," July 2014. http://www.ofcom.org.uk/files/2014/07/annrep1314.pdf.

Ofcom. "The Office of Communications, Annual Report and Accounts for the Period 1 April 2015 to 31 March 2016," July 2016. http://www.ofcom.org.uk/content/about/annual-reports-plans/annual-reports/annual-report-15-16/Ofcom_Annual_Report_2015-2016.pdf.

Ofcom. "The Regulation of Video on Demand Services, Statement," December 18, 2009. http://stakeholders.ofcom.org.uk/binaries/consultations/vod/statement/vodstatement.pdf.

Ofcom. "UK Audience Attitudes to the Broadcast Media," July 5, 2013. http://stakeholders.ofcom.org.uk/market-data-research/other/tv-research/attitudes-broadcast-media/.

Ofcom. "Who Needs to Notify, Guidance Notes on Who Needs to Notify an on-Demand Programme Service to Ofcom," December 18, 2015. http://stakeholders.ofcom.org.uk/binaries/broadcast/on-demand/rules-guidance/Guidance_on_who_needs_to_notify.pdf.

Ofcom, and ATVOD. "Regulatory Fees for Video on Demand Services for the Period up to 31 March 2011, Joint Statement," June 17, 2010.

# Table of Cases

*Court of Justice of the European Union*

| | | |
|---|---|---|
| 22/70 | Commission of the European Communities v Council of the European Communities, European Agreement on Road Transport (AETR) | EU:C:1971:32 |
| 36/74 | Walrave and Koch v Association Union Cycliste Internationale | EU:C:1974:140 |
| 155/73 | Giuseppe Sacchi | EU:C:1974:40 |
| 33/74 | Van Binsbergen v Bedrifsvereniging voor de Metallnijverheid | EU:C:1974:131 |
| 52/79 | Procureur du Roi v Marc J. V. C. Debauve a.o. | EU:C:1980:83 |
| 62/79 | SA Compagnie générale pour la diffusion de la télévision, Coditel, a.o. v Ciné Vog Films a.o. | EU:C:1980:84 |
| 352/85 | Bond van Adverteerders and others v The Netherlands State | EU:C:1988:196 |
| 68/88 | Commission of the European Communities v Hellenic Republic | EU:C:1989:339 |
| C-221/89 | The Queen vs. Secretary of State for Transport, ex parte Factortame Ltd a.o. | EU:C:1991:320 |
| C-288/89 | Collectieve Antennevoorziening Gouda v Commissariaat voor de Media | EU:C:1991:323 |
| C-353/89 | Commission v Netherlands | EU:C:1991:325 |
| C-148/91 | Veronica Omroep Organisatie v Commissariaat voor de Media | EU:C:1993:45 |
| C-23/93 | TV 10 SA v Commissariaat voor de Media | EU:C:1994:362 |
| C-384/93 | Alpine Investments BV v Minister van Financiën | EU:C:1995:126 |
| C-55/94 | Reinhard Gebhard v Consiglio dell'Ordine degli Avvocati e Procuratori di Milano | EU:C:1995:411 |
| C-222/94 | Commission of the European Communities v United Kingdom of Great Britain and Northern Ireland | EU:C:1996:314 |
| C-11/95 | Commission of the European Communities v Kingdom of Belgium | EU:C:1996:316 |
| C-34-36/95 | Konsumentombudsmannen v De Agostini, Förlag AB and TV-Shop I Sverige AB | EU:C:1997:344 |

| | | |
|---|---|---|
| C-261/95 | Rosalba Palmisani v Istituto nazionale della previdenza sociale (INPS) | EU:C:1997:351 |
| C-56/96 | VT4 v Vlaamse Gemeenschap | EU:C:1997:284 |
| C-212/97 | Centros v Erhvervs-og Selskabsstyrelsen | EU:C:1999:126 |
| C-6/98 | Arbeitsgemeinschaft Deutscher Rundfunkanstalten (ARD) and PRO Sieben Media AG | EU:C:1999:532 |
| C-466/98 | Commission of the European Communities v United Kingdom of Great Britain and Northern Ireland | EU:C:2002:624 |
| C-467/98 | Commission of the European Communities v. Kingdom of Denmark | EU:C:2002:625 |
| C-468/98 | Commission of the European Communities v Kingdom of Sweden | EU:C:2002:626 |
| C-469/98 | Commission of the European Communities v Republic of Finland | EU:C:2002:627 |
| C-471/98 | Commission of the European Communities v Kingdom of Belgium | EU:C:2002:628 |
| C-472/98 | Commission of the European Communities v Grand Duchy of Luxembourg | EU:C:2002:629 |
| C-475/98 | Commission of the European Communities v Republic of Austria | EU:C:2002:630 |
| C-476/98 | Commission of the European Communities v Federal Republic of Germany | EU:C:2002:631 |
| C-17/00 | François De Coster v Collège des bourgmestre et échevins de Watermael-Boitsfort | EU:C:2001:651 |
| T-33/01 | Infront WM AG v Commission of the European Communities | EU:T:2005:461 |
| C-245/01 | RTL Television GmbH v Niedersächsische Landesmedienanstalt für Privaten Rundfunk (NML) | EU:C:2003:580 |
| C-422/01 | Försäkringsaktiebolaget Skandia (publ) and Ola Ramstedt v Riksskatteverket | EU:C:2003:380 |
| C-262/02 | Commission of the European Communities v French Republic (Loi Evin) | EU:C:2004:431 |
| C-429/02 | Bacardi France SAS v Télévision francaise 1 (TF1) and Others | EU:C:2004:432 |
| C-89/04 | Mediakabel BV v Commissariaat voor de Media | EU:C:2005:348 |
| C-125/06 P | Commission of the European Communities v Infront WM AG | EU:C:2008:159 |
| C-195/06 | Kommunikationsbehörde Austria (KkommAustria) v Österreichischer Rundfunk (ORF) | EU:C:2007:613 |

| | | |
|---|---|---|
| C-244/06 | Dynamic Medien Vertriebs GmbH v Avides Media AG, | EU:C:2008:85 |
| T-385/07 | Fédération Internationale de Football Association (FIFA) v European Commission | ECR:T:2011:42 |
| T-55/08 | Union des associations européennes de football (UEFA) v European Commission | EU:T:2011:43 |
| T-68/08 | Fédération Internationale de Football Association (FIFA) v European Commission | EU:T:2011:44 |
| C-279/09 | DEB Deutsch Energiehandels- und Beratungsgesellschaft mbH v Bundesrepublik Deutschland | EU:C:2010:811 |
| C-281/09 | European Commission v Kingdom of Spain, Judgment of 24.11.2011 | EU:C:2011:767 |
| C-517/09 | RTL Belgium | EU:C:2010:821 |
| C-244-245/10 | Mesopotamia Broadcast A/S METV and Roy TV A/S v Germany | EU:C:2011:607 |
| C-617/10 | Åklagaren v Hans Åkerberg Fransson | EU:C:2013:105 |
| C-201/11 P | UEFA v European Commission | EU:C:2013:519 |
| C-204/11 P | FIFA v European Commission | EU:C:2013:477 |
| C-205/11 P | FIFA v European Commission | EU:C:2013:478 |
| C-283/11 | Sky Österreich GmbH v Österreichischer Rundfunk (ORF) | EU:C:2013:28 |
| C-399/11 | Stefano Melloni v Ministerio Fiscal | EU:C:2013:107 |
| C-234/12 | Sky Italia srl v Autorità per le Garanzie nelle Comunicazioni (AGCOM) | EU:C:2013:496 |
| C-370/12 | Pringle v Government of Ireland, Ireland and the Attorney General | EU:C:2012:756 |
| C-291/13 | Sotiris Papasavvas v. O Fileleftheros Dimosia Etaireia Ltd a.o. | EU:C:2014:2209 |
| C-314/14 | Sanoma Media Finland Oy/Nelonen Media, Helsinki | EU:C:2016:89 |
| C-347/14 | New Media Online GmbH v Bundeskommunikationssenat | EU:C:2015:434 |
| C-362/14 | Maximilian Schrems v Data Protection Commissioner | EU:C:2015:650 |

*European Court of Human Rights*

| | | |
|---|---|---|
| Handyside v United Kingdom | Judgment of 07.12.1976 | Application no. 5493/72 |
| Lingens v Austria | Judgment of 08.06.1986 | Application no. 9815/82 |

| | | |
|---|---|---|
| Groppera Radio AG a.o. v Switzerland | Judgment of 28.03.1990 | Application no. 10890/84 |
| Otto-Preminger Institut v Austria | Judgment of 20.09.1994 | Application no. 13470/87 |
| Jersild v Denmark | Judgment of 23.09.1994 | Application no. 15890/89 |
| Verein gegen Tierfabriken v Switzerland | Judgment of 28.06.2001 | Application no. 24699/94 |
| Murphy v Ireland | Judgment of 03.12.2003 | Application no. 44179/98 |
| Informationsverein Lentia a.o. v Austria | Judgment of 24.11.1993 | Applications nos. 13914/88; 15041/89; 15717/89; 15779/89; 17207/90 |
| Manole a.o. v Moldova | Judgment of 17.12.2009 | Application no. 13936/02 |
| Times Newspapers Ltd v United Kingdom | Judgment of 10.03.2009 | Applications nos. 3002/03; 23676/03 |
| Dubus SA v France | Judgment of 11.09.2009 | Application no. 5242/04 |
| Mouvement Raelien Suisse v Switzerland | Judgment of 13.01.2013 | Application no. 16354/06 |
| Centro Europa 7 S.R.L. and Di Stefano v Italy | Judgment of 07.06.2012 | Application no. 38433/09 |
| Delfi AS v Estonia | Judgment of 16.06.2015 | Application no. 64569/09 |

*National Courts*

*Germany*
*Federal courts*

| | | |
|---|---|---|
| BGH | Judgment of 22.07.1969 | 1 StR 456/68 |
| BGH | Judgment of 22.05.2003 | 1 StR 70/03 |
| BGH | Judgment of 19.07.2007 | I ZR 137/04 |
| BGH | Judgment of 18.10.2007 | I ZR 102/05 |
| BGH | Judgment of 30.04.2015 | I ZR 13/14 |
| BVerfG | Judgment of 18.02.1961 | 2 BvG 1 u. 2/60 |
| BVerfG | Judgment of 27.07.1971 | 2 BvF 1/68; 2 BvR 702/68 |

| | | |
|---|---|---|
| BVerfG | Judgment of 05.06.1973 | 1 BvR 536/72 |
| BVerfG | Judgment of 16.06.1981 | 1 BvL 89/78 |
| BVerfG | Judgment of 04.11.1986 | 1 BvF 1/84 |
| BVerfG | Judgment of 24.03.1987 | 1 BvR 147/86; 1 BvR 478/86 |
| BVerfG | Order of 27.11.1990 | 1 BvR 402/87 |
| BVerfG | Order of 22.02.1994 | 1 BvL 30/88 |
| BVerfG | Judgment of 22.03.1995 | 2 BvG 1/89 |
| BVerfG | Order of 24.09.2009 | 1 BvR 1231/04 |
| BVerfG | Judgment of 20.02.2002 | 6 C 13/01 |

*State courts*

| | | |
|---|---|---|
| BayVGH | Judgment of 28.10.2009 | 7 N 09.1377 |
| BayVGH | Judgment of 23.03.2011 | 7 BV 09.2517 |
| KG Berlin | Judgment of 26.04.2004 | (5) 1 Ss 436/03 |
| LG Düsseldorf | Judgment of 28.07.2004 | 12 O 19/04 |
| LG Köln | Judgment of 27.09.2012 | 31 O 360/11 |
| OLG Düsseldorf | Judgment of 24.05.2005 | I-20 U 143/04 |
| OLG Köln | Judgment of 20.12.2013 | 6 U 188/12 |
| VG Berlin | Judgment of 06.07.2006 | 27 A 236.04 |
| VG München | Judgment of 04.11.2004 | M 17 K 02.5297 |

*France*

| | | | |
|---|---|---|---|
| Cour constitutionnel | Judgment of 16.07.1971 | n° 71-44 DC | FR:CC:1971:71.44.DC Official Journal of 18.07.1971, p. 7114 |
| Cour constitutionnel | Judgment of 27.07.1982 | n° 82-141 DC | FR:CC:1982:82.141.DC Official Journal of 29.07.1982, p. 2422 |
| Cour constitutionnel | Judgment of 25.07.1984 | n° 84-176 DC | FR:CC:1984:84.176.DC Official Journal of 28.07.1984, p. 2492 |

| | | | |
|---|---|---|---|
| Cour constitutionnel | Judgment of 18.09.1986 | n° 86-217 DC | FR:CC:1986:86. 217.DC Official Journal of 19.09.1986, p. 11294 |
| Cour constitutionnel | Judgment of 17.01.1989 | n° 88-248 DC | FR:CC:1989:88. 248.DC Official Journal of 18.01.1989, p. 754 |
| Cour constitutionnel | Judgment of 03.03.2009 | n° 2009-576 | FR:CC:2009:2009. 576.DC Official Journal of 07.03.2009, p. 4336 |
| Cour constitutionnel | Judgment of 03.03.2009 | n° 2009-577 DC | FR:CC:2009:2009. 577.DC Official Journal of 07.03.2009, p. 4336 |
| Cour constitutionnel | Judgment of 12.10.2012 | n° 2012-280 QPC | FR:CC:2012:2012. 280.QPC Official Journal of 1.10.2012, p. 16031 |
| Conseil d'Etat | Judgment of 26.05.2010 | n° 320863 | FR:CESSR:2010: 320863:20100526 |
| Conseil d'Etat | Judgment of 30.06.2000 | n° 222194 ; n° 222195 | FR:CESJS:2000: 222194.20000630 |
| Conseil d'Etat | Judgment of 14.06.2002 | n° 237910 | FR:CESSR:2002: 237910.20020614 |
| Conseil d'Etat | Jugment of 04.02.3004 | n°261804 | FR:CESSR:2004: 261804.20040204 |
| Conseil d'Etat | Judgment of 17.05.2006 | n° 263081 | FR:CESSR:2006: 263081.20060517 |
| Conseil d'Etat | Judgment of 06.10.2008 | n° 311017 | FR:CESSR:2008:3 11017.20081006 |
| Conseil d'Etat | Judgment of 18.12.2009 | n° 310646 | FR:CESSR:2009: 310646.20091218 |
| Conseil d'Etat | Judgment of 22.09.2010 | n° 341064 | FR:CESSR:2010: 341064.20100922 |
| Conseil d'Etat | Judgment of 06.12.2010 | n° 344567 | FR:CEORD:2010: 344567.20101206 |

| | | | |
|---|---|---|---|
| Conseil d'Etat | Judgment of 01.06.2015 | n° 372057 | FR:CESSR:2015:372057:20150601 |

*USA*

| | |
|---|---|
| Palko v. Connecticut | 302 U.S. 319 (1937) |